The Oxford Handbook of Evolutionary Perspectives on Violence, Homicide, and War

OXFORD LIBRARY OF PSYCHOLOGY

EDITOR-IN-CHIEF

Peter E. Nathan

AREA EDITORS:

Clinical Psychology
David H. Barlow

Cognitive Neuroscience
Kevin N. Ochsner and Stephen M. Kosslyn

Cognitive Psychology
Daniel Reisberg

Counseling Psychology
Elizabeth M. Altmaier and Jo-Ida C. Hansen

Developmental Psychology
Philip David Zelazo

Health Psychology
Howard S. Friedman

History of Psychology
David B. Baker

Methods and Measurement
Todd D. Little

Neuropsychology
Kenneth M. Adams

Organizational Psychology
Steve W. J. Kozlowski

Personality and Social Psychology
Kay Deaux and Mark Snyder

OXFORD LIBRARY OF PSYCHOLOGY

Editor in Chief PETER E. NATHAN
Editor, Organizational Psychology STEVE W. J. KOZLOWSKI

The Oxford Handbook of Evolutionary Perspectives on Violence, Homicide, and War

Edited by
Todd K. Shackelford
Viviana A. Weekes-Shackelford

OXFORD
UNIVERSITY PRESS

Oxford University Press, Inc., publishes works that further
Oxford University's objective of excellence
in research, scholarship, and education.

Oxford   New York
Auckland   Cape Town   Dar es Salaam   Hong Kong   Karachi
Kuala Lumpur   Madrid   Melbourne   Mexico City   Nairobi
New Delhi   Shanghai   Taipei   Toronto

With offices in
Argentina   Austria   Brazil   Chile   Czech Republic   France   Greece
Guatemala   Hungary   Italy   Japan   Poland   Portugal   Singapore
South Korea   Switzerland   Thailand   Turkey   Ukraine   Vietnam

Copyright © 2012 by Oxford University Press, Inc.

Published by Oxford University Press, Inc.
198 Madison Avenue, New York, New York 10016
www.oup.com

Oxford is a registered trademark of Oxford University Press

All rights reserved. No part of this publication may be reproduced,
stored in a retrieval system, or transmitted, in any form or by any means,
electronic, mechanical, photocopying, recording, or otherwise,
without the prior permission of Oxford University Press

Library of Congress Cataloging-in-Publication Data
The Oxford handbook of evolutionary perspectives on violence, homicide, and war / edited by Todd K.
Shackelford, Viviana A. Weekes-Shackelford.
   p. cm. — (Oxford library of psychology)
ISBN 978-0-19-973840-3
 1. Violence—Psychological aspects.   2. Homicide—Psychological aspects.   3. War—Psychological
aspects.   4. Evolutionary psychology.   I. Shackelford, Todd K. (Todd Kennedy), 1971-
II. Weekes-Shackelford, Viviana A.
 BF575.A3O94 2012
 155.7—dc23
 2011047400

SHORT CONTENTS

Oxford Library of Psychology vii–viii

About the Editors ix

Contributors xi–xii

Table of Contents xiii–xv

Chapters 1–524

Index 525

OXFORD LIBRARY OF PSYCHOLOGY

The *Oxford Library of Psychology*, a landmark series of handbooks, is published by Oxford University Press, one of the world's oldest and most highly respected publishers, with a tradition of publishing significant books in psychology. The ambitious goal of the *Oxford Library of Psychology* is nothing less than to span a vibrant, wide-ranging field and, in so doing, to fill a clear market need.

Encompassing a comprehensive set of handbooks, organized hierarchically, the *Library* incorporates volumes at different levels, each designed to meet a distinct need. At one level are a set of handbooks designed broadly to survey the major subfields of psychology; at another are numerous handbooks that cover important current focal research and scholarly areas of psychology in depth and detail. Planned as a reflection of the dynamism of psychology, the *Library* will grow and expand as psychology itself develops, thereby highlighting significant new research that will impact on the field. Adding to its accessibility and ease of use, the *Library* will be published in print and, later on, electronically.

The *Library* surveys psychology's principal subfields with a set of handbooks that capture the current status and future prospects of those major subdisciplines. This initial set includes handbooks of social and personality psychology, clinical psychology, counseling psychology, school psychology, educational psychology, industrial and organizational psychology, cognitive psychology, cognitive neuroscience, methods and measurements, history, neuropsychology, personality assessment, developmental psychology, and more. Each handbook undertakes to review one of psychology's major subdisciplines with breadth, comprehensiveness, and exemplary scholarship. In addition to these broadly conceived volumes, the *Library* also includes a large number of handbooks designed to explore in depth more specialized areas of scholarship and research, such as stress, health and coping, anxiety and related disorders, cognitive development, or child and adolescent assessment. In contrast to the broad coverage of the subfield handbooks, each of these latter volumes focuses on an especially productive, more highly focused line of scholarship and research. Whether at the broadest or most specific level, however, all of the *Library* handbooks offer synthetic coverage that reviews and evaluates the relevant past and present research and anticipates research in the future. Each handbook in the *Library* includes introductory and concluding chapters written by its editor to provide a roadmap to the handbook's table of contents and to offer informed anticipations of significant future developments in that field.

An undertaking of this scope calls for handbook editors and chapter authors who are established scholars in the areas about which they write. Many of the nation's and world's most productive and best-respected psychologists have agreed to edit *Library* handbooks or write authoritative chapters in their areas of expertise.

For whom has the *Oxford Library of Psychology* been written? Because of its breadth, depth, and accessibility, the *Library* serves a diverse audience, including graduate students in psychology and their faculty mentors, scholars, researchers, and practitioners in psychology and related fields. Readers will find in the *Library* the information they seek on the subfield or focal area of psychology in which they work or are interested.

Befitting its commitment to accessibility, each handbook includes a comprehensive index, as well as extensive references to help guide research. And because the *Library* was designed from its inception as an online as well as a print resource, its structure and contents will be readily and rationally searchable online. Further, once the *Library* is released online, the handbooks will be regularly and thoroughly updated.

In summary, the *Oxford Library of Psychology* will grow organically to provide a thoroughly informed perspective on the field of psychology, one that reflects both psychology's dynamism and its increasing interdisciplinarity. Once published electronically, the *Library* is also destined to become a uniquely valuable interactive tool, with extended search and browsing capabilities. As you begin to consult this handbook, we sincerely hope you will share our enthusiasm for the more than 500-year tradition of Oxford University Press for excellence, innovation, and quality, as exemplified by the *Oxford Library of Psychology*.

Peter E. Nathan
Editor-in-Chief
Oxford Library of Psychology

ABOUT THE EDITORS

Todd K. Shackelford
Todd K. Shackelford is professor and chair of psychology at Oakland University in Rochester, Michigan. Much of his research addresses sexual conflict in humans, including violence, rape, and homicide (see www.ToddKShackelford.com).

Viviana A. Weekes-Shackelford
Viviana A. Weekes-Shackelford is special lecturer in psychology at Oakland University in Rochester, Michigan. She received her PhD in evolutionary developmental psychology working with David Bjorklund at Florida Atlantic University. Her research focuses on conflict in parent–child and other familial relationships.

CONTRIBUTORS

Candace S. Alcorta
Department of Anthropology
University of Connecticut
Storrs, CT

Jay Belsky
Human and Community Development
University of California
Davis, CA

R. Michael Brown
Department of Psychology
Pacific Lutheran University
Tacoma, WA

Ryan P. Brown
Department of Psychology
The University of Oklahoma
Norman, OK

Stephanie L. Brown
Center for Medical Humanities, Compassionate Care, and Bioethics
Stony Brook University
Stony Brook, NY

Kingsley R. Browne
Wayne State University Law School
Detroit, MI

Joseph A. Camilleri
Department of Psychology
Westfield State University
Westfield, MA

Anne Campbell
Department of Psychology
Durham University
Durham, England, UK

Joseph Carroll
Department of English
University of Missouri, St. Louis
St. Louis, MO

Catharine Cross
Department of Psychology
Durham University
Durham, England, UK

Andrew Dane
Department of Psychology
Brock University
Hamilton, Ontario, Canada

Andrea M. den Boer
School of Politics and International Relations
University of Kent
Canterbury, Kent, UK

Nancy K. Dess
Department of Psychology
Occidental College
Los Angeles, CA

Corey L. Fincher
School of Psychology
The University of Aberdeen
Aberdeen, Scotland, UK

Carey J. Fitzgerald
Department of Psychology
Central Michigan University
Mount Pleasant, MI

Aaron T. Goetz
Department of Psychology
California State University, Fullerton
Fullerton, CA

Gregory Gorelik
Department of Psychology
Florida Atlantic University
Boca Raton, FL

Grant T. Harris
Queen's University,
University of Toronto, and
Waypoint CMH, Penetanguishene, Canada

John Hartung
Department of Anesthesiology
State University of New York
Brooklyn, NY

Valerie M. Hudson
The Bush School of Government and Public Service
Texas A&M University
Texas

xi

Daniel J. Kruger
School of Public Health
University of Michigan
Ann Arbor, MI

Patricia M. Lambert
Department of Anthropology
Utah State University
Logan, UT

Kenneth Letendre
Departments of Biology and Computer Science
The University of New Mexico
Albuquerque, NM

Marieke C.A. Liem
Department of Criminology and Criminal Law
Leiden University
Leiden, The Netherlands

James R. Liddle
Department of Psychology
Florida Atlantic University
Boca Raton, FL

Zopito Marini
Department of Child and Youth Studies
Brock University
Hamilton, Ontario, Canada

Nicholas E. Newton-Fisher
School of Anthropology & Conservation
University of Kent
Canterbury, Kent, UK

Lindsey L. Osterman
Department of Psychology
The University of Oklahoma
Norman, OK

Emily G. Patterson-Kane
American Veterinary Medical Association
Schaumburg, IL

Gregory S. Paul
Baltimore, MD

Erika J. Phillips
Department of Anthropology
University of Connecticut
Storrs, CT

Heather Piper
Education and Social Research Institute
Manchester Metropolitan University
Manchester, UK

Marnie E. Rice
Queen's University,
University of Toronto, and
Waypoint CMH, Penetanguishene, Canada

Gorge A. Romero
Department of Psychology
University of California, Fullerton
Fullerton, CA

Catherine Salmon
Department of Psychology
University of Redlands
Redlands, CA

Todd K. Shackelford
Department of Psychology
Oakland University
Rochester, MI

Hogan M. Sherrow
Department of Sociology & Anthropology
Hominid Behavior Research Project
Ohio University

David Livingstone Smith
Department of Philosophy
University of New England
Armidale, New South Wales, Australia

Richard Sosis
Department of Anthropology
University of Connecticut
Storrs, CT

Melissa Emery Thompson
Department of Anthropology
University of New Mexico
Albuquerque, NM

Randy Thornhill
Department of Biology
The University of New Mexico
Albuquerque, NM

Mark Van Vugt
VU University Amsterdam, the Netherlands
University of Oxford
Oxford, UK

Anthony Volk
Department of Child and Youth Studies
Brock University
Hamilton, Ontario, Canada

Viviana A. Weekes-Shackelford
Department of Psychology
Oakland University
Rochester, MI

CONTENTS

Part One • Introduction to Evolutionary Perspectives on Violence, Homicide, and War

1. Evolutionary Perspectives on Violence, Homicide, and War   3
   James R. Liddle, Todd K. Shackelford, and *Viviana A. Weekes-Shackelford*
2. Violence Across Animals and Within Early Hominins   23
   Hogan M. Sherrow
3. Comparative Evolutionary Perspectives on Violence   41
   Nicholas E. Newton-Fisher and *Melissa Emery Thompson*

Part Two • Evolutionary Perspectives on Familial Violence and Homicide

4. Intimate Partner Violence: War at Our Doorsteps   63
   Aaron T. Goetz and *Gorge A. Romero*
5. Chastity, Fidelity and Conquest: Biblical Rules for Women and War   77
   John Hartung
6. Filicide and Child Maltreatment: Prospects for Ultimate Explanation   91
   Grant T. Harris and *Marnie E. Rice*
7. Siblicide in Humans and Other Species   106
   Catherine Salmon
8. Familial Homicide-Suicide   117
   Marieke C. A. Liem
9. Suicide   132
   R. Michael Brown and *Stephanie L. Brown*
10. Evolutionary Perspectives on Male-Male Competition, Violence, and Homicide   153
    Daniel J. Kruger and *Carey J. Fitzgerald*

Part Three • Evolutionary Perspectives on Extrafamilial Violence and Homicide

11. Evolutionary Psychological Perspectives on Sexual Offending: From Etiology to Intervention   173
    Joseph A. Camilleri
12. Women and Aggression   197
    Anne Campbell and *Catharine Cross*

13. Culture of Honor, Violence, and Homicide   218
    Ryan P. Brown and *Lindsey L. Osterman*
14. Sacrifice and Sacred Values: Evolutionary Perspectives on Religious Terrorism   233
    Richard Sosis, Erika J. Phillips, and *Candace S. Alcorta*
15. Animal Abuse and Cruelty   254
    Emily G. Patterson-Kane and Heather Piper
16. If, When, and Why Adolescent Bullying Is Adaptive   270
    Anthony Volk, Joseph A. Camilleri, Andrew Dane, and *Zopito Marini*

Part Four • Evolutionary Perspectives on War

17. The Male Warrior Hypothesis: The Evolutionary Psychology of Intergroup Conflict, Tribal Aggression, and Warfare   291
    Mark Van Vugt
18. A Feminist Evolutionary Analysis of the Relationship Between Violence Against and Inequitable Treatment of Women, and Conflict Within and Between Human Collectives, Including Nation-States   301
    Valerie M. Hudson and *Andrea M. den Boer*
19. War Histories in Evolutionary Perspective: Insights From Prehistoric North America   324
    Patricia M. Lambert
20. War, Evolution, and the Nature of Human Nature   339
    David Livingstone Smith
21. Parasite Stress, Collectivism, and Human Warfare   351
    Kenneth Letendre, Corey L. Fincher, and *Randy Thornhill*
22. Band of Brothers or Band of Siblings?: An Evolutionary Perspective on Sexual Integration of Combat Forces   372
    Kingsley R. Browne
23. An Evolutionary Perspective on Child Development in the Context of War and Political Violence   393
    Jay Belsky

Part Five • Conclusions and Future Directions for Evolutionary Perspectives on Violence, Homicide, and War

24. The Extremes of Conflict in Literature: Violence, Homicide, and War   413
    Joseph Carroll
25. Why Religion Is Unable to Minimize Lethal and Nonlethal Societal Dysfunction Within and Between Nations   435
    Gregory S. Paul

26. Peace and the Human Animal: Toward Integration of Comparative Evolutionary Psychology and Peace Studies 471
    Nancy K. Dess
27. Resource Acquisition, Violence, and Evolutionary Consciousness 506
    Gregory Gorelik, Todd K. Shackelford, and *Viviana A. Weekes-Shackelford*

Index   525

PART 1

Introduction to Evolutionary Perspectives on Violence, Homicide, and War

CHAPTER
1 Evolutionary Perspectives on Violence, Homicide, and War

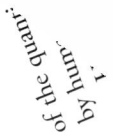

James R. Liddle, Todd K. Shackelford, *and* Viviana A. Weekes-Shackelford

Abstract

We review and discuss the evolutionary psychological literature on violence, homicide, and war in humans and nonhumans, and in doing so we argue that an evolutionary perspective can substantially enhance our understanding of these behaviors. We provide a brief primer on evolutionary psychology, describing basic tenets of the field. The theories of sexual selection and parental investment are explained and subsequently used to highlight the evolutionary logic underlying the use of violence by humans and other animals. Our examination of violent behavior begins with a focus on nonhuman animals, reviewing the different contexts in which violence occurs and discussing how an evolutionary perspective can explain why it occurs in these contexts. We then examine violence in humans and illustrate the similarities and differences between human and nonhuman violence. Finally, we summarize what an evolutionary perspective can offer in terms of understanding violence, homicide, and war, and we discuss directions for future research.

Key Words: evolution, evolutionary psychology, sexual selection, parental investment, aggression, violence, homicide, war

Introduction

Violence, defined by the World Health Organization as "the intentional use of physical force or power, threatened or actual, against oneself, another person, or against a group or community, that either results in or has a high likelihood of resulting in injury, death, psychological harm, maldevelopment or deprivation" (Dahlberg & Krug, 2002, p. 5), is a ubiquitous characteristic of human societies, both past and present. For example, although crime rates in the United States have decreased in recent years, there were 13,636 homicides and 1,318,398 violent crimes reported in 2009 (U. S. Department of Justice, 2010). Lifetime prevalence estimates of the rape of women in Western samples reach as high as 13%, which may actually be an underestimate (see McKibbin & Shackelford, 2011), and between 10% and 26% of women experience rape in marriage (Goetz, Shackelford, Starratt, & McKibbin, 2008). The suicide rate in the United States stands at roughly 11 per 100,000, which is lower than the global average of 14.5 per 100,000 (Brown & Brown, Chapter 9, this volume) but still translates into approximately 34,100 deaths per year. Around the world, roughly 87,500,000 people have died as a result of wars in the 20th century, with 54,000,000 of these being civilian deaths (Smith, 2007, p. 18). Among hunter-gatherer tribes, an average of 13% (based on archaeological data) to 15% (based on ethnographic data; Bowles, 2006) of men die due to warfare, and roughly 20%–30% of men die from tribal violence among the Yanomamö (Chagnon, 1988). This collection of statistics is by no means complete; it merely scratches the surface

This chapter is based on Liddle, Shackelford, and Weekes-Shackelford (2012).

...ty and quality of violence perpetrated ...ns.

How can we explain these phenomena? Although some violent episodes can be attributed to substance abuse, mental illnesses or disorders, and so forth, the majority of violent behavior in our species, as well as in other species, cannot be dismissed as an aberration. Violent behavior, including homicide and war, requires a deeper explanation, which can be provided by adopting an evolutionary perspective.

An Evolutionary Psychological Perspective

> In the distant future I see open fields for more important researches. Psychology will be based on a new foundation, that of the necessary acquirement of each mental power and capacity by gradation. Light will be thrown on the origin of man and his history.
> —*Charles Darwin*, 1859, p. 488

Evolutionary psychology represents the "new foundation" of psychology that Darwin envisioned, in which the evolution of the mind is not only acknowledged, but the theory of evolution is applied to the study of the mind. Evolutionary psychology is not a subdiscipline of psychology, but instead it represents a unifying approach to psychology in which the theory of evolution can be—and has been to varying degrees—applied to all psychological subdisciplines (see Buss, 2011). For example, much progress has been made in incorporating evolutionary theory into the subdisciplines of social psychology (Kenrick, Neuberg, & Cialdini, 2009), developmental psychology (Ellis & Bjorklund, 2005), cognitive psychology (Pinker, 2009), abnormal psychology (Wakefield, 1992), and personality psychology (Buss, 2009).

Specifically, evolutionary psychologists posit that the human brain is composed of a large number of domain-specific information-processing mechanisms (i.e., evolved psychological mechanisms; Buss, 2011) that were selected over deep evolutionary history in response to the specific and recurrent adaptive problems faced by our ancestors, such as finding food and shelter, avoiding predators, finding a mate, and protecting and providing for one's children—in short, problems related to survival and reproduction (Tooby & Cosmides, 2005). The existence and role of domain-general mechanisms (e.g., fluid intelligence) are currently debated, but evolutionary psychologists maintain that the brain is predominantly comprised of domain-specific mechanisms.

Evolved psychological mechanisms function by registering specific types of input (e.g., environmental stimuli, physiological activity, output from other psychological mechanisms), processing this information, and generating a specific output (i.e., physiological activity, information for other psychological mechanisms, or manifest behavior; Buss, 2011). As a result of this process, evolved psychological mechanisms may generate maladaptive behavior in contemporary societies due to novel inputs. For example, a mechanism that generates a preference for fatty foods is likely to have been adaptive for much of our evolutionary history due to the scarcity of food in general, but this mechanism can result in serious health problems in contemporary societies where fatty foods are cheap and plentiful. Similarly, humans often experience fear in response to stimuli that are likely to have been potent threats throughout our evolutionary history (e.g., snakes and spiders), even if they no longer represent realistic threats in contemporary environments. However, stimuli that *do* represent threats in such environments (e.g., automobiles, electrical outlets, and other novel sources of injury or death) rarely elicit similar levels of fear because they have not existed long enough for psychological mechanisms to be selected for in response to these threats (Öhman & Mineka, 2001).

Given the view of the mind outlined earlier, evolutionary psychologists proceed to generate hypotheses about what types of psychological mechanisms exist based on defensible assumptions about the selection pressures faced throughout human evolutionary history. These hypotheses include predictions regarding the outputs that are expected to be generated in contemporary environments (i.e., environments that provide novel inputs that did not exist when these mechanisms evolved). As we will see later in this chapter, the approach described earlier has significantly expanded our understanding of violence, homicide, and war.

However, before one can fully appreciate the contribution that an evolutionary perspective has made toward understanding these behaviors, it is important to note that evolutionary psychologists do not contend that such behaviors are inevitable. Despite the increased incorporation of an evolutionary perspective into mainstream psychology over recent years (see Cornwell, Palmer, Guinther, & Davis, 2005), evolutionary psychology continues to be met with criticisms that largely stem from misconceptions of the field, such as the idea that evolutionary psychology implies genetic determinism (e.g., Coyne, 2009). Since there have already been several rebuttals published in response to this and other criticisms (e.g., Bryant, 2006; Confer et al., 2010; Geher, 2006; Hagen, 2005; Kurzban, 2002; Liddle, Bush, & Shackelford, 2011; Liddle & Shackelford, 2009; Sell, Hagen, Cosmides, & Tooby, 2003), we will not provide an in-depth review here. We will, however, note that evolutionary psychologists acknowledge the important interactions that take place between one's genes and one's environment.

Furthermore, evolutionary psychologists do not argue that *behaviors* have evolved but rather that psychological mechanisms have evolved. Many of these mechanisms produce behavior, but only in response to specific environmental inputs. Without the appropriate input, a particular psychological mechanism will not produce any output. In fact, since violent behaviors are potentially very costly, evolutionary accounts suggest that we should only expect these behaviors under very specific conditions (i.e., in response to a specific and limited set of environmental inputs). The remainder of this chapter expands upon this premise, and we begin by examining violence in nonhuman animals.

Red in Tooth and Claw: Violence in Nonhuman Animals

The animal kingdom is not a peaceful kingdom. Aside from the obvious violence that occurs between species as predators attempt to make a meal out of their prey (see also Patterson-Kane & Piper, Chapter 15, this volume, for another form of interspecies violence: animal abuse by humans), a substantial amount of violence occurs *within* species as well, and an evolutionary perspective can help explain why this occurs. A large portion of this violence, and the conditions in which it is expected to occur, can be explained by relying on two evolutionary theoretical models: sexual selection and parental investment theory.

Sexual Selection

The concept of sexual selection (Darwin, 1871) provides an important addendum to the theory of evolution by natural selection. Natural selection explains the evolution of complex traits as a result of heritable variations that influence differential survival. In any given population, some organisms are more likely to survive and subsequently pass on their genes than are others, and to the extent that heritable variations among organisms account for these differences in survival and reproduction, those variations will be selected for. Through this process, complex adaptations emerge as slight improvements in particular traits and continue to be selected for over thousands of generations. For example, computer simulations have indicated that a patch of light-sensitive cells can evolve into a complex eye through intermediate steps taking place over fewer than 400,000 generations, a brief period on an evolutionary timescale (Nilsson & Pelger, 1994).

Although survivability is important, this is not the sole determinant of one's fitness (i.e., one's success in passing on his or her genes to the next generation), at least among sexually reproducing organisms. A sexually reproducing organism that lives for hundreds of years but never produces offspring will be no more successful, evolutionarily speaking, than an organism that dies immediately after birth. Therefore, selection will operate not only on traits that affect one's chances of survival but also on traits that affect one's reproductive potential. This fact can explain, for example, the evolution of the peacock's tail, a trait that initially tormented Darwin because it seemingly contradicted his theory of evolution by natural selection. The large, colorful tail is not only metabolically wasteful to produce but cumbersome as well, making it more difficult for peacocks to escape from predators. Natural selection would seemingly select *against* such a trait, since it is likely to have a negative impact on survival. However, Darwin (1871) came to realize that if peahens preferentially mate with peacocks that possess large tails, the cost to survival will be outweighed by the benefit to reproductive potential, and thus the trait will be *sexually selected*. In fact, the peacock's tail is likely preferred by peahens precisely *because* it is a harmful trait to possess, and any peacock that is capable of surviving with such a "handicap" is providing an honest signal that he possesses good genes (Zahavi & Zahavi, 1996).

Sexual selection operates by two primary means: intrasexual competition and intersexual selection (Buss, 2011). The peacock's tail is an example of a trait produced by intersexual selection, in which a trait is selected for because it is preferred by the opposite sex. Intrasexual competition refers to competition between same-sex rivals for access to mating opportunities, and traits that improve one's chances of succeeding in such competition will be selected for. As we will see, both of these components of sexual selection, especially intrasexual competition, can help explain much of the violence that occurs within species. However, sexual selection alone provides us with an incomplete understanding of violent behavior. For example, in most species males are much more likely to engage in physically violent intrasexual competition than are females. To explain this robust sex difference, we must refer to parental investment theory.

Parental Investment Theory

Parental investment (Trivers, 1972) refers to the allocation of resources to offspring, at the expense of other potential sources of resource allocation (e.g., survival, mating effort, additional offspring). A key component of parental investment theory is that there is often a large discrepancy in the minimum obligatory parental investment provided to offspring by males and females, and this discrepancy can explain sex differences in regard to reproductive strategies, such as engaging in risky competition (e.g., physical violence) for mates.

In all mammals, females exhibit greater minimum obligatory parental investment than males. Females must devote considerable time and energy to their offspring due to internal fertilization and gestation, which is often followed by a period of nursing, whereas the minimum obligatory investment by males is the contribution of sperm. This results in females being far more discriminating when choosing a male to mate with, because there are much greater costs associated with not choosing wisely, such as potentially investing a great deal of resources into offspring with low prospects of survival due to bad genes. Therefore, females represent a limiting factor for male reproductive success, and as Ketelaar and Ellis (2000) describe, "Males should thus be selected to be more risk-taking and aggressive than females in pursuing sexual contacts, and to allocate more competitive effort toward monopolizing sexual access" (p. 7). Additionally, since greater maternal investment means that offspring rely on their mothers more than their fathers for survival, the costs of engaging in violent behavior are potentially much greater for females than for males. If a female is seriously injured or killed, any offspring that were being cared for by her, especially very young offspring, will be unlikely to survive (Sear & Mace, 2008), and this would act as a strong selection pressure *against* predispositions to violence among females (see Campbell & Cross, Chapter 12, this volume). The males of most species, since they provide little to no care to their offspring in the first place, have not been exposed to a similar selection pressure.

In summary, parental investment theory predicts that the sex that exhibits lesser obligatory parental investment (typically males) should be predisposed to violence because of the benefits of successfully competing with same-sex rivals (i.e., access to the "choosier" sex for mating), and the sex that exhibits greater obligatory investment (typically females) should be predisposed to *avoid* violence because of the costs associated with injury and death (i.e., being unable to care for one's offspring). The fact that the males of most animal species, particularly mammals, are overwhelmingly more prone to physical violence than are females (Ghiglieri, 1999) seemingly supports parental investment theory, but the predictive power of this theory is particularly evident when examining certain nonmammalian species in which the discrepancy in minimum parental investment is reversed between the sexes. For example, among certain species of birds, males invest more in their offspring than do females. Ghiglieri (1999) describes the behavioral results of this role reversal among Australian cassowaries:

> ...females are the aggressive (macho) sex.... these six-foot tall birds, armed with a three-inch claw/spike that can disembowel a dingo, battle each other using brutal kicks. A victorious female then mates with as many males as she can find, one after the other. She leaves each with a clutch of her eggs. The males, who are one-third smaller than the females, dutifully incubate the eggs, driving off predators and sometimes going up to fifty days without food to protect the clutch.
> (pp. 10–11)

Other "sex-role-reversed" species include the Mormon cricket, the pipefish seahorse, and the Panamanian poison arrow frog (Trivers, 1985, as cited in Buss, 2011). The males of these species invest more in their offspring than do females, and as parental investment theory predicts, they are more discriminating when choosing which females to mate with, while the females compete with each other, often violently, for access to males.

The theories of sexual selection and parental investment imply that violence among nonhuman animals is not arbitrary or pointless but instead is determined by calculations of costs and benefits. These calculations need not be made consciously, and as Campbell (2005) explains, "...emotionally driven information processing mechanisms have been honed through evolutionary time to trip a decision in a way that can seem automatic and unreflective" (p. 629). In other words, it seems plausible to posit that evolved psychological mechanisms for violence exist in nonhuman animals, and that these mechanisms generate violent behavior in response to specific inputs that indicate that the potential costs of violence are outweighed by the potential benefits. In the sections that follow, we describe what some of these inputs may be and how these inputs influence the cost-benefit calculations that determine the likelihood of engaging in violent behavior.

To the Victor Belong the Spoils

Some degree of violence has been observed in virtually every known animal population, and the majority of this violence exists in the context of resource competition, with one sought-after resource being access to mates (see Sherrow, Chapter 2, this volume). More specifically, it is typically males who engage in intrasexual violence as a way of competing for access to females. The females preferentially mate with the victors of these violent competitions, and the losers are largely, if not completely, excluded from mating opportunities.

The severity of violence can vary considerably, from male Japanese beetles engaging in "shoving matches" for access to mates, with the loser eventually being chased away (Hongo, 2003), to male red deer fighting intensely during the mating season, accounting for 13%–29% of adult male deaths (Clutton-Brock & Albon, 1982). Given the high potential costs associated with violent intrasexual competition (e.g., severe injury or death), many species engage in intrasexual competition consisting of ritualized fighting (Maynard-Smith & Price, 1973; Sherrow, Chapter 2, this volume), in which physical attacks are mostly replaced by violent *displays*. Those engaged in ritualized fighting can rely on several cues to "size up" their opponents (e.g., body size and physical condition; see Newton-Fisher & Thompson, Chapter 3, this volume), thus limiting the need to commit to a fight to the death (or serious injury) if the likely victor can be identified.

This approach to intrasexual competition can be observed within chimpanzee communities. Male chimpanzees occasionally fight and injure each other, but intrasexual competition is more often conducted via displays that serve as cues to competitive ability, thus obviating any physical violence (Goodall, 1986). Ritualized fighting can also be observed among male sierra dome spiders, in which the likely loser can retreat before suffering any severe injuries. However, when a clear victor cannot be identified from ritualized fighting, neither competitor will back down because they both perceive that they may be victorious, and therefore the fighting will become more severe and often lead to serious injury or death (deCarvalho, Watson, & Field, 2004).

One important factor that determines the degree of intrasexual competition in a species is the extent to which the losers of such competition are excluded from mating. The greater the exclusion, the higher the stakes, with the end result being more intense competition. One species that illustrates this concept well is the elephant seal. Mating is highly polygynous, with individual males forming and defending harems of females during breeding season. Males that are capable of defending a harem have exclusive access to the females of that territory, translating into huge reproductive success, whereas males who are incapable of defending a harem or taking over another male's harem are almost completely excluded from any mating opportunities. This reproductive context sets off an evolutionary arms race among males competing intrasexually for mating opportunities, resulting in extreme sexual dimorphism in which males are several times larger than females (Cartwright, 2000). Larger size has been selected for among males because it provides an advantage during violent intrasexual competition. Large size can be useful not only in the context of violent competition, but also it can serve as an honest signal of one's strength and prowess, thereby deterring potential competitions. Indeed, male elephant seals often rely on ritualized fighting displays to settle intrasexual competitions (Sanvito, Galimberti, & Miller, 2007), but since the stakes are so high, violent competitions are not uncommon (Haley, 1994).

This Land Is My Land

The examples of intrasexual competition mentioned thus far illustrate the importance of a particular resource: access to mates. However, mating opportunities mean nothing if you or your offspring do not have access to food, a scarce commodity for many species. Therefore, access to food or feeding territories—when such resources are scarce—represents a likely motivator of violent competition. For example, competition over food is not observed among mountain gorillas, who mostly eat leaves, stems, and piths, because they live in environments in which they are surrounded by potential food (Fossey, 1984), but this is not the case among black-and-white colobus monkeys, who defend valuable feeding territories from rival groups (Harris, 2006).

Unlike access to mates, which is a resource primarily fought for between males, food is an important resource for both males and females, perhaps even more important for females because they often need to provide for their offspring as well. Therefore, we should expect females to be willing to engage in violence to compete for food, although their willingness to engage in violence, relative to males, should still be mitigated by the higher potential costs, as explained by parental investment theory. Indeed, both male and female kangaroo rats engage in intrasexual and intersexual competition over seeds and suitable areas to cache seeds (Blaustein & Risser, 1976). Additionally, female chimpanzees have been observed acting more aggressively than normal, almost approaching male levels of aggression, when food is scarce or feeding territories are at stake (Muller, 2007).

A particular form of competition for food and territory worth highlighting is coalitional violence, in which a group of individuals works together to attack a rival group or individual (see Newton-Fisher & Thompson, Chapter 3, this volume). Since this type of competition requires teamwork, it is primarily observed among social animals, particularly carnivores such as lions (Mosser & Packer, 2009), African wild dogs (Creel & Creel, 2002), hyenas (Boydston, Morelli, & Holekamp, 2001), and wolves (Mech, 1977). Like intrasexual competition for mates, the likelihood of violence between groups is largely determined by the perceived difference in strength between competitors, but the cost-benefit calculations differ in this context. When competing for mates, males are less likely to engage in violence if a victor can be identified through violent displays. This makes sense because escalating the competition would not provide additional benefits to the victor, and the competitors are often males from the same group, which means they are potential allies if attacked by a rival group. But unlike competitors for mates within the group, rival groups that compete for food and territory represent a long-term threat, and the elimination of such threats whenever possible is desirable. Eliminating rival groups can produce long-term benefits, such as increased territory size, which translates into increased access to food and other resources. Therefore, the greater the perceived difference in strength between groups, the *more* likely the stronger group is to engage in violent competition. For example, among wolves, in which 25%–65% of adult deaths are due to coalitional violence, death is most likely when a lone wolf is confronted on the outskirts of their territory by a rival pack (Mech, Adams, Meier, Burch, & Dale, 1998). A similar pattern is found among African lions, in which lethal violence is most likely when a pack comes into contact with a lone rival (Grinnell, Packer, & Pusey, 1995).

The coalitional violence observed among male chimpanzees is especially noteworthy in that it most closely resembles human warlike behaviors. Male chimpanzees have been observed forming "raiding parties," in which a group of males stealthily investigates areas beyond their own group's territory, seemingly on the lookout for isolated (i.e., vulnerable) males from rival groups. Again, the difference in strength that so often mitigates violence during mate competition actually fuels violence in this context. This type of behavior was first observed by Goodall (1979) within 2 years of no longer giving chimpanzees at Gombe 600 bananas a day to habituate them to the presence of humans. Within this time period, the chimps at Gombe split into the Kasakela community (with roughly 35 members) in the north and the Kahama community (with roughly 15 members) in the south. There were seven males in the Kahama community, and at least five of them were systematically killed by male coalitions from the Kahama community, while the remaining two disappeared due to unknown causes. These murders were brutal and seemingly premeditated, and based on the severity of the wounds inflicted, it is clear that the goal was to kill rather than to injure the victims (Ghiglieri, 1999).

Although the events described earlier may have initially been viewed as anomalous behavior, a similar "war" was launched a decade later by chimpanzees in the Mahale Mountains, and as Ghiglieri (1999) describes, "...males of Nishida's huge M-Group (more than eighty chimps) systematically stalked and murdered the six adult males of the smaller, neighboring K-Group, which contained twenty-two chimps at the onset of hostilities" (p. 173). Among the chimpanzees of Kibale, three adult males of the Kanyawara community were killed by males of the Wantabu community between 1988 and 1994, an important finding because these chimps were never given food by observers, eliminating the possibility that previous observations of raiding were merely the result of altered lifestyles due to human involvement. Over the years, these observations have been supplemented by dozens of similar accounts observed among chimpanzees throughout Africa (see Newton-Fisher & Thompson, Chapter 3, this volume).

Importantly, in the majority of cases of raiding and eliminating rival males, the victorious chimps benefitted from expanded territories (which provides additional food resources) and the assimilation of females from the defeated group (Ghiglieri, 1999). At the very least, victorious chimps benefit by no longer having to defend their resources from the eliminated rivals. It is also worth noting that when neighboring groups are roughly equal in size, raiding is rare, if it occurs at all (Ghiglieri, 1999). Given the large benefits and the low risks associated with violence when the target is outnumbered, it is not difficult to see why chimpanzees, under the proper conditions, are willing to engage in what can arguably be defined as warfare.

Infanticide

An additional form of violence among nonhuman animals that warrants our attention is infanticide, or the killing of same-species infants, which has been observed among many species of mammals (Hrdy, 1977, 1979; Janson & van Schaik, 2000). Like other forms of violence, there appears to be an underlying evolutionary logic to infanticide, with both males and females engaging in this behavior but in different contexts. When males commit infanticide, it is almost exclusively unrelated infants who are killed, and the primary benefit of this act appears to be increased mating opportunities. More specifically, many female mammals who are nursing infants experience lactational amenorrhea and do not ovulate, but if the infant is killed, the female begins to cycle again (Hrdy, 1979). In other words, the female becomes available for mating following infanticide, and such females will often mate with the male who committed the infanticide. This type of infanticide is often observed in polygynous species, such as lions, when a new male comes into power and monopolizes mating opportunities after killing any unrelated infants (Newton-Fisher & Thompson, Chapter 3, this volume; Pusey & Packer, 1994).

When females commit infanticide, the target infant may either be related or unrelated, with a different evolutionary logic underlying the two scenarios. Females may kill unrelated infants when such behavior results in reduced present and future resource competition faced by her and her own offspring (see Sherrow, Chapter 2, this volume). An environment with scarce resources is not enough to evoke this type of infanticide; there must be intragroup competition for resources, and the elimination of unrelated infants must potentially result in increased access to these resources (Leland, Struhsaker, & Butynski, 1984). This type of infanticide, along with the predicted prerequisite conditions, has been observed among ground squirrels (Waterman, 1984) and several species of birds (Mock, 1984).

Females also kill their own offspring, which may seem maladaptive from an evolutionary perspective, but it is important to keep in mind that the females of most species, particularly mammals, must invest substantially in their offspring. Given the high costs of parental investment faced by females, there are occasionally situations in which it is in the best interest of the female (in terms of her fitness) to forego paying those costs. For example, when resources are scarce and a female already has offspring, additional offspring may result in a lack of adequate distribution of resources among all of the offspring. In this case, it would be in the mother's interests to either directly or indirectly (via neglect) kill the new infant in order to increase the survival chances of her other offspring in whom she already has invested substantially (Hrdy, 2000; see also Harris & Rice, Chapter 6, this volume). In short, infanticide among nonhuman animals can occur for many reasons, none of which are arbitrary, at least when considered from an evolutionary perspective.

Summary

The examples of violence among nonhuman animals described earlier illustrate that violence is not random or aberrant but functional. Violent behavior serves a purpose and is likely the result of evolved psychological mechanisms that, based on particular environmental inputs, calculate whether the costs of violence are outweighed by the potential benefits. These inputs include the availability of resources, including food, territory, and access to mates; the strength of one's opponent, which may be assessed via ritualized fighting displays; and the number of opponents, which is an important factor for determining the likelihood of coalitional violence against rival groups. Even when one's "opponent" does not represent a threat in terms of retaliation, as is the case with infants, the use of violence still relies on the calculation of costs and benefits to one's fitness, such as when a mother engages in infanticide to increase the survival prospects of her other offspring or her future offspring. But an important question remains: Is *human* violence similarly purposeful?

The Most Dangerous Animal: Violence in Humans

"Me against my brother," goes the old Arab proverb; "me and my brother against my cousins; me, my brother and my cousins against our nonrelatives; me, my brother, cousins and friends against our enemies

in the village, all of these and the whole village against the next village."
—*Ghiglieri*, 1999, p. 170

The violent behaviors humans engage in may often seem senseless, particularly when one hears reports of school shootings, war atrocities, mass murders, and so forth. However, the preceding account of nonhuman animals suggests that violent behaviors are produced in order to solve particular adaptive problems, and therefore it is not unreasonable to conceive of an evolutionary functionality underlying many cases of violence among *Homo sapiens*. But the ubiquity and apparent functionality of violence throughout the animal kingdom is not the only line of evidence suggesting that violence serves a purpose in humans. Additional support for this idea comes from the evidence of violence committed by humans throughout our evolutionary history, which we examine next.

A History of Violence

Although there is much that we still do not know about the evolutionary history of humans (e.g., the emergence of language), the archaeological evidence for violence between early humans is indisputable. For example, human skeletons from the upper Paleolithic period have been found with projectile points imbedded in them and skeletal trauma that appears to have been caused by clubbing (Ferguson, 1997; Smith, Chapter 20, this volume). Smith (2007) describes several more examples of such violence:

> A Neanderthal man who lived in a cave in Shanidar, Iraq, was stabbed in the side in what was probably a face-to-face confrontation; a young child was killed 30,000 years ago in what is now Grimaldi, Italy, when a spear pierced his tiny body and lodged deep in his spine; an Egyptian man met his death 20,000 years ago when two arrows entered his abdomen and a third lodged in his upper arm. (p. 45)

A cemetery at Jebel Sahaba in Northern Sudan dating back roughly 13,000 years provides particularly strong evidence of violence, and perhaps war, between early humans. Among the 59 bodies discovered there, almost half appear to have been killed by weapons, because arrowheads and barbs were discovered in and around their bones (see Smith, Chapter 20, this volume). Among the children buried there who met a violent end, the wounds indicate that they were executed, with arrows shot into their necks at close range (Smith, 2007). Similar examples of mass killings include mass burial sites in Germany, Bavaria, and France, all of which contain the skeletons of individuals who appear to have been killed violently, often by blows to the head (Keeley, 1996). Taken together, the archaeological findings discussed thus far represent the most direct evidence for violence between early humans.

Given the difficulty with finding skeletal remains from our early evolutionary history, it is likely that acts of violence were more common than what the archaeological evidence described earlier suggests. Fortunately, there are other pieces of evidence that highlight the violence that may have occurred between early humans. For example, the crafting of tools necessary for inflicting severe violence on other humans, such as stone axes and wooden spears, began at least 400,000 years ago (Smith, 2007), although such tools were clearly useful for other tasks as well, such as hunting. Additional evidence for the possibility of violence among early humans comes from Late Paleolithic paintings found in France, Spain, and Italy depicting humans being killed with arrows and spears (Smith, 2007). Moving ahead in our evolutionary history, the early writings of many civilizations provide additional details of human violence, particularly large-scale violence. Such writings come from a variety of societies, such as Egypt, Sumer, Greece, Rome, India, and Mesoamerica (Keeley, 1996). In particular, the Old Testament and Homer's *Iliad* provide extensive and graphic details of warfare (Carroll, Chapter 24, this volume; Gottschall, 2008), and although some of the violent stories depicted in these works are either clearly fictional or dubious, it seems likely that the authors were inspired by first- or secondhand accounts of similar violence.

Finally, the transition from nomadic lifestyles to permanent settlements beginning in the Neolithic period roughly 10,000 years ago provides further evidence that violence between humans represented an ongoing threat for our ancestors. This transition took place initially in the Fertile Crescent and was primarily driven by the advent of agriculture and the domestication of animals, which required humans to stay in one place to cultivate the land for food (Diamond, 1997). This new way of life led to larger populations, technological advancements, and, importantly, the stockpiling of resources, which made permanent settlements the focal points for violence between groups of humans. The fact that such violence occurred, or that it was at least a realistic threat, is evidenced by the architecture of early settlements. More specifically, those who built permanent settlements made sure to build protective walls, and as settlements grew in size and technology advanced, the fortifications became more elaborate and extensive (Smith, 2007). Given the labor and resources necessary to fortify settlements, it seems likely that attacks by other humans constituted a serious threat, a conclusion that is strengthened when the other evidence for violence described earlier is taken into account.

In summary, the evidence of violence throughout human evolutionary history serves as a powerful reminder that contemporary violence is not a new phenomenon. Although we cannot ascertain with any certainty the contexts in which most violence took place between our ancestors, our history suggests that we should not blame violent video games and other media as the sole or primary source of the violence we see in contemporary societies. Although certain novel aspects of contemporary environments may influence violent behavior (but see Ferguson & Kilburn, 2009, for a meta-analysis indicating little to no effect of violent media on violent behavior), we believe that researchers should also focus on environmental factors that have been recurrent throughout our evolutionary history, as well as the recurrent adaptive problems that our ancestors faced, particularly those that could have been solved through violence. As we will see, mating represents one potential source for many of these types of adaptive problems.

In the Name of Love

As with many other animals, mating can serve as a direct or indirect catalyst for violence among humans, and the theories of sexual selection and parental investment can help explain why this occurs. Humans are unique among most species in terms of the typically large amount of paternal investment in offspring, but women still exhibit greater obligatory investment and thus represent a limiting factor for male reproductive success. Furthermore, men are roughly 120%–130% the weight of females (Ghiglieri, 1999), and this sexual dimorphism suggests a history of effective polygyny in which some men secure a greater number of mating opportunities at the expense of other men, thus increasing the variability of male reproductive success (Buss & Shackelford, 1997).

As in other species, increased variability in reproductive success and lower obligatory parental investment relative to the opposite sex translate into fiercer and riskier intrasexual competition for mating opportunities (Campbell, 2005). Therefore, it is not surprising that men around the world are substantially more physically violent than are women. In the United States, roughly 87% of those who commit homicide, and 75% of those who fall victim to homicide, are men (Lester, 1991), a statistic that is similar, if not even more male biased, in other countries (Buss, 2005; Daly & Wilson, 1988; Ghiglieri, 1999). Additionally, the levels of mortality from violence are highest in young adulthood and decrease considerably as men marry, start families, and invest in their children, that is, when the search and competition for mating opportunities decreases (Kruger & Fitzgerald, Chapter 10, this volume; Kruger & Nesse, 2006). Although other factors may play a role in the high rates of violence among young men, the consistently higher mortality rate across the lifespan for men who have never married compared with men who have supports the idea that intrasexual competition is an important factor at any age in which a man is looking for a mate.

But how does violence translate into mating opportunities? It seems that both intrasexual competition and intersexual selection play important roles, in that intrasexual competition between men is often directly related to status or reputation, and women preferentially choose partners of high status, most likely because high status has historically translated into having access to more food, better territory, and greater social support, thus serving as an honest signal of a man's ability (but not necessarily *intent*) to provide for a woman and her offspring (Buss, 2005). Among the Yanomamö, Chagnon (1988) documented that roughly 40% of the men had participated in homicide, and these men had higher social status, as well as more wives, than those who had not participated in homicide. Nonlethal fights with clubs are also common among Yanomamö men, and they often take place in the context of competition over mates (Chagnon, 1992). Although the frequency of violence among the Yanomamö is higher than that found in many other tribal societies, the reasoning behind the violence is not unique. Indeed, many tribal societies bestow increased status and honor to men who have committed homicide (Daly & Wilson, 1988). This phenomenon can even be found in the United States, particularly among gangs, in which the most violent gang members often have the highest status (Campbell, 1993) and the most sexual partners (Buss, 2011; Ghiglieri, 1999; Palmer & Tilly, 1995). Even among children and adolescents who do not engage in criminal behavior, the importance of intrasexual competition over status can be observed in the context of bullying (see Volk, Camilleri, Dane, & Marini, Chapter 16, this volume). Male bullies who pick on weaker individuals are able to acquire higher status (Vaillancourt, Hymel, & McDougall, 2003), resources ranging from lunch money and books to leather jackets and designer sneakers (Buss, 2011; Olweus, 1978), and dating or mating opportunities (Connolly, Pepler, Craig, & Taradash, 2000).

The importance that men place on status, and perceived threats to one's status, makes sense when we consider the small groups in which humans lived for the majority of our evolutionary history. We have inherited psychological mechanisms that evolved in response to a type of group living in which anonymity was mostly lacking, if not entirely absent. In other words, groups were small enough that everyone likely knew and repeatedly interacted with each other. In such an environment, failure to defend one's status or reputation when provoked by a rival would have been very costly, particularly for men, because of the message it would send to the rest of the community: "I am weak and exploitable." Such a message would have a severe impact on one's mating potential. With such high costs, violence could emerge as a viable strategy for defending one's status, or for ascending the status hierarchy, which would provide substantial benefits. Although the adaptive problem of status maintenance differs in large modern societies involving many interactions with people we may never see again, we still carry with us psychological mechanisms that are sensitive to perceived status threats. As Buss (2005) explains:

> Though we may like to believe that societies today respect a man more for walking away from an insult or threat than for confronting it, such insults have powerful consequences, because of the deeply ingrained messages they send, messages our brains have evolved to read. An insult taken without retaliation sends a signal first to the one who hurled the words that he can get away with dominating the one he's offended.... it tells the challenger that he can tread on his victim's turf..., take over his territory, and he can come on to his wife or girlfriend if he chooses.... A challenge left unmet unfortunately also sends these messages to the crowd watching...Witnesses to the challenge may view the insulted person as exploitable, encouraging further infringements on his interests.
> (p. 207)

In short, our evolutionary history has equipped men with a heightened sensitivity to perceived affronts to status and reputation. It is therefore not surprising to see that many male-on-male homicides result from seemingly "trivial altercations" that are best viewed as status contests (Buss, 2005; Daly & Wilson, 1988). These altercations typically involve a man perceiving a slight to his status from another man who refuses to apologize, thus leading to an escalation of violence and, in some cases, homicide (Campbell, 2005).

Despite the overrepresentation of men in statistics regarding violent behavior, it is important to recognize that violence is not an exclusively male behavior. If it were, then we may expect, for example, that only men have homicidal fantasies. In reality, although a greater percentage of male college students in the United States admit to such fantasies (80%), studies have shown that 60% of women admit to having homicidal fantasies as well (Buss, 2005; Kenrick & Sheets, 1993). But the inclusion of women in the world of violence is not limited to fantasies. Although women represent the choosier sex due to their greater parental investment, they still engage in intrasexual competition for the highest quality mates (e.g., men with good genes, men likely to invest in offspring). This intrasexual competition is further necessitated by ecologically or socially imposed monogamy, which increases the choosiness of men looking for mates, particularly when they are looking for long-term mates (Campbell, 2005).

Since the potential costs associated with physical violence are often higher for women than for men, women often opt for other forms of violence when competing for mates. Female intrasexual competition for mates typically involves *indirect* or *relational aggression*, which consists of verbal derogation, gossip, spreading rumors, and other nonphysical forms of ostracism and stigmatization in which the victim is often "attacked" indirectly, thereby reducing the likelihood of retaliation (Björkqvist, Österman, & Lagerspetz, 1994; Campbell & Cross, Chapter 12, this volume). Although a meta-analysis by Archer (2004) suggests that there is little to no sex difference in the use of indirect aggression, the specific contexts in which this aggression is used do seem to differ. For example, women are more likely to gossip negatively about the physical appearance of intrasexual rivals than are men (Brown, 1998; Buss & Dedden, 1990; Simmons, 2002). Given the priority that men place on physical attractiveness in potential mates (Buss, 2003), this proves to be a very effective strategy for derogating one's rivals. Women are also more likely to spread rumors about, or draw attention to, the sexual promiscuity of other women (Campbell, 1982; Campbell & Cross, Chapter 12, this volume). This can be costly for the victim of such indirect aggression because sexual promiscuity serves as a cue to potential infidelity and is therefore an unattractive trait to men looking for a long-term partner. In summary, when women engage in intrasexual competition via indirect aggression, they specifically target traits in their rivals that will decrease their attractiveness to men looking for mates, particularly long-term mates.

Not all violence in the context of mating occurs intrasexually. Male violence directed at women, most often intimate partners, is a phenomenon that must be addressed. Every year, more than half a million women in the United States report being attacked violently by current or former intimate partners, and annual rates of violent victimization of women range from 14% to 16% (Buss & Duntley, 2011). An evolutionary perspective can help explain why such violence occurs (see Camilleri, Chapter 11, this volume; Goetz & Romero, Chapter 4, this volume). As mentioned earlier, humans are unique in the animal kingdom in terms of the substantial investment that men often make in their offspring. However, until the very recent possibility of DNA testing, men could never be certain that their putative offspring were genetically their own. Therefore, the possibility of cuckoldry (i.e., having an unfaithful partner and subsequently investing in genetically unrelated offspring) has represented a serious adaptive problem for men throughout our evolutionary history.

The costs of cuckoldry are severe; not only would a cuckold be increasing the fitness of a rival by investing in his offspring, but the cuckold's own fitness would also suffer as he continues to spend resources that could be allocated to his genetically related offspring (if he has any) or to future offspring. Given contemporary estimates of worldwide cuckoldry that range from 1% to 30% (Goetz, Shackelford, Platek, Starratt, & McKibbin, 2008), it is likely that cuckoldry occurred often enough throughout our evolutionary history to have imposed strong selection pressures on men. Therefore, we should expect male psychology to have been shaped by this adaptive problem, resulting in psychological mechanisms for detecting and preventing cuckoldry. And as we have seen throughout this chapter, when an adaptive problem carries such extraordinary costs, violence may emerge as a viable solution.

To prevent cuckoldry, men are extremely sensitive to the possibility of female sexual infidelity, and cues to infidelity serve as powerful inputs to the psychological mechanisms that evolved in response to this adaptive problem. In fact, men exhibit an overperception of partner infidelity, in that they are generally more likely than women to judge their partners as being unfaithful in the future (Goetz & Causey, 2009). Since false positives (perceiving infidelity when it has not occurred) are less costly to men's fitness than false negatives (not perceiving infidelity when it has occurred), men have evolved mechanisms that generate overperceptions of the possibility of partner infidelity.

Simply perceiving cues to infidelity is not enough to prevent cuckoldry. Such cues initiate sexual jealousy, which in turn motivates behaviors that function to eliminate the threat of cuckoldry. Unfortunately, the behaviors that are motivated can often be violent. Indeed, one of the most frequently cited causes of intimate partner violence, as well as homicide, is male sexual jealousy (Goetz, Shackelford, Romero, Kaighobadi, & Miner, 2008), and men's partner-directed violence is often predicted by men's perceived risk of partner infidelity (Kaighobadi & Shackelford, 2009). Violence can effectively restrict an intimate partner's behavior, thus limiting the possibility of infidelity (Goetz, Shackelford, Romero, et al., 2008). If it is suspected that sexual infidelity occurred recently, men may engage in sexual coercion, thereby minimizing the risk of cuckoldry via sperm competition. This hypothesis is supported by research indicating that men are more likely to engage in sexual coercion when the perceived risk of cuckoldry is high (Goetz & Shackelford, 2006; Lalumière, Harris, Quinsey, & Rice, 2005; Thornhill & Palmer, 2000; Wilson & Daly, 1992). Although these behaviors are clearly abhorrent, they do not appear to be arbitrary or merely a manifestation of men's desire for power and dominance. Rather, they ultimately stem from selection pressures acting on men throughout evolutionary history to minimize the possibility of female sexual infidelity and subsequent cuckoldry.

All in the Family

Of course, not all violence among humans is restricted to the context of mating. As in other species, additional resources besides access to mates (e.g., food, one's time and energy) serve as sources of conflict, and one arena in which such conflicts may occur is within the family. But when discussing violence within families, it is important to consider the genetic relatedness of family members. According to kin selection theory (Hamilton, 1964), organisms should be more altruistic and less competitive toward others as a function of their genetic relatedness. Helping a genetic relative and increasing that person's fitness, even at a cost to oneself, can ultimately be beneficial to the altruist because of the genes he or she shares with the beneficiary. In other words, increasing a genetic relative's fitness will result in some of one's own genes being passed on to future generations, thereby increasing one's *inclusive fitness*. With this important caveat in mind, it is no surprise that a substantial proportion of violence, particularly homicides, within families takes place between individuals who are *not* genetically related (Campbell, 2005). For example, among 508 Detroit homicides in 1972, 25% occurred between relatives, but only 6.3% involved genetic relatives, a pattern found consistently across societies and time periods (Daly & Wilson, 1988). However, even though these findings are consistent with kin selection theory, they also illustrate that genetic relatedness does not always prevent violence.

Despite the lower levels of competition between genetic relatives predicted by kin selection theory, competition and violence do occur. Since genetic relatives (identical twins notwithstanding) only share a portion of their genes with each other, conflicts of interest are expected, with violence sometimes occurring as a result. One example of such conflict is that between siblings. Sibling violence is the most common type of nonlethal violence within families (Wiehe, 1997). Siblings compete with each other for limited parental resources. Throughout human evolutionary history, and in many other species, the primary resource competed over would be food, but in contemporary societies siblings most often compete for time, attention, and money (see Salmon, Chapter 7, this volume). This competition can often turn violent, with 74% of children pushing and shoving their siblings and 42% kicking, biting, or punching their siblings, according to a recent national study of family violence (Straus, Gelles, & Steinmetz, 2006). Violence between siblings is more likely to occur the closer they are to each other in terms of age, and also if they are the same sex (Sulloway, 1996). This may be due to the fact that siblings of the same sex and similar age desire similar resources. Violence between siblings, especially older male siblings, can sometimes escalate to homicide, although the murder of a sibling (i.e., siblicide) is rare, accounting for roughly 1% of homicides in the United States (Underwood & Patch, 1999).

Another form of within-family violence occurs between parents and offspring. As explained earlier, women must invest heavily in their offspring, and this investment is obligatory. The high costs of maternal investment can also help explain a particularly abhorrent example of within-family violence: filicide (see Harris & Rice, Chapter 6, this volume). The murder of one's children, particularly newborns (i.e., infanticide), is one of the few cases of extreme violence that is perpetrated by women more often than men (Bourget, Grace, & Whitehurst, 2007). Given the high costs associated with investing in offspring, female psychology is likely to have been shaped in such a way as to forego paying these costs when the desired outcome of investment (i.e., a reproductively capable adult) is unlikely to occur. Examples of such a situation include low infant quality (e.g., deformities or illness) or a lack of adequate resources for investment (e.g., poverty, absence of male support, investment in older offspring), and Daly and Wilson (1988) have found that these contexts predict maternal infanticide across cultures.

As children get older, the possibility of filicide being perpetrated by the mother decreases substantially, which makes sense given how much the mother has already invested in the child. Indeed, women who kill their older children are often diagnosed with mental illness (Harris, Hilton, Rice, & Eke, 2007). However, children are still at risk from other members of the family, particularly stepparents. Although most stepparents do not perpetrate violence against their stepchildren, the presence of a stepparent in the home is the single largest predictor of child abuse and filicide, with preschool-aged stepchildren suffering from a risk of filicide that is 40 to 100 times higher than children living with their genetic parents (Daly & Wilson, 1988). The lack of genetic relatedness most likely plays an important role, and this finding powerfully illustrates the importance of applying an evolutionary perspective to violence, since the presence of stepparents was not identified as a risk factor until child abuse was studied by evolutionary psychologists (Buss, 2011).

Finally, perhaps the most difficult violence to explain from an evolutionary perspective occurs when there are seemingly no conflicts of interest: taking one's own life. Admittedly, some cases of suicide, particularly those committed after perpetrating familial homicide, can best be explained as a result of mental illness (see Liem, Chapter 8, this volume). However, even though there initially appears to be no evolutionary logic underlying suicide, this assumption falls apart upon closer inspection (see Brown & Brown, Chapter 9, this volume). For example, *attempted* suicide is often described as "a cry for help," and it is feasible that such behavior may have been selected for as a strategy for leveraging resources and help from social partners (Watson & Andrews, 2002) or investment from parents in the case of adolescents (Andrews, 2006). The costliness of such a strategy may be advantageous in that it serves as an honest signal of one's need for help. Evidence consistent with this hypothesis includes the observations that those who deliberately harm themselves often have needs that have been unmet, have difficulty communicating their needs to others, and ultimately benefit from self-harm by receiving more attention and help from others (Hagen, Watson, & Hammerstein, 2008).

As for those who go beyond self-harm and commit suicide, there is clearly no direct benefit to the individual, but this behavior could have been selected for based on benefits to one's inclusive fitness. If one's reproductive potential is very low, then the possibility of passing on one's genes depends on the reproductive success of one's genetic relatives. However, if one also happens to be a burden to genetic relatives, his or her potential for reproductive success may be diminished. Therefore, the combination of low reproductive potential and burdensomeness to genetic relatives represents a scenario in which suicide may increase the potential for a portion of one's genes to be passed on to future generations (deCatanzaro, 1986). In short, suicide may improve inclusive fitness in specific situations, thereby leading to the selection of genes involved in the act of suicide, which has a heritability of roughly 40% (McGuffin, Marusic, & Farmer, 2001). Consistent with this hypothesis, many studies of suicide and the risk of suicide have discovered an association with factors related to low reproductive potential (e.g., old age, low family income, low fertility) and burdensomeness to genetic relatives (e.g., as self-reported, as rated by clinicians, as documented in suicide notes) (Calzeroni, Conte, Pennati, & Vita, 1990; Goodman, 1999; Joiner et al., 2002, 2003; Motto & Bostrom, 1990; World Health Organization, 2010).

That Atrocity of Atrocities, War

Man is the only animal that deals in that atrocity of atrocities, War. He is the only one that gathers his brethren about him and goes forth in cold blood and calm pulse to exterminate his kind. He is the only animal that for sordid wages will march out... and help to slaughter strangers of his own species who have done him no harm and with whom he has no quarrel.... And in the intervals between campaigns he washes the blood off his hands and works for "the universal brotherhood of man"—with his mouth.
—*Mark Twain*, 1896/1992, p. 210

Any comprehensive discussion of human violence would be incomplete without an analysis of war. Although it is difficult to determine when humans began engaging in warfare, the raiding behavior of chimpanzees suggests that warlike behaviors have been a part of the human behavioral repertoire for the majority of, if not the entirety of, our evolutionary history. However, as the Twain quote illustrates, humans engage in warfare on a scale that is unmatched throughout the rest of the animal kingdom. This increase in scale was likely set into motion when humans shifted from nomadic lifestyles to living in permanent settlements. As settlements and their stockpiled resources grew, the benefits of conquering neighboring settlements increased, as did the potential costs associated with increasing defenses. Indeed, archaeological evidence of Native American settlements indicates that increased defense was related to geographic regions and time periods marked by resource scarcity and climatic unpredictability, factors that would have served as an impetus for warfare in order to plunder precious resources from rival settlements (Lambert, Chapter 19, this volume; LeBlanc, 1999).

Engaging in war, whether it occurs between tribes or countries, is almost exclusively a male enterprise (see Browne, Chapter 22, this volume; Van Vugt, Chapter 17, this volume). There are several factors that can help explain this, such as the differential costs of violence for men and women due to differences in parental investment, increased mating opportunities that result from controlling resources and territory (van der Dennen, 1995), and access to mates from the defeated rival's community (Campbell, 2005). The link between warfare and mating is further supported by the recent finding that men, but not women, are more likely to endorse war-supporting statements when exposed to photographs of attractive members of the opposite sex (Chang, Lu, Li, & Li, 2011). In short, the potential benefits of warfare have been greater for men than for women throughout our evolutionary history, whereas the potential costs have been greater for women than for men. This created a selection pressure for men to be capable of forming alliances with other men in order to engage in coalitional aggression, with the goal of acquiring or defending resources relevant to survival and reproduction.

The ability to form cohesive male coalitions and successfully attack rivals is also dependent on a clearly perceived distinction between the ingroup and outgroup, along with ingroup amity and outgroup enmity (Durrant, 2011). Humans likely inherited this capacity from a much earlier ancestor, because as Smith (2007) explains, "Contact with a stranger of the same species is the most potent trigger for aggressive behavior among nonhuman animals, and it has been observed in virtually every species with complex social lives" (p. 74). However, studies indicate that men are more likely to display racism and xenophobia than women, particularly in threatening situations (Gerard & Hoyt, 1974; Schaller, Park, & Mueller, 2003).Thus, male perceptions of outgroups seem to be particularly tuned to facilitate intergroup aggression.

Despite the potential benefits of engaging in war and male psychological predispositions that facilitate going to war, the potential injury and loss of life still represent substantial costs that are likely to select against such behavior unless certain conditions are met to offset these costs. Tooby and Cosmides (1988) have argued that there are at least four such conditions: (1) average long-term gains in reproductive resources outweigh the reproductive costs of war; (2) the belief that one's group will be victorious; (3) receiving benefits commensurate with one's contribution and degree of risk taken; and (4) an inability to accurately predict which group members will live or die. In short, conditions that increase the perceived benefits and decrease the perceived costs will facilitate the willingness of men to engage in warfare.

Individual and Cultural Differences in Violence

The evolutionary accounts of human violence discussed thus far have not adequately addressed the issue of individual differences. For example, even though men are more predisposed to behave violently than women in particular contexts, it is not the case that *every* man will react with violence when insulted in public or when catching his partner with another man. Evolutionary psychology is often focused on identifying adaptations that are either "universal" among humans or sex specific, and for a long time individual differences were ignored or viewed as unimportant. In recent years, however, evolutionary psychologists have begun to acknowledge the importance of individual differences. Progress is being made in regard to explaining individual differences from an evolutionary perspective (see Buss, 2009), and this progress also applies to individual differences in violent behavior.

Life history theory provides a powerful framework for understanding individual differences from an evolutionary perspective, and it is based on the premise that organisms face trade-offs when deciding how to allocate their time, energy, and other resources to various aspects of survival and reproduction, because these resources are finite (Kruger & Fitzgerald, Chapter 10, this volume; Stearns, 1992). There is no single strategy of allocation that is optimal, and thus individual differences are to be expected as a result of different ecological conditions and ontogenetic experiences. The trade-offs most relevant to understanding individual differences in violence are those between current and future reproduction, and between quantity of offspring and investment in offspring. When organisms opt to produce a large quantity of offspring with little investment in each, they are also prone to engage in riskier behavior, including violence, in order to successfully compete with intrasexual rivals and secure mating opportunities. Not surprisingly, the males of most species are more likely to engage in this "r-selected," or fast, life history strategy, than females, who generally provide greater obligatory investment in offspring and thus engage in a "K-selected," or slow, life history strategy by default (Stearns, 1992).

These strategies are not fixed across an organism's life span. For example, men are most likely to engage in a fast strategy during young adulthood, defined by the peak of risky and violent behavior in this age group (Kruger & Nesse, 2006). Across species, the preferred strategy varies as a function of unpredictability in the environment, with uncertain conditions fostering a fast strategy. The logic behind this is that one's prospects for reproductive success in the future are uncertain, so the best strategy is to allocate resources to mating effort now. This logic can also explain individual differences in human violence, particularly among men. In the United States, the sex difference in mortality rates is higher for those in lower income groups and those with low educational attainment, both factors that influence one's certainty of future success (Kruger & Nesse, 2006). Across societies, male mortality is disproportionally higher when economic inequality is greater (Kruger, 2010). The effect of an uncertain future on violence can also be seen when examining the economic transitions that took place in Central and Eastern Europe in the 1990s. The transition from the socialist period to market economies resulted in greater variance in social status and resource acquisition, and it also resulted in increased sex differences in mortality rates (Kruger & Nesse, 2007). When the future is uncertain, men seem to engage in more risky and violent behavior, which suggests that they are engaging in greater intrasexual competition in order to increase their current reproductive success.

As some of the earlier examples illustrate, environmental conditions can produce differences in violence at the societal level. Another environmental factor that can help explain differences in violence, particularly intergroup violence, between societies is parasite prevalence (see Letendre, Fincher, & Thornhill, Chapter 21, this volume). Throughout our evolutionary history, parasites have constituted a serious adaptive problem, resulting in an evolutionary arms race between the ability of humans to resist infection from local parasites and the ability of local parasites to bypass this resistance. The adaptive problem of parasites has additionally resulted in selection pressures on human psychology to produce behaviors that help one avoid infection. Fincher, Thornhill, and colleagues have developed the parasite stress model, which posits evolved psychological mechanisms that assess parasite prevalence in the surrounding region and, based on this assessment, motivate behaviors that manage the risk of exposure. More specifically, in regions of high parasite stress, humans are likely to embrace values that minimize interaction with outgroup members, such as collectivism, ethnocentrism, and xenophobia (Fincher, Thornhill, Murray, & Schaller, 2008).

Unfortunately, this adaptive response reduces the possibility of cooperation between groups in regions of high parasite stress and increases the likelihood of autocracies (Thornhill, Fincher, & Aran, 2009; Thornhill, Fincher, Murray, & Schaller, 2010). As a result, such collectivist societies often suffer from poverty and inequality, which leads to within-state fractionation and violence in competition for resources. An analysis of two data sets on intrastate armed conflict around the world confirmed that pathogen stress positively predicts the frequency of such violence, from small-scale conflicts to large-scale civil wars (Letendre, Fincher, & Thornhill, 2010; Letendre et al., Chapter 21, this volume).

Cultural values can play an important role in societal differences in violence, and another example of this effect can be found among "cultures of honor" (see Brown & Osterman, Chapter 13, this volume).

In cultures of honor, which have been documented throughout the world (Daly & Wilson, 1988), the male predisposition to defend one's status and reputation with violence is strengthened. Men from cultures of honor are not more violent in general, but they are more likely to resort to violence when they perceive an intrasexual threat to their status (Cohen & Nisbett, 1994).

A prime example of the culture of honor consists of White men from the southern United States, who exhibit a higher homicide rate than White Northerners in relation to "trivial altercations" concerning one's reputation (Nisbet, 1993). White Southern males are primarily descended from Ulster Scots, who settled in the region during the 18th and 19th centuries. Cultures of honor are most likely to manifest in response to long periods of resource deprivation, a strong likelihood of a man's resources being thieved by other men, and the lack of a strong governing body or law enforcement to prevent thievery (Shackelford, 2005). Ulster Scots suffered these conditions between roughly 1000 and 1750 A.D. (Fischer, 1989). They also faced similar conditions in the southern United States because they primarily engaged in herding, which involved a greater potential for theft compared to the northern emphasis on farming. Furthermore, the South was marked by weak law enforcement and state power well into the 19th century (Shackelford, 2005). Although these facts can explain why the culture of honor originated in the South, additional research is needed to better understand why these cultural values persist in the present day.

Another aspect of culture that deserves consideration when discussing societal differences in violence is religion. Although a discussion of whether religion is ultimately a positive or negative influence on humanity is beyond the scope of this chapter, we would be remiss if we did not reference the extreme acts of violence that have been committed in the name of one religion or another throughout human history, such as the Crusades and other military conquests, the Inquisitions, subjugation and oppression of women (see Hartung, Chapter 5, this volume), and acts of terrorism that are often motivated, at least in part, by religious beliefs (Liddle et al., 2010; Sosis, Phillips, & Alcorta, Chapter 14, this volume). In addition to these examples, it is important to note that one's religion often serves as a powerful source of ingroup identity, thus marking all of those who do not share one's beliefs as the outgroup. Although this can result in increased prosociality among ingroup members, it is unlikely to increase prosociality toward outgroup members unless one can improve his or her reputation by engaging in such behavior (Norenzayan & Shariff, 2008). Despite certain religious scriptures that may profess the unity of all humankind, our psychological predispositions to ingroup amity and outgroup enmity are difficult to override (see Cikara, Bruneau, & Saxe, 2011). This heightened perception of the ingroup and outgroup may partially explain why largely irreligious societies are less likely to go to war, especially unprovoked war (see Paul, Chapter 25, this volume), although additional research must be done to determine whether there is any causal relationship.

Conclusion

Violence exists in a variety of forms and is elicited by a variety of contexts and inputs. Violent behaviors in humans and other animals are not arbitrary; rather, they appear to have been selected for to solve particular adaptive problems. In a broad sense, violence can be viewed as a strategy employed in the competition for resources. The scope and severity of violent behaviors are largely dependent on what resource is being competed for, who the competitors are, and the costs and benefits of engaging in violence in the particular context. Although this is an oversimplification, it illustrates that there is an evolutionary logic to be found behind most acts of violence, and acknowledging this is an important step toward better understanding why violence occurs.

Despite the accounts of violence described throughout this chapter, it should be noted that humans and many other species also have a tremendous capacity for cooperation. Far more time is spent engaging in cooperation, or at least peaceful coexistence, than is spent engaging in violence. But when violence does occur, it can often overshadow our altruistic side. This should not be misinterpreted as suggesting that we are "naturally good" and that violence represents a deviation from human nature. We are not naturally good or naturally evil; we are both. Our ancestors, the unbroken line of individuals who successfully passed on their genes to future generations eventually leading to us, are those who successfully used violence *and* cooperation to solve specific adaptive problems. Violence and cooperation, in their myriad forms, represent the output of evolved psychological mechanisms.

It is important to keep in mind that just because violence may be "natural," that does not serve as a justification for such behavior. We must avoid committing the naturalistic fallacy and concluding that people today ought to be violent because it served an adaptive purpose for our ancestors, or even if it continues to serve an adaptive purpose today. We also need to remember that an evolutionary explanation for violence does not imply that such behavior is inevitable or impossible to prevent. By studying violence from an evolutionary perspective, analyzing the contexts in which it occurs and the stimuli that influence its occurrence, we can gain a better understanding of the mechanisms that produce violence, thus putting us in a better position to limit the activation of such mechanisms.

Future Directions

Studying violence from an evolutionary perspective requires focusing on a multitude of contexts in an attempt to pinpoint the specific inputs that are likely to activate the psychological mechanisms that generate violent behaviors. Given the variety of violent behaviors in which humans and other animals engage, along with the various stimuli that elicit these behaviors, the possibilities for future research are vast. In regard to the examples of violence that were addressed throughout this chapter, the evolutionary explanations offered here are by no means the final say on why these specific acts of violence occur. Additional research is needed to understand the specific inputs that activate violence-producing mechanisms and to unravel the complex interactions between environmental stimuli (including one's experiences throughout development) and one's genotype. Furthermore, it is important to gain a better understanding of how violence affects those who witness it, particularly the developmental effects of exposure to violence (see Belsky, Chapter 23, this volume).

Although male violence against intimate partners has garnered more attention by evolutionary psychologists and the social sciences in general, female violence against intimate partners must also be addressed (see Campbell & Cross, Chapter 12, this volume). In fact, women initiate both verbal and physical attacks on their partners at higher rates than do men (DeMaris, 1992; de Weerth & Kalma, 1993). The evolutionary logic behind this behavior must diverge to some degree from male-perpetrated intimate partner violence, which is driven in large part by paternity uncertainty and the threat of cuckoldry. Therefore, researchers must focus on identifying the contexts in which female-perpetrated intimate partner violence takes place and determining whether such behavior serves (or may have served at some point in our evolutionary history) an adaptive purpose.

The issue of whether violence constitutes an adaptation is particularly contentious with regard to homicide. Although some evolutionary psychologists have attempted to explain homicide as a "slip up" of psychological mechanisms designed to produce nonlethal violence (Daly & Wilson, 1988; Kenrick & Sheets, 1993), others argue that some homicides are the result of mechanisms designed specifically for producing lethal violence (Duntley & Buss, 2011). Although both camps agree that neither explanation can apply to *all* cases of homicide, additional research must be conducted to determine which homicides perpetrated by humans support the by-product theory and which support the adaptation theory. One potential method may be to investigate any genetic differences between individuals who have committed a particular form of violent behavior and those who have not. Although it is difficult to uncover the genetic foundations of complex behaviors, researchers have had some success in linking genes to violence, aggression, and other antisocial behaviors (see Ferguson & Beaver, 2009).

Finally, as important as it is to apply an evolutionary perspective to violence, we must also work toward an evolutionary psychological understanding of peace (see Dess, Chapter 26, this volume). As we noted earlier, despite the human capacity for violence, we also have a capacity for cooperation and peace, and we should attempt to gain a better understanding of the psychological mechanisms that generate such behavior, particularly by identifying the contexts in which peaceful coexistence is most likely to occur. For example, the weakening of male dominance hierarchies appears to play an important role in diminishing intergroup conflicts, presumably by weakening the control and coercion of females and promoting the development of democracy (see Hudson & den Boer, Chapter 18, this volume). By further investigating this phenomenon and other factors that appear to be related to the emergence of peace, we may learn what global changes are needed to increase the likelihood of peaceful interactions throughout the world.

References

Andrews, P. W. (2006). Parent-offspring conflict and cost-benefit analysis in adolescent suicidal behavior: Effects of birth order and dissatisfaction with mother on attempt incidence and severity. *Human Nature, 17*, 190–211.

Archer, J. (2004). Sex differences in aggression in real world settings: A meta-analytic review. *Review of General Psychology, 8*, 291–322.

Björkqvist, K., Österman, K., & Lagerspetz, K. M. J. (1994). Sex differences in covert aggression among adults. *Aggressive Behavior, 20*, 27–33.

Blaustein, A. R., & Risser, A. C. (1976). Interspecific interactions between three sympatric species of kangaroo rats (*Dipodomys*). *Animal Behaviour, 24*, 381–385.

Bourget, D., Grace, J., & Whitehurst, L. (2007). A review of maternal and paternal filicide. *Journal of the American Academy of Psychiatry and Law, 35*, 74–82.

Bowles, S. (2006). Group competition, reproductive leveling, and the evolution of human altruism. *Science, 314*, 1569–1572.

Boydston, E. E., Morelli, T. L., & Holekamp, K. E. (2001). Sex differences in territorial behavior exhibited by the spotted hyena (*Hyeanidae, Crocuta crocuta*). *Ethology, 107*, 369–385.

Brown, L. M. (1998). *Raising their voices: The politics of girls' anger*. London: Harvard University Press.

Bryant, G. A. (2006). On hasty generalization about evolutionary psychology: A review of David Buller, *Adapting minds: Evolutionary psychology and the persistent quest for human nature*. *American Journal of Psychology, 119*, 481–487.

Buss, D. M. (2003). *The evolution of desire: Strategies of human mating* (Rev. ed.). New York: Basic Books.

Buss, D. M. (2005). *The murderer next door: Why the mind is designed to kill*. New York: Penguin.

Buss, D. M. (2009). How can evolutionary psychology successfully explain personality and individual differences? *Perspectives on Psychological Science, 4*, 359–366.

Buss, D. M. (2011). *Evolutionary psychology: The new science of the mind* (4th ed.). Boston: Pearson.

Buss, D. M., & Dedden, L. A. (1990). Derogation of competitors. *Journal of Personal and Social Relationships, 7*, 395–422.

Buss, D. M., & Duntley, J. D. (2011). The evolution of intimate partner violence. *Aggression and Violent Behavior, 16*, 411–419.

Buss, D. M., & Shackelford, T. K. (1997). Human aggression in evolutionary psychological perspective. *Clinical Psychology Review, 17*, 605–619.

Calzeroni, A., Conte, G., Pennati, A., & Vita, A. (1990). Celibacy and fertility rates in patients with major affective disorders: The relevance of delusional symptoms and suicidal behavior. *Acta Psychiatrica Scandinavia, 82*, 309–310.

Campbell, A. (1982). Female aggression. In P. Marsh & A. Campbell (Eds.), *Aggression and violence* (pp. 137–150). Oxford, England: Blackwell.

Campbell, A. (1993). *Men, women, and aggression*. New York: Basic Books.

Campbell, A. (2005). Aggression. In D. M. Buss (Ed.), *The handbook of evolutionary psychology* (pp. 628–652). Hoboken, NJ: Wiley.

Cartwright, J. (2000). *Evolution and human behavior: Darwinian perspectives on human nature*. Cambridge, MA: MIT Press.

Chagnon, N. A. (1988). Life histories, blood revenge, and warfare in a tribal population. *Science, 239*, 985–992.

Chagnon, N. A. (1992). *Yanomamö* (4th ed.). Fort Worth, TX: Harcourt Brace Jovanovich.

Chang, L., Lu, H. J., Li, H., & Li, T. (2011). The face that launched a thousand ships: The mating-warring association in men. *Personality and Social Psychology Bulletin, 37*, 976–984.

Cikara, M., Bruneau, E. G., & Saxe, R. R. (2011). Us and them: Intergroup failures of empathy. *Current Directions in Psychological Science, 20*, 149–153.

Clutton-Brock, T. H., & Albon, S. D. (1982). Winter mortality in red deer (*Cervus elaphus*). *Journal of Zoology, 198*, 515–519.

Cohen, D., & Nisbett, R. E. (1994). Self-protection and the culture of honor: Explaining Southern homicide. *Personality and Social Psychology Bulletin, 20*, 551–567.

Confer, J. C., Easton, J. E., Fleischman, D. S., Goetz, C., Lewis, D. M., Perilloux, C., & Buss, D. M. (2010). Evolutionary psychology: Controversies, questions, prospects, and limitations. *American Psychologist, 65*, 110–126.

Connolly, J., Pepler, D., Craig, W., & Taradash, A. (2000). Dating experiences of bullies in early adolescence. *Child Maltreatment, 5*, 299–310.

Cornwell, R. E., Palmer, C., Guinther, P. M., & Davis, H. P. (2005). Introductory psychology texts as a view of sociobiology/evolutionary psychology's role in psychology. *Evolutionary Psychology, 3*, 355–374.

Coyne, J. (2009). *Why evolution is true*. New York: Viking Penguin.

Creel, S., & Creel, N. M. (2002). *The African wild dog: Behavior, ecology, and conservation*. Princeton, NJ: Princeton University Press.

Dahlberg, L. L., & Krug, E. G. (2002). Violence—a global public health problem. In E. G. Krug, L. L. Dahlberg, J. A. Mercy, A. B. Zwi, & R. Lozano (Eds.), *World report on violence and health* (pp. 1–22). Geneva, Switzerland: World Health Organization.

Daly, M., & Wilson, M. (1988). *Homicide*. New York: Aldine de Gruyter.

Darwin, C. (1859). *On the origin of species by means of natural selection*. London: John Murray.

Darwin, C. (1871). *The descent of man, and selection in relation to sex*. London: John Murray.

deCarvalho, T. N., Watson, P. J., & Field, S. A. (2004). Costs increase as ritualized fighting progresses within and between phases in the sierra dome spider, *Neriene litigiosa*. *Animal Behaviour, 68*, 473–482.

deCatanzaro, D. (1986). A mathematical model of evolutionary pressures regulating self-preservation and self-destruction. *Suicide and Life-Threatening Behavior, 16*, 166–181.

DeMaris, A. (1992). Male versus female initiation of aggression. In E. C. Viano (Ed.), *Intimate violence: International perspectives* (pp. 111–120). Washington, DC: Hemisphere.

de Weerth, C., & Kalma, A. P. (1993). Female aggression as a response to sexual jealousy: A sex role reversal? *Aggressive Behavior, 19*, 265–279.

Diamond, J. (1997). *Guns, germs, and steel: The fates of human societies*. New York: W.W. Norton.

Duntley, J. D., & Buss, D. M. (2011). Homicide adaptations. *Aggression and Violent Behavior, 16*, 399–410.

Durrant, R. (2011). Collective violence: An evolutionary perspective. *Aggression and Violent Behavior, 16*, 428–236.

Ellis, B. J., & Bjorklund, D. F. (Eds.) (2005). *Origins of the social mind: Evolutionary psychology and child development*. New York: Guilford Press.

Ferguson, C. J., & Beaver, K. M. (2009). Natural born killers: The genetic origins of extreme violence. *Aggression and Violent Behavior, 14*, 286–294.

Ferguson, C. J., & Kilburn, J. (2009). The public health risks of media violence: A meta-analytic review. *The Journal of Pediatrics, 154*, 759–763.

Ferguson, R. B. (1997). Violence and war in prehistory. In D. L. Martin & D. W. Frayer (Eds.), *Troubled times: Violence and war in the past. War and society* (Vol. 3, pp. 321–356). Amsterdam: Gordon Breach.

Fincher, C. L., Thornhill, R., Murray, D. R., & Schaller, M. (2008). Pathogen prevalence predicts human cross-cultural variability in individualism/collectivism. *Proceedings of the Royal Society of London B, 275*, 1279–1285.

Fischer, D. H. (1989). *Albion's seed: Four British folkways in America*. New York: Oxford University Press.

Fossey, D. (1984). Mountain gorilla research, 1977–1979. *National Geographic Society Research Reports, 1976 Projects*, 363–412.

Geher, G. (2006). Evolutionary psychology is not evil! (... And here's why...). *Psychological Topics, 15*, 181–202.

Gerard, H., & Hoyt, M. F. (1974). Distinctiveness of social categorization and attitude toward in-group members. *Journal of Personality and Social Psychology, 29*, 836–842.

Ghiglieri, M. P. (1999). *The dark side of man: Tracing the origins of male violence*. New York: Basic Books.

Goetz, A. T., & Causey, K. (2009). Sex differences in perceptions of infidelity: Men often assume the worst. *Evolutionary Psychology, 7*, 253–263.

Goetz, A. T., & Shackelford, T. K. (2006). Sexual coercion and forced in-pair copulation as sperm competition tactics in humans. *Human Nature, 17*, 265–282.

Goetz, A. T., Shackelford, T. K., Platek, S. M., Starratt, V. G., & McKibbin, W. F. (2008). Sperm competition in humans: Implications for male sexual psychology, physiology, anatomy, and behavior. *Annual Review of Sex Research, 18*, 1–22.

Goetz, A. T., Shackelford, T. K., Romero, G. A., Kaighobadi, F., & Miner, E. J. (2008). Punishment, proprietariness, and paternity: Men's violence against women from an evolutionary perspective. *Aggression and Violent Behavior, 13*, 481–489.

Goetz, A. T., Shackelford, T. K., Starratt, V. G., & McKibbin, W. F. (2008). Intimate partner violence. In J. D. Duntley & T. K. Shackelford (Eds.), *Evolutionary forensic psychology: Darwinian foundations of crime and law* (pp. 65–78). New York: Oxford University Press.

Goodall, J. (1979). Life and death at Gombe. *National Geographic, 155*, 592–621.

Goodall, J. (1986). *The chimpanzees of Gombe*. Boston: Houghton Mifflin.

Goodman, E. (1999). The role of socioeconomic status gradients in explaining differences in US adolescents' health. *American Journal of Public Health, 89*, 1522–1528.

Gottschall, J. (2008). *The rape of Troy: Evolution, violence, and the world of Homer*. Cambridge, MA: Cambridge University Press.

Grinnell, J., Packer, C., & Pusey, A. (1995). Cooperation in male lions: Kinship, reciprocity or mutualism? *Animal Behaviour, 49*, 95–105.

Hagen, E. H. (2005). Controversial issues in evolutionary psychology. In D. M. Buss (Ed.), *The handbook of evolutionary psychology* (pp. 145–173). Hoboken, NJ: Wiley.

Hagen, E. H., Watson, P. J., & Hammerstein, P. (2008). Gestures of despair and hope: A view on deliberate self-harm from economics and evolutionary biology. *Biological Theory, 3*, 123–138.

Haley, M. P. (1994). Resource-holding power asymmetries, the prior residence effect, and reproductive payoffs in male northern elephant seal fights. *Behavioral Ecology and Sociobiology, 34*, 427–434.

Hamilton, W. D. (1964). The genetical evolution of social behaviour, I and II. *Journal of Theoretical Biology, 7*, 1–52.

Harris, G.T., Hilton, N.Z., Rice, M.E., & Eke, A.W. (2007). Children killed by genetic parents versus stepparents. *Evolution and Human Behavior*, 28, 85–95.

Harris, T. R. (2006). Between-group contest competition for food in a highly folivorous population of black and white colobus monkeys (*Colobus guereza*). *Behavioral Ecology and Sociobiology*, 61, 317–329.

Hongo, Y. (2003). Appraising behaviour during male-male interaction in the Japanese horned beetle *Trypoxylus dichotomus septentrionalis* (Kono). *Behaviour*, 140, 501–517.

Hrdy, S. B. (1977). Infanticide as a primate reproductive strategy. *American Scientist*, 65, 40–49.

Hrdy, S. B. (1979). Infanticide among animals: A review, classification, and examination of the implications for the reproductive strategies of females. *Ethology and Sociobiology*, 1, 13–40.

Hrdy, S. B. (2000). *Mother nature: Maternal instincts and how they shape the human species*. New York: Ballantine Books.

Janson, C. H., & van Schaik, C. P. (2000). The behavioral ecology of infanticide by males. In C. P. van Schaik & C. H. Janson (Eds.), *Infanticide in males and its implications* (pp. 469–494). Cambridge, MA: Cambridge University Press.

Joiner, T. E., Pettit, J. W., Walker, R. L., Voelz, Z. R., Cruz, J., Rudd, M. D., & Lester, D. (2002). Perceived burdensomeness and suicidality: Two studies on the suicide notes of those attempting and those completing suicide. *Journal of Social and Clinical Psychology*, 21, 531–545.

Joiner, T. E., Steer, R. A., Brown, G., Beck, A. T., Pettit, J. W., & Rudd, M. D. (2003). Worst-point suicidal plans: A dimension of suicidality predictive of past suicidal attempts and eventual death by suicide. *Behaviour Research and Therapy*, 41, 1469–1480.

Kaighobadi, F., & Shackelford, T. K. (2009). Suspicions of female infidelity predict men's partner-directed violence. *Behavioral and Brain Sciences*, 32, 281–282.

Keeley, L. H. (1996). *War before civilization: The myth of the peaceful savage*. New York: Oxford University Press.

Kenrick, D. T., Neuberg, S. L., & Cialdini, R. B. (2009). *Social psychology: Goals in interaction* (5th ed.). Boston: Allyn & Bacon.

Kenrick, D. T., & Sheets, V. (1993). Homicidal fantasies. *Ethology and Sociobiology*, 14, 231–246.

Ketelaar, T., & Ellis, B. J. (2000). Are evolutionary explanations unfalsifiable? Evolutionary psychology and the Lakatosian philosophy of science. *Psychological Inquiry*, 11, 1–21.

Kruger, D. J. (2010). Socio-demographic factors intensifying male mating competition exacerbate male mortality rates. *Evolutionary Psychology*, 8, 194–204.

Kruger, D. J., & Nesse, R. M. (2006). An evolutionary life-history framework for understanding sex differences in human mortality rates. *Human Nature*, 17, 74–97.

Kruger, D. J., & Nesse, R. M. (2007). Economic transition, male competition, and sex differences in mortality rates. *Evolutionary Psychology*, 5, 411–427.

Kurzban, R. (2002). Alas poor evolutionary psychology: Unfairly accused, unjustly condemned. *Human Nature Review*, 2, 99–109.

Lalumière, M. L., Harris, G. T., Quinsey, V. L., & Rice, M. E. (2005). *The causes of rape: Understanding individual differences in male propensity for sexual aggression*. Washington, DC: APA Press.

LeBlanc, S. A. (1999). *Prehistoric warfare in the American Southwest*. Salt Lake City: University of Utah Press.

Leland, L., Struhsaker, T. T., & Butynski, T. M. (1984). Infanticide by adult males in three primate species of the Kibale forest, Uganda: A test of hypotheses. In G. Hausfater & S. Hrdy (Eds.), *Infanticide: Comparative and evolutionary perspectives* (pp. 151–172). New York: Aldine.

Lester, D. (1991). *Questions and answers about murder*. Philadelphia: Charles Press.

Letendre, K., Fincher, C. L. & Thornhill, R. (2010). Does infectious disease cause global variation in the frequency of intrastate armed conflict and civil war? *Biological Reviews*, 85, 669–683.

Liddle, J. R., Bush, L. S., & Shackelford, T. K. (2011). An introduction to evolutionary psychology and its application to suicide terrorism. *Behavioral Sciences of Terrorism and Political Aggression*, 3, 176–197.

Liddle, J. R., & Shackelford, T. K. (2009). Why evolutionary psychology is "true." A review of Jerry Coyne, *Why evolution is true*. *Evolutionary Psychology*, 7, 288–294.

Liddle, J. R., Shackelford, T. K., & Weekes-Shackelford, V. A. (2012). Why can't we all just get along? Evolutionary perspectives on violence, homicide, and war. *Review of General Psychology*, 16, 24-36.

Maynard-Smith, J., & Price, G. R. (1973). The logic of animal conflict. *Nature*, 246, 15–18.

McGuffin, P., Marusic, A., & Farmer, A. (2001). What can psychiatric genetics offer suicidology? *Crisis*, 22, 61–65.

McKibbin, W. F., & Shackelford, T. K. (2011). Women's avoidance of rape. *Aggression and Violent Behavior*, 16, 437–433.

Mech, L. D. (1977). Productivity, mortality, and population trends of wolves in northeastern Minnesota. *Journal of Mammalogy*, 58, 559–574.

Mech, L. D., Adams, L. G., Meier, T. J., Burch, J. W., & Dale, B. W. (1998). *The wolves of Denali*. Minneapolis: University of Minnesota Press.

Mock, D. W. (1984). Infanticide, siblicide, and avian nesting mortality. In G. Hausfater & S. Hrdy (Eds.), *Infanticide: Comparative and evolutionary perspectives* (pp. 3–30). New York: Aldine.

Mosser, A., & Packer, C. (2009). Group territoriality and the benefits of sociality in the African lion, Panthera leo. *Animal Behaviour*, 78, 359–370.

Motto, J. A., & Bostrom, A. (1990). Empirical indicators of near-term suicide risk. *Crisis*, 11, 52–59.

Muller, M. (2007). Chimpanzee violence: Femmes fatales. *Current Biology*, 17, R365–R366.

Nilsson, D. E., & Pelger, S. (1994). A pessimistic estimate of the time required for an eye to evolve. *Proceedings of the Royal Society of London B*, 256, 53–58.

Nisbett, R. E. (1993). Violence and U. S. regional culture. *American Psychologist*, 48, 441–449.

Norenzayan, A., & Shariff, A. F. (2008). The origin and evolution of religious prosociality. *Science*, 322, 58–62.

Öhman, A., & Mineka, S. (2001). Fears, phobias, and preparedness: Toward an evolved module of fear and fear learning. *Psychological Review*, 108, 483–522.

Olweus, D. (1978). *Aggression in schools*. New York: Wiley.

Palmer, C. T., & Tilly, C. F. (1995). Sexual access to females as a motivation for joining gangs: An evolutionary approach. *Journal of Sex Research*, 32, 213–217.

Pinker, S. (2009). *How the mind works* (reissue ed.). New York: W. W. Norton.

Pusey, A. E., & Packer, C. (1994). Infanticide in lions: Consequences and counterstrategies. In S. Parmigiani & F. S. vom Saal (Eds.), *Infanticide and parental care* (pp. 277–300). Langhorne, PA: Harwood Academic Publishers.

Sanvito, S., Galimberti, F., & Miller, E. H. (2007). Vocal signaling of male southern elephant seals is honest but imprecise. *Animal Behaviour, 73*, 287–299.

Schaller, M., Park, J. H., & Mueller, A. (2003). Fear of the dark: Interactive effects of beliefs about danger and ambient darkness on ethnic stereotypes. *Personality and Social Psychology Bulletin, 29*, 637–649.

Sear, R., & Mace, R. (2008). Who keeps children alive? A review of the effects of kin on child survival. *Evolution and Human Behavior, 29*, 1–18.

Sell, A., Hagen, E., Cosmides, L., & Tooby, J. (2003). Evolutionary psychology: Applications and criticisms. In *Encyclopedia of cognitive science* (pp. 47–53). London: Macmillan.

Shackelford, T. K. (2005). An evolutionary psychological perspective on cultures of honor. *Evolutionary Psychology, 3*, 381–391.

Simmons, R. (2002). *Odd girl out: The hidden culture of aggression in girls*. London: Harcourt.

Smith, D. L. (2007). *The most dangerous animal. Human nature and the origins of war*. New York: St. Martin's.

Stearns, S. C. (1992). *The evolution of life histories*. Oxford, England: Oxford University Press.

Straus, M., Gelles, R. J., & Steinmetz, S. K. (2006). *Behind closed doors: Violence in the American family*. Piscataway, NJ: Transaction Publishers.

Sulloway, F. J. (1996). *Born to rebel*. New York: Pantheon.

Thornhill, R., Fincher, C. L., & Aran, D. (2009). Parasites, democratization, and the liberalization of values across contemporary countries. *Biological Reviews, 184*, 113–131.

Thornhill, R., Fincher, C. L., Murray, D. R. & Schaller, M. (2010). Zoonotic and non-zoonotic diseases in relation to human personality and societal values: Support for the parasite-stress model. *Evolutionary Psychology, 8*, 151–169.

Thornhill, R., & Palmer, C. T. (2000). *A natural history of rape*. Cambridge, MA: MIT Press.

Tooby, J., & Cosmides, L. (1988). *The evolution of war and its cognitive foundations*. Institute for Evolutionary Studies Technical Report #88-1. Retrieved November 2011, from http://www.psych.ucsb.edu/research/cep/papers/Evolofwar.pdf

Tooby, J., & Cosmides, L. (2005). Conceptual foundations of evolutionary psychology. In D. M. Buss (Ed.), *The handbook of evolutionary psychology* (pp. 5–67). Hoboken, NJ: Wiley.

Trivers, R. L. (1972). Parental investment and sexual selection. In B. Campbell (Ed.), *Sexual selection and the descent of man 1871–1971* (pp. 136–179). Chicago: Aldine.

Twain, M. (1992). Man's place in the animal world. In L. J. Budd (Ed.), *Mark Twain: Collected tales, sketches, speeches, and essays. Volume 2: 1891–1910* (pp. 207–216). New York: Literary Classics of the United States. (Original work published 1896)

Underwood, R. C., & Patch, P. C. (1999). Siblicide: A descriptive analysis of sibling homicide. *Homicide Studies, 3*, 333–348.

US Department of Justice, Federal Bureau of Investigation, Criminal Justice Information Services Division. (2010, September). *Crime in the United States, 2009*. Retrieved June 2011, from http://www2.fbi.gov/ucr/cius2009/index.html

Vaillancourt, T., Hymel, S., & McDougall, P. (2003). Bullying is power: Implications for school-based intervention strategies. *Journal of Applied School Psychology, 19*, 157–176.

van der Dennen, J. M. G. (1995). *The origin of war: The evolution of a male-coalitional reproductive strategy*. Gronigen, The Netherlands: Origin Press.

Wakefield, J. C. (1992). The concept of mental disorder: On the boundary between biological facts and social values. *American Psychologist, 47*, 373–388.

Waterman, J. (1984). Infanticide in the Columbian ground squirrel, *Spermophilus columbianus*. *Journal of Mammalogy, 65*, 137–138.

Watson, P. J., & Andrews, P. W. (2002). Toward a revised evolutionary adaptationist analysis of depression: The social navigation hypothesis. *Journal of Affective Disorders, 72*, 1–14.

Wiehe, V. R. (1997). *Sibling abuse*. Thousand Oaks, CA: Sage Publications.

Wilson, M., & Daly, M. (1992). The man who mistook his wife for a chattel. In J. H. Barkow, L. Cosmides, & J. Tooby (Eds.), *The adapted mind* (pp. 289–322). New York: Oxford University Press.

World Health Organization. (2010). *Suicide prevention*. Retrieved June 2011, from http://www.who.int/mental_health/prevention/suicide/suicideprevent/en/index.html

Zahavi, A., & Zahavi, A. (1996). *The handicap principle*. New York: Oxford University Press.

CHAPTER 2

Violence Across Animals and Within Early Hominins

Hogan M. Sherrow

Abstract

Violence is common among animal populations, but the term is rarely used in modern behavioral ecology studies and is instead typically reserved for aberrant human behaviors. Despite this, there are virtually no animal populations in which violence, to some degree, has not been observed. Instead, organisms have elaborate behaviors that allow them to mitigate violence when it does occur or attempt to avoid it all together. Here I review two separate, but not mutually exclusive, views on the evolution of violence across animals. I then characterize violence across animals, with special emphasis on apes, including humans. Finally, I present a model for violence in our earliest hominin ancestors.

Key Words: violence, evolution, resource competition, coalitions

Introduction

October 2004, Ngogo, Kibale National Park, Uganda
The three males rushed, screaming excitedly, hair on end, into the undergrowth, pursuing the female and her offspring. She was old, weak, and missing much of her hair, with one arm draped over the body and head of her infant, she turned to face her attackers. They jumped on her, kicking her, pulling at her arms, trying to dislodge the infant from them. Screaming she lunged back with her one free arm and slapped at the males, alarm calls flowing from her mouth signaling her distress. The males tried again, but the old female continued to deflect their attacks, protecting her infant. Suddenly, a female screamed from above them in the canopy as several of the males' allies caught up with her. The three males were distracted and turned back to join the attack on the arboreal female. As they did so, the old female on the ground seized the opportunity and fled into the undergrowth, saving the life of her young infant.

—Sherrow and Amsler (2007)

Violence is common among many living organisms (Williams, 1966) and probably has roots that stretch back to the time of the first noncloned life forms that were capable of physical interaction. The term "violence" is often used interchangeably with "aggression" or "agonism," but it differs in its precision, and that difference is worth recognizing. While "aggression" is normally defined as any behavior relating to attack, threat, or defense, and "agonism" includes all of those behaviors plus fleeing (Immelmann & Beer, 1989), "violence" is more specific. "Violence" is defined as one or more individuals physically attacking one or more other individuals (Immelmann & Beer, 1989). The term "violence" is typically used in a negative, antisocial context, especially regarding humans. I did a brief survey of the scientific literature over the past 4 years and found no articles that used the term "violence" when referring to animal behavior. Instead, the term was reserved for human behavior and typically for behaviors that are categorized as delinquent or antisocial.

In the natural world, however, violence does occur in many degrees of severity. It can be as mild as two Japanese beetles "shoving" each other during mating competition, in which neither combatant is usually hurt, and the loser is simply chased off (Hongo, 2003), or it can be as severe as a male mountain gorilla eviscerating an unrelated infant in an attempt to mate with its mother (Watts, 1989).

Regardless of the nature of the violence itself, it most often occurs in nonhuman animals in the context of resource or mate competition (Archer, 1988). In the natural world, especially among mammals, access to food is paramount for female reproductive success, and access to mates is the most important factor impacting male fitness (Emlen & Oring, 1977; Wrangham, 1980). Among our own species, violence is often divorced from direct competition over resources or mates, and it has reached new heights of severity, resulting in the deaths of millions in wars, terrorist attacks, colonialism, and the Holocaust (Keegan, 1993). If we hope to understand violence, we need to understand its long evolutionary history and significance, and how it is expressed in individuals across various taxa, particularly our closest relatives.

Research on the origins and significance of violence has come primarily from two competing, though not mutually exclusive, perspectives. The first perspective focuses on the facts that violence is relatively rare, even among the most belligerent species, and that most organisms are violent only in certain contexts. Proponents of this perspective point out that most organisms spend very little time engaged in agonistic behaviors of any kind, and even less time engaged in violence (e.g., Sussman, Garber, & Cheverud, 2005).

Instead, these authors point out that cooperative and affiliative behaviors are far more common in nature than are competitive and agonistic behaviors. Their observations have led many of them to conclude that violence is an aberrant behavior that is not typical or normal for most organisms but is, instead, the result of specific conditions, such as habitat disturbance (Dohlinow, 1977), overcrowding (Calhoun, 1962), or chemical imbalance (Hendricks et al, 2003). Still other researchers who adopt this perspective see violence as a natural, but relatively insignificant, behavior among animal populations (Sussman et al., 2005).

The second perspective taken by researchers focused on the origins and significance of violence acknowledges that violence is relatively rare among most animal populations. However, these same researchers point out that an event does not have to happen frequently to be evolutionarily significant, provided it impacts fitness severely enough when it does occur. An example of this is predation. Predation is a relatively rare event, but when it occurs it impacts fitness drastically and, therefore, can be a strong selective force impacting animal populations. Researchers who take this perspective assert that violence is similar to predation in that while it may be rare, when it occurs it has the potential to drastically alter the fitness of the individuals involved (e.g., Mech, 1977) and, therefore, can be a strong selective force. Furthermore, they suggest that while violence may not be a common behavior of the organisms in question, it is one of the strategies employed by individuals to gain access to resources and to compete successfully (e.g., Wrangham, 1999).

Researchers who have suggested that violence is either aberrant or not significant often refer to what I term the "myth of restraint" as evidence supporting their position. The myth of restraint stems from recognition in early ethological studies that animal combatants rarely inflicted mortal wounds on each other, even when it was obvious that they were capable of doing so. This was most clearly advocated by the great ethologist Konrad Lorenz, who, in his landmark book *King Solomon's Ring*, provided strong evidence in support of general mechanisms of restraint, which he claimed inhibited severe violence in many species (Lorenz, 1959). While his reasoning was sound, and his observations were objective in nature, Lorenz made the error of equating actions with intentions. He concluded that because individuals were rarely if ever seriously injured or killed during violent interactions that the species had evolved inhibitions against such behaviors and tried to avoid them, primarily through ritualized fighting (Lorenz, 1963).

Ritualized fighting has been observed in taxa ranging from mantis shrimp (Taylor & Patek, 2010) to gray wolves (Mech, 1977) to humans (Chagnon, 1997) and has been shown to decrease the potential for serious injury or death among combatants. Despite its positive impact on survivorship, ritualized fighting need have nothing to do with inhibitions toward killing, or restraint during fighting. Ritualized fighting could have evolved across numerous taxa as an evolutionarily stable strategy (ESS) in response to the costs associated with lethal aggression (Maynard-Smith & Price, 1973). If inflicting serious wounds or killing a rival presents too high of a cost, and the winner in a contest over mates or resources can still reap the fitness benefits associated with winning, without doing either of those things, ritualized fighting could be selected for.

Results from studies on male contests over mates in the sierra dome spider (*Neriene litigiosa*) support this hypothesis (de Carvalho et al., 2003). Among sierra dome spiders, males engage in a stereotypical pattern of ritualized fighting. If at any point during the contest one male determines that the costs are too high, it can retreat and will suffer no further damage from the victor. If, however, both males determine that the costs of competing are low enough, or that the costs of retreating and losing a mating opportunity are too high, they will engage in violent competition, which often results in severe injury or death (de Carvalho et al., 2003).

A similar cost-benefit analysis is applicable to chimpanzees, which along with bonobos, are our closest living relatives. While chimpanzees do not have ritualized fights nearly as elaborate or rigid as sierra dome spiders, they do engage in ritual-like behaviors associated with fighting over mates and resources. Within communities, males frequently avoid violent interactions by recognizing disparities in competitive abilities via displays (Goodall, 1986). When the mechanisms designed to reduce violence and aggression break down, male chimpanzees often fight and can injure each other, sometimes severely (e.g. Fawcett & Muhumuza, 2000; Watts, 2004).

Male chimpanzees regularly engage in territorial behaviors with males from other communities (intercommunity encounters [ICEs]), which include, but are not limited to, aural and visual displays, incursions, raids, lethal intercommunity coalitions (LICs), and battles (Goodall, 1986; Muller, 2002; Sherrow, unpublished data; Sherrow & Amsler, 2007; Watts & Mitani, 2001). During ICEs, males choose to reduce or escalate conflicts based on the costs involved, particularly the number of potential enemy combatants present. Wilson et al. (2001) have shown that male chimpanzees are more likely to seek out ICEs when they assess a numerical advantage over their rivals.

Regardless of whether ritualized fighting has evolved as part of an ESS, its prevalence across taxa, ranging from arachnids to hominids, indicates that it is not a shared, derived characteristic but instead a common behavioral strategy employed by organisms during contests over resources. Furthermore, its presence indicates that violence is common among many animals, providing the behavioral milieu for selection to act upon.

It appears that animals do not possess a restraint against violence but instead have effective mechanisms for reducing the costs associated with behaving violently.

Despite the fact that the evidence overwhelmingly supports the position that violence is a natural, common behavior, it does not mean that it happens at high frequencies within populations. Instead, when it does occur, violence has the potential to result in extreme fitness costs, resulting in strong selection for behaviors that manage or minimize its occurrence and impact. Ritualized fighting is one of the behaviors most commonly used among nonhuman animals. Humans not only employ ritualized fighting but also diplomacy, treaties, intermixing of families through arranged marriage, long-term alliances, and many other behaviors to mitigate violence. Ours is a more complex, but not atypical, mammalian strategy for reducing potential costs associated with violence.

De Carvalho et al.'s (2003) study on sierra dome spiders provides data that indicate that when the costs of competition increase, the intensity of competition between individual spiders increases, often leading to violence. If those results are applicable across animal taxa, and the principles appear to hold, then we should expect to see competition increasing and becoming more intense among animal populations when those populations are under resource stress of some kind. Calhoun (1962), Hendricks et al. (2003), Dohlinow (1977), and Sussman et al. (2005) provide data that support this hypothesis.

Beyond the general support these studies provide for resource stress as a major cause of animal violence, they bring an important perspective on studies of violence as well. First, by providing an alternative hypothesis to the dominant paradigm, these studies have propelled the study of violence forward by compelling researchers to collect more data, on more taxa, and to further test assumptions and established results. Second, these studies provide support for the hypothesis that violence is not a frequent occurrence in most populations and that it is intensified by external factors such as predation pressure, habitat disturbance, and stress. However, this does not mean that violence is abnormal or insignificant for the populations in question.

It was my original intention when writing this chapter to compile an exhaustive list of known species in which violence has been recorded. However, after conducting extensive research on the topic, one trend is clear: There are very few, if any, species in which violence of some sort has not been recorded. Across all animal taxa, ranging from butterflies (Kemp & Wiklund, 2001) to muriqui (Talebi, Beltrao-Mendes, & Lee, 2009) to social fish (Wong & Balshine, 2011), violence has been observed. Despite the fact that many species spend the majority of their time in a social context cooperating with or ignoring conspecifics (Sussman et al., 2005), most still engage in violence of some sort at some point.

Fashing (2001a) observed no intragroup agonism in over 16,000 scans, taken over a 12-month period, on black-and-white colobus monkeys (*Colobus guereza*) in the Kakamega Forest in Kenya. However, he did observe 136 intergroup encounters during the same period, most of which were aggressive in nature, some involving violence between rival individuals and groups (Fashing, 2001b). Black-and-white colobus monkeys are characterized by low within-group feeding competition, but they defend feeding areas against extragroup conspecifics (Harris, 2006), and violence is one method they use to defend those feeding areas.

The data on black-and-white colobus monkeys reinforce the emerging pattern of occasional violence observed across animal populations. What is more, the combination of ubiquity and low frequency, with mitigating mechanisms, suggests that violence has been a strong selective force throughout the evolutionary history of most animal species. It now appears that the debate over whether violence is the result of nature or nurture has been settled. Organisms are naturally aggressive, and occasionally violent, and that violence can be mitigated or enhanced depending on the social context in which those organisms develop and operate as adults. Instead of rehashing this debate, I will focus on the patterns of violence observed within and between the sexes across mammals, with a special emphasis on the hominoids, or apes. At the end of the chapter, I will present one potential model regarding the behavior of our earliest hominin ancestors and the potential for violence in those early bipedal ape populations.

Violence Across Animals

Mammals occupy a wide range of ecological niches and display a wide array of social structures and mating strategies. Ranging from solitary granivores to social carnivores, mammals are anything but a homogenous group. Despite this great diversity, all mammals require access to food and mates and defense against predation. Because potential food and mates are finite and predator defense varies depending on position within a social group and access to food, these represent contestable resources and conditions. During competition over these resources, mammals can engage in two general types of violence: nonlethal and lethal.

Nonlethal Violence

The most common form of violence among mammals is nonlethal violence (NLV). NLV does not result in the death of either participant, and it usually includes grabbing, hitting, kicking, biting, and other forms of physical aggression that do not inflict fatal wounds. NLV is common across mammals and has been observed in both solitary and group living species. Kangaroo rats (*Dipodomys* spp.) are solitary mammals that cache seeds in open habitats (Swartz, Maryke, & Ned, 2010). Seeds and suitable microenvironments in which to cache them are limited resources, and both male and female kangaroo rats engage in intrasexual and intersexual competition over these areas (Blaustein & Risser, 1976). While territorial contests in kangaroo rates consist mostly of displays, they can result in aggressive behaviors, including nonlethal fighting and violence (Shier & Randall, 2007).

Male elephant seals (*Mirounga* spp.) are well known for their violent, often bloody contests over stretches of beach and the sexual access to females that come with being a "beach master" (Bester, 1988). Elephant seals are seasonal breeders that form harems dominated by a single male who monopolizes all breeding with the females within his territory by defending and coercing them, as well as attacking any male interlopers (Bester, 1988). The result of monopolization of fertile females by a few powerful males is high reproductive skew, meaning that few males gain reproductive opportunities in any given breeding season.

Despite their violent reputations, most male elephant seals rely on ritualized displays and honest vocal signals to assess the relative condition of their rivals before deciding whether to attack (Sanvito, Galimberti, & Miller, 2007). Like most contests between mammals over resources, male elephant seal contests are dyadic interactions, meaning they take place between two individuals. As a result, for male elephant seals, like most adult mammals, the costs associated with attacking, injuring and potentially killing a rival are often extremely high. Without allies to help them fight, male elephant seals risk being killed themselves in a lethal attack (Wrangham, 1999). Despite the potential costs of launching a violent attack, competition over access to mates is so intense and the subsequent costs of losing mating opportunities are so high, that male elephant seals still routinely engage in intrasexual and intersexual violence (Haley, 1994).

The patterns observed in kangaroo rats and elephant seals are typical across many mammal populations. Much like sierra dome spiders, the intensity of their competition and the probability that they will engage in violence depend on the costs involved in such activities, on both sides of the equation. Even if the costs of violence are high, they can be offset by even higher costs associated with losing contests or not competing at all. In the case of kangaroo rats that have incredibly high-energy demands relative to body size, the loss of seed caches could result in starvation or reduced physical condition (Shier & Randall, 2007) that would make them more vulnerable to disease and predation and less attractive as potential mates. For male elephant seals, losing in contests over territories or losing control over females often results in total exclusion from breeding (Carrick & Ingham, 1962).

Despite the need to engage in violence, both kangaroo rats and elephant seals usually find ways to minimize the potential costs, a common practice across mammals. Because individuals have developed strategies to reduce costs associated with violent behavior, NLV is found in every one of the 29 orders (Wilson & Reeder, 2005) of living mammals. While researchers typically focus on NLV that occurs between males during mating competition (e.g., roe deer, *Caprealus caprealus*, Melis, Hoem, Linnell, & Andersen, 2005), NLV also occurs between males and females (e.g., lions, *Panthera leo*, Schaller, 1972) and between females (e.g., rhesus macaques, *Macaca mulatta*, Bernstein, Gordon, & Rose, 1974). The overall picture is that NLV is common across mammals and is an effective strategy during some forms of resource competition.

Lethal Violence

Far rarer than NLV is lethal violence (LV), which results in the death of one or more combatants. LV is rare among mammals because it is difficult for most adult animals to inflict fatal wounds on rivals who are similarly equipped for combat. As a result, the risks and associated costs of LV are too high for potential attackers in most species to reap the benefits associated with eliminating rivals. Despite these risks, as in the sierra dome spider, when competition is intense and survival or reproduction is at stake, or when the risks are mitigated in some way, mammals are not hesitant about killing conspecifics (Enquist & Leimar, 1990; Wrangham, 1999). When LV occurs, it is typically intrasexual in nature, though there have been reports of intersexual lethal violence among adult chimpanzees, *Pan troglodytes* (Goodall, 1986).

In several mammalian species, dyadic contests between adults can lead to fatal injuries (e.g., red deer, *Cervus elaphus*, Clutton-Brock, Guinness, & Albon, 1982), pronghorn (*Antilocapra americana*, Byers, 1997), wedge-capped capuchins (*Cebus olivaceous*, Miller, 1998) and white-faced capuchins (*Cebus capucinus*, Gros-Louis, Perry, & Manson, 2003). Additionally, infanticide, mostly by adult males, occurs in many primate taxa (reviewed in van Schaik, 2000). In contrast, the killing of conspecifics other than infants by coalitions of multiple individuals is known only in a few social carnivores (e.g., lions, *Panthera leo*, Grinnell, Packer, & Pusey, 1995; African wild dogs, *Lycaon pictus*, Creel & Creel, 2002), and wolves (Mech & Boitani, 2003), and a few primate species (e.g., western red colobus, *Procolobus badius temmincki*, Starin, 1994), diana monkeys (*Cercopithecus diana*, McGraw, Plavcan, & Adachi-Kanazawa, 2002), white-faced capuchins (Gros-Louis et al., 2003), and chimpanzees (*Pan troglodytes*, Wilson & Wrangham, 2003).

One group of mammals that is equipped to inflict fatal wounds during fights, and in which death occurs on a relatively regular basis, are the ruminants, particularly deer and antelope. Red deer males, *Cervus elaphus*, compete intensely over access to mates, fighting during the mating season, called the rut, with losers of contests completely excluded from mating (Clutton-Brock et al., 1982). Clutton-Brock et al. (1982) found that 13%–29% of adult male deaths were the result of rut fighting. Similarly, male pronghorn antelope, *Antilocapra americana*, fight intensely over females during a breeding season and losers are excluded from mating. In one study, 12% of the fights observed led to the death of one or both combatants (Byers, 1997).

Researchers have reported comparable results among nonruminant species ranging from mountain gorillas (Watts, 1988) to elephant seals, discussed earlier (Bester, 1988). The consistent pattern that emerges among these species is that when LV occurs, it is highly dangerous for both combatants and is never coalitional in nature (Wrangham, 1999). Coalitions are formed between individuals when they support each other in agonistic interactions (Harcourt & de Waal, 1992). The majority of LV observed in mammal populations is coalitional in nature and occurs in species that form bonds within social groups (Wrangham, 1999).

A group of mammals that is well equipped to kill and regularly forms intense bonds is the social carnivores. Not surprisingly, most cases of coalitional LV, outside the primates, have been observed in this group. Coalitional LV has been observed in lions, *Panthera leo* (Packer et al., 1988), cheetahs, *Acinonyx jubatus* (Caro & Collins, 1986), spotted hyenas, *Crocuta crocuta* (Kruuk, 1972), African wild dogs, *Lycaon pictus* (Creel & Creel, 2002), and gray wolves, *Canis lupis* (Mech, Adams, Meier, Burch, & Dale, 1998). Data for mortality rates in lions, cheetahs, and hyenas are lacking, but Mech et al. (1998) found that mortality due to coalitional LV in three different gray wolf populations ranged from 39% to 65% (Mech et al., 1998). They concluded that mortality due to coalitional LV is normal among gray wolves and can have a significant impact on those populations.

One of the advantages gained through coalitional attacks is risk reduction for the attackers (Wrangham, 1999). If groups of bonded animals can reduce the costs associated with combat by outnumbering their rivals, they can gain by eliminating them through coalitional LV. This prediction is often associated with the imbalance-of-power hypothesis, which was formally introduced by Manson and Wrangham (1991) and has to do with group or community competition: "The imbalance-of-power hypothesis proposes that the function of unprovoked intercommunity aggression (i.e., deep incursions and coalitionary attacks) is intercommunity dominance" (Wrangham, 1999, p. 12).

Several studies support the imbalance-of-power hypothesis among chimpanzees (e.g., Mitani, Watts, & Amsler, 2010; Sherrow & Amsler, 2007; Wilson et al., 2001), and the data available for social carnivores appear to provide additional support (Mech et al., 1998). Groups of bonded animals engage in coalitional LV during competition with extragroup conspecifics. In other words, individuals within groups of social carnivores and some primate species use coalitional LV to gain advantages in competition with individuals from other groups over territory and resources. By using numerical advantage to overwhelm their rivals, successful individuals are able to reduce the risks normally associated with lethal attacks (Wrangham, 1999).

The family *Delphinidae*, the true dolphins, which includes bottlenose dolphins (*Tursiops* spp.) and orcas (*Orcinus* spp.) is a group of mammals that shares many characteristics with the social carnivores, including strong social bonds and heavy competition over mates and resources. While coalitional LV on adults has not been observed in dolphins, coalitional violence, including infanticide, has (Dunn, Barco, Pabst, & McLellan, 2002). It may be that coalitional LV toward adults just has not yet been observed in dolphins. Alternatively, the added dimension of an aquatic environment may make it difficult for a group of attackers to restrain a victim long enough and securely enough to inflict fatal wounds.

Infanticide: One Form of Lethal Violence

Infanticide is one form of LV that happens in both dyadic interactions and via coalitions. Infanticide is the killing of same-species infants by adults, and it is widespread across mammals (Janson & van Schaik, 2000). For centuries, stories have circulated about how males from some species will kill infants of their species if given the chance. One of the first pieces of knowledge any aspiring naturalist, or hiker, in the Pacific Northwest of the United States learns about bears is that males will kill cubs if given the chance, and that is one of the main reasons females with cubs are so vigilant and so dangerous.

In 1974, Hrdy provided the first systematic observations of infanticide in mammals and identified a potential causal factor for the behavior. Hrdy (1974) observed that male langurs (*Presbytis* spp.) committed infanticides when they could not be the fathers of the targets of their aggression. Furthermore, females became sexually receptive shortly after their dependent infants were killed and they often chose to mate with the infanticidal male (Hrdy, 1974). Hrdy's conclusion was that infanticide is a reproductive strategy employed by males to increase mating opportunities and reduce competition for their offspring.

Since Hrdy's groundbreaking study, data on infanticides committed by adults on unrelated infants from mammal taxa ranging from California ground squirrels, *Otospermophilus beecheyi* (Trulio, Loughry, Hennessy, & Owings, 1986), to brown bears, *Ursus arctos* (Fernandez-Gil et al., 2010), have continued to be reported by researchers around the world. To date, infanticide committed by male and female adult animals on unrelated infants has been reported in over 100 species of mammals (Agrell, Wolff, & Ylonen, 1998), including 39 species of primates (van Schaik, 2000). Females use infanticide to reduce present and future competition for their offspring, while securing calories by cannibalizing the infant.

Males use infanticide for much the same reasons, but experience an added benefit in increased mating opportunities. Many female mammals experience lactational ammenorhea and do not begin ovulating as long as they have a nursing infant (Hausfater & Hrdy, 1984). By killing dependent infants, males thereby indirectly stimulate females to begin cycling again by removing the energy demand the infant represents (Hrdy, 1979).

The most common pattern of infanticide observed across mammals is one in which adult males or females act alone and attack and kill an unrelated infant (Janson & van Schaik, 2000). However, in species in which strong bonds are formed, such as the social carnivores and the Delphinids, coalitional infanticides occur. Among the *Delphinidae* coalitional infanticides are one of the strategies males use to increase their reproductive access to females (Dunn et al., 2002). Similarly, male lions regularly kill all dependent offspring when they take over a pride, providing them with greater access to females as they reenter estrous after the loss over their dependent cubs (Packer & Pusey, 1983).

Infanticide does not generally incur the same risks as attacking adult conspecifics; infants are weaker, less equipped for fighting, and generally ineffective in defending themselves. At the same time, infanticide can have severe impacts on the reproductive success of individuals and the genotypes of populations by acting as a selective force, favoring certain germ lines over others. The result is that male mammals ranging from rats (Menella & Moltz, 1988) to hanuman langurs (Hrdy, 1974) to bottlenose dolphins (Patterson, Reid, Wilson, Ross, & Thompson, 1998) engage in infanticide as a reproductive strategy. The effect is so strong in primates that infanticide has been suggested as a driving force in the formation of social groups in our order (Sterck, Watts, & van Schaik, 1997).

Nonlethal Violence Among the Apes

While some primates rarely engage in NLV (e.g., ruffed lemurs, *Varecia variegate*; Vasey, 1997), all species appear to do so under certain conditions (Sussman et al., 2005).

Unlike the pattern observed among ruffed lemurs and some other Strepsirrhines, NLV is common among the monkeys and apes and varies in intensity across species and contexts (Sussman et al., 2005). NLV has been reported in all of the extant apes with males typically, but not always, acting as the aggressors (humans, *Homo sapiens*, Daly & Wilson, 1988; chimpanzees, *Pan troglodytes*, Goodall, 1986; bonobos, *Pan paniscus*, White & Wood, 2007; gorillas, *Gorilla* spp., Fossey, 1984; orangutans, *Pongo* spp., Knott et al., 2010; and gibbons, *Hylobates* spp., Carpenter, 1938). Another common pattern of NLV observed in apes is the targeting of immature animals for violence, which is rarely severe (but see Arcadi & Wrangham, 1999; Daly & Wilson, 1988; and Watts, 1989).

Intersexual NLV is common in the nonhuman apes and usually involves males attacking females in an attempt to control or coerce them (e.g., Knott, Emery-Thompson, Stumpf, & McIntyre, 2010; Muller, Kahlenberg, Emery-Thompson, & Wrangham, 2007; Smuts & Smuts, 1993; Stumpf & Boesch, 2010). For example, Knott et al. (2010) reported that prime male orangutans used some form of sexual coercion in 86% of their copulations, which included violent behaviors such as pulling and restraining. However, there have been reports of female apes attacking males in an attempt to police their behavior (Newton-Fisher, 2006). Despite the commonness of intersexual NLV in the apes, intrasexual NLV is often more common and can have even greater impacts on the fitness of individuals across populations.

Male and female apes routinely engage in intrasexual NLV, with varying degrees of intensity. Competition over resources among the apes ranges from relatively relaxed in female mountain gorillas, *Gorilla berengei* (Watts, 1994), and chimpanzees, *Pan troglodytes* (Goodall, 1986), to intense among adult male orangutans, *Pongo pygmaeus* (Knott et al., 2010), and gorillas (Fossey, 1984). Variation in competitive intensity is correlated with whether the resources in question can be monopolized (Wrangham, 1980). Intensity in competition and the associated costs of violence help determine whether individuals engage in violence on a regular basis.

Female mountain gorillas and chimpanzees experience reduced competition for different ecological reasons. Mountain gorillas are folivorous, relying heavily on terrestrial herbaceous vegetation, stems, and piths (Fossey, 1984), while chimpanzees are frugivorous omnivores, eating primarily ripe fruits, as well as other plant and some animal material (Goodall, 1986). Gorillas live in what some researchers have characterized as a "giant salad bowl" (Watts, personal communication), surrounded by potential food, making it impossible to monopolize food sources. Chimpanzee food sources, on the other hand, are distributed unevenly throughout their environment, resulting in the need for females to practice "scramble" competition, in which the first individual at a food source enjoys an advantage in access to it (Wrangham, 1980). Both conditions have resulted in weak selective pressures for females to form strong hierarchies and a more relaxed social condition than that observed in some other primates, such as rhesus macaques (Bernstein et al., 1974).

Male orangutans and gorillas practice mating strategies that are superficially similar to that seen in elephant seals. Body size dimorphism is extreme in all three species and males compete intensely to control access to multiple females. Female orangutans and gorillas, like female elephant seals (Bester, 1988), are preferentially attracted to fully adult males and employ strategies to attempt to mate only with those males (orangutans: Knott et al., 2010; gorillas: Watts, 1988). Orangutans live mostly solitary lives, coming together to mate and when there is localized fruit abundance (Knott et al., 2010). Males maintain large home ranges that overlap those of multiple females, and they attempt to exclude all other males from those ranges (Singleton & van Schaik, 2001). Gorillas typically live in single-male groups in which multiple females and their offspring are bonded to the same male and stay with that male throughout the day (Fossey, 1984).

While male orangutans have a more difficult time defending a home range and the females in it in the forest canopy than male gorillas do defending females in the forest, or than elephant seals do defending territories on open beaches, the underlying variables are the same. The result is that orangutan and gorilla males behave in ways that are similar to male elephant seals, using displays and vocalizations to demonstrate physical condition and willingness to engage in violence. Like male elephant seals, male gorillas and orangutans compete on a dyadic level, resulting in high costs for engaging in violent behaviors, and even higher potential costs for inflicting lethal wounds during that violence.

The overall pattern of NLV in the apes, including humans, is varied but generally consistent across species. Both males and females engage in intersexual and intrasexual NLV, with other adults and with immature animals (Appendix A.1). The intensity of violence within the apes, and their overall belligerence as a species, is correlated with how they compete for resources within their ecological niches (Wrangham, 1980). While NLV is common among the apes and is not absent in any of the extant species, LV is far rarer.

Lethal Violence Among the Apes

LV is much less common than NLV across primates and within the apes, and it has not been reported in either orangutans or bonobos. However, Knott (2000) suggested that male orangutans are potentially lethal in their aggression toward one another, and Knott et al. (2010) have suggested that female orangutans employ behavioral strategies to protect against infanticide. It could be that LV has just not been observed in wild orangutan populations. Even if LV does not occur in these two species, it has been reported in all of the other apes (humans: Daly & Wilson, 1988; chimpanzees: Goodall, 1986, Wilson & Wrangham, 2003; gorillas: Watts, 1988, 1989; and gibbons: Alfred & Sati, 1991; Palombit, 1993). Humans (Daly & Wilson, 1988), chimpanzees (Arcadi & Wrangham, 1999; Goodall, 1986), and gibbons (Alfred & Sati, 1991; Palombit, 1993) engage in lethal violence against both adults and infants while gorillas have only been observed committing infanticide (Watts, 1989).

Gibbons typically live in socially and reproductively monogamous groups (Borries, Savini, & Koenig, 2011; but see Fuentes, 2000). Males and females are monomorphic and cooperatively defend territories, through a combination of coordinated songs called duets (Geissmann, 2002) and aggression that is typically nonlethal in nature (Reichard & Sommer, 1997). In 1991, Alfred and Sabati reported a single instance of infanticide in hoolock gibbons (*Hylobates hoolock*) when an adult male attacked an infant from within his own group. The infant was bitten and dropped to the forest floor and later died from its wounds. In 1993, Palombit reported a single instance of lethal intergroup violence between two adult males from separate groups of white-handed gibbons (*Hylobates lar*). During that interaction, one of the males was severely wounded on the back and weeks later succumbed to infection brought on from his injuries. The other male suffered superficial wounds only. While the victim's death was not immediate, it did appear to be a direct consequence of the injury he suffered during the intergroup interaction. While these two observations indicate that lethal violence against adults and infants does occur among the gibbons, they also indicate that this behavior is most likely rare.

Gorillas usually live in single-male, multiple-female groups that are cohesive in nature (as described earlier). Males compete intensely over mating opportunities, and losers of those contests are usually excluded from mating (Yamagiwa,

1987). Lethal male-male violence has been reported for this species, but it appears to be rare (Watts, 1988). The lack of female-female LV in gorillas can be attributed to the relatively relaxed feeding competition, discussed earlier. Similarly, the absence of intrasexual LV in gorillas is fairly straightforward; female gorillas have almost no chance of killing adult males, even if it was advantageous for them to do so, and males have little to gain by killing potential or actual mates.

The lack of male-male LV in gorillas is somewhat more difficult to understand. Male gorillas are the largest of all the living primates and are well equipped for battle. They have heavily muscled bodies, with large, projecting canines (Gregory, 1950) that make effective weapons, and when adult males fight, it can be very intense (Fossey, 1984) and losers usually suffer heavy reproductive costs (Fossey, 1984; Watts, 1989; Yamagiwa, 1987). Still, lethal attacks between male gorillas have never been observed. Instead, adult males typically use displays such as chest beating and bluff charges during aggressive encounters with each other (Schaller, 1963). It may be that the risks are too high for lone male gorillas to carry out lethal attacks on other males. Even a young adult male is large and powerful and would be difficult for a single male to inflict lethal wounds on.

Instead of incurring the costs associated with violent attacks on adult rivals, male gorillas employ infanticide as a strategy to simultaneously increase mating opportunities with females, while reducing present and future competition for them and their offspring (Watts, 1989). Harcourt and Greenberg (2001) reported that, within the Karisoke mountain gorilla population, there is a 14% chance that a given infant will be the victim of infanticide. As a result, infanticide is a significant source of mortality among infant gorillas at Karisoke, accounting for 37% of all deaths before the age of 4 years (Watts, 1989). Fitting the typical pattern observed in other mammal species (Agrell et al., 1998), infanticides in gorillas usually occur during intercommunity encounters or takeovers and are committed by unrelated adult males, acting alone (Watts, 1989).

LV in chimpanzees and humans is much more common and varied than that seen in gorillas and gibbons, with males and females from both species participating. Infanticidal attacks by males and females have been reported in chimpanzees (for a review, see Arcadi & Wrangham, 1999) and humans (for a review, see Daly & Wilson, 1988). While female chimpanzees have not been observed committing LV against adult conspecifics, human females have been known to kill other adult humans, though the rate is staggeringly low when compared to rates of human male LV (Daly & Wilson, 1988). In their landmark study, Daly and Wilson (1988) found that the average rate of intrasexual LV among males across 35 different populations was 19.7 times higher than that observed among females—a difference that was even larger when relatedness and age of victim were controlled. In Canada, for example, once age and relatedness were controlled, the rate of intrasexual LV among males was 38.9 times higher than that observed in females (Daly & Wilson, 1988).

An overview of the literature on LV in chimpanzees reveals a similar pattern to that observed in humans. Males are far more likely than females to commit acts of LV against infants and adults. Out of 95 cases of known, inferred, or suspected LV across five different chimpanzee study sites, 88 were perpetrated by males, 2 by males and females, and 5 by females alone (Boesch et al., 2007; Mitani et al., 2010; Pusey et al., 2008; Sherrow & Amsler, 2007; Watts et al, 2002; Watts et al, 2006; Williams et al., 2008; Wrangham, Wilson, & Muller, 2006). In other words, among wild chimpanzees, males engage in LV at a rate that is 17.6 times higher than females. The difference is even more pronounced if infanticide is removed from the equation. Female chimpanzees have never been observed lethally attacking an adult conspecific of either sex. Among chimpanzees, LV that targets adults is exclusively a male behavior.

Even infanticides are far more likely to be committed by males than females. Of the 40 cases of known, inferred, or suspected infanticide across the same study sites, during the same time period, adult males committed 30, or 75%. Mixed-sex parties and females committed five infanticidal attacks each, or 12.5% each. In all, male chimpanzees committed infanticide 6 times more often than females (Boesch et al., 2007; Mitani et al., 2010; Pusey et al., 2008; Sherrow & Amsler, 2007; Williams et al., 2008; Wrangham et al., 2006).

Interestingly, the only recorded case of a female participating in intercommunity LV was of a seemingly postreproductive female from the Ngogo community in Kibale National Park, Uganda (Sherrow & Amsler, 2007). Every other case of infanticide occurred within a community, and most involved females and their daughters as part of a coalition (Pusey et al., 2008; but see Arcadi & Wrangham, 1999). The available data, which represent hundreds of study-years and thousands of hours of observation, at multiple sites across Africa, point to one undeniable conclusion: Male chimpanzees are more violent than their female counterparts.

Bonobos, chimpanzees, and humans all live in fission-fusion societies, providing the opportunity for individuals to be caught alone (Wrangham & Peterson, 1996). The critical difference between the social structures of chimpanzees and humans as contrasted with most of the other apes, including bonobos, is the strength of male bonds. Both species can be characterized as male bonded (van Hoof & van Schaik, 1994; Manson & Wrangham, 1991), and male chimpanzees and humans exhibit strong preferences for each other as social partners. Though human social systems are not as rigid as those of chimpanzees (Boehm, 1999), and adult human males and females typically form pair bonds that last multiple years, in communities that are not always kin based (Hill et al., 2011), there are basal similarities between the social structures of both chimpanzees and humans.

Chimpanzees live in multimale, multifemale, fission-fusion communities in which males are philopatric and females usually emigrate at adolescence (Goodall, 1986). Adult females are less gregarious than males (Pepper, Mitani, & Watts, 1999; Wrangham, 2000) and establish core areas within a community's territory in which they are often accompanied by dependent offspring (Goodall, 1986). Adult male chimpanzees form long-lasting social bonds with each other (Mitani, 2009) that have been characterized as friendships (Nishida & Hosaka, 1996). Some males form alliances that have an important impact on the acquisition and maintenance of dominance rank (de Waal, 1982; Nishida & Hosaka, 1996), and rank influences access to fertile females and male reproductive success (Constable, Ashley, Goodall, & Pusey, 2001; de Waal, 1982; Tutin, 1979; Vigilant, Hofreiter, Siedel, & Boesch, 2001; Watts, 1998, 2004). While adult males in a chimpanzee community compete for access to mates, they cooperate to defend the community territory and exclude extracommunity males (Boesch & Boesch-Achermann, 2000; Goodall, 1986; Mitani & Watts, 2005; Mitani et al., 2010; Watts & Mitani, 2001; Wilson & Wrangham, 2003; Wrangham, 1999).

Chapais (2008) recently suggested that the ancestral human social condition was based on pair bonding, within a larger social system of hunters and gatherers. It is well accepted that humans lived as hunters and gatherers until the Holocene, and so that condition is thought to provide greater insight into ancestral human social conditions than others (Marlowe, Apicella, & Reed, 2005). In a recent study of residence patterns in hunter and gatherer societies, Hill et al. (2011) found support for Chapais' hypothesis. They used published data from 32 societies and determined that hunter and gatherer populations are characterized by bisexual dispersal and philopatry, with a high incidence of brother/sister coresidence. Hill et al.'s findings led them to hypothesize that "monogamous pair bonding, paternal recognition within cooperatively breeding social units, and bisexual dispersal facilitate frequent and friendly intergroup relations and migration and low group genetic relatedness of ban co-residents" (p. 1288).

While Hill et al. (2011) did not find a bias for parents residing with offspring among human groups, they did find a statistically significant pattern of male relatives residing in these societies. This finding by Hill et al. is important and supports earlier cross-cultural studies, which suggested that the majority of human populations were patrilocal and male bonded (Manson & Wrangham, 1991; Smuts, 1995). Groups of related males maintain social and political affiliations over multiple generations, whereas females usually transfer to new groups for mating opportunities (Manson & Wrangham, 1991). Within any given social system males compete with one another for dominance, or status, and access to mates (Chagnon & Irons, 1979; Mazur & Booth, 1998), and competition over females can be severe (e.g., Chagnon, 1988; Hill & Hurtado, 1996).

Coalition building and alliance formation are commonplace among human males as they strive for dominance and status. Males with more, long-lasting alliances achieve higher status, and status leads to greater reproductive opportunities (Hill & Hurtado, 1996). Despite competition over status and access to mates, all males within a community work together to defend a territory against outsiders and to exclude extracommunity conspecifics (Cioffi-Revilla, 1996; Manson & Wrangham, 1991; Singer, 1981; Wilson & Wrangham, 2003). While this pattern applies to the majority of human societies, there is variation in how it is expressed.

The basic pattern observed in chimpanzees and humans is one of intense, long-lasting male bonds that impact dominance and status within the group and allow groups of related males to work together to exclude other males, especially extracommunity males, from resources of different kinds. Male bonding is important for LV in chimpanzees and humans for two reasons; (1) the vast majority of cases of LV in both species is perpetrated by males, and (2) male bonding promotes cooperation and concerted actions by males, making it easier for them to gang up on potential victims and minimize the risks associated with LV.

In our own species, male bonding and LV is taken to extremes, with whole populations of related males, or males who identify as part of the same group, eliminating smaller groups of similarly bonded males (Keegan, 1993). In both chimpanzees and humans most LV is intercommunal in nature, with groups of males targeting infants and adults from other communities (chimpanzees: Mitani et al., 2010; Pusey et al., 2008; Williams et al., 2008; Wrangham et al., 2006; humans: Chagnon, 1988; Livingstone Smith, 2007; Wrangham & Peterson, 1996). However, there have been a few cases in which infants and adult males from within communities have been attacked and killed by coalitions of adult males (for review, see Wrangham et al., 2006) and adult females (see earlier discussion).

The overall picture of violence among the apes is that it is, primarily, a male behavior, especially when that violence turns lethal (Wrangham & Peterson, 1996). While both males and females engage in NLV ranging from chasing, to charging, to hitting, male apes are far more likely to engage in LV than are females. This pattern is consistent with the pattern observed across mammals, and it is observed in humans as well. These basic data on apes can provide insights into the presence or absence of violence, especially LV in the earliest hominin populations.

Violence in Early Hominins

The question of whether the earliest hominins were characterized by violence has been debated since Darwin first suggested in his 1871 volume, *The Descent of Man and Selection in Relation to Sex*, that the need to carry weapons associated with violent conflict may have been related to the evolution of bipedalism. There are essentially two camps in this protracted debate, which mirrors the larger discussion of violence as a natural behavior, chronicled at the beginning of this chapter. It is important to note that while some generalizations can be made about each camp, neither is a homogeneous group, and there are differing opinions, hypotheses, and theories among the researchers involved. Despite the variation in both groups, there are two basic positions in the debate.

One group has taken the position that ours is a naturally cooperative, peaceful species that only engages in violence, especially violence that is lethal in nature, when a natural balance or equilibrium has been disrupted (e.g., de Waal, 1997, 2009; Fry, 2007; Hart & Sussman, 2005; Kelly, 2000; Lorenz, 1963). Researchers who adopt this position tend to minimize competition over resources and, instead, stress the ability of humans to cooperate at extraordinary levels (e.g., Fry, 2007). They also tend to overlook the pervasiveness of violence across all taxa, including the primates. While most recognize the apparent universality of violence across primates and the other animal orders, they tend to minimize the importance of violence, especially LV, in shaping the social systems those species operate in (e.g., Hart & Sussman, 2005).

On the other side of the debate over violence in our evolutionary past are researchers who view the ubiquity of violence across human cultures and in our primate relatives, combined with the basic similarities of violence in human and chimpanzee populations, to indicate a deep evolutionary history of this behavior within our lineage (e.g., Boehm, 1999; Davie, 1929; Gat, 2006; Keeley, 1996; LeBlanc & Register, 2003; Livingstone Smith, 2007; Otterbein, 1973; Wrangham & Peterson, 1996). Researchers who take this perspective tend to focus on competition over resources and the fitness advantages that targeted violence can provide individuals during such competition.

It is generally agreed upon by researchers who have taken the position of early hominins as inherently peaceful that NLV was present in these populations (e.g., Hart & Sussman, 2005). However, most of those same researchers contend that LV was incredibly rare (de Waal, 1997) or absent (Hart & Sussman, 2005) in early hominin populations. Their conclusions stem from several different perspectives and data sets. First, researchers who take the position that early hominins were inherently peaceful point out that LV has never been observed in one of our closest living relatives, the bonobo (de Waal, 1997). Bonobos have been studied in the wild for over 30 years, in multiple locations, by multiple researchers, with differing levels of habituation and provisioning. There has not been a single case of LV reported in the literature at any of those locations. Despite regular female coalitions against males (e.g., de Waal, 1997; Kano, 1992; Parish, 1994, 1996;

Parish & de Waal, 2000; White & Wood, 2007) and agonistic interactions between males from separate communities (Hohmann, 2001; Ihobe, 1992), LV appears to be absent in bonobos.

Second, researchers who take the position that early hominins were inherently peaceful highlight the cooperative nature of the human species, and the universal morals humans exhibit, which reinforce that cooperation. The complexity of human relationships, networks, and societies surpasses any other animal species, including those of the Delphinids and our closest living relatives. Evidence supports that one of the results of such complexity is increased encephalization (Byrne & Whiten, 1988). Such a large and complex brain allows humans to cooperate in ways that no other species is capable of Humans' complex brains are also ideal for developing behaviors like universal morals and norms (de Waal, 1997). As a result, humans are the most cooperative mammals that have ever existed, capable of forming intense bonds with kin and nonkin, which are reinforced through shared understandings of norms and morals (Boehm, 1999; Hill et al., 2011; de Waal, 1997). Those bonds and social rules allow individuals to cooperate at levels that have never been seen in any animal species, resulting in everything from egalitarian societies in hunter and gatherer populations (Boehm, 1999) to historical and modern-day cities (Mumford, 1961). There is little doubt that cooperation, reinforced through universal norms and morals, is a species-typical behavior exhibited by modern humans.

The data on human cooperation and norms, combined with the lack of LV in bonobos, is compelling evidence for some that early hominins were inherently peaceful (Hart & Sussman, 2005). However, cooperation and norms that reinforce it and LV are not mutually exclusive. In fact, in many human cultures males utilize their cooperative relationships with other community members to engage in LV against males from other communities (Livingstone Smith, 2007). Furthermore, the universality of norms and morals that prohibit and limit LV between community members indicates that humans have been subjected to strong selective forces favoring the mitigation of such behaviors (Boehm, 1999). Such selective forces could only come into play if violence was prevalent in early human populations.

The lack of LV in bonobos provides important information about the behavioral ecology of this species and behavioral variation in the genus *Pan*. However, by itself, the lack of LV in bonobos does not provide much information on the behavior of early hominins. The reason for this is that it is a single data set from one species, and no species can serve as a surrogate for the behavior of early hominins. Instead, the most parsimonious approach to reconstruct the social behaviors of early hominins is to use a phylogenetically conservative approach (sensu Wrangham, 1987). Wrangham's premise is simple: Behaviors that are observed in more than one living ape most likely evolved once and not multiple times, and therefore represent shared traits inherited from a common ancestor.

When this methodology is applied to the question of whether early hominins engaged in NLV and LV, the results are relatively straightforward (Appendix 1). While I have expanded the database to include data on all of the living apes, in an effort to provide a more complete picture of violence across the Hominoids, I have weighted the data on humans, chimpanzees, and bonobos more heavily than the others. If a behavior has been observed in two of those three species, I have considered it likely to been present in early hominins as well. If it is absent in one of the three species, it is likely a unique characteristic of that species, and not representative of the primitive condition for all three.

The data presented here indicate that it is likely that early hominins engaged in intrasexual and intersexual NLV against adult and immature conspecifics that ranged from chasing, to hitting, to biting, but did not result in fatalities. Furthermore, the data indicate that early hominins probably engaged in intrasexual and intersexual LV against adult and immature conspecifics as well. While there is more variation across the living apes in the type of LV observed, research suggests that bonobos are anomalous in not engaging in this activity. Furthermore, the observation of LV in humans and chimpanzees that covers the spectrum indicates that this behavior is not unique to either species and was likely present in the last common ancestor of both and the earliest hominins. LV was probably made less costly and more easily achieved thanks to the likely social structure of fission-fusion communities in which males were bonded with each other, collectively defended territories, and occasionally enjoyed imbalances of power in competition with extra-group conspecifics..

The overall picture that emerges from these data is the presence of both NLV and LV in early hominins, ranging from within-community fights to infanticides and other lethal attacks on conspecifics (but see Suwa et al., 2009). Early hominins were medium-sized apes that lived in woodland/forested ecologies (White et al., 2009). Given their body size and general ecology, it is likely that these bipedal apes were omnivorous frugivores that lived in fission-fusion communities as part of female competitive strategies over food resources. Early hominins were most likely male bonded and territorial and practiced fission-fusion grouping patterns, resulting in the occasional isolation of individuals and the potential for imbalances of power (Wrangham, 1999; but see Suwa et al., 2009).

Conclusion

Violence is widespread across living organisms and is prevalent in animal taxa ranging from insects to hominins. As such, violence has a long evolutionary history and is just one of the strategies that organisms use to successfully compete for resources in varying contexts. There are two broad categories of violence, nonlethal violence (NLV) and lethal violence (LV). The primary distinction between the two categories is that LV leads to the death of one or more actors participating in violence, and it can inflict high costs on the individuals involved. LV is rarer than NLV and there is controversy over whether it is a natural behavior for those species in which it has been observed.

The preponderance of evidence suggests that both NLV and LV are natural behaviors that are carried out by individuals in wild populations when the contexts they find themselves in favor such behavior (e.g., mating competition in sierra dome spiders; de Carvalho et al., 2003). NLV typically includes chasing, hitting, biting and other nonlethal forms of aggression. It is ubiquitous across mammals and appears to be a regular part of social interaction. Within the primates, NLV has been reported in almost, if not every, known species (Hart & Sussman, 2005).

LV is much less common across mammals, but it is still widespread. Ranging from male red deer deaths during mating competition (Clutton-Brock et al., 1982) to infanticide in bottlenose dolphins (Dunn et al., 2002) to mass killings during wartime in humans (Keegan, 1993), LV takes many forms in mammals. LV directed toward adults is rare in primates, but it has been observed in several species, including western red colobus (Starin, 1994), diana monkeys (McGraw et al., 2002), wedge-capped capuchins (Miller, 1998), white-faced capuchins (Gros-Louis et al., 2003), chimpanzees (Wrangham et al., 2003), gibbons (Palombit, 1993), and humans (Boehm, 1999; Daly & Wilson, 1988). Furthermore, adult-adult LV has been suggested in orangutans (Knott, 2000).

Infanticide is the killing of same-species infants by one or more adults and is more common among primates than adult-adult LV. To date, infanticide has been reported in at least 39 primate species (reviewed in van Schaik, 2000) and has been suggested as a major force in the evolution of female primate social relationships (Sterck et al., 1997). Infanticide has been reported (gibbons, Alfred & Sati, 1991; gorillas, Fossey, 1984; chimpanzees, Goodall, 1986; humans, Daly & Wilson, 1988) or suggested (orangutans, Knott et al., 2010) in all of the apes, except bonobos. Among the apes, it appears that only bonobos lack LV directed toward adults and infanticide, suggesting that their unique behavioral pattern is just that, unique to their species.

The patterns of violence observed in the apes, including humans, are consistent with those observed across other animals. NLV is not exclusively a male activity, and both females and males engage in NLV as part of normal social interactions, which include contests over food, territory, and access to mates. LV is almost always a male activity and is usually associated with mating competition. When the costs of losing a mating contest are too high (e.g., elephant seals, Haley, 1994) or the risks associated with killing an adult conspecific are minimized (e.g., chimpanzees, Wrangham, 1999), males will attempt to eliminate rivals. The elimination of rivals is made easier when individuals regularly forage or travel alone, as they do in a fission-fusion social system (Manson & Wrangham, 1991). The risks associated with attacking rivals are further reduced when males bond together, allowing for coalitions and cooperation and resulting in imbalances of power (Wrangham, 1999).

While no single species represents an accurate model for early hominin behavior, their behavior can be modeled using a phylogenetically conservative approach (Wrangham, 1987). Applying this approach to a combination of new and synthesized data indicates that early hominins displayed behaviors typical of the ape pattern. It is almost certain that early hominins, like every other ape species, including bonobos, engaged in NLV that was directed at adults and immatures. Furthermore, the data presented in Table 2.1 indicate that the earliest hominins engaged in LV that was made advantageous through the combination of a fission-fusion social system and male bonding. Given the patterns observed in humans and the other apes, excluding bonobos, early hominins probably committed acts of intrasexual and intersexual LV and infanticide via coalitions, reducing the risks associated with such attacks.

Future Directions

There are several key areas that need to be addressed in the future to expand and illuminate studies on the evolution of violence. First, comparative studies that synthesize data on human and nonhuman primates and other animals are lacking, for one primary reason. As discussed earlier, the term "violence" is rarely used in studies on nonhuman animals. Instead, the term "aggression," a more generalized term, is used with various qualifiers, such as lethal and nonlethal. The term "violence" is generally only used in studies on humans, and typically it only refers to aberrant, illegal, or antisocial behaviors. While this typically suffices for psychological, sociological, or criminological studies, the framing of violence as unwanted behavior makes it difficult, if not impossible, to use the term for comparative studies of humans and other animals. Violence needs to be decoupled from aberrant behaviors to allow for the comparison of this behavior across all taxa, including humans.

Second, while NLV appears to be universal, we still do not have a clear sense of how many species engage in LV. Lethal violence is suspected in several species (e.g., orangutans—Knott, 2000) but has not been confirmed. Among several of the species in which we have confirmed LV, we still do not have complete data on their social structures, mating systems, or life histories. Concerted efforts should be made to collect those data and report on them in the literature. As we compile a more comprehensive database on LV across animal populations, we will be better positioned to analyze it in our own species and our hominin ancestors.

Third, our understanding of the behavioral ecology of hominins is limited due to incomplete data in the fossil record, combined with uncertainty over the specific characteristics of known hominins. Even though research continues to increase our understanding of the hominin fossil record, it will remain incomplete for the foreseeable future. However, we can increase our understanding of the characteristics of known hominins and our ability to model the behavior of those organisms. With continued research on the known fossil record that includes the application of biological principles, we can further refine our conclusions about hominins. The methods introduced by Wrangham (1987) and expanded upon here provide objective approaches to modeling hominin behavior, based on observed behaviors in relevant species. The continued and expanded application of this method will further our ability to model hominin behavior effectively.

References

Agrell, J., Wolff, J. O., & Ylonen, H. (1998). Counterstrategies to infanticide in mammals: cost and consequences. *Oikos, 83*, 507–517.

Alfred, J. R. B., & Sati, J. P. (1991). On the first record of infanticide in the hoolock gibbon- *Hylobates hoolock* in the wild. *Records of the Zoological Survey of India, 89*(1–4), 319–321.

Arcadi, A. C., & Wrangham, R. W. (1999). Infanticide in chimpanzees: Review of cases and a new within group observation from the Kanyawara study group in Kibale National Park. *Primates, 40*, 337–351.

Archer, J. (1988). *The behavioral biology of aggression*. New York: Cambridge University Press.

Bernstein, I. S., Gordon, T. P., & Rose, R. M. (1974). Aggression and social controls in rhesus monkey (Macaca mulatta) groups revealed in group formation studies. *Folia Primatologica, 21*, 81–107.

Bester, M. N. (1988). Marking and monitoring studies of the Kerguelen stock of southern elephant seals, (*Mirounga leonine*), and their bearing on biological research in the Vestfold Hills. *Hydrobiologia, 165*, 269–277.

Blaustein, A. R., & Risser, A. C., J. R. (1976). Interspecific interactions between three sympatric species of kangaroo rats (Dipodomys). *Animal Behaviour, 24*, 381–385.

Boehm, C. (1999). *Hierarchy in the forest: The evolution of egalitarian behavior*. Cambridge, MA: Harvard University Press.

Boesch, C., & Boesch-Achermann, H. (2000). *The Chimpanzees of the Tai forest: Behavioural ecology and evolution*. Oxford, England: Oxford University Press.

Boesch, C., Head, J., Tagg, N., Arandjelovic, M., Vigilant, L., & Robbins, M. M. (2007). Fatal chimpanzee attack in Loango National Park, Gabon. *International Journal of Primatology, 28*(5), 1025–1034.

Borries, C., Savini, T., & Koenig, A. (2011). Social monogamy and the threat of infanticide in larger mammals. *Behavioral Ecology and Socibiology, 65*(4), 685–693.

Byers, J. A. (1997). *American pronghorn: Social adaptations and the ghosts of predators past*. Chicago: University of Chicago Press.

Byrne, R., & Whiten, A. (1988). *Machiavellian intelligence*. New York: Oxford University Press.

Calhoun, J. B. (1962). Population density and social pathology. *Scientific American, 206*, 139–148.

Caro, T. M., & Collins, D. A. (1986). Male cheetahs of the Serengeti. *National Geographic Research, 2*, 75–86.

Carpenter, C. R., (1938). A survey of wildlife conditions in Atjeh, North Sumatra. *Netherlands Committee for International Nature Protection, 12*, 1–33.

Carrick, R., & Ingham, S. E. (1962). Studies of the southern elephant seal *Mirounga leonina* (L.). V. Population dynamics and utilization. *CSIRO Wildlife Research, 7*, 198–206.

Chagnon, N. A. (1988). Life histories, blood revenge, and warfare in a tribal population. *Science, 239*, 985–992.

Chagnon, N. (1997). *Yanomamo* (5th ed.). New York: Harcourt Brace.

Chagnon, N., & Irons, W. (1979). *Evolutionary biology and human social behavior*. Pacific Grove, CA: Duxbury Press.

Chapais, B. (2008). *Primeval kinship: How pair-bonding gave birth to human society*. Cambridge, MA: Harvard University Press.

Cioffi-Revilla, C. (1996). Origins and evolution of war and politics. *International Studies Quarterly, 40*, 1–22.

Clutton-Brock, T. H., Guinness, F. E., & Albon, S. A. (1982). *Red deer: Behavior and ecology of two sexes*. Chicago: University of Chicago Press.

Constable, J. L., Ashley, M. V., Goodall, J., & Pusey, A. E. (2001). Noninvasive paternity assignment in Gombe chimpanzees. *Molecular Ecology, 10*(5), 1279–1300.

Creel, S., & Creel, N. M. (2002). *The African wild dog: Behavior, ecology, and conservation*. Princeton, NJ: Princeton University Press.

Daly, M., & Wilson, M. (1988). *Homicide*. Hawthorne, NY: Aldine de Gruyter.

Darwin, C. (1871). *The descent of man, and selection in relation to sex*. London: John Murray.

Davie, M. R. (1929). *The evolution of war: A study of its role in early societies*. New Haven, CT: Yale University Press.

De Carvalho, T. N., Watson, P. J., & Field, S. A. (2003). Costs increase ritualized fighting progresses within and between phases in the sierra dome spider, Neriene litigiosa. *Animal Behaviour, 68*, 473–482.

De Waal, F. B. M. (1982). *Chimpanzee politics: Power and sex among apes*. Baltimore: Johns Hopkins University Press.

De Waal, F. B. M. (1997). *Good natured: The origins of right and wrong in humans and other animals*. Cambridge, MA: Harvard University Press.

De Waal, F. B. M. (2009). *The age of empathy: Nature's lessons for a kinder society*. New York, NY: Crown.

Dohlinow, P. (1977). Normal monkeys? *American Scientist, 65*, 266.

Dunn, D. G., Barco, S. G., Pabst, D. A., & McLellan, W. A. (2002). Evidence for infanticide in wild bottlenose dolphins of the western north Atlantic. *Journal of Wildlife Diseases, 38*, 505–510.

East, M. L., & Hofer, H. (2001). Male spotted hyenas (crocuta crocuta) queue for status in social groups dominated by females. *Behavioral Ecology, 12*(5), 558–568.

Emlen, S. T., & Oring, L. W. (1977). Ecology, sexual selection, and the evolution of mating systems. *Science, 197*, 215–223.

Enquist, M., & Leimar, O. (1990). The evolution of fatal fighting. *Animal Behaviour, 39*, 1–9.

Fashing, P. J. (2001a). Activity and ranging patterns of guerezas in the Kakamega Forest: Intergroup variation and implications for intragroup feeding competition. *International Journal of Primatology, 22*, 549–577.

Fashing, P. J. (2001b). Feeding ecology of guerezas in the Kakamega Forest: The importance of Moraceae fruit in their diet. *International Journal of Primatology, 22*, 579–609.

Fawcett, K., & Muhumuza, G. (2000). Death of a wild chimpanzee community member: Possible outcome of intense sexual competition. *American Journal of Primatology, 51*(4), 243–247.

Fernandez-Gil, A., Swenson, J. E., Granda, C., Perez, T., Dominguez, A., Ordiz, A., ... Delibes M., (2010). Evidence of sexually selected infanticide in an endangered brown bear population. *Animal Behaviour, 79*, 521–527.

Fossey, D. (1984). *Gorillas in the mist*. New York: Houghton Mifflin.

Fry, D. P. (2007). *Beyond war*. New York: Oxford University Press.

Fuentes, A. (2000). Hylobatid communities: Changing views on pair bonding and social organization in hominoids. *Yearbook of Physical Anthropology, 43*, 33–60.

Gat, A. (2006). *War in human civilization*. New York: Oxford University Press.

Geissmann, T. (2002). Duet-splitting and the evolution of gibbon songs. *Biological Reviews, 77(1)*, 57–76.

Goodall, J. (1986). *The chimpanzees of Gombe: Patterns of behavior*. New York: Cambridge University Press.

Gregory, W. K. (1950). *The anatomy of the gorilla*. New York: Columbia University Press.

Grinnell, J., Packer, C., & Pusey, A. E. (*1995*). Cooperation in male *lions*: Kinship, reciprocity or mutualism? *Animal Behaviour, 49*, 95–105.

Gros-Louis, J., Perry, S., & Manson, J. H. (2003). Violent coalitionary attacks and intraspecific killing in wild white-faced capuchin monkeys (Cebus capucinus). *Primates, 44*, 341–146.

Haley, M. P. (1994). Resource-holding power asymmetries, the prior residence effect, and reproductive payoffs in male northern elephant seal fights. *Behavioral Ecology and Sociobiology, 34*(6), 427–434.

Harcourt, A. H., & de Waal, F. B. (1992). *Coalitions and alliances in humans and other animals*. New York: Oxford University Press.

Harcourt, A., & Greenberg, J. (2001). Do gorilla females join males to avoid infanticide? A quantitative model. *Animal Behaviour, 62*, 905–915.

Harris, T. R. (2006). Between-group contest competition for food in a highly folivorous population of black and white colobus monkeys (Colobus guereza). *Behavioral Ecology and Sociobiology, 61*, 317–329.

Hart, D., & Sussman, R. (2005). *Man the hunted: Primates, predators, and human evolution*. New York: Basic Books.

Hausfater, G., & Hrdy, S. B. (1984). *Infanticide: Comparative and evolutionary perspectives*. Foundations of Human Behavior Series. Hawthorne, NY: Aldine de Gruyter.

Hendricks, T. J., Fyodorov, D. V., Wegman, L. J., Lelutiu, N. B., Pehek, E. A., Yamamoto, B., Deneris, E. S. (2003) Pet-1 ETS gene plays a critical role in 5-HT neuron development and is required for normal anxiety-like and aggressive behavior. *Neuron, 37*(2), 233–247.

Hill, K. R., & Hurtado, A. M. (1996). *Aché life history*. Hawthorne, NY: Aldine de Gruyter.

Hill, K. R., Walker, R. S., Bozicevic, M., Eder, J., Headland, T., Hewlett, B., Hurtado, A. M., ... Wood, B. (2011). Co-Residence patterns in hunter-gatherer societies show unique human social structure. *Science, 331*(6022), 1286–1289.

Hohmann, G. (2001). Association and social interactions between strangers and residents in bonobos (*Pan paniscus*). *Primates, 42*(1). 91–99.

Hongo, Y. (2003). Appraising behaviour during male-male interaction in the Japanese horned beetle *Trypoxylus dichotomus spetentrionalis* (Kono). *Behaviour,140*, 501–517.

Hrdy, S. B. (1974). Male-male competition and infanticide among langurs (presbytis-entellus) of abu, rajasthan. *Folia Primatologica, 22*(1), 19–58.

Hrdy, S. B. (1979). Infanticide among animals—review, classification, and examination of the implications for the reproductive strategies of females. *Ethology and Sociobiology, 1*(1), 13–40.

Ihobe, H. (1992). Observations on the meat-eating behavior of wild bonobos (*Pan paniscus*) at Wamba, Republic of Zaire. *Primates, 33*(2), 247–250.

Immelmann, K., & Beer, C. (*1989*). *A dictionary of ethology*. Cambridge, MA: Harvard University Press.

Janson, C., & van Schaik, C. P. (2000). *Infanticide by males and its implications*. Cambridge, England: Cambridge University Press.

Kano, T. (1992). *The last ape: Pygmy chimpanzee behavior and ecology*. Stanford, CA: Stanford University Press.

Keegan, J. (1993). *A history of warfare*. New York: Vintage Press.

Keeley, L. H. (1996). *War before civilization: The myth of the peaceful savage*. New York: Oxford University Press.

Kelly, R. C. (2000). *Warless societies and the origin of war*. Ann Arbor: University of Michigan Press.

Kemp, D. J., & Wiklund, C. (2001). Fighting without weaponry: A review of male-male contest competition in butterflies. *Behavioral Ecology Sociobiology, 49*, 429–442.

Knott, C. D. (March, 2000). *Testosterone and behavioral differences in fully developed and undeveloped wild Bornean orangutans (Pongo pygmaeus pygmaeus)*. Paper presented at the American Association of Physical Anthropologists Annual Meeting, San Antonio, TX.

Knott, C. D., Emery-Thompson, M., Stumpf, R. M., & McIntyre, M. H. (2010). Female reproductive strategies in orangutans, evidence for female choice and counterstrategies to infanticide in a species with frequent sexual coercion. *Proceedings of the Royal Society B, 277*, 105–113.

Kruuk, H. (1972). *The spotted hyena. A study of predation and social behavior*. Chicago: University of Chicago Press.

LeBlanc, S. A., & Register, K. E. (2003). *Constant battles: Why we fight*. New York: Macmillan.

Livingstone Smith, D. (2007). *The most dangerous animal: Human nature and the origins of war*. New York: St. Martin's Press.

Lorenz, K. (1959). *King Solomon's ring: New light on animals' ways*. New York, NY: Crowell.

Lorenz, K. (1963). *On aggression*. London, UK: Methuen.

Manson, J. H., & Wrangham, R. W. (1991). Intergroup aggression in chimpanzees and humans. *Current Anthropology, 32*, 369–390.

Marlowe, F., Apicella, C., & Reed, D. (2005). Men's preferences for women's profile waist-to-hip ratio in two societies. *Evolution and Human Behavior, 26*(6), 458–468.

Maynard-Smith, J., & Price, G. R. (1973). The logic of animal conflict. *Nature, 246*, 15–18.

Mazur, A., & Booth, A., (1998). Testosterone and dominance in men. *Behavioral Brain Science, 21*, 353–397.

McGraw, W. S., Plavcan, J. M., & Adachi-Kanazawa, K. (2002). Adult female Cercopithecus diana employ canine teeth to kill another adult female. *International Journal of Primatology, 23*, 1301–1308.

Mech, L. D. (1977). Productivity, mortality, and population trends of wolves in Northeastern Minnesota. *Journal of Mammology, 58*(4), 559–574.

Mech, L. D., Adams, L. G., Meier, T. J., Burch, J. W., & Dale, B. W., (1998). *The wolves of Denali*. Minneapolis: University of Minnesota Press.

Mech, L. D. & Boitani, L. (2003). *Wolves: Behavior, ecology, and conservation*. Chicago: University of Chicago Press.

Melis, C., Hoem, S. A., Linnell, J. D. C., & Andersen, R. (2005). Age-specific reproductive behaviours in male roe deer capreolus capreolus. *Acta Theriologica, 50*(4), 445–452.

Menella, J. A., & Moltz, H. (1988). Infanticide in rats: Male strategy and female counter strategy. *Physiology and Behavior, 42*, 19–28.

Miller, L. E. (1998). Fatal attack among wedge-capped capuchins. *Folia Primatologica, 69*, 89–92.

Mitani, J. C. (2009). Male chimpanzees form enduring and equitable social bonds. *Animal Behaviour, 77*(3), 633–640.

Mitani, J.C. and D. Watts. 2005. Correlates of territorial boundary patrol behavior in wild chimpanzees. *Animal Behaviour* 70: 1079–1086.

Mitani, J. C., Watts, D. P., & Amsler, S. J. (2010). Lethal intergroup aggression leads to territorial expansion in wild chimpanzees. *Current Biology, 20*, 507–508.

Muller, M. N. (2002). Agonistic relations among Kanyawara chimpanzees. In C. Boesch, G. Hohmann, & L. Marchant (Eds.), *Behavioral diversity in chimpanzees and bonobos* (pp. 112–124). Cambridge, England: Cambridge University Press.

Muller, M. N., Kahlenberg, S. K., Emery-Thompson, M., & Wrangham, R. W. (2007). Male coercion and the costs of promiscuous mating in chimpanzees. *Proceedings of the Royal Society B, 274*, 1009–1014.

Mumford, L. (1961). *The city in history: Its origins, its transformations, and its prospects*. New York; Harcourt, Brace & World.

Newton-Fisher, N. E. (2006). Female coalitions against male aggression in wild chimpanzees of the Budongo forest. *International Journal of Primatology, 27*, 1589–1599.

Nishida, T., & Hosaka, K. (1996). Coalition strategies among adult male chimpanzees of the Mahale Mountains, Tanzania. In W. C. McGrew, L. F. Marchant, & T. Nishida (Eds.), *Great ape societies* (pp. 114–134). New York: Cambridge University Press.

Otterbein, K. (1973). The anthropology of war. In J. J. Honigmann (Ed.), *Handbook of social and cultural anthropology* (pp 923–958). New York, NY: Rand McNally.

Packer, C., & Pusey, A. E., (1983). Adaptations of female lions to infanticide by incoming males. *American Naturalist, 121*, 716–728.

Packer, C., Herbst, L., Pusey, A. E., Bygott, J. D., Cairns, S. J., Hanby, J. P., & Borgerhoff-Mulder, M. (1988). Reproductive success of lions. In T. H. Clutton Brock (Ed.), *Reproductive success* (pp. 363–383). Chicago: University of Chicago Press.

Palombit, R. (1993). Lethal territorial aggression in a white-handed gibbon. *American Journal of Primatology, 31*(4), 311–318.

Parish, A. (1994). Sex and food control in the uncommon chimpanzee—how bonobo females overcome a phylogenetic legacy of male dominance. *Ethology and Sociobiology, 15*(3), 157–179.

Parish, A. R. (1996). Female relationships in bonobos (*Pan paniscus*): evidence for bonding, cooperation, and female dominance in a male-philopatric species. *Human Nature*, 7:61–96.

Parish, A., & De Waal, F. B. M. (2000). The other "closest living relative"—How bonobos (*Pan paniscus*) challenge traditional assumptions about females, dominance, intra- and intersexual interactions, and hominid evolution. *Annals of the New York Academy of Sciences, 907*, 97–113

Patterson, I. A. P., Reid, R. J., Wilson, B., Ross, H. M., & Thompson, P. M. (1998). Evidence for infanticide in bottlenose dolphins: An explanation for violent interactions with harbour porpoises? *Proceedings of the Royal Society London B, 265*, 1167–1170.

Pepper, J. W., Mitani, J. C., & Watts, D. P. (1999). General gregariousness and specific social preferences among wild chimpanzees. *International Journal of Primatology, 20*(5), 613–632.

Pusey, A. E., Murray, C., Wallauer, W., Wilson, M., Wroblewski, E., & Goodall, J. (2008). Severe aggression among female *Pan troglodytes schweinfurthii* at Gombe National Park, Tanzania. *International Journal of Primatology, 29*, 949–973.

Reichard, U., & Sommer, V. (1997). Group encounters in wild gibbons (*Hylobates lar*): Agonism, affiliation, and the concept of infanticide. *Behaviour, 134*, 1135–1174.

Sanvito, S., Galimberti, F., & Miller, E. H. (2007). Vocal signalling of male southern elephant seals is honest but imprecise. *Animal Behaviour, 73*(2), 287–299.

Schaller, G. B. (1963). *The mountain gorilla: Ecology and behavior*. Chicago: University of Chicago Press.

Schaller, G. B. (1972). *The Serengeti lion: A study of predator-prey relations*. Chicago: University of Chicago Press.

Sherrow, H. M., & Amsler, S. J. (2007). New cases of intercommunity infanticides by the chimpanzees of Ngogo, Kibale National Park, Uganda. *International Journal of Primatology, 28*(1), 9–22.

Shier, D. M., & Randall, J. A. (2007). Use of different signaling modalities to communicate status by dominant and subordinate heermann's kangaroo rats (Dipodomys heermanni). *Behavioral Ecology and Sociobiology, 61*(7), 1023–1032.

Singer, P. (1981). *The expanding circle: Ethics and sociobiology*. New York: Oxford University Press.

Singleton, I., & van Schaik, C. P. (2001). Orangutan home range size and its determinants in a Sumatran swamp forest. *International Journal of Primatology, 22*(6), 877–911.

Smuts, B. B. (1995). The evolutionary origins of patriarchy. *Human Nature, 6*(1), 1–32.

Smuts, B. B., & Smuts, R. W. (1993). Male aggression and sexual coercion of females in nonhuman primates and other mammals: Evidence and theoretical implications. *Advances in the Study of Behavior, 22*, 1–63.

Starin, E. D. (1994). Philopatry and affiliation among red colobus. *Behaviour, 130*, 253–270.

Sterck, E. H. M., Watts, D. P., & van Schaik, C. P. (1997). The evolution of female social relationships in nonhuman primates. *Behavioral Ecology and Sociobiology, 41*, 291–309.

Stumpf, R. M., & Boesch, C. (2010). Male aggression and sexual coercion in wild West African chimpanzees (*Pan troglodytes verus*). *Animal Behaviour, 79*, 333–342.

Sussman, R. W., Garber, P. A., & Cheverud, J. (2005). The importance of cooperation and affiliation in the evolution of primate sociality. *American Journal of Physical Anthropology, 128*, 84–97.

Suwa, G., Kono, R. T., Simpson, S. W., Asfaw, B., Lovejoy, C. O., & White, T. D. (2009). Paleobiological implications of the *Ardipithecus ramidus* dentition. *Science, 326*, 94–99.

Swartz, J. D., Maryke, J. S., & Ned, A. (2010). Coexisting desert rodents differ in selection of microhabitats for cache placement and pilferage. *Journal of Mammalogy, 91*, 1261–1268.

Talebi, M. G., Beltrao-Mendes, R., & Lee, P. C. (2009). Intracommunity coalitionary lethal attack of an adult male southern muriqui (Brachyteles arachnoides). *American Journal of Primatology, 71*(10), 860–867.

Taylor, J. R. A., & Patek, S. N. (2010). Ritualized fighting and biological armor: The impact mechanics of the mantis shrimp's telson. *Journal of Experimental Biology, 213*, 3496–3504.

Trulio, L. A., Loughry, W. J., Hennessy, D. F., & Owings, D. H. (1986). Infanticide in California ground-squirrels. *Animal Behaviour, 34*, 291–294.

Tutin, C. E. G. (1979). Mating patterns and reproductive strategies in a community of wild chimpanzees (*Pan troglodytes schweinfurthii*). *Behavioral Ecology and Sociobiology, 6*(1), 29.

Van Hoof, J. A. R. A. M., & van Schaik, C. P. (1994). Male bonds: Afilliative relationships among nonhuman primate males. *Behaviour, 130*(3–4), 143–151.

Van Schaik, C. P. (2000). Infanticide by male primates: The sexual selection hypothesis revisited. In C. P. van Schaik & C. H. Janson (Eds.), *Male infanticide and its implications* (pp. 27–60). New York: Cambridge University Press.

Vasey, N. (1997). *Community ecology and behavior of varecia variegata rubra and lemur fulvus albifrons, on the Masoala Peninsula, Madagascar*. Unpublished Ph.D. dissertation, Washington University, St. Louis, MO.

Vigilant, L., Hofreiter, M., Siedel, H., & Boesch, C. (2001). Paternity and relatedness in wild chimpanzee communities. *Proceedings of the National Academy of Sciences USA, 98*(23), 12890–12895.

Watts, D. P. (1988). Environmental influences on mountain gorilla time budgets. *American Journal of Primatology, 15*, 195–211.

Watts, D. P. (1989). Infanticide in mountain gorillas—new cases and a reconsideration of the evidence. *Ethology, 81*(1), 1–18.

Watts, D. P. (1994). The influence of male mating tactics on habitat use in mountain gorillas (*Gorilla gorilla beringei*). *Primates, 35*(1), 35–47.

Watts, D. P. (1998). Coalitionary mate guarding by male chimpanzees at Ngogo, Kibale National Park, Uganda. *Behavioral Ecology and Sociobiology, 44*(1), 43–55.

Watts, D. P. (2004). Intracommunity coalitionary killing of an adult male chimpanzee at Ngogo, Kibale National Park, Uganda. *International Journal of Primatology, 25*, 507–521.

Watts, D. P., & Mitani, J. C. (2001). Boundary patrols and intergroup encounters in wild chimpanzees. *Behaviour, 138*, 299–327.

Watts, D. P., Mitani, J. C., & Sherrow, H. M. (2002). New Cases of Inter-community Infanticide by Male Chimpanzees at Ngogo, Kibale National Park, Uganda. *Primates. 43*(3), 263–270.

Watts, D. P., Muller, M., Amsler, S. J., Mbabazi, G., & Mitani, J. C. (2006). Lethal intergroup aggression by chimpanzees in Kibale National Park, Uganda. *American Journal of Primatology, 68*(2), 161–180.

White, F. J., & Wood, K. D. (2007). Female feeding priority in bonobos, Pan paniscus, and the question of female dominance. *American Journal of Primatology, 69*, 1–14.

White, T. D., Asfaw, B., Beyene, Y. Haile-Selassie, Y., Lovejoy, C. O., Suwa, G., & WoldeGabriel, G. (2009). *Ardipithecus ramidus* and the paleobiology of early hominids. *Science, 329*, 75–86.

Williams, G. C. (1966). *Adaptation and evolution*. Princeton, NJ: Princeton University Press.

Williams, J. M., Lonsdorf, E. V., Wilson, M. L., Schumacher-Stankey, J., Goodall, J., & Pusey, A. E. (2008). Causes of death in the kasekela chimpanzees of Gombe National Park, Tanzania. *American Journal of Primatology, 70*(8), 766–777.

Wilson, D. E., & Reeder, D. M. (2005). *Mammal species of the world. A taxonomic and geographic reference* (3rd ed.). Baltimore: Johns Hopkins University Press.

Wilson, M. L., Hauser, M. D., & Wrangham, R. W. (2001). Does participation in intergroup conflict depend on numerical assessment, range location, or rank for wild chimpanzees? *Animal Behaviour, 61*, 1203–1216.

Wilson, M. L., & Wrangham, R. W. (2003). Intergroup relations in chimpanzees. *Annual Review of Anthropology, 32*, 363–392.

Wong, M., & Balshine, S. (2011). Fight for your breeding right: Hierarchy re-establishment predicts aggression in a social queue. *Biology Letters, 7*(2), 190–193.

Wrangham, R. W. (1980). An ecological model of the evolution of female-bonded groups of primates. *Behaviour, 75,* 262–300.

Wrangham, R. W. (1987). The significance of African apes for reconstructing human social evolution. In W. G. Kinzey (Ed.), *Primate models of hominid evolution* (pp. 51–71). New York: SUNY Press.

Wrangham, R. W. (1999). Evolution of coalitionary killing. *Yearbook of Physical Anthropology, 42,* 1–30.

Wrangham, R. W. (2000). Why are male chimpanzees more gregarious than mothers? A scramble competition hypothesis. In P. M. Kappeler (Ed.), *Primate males: Causes and consequences of variation in group composition* (pp. 248–257). New York: Cambridge University Press.

Wrangham, R. W. & Peterson, D. (1996). *Demonic males: Apes and the origins of human violence.* London: Bloomsbury.

Wrangham, R. W., & Wilson, M. L. (2004). Collective violence—comparisons between youths and chimpanzees. *Youth Violence: Scientific Approaches to Prevention, 1036,* 233–256.

Wrangham, R. W., Wilson, M. L., & Muller, M. N. (2006). Comparative rates of violence in chimpanzees and humans. *Primates, 47*(1), 14–26.

Yamagiwa, J. (1987). Intragroup and intergroup interactions of an all-male group of Virunga mountain gorillas (*Gorilla gorilla berengei*). *Primates, 28*(1), 1–30.

Appendix A.1 The Likelihood That Early Hominins Engaged in Nonlethal Violence and Lethal Violence Based on Applying Wrangham's Methodology (1987) to Data on the Living Apes

	Hylobates spp.	Pongo spp.	Gorilla spp.	Pan paniscus	Pan troglodytes	Homo sapiens	Early Hominins
Nonlethal violence (NLV)	Yes	Yes	Yes	Yes	Yes	Yes	Yes
Intrasexual NLV	Yes	Yes	Yes	Yes	Yes	Yes	Yes
Intersexual NLV	Yes	Yes	Yes	Yes	Yes	Yes	Yes
NLV toward immatures	Yes	Yes	Yes	Yes	Yes	Yes	Yes
Lethal violence (LV)	Yes	?*	Yes	No	Yes	Yes	Yes
Intrasexual LV	Yes	?*	No	No	Yes	Yes	Yes
Intersexual LV	No	No	No	No	Yes	Yes	Yes
Infanticide	Yes	?**	Yes	No	Yes	Yes	Yes
Fission-fusion	No	Yes	No	Yes	Yes	Yes	Yes
Male bonded	No	No	No	No	Yes	Yes	Yes
Territorial	Yes	No	No	No	Yes	Yes	Yes

Note. Early hominins, humans, chimpanzees, and bonobos are in bold type to recognize the importance of using humans, chimpanzees, and bonobos to reconstruct the behavior of early hominins.
* Knott, 2000.
** Knott et al., 2010.

CHAPTER 3
Comparative Evolutionary Perspectives on Violence

Nicholas E. Newton-Fisher *and* Melissa Emery Thompson

Abstract

Perhaps more than for any other human behavior, the evolutionary heritage of violence has been the subject of vigorous debate: whether shared patterns of intraspecific aggression between humans and other species doom us to a bloody existence. This chapter reviews intraspecific aggression and violence among mammalian species, focusing on primates. It highlights three themes: (1) aggression is a part of everyday life for most social animals, (2) the vast majority of conflicts in animal societies are of low intensity, and (3) there are extraordinary examples within the broad spectrum of aggressive behaviors seen in nonhumans that conform to even the most anthropocentric definitions of violence. To illustrate this third theme, the chapter reviews violence in chimpanzees, the extant species most closely related to humans and that, next to humans, exhibits the most spectacularly gruesome and varied aggressive repertoire in mammals.

Key Words: chimpanzee, *Pan troglodytes*, primate, mammal, lethal, aggression, comparative, gang assault, imbalance of power, infanticide

Introduction

Perhaps more than for any other human behavior, the evolutionary heritage of violence has been the subject of vigorous debate (Adams, 1989; De Waal, 1992; Knauft, 1991; Sussman & Marshack, 2010; Wrangham & Peterson, 1996). At the root of this debate is not the fact of human violence but whether shared patterns of intraspecific aggression between humans and other animal species doom us to a bloody existence. Yet it is those who find close parallels between human and nonhuman aggression who emphasize the ways in which aggression coexists with cooperation and stress that the challenge of controlling violence lies in understanding its adaptive contexts (de Waal, 2000; Wrangham & Peterson, 1996).

In this chapter, we review intraspecific aggression and violence among mammalian species, identifying guiding principles and common patterns that can inform the study of human violence. In doing so, we recognize the difficulties of making direct analogies within a category of behavior that is at once pervasive, exceptionally variable, and difficult to define. We cast a wide comparative net but focus on primate species. Our review highlights three major themes. First, aggression is a part of everyday life for most social animals. Rather than a violation of the social contract, aggressive episodes are essential in creating and maintaining social order (de Waal, 2000). Second, the vast majority of conflicts in animal societies, even within those that could be rated as highly aggressive, are of low intensity. In fact, animals have a variety of behavioral and physical adaptations that help to deter escalated conflicts. Third, within the broad spectrum of aggressive behaviors seen in nonhumans are extraordinary examples that conform to even the most anthropocentric definitions of violence. This third theme is clearest in our substantial treatment of violence in one particular primate species, the chimpanzee (*Pan troglodytes*).

Defining Violence and Aggression

Aggression and violence are difficult concepts to define, particularly when comparing animals and humans (Blanchard & Blanchard, 2003; Lederhendler, 2003; Natarajan & Caramaschi, 2010; Silverberg & Gray, 1992; Tolan, 2007). The usage of the term "violence" often contains an implicit value judgment about the appropriateness of aggression (Brain, 1994). Yet the two terms are typically used interchangeably in the human literature, perhaps because any aggressive behavior is generally considered to violate social norms. Behaviors such as hitting, biting, or threatening another individual are rarely referred to as violent when they occur with regularity in animal groups. A recent search of the prominent database Zoological Record returned only 34 references with the keyword "violence" that contain direct observations of the behavior of nonhuman animals (as opposed to impacts of human violence on animals). In comparison, the database PsychInfo returned nearly 30,000 references on violence in humans.

One perspective on defining aggression and violence focuses on underlying emotional states, particularly anger, a contextualization that poses a significant challenge for comparative work (Blanchard & Blanchard, 2003). This framework contrasts emotionally driven, or "affective," aggression with goal driven, or "instrumental," aggression (Blanchard & Blanchard, 2003; Houston & Stanford, 2005; Moyer, 1976; Stanford, Houston, Villemarette-Pittman, & Greve, 2003). Some scholars place a close concordance between affective aggression in humans and aggression in other animals, while seeing "instrumental" aggression as requiring greater cognitive complexity than most species possess (Blanchard & Blanchard, 2003). The paired implications are that humans who lack proper control of emotions and natural impulses revert to their animal instincts, and that nonhuman animals are incapable of conceptualizing how their aggressive actions could facilitate a desired goal. This is puzzling for a number of reasons, not the least of which is that Moyer's (1976) original conception of instrumental aggression pointed to prior experience as a simple way for aggression to become cognitively linked to a reward. Strangely, affective aggression is often referred to as "hostile" or "offensive" aggression, with the intent of inflicting harm, and simultaneously as a response to provocation or direct challenge to something important for the aggressor. As the intent to harm is frequently used to define violence (Krug, Dahlberg, Mercy, Zwi, & Lozano, 2002; Tolan, 2007), the instrumental/affective paradigm would seem to attribute most agonism in animal groups to violence, while excluding the premeditated, predatory attacks that human legal systems find most egregious. In general, it can be difficult to reconcile the conflation of proximate psychological states with the potential functions of aggression (Archer, 1988; Bushman & Anderson, 2001).

What, if any, types of animal aggression are most appropriate to a discussion of violence? Broad definitions of violence incorporate any aggression that results in direct physical contact. This definition has the advantage of being empirically precise, although overly general. Under this perspective, violent behavior is not distinguished by the underlying motivation but by the escalation of conflict. This contrasts with a common perspective in the human literature, which necessitates the actor's intention to harm but does not necessarily require consummation of physical attack (Krug et al., 2002; Tolan, 2007). The latter definition is complicated by the fact that animal intentions typically elude us, while the former definition does not allow us to distinguish particular behavioral contexts as violent, since any type of conflict could escalate. For our purposes, we adhere to the spirit of both of these definitions. After addressing the contexts of aggression generally, we will discuss why aggression sometimes escalates to the point of injury to the participants, and then we will highlight examples in which aggression seems unusually likely to lead to injury or death or in which animals appear motivated to inflict maximum damage, even against a retreating opponent. The point is not that we should restrict our animal-human comparisons to these extreme examples, but that human violence falls, not to either extreme, but within the broad range of variation exhibited by nonhuman animals. Furthermore, studies of violence in nonhumans, particularly in our close ape relatives, provide a framework for understanding how extreme expressions of aggression can emerge through adaptive processes.

Animal Models of Aggression

Aggressive conflicts are common whenever individuals come into frequent contact with one another. As a general rule, since fighting costs time and energy, and could potentially lead to injuries, natural selection is expected to have shaped organisms such that they only engage in aggression when the benefits to be gained through conflict exceed the perceived costs of fighting (Maynard Smith & Parker, 1976; Maynard Smith & Price, 1973; Popp & DeVore, 1979). Thus, aggression is expected to relate directly or indirectly to access to limited resources. Evolutionarily speaking, reproductive success in females is limited by the availability of energy by which to afford the costly process of reproduction (Trivers, 1972; Wrangham, 1980). In males, reproductive success is primarily limited by access to fertile mates (Bateman, 1948; Emlen & Oring, 1977; Trivers, 1972). Therefore, it is not surprising that conflicts among females are frequently about immediate access to food resources or concern the security of their offspring, whereas conflicts among males are frequently about their sexual access to females. Conflicts between the sexes tend to emerge when reproductive interests differ, such as when a female refuses mating attempts or strays too far from an interested male (Arnqvist & Rowe, 2005; Clutton-Brock & Parker, 1995; Parker, 1979; Smuts & Smuts, 1993). To be clear, these are only broad generalizations about the nature of interindividual conflicts, and there are myriad variations. Importantly, aggressive contests may occur between unfamiliar individuals, but they are also common between individuals with long-term social relationships, including close relatives.

A special case of aggression emerges when animals conflict not over immediate access to a particular resource but over long-term access. Territorial aggression occurs when an individual (or group of individuals) defends a particular location, and the resources within, from intruders. The resource defended might be food, mates, various types of shelter, and locations of reproductive activity, such as display sites (Wilson, 1975). Territorial aggression seems particular likely to lead to escalation of aggression, perhaps because the contestants lack any type of valuable social relationship or because conflicts over territory concern benefits that are greater and longer lasting than most conflicts over immediate resource patches. On the other hand, sporadic territorial disputes can be less costly than contesting repeatedly over the individual resources within the territory (Wilson, 1975).

In social species, a large proportion of aggressive events occur independently of a contested resource. Where individuals face persistent competition for resources with the same competitors, such conflicts can help negotiate and reinforce status relationships that affect future resource access. At one level, preexisting knowledge of the fighting ability and motivation of a competitor help an individual assess the relative costs of fighting and probability of winning a contest (Carpenter, 1942; Popp & DeVore, 1979; van Rhijn & Vodegel, 1980). Thus, dominance relationships can theoretically help reduce the frequency and intensity of future conflicts. At another level, if high dominance rank leads to predictable rewards, status itself can be the contested resource and can incite intense aggression.

Negotiating formal status relationships is just one mechanism by which animals reduce the risks associated with aggression. It is striking that, even among species considered most aggressive, the vast majority of conflicts are resolved without physical contact. Even where competitors lack prior experience of each other's fighting ability, it pays to be able to accurately interpret cues of an opponent's probability of winning a contest, its "resource-holding potential" (RHP) (Archer, 1988; Parker, 1974). Body size, development of weaponry, and physical condition can be essential cues that individuals flaunt and evaluate in ritualized displays prior to initiating fights. Scent marking and auditory displays can perform a similar role in the absence of face-to-face assessments, potentially carrying information about the physiological status of the signaller, its identity (association with past aggressive encounters), the probability of encountering it, the number of territory holders, and the motivation to defend a territory (Gosling & Roberts, 2001; Johnson, 1973; Kitchen, 2004; Ralls, 1971; Wilson, Hauser, & Wrangham, 2001). Regardless of the modality, displays offer the weaker competitor the opportunity to retreat without injury.

The logic for how animals avoid costly fighting also provides clear predictions as to how conflicts can escalate into serious, and even fatal, combat (Archer, 1988; Archer & Huntingford, 1994; Maynard Smith & Parker, 1976; Maynard Smith & Price, 1973). Escalated conflict is most likely to develop when (a) the resource is of non trivial value to the winner's reproductive success, and (b) competitors are similar in RHP. A variety of contextual factors can also play a role in modifying the costs and benefits of aggression, affecting one or both competitors' willingness to engage (Archer, 1988; Dugatkin & Dugatkin, 2007; Enquist & Leimar, 1990; Maynard Smith & Parker, 1976; Parker, 1974). For example, a resource may have greater incremental value to one of the competitors (e.g., a hungry individual), increasing its tolerance for the costs of fighting. Individuals may fight harder to protect a resource they currently hold than to usurp the control of another individual. Individuals with few alternative opportunities for resource gain, such as older males lacking future breeding opportunities, may continue to fight even with the odds firmly against them. On the other hand, within social groups in which individuals rely on one another as allies, the risk of damaging a beneficial relationship can mitigate the intensity of aggression between group members. Finally, all of the aforementioned calculations become vastly more complex when groups of competitors, as opposed to individuals, are involved in conflicts.

Lethal Aggression
INFANTICIDE

The most widespread form of lethal aggression in mammals is infanticide (Hrdy, 1977, 1979; van Schaik & Janson, 2000). Our discussion here is brief, because infanticide does not fit within the general framework for escalated aggression. While infanticide by related and unrelated females does occur (Packer & Pusey, 1984), most cases are perpetrated by males and are attributable to sexual selection on males with limited periods of breeding opportunity (Hrdy, 1979; van Schaik, 2000). Infanticide exploits the fact that, due to the alleviation of the energetic burden of lactation, females who lose a suckling infant come back into breeding condition earlier than they would have with the infant intact. When male reproductive skew is high, and tenure as the breeding male is brief compared with female interbirth interval, this added time is critical for male reproductive success. Infanticide is most often seen when an outside male, thus one unlikely to have fathered the infants, takes over the key breeding position in a group of females (Hanuman langurs, *Semnopithecus entellus*: Borries et al., 1999; lions, *Panthera leo*: Pusey & Packer, 1994). Under these conditions, infanticides can account for a large proportion of infant mortality. However, infanticide occurs within a broad range of social contexts, suggesting that infants are vulnerable whenever paternity certainty is very low. We return to infanticide later, in our discussion of violence in chimpanzees.

DYADIC AGGRESSION

In highly polygynous species, winners of aggressive contests can gain substantial and immediate fitness benefits. Under such conditions, sexual selection has favored large body size and elaboration of morphological weaponry in males (Alexander et al., 1979; Berglund, Bisazza, & Pilastro, 1996; Clutton-Brock, 1982; Mitani, Gros-Louis, & Richard, 1996). Not surprisingly, where dyadic male contests over mates are particularly intense, significant wounding and mortality can occur; we are unaware of any mammalian species in which such lethal "duels" occur between females.

Despite elaborate displays that appear to reduce the frequency of escalated conflict, serious injuries and deaths are common during the rutting season of male herbivores. Among red deer (*Cervus elaphus*), for example, approximately 6% of rutting stags are permanently injured (e.g., blinding, lameness) each year, with 20%–30% sustaining such injuries over their lifetime (Clutton-Brock, Albon, Gibson, & Guinness, 1979; Clutton-Brock, Guinness, & Albon, 1982). These rutting injuries comprise a significant source (5%–29%) of adult male mortality (Clutton-Brock et al., 1982; Heptner, Nasimovitsch, & Bannikov, 1961). Similarly grim statistics from male duelling are reported for mule deer (*Odocoileus hemionus*; Geist, 1974), caribou (*Rangifer tarandus*; Bergerud, 1973), moose (*Alces alces*; Pielowski, 1969 in Clutton-Brock, 1982), pronghorn (*Antilocapra americana*; Byers, 1997), and musk oxen (*Ovibos moschatus*; Wilkinson & Shank, 1976). Although less pervasive, mortality and serious wounding have also been documented during mating or territorial disputes in elephant seals (*Mirounga angustirostris*; Le Boeuf & Reiter, 1988), African elephants (*Loxodonta africana*; Poole, 1989), and Indian rhinoceros (*Rhinoceros unicornis*; Laurie, 1982; Yadav, 2000).

Among male primates, canines rather than horns or antlers present a significant risk of injury when male-male competition escalates. Gelada (*Theropithecus gelada*) have among the most elaborated canines in the primates (Plavcan & van Schaik, 1992), indicative of the intense competition to control harems of females. Approximately one in four fights among males result in severe injury (Dunbar, 1984). In mandrills (*Mandrillus sphinx*; Setchell & Wickings, 2005) and yellow baboons (*Papio cynocephalus*; Drews, 1996), less than 1% of male conflicts lead to injury, but conflicts are frequent enough that injuries, primarily canine slashes that take several weeks to heal, are a persistent threat to male fitness. Despite this, direct killings in these conflicts are remarkably rare.

COALITIONAL AGGRESSION

Lethal coalitional aggression usually occurs between members of different social groups. Some exceptions can be found within groups of primates in which competition for breeding positions is intense and many individuals have a vested interest in the outcome of competition. Examples include the fatal overthrow of an alpha male capuchin monkey (*Cebus capucinus*) by a coalition of male and female group members (Gros-Louis, Perry, & Manson, 2003) and lethal attacks by coalitions of adult males on subadult male spider monkeys (*Ateles geoffroyi*) during times of heightened reproductive competition (Campbell, 2006; Valero, Schaffner, Vick, Aureli, & Ramos-Fernandez, 2006). Such attacks are often lengthy or in series, with victims held down while multiple individuals hit and inflict severe bites.

The primary context of lethal coalitional aggression is competition between groups, with larger groups having greater competitive advantage over smaller groups or individuals who are temporarily separated from the group. Group size might be thought to operate in an analogous way to individual RHP. However, unlike dyadic conflicts, in which large differences in RHP deter escalated conflicts, numerical advantage in some forms of group territorial conflicts increases the lethality of aggression.

Among African wild dogs (*Lycaon pictus*), encounters between two packs invariably lead to chases or fights, with the larger pack on the offensive (Creel & Creel, 2002). Although individuals are usually not killed directly in these conflicts, severe bite injuries occur in a large proportion (~38%) of attacks and can lead to death. Hyena (*Crocuta crocuta*) groups not only conflict over prey carcasses (Hofer & East, 1993) but also actively patrol their territorial borders with the apparent purpose of detecting incursions from neighboring clans (Boydston, Morelli, & Holekamp, 2001). When intruders are detected near or within the territory, the home group launches a cooperative defense. These "clan wars," led by the dominant female members of the group, are usually low in intensity, with both sides rushing at one another repeatedly. However, when physical contact does occur, it can lead to severe injury or death. Kruuk (1972, p. 256) describes such an event at a kill:

> The Scratching Rock hyenas...grabbed one of the Mungi males and bit him wherever they could...[he] was literally pulled apart, and when I later studied the injuries more closely, it appeared that his ears were bitten off and so were his feet and testicles, he was paralyzed by a spinal injury, had large gashes in the hind legs and belly, and subcutaneous hemorrhages all over.

Coalitional aggression is a common cause (25%–65%) of adult mortality in wolves (*Canis lupus*), occurring most often when lone wolves stray outside of their home territory or into border zones and meet neighboring packs (Mech, 1977; Mech, Adams, Meier, Burch, & Dale, 1998). Similar intraspecific aggression is implicated in an estimated 3%–7% of red fox (*Vulpes vulpes*) deaths (Harris & Smith, 1987). In African lions, coalitions of males attack and sometimes kill both male and female members of neighboring groups (Grinnell, Packer, & Pusey 1995; Mosser & Packer, 2009). Prey-rich territories engender greater competition and higher rates of mortality and wounding. Latency to attack is reduced and lethality increased when a coalition of males meets a lone individual (Grinnell et al., 1995); thus, individuals are less likely to travel alone when neighboring a group with a large male coalition (Mosser & Packer, 2009).

Lethal intergroup aggression is less consistently manifest in primate social groups. Coalitional attacks have been observed against extragroup males, presumed to be potential immigrants, in both capuchins (Gros-Louis et al., 2003) and red colobus monkeys (*Procolobus badius temminckii*) (Starin, 1994). Incidents involve both male and female attackers and can be brutal, consisting of severe bites (removing chunks of flesh or opening the abdominal cavity), hitting, dragging, and throwing of the victim. Unlike the carnivore examples, these cases suggest not defense of territory but defense of offspring, because immigrant males pose a threat of infanticide. Severe aggression does appear to serve a territorial function in spider monkeys, although fatalities have not been directly observed (Aureli, Schaffner, Verpooten, Slater, & Ramos-Fernandez, 2006). As in chimpanzees (see next section), large subgroups composed primarily of males not only patrol territory boundaries but also make incursions into neighboring territories, with the apparent purpose of inciting aggression against vulnerable individuals. This conclusion is reinforced by the differences in behavior between "raiding" and foraging parties, by the fact that raiding parties return to their home territory without having exploited resources within the trespassed area, and by the severe aggression initiated when a stranger is encountered.

These examples suggest that intergroup conflicts are particularly prone to lethal violence. The function of such aggression is not always clear and may vary by species or even within species. For example, in hyenas, defense of food resources appears to be a major cause of territorial aggression, since severe conflicts are most likely near prey carcasses and are not predicted by the reproductive state of the females involved or the proximity of the den (Boydston et al., 2001; Hofer & East, 1993). On the other hand, male hyenas are particularly active in attacking male intruders, suggesting that they may have interests in mate defense as well (Boydston et al., 2001). Similarly in wild dogs, group members usually attack individuals of the same sex, even running past opposite-sex opponents to get to them (Creel & Creel, 2002). Breeding competition appears to be a weak explanation, however, since nonbreeding individuals in these groups participate actively in defense (Boydston et al., 2001) and both breeding and nonbreeding individuals may be attacked (Mech et al., 1998). In these species where reproductive success is tightly dependent on territory size and group size strongly predicts the ability to hold a territory, the function of aggression may go beyond territorial *defense*, to achieving territorial *dominance* over neighboring groups. One means of doing so may be through the violent elimination of members of these groups (Manson & Wrangham, 1991; Mosser & Packer, 2009; Wrangham, 1999a, 1999b). This may be most clearly seen in one of human's closest extant relatives, the chimpanzee, in which coalitional violence is particularly purposeful and severe.

Violence in Chimpanzees

In this section, we consider chimpanzees as a case study of violence in animals. Chimpanzees are worth particular consideration both because of their close phylogenetic relationship to humans and because they exhibit an unusual severity and diversity of escalated aggressive behaviors.

Intercommunity Violence Between Adult Males

The earliest accounts come from the Gombe National Park, Tanzania, and these examples are indicative of the nature of the violence. Goodall et al. (1979) reported how, on January, 7, 1974, six adult males of the *Kasakela* community launched a brutal gang assault on a lone male from the neighbouring *Kahama* community. This attack lasted 10 minutes and left the victim beaten, bitten, and bloody. Although he was still alive when his attackers left, he was never seen again. Exactly 1 month later, another group of six *Kasakela* males, including two of the previous attackers, launched a longer, more brutal attack on another adult male from the *Kahama* community. For close to 20 minutes, the victim was beaten, pounded, and bitten. He was left severely wounded, shaking, and unable to sit. He also was never seen again. In both cases, one of the attackers had pinned the victim to the ground while the others inflicted blows (Goodall et al., 1979).

While Goodall's initial observations of lethal violence were a shock to the scientific community, dozens of similar events have been documented from chimpanzee communities throughout Africa (Boesch et al., 2007, 2008; Goodall, 1986; Goossens et al., 2005; Mitani, Watts, & Amsler, 2010; J. Mitani, personal communication; Muller, 2002; Nishida, Hiraiwa-Haegawa, Hasegawa, & Takahata, 1985; Watts, Muller, Amsler, Mbabazi, & Mitani, 2006; Wilson, Wallauer, & Pusey, 2004; Wrangham, 1975, 1999b; Wrangham, Wilson, & Muller, 2006). Some of the accounts are even more brutal than those reported for the Gombe chimpanzees. One such example comes from the Taï Forest, Cote D'Ivoire, where on March 1, 2005, a group of four adult males, three adult females, and two adolescent males from the *South Group* community launched a sustained, brutal attack against a lone male from the *East Group* community. The initial assault lasted 22 minutes. After a 7-minute break during which the victim was just about able to sit, three of the adult males attacked again, delivering a vicious onslaught that lasted a full minute. As a result of these attacks, the victim received injuries that included a broken arm, bite wounds, a 10 cm gash to his throat, and having his penis and testicles torn from his body. He suffered such facial disfigurement that his identity could not be confirmed (Boesch et al., 2008).

Across the geographic range of chimpanzees, the pattern of violence is the same. The vast majority of attacks involve a group—or gang—from one community targeting a lone member of a neighboring community for a sustained attack. Targets are usually adult males, although females have also been killed. Deep bite wounds and broken limbs are typical, as are some specific injuries: traumatic damage to the throat, removal of some or all of the genitalia, and disfiguring of the face. Wounds are typically so severe that deaths cannot be viewed as merely incidental but as the intended outcome of the attack. Wrangham (1999b) estimated that the rate of lethal attacks on adult chimpanzees alone averages 0.25 per year for each community of East African chimpanzees, making lethal violence from other chimpanzees a major source of adult mortality (Mitani et al., 2010; Nishida et al., 2003; Williams et al., 2008; Wrangham et al., 2006), although perhaps less so among the West African subspecies (Boesch et al., 2008).

Chimpanzee communities are relatively stable groups of multiple males and females occupying home ranges that, in forested habitats, vary in size from around 6–7 km^2 (Goodall, 1986; Newton-Fisher, 2002a, 2003) to over 20 km^2 (Herbinger, Boesch, & Rothe, 2001; Wilson et al., 2001). Individuals forage across these communal home ranges in subgroups ("parties": Sugiyama, 1968) that are variable in both size and composition. Female chimpanzees are typically less gregarious than males, probably in an effort to optimize feeding efficiency in the face of competition (Wrangham, 1986). Most long-term studies of chimpanzee have been conducted in forest or woodland habitats, the dominant habitat type for this species. Chimpanzees living in savannah habitats have much larger home ranges (e.g., 63 km^2: Pruetz, 2006; 228 km^2: Tutin, McGrew, & Baldwin, 1983), and it is not clear whether they are strictly territorial; theoretical considerations, specifically the ability to effectively patrol such large areas (Lowen & Dunbar, 1994; Mitani & Rodman, 1979), suggest otherwise.

The primary benefit of aggressive territoriality appears to be intercommunity dominance and, consequently, territorial security and range expansion (Crofoot & Wrangham, 2010; Mitani et al., 2010). The males of the *Kasakela* community, the aggressors in the first example, are thought to have continued their lethal attacks over a 3-year period. During this time, all males of the *Kahama* community disappeared; some attacks were observed, and others were inferred (Goodall, 1986). Similarly, males of Mahale *M-group* community in Tanzania are thought to have systematically killed most if not all of the males of the neighboring *K-group* community (Nishida et al., 1985). In both cases, the victorious males were able to expand their range (Gombe: Goodall, 1986, Figure 9.6 *contra* Manson & Wrangham, 1991; Mahale: Nishida et al., 1985). More recently, the chimpanzees of the *Ngogo* community in the Kibale forest, Uganda, have expanded their range by one-fifth following a sustained period of aggressive territoriality and lethal violence (Mitani et al., 2010). In each of these cases, the violence and range expansion has been targeted and directional: Chimpanzees enlarge their home ranges by advancing into particular areas. Recent research in Kibale suggests that the timing and location of incursions there are related to the availability of valuable seasonal food resources (Wilson, Wells, Kahlenberg, & Wrangham, 2010). Increasing ranging area provides access to additional food resources and reduces the local population density, decreasing feeding competition. This translates into increased body weight (Pusey, Oehlert, Williams, & Goodall, 2005) and faster birth rates, suggesting that range expansion improves reproductive success of community members (Williams, Oehlert, Carlis, & Pusey, 2004). Reduced feeding competition may also allow larger parties to be sustained for longer periods, in turn providing more effective border patrolling and success in territorial encounters.

As part of territorial defense, groups of males engage in patrolling behavior both along and beyond territorial boundaries. Patrols are characterised by silent, determined travel, with pauses during which the chimpanzees sit quietly and appear to listen for sounds of other chimpanzees or inspect signs of chimpanzees such as nests, feces, or food remains (Goodall, 1986). The frequency with which chimpanzees patrol the boundaries of their home range varies, but such patrols are a common aspect of chimpanzee behavior (Wrangham, 1999b). Lone chimpanzees tend to avoid border areas, and even when with companions chimpanzees often show extreme wariness when in border areas, particularly when presented with indications of the proximity of neighboring chimpanzees (Wilson, Hauser, & Wrangham, 2007). Boundary patrols sometimes develop into raids (Goodall et al., 1979; Goodall, 1986; Manson & Wrangham, 1991), in which groups of males make incursions deep into neighboring territories. These males do not typically exploit resources found in the rival territory but instead appear determined to locate and attack isolated rivals.

The response of chimpanzees on encountering neighbors appears strongly contingent on party size and the number of adult males. Larger parties are more likely to threaten or attack, and smaller parties to flee (Boesch & Boesch-Achermann, 2000; Bygott, 1974; Wrangham, 1975), although it is not always so clear cut (Watts & Mitani, 2001b). Aggressive confrontations are more likely when there is an imbalance in power between two parties, specifically in the number of adult males present (Boesch & Boesch-Achermann, 2000). Experimental playbacks of a single male vocalizing resulted in parties with three or more males moving rapidly, and loudly, toward the location of the call, while parties with one or two males remained silent and either avoided the (imagined) caller or approached cautiously (Wilson et al., 2001). All observations of intercommunity lethal violence between adult males involve at least four attackers against a single victim, and the probability that an encounter by strangers will lead to escalated attack and injury is highest when one side is greatly outnumbered. This is an important contrast to the models for escalated aggression between individuals, in which escalation is least likely when one opponent is clearly outmatched. Attacking chimpanzees often do not accept surrender of their opponent as the end to a territorial conflict but pursue them as they flee.

The imbalance-of-power hypothesis has been advanced to address this unexpected pattern of escalated aggression (Bygott, 1979; Manson & Wrangham, 1991; Wrangham, 1999b). While some species engage in territorial battles in which whole groups of individuals face off against one another, escalation to violence is very rare because the risks associated with escalation could be substantial. In chimpanzees, as well as spider monkeys and many social carnivores, the flexible association patterns of individuals that result in parties of varying size and composition create opportunities for an imbalance of power, should two such parties encounter one another. The imbalance-of-power hypothesis proposes that under some circumstances lethal violence is favored by natural selection *because* its cost is low: Victims are outnumbered such that aggressors are at minimal risk of injury. How low remains an unanswered question. Patrolling incurs time, opportunity, and energy costs (Watts & Mitani, 2001b), and attacking other chimpanzees is not risk free: Even during gang assaults, attackers can be wounded (Boesch et al., 2008; Fawcett & Muhumuza, 2000).

But why *lethal* violence? Dominance within communities is settled without recourse to lethal aggression (Goodall, 1986; Muller, 2002; Newton-Fisher, 2002b, 2004; Nishida & Hosaka, 1996), and other primate species engage in intergroup aggressive dominance contests (Crofoot & Wrangham, 2010) without the lethal violence practiced by chimpanzees. Encounters between neighboring chimpanzee communities can be resolved with non lethal aggression (Boesch & Boesch-Achermann, 2000), and there is evidence that dominant communities can displace their neighbors: *K-group* in Mahale was seasonally displaced by *M-group* from around half of their home range for at least 5 years before *K-group* started to lose adults males to assumed intercommunity violence (Nishida, 1979; Nishida et al., 1985). In Budongo, the *Sonso* community has in recent years shifted its range in the absence of lethal violence, with areas previously part of its range now home to chimpanzees from another community (Newton-Fisher, unpublished data). The models for aggression that hold up well for other species imply that the outcomes of non lethal aggressive encounters and the consequent intimidation of individuals in other communities should be sufficient to produce intergroup dominance and its associated benefits (Wilson et al., 2004).

The original formulations of the imbalance-of-power hypothesis laid out the necessary conditions for coalitional attacks to evolve, but they did not address the benefits that could form a complete explanation for the evolution of such an unusual behavioral pattern. Elaborated versions of the hypothesis have proposed that the lethality of territorial aggression functions specifically to slowly reduce the relative coalitional power of neighbouring groups, thus increasing the probability of winning future encounters (Boone, 1991; Wrangham, 1999a, 1999b). Thus chimpanzees, and a select number of species, have both the opportunity to eliminate isolated rivals and the incentive to do so.

Faced with a high threat of attack by neighbors, chimpanzees might be expected to adopt counterstrategies, chiefly avoidance of small party sizes that make them vulnerable to imbalances of power. However, given that their flexible social structure is apparently an adaptation to limited, clumped food resources, this may not be a viable long-term strategy if the regular energetic costs associated with foraging in larger parties outweigh the sporadic risk of attack. Additionally, those communities who have faced territorial losses to neighboring groups may be least able to afford to forage in larger parties. In the face of aggressive territoriality, this might in turn increase the mortality risk to individuals as well as accelerating the collapse of communities.

Under traditional game-theoretical models of aggression, the severity of aggression is kept in check by the costs associated with escalated conflicts, maintaining an evolutionarily stable level of aggression. The imbalance-of-power hypothesis proposes that unrestrained violence occurs when the costs and benefits of escalation are dramatically altered by social conditions. While a key component of many evolutionarily stable aggression models is the ability of the weaker individual to avoid conflict or cut its losses and escape, isolated chimpanzees can be victims regardless of their own choice of strategy. These conditions suggest the possibility for runaway selection on competition between groups, in which the selective advantages of escalated aggression run untempered by costs until lethal behaviors emerge.

Once such a trait has spread, the costs are felt in increased mortality rates, estimated at 0.4%–1.4% per year for adult and adolescent males (Wrangham et al., 2006). However, because *any* isolated individual can become a victim, the costs are born regardless of participation in lethal conflict. This means that the violent strategy would not experience specific negative selection provided that the majority of the violent individuals continue to reap reproductive benefits, and a peaceful strategy would have little opportunity to invade. Is lethal violence as currently observed an evolutionarily stable strategy for chimpanzees? Or is there potential for the incursion of more elaborated strategies of violence or effective counterstrategies? These questions have important ramifications for understanding the similar types of coalitional violence in humans, but new evolutionary models are needed to understand the evolution and persistence of this trait. There is much we have yet to discover about territoriality and lethal violence in chimpanzees, and many unanswered questions, for example: How do energetic and opportunity costs of territorial behavior counterbalance the potential benefits of increased territory? How are the costs and benefits distributed across males? How large a territory can males successfully defend? How often are male cohorts eliminated? How strongly do stochastic events, such as disease epidemics, habitat disturbance, and male-biased births, impact the balance of power between communities?

Intracommunity Violence Between Adult Males

Given the level of violence observed between communities, the amount of restraint observed between males within communities is remarkable: Males in the same group present a much more immediate threat to reproductive opportunities, and males capable of killing chimpanzees in other communities should be as capable of doing the same to members of their own community. Most aggression between adult males, however, takes the form of threatening gestures, vocalizations, and charging displays: bluff attacks without physical contact (Bygott, 1979; Goodall, 1986; Nishida, Kano, Goodall, McGrew, Nakamura, 1999). Physical attacks are a minority of agonistic interactions, and attacks resulting in wounding are even less common. When it does occur, violence is mostly restricted to dyadic interactions, but it can escalate and involve coalitions of males whose interests coalesce. There are even a few accounts of non lethal gang attacks that are otherwise similar to intercommunity attacks (Goodall, 1992; Nishida & Hosaka, 1996; Nishida, Hosaka, Nakamura, & Hamai, 1995; Watts, 2004). Only a handful of cases of *lethal* violence between adult males of the same community have been documented, however, despite decades of detailed observations of chimpanzees (Fawcett & Muhumuza, 2000; Kaburu, Inoue, & Newton-Fisher, in prep; Nishida, 1996; Mjungu, 2010; Terio et al., 2011; Watts, 2004). Of five known cases, one was inferred from circumstantial evidence while four were observed directly. Each observation describes a sustained attack by a group of adult males against a single victim who suffers trauma from prolonged beating in addition to multiple, severe bite wounds. In at least one case, chunks of the victim's flesh were found in the feces of the attackers (Fawcett & Muhumuza, 2000).

Male tolerance of reproductive competition from other males in their community is likely to be contingent on benefits that competitors can provide to offset the cost of tolerance. The most obvious of these is the protection from intercommunity violence accorded by the presence and cooperation of other adult males. The more adult males within a community, the larger the potential size of parties patrolling boundary areas and, consequently, the lower risk both of injury when patrolling and of losing territory to neighbors. Additionally, within the community, other males can be valuable coalition partners, providing status, nutritional, and mating benefits that individuals could not obtain alone (Watts, 1998, 2002; Watts & Mitani, 2001a). Males may trade limited reproductive tolerance for the advantages that coalition partners confer on fitness, although such a trade-off should be sensitive to the risk of lethal violence from neighboring communities. Males facing greater risk should be less violently aggressive toward one another, while increased levels of intracommunity violence would be expected where risk of lethal intercommunity violence is decreased. Within-community gang violence and lethal violence should also be skewed toward the least "valuable" individuals: those least useful as coalition (Boesch & Boesch-Achermann, 2000; Goodall, 1986; Nishida & Hosaka, 1996) or hunting (Boesch & Boesch, 1989; Mitani & Watts, 1999) partners, or who can offer few benefits in exchanges of social services such as grooming (Newton-Fisher & Lee, 2011), may not be worth tolerating as reproductive competitors. When a male offers little value to the others in his cohort, where converging interests within the cohort allow an imbalance of power to develop, and the costs to other males—themselves set by the current intercommunity context—associated with his death are small, that individual may be at high risk of receiving violent, perhaps lethal, aggression.

In support of this hypothesis, in four of the five cases of lethal aggression between adult males, the individual killed was low ranking, and to some extent, socially peripheral. In both the *Sonso* (Fawcett & Muhumuza, 2000) and *Ngogo* (Watts, 2004) communities, the victim was a young adult male, while in Mahale's *M-group* (Nishida, 1996; Nishida, 2011) and Gombe's *Mitumba* community (Mjungu, 2010; Terio et al., 2011), the victim was a previous deposed alpha male. In contrast, however, the most recent observations from Mahale's *M-group* concern the killing of the incumbent alpha male (Kaburu et al., in prep). Clearly, we still have much to learn about the dynamics of within-community violence between adult males.

Violence Between Males and Females

Chimpanzee females habitually disperse from their natal communities at sexual maturity. In doing so, females typically avoid attacks by the "stranger" males in their new community. It has been suggested that females initiate contact with a new community while showing the large genital swelling characterizing sexual receptivity, advertising their value to males as mates (Nishida, 1979; Pusey, 1979). Reproductive rates in chimpanzees are very low, with interbirth intervals of approximately 5–7 years (Emery Thompson et al., 2007a) rivalling the longest interbirth intervals among animals. Factoring in infant mortality, most females wean only 1–2 offspring (Hill et al., 2001; Nishida et al., 2003). Thus, while new females create an increase in resource pressure within the community, they represent valuable reproductive opportunities, and males likely gain more by allowing females into their community than by excluding them.

Yet, as with male chimpanzees, adult females are at risk from intercommunity violence, although the risk appears reduced for females exhibiting sexual swellings. In intercommunity encounters at Gombe, *Kasakela* community males were more likely to direct aggression toward non swollen females (Williams et al., 2004), and such attacks were often violent, leading to wounding and even death. Goodall (1986) reports 20 severe attacks by males on such females: In 13 of 14 cases where the female was clearly observed, she was left seriously injured. Aggression against swollen females is less common (13% of observed encounters between *Kasakela* males and extracommunity females: Williams et al., 2004), but when it occurs it can be severe (at least two of the three observed encounters: Williams et al., 2004).

If lethal violence is the result of a strategy of eliminating rival male coalitions, why should male chimpanzees direct violent, potentially lethal, aggression toward females? If access to new sexual partners is an important secondary function of male intercommunity aggression, as has been suggested (Boesch & Boesch-Achermann, 2000; Manson & Wrangham, 1991; Wrangham, 1979; Wrangham & Peterson, 1996), such aggression seems particularly counterproductive. One possibility is that males use violence in an attempt to coerce females to join their community (Boesch & Boesch-Achermann, 2000; Williams et al., 2004). If this were the case, however, swollen females would seem the most obvious mating partners and so the probable targets of aggression, but instead they receive less aggression than do non swollen females. Aside from the obvious consequence of eliminating potential mates, targeting females for intercommunity aggression should also have the effect of causing at least some females to adjust their ranging patterns to avoid areas of intercommunity conflict, making them less available to males expanding their territory (Williams, Pusey, Carlis, Farm, & Goodall, 2002). Alternatively, it has been suggested that male aggression against females can be explained as a form of resource defense (Boone, 1991; Goodall, 1990; Nishida, 1991; Williams et al., 2004); males are aggressive to any and all individuals that they encounter from neighboring communities, attempting to keep them out of the home range that provides the resource base for themselves, their infants, and the mothers of these infants. Such resource defense may also be the case for some social carnivores, although in those cases—and unlike chimpanzees—females are active participants in territorial aggression.

Not all females are victims of violence. While those most at risk are non cycling, parous females—mothers with dependent offspring—such females are not always subject to violent aggression (Williams et al., 2004), and may successfully transfer into a new community (Emery Thompson, Newton-Fisher, & Reynolds, 2006; Nishida et al., 1985; Williams, 2000). Following the virtual extinction of the Mahale *K-group*, all fertile, cycling females from *K-group* joined *M-group*, adjusting their ranging patterns and associating with the males of *M-group* (Nishida et al., 1985). Females may be driven to transfer by the collapse of community integrity through the loss of adult males to intercommunity violence, poaching, predation or disease, or drawn to an area with a relatively greater resource supply (Emery Thompson et al., 2006), but this does not explain why they are tolerated by males, particularly if male territoriality functions as resource defense.

Such tolerance is only going to benefit males if the females transfer into their communities and make themselves available as mates. Males should therefore distinguish between the two "types" of females, *transferring* and *non transferring*. Given that judging intentions may be impossible, or at best unreliable, the parsimonious mechanism might be a simple spatially based decision rule: When encountering extracommunity females, attack if at or beyond the borders of the community's home range; tolerate if within the core area. Such a rule, and the functional logic for it, could explain why females are able to transfer successfully but why boundary zones between communities remain hazardous to them while attempting to do so. In the context of the resource-defense hypothesis for chimpanzee territoriality (and territorial expansion), males gain additional mates not by annexing their core areas but by holding a resource base that is attractive to females.

SEXUAL COERCION

It is worth noting that once integrated into a community, females are not free from violence. Male aggression toward females is a consistent aspect of chimpanzee society (Goodall, 1986) and, although much consists of mild threats, attacks can vary from a kick or slap to prolonged bouts of violent aggression, including biting, pounding, dragging, and slamming into the ground (Goodall, 1986; Muller, Kahlenberg, & Wrangham, 2009a). At times males may also employ vegetation as weapons, ranging from flailing at the female with the leafy branches of an understory sapling to the use of wooden clubs, which are not used in male-male aggression (Linden, 2002; Muller et al., 2009a). As female chimpanzees are universally subordinate to adult males and usually attempt to flee an attacking male, this represents a type of conflict that is escalated beyond apparently necessary levels; indicative, by most definitions, of violence. Females receive aggression from males far more frequently when cycling and maximally swollen than at other times (Muller, Kahlenberg, Emery Thompson, & Wrangham, 2007). While the use of aggressive force as a direct means to obtain copulations is extremely rare in chimpanzees, evidence suggests that aggression serves a sexually coercive function, increasing the aggressive male's mating success relative to others while inflicting a cost upon the female (Muller et al., 2009a; Muller, Kahlenberg, & Wrangham, 2009b). It is likely that sexual aggression serves *harassment* and *intimidation* functions (Clutton-Brock & Parker, 1995), increasing the costs of resisting the aggressive male's mating attempts and reducing the probability of future resistance. There are also clear cases of punishment, whereby mate-guarding males attack a female for approaching a rival male while sexually receptive. Males have higher mating success with the females whom they are most aggressive toward, and these females will selectively approach their tormentors at the times when they are most likely to conceive (Muller et al., 2007; Muller, Emery Thompson, Kahlenberg, & Wrangham, 2011). The amount of aggression received is a strong predictor of female stress hormone levels (Emery Thompson, Muller, Wrangham, Lwanga, & Potts, 2009).

Not all aggression by male chimpanzees toward females of their own community functions as sexual coercion. Mild threats given when foraging within a food patch, such as the crown of a fruiting tree, may be due to contest competition over food; some females may be struck by a passing male as he displays through a party, scattering its members, inadvertent victims of a display aimed at other males; or a female may be the intended target of aggression from one or more males intervening in fights, such as when males defend immigrant females from the attacks of resident females (Kahlenberg, Emery Thompson, Muller, & Wrangham, 2008a; Pusey, 1980). A female may even be picked up and slammed into the ground for failing to give a submissive pant-grunt vocalization when approaching a high-ranking male (Newton-Fisher, personal observation). The consequences of such aggression have not been investigated systematically, however, and we cannot exclude the possibility that, particularly as the level of violence increases, such aggression contributes toward the intimidation of females. *Intimidation* in general has been poorly studied in chimpanzees, although it may be behind much of the aggression—and violence—directed by male chimpanzees toward females (Muller et al., 2009a).

Infanticide by Males

The killing, and often cannibalism, of infants by adult males has been reported from seven different communities across four separate populations (Arcadi & Wrangham, 1999; Goodall, 1977; Hamai, Nishida, Takasaki, & Turner, 1992; Kutsukake &

Matsusaka, 2002; Murray, Wroblewski, & Pusey, 2007; Newton-Fisher, 1999; Nishida, Uehara, & Nyundo, 1979; Watts, 1998; Watts & Mitani, 2000; Watts, Mitani, & Sherrow, 2002; Wilson et al., 2004). Over 30 cases of infanticide by males have now been reported (Murray et al., 2007).

In the context of intercommunity violence, it has been suggested that male attacks on parous females are aimed at killing their infants in order to end the mothers' lactational amenorrhea, so speeding the resumption of cycling, and perhaps to encourage the female to transfer into the aggressors community by demonstrating the inability of the female's community males to prevent the infanticide (Hiraiwa-Hasegawa & Hasegawa, 1994). This "sexual selection" hypothesis for infanticide in primates and other animals (Hrdy, 1977) appears to be well supported for a number of primate species (van Schaik, 2000), but it is unconvincing as an explanation of between-community infanticide in chimpanzees (Wilson et al., 2004). Although some attacks appear focused on seizing and killing the infant (e.g., Newton-Fisher, 1999), in others infanticide seems to be incidental to violent attacks on the mother (Goodall, 1986, 1990). Furthermore, in contrast to many other species, there is no evidence that infanticidal males gain matings, let alone paternity, from the mothers of their victims (Goodall, 1986; Hiraiwa-Hasegawa & Hasegawa, 1994; Pusey, 2001).

An alternate hypothesis is that infanticide by males functions to reduce the future strength of rival male coalitions who hold neighboring territories (Arcadi & Wrangham, 1999; Hiraiwa-Hasegawa & Hasegawa, 1994; Newton-Fisher, 1999; Takahata, 1985). Intercommunity infanticide appears to be male biased (Wrangham et al., 2006), and that it is not exclusively directed at male infants may simply be due to the low cost of making a mistake—killing a female infant instead of a male (Wilson et al., 2004). With such small sample sizes, however, it is difficult to be sure the bias toward male infants is real, and not an artifact of sampling (Wilson & Wrangham, 2003). Other suggestions include infanticide as a by-product of male aggression (Bartlett, Sussman, & Cheverud, 1993), which might explain infants killed incidentally during attacks on their mothers but does not account for those attacks that appear to target the infant specifically. Such attacks are more similar to predatory attacks on monkeys, which, in East African chimpanzees at least, are often aimed at seizing infants from their mothers (Stanford, 1998); the subsequent cannibalism, and the patterns of begging and sharing, might support predation as a hypothesis, but the degree of consumption is variable and not all infants killed are consumed. Under the resource-defense hypothesis for intergroup territoriality and male aggression, infanticide is functionally equivalent to the killing of adults, and it requires no distinct explanation (Wilson et al., 2004).

In contrast to that committed during intercommunity encounters, within-community infanticide by male chimpanzees is largely consistent with the sexual selection hypothesis (van Schaik, 2000). Infants are typically killed by males unlikely to be their fathers, and those who can gain subsequent sexual access to the females. Infanticide also reduces subsequent interbirth intervals. The number of these infanticides is small (nine observations in Murray et al., 2007: Table 1), however, and consequently it is not clear whether infanticidal males benefit directly from subsequent resumption of cycling. Furthermore, in at least one case the probable father of the killed infant was involved in the attack (Takahata, 1985).

Other proposed adaptive hypotheses are difficult to exclude. Predation remains a possibility, as infants were cannibalised whenever the mother was not able to retrieve the infant (Goodall, 1977; Hamai et al., 1992). Resource competition has also been suggested, with males seeking to eliminate future rivals for mating competition (Nishida & Kawanaka, 1985). In support of this, all of the infants killed by adult males in within-community violence have been male (Wrangham et al., 2006), although most of these were from a single community, *M-group* in Mahale. One significant problem with this future-rivals hypothesis is that the reproductive careers of the killer and the victim are unlikely to overlap: Male chimpanzees rarely father offspring before the age of 15 (Boesch, Kohou, Neen, & Vigilant, 2006; Newton-Fisher et al., 2010) and can expect a reproductive career—and life span—from that point of less than 15 years (Hill et al., 2001). While resource competition may be a good explanation for infanticide in intercommunity encounters, it seems unlikely to account for within-community infanticide by males.

An alternative possibility is that within-community infanticide by males functions as sexual coercion, encouraging the victim's mother to bias her mating activity toward the infanticidal male, thereby compromising her promiscuous mating strategy (Hamai et al., 1992; Muller et al., 2009a; van Schaik, Pradhan, & van Noordwijk, 2004).

Such an explanation could also account for the killing by adult males of older infants and juveniles, whose deaths would not shorten their mothers' interbirth intervals (Hamai et al., 1992; Murray et al., 2007).

Violence Between Adult Females

Adult female chimpanzees are less obviously and less spectacularly aggressive to one another than are adult males. This sex difference is consistent with the general pattern observed across mammals and with theoretical considerations, which set the potential risks to infants against the marginal gains from conflicts over individual resources. However, in most other species that engage in lethal coalitional attacks, females are active participants, which is in accord with evidence that female reproductive interests are strongly influenced by intercommunity resource competition. Given the strong influences of resource access on female reproductive success in chimpanzees (Emery Thompson, Kahlenberg, Gilby, & Wrangham, 2007b; Williams et al., 2002), it is therefore surprising that females do not engage in intergroup conflicts in the same way that hyenas do. The reason may lie in the peculiar type of feeding competition occurring within chimpanzee communities, in which females conduct their own variation of territorial defense within the larger home range. While rarely fighting over individual food resources, female chimpanzees appear to compete for preferential access to high-quality food resources within spatially restricted areas, which then become the core of their ranging areas (Pusey et al., 2008). High-ranking females occupy core areas with higher quality food resources than low-ranking females, at least in the two communities where this has been investigated (Kahlenberg, Emery Thompson, & Wrangham, 2008b; Murray, Eberly, & Pusey, 2006), and females with high-quality core areas have decreased interbirth intervals and increased infant survival (Emery Thompson et al., 2007b). Aggression between females may therefore serve to negotiate access to these core areas, with important fitness consequences.

Consistent with the core-area-competition hypothesis, aggression is most frequent and severe when new females attempt to immigrate into the community (Goodall, 1986; Kahlenberg et al., 2008a; Nishida, 1989; Pusey et al., 2008; Pusey, 1980). Immigrants are often threatened or attacked by resident females acting alone or in coalitions. Severe injuries can result, and females are sometimes convinced to return from whence they came (Pusey et al., 2008). Females show strong fidelity to core areas once established (Emery Thompson et al., 2007b; Williams et al., 2002), and so the process of immigration represents a period of heightened female competition (Kahlenberg et al., 2008a). Increasing numbers of females leads to greater feeding competition within a community, the impact of which will be particularly marked for any female who has to share parts of her core area (and the resources therein) with an additional female. Aggression by residents toward immigrants therefore appears to function to reduce long-term feeding competition by encouraging would-be immigrants to establish core areas elsewhere within the community home range or in another community altogether (Williams, 2000). Even though female resource access is threatened by territorial disputes with neighboring groups, they seem to limit their efforts to protecting the particular areas most important for their individual reproductive success. There are a few accounts of adult females participating in violent attacks on resident females from other communities (i.e., between-community violence), but this appears to be supplemental to concurrent violence by adult males (Arcadi & Wrangham, 1999; Goodall, 1986).

INFANTICIDE BY FEMALES

Resource competition among females can take a deadly turn when female attacks are targeted at the infants of their rivals. Infanticide by females is rare among primates but known from other resource-limited and territorial species, such as wild dogs (van Lawick, 1973) and hyenas (White, 2005). Multiple cases of infanticide by adult females have been reported from chimpanzee populations of Gombe (Goodall, 1986; Pusey et al., 2008) and Budongo (Townsend, Slocombe, Emery Thompson, & Zuberbuhler, 2007). In the Gombe *Kasakela* community, between 1975 and 1978, an adult female and her adolescent daughter (Passion and Pom) killed between three and eight infants and were seen attempting to kill two more. In one case, a 10-minute violent fight during which the mother was held down by one of the attackers resulted in severe multiple bite wounds that took a month to heal (Goodall, 1977, 1986). More recently, a second mother-daughter pair (Fifi and Fanni) led persistent but unsuccessful attacks against the infants of another resident female, and a suspected female infanticide occurred in the neighboring *Mitumba* community (Pusey et al., 2008). In the Budongo Forest's *Sonso* community, three cases of infanticide were documented between 2004 and 2006, in which a group of adult females killed (one case), or were strongly suspected of killing (two cases), the infant (Townsend et al., 2007). In both Gombe and Budongo, additional unexplained disappearances or mutilated infant corpses during the same time frame suggested that the extent of female infanticides may have been greater.

While once thought to be the aberrant behavior of a few disturbed individuals or the misplaced desire to obtain meat, female infanticide in chimpanzees is currently regarded as an extreme consequence of resource competition between females. Infanticide may encourage mothers of the slain infants to locate their foraging ranges away from violent females, or it may be a specific strategy to eliminate future competitors when they are most vulnerable (Pusey, 1983; Pusey et al., 2008). Core areas overlap substantially, and so the fewer nonrelatives exploiting the resources therein, the better; particularly as strong site fidelity means that females and their offspring will rely on the resources during periods of food shortage. The possibility of predation as an explanation (Goodall, 1986) cannot be entirely eliminated: The three infants killed by the adult female Passion were consumed during lengthy feeding bouts. The behavior seen in the *Sonso* community was different, however, with clear evidence of no cannibalism in at least two of the cases (the third is ambiguous; Townsend et al., 2007). A variety of evidence points to competitive influences. All of the attackers from the different communities occupied very high dominance ranks. Two of the three attacks at *Sonso* involved the infants of immigrant females, while the third involved a female who very rarely interacted with the group, suggesting that she was either highly peripheral or had been visiting other communities (Townsend et al., 2007). These attacks occurred following an unusually large influx of females, which would have increased the resource pressure on the relatively small *Sonso* home range. The Gombe attacks were against the infants of resident females whose core areas were highly overlapping with the attackers (Pusey et al., 2008). In accordance with the hypothesis of resource competition, the high incidence of infanticide at Gombe may be related to the limits on female dispersal there. The *Kasakela* community occupies the majority of an isolated forest block, with two smaller communities at the northern and southern margins. Females are less likely to emigrate there than elsewhere, and females inherit the core areas of their mothers, meaning that an infant born into the community represents a permanent burden on already limited resources (Pusey et al., 2008).

Conclusion

Comparisons of human and nonhuman violence are hindered by widely varying and overly limiting definitions, many of which rely on proximate psychological mechanisms. Here, we provide a review of theoretical and empirical data on aggression in mammals, focusing on functional and adaptive aspects of aggression. While aggression is a pervasive feature of animal societies, the majority of aggression is low in intensity and directed at resolving short- or long-term access to resources. Conflict escalation and the possibility of injury or death occur under a limited range of circumstances in which individual strengths and incentives are closely matched or the resource being contested is particularly valuable. When groups, rather than individuals, engage in resource competition, these dynamics can change in important ways and conflicts are more likely to escalate to violence. Some of the most directly lethal forms of aggression occur in competitions between groups of individuals whose reproductive success hinges on maintenance of territory and numerical superiority over groups of rivals. In this chapter, we directed particular attention to lethal coalitional aggression in chimpanzees, the extant species most closely related to humans and that, next to humans, exhibits the most spectacularly gruesome and varied aggressive repertoire observed in mammals. The lethality of intergroup conflicts in chimpanzees is likely to be strongly influenced by their grouping patterns, which allows isolated individuals to fall victim to large coalitions of rival males. Predominant hypotheses suggest that the reproductive success of chimpanzees is significantly influenced by their access to territory and the food resources within. Under intense competition and low costs to escalated aggression, males may benefit not only by dominating but also by eliminating males from rival groups. However, other forms of lethal and nonlethal violence are particularly notable in chimpanzees, including lethal coalitional attacks on within-group males, severe attacks between resident and immigrant females, and infanticides by both male and female attackers against both inter- and intracommunity targets. As in certain other species, such as some social carnivores, chimpanzees face pervasive resource competition and tread a delicate balance between the benefits of allies and the costs of competitors.

Future Directions

1. A greater use of comparative studies of violence, and the use of compatible definitions and terminology. The study of violence in humans is complicated by myriad uses of the term, from the violence of nation states to emotional violence. Animal models have much to offer the study of human behavior, and perspectives from human studies can likewise foster research on nonhumans (Brosnan, Newton-Fisher, & van Vugt, 2009). Adopting an approach based on observed behavior, rather than inferred mental or emotional states for interpersonal, dyadic, and small-group interactions, allows results to be understood from a broad comparative perspective. To be clear, this does not mean importing an explanation from one species and imposing it on another, but it does allow the use of well-developed theory that holds across multiple taxa and provides a broad basis for the testing of hypotheses. Such an approach would allow analysis of the behavior to be independent of investigation of emotion or intent. Separating the function of the behavior from the intrinsic and extrinsic causal factors will allow both a clearer understanding of violence in humans and a better appreciation of the commonalities it has with similar behavior in other species.

2. A more complete understanding of intergroup lethal coalitional violence in chimpanzees and other species, including humans. Our review of intergroup lethal violence in chimpanzees has highlighted numerous questions for which we have no answers. For instance, the additional mortality risk among adult and adolescent males generated by lethal intergroup violence is a cost currently unaccounted for in existing models. It is not clear whether the indirect benefits that flow from territorial enlargement are sufficient to offset this cost. We raise the possibility that lethal violence may persist as an evolutionary stable strategy, and this would seem an interesting avenue to explore. We also know little about the ways costs and benefits are distributed across individuals. Increased mortality risk seems to be distributed among individuals relatively uniformly, unlike the benefits that are skewed by male rank. Why should individuals likely to receive few benefits assist those likely to receive the majority, which in chimpanzees might be only the alpha and one or two other males? Is eliminating members of rival coalitions a way to reduce the mortality risk such coalitions impose, with this risk reduction driving participation in patrols, gang assaults, and lethal aggression? Finally, the extreme violence described for chimpanzees is notably absent in their sister species, the bonobo (*Pan paniscus*), in which intergroup encounters can be either tolerant or hostile. The reasons for such variation, and those for the lack of escalation in either inter- and intragroup interactions, are not fully understood.

References

Adams, D. (1989). The Seville statement on violence: A progress report. *Journal of Peace Research, 26*, 113–121.

Alexander, R., Hoogland, J., Howard, R., Noonan, K., & Sherman, P. (1979). Sexual dimorphism and breeding systems in pinnipeds, ungulates, primates, and humans. In N. Chagnon & W. Irons (Eds.), *Evolutionary biology and human behavior* (pp. 402–435). North Scituate, MA: Duxbury.

Arcadi, A. C., & Wrangham, R. W. (1999). Infanticide in chimpanzees: Review of cases and a new within-group observation from the Kanyawara study group in Kibale National Park. *Primates, 40*, 337–351.

Archer, J. (1988). *The behavioural biology of aggression*. New York: Cambridge University Press.

Archer, J., & Huntingford, F. (1994). Game theory models and escalation of animal fights. In M. Potegal & J. F. Knutson (Eds.), *The dynamics of aggression: Biological and social processes in dyads and groups* (pp. 3–32). Hillsdale, NJ: Erlbaum.

Arnqvist, G., & Rowe, L. (2005). *Sexual conflict*. Princeton, NJ: Princeton University Press.

Aureli, F., Schaffner, C. M., Verpooten, J., Slater, K., & Ramos-Fernandez, G. (2006). Raiding parties of male spider monkeys: Insights into human warfare? *American Journal of Physical Anthropology, 131*, 486–497.

Bartlett, T. Q., Sussman, R. W., & Cheverud, J. M. (1993). Infant killing in primates: A review of observed cases with specific reference to the sexual selection hypothesis. *American Anthropologist, 95*, 958–990.

Bateman, A. J. (1948). Intra-sexual selection in *Drosophila*. *Heredity, 2*, 349–368.

Bergerud, A. T. (1973). Movement and rutting behavior of caribou (*Rangifer tarandus*) at Mount Alberta, Quebec. *Canadian Field-Naturalist, 87*, 357–369.

Berglund, A., Bisazza, A., & Pilastro, A. (1996). Armaments and ornaments: An evolutionary explanation of traits of dual utility. *Biological Journal of the Linnean Society, 58*, 385–399.

Blanchard, D. C., & Blanchard, R. J. (2003). What can animal aggression research tell us about human aggression? *Hormones and Behavior, 44*, 171–177.

Boesch, C., & Boesch, H. (1989). Hunting behavior of wild chimpanzees in the Taï National Park. *American Journal of Physical Anthropology, 78*, 547–573.

Boesch, C., & Boesch-Achermann, H. (2000). *The chimpanzees of the Tai forest*. Oxford, England: Oxford University Press.

Boesch, C., Crockford, C., Herbinger, I., Wittig, R., Moebius, Y., & Normand, E. (2008). Intergroup conflicts among chimpanzees in Tai National Park: Lethal violence and the female perspective. *American Journal of Primatology, 70*, 519–532.

Boesch, C., Head, J., Tagg, N., Arandjelovic, M., Vigilant, L., & Robbins, M. M. (2007). Fatal chimpanzee attack in Loango National Park, Gabon. *International Journal of Primatology, 28*, 1025–1034.

Boesch, C., Kohou, G., Nene, H., & Vigilant, L. (2006). Male competition and paternity in wild chimpanzees of the Tai forest. *American Journal of Physical Anthropology, 130,* 103–115.

Boone, J. L. (1991). Comments on Manson, J. H., & Wrangham, R. W. "Intergroup aggression in chimpanzees and humans." *Current Anthropology, 32,* 377.

Borries, C., Launhardt, K., Epplen, C., Epplen, J. T., & Winkler, P. (1999). DNA analyses support the hypothesis that infanticide is adaptive in langur monkeys. *Proceedings of the Royal Society of London Series B: Biological Sciences, 266,* 901–904.

Boydston, E. E., Morelli, T. L., & Holekamp, K. E. (2001). Sex differences in territorial behavior exhibited by the spotted hyena (Hyeanidae, *Crocuta crocuta*). *Ethology, 107,* 369–385.

Brain, P. F. (1994). Hormonal aspects of aggression and violence. In A. J. Reiss, K. A. Miczek, & J. A. Roth (Eds.), *Understanding and preventing violence: Biobehavioral influences* (pp. 173–244). Washington, DC: National Academy of Sciences.

Brosnan, S. F., Newton-Fisher, N. E., & van Vugt, M. (2009). A melding of the minds: When primatology meets personality and social psychology. *Personality and Social Psychology Review, 13,* 129–147.

Bushman, B. J., & Anderson, C. A. (2001). Is it time to pull the plug on the hostile versus instrumental aggression dichotomy? *Psychological Review, 108,* 273–279.

Byers, J. A. (1997). *American pronghorn: Social adaptation and the ghosts of predators past.* Chicago: Chicago University Press.

Bygott, J. D. (1974). *Agonistic behaviour and dominance in wild chimpanzees.* Unpublished Ph.D. dissertation, University of Cambridge, Cambridge, England.

Bygott, J. D. (1979). Agonistic behaviour, dominance, and social structure in wild chimpanzees of the Gombe National Park. In D. A. Hamburg & E. R. McCown (Eds.), *The great apes* (pp. 405–428). Menlo Park, CA: Benjamin/Cummings Publishing Company.

Campbell, C. J. (2006). Lethal intragroup aggression by adult male spider monkeys (*Ateles geoffroyi*). *American Journal of Primatology, 68,* 1197–1201.

Carpenter, C. R. (1942). Societies of monkeys and apes. *Biological Symposia, 8,* 177–204.

Clutton-Brock, T. (1982). The functions of antlers. *Behaviour, 79,* 108–124.

Clutton-Brock, T., Albon, S. D., Gibson, R. M., & Guinness, F. E. (1979). Adaptive aspects of fighting in red deer (*Cervus elaphus* L.). *Animal Behaviour, 27,* 211–225.

Clutton-Brock, T., Guinness, F. E., & Albon, S. D. (1982). *Red deer: Behavior and ecology of two sexes.* Chicago: University of Chicago Press.

Clutton-Brock, T. H., & Parker, G. A. (1995). Sexual coercion in animal societies. *Animal Behaviour, 49,* 1345–1365.

Creel, S., & Creel, N. M. (2002). *The African wild dog: Behavior, ecology, and conservation.* Princeton, NJ: Princeton University Press.

Crofoot, M. C., & Wrangham, R. W. (2010). Intergroup aggression in primates and humans: The case for a unified theory. In P. M. Kappeler & J. Silk (Eds.), *Minding the gap: Tracing the origins of human universals.* (pp. 171–195). Berlin: Springer.

de Waal, F. B. M. (1992). Aggression as a well-integrated part of primate social relationships: A critique of the Seville Statment on Violence. In J. Silverberg & J. P. Gray (Eds.), *Aggression and peacefulness in humans and other primates* (pp. 37–56). New York: Oxford University Press.

de Waal, F. B. M. (2000). Primates—a natural heritage of conflict resolution. *Science, 289,* 586–590.

Drews, C. (1996). Contexts and patterns of injuries in free-ranging male baboons (*Papio cynocephalus*). *Behaviour, 133,* 443–474.

Dugatkin, L. A., & Dugatkin, A. D. (2007). Extrinsic effects, estimating opponents' RHP, and the structure of dominance hierarchies. *Biology Letters, 3,* 614–616.

Dunbar, R. I. M. (1984). *Reproductive decisions: An economic analysis of Gelada baboon social strategies.* Princeton, NJ: Princeton University Press.

Emery Thompson, M., Jones, J. H., Pusey, A. E., Brewer-Marsden, S., Goodall, J., Marsden, D.,...Wrangham, R. W. (2007a). Aging and fertility patterns in wild chimpanzees provide insights into the evolution of menopause. *Current Biology, 17,* 2150–2156.

Emery Thompson, M., Kahlenberg, S. M., Gilby, I. C., & Wrangham, R. W. (2007b). Core area quality is associated with variance in reproductive success among female chimpanzees at Kibale National Park. *Animal Behaviour, 73,* 501–512.

Emery Thompson, M., Muller, M. N., Wrangham, R. W., Lwanga, J. S., & Potts, K. B. (2009). Urinary C-peptide tracks seasonal and individual variation in energy balance in wild chimpanzees. *Hormones and Behavior, 55,* 299–305.

Emery Thompson, M., Newton-Fisher, N. E., & Reynolds, V. (2006). Probable community transfer of parous adult female chimpanzees in the Budongo forest, Uganda. *International Journal of Primatology, 27,* 1601–1617.

Emlen, S. T., & Oring, L. W. (1977). Ecology, sexual selection, and the evolution of mating systems. *Science, 197,* 215–223.

Enquist, M., & Leimar, O. (1990). The evolution of fatal fighting. *Animal Behaviour, 39,* 1–9.

Fawcett, K., & Muhumuza, G. (2000). Death of a wild chimpanzee community member: Possible outcome of intense sexual competition. *American Journal of Primatology, 51,* 243–247.

Geist, V. (1974). On fighting strategies in animal combat. *Nature, 250,* 354.

Goodall, J. (1977). Infant killing and cannibalism in free-living chimpanzees. *Folia Primatologica, 28,* 259–282.

Goodall, J. (1986). *The chimpanzees of Gombe: Patterns of behavior.* Cambridge, MA: Belknap Press.

Goodall, J. (1990). *Through a window: My thirty years with the chimpanzees of Gombe.* London: Goerge Weidenfeld & Nicolson Ltd.

Goodall, J. (1992). Unusual violence in the overthrow of an alpha male chimpanzee at Gombe. In T. Nishida, W. C. McGrew, R. P. Marle, M. Pickford, & F. B. M. deWaal (Eds.), *Topics in primatology: Human origins* (pp. 131–142). Tokyo: University of Tokyo Press.

Goodall, J., Bandora, A., Bergmann, E., Busse, C., Matama, H., Mpongo, E.,...Riss, D. (1979). Intercommunity interactions in the chimpanzee population of the Gombe National Park. In D. A. Hamburg & E. R. McCown (Eds.), *The great apes* (pp. 13–53). Menlo Park, CA: Benjamin/Cummings.

Goossens, B., Setchell, J. M., Tchidongo, E., Dilambaka, E., Vidal, C., Ancrenaz, A., & Jamart, A. (2005). Survival, interactions with conspecifics and reproduction in 37 chimpanzees released into the wild. *Biological Conservation, 123,* 461–475.

Gosling, L. M., & Roberts, S. C. (2001). Scent-marking by male mammals: Cheat-proof signals to competitors and mates. *Advances in the Study of Behavior, 30,* 169–217.

Grinnell, J., Packer, C., & Pusey, A. (1995). Cooperation in male lions: Kinship, reciprocity or mutualism? *Animal Behaviour, 49*, 95–105.

Gros-Louis, J., Perry, S., & Manson, J. (2003). Violent coalitionary attacks and intraspecific killing in wild white-faced capuchin monkeys (*Cebus capucinus*). *Primates, 44*, 341–346.

Hamai, M., Nishida, T., Takasaki, H., & Turner, L. A. (1992). New records of within-group infanticide and cannibalism in wild chimpanzees. *Primates, 33*, 151–162.

Harris, S., & Smith, G. C. (1987). Demography of two urban fox (*Vulpes vulpes*) populations. *Journal of Applied Ecology, 24*, 75–86.

Heptner, W. A., Nasimovitsch, A. A., & Bannikov, A. G. (1961). *Mammals of the Soviet Union*. Jena, Germany: Fischer-Verlag.

Herbinger, I., Boesch, C., & Rothe, H. (2001). Territory characteristics among three neighboring chimpanzee communities in the Taï National Park, Cote d'Ivoire. *International Journal of Primatology, 22*, 143–167.

Hill, K., Boesch, C., Goodall, J., Pusey, A., Williams, J., & Wrangham, R. (2001). Mortality rates among wild chimpanzees. *Journal of Human Evolution, 40*, 437–450.

Hiraiwa-Hasegawa, M., & Hasegawa, T. (1994). Infanticide in non-human primates: sexual selection and resource competition. In S. Parmigiani & F. S. vom Saal (Eds.), *Infanticide and parental care* (pp. 137–153). Chur, Switzerland: Harwood.

Hofer, H., & East, M. L. (1993). The commuting system of Serengeti spotted hyenas: How a predator copes with migratory prey II: Intrusion pressure and commuters' space-use. *Animal Behaviour, 46*, 575–589.

Houston, R. J., & Stanford, M. S. (2005). Characterization of aggressive behavior and phenytoin response. *Aggressive Behavior, 32*, 1–6.

Hrdy, S. B. (1977). Infanticide as a primate reproductive strategy. *American Scientist, 65*, 40–49.

Hrdy, S. B. (1979). Infanticide among animals: A review, classification, and examination of the implications for the reproductive strategies of females. *Ethology and Sociobiology, 1*, 13–40.

Johnson, R. P. (1973). Scent marking in mammals. *Animal Behaviour, 21*, 521–555.

Kaburu, S. S. K., Inoue, S., & Newton-Fisher, N. E. (in prep). Death of the alpha: within community lethal violence among chimpanzees of the Mahale Mountains, National Park.

Kahlenberg, S. M., Emery Thompson, M., Muller, M. N., & Wrangham, R. W. (2008a). Immigration costs for female chimpanzees and male protection as an immigrant counterstrategy to intrasexual aggression. *Animal Behaviour, 76*, 1497–1509.

Kahlenberg, S. M., Emery Thompson, M., & Wrangham, R. W. (2008b). Female competition over core areas in *Pan troglodytes schweinfurthii*, Kibale National Park, Uganda. *International Journal of Primatology, 29*, 931–947.

Kitchen, D. M. (2004). Alpha male black howler monkey responses to loud calls: Effect of numeric odds, male companion behaviour and reproductive investment. *Animal Behaviour, 67*, 125–139.

Knauft, B. M. (1991). Violence and sociality in human evolution. *Current Anthropology, 32*, 391–409.

Krug, E. G., Dahlberg, L. L., Mercy, J. A., Zwi, A. B., & Lozano, R. (2002). World report on violence and health. Geneva: World Health Organization.

Kruuk, H. (1972). *The spotted hyena. A study of predation and social behavior*. Chicago: University of Chicago Press.

Kutsukake, N., & Matsusaka, T. (2002). Incident of intense aggression by chimpanzees against an infant from another group in Mahale Mountains National Park, Tanzania. *American Journal of Primatology, 58*, 175–180.

Laurie, A. (1982). Behavioural ecology of the greater one-horned rhinoceros (*Rhinoceros unicornis*). *Journal of Zoology, 196*, 307–341.

Le Boeuf, B. J., & Reiter, J. (1988). Lifetime reproductive success in Northern elephant seals. In T. H. Clutton-Brock (Ed.), *Reproductive success: Studies of individual variation in contrasting breeding systems* (pp. 344–362). Chicago: University of Chicago Press.

Lederhendler, I. I. (2003). Aggression and violence: Perspectives on integrating animal and human research approaches. *Hormones and Behavior, 44*, 145–160.

Linden, E. (2002). The wife beaters of Kibale. *Time, 160*, 56–57.

Lowen, C., & Dunbar, R. I. M. (1994). Territory size and defendability in primates. *Behavioral Ecology and Sociobiology, 35*, 347–354.

Manson, J. H., & Wrangham, R. W. (1991). Intergroup aggression in chimpanzees and humans. *Current Anthropology, 32*, 369–390.

Maynard Smith, J., & Parker, G. A. (1976). The logic of asymmetric contests. *Animal Behaviour, 24*, 159–175.

Maynard Smith, J., & Price, G. R. (1973). Logic of animal conflicts. *Nature, 246*, 15–18.

Mech, L. D. (1977). Productivity, mortality, and population trends of wolves in northeastern Minnesota. *Journal of Mammalogy, 58*, 559–574.

Mech, L. D., Adams, L. G., Meier, T. J., Burch, J. W., & Dale, B. W. (1998). *The wolves of Denali*. Minneapolis: University of Minnesota Press.

Mitani, J. C., Gros-Louis, J., & Richard, A. F. (1996). Sexual dimorphism, the operational sex ratio, and the intensity of male competition in polygynous primaes. *The American Naturalist, 147*, 966–980.

Mitani, J. C., & Rodman, P. S. (1979). Territoriality: The relation of ranging patterns and home range size to defendibility, with an analysis of territoriality among primate species. *Behavioral Ecology and Sociobiology, 5*, 241–251.

Mitani, J. C., & Watts, D. P. (1999). Demographic influences on the hunting behavior of chimpanzees. *American Journal of Physical Anthropology, 109*, 439–454.

Mitani, J. C., Watts, D. P., & Amsler, S. J. (2010). Lethal intergroup aggression leads to territorial expansion in wild chimpanzees. *Current Biology, 20*, R507-R508.

Mjungu, D. C. (2010). *Dynamics of intergroup competition in two neighboring chimpanzee communities*. Unpublished Ph.D. dissertation, University Of Minnesota, Minneapolis.

Mosser, A., & Packer, C. (2009). Group territoriality and the benefits of sociality in the African lion, *Panthera leo*. *Animal Behaviour, 78*, 359–370.

Moyer, K. E. (1976). *The psychology of aggression*. New York: Harper & Row.

Muller, M. N. (2002). Agonistic relations among Kanyawara chimpanzees. In C. Boesch, G. Hohmann, & L. F. Marchant (Eds.), *Behavioral diversity in chimpanzees and bonobos* (pp. 112–124). Cambridge, England: Cambridge University Press.

Muller, M. N., Emery Thompson, M., Kahlenberg, S., & Wrangham, R. W. (2011). Sexual coercion by male chimpanzees shows that female choice may be more apparent than real. *Behavioral Ecology and Sociobiology, 65*, 921–933.

Muller, M. N., Kahlenberg, S. M., Emery Thompson, M., & Wrangham, R. W. (2007). Male coercion and the costs of promiscuous mating for female chimpanzees. *Proceedings of the Royal Society B: Biological Sciences, 274*, 1009–1014.

Muller, M. N., Kahlenberg, S. M., & Wrangham, R. W. (2009a). Male aggression against females and sexual coercion in chimpanzees. In M. N. Muller & R. W. Wrangham (Eds.), *Sexual coercion in primates and humans* (pp. 184–217). Cambidge, MA: Harvard University Press.

Muller, M. N., Kahlenberg, S. M., & Wrangham, R. W. (2009b). Male aggression and sexual coercion of females in primates. In M. N. Muller & R. W. Wrangham (Eds.), *Sexual coercion in primates and humans* (pp. 3–22). Cambridge, MA: Harvard University Press.

Murray, C. M., Eberly, L. E., & Pusey, A. E. (2006). Foraging strategies as a function of season and rank among wild female chimpanzees (*Pan troglodytes*). *Behavioral Ecology, 17*, 1020–1028.

Murray, C. M., Wroblewski, E., & Pusey, A. E. (2007). New case of intragroup infanticide in the chimpanzees of Gombe National Park. *International Journal of Primatology, 28*, 23–37.

Natarajan, D., & Caramaschi, D. (2010). Animal violence demystified. *Frontiers in Behavioral Neuroscience, 4*, 1–16.

Newton-Fisher, N. E. (1999). Infant killers of Budongo. *Folia Primatologica, 70*, 167–169.

Newton-Fisher, N. (2002a). Ranging patterns of male chimpanzees in the Budongo Forest, Uganda: Range structure and individual differences. In C. S. Harcourt & B. R. Sherwood (Eds.), *New Perspectives in Primate Evolution and Behaviour* (pp. 287–308). Otley, England: Westbury.

Newton-Fisher, N. E. (2002b). Relationships of male chimpanzees in the Budongo forest, Uganda. In C. Boesch, G. Hohmann, & L. F. Marchant (Eds.), *Behavioural diversity in chimpanzees and bonobos* (pp. 125–137). Cambridge, England: Cambridge University Press.

Newton-Fisher, N. E. (2003). The home range of the Sonso community of chimpanzees from the Budongo Forest, Uganda. *African Journal of Ecology, 41*, 151–156.

Newton-Fisher, N. E. (2004). Hierarchy and social status in Budongo chimpanzees. *Primates, 45*, 81–87.

Newton-Fisher, N. E., Emery Thompson, M., Reynolds, V., Boesch, C., & Vigilant, L. (2010). Paternity and social rank in wild chimpanzees (*Pan troglodytes*) from the Budongo Forest, Uganda. *American Journal of Physical Anthropology, 142*, 417–428.

Newton-Fisher, N. E., & Lee, P. C. (2011). Grooming reciprocity in wild male chimpanzees. *Animal Behaviour, 81*, 439–446.

Nishida, T. (1979). The social structure of chimpanzees of the Mahale Mountains. In D. A. Hamburg & E. R. McCown (Eds.), *The great apes* (pp. 73–122). Menlo Park, CA: Benjamin/Cummings.

Nishida, T. (1989). Social interactions between resident and immigrant female chimpanzees. In P. G. Heltne & L. A. Marquardt (Eds.), *Understanding chimpanzees* (pp. 68–89). Cambridge, MA: Harvard University Press.

Nishida, T. (1991). Comments on Manson, J. H., & Wrangham, R. W. "Intergroup aggression in chimpanzees and humans." *Current Anthropology, 32*, 381–382.

Nishida, T. (1996). The death of Ntologi, the unparalleled leader of M group. *Pan Africa News, 3*, 4.

Nishida, T. (2011). *Chimpanzees of the lakeshore: Natural history and culture at Mahale.* Cambridge: Cambridge University Press.

Nishida, T., Corp, N., Hamai, M., Hasegawa, T., Hiraiwa-Hasegawa, M., Hosaka, K.,...Zamma, K. (2003). Demography, female life history, and reproductive profiles among the chimpanzees of Mahale. *American Journal of Primatology, 59*, 99–121.

Nishida, T., Hiraiwa-Hasegawa, M., Hasegawa, T., & Takahata, Y. (1985). Group extinction and female transfer in wild chimpanzees in the Mahale National Park, Tanzania. *Z. Tierpsychol., 67*, 284–301.

Nishida, T., & Hosaka, K. (1996). Coalition strategies among adult male chimpanzees of the Mahale Mountains, Tanzania. In W. C. McGrew, L. F. Marchant, & T. Nishida (Eds.), *Great ape societies* (pp. 114–134). Cambridge, England: Cambridge University Press.

Nishida, T., Hosaka, K., Nakamura, M., & Hamai, M. (1995). A within-group gang attack on a young-adult male chimpanzee—ostracism of an ill-mannered member. *Primates, 36*, 207–211.

Nishida, T., Kano, T., Goodall, J., McGrew, W. C., & Nakamura, M. (1999). Ethogram and ethnography of Mahale chimpanzees. *Anthropological Science, 107*, 141–188.

Nishida, T., & Kawanaka, K. (1985). Within-group cannibalism by adult male chimpanzees. *Primates, 26*, 274–285.

Nishida, T., Uehara, S., & Nyundo, R. (1979). Predatory behavior among wild chimpanzees of the Mahale Mountains. *Primates, 20*, 43831.

Packer, C., & Pusey, A. E. (1984). Infanticide in carnivores. In G. Hausfater & S. B. Hrdy (Eds.), *Infanticide: Comparative and evolutionary perspectives* (pp. 31–42). New York: Aldine.

Parker, G. A. (1974). Assessment strategy and the evolution of fighting behaviour. *Journal of Theoretical Biology, 47*, 223–243.

Parker, G. A. (1979). Sexual selection and sexual conflict. In M. S. Blum & N. A. Blum (Eds.), *Sexual selection and reproductive competition* (pp. 123–166). New York: Academic Press.

Plavcan, J. M., & van Schaik, C. P. (1992). Intrasexual competition and canine dimorphism in anthropoid primates. *American Journal of Physical Anthropology, 87*, 461–477.

Poole, J. H. (1989). Announcing intent: The aggressive state of musth in African elephants. *Animal Behaviour, 37*, 140–152.

Popp, J. L., & DeVore, I. (1979). Aggressive competition and social dominance theory: synopsis. In D. A. Hamburg & E. R. McCown (Eds.), *The great apes* (pp. 316–338). Menlo Park, CA: Benjamin/Cummings.

Pruetz, J. D. (2006). Feeding ecology of savanna chimpanzees (*Pan troglodytes verus*) at Fongoli, Senegal. In G. Hohmann, M. M. Robbins, & C. Boesch (Eds.), *Feeding ecology in apes and other primates. Ecological, physical and behavioral aspects* (pp. 161–182). Cambridge, England: Cambridge University Press.

Pusey, A., Murray, C., Wallauer, W., Wilson, M., Wroblewski, E., & Goodall, J. (2008). Severe aggression among female *Pan troglodytes schweinfurthii* at Gombe National Park, Tanzania. *International Journal of Primatology, 29*, 949–973.

Pusey, A. E. (1979). Intercommunity transfer of chimpanzees in the Gombe National Park. In D. A. Hamburg &

E. R. McCown (Eds.), *The great apes* (pp. 465–480). Menlo Park, CA: Benjamin/Cummings.

Pusey, A. E. (1980). Inbreeding avoidance in chimpanzees. *Animal Behaviour, 28*, 543–552.

Pusey, A. E. (1983). Mother-offspring relationships in chimpanzees after weaning. *Animal Behaviour, 31*, 363–377.

Pusey, A. E. (2001). Of genes and apes: chimpanzee social organisation and reproduction. In F. B. M. de Waal (Ed.), *Tree of origin* (pp. 11–37). Cambridge, MA: Harvard University Press.

Pusey, A. E., Oehlert, G. W., Williams, J. M., & Goodall, J. (2005). Influence of ecological and social factors on body mass of wild chimpanzees. *International Journal of Primatology, 26*, 3–31.

Pusey, A. E., & Packer, C. (1994). Infanticide in lions: Consequences and counterstrategies. In S. Parmigiani & F. S. vom Saal (Eds.), *Infanticide and parental care* (pp. 277–300). Langhorne, PA: Harwood Academic Publishers.

Ralls, K. (1971). Mammalian scent marking. *Science, 171*, 443–449.

Setchell, J. M., & Wickings, E. J. (2005). Dominance, status signals and coloration in male mandrills (*Mandrillus sphinx*). *Ethology, 111*, 25–50.

Silverberg, J., & Gray, J. P. (1992). Violence and peacefulness as behavioral potentialities of Primates. In J. Silverberg & J. P. Gray (Eds.), *Aggression and peacefulness in humans and other primates* (pp. 1–36). New York: Oxford University Press.

Smuts, B. B., & Smuts, R. W. (1993). Male aggression and sexual coercion of females in nonhuman primates and other mammals: Evidence and theoretical implications. *Advances in the Study of Behavior, 22*, 1–63.

Stanford, C. B. (1998). *Chimpanzee and red colobus*. Cambridge, MA: Harvard University Press.

Stanford, M. S., Houston, R. J., Villemarette-Pittman, N. R., & Greve, K. W. (2003). Premeditated aggression: Clinical assessment and cognitive psychophysiology. *Personality and Individual Differences, 34*, 773–781.

Starin, E. D. (1994). Philopatry and affiliation among red colobus. *Behaviour, 130*, 253–270.

Sugiyama, Y. (1968). Social organisation of chimpanzees in the Budongo Forest, Uganda. *Primates, 92*, 225–258.

Sussman, R. W., & Marshack, J. L. (2010). Are humans inherently killers? *Global Nonkilling Working Papers*, 1.

Takahata, Y. (1985). Adult male chimpanzees kill and eat a male newborn infant: Newly observed intragroup infanticide and cannibalism in Mahale Mountains National Park, Tanzania. *Folia Primatologica, 44*, 161–170.

Terio, K. A., Kinsel, M. J., Raphael, J., Mlengeya, T., Lipende, I., Kirchhoff, C. A., ... Lonsdorf, E. V. (2011). Pathologic Lesions in Chimpanzees (*Pan troglodytes schweinfurthii*) from Gombe National Park, Tanzania, 2004–2010. *Journal of Zoo and Wildlife Medicine, 42*, 597–607.

Tolan, P. H. (2007). Understanding violence. In D. J. Flannery, A. T. Vazsonyi & I. D. Waldman (Eds.), *The Cambridge handbook of violent behavior and aggression* (pp. 5–18). New York: Cambridge University Press.

Townsend, S. W., Slocombe, K. E., Emery Thompson, M., & Zuberbuhler, K. (2007). Female-led infanticide in wild chimpanzees. *Current Biology, 17*, R355–R356.

Trivers, R. L. (1972). Parental investment and sexual selection. In B. Campbell (Ed.), *Sexual selection and the descent of man: 1871–1971* (pp. 136–179). Chicago: Aldine.

Tutin, C. E. G., McGrew, W. C., & Baldwin, P. J. (1983). Social organisation of savanna dwelling chimpanzees *Pan troglodytes verus*, at Mt. Assirik, Senegal. *Primates, 24*, 154–173.

Valero, A., Schaffner, C. M., Vick, L. G., Aureli, F., & Ramos-Fernandez, G. (2006). Intragroup lethal aggression in wild spider monkeys. *American Journal of Primatology, 68*, 732–737.

van Lawick, H. (1973). *Solo: The story of an African wild dog*. Glasgow: Collins.

van Rhijn, J. G., & Vodegel, R. (1980). Being honest about one's intentions: An evolutionary stable strategy for animal conflicts. *Journal of Theoretical Biology, 85*, 623–641.

van Schaik, C. P. (2000). Infanticide by male primates: The sexual selection hypothesis revisited. In C. P. van Schaik & C. H. Janson (Eds.), *Infanticide by males and its implications* (pp. 27–60). Cambridge, England: Cambridge University Press.

van Schaik, C. P., & Janson, C. H. (2000). *Infanticide by males and its implications*. Cambridge, England: Cambridge University Press.

van Schaik, C. P., Pradhan, G. R., & van Noordwijk, M. A. (2004). Mating conflict in primates: Infanticide, sexual harassment and female sexuality. In P. M. Kappeler & C. P. van Schaik (Eds.), *Sexual selection in primates* (pp. 131–150). Cambridge, England: Cambridge University Press.

Watts, D. P. (1998). Coalitionary mate guarding by male chimpanzees at Ngogo, Kibale National Park, Uganda. *Behavioral Ecology and Sociobiology, 44*, 43–55.

Watts, D. P. (2002). Reciprocity and interchange in the social relationships of wild male chimpanzees. *Behaviour, 139*, 343–370.

Watts, D. P. (2004). Intracommunity coalitionary killing of an adult male chimpanzee at Ngogo, Kibale National Park, Uganda. *International Journal of Primatology, 24*, 507–521.

Watts, D. P., & Mitani, J. C. (2000). Infanticide and cannibalism by male chimpanzees at Ngogo, Kibale National Park, Uganda. *Primates, 41*, 357–365.

Watts, D. P., & Mitani, J. C. (2001a). Male chimpanzee boundary patrolling and social bonds. *American Journal of Physical Anthropology, 114*(S32), 160–161.

Watts, D. P., & Mitani, J. C. (2001b). Boundary patrols and intergroup encounters in wild chimpanzees. *Behaviour, 138*, 299–327.

Watts, D. P., Mitani, J. C., & Sherrow, H. M. (2002). New cases of inter-community infanticide by male chimpanzees at Ngogo, Kibale National Park, Uganda. *Primates, 43*, 263–270.

Watts, D. P., Muller, M., Amsler, S. J., Mbabazi, G., & Mitani, J. C. (2006). Lethal intergroup aggression by chimpanzees in Kibale National Park, Uganda. *American Journal of Primatology, 68*, 161–180.

White, P. A. (2005). Maternal rank is not correlated with cub survival in the spotted hyena, *Crocuta crocuta*. *Behavioral Ecology, 16*, 606–613.

Wilkinson, P. F., & Shank, C. C. (1976). Rutting-fight mortality among musk oxen on Banks Island, Northwest Territories, Canada. *Animal Behaviour, 24*, 756–758.

Williams, J. M. (2000). *Female strategies and the reasons for territoriality in chimpanzees: Lessons from three decades of research at Gombe*. Unpublished Ph.D. dissertation, University of Minnesota, Minneapolis.

Williams, J. M., Lonsdorf, E. V., Wilson, M. L., Schumacher-Stankey, J., Goodall, J., & Pusey, A. E. (2008). Causes of death in the Kasekela chimpanzees of Gombe National Park, Tanzania. *American Journal of Primatology, 70,* 766–777.

Williams, J. M., Oehlert, G. W., Carlis, J. V., & Pusey, A. E. (2004). Why do male chimpanzees defend a group range? *Animal Behaviour, 68,* 523–532.

Williams, J. M., Pusey, A. E., Carlis, J. V., Farm, B. P., & Goodall, J. (2002). Female competition and male territorial behaviour influence female chimpanzees' ranging patterns. *Animal Behaviour, 63,* 347–360.

Wilson, E. O. (1975). *Sociobiology: The new synthesis.* Cambridge, MA: Harvard University Press.

Wilson, M. L., Hauser, M. D., & Wrangham, R. W. (2001). Does participation in intergroup conflict depend on numerical assessment, range location, or rank for wild chimpanzees? *Animal Behaviour, 61,* 1203–1216.

Wilson, M. L., Hauser, M. D., & Wrangham, R. W. (2007). Chimpanzees (*Pan troglodytes*) modify grouping and vocal behaviour in response to location-specific risk. *Behaviour, 144,* 1621–1653.

Wilson, M. L., Wallauer, W. R., & Pusey, A. E. (2004). New cases of intergroup violence among chimpanzees in Gombe National Park, Tanzania. *International Journal of Primatology, 25,* 523–549.

Wilson, M. L., Wells, M., Kahlenberg, S., & Wrangham, R. W. (2010). Food resources affect the timing of intercommunity interactions in the Kanyawara community of chimpanzees, Kibale National Park, Uganda. *American Journal of Physical Anthropology, 41,* 246–246.

Wilson, M. L., & Wrangham, R. W. (2003). Intergroup relations in chimpanzees. *Annual Review of Anthropology, 32,* 363–392.

Wrangham, R. (1999a). Is military incompetence adaptive? *Evolution and Human Behavior, 20,* 3–17.

Wrangham, R., & Peterson, D. (1996). *Demonic males: Apes and the origins of human violence.* New York: Mariner Books.

Wrangham, R. W. (1975). *The behavioural ecology of chimpanzees in the Gombe National Park, Tanzania.* Unpublished Ph.D. dissertation, Cambridge University, Cambridge, England.

Wrangham, R. W. (1979). Sex differences in chimpanzee dispersion. In D. A. Hamburg & E. R. McCown (Eds.), *The great apes* (pp. 481–490). Menlo Park, CA.: Benjamin/Cummings.

Wrangham, R. W. (1980). An ecological model of female-bonded primate groups. *Behaviour, 75,* 262–299.

Wrangham, R. W. (1986). Ecology and social relationships in two species of chimpanzee. In D. I. Rubenstein & R. W. Wrangham (Eds.), *Ecology and social evolution: Birds and mammals* (pp. 352–378). Princeton, NJ: Princeton University Press.

Wrangham, R. W. (1999b). Evolution of coalitionary killing. *Yearbook of Physical Anthropology, 42,* 1–30.

Wrangham, R. W., Wilson, M. L., & Muller, M. N. (2006). Comparative rates of violence in chimpanzees and humans. *Primates, 47,* 14–26.

Yadav, V. K. (2000). Male-male aggression in *Rhinoceros unicornis*—case study from North Bengal, India. *Indian Forester, 126,* 1030–1034.

PART 2

Evolutionary Perspectives on Familial Violence and Homicide

CHAPTER 4

Intimate Partner Violence: War at Our Doorsteps

Aaron T. Goetz *and* Gorge A. Romero

Abstract

Violence between intimate partners transcends culture and time. This chapter synthesizes several fronts of evolutionary-based research in order to describe and explain the primary causes of female-directed violence. Sexual conflict between men and women suggests that the sexes have unique avenues to reproductive success. Women's mating strategies, coupled with men's inability to ensure that the offspring they invest in are genetically their own, generated selective pressures for men to evolve tactics to eliminate threats to valued relationships. This chapter details how some of these tactics—executed by psychological mechanisms—lead to the violence, rape, and homicide observed among intimate partners. Using evolutionary theory, we seek to provide insight on ultimate explanations for intimate partner violence. Through this and through efforts made to understand proximate explanations of men's violence against women, we hope to contribute to a complete understanding of men's use of aggression in the relationships they value most.

Key Words: intimate partner violence, sexual conflict, paternity uncertainty, infidelity, sexual jealousy

Introduction

Waking up from a nap, Fakhra Khar hears the voice of her husband calling her name. As she opens her eyes, she wonders why she is hearing his voice. Khar had left her husband days earlier to work as a dancing girl and prostitute in the red-light district of the city where she was raised. Although still disoriented, Khar sees her husband standing over her. He puts his hand on her head, tilting it upward, and then proceeds to pour hydrochloric acid over her face. This attack left Khar disfigured in her face and upper body, with her lips fused together and her hair melted away (Lahore, 2001). *Karo-kari* is the phrase used in Urdu, a Hindustani language, to refer to the traditional use of violence primarily utilized by men against partners suspected of infidelity, and Khar had become a victim of this punishment (Patel & Gadit, 2008). Although *karo-kari* may be an unfamiliar phrase to the West, its implications are not. After recently becoming engaged, Linda Riss received a knock on her door from a man delivering a package. Excited, Riss hoped it was a present from her fiancé, but what she received was a splash of sodium hydroxide, a corrosive liquid that left Riss disfigured and blind. Motivated by jealousy, Riss's previous partner had hired a man to carry out the attack (Fass, 2004). After some time had passed from their respective incidents, both Khar and Riss returned to the partners that left them disfigured. Considering that 30% of homicides against women in the United States are instigated by intimate partners (Catalano, 2006) and that across cultures the prevalence for women succumbing to the violence of intimate partners falls between 19% and 75% (Garcia-Moreno, Jansen, Ellsberg, Heise, & Watts, 2006), men's violence against women is not isolated to any particular region of the world.

Intimate partner violence (IPV) has manifested itself not only across cultures but has transcended through time. Intimate partner violence and, specifically, men's violence against women, has been addressed from evolutionary perspectives as rooted deeply in a key adaptive problem men faced over evolutionary history: ensuring that the children they invest in are genetically their own. Cuckoldry, the unwitting investment in genetically unrelated children, effectively eliminated men who could not counter women's strategies of receiving material and genetic resources from more than one partner. The threat of cuckoldry is so devastating that its consequences are perhaps only rivaled by parasitic threats (Goetz, Shackelford, Romero, Kaighobadi, & Miner, 2008). Couple this threat with estimates of nonpaternity ranging from 2% to 10% (Anderson, 2006; Bellis, Hughes, Hughes, & Ashton, 2005), and it is clear that a selection force for anticuckoldry tactics must have shaped ancestral men to detect and eliminate threats to their reproductive success.

In this chapter, we take an evolutionary stance on female-directed IPV, the same violence that afflicted Fakhra Khar, Linda Riss, and that has afflicted many women throughout evolutionary history. This effort requires the initial exploration of the source of all forms of IPV: paternity uncertainty. Because perceived risk of partner infidelity moderates female-directed violence (Kaighobadi et al., 2009) and because research has suggested a progressive unraveling from nonviolent to violent tactics (Kaighobadi, Starratt, Shackelford, & Popp, 2008), we elaborate on two general tactics men use to defend their reproductive fitness: psychological tactics (e.g., sexual jealousy and partner insults) and physical tactics (e.g., the severity of female-directed violence and forced copulation). Some of the tactics, as we shall see, have strong evidence to support them as adaptations to sexual conflict (e.g., mate guarding), while others are currently lacking evidence to imply adaptive benefits (e.g., uxoricide or wife killing). Nonetheless, it is important to emphasize that our review of these tactics is scientific and is not meant to provide justification for such abhorrent behavior. The prevalence of IPV is not something to take lightly, and it will be through the understanding of both the natural history of its existence in addition to the proximate causes that manifest it that societies will be able to ameliorate the impact it has in the lives of women.

Biology: The Source of Paternity Uncertainty

Ancestral women without a doubt knew that their child was their own genetic product. Internal fertilization and gestation in mammals have reassured females that the investments they give a fetus in utero, an infant through lactation, and a developing offspring through nurturing are to the benefit of her own reproductive success. Men encounter a different biological situation. The manufacturing of sperm is cost effective when considering energetics and somatic resource allocation (Ellison, 2003). In fact, the donation of sperm in a fertile woman's reproductive tract is literally the minimal investment that men need to contribute to produce offspring. Without incurring the costs of a 9-month pregnancy, men could potentially move from partner to partner in attempts to maximize reproductive output. The freedom from extended investment that male biology brings loses some appeal when considering that, with other men interested in the benefit of their own reproductive success, a child born to a sexual partner may not be the genetic product of the man who invests in the offspring. This is the threat of cuckoldry and, as mentioned earlier, it is responsible for the genetic demise of men who could not retain a faithful partner with whom to produce offspring. Even without direct observation of the ancestral environment, we can infer that men faced the threat of cuckoldry. When considering (a) cross-cultural infidelity and paternal discrepancy rates; (b) the cross-cultural ubiquity and power of men's sexual jealousy (e.g., Buss, 2000; Daly, Wilson, & Weghorst, 1982); (c) women's fertile-phase sexuality, which functions primarily in the context of extrapair mating (e.g., Gangestad & Thornhill, 1998, 2008; Penton-Voak et al., 1999); (d) men's overperception of female infidelity (Andrews, Gangestad, Miller, Haselton, & Neale, 2008; Goetz & Causey, 2009); (e) adaptations associated with sperm competition in humans (e.g., Goetz & Shackelford, 2006; Shackelford & Goetz, 2007); (f) the matrilateral bias associated with grandparental and avuncular investment (e.g., Euler & Weitzel, 1996; Gaulin, McBurney, & Brakeman-Wartell, 1997; Jeon & Buss, 2007); and (g) paternity inferences and willingness to invest associated with paternal resemblance (Platek, Burch, Panyavin, Wasserman, & Gallup, 2002; Platek et al., 2003, 2004; Platek, Keenan, & Mohamed, 2005), it is evident that women's infidelity and men's susceptibility to cuckoldry were recurrent facets of human evolutionary history.

Accumulating some of the costs of cuckoldry reveals that the loss of time, effort, and resources spent on attracting a partner, resources directed at raising a rival's offspring, and reputational damage faced if the incident became public likely selected for men's sensitivity to and prevention of a partner's infidelity. This has resulted in the shaping of an integrated mental system that processes, assesses, and executes behavior to manage threats of cuckoldry—that is, cuckoldry has led to the evolution of specialized psychological mechanisms, neural-based features of human psychology designed by natural selection to solve specific adaptive problems. The first step to maintaining a secure relationship, one might argue, is to consistently monitor for threats. This is exactly what the functional emotion of sexual jealousy seeks to detect and in the next section, the purpose of jealousy is elucidated and discussed as a precursor to IPV.

Psychological Mechanisms Designed to Reduce Paternity Uncertainty
Men's Sexual Jealousy

Emotions function to elicit mechanisms that in turn guide specific behavior (Cosmides & Tooby, 2000). Emotions, as Nesse (1998) argues, are not designed to maximize happiness but rather for the benefit of the individual's reproductive success. Jealousy is an ideal exemplar for Nesse's description of emotions because it is generally associated with negative dispositions, but regardless of how pleasant our experience of jealousy might be, its universality among humans is attributed to its functionality. Jealousy overwhelms men and women when a valued relationship is threatened by a real or imagined rival, and it generates contextually contingent responses aimed at reducing or eliminating the threat. Jealousy may not be a pleasant state, but it is a state that allows individuals to become socially adept at recognizing when a relationship of interest is compromised. Jealousy functions to produce behavior aimed to prevent the derailment of a relationship. When aroused, jealousy motivates behavior in an attempt to deter mates from infidelity or departure from the relationship (Buss, Larsen, Westen, & Semmelroth, 1992; Daly et al., 1982; Symons, 1979).

Men and women express jealousy similarly in regard to frequency and intensity (Shackelford, LeBlanc, & Drass, 2000; White, 1981); however, research has repeatedly demonstrated that sex differences emerge in light of sexual and emotional jealousy (e.g., Buss, 2000; Symons, 1979). These differences are rooted in the divergent adaptive problems faced by men, that is, ensuring paternity certainty by eliminating threats of cuckoldry, and women, that is, sustaining continuous investment from her partner exclusively in her and her offspring. The evidence for these sex differences has been established on several research fronts, including experimental data (e.g., Schützwohl & Koch, 2004), physiological data (Buss et al., 1992), patterns of relationship termination (Betzig, 1989; Shackelford, Buss, & Bennett, 2002), and the behavioral output of jealousy (e.g., Buss & Shackelford, 1997). Men's sexual jealousy alone cannot prevent cuckoldry. Detection of a threat is only the beginning; managing the threat must follow from jealousy-directed behavior.

Postthreat Detection Behavior: Nonviolent Tactics

Being aware of threats allows men to deploy mate-retention behaviors derived from jealousy. Buss (1988) noted several mate guarding tactics, such as enhanced vigilance of partner whereabouts, concealment of a partner from potential rivals in social settings, and efforts to monopolize a partner's time. These tactics, as we will see, are a first line of defense that serves to help reduce threats of cuckoldry and in turn secure reproductive success. Buss and Shackelford (1997) demonstrated that men tend to monitor their partners more closely when they are of greater reproductive value (an indicator that may reflect a higher likelihood to be poached) and when the perceived probability of extrapair copulation is higher. Additionally, men who are mated to women who possess characteristics that make them more likely to commit sexual infidelity guard their partners more intensely (Goetz et al., 2005). Men also guard their partners more intensely after spending a greater proportion of time apart from them—a situation that increases the likelihood of female sexual infidelity (Starratt, Shackelford, Goetz, & McKibbin, 2007)—and when she is near ovulation, a time when a sexual infidelity would be most detrimental (Gangestad, Thornhill, & Garver, 2002). When enhanced monitoring is not sufficient, for example, when a man has low mate value, turning to verbal insults in order to implant resonating thoughts in his partner's mind that she is unattractive or has been unfaithful might be integrated with mate guarding (Miner, Shackelford, & Starratt, 2009; Starratt, Goetz, Shackelford, McKibbin, & Stewart-Williams, 2008). Protective guarding of partners from poachers might serve as an effective means to secure a relationship, but this is not always the case. When a man feels that his relationship may have been put in jeopardy, violence (aroused from anger and directed by jealousy) sometimes erupts between intimate partners and, as the next section details, this violence is aimed to punish a defecting partner.

Intimate Partner Violence
Jealousy's Interaction With Anger

In essence, men's history of violence suggests that there are at least two recurrent settings for dyadic conflict: status contests and IPV (Goetz, 2010). Intrasexual competition among men is more intense, direct, and involves more physical violence than female intrasexual competition (Benenson, 2009). Androgens function to regulate muscle mass and shape sexually dimorphic characteristics among men (Bhasin, 2003; Penton-Voak, & Chen, 2004). This leads to men carrying 61% more muscle mass than women (Lassek & Gaulin, 2009), the majority of which is located in the upper body (Abe, Kearns, & Fukunaga, 2003)—an indication that upper body strength is relevant to men's formidability (Sell et al., 2008). Put succinctly, men's phenotypes are indicative of the ancestral need to physically out-compete rivals in order to directly deal with threats to reproductive fitness. This facet of men's evolutionary history might explain why aggression is more appealing to men than women (Campbell, 1999; Vandello, Random, Hettinger, & Askew, 2009).

Although intrasexual competition is not the focus of this chapter, it is relevant to understanding IPV. In the previous section, we reviewed some of the nonviolent tactics men use to secure their relationships. These were primarily driven through jealousy, but at what point does jealousy drive violence against partners? Complex behavior requires the interaction of psychological mechanisms and here we argue that the interaction of the emotion anger with jealousy directs men's violence against women. If, as Western culture has expressed, jealousy is a green-eyed monster, then anger is responsible for readying the monster and jealousy provides the eyes to detect threats and direct attacks. Like jealousy, anger may not be a pleasant emotion, but it is functional nonetheless. Anger serves as a bargaining tactic in interpersonal conflicts and is used to negotiate outcomes that are in favor of the angered person (Sell, Tooby, & Cosmides, 2010). Those who are stronger or more formidable, as men are on average compared to women, are in a better position to negotiate conflict and are thus more prone to anger.

With anger and jealousy aroused in men, IPV may erupt to negotiate an outcome in the favor of men's reproductive fitness.

Anger might be so intertwined with violence that it is conveniently overlooked in proximate explanations of IPV, such that the circumstantial factors of alcohol abuse (Stith, Smith, Penn, Ward, & Tritt, 2004), feelings of patriarchy (Watts & Zimmerman, 2002), and lack of communication skills (Babcock, Waltz, Jacobson, & Gottman, 1993) become the focus of research. However, research shows that the salience of these risk factors is not as compelling when taking into account the ultimate explanations for this violence. For example, Foran and O'Leary (2008) found that the relationship between alcohol use and IPV is moderated by feelings of jealousy, such that nonsevere forms of physical aggression are primarily rooted in feelings of jealousy. Alcohol use increases the frequency of severe forms of physical aggression only when men reported (or were reported by their partner to have) stronger feelings of jealousy. Evolutionary explanations, as we note here, yield the ability to parse out otherwise neglected motivations like jealousy and anger in IPV contexts. Appreciating "ultimate" causes in investigating IPV can help elucidate research as an alternative, but compatible, approach to understanding proximate causes. IPV was a recurrent setting for violence over evolutionary history and, as we argue in the next section, violence functions to defend reproductive fitness in an intersexual context much like status concerns function to defend reproductive fitness in an intrasexual context.

Violence Is Punishment

It seems paradoxical that a biparental species marked by high paternal investment can have female-directed IPV as commonplace behavior. The prevalence rates of IPV listed earlier in this chapter leave no question about the occurrence of female-directed IPV in humans. Regardless of the proximate reasons, why does partner-directed violence manifest in the first place? This is an evolutionary question, and the answer lies in ancestral men's challenge of ensuring that partners remain cooperative with their fitness interests. Female-directed IPV is a form of punishment that is designed to negotiate fitness costs presented by past partner infidelity and facilitates the deterrence of suspected future female infidelity (Goetz et al., 2008). Clutton-Brock and Parker (1995) argued that punishment is a functional behavior aimed at reducing conflicts of interest with individuals expressing fitness-threatening behaviors to the aggressor. Keeping in mind that anger is an emotion that is used to negotiate a position during conflict, it becomes evident how both anger and jealousy can drive physical punishment among intimate partners.

Clutton-Brock and Parker's (1995) framework of punishment suggests that the severity of violence used against intimate partners is contingent on men's perceptions of how detrimental a partner's behavior is to their fitness. In line with this, research has found that men's violence against their intimate partners varies according to how serious a threat was perceived (e.g., Fitness, 2001; Fitness & Peterson, 2008). Fitness (2001) documented that punishment in a relationship varied with the perceived seriousness of the offense, such that retaliation for sexual infidelity received the most severe punishment, followed by less critical offenses such as trivial lying. Although the propensity to engage in physical violence was influenced by whether a partner was forgiven for the offense, it was the severity of betrayal that largely determined whether a partner would be forgiven. Upon these foundations, researchers are now beginning to appreciate that the costs that cuckoldry poses to men's fitness allows one to predict that the occurrence of IPV should be related to perceptions of threats to fitness, such as sexual infidelity and relationship termination (Goetz et al., 2008).

Punishment can be costly to those who institute it and, thus, we can expect to see it explicitly used under specific contexts in which the behavior of others is noncooperative. IPV could have posed costs to ancestral men in the form of reputational damage and retaliation from a female's nearby male kin, for example. Figueredo et al. (2001) presented evidence for this latter prediction by demonstrating that women who lived near several of their male kin were physically abused less often by their partners. Nevertheless, punishment is still utilized, and although there are costs associated with its use, punishment may prove to be effective at reducing the occurrence of cuckoldry. To make predictions about the effectiveness of punishment, we look to research performed in game theory to assess its potential functionality.

Game theory acknowledges that an individual's social behavior does not occur in a vacuum, but rather it must be considered in conjunction with the behavior of others. Evolutionary game theory (Fisher, 1930; Maynard-Smith, 1982) magnifies this logic by generations to show that the evolution of a trait depends on how it interacts with other extant and evolving traits. Because game theory considers the cost and benefits of interactions between competing strategies (e.g., people), it has relevance for the understanding of punishment as a male tactic against intimate partners. Given competing interests of the individuals involved in an interaction, game theory can evaluate competing strategies to determine the most effective approach to a particular interaction.

As previously reviewed, much evidence suggests that female infidelity and cuckoldry were recurrent features of our evolutionary history. Women's sexual infidelity is in direct conflict with men's evolutionary interests, setting the stage for a game theoretical analysis. If a woman's sexual infidelity goes without retaliation, it is probable that future defection will occur (Axelrod & Hamilton, 1981) and the man will continue to incur costs. With this in mind, punishment (i.e., IPV) can be viewed as retaliation against a defecting partner. Game theoretical studies examining the practicality of punishment as retaliatory strategy suggest that, even with the accrued costs from punishing over time, defection is effectively reduced (Fehr & Gächter, 1999; Gächter, Renner, & Sefton, 2008). Using game theory, we can argue that IPV might have served as an effective form of punishment by limiting the benefits gained from defecting from a relationship, deterring the occurrence of future defecting behavior, and preventing defection from occurring in the first place by establishing and promoting severe punishment as a consequence for defection (Fehr & Gächter, 1999; Hauert, Traulsen, Brandt, Nowak, & Sigmund, 2007; Rauhut & Junker, 2009).

Men's Proprietariness and Violence

Men's sexual jealousy or sexual proprietariness (Daly et al., 1982) is frequently found to be one of the key causes of IPV, both physical and sexual (e.g., Buss, 2000; Daly & Wilson, 1988; Dobash & Dobash, 1979; Dutton, 1998; Frieze, 1983; Gage & Hutchinson, 2006). Moreover, suspicion or knowledge of infidelity reliably provokes violent behavior (Goetz & Shackelford, 2006, 2009; Kaighobadi et al., 2008; McKibbin, Starrratt, Shackelford, & Goetz, 2011). Recognizing that men's mate-retention behaviors are manifestations of elicited sexual jealousy, Shackelford, Goetz, Buss, Euler, and Hoier (2005) investigated associations between men's mate-retention behaviors and IPV. Shackelford and colleagues found across three studies that male use of specific mate-retention behaviors was related to partner violence in a predictable fashion. For example, men who dropped by unexpectedly to see what their partner was doing or who told their partner that they would "die" if she ever left him were most likely to use serious violence against their partners, whereas men who attempted to retain their partners by expressing affection and displaying resources were least likely to use violence against their partners. These findings corroborated those by Wilson, Johnson, and Daly (1995), who found that women who affirmed that their partner insisted on knowing their whereabouts or limited their social contacts were twice as likely to have experienced serious violence at the hands of their partners.

Physical violence has been identified as a tactic used by men to restrict an intimate partner's behavior, especially her sexual behavior outside the intimate relationship (Daly & Wilson, 1988; Goetz & Steele, 2009; Wilson & Daly, 1996) and is best understood in the context of female infidelity. Goetz (2007) hypothesized that men possess evolved psychological mechanisms dedicated to generating risk assessments of a partner's sexual infidelity, and that these mechanisms selectively process information associated with assessments of time spent apart from the partner, the presence of potential mate poachers, the partner's reproductive value and fertility, and the partner's personality characteristics. Moreover, mechanisms designed to detect the likelihood of sexual infidelity in men seem to overestimate the probability of its occurrence (Goetz & Causey, 2009). Together with risk assessment of a partner's sexual infidelity, contextual factors—such as social and reputational costs, proximity of the partner's kin capable of retaliation, and economic dependency (Figueredo & McCloskey, 1993; Wilson & Daly, 1993)—are processed during decisions to inflict violence on a partner.

Evolutionary perspectives appreciate that IPV is not sex specific and is not isolated to human relationships (e.g., Goetz et al., 2008). The role of men's sexual jealousy in IPV in humans is significant and is sometimes ignored or is undervalued by alternative approaches to studying partner violence (e.g., Felson & Outlaw, 2007; Graham-Kevan & Archer, 2009). Multiple factors contribute to the occurrence of IPV; however, we argue that paternity uncertainty is an important facet to understanding and predicting female-directed violence. As we will discuss in the following section, conceptualizing IPV from an evolutionary perspective of men's prioprietariness allows us to explain several cases of partner violence and to predict the severity of violence based on detection of a threat to fitness.

Manifestations of Violence

When unrelated offspring, such as stepchildren, coreside with an adult male parent substitute, such as a stepfather, male jealousy progressively elevates. Men may become less willing to allocate resources toward nongenetic offspring, as compared to the biological mother, and the resulting inequality of investment can transcend from minor conflict to violence (Brewer & Paulsen, 1999; Daly, Wiseman, & Wilson, 1997). Documented cases of domestic violence feature an overwhelming proportion of women who reside with offspring sired by former partners (Brownridge, 2004; Daly, Singh, & Wilson, 1993; Figueredo & McCloskey, 1993). Using archival data spanning a 20-year period, Daly and colleagues (1997) documented that women with offspring sired by former partners were over 12 times more likely to be killed by subsequent partners (relative to women without offspring sired by former partners). Furthermore, women residing in stepfamilies have an increased probability of experiencing severe expressions of physical violence (Brownridge, 2004). Even in the most extreme case of uxoricide, women residing with offspring unrelated to their current partner are at a higher risk of being killed as compared with women who have offspring with their current partner (Brewer & Paulsen, 1999; Daly et al., 1997).

Relationships that potentially lack commitment, such as those seen among cohabitating couples as compared to married couples, also agitate men's sexual jealousy. Unwed women residing with their partners have been found to be at an elevated risk for female-directed violence when compared to married women (Brownridge, 2008; Shackelford, 2001; Shackelford & Mouzos, 2005; Wilson, Daly, & Wright, 1993; Wilson, Johnson, & Daly, 1995). Notwithstanding, cohabitation as a risk factor for female-directed violence may be receding in impact as unwed intimate relationships become more prevalent (Brownridge, 2008). Although we see that the escalation and severity of violence can be influenced by a number of factors, we next turn to focus on the most serious form of female-directed violence— partner killing—and attempt to understand the role that men's psychology plays in motivating partner killing.

Men's Instigation of Uxoricide

Of the 3,122 reported homicides of females that occurred in the United States alone in 2009, 35% of them were perpetrated by a husband or boyfriend (US Department of Justice, 2010), and as research has established, the killing of an intimate partner is often associated with men's sexual jealousy (Daly & Wilson, 1988; Serran & Firestone, 2004). As mentioned earlier, inflicting punishment on a partner can be costly; consequently, we can assume that the killing of an intimate partner will be met with severe repercussions. With this in mind, it is worth analyzing whether partner killing could have been substantially beneficial for men, so that selection pressures operated to favor those who carried out intimate femicide. Wilson and Daly (Daly & Wilson, 1988; Wilson & Daly, 1998; Wilson, Daly, & Daniele, 1995) address this question by proposing that partner killing is likely to be an unintended by-product of evolved mechanisms designed to influence and restrict a partner's behavior. This by-product hypothesis, otherwise known as the slipup hypothesis, does not view partner killing as adaptive behavior and, hence, suggests that selection would not favor the development of this behavior as a part of evolved male psychology. Altercations between intimate partners that result in men killing their partner therefore represent instances of misapplied control tactics. Arguing that many partner homicides are premeditated and not accidental, Buss and Duntley (1998, 2003; see also Buss, 2005) have suggested that many instances of lethal IPV are produced by evolved psychological mechanisms specifically designed to motivate killing a partner under certain conditions. Discovering a partner's sexual infidelity, Buss and Duntley argue, is a special circumstance that might trigger specialized psychology in men. Homicide adaptation theory does not argue that discovering a partner's infidelity invariantly leads to partner killing, but that this situation activates evolved mechanisms associated with weighing the costs and benefits of homicide, and that under certain circumstances, partner killing by men might be the designed outcome (Buss, 2005). Wilson and Daly's (1998; Wilson, Johnson, & Daly, 1995) and Buss and Duntley's (1998, 2003) contrasting hypotheses have not yet been tested concurrently, so that a single hypothesis remains to be found that best accounts for the data. Recent research has critiqued the proposition that the killing of an intimate partner is the result of an evaluation from adaptive mechanisms. Durrant (2009) argued that ancestral societies upheld sanctions against killing that would have made partner killing too costly to be adaptive. Durrant also highlights many shortcomings in using comparative research as support for homicide adaptation theory and suggests that understanding partner killing from a by-product standpoint is more parsimonious until further evidence is provided to support the existence of evolved mechanisms associated with partner killing. Although we appreciate, as do Buss and Duntley, that assuming a priori that a trait may be an adaptation is a heuristic that guides research questions and methods, an adaptationist's hypothesis is merely a starting point. Nevertheless, we turn once again to evolutionary game theory and consider the costs associated with lethal IPV, in an effort to further inform the ongoing debate.

As game theory is the study of multiple competing strategies, we consider a simplified model of lethal IPV to see how it performs against similar strategies. Consider, first, the consequences of an ancestral man killing an intimate partner after discovering her infidelity. Given an ancestral group size of 150 individuals (Dunbar, 1993), a roughly equal sex ratio, and given that approximately 50% of the population would be of reproductive age, this reduces the pool of reproductive aged men and women to 38 each. Just one case of lethal IPV results in nearly a 3% reduction in the available mating pool (from 38 potential mates to 37). Thus, the man's action to eliminate his partner is more costly to him than if he would have not eliminated her and simply terminated the relationship. By eliminating his partner, other males' options have become limited also, because the 38 men are now competing for 37 women. If, however, the man terminates the relationship instead, there remain 38 men competing for 38 women. Thus, the action of just one man killing his partner decreases the pool of available mates and, more important, intensifies mating competition for himself. This simplified model did not assume other parameters (e.g., polygyny) that would have exacerbated these results. Furthermore, the calculations were based on Dunbar's (1993) research arguing that our ancestors evolved in groups of roughly 150 individuals, but note that the results change by only 1% for every change in 50 members. Moreover, the mating competition intensification is exponentially greater when applied to an entire community of men who eliminate cheating partners. Other costs associated with killing an intimate partner include incurring the wrath of her kin and the local community, experiencing a significant decrease in mate value (e.g., Burkett & Kirkpatrick, 2006), and if they had children together, depriving the children of maternal investment.

Thus, given the simplified game theoretical analysis, the many costs associated with killing an intimate partner, the absence of research identifying the computational mechanisms underlying intimate partner homicide, and Durrant's (2009) other criticisms, Wilson and Daly's (1998; Wilson, Daly, & Daniele, 1995) by-product hypothesis remains the most parsimonious explanation for intimate femicide. Future research, of course, is needed to test the adaptation and by-product hypotheses concurrently.

Sexual Coercion

Between 10% and 26% of women experience rape in marriage (Abrahams, Jewkes, Hoffman, & Laubscher, 2004; Dunkle et al., 2004; Finkelhor & Yllo, 1985; Hadi, 2000; Painter & Farrington, 1999; Russell, 1982; Watts, Keogh, Ndlovu, & Kwaramba, 1998). Rape also occurs in nonmarital intimate relationships. Goetz and Shackelford (2006) secured prevalence estimates of rape in intimate relationships from a sample of young men and from an independent sample of young women in a committed relationship for at least 1 year, but not necessarily married. Goetz and Shackelford documented that 7.3% of men admitted to raping their current partner at least once, and 9.1% of women reported that they had experienced at least one rape by their current partner. Although these percentages are astonishingly high, they likely do not reflect the true incidence of partner rape. Questions concerning sexual coercion and rape in relationships are emotionally loaded and can be subject to social desirability; therefore, such percentages may be underestimates of the prevalence of rape in intimate relationships among young men and women. Several hypotheses have been proposed to explain why, across cultures, reliable percentages of women are sexually coerced by their partners. Here we highlight two approaches: (a) viewing sexual coercion as a result of men's desire for domination and control and (b) understanding sexual coercion as a result of paternity uncertainty.

Some researchers have hypothesized that sexual coercion in intimate relationships is motivated by men's attempts to dominate and control their partners (e.g., Basile, 2002; Bergen, 1996; Frieze, 1983; Gage & Hutchinson, 2006; Gelles, 1977; Meyer, Vivian, & O'Leary, 1998; Watts et al., 1998) and that this expression of power is the product of men's social roles (e.g., Brownmiller, 1975; Johnson, 1995; Yllo & Straus, 1990). Results relevant to this hypothesis are mixed. Several studies have found that physically abusive men are more likely than nonabusive men to sexually coerce their female partners (Apt & Hurlbert, 1993; DeMaris, 1997; Donnelly, 1993; Finkelhor & Yllo, 1985; Koziol-McLain, Coates, & Lowenstein, 2001; Shackelford & Goetz, 2004), supporting the domination and control hypothesis. Gage and Hutchinson (2006), however, found that women's risk of sexual coercion by their partners is not related to measures assessing the relative dimensions of power in a relationship, such as who maintains control over decision making. That is, women mated to men who hold the dominant position in the relationship are not more likely to experience sexual coercion than are women mated to men who do not hold the dominant position in the relationship, thus contradicting the domination and control hypothesis. Although many researchers agree that individual men may sexually coerce their partners to maintain dominance and control, proponents of the domination and control hypothesis often argue that men are motivated as a group to exercise "patriarchal power" or "patriarchal terrorism" over women (e.g., Brownmiller, 1975; Johnson, 1995; Yllo & Straus, 1990).

An alternative hypothesis has been advanced by researchers studying sexual coercion from an evolutionary perspective: Sexual coercion in intimate relationships may be related to paternity uncertainty, with its occurrence related to a man's suspicions of his partner's sexual infidelity (Camilleri, 2004; Goetz & Shackelford, 2006; Goetz, Shackelford, & Camilleri, 2008; Lalumière, Harris, Quinsey, & Rice, 2005; Thornhill & Thornhill, 1992; Wilson & Daly, 1992). Sexual coercion in response to cues of his partner's sexual infidelity might function to introduce a man's sperm into his partner's reproductive tract at a time when there is a high risk of cuckoldry (i.e., when his partner has recently been inseminated by a rival male). This sperm competition hypothesis was proposed following recognition that forced in-pair copulation (i.e., partner rape) in nonhuman species followed female extra-pair copulations (e.g., Barash, 1977; Cheng, Burns, & McKinney, 1983; Lalumière et al., 2005; McKinney, Cheng, & Bruggers, 1984) and that sexual coercion and rape in human intimate relationships often followed accusations of female infidelity (e.g., Finkelhor & Yllo, 1985; Russell, 1982). We turn our discussion to research that has focused on establishing evidence for the occurrence of forced in-pair copulation (FIPC) in humans.

Forced Copulation

Wilson and Daly (1992) suggested that "sexual insistence" in the context of a relationship might act as a sperm competition tactic in humans as well. Thornhill and Thornhill (1992) also hypothesized that FIPC may be an anticuckoldry tactic designed over human evolutionary history by selective pressures associated with sperm competition. Thornhill and Thornhill argued that a woman who resists or avoids copulating with her partner might thereby be signaling to him that she has been sexually unfaithful and that the FIPC functions to decrease his paternity uncertainty. Thornhill and Thornhill argued that the fact that the rape of a woman by her partner is more likely to occur during or after a breakup—times in which men express great concern about female sexual infidelity—provides preliminary support for the hypothesis. Thornhill and Thornhill also cited research by Frieze (1983) indicating that women who were physically abused and raped by their husbands rated them to be more sexually jealous than did women who were abused but not raped.

Similar arguments presented by Thornhill and Palmer (2000) and Lalumière et al. (2005) suggest that men who suspect that their female partner has been sexually unfaithful may be motivated to engage in FIPC. Both indirect and direct empirical evidence supporting this hypothesis has been documented. Frieze (1983) and Gage and Hutchinson (2006), for example, found that husbands who raped their wives were more sexually jealous than husbands who did not rape their wives. Shields and Hanneke (1983) documented that victims of FIPC were more likely to have reported engaging in extramarital sex than women who were not raped by their in-pair partner. Studying men's partner-directed insults, Starratt, Goetz, Shackelford, McKibbin, and Stewart-Williams (2008) found in two studies that a reliable predictor of a man's sexual coercion is his accusations of his partner's sexual infidelity. Specifically, men who accuse their partners of being unfaithful (nominating items such as "I accused my partner of having sex with many other men" and "I called my partner a 'whore' or a 'slut'") were more likely to be sexually coercive. Direct empirical evidence supporting this hypothesis is accumulating. Camilleri (2004), for example, found that risk of a partner's infidelity predicted the use of sexual coercion by male participants but not female participants. Goetz and Shackelford (2006) documented in two studies that a man's sexual coercion in the context of an intimate relationship is related positively to his partner's infidelities. According to men's self-reports and women's partner reports, men who used more sexual coercion in their relationship were mated to women who had been or were likely to be unfaithful, and these men also were likely to use more mate-retention behaviors. In a forensic sample, Camilleri and Quinsey (2009) found that convicted partner rapists, compared to nonsexual partner abusers, experienced more cuckoldry risk events prior to committing their offense; and in a second study involving a community sample, direct and recent cues to female infidelity predicted men's self-reported propensity for sexual coercion. Goetz and Shackelford (2009) collected data on the proximate and ultimate causes of men's sexual coercion in intimate relationships to explore how these variables interact. In two studies involving men's self-reports and women's partner reports, men's sexual coercion of their partners was consistently predicted by female infidelity even after controlling for men's dominate personalities and men's controlling behavior. Because cuckoldry poses a substantial reproductive cost for males of paternally investing species, men are expected to have evolved a host of adaptations to confront the adaptive problem of paternity uncertainty. One such adaptation may be a sperm competition tactic whereby sexual coercion and FIPC function to increase likelihood that the in-pair male, and not a rival male, sires the offspring that his partner might produce. It may be that a proportion of sexually coercive behaviors (in the context of an intimate relationship) are performed by antisocial men who aim to punish, humiliate, or control their partners, independent of their perception of cuckoldry risk. We are not arguing that all sexual coercion and FIPCs are the output of evolved psychological mechanisms designed to reduce the risk of being cuckolded. Instead, we are suggesting that sexual coercion might sometimes be the result of men's evolved psychology associated with men's sexual jealousy.

Conclusion

Female-directed violence, homicide, coercion, and rape have plagued intimate relationships over human evolutionary history. Because violence plagues a surprising percentage of relationships, it is paramount to understand why it resides in the relationships valued intensely by much of humanity. The prevalence of IPV suggests that there is a war at the doorsteps of many of our homes. It is a war fueled by the propensity of individuals to act in the evolutionary interests of their genes through the activation of ancient psychological programs that execute behaviors that were once effective at securing an opportunity of introducing offspring into subsequent generations. Evolutionary psychologists have elucidated mechanisms in men that are primarily responsible for the eruption of IPV. Although this exploration into human nature reveals aspects about men that are not socially desirable in modern society, it is crucial to acknowledge the influence of past selection pressures on present behavior. If society's interests are aimed at ending the war at home, it will only succeed by embracing both ultimate and proximate explanations of human behavior.

Future Directions

1. Our game theoretical analysis of Buss and Duntley's (1998, 2003) homicide adaptation theory suggests that uxoricide was not likely adaptive for ancestral men. However, because a psychological mechanism directing the killing of an intimate partner is likely to be contextually contingent, future research might consider analyzing the benefits men receive from partner killing under biosocial pressures. Analyses of the reproductive success of men in societies in which honor killings are instituted might elucidate circumstances in which men could benefit from killing an intimate partner. Patel and Gadit (2008) found that honor killings are primarily performed by men against their intimate partners who had been suspected of infidelity. Moreover, approval of honor killings seems to be rooted in the restoration of valor and respect for men (Plant, 2005). This restoration of respect might be an avenue for men in these societies to sustain status (a means to manage intrasexual competition) or perhaps as a signal of righteous behavior that may be attractive to women, who sometimes participate in honor killings.

2. Female-directed IPV is unlike other manifestations of men's aggression; the severity of violence varies with perceived risk of cuckoldry, and there are numerous tactics used in its occurrence that may be unique to the behavior (e.g., slapping). Researchers should consider that attacks on women might be strategically placed. Visible bruises, lacerations, or as in the extreme examples illustrated in the introduction to this chapter, intentional disfigurement of the face, might serve to deter rivals either through an indirect display of formidability or to control how attractive other men might view their partner. Saddki, Suhaimi, and Daud (2010) found that women who sought medical treatment after an occurrence of IPV were primarily injured on the face. This research suggests that men who suspect infidelity or potential defection from a relationship might direct their attacks to publicly visible areas such as the face to ward rivals away.

3. Although several of the implications of technologies like hormonal birth control for women might be too evolutionarily novel for men to understand, a woman who does not become pregnant after repeated intercourse might frustrate some men. Women who did not become pregnant in the ancestral environment were infertile or might have been attempting to sabotage pregnancy from their partners. Moreover, a woman who was not pregnant or lactating in the ancestral environment was allocating resources toward future reproductive success (Bribiescas & Ellison, 2008) and was at a higher risk of being poached. Thus, it might be the case that jealous men might use sexual and verbal coercion to directly communicate their desire to have offspring with their partners. Men might communicate their desire to become a father more when they are jealous in order to encourage pregnancy, direct a woman's investments into his offspring, and assure continued investment in the relationship if she conceives. This might confer more mating opportunities for a man, and if over time his partner does not conceive after his expressed interest in having offspring, coercion might elevate to threaten investment in other women.

References

Abe, T., Kearns, C. F., & Fukunaga, T. (2003). Sex differences in whole body skeletal muscle mass measured by magnetic resonance imaging and its distribution in young Japanese adults. *British Journal of Sports Medicine, 37*, 436–440.

Abrahams, N., Jewkes, R., Hoffman, M., & Laubscher, R. (2004). Sexual violence against intimate partners in Cape Town: Prevalence and risk factors reported by men. *Bulletin of the World Health Organisation, 82*, 330–337.

Anderson, K. G. (2006). How well does paternity confidence match actual paternity? Results from worldwide nonpaternity rates. *Current Anthropology, 48*, 511–518.

Andrews, P. W., Gangestad, S. W., Miller, G. F., Haselton, M. G., & Neale, M. C. (2008). Sex differences in detecting sexual infidelity: Results of a maximum likelihood method for analyzing the sensitivity of sex differences to underreporting. *Human Nature, 19*, 347–373.

Apt, C., & Hurlbert, D. F. (1993). The sexuality of women in physically abusive marriages: Comparative study. *Journal of Family Violence, 8*, 57–69.

Axelord, R., & Hamilton, W. D. (1981). The evolution of cooperation. *Science, 211*, 1390–1396.

Babcock, J. C., Waltz, J., Jacobson, N. S., & Gottman, J. M. (1993). Power and violence: The relation between communication patterns, power discrepancies, and domestic violence. *Journal of Consulting and Clinical Psychology, 61*, 40–50.

Barash, D. P. (1977). Sociobiology of rape in mallards (Anas platyrhynchos): Response of the mated male. *Science, 197*, 788–789.

Basile, K. C. (2002). Prevalence of wife rape and other intimate partner sexual coercion in a nationally representative sample of women. *Violence and Victims, 17*, 511–524.

Bellis, M. A., Hughes, K., Hughes, S., & Ashton, J. R. (2005). Measuring paternal discrepancy and its public health consequences. *Journal of Epidemiology and Community Health, 59*, 749-754.

Benenson, J. F. (2009). Dominating versus eliminating the competition: Sex differences in human intrasexual aggression. *Behavioral and Brain Sciences, 32*, 268–269.

Bergen, R. K. (1996). *Wife rape: Understanding the response of survivors and service providers.* Thousand Oaks, CA: Sage.

Betzig, L. (1989). Causes of conjugal dissolution: A cross-cultural study. *Current Anthropology, 30*, 654–676.

Bhasin, S. (2003). Regulation of body composition by androgens. *Journal of Endocrinology Investigation, 26*, 814–822.

Brewer, V. E., & Paulsen, D. J. (1999). A comparison of US and Canadian findings on uxoricide risk for women with children sired by previous partners. *Homicide Studies, 3*, 317–332.

Bribiescas, R. G., & Ellison, P. T. (2008). How hormones mediate trade-offs in human health and disease. In S. C. Stearns & J. C. Koella's (Eds.), *Evolution in health and disease* (pp. 77- 93). Oxford: Oxford University Press.

Brownmiller, S. (1975). *Against our will: Men, women, and rape.* New York: Simon & Schuster.

Brownridge, D. A. (2004). Male partner violence against women in stepfamilies: An analysis of risk and explanations in the Canadian milieu. *Violence and Victims, 19*, 17–36.

Brownridge, D. A. (2008). The elevated risk for violence against cohabitating women: A comparison of three nationally representative surveys of Canada. *Violence Against Women, 14*, 809–832.

Burkett, B. N., & Kirkpatrick, L. A. (2006, June 10). *What are deal breakers in a mate: Characteristics that are intolerable in a potential mate.* Paper presented at the Annual Meeting of the Human Behavior and Evolution Society, Philadelphia, PA.

Buss, D. M. (1988). From vigilance to violence: Tactics of mate retention in American undergraduates. *Ethology and Sociobiology, 9*, 291–317.

Buss, D. M. (2000). *The dangerous passion.* New York: The Free Press.

Buss, D. M. (2005). *The murderer next door.* New York: The Penguin Press.

Buss, D. M., & Duntley, J. D. (1998, July 10). *Evolved homicide modules.* Paper presented at the Annual Meeting of the Human Behavior and Evolution Society, Davis, CA.

Buss, D. M., & Duntley, J. D. (2003). Homicide: An evolutionary perspective and implications for public policy. In N. Dress (Ed.), *Violence and public policy* (pp. 115–128). Westport, CT: Greenwood.

Buss, D. M., Larsen, R. J., Westen, D., & Semmelroth, J. (1992). Sex differences in jealousy: Evolution, physiology and psychology. *Psychological Science, 3*, 251–255.

Buss, D. M., & Shackelford, T. K. (1997). From vigilance to violence: Mate retention tactics in married couples. *Journal of Personality and Social Psychology, 72*, 346–361.

Camilleri, J. (2004). *Investigating sexual coercion in romantic relationships: A test of the cuckoldry risk hypothesis.* Unpublished Master's thesis, University of Saskatchewan, Saskatoon, Saskatchewan, Canada.

Camilleri, J. A., & Quinsey, V. L. (2009). Testing the cuckoldry risk hypothesis of partner sexual coercion in forensic and community samples. *Evolutionary Psychology, 7*, 164–178.

Campbell, A. (1999). Staying alive: Evolution, culture, and women's intrasexual aggression. *Behavioral and Brain Sciences, 22*, 203–252.

Catalano, S. (2006). *Intimate partner violence in the United States.* Washington, DC: Bureau of Justice Statistics, US Department of Justice.

Cheng, K. M., Burns, J. T., & McKinney, F. (1983). Forced copulation in captive mallards III. Sperm competition. *The Auk, 100*, 302–310.

Clutton-Brock, T. H., & Parker, G. A. (1995). Punishment in animal societies. *Nature, 373*, 209–216.

Cosmides, L., & Tooby, J. (2000). Evolutionary psychology and the emotions. In M. Lewis & J. M. Haviland-Jones (Eds.), *Handbook of emotions* (2nd ed., pp. 91–115). New York: Guilford Press.

Daly, M., Singh, L. S., & Wilson, M. (1993). Children fathered by previous partners: A risk factor for violence against women. *Canadian Journal of Public Health, 84*, 209–210.

Daly, M., & Wilson, M. (1988). *Homicide.* Hawthorne, NY: Aldine de Gruyter.

Daly, M., Wilson, M., & Weghorst, J. (1982). Male sexual jealousy. *Ethology and Sociobiology, 3*, 11–27.

Daly, M., Wiseman, K. A., & Wilson, M. I. (1997). Women with children sired by previous partners incur excess risk of uxoricide. *Homicide Studies, 1*, 61–71.

DeMaris, A. (1997). Elevated sexual activity in violent marriages: Hypersexuality or sexual extortion? *Journal of Sex Research, 34*, 361–373.

Dobash, R. E., & Dobash, R. P. (1979). *Violence against wives.* New York: The Free Press.

Donnelly, D. A. (1993). Sexually inactive marriages. *The Journal of Sex Research, 30*, 171–179.

Dunbar, R. I. M. (1993). Coevolution of neocortical size, group size and language in humans. *Behavioral and Brain Sciences, 16*, 681–735.

Dunkle, K. L., Jewkes, R. K., Brown, H. C., Gray, G. E., McIntyre, J. A., & Harlow, S. D. (2004). Gender-based violence, relationship power and risk of prevalent HIV infection among women attending antenatal clinics in Soweto, South Africa. *Lancet, 363*, 1415–1421.

Durrant, R. (2009). Born to kill? A critical evaluation of homicide adaptation theory. *Aggression and Violent Behavior, 14*, 374–381.

Dutton, D. G. (1998). *The abusive personality.* New York: Guilford Press.

Ellison, P. T. (2003). Energetics and reproductive effort. *American Journal of Human Biology, 15*, 342–351.

Euler, H. A. & Weitzel, B. (1996). Discriminative grandparental solicitude as reproductive strategy. *Human Nature: An Interdisciplinary Biosocial Perspective, 7*, 39–59.

Fass, M. (2004, March 21). Citypeople; A sort of love story. *The New York Times.* Retrieved November 2011, from http://www.nytimes.com/2004/03/21/nyregion/citypeople-a-sort-of-love-story.html?pagewanted=1

Fehr, E., & Gächter, S. (1999). Cooperation and punishment in public goods experiments. *American Economic Review, 90*, 980–994.

Felson, R., & Outlaw, M. C. (2007). The control motive and marital violence. *Violence and Victims, 22*, 387–407.

Figueredo, A. J., Corral-Verduogo, V., Frías-Armenta, M., Bachar, K. J., White, J., McNeill, P. L.,...del PilarCastell-Ruiz, I. (2001). Blood, solidarity, status, and honor: The sexual balance of power and spousal abuse in Sonora, Mexico. *Evolution and Human Behavior, 22*, 295–328.

Figueredo, A. J., & McCloskey, L. A. (1993). Sex, money, and paternity: The evolution of domestic violence. *Ethology and Sociobiology, 14*, 353–379.

Finkelhor, D., & Yllo, K. (1985). *License to rape: Sexual abuse of wives.* New York: Holt, Rinehart, & Winston.

Fisher, R. A. (1930). *The genetical theory of natural selection.* Oxford, England: Clarendon Press.

Fitness, J. (2001). Betrayal, rejection, revenge and forgiveness: An interpersonal script. In M. Leary (Ed.), *Interpersonal rejection* (pp. 73–103). New York: Oxford University Press.

Fitness, J., & Peterson, J. (2008). Punishment and forgiveness in close relationships: An evolutionary, social-psychological perspective. In J. P. Forgas & J. Fitness (Eds.), *Social relationships: Cognitive, affective, and motivational processes* (pp. 255–270). New York: Psychology Press.

Foran, H. M., & O'Leary, K. D. (2008). Problem drinking, jealousy, and anger control: Variables predicting physical aggression against a partner. *Journal of Family Violence, 23*, 141–148.

Frieze, I. H. (1983). Investigating the causes and consequences of marital rape. *Signs: Journal of Women in Culture and Society, 8*, 532–553.

Gage, A. J., & Hutchinson, P. L. (2006). Power, control, and intimate partner sexual violence in Haiti. *Archives of Sexual Behavior, 35*, 11–24.

Gächter, S., Renner, E., & Sefton, M. (2008). The long-run benefits of punishment. *Science, 322*, 1510.

Gangestad, S. W., & Thornhill, R. (1998). Menstrual cycle variation in women's preferences for the scent of symmetrical men. *Proceedings of the Royal Society B, 265*, 927–933.

Gangestad, S. W., & Thornhill, R. (2008). Human oestrus. *Proceedings of the Royal Society B, 275*, 991–1000.

Gangestad, S. W., Thornhill, R., & Garver, C. E. (2002). Changes in women's sexual interests and their partner's mate-retention tactics across the menstrual cycle: Evidence for shifting conflicts of interest. *Proceedings of the Royal Society of London, 269*, 975–982.

Garcia-Moreno, C., Jansen, H., Ellsberg, M., Heise, L., & Watts, C. H. (2006). Prevalence of intimate partner violence: Findings from the WHO multi-country study on women's health and domestic violence. *Lancet, 368*, 1260–1269.

Gaulin, S. J. C., McBurney, D. H., & Brakeman-Wartell, S. L. (1997). Matrilateral biases in the investment of aunts and uncles: A consequence of measure of paternity uncertainty. *Human Nature: An Interdisciplinary Biosocial Perspective, 8*, 139–151.

Gelles, R. (1977). Power, sex and violence: The case of marital rape. *Family Coordinator, 26*, 339–347.

Goetz, A. T. (2007). Violence and abuse in families: The consequences of paternal uncertainty. In C. Salmon & T. K. Shackelford (Eds.), *Family relationships: An evolutionary perspective* (pp. 259–274). New York: Oxford University Press.

Goetz, A. T. (2010). The evolutionary psychology of violence. *Psicothemia, 22*, 15–21.

Goetz, A. T., & Causey, K. (2009). Sex differences in perceptions of infidelity: Men often assume the worst. *Evolutionary Psychology, 7*, 253–263.

Goetz, A. T., & Shackelford, T. K. (2006). Sexual coercion and forced in-pair copulation as sperm competition tactics in humans. *Human Nature, 17*, 265–282.

Goetz, A. T., & Shackelford, T. K. (2009). Sexual coercion in intimate relationships: A comparative analysis of the effects of women's infidelity and men's dominance and control. *Archives of Sexual Behavior, 38*, 226–234.

Goetz, A. T., Shackelford, T. K., & Camilleri, J. A. (2008). Proximate and ultimate explanations are required for a comprehensive understanding of partner rape. *Aggression and Violent Behavior, 13*, 119–123.

Goetz, A. T., Shackelford, T. K., Romero, G. A., Kaighobadi, F., & Miner, E. J. (2008). Punishment, proprietariness, and paternity: Men's violence against women from an evolutionary perspective. *Aggression and Violent Behavior, 13*, 481–489.

Goetz, A. T., & Steele, K. (2009, February 27). *Men's proprietary view of their romantic partners is specific to sexuality: An experimental study.* Paper presented at the 3rd International Conference on the Evolution of Human Aggression: Lessons for today's conflicts, Salt Lake City, UT.

Goetz, A. T., Shackelford, T. K., Weekes-Shackelford, V. A., Euler, H. A., Hoier, S., Schmitt, D. P., & LaMunyon, C. W. (2005). Mate retention, semen displacement, and human sperm competition: A preliminary investigation of tactics to prevent and correct female infidelity. *Personality and Individual Differences, 38*, 749–763.

Graham-Kevan, N., & Archer, J. (2009). Control tactics and partner violence in heterosexual relationships. *Evolution and Human Behavior, 30*, 445–452.

Hauert, C., Traulsen, A., Brandt, H., Nowak, M. A., & Sigmund, K. (2007). Via freedom to coercion: The emergence of costly punishment. *Science, 316*, 1905–1907.

Hadi, A. (2000). Prevalence and correlates of the risk of martial sexual violence in Bangladesh. *Journal of Interpersonal Violence, 15*, 787–805.

Jeon, J., & Buss, D. M. (2007). Altruism towards cousins. *Proceedings of the Royal Society B, 274*, 1181–1187.

Johnson, M. P. (1995). Patriarchal terrorism and common couple violence: Two forms of violence against women. *Journal of Marriage and the Family, 57*, 283–294.

Kaighobadi, F., Starratt, V. G., Shackelford, T. K., & Popp, D. (2008). Male mate retention mediates the relationship between female sexual infidelity and female-directed violence. *Personality and Individual Differences, 44*, 1422–1431.

Kaighobadi, F., Shackelford, T. K., Popp, D., Moyer, R. M., Bates, V. M., & Liddle, J. R. (2009). Perceived risk of female infidelity moderates the relationship between personality and partner-directed violence. *Journal of Research in Personality, 43*, 1033–1039.

Koziol-McLain, J., Coates, C. J., & Lowenstein, S. R. (2001). Predictive validity of a screen for partner violence against women. *American Journal of Preventative Medicine, 21*, 93–100.

Lahore, H. B. (2001, August 20). The evil that men do. *Time.* Retrieved November 2011, from http://www.time.com/time/magazine/article/0,9171,170879,00.html

Lalumière, M. L., Harris, G. T., Quinsey, V. L., & Rice, M. E. (2005). *The causes of rape: Understanding individual differences in male propensity for sexual aggression.* Washington, DC: APA Press.

Lassek, W. D., & Gaulin, S. J. C. (2009). Costs and benefits of fat-free muscle mass in men: Relationship to mating success, dietary requirements, and native immunity. *Evolution and Human Behavior, 30*, 322–328.

Maynard Smith, J. (1982). *Evolution and the theory of games*. Cambridge, England: Cambridge University Press.

McKinney, F., Cheng, K. M., & Bruggers, D. J. (1984). Sperm competition in apparently monogamous birds. In R. L. Smith (Ed.), *Sperm competition and evolution of animal mating systems* (pp. 523–545). New York: Academic Press.

McKibbin, W. F., Starratt, V. G., Shackelford, T. K., & Goetz, A. T. (2011). Perceived risk of female infidelity moderates the relationship between objective risk of female infidelity and sexual coercion in Humans (*Homo sapiens*). *Journal of Comparative Psychology, 125*, 370–373.

Meyer, S., Vivian, D., & O'Leary, K. D. (1998). Men's sexual aggression in marriage: Couple's reports. *Violence Against Women, 4*, 415–435.

Miner, E. J., Shackelford, T. K., & Starratt, V. G. (2009). Mate value of romantic partner predicts men's partner-directed verbal insults. *Personality and Individual Differences, 46*, 135–139.

Nesse, R. (1998). Emotional disorders in evolutionary perspective. *British Journal of Medical Psychology, 71*, 397–415.

Painter, K., & Farrington, D. P. (1999). Wife rape in Great Britain. In R. Muraskin (Ed.), *Women and justice: Development of international policy* (pp. 135–164). New York: Gordon and Breach.

Patel, S., & Gadit, A. M. (2008) Karo-kari: A form of honour killing in Pakistan. *Transcultural Psychiatry, 45*, 683–694.

Penton-Voak, I. S., & Chen, J. Y. (2004). High salivary testosterone is linked to masculine male facial appearances in humans. *Evolution and Human Behavior, 25*, 229–241.

Penton-Voak, I. S., Perrett, D. I., Castles, D. L., Kobayashi, T., Burt, D. M., Murray, L. K., & Minamisawa, R. (1999). Female preference for male faces changes cyclically. *Nature, 399*, 741–742.

Plant, V. (2005). Honor killings and the asylum gender gap. *Journal of Transnational Law and Policy, 15*, 109–129.

Platek, S. M., Burch, R. L., Panyavin, I. S., Wasserman, B. H., & Gallup, G. G. (2002). Reactions to children's faces: Resemblance matters more for males than females. *Evolution and Human Behavior, 23*, 159–166.

Platek, S. M., Critton, S. R., Burch, R. L., Frederick, D. A., Myers, T. E., & Gallup, G. G. (2003). How much resemblance is enough? Sex difference in reactions to resemblance, but not the ability to detect resemblance. *Evolution and Human Behavior, 24*, 81–87.

Platek, S. M., Keenan, J. P., & Mohamed, F. B. (2005). Sex differences in neural correlates of child facial resemblance: An event-related fMRI study. *NeuroImage, 25*, 1336–1344.

Platek, S. M., Raines, D. M., Gallup, G. G., Mohamed, F. B., Thomson, J. W., Myers, T. E., ...Arigo, D. R. (2004). Reactions to children's faces: Males are still more affected by resemblance than females are, and so are their brains. *Evolution and Human Behavior, 25*, 394–405.

Rauhut, H., & Junker, M. (2009). Punishment deters crime because humans are bounded in their strategic decision-making. *Journal of Artificial Societies and Social Simulation, 12*, 1.

Russell, D. E. H. (1982). *Rape in marriage*. New York: Macmillan Press.

Saddki, N., Suhaimi, A. A., & Daud, R. (2010). Maxillofacial injuries associated with intimate partner violence in women. *BioMed Central Public Health, 10*, 1–6.

Schützwohl, A., & Koch, S. (2004). Sex differences in jealousy: The recall of cues to sexual and emotional infidelity in personally more and less threatening context conditions. *Evolution and Human Behavior, 25*, 249–257.

Sell, A., Cosmides, L., Tooby, J., Sznycer, D., von Rueden, C., & Gurven, M. (2008). Human adaptations for the visual assessment of strength and fighting ability from the body and face. *Proceedings of the Royal Society B, 276*, 575–584.

Sell, A., Tooby, J., & Cosmides, L. (2010). Formidability and the logic of human anger. *Proceedings of the National Academy of Sciences USA, 106*, 15073–15078.

Serran, G., & Firestone, P. (2004). Intimate partner homicide: A review of the male proprietariness and the self-defense theories. *Aggression and Violent Behavior, 9*, 1–15.

Shackelford, T. K. (2001). Cohabitation, marriage, and murder: Woman-killing by male romantic partners. *Aggressive Behavior, 27*, 284–291.

Shackelford, T. K., Buss, D. M., & Bennett, K. (2002). Forgiveness or breakup: Sex differences in responses to a partner's infidelity. *Cognition and Emotion, 16*, 299–307.

Shackelford, T. K., & Goetz, A. T. (2004). Men's sexual coercion in intimate relationships: Development and initial validation of the Sexual Coercion in Intimate Relationships Scale. *Violence and Victims, 19*, 21–36.

Shackelford, T. K., & Goetz, A. T. (2006). Comparative psychology of sperm competition. *Journal of Comparative Psychology, 120*, 139–146.

Shackelford, T. K., & Goetz, A. T. (2007) Adaptation to sperm competition in humans. *Current Directions in Psychological Science, 16*, 47–50.

Shackelford, T. K., Goetz, A. T., Buss, D. M., Euler, H. A., & Hoier, S. (2005). When we hurt the ones we love: Predicting violence against women from men's mate retention tactics. *Personal Relationships, 12*, 447–463.

Shackelford, T. K., LeBlanc, G. J., & Drass, E. (2000). Emotional reactions to infidelity. *Cognition and Emotion, 14*, 643–659.

Shackelford, T. K., & Mouzos, J. (2005). Partner killing by men in cohabitating and marital relationships: A comparative, cross-national analysis of data from Australia and the United States. *Journal of Interpersonal Violence, 20*, 1310–1324.

Shields, N. M., & Hanneke, C. R. (1983). Battered wives' reactions to marital rape. In R. Gelles, G. Hotaling, M. Straus, & D. Finkelhor (Eds.), *The dark side of families* (pp. 131–148). Beverly Hills, CA: Sage.

Starratt, V. G., Goetz, A. T., Shackelford, T. K., McKibbin, W. F., & Stewart-Williams, S. (2008). Men's partner-directed insults and sexual coercion in intimate relationships. *Journal of Family Violence, 23*, 315–323.

Starratt, V. J., Shackelford, T. K., Goetz, A. T., & McKibbin, W. F. (2007). Male mate retention behaviors vary with risk of female infidelity and sperm competition. *Acta Psychologica Sinica, 39*, 523–527.

Stith, S. M., Smith, D. B., Penn, C. E., Ward, D. B., & Tritt, D. (2004). Intimate partner physical abuse perpetration and victimization risk factors: A meta-analytic review. *Aggression and Violent Behavior, 10*, 65–98.

Symons, D. (1979). *The evolution of human sexuality*. New York: Oxford University Press.

Thornhill, R., & Palmer, C. T. (2000). *A natural history of rape*. Cambridge, MA: MIT Press.

Thornhill, R., & Thornhill, N. W. (1992). The evolutionary psychology of men's coercive sexuality. *Behavioral and Brain Sciences, 15*, 363–421.

US Department of Justice, Federal Bureau of Investigation. (2010). *Crime in the United States*, 2009. Retrieved

November 2011, from http://www2.fbi.gov/ucr/cius2009/offenses/expanded_information/data/shrtable_10.html

Vandello, J. A., Ransom, S., Hettinger, V. E., & Askew, K. (2009). Men's misperceptions about the acceptability and attractiveness of aggression. *Journal of Experimental Social Psychology, 45*, 1209–1219.

Watts, C., Keogh, E., Ndlovu, M., & Kwaramba, R. (1998). Withholding of sex and forced sex: Dimensions of violence against Zimbabwean women. *Reproductive Health Matters, 6*, 57–65.

Watts, C., & Zimmerman, C. (2002). Violence against women: Global scope and magnitude. *The Lancet, 359*, 1232–1237.

White, G. L. (1981). Some correlates of romantic jealousy. *Journal of Personality, 49*, 129–147.

Wilson, M., & Daly, M. (1992). The man who mistook his wife for a chattel. In J. H. Barkow, L. Cosmides, & J. Tooby (Eds.), *The adapted mind* (pp. 289–322). New York: Oxford University Press.

Wilson, M., & Daly, M. (1993). An evolutionary psychological perspective on male sexual proprietariness and violence against wives. *Violence and Victims, 8*, 271–294.

Wilson, M., & Daly, M. (1996). Male sexual proprietariness and violence against women. *Current Directions in Psychological Science, 5*, 2–7.

Wilson, M., & Daly, M. (1998). Lethal and nonlethal violence against wives and the evolutionary psychology of male sexual proprietariness. In R. E. Dobash, & R. P. Dobash (Eds.), *Rethinking violence against women* (pp. 199–230). Thousand Oaks, CA: Sage.

Wilson, M., Daly, M., & Daniele, A. (1995). Familicide: The killing of spouse and children. *Aggressive Behavior, 21*, 275–291.

Wilson, M., Daly, M., & Wright, C. (1993). Uxoricide in Canada: Demographic risk patterns. *Canadian Journal of Criminology, 37*, 331–361.

Wilson, M., Johnson, H., & Daly M. (1995). Lethal and nonlethal violence against wives. *Canadian Journal of Criminology, 37*, 331–361.

Yllo, K., & Straus, M. A. (1990). Patriarchy and violence against wives: The impact of structural and normative factors. In M. A. Straus & R. J. Gelles (Eds.), *Physical violence in American families: Risk factors and adaptations to violence in 8145 families* (pp. 383–399). New Brunswick, NJ: Transaction.

CHAPTER 5

Chastity, Fidelity, and Conquest: Biblical Rules for Women and War

John Hartung

> **Abstract**
> The Bible instructs men to take a proactive approach to their problem with paternity – the possibility that a man's putative child may be another man's genetic offspring – by stoning brides who do not bleed on first penetration, by burning women who have become pregnant out of wedlock, by torturing and poisoning wives who are suspected of adultery, by executing women who have committed adultery and by murdering female prisoners of war who are not virgins. In addition to enhancing men's assurance of paternity, control of women reduces conflict between men over women, which enhances male-male solidarity and thus a society's capacity for military conquest. Concomitant to instructions for controlling women, the Bible commands adherents to commit absolute genocide against people whose land they wish to occupy, kill men in surrounding nations unless they agree to be slaves, and take their virgin women and girls as booty.
> Although some non-Western cultures also sanctify such practices, in other traditional societies women have been "very free and at liberty in doing what they please with themselves" (Barbosa, 1500/1866) and military conquest has not been a religious obligation. It follows that the Bible's dark legacy is not a requirement of human nature.
>
> **Key Words:** adultery, anal intercourse, Bible, Canaan, chastity, Christianity, Codes of Maimonides, fidelity, genocide, Greater Israel, human sacrifice, Israel, Judaism, Muslim civilization, Midrash Rabbah, murder, Onanism, One State Solution, paternity, Palestine, rape, sexual repression, slavery, Talmud, Torah, Two State Solution, torture, virginity testing, war, War Against Terrorism, Western civilization, World War III, Zionism.

Introduction: Blood and Stone

There are passages in the Bible that should make every woman wary...and tell every man who has plumbed the darkness of his soul how close he came to fathoming its bottom. For example, consider Deuteronomy 22:13–21,[1] which can be better understood by knowing that "tokens of virginity" are stains on bed linen that have been made by breaking a bride's hymen:

> If any man takes a wife, and goes in to her, and then spurns her, and charges her with shameful conduct, and brings an evil name upon her, saying, "I took this woman, and when I came near her, I did not find in her the tokens of virginity," then the father of the young woman and her mother shall take and bring out the tokens of her virginity...and they shall spread the garment before the elders of the city...but if the thing is true, that the tokens of virginity were not found in the young woman, then they shall bring out the young woman to the door of her father's house, and the men of her city shall stone her to death with stones, because she has wrought folly in Israel by playing the harlot in her father's house; so you shall purge the evil from the midst of you.

Bloodied sheets are still nailed to brides' fathers' doors,[2] and in other contexts, the god of the Bible still inspires some of his followers to stone people to death ("Israeli admits...," 1991).

Judah and Tamar

Newlywed women notwithstanding, the precedent for executing a prospective wife who might be pregnant by a man other than her fiancé was set by Jacob's son Judah, whose descendants' religious sect, Judahism, was amalgamated into Judaism while its adherents lived in Babylon (Iraq, the homeland of Abraham, from whom Judaism, Islam and Christianity claim spiritual descent). Tamar was the mother of Judah's twin sons, Perez and Zerah, but Tamar was not Judah's wife. She was his daughter-in-law, twice over, with plans for a third. That is, Judah had three sons when he arranged to have Tamar marry his first son, Er. Unfortunately, according to the Talmud, Er had such a persistent predilection for anal intercourse that Tamar was prevented from becoming pregnant (Talmud: Yebamoth 34b; cf. 59b w/note 17, p. 396).[3] This circumstance caused Israel's god to strike Er dead (Genesis 38:7), whereupon Judah implored his second son, Onan, to engage in the common tradition of levirate marriage – a marriage that ended badly (Genesis 38:8–11):

> "Go in to your brother's wife, and perform the duty of a brother-in-law to her, and raise up offspring for your brother." But...when he went in to his brother's wife he spilled the semen on the ground...And what he did was displeasing in the sight of the LORD, and he slew him also. Then Judah said to Tamar his daughter-in-law, "Remain a widow in your father's house, till Shelah my [third] son grows up"...So Tamar went and dwelt in her father's house.

Judah did not keep his word regarding Shelah, which eventually caused him great embarrassment and almost cost Tamar her life, but she was clever and things ended well (Genesis 38:13–19 and 24–27):

> And when Tamar was told, "Your father-in-law is going up to Timnah to shear his sheep," she put off her widow's garments, and put on a veil, wrapping herself up, and sat at the entrance to Enaim, which is on the road to Timnah; for she saw that Shelah was grown up, and she had not been given to him in marriage. When Judah saw her, he thought her to be a harlot, for she had covered her face. He went over to her at the road side, and said, "Come, let me come in to you," for he did not know that she was his daughter-in-law. She said, "What will you give me, that you may come in to me?" He answered, "I will send you a kid from the flock." And she said, "Will you give me a pledge, till you send it?" He said, "What pledge shall I give you?" She replied, "Your signet and your cord, and your staff that is in your hand." So he gave them to her, and went in to her, and she conceived by him. Then she arose and went away, and taking off her veil she put on the garments of her widowhood.
>
> ...About three months later Judah was told, "Tamar your daughter-in-law has played the harlot; and moreover she is with child by harlotry." And Judah said, "Bring her out, and let her be burned." As she was being brought out, she sent word to her father-in-law, "By the man to whom these belong, I am with child." And she said, "Mark, I pray you, whose these are, the signet and the cord and the staff." Then Judah acknowledged them and said, "She is more righteous than I, inasmuch as I did not give her to my son Shelah." And he did not lie with her again. When the time of her delivery came, there were twins in her womb [Perez and Zerah].

A Virgin Marry

Every man knows two things about every virgin – she is not pregnant and she will not know how he stacks up as a lover. The latter reality is not discussed, but the former issue inspires customs, rules and laws in most traditional (read "anthropological") societies. Where men bequeath wealth primarily to their putative children by their wife (patrilineally; Hartung 1976, 1982), as distinct from leaving wealth to their sisters' children (matrilineally; Hartung 1981, 1985), they tend to be concerned about, if not hysterically obsessed over, the sexual fidelity of their mates (Buss, 2000; Easton & Shackelford, 2009; Kaighobadi, Shackelford, & Goetz, in press; Kaighobadi & Shackelford, 2012; McKibbin, Starratt, Shackelford, & Goetz, 2011; Platek & Shackelford, 2006).[4] Thus, we have practices like infibulation (near total surgical closure of the vulva), claustration, footbinding, chastity belts, psychosocial sexual terrorism and a husband's right to murder his wife for infidelity (Leviticus 20:10; Deuteronomy 22:22–23).[5] A grip on the nether reaches of this reality can be gained by contemplating current practices among some tradition-bound people whose Christianity and Judaism go back more than a millennium – among Christians in Ethiopia, among Ethiopian Jews in Ethiopia and Israel, and among some Coptic Christians in Egypt – where control of women is facilitated by cutting out their clitoris, traditionally with a shard of glass, but more recently with a razor blade.[6]

Even contemporary First World patrilineal societies evidence stark symptoms of biblical sexual repression. From the widespread sentiment that AIDS is their god's punishment for promiscuity and homosexuality[7] to an American church group that thanks its god for killing US soldiers in Iraq and Afghanistan as punishment for their nation's "immorality and tolerance of homosexuality and abortion" ("US military funeral...," 2010; Walsh, 2011), one can see a connection between the roots and the branches – between what is written in the Bible and the way that many people think today.

Nevertheless, even in traditional patrilineal societies, exceptional arrangements and rules allow for the marriage of women who are known to be non-virgins. The ancient Israelites were sophisticated in that regard. Based on the account that three months elapsed between Tamar's intercourse with her father-in-law and the discovery that she was pregnant, the rabbis of the Talmud made the following provision, as summarized by Maimonides (1195/1972: 2:11:18),[8] whose 12th-century synopses of the Bible and the Talmud are generally regarded as most authoritative: "A divorcee or widow may not become betrothed without waiting ninety days... in order to determine whether she is or is not pregnant, and in order to distinguish between the seed of the first husband and the seed of the second." The following clarification is added in the Talmud (Yebamoth 42a): "A woman conceals the fact [of her pregnancy] in order that her child may inherit his share in her second husband's estate," with further explanation in an editor's footnote: "She makes every effort to conceal all signs of pregnancy which might lead to the discovery that the child's father was her first husband."[9]

The rabbis of the Talmud (traditionally called The Sages) were keenly aware that men's aversion to raising children born of cuckoldry could jeopardize those children's and their mother's lives, as remains the case today (Daly & Wilson, 1988; Miner, Shackelford, Block, Starratt, & Weekes-Shackelford, in press). Accordingly, no accommodation could be made to marry a pregnant or nursing woman unless the prospective groom was the brother of her deceased husband, in which case the child would be genetically half his (Maimonides 1195/1972: 2:11:25–27):

> The Sages have also enacted that a man should not marry another man's pregnant or nursing [previous] wife, even though it is known who had impregnated her, lest the child should be harmed during subsequent intercourse, since the child not being his, he will not take proper precautions. [A clarification is added in the Talmud (Yebamoth 42a): "This is a preventive measure against turning the foetus into a *sandal* (an abortus)... due to intercourse or abdominal pressure."] In the case of a nursing woman [a man should not marry], lest her milk should spoil, since he will not take care to remedy the milk with such things as are helpful in such an event.

As is often the case, the devil was in the details. At this juncture in the Talmud, a student of The Sages asked about the conjectured woman with spoiled milk whose husband would not help correct the problem: "His own child [his by her] she would sustain with eggs and [purchased] milk. Would she not sustain her own child [hers, not his] with eggs and milk?" The answer came back, "Her husband would not give her the means" (Talmud: Yebamoth 42a).

The Law of Divorce

Whether in a tenement or in a temple, "Her husband would not give her the means" is key to understanding the hollowness that grips women who have a starving child, or face divorce, and have no opportunity to make a living. As stipulated in Deuteronomy 24:1–5, a man could divorce his wife at any time for any reason (in distinction, a woman could not divorce her husband for any reason, as remains largely the case in Israel today): "When a man takes a wife and marries her, if then she finds no favor in his eyes because he has found some indecency in her, he writes her a bill of divorce and puts it in her hand and sends her out of his house." The Talmud put a point on this (Gittin 90a): "He may divorce her even if she has merely spoilt his food, since it says, because he hath found some unseemly thing in her. He may divorce her even if he finds another woman more beautiful than she is, as it says, it cometh to pass, if she find no favor in his eyes."

Fortunately, women had some legal safeguards under biblical law. A one-time alimony payment called *kethubah* was stipulated in premarital agreements. The standard agreement for a virgin was 200 *zuz* (gold coins), and 100 *zuz* for a nonvirgin (widow or divorcee at the time of marriage). A wealthy man could afford to keep a less desired wife and still marry "another woman more beautiful than she," but a common man could not support two wives, and 200 *zuz* was enough to prevent him from divorcing his wife on a whim. But not to worry, if she was not performing her wifely duties, he could beat her (Maimonides 1195/1972: 1:21:7 and 10):

> There are five kinds of work that any wife must perform for her husband: she must spin, wash his face, hands, and feet, pour his cup, spread his couch, and wait on him. And there are also six kinds of work that some wives must, and some need not, perform [depending upon whether their husband retained female slaves or maidservants]: attend to the grinding, cook, bake, launder, nurse, and give fodder to his mount...A wife who refuses to perform any kind of work that she is obligated to do, may be compelled to perform it, even by scourging her with a rod.

However, for the man who had a sustained desire for divorce, but did not have, or did not want to part with, the required sum of money, there was an alternate route: "A woman who is divorced on the ground of ill repute takes only what is hers and departs" (Talmud: Kethuboth 101a). The operative clause in this most operative sanction is "on the grounds of ill repute." Only the charge of infidelity, only a feeling of jealousy on the part of a husband, was required to make a woman forgo her *kethubah*, or undergo an ordeal that might cost her life.

The Law of Jealousy

> And the LORD said to Moses, "Say to the people of Israel, If any man's wife goes astray and acts unfaithfully against him...and if the spirit of jealousy comes upon him, and he is jealous of his wife who has defiled herself; or if the spirit of jealousy comes upon him, and he is jealous of his wife, though she has not defiled herself; then the man shall bring his wife to the priest...and the priest shall bring her near, and set her before the LORD...and in his hand the priest shall have the water of bitterness that brings the curse. Then the priest shall make her take an oath, saying, "If no man has lain with you, and if you have not turned aside to uncleanness, while you were under your husband's authority, be free from this water of bitterness that brings the curse. But if you have gone astray, though you are under your husband's authority, and if you have defiled yourself, and some man other than your husband has lain with you, then...may this water that brings the curse pass into your bowels and make your body swell and your thigh fall away." And the woman shall say, "Amen, Amen." Then the priest shall...make the woman drink the water of bitterness that brings the curse, and the water that brings the curse shall enter into her and cause bitter pain...then, if she has defiled herself and has acted unfaithfully against her husband...her body shall swell, and her thigh shall fall away, and the woman shall become an execration among her people. But if the woman has not defiled herself and is clean, then she shall be free and shall conceive children.
> (Numbers 5:11–28)

Detailed accounts of the this procedure are scattered throughout the Talmud and the Midrash Rabbah (The Great Exposition, a compendium of biblical exegeses that is less extensive but not less authoritative than the Talmud). Again, the devil is in those details, and being appraised of them would not only have discouraged sexual infidelity, it would have compelled women to constantly reassure their husbands in that regard. Indeed, according to the Midrash, a woman could be guilty without having touched another man...she could even commit adultery while having sexual intercourse with her husband: "When a woman is secluded with her husband and is engaged in intercourse with him, and at the same time her heart is with another man whom she has seen on the road, there is no adultery greater than this" (Midrash Rabbah: Numbers 9:34).

The Details

Maimonides pieced together a description of the ordeal, leaving out, as was his habit, instructions that were not politically correct even by 12th-century standards. What follows is from Maimonides (1195: 5:3:1–16) with explanatory inserts from The Midrash Rabbah (underlined, Numbers 9:14–33) and the Talmud (in italic type, Sotah 19b):

> The Great Court seated the woman in their midst, and with her husband absent, endeavored to inspire her with great awe, in order to avoid having her drink of the water. They said to her: "My daughter, much is wrought by wine, much by levity, much by childishness, and much by evil neighbors...They said to her further: "My daughter, many have preceded thee, and have been swept away. Great and worthy men have been overcome by their inclination to evil, and have stumbled." They then recited to her the story of Judah and Tamar...All this in order to ease the way for her, so that she might confess.
>
> If she thereupon said, "Yea, I have been defiled," she was dismissed without her kethubah, and went her way.
>
> If she stood upon her plea that she was innocent, they took her to the East gate of the Temple Court, which is opposite the Holy of Holies, made her go up and down from place to place, and led her around, in

order to tire her out so much that she might become sick of it and perchance confess... They then gathered a great throng of women around her, for all women who were there were in duty bound to behold her, as it is said, "that all women may be taught not to do after your lewdness" (Ezekiel 23:48). Also any man who wished to come and behold her, was allowed to do so. The while she stood among them stripped of wrap and kerchief, and clad only in her body clothes and head cap, like a woman in the privacy of her home... Thereupon one of the priests of the Temple Court approached her, grasped her garments at the front, and ripped them apart until he laid bare her bosom. He then uncovered her hair and loosened her tresses, after which he fetched an Egyptian rope, to remind her of the Egyptian doing that she had committed, and tied it above her breasts... He then brought a tenth of an ephah of barley flour, provided by the husband, put it in an Egyptian basket and placed it in her hands in order to make her weary.

During all the time that the woman's head was uncovered and the tenth of an ephah held in her hands, the water of bitterness was in the vessel held by the priest, so that she would be made to see the water... <u>He must let her see the water so as to instill terror into her</u>... He then made her drink the water... <u>if she says "I will not drink," they beat her with the flat side of a sword and chide her and make her drink by force</u>... They insert iron tongs into her mouth, so that if she says "I refuse to drink," they exert influence upon her and make her drink by force.

If the woman was innocent, she came out and went her way, remaining permitted to her husband. If she was defiled, her face immediately turned pale, her eyes bulged, and her veins filled up... <u>her mouth would emit an evil odour; her neck would swell; her flesh would decay</u>... And all those present cried, "Away with her, away with her!," lest her menstrual blood should start flowing, seeing that a menstruating woman would cause the women's section of the Temple Court to become unclean. Thereupon she was removed from that section, where she was standing. After this, first her belly became swollen, then her thighs fell away, and finally she died.

A woman who survived The Ordeal of Bitter Waters was still in jeopardy (Maimonides 1195/1972: 5:3:23): "If after she had drunk of the water witnesses came forth to testify to her defilement, she was dismissed without her ketubbah... even if none of the aforementioned tokens of guilt had manifested themselves in her." Indeed, as stipulated by commandments given in the Torah (first five books of the Bible) and illustrated by examples given throughout the Holy Scriptures, an overall approach to women's moral status was summarized in the Talmud (Sotah 28b): "A woman about whom there is doubt whether she is immoral is treated like an immoral woman," and a mother of this invention was men's concern about paternity. That is, if reproduction was not at issue, a woman could be divorced at no cost and without ceremony (parenthesis not added, Sotah 24a): "A woman incapable of conception, one too old to bear children, and one who is unfit to bear children (by taking some drug and not just barren or too old to bear children) do not receive the marriage-settlement and do not drink."

Every Woman Who Has Known

The first mass murder of nonvirgin captive women was inflicted upon the Midianites – people who invented the god adopted by Moses on instruction from one of his fathers-in-law, Jethro, who was a Midianite priest (see Exodus 2–3 and 18). Since gods of that era were worshipped first and foremost for their ability to confer victory in war, having exclusive access to a powerful god was a requirement for conquering Palestine and establishing Israel's prophesied dominion over surrounding nations (e.g., Psalms 2:8–9, Isaiah 14:2, 45:14, 60:1–12). The destruction of the Midianites made the Israelites their god's only people – a jealous god for a jealous people (truncated from Numbers 31:7–35):

> They warred against Midian, as the LORD commanded Moses, and slew every male... And the people of Israel took captive the women of Midian and their little ones... Then they brought the captives and the booty and the spoil to Moses... And Moses was angry with the officers of the army, the commanders of thousands and the commanders of hundreds, who had come from service in the war. Moses said to them, "Have you let all the women live?... now kill every woman who has known man by lying with him. But all the young girls who have not known man by lying with him, keep alive for yourselves"[10]... the booty remaining of the spoil that the men of war took was... thirty-two thousand persons in all, women who had not known man by lying with him.

Only 31,968 of those virgins could be made available to Israelite men because 32 of them were given "to Eleazar the priest" as an "offering for the Lord," that is, for human sacrifice (Numbers 31). These "young girls" were to be "an heave offering" (see Numbers 31:29 and 41, King James translation), which means that after dismemberment, their body parts were to be "heaved up," or thrown in the air, in celebration.[11] To this day, in their daily morning prayer, observant Orthodox Jewish men thank their god for having not made them a non-Jew ("Baruch shelo as ani goy" – "Blessed is He that did not make me a non-Jew") and for having not made them a woman ("Baruch shelo as aniisha" – "Blessed is He that did not make me a woman"). No wonder.

Heave offerings aside, if there were 32,000 virgins, it seems reasonable to assume that there were a large number of nonvirgins. Sorting out who to keep and who to kill would have been a major undertaking. In a tale too fanciful to warrant discussion of its plausibility,[3] but one that clearly reveals prevailing attitudes, the rabbis of the Talmud explained how the necessary virginity testing was accomplished. Anatomy not being the forte of these 3rd-to- 6th-century exegetes, the diagnostic procedure was to have the woman in question straddle a cask of wine so that her vagina covered the hole in the side of the cask. According to Rabbi Kahana, son of Rabbi Nathan, one only needed to smell the woman's breath to decipher whether her hymen was sufficiently intact to prevent a bouquet from rising (Talmud: Yebamoth 60b): "They made them sit upon the mouth of a wine-cask. Through anyone who had had previous intercourse, the odour penetrated; through a virgin, its odour did not penetrate."

This simplified matters: Smell wine, pull the woman off the cask and cut her throat…or don't smell wine, pull the girl off the cask and rape her. Putting 60-some thousand women through this process in a reasonable amount of time would have required far more casks of wine than the Israelites would have brought with them on a military campaign, but there was no limit to the imaginations of The Sages of the Talmud. Nevertheless, as American soldiers who rape and murder captive Muslim civilians ("Ex-US soldier…," 2009; "US court hears…," 2006; *Hammer*, 2010) have proven, The Sages were right to assume that such levels of brutality are within the male repertoire ("Iraqi medic…," 2006):

> An Iraqi medic who responded to a home where U.S. soldiers allegedly raped and killed a teenage Iraqi girl and murdered her sister and parents described on Sunday a display of carnage so horrific he said it made him sick for two weeks. In the opening day of testimony in a military hearing in Baghdad to determine whether there is enough evidence to hold a court-martial for five U.S. soldiers, the medic, whose name was withheld for security reasons, testified that he saw smoke when he arrived at the family's home in Mahmudiyah on the afternoon of March 12. Inside, on the floor of the living room by the window, a teenage girl lay dead on her back, her legs spread, her clothes torn off, her body burned from her waist to her head, a single bullet hole under her left eye, he said.

> Her mother also lay dead on the floor with bullet wounds in her chest and abdomen, he said.

> In another room, the medic found what remained of the girl's father in a pool of blood. "The brain was on the floor and parts of the head were all over the place," the medic said. Next to him was his other daughter, who was about 6 years old. It appeared to him as if a bullet had "entered the front of her face and out the back of her head," he said.

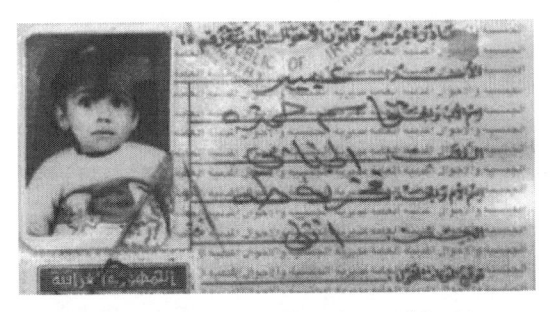

Iraqi ID card issued in 1993 to Abeer Qassim al-Janabi.

Abeer, age 7.

Abeer, age 9.

And sometimes, after a plea bargain to avoid the death penalty, they confess without feeling that they have done something wrong ("I hate Iraqis....," 2006):

> One of four U.S. soldiers accused of raping a 14-year-old Iraqi girl last spring showed little remorse and even smiled during a confession to charges he conspired to kill her and her family.
>
> Even before the hearing Wednesday to announce a plea agreement, Spc. James P. Barker, 23, slapped hands with other soldiers and grinned as he smoked a cigarette in the rain. A bailiff scolded him. And when he described for the judge the assault in his own words, he gave vivid details of the rape with a deadpan delivery.
>
> "That's pretty much all I have to say," Barker muttered with a shrug after describing raping the screaming girl.
>
> Barker agreed to plead guilty to the charges to avoid the death penalty, his civilian attorney David Sheldon said. The agreement requires him to testify against three other soldiers and a former Army private also accused in the March 12 attack in Mahmoudiya, 20 miles south of Baghdad.

So What?

Unlike Joseph Kony and his Lord's Resistance Army, it seems unlikely that any of these VFW murdering rapists took license directly from the Bible. Nevertheless, they were raised in a culture that diminishes, entirely ignores, or celebrates offenses that it commits against non-Judeo-Christian nations – whether the commandment to vanquish the original inhabitants of Canaan (Deuteronomy 20:16–18), the Crusades, or the re-creation of Israel at the expense of Palestinians – while continuously propagandizing offenses committed against it in retaliation.[12] Under that condition, for the simplistic-minded, and especially the simple-minded simplistic-minded, having been told who the "bad guys" are, and that they are the "good guys," is all that is needed to drive a connection between the Bible, the cultures that it has spawned, and the moral disinhibition that disinhibited the gang rape and murder of Abeer Qassim al-Janabi.

Regardless of its ontogeny or etiology, rape and murder are wrong – but rape and murder are not evil in and of themselves. There is a distinction between what is wrong and what is evil. Evil is committed when clarity is taken away from what is clearly wrong, allowing wrong to be seen as less wrong, excusable, right, or an obligatory commandment of a Lord God Almighty. The god of the ancient Israelites was a conceptualization of men. Those men's attitudes toward women were common and remain common, in both senses of the word. Then as now, the perception of women as sexual outlets whose behavior must be controlled by overwhelming force wells up from the dregs of a fetid hole into which any man can sink.

Israelite women and women captured by Israelite men were not worse off than most women in the ancient Levant, but Israelite men were ahead of their time in extensively codifying the regulation of women into written laws attributed to their god. Recording and sanctifying rules that promote the interests of rulers at the expense of the ruled gives inertia to injustice. So it matters that rules for torturing and murdering women are promulgated in the Torah, which lies at the heart of the Bible, which lies at the heart of Judaism, which lies at the heart of Christianity. A wolf, no matter how big and bad, cannot be evil. In distinction, a wolf in sheep's clothing is pure evil.

Another Mother of This Invention

In addition to serving men's reproductive interests, laws that increase chastity and fidelity facilitate male-male solidarity by reducing a major source of within-group adversity among all fundamentally polygynous primates – competition between males over females who would otherwise have some capacity to choose their mates (Buss, 2000; Chagnon, 1968, 1979, 1988;Daly & Wilson, 1988). Male solidarity was critically important for accomplishing the biblical commandment to subjugate people in surrounding nations and annihilate the native inhabitants of the Israelites' to-be-conquered homeland – making Israel a land without a people for a people without a land, as was attempted again in 1948. That original Zionism is the overarching theme of the Torah (Deuteronomy 20:10–18)[13]:

> When you draw near to a city to fight against it, offer terms of peace to it. And if its answer to you is peace and it opens to you, then all the people who are found in it shall do forced labor for you and shall serve you.[14] But if it makes no peace with you, but makes war against you, then you shall besiege it; and when the LORD your God gives it into your hand you shall put all its males to the sword, but the women and the little ones, the cattle, and everything else in the city, all its spoil, you shall take as booty for yourselves; and you shall enjoy the spoil of your enemies, which the LORD your God has given you. Thus you shall do to all the cities which are very far from you, which are not cities of the nations here.
>
> But in the cities of these peoples that the LORD your God gives you for an inheritance you shall save alive nothing that breathes, but you shall utterly destroy them, the Hittites and the Amorites, the Canaanites and the Perizzites, the Hivites and the Jebusites [the people of Jerusalem], as the LORD your God has commanded; that they may not teach you to do according to all their abominable practices which they have done in the service of their Gods, and so to sin against the LORD your God.

The implications of this original Zionism for contemporary Zionism are correctly perceived by more than a few contemporary rabbis, but only a small number of them have had the courage to commit those implications to writing (Estrin, 2010; Popper, 2009). Nevertheless, this proves that Zionism is not racism only in the sense that Zionism makes racism look like a transgression of etiquette.

Evidence that laws regulating the behavior of women can also subserve the territorial ambitions of a state comes from examples in which women are excused from those regulations for the good of the state. Citing the biblical precedents of Ester and Yael, Rabbi Ari Shvat recently formulated the ruling that "Illicit sex for the sake of national security" is permitted to female Mossad agents (Israel's secret service; "Israeli rabbi: Honey-pot…," 2010; Kalman, 2010).[15]

Future Directions

Humans have invented hundreds of gods over the past several thousand years. Those gods were designed to serve their inventors' purposes. Those purposes have often included vicious control of women and the correlate objective of military conquest. The reigning god of Western civilization, the god that Jesus prayed to,[16] commanded his followers to stone nonvirgin brides, torture wives suspected of adultery, murder captured non-virgin women, perform ritual human sacrifice of captured virgin women, enslave distant nations of people, exact tribute from those enslaved people, and commit absolute genocide in pursuit of land and resources.

Although modern cultures seldom invent new gods to help shape public policy, many of them are saddled with religious legacies that reinforce the darker inclinations of human nature. Whether the barbarity of cultural ancestors is manifest today in unequal pay for equal work (which wreaks profound psychological havoc, Hartung, 1988), or the inchoate notion that it is acceptable to make Palestinians pay for what Germans did to Jews during World War II (which also wreaks profound psychological havoc – most Arab terrorists being crazy because we have driven them crazy), ongoing reverence for the god of the Bible increases the probability that humans will self-destruct.

The gender inequality issue requires strengthening and enforcing laws that are on the books of most Western nations and encouraging their extension and enforcement around the world. Unfortunately, in that regard, the world is currently in a state that is analogous to the time when some of its dominant cultures realized that slavery and indentured servitude are immoral, but none of them had rid themselves of both. So until we develop some G7-size shining examples, gender equality will be a hard sell. Somewhat paradoxically, that means we need to focus most forcefully on areas where the most progress has already been made…and avoid acquiescing to critics who would have that pressure reduced on grounds that conditions for women are worse in many Third World nations.

The Middle East issue requires Western civilization to stop perpetrating the crime that Harry Truman initiated in 1947 and was, per John Kennedy's account to Gore Vidal, rewarded for in 1948.[17] Just as the Treaty of Versailles invited World War II, so the re-creation of Israel invited the 1948 Arab-Israeli War, the Sinai War, the Six-Day War, the War of Attrition, the Yom Kippur War, the First and Second Lebanon Wars, the Gaza War, the Gulf War, the Iraq War, the war in Afghanistan, the war in Libya, the drumbeat for war against Iran (Chomsky, 2011a) and the amorphous War Against Terrorism – whose efforts range from America aping Israel by celebrating extrajudicial assassinations (Chomsky, 2011b) and by torturing prisoners…to removing shoes in airports.[18]

That string of comparatively small wars seems likely to lengthen and points toward World War III. If World War III should occur within the next 20 years, civilization (humanity's capacity to preserve, implement and extend knowledge thus far accumulated) would almost certainly survive because the world's arsenal of nuclear weapons has been substantially reduced over the past 20 years. However, if World War III occurs subsequent to the much-sought-after technological breakthrough that will lower the cost of nuclear bombs by a game-changing magnitude, scores of nations will have them, delivery systems will range from ICBM's to trucks, and World War III could damage civilization beyond repair. Even if civilization could be salvaged after such a war, in the Middle East, even if the Zionist-to-Arab kill ratio were 1:10, only Israelis (Zionist and non-Zionist alike) would face annihilation. As such, now is the time to dissuade people who claim a right to behave in a barbarous manner because barbaric instructions are given to them by a god invented by their ancestors to serve the same purposes today that he served back then: theft of other people's liberty, lives and land ("Book about killing…," 2009; "West Bank rabbi…," 2009). Christians and Jews should "purge the evil"[19] that lies at their foundation and advocate the One State Solution for Israelis and Palestinians…a One State Solution that offers expedited citizenship and help finding homes, schools and jobs for Israeli Jews who would prefer to live in the United States (Hartung, 1997b, 1097c, 1997d, 1998, 2006).

The Two State Solution is simply "Reformed Zionism" – a matter of somewhat more subtle injustice so steeped in self-righteousness that it is not less evil than the Zionism of Moses. Contemporary Orthodox Zionists (as distinct from Reformed Zionists) call for disabling and expelling Palestinians in order to steal everything they have. In distinction, Reform Judaism encourages the Two State Solution, which, self-righteousness aside, amounts to the following: "Don't disable the Palestinians completely. Give them a 'country' under our control and leave them just enough to survive. After all, Israel needs an underclass to do the scut work and heavy lifting,[13] like the Gibeonites in Joshua's time (Joshua 9:27)… and what could be better than having them go home each evening to a different 'country'?" In complicity, contemporary Reformed Zionist Christians (Barack Obama, 2011) view the prospect of "giving" the Palestinians 22% of what should be theirs (Abbas, 2011) as noblesse oblige…but Reformed Zionism, whether promoted by Christians or Jews, is ultimately as much an oxymoron as "Reformed Fascism,"… so abject betrayal of Palestinians by Reformed Zionists like Barack Obama, Hillary Clinton and Susan Rice, should come as no surprise (Ephron, 2011; Falk, 2011). And whether Reformed Zionism brings World War III in 20 years, 40 years, or 80 years – whether before the implementation of a Two State Solution, during its implementation, or after its failure – the hatred necessarily generated by any form of Zionism is cumulative, irreducible and inescapable.

Whether foundational texts advocate persecution of women or serial genocide, we cannot combat evil and simultaneously give it sanctuary. We should not give evil a place to hide – not in the Bible, not in the tortuous discourse of the Talmud, not in the propaganda of people who disguise an assumption of divine privilege behind a presumption of bequeathed victimhood (Etkes, 2006; Finkelstein, 2003, 2005; Hartung n.d.c; Levy, 2010, 2012), not in the blather of Christians who imagine that they will bring heaven to earth if they support those claims, and not in the fatuous speech of politicians who pander to those people (Lederer, 2011).

Western civilization cannot be the "light unto the nations" that it fancies itself to be – whether through Moses or Jesus – nor even a respectable example of a civilization that upholds human rights, until women have full equality of opportunity, until we stop violating the rights of Palestinians as a special case, and until we stop violating much of the Muslim world in secondary consequence. To break cleanly into an enlightened future (Hartung, 1996), a future that is free of gods, clerical goblins and their attendant scriptures, we need to break cleanly from a fettered past (Dawkins, 2006; Hartung, 1995, 1996, 2006; Hitchens, 2007; Paine, 1794).

Notes

1. Except where otherwise noted, all biblical quotations are from The Revised Standard Version.

2. Traditional Christian families in Ethiopia still display this sheet on the door of a bride's father's house for several days after her wedding as an advertisement of his family's honor—that is, that they delivered an intact bride in exchange for her brideprice (personal observation).

3. The historical/empirical veracity of biblical/talmudic/midrashic stories, or of any story told in earnest, is independent of the messages, both implicit and explicit, that they convey. Throughout this chapter, those messages are considered to contain valid information about prevailing attitudes, mores, and perspectives. References to the Talmud are given by Tractate and Folio number. All quotations are from the Soncino Press translation.

4. For additional Darwinian interpretations of male sexual jealousy, see Buss (1988); Buss et al. (1992); Daly, Wilson, and Weghorst (1982); Dickemann (1981); Flinn (1988); and Geary et al. (1995). For additional perspectives on matrilineal versus patrilineal inheritance, see Alexander (1974); Flinn(1981); Gaulin and Schlegel (1980); Green (1978); and Kurland (1979).

5. Read out of context, the rule given in the Torah for adultery appears to be symmetrical, for example, Leviticus 20:10: "If a man commits adultery with the wife of his neighbor, both the adulterer and the adulteress shall be put to death," but a woman was guilty of adultery if she had sexual intercourse with any man other than her husband while a man was only guilty if he had intercourse with the wife of a fellow Israelite ("neighbor" = Israelite, cf. Hartung, 1995).

6. I recall an Ethiopian woman's explanation that a properly curved shard from a shattered Coke bottle is preferable to a razor blade because, skillfully used, it minimizes inclusion of nonclitoral tissue (circa 1969, personal communication). The suggestion that clitoridectomy is a paternity strategy (Hartung, 1976) is denied by the duly enculturated, who refer to it as female circumcision and explain the practice as sexually egalitarian, that is, "something for the girls," despite knowing that the clitoris is anatomically and neurologically analogous to the glans penis rather than the foreskin of the penis. Although many Christians and Jews are under the impression that female genital mutilation is primarily a Muslim practice, because it currently occurs most frequently in Muslim cultures and is not mentioned in the Bible, there is also no mention of any such ritual in the Koran (Hartung, 1997a). Nevertheless, Muslims, Christians and Jews who clitoridectomize consider the practice to be a religious obligation—undoubtedly because the practice existed as a paternity tactic long before the invention of Abrahamic religions.

7. While sexual behavior between women seems to have been beyond the imaginations of the men who crafted the laws that they ascribed to their deity, the ancient Israelites were typically decisive about sexual behavior between men: "If a man lies with a male as with a woman, both of them have committed an abomination; they shall be put to death, their blood is upon them" (Leviticus 20:13). Nevertheless, according to the Talmud, men were deemed not punishable for pederasty with a boy under 9 years of age (cf. Hartung, n.d.b).

8. Citations to Maimonides's *Book of Women* are given by Treatise, Chapter, and Section.

9. One wonders whether women, like female Langur monkeys in this predicament (Hrdy, 1977), increase solicitation of sexual intercourse with their new mate as a facultative response that would be naturally selected because it could cause the would-be father to behave like a genetic father.

10. Several sacred Jewish texts written subsequent to the compilation of the Torah express second thoughts about the genocide of the Midianites—not because of the colossal evil of the deed but because the sudden influx of so many shiksas was perceived to have had dysgenic effects (Hartung, n.d.b).

11. Stories of sacrifice of Canaanites, Midianites, and other non-Israelites by Israelites were common (for a poignant example, see 1st Samuel 15:31–32), but sacrifice of Israelites by Israelites in order to appease or cajole their god was rare subsequent to rescission of the commandment to sacrifice all first-born children (cf. Exodus 13:2; 22:29–30 and Leviticus 27:28–29 with Exodus 13:13 and 34:20), a commandment for which the god of the Israelites eventually apologized (Ezekiel 20:26). Nevertheless, ritual sacrifice of a virgin Israelite woman was still well received and well rewarded (e.g., Judges 11:12 through 12:8).

12. We have all heard stories of torture, rape, and murder committed by Arab regimes. An entirely fabricated and exceedingly effective story about Iraqi soldiers murdering babies in Kuwait was used to "manufacture consent" (Herman & Chomsky, 2002) for the Gulf War (http://en.wikipedia.org/wiki/Nayirah_(testimony)#Incubator_allegations), but we seem to be at peace with biblical stories about Israelites murdering the babies of their enemies (Psalms 137:9, Hosea 13:16, Isaiah 13:15–18, 2 Kings 15:16). Although some reports of torture, rape, and murder committed by potential Muslim adversaries are true, what every American needs to remember is that we too have committed torture, rape, and murder. And on a grander scale, we need to realize that each of us, Zionist and anti-Zionist alike, is responsible for the torture and/or murder of every Palestinian who has been tortured or murdered by Israel and every Muslim of any ilk who has been tortured and/or murdered by the United States (including Samir Kahn as collateral damage during the murder of Anwar Al-Awlaki, both of whom were American citizens).

13. For additional examples of the commandment to commit genocide and boasts of having done so, see Numbers 21:2–3; 21:34–35; 24:8; 24:19–20; Deuteronomy 2:34; 3:2–6; 3:21; 7:12; 7:16; 7:23–24; 9:3; 11:24–25; 31:35; 33:27; Joshua 2:10; 6:21; 8:2; 8:24–26; 10:1; 10:28; 10:35; 10:37; 10:39–40; 11:11–14; 11:20–21; Judges 1:17; 3:29; I Samuel 15:3; 15:8; 15:15; 15:18; 15:20; and I Chronicles 4:41. See also Hartung (1995).

14. One of Israel's highest ranking religious authorities, Rabbi Ovadia Yosef, reiterated the precept that "Goyim [non-Jews] were born only to serve us. Without that, they have no place in the world—only to serve the People of Israel" (Mozgovaya, 2010a; "Poll: Youth name...," 2006). This point of view is iterated throughout the Bible, reiterated throughout the Talmud, and at least partially subscribed to by most post-Roosevelt US Congress people and, with the exception of Eisenhower and post-term Carter, most US Presidents.

15. There was no conflict between the commandment "Thou shalt not kill" and the commandment to commit genocide. In distinction, the former facilitated the latter (Hartung, 1995). An original Torah scroll required about 70 goat skins and a great deal of manual labor. Because page space was such a primary concern, the only punctuation marks developed by phonetic languages of that time were small, subscript tick marks, as required, to designate where one word stopped and the next word began. Otherwise, ancient Hebrew writing was a continuous set of block letters (all caps) read right-to-left. There were no periods, no commas, no first-word capitalization and no paragraph breaks. In modern translations, decisions about where sentences and paragraphs begin and end are courtesy of the translator. Accordingly, instead of being spaced as five separate paragraphs of one sentence each (the only place in the Bible where this short-sentence-paragraphing occurs), highlighting what has come to be interpreted as five of the Big Ten out of 613 commandments, as follows:

Thou shalt not kill.
Neither shalt thou commit adultery.

Neither shalt thou steal.
Neither shalt thou bear false witness against thy neighbor.
Neither shall you covet your neighbor's wife and you shall not desire your neighbor's house, his field, or his manservant, or his maidservant, his ox, or his ass, or anything that is your neighbor's.

Without changing any of the words, Deuteronomy 5:17–21 should be translated:

Thou shalt not kill, neither shalt thou commit adultery, neither shalt thou steal, neither shalt thou bear false witness against thy neighbor. Neither shall you covet your neighbor's wife, and you shall not desire your neighbor's house, his field, or his manservant, or his maidservant, his ox, or his ass, or anything that is your neighbor's.

In this translation, the question, "Thou shalt not kill who?" is answered by the "Love Commandment." Here are four translations of Leviticus 19:18:

• Thou shalt not avenge, nor bear any grudge against the children of thy people, but thou shalt love thy neighbor as thyself. (First Jewish Publication Society translation, 1917, and the King James Version)
• You shall not take vengeance or bear any grudge against the sons of your own people, but you shall love your neighbor as yourself. (Revised Standard Version)
• You shall not take vengeance or bear a grudge against your countrymen. Love your fellow as yourself. (Tanakh, 1985)

In context, the word translated as *neighbor* meant "the children of thy people," "the sons of your own people," "your countrymen"—in other words, fellow Israelites—and "Thou shalt not kill" meant "Thou shalt not kill thy neighbor—the children of thy people, your countrymen," your fellow Israelites, because, among other objectives, just as modern Zionists need to cooperate in order to accomplish Greater Israel, ancient Zionists needed to cooperate with each other in order to fulfill the genocide commandments. (For details and corroborative interpretations in the rest of the Bible, the Talmud, and from Maimonides, see Hartung, 1995.)

16. When Jesus prayed "Our Father who art in heaven," he was not talking to himself. Vermes (1973) has presented persuasive evidence and arguments that Jesus had on-days and off-days regarding his confidence that he was the Jewish Messiah. Although the Christian Church invented the Nicene Creed (3 is 1 and 1 is 3) some 300 years after Jesus's death in order to resolve Christian adherence to the First Commandment, Jesus never had an "on" day regarding whether he was the god that he prayed to. Indeed, he would have considered the question, let alone the assertion, to be blasphemous.

In Jesus's time, the job of the Jewish Messiah was to re-create the Kingdom of David . . . a time when Jews had complete dominion over Greater Israel and reputed themselves to have received spectacular amounts of tribute (protection money) from all surrounding nations (e.g., 666 talents of gold [I Kings 10:14–15] is about 60,000 pounds—almost certainly an exaggeration of biblical proportions, and three times the amount that Attila the Hun was able to extort from Rome per annum prior to sacking it for late payment). Although Jesus was only one in a long line of Messiah candidates (having been preceded, for example, by John the Baptist and most recently succeeded by Menachem Schneerson [http://www.rickross.com/reference/lubavitch/lubavitch1.html]), his modus operandi may have been unique. Jesus's strategy was to create brotherly love among all sects of Jews—right down to the Samaritans—in order to provide a united front against Roman colonialism. This love did not extend to goyim unless they served Israel in some extraordinary individual capacity (as in "but some of my best friends are goy!"; see Luke 7:1–10 for an example), and he only blessed a leftover Canaanite woman because she was willing to accept herself and her kind as having the status of dogs in comparison to Israelites (see Matthew 15:21–28 and Hartung, 1995). It should be noted that, thanks to Saul of Tarsus (Saint Paul), Jesus accomplished his "on-day" objective—except that the enormous tribute paid to the reconstituted Israel comes from the United States instead of being sent by surrounding nations.

Anyone who doubts the depth of Christian allegiance to Zionism, or thinks that it only pertains to right-wing fundamentalist Christians, should contemplate the conflict between the drive to "stabilize" world oil prices (Chomsky, 2011a) and allegiance to Israel. These two pursuits are antithetical, but for most Christians and Jews—that is, the vast majority of Americans—Zionism even trumps oil.

17. Gore Vidal and John F. Kennedy were great friends. Vidal recounted Kennedy's account of Truman's reward for his support of Israel in the foreword to the late Israel Shahak's *Jewish History, Jewish Religion: The Weight of Three Thousand Years* (1994) as follows (also available at: http://www.abbc.net/historia/shahak/english.htm#foreword):

Sometime in the late 1950s, that world-class gossip and occasional historian, John F. Kennedy, told me how, in 1948, Harry S. Truman had been pretty much abandoned by everyone when he came to run for president. Then an American Zionist brought him two million dollars in cash, in a suitcase, aboard his whistle-stop campaign train. "That's why our recognition of Israel was rushed through so fast." As neither Jack nor I was an anti-Semite (unlike his father and mygrandfather) we took this to be just another funny story about Truman and the serene corruption of American politics.

Unfortunately, the hurried recognition of Israel as a state has resulted in forty-five years of murderous confusion, and the destruction of what Zionist fellow travelers thought would be a pluralistic state—home to its native population of Muslims, Christians and Jews, as well as a future home to peaceful European and American Jewish immigrants, even the ones who affected to believe that the great realtor in the sky had given them, in perpetuity, the lands of Judea and Sameria. Since many of the immigrants were good socialists in Europe, we assumed that they would not allow the new state to become a theocracy, and that the native Palestinians could live with them as equals. This was not meant to be. I shall not rehearse the wars and alarms of that unhappy region. But I will say that the hasty invention of Israel has poisoned the political and intellectual life of the USA, Israel's unlikely patron.

Unlikely, because no other minority in American history has ever hijacked so much money from the American taxpayers in order to invest in a "homeland." It is as if the American taxpayer had been obliged to support the Pope in his reconquest of the Papal States simply because one third of our people are Roman Catholic. Had this been attempted, there would have been a great uproar and Congress would have said no. But a religious minority of less than two per cent has bought or intimidated seventy senators (the necessary two thirds to overcome an unlikely presidential veto) while enjoying support of the media.

In a sense, I rather admire the way that the Israel lobby has gone about its business of seeing that billions of dollars, year after year, go to make Israel a "bulwark against communism." Actually, neither the USSR nor communism was ever much of a presence in the region. What America did manage to do was to turn the once friendly Arab world against us. Meanwhile, the misinformation about what is going on in the Middle East has got even greater and the principal victim of these gaudy lies—the American taxpayer to one side—is American Jewry, as it is constantly bullied by such professional terrorists as Begin and Shamir. Worse, with a few honorable exceptions, Jewish-American intellectuals abandoned liberalism for a series of demented alliances with the Christian (antisemitic) right and with the Pentagon-industrial complex. In 1985 one of them blithely wrote that when Jews arrived on the American scene they "found liberal opinion and liberal politicians more congenial in their attitudes, more sensitive to Jewish concerns" but now it is in the Jewish interest to ally with the Protestant fundamentalists because, after all, "is there any point in Jews hanging on dogmatically, hypocritically, to their opinions of yesteryear?" At this point the American left split and those of us who criticized our onetime Jewish allies for misguided opportunism, were promptly rewarded with the ritual epithet "anti-Semite" or "self-hating Jew."

Fortunately, the voice of reason is alive and well, and in Israel, of all places. From Jerusalem, Israel Shahak never ceases to analyze not only the dismal politics of Israel today but the Talmud itself, and the effect of the entire rabbinical tradition on a small state that the right-wing rabbinate means to turn into a theocracy for Jews only. I have been reading Shahak for years. He has a satirist's eye for the confusions to be found in any religion that tries to rationalize the irrational. He has a scholar's sharp eye for textual contradictions. He is a joy to read on the great Gentile-hating Dr. Maimonides.

Needless to say, Israel's authorities deplore Shahak. But there is not much to be done with a retired professor of chemistry who was born in Warsaw in 1933 and spent his childhood in the concentration camp at Belsen. In 1945, he came to Israel; served in the Israeli military; did not become a Marxist in the years when it was fashionable. He was—and still is—a humanist who detests imperialism whether in the names of the God of Abraham or of George Bush. Equally, he opposes with great wit and learning the totalitarian strain in Judaism. Like a highly learned Thomas Paine, Shahak illustrates the prospect before us, as well as the long history behind us, and thus he continues to reason, year after year. Those who heed him will certainly be wiser and—dare I say?—better. He is the latest, if not the last, of the great prophets.

Whether Truman was promised that suitcase of cash in advance remains unknown, but that he squandered America's supreme post–World War II influence by twisting every arm at the United Nations to force the re-creation of Israel has been copiously documented.

Issue should be taken with Vidal's perception that "a religious minority of less than 2% has bought or intimidated seventy senators (the necessary two thirds to overcome an unlikely presidential veto) while enjoying support of the media." Zionist Jews, who number far fewer than 16 million, are the sparkplugs of Zionism,—but the rest of the engine is drawn from 2.2 billion Christians, most of whom range from vaguely philo-Semitic (Mead, 2008) to frank Zionists (Mozgovaya, 2010b). Many Christians have difficulty appreciating this, but it should be kept in mind that the Jewish Bible comprises about two-thirds of the Christian Bible and Christians worship the god of the Jews (the god that Jesusworshipped) and Jesus himself (who was a Jew and, with the help of Saul of Tarsus, the most effective Zionist in history).

18. More than a few talking-head apologists for Zionism have argued that Israel is not a primary cause of America's wars against Muslims by conjecturing that if Israel were to disappear, those wars would continue. That conjecture is overstated but largely true because those wars have taken on a life of their own. However, just because a cancer metastasis generates a new primary tumor that sends out its own metastases, it does not follow that the mother tumor stops generating metastases.

19. The Bible is not evil by virtue of its barbaric objectives or even its glorification of cruelty, murder, rape, and genocide (Hartung, n.d.b). Many ancient works do that—the *Iliad*, the Icelandic Sagas, the tales of the ancient Syrians, and the inscriptions of the ancient Mayans, for example—but no one is selling or buying the *Iliad* as a foundation for morality. Therein lies the problem. The Bible is sold and bought as a guide to how people should live their lives. And it is, by far, the world's all-time bestseller. But the effort to make the Bible a universal guide to morality is impossible, because only orally transmitted myths can make 180-degree turns across a series of generations and get away with claims to authority based on antiquity. In distinction, distortions and selective dismissals of written myths can only, at best, fool some of the people most of the time or most of the people some of the time...such that deep-seated cultural reinforcement of evil perpetuates evil behavior beyond where it would go without that reinforcement.

References

Abbas, M. (2011, May 16). The long overdue Palestinian state. *The New York Times*. Retrieved November 2011, from http://www.nytimes.com/2011/05/17/opinion/17abbas.html?_r=1&scp=2&sq%20=mahmoud%20abbas&st=cse

Alexander, R. D. (1974). The evolution of social behavior. *Annual Review of Ecology and Systematics, 5*, 325–383.

Barbosa, D. (1866). *East Africa and Malabar*. London: H. E. J. Stanley.

Book about killing gentile children becomes bestseller in Israel. (2009, November 11). *European Union Times*. Retrieved November 2011, from http://www.eutimes.net/2009/11/book-about-killing-gentile-children-becomes-bestseller-in-israel/

Buss, D. (1988). From vigilance to violence: Tactics of mate retention in American undergraduates. *Ethology and Sociobiology, 9*, 291–317.

Buss, D. (2000). *The dangerous passion: Why jealousy is as necessary as love and sex*. New York: Free Press.

Buss, D., Larsen, R. J., Westen, D., &Semmelroth, J. (1992). Sex differences in jealousy: Evolution, physiology, and psychology. *Psychological Science, 3*, 252–255.

Chagnon, N. A. (1968). *Yanamamo: The fierce people*. Austin, TX: Holt, Rinehart & Winston.

Chagnon, N. A. (1979). Mate competition, favoring close kin, and village fissioning among the Yanomamo Indians. In N. Chagnon & W. Irons (Eds.), *Evolutionary biology and human social behavior* (pp. 86–131). North Scituate, MA: Duxbury.

Chagnon, N. A. (1988). Life histories, blood revenge, and warfare in a tribal population. *Science, 239*, 985–992.

Chomsky, N. (2011a). The Iranian threat. *Aljazeera*. Retrieved January 2012, from http://www.aljazeera.com/indepth/opinion/2011/11/20111122142555908626.html

Chomsky, N. (2011b). 9/11 – Was there an alternative? *Aljazeera*. Retrieved November 2011, from http://english.aljazeera.net/indepth/opinion/2011/09/20119775453842191.html

Daly, M., & Wilson, M. (1988). *Homicide*. Hawthorne, NY: Aldine de Gruyter.

Daly, M., Wilson, M., & Weghorst, S. J. (1982). Male sexual jealousy. *Ethology and Sociobiology*, 3, 11–27.

Dawkins, R. (2006). *The god delusion*. New York: Bantam Books.

Dickemann, M. (1981). Paternal confidence and dowry competition: A biocultural analysis of purdah. In R. D. Alexander & D. W. Tinkle (Eds.), *Natural selection and social behavior* (pp. 417–438). New York: Chiron.

Ephron, D. (2011, April 24). Mahmous Abbas: A president speaks out. *The Daily Beast*. Retrieved November, 2011, from http://www.thedailybeast.com/articles/2011/04/24/palestinian-president-mahmoud-abbas-speaks-out-about-obamas-betrayal-and-more.html

Easton, J. A., & Shackelford, T. K. (2009). Morbid jealousy and sex differences in partner-directed violence. *Human Nature*, 20, 342–350.

Estrin, D. (2010, January 20). Rabbinic text or call to terror? *The Jewish Daily Forward*. Retrieved November 2011, from http://www.forward.com/articles/123925/

Etkes, D. (2006, December 23). Holocaust as alibi. Haaretz. Retrieved January 2012 from http://www.haaretz.com/print-edition/opinion/holocaust-as-alibi-1.207871

Ex-US soldier guilty of Iraq deaths. (2009, May 8). *Aljazeera*. Retrieved MONTH, from Accessed January 12, 2012 at http://english.aljazeera.net/news/americas/2009/05/200957214557803392.html

Falk, R. (2011, May 25). Obama's AIPAC speech: A further betrayal of the Palestinian people. *Intifada*. Retrieved November 2011, from http://www.intifada-palestine.com/2011/05/richard-falk-obama's-aipac-speech-a-further-betrayal-of-the-palestinian-people/

Finkelstein, N. G. (2003). *The Holocaust industry: Reflections on the exploitation of Jewish suffering* (2nd ed.). London: Verso.

Finkelstein, N. G. (2005). *Beyond chutzpah: On the misuse of anti-Semitism and the abuse of history*. Berkeley: University of California Press.

Flinn, M. (1981). Uterine vs. agnatic kinship variability and associated cousin marriage preferences an evolutionary biological analysis. In R. D. Alexander & D. W. Tinkle (Eds.), *Natural selection and social behavior* (pp. 439–475). New York: Chiron.

Flinn, M. (1988). Mate guarding in a Caribbean village. *Ethology and Sociobiology*, 9, 1–28.

Full text of Colin Powell's speech. (2003, February 5). Guardian. Retrieved April 2012, from http://www.guardian.co.uk/world/2003/feb/05/iraq.usa

Gaulin, S. J. C., & Schlegel, A. (1980). Paternal confidence and paternal investment: A cross cultural test of a sociobiological hypothesis. *Ethology and Sociobiology*, 1, 301–309.

Geary, D. C., Rumsey, M., Bow-Thomas, C. C., & Hoard, M. K. (1995). Sexual jealousy as a facultative trait: Evidence from the pattern of sex differences in adults from China and the United States. *Ethology and Sociobiology*, 16, 355–383.

Green, P. J. (1978). Promiscuity, paternity and culture. *American Ethnologist*, 5, 151–159.

Hammer, J. (2010, March 11). Death squad. New York Times Sunday Book Review. Retrieved January 2012 from http://www.nytimes.com/2010/03/14/books/review/Hammer-t.html?scp=3&sq=Steven+Green&st=nyt

Hartung, J. (1976). On natural selection and inheritance of wealth. *Current Anthropology*, 17, 607–622.

Hartung, J. (1981). Paternity and inheritance of wealth. *Nature*, 291, 652–54.

Hartung, J. (1982). Polygyny and inheritance of wealth. *Current Anthropology*, 23, 1–12.

Hartung, J. (1985). Matrilineal inheritance: New theory and analysis. *Behavioral and Brain Sciences*, 8, 661–688.

Hartung, J. (1988). Deceiving Down: Conjectures on the Management of Subordinate Status. In: Lockard, J. & Paulus, D., Eds. Self-Deceit: An Adaptive Mechanism (pp170–185). Englewood Cliffs: Prentice-Hall.

Hartung, J. (1995). Love thy neighbor: The evolution of in-group morality. *Skeptic*, 3, 86–99.

Hartung, J. (1996). Prospects for existence: Morality and genetic engineering. *Skeptic*, 4, 62–71.

Hartung, J. (1997a, January 3). Religion and mutilation. *New York Times*, p A26.

Hartung, J. (1997b, October). The final settlement. *Palestine Times*. Retrieved January 2012, from http://www.strugglesforexistence.com/?p=article_p&id=6

Hartung, J. (1997c, November). Know your enemy: Netanyhu. *Palestine Times*. Retrieved January 2012, from http://www.strugglesforexistence.com/?p=article_p&id=11

Hartung, J. (1997d, December). Thou shalt not kill whom? *Palestine Times*. Retrieved January 2012, from http://www.strugglesforexistence.com/?p=article_p&id=10

Hartung, J. (1998, February). The virtues of violence against property: Advice for the new intifadah. *Palestine Times*. Retrieved January 2012, from http://www.strugglesforexistence.com/?p=article_p&id=9

Hartung, J. (2006). *Bring Them Here: A One State Solution for Israel and Palestine*. Retrieved March 2012, from http://www.strugglesforexistence.com/?p=video_p&id=2

Hartung, J. (n.d.a). *Rape: Biblical roots of the long leash on men*. Retrieved November 2011, from http://www.strugglesforexistence.com/?p=article_p&id=5

Hartung, J. (n.d.b). *Shiksa: Biblical roots of racism*. Retrieved November 2011, from http://strugglesforexistence.com/?p=article_p&id=16

Hartung, J. (n.d.c). *Passover: Caveat emptor*. Retrieved November 2011, from http://www.strugglesforexistence.com/?p=article_p&id=14

Herman, E. S., & Chomsky, N. (2002). *Manufacturing consent: The political economy of the mass media*. New York: Pantheon.

Hitchens, C. (2007). *God is not great: How religion poisons everything*. New York: Twelve Books.

Hrdy, S. (1977). *The langurs of Abu*. Cambridge, MA: Harvard University Press.

I hate Iraqis, rape accused tells military court. (2006, November 17). *Information Clearing House*. Retrieved November 2011, from http://www.informationclearinghouse.info/article15649.htm

Iraqi medic describes carnage (2006, August 7). *Washington Post*. Retrieved November 2011, from http://www.washingtonpost.com/wp-dyn/content/article/2006/08/06/AR2006080600803.html

Israeli admits stoning Arabs to death. (1991, June 21, p. 9). *New York Post*.

Israeli rabbi: Honey-pot sex is kosher for female Mossad agents. (2010, October 5). *Haaretz*. Retrieved November 2011, from http://www.haaretz.com/jewish-world/israeli-rabbi-honey-pot-sex-is-kosher-for-female-mossad-agents-1.317288

Kaighobadi, F., & Shackelford, T. K. (2012). Vigilance, violence, and murder in mateships. In M. DeLisi & P. Conis (Eds.), *Violent offenders: Theory, research, policy, and practice* (pp. 125–142). Boston: Jones and Bartlett.

Kaighobadi, F., Shackelford, T. K., & Goetz, A. T. (2011). Sexual conflict in mateships: From mate retention to murder. In T. K. Shackelford & A. T. Goetz (Eds.), *Oxford handbook of sexual conflict in humans* (pp. 269–279). New York: Oxford University Press.

Kalman, M. (2010, October 5) Mossad's seductive "honey trap" is kosher, rabbi finds. *AOL News*. Retrieved November 2011, from http://www.aolnews.com/world/article/mossads-seductive-honey-trap-is-kosher-rabbi-finds/19659690

Kurland, J. A. (1979). Paternity, mother's brother, and human sociality. In N.A. Chagnon & W. Irons (Eds.), *Evolutionary biology and human social behavior* (pp. 145–170). North Scituate, MA: Duxbury.

Lawrence, J. (2003, January 29). Bush's agenda walks the church-state line. USA Today. Retrieved April 2012, from http://www.usatoday.com/news/washington/2003-01-29-bush-religion_x.htm

Lederer, E. M. (2011, February 18). US vetoes Israel settlement UN resolution. *Associated Press*. Retrieved November 2011, from http://www.huffingtonpost.com/2011/02/18/us-vetoes-israel-settlement_n_825391.html

Levy, G. (2010, January 28). Holocaust remembrance is a boon for Israeli propaganda. Retrieved January 2012, from http://www.haaretz.com/print-edition/opinion/holocaust-remembrance-is-a-boon-for-israeli-propaganda-1.262235

Levy, G. (2012, January 29). God rules all in 2012 Israel, even the state. Haaretz. Retrieved January 2012 from http://www.haaretz.com/print-edition/opinion/god-rules-all-in-2012-israel-even-the-state-1.409739

Maimonides, M. (1972). *The book of women: The code of Maimonides* (H. Klein, Trans.) New Haven, CT: Yale University Press.(Original work published 1195).

McKibbin, W. F., Starratt, V. G., Shackelford, T. K., & Goetz, A. T. (2011). Perceived risk of female infidelity moderates the relationship between objective risk of female infidelity and sexual coercion in Humans (Homo sapiens). *Journal of Comparative Psychology*, *125*, 370–373.

Mead, W. R. (2008, June 19). Promised lands: Israel's broad American base. *New York Times*. Retrieved November 2011, from http://www.nytimes.com/2008/06/19/opinion/19iht-edmead.1.13829788.html

Midrash Rabbah, The 400 BCE-1200 CE (circa) The Midrash Rabbah. Freedman, H. & Simon, M. (eds.) New York: Soncino Press (1983).

Miner, E. J., Shackelford, T. K., Block, C. R., Starratt, V. G., & Weekes-Shackelford, V. A. (in press). Risk of death or life-threatening injury for women with children not sired by the abuser. *Human Nature*.

Mozgovaya, N. (2010a, October 10). ADL slams Shas spiritual leader for "Goyim were born to serve Jews" comment. *Haaretz*. Retrieved November 2011, from http://www.haaretz.com/jewish-world/adl-slams-shas-spiritual-leader-for-saying-non-jews-were-born-to-serve-jews-1.320235

Mozgovaya, N. (2010b, July 22). Focus U.S.A. / Whatever happens, Israel can always count on U.S. evengelicals. *Haaretz*. Retrieved November 2011, from http://www.haaretz.com/blogs/focus-u-s-a/focus-u-s-a-whatever-happens-israel-can-always-count-on-u-s-evangelicals-1.303452

New York Times. (2011, October 12). *Justifying the killing of an American*. Editorial. Retrieved January 2012, from http://www.nytimes.com/2011/10/12/opinion/justifying-the-killing-of-an-american.html

Obama, B. (2011, May 19). Remarks by the President on the Middle East and North Africa. Retrieved November 2011, from http://www.whitehouse.gov/the-press-office/2011/05/19/remarks-president-middle-east-and-north-africa

Paine, T. (1984/1794). *The age of reason*. Buffalo, NY: Prometheus Books.

Platek, S. M., & Shackelford, T. K. (2006). *Female infidelity and paternal uncertainty: Evolutionary perspectives on male anti-cuckoldry tactics*. Cambridge, England: Cambridge University Press.

Poll: Youth name Ovadia Yosef as most influential Israeli. (2006, November 7). *Haaretz*. Retrieved November 2011, from http://www.haaretz.com/news/poll-youth-name-ovadia-yosef-as-most-influential-israeli-1.204517

Popper, N. (2009, June 9). Chabad rabbi: Jews should kill Arab men, women and children during war. *Haaretz*. Retrieved November 2011, from http://www.haaretz.com/news/chabad-rabbi-jews-should-kill-arab-men-women-and-children-during-war-1.277616

Shahak, I. (1994). *Jewish history, Jewish religion: The weight of three thousand years*. London: Pluto Press.

Talmud, The 400 CE (circa) The Babylonian Talmud. Quincentenary Edition, Epstein, I. (ed). London: Soncino Press (1978).

US court hears Iraq rape case. (2006, August 6). *Aljazeera*. Retrieved January 15, 2012, from http://english.aljazeera.net/archive/2006/08/200841015713338135.html

US military funeral protest case opens in supreme court. (2010, October 7). *Guardian*. Retrieved November 2011, from http://www.guardian.co.uk/law/2010/oct/07/us-military-funeral-protest-supreme-court

Vermes, G. (1973). *Jesus the Jew: A historian's reading of the gospels*. Philadelphia: Fortress Press.

Walsh, T. (2011, January 29). Chaos erupts at funeral of Ugandan gay rights activist. *CNN*. Retrieved November 2011, from http://edition.cnn.com/2011/WORLD/africa/01/29/uganda.gay.activist.funeral/

West Bank rabbi: Jews can kill gentiles who threaten Israel. (2009, September 11). *Haaretz*. Retrieved November 2011, from http://www.haaretz.com/jewish-world/news/west-bank-rabbi-jews-can-kill-gentiles-who-threaten-israel-1.4496

CHAPTER 6

Filicide and Child Maltreatment: Prospects for Ultimate Explanation

Grant T. Harris *and* Marnie E. Rice

Abstract

The clinical literature on human filicide and child maltreatment lacks a comprehensive explanation both for perpetration and its effects. In this chapter, we outline how evolutionary, selectionist thinking can help make sense of the data on the perpetrators of child maltreatment and filicide, and potentially also help make sense of the effects of maltreatment on its victims. At the proximate level, filicide and child maltreatment seem pathological or inexplicable by natural causes. At the ultimate level, however, we explore how things that seem deviant, disturbed, and even self-destructive can be understood as adaptive or as side effects of adaptations. In addition to leading to scientific hypotheses that can further our theoretical understanding, an evolutionary explanation might help efforts to assess the risk of these troubling behaviors, prevent them, and remedy the effects.

Key Words: filicide, infanticide, child homicide, child maltreatment, child abuse, stepparents, parental investment, parental solicitude

Introduction

Humans are remarkable among species for their parental investment. Those human parents who were indifferent to the welfare of their offspring would have had fewer descendants who themselves lived to reproduce. Thus, everyone alive now is descended from a long line of humans who ensured the survival and well-being of their children. Parental solicitude seems to require little explanation. What does seem to demand explanation is why parents would ever neglect, mistreat, harm, or kill their children. Contemporary evidence indicates that children who experience mistreatment or neglect suffer long-term psychological damage as a result. On the other hand, at least some kinds of childhood adversity would have been a common feature of human history. In this chapter, we review these effects of child maltreatment and explore whether ultimate (selectionist, evolutionary) explanations can deepen our understanding of these phenomena, and whether humans have evolved facultative responses to adverse childhood events.

The ultimate or selectionist thinking underpinning this chapter involves three interrelated theories from evolutionary biology that we will rely on throughout the discussion:

Life History Theory is about the trade-offs, shaped by evolutionary forces, in the timing and allocation of energy made by organisms in development, reproduction, parental care, and longevity. Such allocations usually depend both on environmental circumstance and the organism's own individual condition. Central to ideas presented here is that there are individual differences in the life history strategies people pursue and that these are relatively stable across the life course.

Parental Investment Theory, which may be understood as a corollary of life history theory, refers to how parents allocate the expenditure of energy in a single offspring against costs to their investment in other aspects of fitness (including other offspring, other genetic relatives, and other reproductive opportunities). Generally, the sex that makes the greater mandatory parental investment (in gestation, lactation, and care) is the discriminating one in mating, while the other sex competes more for sexual access to the higher investing sex. Because, in humans, the lesser investing sex nevertheless does generally make substantial parental investment, this has created selection pressure to ensure that the investment is not made indiscriminately.

Inclusive Fitness Theory, or kin selection theory, states that reproductive fitness depends on the survival of an organism's own genes plus the survival of copies of those genes carried by others, especially close genetic relatives. Most obviously, human parents often act to enhance the survival of offspring even at the cost of their own survival and potential future reproductive opportunities. And, as we discuss here, sometimes they do not.

The Effects of Maltreatment and Abuse

The literature on child maltreatment is voluminous with two entire fields of social policy (mental health and child welfare) and several scholarly journals devoted entirely to the topic (Chaffin, 2006). Briefly, the sequelae of childhood maltreatment fall into two broad categories: subsequent internalizing and externalizing problems. Externalizing characteristics, including hyperactivity, impulsivity, sensation seeking, delinquency, and violence are frequently associated with childhood maltreatment. There are well-established associations between childhood maltreatment and criminality (Kaplow & Widom, 2007; Kingree, Phan, & Thompson, 2003; McGloin & Widom, 2001; Smith & Thornberry, 1995; Stouthamer-Loeber, Loeber, Homish, & Wei, 2001), aggression (Duke, Pettingell, McMorris, & Borowsky, 2010; Felson & Lane, 2009; Huizinga et al., 2006; Lansford et al., 2007; Manly, Kim, Rogosch, & Cicchetti, 2001), substance abuse (Clark, Thatcher, & Martin, 2010; Lansford, Dodge, Pettit, & Bates, 2010; Stein, Leslie, & Nyamathi, 2002; Topitzes, Mersky, & Reynolds, 2009), decelerated autonomic response to stress (Ford, Fraleigh, Albert, & Connor, 2010; Kim & Cicchetti, 2010), risky sexuality (Senn & Carey, 2010; Wilson & Widom, 2008), personality disorder (Johnson, Cohen, Brown, Smailes, & Bernstein, 1999; Kim, Cicchetti, Rogosch, & Manly, 2009; Natsuaki, Cicchetti, & Rogosch, 2009), and psychopathy (Gao, Raine, Chan, Venables, & Mednick, 2010).

Childhood abuse and maltreatment are also associated with later internalizing problems, including depression, anxiety, and social withdrawal (van Harmelen et al., 2010; Kaplow & Widom, 2007; Manly et al., 2001; Stein et al., 2002); low self-esteem (Stein et al., 2002); and heightened hormonal response to stress (Clark et al., 2010). Finally, childhood maltreatment is also associated with later poor health (Lanier, Jonson-Reid, Stahlschmidt, Drake, & Constantino, 2010; Topitzes et al., 2009); and poor school, vocational, and economic adjustment (Veltman & Browne, 2001; Zielinski, 2009).

Externalizing symptoms are often thought to have a social learning basis. The intergenerational transmission of violence perspective is that parents who use violence to resolve interpersonal conflict (including that involved in child rearing) inadvertently "teach" their children to use aggression as they encounter conflict with others. Another view is that as children are abused and neglected by their parents, they "learn" they have low value and this is reflected in their later intrapersonal experiences (feeling worthless, fearful, etc.). However, behavior genetic studies reveal that externalizing (and to some extent, internalizing) problems exhibit considerable heritability (Harris, Hilton, & Rice, 2011), which is inconsistent with a simple social learning interpretation of the effects of childhood maltreatment. Parents and children might resemble each other in the temperamentally based tendency to engage in maltreatment and externalizing traits, respectively, due to both being underlain by a common set of genetic factors. Thus, behavioral genetic research suggests that childhood maltreatment might not cause later externalizing problems at all; both might be due to a third cause, although to date such a cause has not been identified. One possibility is that the most extreme forms of externalizing problems comprise an alternative, obligate life history strategy due to frequency-dependent selection. We will discuss this in more detail later.

A third possible interpretation of the effects of child abuse is that causation works in the opposite direction. That is, parents of aggressive, difficult-to-parent children might turn to ever harsher, even abusive, tactics in efforts to gain compliance and cooperation from such children. Or perhaps fearful, socially withdrawn behavior induces some parents to employ harsh and self-defeating tactics to "toughen" children up and make them more resilient. Several lines of evidence fail to support reverse or spurious causation, however. First, experimental nonhuman animal research yields results consistent with the hypothesis that maltreatment causes adverse outcomes (e.g., Nelson et al., 2009). Second, longitudinal studies yield patterns of results more parsimoniously attributing internalizing and externalizing traits to earlier maltreatment (e.g., Caspi et al., 2002; Kim & Cicchetti, 2010). Third, behavioral genetic studies come close to ruling out common inheritance as the sole source of the association between early abuse and later antisociality (e.g., Caspi et al., 2002; Jonson-Reid et al., 2010). Lastly, the effects of maltreatment appear to be moderated by genetic factors such that some monoamine oxidase alleles are associated, given early maltreatment, with externalizing outcomes (e.g., Beach et al., 2010; Beaver, Mancini, DeLisi, & Vaughn, 2010). Other physiological measures appear to confer additional risk or protective effects of childhood maltreatment (Briere & Jordan, 2009; Cicchetti & Rogosch, 2001; Cicchetti, Rogosch, Gunnar, & Toth, 2010; also see Tyrka et al., 2009).

In summary, psychological and behavioral genetic research provides evidence that the effects of child maltreatment are not entirely socially caused, and heritable processes are implicated, thus opening the door to selectionist explanations. In the remainder of this chapter, we will review the existing literature on child maltreatment and filicide among humans and explore how selectionist accounts help make sense of the evidence, drawing also from selectionist contributions to domestic violence and sexual coercion.

Parental Perpetrators of Filicide and Maltreatment

Homicide and fatal neglect by family members is a common cause of death among children (Adinkrah, 2001, 2003; Boudreaux, Lord, & Jarvis, 2001; Goetting, 1988; Koenen & Thompson, 2008; Lee & Lathrop, 2010; Lord, Boudreaux, Jarvis, Waldvogel, & Weeks, 2002; Pritchard & Butler, 2003). The risk of filicide decreases with the age of the child (Adinkrah, 2001; Boudreaux et al., 2001; Finkelhor, 1997; Hicks & Gaughan, 1995; Kunz & Bahr, 1996; Lee & Lathrop, 2010; Lord et al., 2002; McClain, Sacks, Froehlke, & Ewigman, 1993). Among the youngest children, mothers are the most likely perpetrators (Adinkrah, 2003; Boudreaux et al., 2001; Bourget, Grace, & Whitehurst, 2007; d'Orban, 1979; Finkelhor, 1997; Holden, Burland, & Lemmen, 1996; Klevens & Leeb, 2010; Kunz & Bahr, 1996; Lord et al., 2002; Xie & Yamagami, 1995). As children age, however, there is greater risk of fatal harm from fathers and unrelated male members of the household (Adinkrah, 2001, 2003; Alexandre, Nadanovsky, Moraes, & Reichenheim, 2010; Bourget et al., 2007; Finkelhor, 1997; Goetting, 1988; Kaplun & Reich, 1976; Kasim, Cheah, & Shafie, 1995; Kunz & Bahr, 1996; Lord et al., 2002; Lucas et al., 2002; Lyman et al., 2003; Marleau, Poulin, Webanck, Roy, & Laporte, 1999; Smithey, 1998; Somander & Rammer, 1991; Stiffman, Schnitzer, Adam, Kruse, & Ewigman, 2002; Strang, 1996; Temrin, Nordlund, & Sterner, 2004).

Most clinical and professional discussions of filicide emphasize such socioeconomic stressors as poverty and unemployment (e.g., Belsky, 1993; Finkelhor, 1997; Goetting, 1988), mental illness (Bourget & Gagné, 2002; Goetting, 1988; Marleau et al., 1999; Resnick, 1969; Stroud & Pritchard, 2001; Wilczynski, 1995; Xie & Yamagami, 1995), and marital discord (Adinkrah, 2003; Somander & Rammer, 1991; Stanton & Simpson, 2002). In a study of lay explanations of child maltreatment, prevalent opinions about causes were very similar to those usually advanced by clinical experts: poverty and family instability, intoxication, stress, moral ignorance, and individual pathology (Korbin, Coulton, Lindstrom-Ufuti, & Spilsbury, 2000)—but these explanations are insufficiently constrained; for example, how poverty or family breakup causes some parents, but not most, to neglect, abuse, or kill their offspring is not specified. There is evidence that mothers, fathers, and stepparents who mistreat or kill their children do so for different reasons (Dufour, Lavergne, Larrivée, & Trocmé, 2008; Kauppi, Kumpulainen, Karkola, Vanamo, & Merikanto, 2010; Liem & Koenraadt, 2010; Porter & Gavin, 2010), so we will discuss them separately.

PATERNAL PERPETRATORS

Paternal investment is unusual among mammals (Geary, 2000) and even in humans, it is highly conditional. Paternal investment appears to be the inverse of paternal maltreatment (Herring, 2009) and maltreatment (including fatal maltreatment and even accidental fatalities; Janson & van Schaik, 2000; Tooley, Karakis, Stokes, & Ozanne-Smith, 2006; van Schaik & Janson, 2000) is associated with degree of genetic relatedness (Cavanagh, Dobash, & Dobash, 2007; Daly & Wilson, 1994; Harris, Hilton, Rice, & Eke, 2007; Herring, 2009;

Weekes-Shackelford & Shackelford, 2004). Fathers who kill their children also are likely to commit suicide and many seem to have acted out of vengeful anger (Adinkrah, 2001, 2003; Cavanagh et al., 2007; Goetting, 1988; Harris, Hilton et al., 2007; Kaplun & Reich, 1976; Kasim et al., 1995; Lyman et al., 2003; Smithey, 1998). Such filicides seem to be characterized by sexual jealousy, marital disharmony, marital separation, and even uxoricide (killing one's wife; Adinkrah, 2001, 2003; Harris, Hilton et al., 2007; Lucas et al., 2002; Marleau et al., 1999; Strang, 1996). Investigators have coined the term "familicide" to describe the killing of children and their mother by the father/husband, often accompanied by a completed or attempted suicide (Adinkrah, 2001, 2003; Daly & Wilson, 1988a, 1988b; Harris, Hilton et al., 2007). It is rare for women to commit mass family murder (Harris, Hilton et al., 2007; Wilson, Daly, & Daniele, 1995). Overall, men who kill their children are reported to have worse histories of criminal, antisocial, and substance-abusing behavior (Goetting, 1988; Harris, Hilton et al., 2007; Kaplun & Reich, 1976; Kasim et al., 1995; Pitt & Bale, 1995) than the male population at large, and this is especially true for stepfathers, who act in a paternal role but are not genetically related to the victim (Goetting, 1988; Harris, Hilton et al., 2007; Hicks & Gaughan, 1995; Kaplun & Reich, 1976; Kasim et al., 1995; Lucas et al., 2002; Lyman et al., 2003).

Among humans, data showing that filicide is associated with circumstances related to net ancestral reproductive fitness would argue for interpretations reflecting manipulation or sexual selection. These two ideas depend in turn on the selectionist concepts outlined in inclusive fitness theory and parental investment theory. That is, the evolution of human reproduction has left males with the benefits of paternal investment in dynamic tension with the risks of inadvertent investment in the offspring of others. By this account, modern men are descended from ancestral males who exhibited considerable parental solicitude and investment in children, but not those who did so indiscriminately. Such selectionist accounts hypothesize that male reproductive fitness has been associated with proprietary behavior toward their mates. Some degree of coercion by men toward women and suspicion regarding their offspring is explicable on the grounds that ancestral males who engaged in some form of coercion, threat, and even force to discourage their mates from sexual behavior with other men would be less likely to raise young who were not their own. Threats the perpetrator was demonstrably willing and able to carry out (in contrast to deliberate bluffing) would have the most potent effects (Daly & Wilson, 1988a, 1994, 1996; Wilson, Daly, & Daniele, 1995).

MATERNAL PERPETRATORS

Because uncertainty about maternity is so unlikely among humans, maternal investment is less conditional than paternal investment. A mother's killing of her infant is related to being young and lacking experience, and to such stressors as uncertainty about which sexual partner is the father of the infant, poverty, and lack of interpersonal supports (Adinkrah, 2001; 2003; Boudreaux et al., 2001; Haapasalo & Petaja, 1999; Hicks & Gaughan, 1995). Mothers who kill older children are usually evaluated as having done so due to the mother's severe mental illness (Adinkrah, 2001; Bourget & Gagné, 2002; d'Orban, 1979; Haapasalo & Petaja, 1999; Harris, Hilton et al., 2007; Holden et al., 1996; Kunz & Bahr, 1996; Lewis, Baranoski, Buchanan, & Benedek, 1998; Silverman & Kennedy, 1988; Strang, 1996; Stroud, 1996; Tuteur & Glotzer, 1959; Wilczynski, 1995; Xie & Yamagami, 1995) and, in Canada, are often charged with the lesser crime of infanticide rather than murder. Infanticide is defined in the Canadian Criminal Code as the killing by a mother of her newborn child when she is mentally disturbed due either to lack of recovery from childbirth or to the effect of lactation (Criminal Code, R.S., c.C., 1985, Part VIII-34, s.216), and it carries considerably milder sanctions. Compared to all other child homicide perpetrators, genetic mothers who kill their noninfant children are more likely to be diagnosed with serious mental disorder and be excused on account of insanity (Harris, Hilton et al., 2007). In this context, offense details, though often horrific, do not typically imply antagonism toward victims. Indeed, the mother may be trying to effect a tragic "rescue" by taking the child with her when she ends her own life (Adinkrah, 2001; Harris, Hilton et al., 2007; Silverman & Kennedy, 1988).

What might be the most puzzling case—a mother who kills her own young child—is, in the selectionist literature, explained as having had direct adaptive benefit. The selectionist account arises from the well-established finding that maternal filicides exhibit a greater inverse relationship with age than child homicides perpetrated by anyone else. The age of a child represents more "sunken" investment for a mother than for any other relative; thus, a mother stands to lose more by the death of an older child and least by the death of a newborn. Studies of humans and nonhumans (Hausfater & Hrdy, 1984; Hrdy, 1979, 1999; Scrimshaw, 1984) have identified three possible adaptive bases for filicide by mothers. The most relevant to human maternal filicide is manipulation—killing that directly improves the mother's overall inclusive fitness (e.g., killing newborns that would draw scarce resources away from older or future offspring, thus enabling the others to survive). The others are direct resource competition (e.g., there is insufficient food for both mother and offspring to survive but there are reasonable prospects for improvement in supply) and resource exploitation (e.g., cannibalism). Ultimate, selectionist explanations (Hrdy, 1999) point to parental manipulation as relevant to human filicide. Mothers are obliged to invest much in each offspring through gestation, lactation, and the consequent sacrifice of opportunities to produce later offspring. Ancestral mothers stood to lose much by investing in offspring who would not thrive as well as might later children. The occasions on which the mother of an infant elects to let or cause the child to die, according to selectionist theory, would most likely be when the child is an infant (relatively fewer resources have already been expended), the mother is young (she has prospects for later successful reproduction), her resources are scarce, paternal support is undependable for any reason, or the infant has obvious health problems. These would all be circumstances in which women's ancestral reproductive fitness might have been enhanced by parental manipulation; killing her child allowed her to devote more resources to older offspring or to delay reproduction until more favorable circumstances were likely to occur. Each of these circumstances—infant victim, young mother, poor resources, unhealthy child, and absent paternal support—is empirically associated with maternal filicide (Harris, Hilton et al., 2007). The killing of healthy children after the first year of life by genetic mothers is commonly associated with true pathology or disorder (Daly & Wilson, 1988a), in the sense that a pathology is the failure of a mechanism to perform the function for which it was designed by natural selection (e.g., Wakefield, 1992).

STEPPARENTAL PERPETRATORS

Filicide by stepparents (male and female) may be unlikely to carry direct adaptive advantages (Forbes, 2005), but the clearest example of parents' reproductive interests not coinciding with the child's occurs in stepparenting relationships. Although it may not have been the case throughout much of human history, step\fatherhood is very much more common today than stepmotherhood (Harris, Hilton et al., 2007). And, although filicide and child maltreatment may be as common among stepmothers as among stepfathers, the fact that stepfatherhood is so much more prevalent means that stepfathers account for the majority of cases of filicide and child maltreatment by stepparents. In historic times, stepfamilies in America and Europe were more often formed after death than divorce. Mothers of young children incurred substantial mortality due to childbirth, and widowers often kept the children and brought in a stepmother. Many, if not most, stepparent relationships are loving and solicitous. Indeed, on selectionist grounds, prospective partners can be expected to exhibit some stepparental solicitude as a hard-to-fake aspect of mating effort. Despite its archetypal representation in folklore, the association between stepparenthood and child maltreatment and filicide has only rather recently been examined empirically (Wilson, Daly, & Weghorst, 1980). Research motivated by selectionist thinking has established that stepparents represent a much greater risk of violence and death to children than do genetic parents, independent of parental age and poverty (Daly & Wilson, 1998a; Harris, Hilton et al., 2007).

There has been very little research on stepmaternal maltreatment and filicide specifically. Because the risks to reproductive success associated with indiscriminant stepparental solicitude are greater for women (who experience much less variability in reproductive success) than for men, selectionist theory would predict that they would exhibit even greater differences in levels of parental solicitude as a function of their status as either genetic mothers or stepmothers. Furthermore, all human fatherhood entails more parental uncertainty than motherhood (due to extrapair mating, concealed ovulation, and internal gestation) such that parental solicitude would be expected to be more similar among fathers and stepfathers than between mothers and stepmothers. Some recent research (Harris, Hilton et al., 2007) confirms these expectations. This study also reported that those stepmothers who committed filicide (though only 25% as prevalent as stepfather filicide perpetrators) engaged in much worse prior maltreatment and neglect, especially if she also had genetic children, than any other class of parental filicide perpetrator.

THE RELEVANCE OF ULTIMATE EXPLANATION

Thinking about human evolutionary history helps make sense of many aspects of this literature.

To be sure, the proximal bases of severe child maltreatment are of the greatest interest to most laypeople and policy makers who want answers to such questions as: What can be done to provide early detection and treatment for new mothers experiencing postpartum depression? Would parenting skill training and anger management therapy ameliorate dangerously abusive behavior of some fathers? Would multisystemic treatment help families build material and interpersonal supports so as to avoid serious neglect of children in their care? Answers to these questions depend critically on valid proximal accounts. For scientists, however, it is also important to understand when and why new mothers might experience a mental disorder so severe that a newborn's life is at risk. When and why would a father (or "surrogate") be so indifferent to or angry toward a child that serious harm or death might result? When and why does a family's composition actually constitute a risk of mortality to its youngest members? An appreciation of ultimate causation helps tackle these questions, and selectionist thinking illuminates several explanatory themes.

Human Life History Strategies Vary Sensibly

Human males and females have clear differences in reproductive strategies. These are best articulated in parental investment theory (Trivers, 1972). Due to fundamental sex differences in minimal parental investment and the inescapable consequences of internal fertilization, male and females exhibit fundamental differences in psychological characteristics associated with both intersex and intrasex relationships. Females can be certain that an offspring is genetically their own, but ancestral males who were indifferent to the risk of sexual infidelity and cuckoldry, the loss of mates to other males, and to the possibility of their own material resources supporting offspring other than their own experienced, on average, impaired reproductive success. Thus, human males are all descended from men who were alert to such risks—sexual proprietariness, sexual jealousy, and the use of violence or the threat of violence to enforce fidelity are to be expected by this consideration of how male psychology evolved. The result is that human male psychology has evolved mechanisms to regard the sexual alienation of a spouse as a catastrophic loss to be resisted via aggressive, high-stakes tactics that usually succeed, but that occasionally backfire, resulting in a loss of reproductive fitness. Apparently maladaptive behavior could "represent the tail of some motivational distribution" (Daly & Wilson, 1998a, p. 443).

Media reports tell us that a father can be so irrationally distraught or angered by his wife's leaving him for another man that he kills her and her children and even himself. The selectionist approach both affords a possible source for such an extreme emotional reaction and explains why such lethal behavior is so uncommon in response to even the most extreme of life's other tribulations, or among mothers under any circumstances (Liem, de Vet, & Koenraadt, 2010).

There are also individual differences in male life history strategies in response to male-male competition. Thus, processes underlying competitive aggression, risk taking, mating effort, impulsivity, conscientiousness, and antisociality can be understood as features of differing male reproductive strategies. Many males adopt an approach to life characterized by high degrees of compromise with female reproductive strategy, and thus exhibit considerable paternal investment, reciprocal altruism, and interpersonal cooperation. Such life history strategies by a majority, however, create a behavioral niche for an alternative strategy characterized by interpersonal exploitation, social parasitism, irresponsibility, emotional callousness, violence, and coercion (Hare, 2003; Harris, Rice, Hilton, Lalumière, & Quinsey, 2007; Lalumière, Mishra, & Harris, 2008; Mealey, 1995). This strategy, associated with the clinical condition known as psychopathy, exhibits high heritability in behavioral genetic studies and, therefore, is probably substantially an obligate strategy (Lalumière et al., 2008). Such males, of course, engage in criminal and violent behavior greatly out of proportion to their numbers and represent disproportionate levels of risk of nonlethal violence and lethal violence to both their mates and their offspring (Annerback, Svedin, & Gustafsson, 2007; Bourget et al., 2007; Colman, Mitchell-Herzfeld, Kim, & Shady, 2010; Flynn, Shaw, & Abel, 2007; Harris, Rice et al., 2007; Hilton, Harris, & Rice, 2010; Kauppi et al., 2010).

Parental Solicitude Varies Sensibly

In mammalian species especially, high levels of parental solicitude represent an obvious and important aspect of reproductive fitness. Within that general tendency, however, a parent's reproductive interests are not isomorphic with those of each offspring. Selectionist work on infanticide (e.g., Hrdy, 1979, 1992, 1999) demonstrates that modern human mothers are descended from females who ensured that the interests of any single child did not risk the net interests of her present and future offspring. The proximal result in response to such a risk is expected to be a relative absence of parental solicitude toward offspring who carry such risks. In a world of limited resources, stepparental investment entails greater reproductive cost (and smaller reproductive benefit) than genetic-parental solicitude. The greater tendency of stepparents to beat children to death in a rage (Daly & Wilson, 1988a, 1994; Harris, Hilton et al., 2007; Weekes-Shackelford & Shackelford, 2004) suggests a failure of solicitude (as distinct from a direct adaptive advantage to homicidal behavior) compared to comparatively painless, planned filicides by gunshot or asphyxia by genetic parents (Harris, Hilton et al., 2007; Weekes-Shackelford & Shackelford, 2004).

Selection Cannot Optimize for the Future

Finally, we return to the interesting findings that abuse and fatal maltreatment sometimes characterize stepparenting, but perhaps less often characterize adoptive relationships. Interestingly, the details of household composition as a risk for lower solicitude and maltreatment might be important: Data also suggest that two-adoptive parent families might not represent risk of maltreatment and filicide while stepparental families do (Hamilton, Cheng, & Powell, 2007; Ijzendoorn, Euser, Prinzie, Juffer, & Bakermans-Kranenburg, 2009). Perhaps human evolutionary history simply lacked the conditions necessary for discriminative parental solicitude under the conditions typical of modern adoption. That is, if raising completely unrelated children by an intact mating pair was rare (or uniquely associated with having no genetically related offspring) among ancestral humans, then any psychological tendency toward lower investment and lesser parental solicitude had no opportunity to evolve (also see Lawler, 2008).

SUMMARY OF PERPETRATORS OF FILICIDE AND CHILD MALTREATMENT

We contend that selectionist approaches can help provide a complete account for the empirical findings about filicide and child maltreatment. Although proximate accounts such as stress and marital disharmony could partially explain the prevalence of filicide and child maltreatment by step versus genetic parents, selectionist theory can provide a compelling account why it is so very much more common among stepparents. Poverty and social stress could explain infanticide by young genetic mothers, but they cannot in themselves account for such findings as greater mental illness and legal insanity of genetic mothers compared to other perpetrators, or greater anger, rage, hostility, and death by beating by stepparents rather than genetic parents. Mental illness is consistent with many present findings (especially the rare cases of filicide of older children by genetic mothers), but it cannot account for the observation that suicide, spousal homicide, familicide, and high levels of marital discord and conflict uniquely characterize filicide by fathers, or that death by beating especially characterizes filicide by stepparents. Marital disharmony could be a proximal cause of familicide especially, but it cannot itself account for the finding that quicker methods of killing are used by genetic parents than by stepparents. The present findings are most consistent with human filicide as evolved forms of parental manipulation—parental actions designed to seize control of reproduction by affecting resource allocation among offspring or by affecting the reproductive behavior of mates. Selection has shaped human male psychology toward highly aggressive responses to spousal alienation, resulting in extreme cases in maladaptive behaviors such as killing his own children. Filicide by genetic mothers most commonly occurs among young mothers of infant children, a finding best explained by the selectionist account of it having had a direct adaptive benefit. Maternal filicide of older children can be explained by the nonselectionist explanation of mental illness, but its rarity is most consistent with a selectionist explanation.

Externalizing and Internalizing Traits as Facultative Responses to Adversity: The Theory and Its Implications

A short-term, impulsive, risk-prone, high mating effort life strategy can be understood as a viable (though morally questionable) alternative life strategy. Also as suggested earlier, we propose that, at the extreme, psychopathy comprises a substantially obligate life strategy that has been maintained in the human population by frequency dependent selection. Short of that extreme, however, there is considerable evidence that antisocial (externalizing) traits comprise an at least partially facultative or conditional response to early adversity (e.g., Neugebauer, Hoek, & Susser, 1999). Thus, there are findings in which personal traits (e.g., impulsivity) that yield main effects also interact with neighborhood disadvantage such that the personal traits appear to exert greater influence in relatively disadvantaged neighborhoods (Lynam et al., 2000; also see Caspi et al., 2002; Dumont, Widom, & Czaja, 2007; Slep & O'Leary, 2005; for similar examples).

Elsewhere (Lalumiére, Harris, Quinsey, & Rice, 2005), we developed a three-path model to explain the prevalence of sexual coercion. In this context, the path associated with competitive disadvantage (i.e., comparatively few personal resources, abilities, and skills) and early adversity are hypothesized to engage an early-starting and enduring strategic response characterized by short horizons, risk taking, and interpersonal exploitation (Daly & Wilson, 1985, 1994). The degree to which this facultative strategy is modifiable based on conditions later than early childhood is unknown. Nevertheless, we suggest that the effects of treatment and rehabilitation programs for offenders are best understood as interventions that induce them to modify these life history strategies (Harris & Rice, 2006; Lalumiére et al., 2005; Rice & Harris, 1997). Moreover, we suggest that these considerations might suggest novel treatment targets and styles of intervention. The point, however, is that these would be thought of as altering people's life strategies.

Although less thoroughly documented, there is also evidence that childhood maltreatment is causally related to later depression and anxiety. And similar to the literature on externalizing traits as a facultative response to adverse childhood environments, there are suggestions that internalizing conditions can be understood in the same way. Thus, social withdrawal, risk aversion, and reduced physical activity can be seen as the modern results of an evolved human conditional response to social or material loss (Price et al., 2007; Sloman, 2008), risk of infection (Kinney & Tanaka, 2009), and other physical and emotional threats (Keller & Nesse, 2006; Nettle, 2004; Nesse & Ellesworth, 2009). A fundamental question pertains to why the same adversity should induce a facultative externalizing response in some people and a facultative internalizing response in others. It appears that this distinction can be attributed to aspects of the genome (Beach et al., 2010), although how evolution led to these two distinct genomes is unknown. Nevertheless, the existence of those two genomes can explain why internalizing and externalizing traits exhibit substantial heritability in behavioral genetic studies and simultaneously have the properties of conditional strategies.

Our aim is not to advocate for one particular hypothesis about internalizing and externalizing traits having had adaptive significance in human evolution. The heritability observed in behavioral genetic studies precludes the possibility that internalizing and externalizing traits are fully or completely facultative (i.e., occur purely in response to environmental conditions). Our argument is that they are substantially or partially facultative strategies. We suggest that selectionist thinking can illuminate the distinction between proximate and ultimate causes. At the proximate level, childhood maltreatment can seem pathological in its causes and effects, while at the ultimate level, selectionist thinking can reveal that organisms usually evolve adaptive responses to the survival and reproductive problems that life presents (interestingly, childhood abuse and neglect have been reported to be unrelated to longevity; White & Widom, 2003). Because some children throughout human history certainly faced physical and emotional adversity (some at the hands of adults in their family groups), this line of thinking helps us seek new ways of understanding these phenomena.

NOVEL HYPOTHESES FOR RISK ASSESSMENT AND INTERVENTION

Research suggests that men who commit uxoricide yield high scores on actuarial assessments for the assessment of the general risk of domestic violence (Eke, Hilton, Harris, Rice, & Houghton, 2011; Hilton & Harris, 2005), and that many paternal filicides are occasioned by domestic conflict and marital discord. However, because of their frequent general lack of criminal history, many genetic fathers who kill their children do not exhibit high scores on standardized risk assessments for violence (Hilton & Harris, 2005). We suggest that research informed by selectionist hypotheses might profitably examine the empirical predictors of filicide and maltreatment with a view to enhancing the validity of available risk assessments. It is interesting to examine current assessments with some established predictive validity in light of selectionist ideas about ultimate causation.

The Child Abuse Potential inventory (Milner & Wimberly, 1980; see also Ondersma, Chaffin, Mullins, & LeBreton, 2005) is a self-report scale with items reflecting parents' anger, emotional instability, depression, unhappiness, and feelings of isolation. In addition, items reflect rigidity, punitiveness, general family conflict, and the attitude that the child is a problem. As proximal manifestations of some selectionist-inspired, ultimate explanations of maltreatment, most of these make sense. However, might items more directly tapping such potential risk factors as low parental solicitude (e.g., "I dislike spending time with this child" or "I don't have the energy to care for this child"), paternity uncertainty (e.g., "I'm not sure who is this child's actual father"), jealousy, and real or suspected cuckoldry (e.g., "I suspect my partner is or might be unfaithful," or "Our relationship is breaking up/has broken up because of sexual infidelity") improve the predictive validity of such an inventory?

Actuarial risk assessments are based on follow-up research (c.f., Hilton et al., 2004, 2010; Quinsey, Harris, Rice, & Cormier, 2006) and, because items identified predict the outcome, they must be consilient with its correct ultimate and proximate explanations. One of the most well-established such actuarials for assessing risk of serious child maltreatment (Baird & Wagner, 2000) is interesting in this regard. Items are assessed by evaluators based on records, collateral informants, and interviews. We suggest its items reflect parental solicitude (current and prior neglect, child's disability or health problems), parents' life history strategy (mental health problems, number of children, substance abuse, criminal records, violence, failure to comply with court conditions), and child's life history strategy (delinquency). Based on the selectionist thinking outlined in this chapter, we suggest other important variables to consider might include competitive disadvantage (as opposed to poverty per se) on the part of parent(s); the presence of half-siblings; actual or anticipated marital separation or breakup; sexual jealousy; and living with a stepparent, perhaps especially a parent's new boyfriend or girlfriend, and especially if he or she has externalizing traits.

In terms of intervention for the victims of severe childhood maltreatment (see Shackelford, Weekes-Shackelford, & Schmitt, 2005 for an example in a similar domain), we would advocate empirically supported therapies for those adult and juvenile survivors of abuse and maltreatment who experience anxiety, depression, and posttraumatic stress (Baker, McFall, & Shoham, 2008), even though theories upon which such treatments are based are silent with respect to ultimate explanations. On the other hand, it has been much more difficult to identify effective treatments for externalizing problems, especially among the most serious adult offenders (Harris & Rice, 2006; Rice & Harris, 1997). There is persuasive evidence that particular interventions are effective for juveniles who have exhibited antisocial and externalizing problems. Indeed, the largest ameliorative effects are obtained with the most aggressive children and more serious juvenile offenders (Lipsey, Wilson, & Cothern, 2000; Wilson & Lipsey, 2007). We suggest that the most effective interventions for such young people—interpersonal skills training and behavioral programs—can be seen as inducing a facultative switch in life history strategy (Lalumière et al., 2005; Quinsey et al., 2006; Rice & Harris, 1997). Thus, potential might lie in other suggestions to invoke altered facultative strategies (Lalumière et al., 2005; Quinsey et al., 2006) that might improve effectiveness, especially among adults.

OTHER SELECTIONIST-INSPIRED PUZZLES
Spiteful Strategies

The study of child maltreatment and filicide can examine alternative selectionist hypotheses about externalizing conditions that address aspects not otherwise well explained. Earlier, we discussed the hypothesis that psychopathy comprises a substantially obligate alternative life history strategy (Harris, Skilling, & Rice, 2001; Lalumière et al., 2005; Lalumière, Harris, & Rice, 2001; Lalumière, Mishra, & Harris, 2008; Rice & Harris, in press). Psychopaths are especially likely to engage in physical violence (e.g., Harris, Rice, & Cormier, 1991; Serin, 1991), for example, by selectively harming unrelated males (Williamson, Hare, & Wong, 1987). It is unclear, however, what could have been gained from such violence, as retaliation would likely have been very costly in ancestral (and current) environments. As well, psychopaths are relatively unaffected by the threat or application of punishment and recidivate at considerably higher rates than nonpsychopathic offenders (Harris et al., 1991). Might psychopaths' filicide and maltreatment (especially toward stepchildren) exhibit remnants of sexual selection—enhancing reproductive capacity by killing the offspring of other males—as an aspect of mating effort? Some aspects of filicide by stepfathers resemble sexually selected and spiteful tactics (Hrdy, 1999).

Purely selfish strategies do not impose pointless (i.e., of no benefit to the perpetrator) harm on nonrelatives nor incur large costs of pointless actions. Such tactics, however, are characteristics of *spiteful* strategies (Hamilton, 1970). Spiteful strategies may evolve when costs can be imposed upon those significantly less likely than chance to bear copies of the alleles associated with the behavior (negative relatives) by decreasing the reproductive success of rival genes (Gardner & West, 2004). Thus, indirect fitness benefit can occur by reducing the fitness of rival genes, thereby increasing the relative success of copies of spiteful individuals' genes. Selection could have favored tactics that carried survival and reproductive costs if indirect fitness benefits outweighed direct fitness costs (Hamilton, 1964, 1970). Perhaps psychopaths have executed a blended strategy as opposed to simple selfishness: Where they could have improved their own lot, they behaved selfishly, engaging for example in sexual coercion; where they could wreak havoc, they did so spitefully, doing harm to negative relatives via spiteful filicide observed in other species (Dobson, Chesser, & Zinner, 2000).

Epigenetics and the Acquisition of Inherited Traits

Intriguing new research has implications for the ways in which child maltreatment might be maintained in the human population. Epigenetics refers to ways in which gene expression is affected by mechanisms outside the genome itself, that is, independent of the DNA sequence. These mechanisms can persist throughout the life of the individual and across generations and yet be environmental in origin (Masterpasqua, 2009). Thus, research in humans and other animals suggests that certain aspects of the early environment, including the parent–offspring relationship, can, via modifications to the epigenome, have profound effects upon gene expression. These modifications can therefore yield alterations in behavior and affect that persist through the life span and into succeeding generations (Champagne, 2010; McGowan, Meaney, & Szyf, 2008; Szyf, McGown, & Meaney, 2008). Especially interesting in the present context is that many influential aspects of the physical and social environment in this epigenomic research resemble various forms of child maltreatment (Champagne, 2010). Particularly relevant for selectionist thinking is that some of these mechanisms of intergenerational transmission are behaviorally mediated (Champagne & Meaney, 2007; Diorio & Meaney, 2007) and are also potentially reversible through behavioral interventions. If so, psychosocial interventions that reduce child maltreatment in one generation might be reflected in succeeding generations but via mechanisms quite different from the social learning or cultural influences usually invoked. Although we are just beginning to understand the role of epigenetics in human evolution (Jablonka & Raz, 2009), it is clear that it holds much promise for the amelioration of the effects of child maltreatment and its decline across subsequent generations.

Conclusion

The empirical literatures on filicide and child maltreatment are remarkably consistent with a selectionist analysis first provided by Daly and Wilson (1988a, 1988b, 1996; Wilson et al., 1980) decades ago. The evidence is most consistent with human filicide and child maltreatment as reflecting various forms of parental manipulation—parents affecting resource allocation among offspring in such a way as to increase the reproductive ability of genetic offspring or by affecting the reproductive behavior of mates in such a way as to increase the number of and viability of genetic offspring. The explanatory utility of a selectionist account lies in its ability to make sense of the overall pattern of child maltreatment and filicide by humans, including comparisons between male and female perpetrators, between genetic and stepparental perpetrators, and even between maternal perpetrators of infants versus older children. It can account for Cinderella's treatment at the hands of her stepmother (Daly & Wilson, 1998b) but also uniquely predicts how Cinderella (and other stepchildren) would be treated differently by her mother, father, or stepfather, or indeed by her stepmother had there been no stepsiblings. In addition, this chapter suggested that selectionist thinking and ultimate explanation can shed light on the effects of serious child maltreatment on its victims. That is, we suggest that adverse social environments do not necessarily cause pathology (in the biological sense). Rather, adversity might be seen as inducing alteration in reproductive or life history strategies. To be sure, these strategies (if they are that) are the cause of much more unhappiness and suffering. Selectionist-inspired research might also help develop better ways to identify those at greatest risk and prompt further strategic shifts leading to less maltreatment and filicide (and greater happiness for all) in succeeding generations. More generally, our understanding of much seemingly aberrant human behavior can be furthered by considering them as aspects of intrasex (e.g., sexually selected maltreatment and filicide of nongenetic children by antisocial stepfathers) or intersex (e.g., familial violence as explicit or implicit coercion designed to decrease the risk of cuckoldry) reproductive competition (Lalumière et al., 2005).

FUTURE DIRECTIONS

In addition to further empirical study of all the implications of ultimate explanations (including selectionist-inspired puzzles) outlined in the previous section, we briefly suggest two other possible avenues. First, not everyone exposed to childhood maltreatment seems to be affected by it. Although some factors associated with resilience have been studied (e.g., Collishaw et al., 2007; Mrazek &

Mrazek, 1987; Wingo et al., 2010), it remains an understudied area. An open question is whether resilience (or "protective" factors) is anything other than "risk" factors expressed positively (e.g., positive self-worth vs. low self-esteem, ego control vs. ego-undercontrol, family stability vs. family instability, etc.; Heller, Larrieu, D'Imperio, & Boris, 1999; Walsh, Dawson, & Mattingly, 2010). One intriguing possibility is that an apparent protective mechanism—dissociation (absence of specific cognitive or affective memory for repeated traumatic events)—might simultaneously be a risk factor for later posttraumatic mental disorder (Goodman, Quas, & Ogle, 2010). Might selectionist thinking and an appreciation for ultimate explanations help inform future research on post-traumatic disorders, especially toward helping with treatment?

Second, also pertaining to intervention, selectionist thinking has been incorporated into designing programs to enhance parental performance. Compared to traditional services, a "cognitively enhanced" service (aimed at improving material and personal parental resources) increased investment in high-risk offspring (Bugental, Beaulieu, & Silbert-Geigert, 2010). An obvious extension is to test similar selectionist-informed interventions with parents already identified as at risk (or perhaps even adjudicated) for maltreatment of their children.

References

Adinkrah, M. (2001). When parents kill: An analysis of filicides in Fiji. *International Journal of Offender Therapy and Comparative Criminology, 45*, 144–158.

Adinkrah, M. (2003). Men who kill their own children: Paternal filicide incidents in contemporary Fiji. *Child Abuse and Neglect, 27*, 557–568.

Alexandre, G. C., Nadanovsky, P., Moraes, C. L., & Reichenheim, M. (2010). The presence of a stepfather and child physical abuse, as reported by a sample of Brazilian mothers in Rio de Janeiro. *Child Abuse and Neglect, 34*, 959–996.

Annerbäck, E. M., Svedin, C. G., & Gustafsson, P. A. (2009). Characteristic features of severe child physical abuse—A multi-informant approach. *Journal of Family Violence, 25*, 165–172.

Baird, C., & Wagner, D. (2000). The relative validity of actuarial-and consensus-based risk assessment systems. *Children and Youth Services Review, 22*, 839–871.

Baker, T. B., McFall, R. M., & Shoham, V. (2009). Current status and future prospects of clinical psychology. *Psychological Science in the Public Interest, 9*, 67–103.

Beach, S. R., Brody, G. H., Gunter, T. D., Packer, H., Wernett, P., & Philibert, R. A. (2010). Child maltreatment moderates the association of MAOA with symptoms of depression and antisocial personality disorder. *Journal of Family Psychology, 24*, 12–20.

Beaver, K. M., Mancini, C., DeLisi, M., & Vaughn, M. G. (2010). Resiliency to victimization: The role of genetic factors. *Journal of Interpersonal Violence, 30*, 1–25.

Belsky, J. (1993). Etiology of child maltreatment: A developmental-ecological analysis. *Psychological Bulletin, 114*, 413–434.

Boudreaux, M. C., Lord, W. D., & Jarvis, J. P. (2001). Behavioral perspectives on child homicide. *Trauma, Violence, and Abuse, 2*, 56–78.

Bourget, D., & Gagné, P. (2002). Maternal filicide in Québec. *Journal of the American Academy of Psychiatry and Law, 30*, 345–351.

Bourget, D., Grace, J., & Whitehurst, L. (2007). A review of maternal and paternal filicide. *Journal of the American Academy of Psychiatry and Law, 35*, 74–82.

Briere, J., & Jordan, C. E. (2009). Childhood maltreatment, intervening variables, and adult psychological difficulties in women. *Trauma, Violence, and Abuse, 10*, 375–388.

Bugental, D. B., Beaulieu, D. A., & Silbert-Geiger, A. (2010). Increases in parental investment and child health as a result of an early intervention. *Journal of Experimental Child Psychology, 106*, 30–40.

Caspi, A., McClay, J., Moffitt, T. E., Mill, J., Martin, J., Craig, I. W.,... Poulton, R. (2002). Role of genotype in the cycle of violence in maltreated children. *Science, 297*, 851–854.

Cavanagh, K., Dobash, R. E., & Dobash, R. P. (2007). The murder of children by fathers in the context of child abuse. *Child Abuse and Neglect, 31*, 731–746.

Chaffin, M. (2006). The changing focus of child maltreatment research and practice within psychology. *Journal of Social Issues, 62*, 663–684.

Champagne, F. A. (2010). Early adversity and developmental outcomes: Interaction between genetics, epigenetics, and social experiences across the life span. *Perspectives on Psychological Science, 5*, 564–574.

Champagne, F. A., & Meaney, M. J. (2007). Transgenerational effects of social environment on variations in maternal care and behavioral response to novelty. *Behavioral Neuroscience, 121*, 1353–1363.

Cicchetti, D., & Rogosch, F. A. (2001). The impact of child maltreatment and psychopathology on neuroendocrine functioning. *Development and Psychopathology, 13*, 783–804.

Cicchetti, D., Rogosch, F. A., Gunnar, M. R., & Toth, S. L. (2010). The differential impacts of early physical and sexual abuse and internalizing problems on daytime cortisol rhythm in school-aged children. *Child Development, 81*, 252–269.

Clark, D. B., Thatcher, D. L., & Martin, C. S. (2010). Child abuse and other traumatic experiences, alcohol use disorders, and health problems in adolescence and young adulthood. *Journal of Pediatric Psychology, 35*, 499–510.

Collishaw, S., Pickles, A., Messer, J., Rutter, M., Shearer, C., & Maughan, B. (2007). Resilience to adult psychopathology following childhood maltreatment: Evidence from a community sample. *Child Abuse and Neglect, 31*, 211–229.

Colman, R. A., Mitchell-Herzfeld, S., Kim, D. H., & Shady, T. A. (2010). From delinquency to the perpetration of child maltreatment: Examining the early adult criminal justice and child welfare involvement of youth released from juvenile justice facilities. *Children and Youth Services Review, 32*, 1410–1417.

d'Orban, P. T. (1979). Women who kill their children. *British Journal of Psychiatry, 134*, 560–571.

Daly, M., & Wilson, M. (1985). Child abuse and other risks of not living with both parents. *Ethology and Sociobiology, 6*, 197–210.

Daly, M., & Wilson, M. (1988a). Evolutionary social psychology and family homicide. *Science, 242*, 519–524.

Daly, M., & Wilson, M. (1988b). *Homicide*. Hawthorne, NY: Aldine de Gruyter.

Daly, M., & Wilson, M. (1994). Some differential attributes of lethal assaults on small children by stepfathers versus genetic fathers. *Ethology and Sociobiology, 15*, 207–217.

Daly, M., & Wilson, M. (1994). Some differential attributes of lethal assaults on small children by stepfathers versus genetic fathers. *Ethology and Sociobiology, 15*, 207–217.

Daly, M., & Wilson, M. (1998a). The evolutionary social psychology of family violence. In. C. Crawford & D. L. Krebs (Eds.), *Handbook of evolutionary psychology* (pp. 431–456). Mahwah, NJ: Erlbaum.

Daly, M., & Wilson, M., (1998b). *The truth about Cinderella: A Darwinian view of parental love*. New Haven, CT: Yale University Press.

Daly, M., & Wilson, M. I. (1996). Violence against stepchildren. *Current Directions in Psychological Science, 5*, 77–81.

Diorio, J., & Meaney, M. J. (2007). Maternal programming of defensive responses through sustained effects on gene expression. *Journal of Psychiatry and Neuroscience, 32*, 275–284.

Dobson, F. S., Chesser, R. K., & Zinner, B. (2000). The evolution of infanticide: Genetic benefits of extreme nepotism and spite. *Ethology Ecology and Evolution, 12*, 131–148.

Dufour, S., Lavergne, C., Larrivée, M. C., & Trocmé, N. (2008). Who are these parents involved in child neglect? A differential analysis by parent gender and family structure. *Children and Youth Services Review, 30*, 141–156.

Duke, N. N., Pettingell, S. L., McMorris, B. J., & Borowsky, I. W. (2010). Adolescent violence perpetration: Associations with multiple types of adverse childhood experiences. *Pediatrics, 125*, e778-e786.

Dumont, K. A., Widom, C. S., & Czaja, S. J. (2007). Predictors of resilience in abused and neglected children grown-up: The role of individual and neighborhood characteristics. *Child Abuse and Neglect, 31*, 255–274.

Eke, A. W., Hilton, N. Z., Harris, G. T., Rice, M. E., & Houghton, R. E. (2011). Intimate partner homicide: Risk assessment and prospects for prediction. *Journal of Family Violence, 26*, 211–216.

Felson, R. B., & Lane, K. J. (2009). Social learning, sexual and physical abuse, and adult crime. *Aggressive Behavior, 35*, 489–501.

Finkelhor, D. (1997). The homicides of children and youth. In G. Kaufman Kantor & J. Jasinski (Eds.), *Out of the darkness: Contemporary perspectives on family violence* (pp. 17–34). Thousand Oaks, CA: Sage Publications.

Flynn, S. M., Shaw, J. J., & Abel, K. M. (2007). Homicide of infants: A cross-sectional study. *Journal of Clinical Psychiatry, 68*, 1501–1509.

Forbes, S. (2005). *A natural history of families*. Princeton, NJ: Princeton University Press.

Ford, J. D., Fraleigh, L. A., Albert, D. B., & Connor, D. F. (2010). Child abuse and autonomic nervous system hyporesponsivity among psychiatrically impaired children. *Child Abuse and Neglect, 34*, 507–515.

Gao, Y., Raine, A., Chan, E., Venables, P. H., & Mednick, S. A. (2010). Early maternal and paternal bonding, childhood physical abuse and adult psychopathic personality. *Psychological Medicine, 40*, 1007–1016.

Gardner, A., & West, S. A. (2004). Spite and the scale of competition. *Journal of the Evolutionary Biology, 17*, 1195–1203.

Geary, D. C. (2000). Evolution and proximate expression of human paternal investment. *Psychological Bulletin, 126*, 55–77.

Goetting, A. (1988). When parents kill their young children: Detroit 1982–1986. *Journal of Family Violence, 3*, 339–346.

Goodman, G. S., Quas, J. A., & Ogle, C. M. (2010). Child maltreatment and memory. *Annual Review of Psychology, 61*, 325–351.

Haapasalo, J., & Petaja, S. (1999). Mothers who killed or attempted to kill their child: Life circumstances, childhood abuse, and types of killing. *Violence and Victims, 14*, 219–239.

Hamilton, L., Cheng, S., & Powell, B. (2007). Adoptive parents, adaptive parents: Evaluating the importance of biological ties for parental investment. *American Sociological Review, 72*, 95–116.

Hamilton, W. D. (1964). The genetical evolution of social behaviour (I and II). *Journal of Theoretical Biology, 7*, 1–52.

Hamilton, W. D. (1970). Selfish and spiteful behaviour in an evolutionary model. *Nature, 228*, 1218–1220.

Hare, R. D. (2003). *The revised Psychopathy Checklist*. Toronto: Multi-Health Systems.

Harris, G.T., Hilton, N.Z., & Rice, M.E. (2011). Explaining the frequency of intimate partner violence by male perpetrators: Do attitude, relationship, and neighborhood variables add to antisociality? *Criminal Justice and Behavior, 38*, 309–331.

Harris, G. T., Hilton, N. Z., Rice, M. E., & Eke, A. W. (2007). Children killed by genetic parents versus stepparents. *Evolution and Human Behavior, 28*, 85–95.

Harris, G. T., & Rice, M. E. (2006). Treatment of psychopathy: A review of empirical findings. In C. Patrick (Ed.), *The handbook of psychopathy* (pp. 555–572). New York: Guilford Press.

Harris, G.T., Rice, M.E., & Cormier, C.A. (1991). Psychopathy and violent recidivism. *Law and Human Behavior, 15*, 625–637.

Harris, G. T., Rice, M. E., Hilton, N. Z., Lalumière, M. L., & Quinsey, V. L. (2007). Coercive and precocious sexuality as a fundamental aspect of psychopathy. *Journal of Personality Disorders, 21*, 1–29.

Harris, G. T., Skilling, T. A., & Rice, M. E. (2001). The construct of psychopathy. In M. Tonry (Ed.), *Crime and justice: An annual review of research* (pp. 197–264). Chicago: University of Chicago Press.

Hausfater, G. & Hrdy, S. B. (1984). *Infanticide*. Hawthorne, NY: Aldine de Gruyter.

Heller, S. S., Larrieu, J. A., D'Imperio, R., & Boris, N. W. (1999). Research on resilience to child maltreatment: Empirical considerations. *Child Abuse and Neglect, 23*, 321–338.

Herring, D. J. (2009). Fathers and child maltreatment: A research agenda based on evolutionary theory and behavioral biology research. *Children and Youth Services, 31*, 935–945.

Hicks, R. A., & Gaughan, D. C. (1995). Understanding fatal child abuse. *Child Abuse and Neglect, 19*, 855–863.

Hilton, N. Z. & Harris, G. T. (2005). Predicting wife assault: A critical review and implications for policy and practice. *Trauma, Violence, and Abuse, 6*, 3–23.

Hilton, N. Z., Harris, G. T., & Rice, M. E. (2010). *Risk assessment for domestically violent men: Tools for criminal justice, offender intervention, and victim services*. Washington, DC: American Psychological Association.

Hilton, N. Z., Harris, G. T., Rice, M. E., Lang, C., Cormier, C. A., & Lines, K. J. (2004). A brief actuarial assessment for the prediction of wife assault recidivism: The Ontario

Domestic Assault Risk Assessment. *Psychological Assessment, 16,* 267–275.

Holden, C. E., Burland, A. S., & Lemmen, C. A. (1996). Insanity and filicide: Women who murder their children. In E. Benedek (Ed.), *Emerging issues in forensic psychiatry: From the clinic to the courthouse* (pp. 25–34). San Francisco: Jossey-Bass.

Hrdy, S. B. (1979). Infanticide among animals: A review, classification, and examination of the implications for the reproductive strategies of females. *Ethology and Sociobiology, 1,* 13–40.

Hrdy, S. B. (1992). Fitness tradeoffs in the history and evolution of delegated mothering with special reference to wet-nursing, abandonment, and infanticide. *Ethology and Sociobiology, 13,* 409–442.

Hrdy, S.B. (1999). *Mother nature: A history of mothers, infants, and natural selection.* Toronto: Random House.

Huizinga, D., Haberstick, B. C., Smolen, A., Menard, S., Young, S. E., Corley, R. P., ... Hewitt, J. K. (2006). Childhood maltreatment, subsequent antisocial behavior, and the role of monoamine oxidase a genotype. *Biological Psychiatry, 60,* 677–683.

IJzendoorn, M. H., Euser, E. M., Prinzie, P., Juffer, F., & Bakermans-Kranenburg, M. J. (2009). Elevated risk of child maltreatment in families with stepparents but not with adoptive parents. *Child Maltreatment, 14,* 369–375.

Jablonka, E., & Raz, G. (2009). Transgenerational epigenetic inheritance: Prevalence, mechanisms, and implications for the study of heredity and evolution. *The Quarterly Review of Biology, 84,* 131–176.

Janson, C. H., & van Schaik, C. P. (2000). The behavioral ecology of infanticide by males. In C.P. van Schaik & C.H. Janson (Eds.), *Infanticide by males and its implications* (pp. 469–494). Cambridge, England: Cambridge University Press.

Johnson, J. G., Cohen, P., Brown, J., Smailes, E. M., & Bernstein, D. P. (1999). Childhood maltreatment increases risk for personality disorders during early adulthood. *Archives of General Psychiatry, 56,* 600–606.

Jonson-Reid, M., Pesnall, N., Drake, B., Fox, L., Bierut, L., Reich, W., Kane, P., ... Constantino, J. N. (2010). Effects of child maltreatment and inherited liability on antisocial development: An official records study. *Journal of the American Academy of Child and Adolescent Psychiatry, 49,* 321–332.

Kaplow, J. B., & Widom, C. S. (2007). Age of onset of child maltreatment predicts long-term mental health outcomes. *Journal of Abnormal Psychology, 116,* 176–187.

Kaplun, D., & Reich, R. (1976). The murdered child and his killers. *American Journal of Psychiatry, 133,* 809–813.

Kasim, M. S., Cheah, I., & Shafie, H. M. (1995). Childhood deaths from physical abuse. *Child Abuse and Neglect, 19,* 847–854.

Kauppi, A., Kumpulainen, K., Karkola, K., Vanamo, T., & Merikanto, J. (2010). Maternal and paternal filicides: A retrospective review of filicides in Finland. *Journal of the American Academy of Psychiatry and Law, 38,* 229–238.

Keller, M. C., & Nesse, R. M. (2006). The evolutionary significance of depressive symptoms: Different adverse situations lead to different depressive symptom patterns. *Journal of Personality and Social Psychology, 91,* 316–330.

Kim, J., & Cicchetti, D. (2010). Longitudinal pathways linking child maltreatment, emotion regulation, peer relations, and psychopathology. *The Journal of Child Psychology and Psychiatry, 51,* 706–716.

Kim, J., Cicchetti, D., Rogosch, F. A., & Manly, J. T. (2009). Child maltreatment and trajectories of personality and behavioral functioning: Implications for the development of personality disorder. *Development and Psychopathology, 21,* 889–912.

Kingree, J. B., Phan, D., & Thompson, M. (2003). Child maltreatment and recidivism among adolescent detainees. *Criminal Justice and Behavior, 30,* 623–643.

Kinney, D. K., & Tanaka, M. (2009). An evolutionary hypothesis of depression and its symptoms, adaptive value, and risk factors. *The Journal of Nervous and Mental Disease, 197,* 561–567.

Klevens, J., & Leeb, R. T. (2010). Child maltreatment fatalities in children under 5: Findings from the national violence death reporting system. *Child Abuse and Neglect, 34,* 262–266.

Koenen, M. A., & Thompson, J. W. (2008). Filicide: Historical review and prevention of child death by parent. *Infant Mental Health Journal, 29,* 61–75.

Korbin, J. E., Coulton, C. J., Lindstrom-Ufuti, H., & Spilsbury, J. (2000). Neighborhood views on the definition and etiology of child maltreatment. *Child Abuse and Neglect, 24,* 1509–1527.

Kunz, J., & Bahr, S. J. (1996). A profile of parental homicide against children. *Journal of Family Violence, 11,* 347–362.

Lalumière, M. L., Harris, G. T., Quinsey, V. L., & Rice, M. E. (2005). *The causes of rape: Understanding individual differences in the male propensity for sexual aggression.* Washington, DC: American Psychological Association.

Lalumière, M. L., Harris, G. T., & Rice, M. E. (2001). Psychopathy and developmental instability. *Evolution and Human Behavior, 22,* 75–92.

Lalumière, M. L., Mishra, S., & Harris, G. T. (2008). In cold blood: The evolution of psychopathy. In J. Duntley & T. K. Shackelford (Eds.), *Evolutionary forensic psychology* (pp. 176–197). New York: Oxford University Press.

Lanier, P., Jonson-Reid, M., Stahlschmidt, M. J., Drake, B., & Constantino, J. (2010). Child maltreatment and pediatric health outcomes: A longitudinal study of low-income children. *Journal of Pediatric Psychology, 35,* 511–522.

Lansford, J. E., Dodge, K. A., Pettit, G. S., & Bates, J. E. (2010). Does physical abuse in early childhood predict substance use in adolescence and early adulthood? *Child Maltreatment 15,* 190–194.

Lansford, J. E., Miller-Johnson, S., Berlin, L. J., Dodge, K. A., Bates, J. E., & Pettit, G. S. (2007). Early physical abuse and later violent delinquency: A prospective longitudinal study. *Child Maltreatment, 12,* 233–245.

Lawler, J. J. (2008). Maltreated children's emotional availability with kin and non-kin foster mothers: A sociobiological perspective. *Children and Youth Services Review, 30,* 1131–1143.

Lee, C. K., & Lathrop, S. L. (2010). Child abuse-related homicides in New Mexico: A 6-year retrospective review. *Journal of Forensic Sciences, 55,* 100–103.

Lewis, C. F., Baranoski, M. V., Buchanan, J. A., & Benedek, E. P. (1998). Factors associated with weapon use in maternal filicide. *Journal of Forensic Sciences, 43,* 613–618.

Liem, M., deVet, R., & Koenraadt, F. (2010). Filicide followed by parasuicide: A comparison of suicidal and non-suicidal child homicide. *Child Abuse and Neglect, 34,* 558–562.

Liem, M., & Koenraadt, F. (2008). Filicide: A comparative study of maternal versus paternal child homicide. *Criminal Behaviour and Mental Health, 18,* 166–176.

Lipsey, M. W., Wilson, D. B., & Cothern, L. (2000, April). *Effective intervention for serious juvenile offenders*. Juvenile Justice Bulletin. Washington, DC: US Department of Justice, Office of Justice Programs.

Lord, W. D., Boudreaux, M. C., Jarvis, J. P., Waldvogel, J., & Weeks, H. (2002). Comparative patterns in life course victimization. *Homicide Studies*, 6, 325–347.

Lucas, D. R., Wezner, K. C., Milner, J. S., McCanne, T. R., Harris, I. N., Monroe-Possey, C., & Nelson, J. P. (2002). Victim, perpetrator, family, and incident characteristics of infant and child homicide in the United States Air Force. *Child Abuse and Neglect*, 26, 167–186.

Lyman, J. M., McGwin, G., Malone, D. E., Taylor, A. J., Brissie, R. M., Davis, G., & Rue, L. W., III. (2003). Epidemiology of child homicide in Jefferson County, Alabama. *Child Abuse and Neglect*, 27, 1063–1073.

Lynam, D. R., Caspi, A., Moffit, T. E., Wikström, P., Loeber, R., & Novak, S. (2000). The interaction between impulsivity and neighborhood context on offending: The effects of impulsivity are stronger in poorer neighborhoods. *Journal of Abnormal Psychology*, 109, 563–574.

Manly, J. T., Kim, J. E., Rogosch, A., & Cicchetti, D. (2001). Dimensions of child maltreatment and children's adjustment: Contributions of developmental timing and subtype. *Development and Psychopathology*, 13, 759–782.

Marleau, J., Poulin, B., Webanchk, T., Roy, R., & Laporte, L. (1999). Paternal filicide: A study of 10 men. *Canadian Journal of Psychiatry*, 44, 57–63.

Masterpasqua, F. (2009). Psychology and epigenetics. *Review of General Psychology*, 13, 194–201.

McClain, P. W., Sacks, J. J., Froehlke, R. G., & Ewigman, B. G. (1993). Estimates of fatal child abuse and neglect, United States, 1979 through 1988. *Pediatrics*, 91, 338–343.

McGloin, J. M., & Widom, C. S. (2001). Resilience among abused and neglected children grown up. *Development and Psychopathology*, 13, 1021–1038.

McGowan, P. O., Meaney, M. J., & Szyf, M. (2008). Diet and epigenetic (re)programming of phenotypic differences in behavior. *Brain Research*, 1237, 12–24.

Mealey, L. (1995). The sociobiology of sociopathy: An integrated evolutionary model. *Behavioral and Brain Sciences*, 18, 523–599.

Milner, J. S., & Wimberley, R. C. (1980). Prediction and explanation of child abuse. *Journal of Clinical Psychology*, 36, 875–880.

Mrazek, P. J., & Mrazek, D. A. (1987). Resilience in child maltreatment victims: A conceptual exploration. *Child Abuse and Neglect*, 11, 357–366.

Natsuaki, M. N., Cicchetti, D., & Rogosch, F. A. (2009). Examining the developmental history of child maltreatment, peer relations, and externalizing problems among adolescents with symptoms of paranoid personality disorder. *Development and Psychopathology*, 21, 1181–1193.

Nelson, E. E., Herman, K. N., Barrett, C. E., Noble, P. L., Wojteczko, K., Chisholm, K., … Pine, D. S. (2009). Adverse rearing experiences enhance responding to both aversive and rewarding stimuli in juvenile rhesus monkeys. *Biological Psychiatry*, 66, 702–704.

Nesse, R. M., & Ellsworth, P. C. (2009). Evolution, emotions, and emotional disorders. *American Psychologist*, 64, 129–139.

Nettle, D. (2004). Evolutionary origins of depression: a review and reformulation. *Journal of Affective Disorders*, 81, 91–102.

Neugebauer, R., Hoek, H. W., & Susser, E. (1999). Prenatal exposure to wartime famine and development of antisocial personality disorder in early adulthood. *Journal of the American Medical Association*, 282, 455–462.

Ondersma, S. J., Chaffin, M. J., Mullins, S. M., & LeBreton, J. M. (2005). A brief form of the child abuse potential inventory: Development and validation. *Journal of Clinical Child and Adolescent Psychology*, 34, 301–311.

Pitt, S. E., & Bale, E. M. (1995). Neonaticide, infanticide, and filicide: A review of the literature. *Bulletin of the American Academy of Psychiatry and Law*, 23, 375–385.

Porter, T., & Gavin, H. (2010). Infanticide and neonaticide: A review of 40 years of research literature on incidence and causes. *Trauma, Violence, and Abuse*, 11, 99–112.

Price, J. S., Gardner, R., Wilson, D. R., Sloman, L., Rohde, P., & Erickson, M. (2007). Territory, rank and mental health: The history of an idea. *Evolutionary Psychology*, 5, 531–554.

Pritchard, C., & Butler, A. (2003). A comparative study of children and adult homicide rates in the USA and the major western countries 1974–1999: Grounds for concern? *Journal of Family Violence*, 18, 341–350.

Quinsey, V. L., Harris, G. T., Rice, M. E., & Cormier, C. A. (2006). *Violent offenders: Appraising and managing risk* (2nd ed.). Washington, DC: American Psychological Association.

Resnick, P. J. (1969). Child murder by parents: A psychiatric review of filicide. *American Journal of Psychiatry*, 126, 73–82.

Rice, M. E., & Harris, G. T. (1997). Treatment of adult offenders. In D. Stoff, J. Breiling, & J. D. Maser (Eds.), *Handbook of antisocial behavior* (pp. 425–435). New York: Wiley.

Rice, M.E., & Harris, G.T. (in press). Psychopathy and violent recidivism. In K.A. Kiehl & W. Sinnott-Armstrong (Eds.) *Handbook on psychopathy and law*. New York: Oxford University Press.

Scrimshaw, S. C. M. (1984). Infanticide in human populations: Societal and individual concerns. In G. Hausfater & S. Blaffer Hrdy (Eds.), *Infanticide* (pp. 439–502). Hawthorne, NY: Aldine de Gruyter.

Senn, T. E., & Carey, M. P. (2010). Child maltreatment and women's adult sexual risk behavior: Childhood sexual abuse as a unique risk factor. *Child Maltreatment*, 15, 324–335.

Serin, R. C. (1991). Psychopathy and violence in criminals. *Journal of Interpersonal Violence*, 6, 423–431.

Shackelford, T. K., Weekes-Shackelford, V. A., & Schmitt, D. P. (2005). An evolutionary perspective on why some men refuse or reduce their child support payments. *Basic and Applied Social Psychology*, 27, 297–306.

Silverman, R. A., & Kennedy, L. W. (1988). Women who kill their children. *Violence and Victims*, 3, 113–127.

Slep, A. M., & O'Leary, S. G. (2005). Parent and partner violence in families with young children: Rates, patterns, and connections. *Journal of Consulting and Clinical Psychology*, 73, 435–444.

Sloman, L. (2008). A new comprehensive evolutionary model of depression and anxiety. *Journal of Affective Disorders*, 106, 219–228.

Smith, C., & Thornberry, T. P. (1995). The relationship between childhood maltreatment and adolescent involvement in delinquency. *Criminology*, 33, 451–481.

Smithey, M. (1998). Infant homicide: Victim/offender relationship and causes of death. *Journal of Family Violence*, 13, 285–297.

Somander, L. K., & Rammer, L. M. (1991). Intra- and extrafamilial child homicide in Sweden 1971–1980. *Child Abuse and Neglect, 15,* 45–55.

Stanton, J., & Simpson, A. (2002). Filicide: A review. *International Journal of Law and Psychiatry, 25,* 1–14.

Stein, J. A., Leslie, M. B., & Nyamathi, A. (2002). Relative contributions of parent substance use and childhood maltreatment to chromic homelessness, depression, and substance abuse problems among homeless women: Mediating roles of self-esteem and abuse in adulthood. *Child Abuse and Neglect, 26,* 1011–1027.

Stiffman, M. N., Schnitzer, P. G., Adam, P., Kruse, R. L., & Ewigman, B. G. (2002). Household composition and risk of fatal child maltreatment. *Pediatrics, 109,* 615–621.

Stouthamer-Loeber, M., Loeber, R., Homish, D. L., & Wei, E. (2001). Maltreatment of boys and the development of disruptive and delinquent behavior. *Development and Psychopathology, 13,* 941–955.

Strang, H. (1996). Children as victims of homicide. *Australian Institute of Criminology, 53,* 1–6.

Stroud, J. (1996). Mental disorder and the homicide of children: A review. *Social Work and Social Sciences Review, 6,* 149–162.

Stroud, J., & Pritchard, C. (2001). Child homicide: Psychiatric disorder and dangerousness: A review and an empirical approach. *British Journal of Social Work, 31,* 249–269.

Szyf, M., McGowan, P., & Meaney, M. J. (2008). The social environment and the epigenome. *Environmental and Molecular Mutagenesis, 49,* 46–60.

Temrin, H., Nordlund, J., & Sterner, H. (2004). Are stepchildren over-represented as victims of lethal parental violence in Sweden? *Proceedings of the Royal Society of London, 271,* S124–S126.

Tooley, G. A., Karakis, M., Stokes, M., & Ozanne-Smith, J. (2006). Generalising the Cinderella effect to unintentional childhood fatalities. *Evolution and Human Behavior, 27,* 224–230.

Topitzes, J., Mersky, J. P., & Reynolds, A. J. (2009). Child maltreatment and adult cigarette smoking: A long-term developmental model. *Journal of Pediatric Psychology, 35,* 484–498.

Trivers, R. L. (1972). Parental investment and sexual selection. In B. Campbell (Ed.), *Sexual selection and the descent of man* (pp. 139–179). Chicago: Aldine.

Tuteur, W., & Glotzer, J. (1959). Murdering mothers. *American Journal of Psychiatry, 116,* 447–452.

Tyrka, A. R., Price, L. H., Gelernter, J., Schepker, C., Anderson, G. M., & Carpenter, L. L. (2009). Interaction of childhood maltreatment with the corticotrophin-releasing hormone receptor gene: Effects on hypothalamic-pituitary-adrenal axis reactivity. *Biological Psychiatry, 66,* 681–685.

van Harmelen, A. L., deJong, P. J., Glashouwer, K. A., Spinhoven, P., Penninx, B. W., & Elzinga, B. M. (2010). Child abuse and negative explicit and automatic self-associations: The cognitive scars of emotional maltreatment. *Behaviour Research and Therapy, 48,* 486–494.

van Schaik, C. P., & Janson, C. H. (2000). *Infanticide by males and its implications.* Cambridge, England: Cambridge University Press.

Veltman, M. W., & Browne, K. D. (2001). Three decades of child maltreatment research: Implications for the school years. *Trauma, Violence, and Abuse, 2,* 215–239.

Wakefield, J. C. (1992). Disorder as harmful dysfunction: A conceptual critique of DSM-III-R's definition of mental disorder. *Psychological, 99,* 232–247.

Walsh, W. A., Dawson, J., & Mattingly, M. J. (2010). How are we measuring resilience following childhood maltreatment? Is the research adequate and consistent? What is the impact on research, practice, and policy? *Trauma, Violence, and Abuse, 11,* 27–41.

Weekes-Shackelford, V. A., & Shackelford, T. K. (2004). Methods of filicide: Stepparents and genetic parents kill differently. *Violence and Victims, 19,* 75–81.

White, H. R., & Widom, C. S. (2003). Does childhood victimization increase the risk of early death? A 25-year prospective study. *Child Abuse and Neglect, 27,* 841–853.

Wilczynski, A. (1995). Child killing by parents: A motivational model. *Child Abuse Review, 4,* 365–370.

Wilczynski, A. (1997). Prior agency contact and physical abuse in cases of child homicide. *British Journal of Social Work, 27,* 241–253.

Williamson, S., Hare, R. D., & Wong, S. (1987). Violence: Criminal psychopaths and their victims. *Canadian Journal of Behavioural Science, 19,* 454–462.

Wilson, H. W., & Widom, C. S. (2008). An examination of risky sexual behavior and HIV in victims of child abuse and neglect: A 30-year follow-up. *Health Psychology, 27,* 149–158.

Wilson, M., Daly, M., & Daniele, A. (1995). Familicide: The killing of spouse and children. *Aggressive Behavior, 21,* 275–291.

Wilson, M. I., Daly, M., & Weghorst, S. J. (1980). Household composition and the risk of child abuse and neglect. *Journal of Biosocial Science, 12,* 333–340.

Wilson, S. J., & Lipsey, M. W. (2007). School-based interventions for aggressive and disruptive behavior: Update of a meta-analysis. *American Journal of Preventative Medicine, 33,* S130–S143.

Wingo, A. P., Wrenn, G., Pelletier, T., Gutman, A. R., Bradley, B., & Ressler, K. J. (2010). Moderating effects of resilience on depression in individuals with a history of childhood abuse or trauma exposure. *Journal of Affective Disorders, 126,* 411–414.

Xie, L., & Yamagami, A. (1995). How much of the child murder in Japan is caused by mentally disordered mothers? *International Medical Journal, 2,* 309–313.

Zielinski, D. S. (2009). Child maltreatment and adult socioeconomic well-being. *Child Abuse and Neglect, 33,* 666–678.

CHAPTER 7

Siblicide in Humans and Other Species

Catherine Salmon

Abstract

Sibling conflict is common across a wide variety of species, including humans. It is an expected process because offspring compete for dominance as well as food resources (most common in nonhuman species) and also for parental attention, money, and other personal resources in the case of human children. While most conflict in humans has no long lasting effects, under some circumstances, sibling conflict can turn violent and even result in death, what is commonly referred to as siblicide. While siblicide is quite rare in humans, from an evolutionary perspective, we would expect it to be influenced by some of the same factors as less intense sibling conflict. Such factors include sex of sibling, resource availability, birth spacing, and relatedness. These factors will be discussed with respect to research on sibling conflict and siblicide in human and nonhuman species.

Key Words: parental investment, sibling conflict, parent–offspring conflict, primogeniture

For he today that sheds his blood with me, Shall be my brother.
—*Henry V* (4:3)

And Cain talked with Abel his brother and it came to pass, when they were in the field, that Cain rose up against Abel his brother, and slew him.
—*Genesis* 4:8

There is no friend like a brother: there is also no enemy like a brother.
—*Bengali* proverb

Introduction

How do we reconcile the preceding quotes, each touching on the nature of brotherhood? The first, the band of brothers speech from *Henry V*, emphasizes the shared interests of siblings, implying that one brother's best interests are those of his siblings as well. Here brothers are a united front. And yet in the passage from Genesis, one brother kills another; clearly Cain did not care about his brother's interests at all, only himself. A united front or deadly enemies—what factors influence how sibling relations play out? This chapter will explore the root causes of sibling unity and conflict, both in other species and in humans. In particular, I will focus on the circumstances that can lead to siblicide, the most extreme outcome of sibling competition.

Siblicide is the killing of one sibling by another and includes both fratricide (the killing of one's brother) and sororicide (the killing of one's sister). Sibling violence is the most frequent type of familial nonlethal violence (Wiehe, 1997). But siblicides themselves are relatively rare and, as a result, infrequently studied. The majority of research attention on familial homicide has focused on spousal violence and homicide and child abuse and infanticide. Siblicide accounts for approximately 1% of homicides in the United States and 7.6% of familial homicides (Underwood & Patch, 1999), while in Canada, siblicides account for around 2% of familial homicides (Statistics Canada, 2004).

As the second quote illustrates, historical data and fictional stories (e.g., Sultan Mehmet II of the Ottoman empire who imprisoned his brothers and then killed them all once he had produced an heir; Cain who slew his brother Abel after God preferred Abel's animal offerings to Cain's crops; and Romulus and Remus, twins born of a human and a god who founded Rome— Romulus killed Remus in a dispute over where to build the city) have illustrated siblicidal conflict, despite the fact that the majority of family violence and homicide research has largely ignored it. When sibling conflict is examined in humans, it is mostly of the nonlethal variety, which of course is also more common.

Evolutionary perspectives have been productively applied to the study of homicide in a variety of contexts, including spousal homicide (Daly & Wilson, 1988; Wilson & Daly, 2004), infanticide (Daly & Wilson, 1984, 1994), male-male conflicts (Daly & Wilson, 1988; Daly, Wilson, & Vasdev, 2001; Duntley & Buss, 2005), and siblicide (Daly, Wilson, Salmon, Hiraiwa-Hasegawa, & Hasegawa, 2001; Michalski, Russell, Shackelford, & Weekes-Shackelford, 2007). It has also been applied to the study of many accounts of siblicide in a variety of other species. In the rest of this chapter, I open with a discussion of an evolutionary perspective on sibling conflict, followed by a discussion of siblicide in several other animal species before turning to our own.

Sibling Conflict Theory

Sibling relationships are some of the most long-lasting in our human lives. But in both humans and other animals, siblings present the potential for great solidarity and great strife. Aspects of our personalities are shaped by the presence of siblings. Frank Sulloway (1996, 2007; Sulloway & Zweigenhaft, 2010), among others (Salmon, 1999, 2003), have elegantly outlined the ways in which birth order (your position in your sibship) influences differences in a variety of traits, including the "Big Five" personality dimensions (extraversion, conscientiousness, agreeableness, openness, and neuroticism). While the quote from *Henry V* illustrates the solidarity of brothers, the shared interests, the biblical tale referenced is one of conflict over, at its heart, "parental" investment.

At the core of Hamilton's (1964) inclusive fitness theory is the idea that kin are valuable, that they share a commonality of interest. From this perspective, natural selection favors not only traits that promote individual survival and reproduction but also traits that increase the reproductive success of one's kin. In a genetic sense, what enhances the fitness of one's kin enhances one's own inclusive fitness. And the more closely related two kin are, the more common their genetic cause. But an inherent property of social behavior is that the interests of interacting individuals invariably conflict to some degree. Each individual behaves so as to increase its own inclusive fitness, even when it reduces the inclusive fitness of others. Social interactions inevitably entail competition, even during cooperative interactions. The interaction between parents and offspring involves a high level of cooperation but is not free of conflict. They have a shared objective in the enhancement of offspring survival, but they may disagree on how important individual offspring are relative to other options. Likewise, siblings disagree over how important each other is and the optimal allocation of parental resources.

Being closely related does not mean that one's interests are identical. As much as the degree of genetic similarity is a source of common interests, the degree of genetic nonidentity can raise the potential for conflict. This becomes obvious when individuals are competing for some scarce resource such as mates, food, or territory. But such conflicts can also be acted out in cooperative ventures, including those between parent and offspring, since they are not genetically identical (Trivers, 1974), despite offspring being the vehicles of their parents' fitness. This also applies to siblings, who share a common genetic heritage but who are not genetically identical (except in the case of identical twins; for a discussion of their unique closeness, see Segal, 2005).

Parent–offspring conflict can arise because some actions that advance the fitness of an offspring can potentially reduce the lifetime success of the parent and vice versa. Siblicide in some seabirds illustrates this conflict and how it plays out in two closely related species. Siblicide is common in some boobies, colonially nesting seabirds. Typically, the older, or "A," chick disposes of its younger "B" chick sibling within the first few days after it hatches. Forced out of the nest, the younger, smaller chick will die of exposure or starvation. Masked booby (*Sula dactylatra*) parents tolerate siblicide, presumably either because they are unable to prevent it or because it is in the best interests of the parents themselves as well as the surviving "A" chick. However, there is much less siblicide in the blue-footed booby (*Sula nebouxii*), which could be due to differences in chick or parent behavior. In fact, when blue-footed booby chicks are placed in a masked booby nest, the "A" chick will kill its sibling (Lougheed & Anderson, 1999). However, when masked chicks are placed in a blue-footed nest, the foster parents seem to prevent siblicide from occurring (presumably because in this species, the benefits to parents of having both chicks survive outweighs the cost to the A chick, from the parental fitness perspective).

In general, we expect parents to allocate their parental investment among their offspring in ways that optimize their own inclusive fitness. All other things equal (no misattributed paternity, etc.), parents are equally related to all their offspring. However, we expect offspring to have a somewhat different take on that matter. They are more closely related to themselves than to their siblings (Trivers, 1974). As a result, we might expect each offspring to want to extract more than its share of parental investment. Conflicts arise over the level of investment each party considers is appropriate. One result is parent–offspring conflict. Another is sibling conflict. Parent–offspring conflict theory (Salmon, 2007; Trivers, 1974) predicts that offspring will covet more resources for themselves from parents than parents are willing to give and that parents will encourage offspring to value their siblings more than the siblings will be naturally inclined to value each other. Siblings are each other's primary competitors for parental resources and, as a result, mechanisms have been selected in offspring that increase investment in themselves relative to their siblings. Siblicide can be seen as an infrequent outcome of this process in humans. However, in other species, it is much more common.

Sibling Competition in Nonhumans

Sibling competition in nonhumans plays out in various ways. Before discussing its most extreme form, siblicide, it is useful to look at several examples of how nonlethal sibling conflict plays out. Based on inclusive fitness theory, we expect greater levels of conflict between nonkin than between kin over resources such as food or territory and perhaps greater conflict between more distant kin than close kin. One study that examined the impact of kinship on reducing levels of aggression investigated territorial aggression in female Belding's ground squirrels (*S. beldingi*). Female ground squirrels tend to live close to their natal burrow so that sisters often hold adjacent territories. Holmes and Sherman (1982) found that half-sisters exhibited more aggression toward each other than did full siblings and were also less likely to help defend one another's burrow from nonkin, even though they shared the same natal nest (same mother). Full sisters are more cooperative and less antagonistic than half-sisters.

Scramble competition between siblings also occurs in many mammals over access to milk. In guinea pigs (*Cavia aperea f. porcellus*), the number of offspring influences this competition. When litters are manipulated to have more or fewer offspring (Fey & Trillmich, 2008), the pups from larger litters had lower growth rates due to competition for milk, and they had to wait longer for access to teats. Aggression toward siblings was seen only in the larger litters.

Such competition for milk also occurs in domestic pigs. Piglets compete directly for access to the sow's teats and, in fact, the piglets' dentition is specialized to facilitate aggressive attacks on each other. Sometimes low birth weight piglets die as a result of this competition. Piglets also compete indirectly for milk, by stimulating milk production at the teats that they habitually use, with the result being less milk production by other teats (Drake, Fraser, & Weary, 2008). Food shortages increase the intensity of the aggressive competition.

Siblicide in many species is the result of acute resource shortages resulting in extreme levels of sibling competition. Both the degree of relatedness between offspring and the impact of such intense competition on parental fitness can influence the final outcome. Researchers also distinguish between species in which aggression between siblings is almost always fatal to subordinates (obligate siblicide) and those in which the consequences of aggression are highly variable, influenced by environmental conditions (facultative siblicide).

One might ask, "Why do parents produce more offspring than they are able to raise?" There are several ways in which overproduction can result in increased parental fitness. "Overproduction allows: (1) efficient 'resource-tracking' (where the extra offspring actually turn out to be affordable because of an unpredictable upswing in ecological conditions); (2) the possibility of 'sibling facilitation' (e.g. some offspring serving as helpers or critical meals for others); and/or (3) the use of extras as 'replacement offspring' when one or more members of the core brood proves defective or happens to die" (Mock & Parker, 1998, p. 2). Parents may also be able to care for all offspring but choose to keep some resources in reserve for other uses, including future reproductive opportunities (Williams, 1966). There are also cases in which parents not only do not prevent siblicide but may also facilitate brood reduction through asynchronous hatching, selective care of offspring, or infanticide (St Clair, Waas, St Clair, & Boag, 1995). Some researchers have suggested that we should expect obligate siblicide or aggression to evolve where resources are routinely limited and siblings can present a serious resource threat, while facultative siblicide will evolve in circumstances in which resources are not always limited (Mock, Drummond, & Stinson, 1990). In the first case, the extra sibling can serve as a replacement if the first one dies; in the second case, the extra sibling will survive and contribute to parental and sibling fitness when conditions are good.

Studies of Siblicide in Nonhumans

There are numerous studies of siblicide and sibling aggression in a variety of species, many of them avian. In many animal species, parents produce more offspring than they can actually afford to raise (Mock & Parker, 1998). In most species, brood reduction occurs through differential starvation. In other cases, brood reduction takes place by siblicide, the elder "A" chick either killing its younger "B" sibling directly or ejecting it from the nest. The assumption is that food availability is the resource that drives the conflict. Much of the sibling aggression research has been focused on bird species for a variety of reasons, including the fact that nestmates are in a small confined area, dependent on parents delivering packets of food that are often easily quantified, and their nests are often in places that make them observable (albeit with the aid of blinds, in many cases).

Kittiwakes

There have been a number of studies testing the food amount hypothesis (FAH), which suggests that sibling aggression is negatively correlated with the amount of food given to the aggressor (Mock, 1987). Field studies have provided supporting evidence in a number of species (including cattle egrets, discussed later), and experimental evidence is accumulating in facultative species such as osprey (Machmer & Ydenberg, 1998) and the black-legged kittiwake.

A study testing the FAH in black-legged kittiwakes was conducted at a colony nesting on an island in the Gulf of Alaska. The amount of food available to the parents over the season was manipulated as part of a large-scale food supplementation project designed to study the impact of food supply on kittiwake breeding. Breeding pairs raising two chicks were split into two groups, one that was given supplemental food (fish, their natural prey) and one that was not. Supplemental feeding began about a month before hatching and ceased when most chicks had fledged. This population had been experiencing a long-term food shortage.

The "A" chicks were fed significantly more by the fed parents than by the unfed parents and gained significantly more weight. There was no significant difference in the feeding rate of the "B" chicks. The "A" chicks in both groups became less aggressive over time, but the "A" chicks in the fed group were significantly less aggressive both in terms of frequency and intensity than those in the unfed group (White et al., 2010). This experimental result echoes the observations made in the field that chick aggression is higher in years of food shortages (Irons, 1992) and also provides evidence for the adaptive nature of sibling aggression.

Boobies

A variety of species of boobies have been examined with regard to siblicide. I will briefly discuss two examples. The Nazca booby (*Sula granli*), a seabird, fledges a maximum of one nestling regardless of the clutch size. The elder chick always eliminates its younger rival. As such, this is an obligate siblicidal species (Anderson, 1990). The Insurance Egg Hypothesis has been advanced as an explanation for the fact that more eggs, typically two, are laid, while only one survives to fledge. The idea behind this surplus production of offspring is that the second egg can serve as a replacement, or insurance, in case the first egg fails to hatch or the first chick dies soon after hatching. In other words, booby parents who produce two eggs will have greater reproductive success than those that lay just the one egg.

This hypothesis was tested by Clifford and Anderson (2000) by manipulating the clutch sizes of parents. They enlarged natural one-egg clutches to two-egg clutches and found that the parents produced more hatchlings and fledglings than control one-egg clutches. They also took natural two-egg clutches and reduced them to one-egg clutches and found that the parents produced fewer hatchlings and fledglings than the control two-egg clutches. So there clearly was an insurance benefit to the two-egg clutch size, with higher parental reproductive success. One might then ask, "Why do all the natural clutches not consist of two eggs?" The most likely answer is a proximate one. Parents who are limited in terms of food availability or their own resources are only able to produce the one egg.

Interestingly, some studies have looked at the mechanisms that may facilitate obligate versus facultative siblicide. Muller and colleagues (2008) examined perinatal androgen levels in two species of booby, the previously mentioned obligate Nazca and the facultative blue-footed booby (*Sula nebouxii*), which, unlike the Nazca, often raises more than one chick. Blue-footed boobies will preferentially feed the largest chick if there is a shortage of food, but the patterns of chick aggression are quite different. The Nazca elder chick unconditionally attacks its smaller sibling and will eject it from the nest. Blue-footed chicks do exhibit aggression, but it is conditional on food availability, is concentrated in attempts to get (or prevent a sibling from getting) whatever food is available, and typically occurs much later in the nesting period. Muller and his colleagues found that Nazca chicks hatch with higher circulating androgen levels than the facultative blue-footed chicks. As I will discuss later, androgens are also associated with the high degree of sibling aggression in hyenas.

Black Eagles

The black eagle (*Aquila verreauxi*) is found in the mountains of southern and northeastern Africa as well as parts of the Middle East. They build their nests on cliff ledges and lay two eggs, which hatch asynchronously about 3 days apart. As a result, the "A" chick is larger, typically attacking the "B" chick from the day it hatches. The chicks have very sharp beaks and will peck at each other, the older one often keeping the smaller away from food until it withers and dies. It is very rare for more than one chick to fledge from the nest (Simmons, 1988), with most evidence supporting the insurance policy theory for overproduction. If the A chick survives, the B chick will die. Thus, this is a species with obligate siblicide.

Cattle Egrets

The widespread cattle egret (*Bubulcus ibis*) is a type of heron that, unlike most herons, typically feeds in fields and dry grassy habitats. Their clutch size can be one to five eggs, but three is typical. Most often, the third and fourth chicks do not survive and broods are characterized by intense sibling rivalry. In a brood of three, the "A," "B," and "C" chicks will hatch asynchronously, again giving the "A" chick the size advantage. The "A" chick usually wins a few early fights and then sits back to enjoy its dominant position, getting first grab at any food delivered. The "C" chick gets about half the food of its older siblings and loses the majority of fights to the "B" chick. When very young, the pecks do not inflict much physical damage but as they get larger, they raise their heads up and drive down, drawing blood. Eventually the "C" chick concedes by lowering its head (a disadvantage when food comes from the beak of a parent above). The "C" chick loses weight and strength in the absence of enough food (which is monopolized by the "A" and "B" chicks; fighting is most intense when food is arriving). By their third week, one-third to one-half of the "C" chicks have died (Mock, 2004). In those nests where a senior chick is lost (due to defect, disease, predation, etc.), the "C" chick is more likely to survive to fledge.

Laughing Kookaburras

The laughing kookaburra (*Dacelo novaeguineae*) is an Australian cooperatively breeding species, a member of the kingfisher family. They are carnivorous and live in forested areas. They live in a type of family group with a monogamous pair breeding, supported by older offspring. They typically lay three eggs at 2-day intervals, which then hatch asynchronously, again giving an advantage to the older, larger chick. The chicks have a hooked bill (the hook disappearing by the time they fledge), which they use in competition with their nestmates to grasp and shake their opponent. Such competition is very common when the food supply is not sufficient and there is typically a wave of "C" chick deaths in their first week (due to physical damage). A week or two later another wave of deaths often occurs with less visible injuries, usually due to starvation (Legge, 2000; Legge & Cockburn, 2000).

Spotted Hyenas

As one of the few mammals in which siblicide has been documented, the spotted hyena (*Crocuta crocuta*) has been the focus on much attention, some of it focused on whether siblicide in this species is obligate or facultative. Early studies suggested that siblicide siblings kill approximately one-quarter of cubs, half of those born to same-sex litters (Frank, Glickman, & Licht, 1991). Spotted hyenas are found in sub-Saharan Africa and the cubs are born in underground dens. The species is also well known for the strong degree to which the females are masculinized, both anatomically and behaviorally, by exposure to high levels of androgens during development. These elevated androgen levels are also seen in neonates. The cubs show precocial motor development, their eyes are open, and they have fully erupted front teeth at birth. These teeth are used to bite and shake their sibling competitors. Typically, spotted hyenas give birth to pairs of cubs, who fight most aggressively during the 48 hours right after birth (Frank et al., 1991; Smale, Holekamp, Weldele, Frank, & Glickman, 1995). Dominance is clearly established and in same-sex litters the subordinate offspring may perish. In mixed-sex litters, both usually survive. When three cubs are born, the third almost always perishes. Initially, the suggestion was that this was obligate siblicide, but more recent evidence of wild and captive populations suggests that it is more likely facultative siblicide (Smale, Holekamp, & White, 1999; Wahaj, Place, Weldele, Glickman, & Holekamp, 2007). The early aggression to establish dominance will have detrimental consequences for the subordinate cub if resources are insufficient, because the dominant cub is likely to monopolize the food supply.

Galapagos Fur Seals

The Galapagos fur seal (*Arctocephalus galapagooensis*) is another species, like the hyena, with high resource uncertainty. They also wean late and as a result often have overlapping successive young. In fact, 5% to 23% of pups (the range varies by year) are born while the older sibling is still being nursed. These younger siblings are also born at a lower weight than those without older and still dependent siblings and grow less and suffer higher early mortality. Many of these siblings will also be half-siblings rather than full siblings, sharing a mother but with different sires. Approximately half the older siblings will harass the younger one, biting them and/or chasing them away from the mother (Trillmich & Wolf, 2008). Most mothers interfere in such conflicts, using threats or biting the older offspring to get it to leave the younger offspring alone. But even in the absence of direct attacks, scramble competition for milk can be lethal, with the older pup leaving little milk for the younger pup after it has finished sucking.

Meerkats

Unlike the previously mentioned species, meerkats (*Suricata suricatta*) are not siblicidal. But as juveniles, they do commonly engage in aggression between littermates that can be fierce, though rarely resulting in serious injury and never lethal (Hodge, Flower, & Clutton-Brock, 2007). The factors that influence aggression in this species are informative for understanding human sibling conflict, in turn.

In meerkats, reproduction is largely monopolized by one female in each group. She will average three to four litters of pups per year, and those litters will consist of an average of four pups, though there can be as few as one and as many as seven (Hodge, Manica, Flower, & Clutton-Brock, 2008). Initially, the pups are fed in their burrows, but as they get older, they will travel with the adults in the group, begging for food from helpers. Meerkats are cooperative breeders with nonreproductive adults helping to feed and protect offspring. A pup in close proximity to a helper will benefit if there are no other pups around, as the helpers typically feed whichever begging pup is closest. As a result, pups try to defend access to their helper and will attack littermates who approach them. Typically a few snaps and lunges will drive another pup off, but occasionally fights occur and the loser will retreat.

In this system, aggression between littermates increases when rain and helper number are low, as both of these factors influence food availability for the pups. Hodge and colleagues (2008) examined the role of food availability on sibling aggression via short-term feeding experiments in which they decreased a pup's hunger by provisioning with a small amount of food before a foraging excursion. Pups that had been fed exhibited less aggression during foraging/begging than the unfed control pups. This sibling conflict over resources is echoed in cases of sibling conflict in humans (see later). And as in meerkats, most human sibling conflict happens as juveniles and dissipates over time. Occasionally, however, unlike the meerkats, it can explode into violence and death, more often in the case of adults.

Sibling Conflict in Humans

In most nonhuman animal species, we see at the heart of sibling conflict, whether mild aggression or siblicide, conflict over resources, especially food. Sibling conflict in humans is also over resources in the form of parental investment (which could involve food and shelter in the ancestral past and in most Western societies today involves time/attention and money). However, there are several relevant differences between humans and many nonhuman species. Humans generally have one offspring at a time, so it is not quite the same as having several chicks/pups to feed at one time, unless one has twins. On the other hand, human offspring stay at "the nest" for a longer period of time and so parents typically do have to juggle the needs and demands of several children at once. Having children closely spaced in age seems to increase the degree of sibling conflict, especially when they are of the same sex (Sulloway, 1996). While animal parents often seem to ignore sibling aggression, human parents often vigorously discourage it and try to convince their children to value each other more highly than they seem inclined to value each other. Interestingly, when it comes to siblicide, in animals this happens when offspring are extremely young, for example, in nestlings. In humans, siblicide is more frequent among adults, though it is quite rare in either case.

Although siblicide in humans is rare, sibling aggression is the most frequent form of nonlethal familial violence (Wiehe, 1997). While siblings can be our playmates and companions, an essential part of our socialization, they can also be our competitors for limited parental time and attention. Differential parental investment is associated with higher levels of conflict between siblings (Brody, Stoneman, & Burke, 1987). Cicirelli (1995) also notes that siblings whose ages differ by less than 2 years quarrel more as coresiding children than those whose ages differ more, because those close in age tend to share similar needs. While baby animals fight to establish dominance or gain access to scarce food resources, human children tend to fight not only over who gets the bigger piece of cake but also over what they will watch on television, what they will play on the Wii, who takes out the garbage, and who mom loves best.

Studies that examine children's perceptions of conflict with their siblings yield interesting results. One study of sibling pairs (average ages 11 years and 8 years) reported that disagreements and conflict focused on the sharing of personal possessions (e.g., a bike) and physical aggression (e.g., hitting, biting, throwing things) rather than parental favoritism. The majority of conflicts ended with parental intervention (McGuire, Manke, Eftekhari, & Dunn, 2000). Older children also tend to dominate and win many of these early conflicts (Ross, Filyer, Lollis, Perlman, & Martin, 1994). While the majority of these conflicts are often seen as minor, a national study of family violence (Straus, Gelles, & Steinmetz, 2006) reported that 74% of children had pushed or shoved a sibling and 42% had kicked, bitten, or punched a sibling. As the feelings that siblings develop toward one another in childhood can persist into adulthood (Ross & Milgram, 1982), it should not be surprising that some early conflicts (though certainly not all) fail to dissipate when children grow up and leave the home, and that more extreme sibling violence is more typically seen in adults than in children.

Siblicide in Humans

Early research into the causes of homicide focused on the role of proximity, the idea that those who are in frequent contact have the opportunity and perhaps the motivation (arguments, etc.) for murder. In many cultures, there are myths and stories about familial homicide, with fratricide being a common theme. And yet kin are killed much less frequently than "acquaintances" or strangers. In a report of closed case Detroit homicides during 1972, in which the relationship between victim and offender was known, 47.8% were unrelated acquaintances, 27.2% were strangers, and 25.0% were relatives (Daly & Wilson, 1982). However, most of the murdered relatives were spouses (and thus not genetically related). Just 1.9% of the total homicides were siblicides. More recent reports give similar figures—around 1% of homicides in the United States involve siblings (Underwood & Patch, 1999). This is quite a low number when we consider how much time siblings spend together.

There is, in fact, a surprising lack of research on siblicide in humans. Or perhaps this is not so surprising, considering the relatively few homicides there are and then again the small number that involve brothers and the even smaller number that involve sisters. But if siblicide is the extreme end of the sibling rivalry continuum, it is worth considering what researchers have discovered by examining the data that do exist.

An excellent anthropological source of information can be found in Elwin's (1950) account of homicide in the Bison Horn Maria of India between 1920 and 1941. This population at the time was living a traditional slash-and-burn horticulture existence with a patrilineal descent system. Men purchased their wives with the help of their kinsmen and could have more than one wife. This is rather different from the Detroit population previously discussed, and there is another difference in addition to lifestyle. In the Bison Horn Maria, 31.8% of homicide victims were killed by blood relatives. While some of this could be due to access to kin, in such traditional patrilineal societies most men interact mainly with their own relatives, and sibling rivalry is likely to be an important context for homicide. Because land and other resources are held by families, brothers and other kin are not only your support, they are also your competition for control of those resources. At the root of the fatal disputes between genetic kin was conflict over control of familial property. An illustrative example is reported from Elwin by Daly and Wilson (1988):

> Upon their father's death, the elder Buti had inherited the family farm. Like many a disenfranchised younger brother throughout human history, Chule left home to seek his fortune. He did not find it, and so, after several years, the prodigal Chule returned to his father's land, there to rent a plot from his brother and farm it. So he did, but only for one year. When the lease came up for renewal, Buti at first doubled the rent, and then reneged on the agreement altogether, in order to bestow the land on a third brother. Defeated, Chule again moved away, but on a return visit to collect his possessions, he was confronted by Buti brandishing a knife. To be thus run off his natal farm was too much for the propertyless Chule, whose resentment at last exploded. Close at hand was an ax.
>
> (pp. 29–30)

Conflicts between brothers like this one would be quite unlikely in foraging societies in which there is little property to hold onto and defend and in which your kin are your most valuable asset. But in a situation like Buti and Chule's, extreme conflict is much more likely, because land is typically not seen as property that is divisible (at some point it becomes too small to be useful when divided). In many agricultural societies, one brother will get the farm and the rest have to fend for themselves. In such cases, other, typically younger brothers, will come into conflict over the property or the elder brother's authority over it and them. In fact, feudal societies, in which kin are not a significant source of power or resources, are characterized by fraternal violence in royal lineages as brotherly affections are swamped by the opportunity to rule (Goody, 1966), such as when Aethelred became King of Saxon Britain by murdering his older half-brother Edward.

Are Some Individual Humans More Likely to Kill Siblings Than Others?

There are several factors that an evolutionary-minded thinker might expect to influence the answer to this question. They include gender, birth order, and relatedness (e.g., Is this a full sibling or half-sibling?). There are also possible proximate influences such as substance abuse, poverty, social disorganization, and mental illness (Diem & Pizarro, 2010), but here I focus on the evolutionary or ultimate influences.

The issue of gender (male, female) is straightforward. Men (especially young men) are far more likely to commit homicides overall in comparison to women (Daly & Wilson, 1988). One would expect same-sex sibling rivalry (a more direct competition for the same resources and attention when close in age) to be more intense than the rivalry between brother and sister. The authority and favored status of an eldest boy may also be a particular source of frustration and resentment to younger brothers in comparison to sisters. In fact, the majority of siblicides are committed by males against a brother. This was true in the Detroit sample discussed in Daly and Wilson (1982), as well as in several other US and Canadian samples (Gebo, 2002; Marleau & Saucier, 1998; Underwood & Patch, 1999): 73.0%–87.7% of siblicides involved pairs of brothers.

Sulloway (1996), in his book *Born to Rebel*, suggested that birth order might play a role in siblicidal conflict. This was based on the following Darwinian reasoning:

> Because firstborns tend to reproduce first, later-borns have more to lose by committing homicide against an older sibling. A younger sibling's inclusive fitness will be enhanced by any offspring produced by older siblings. If a younger sibling kills an older sibling, this act may endanger the survival prospects of nieces and nephews already born to the older sibling. If there is a difference in fratricide rates by birth order, the prediction must be that firstborns are more fratricidal.
>
> (p. 437)

Marleau and Saucier (1998) used Statistics Canada's database of homicides known to Canadian police to test Sulloway's prediction and found disconfirming evidence. In their sample, the offender was the younger of the two siblings in 56% of the cases, a slight difference. This means firstborns are not disproportionally the killers. However, their data did not answer questions about whether pubertal status plays a role, whether the age spacing between siblings is important, or whether specific birth order (first, middle, last) might be a more relevant factor. Daly, Wilson, Salmon, Hiraiwa-Hasegawa, and Hasegawa (2001) attempted to examine some of these other factors by analyzing national homicide data from Canada, Great Britain, and Japan, as well as city-level data from Chicago. Overall, there was a slightly greater likelihood for the killer to be the younger sibling, 55.2% in Canada (1979–1990), 60.0% in England and Wales (1977–1990), 46.7% in Japan (1950s), and 57.0% in Chicago (1964–1994). Not only were the majority of cases brother-brother killings, but same-sex cases (brother-brother and sister-sister) were more numerous than would be expected if killer's sex and victim's sex were independent. This is more evidence that siblicide is the extreme end of the continuum of sibling rivalry, which tends to be more intense within than between the sexes. The Japanese data set was the only one that provided actual birth order information about killer and victim, but the data provided no support for the hypothesis that specific birth order is strongly related to committing, or being the victim of, siblicide.

One point worth mentioning is that Sulloway's (1996) hypothesis focuses on the concept that older siblings would have greater reproductive value than younger ones in the environments in which human psychological adaptations evolved. This leads to asymmetrical contributions to the inclusive fitness of one child versus the other (as well as predictions about expected contributions to parental fitness that lead to the assumption of favoritism toward firstborns). However, this would only apply to children because this is when such reproductive disparity occurs. Once siblings have reached older ages, expected future reproduction is actually higher in the younger sibling. If this is the case, Sulloway's hypothesis might work out if we confined the analysis to younger children. When Daly et al. (2001) did this, analyzing the small sample of siblicides involving those under 14 years of age, a significantly larger number were committed by the older sibling. Gebo (2002), using the US Federal Bureau of Investigation Uniform Crime Reports Supplementary Homicide Reports, found the same pattern. However, this is not unique to sibling homicides because the likelihood of killing anyone increases with age through late childhood and adolescence. When juvenile homicides involving nonrelatives were compared to siblicides, the age pattern was the same, suggesting that the fact that older children kill more often than younger ones accounts for the fact that siblicide in childhood is asymmetrical to adulthood with respect to seniority.

Like Holmes and Sherman's (1982) study of the impact of half-sibship on aggression in female ground squirrels, Michalski, Russell, Shackelford, and Weekes-Shackelford (2007) examined the impact of genetic relatedness on siblicide using data from the Chicago Historical Homicide Project (which contains data on over 11,000 homicides in Chicago from 1870 to 1930). They found a very small relationship for siblicides as a whole but did find a stronger relationship in terms of accidental deaths (playing with gun, gun dropped and went off) being more common when the brothers involved were full siblings.

There are also theoretical reasons to expect age disparity to play a role in sibling conflict. A number of researchers have noted that successive births within 3 years or less are too soon from the perspective of the older child (Blurton Jones & daCosta, 1987; Mock & Parker, 1997). In the ancestral environment (with no handy substitutes for mother's milk), children typically nursed for several years with corresponding 3- to 6-year birth intervals. Children close in age and developmental stage with similar needs are more likely to experience intense competition for parental attention and other resources. To examine this, Daly et al. (2001) analyzed their Canadian data with regard to the age intervals between brothers involved in a siblicide and found that it was not an expected predictor. However, they did note that the tendency for the killer to be younger was stronger when the ages were closer: Though it was not significant in any one data set, it was an apparent trend in the three largest sets.

Why are fratricides committed more often by the younger sibling? Case accounts often reflect a power struggle between older and younger brother that culminates in violence and death (Ewing, 1997). It is not always the younger that initiates the aggression, but his defiance of the elder's authority may be what leads to a conflict ending in death. The Chicago police files' descriptions (Daly et al., 2001) echo the idea of a younger sibling's defiance (refusal to help his older brother eliminate a rival) and conflicts over money. Sulloway (1996) referenced Cain and Abel as an example of the older brother killing the younger brother, but that case is unusual in that it was the younger Abel who was favored by their parents and god and the elder Cain who was resentful of that state of affairs. It is much more common to read of tales in which the elder brother is favored and eventually killed by his younger brother, as in the Japanese epic *The Exploits of Prince Yamoto*, who begins his story by killing his overbearing older brother.

Conclusions

Although rare in humans, siblicide can be viewed as the extreme outcome of sibling conflict, played out to a final end. Like facultative siblicide in nonhumans, it seems to be influenced to some extent by concerns over resource availability. However, human siblicide is different from nonhuman siblicide in that it is more likely to occur between adults than between children. As such, it not only can involve relatively direct conflict over money, it also tends to involve clashes of dominance with younger same-sex siblings (usually brothers) unwilling to accept the authority of their elder sibling. In nonhumans, the elder (or larger sibling) is almost always the victor. In humans, it is slightly more often the younger brother who kills.

Future Directions

1. Siblicide in humans is an area of homicide research that has been largely ignored in favor of focusing on spousal homicide and infanticide. More complete studies of the circumstances surrounding siblicides, in particular childhood relationships with parents and siblings, would be informative.

2. While a greater number of siblicides are fratricides, sororicides do occur, and it would be helpful to know whether they are different in motive or circumstance from the more common brother-brother siblicide.

3. More data need to be gathered in non-Western societies to better examine the variety of factors (patrilineal inheritance, preference for one sex versus the other, etc.) that may influence which siblings are more likely to kill.

4. More human data need to be collected on how relatedness impacts siblicide, including studies of stepsibling and half-sibling homicides as well as adoptive siblings.

References

Anderson, D. J. (1990). Evolution of obligate siblicide in boobies. I. A test of the insurance-egg hypothesis. *American Naturalist*, *135*, 334–350.

Blurton Jones, N.G., & daCosta, E. (1987). A suggested adaptive value of toddler night waking: Delaying the birth of the next sibling. *Ethology and Sociobiology*, *8*, 135–142.

Brody, G. H., Stoneman, Z, & Burke, M. (1987). Child temperaments, maternal differential behavior, and sibling relationships. *Developmental Psychology*, *23*, 354–362.

Cicirelli, V. G. (1995). *Sibling relationships across the life span*. New York: Plenum.

Clifford, L. D., & Anderson, D. J. (2000). Experimental demonstration of the insurance value of extra eggs in an obligately siblicidal seabird. *Behavioral Ecology*, *12*, 340–347.

Daly, M., & Wilson, M. (1982). Homicide and kinship. *American Anthropologist*, *84*, 372–378.

Daly, M., & Wilson, M. (1984). A sociobiological analysis of human infanticide. In G. Hausfater & S. B. Hrdy (Eds.), *Infanticide: Comparative and evolutionary perspectives* (pp. 487–502). New York: Aldine Press.

Daly, M., & Wilson, M. (1988). *Homicide*. Hawthorne, NY: Aldine.

Daly, M., & Wilson, M. (1994). Some differential attributes of lethal assaults on small children by stepfathers versus genetic fathers. *Ethology and Sociobiology*, *15*, 207–217.

Daly, M., Wilson, M., Salmon, C. A., Hiraiwa-Hasegawa, M., & Hasegawa, T. (2001). Siblicide and seniority. *Homicide Studies*, *5*, 30–45.

Daly, M., Wilson, M., & Vasdev, S. (2001) Income inequality and homicide rates in Canada and the United States. *Canadian Journal of Criminology*, *43*, 219–236.

Diem, C., & Pizarro, J. M. (2010). Social structure and family homicides. *Journal of Family Violence*, *25*, 521–532.

Drake, A., Fraser, D., & Weary, D. M. (2008). Parent-offspring resource allocation in domestic pigs. *Behavioral Ecology and Sociobiology*, *62*, 309–319.

Duntley, J. D., & Buss, D. M. (2005). The plausibility of adaptations for homicide. In P. Carruthers, S. Laurence, & S. Stich (Eds.), *The innate mind: Structure and contents* (pp. 291–304). New York: Oxford University Press.

Elwin, V. (1950). *Maria murder and suicide*. (2nd ed). Bombay, India: Oxford University Press.

Ewing, C. P. (1997). *Fatal families: The dynamics of intrafamilial homicide*. London: Sage Publications.

Fey, K., & Trillmich, F. (2008). Sibling competition in guinea pigs (Cavia aperea f. porceilus): scrambling for mother's teats is stressful. *Behavioral Ecology and Sociobiology*, *62*, 321–329.

Frank, L. G., Glickman, S. E., & Licht, P. (1991). Fatal sibling aggression, precocial development, and androgens in neonatal spotted hyaenas. *Science*, *252*, 702–704.

Gebo, E. (2002). A contextual exploration of siblicide. *Violence and Victims*, *17*, 157–168.

Goody, J. (1966). *Succession to high office*. Cambridge, England: Cambridge University Press.

Hamilton, W. D. (1964). The genetical evolution of social behavior. I. *Journal of Theoretical Biology*, *7*, 1–16.

Hodge, S. J., Flower, T. P., & Clutton-Brock, T. H. (2007). Offspring competition and helper associations in cooperative meerkats. *Animal Behaviour*, *74*, 957–964.

Hodge, S. J., Manica, A., Flower, T. P., & Clutton-Brock, T. H. (2008). Determinants of reproductive success in dominant female meerkats. *Journal of Animal Ecology*, *77*, 92–102.

Holmes, W. G., & Sherman, P. W. (1982). The ontogeny of kin recognition in two species of ground squirrels. *American Zoologist*, *22*, 491–517.

Irons, D. B. (1992). *Aspect of foraging behavior and reproductive biology of the black-legged kittiwake.* Unpublished Ph.D. dissertation, University of California, Irvine.

Legge, S. (2000). Siblicide in the cooperatively breeding laughing kookaburra (*Dacelo novaeguineae*). *Behavioral Ecology and Sociobiology, 48,* 293–302.

Legge, S., & Cockburn, A. (2000). Social and mating system of cooperatively breeding laughing kookaburra (*Dacelo novaeguineae*). *Behavioral Ecology and Sociobiology, 47,* 220–229.

Lougheed, L. W., & Anderson, D. J. (1999). Parent blue-footed boobies suppress siblicidal behavior of offspring. *Behavioral Ecology and Sociobiology, 45,* 11–18.

Machmer, M. M., & Ydenberg, R. C. (1998). The relative roles of hunger and size asymmetry in sibling aggression between nestling ospreys, *Pandion haliaetus. Canadian Journal of Zoology, 76,* 181–186.

Marleau, J. D., & Saucier, J. F. (1998). Birth order and fratricidal behavior in Canada. *Psychological Reports, 82,* 817–818.

McGuire, S., Manke, B., Eftekhair, A., & Dunn, J. (2000). Children's perceptions of sibling conflict during middle childhood: Issues and sibling (dis)similarity. *Social Development, 9,* 173–190.

Michalski, R. L., Russell, D. P., Shackelford, T. K., & Weekes-Shackelfrod, V. A. (2007). Siblicide and genetic relatedness in Chicago, 1870–1930. *Homicide Studies, 11,* 231–237.

Mock, D. W. (1987). Siblicide, parent-offspring conflict, and unequal parental investment by egrets and herons. *Behavioral Ecology and Sociobiology, 20,* 247–256.

Mock, D. W. (2004). *More than kin and less than kind: The evolution of family conflict.* Cambridge, MA: Belknap Press.

Mock, D. W., Drummond, H., & Stinson, C. H. (1990). Avian siblicide. *American Scientist, 78,* 438–449.

Mock, D. W., & Parker, G. A. (1997). *The evolution of sibling rivalry.* Oxford, UK: Oxford University Press.

Mock, D. W., & Parker, G. A. (1998). Siblicide, family conflict, and the evolutionary limits of selfishness. *Animal Behaviour, 56,* 1–10.

Muller, M. S., Brennecke, J. F., Porter, E. T., Ottinger, M. A., & Anderson, D. J. (2008). Perinatal androgens and adult behavior vary with nesting social system in siblicidal boobies. *PLoS One, 3,* e2460. doi:10.1371/journal.pone.0002460

Ross, H. S., Filyer, R. E., Lollis, S. P., Perlman, M., & Martin, J. L. (1994). Administering justice in the family: Special section: Siblings, family relationships, and child development. *Journal of Family Psychology, 8,* 254–273.

Ross, H. G., & Milgram, J. (1982). Important variables in adult sibling relationships: A qualitative study. In M. E. Lamb & B. Sutton Smith (Eds.), *Sibling relationships: Their nature and significance across the lifespan* (pp. 225–247). Hillsdale, NJ: Erlbaum.

St Clair, C. C., Waas, J. R., St Clair, R. C., & Boag, P. T. (1995). Unfit mothers? Maternal infanticide in royal penguins. *Animal Behaviour, 50,* 1177–1185.

Salmon, C. A. (1999). On the impact of sex and birth order on contact with kin. *Human Nature, 10,* 183–197.

Salmon, C. A. (2003). Birth order and relationships: Family, friends, and sexual partners. *Human Nature, 14,* 73–88.

Salmon, C. A. (2007). Parent-offspring conflict. In C. A. Salmon & T. K. Shackelford (Eds.), *Family relationships: An evolutionary perspective* (pp. 145–161). New York: Oxford University Press.

Segal, N. L. (2005). Evolutionary studies of cooperation, competition, and altruism: A twin-based approach. In R. L. Burgess & K. B. MacDonald (Eds.), *Evolutionary perspectives on human development* (2nd ed., pp. 265–304). Thousand Oaks, CA: Sage.

Simmons, R. (1988). Offspring quality and the evolution of Cainism. *Ibis, 130,* 339–357.

Smale, L., Holekamp, K. E., Weldele, M., Frank, L. G., & Glickman, S. E. (1995). Competition and cooperation between littermates in the spotted hyaena, *Crocuta crocuta. Animal Behaviour, 50,* 671–682.

Smale, L., Holekamp, K. E., & White, P. A. (1999). Siblicide revisted in the spotted hyaena: Does it conform to obligate or facultative models? *Animal Behaviour, 58,* 545–551.

Statistics Canada. (2004). *Homicide in Canada, 2004.* Ottawa, ON: Canadian Centre for Justice Statistics, Catalogue 85-002-XPE 25(6), 2005.

Straus, M., Gelles, R. J., & Steinmetz, S. K. (2006). *Behind closed doors: Violence in the American family.* Piscataway, NJ: Transaction Publishers.

Sulloway, F. J. (1996). *Born to rebel.* New York: Pantheon.

Sulloway, F. J. (2007). Birth order. In C. A. Salmon & T. K. Shackelford (Eds.), *Family relationships: An evolutionary perspective* (pp. 162–182). New York: Oxford University Press.

Sulloway, F. J., & Zweigenhaft, R. L. (2010). Birth order and risk taking in athletics: A meta-analysis and study of major league baseball players. *Personality and Social Psychology Review, 14,* 402–416.

Trillmich, F., & Wolf, J. B. W. (2008). Parent-offspring and sibling conflict in the Galapagos fur seals and sea lions. *Behavioral Ecology and Sociobiology, 62,* 363–375.

Trivers, R. L. (1974). Parent-offspring conflict. *American Zoologist, 14,* 249–264.

Underwood, R. C., & Patch, P. C. (1999). Siblicide: A descriptive analysis of sibling homicide. *Homicide Studies, 3,* 333–48.

Wahaj, S. A., Place, N. J., Weldele, M. L., Glickman, S. E., & Holekamp, K. E. (2007). Siblicide in the spotted hyena: Analysis with ultrasonic examination of wild and captive individuals. *Behavioral Ecology, 18,* 974–984.

White, J., Leclaire, S., Kriloff, M., Mulard, H., Hatch, S. A., & Danchin, E. (2010). Sustained increase in food supplies reduces broodmate aggression in black-legged kittiwakes. *Animal Behaviour, 79,* 1095–1100.

Wiehe, V. R. (1997). *Sibling abuse.* Thousand Oaks, CA: Sage Publications.

Williams, G. C. (1966). Natural selection, the costs of reproduction, and a refinement of Lack's principle. *American Naturalist, 100,* 687–690.

Wilson, M., & Daly, M. (2004). Marital cooperation and conflict. In C. B. Crawford & C. A. Salmon (Eds.), *Handbook of evolutionary psychology* (pp. 197–215). New York: Erlbaum.

CHAPTER 8

Familial Homicide-Suicide

Marieke C. A. Liem

Abstract

Homicide followed by suicide constitutes a severe form of lethal violence that leads to shock and incomprehension. These acts of interpersonal violence mainly occur in partnerships and families, involving male perpetrators and female and child victims. This chapter delineates the present state of knowledge regarding homicide-suicide by addressing the nature and incidence of these acts and the characteristics of subtypes of homicide-suicide. Specific attention is paid to the main theoretical underpinnings used to explain the homicide-suicide phenomenon, with a particular focus on evolutionary psychological perspectives.

Key Words: homicide-suicide, murder-suicide, homicide, suicide, familicide, filicide, intimate partner homicide, uxoricide, evolution

Introduction

"Homicide-suicide" is a generic term referring to a homicide and a subsequent suicide by the same actor. These events are a significant public health concern, victimizing not only those directly involved in the act but also relatives, friends, and acquaintances. Given the fact that multiple victims are involved, the degree of secondary victimization tends to spread drastically.

While homicide and suicide are two well-defined phenomena, there is no standard legal description of the homicide-suicide phenomenon (Palermo, 1994), because cases typically do not result in a criminal charge or trial (Felthous & Hempel, 1995). Although homicide-suicide is often referred to as murder-suicide, "murder" denotes the legal aspect of intentional homicide, whereas "homicide" includes both murder and manslaughter and is therefore the preferred, more encompassing, term (Milroy, Drastas, & Ranson, 1997).

There are broad variations in operational criteria for the homicide-suicide act. Some researchers rely on a time span of 24 hours (Barber et al., 2008; Carcach & Grabosky, 1998; Cohen, Llorente, & Eisdorfer, 1998; Harper & Voigt, 2007; Logan et al., 2008) or several days (Cohen et al., 1998; Felthous & Hempel, 1995) between the homicide and the suicide of the perpetrator; others use a week as an inclusion criterion (Campanelli & Gilson, 2002; Chan, Beh, & Broadhurst, 2003; Comstock et al., 2005; Marzuk, Tardiff, & Hirsch, 1992); and still others do not use a time line at all (Berman, 1979; Dettling, Althaus, & Haffner, 2003; Hata et al., 2001). It can be argued that the longer the time line between the homicide and the subsequent suicide of the perpetrator, the less likely the motive for suicide is related to the preceding homicide, but rather to circumstances related to incarceration and associated feelings of isolation and helplessness. In this chapter, a homicide-suicide incident is defined as an incident involving one or more homicides followed by the suicide of the suspected perpetrator within 24 hours, a definition used in several previous studies (Barber et al., 2008; Carcach & Grabosky, 1998;

Cohen et al., 1998; Harper & Voigt, 2007; Logan et al., 2008).

Incidence

A review of recent international epidemiological studies reveals that, overall, homicide-suicide is a relatively rare event, but it also reveals that substantial cross-national differences exist. Ever since West (1965) conducted his early study on homicide-suicide in London, many epidemiological studies have been conducted, mapping the incidence and prevalence of homicide-suicide in different regions (Table 8.1). While homicide-suicide incidents make up a relatively small proportion of homicides overall, certain subtypes of homicide—notably men who kill an intimate partner with a firearm—make up over half of all homicide incidents (Barber et al., 2008; Easteal, 1993; Liem, Postulart, &

Table 8.1 Recent Comparative Frequencies and Rates of Homicide-Suicide.

Country	Study	Period	Homicide-Suicides N	%	Rate per 100.000
Australia	Carcach and Grabosky (1998)	1989–1996	144	5.5	0.22
England and Wales	Barraclough and Clare Harris (2002)	1988–1992	144	1.0	NA
England and Wales	Flynn et al. (2009)	1996–2005	203	3.8	0.05
Finland	Kivivouri and Lethi (2003)	1960–2000	166	8.0	0.17
France	Saint Martin et al. (2008)	2000–2005	10	11.0	1.55
Hong Kong	Chan (2007)	1989–2003	88	NA	0.18
Hong Kong	Chan, Beh, and Broadhurst (2003)	1989–1997	49	6.0	0.09
Japan, Toyama	Hata et al. (2001)	1986–1995	25	25.3	0.15
Japan, Sapporo	Hata et al. (2001)	1986–1995	21	20.6	0.06
Netherlands	Liem, Postulart et al. (2009)	1992–2006	103	4.0	0.05
New Zealand	Moskowitz et al. (2006)	1991–2000	33	NA	0.08
South Africa, Durban	Roberts et al. (2010)	2000–2001	21	0.9	0.89
Switzerland, Geneva	Shiferaw et al. (2010)	1956–2005	23	10.0	NA
Turkey, Konya	Dogan et al. (2010)	2000–2007	10	2.9	NA
United States	Logan et al. (2008)	2001–2002	408	6.6	0.19
United States	Barber et al. (2008)	2003–2005	74	4.9	NA
United States	Bridges and Lester (2010)	1968–1975	2,215	1.8	0.134
United States, Chicago	Stack (1997)	1965–1990	267	1.6	NA
United States, Florida	Cohen et al. (1998)	1988–1994	171	2.5–12.0	0.5–0.7
United States, New Hampshire	Campanelli and Gilson (2002)	1995–2000	16	14.7	0.26
United States, Oklahoma	Comstock et al. (2005)	1994–2001	73	4.0	0.30

Note. To give a reliable representation of figures, only recent studies were included. The publication year 1995 was used as a cutoff point. NA, data not available.

Nieuwbeerta, 2009; Lund & Smorodinsky, 2001; Walsh & Hemenway, 2005).

In recent years, the rate of homicide-suicides has ranged from as low as 0.05 per 100,000 persons per year in England and Wales (Flynn et al., 2009) and in the Netherlands (Liem, Postulart et al., 2009) to 0.89 per 100,000 in the Durham region in South Africa (Roberts, Wassenaar, Canetto, & Pillay, 2010). In comparison to England and Wales, the United States has a relatively high homicide-suicide rate. Recent accounts report the homicide-suicide rate to vary from 0.27 per 100,000 persons per year in Kentucky (Walsh & Hemenway, 2005) to 0.38 per 100,000 persons per year in central Virginia (Hannah, Turf, & Fierro, 1998). In Australia and New Zealand, the homicide-suicide rate ranges from 0.07 per 100,000 persons per year (Moskowitz, Simpson, McKenna, Skipworth, & Barry-Walsh, 2006) to 0.11 per 100,000 persons per year (Carcach & Grabosky, 1998). Marzuk et al. (1992) placed the homicide-suicide mortality rate in the United States, based on 1,000 to 1,500 deaths per year, on par with diseases such as tuberculosis (1,467 deaths), viral hepatitis (1,290 deaths), influenza (1,943 deaths), and meningitis (1,156 deaths) (Marzuk et al., 1992).

Several studies have found that the rate of homicide-suicide remains relatively stable over time (e.g., Coid, 1983; Felthous & Hempel, 1995), despite a fluctuation in the overall homicide rate. Felthous and Hempel held that, since homicide-suicides involve predominantly intimate (family) victims, and the rates of these killings fluctuate less than the suicide and homicide rates do independently, homicide-suicide rates are subject to similar influences and are of comparable stability as the rate of intimate homicide. Others point to the role of mental disorder among homicide-suicide perpetrators in order to explain its relative stability: Even though the homicide rate fluctuates over time, the rate of homicides attributable to mental disorder—such as of the majority of homicide-suicides—remains relatively stable. This observation has been attributed to the so-called survivor effect. This means that as the homicide rate increases above a certain point, the homicide-suicide rates increase less rapidly because the number of potential offenders is exhausted (Large, Smith, & Nielssen, 2009). Although the rates of homicide-suicide appear to be relatively stable across nations, sociocultural influences lead to varying characteristics. For example, as Nock and Marzuk (1999) pointed out, most homicide-suicides in the United States are perpetrated by men against their (estranged) intimate partners, whereas in Japan the majority of homicide-suicides take place between mothers and their children.

While some studies found relative stability in the homicide-suicide rate, others found no evidence for such stability. Milroy (1995a), for example, found a decline in the proportion of homicide offenders who committed suicide. A similar decline was found by Kivivouri and Lethi (2003), who analyzed homicide-suicide rates in Finland between 1960 and 2000 and by Gartner and McCarthy (2008), who studied homicide-suicide trends between 1900 and 1990 in four North American cities. The latter research ascribed the decline in homicide-suicide trends in the course of the 20th century to an overall decline in homicides involving intimate partners and children. This is believed to be due to a growing availability of contraceptives, smaller families, greater access to and social acceptance of divorce, increased social and economic support for single-parent families, improved access to counselling, and advances in diagnosing and treating mental health problems. Ascribing the decline in homicide-suicide to improved social conditions has been supported by others as well (Large et al., 2009). In addition, Gartner and McCarthy (2008) proposed that a decrease in suicides after spouse killings and child killings reflects an increasing individualization over time, whereby people are able to more easily separate themselves—psychologically and emotionally—from other family members. From this perspective, the family's power as a "master status" or cornerstone of identity diminished over time, resulting in a decline in homicide-suicides.

The Nature of Homicide-Suicide

Several studies have compared homicide-suicides to homicides not followed by suicides. One of the first studies on homicide-suicide, conducted by West (1965), relied on London city-level data. He found "an overwhelming domestic nature" of homicide-suicide in almost all comparisons made. Another early study, performed by Stack (1997), was based on city-level data from Chicago. He found that homicide was more likely to be followed by suicide if the relational distance between perpetrator and victim was smaller. Carcach and Grabosky (1998) compared homicide-suicides to homicides using Australian data. They found that the odds for homicide-suicides are greater when victim and offender are Caucasian and a firearm is used in the offence. These findings were replicated in a recent study based on nationwide data from the Netherlands (Liem, Postulart et al., 2009).

The first scholar who conducted a comparison between homicide-suicides and other suicides was Ruth Cavan (1928) in a qualitative analysis of Chicago data (Cavan, 1928). In a second study, based on Denver and Los Angeles coroners' reports, Selkin (1976) quantitatively compared 13 homicide-suicides to 13 suicides and found that none of the homicide-suicide cases included old, alone individuals at a declining stage in their lives. He concluded that individuals committing suicide bore little resemblance to homicide-suicide perpetrators, a finding later corroborated by Berman (1979). Studying police and coroner's reports in Philadelphia, Baltimore, and Washington D.C., Berman found that, compared to suicides, homicide-suicides were more likely to be committed by males, take place in the bedroom, and involve a gun. More recently, Malphurs et al. (2001) and Malphurs and Cohen (2005) compared a sample of homicide-suicides by older persons to a control group of other suicides in Florida, finding a caregiving strain to be a predominant factor among older homicide-suicide perpetrators compared to those "only" committing suicide. Finally, Barber et al. (2008) recently compared the presence of antidepressants in suicide perpetrators to homicide-suicide perpetrators and found no difference between the two groups.

So far, few studies have conducted simultaneous bilateral comparisons of homicide-suicides versus homicides *and* suicides. Conducting such a comparison based on data from 17 US states, Logan et al. (2008) found that homicide-suicide perpetrators were more likely to belong to an older age group and to be Caucasian compared to homicide perpetrators. In contrast to suicides, however, homicide-suicide perpetrators were less likely to be Caucasian. Similar findings were reported for the Netherlands by Liem and Nieuwbeerta (2010). The authors also found homicide-suicide perpetrators to be older than homicide perpetrators, but overall younger compared to those committing suicide. A recent study by Flynn et al. (2009), based on data from England and Wales, reported that fewer perpetrators of homicide-suicide compared with homicide or suicide only had been in contact with mental health services. In short, both unilateral and bilateral comparisons of homicide-suicide with other types of lethal violence reveal that these acts cannot easily be equated with either homicide or suicide.

Because of the extreme nature of the homicide-suicide event relative to homicide or suicide alone, several researchers have pointed to the influence of mental disorder in homicide-suicide. The most frequently cited types of psychopathology include depression (Bourget, Gagne, & Moamai, 2000; Chan et al., 2003; Easteal, 1993; Hatters Friedman, Holden, Hrouda, & Resnick, 2008; Léveillée, Marleau, & Dubé, 2007; Lewis & Bunce, 2003; Okumura & Kraus, 1996; Polk, 1994; Rohde et al.1998), morbid jealousy, and paranoid ideation (Felthous & Hempel, 1995; Milroy, 1995a), as well as personality disorders and psychotic disorders (Liem, Hengeveld, & Koenraadt, 2009).

Classifying Homicide-Suicide

Over time, several scholars have proposed a classification system of homicide-suicide. Berman (1979) generated a typology in which he included subclasses of suicide pacts and so-called exhibitionistic suicides, such as assassination followed by suicide and terrorist suicide missions. Later, Wallace (1986) generated four etiological models of homicide-suicide based on motive, conflict, altruism, and mental abnormality.

Marzuk, Tardiff, and Hirsch (1992) were the first to develop a classification system that categorized homicide-suicide according to the relationship between victim and perpetrator. The four most common types of homicide-suicide in this classification were spousal homicide-suicide, child-suicide, familicide-suicide, and extrafamilial homicide-suicide. Familicide-suicide constitutes an overlap of both spousal homicide-suicide and child homicide-suicide. Extrafamilial homicide-suicides involve victims outside the family realm.

Hanzlick and Koponen (1994) adapted Marzuk et al.'s (1992) classification system by delineating sociodemographic variables, event-related characteristics, as well as precipitating stressors. Felthous and Hempel (1995) proposed to connect Marzuk et al.'s (1992) classification to one based on psychopathology. Palermo et al. (1997) distinguished three forms of homicide-suicide, the first type consisting of homicide combined with a self-destructive act rising out of anger or paranoia. The second type of homicide-suicide includes perpetrators who commit suicide motivated by fear of detection and exposure. For the third type, the authors distinguished "kamikaze"-like terrorist acts where the perpetrator dies as a by-product of the homicidal act. Harper and Voigt (2007) recently proposed a classification system involving "intimate or domestic lethal violence-suicide," "family annihilation-suicide," "mercy killing-suicide," "public killing spree-suicide," and a category consisting of "mistaken or accidental homicide-suicide."

In further examining the different homicide-suicide subtypes, Marzuk et al.'s (1992) classification scheme will be used as a taxonomy. This system has been used by many others throughout the years in both the presentation of case study material as well as in further analysis of homicide-suicide acts (Chan et al., 2003; Liem, Postulart et al., 2009; Logan et al., 2008). Next, the general characteristics of homicide-suicide will be reviewed according to these different subtypes.

In the remainder of this chapter, the focus will be on *familial* homicide-suicide. Extrafamilial homicide-suicides such as terrorist suicide missions and mass shootings by disgruntled individuals are often extensively reported on in the media, probably due to their shocking effect. These types of killings are, however, very rare (Liem & Koenraadt, 2007; Liem, Postulart et. al., 2009). As we will observe later, the motives and characteristics underlying extrafamilial homicide-suicide are drastically different from familial types of homicide-suicide. Therefore, the chapter at hand focuses on the most common types of homicide-suicide, namely those taking place within the family, involving partner killing (the killing of an intimate partner or an estranged intimate partner), filicides (the killing of a child by a parent), familicides (the killing of an intimate partner and children) as well as "other" homicide-suicides within the family: parricides (the killing of a parent) and siblicides (the killing of a sibling).

Subtypes of Homicide-Suicide
Intimate Partner Homicide-Suicide

The killing of an intimate partner is not only the most common type of domestic homicide but also the most common type of homicide-suicide (Barber et al., 2008; Bossarte, Simon, & Barker, 2006; Bourget et al., 2000; Comstock et al., 2005; Dutton & Kerry, 1999; Malphurs & Cohen, 2002; Marzuk et al., 1992; Saleva, Putkonen, Kiviruusu, & Lönnqvist, 2007). In Marzuk et al.'s (1992) classification system, a two-fold division in cases of intimate partner homicide-suicide is made. The first focuses on a pathological type of possessiveness, and the latter clusters around a theme of old age and ill health.

Both types of intimate partner homicide-suicide are predominantly committed by men. Women who murder their partner hardly ever commit suicide (Belfrage & Rying, 2004; Bourget et al., 2000; Dawson, 2005; Easteal, 1993; Hanzlick & Koponen, 1994; Harper & Voigt, 2007; Stack, 1997). Swatt and He (2006) suggested that the lack of suicidal behavior can be explained by the liberation women feel after having killed their tormentor, rather than a feeling of guilt and a wish to be reunited with the victim in death. With regard to age characteristics, suicidal perpetrators are older than those not committing suicide (Belfrage & Rying, 2004; Lund & Smorodinsky, 2001). Reasoning that homicide-suicides involve a high proportion of mental disorders, Felthous and Hempel (1995) argue that an older age is accompanied by mental disorders, in particular that depressive and paranoid conditions are more likely to occur with older age. In addition, they hold that an older perpetrator will have had time to establish an intimate relationship lasting long enough for bonding, dependence, turmoil, and instability to develop. Others have reported cross-culturally a high prevalence of previous physical abuse by homicide-suicide perpetrators (Harper & Voigt, 2007; Koziol-McLain et al., 2006; Lindqvist & Gustafsson, 1995; Malphurs & Cohen, 2005; Morton et al., 1998; Palermo, 1994; Rosenbaum 1990; Stack, 1997; Starzomski & Nussbaum, 2000).

Concerning the homicide-suicide event, research shows that the homicide and suicide methods are typically violent. In countries other than the United States, shooting is the most frequent method (e.g., Barraclough & Clare Harris, 2002; Bourget et al., 2000; Easteal, 1993; Koziol-McLain et al., 2006; Lecomte & Fornes, 1998; Milroy, 1993; Moskowitz et al., 2006; Saleva et al., 2007). A study by Dawson (2005), who compared "simple" intimate partner homicides to intimate partner homicide-suicides, found that the first were more likely to involve a premeditative component. In addition, perpetrators motivated by jealousy, ill health, and other life stresses were more likely to kill themselves after killing their spouse than those prompted by other factors. Among the subgroup of ailing spouses, researchers have pointed to the role of financial stress (Milroy, 1995b) as well as changing health in one or both of the partners. In these cases, one of the partners—usually the male—acts as a caregiver for the other, not infrequently creating a special, inseparable unit. The homicide-suicide occurs when this unit is threatened with dissolution (Cohen et al., 1998).

Intimate partner homicide-suicide perpetrators are often found to suffer from mental illness, with depression being the most commonly cited disorder (Bourget et al., 2000; Rosenbaum, 1990). In regard to personality characteristics, men who commit intimate partner homicide-suicide are reported to be controlling and dependent. What these men seem to have in common is a profound emotional dependency on their intimate partner, regarding her as fundamental to their existence (Liem & Roberts, 2009). When the continuation of the relationship is threatened, a breakthrough of aggression takes the shape of a homicide-suicide (Dutton & Kerry, 1999; Palermo, 1994). This finding challenges Marzuk et al.'s definition of the subgroup of amorous jealousy, emphasizing jealous beliefs to constitute the underlying reason for the intimate partner homicide-suicide, rather than acknowledging additional factors such as interpersonal dependency. What both the "jealous" perpetrator in Marzuk et al.'s classification scheme and the "dependent" perpetrator in empirical studies have in common is the trigger leading up to the event: the female partner's rejection and an immediate threat of withdrawal and estrangement.

Child Homicide-Suicide

The killing of a child by a parent followed by suicide of the perpetrator is the second most common type of homicide-suicide (Barraclough & Clare Harris, 2002; Harper & Voigt, 2007; Malphurs & Cohen, 2002; Marzuk et al., 1992; Milroy, 1993; Stack, 1997). Both men and women are involved in child homicide-suicide. Depending on the nature of the sample, some find an overrepresentation of men (Byard, Knight, James, & Gilbert, 1999; Cooper & Eaves, 1996; Shackelford, Weekes-Shackelford, & Beasley, 2005), others of women (Goldney, 1977; Logan et al., 2008). Overall, genetic parents who kill their child are more likely to commit suicide than are stepparents who kill their stepchild (Daly & Wilson, 1988, 1994; O'Connor & Sheehy, 2000). In addition, previous studies found suicidal parents to be older than those not committing suicide following the homicide (Shackelford et al., 2005). Accordingly, the victims in child homicide-suicide tend to be older as well (Hatters Friedman et al., 2008; Krischer, Stone, Sevecke, & Steinmeyer, 2007; Shackelford et al., 2005). Suicide is uncommon when mothers kill a child less than 1 year of age (Felthous & Hempel, 1995; Krischer et al., 2007).

With regard to the homicide methods used in the offence, Dettling et al. (2003) found child victims of homicide-suicide to present patterns usually found in suicides. Women are reported to use relatively nonviolent methods compared to men, as women tend to poison or smother their children rather than killing them with firearms or other weapons (Byard et al., 1999; Milroy, 1993). The main intention of parents killing themselves and their children is reported to be their own self-destruction, with the children being killed as part of an "extended suicide," a phenomenon first described by Näcke (1908). In such a constellation, the parent considers the child as an "extension" of the self that should be taken along in death, because they are convinced that there would be no one else to care for the child after having committed suicide (Marleau, Poulin, Webanck, Roy, & Laporte, 1999; Messing & Heeren, 2004; Milroy, 1995b; Somander & Rammer, 1991). Others point out that a child might be in danger of becoming a part of a homicide-suicide when the perpetrator's primary aggression is directed toward an estranged spouse. Here, the child is killed in order to hurt the estranged intimate partner (Okumura & Kraus, 1996).

On an international level, concerning the role of mental illness in such cases, depression (with and without psychotic features) is the most prevalent disorder in these perpetrators (Chan et al., 2003; Hatters Friedman et al., 2008; Léveillée et al., 2007; Lewis & Bunce, 2003; Polk, 1994; Rohde et al., 1998). A history of psychiatric treatment is prevalent in many cases (Malphurs & Cohen, 2002). Regarding the role of psychosis, Lewis and Bunce (2003) found in a sample of forensic psychiatric evaluations that psychotic women were more likely to kill multiple victims and to attempt suicide at the time of the offence than nonpsychotic women who killed their children.

Familicide-Suicide

Compared to spousal homicide-suicide and child homicide-suicide, familicide-suicide is relatively rare (e.g., Carcach & Grabosky, 1998; Liem et al., 2009; Logan et al., 2008). Familicide-suicides are almost exclusively committed by men (Byard et al., 1999; Marleau et al., 1999; Somander & Rammer, 1991). Within the research literature, no specific distinction is made between suicidal and nonsuicidal familicide perpetrators. American research by Ewing (1997) points out that the typical familicide perpetrator is a White male in his 30s or 40s. With regard to the modus operandus in familicide-suicides, studies conducted in Canada, England and Wales, the United States, and Switzerland have found that the killings as well as the subsequent suicide are typically committed with a firearm that belongs to the perpetrator and has been present in the home for some time (Barber et al., 2008; Ewing, 1993; Killias, Dilitz, & Bergerioux, 2006; Wilson, Daly, & Daniele, 1995).

Drawing from over 300 American case studies of familial homicides, Websdale (1999) found that, compared to single intimate homicides, those who commit familicides have fewer criminal records and more economic resources (Websdale, 1999). Other studies conducted in the United States report the contrary, pointing toward the perpetrator's loss of a job, continuous unemployment, and the subsequent inability to support his family (Ewing, 1997; Palermo et al., 1997). When trapped by the breakdown of economic dreams, the familicidal man does not see another option but to "protect" his family from the fate that would befall them without his support. Others point out that perpetrators are motivated by a loss of control, most commonly associated with loss of control over the intimate partner (Marzuk et al., 1992; Wilson et al., 1995). In this light, familicide-suicides resemble intimate partner homicide-suicides, in that the primary object of the man's actions is the spouse rather than the children.

In sum, the literature indicates that there are two main types of familicidal perpetrators. Frazier (1975) describes these as the "murder by proxy" type and as the "suicide by proxy" type (Frazier, 1975). "Murder by proxy" applies to cases in which victims are chosen because they are identified with a primary target against which revenge is sought. A man might kill all of his children because he regards them as an extension of his wife, and he seeks to get even with her. Fear of consequences, guilt, or shame may cause him to subsequently end his own life. "Suicide by proxy" refers to a husband and father who feels despondent over the fate of the family and does not only take his own life but also that of his children and spouse, in order to protect them from perceived future pain and suffering.

Similar to other types of homicide-suicide, in familicide-suicide the role of depression is reported to be pronounced (Polk, 1994; Schlesinger, 2000). On the basis of coroner and police files in British Columbia, Canada, Cooper and Eaves (1996) compared familicidal perpetrators who committed suicide to those not committing suicide and found that the former suffered from more severe psychopathology than the latter (Cooper & Eaves, 1996). The latter were not only considered to be dangerous to family members but also to others outside of the family.

"Other" Homicide-Suicides

This final category involves homicide-suicide of parents, siblings, and other family members. While the killing of parents (parricide) and the killing of siblings (siblicide) are infrequent events, such killings followed by suicide are even more uncommon. A review of the literature shows that in samples of parricide perpetrators, none or very few commit or attempt to commit suicide after the offence (Bourget, Gagne, & Labelle, 2007; Marleau, Auclair, & Millaud, 2006; Millaud, 1996; Mouzos & Rushforth, 2003). The same holds for empirical studies on siblicide (Marleau, 2003). The relative absence of suicidal behavior following parricide has been attributed to the so-called him-or-me dilemma (Crimmins, 1993). In such cases, adolescents may either proceed to suicide or opt for homicide. Both homicide and suicide emerge as a desire for escape from an intolerable situation characterized by abuse (Dutton & Yamini, 1995). Others (Crimmins, 1993) hold that the killing of the self *or* the parent is the only way to separate successfully from the parent. In this process, the conflict stems from the separation-individuation phase of development and can only be resolved by annihilating the self *or* the other, rather than a combination thereof. In many ways, reasons for the absence of suicide following a siblicide resemble those in parricide, since the aggression is primarily aimed at the other rather than at the self. Medlicott (1970; cf. Marleau, 2003) has pointed out that the absence of suicidal behavior among siblicide perpetrators can be ascribed to the symbolic destruction of part of the self in the killing of a brother and/or sister. In this view, suicide is, in a way, already accomplished.

Theoretical Perspectives

Several theoretical notions have been applied in relation to homicide-suicide. Among these theories, however, there is an overall lack of comprehensive *criminological* theories that explain this type of lethal violence. This could be due to the fact that, as Levi and Maguire (2007) pointed out, criminologists generally tend to ignore violent crime. Much of the criminological literature that attempts to explain violent crime takes as its field of enquiry the "conventional" kinds of assault that dominate the "offences against persons" recorded in national crime statistics, rather than extremes of interpersonal violence such as homicide. Because of its noncriminal nature, suicide has remained outside of criminological analyses entirely. Previous theories that have been used to explain homicide-suicide can be divided into three parts, varying from the origin of aggressive behavior (strain theories) and the direction of aggression (stream analogy for lethal violence) to the outcome of aggression (psychodynamic theory, social integration theory, and evolutionary psychological theory), resulting in a homicide-suicide. Following, these theories will briefly be discussed. Given the specific focus of this handbook, close attention will be paid to the evolutionary analyses of familial homicide-suicide.

One of the theories used to explain the homicide-suicide phenomenon is Merton's (1968) strain theory. This theory provides insight into the *origin* of aggressive behavior. Drawing on Durkheim's (2002) concept of anomie, Merton holds that a state of "anomie," or a personal feeling of a lack of social norms, arises when certain groups are restricted in attaining a cultural value (e.g., wealth) through institutionalized means (e.g., work). In Merton's theory there are various ways in which an individual can respond to the problem of anomie: by conformity, innovation, ritualism, retreatism, or rebellion. The latter two coping mechanisms have been used to explain the direction of aggression in both suicide and homicide: The retreating individual withdraws or seeks to isolate himself or herself from the social structure—the most extreme and permanent form of aggression being suicide. In rebellion, on the other hand, the individual responds to frustrations by striking out against social structures and their participants—the most extreme form of aggression constituting homicide (Palmer & Linsky, 1972; cf. Unnithan et al., 1994).

Later scholars, such as Agnew (1992), have interpreted Merton's concept of strain as personal strain, rather than as societal strain. Agnew's theory focuses on relationships in which the person is presented with a "noxious" situation. These situations range from preventing an individual from achieving positively valued goals, removing or threatening to remove positively valued stimuli, and presenting or threatening to present an individual with noxious or negatively valued stimuli. This condition generates a variety of negative emotions, such as disappointment, depression, fear, and anger. Violent behavior, then, becomes a means to cope with frustration and interpersonal problems. Agnew's theory of social stress and strain has been applied to homicide-suicide by Harper and Voigt (2007). Based on findings from previous literature as well as findings from their sample of 42 homicide-suicides in New Orleans, factors such as loss of a job, financial problems, and loss of or rejection by a sexual partner were prevalent among the predictors of homicide-suicide. In this light, inability to achieve positively valued goals includes the withdrawal from an intimate partner and/or children. The presentation of negatively valued stimuli corresponds to interpersonal rejection or abandonment (Harper & Voigt, 2007). From this point of view, homicide-suicide occurs when an individual is faced with the inability to achieve positively valued goals combined with the occurrence of negatively valued stimuli.

A second theoretical approach used to explain homicide followed by suicide includes the stream analogy for lethal violence. Rather than considering the *origin* of aggression, the stream analogy addresses the *direction* of aggressive impulses. Underpinnings of this theory can be traced back to Henry and Short (1954), who held that both homicide and suicide are alternative aggressive responses to frustration. This understanding was revived with the introduction of the stream analogy for lethal violence by Whitt et al. (in Unnithan, Huff-Corzine, Corzine, & Whitt, 1994), describing lethal violence as a stream with two distinct currents flowing through time: the homicide current and the suicide current. The combined currents comprise the overall amount of lethal violence. To explain the choice between homicide and suicide, the stream analogy uses concepts from attribution theory, the choice between homicide and suicide depending on attributional concerns: A higher tendency of external blame in response to frustration will result in a higher homicide rate relative to the suicide rate (Batton, 1999; cf. Wu, 2003). Conversely, factors that increase the internal attribution of blame in response to frustration increase the risk of suicide relative to homicide. In this model, individuals in both groups have a hopeless perspective on their prospects for the future. This theory does not, however, discuss conditions under which homicide and suicide occur simultaneously in a homicide-suicide. Homicide-suicide blurs the clear lines between homicidal and suicidal behavior—homicide being outwardly directed while suicide is inwardly directed. Stack (1997) attempted to apply the stream analogy to homicide-suicide in a study of Chicago homicides. He concluded that the principal source of frustration in homicide-suicide stems from the perpetrator's inability to live *with* or *without* the victim. He argued that the homicide act overcomes a sense of helplessness, but that the ensuing guilt causes suicide. Stack suggested viewing homicide-suicide as containing both inward and outward attribution: homicide resulting from external blame attribution, followed by an internal attribution resulting in a suicide. In a similar vein, Liem and Roberts (2009) found perpetrators of intimate partner homicides who committed a serious suicide attempt to have a high prevalence of unemployment, depressive disorder, previous suicide threats, and suicide plans in line with suicide victims. These findings suggest that intimate partner homicide-suicide favors the suicide current over the homicide current.

A third approach represented in the empirical literature on homicide-suicide includes theories that focus on the *outcome* of aggression—as opposed to the aforementioned theories dealing with the origin or direction of aggression. One of the main theories within this framework is the psychodynamic approach. This approach can be traced back to Freud's (1917 [1961]) theories on aggression, in which he considered suicide an impulse to commit murder turned inward upon the self. In this light, suicide is essentially hostility directed toward the introjected hated object. Menninger (1938) incorporated Freud's concepts of the interchangeability of self-directed and other-directed aggression in his work, postulating that suicide is a wish to kill, a wish to be killed, and a wish to die. Menninger held that homicide-suicide was a two-stage process in which he described homicide as the angry, aggressive component that comes before a suicide: the wish to kill or to destroy.

Other Freudian elements key to the understanding of both homicide and suicide are the concepts of the ego, the superego, and the id (Freud, 1949). In this psychodynamic model, the ego is battling with the id, the superego, and the outside world—concepts later incorporated by theorists such as Henry and Short (1954). In addition to taking on a sociological point of view to explain both homicidal and suicidal behavior as described before, they also incorporated psychodynamic factors in their explanatory model. Henry and Short (1954) postulated that suicide is a function of an excessively strict superego or an internalized restraining mechanism of the personality, which prohibits the outward expression of aggression. From these theoretical underpinnings it can be deduced that, when a person with a strong superego formation kills, he or she is more likely to commit suicide after the killing than someone who does not have an internalized prohibition against the outward expression of aggression. Suicide can thus be considered as self-punishment by the superego for having resorted to violent behavior (and thereby constituting an act motivated by guilt and self-blame). In addition, Henry and Short held that the homicide victim in a homicide-suicide not only represents a source of frustration but also a source of nurturance. When the source of frustration (i.e., the victim) is destroyed in a homicide, the source of nurturance is also lost. Hence, the killing of the victim can restore or even increase frustration over the loss of a loved object. The self then becomes a legitimate target of aggression in the form of suicide.

Finally, in addition to the psychodynamic approach, social integration theory has been used to explain homicide-suicide by focusing on the *outcome* of aggression. Social integration theory holds that both homicide and suicide are social facts, which can be explained by other social facts as precipitated by Durkheim (1897/2002). In his writings, Durkheim asserted that variations in the suicide rate of any society depend on the type and extent of social organizations and integration. Suicide is more likely to occur when the attachment between the individual and society is weak. Thus, there are few social ties to keep the individual from taking his or her life. From a social integration perspective, the likelihood of homicide-suicide over suicide increases as social disintegration increases. Homicide-suicide thereby represents an extreme variation of suicidal behavior, resulting from extreme social disintegration. The findings from empirical research, showing social isolation as a contributing factor in homicide-suicides, are in line with these ideas (Cohen et al., 1998; Haenel & Elsässer, 2000).

Evolutionary Perspectives on Homicide-Suicide

In short, according to evolutionary perspectives on lethal violence, certain types of homicide, in particular, domestic homicides such as intimate partner homicide and filicide (the killing of a child by a parent) can be explained by the Darwinian concepts of reproductive fitness and natural selection. The main assumption underlying these theoretical constructs is that psychological processes have been shaped by selection in order to make adaptive decisions that will promote the individual's fitness and, hence, survival. In the context of evolutionary perspectives, reproductive success by natural selection will cause flourishing traits to survive across generations (Daly & Wilson, 1988). From an evolutionary point of view, however, suicide following a homicide appears to be "spiteful": The actor carries out a course of action that is devastating to his or her own reproductive and survival interests. Relatedly, it has been argued that the more a homicide opposes reproductive and survival interests, the more likely it is to be "abnormal." This notion is supported by empirical research. First, previous studies document that homicide-suicide is a rare event cross-culturally. Secondly, the relative "abnormality" of the homicide-suicide might be explained, in part, by the influence of mental illness: Previous studies found that individuals who committed a homicide-suicide were more likely to suffer from severe psychopathology compared to those who "only" engaged in homicidal behavior (Dawson, 2005; Liem, Hengeveld et al., 2009). Indirect measures of mental illness are also in line with these findings: Previous research suggests that psychiatric problems increase with age, pointing to greater prevalence of mental disorder (particularly depression) among older individuals (Bijl, Ravelli, & Zessen, 1998; DeLeo & Spathonis, 2004). Following this line of reasoning, individuals committing homicide-suicide are older—and thus more likely to suffer from certain types of psychopathology—than individuals engaging in homicide not followed by suicide, a finding supported cross-culturally (Belfrage & Rying, 2004; Liem, Hengeveld et al., 2009; Liem & Nieuwbeerta, 2010; Logan et al., 2008; Lund & Smorodinsky, 2001). Following, I will examine the role of evolutionary perspectives when applied to the most common types of familial homicide-suicide: intimate partner homicide-suicide and child homicide-suicide.

INTIMATE PARTNER HOMICIDE FOLLOWED BY SUICIDE

From a biological perspective, women possess reproductive resources that can be owned and exchanged by men (Daly & Wilson, 1988). In this light, men exercise control over women's sexuality and reproductive capacity—control that is rooted in evolutionary responses to misattributed parenthood and male-male rivalry (Daly & Wilson, 1988). When control over the woman's sexuality is threatened, for example, by her infidelity or her estrangement, the would-be cuckold sometimes responds with violence (Daly & Wilson, 1988, 1995; Wilson & Daly, 1992; Wilson et al., 1995). Violence, and particularly intimate partner violence, is thus used to exercise control. According to this evolutionary approach, homicide of an intimate partner is an unintended "by-product" of violence. Daly & Wilson (1988) have argued that sublethal use of coercive violence can serve husbands' interests by deterring wives' autonomy. Men who kill their wives may thus "overstep" the bounds of utility. Intimate partner homicide followed by suicide, then, opposes evolutionary interests, according to this perspective: Not only has the perpetrator killed his "vehicle" to reproduce, by committing suicide he has stopped the possibilities to reproduce altogether. This evolutionary perspective therefore might lead to the argument that that the more a homicide appears to oppose evolutionary interests, the more likely it is to be classified as "abnormal," and this includes homicides attributable to mental illness and/or homicides followed by suicide.

Another way to interpret the counterevolutionary nature of intimate partner homicide-suicide is not to regard the act as primarily homicidal, but rather as a primarily suicidal or as a separate phenomenon entirely (Liem, 2010a). Seeing these types of homicides as primarily suicidal, the main aim of the perpetrator is to end his own life. In such cases, the intimate partner is "taken along" in the suicide of the perpetrator when he comes to realize that the bond between he and his intimate partner will be broken after he has committed suicide. Not infrequently, in these cases the perpetrator and victim are deeply dependent on one another (Liem, 2010a). The victim is, as it were, integrated in the perpetrator's self. Conversely, one could also consider intimate partner homicide-suicide as constituting a separate phenomenon altogether. Here, the perpetrator considers homicide-suicide to be a total solution; either "only" killing his intimate partner or committing suicide "alone" is not seriously considered. In these cases, the perpetrator's self-concept is strongly determined by the intimate partner. Feelings of dependency prevail—sometimes evolving to such an extent that there is a symbiotic relationship between the perpetrator and the victim (Liem, 2010a). Because the perpetrator's self-concept is contingent on that of the intimate partner, his self threatens to disintegrate when his (dependent) relationship with her breaks down, for example, in the case of her withdrawal or estrangement. In this light, the homicide-suicide has an ego-protective function, as it serves to preserve the perpetrator's concept of self as an intimate partner. In these cases there is no developed suicide plan, but rather a developed homicide-suicide plan through which the symbiotic bond with the victim can be restored or maintained.

CHILD HOMICIDE FOLLOWED BY SUICIDE

Similar to intimate partner homicide, evolutionary perspectives also may shed light on homicides involving children. From an evolutionary perspective on parental psychology, parents have a stake in their children's survival and reproductive success, given that they are vehicles of their genetic success (Daly & Wilson, 1988). This fact is central to the explanation of certain types of child homicide.

First, evolutionary approaches have been used to explain the overrepresentation of stepparents as perpetrators of child homicide, in particular focusing on factors such as a lack of genetic relatedness. According to this approach, children are more likely to be killed by their stepparents than by their biological parents due to the lack of a genetic link between perpetrator and victim. By destroying stepchild(ren), and thereby doing away with the genetic material of competitors, the stepparent may increase the survival of his or her own, biological, descendants. Stepparental psychology thus motivates behaviors such as filicide to dispose of a resource-draining ward to which the person is not genetically related (Shackelford et al., 2005). From this view, when stepparents kill their stepchild, a burden upon their fitness is lifted, while biological parents generally lose a substantial investment. Stepparents who engage in suicidal behavior following the child homicide, however, seem to counteract evolutionary interests, as they cannot reap the benefits of the filicide. Previous empirical studies support this notion, finding that stepparents are less likely to engage in suicidal behavior subsequent to filicide than are biological parents (Daly & Wilson, 1988; Nordlund & Temrin, 2007; Shackelford et al., 2005; Shackelford, Weekes-Shackelford, & Beasley, 2008; Wilson et al., 1995).

Second, evolutionary perspectives indicate that parents value offspring more as that offspring ages and approaches reproductive maturity. Once a child has reached reproductive age, the child is able to pass on the parent's genes. Younger offspring may thus be killed to increase the chances of survival of older offspring. From this perspective, filicide of an older child, who is closer to reproductive maturity, is counteracting evolutionary interests and, hence, may be attributable to the parent's abnormal psychological functioning. Accordingly, child homicides involving an older victim are thus more likely to be followed by a suicide—a notion supported by empirical research (Hatters Friedman et al., 2008; Liem, De Vet, & Koenraadt, 2010; Shackelford et al., 2005).

Third, as mentioned previously, the more a homicide opposes evolutionary interests, the more likely it is to be accompanied by mental illness. From this point of view, perpetrators who commit suicide after the child homicide are more likely to suffer from mental illness compared to those "only" killing their children. This presumption has been supported by several empirical studies (Holden, Burland, & Lemmen, 1996; Léveillée et al., 2007; Lewis & Bunce, 2003), finding depressive and/or psychotic disorders to be most prevalent.

Fourth, evolutionary perspectives provide insight into the killing of multiple family members. Daly and Wilson (1988) argued that killers who perpetrate homicides that are especially damaging to their fitness interests, such as homicides involving multiple family members, are more likely to be suicidal or mentally ill. Other research corroborates these presumptions, finding that familial homicide followed by suicide are indeed more likely to result in the suicide of the perpetrator compared to single-victim homicides (Shackelford et al., 2005, 2008; Wilson et al., 1995).

In sum, the findings from previous international studies supporting these evolutionary perspectives suggest that filicide followed by suicidal behavior shares universal characteristics.

Conclusion

From an evolutionary point of view, homicide followed by suicide appears to be counter to the perpetrator's reproductive and survival interests. Several evolutionary theories therefore point to the role of mental illness to explain homicide-suicide. Another way to address this apparently counterreproduction, countersurvival aspect of these cases is to consider homicide-suicide as primarily suicidal or to consider it as a separate type of lethal violence that can be explained by different theoretical perspectives, particularly related to the influence of interpersonal dependency.

Future Directions

Based on a review of previous work performed in the field of homicide-suicide as presented in this chapter, as well as the shortcomings of studies conducted in this field, at least four directions for future research can be outlined:

1. Within the body of research on the homicide-suicide phenomenon, theory formation and theory testing are relatively rare. Existing theories consider homicide-suicide either as a variant of homicidal behavior or as a variant of suicidal behavior. As outlined earlier, empirical research indicates that homicide-suicide might constitute a phenomenon separate from both homicide and suicide. Our theoretical understanding of these types of lethal violence might be in need of revision.

2. Second, previous research on homicide-suicide has been restricted to a few Western countries and has often relied on small samples (Liem, 2010b). To overcome this shortcoming, several initiatives have been raised to conduct multicenter studies, one of which is the European Homicide-Suicide Study (EHHS). The empirical cornerstone of this project is the collection of complete national samples of homicide-suicide from six European countries across a full decade (Oberwittler, 2008). This uniform, large-scale data set allows for the systematic and cross-national analysis of homicide-suicide. The first results of this study are expected in due course (http://ehss.mpicc.de).

3. Third, because of the nature of homicide-suicide, both perpetrator and victim die in these events. Hence, the data sources used in previous studies typically lack detailed information on the dynamics underlying the event, the motives involved, and the role of other precipitating factors. Several researchers have therefore called for the studying of survivors of these acts (Berman, 1996; Brett, 2002; Hillbrand, 2001). It has been suggested that in homicides followed by a failed suicide, the nonlethal outcome of the act may be a matter of chance. Therefore, this group is likely to have similar characteristics as the homicide-suicide group. Studies following this approach are able to provide a large amount of new details (Liem, Hengeveld, et al., 2009).

4. To overcome the limitation of having limited information available on perpetrators and victims, future research could make use of the so-called psychological autopsy method (Shneidman, 1981). This method is based upon a combination of interviews of those closest to the deceased and an examination of corroborating evidence from sources such as hospital reports and criminal records. From this information, an assessment is made of the suicide victim's mental and physical health, personality, experiences with social adversity, and social integration (Cavanagh, Carson, Sharpe, & Lawrie, 2003). The psychological autopsy method has been useful in the study of suicide (Conwell et al., 1996; Isometsä, 2001) and could be applied to perpetrators and victims of a homicide-suicide in order to get a more extensive view of the psychopathological, motivational, and circumstantial characteristics of the perpetrator.

References

Agnew, R. (1992). Foundation for a general strain theory of crime and delinquency. *Criminology, 30,* 47–87.

Barber, C. W., Azrael, D., Hemenway, D., Olson, L. M., Nie, C., Schaechter, J., & Walsh, S. (2008). Suicides and Suicide Attempts Following Homicide. *Homicide Studies, 12*(3), 285–297.

Barraclough, B. M., & Clare Harris, E. (2002). Suicide preceded by murder: The epidemiology of homicide-suicide in England and Wales 1988–92. *Psychological Medicine, 32,* 577–584.

Belfrage, H., & Rying, M. (2004). Characteristics of spousal perpetrators: A study of all cases of spousal homicide in Sweden 1990–1999. *Criminal Behaviour and Mental Health, 14,* 121–133.

Berman, A. L. (1979). Dyadic death: Homicide-suicide. *Suicide and Life-Threatening Behavior, 9,* 15–23.

Berman, A. L. (1996). Dyadic death: A typology. *Suicide and Life Threatening Behaviour, 26,* 342–350.

Bijl, R. V., Ravelli, A., & Zessen, V. G. (1998). Prevalence of psychiatric disorder in the general population: Results of the Netherlands Mental Health Survey and Incidence Study (NEMESIS). *Social Psychiatry and Psychiatric Epidemiology, 33,* 587–595.

Bossarte, R. M., Simon, T. R., & Barker, L. (2006). Characteristics of homicide followed by suicide incidents in multiple states, 2003–04. *Injury Prevention, 12,* 33–38.

Bourget, D., Gagne, P., & Labelle, M. E. (2007). Parricide: A comparative study of matricide versus patricide. *Journal of American Academy of Psychiatry and Law, 35*(12), 306–312.

Bourget, D., Gagne, P., & Moamai, J. (2000). Spousal homicide and suicide in Quebec. *Journal of the American Academia for Psychiatry and Law, 28,* 179–182.

Brett, A. (2002). Murder-parasuicide: A case series in Western Australia. *Psychiatry, Psychology and Law, 9,* 96–99.

Bridges, F. S., & Lester, D. (2010). Homicide-suicide in the United States, 1968–1975. *Forensic Science International, 206,* 185–189.

Byard, R., Knight, D., James, R. A., & Gilbert, J. (1999). Murder-suicides involving children: A 29-year study. *American Journal of Forensic Medicine and Pathology, 20,* 232–327.

Campanelli, G., & Gilson, T. (2002). Murder-suicide in New Hampshire, 1995–2000. *American Journal of Forensic Medicine and Pathology, 23,* 248–251.

Carcach, C., & Grabosky, P. N. (1998). *Murder-suicide in Australia.* Report No. 82. Australian Institute of Criminology Trends and Issues in Crime and Criminal Justice. Canberra, Australia.

Cavan, R. (1928). *Suicide.* Chicago: University of Chicago Press.

Cavanagh, J. T. O., Carson, A. J., Sharpe, M., & Lawrie, S. M. (2003). Psychological autopsy studies of suicide: A systematic review. *Psychological Medicine, 33,* 395–405.

Chan, C. Y. (2007). Hostility in homicide-suicide events: A typological analysis with data from a Chinese society, Hong Kong, 1989–2003. *Asian Criminology, 2,* 1–18.

Chan, C. Y., Beh, S. L., & Broadhurst, R. G. (2003). Homicide-suicide in Hong Kong 1989–1998. *Forensic Science International, 137,* 165–171.

Cohen, D., Llorente, M., & Eisdorfer, C. (1998). Homicide-suicide in older persons. *American Journal of Psychiatry, 155,* 390–396.

Coid, J. (1983). The epidemiology of abnormal homicide and murder followed by suicide. *Psychological Medicine, 13*, 855–860.

Comstock, R. D., Mallonnee, S., Kruger, E., Rayno, K., Vance, A., & Jordan, F. (2005). Epidemiology of homicide-suicide events: Oklahoma, 1994–2001. *American Journal of Forensic Medicine and Pathology, 26*, 229–235.

Conwell, Y., Duberstein, P. R., Cox, C., Herrmann, J. H., Forbes, N. T., & Caine, E. D. (1996). Relationships of age and Axis I diagnosis in victims of completed suicide: A psychological autopsy study. *American Journal of Psychiatry, 153*, 1001–1008.

Cooper, M., & Eaves, D. (1996). Suicide following homicide in the family. *Violence and Victims, 11*, 99–112.

Crimmins, S. (1993). Parricide vs suicide: The dilemma of them or me. In A. V. Wilson (Ed.), *Homicide: The victim/offender connection* (pp. 115–134). Cincinatti, OH: Anderson.

Daly, M., & Wilson, M. I. (1988). *Homicide*. New York: Aldine de Gruyter.

Daly, M., & Wilson, M. I. (1994). Some differential attributes of lethal assaults on small children by stepfathers versus genetic fathers. *Ethology and Sociobiology, 15*, 207–217.

Daly, M., & Wilson, M. I. (1995). Familicide: The killing of spouse and children. *Aggressive Behavior, 21*, 275–291.

Dawson, M. (2005). Intimate femicide followed by suicide: Examining the role of premeditation. *Suicide and Life-Threatening Behavior, 35*, 76–90.

DeLeo, D., & Spathonis, K. (2004). Suicide and suicidal behaviour in late-life. In D. De Leo, U. Bille-Brahe, A. Kerkhof, & A. Schmidtke (Eds.), *Suicidal behaviour. Theories and research findings*. Göttingen, Germany: Hogrefe & Huber.

Dettling, A., Althaus, L., & Haffner, H. T. (2003). Criteria for homicide and suicide on victims of extended suicide due to sharp force injury. *Forensic Science International, 134*, 142–146.

Dogan, K. H., Demirci, S., Gunaydin, G., & Buken, B. 2010. Homicide-suicide in Konya, Turkey between 2000 and 2007. *Journal of Forensic Sciences, 55*(1), 110–115.

Durkheim, E. (1897/2002). *Suicide*. Abingdon, England: Routledge. (Original work published 1897).

Dutton, D., & Kerry, G. (1999). Modus operandi and personality disorder in incarcerated spousal killers. *International Journal of Law and Psychiatry, 22*, 287–299.

Dutton, D., & Yamini, S. (1995). Adolescent parricide: An integration of social cognitive theory and clinical views of projective-introjective cycling. *American Journal of Orthopsychiatry, 65*, 1367–1386.

Easteal, P. W. (1993). *Killing the beloved*. Canberra, Australia: Australian Institute of Criminology.

Ewing, C. P. (1993). *Kids who kill: Juvenile murder in America*. London: Lexington Books.

Ewing, C. P. (1997). *Fatal families*. London: Sage.

Felthous, A. R., & Hempel, A. G. (1995). Combined homicide-suicides: A review. *Journal of Forensic Sciences, 40*, 846–857.

Flynn, S., et al. (2009). Homicide followed by suicide: A cross-sectional study. *The Journal of Forensic Psychiatry and Psychology, 20*(2), 306–321.

Frazier, S. H. (1975). Violence and social impact. In J. C. a. G. Schoolar (Ed.), *Research and the psychiatric patient*. New York: Brunner and Mazel.

Freud, S. (1917). Mourning and melancholia. In J. Strachey (Ed.), *The complete psychological works of Sigmund Freud* (pp. 237-260, Volume 14). London: Hogarth Press.

Freud, S. (1949). *The ego and the id*. London: The Hogarth Press.

Gartner, R., & McCarthy, B. (2008). Twentieth-century trends in homicide followed by suicide in four North American cities. In J. Weaver & D. Wright (Eds.), *Histories of suicide: International perspectives on self-destruction in the modern world*. Toronto: University of Toronto Press.

Goldney, R. D. (1977). Family murder followed by suicide. *Forensic Science International, 3*, 219–228.

Haenel, T., & Elsässer, P. N. (2000). Double suicide and homicide-suicide in Switzerland. *Crisis, 21*, 122–125.

Hannah, S. G., Turf, E. E., & Fierro, M. F. (1998). Murder-suicide in central Virginia: A descripitive epidemiologic study and empiric validation of the Hanzlick-Koponen typology. *American Journal of Forensic Medicine and Pathology, 19*, 275–283.

Hanzlick, R., & Koponen, M. (1994). Murder-suicide in Fulton County, Georgia: Comparison with a recent report and proposed typology. *American Journal for Medical Pathology, 15*, 168–175.

Harper, D. W., & Voigt, L. (2007). Homicide followed by suicide. An integrated theoretical perspective. *Homicide Studies, 11*(4), 295–318.

Hata, N., Komanito, Y., Shimada, I., Takizawa, H., Fujikura, T., Morita, M., et al. (2001). Regional differences in homicide patterns in five areas of Japan. *Legal Medicine, 3*, 44–55.

Hatters Friedman, S., Holden, C. E., Hrouda, D. R., & Resnick, P. J. (2008). Maternal filicide and its intersection with suicide. *Brief Treatment and Crisis Intervention, 0*(1), 1–9.

Henry, A., & Short, J. (1954). *Suicide and homicide*. Glencoe, IL: The Free Press.

Hillbrand, M. (2001). Homicide-suicide and other forms of co-occurring aggression against self and against others. *Professional Psychology: Research and Practice, 32*, 626–635.

Holden, C. E., Burland, A. S., & Lemmen, C. A. (1996). Insanity and filicide: Women who murder their children. *New Directions for Mental Health Services, 69*(25–34).

Isometsä, E. T. (2001). Psychological autopsy studies—a review. *European Psychiatry, 16*, 379–385.

Killias, M., Dilitz, C., & Bergerioux, M. (2006). Drames familiaux—un "Sonderfall" suisse. *Crimiscope, 33*, 1–8.

Kivivouri, J., & Lethi, M. (2003). Homicide followed by suicide in Finland: Trend and social focus. *Journal Scandinavian Study in Criminology and Crime Prevention, 4*, 223–230.

Koziol-McLain, J., Webster, D., McFarlane, J., et al. (2006). Risk factors for femicide-suicide in abusive relationships: Results from a multisite study. *Violence and Victims, 21*, 3–21.

Krischer, M. K., Stone, M. H., Sevecke, K., & Steinmeyer, E. M. (2007). Motives for maternal filicide: Results from a study with female forensic patients. *International Journal of Law and Psychiatry, 30*, 191–200.

Large, M., Smith, G., & Nielssen, O. (2009). The epidemiology of homicide followed by suicide: A systematic and quantitative review. *Suicide and Life-Threatening Behavior, 39*, 294–306.

Lecomte, D., & Fornes, P. (1998). Homicide followed by suicide: Paris and its suburbs, 1991–1996. *Journal of Forensic Sciences, 43*, 760–764.

Léveillée, S., Marleau, J. D., & Dubé, M. (2007). Filicide: A comparison by sex and presence of absence of self-destructive behaviour *Journal of Family Violence, 22*, 287–295.

Levi, M., Maguire, M., & Brookman, F. (2007). Violent crime. In M. Maguire, R. Morgan, & R. Reiner (Eds.), *The Oxford handbook of criminology* (3rd ed., pp. 687–732). Oxford, England: Oxford University Press.

Lewis, C. F., & Bunce, S. C. (2003). Filicidal mothers and the impact of psychosis on maternal filicide. *Journal of the American Academia for Psychiatry and Law, 31*, 459–470.

Liem, M. (2010a). Homicide-parasuicide: A qualitative comparison with homicide and parasuicide. *Journal of Forensic Psychiatry and Psychology, 21*, 247–263.

Liem, M. (2010b). Homicide followed by suicide: A review. *Aggression and Violent Behavior, 15*(3), 153–161.

Liem, M., De Vet, R., & Koenraadt, F. (2010). Filicide followed by parasuicide: A comparison of suicidal and non-suicidal child homicide. *Child Abuse and Neglect, 34*, 558–562.

Liem, M., Hengeveld, M. W., & Koenraadt, F. (2009). Domestic homicide followed by parasuicide. *International Journal of Offender Therapy and Comparative Criminology, 53*(5), 497–516.

Liem, M., & Koenraadt, F. (2007). Homicide-suicide in the Netherlands: A study of newspaper reports, 1992–2005. *The Journal of Forensic Psychiatry & Psychology, 18*(4), 482–493.

Liem, M., & Nieuwbeerta, P. (2010). Homicide followed by suicide: A comparison with homicide and suicide. *Suicide and Life Threatening Behavior, 404*, 133–145.

Liem, M., Postulart, M., & Nieuwbeerta, P. (2009). Homicide-suicide in the Netherlands: An epidemiology. *Homicide Studies, 13*, 99–123.

Liem, M., & Roberts, D. (2009). Intimate partner homicide by presence or absence of a self-destructive act. *Homicide Studies, 13*, 339–354.

Lindqvist, P., & Gustafsson, L. (1995). Homicide followed by the offenders suicide in Northern Sweden. *Nordic Journal of Psychiatry, 49*, 17–24.

Logan, J., Hill, H. A., Lynberg Black, M., Crosby, A., Karcg, D. L., Barnes, J. D., & Lubell, K. M. (2008). Characteristics of perpetrators in homicide-followed-by-suicide incidents: National Violent Death Reporting System—17 US States, 2003–2005. *American Journal of Epidemiology, 168*, 1056–1064.

Lund, L. E., & Smorodinsky, S. (2001). Violent death among intimate partners: A comparison of homicide and homicide followed by suicide in California. *Suicide and Life Threatening Behaviour, 31*, 451–459.

Malphurs, J. E., & Cohen, D. (2002). A newspaper surveillance study of homicide-suicide in the United States. *The American Journal of Forensic Medicine and Pathology, 23*, 142–148.

Malphurs, J. E., & Cohen, D. (2005). A statewide case-control study of spousal homicide-suicide in older persons. *American Journal of Geriatric Psychiatry, 13*, 211–217.

Malphurs, J. E., Eisdorfer, C., & Cohen, D. (2001). A comparison of antecedents of homicide-suicide and suicide in older married men. *American Journal of Geriatric Psychiatry, 9*, 49–57.

Marleau, J. D. (2003). Fratricide et sororicide: synthèse de la littérature. *Criminologie, 36*, 157–175.

Marleau, J. D., Auclair, N., & Millaud, F. (2006). Comparison of factors associated with parricide in adults and adolescents. *Journal of Family Violence, 21*, 321–325.

Marleau, J. D., Poulin, B., Webanck, T., Roy, R., & Laporte, L. (1999). Paternal filicide: A study of 10 men. *Canadian Journal of Psychiatry, 44*, 57–63.

Marzuk, P. M., Tardiff, K., & Hirsch, C. S. (1992). The epidemiology of murder-suicide. *Journal of the American Medical Association, 267*, 3179–3183.

Menninger, K. A. (1938). *Man against himself.* New York: Harcourt & Brace.

Merton, R. K. (1968). *Social theory and social structure.* Glencoe, IL: The Free Press.

Messing, J. T., & Heeren, J. W. (2004). Another side of multiple murder. *Homicide Studies, 8*, 123–158.

Millaud, F. (1996). Parricide and mental illness. *International Journal of Law and Psychiatry, 19*, 173–182.

Milroy, C. M. (1993). Homicide followed by suicide (dyadic death) in Yorkshire and Humbershire. *Medicine, Science and the Law, 33*, 167–171.

Milroy, C. M. (1995a). The epidemiology of homicide-suicide (dyadic death). *Forensic Science International, 71*, 117–122.

Milroy, C. M. (1995b). Reasons for homicide and suicide in episodes of dyadic death in Yorkshire and Humbershire. *Medicine, Science and the Law, 35*, 213–217.

Milroy, C. M., Drastas, M., & Ranson, D. (1997). Homicide-suicide in Victoria, Australia. *The American Journal of Forensic Medicine and Pathology, 18*, 369–373.

Morton, E., Runyan, C. W., Moracco, K. E., et al. (1998). Partner homicide-suicide involving female homicide victims: A population-based study in North Carolina, 1988–1992. *Violence and Victims, 13*, 91–106.

Moskowitz, A., Simpson, A. I. F., McKenna, B., Skipworth, J., & Barry-Walsh, J. (2006). The role of mental illness in homicide-suicide in New Zealand, 1991–2001. *The Journal of Forensic Psychiatry and Psychology, 17*, 417–430.

Mouzos, J., & Rushforth, C. (2003). *Family homicide in Australia.* Report No. 225. Australian Institute of Criminology Trends and Issues in Crime and Criminal Justice, Canberra, Australia.

Näcke, P. (1908). Der Familienmord in gerichtlich-psychiatrischer Beziehung. *Zeitung Gerichtliche Medizin, 35*, 137–157.

Nock, M. K., & Marzuk, P. M. (1999). Murder-suicide. In D. G. Jacobs (Ed.), *The Harvard Medical School guide to suicide assessment and intervention* (pp. 188–209). San Francisco: Jossey-Bass.

Nordlund, J., & Temrin, H. (2007). Do characteristics of parental child homicide in Sweden fit evolutionary predictions? *Ethology, 113*, 1029–1037.

O'Connor, R., & Sheehy, N. (2000). *Understanding suicidal behaviour.* Leicester, England: British Psychological Society.

Oberwittler, D. (2008). The "European Homicide-Suicide Study" (EHHS)—a new collaborative research effort. *The Criminologist, May/June 2008*.

Okumura, Y., & Kraus, A. (1996). Zwölf Patientinnen mit erweiterter Selbsttötung—Psychologie, Persönlichkeit, Motivation, Vorgeschichte und psychosoziale Konfliktsituation. *Fortschritte der Neurologie Psychiatrie, 64*, 184–191.

Palermo, G. B. (1994). Murder-suicide—an extended suicide. *International Journal of Offender Therapy and Comparative Criminology, 10*, 106–118.

Palermo, G. B., Smith, M. B., Jenzten, J. M., Henry, T. E., Konicek, P. J., Peterson, G. F., et al. (1997). Murder-suicide of the jealous paranoia type: A multicenter statistical pilot study. *American Journal of Forensic Medicine and Pathology, 18*, 374–383.

Polk, K. (1994). *When men kill: Scenarios of masculine violence.* Cambridge, England: Cambridge University Press.

Roberts, K., Wassenaar, D., Canetto, S. S., & Pillay, A. (2010). Homicide-suicide in Durban, South Africa. *Journal of Interpersonal Violence, 25*(5), 877–899.

Rohde, A., Raic, D., Varchmin-Schultheiß, K., & Marneros, A. (1998). Infanticide: Sociobiological background and motivational aspects. *Archives of Women's Mental Health, 1*, 125–130.

Rosenbaum, M. (1990). The role of depression in couples involved in murder-suicide and homicide. *American Journal of Psychiatry, 147*, 1036–1039.

Saleva, O., Putkonen, H., Kiviruusu, O., & Lönnqvist, J. (2007). Homicide-suicide—an event hard to prevent and separate from homicide or suicide. *Forensic Science International, 166*, 204–208.

Saint-Martin, P., Bouyssy, M., & O'Byrne, P. (2008). Homicide-suicide in Tours, France (2000–2005)—description of 10 cases and a review of the literature. *Journal of Forensic and Legal Medicine, 15*, 104–109.

Schlesinger, L. B. (2000). Familicide, depression and catathymic process. *Journal of Forensic Sciences, 45*, 200–203.

Selkin, J. (1976). Rescue fantasies in homicide-suicide. *Suicide and Life-Threatening Behavior, 6*, 79–85.

Shackelford, T. K., Weekes-Shackelford, V. A., & Beasley, S. L. (2005). An explanatory analysis of the contexts and circumstances of filicide-suicide in Chicago, 1965–1994. *Aggressive Behavior, 31*, 399–406.

Shackelford, T. K., Weekes-Shackelford, V. A., & Beasley, S. L. (2008). Filicide-suicide in Chicago, 1870–1930. *Journal of Interpersonal Violence, 23*, 589–599.

Shiferaw, K., Burkhardt, S., Lardi, C., Mangin, P., & Harpe, R. L. (2010). A half century retrospective study of homicide-suicide in Geneva—Switzerland: 1956–2005. *Journal of Forensic and Legal Medicine, 17*(2), 62–66.

Shneidman, E. S. (1981). The psychological autopsy. *Suicide and Life-Threatening Behavior, 11*, 325–340.

Somander, L. K. H., & Rammer, L. M. (1991). Intra- and extrafamilial child homicide in Sweden 1971–1980. *Child Abuse and Neglect, 15*, 45–55.

Stack, S. (1997). Homicide followed by suicide: An analysis of Chicago data. *Criminology, 35*, 435–454.

Starzomski, A., & Nussbaum, D. (2000). The self and the psychology of domestic homicide-suicide. *International Journal of Offender Therapy and Comparative Criminology, 44*, 468–479.

Swatt, M., & He, N. (2006). Exploring the difference between male and female intimate partner homicides. *Homicide Studies, 10*, 279–292.

Unnithan, N. P., Huff-Corzine, L., Corzine, J., & Whitt, H. P. (1994). *The currents of lethal violence: An integrated model of suicide and homicide.* New York: State University of New York Press.

Wallace, A. (1986). *Homicide the social reality.* Sydney, Australia: New South Wales Bureau of Crime Statistics and Research.

Walsh, S., & Hemenway, D. (2005). Intimate partner violence: Homicides followed by suicides in Kentucky. *Journal of the Kentucky Medical Association, 103*, 10–13.

Websdale, N. (1999). *Understanding domestic homicide.* Boston: Northeastern University Press.

West, D. J. (1965). *Murder followed by suicide.* Cambridge, MA: Harvard University Press.

Wilson, M., & Daly, M. I. (1992). Till death us do part. In J. Radford & D. E. H. Russell (Eds.), *Femicide: The politics of woman killing* (pp. 83–98). Buckingham, England: Open University Press.

Wilson, M., Daly, M. I., & Daniele, A. (1995). Familicide: The killing of spouse and children. *Aggressive Behavior, 21*, 275–291.

Wu, B. (2003). Testing the stream analogy for lethal violence: A macro study of suicide and homicide. *Western Criminology Review, 4*(3), 215–225.

CHAPTER 9

Suicide

R. Michael Brown *and* Stephanie L. Brown

Abstract

The focus of this chapter is suicide, with emphasis on two evolutionary explanations. One views suicide as a by-product of states, traits, or predispositions that may have been adaptive in ancestral environments. The other views suicide as an evolved response that is conditioned on rare but well-specified environmental circumstances. The chapter considers this second approach—an inclusive fitness model of self-destructive motivation—in some detail. This model identifies circumstances under which self-preservation might be expected to break down—namely, the coupling of low individual reproductive potential with a sense of being a burden to close kin (burdensomeness). Although the model was designed to show how self-destructive phenomena might have evolved in ancestral environments, there is growing evidence to suggest that it is also capable of predicting instances of suicidal thinking and behavior in the present. We review that evidence and include a description of our own program of research that has tested and extended the model.

Key Words: suicide, suicidal thinking, suicidal behavior, evolutionary, inclusive fitness, burdensomeness, reproductive potential, self-destructive

Introduction

In this chapter we consider suicide, with special emphasis on evolutionary considerations. We begin with an introduction to the topic of suicide, followed by a discussion of proximate factors thought to play a role in this troubling phenomenon. The remainder of the chapter presents evolutionary accounts of suicidal thinking and behavior.

The Nature and Extent of Suicide

Suicide, often characterized as the intentional taking of one's life (Mayo, 1992), has a long history, despite the fact that the term "suicide" does not appear until the early 17th century in the writings of Thomas Browne (Minois, 1999). As historians of suicide have noted, suicidal acts were depicted in the Old Testament; described (sometimes with great admiration) in Greek and Roman times; condemned in Judeo-Christian, Islamic, and Hindu religious traditions; tolerated under certain conditions (e.g., euthanasia) in Buddhist writings; defended by some influential Renaissance and Enlightenment figures (e.g., Erasmus, Thomas More, John Donne, David Hume); and romanticized by others, such as Goethe in *Young Werther's Sufferings* (Minois, 1999; van Hoof, 2000). Later, in response to both 19th-century social science research and psychoanalytic theory, suicidal behavior would be considered variously as a multifaceted product of social conditions (Durkheim, 1897/1951) and/or as part and parcel of mental illness (e.g., Freud, 1917/1963; Menninger, 1938/1985). Indeed, these two early 20th-century views of suicide were seminal forces in shaping contemporary suicidology in the United States and other Western countries (van Hoof, 2000).

Though coroners, medical examiners, and many suicidologists insist on intent as a criterion for classifying a death as suicide, there can be considerable difficulty inferring, before or after the fact, an individual's true intentions. Only 15%–30% of individuals whose deaths are classified as suicides leave notes (Maris, Berman, & Silverman, 2000a), and not all notes make it clear that the intent of the individual was to actually end his or her life (Linsley, Schapira, & Kelly, 2001). No doubt, some deaths ruled to be suicides are not intentional, but the converse is also reasonable and perhaps more likely—some cases of intentional self-termination may be misclassified as accidental or indeterminate deaths. This latter possibility has been given more weight because coroners/medical examiners may be reluctant to classify a death as suicide without clear evidence of intent, leading some investigators to propose that classification criteria for suicide should be broadened to include deaths that are self-inflicted, irrespective of intent (e.g., Rockett et al., 2010).

Suicide is evident in all cultures that have been studied, regardless of degree of technological advancement, including those in Africa, the South Pacific, and aboriginal India and North and South America (deCatanzaro, 1987). In the United States in 2007, the most recent year for which complete statistics are available, suicide ranked eleventh among all causes of death, the overall rate standing at just over 11 per 100,000 people (Centers for Disease Control, 2010). Based on World Health Organization statistics (Krug, Dahlberg, Mercy, Zwi, & Lozano, 2002), the US rate is lower than the global average of 14.5 per 100,000, and decidedly lower than rates in eastern European countries, such as Belarus (41.5), the Russian Federation (43.1), and Lithuania (51.6). The overall rate of suicide in the United States and many other countries has not varied much over long periods of time (e.g., 1955–2005 in the United States), but not all countries surveyed are similar. Moreover, the relative steadiness of the overall rate of suicide within a country can obscure substantial change in certain demographic groups. For example, from 1950 to 1990 in the United States there was a four-fold increase in suicide rates for individuals 15–19 years of age but a decline of 38% during the next 17 years in this same age category (Centers for Disease Control, 2009).

The rate of suicide varies systematically with certain demographic factors, especially gender and age. In the United States more males complete suicide than females, a ratio of close to 4:1, but females attempt suicide two to three times as often as males. The higher rate of fatal suicide for males in the United States is, for the most part, found globally as well, with the male-female ratio ranging from 1.0:1 in China to 10.4:1 in Puerto Rico; the average is about 3:1 globally (Krug et al., 2002). As for age, suicides increase with age generally, but especially among males. This trend is apparent not only in the United States but also globally. However, it is not clear the extent to which the age-related suicide trend is accounted for by cohort (time of birth) effects rather than age itself, especially large cohort size and higher rates of out-of-wedlock birth (Stockard & O'Brien, 2002). These cohort effects may also contribute to the dramatic time-related increases and subsequent declines in youth suicide rates noted earlier.

Because suicide is an infrequently occurring phenomenon, and for obvious practical reasons, most research investigating suicide does not focus on completions but rather on suicidal thinking (ideation, planning) and behavior (e.g., nonfatal attempts). There are sound reasons to assume a continuum ranging from suicidal ideation to plans to attempts to completions (Kachur, Potter, Powell, & Rosenberg, 1995; Maris, 1992), and, indeed, many suicide prevention guidelines and programs are designed with this assumption in mind (e.g., Suicide Prevention Resource Center, 2004).[1] That said, there are also data to suggest discontinuities, especially between nonfatal attempts and suicide completions (e.g., Kreitman, 1977; Tanney, 2000). And, although measures of suicidal thinking and behavior are intercorrelated, the fact remains that the vast majority of suicide ideators do not attempt or complete suicide, and the majority of attempters do not complete (Maris et al., 2000b). Therefore, caution must be observed in making generalizations about completed suicide from studies restricted to suicidal thinking and nonfatal suicidal behavior.

Proximate Factors in Suicidal Thinking and Behavior

Suicidal phenomena are complex, likely resulting from interplay among a variety of social, economic, biological, and psychological factors. Durkheim's (1897/1951) seminal work was the first systematic attempt to classify and explain suicide, and his causal focus was squarely on societal conditions and events, especially degree of social integration (e.g., shared beliefs, interdependence, strong social bonds) and social upheavals (e.g., transitions from prosperity to poverty and vice versa). According to Durkheim, low levels of integration ("excessive individuation") can lead to what he called *egoistic suicide*, while very high levels ("rudimentary individuation") can result in *altruistic suicide*. Social upheaval, resulting in a disruption of society's ability to regulate outcomes for individuals, produces *anomic suicide*.

THE ROLE OF PSYCHOLOGICAL DISTURBANCE
> The best proof of madness...is the fact of having killed oneself. Hence all suicides are by definition insane.
> (*Minois*, 1999, p. 138, paraphrasing Chaline, 1665)

Despite Durkheim's emphasis on societal influences, and his dismissal of "insanity," "psychopathic states," or "alcohol consumption" as sufficient explanations of suicide on empirical grounds, much of the theoretical and research activity that followed has stressed the role of such factors, especially mood disorders, schizophrenia, substance abuse, feelings of hopelessness, and impulsive/aggressive traits. The idea, stemming directly from 19th-century views of suicide (van Hoof, 2000), is that such factors either establish vulnerability or serve as triggers for self-destructive thinking and behavior.[2] Contemporary variants of this view include Brent and Mann's (2006) "familial" model and Wenzel and Beck's (2008) cognitive model of suicidal thinking and behavior. In Brent and Mann's model, which focuses on adolescent suicide, allowance is made for familial transmission of vulnerability to suicidal behavior that is independent of transmission of mental disorder. However, major contributors to suicidal behavior are mood disorders and impulsive aggression. The Wenzel and Beck model assumes "psychiatric disturbance" as a major driver of suicidal thinking (especially a sense of hopelessness), and the existence of dispositional factors (e.g., "the confluence of aggression, hostility, and impulsivity") that make individuals vulnerable to both psychological disturbance and suicidal thinking and behavior.

Both retrospective and prospective studies provide empirical support for these and other variants of the psychological disturbance model of suicide. For example, there are data to show that as many as 9 of 10 individuals who commit suicide appear to have been suffering from some form of psychopathology at the time of their death (Arsenault-Lapierre, Kim, & Turecki, 2004; Harris & Barraclough, 1997). And, although most individuals who are diagnosed with a disorder do not commit suicide, they are more likely than the general public to do so. For example, Guze and Robins (1970) reported a 15% lifetime risk of suicide in patients suffering from major depression. Moreover, there is now a sizeable literature that implicates impulsivity/aggression in suicide, especially suicide attempts (Turecki, 2005).

Such findings have stimulated (a) large-scale research initiatives guided by the psychological disturbance model of suicide, including investigations of neurochemical and genetic correlates of suicide (see McGowan et al., 2008 for a recent example, and Mann, 2003 for a review of earlier studies); and (b) treatment/prevention programs premised on the psychological disturbance model (Goldney, 2005). Indeed, it is not unusual to find endorsements of the model like the one provided by Tanney (2000):

> The findings of comorbidity studies of a positive relationship between suicidal acts and the number of mental disorders (Axis I and Axis II) strongly suggests a role for mental disorders in the causation of suicidal acts...The evidence is coherent and convincing that mental disorders can have an impact on numerous faculties and competencies of "mind" to the extent that persons with such disorders are rendered not responsible for certain actions, including their own self-termination.
> (pp. 340–341).

However compelling these arguments and data may seem, there are sound reasons for suspecting that the causal role of mental disorders in suicide may have been overstated, including the following:

• Mental disorders are not unique risk factors for suicide; they are also associated with *nonsuicidal* deaths, including homicides (Herjanic & Meyer, 1976), and deaths by natural causes and accidents (Joukamaa et al., 2001). For example, Holding and Barraclough (1977) found that 60% of those who died in accidents in the United Kingdom were classified as suffering from mental disorders prior to death, and the figure was close to 75% for three Taiwanese groups whose deaths were ruled accidental (Gau & Cheng, 2004). If psychological disturbance is implicated in both suicidal and nonsuicidal deaths, then it lacks discriminant validity and, therefore, theoretical value or even practical utility as a "risk factor" for any particular kind of death, including suicide.

• Patient status and measurement variables can inflate estimates of lifetime risk of suicide in psychiatric populations. For example, as noted previously, Guze and Robins (1970) reported a 15% lifetime risk of suicide in patients suffering from major depression. However, this figure was based mainly on retrospective studies of *hospitalized* patients. Bostwick and Pankratz (2000) reanalyzed the Guze and Robins meta-analysis and demonstrated that hospitalization nearly doubles lifetime suicide risk—4.0% hospitalized versus 2.2% never hospitalized. Note that neither of these figures is close to the 15% estimate for depressed patients reported by Guze and Robins. Why? Because Bostwick and Pankratz used a "case fatality" measure of lifetime risk, as opposed to Guze and Robins's "proportionate mortality" measure. Case fatality estimates reflect the percentage of a depressed sample that died by suicide. Proportionate mortality estimates reflect the percentage of the dead in a depressed sample that died by suicide. Both measures will yield the same result, so long as each patient is followed over his or her entire lifetime. But if follow-up periods are short—as they were in the studies Guze and Robins reviewed—the proportionate mortality measure will overestimate suicide risk. As Bostwick and Pankratz note, the overestimation occurs because suicide is overrepresented among younger individuals, and because suicides tend to peak just after hospital admission, and then again shortly after discharge (Qin & Nordentof, 2005).

- Diagnostic criteria for mental disorders (especially depression), based on the *Diagnostic and Statistical Manual of Mental Disorders* (*DSM*) have changed from the 1970s to present day (*DSM-II* through *DSM-IV*), dramatically increasing the numbers of individuals who are classified as depressed (Klein & Thase, 1997) and, therefore, the odds that deaths classified as suicides will have a history of mental disorder.
- Confounding of mood disorders (especially depression) with suicide. Depression is diagnosed, in part, because reports of suicidal ideation, planning, and a history of attempts are considered symptomatic of the disorder. This is a problem for both prospective and cross-sectional investigations of the relationship between mental disorders and suicide.
- Selection bias. It is often suicidal or homicidal tendencies (danger to self or others) that drive psychiatric hospitalization (Mellesdal et al., 2010). Once admitted, patients are typically diagnosed with a mental disorder. Therefore, rather than acting as a causal force, diagnosed mental disorders may serve as proxies for past suicidal thinking and behavior, which are arguably the best predictors of future suicidal behavior, even when otherwise robust correlates such as hopelessness and symptoms of mental disorders are controlled (Joiner et al., 2005).
- Problems associated with psychological autopsies, the method commonly used to determine whether mental disorders were involved in a given suicide (e.g., Pouliot & De Leo, 2006). Limitations include inaccuracy of coroner/medical examiner decisions in the case of equivocal deaths, selection bias, recall bias, confirmation bias, lack of reliability, and heavy reliance on informants who have a stake in the outcome of the psychological autopsy.

GENETIC FACTORS AND NEUROCHEMICAL CORRELATES

Family Studies of Genetic Influence Investigation of genetic influence on human phenotypic traits typically begins with studies of family resemblance, and suicide is no exception. Such studies have shown that suicidal thinking and behavior aggregate in families. Individuals who have attempted or completed suicide are more likely to have first-degree relatives (e.g., parents, children) who have done the same, and the similarity is considerably higher than it is for unrelated members of the general population. The same case can be made for mental disorders that are associated with suicide, especially those involving major depression (Sullivan, Neale, & Kendler, 2000), raising the possibility that depression or some other risk factor is responsible for the family resemblance in suicidality. However, those studies that have controlled statistically for depression still report a familial effect for suicide (see McGirr et al., 2009, for a recent example, and Brent & Melhem, 2008, for a review of earlier studies).

Twin studies have typically shown higher concordance ratios for suicidality in identical as opposed to fraternal twins, consistent with the hypothesis that suicide has genetic underpinnings. For example, Roy and colleagues (as reviewed in Roy, 1992) pooled completed suicide data from their own and earlier studies, yielding 399 twin pairs. Results showed that concordance for identical twins was over 18 times that of fraternals. More recent studies focusing on nonfatal suicidal attempts have replicated the finding of higher concordance for identicals than fraternals, independent of mental disorders (Brent & Mann, 2005; Mann et al., 2009).

Evidence from studies of family resemblance and twin studies is consistent with the hypothesis that genetic differences contribute to variation (individual differences) in suicidal thinking and behavior, independent of psychological disturbance. Such studies have yielded heritability estimates of slightly over 40% for completed suicide (McGuffin, Marusic, & Farmer, 2001), and 17%–55% for suicidal thinking, plans, and nonfatal attempts (Brent

& Mann 2005; Voracek & Loibl, 2007). It should be noted, however, that twin studies published to date have not included twins reared apart, essential for gauging relative contributions of genetic and environmental variation to individual differences in suicidality.

Adoption studies represent a potentially powerful method of assessing the relative contributions of genetic variation to a given trait. The most impressive adoption studies of suicide to date are those conducted by Kety and colleagues using a registry of over 5,000 adoptions that took place in Denmark during the years 1924–1947 (Schulsinger, Kety, Rosenthal, & Wender, 1979; Wender, Kety, Rosental, & Schulsinger, 1986). In one of these studies 57 adoptees had committed suicide. Of these 57, 4.5% of their *biological* (genetic) relatives had also done so; less than 1% of the biological relatives of a carefully matched group of adopted controls (who had not committed suicide) died of suicide. Importantly, *none* of the adopted (nongenetic) relatives of adoptees in either group died of suicide, raising the possibility that rearing environment contributes less than genetic factors to variation in suicidal thinking and behavior. Findings did not appear to be driven primarily by psychological disturbance, but neither did they rule it (especially impulsivity) out as an independent or additive predisposing condition for suicide.

Neurochemical Correlates and Specific Gene Effects The pioneering work of Asberg and colleagues (Åsberg, Träskman, & Thorén, 1976) stimulated a body of research devoted to understanding the neurobiological bases of suicide, and traits that may predispose suicide, especially aggression and impulsivity. Asberg, et al. found abnormally low levels of a metabolite of serotonin—5HIAA—in the cerebral spinal fluid (CSF) of depressed suicide victims. Their findings have proven to be reliable and have led to further investigations of the functions of the serotonergic system in relation to suicide, mood disorders, personality disorders, and schizophrenia, and to specific genes that may play a role. Subsequent studies have found that low concentrations of CSF 5HIAA are associated with violent suicides and highly lethal attempts in particular, and postmortem investigations have found fewer binding sites for serotonin transporter in the ventral prefrontal cortex (Mann et al., 2000). This latter observation appears to be specific to suicide as opposed to major depression (Mann et al., 2000). Compared to matched controls, serotonin transporter binding was lower throughout the dorsal-ventral extent of the prefrontal cortex in individuals with a history of major depression. However, reduced binding in the *ventral* prefrontal cortex was specific to suicide. The finding is important because the ventral prefrontal cortex is thought to play a role in behavioral and cognitive inhibition (Mann, 2003). At least some instances of suicidal behavior may occur because of poor inhibitory control, which could result from low levels of serotonin in the very areas that regulate such control.

Neurotransmitters other than serotonin have been hypothesized to play a role in suicidal behavior, specifically norepinephrine and dopamine, but relevant investigations have produced inconsistent results. A seemingly more productive line of research involves the role of the hypothalamic-pituitary-adrenal (HPA) axis, the system responsible for regulating the stress response. A number of studies have found elevated cortisol (stress hormone) levels and/or dexamethasone resistance in depressed individuals who eventually die of suicide (e.g., Coryell & Schlesser, 2001; Yerevanian, Feusner, Koek, & Mintz, 2004). Dexamethasone is a steroid that normally suppresses cortisol production; its failure to do so suggests dysregulation of the HPA axis, at least at the time of the dexamethasone suppression test (DST). Because there is a complex, bidirectional relationship between the HPA axis and the serotonergic system, it is possible that HPA hyperactivity may play some role in altering serotonin levels in suicidal individuals (Carballo et al., 2009).

A number of attempts have been made to identify specific genes that play a role in suicidal behavior. For the most part, these studies have focused on genes for serotonin transporter, receptors, and enzymes; some investigations have also examined specific genes associated with the relationship between HPA axis hyperactivity and suicidal behavior (Sokolowski & Wasserman, 2009). Some of these investigations constitute valiant longitudinal efforts to identify how single genes, and genes interacting with each other and with rearing environments, might affect serotonergic activity that can influence both suicidal behavior and related disorders (e.g., Brezo et al., 2009). But the challenges for such studies are legion, including the daunting task of determining whether candidate genes are specific to regulation of mental traits/states that predispose mental disorders, suicidal behavior, or both.

It is also possible that identifying modes of inheritance beyond DNA sequencing—*epigenetics*—will illuminate the role of gene expression in predisposing suicidal thinking and behavior via effects on both the serotonergic system and HPA axis activity (Autry & Monteggia, 2009). Epigenetic influences consist of chemical regulatory processes that switch genes on or off, either by acting on a gene promoter (a segment of DNA affecting the expression of a particular DNA sequence) or by altering the structure of chromatin (coils of DNA bound to protein). Epigenetic changes do not result in a change in genetic instruction—the arrangement of the base pairs in a DNA molecule—only a change in gene expression. In some cases epigenetic changes can be transmitted to subsequent generations.

Recent work examining suicide victims indicates that those with a history of child abuse show evidence of epigenetic effects on HPA axis activity, paralleling findings from rodent studies that link deficits in maternal caregiving to epigenetically induced stress in offspring (McGowan et al., 2009). This exciting finding may help us better understand how child abuse might produce vulnerability to self-destructive behavior. Nevertheless, there are alternative (nonepigenetic) interpretations, and the caveats associated with gene-association studies of suicide apply to epigenetic studies as well.

Evolutionary Accounts

> It is hard to imagine a behavior that is less likely to maximize an individual's contribution to his or her gene pool than suicide... Even if suicidal behavior in an individual somehow conveyed an advantage to the species as a whole, genetically determined suicidal behavior would rapidly be selected against as individuals who displayed it killed themselves before being able to increase the frequency of these "suicidal" genes in the population by reproducing... Suicide (and hence severe depression) can thus only be seen as a disease state that conveys no benefits to an individual.
>
> (*Feder*, 2001, p. 1084)

It is not uncommon to read or hear comments like Feder's made in response to appeals for the evolutionary significance of suicidal thinking and behavior. Such comments identify a potential problem for a Darwinian explanation of self-destruction: If survival is essential to reproduction, and reproduction is the "engine of the evolutionary process" (Buss, 2004), how could a "gene for suicide" have evolved?[3] Feder's conclusion is that such a gene could never have evolved for the simple reason that its expression would produce a reproductive dead end.

Although intuitively appealing to some, Feder's remarks appear to be uninformed by 20th-century advances in genetics and evolutionary thinking, especially the existence of genetic complexities that could account for the transmission of a suicide gene. Consider the case of gene *pleiotropy*—a given gene resulting in two or more phenotypic outcomes, sometimes in opposite directions—beneficial *and* deleterious (antagonistic pleiotropy). For example, the same gene that codes for traits that enhance mating success during adolescence and young adulthood conceivably might contribute to disease or death at later points in development (Williams, 1957). Such a gene survives over generations because selection becomes weaker with increasing age—the gene's early fitness-enhancing effects outweigh its later deleterious effects. Pleiotropy, even antagonistic pleiotropy, does not have to be age dependent. So long as the adaptive benefits of the expression of a given allele outweigh its maladaptive consequences, it will be transmitted to subsequent generations.

Feder's argument also assumes that "reproducing" is the only way to transmit copies of genes to subsequent generations, a position that is uninformed by the monumental and paradigm-shifting contributions of Hamilton's (1964) inclusive fitness theory. Inclusive fitness theory holds that genes are transmitted to future generations not only through an individual's sexual reproduction but also through that individual's efforts to help genetic relatives reproduce. As Dawkins (1982) put it, for any given individual, inclusive fitness = the individual's reproductive success + that individual's effects on the reproductive success of his or her relatives, weighted by degree of genetic relatedness. Thus, even though a gene for suicide may not be transmitted directly to offspring via sexual reproduction, it could show up in succeeding generations through the mechanism of *kin selection*. Even genes that cause an individual not to reproduce can be favored by natural selection, so long as they enhance the reproduction of genetic relatives.

Suicide as a By-Product of Depression

Evolutionary theories of psychopathology, especially depression, have proliferated since the mid-1990s (Allen & Badcock, 2006), though the basic idea was in play much earlier (e.g., Averill, 1968; Bowlby, 1980; Brown & Cook, 1986; Hoyenga & Hoyenga, 1984). The feature common to these theories is that they do not consider all manifestations of depression to be dysfunctional, in sharp contrast to traditional medical and psychiatric conceptualizations (Andrews & Thomson, 2009). Rather, depression is hypothesized to have had adaptive value in ancestral environments. So-called low mood (mild depression) may have prompted affected individuals to disengage from fitness-depleting social interactions (e.g., Price, Sloman, Gardner, Gilbert, & Rohde, 1994) or goal-directed behaviors that are likely to be unattainable (Nesse, 2000). Depressive reactions in response to separation from a loved one may have motivated reestablishment of proximity or functioned as a signal for obtaining support from others (Averill, 1968; Bowlby, 1980). Even symptoms of major depression may have (a) improved the odds of gaining access to social relationships that enhance fitness or escaping from those that threaten it (Watson & Andrews, 2002); (b) enhanced the analysis of problems that threaten fitness (Andrews & Thomson, 2009); or (c) served to increase resistance to infections (Kinney & Tanaka, 2009).

As for suicide, evolutionary theories of depression either say very little about suicide or give little credence to the possibility that suicide could have enhanced fitness, other than in the case of the elderly (Hagen, 2003). Suicide is viewed either as a maladaptive by-product, perhaps triggered by evolutionarily novel circumstances (Confer et al., 2010), or as a necessary cog in the wheel of a depressive suicide signaling/bargaining strategy—"the cost of maintaining a credible threat" (Hagen, 2003):

> Suicide attempts are necessary to underwrite the credibility of suicide threats and must therefore entail a genuine risk of serious injury or death. Failed attempts resulting in injury can still impose costs on group members and indicate the seriousness of future attempts. Completed suicides are the cost of maintaining a credible threat. A suicidal signaling/bargaining strategy could evolve if it involved warning others beforehand (allowing them to respond to the suicidal person's needs), if the rate of threats were much higher than the rate of attempts, and if the rates of attempts were much higher than the rate of completions. Under these circumstances, the average benefits received over many generations by genes coding for this strategy, when group members were successfully influenced, could exceed the average costs suffered by those genes when suicide attempts succeeded.
> (p. 113)

Some evolutionary accounts of depression do, however, maintain that nonfatal suicidal attempts or self-injurious behaviors may have direct selective value. Watson and Andrews (2002) hypothesize that nonfatal suicide attempts, because of their potential high cost, represent honest signals designed by evolution to motivate social partners to provide help. Extending this logic and applying it to adolescent suicidal behavior, Andrews (2006) has argued that adolescents may use suicide attempts to leverage investment from their parents:

> The *leveraging* hypothesis proposes that desperate offspring may take risks that endanger their lives to leverage extra investment from their parents, whose interest in the continued existence of their offspring is put in jeopardy.... This strategy gets its leveraging power by virtue of the fact that each attempt jeopardizes the parents' genetic interests in offspring survival. Since parents are always exposed to some risk that their offspring will die, the probability of death must be great enough to force the parent to give up the resource.
> (pp. 191–192)

And Hagen, Watson, and Hammerstein (2008) use a similar rationale—the social bargaining model of depression (Hagen, 2003)—to argue that "deliberate self-harm" (DSH) can be adaptive:

> ...Although the bargaining model sees DSH as harmful and well worth treating, it does not see DSH as a brain dysfunction, and the focus is not on the putative psychopathology of the self-harmer.... In the bargaining model, the focus is on genuine unmet needs, real and perhaps intractable conflict, and the ability of DSH to credibly communicate these needs to others in a sometimes-fruitful attempt to obtain essential benefits that would otherwise not be forthcoming. Under the bargaining hypothesis, DSH is a "rational" aspect of human psychology.
> (p. 136)

It should be emphasized that it is the extreme cost of deliberate self-injurious behavior that compels others to take notice and provide those "essential benefits."

Evidence

Several findings are consistent with the argument that nonfatal suicide attempts and deliberate self-harm may function as signals to communicate need and elicit help from others. For example, data from traditional kin-based societies (cited in Hagen, 2003; Hagen et al., 2008) suggest that individuals often use suicide to impose a cost on others (e.g., revenge), and suicide threats to signal hurt or anger, to punish or otherwise pressure others, or to cause others to recognize the harm they have done and to repair it. Beyond these ethnographic accounts of traditional societies, Hagen et al. (2008) have cited evidence from industrialized countries (mainly the United States) that shows that (a) those who engage in deliberate self-harm have unmet needs for help from others, often having come from family environments that are highly stressful and abusive, and filled with interpersonal hostility and conflict; (b) self-harmers have difficulty communicating the intensity of their needs to those in the best position to provide help; and (c) there are potential self-reported benefits associated with self-injurious behavior, including receiving attention from others, elevating one's status, increasing one's control over others, and gaining help from others. There are also data to show that suicide attempts subside once relationships improve (Hawton, Cole, O'Grady, & Osborne, 1982).

To date, there have been few direct tests of the social navigation hypothesis, the social bargaining model, or the leveraging hypothesis vis-à-vis suicidality. One direct test is particularly noteworthy because of its prospective design (Andrews, 2006). In this study, Andrews compared adolescents who were satisfied with their mothers with adolescents who were dissatisfied. Not surprisingly, dissatisfaction with mother at Wave 1 (1994–95) predicted suicidal attempts significantly at Wave 2 (1996). In the highly dissatisfied group, middle-borns made fewer suicide attempts than first- or later-borns, but they made the most serious suicide attempts (those requiring medical treatment). Because middle children may receive less parental investment than first- or later-borns, Andrews interprets these data as providing support for the leveraging hypothesis—middle-borns need to send louder signals to their parents in order to make their needs known:

> The cry-for-help and leveraging hypotheses predict that parental sensitivity to risk will affect adolescent suicidal behavior. Based on evidence that middleborns are in a disfavored birth-order position…, it was suggested that parents might be less sensitive to the risks that their middleborn offspring take. Thus, middleborns might need to take higher risks than first- or lastborns to elicit extra [parental investment], and this should have an inhibitory impact on their decision to make an attempt.
> (p. 205)

To summarize, evolutionary theories of depression do not account for the evolution of suicide; they imply that it is either a maladaptive by-product, or they specifically state that it is the component of a depressive bargaining strategy that maintains the honesty of self-destructive signaling. On the other hand, self-injurious behavior may well have enhanced fitness in ancestral environments. There is considerable evidence that is consistent with this hypothesis but few direct tests of the models that incorporate it.

Suicide as an Evolved Response

From an inclusive fitness perspective, genes that code for behaviors that result in death, however indirectly, can be transmitted to future generations, so long as a consequence of an individual's death is enhancement of the fitness of his or her genetic relatives. This is precisely the rationale Hamilton (1964) provided for understanding the evolution of *altruism* from a gene-centered evolutionary perspective. Genes for altruism could have been transmitted from one generation to the next if costs (c) to the altruist (including his or her death) were outweighed by benefits (b) to the recipient of the altruism, discounted by degree of genetic relatedness between altruist and recipient (r)—Hamilton's rule: $c < rb$. This is also the rationale underlying recent mathematical models of kin selected variations in life span and mortality (e.g., Ronce & Promislow, 2010). In Bourke's (2007) extensive review of kin selection effects on aging, he argues that either accelerated aging or facultative suicide could be favored by natural selection so long as relatives are in a position to gain fitness at the expense of an individual's life:

> There are at least two ways in which a decrease in a focal individual's life span could increase the fitness of another individual. First, in systems of resource inheritance, the death of a resource-holding focal individual releases benefits to its successor… Second, in some social contexts, individuals might be selected to develop specific behaviors or structures for the defense of group members. Defense at times of danger to group members is likely to enhance recipients' fitness while risking the defender's life. If the focal individual nonetheless benefits through increased inclusive fitness, the result could be selection for adaptive suicide. Note that in the first situation outlined above, adaptive suicide would be more likely to involve obligate (programmed) death, whereas in the second, being conditional on a behavioral response to danger, it would be more likely to involve facultative suicide and hence not necessarily aging per se. In both cases, an essential

condition for adaptive suicide under kin selection theory is that the recipients should be relatives.
(p. 115)

Similarly, Lonergan and Travis (2003) have argued that the evolution of a suicide gene is logically and mathematically plausible, so long as it is assumed that (a) individuals become less efficient at utilizing resources with age, (b) individuals possess resources that could enhance the fitness of others, and (c) genetic relatives are aggregated.

> Under these conditions programmed death may be considered an extreme form of altruism, and understood as a special case of Hamilton's rule of inclusive fitness (Hamilton, 1964). Provided that the gene, rather than the individual, is considered as the unit of selection, the evolution of suicide therefore presents no difficulties.
> (p. 775)

Inclusive fitness arguments for suicide are given additional credence by (a) findings from game theoretic methods that show that suicide can become an evolutionarily stable strategy, and that the consequences of suicide are particularly beneficial to kin if the individual who completes suicide is elderly or in poor health (Mascaro, Korb, & Nicholson, 2001); (b) family correlational studies that are consistent with a genetic basis for suicide and suicidal behavior, independent of related psychopathological disorders (Kim et al., 2005; Lieb, Bronisch, Höfler, Schreier, & Wittchen, 2005; Pedersen & Fiske, 2010); (c) well-documented evidence for genetically controlled cell suicide (*apoptosis*, or *programmed cell death*), essential for normal tissue growth and maintenance and triggered by the activation of specific genes (Elmore, 2007); (d) evidence for cell suicide even in *unicellular* organisms, where no fitness benefit is possible other than that of ensuring the viability of neighboring clones (Herker et al., 2004; Knorre, Smirnova, & Severin, 2005); (e) evidence for what appears to be kin-selected suicidal behavior in a variety of animal species, especially in social insects such as worker ants and honeybees (Hölldobler & Wilson,1990; Rueppell, Hayworth, & Ross, 2010; Tofilski et al., 2008; Wilson, 2006) and in certain varieties of aphid (McAllister, Roitberg, & Weldon, 1990; Wu, Bolvin, Brodeur, Giraldeau, & Outreman, 2010); and (f) accounts of apparent altruistic suicide in humans where the cost is death and the mortal consequences are likely understood, if not anticipated, as in the case of certain Inuit groups (e.g., Leighton & Hughes, 1955),

Kamikaze pilots during World War II, and suicide bombers (Pape, 2005).

The best articulated inclusive fitness account of suicide is Denys deCatanzaro's (1986) mathematical model of the evolution of both self-preservative and self-destructive motivational mechanisms in humans and certain other social species (e.g., social *Hymenopterans*). According to this model, self-preservation motivation is variable, ranging from "strong promotion and defense of survival…to outright suicidal tendencies" (deCatanzaro, 1991, p. 16.). Where an individual lies on this continuum is influenced by her expected reproduction over the remainder of her lifetime ("individual reproductive potential," IRP) and by the remaining reproductive value of her genetic relatives ("kin reproductive potential," KRP). In the model, kin reproductive potential is weighted by two factors: degree of genetic relatedness to the individual (r), and the benefit (b) to kin generated by the continuing existence of the individual:

$$\text{Self Preservation Motivation} = \text{IRP} + \sum(\text{KRP} \times r \times b)$$

It should be noted that both individual and kin reproductive potential are calculated from a given point in time forward. That is, they reflect *expected* reproduction and are not counts of existing biological relatives. Degree of genetic relatedness (r) is calculated in the usual way (e.g., 0 = no genetic relatedness; 0.125 = one-eighth, as in one's great grandparent or first cousin; 0.25 = one-quarter, as in one's grandparent, uncle, or niece; 0.5 = one-half, as in one's parent or sibling or child). Most important for our discussion is the "benefit" term, which can be positive or negative. A positive benefit term (b) implies that the individual's continued existence enhances the survival and reproduction of another; a negative benefit term ($-b$) implies that the individual's continued existence interferes with another's survival and reproduction. It is $-b$, typically referred to as *burdensomeness*, that is most relevant to the model's explanation of self-destructive motivation.[4]

At the ultimate level, the model implies that truly self-destructive motivation may have evolved under rare but definable and plausible circumstances: low individual reproductive potential coupled with burdensomeness to genetic relatives. The idea is that in ancestral environments, individuals with extremely poor or nonexistent prospects for reproduction, whose continued existence interfered (however indirectly) with their genetic relatives' reproduction, might have been better off (genetically speaking) if they died. This may seem absurd at first glance, but not from an inclusive fitness perspective. As noted earlier, inclusive fitness theory (Hamilton, 1964) holds that there are two ways of transmitting copies of one's genes to subsequent generations: leave offspring of your own and/or help those who already carry copies of your genes to leave offspring. If you can't reproduce, then helping your genetic relatives reproduce (or at least not interfering with their reproduction) provides the only possible means of leaving a genetic legacy. But if your own prospects for reproduction are limited, and your very existence is an impediment (burden) to close genetic relatives' reproductive success, then staying alive interferes with the only means of genetic transmission available: kin reproduction.

Thus, consistent with inclusive fitness theory, self-destructive tendencies and behaviors that tended to reduce or eliminate burdensomeness altogether could have been preserved by natural selection. Of course, this scenario assumes that, at some level, individuals must be sensitive and responsive to cues for reproductive potential (e.g., perceived health, status, prospects for mating) in themselves and others, and to cues that predict contingencies between behavior and reproductive outcomes.

It is important to emphasize that deCatanzaro's model focuses on *past* recurrent evolutionary contingencies, providing an explanation for the evolution of a capacity for self-destructive motivation in humans and some other highly social species. Considering the nature and extent of post-Pleistocene technological change (e.g., guns) and cultural change (e.g., living in larger social groups consisting mainly of unrelated individuals), there is no particular reason to expect that the model should predict suicidal thinking and behavior in the present; nevertheless, there is increasing evidence to suggest that it does.

Evidence Consistent With the Model

With the exception of our own work (Brown, Dahlen, Mills, Rick, & Biblarz, 1999; Brown et al., 2009), there have been few attempts to directly test deCatanzaro's model. However, data from a variety of sources show that measures reflecting low individual reproductive potential, and perceived burdensomeness, are associated with suicidal thinking and behavior, including risk of completed suicide.

Humans are one among many species in which reproductive value declines with increasing age (Clutton-Brock, 1991). Thus, we might expect suicide rates to increase with age, and indeed there is a global trend in this direction, especially for males (World Health Organization, 2007). Even within an age cohort, reproductive potential can be affected by resource availability, health, dominance (social status), and opportunities for successful mating. Each of these factors has been linked to suicide—for example, low family income (Goodman, 1999) and low fertility (Calzeroni, Conte, Pennati, & Vita, 1990).

As for perceived burdensomeness, researchers operating from diverse theoretical perspectives have argued that it plays a role in self-destructive motivation. For example, some psychoanalytically oriented investigators have proposed that children exposed to messages of rejection may come to see themselves as expendable (Sabbath, 1969) or burdensome (Hendin, 1975; Orbach, 1986; Schrut, 1964) and, if defense mechanisms fail, conclude that they have no right to live (see Wagner, 1997 for a review of this literature). Consistent with both psychodynamic and inclusive fitness perspectives, results of risk assessments have raised the possibility that patient burdensomeness, as rated by clinicians, constitutes a risk factor in adolescent suicide attempts and/or ideation (Woznica & Shapiro, 1990) and in completed suicides in mental health inpatients of various ages (Motto & Bostrom, 1990).

Investigations of reasons for engaging in suicidal behavior (self-reported or rated by others), results of psychological autopsies, and findings from systematic evaluations of suicide notes also highlight a potential role for burdensomeness in self-destructive motivation (Brown, Comtois, & Linehan, 2002; Filiberti et al., 2001; Hedberg, Hopkins, & Kohn, 2003; Joiner et al., 2002; McPherson, Wilson, & Murray, 2007).

To be sure, there are methodological limitations inherent in suicide risk assessment studies (Maris, Berman, & Maltsberger, 1992), psychological autopsies (Clark & Horton-Deutsch, 1992), and the analysis of suicide notes (Joiner et al., 2002; Leenaars, 1992). And stated or rated reasons for suicide may or may not reflect actual motivation for suicidal behavior (Brown et al., 2002). At the same time, there is considerable convergence in the clinical literature that perceived burdensomeness is a potential risk factor for suicidal behavior, and there is a suggestion that burdensomeness is not simply a proxy for negative affect and hopelessness (Joiner et al., 2003; Van Orden, Lynam, Hollar, & Joiner, 2006) or for psychiatric disorder (Hedberg et al., 2003).

Joiner and his colleagues have conducted several studies that highlight the role of perceived burdensomeness in self-destructive motivation—"suicidal desire," in Joiner's terms. For example, Joiner et al. (2002) analyzed the suicide notes of individuals who completed suicide and individuals who survived suicide attempts. Trained raters, blind to which notes belonged to which groups (completers or attempters), evaluated the notes for burdensomeness, hopelessness, and generalized pain. Results showed higher ratings of burdensomeness in the notes of completers than in the notes of attempters who survived. Ratings of hopelessness or emotional pain did not differentiate the two groups. In a second study, ratings of suicide notes of completers showed that perceived burdensomeness was a significant, positive predictor of lethality of the suicide method used. Neither hopelessness nor emotional pain was associated significantly with lethality.

Van Orden et al. (2006) investigated the connection between perceived burdensomeness and self-destructive motivation in a large sample of male and female outpatients from a university psychology clinic. The patients completed well-known measures of suicidal ideation (the Beck Scale for Suicide Ideation) and depression (the Beck Depression Inventory), a single-item measure of hopelessness, and a single-item measure of perceived burdensomeness. Regression analyses revealed that perceived burdensomeness was a significant predictor of both suicidal ideation and past suicide attempts, over and above contributions of depression, hopelessness, and clinical ratings of personality disorder. More recent studies (e.g., Van Orden, Witte, Gordon, Bender, & Joiner, 2008) have confirmed the potency of perceived burdensomeness both as a main effect, and in interaction with a thwarted sense of belongingness, in predicting suicidal ideation in undergraduate participants, independent of participant depression.

Results of these evaluations of the role of perceived burdensomeness, and other data, formed the basis for Joiner's theoretical proposal that perceived burdensomeness, in concert with a failed sense of belongingness, is an important precursor to suicidal motivation (Joiner, 2005; Van Orden et al., 2010) and for the inclusion of perceptions of burden in the 2005 assessment protocol of the National Suicide Prevention Lifeline (Joiner et al., 2007).

Direct Tests of the Model—Main Effects

Direct tests of deCatanzaro's inclusive fitness model have also highlighted the importance of measures of individual reproductive potential and perceived burdensomeness in suicidal thinking and behavior. DeCatanzaro (1995) surveyed samples representing the general public, the elderly, psychiatric patients, criminal psychiatric patients, and homosexuals. Consistent with his model, unstable heterosexual relationships and self-reported burdensomeness to family members predicted suicidal ideation and behavior. Brown et al. (1999) replicated deCatanzaro's findings using a sample of university students. Our major predictors were measured individual reproductive potential (a composite reflecting adequacy of romantic relationships and perceived attractiveness) and perceived benefit to family (a composite reflecting perceived burdensomeness, contributions, and importance to family). Both composite measures were correlated inversely and significantly not only with a measure of suicidal ideation and behavior (as expected) but also with negative affect and hopelessness, each a robust predictor of suicide (Weishaar & Beck, 1992).

Direct Tests of the Model—Interaction Effects

A central prediction from deCatanzaro's model is that effects of perceived burdensomeness are moderated by an individual's residual reproductive potential—an interaction effect. Specifically, limited reproductive prospects due to old age, poor health, inadequate resources, or unsatisfactory relationships with the opposite sex should exacerbate the effects of perceived burdensomeness. By extension, the effects of burdensomeness should also be moderated by characteristics of the person being burdened, such as kin reproductive potential (KRP).

In a series of survey studies employing hierarchical multiple regression techniques, we have shown that effects of perceived burden on suicidal thinking are moderated by (a) measured aspects of participant IRP (self-reported attractiveness, health, and romantic relationship satisfaction), (b) a biological marker of KRP—age of participants' mothers, and (c) a measure of the strength of participant bonds to their parents. We describe the results of four of these studies, conducted with young adolescent and adult university students as participants. In this population suicide is a leading cause of death, usually just behind accidents, and suicidal thinking is prominent (Haas, Hendin, & Mann, 2003). We also describe the results from a fifth study examining suicidal thinking in patients suffering from end-stage renal disease (ESRD) and undergoing dialysis treatment.

STUDY 1

In Study 1 (Brown, Dahlen, Mills, Rick, & Biblarz, unpublished data), we administered the same questionnaire used in Brown et al. (1999) to 97 university students—21 men and 71 women (18 to 24 years)—and conducted hierarchical multiple regressions of the frequency of self-harm ideation. The predictor variables were measures of burden and individual reproductive potential. We ran six separate analyses, regressing self-harm ideation on each of two burden items,[5] in combination with each of three individual reproductive potential items.[6] All regressions were controlled for gender, negative affect, and a well-known measure of hopelessness (Beck, Weissman, Lester, & Trexler, 1974). Results showed the hypothesized moderating effect of individual reproductive potential on burdensomeness. Specifically, self-ratings of burdensomeness to family predicted self-harm ideation significantly, but only when perceived attractiveness was low or hurtfulness of relationships was high.

STUDIES 2 AND 3

The major goal of Studies 2 and 3 (Brown et al., 2009) was to determine whether perceived burdensomeness in adolescents and young adults is moderated by the reproductive potential of the person burdened, specifically, by the age of an individual's mother. Our reason for choosing the mother is that she is, in effect, a potent selection force for her offspring. In particular, she can enhance the inclusive fitness of a child by providing resources necessary for that child's survival and reproduction—calories, warmth, defense, and various forms of assistance, including caring for the child's offspring (Hawkes et al., 1998). A mother can also provide her child with siblings (who carry copies of the child's genes), so long as she remains reproductively viable, mates successfully, and nurtures those siblings. Of course, a mother's ability to provision offspring with siblings is limited by her age. Increasing maternal age is associated with a decline in fertility and fewer mating opportunities (Maestripieri & Carroll 1998).

In ancestral environments, burdening a *young* mother might have compromised the burdensome individual's inclusive fitness by interfering with the mother's continuing mating efforts or by reducing her investment in other (genetically related), and possibly more reproductively capable, offspring. Burdening an older mother would not entail the same level of risk, because an older mother would have been less viable reproductively and, therefore, less able to enhance the burdensome individual's inclusive fitness.

Accordingly, we expected a burden × maternal age interaction, in which perceived burden would be more strongly associated with self-destructive motivation for participants with younger mothers than it would be for participants with older mothers. We assumed that such an interaction, if obtained at the time of data collection, would reflect the effects of earlier ontogenetic experiences and processes. For example, mothers who, because of youth and inexperience, perceive their offspring to be demanding and burdensome may, over time, respond in ways (e.g., neglect, abuse) that bias a child toward internalizing a sense of expendability or burdensomeness (Wagner, 1997). There are certainly animal models consistent with this scenario. Young mothers, in particular, are sensitive to offspring-generated cues for interference with mating and other fitness-enhancing behaviors (Clutton-Brock, 1991; Maestripieri & Carroll, 1998). And observations that young maternal age is associated with poor parenting in humans (US Department of Health and Human Services, 2002), as well as suicide attempts and completions (Mittendorfer-Rutz, Rasmussen, & Wasserman, 2004), are suggestive.

There were 170 participants in Study 2 (42 men and 128 women, 18–24 years) and 180 participants in Study 3 (66 men and 114 women, 18–23 years). In each study we asked participants to rate the extent to which they agreed with each of two burden statements, one of which reflected financial burden and the other demands on time. In Study 2 participants rated their financial and time burdensomeness to "parents" and "family." But in Study 3 participants rated financial and time burdensomeness to *each* member of their immediate family (mother, father, siblings) and to each person they listed as a friend. In both studies we (a) replaced our self-harm ideation measure with a *suicidal ideation* composite that reflected frequency of suicidal thoughts and plans; (b) included a self-report measure of suicide attempt frequency; and (c) included a planned replication of the burden × IRP findings, using perceived health, attractiveness, and romantic relationship satisfaction as separate measures of IRP.

Results of Studies 2 and 3 showed the predicted burden × IRP interactions, replicating and extending findings from our previous studies. Moreover, hierarchical regressions of suicidal ideation and suicide attempts showed that burden effects tended to be stronger for participants whose mothers were younger rather than older. The predicted burden × maternal age interaction materialized for both suicidal ideation and attempts in Study 2, for attempts in Study 3, and for suicidal ideation in Study 3 when measures of participant and sibling reproductive potential were low. These effects—burden × IRP and burden × maternal age—occurred independently of depression and hopelessness; were unique to measures of violent ideation directed toward self, as opposed to others; and (in Study 3) were significant only when those burdened were parents (as opposed to siblings or friends).

The observation in Study 3 that burden interactions were significant only when those burdened were parents warrants elaboration. First, Study 3 was the only one to ask participants about their perceived burden to *each* family member (mother, father, sibling) and to each friend. We employed this strategy in order to evaluate deCatanzaro's prediction that burden effects on self-destructive motivation should be stronger when those burdened are close relatives of the burdensome individual. We were particularly interested in the case of biological parents versus full siblings. According to deCatanzaro's mathematical model, there should be no difference between burdening parents and siblings because genetic relatedness is the same ($r = 0.50$). However, Trivers's (1974) account of parent–offspring conflict holds that siblings compete for parental resources. Thus, burdening siblings could produce fitness *benefits* that burdening parents would not. Consequently, burdening siblings may exert a weaker effect on self-destructive motivation than burdening parents. This is precisely what we found.

STUDY 4

In this fourth study (Brown, Brown, & Nugent, unpublished data) we explored the relationship between perceived burdensomeness and social bonds. Selective Investment Theory (Brown & Brown, 2006) holds that the primary function of social bonds is to motivate us to behave altruistically toward those with whom we are bonded—even when the costs of doing so are extreme. With this in mind, we reasoned that individuals with the strongest bonds would be most sensitive to cues for burdensomeness precisely because of this altruistic motivation generated by the bond. In effect, strongly bonded individuals will consider suicide if they perceive themselves to be a burden because they are highly motivated to place the welfare of the person they are bonded (connected) with above their own. Based on inclusive fitness logic, this relationship is most likely to obtain in the case of close genetic relatives. Burdening a close genetic relative has a greater negative impact on transmitting one's genes to the next generation than burdening a distant relative, or a genetically unrelated individual. Accordingly, we predicted that perceived burden would be more strongly associated with suicidal ideation when bonds to close relatives are strong than when they are weak.

For Study 4 we surveyed 143 university students (52 men and 91 women, 18–29 years). We used the same measures of perceived burden and suicidal ideation as we had used in Study 3, but we added a composite measure of social bond strength (adapted from Brown, 1999) that tapped the following dimensions of affectional bonds (Ainsworth, 1989): feelings of connection, significant and durable feelings of affection, and anticipated distress upon separation. Each participant rated his or her perceived burdensomeness and bond strength, independently, to each parent, sibling, friend, and romantic partner. Control variables were the same as those used in Study 3.

Hierarchical regressions of suicidal ideation revealed a significant burden × bond strength interaction for the parent relationship category only, consistent with our prediction. Specifically, as burden to parents increased, so also did suicidal ideation, but only for participants who had reported having strong bonds to their parents. The interaction remained significant when regressions were controlled for gender, a composite measure of depression-pessimism, other measures of well-being, economic status, relevant family characteristics, and relevant interactions. The burden × bond strength interaction was unique to suicidal ideation, having no effect on violent ideation directed toward others.

STUDY 5

Data from Studies 1–4 are consistent with burden × reproductive potential interactions predicted by deCatanzaro's inclusive fitness model of self-destructive motivation. Yet generalization of these findings (and the model) is limited by the cross-sectional nature of our designs and by restricted samples not at risk for self-destructive behavior. Study 5 (Brown & Brown, unpublished data) is our first attempt to test interactive propositions of the model over time and with a nonstudent population—adults undergoing dialysis therapy for ESRD, a population at risk for emotional problems, including depression (e.g., Hinrichsen, Lieberman, Pollack, & Steinberg, 1989) and self-destructive behavior (e.g., Kimmel, 2000). We focused on the burden × IRP interaction measured at Time 1 (initial assessment) and sought to determine whether IRP moderated any observed burden effects on depression and suicidal ideation measured at Time 2 (1 year later). One hundred and thirteen patients participated in the Time 1 assessment and 60 of these patients provided follow-up data at Time 2. Patients ranged in age from 23 to 81, with a mean age of 55.

The measure of burdensomeness was an eight-item composite that asked patients to indicate whether their illness had created adverse circumstances for their family. IRP was measured in terms of economic status and health. Our measure of depression was the Hopkins Symptom Checklist (Derogatis, Lipman, Rickles, Uhlenhuth, & Covi, 1974), and our measure of suicidal ideation was a composite that reflected both severity and frequency of suicidal thoughts.

To examine whether the burden effect was modified by IRP, we regressed Time 2 depression scores on Time 1 measures of depression, burden, IRP, the interaction of burden and IRP, and other relevant control variables. We did the same for suicidal ideation scores, regressing them on Time 1 measures of suicidal ideation, nonsuicidal symptoms of depression, burden, IRP, the interaction of burden and IRP, and other relevant control variables. The predicted burden × IRP interaction materialized in both cases, significant for depression and marginally significant for suicidal ideation ($p = 0.055$).

Direct Tests of the Model—Other Findings

The same inclusive fitness logic that expects burdening genetic relatives to increase self-destructive motivation dictates that *helping* them should reduce it (Brown, Nesse, Vinokur, & Smith, 2003; deCatanzaro 1986). In Study 3 (described previously) we examined this logic empirically. We included in our survey a measure of perceived contribution to others and hypothesized that it should show predictive patterns with suicidal ideation that are opposite those shown by burdensomeness—specifically, contribution should be inversely correlated with suicidal ideation. We also expected the contribution–suicidal ideation relationship to be most pronounced when those helped are genetic relatives (especially parents) of the person making the contribution. Our findings were consistent with these predictions. Correlations between perceived contribution and suicidal ideation were inverse and significant, and highest when the person helped was a parent.

We replicated this general pattern of findings among dialysis patients in a follow-up of the ESRD patients in Study 4. The procedures and materials were identical, except that we focused on reported contribution to family and friends. Results demonstrated that Time 3 measures of contribution predicted decreased suicidal ideation between Time 3 and Time 4, controlling for depression at Time 3.

One of the most intriguing predictions generated by deCatanzaro's inclusive fitness model is that an individual's self-preservation motivation should vary directly with his or her efforts to help genetic relatives survive and reproduce. Brown et al. (2003) tested this prediction, examining the relationship between giving and mortality. In a sample of 423 married older adults, Brown and her colleagues demonstrated that reports of providing emotional support to a spouse and instrumental support to friends, relatives, and neighbors were each predictive of a 30%–60% decreased risk of mortality over a 5-year period. These results could not be explained by measured health, mental health, health behaviors, personality traits, demographics, or reports of receiving help from relationship partners. Importantly, the inverse relationship between helping and mortality has been replicated (Brown, Smith et al., 2009; Oman, 2007).

Limitations
LIMITATIONS OF THE MODEL

DeCatanzaro was careful to note that his model was intended to explain the possible evolution of self-destructive motivation in rare, well-specified *ancestral* conditions, when humans lived in small and genetically related groups. However, contemporary environments may differ in important ways from those our ancestors occupied, as deCatanzaro (1995) and others (e.g., Tooby & Cosmides, 1992) have noted. Today, many of us live in large, unrelated groups and are often separated by great distances from family and friends. Moreover, modern technology has generated extremely lethal (and readily available) devices for terminating life, as well as communication capabilities that can stoke self-destructive fantasies instantly and repeatedly. Consequently, we should expect that there now exist paths to suicide that are different from those described in the inclusive fitness model of self-destructive motivation. That said, it is important to note that a growing body of evidence, generated from diverse theoretical perspectives, is consistent with a central tenet of deCatanzaro's model—namely, that perceived burdensomeness constitutes an important risk factor for suicidal thinking and behavior.

LIMITATIONS OF THE STUDIES

Generalizations from the results of some of our investigations (Studies 1–4) are limited by virtue of their cross-sectional nature and also by restricted samples of participants—students, largely female, White, middle class, unmarried, at the peak of fertility, in good health, and not suffering from severe psychological disturbance. We doubt that these sample restrictions undermine interpretation of observed burden main effects, which have been replicated across diverse groups (Brown & Brown, 2010; deCatanzarro 1995; Van Orden et al., 2006, 2010), but more work is needed to establish the external validity of the burden *interaction* effects observed in Studies 1–4. At the same time, it is important to note that our hypotheses and measures in these four studies were created specifically for adolescent and young adult participants, limiting generalization to other groups by design.

Implications

DeCatanzaro's model, together with supportive empirical data, has important implications for efforts designed to understand, predict, treat, and prevent suicidal thinking and behavior. Unlike traditional proximate accounts of suicide, the inclusive fitness model does not view suicide as "a disease state that conveys no benefits to an individual" (Feder, 2001, p. 1084) but rather as an evolved, facultative response occasioned by the joint occurrence of low residual reproductive value and perceived burdensomeness. Under these circumstances there *are* benefits conveyed—to the individual's inclusive fitness through enhancement of the fitness of his or her genetic relatives.

The inclusive fitness model does not exclude the possibility that suicide can be triggered by factors other than perceived burdensomeness and low reproductive potential, or the possibility that suicidal behavior can have multiple consequences (adaptive and otherwise). Neither does the model preclude the possibility that depression, hopelessness, impulsivity/aggression, or other proximate factors—biological, psychological, sociocultural—play important mediating roles in orchestrating suicidal thinking and behavior. Indeed, the model is capable of integrating the "almost bewildering array of conditions" (Felner, Adan, & Silverman, 1992, p. 428) linked to suicide into a potentially useful explanatory framework. For example, the vast majority of documented risk factors for suicide might be considered potential threats to inclusive fitness (e.g., parent–child conflict, death of a family member, breakup of a romantic relationship, terminal illness, public humiliation) or reactions to such threats (e.g., substance abuse, affective disorders, conduct disorders).[7] DeCatanzaro's model offers some guidance for evaluating the relative importance of such factors. Specifically, the model holds that predictors of suicide are not sufficient to drive individuals to take their own lives unless they are accompanied by, or are a proxy for, poor or nonexistent prospects for mating success, coupled with intense feelings of burdensomeness to close kin.

Empirical investigation of the constructs specified by deCatanzaro's model has generated results that have important implications for predicting, treating, and preventing suicidal thinking and behavior. For example, findings from investigations of perceived burdensomeness suggest that it should be taken seriously in the clinical assessment of suicide risk (Joiner et al., 2007; Van Orden et al., 2006), regardless of whether such perceptions are accompanied by states of depression or hopelessness. Measures of and proxies for reproductive value should also be considered in conjunction with perceptions of burdensomeness. We have found repeatedly that burden effects are moderated by measures of residual reproductive value, and this argues for their inclusion in assessment protocols (Brown, Brown, et al., 2009).

With respect to intervention, having individuals identify fallacious conclusions of burdensomeness, and focus on contributions made to others, may prove effective in reducing or preventing suicidal thinking and behavior (Brown et al., 1999; Van Orden et al., 2006). Indeed, our finding that perceived contributions are inversely related to suicidal ideation gives reason for optimism concerning the outcomes of such interventions. It may also be important to involve family members in treatment programs, so they "might learn to recognize their roles in communicating overt or subtle messages of burdensomeness...and to appreciate the potentially lethal impact of such communications" (Brown et al., 1999, p. 69).

Conclusions

Our major goal in this chapter has been to explore the possibility that suicidal thinking and behavior may have evolutionary roots. In the interest of providing background, we observed that suicide is a rare but widespread phenomenon, documented cross-culturally and throughout recorded history. We also noted that suicidal thinking and behavior are correlated with psychological disturbance, and this correlation is often interpreted as cause-effect in the medical, psychiatric, and psychological literatures—despite daunting methodological cautions and inconvenient empirical facts. The conflation of suicide with psychological disturbance, and the inference that suicide is a derivative of mental disorder, have each undoubtedly hindered the development of evolutionary theories of self-destruction. If mental disorders and their suicidal derivatives constitute disease-like entities, how could they possibly be considered evolutionarily adaptive?

In this chapter we have taken the bait and tried to answer this rhetorical question. Two evolutionary approaches to understanding suicidal phenomena were examined. One approach views some aspects of mental disorder (e.g., depression) as adaptive, but it considers completed suicide to be either a by-product of depression or a necessary cog in a depressive bargaining strategy (e.g., Hagen, 2003); nonfatal suicidal attempts are viewed as the result of algorithms that function to elicit help from others (e.g., Hagen et al., 2008; Watson & Andrews, 2002). There is evidence consistent with this latter possibility, but few direct tests of the models proposed by Hagen, Watson, and Andrews have been conducted.

The other evolutionary approach to suicide is based on inclusive fitness theory (Hamilton, 1964), and it utilizes the same arguments that demonstrate the plausibility of the evolution of extreme forms of altruism (altruistic suicide) and programmed cell death (apoptosis). This approach holds that suicide could have been adaptive if an individual's reproductive possibilities were poor or nonexistent, and that the individual's continued existence interfered with the reproduction of genetic relatives (deCatanzaro, 1986, 1991).

There is considerable evidence to show that perceived burdensomeness is positively correlated with suicidal thinking and behavior, consistent with deCatanzaro's model. There are direct tests of the model that confirm its central interactive hypothesis: Limited reproductive prospects should magnify the effects of perceived burdensomeness on self-destructive motivation. And there is evidence to suggest that perceived contributions to others show predictive patterns with suicidal ideation that are opposite those shown by burdensomeness; specifically, contribution is inversely correlated with suicidal ideation. Finally, contributions to others also show an inverse relationship with mortality, consistent with deCatanzaro's argument that self-preservation motivation should vary directly with efforts to help others. Of course, much of the relevant evidence comes from cross-sectional studies that use self-report to assess suicidal thinking and behavior. Prospective research designs that evaluate the utility of the inclusive fitness model's constructs as predictors of actual behavior are needed to establish causal pathways.

Comment

Traditional accounts of suicidal phenomena are predicated on the assumption that mental disorders or negative emotions play strong causal roles in determining suicidal intent. However, research generated from such models has yielded little in the way of useful prediction, let alone explanation of suicidal phenomena. A cynical read of the relevant literature might justify the conclusion that the best predictor of suicide is suicidal behavior. Diagnosed mental disorders are clearly implicated in the majority of deaths by suicide, but alas, they are also clearly implicated in accidental deaths, deaths by homicide, and deaths due to natural causes. This fact weakens both the predictive and explanatory value of mental disorders vis-à-vis suicidal thinking and behavior.

Perhaps it is time to at least consider an alternative approach to suicide. Unlike disease models, the evolutionary alternatives described in this chapter identify evolutionarily adaptive consequences of suicidal thinking and behavior, including completed suicide. Moreover, they specify a *limited* set of conditions that would be expected to make such behavior more or less likely. Finally, they accommodate suicidal acts that do not appear to be embedded in psychological disturbance—for example, suicide threats in otherwise normally functioning adolescents, suicide bombings, and so-called rational suicide. Further development and testing of such models may help us improve our understanding of the origins and functions of suicidal thinking and behavior; meaningfully integrate, edit, and evaluate known proximate correlates of suicide; and facilitate efforts to identify and help those at risk. We may even find that some of our most vexing suicidal phenomena—youth suicide, suicide in the military, and suicide terrorism—are easier to predict, understand, and control within this new framework.

Future Directions

The two evolutionary accounts of suicidal thinking and behavior we have described yield highly testable propositions related to the proximate causes and functions of suicidality. For example, the social bargaining model of depression, applied to deliberate self-harm (Hagen et al., 2008), expects first of all the joint occurrence of certain conditions:

> ... (a) the experience of a severe need, inequity, or cost in (b) interdependent social relationships with (c) substantial conflicts of interest, and (d) a relative lack of power to unilaterally improve one's condition. (p. 135)

Beyond this, the social bargaining model holds that key social partners must be aware of self-injurious attempts, must infer that the person making the attempt is in need, and must on at least some occasions help the person in need, following which such attempts should cease. These are well-specified hypotheses that are directly testable through both cross-sectional and prospective means.

The inclusive fitness model we have tested (deCatanzaro, 1986) suggests that cues for burdensomeness play a causal role in producing self-destructive tendencies. But our data do not make clear how this is accomplished. For example, rather than activating self-destructive motivation directly, feelings of burdensomeness may be mediated by negative emotions such as depression. Results of some of our mediational analyses are consistent with this possibility, but cross-sectional research designs are of limited value in identifying the most likely causal sequence. Clearly, prospective studies are needed to help elucidate the role of burdensomeness by itself and in interaction with fitness variables such as health, relationship satisfaction, and strength of social bonds.

Notes

1. Suicide plans and attempts have been established as the most important risk factors for suicide completion (Joiner et al., 2003; Maris, 1992).

2. Durkheim allowed that psychological disturbance could play a predisposing role in suicidal decision making, but not a causal role: "This potentiality of his becomes effective only through the action of other factors which we must discover" (Durkheim, 1951, p. 81).

3. Readers will recognize that Darwin (1871) encountered a similar difficulty in attempting to account for the evolution of altruism: How can it evolve if, by its very nature, altruistic behavior is costly to the altruist, in some cases resulting in self-injury or even death?

4. It is interesting to note the similarity between deCatanzaro's model for suicide and recent inclusive fitness models of aging and mortality. In effect, both sets of models yield equations involving the same causal factors. As Ronce and Promislow (2010, p. 3665) put it: "In the presence of kin competition and limited dispersal, we found that the indicator of the strength of selection on age-specific survival comprises two terms: 'remaining fecundity' (*IRP* in deCatanzaro's model), and 'effects of the focal individual's survival on its relatives' (*b* x *KRP* in deCatanzaro's model)."

5. We tested only two of the six Likert-type burden items separately. The two items chosen were as follows: (a) "I expect that I will always be a burden to my parents or relatives" and (b) "I sometimes feel that my parents or relatives would be better off if I were dead." We selected these two items because they had better face validity than the others, and because they loaded more heavily than the others on a "burden" factor and less heavily on a "dependence-contribution" factor.

6. The three Likert-type IRP items were perceived attractiveness, romantic relationship satisfaction, and romantic relationship hurtfulness.

7. See Plutchik (2000) for a comprehensive list of risk factors for suicidal behavior.

References

Ainsworth, M. D. S. (1989). Attachments beyond infancy. *American Psychologist, 44*, 709–716.

Allen, N. B., & Badcock, P. B. T. (2006). Darwinian models of depression: A review of evolutionary accounts of mood and mood disorders. *Progress in Neuro-Psychopharmacology and Biological Psychiatry, 30*, 815–826.

Andrews, P. W. (2006). Effects of birth order and dissatisfaction with mother on attempt incidence and severity. *Human Nature, 17*, 190–211.

Andrews, P. W., & Thomson, J. A. (2009). The bright side of being blue: Depression as an adaptation for analyzing complex problems. *Psychological Review, 116*, 620–654.

Arsenault-Lapierre, G., Kim, C., & Turecki, G. (2004). Psychiatric diagnoses in 3275 suicides: A meta-analysis. *BMC Psychiatry, 4*, 37–47.

Åsberg M., Träskman L., & Thoren, P. (1976). 5-HIAA in the cerebrospinal fluid. A biochemical suicide predictor? *Archives of General Psychiatry, 33*, 1193–1197.

Autry, A. E., & Monteggia, L. M. (2009). Epigenetics in suicide and depression. *Biological Psychiatry, 66*, 812–813.

Averill J. (1968). Grief: Its nature and significance. *Psychological Bulletin, 70*, 721–748.

Beck, A. T., Weissman, A., Lester, D., & Trexler, L. (1974). The measurement of pessimism: The Hopelessness Scale. *Journal of Consulting and Clinical Psychology, 42*, 861–865.

Bostwick, J. M., & Pankratz, V. S. (2000). Affective disorders and suicide risk: A reexamination. *American Journal of Psychiatry, 157*, 1925–1932.

Bourke, A. F. G. (2007). Kin selection and the evolutionary theory of aging. *Annual Review of Ecology, Evolution, and Systematics, 38*, 103–128.

Bowlby J. (1980). *Attachment and loss. Vol. 3: Loss, sadness and depression.* New York: Basic Books.

Brent, D. A., & Mann, J. J. (2005). Family genetic studies of suicide and suicidal behavior. *American Journal of Medical Genetics, 133C*, 13–24.

Brent, D. A., & Mann, J. J. (2006). Familial pathways to suicidal behavior: Understanding and preventing suicide among adolescents. *New England Journal of Medicine, 355*, 2719–2721.

Brent, D. A., & Melhem, N. (2008). Familial transmission of suicidal behavior. *Psychiatric Clinics of North America, 31*, 157–177.

Brezo, J., Bureau, A., Merette, C., Jomphe, V., Barker, E., D., Vitaro, F., et al. (2010). Differences and similarities in the serotonergic diathesis for suicide attempts and mood disorders: A 22-year longitudinal gene–environment study. *Molecular Psychiatry, 15*, 831–843.

Brown, M. Z., Comtois, K. A., & Linehan, M. M. (2002). Reasons for suicide attempts and nonsuicidal self-injury in women with borderline personality disorder. *Journal of Abnormal Psychology, 111*, 198–202.

Brown, R. M., & Cook, P. P. (1986). *Introductory psychology.* New York: Holt, Reinhart & Winston.

Brown, R. M., Brown S. L., Johnson, A., Melver, K., Olsen, B., & Sullivan, M. (2009). Empirical support for an evolutionary model of self-destructive motivation. *Suicide and Life-Threatening Behavior, 39*, 1–12.

Brown, R. M., Dahlen, E., Mills, C., Rick, J., & Biblarz, A. (1999). Evaluation of an evolutionary model of self-destruction. *Suicide and Life-Threatening Behavior, 29*, 58–71.

Brown, S. L. (1999). The origins of investment: A theory of close relationships. *Dissertation Abstracts International, 60(11-B)*, 5830. (UMI No. 9950232).

Brown, S. L., & Brown, R. M. (2006). Selective Investment Theory: Recasting the functional significance of close relationships. *Psychological Inquiry, 17*, 1–29.

Brown, S. L., Nesse, R., Vinokur, A. D., & Smith, D. M. (2003). Providing support may be more beneficial than receiving it: Results from a prospective study of mortality. *Psychological Science, 14*, 320–327.

Brown, S. L. Smith, D. M., Schulz, R., Kabeto, M., Ubel, P., Yee, J., et al. (2009). Caregiving and decreased mortality in a national sample of older adults, *Psychological Science, 20*, 488–494.

Buss, D. M. (2004). *Evolutionary psychology: The new science of the mind* (2nd ed.). Boston: Allyn & Bacon.

Calzeroni, A., Conte, G., Pennati, A., & Vita, A. (1990). Celibacy and fertility rates in patients with major affective disorders: The relevance of delusional symptoms and suicidal behavior. *Acta Psychiatrica Scandinavia, 82*, 309–310.

Carballo, J. J., Currier, D., Figueroa, A. E., Giner, L., Kelly, S. A., Sublette, M. E., & Oquendo, M. A. (2009). Neurobiological underpinnings of suicidal behavior: Integrating data from clinical and biological studies. *European Journal of Psychiatry, 23*, 243–259.

Centers for Disease Control and Prevention, National Center for Health Statistics. (2009). *Health, United States, 2009.* Hyattsville, MD.

Centers for Disease Control and Prevention, National Center for Injury Prevention and Control. (2010). *Web-based Injury Statistics Query and Reporting System* (WISQARS). Retrieved November 2011, from http://www.cdc.gov/injury/wisqars/index.html

Clark, D. C., & Horton-Deutsch, S. L. (1992). Assessment in absentia: The value of the psychological autopsy method for studying antecedents of suicide and predicting future suicides. In R. W. Maris, A. L. Berman, J. T. Maltsberger, & R. I. Yufit (Eds.), *Assessment and prediction of suicide* (pp. 144–182). New York: The Guilford Press.

Clutton-Brock, T. H. (1991). *The evolution of parental care.* Princeton, NJ: Princeton University Press.

Confer, J. C., Easton, J. A., Fleischman, D. S., Goetz, C. D., Lewis, D. M., Perilloux, C., & Buss, D. M. (2010). Evolutionary psychology: Controversies, questions, prospects, and limitations. *American Psychologist, 65*, 110–126.

Coryell, W., & Schlesser, M. (2001). The dexamethasone suppression test and suicide prediction. *American Journal of Psychiatry, 158*, 748–753.

Darwin, C. (1871). The descent of man, and selection in relation to sex. In E. O. Wilson (Ed.), *From so simple a beginning: The four great books of Charles Darwin* (pp. 783–1248). New York: Norton.

Dawkins, R. (1982). *The extended phenotype.* New York: Oxford University Press.

deCatanzaro, D. (1986). A mathematical model of evolutionary pressures regulating self-preservation and self-destruction. *Suicide and Life-Threatening Behavior, 16*, 166–181.

deCatanzaro, D. (1987). Evolutionary pressures and limitations to self-preservation. In C. Crawford, M. Smith, & D. Krebs (Eds.), *Sociobiology and psychology* (pp. 311–333). Hillsdale, NJ: Erlbaum.

deCatanzaro, D. (1991). Evolutionary limits to self-preservation. *Ethology and Sociobiology, 12*, 13–28.

deCatanzaro, D. (1995). Reproductive status, family interactions, and suicidal ideation: Surveys of the general public and high risk groups. *Ethology and Sociobiology, 16*, 385–394.

Derogatis, L. R., Lipman, R. S., Rickels, K., Uhlenhuth, E. H., & Covi, L. (1974). The Hopkins Symptom Checklist (HSCL): A self-report symptom inventory. *Behavioral Science, 19*, 1–15.

Durkheim, E. (1951). *Suicide: A study in sociology.* New York: The Free Press. (Original work published 1897).

Elmore, S, (2007). Apoptosis: A review of programmed cell death. *Toxicologic Pathology, 35*, 495–516.

Feder, R. (2001). Clinical depression is a disease state, not an adaptation. *Archives of General Psychiatry, 58*, 1084.

Felner, R. D., Adan, A. M., & Silverman, M. M. (1992). Risk assessment and prevention of youth suicide in schools and educational contexts. In R. W. Maris, A. L. Berman, J. T. Maltsberger, & R. I. Yufit (Eds.), *Assessment and prediction of suicide* (pp. 420–447). New York: The Guilford Press.

Filiberti, A, Ripamonti, C., Totis, A., Ventafridda, V. De Conno, F., Contiero, P., & Tamburini, M. (2001*). Journal of Pain and Symptom Management, 22*, 544–553.

Freud, S. (1963). *Mourning and melancholia.* London: Hogarth Press. (Original work published 1917).

Gau, S. S. F., & Cheng, A. T. A. (2004). Mental illness and accidental death. *The British Journal of Psychiatry, 185*, 422–428.

Goldney, R. D. (2005). Suicide prevention: A pragmatic review of recent studies. *Crisis, 26*, 128–140.

Goodman, E. (1999). The role of socioeconomic status gradients in explaining differences in US adolescents' health. *American Journal of Public Health, 89*, 1522–1528.

Guze, S. B., & Robins E. (1970). Suicide and primary affective disorders. *British Journal of Psychiatry, 117*, 437–438

Haas, A. P., Hendin, H., & Mann, J. J. (2003). Suicide in college students. *American Behavioral Scientist, 46*, 1224–1240.

Hagen, E. H. (2003). The bargaining model of depression. In P. Hammerstein (Ed.), *Genetic and cultural evolution of cooperation* (pp. 95–123). Cambridge, MA: MIT Press.

Hagen, E. H., Watson, P. J., & Hammerstein, P. (2008). Gestures of despair and hope: A view on deliberate self-harm from economics and evolutionary biology. *Biological Theory, 3*, 123–138.

Hamilton, W. D. (1964). The genetical evolution of social behavior. *Journal of Theoretical Biology, 7*, 1–16.

Harris, E. C., & Barraclough, B. (1997). Suicide as an outcome for mental disorders: A meta-analysis. *British Journal of Psychiatry, 170*, 205–228.

Hawkes, K., O'Connell, J. F., Blurton Jones, N. G., Charnov, E. L., & Alvarez, H. (1998). Grandmothering, menopause, and the evolution of human life histories. *Proceedings of the National Academy of Sciences USA, 95,* 1336–1339.

Hawton, K., Cole, D., O'Grady, J., & Osborn, M. (1982). Motivational aspects of deliberate self-poisoning in adolescents. *British Journal of Psychiatry, 141,* 286–291.

Hedberg, K., Hopkins, D., & Kohn, M. (2003). Five years of legal physician-assisted suicide in Oregon. *New England Journal of Medicine, 348,* 961–964.

Hendin, H. (1975). Growing up dead: Student suicide. *American Journal of Psychotherapy, 29,* 327–338.

Herjanic, M., & Meyer, D. A. (1976). Psychiatric illness in homicide victims. *American Journal of Psychiatry, 133,* 691–693.

Herker, E., Jungwirth, H., Lehmann, K. A., Maldener, C., Fröhlich, K., Wissing, S., ... Madeo, F. (2004). Chronological aging leads to apoptosis in yeast. *Journal of Cell Biology, 164,* 501–507.

Hinrichsen, G. A., Liberman, J. A., Pollack, S., & Steinberg, H. (1989). Depression in hemodialysis patients. *Psychosomatics, 30,* 284–289.

Holding, T. A., & Barraclough, B. M. (1977). Psychiatric morbidity in a sample of accidents. *British Journal of Psychiatry, 130,* 244–252.

Hölldobler, B., & Wilson, E. O. (1990). *The ants.* Cambridge, MA: Harvard University Press.

Hoyenga, K. B., & Hoyenga, K. T. (1980). *Motivational explanations of behavior: Evolutionary, physiological, and cognitive ideas.* Monterey, CA: Brooks/Cole.

Joiner, T. (2005). *Why people die by suicide.* Cambridge, MA: Harvard University Press.

Joiner, T. E., Pettit, J.W., Walker, R.L., Voelz, Z.R., Cruz, J., Rudd, M.D., & Lester, D. (2002). Perceived burdensomeness and suicidality: Two studies on the suicide notes of those attempting and those completing suicide. *Journal of Social and Clinical Psychology, 21,* 531–545.

Joiner, T. E., Steer, R. A., Brown, G., Beck, A. T., Pettit, J. W., & Rudd, M. D. (2003). Worst-point suicidal plans: A dimension of suicidality predictive of past suicidal attempts and eventual death by suicide. *Behaviour Research and Therapy, 41,* 1469–1480.

Joiner, T. E., Jr., Conwell, Y., Fitzpatrick, K. K., Witte, T. K., Schmidt, N. B., Berlim, M. T., ... Rudd, M. D. (2005). Four studies on how past and current suicidality relate even when "everything but the kitchen sink" is covaried. *Journal of Abnormal Psychology, 114,* 291–303.

Joiner, T., Kalafat, J., Draper, J., Stokes, H., Knudson, M., Berman, A. L., & McKeon, R. (2007). *Suicide and Life-Threatening Behavior, 37,* 353–365.

Joukamaa, M., Heliövaara, M., Knekt, P., Aromaa, A., Raitasalo, R., & Lehtinen, V. (2001). Mental disorders and cause-specific mortality. *The British Journal of Psychiatry, 179,* 498–502.

Kachur, S., Potter, L., Powell, K., & Rosenberg, M. (1995). Suicide: Epidemiology, prevention, treatment. *Adolescent Medicine: State of the Art Review, 6,* 171–182.

Kim, C. D., Seguin, M., Therrien, N., Riopel, G., Chawky, N., Lesage, A. D., & Turecki, G. (2005). Familial aggregation of suicidal behavior: A family study of male suicide completers from the general population. *American Journal of Psychiatry, 162,* 1017–1019.

Kimmel, P. L. (2000). Psychosocial factors in adult end-stage renal disease patients treated with hemodialysis: Correlates and outcomes. *American Journal of Kidney Diseases, 35,* S132–S140.

Kinney, D. K., & Tanaka, M. (2009). An evolutionary hypothesis of depression and its symptoms, adaptive value, and risk factors. *Journal of Nervous and Mental Disorders, 197,* 561–567.

Klein, D. F., & Thase, M. (1997). Medication versus psychotherapy for depression. *Progress Notes (American Society of Clinical Psychopharmacology), 8,* 41–47.

Knorre, D. A., Smirnova, E. A., & Severin, F. F. (2005). Natural conditions inducing programmed cell death in the yeast *Saccharomyces cerevisiae. Biochemistry (Moscow), 70,* 264–266.

Kreitman, N. (Ed.). (1977). *Parasuicide.* London: John Wiley & Sons.

Krug, E. G., Dahlberg, L. L., Mercy, J. A., Zwi, A. B., & Lozano, R. (Eds.). (2002). *World report on violence and health.* Geneva: World Health Organization.

Leenaars, A. A. (1992). Suicide notes, communication, and ideation. In R. W. Maris, A. L. Berman, J. T. Maltsberger, & R. I. Yufit (Eds.), *Assessment and prediction of suicide* (pp. 337–361). New York: The Guilford Press.

Leighton, A. H., & Hughes, C. C. (1955). Notes on Eskimo patterns of suicide. *Southwestern Journal of Anthropology, 11,* 327–338.

Lieb, R., Bronisch, T., Höfler, M., Schreier, A., & Wittchen, H. (2005). Maternal suicidality and risk of suicidality in offspring: Findings from a community study. *American Journal of Psychiatry, 162,* 1665–1671.

Linsley, K. R., Schapira, K., & Kelly, T. P. (2001). Open verdict v. suicide—importance to research. *The British Journal of Psychiatry, 178,* 465–468.

Lonergan, M., & Travis, J. (2003). On the selective advantage of suicide. *The Journals of Gerontology: Biological Sciences, 58,* 775.

Maestripieri, D., & Carroll, K. A. (1998). Child abuse and neglect: Usefulness of the animal data. *Psychological Bulletin, 123,* 211–223.

Mann, J. J. (2003). Neurobiology of suicidal behavior. *Nature Reviews Neuroscience, 4,* 819–828.

Mann, J. J., Huang, Y. Y., Underwood, M. D., Kassir, S. A., Oppenheim, S., Kelly, T. M., ... Arango, V. (2000). A serotonin transporter gene promoter polymorphism (5-HTTLPR) and prefrontal cortical binding in major depression and suicide. *Archives of General Psychiatry, 57,* 729–738.

Mann, J. J., Arango, V. A., Avenevoli, S., Brent, D. A., Champagne, F. A., Clayton, P., ... Wenzel, A. (2009). Candidate endophenotypes for genetic studies of suicidal behavior. *Biological Psychiatry, 65,* 556–563.

Maris, R. W. (1992). The relationship of nonfatal suicide attempts to completed suicides. In R. W. Maris, A. L. Berman, J. T. Maltsberger, & R. I. Yufit (Eds.), *Assessment and prediction of suicide* (pp. 362–380). New York: Guilford.

Maris, R. W., Berman, A. L., & Maltsberger, J. T. (1992). Summary and conclusions: What have we learned about suicide assessment and prediction? In R. W. Maris, A. L. Berman, J. T. Maltsberger, & R. I. Yufit (Eds.), *Assessment and prediction of suicide* (pp. 640–672). New York: Guilford.

Maris, R. W., Berman, A. L., & Silverman, M. (2000a). Suicide notes and communications. In R. W. Maris, A. L. Berman, & M. M. Silverman (Eds.), *Comprehensive textbook of suicidology* (pp. 266–283). New York: The Guilford Press.

Maris, R. W., Berman, A. L., & Silverman, M. (2000b). The empirical foundations of suicidology. In R. W. Maris, A. L. Berman, & M. M. Silverman (Eds.), *Comprehensive textbook of suicidology* (pp. 62–95). New York: The Guilford Press.

Mascaro, S., Korb, K. B., & Nicholson, A. E. (2001). Suicide as an evolutionarily stable strategy. In J. Kelemen & P. Sosik (Eds.), *Proceedings of the 6th European Conference on Advances in Artificial Life, Prague, Czech Republic* (pp. 120–132). London: Springer-Verlag.

Mayo, D. J. (1992). What is being predicted? Definitions of suicide. In R. W. Maris, A. L. Berman, J. T. Maltsberger, & R. I. Yufit (Eds.), *Assessment and prediction of suicide* (pp. 88–101). New York: The Guilford Press.

McAllister, M. K., Roitberg, B. D., & Weldon, L. K. (1990). Adaptive suicide in pea aphids: Decisions are cost sensitive. *Animal Behaviour, 40*, 167–175.

McGirr, A., Alda, M., Seguin, M., Cabot, S., Lesage, A., & Turecki, G. (2009). Familial aggregation of suicide explained by Cluster B traits: A three-group family study of suicide controlling for major depressive disorder. *American Journal of Psychiatry, 166*, 1124–1134.

McGowan, P. O., Sasaki, A., D'Alessio, A. C., Dymov, S., Labonté, B., Szyf, M., et al. (2009). Epigenetic regulation of the glucocorticoid receptor in human brain associates with childhood abuse. *Nature Neuroscience, 12*, 342–348.

McGowan, P. O., Sasaki, A., Huang, T. C. T., Unterberger, A., Suderman, M., Ernst, C., et al. (2008). Promoter-wide hypermethylation of the ribosomal RNA gene promoter in the suicide brain. *PLoS ONE, 3*, e2085.

McGuffin, P., Marusic, A., & Farmer, A. (2001). What can psychiatric genetics offer suicidology? *Crisis, 22*, 61–65.

McPherson, C. J., Wilson, K. G., & Murray, M. A. (2007). Feeling like a burden to others: A systematic review focusing on the end of life. *Palliative Medicine, 21*, 115–128.

Mellesdal, L., Mehlum, L., Wentzel-Larsen, T., Kroken, R., & Jørgensen, H. A. (2010). Suicide risk and acute psychiatric readmissions: a prospective cohort study. *Psychiatric Services 61*, 25–31.

Menninger, K. A. (1985). *Man against himself.* New York: Harcourt Brace Jovanovich. (Original work published 1938).

Minois, G. (1999). *History of suicide: Voluntary death in western culture.* Baltimore: Johns Hopkins University Press.

Mittendorfer-Rutz, E., Rasmussen, F., & Wasserman, D. (2004). Restricted fetal growth and adverse maternal psychosocial and socioeconomic conditions as risk factors for suicidal behaviour of offspring: A cohort study. *Lancet, 364*, 1135–1140.

Motto, J. A., & Bostrom, A. (1990). Empirical indicators of near-term suicide risk. *Crisis, 11*, 52–59.

Nesse, R. M. (2000). Is depression an adaptation? *Archives of General Psychiatry, 57*, 14–20.

Oman, D. (2007). Does volunteering foster physical health and longevity? In S. G. Post (Ed.), *Altruism and health* (pp. 15–32). New York: Oxford Press.

Orbach, I. (1986). The "insolvable problem" as a determinant in the dynamics of suicidal behavior in children. *American Journal of Psychotherapy, 40*, 511–520.

Pape, R. A. (2005). *Dying to win: The strategic logic of suicide terrorism.* New York: Random House.

Pedersen, N. L., & Fiske, A. (2010). Genetic influences on suicide and nonfatal suicidal behavior: Twin study findings. *European Psychiatry, 25*, 264–267.

Plutchik, R. (2000). Aggression, violence, and suicide. In R. W. Maris, A. L. Berman, & M. M. Silverman (Eds.), *Comprehensive textbook of suicidology* (pp. 407–423). New York: The Guilford Press.

Pouliot, L., & De Leo, D. (2006). Critical issues in psychological autopsy studies. *Suicide and Life-Threatening Behavior, 36*, 491–510.

Price, J., Sloman, L. Gardner, R., Gilbert, P., & Rohde, P. (1994). The social competition hypothesis of depression. *British Journal of Psychiatry, 164*, 309–315.

Qin, P., & Nordentof, M. (2005). Suicide risk in relation to psychiatric hospitalization: Evidence based on longitudinal registers. *Archives of General Psychiatry, 62*, 427–432.

Rockett, I. R. H., Hobbs, G., De Leo, D., Stack, S., Frost, J. L., Ducatman, A. M., et al. (2010). Suicide and unintentional poisoning mortality trends in the United States, 1987–2006: Two unrelated phenomena? *BMC Public Health, 10*, 705.

Ronce, O., & Promislow, D. (2010). Kin competition, natal dispersal and the moulding of senescence by natural selection. *Proceedings of the Royal Society B, 277*, 3659–3667.

Roy, A. (1992). Genetics, biology, and suicide in the family. In R. W. Maris, A. L. Berman, J. T. Maltsberger, & R. I. Yufit (Eds.), *Assessment and prediction of suicide* (pp. 574–588). New York: The Guilford Press.

Rueppell, O., Hayworth, M. K., & Ross, N. P. (2010). Altruistic self-removal of health-compromised honey bee workers from their hive. *Journal of Evolutionary Biology, 23*, 1538–1546.

Sabbath, J. C. (1969). The suicidal adolescent: The expendable child. *Journal of the American Academy of Child Psychiatry, 8*, 272–285.

Schrut, A. (1964). Suicidal adolescents and children. *Journal of the American Medical Association, 188*, 1103–1107.

Schulsinger, F., Kety, S. S., Rosenthal, D., & Wender, P. H. (1979). A family study of suicide. In M. Schou & E. Stromgren (Eds.), *Origin, prevention and treatment of affective disorders* (pp. 277–287). New York: Academic Press.

Sokolowski, M., & Wasserman, D. (2009). A review of the neurobiology and genetics of the hypothalamic–pituitary–adrenal axis in suicide. *European Psychiatric Review, 2*, 25–29.

Stockard, J., & O'Brien, R. M. (2002). Cohort effects on suicide rates: International variations. *American Sociological Review, 67*, 854–872.

Suicide Prevention Resource Center. (2004). *Promoting mental health and preventing suicide in college and university settings.* Newton, MA: Education Development Center, Inc.

Sullivan, P. F., Neale, M. C., & Kendler, K. S. (2000). Genetic epidemiology of major depression: Review and meta-analysis. *American Journal of Psychiatry, 157*, 1552–1562.

Tanney, B. L. (2000). Psychiatric diagnoses and suicidal acts. In R. W. Maris, A. L. Berman, & M. M. Silverman (Eds.), *Comprehensive textbook of suicidology* (pp. 311–341). New York: The Guilford Press.

Tofilski, A., Couvillon, M. J., Evison, S. E. F., Helanterä, H., Robinson, E. J. H., & Ratnieks, F. L. W. (2008). Pre-emptive defensive self-sacrifice by ant workers. *American Naturalist, 172*, E239–E243.

Tooby, J., & Cosmides, L. (1992). The psychological foundations of culture. In J. H. Barkow, L. Cosmides, & J. Tooby (Eds.), *The adapted mind: Evolutionary psychology and the generation of culture* (pp. 19–136). New York: Oxford University Press.

Turecki, G. (2005). Dissecting the suicide phenotype: The role of impulsive–aggressive behaviours. *Journal of Psychiatry and Neuroscience, 30*, 398–408.

Trivers, R. L. (1974). Parent-offspring conflict. *American Zoologist, 14*, 249–264.

US Department of Health and Human Services, Administration for Children and Families (2002). *Child Maltreatment 2002*. Washington, DC: Author.

Van Hoof, A. J. L. (2000). A historical perspective on suicide. In R. W. Maris, A. L. Berman, & M. M. Silverman (Eds.), *Comprehensive textbook of suicidology* (pp. 96–123). New York: The Guilford Press.

Van Orden, K. A., Lynam, M. E., Hollar, D., & Joiner, T. E., Jr. (2006). Perceived burdensomeness as an indicator of suicidal symptoms. *Cognitive Therapy and Research, 30*, 457–467.

Van Orden, K. A., Witte, T. K., Cukrowicz, K. C., Braithwaite, S. R., Selby, E. A., & Joiner, T. E., Jr. (2010). The interpersonal theory of suicide. *Psychological Review, 117*, 575–600.

Van Orden, K. A., Witte, T. K., Gordon, K. H., Bender, T. W., & Joiner, T. E., Jr. (2008). Suicidal desire and the capability for suicide: Tests of the Interpersonal-Psychological Theory of Suicidal Behavior among adults. *Journal of Consulting and Clinical Psychology, 76*, 72–83.

Voracek, M., & Loibl, L. M. (2007). Genetics of suicide: A systematic review of twin studies. *Wien Klin Wochenschr, 119*, 463–475.

Wagner, B. M. (1997). Family risk factors for child and adolescent suicidal behavior. *Psychological Bulletin, 121*, 246–298.

Watson, P. J., & Andrews, P. W. (2002). Toward a revised evolutionary adaptation analysis of depression: The social navigation hypothesis. *Journal of Affective Disorders, 72*, 1–14.

Weishaar, M. E., & Beck, A. T. (1992). Hopelessness and suicide. *International Review of Psychiatry, 4*, 177–184.

Wender, P., Kety, S., Rosenthal, D., & Schulsinger, F. (1986). Psychiatric disorders in the biological and adoptive families of adopted individuals with affective disorders. *Archives of General Psychiatry, 43*, 923–929.

Wenzel, A., & Beck, A. T. (2008). A cognitive model of suicidal behavior: Theory and treatment. *Applied and Preventive Psychology, 12*, 189–201.

Williams, G. (1957). Pleiotropy, natural selection, and the evolution of senescence. *Evolution, 11*, 398–411.

Wilson, E. O. (2006). *Nature revealed: Selected writings 1949–2006*. Baltimore: The Johns Hopkins University Press.

World Health Organization. (2007). *Suicide prevention and special programmes*. Retrieved January 2007, from http://www.who.int/mental_health/prevention/suicide/country_reports/en/

Woznica, J. G., & Shapiro, J. R. (1990). An analysis of adolescent suicide attempts: The expendable child. *Journal of Pediatric Psychology, 15*, 789–796.

Wu, G., Boivin, G., Brodeur, J., Giraldeau, L., & Outreman, Y. (2010). Altruistic defence behaviours in aphids. *BMC Evolutionary Biology, 10*, 1–20.

Yerevanian, B. I., Feusner, J. D., Koek, R. J., & Mintz, J. (2004). The dexamethasone suppression test as a predictor of suicidal behavior in unipolar depression. *Journal of Affective Disorders, 83*, 103–108.

CHAPTER 10

Evolutionary Perspectives on Male-Male Competition, Violence, and Homicide

Daniel J. Kruger *and* Carey J. Fitzgerald

Abstract

Aggression and violence are common elements of male mating competition across animal species. The level of violence across species, across human populations, and across individuals within societies corresponds with the intensity of male mating competition. In humans, peak rates of violence and homicide occur as males reach reproductive maturity and contest directly for mates, as well as for the social status and resources that facilitate attraction of prospective partners. In modern societies, levels of mortality from violence decrease considerably as males marry, start families, and undergo a life history shift from mating effort to paternal investment. In other societies, especially those with extended male fertility from additional sequential and/or simultaneous mating partners, risky behaviors including violence persist at higher levels throughout adulthood. Across species, those with higher degrees of male reproductive inequality (polygyny) have higher rates of violence and male mortality. There is a parallel pattern for the degree of polygyny across human populations, as well as for the degree of inequality in social status and resource holdings that are historically tied to male reproductive success. Temporal fluctuations in social stressors such as higher extrinsic mortality and higher socioeconomic inequality also elevate rates of violent behavior and mortality from homicide within societies. Androgen production mirrors the pattern of risky and violent male behavior across the life span, indicating a physiological basis in the mechanisms underlying male sexuality.

Key Words: evolution, sexual selection, sex differences, mating, violence, mortality

Introduction

Life is complicated. The sight of a mother caring for her young offspring generates pleasant feelings and thoughts about the goodness and beauty of nature. Yet in many cases, the conception of the infant was preceded by violent conflict, behaviors that may be as disturbing to human observers as infant care is comforting. The behaviors that humans call violence are an integral part of the cycle of life, occurring in the interactions between predators and prey, as well as in competition between members of the same species for resources, territory, and mates. Across preindustrial societies, almost one in three young men is killed during male competition for resources and social status (Daly & Wilson, 1988).

The technological and cultural features of human civilization distinguish us in many ways from other species, yet our behaviors still often conform to the familiar patterns found throughout the rest of the natural world. Violent behaviors are exhibited by people ranging from foraging tribes only recently contacted by those from the outside world to residents of the affluent suburbs of the world's wealthy nations. Homicide and violence are frequently featured both in local news reports as well as fictive entertainment, perhaps in much greater proportions than would be quantitatively representative of typical patterns. Sensational stories can gain worldwide media attention, yet these are only part of the overall picture. For example, serial killers are often featured in news accounts of homicide, yet they are responsible for only one or two of every hundred homicides in the United States (Ellis & Walsh, 2000). Most of those individuals who commit homicides are actually not much different from most of the people we encounter on a regular basis (Daly & Wilson, 1988). Only in recent decades have researchers studied homicide patterns with tests of hypotheses based on a larger systematic account of human psychology. Psychiatrists defined syndromes of psychopathy based on individual cases, and social scientists created data-driven models based on aggregate statistics. The vague definitions of motivations and circumstances usually found in crime reports did not provide much help in determining risk factors. Prior to the advent of evolutionary psychology, the psychological study of aggression was often fragmented and predictive models were incoherent (Campbell, 2005).

Then, scientists who revitalized the use of evolutionary theory to understand psychology and people's behavior turned their attention to the dark side of human nature. Daly and Wilson (1988) systematically examined patterns of homicide as an outcome of specific types of interpersonal conflicts, predicted from the challenges encountered in natural and sexual selection. There is a wide range of motivations related to violent and homicidal ideation, including mating competition, self-defense, and decreasing the amount of resources expended on others (Buss, 2005). A considerable proportion of specific impulses are related to male reproductive strategies. Although women may also be both the perpetrators and victims of violence, violent aggression does not appear as central a solution to the challenges that females face in reproduction. Men are responsible for the vast majority of violence and homicide across cultures (Daly & Wilson, 1988). For example, men comprise 87% of the perpetrators and 75% of homicide victims in the United States (Lester, 1991). In humans and other primates, competition among males is much more likely to escalate into violence and death than competition among women (Smuts, 1987).

Human aggression and violent behaviors are products of the evolutionary history of our species and the challenges that our ancestors faced, including those posed by their contemporaries. Tinbergen's (1963) four questions may be used as a framework for understanding aggressive and violent behaviors related to male mating competition. These questions include the evolutionary (ultimate) explanations of adaptation (function) and phylogeny (evolution), as well as the proximate explanations of causal mechanisms and ontological development. Such a framework helps illustrate the complex network of relationships between causes emerging at different levels, maintaining an appropriate balance between the reductionism necessary to isolate independent mechanisms and the holistic understanding of the interrelationships among causes and mechanisms.

Evolutionary (Ultimate) Explanations for Male Competition, Violence, and Homicide

Sexual selection and intrasexual competition result in many pervasive differences between men and women. Men and women have somewhat divergent reproductive strategies, with reliable aggregate differences in the psychology and behavior related to reproduction. It is important to consider that such differences are usually more a matter of degree than an opposite kind; there is likely considerable overlap in the male and female distributions across individuals. The basic dynamics of sexual reproduction ultimately illustrate just why there are males and females, and why they differ from each other.

Most complex animals reproduce sexually, as genetic recombination purges harmful mutations and genotypic variability facilitates adaptation to environmental conditions (Williams, 1975), threats from predators and parasites (Williams, 1975), and competition from other species (Bell, 1982), countering the adaptations of prey to predation, and starvation (Bell, 1982).

Sexual reproduction entails the combination of gametes from a pair of parents, and there is disruptive selection for gamete size. Larger gametes give zygotes greater viability; smaller gametes have a quantitative advantage and will be relatively more successful than intermediate sized gametes when large partner gametes are present (Bulmer & Parker, 2002). The biological definition of sex follows from gamete size; females contribute larger gametes than males. Virtually every contrast between females and males follows from this sex difference in investment.

Females usually invest considerably more than males in offspring, often in areas beyond gamete size, and are thus selected to be choosier in considering partners (Bateman, 1948; Trivers, 1972). In humans, women invest the energy and inconveniences of a 9-month pregnancy, undergo risky childbirth, provide nutrition through lactation, and often perform the vast majority of child care, which can last into the offspring's teenage years. Because women invest so substantially in offspring, they should be particularly choosy when evaluating possible mates.

The reproductive success of males depends largely on their ability to secure mating opportunities, both in intrasexual competition with other males that can include fighting for rank or territory, and being chosen by females in intersexual selection because of the attractiveness of their traits and displays (Darwin, 1871). The results include elaborate ornaments such as the peacock's tail and armaments such as the antlers of red deer (Darwin, 1871), all with substantial costs. Males who succeed in these competitions have more offspring; this shapes traits that enhance mating outcomes on average, even if they also increase risk of injury, sickness, and early death (Daly & Wilson, 1978; Møller, Christe, & Lux, 1999). Selection shapes traits not for the welfare of individuals or species, but based on the genes that promote such traits (Dawkins, 1976; Williams, 1966).

Relative to females, the mean optimum balance of investment for males is shifted toward reproductive effort and away from somatic effort (building up the body and maintaining health) and toward mating effort at the expense of parental effort. Women reach diminishing returns in reproductive success from mating effort much more rapidly than men. Men on average have greater height and weight, more upper-body strength, higher metabolic rates, higher juvenile mortality, and later sexual maturity than women (for a review, see Miller, 1998). Such attributes are related to competition for resources, social status, and mates (Wilson & Daly, 1985), competition that can be hazardous, violent, and sometimes fatal (Betzig, 1986; Kaplan & Hill, 1985).

Sex differences in psychology and behavioral tendencies, including the greater male tendencies for risk taking, competitiveness, aggression, and sensitivity to position in social hierarchies, are consequences of sexual selection (Cronin, 1991). Human male mating competition includes potentially lethal violence in conflicts both within and between groups (Chagnon, 1988). Opportunistic raiding is a common feature of foraging societies, perhaps more so than formal battles (Buss, 2006b). In the vast majority of traditional hunter-gatherer, horticultural, pastoral, and agricultural societies, ambushes, raids, and more occasional organized large-scale battles are common between rival groups (Ember, 1978; Keeley, 1996). Motives for these conflicts include retaliation for previous killings, acquiring resources, elevating personal prestige, and acquiring women. Among the Yanomamo, about 40% of men have participated in homicide, and men who have killed have higher social status and more wives than those who have not (Chagnon, 1988). Violent intertribal conflict preceded the 15th-century arrival of Europeans in the Americas; half a thousand individuals were killed in a single incident in the Dakotas around 1325 CE. None of the resulting remains were of young women (Keeley, 1996). In contrast to many fictive depictions, warfare is typically less frequent after contact with modern societies (Keeley, 1996).

Violence may result from competition over access to and control of resources, as well as position in the status hierarchy (Buss & Shackelford, 1997). Paternal investment is much larger in humans than in other primates (Buss & Schmitt, 1993; Geary & Flinn, 2001). This may be related to the high payoffs for large investments in the care and instruction of offspring compared with our primate relatives (Fisher, 1992) and to concealed ovulation in human females and its possible role in decreasing male paternity confidence (Strassmann, 1981, 1996). Children who grow up without an investing father present suffer higher mortality rates (Hill & Hurtado, 1996), and paternal investment in offspring may enhance offspring reproductive success (Geary, 2005). High paternal investment may somewhat decrease the relative importance of direct male violent competition and increase female choosiness and its power to select for certain male characteristics, such as ability and willingness to invest in potential offspring (Low, 2000). This diverts male competitive energies from physical competitions to resource acquisition and display.

Competition with other males can include conflicts over the resources that make them attractive to females as potential providers. Cross-culturally, women value men in terms of social status and economic power (Buss, 1989), and these have a direct relationship to reproductive success across a wide variety of societies (see Hopcroft, 2006). During recent human evolution, males who did not have substantial resources or status may have been unable to establish long-term relationships. In 18th-century Krummhörn, now northwest Germany, nonelite men were four times more likely than elite men to have their genetic lineage die out (Klindworth & Voland, 1995). Sociopolitical arrangements and intergenerational transfers increased variation in male wealth and power across human genetic and cultural coevolution (Smuts, 1995). Men can successfully use violence to elevate their social status and gain respect from others (Campbell, 1993; Chagnon, 1992; Hill & Hurtado, 1996). Greater male risk taking also leads to relatively higher mortality rates from greater nonviolent accidents (Kruger & Nesse, 2004, 2006a, 2006b).

As described earlier, violent aggression is a more prominent component of reproductive strategies for men than for women. Campbell (1999) argues that sex differences in parental investment are the root cause of sex differences in aggression, though she emphasizes the greater potential harm for women's reproductive success as the primary factor rather than the benefits for males who successfully compete. Offspring survival is more severely impacted by the death of a mother than the death of a father. Thus, women would avoid direct physical aggression unless it would be necessary for protecting offspring from harm, or another threat with potentially serious consequences to reproductive success.

Archer's (2000) meta-analysis of spousal aggression indicates that men are more likely to seriously injure and kill their partner than women. Yet women initiate both verbal and physical attacks on their partner at higher rates than men (DeMaris, 1992; De Weerth & Kalma, 1993). Although violence may not be an important component of women's mating effort, it may be related to control of established partners. Because of differences in physiology and strength, men's physical attacks may be more likely to cause injury than attacks by women. The magnitude of the sex difference in violent partner aggression is related to the severity of the attack (Eagly & Steffen, 1986), and women's fear of retaliation from their partner is inversely associated with their likelihood of violent aggression (Eagly & Steffen, 1986).

Rather than emphasizing physical aggression, women compete for long-term mates and resources mainly though relational or informational aggression—gossiping, spreading rumors, stigmatization, ostracism, and punitive friendship termination (Bjorkqvist, Lagerspetz, & Kaukianinen, 1992), actions that are less risky than direct confrontations. Women are more likely to use informational aggression in competition with their peers than men, often making accusations of sexual promiscuity (Brown, 1998; Campbell, 1995). Girls tend to avoid other girls who have a reputation of sexual promiscuity (Lees, 1993) and usually respond to these accusations with denial, rather than challenging the sexual double standard (Lees, 1993). Following from female specialization in parental investment, Taylor et al. (2000) argue that women respond to threats by tending and befriending, forming strong social bonds and protecting the vulnerable, rather than following the typical male pattern of fighting or fleeing from danger.

The overall theme of this work is violence and homicide; thus, these topics are central to the discussions and will be repeated extensively. This should not lead to the misperception that aggression or violence is the dominant response or behavior. Humans are remarkable and perhaps unique not for high levels of violence, but rather for high levels of cooperation with nonrelatives (Trivers, 1971). It is important to remember that men are not biologically predetermined to engage in physical combat or to commit homicide. Aggression is risky and potentially very hazardous, as it reliably leads to further aggression and retaliation (Campbell, 2005). Frank (1988) argues that anger evolved to serve as an honest signal of potential retaliation, and fear may function in part to keep aggression in check (see Campbell, 2005). Just as in other primates, men initially use social displays and rituals to resolve dominance disputes or other social conflicts and turn to physical aggression only when these less costly mechanisms fail (Geary, 1998). Even societies with the highest levels of conflict bestow high social status on those who can effectively make peace (Keeley, 1996). Humans likely evolved mechanisms for deescalating conflicts (Buss, 1995); otherwise very few of our ancestors would have survived by living in social groups.

Phylogenetic Patterns of Violent Male Competition

Tracing phylogenetic patterns can help reconstruct the evolutionary origins and history of attributes and behaviors, aiding the identification of both constraints and factors that promote violent aggression as part of male mating competition. Darwin (1871) noted that males are significantly more physically aggressive than females among mammals and considered the best explanation to be intrasexual competition among males for desired females. Even after Darwin's insights, most explanations of sex differences in human aggression, violence, and mortality were based only on proximate factors. In more recent decades, these explanations have been augmented by evolutionary theory depicting how these differentials emerge from an interaction of characteristics shaped by sexual selection and environmental factors, including human social and cultural patterns (e.g., Daly & Wilson, 1978).

Females outlive males on average in most animal species (Hazzard, 1990). As described earlier, this is because males in many species have been shaped by trade-offs that increase competitive abilities and risk taking, which in turn increase male reproductive success even at the expense of longevity (Daly & Wilson, 1978; Møller, Christe, & Lux 1999). The intensity of sexual selection for each sex depends on features of reproductive patterns. Mammalian males' reproductive successes show more variance and skew than females' because a few males are likely to have many offspring, whereas many males may not mate at all. Most females will rear at least some offspring to maturity.

Higher intensities of male competition are not only harmful to males. In *Drosophila*, males manufacture toxic substances that are transferred to the female during mating, perhaps to reduce the possibility of future copulations with male competitors (Rice, 1996). Female chimpanzees may form a consortship with males to avoid harm and harassment from other males (Palombit, Seyfarth, & Cheney, 1997; Smuts, 1995).

The sex differences in reproductive outcomes are exaggerated in relatively more polygynous species; higher degrees of polygyny correspond with greater male-male competition and risky male behavior (Plavcan, 2000; Plavcan & van Schaik, 1997; Plavcan, van Schaik, & Kappeler, 1995), larger size and armor of males, and higher male mortality rates as compared to females (Leutenegger & Kelley, 1977). The role of the intensity of sexual selection in shaping traits that increase male mating competition and risk taking is demonstrated by the high correlation between excess male mortality and sexual size dimorphism across mammalian taxa, after controlling for the effects of phylogeny (Promislow, 1992).

Most mammal species are polygynous, probably because of the relative male specialization in mating effort and female specialization in infant nutritional provisioning and care (Low, 2003, 2007; Reichard & Boesch, 2003). In highly polygynous species, a few males will have many offspring while many others will have none, thus creating powerful selection for traits that lead to success in mating competition—even if these traits are detrimental to many individuals (Kirkwood & Rose, 1991; Stearns, 1992; Williams, 1957). Clutton-Brock and Isvaran (2007) show that across vertebrate species, the longevity gap between males and females is predominantly for polygynous species. The elephant seal is frequently noted to depict a high degree of polygyny. Elephant seal males compete for dominance of harems of about 30 females and male reproductive success is highly skewed. Male development takes twice as long, and 80% of males die before reproducing (Harvey & Clutton-Brock, 1985).

Humans are far less polygynous than most other primates, but the variation in male reproductive success is still substantially higher than that for females. The vast majority of cultures (84%) documented by anthropologists allow for polygyny (Ember, Ember, & Low, 2007). A few males gain a disproportionately high number of matings, creating a positively skewed distribution of male reproductive success that makes mating competition a potent selection force (Betzig, 1986). Biologists note that the degree of sexual dimorphism is directly related to the level of male mating competition (see Bribiescas, 2006), and human females are on average 80% as large as males (Clutton-Brock, 1985).

Violent Intrasexual Competition Among Male Primates

Wilson and Daly (1985) note the prevalence of violent male conflict across species and its high correlation with rates of male mortality. In langur monkeys, for instance, vicious male-male competition for possession of harems results in high male mortality rates (Hrdy, 1977). As the research on male competition among nonhuman primates displays, males have several aggressive behaviors that are utilized as a means of establishing dominance in order to obtain a mate. In this aspect, humans do not differ from their primate relatives. Male primates compete in intrasexual antagonism to gain access to desirable mates, and females favor males with abundant access to resources and phenotypic cues of gene quality (Buss & Schmitt, 1993; Gangestad & Thornhill, 1997; Lancaster, 1989). Male intrasexual competition includes a wide range of behaviors, including the display of status symbols, provision of resources, and demonstration of strength, including physical violence between males (Buss, 2005). These competitive behaviors are prevalent across many primate species, such as macaques, baboons, and every one of the great apes—including humans.

Aggressive and violent behaviors are common in the service of primate male mating competition. When two or more Barbary macaque males are within close vicinity of an estrous female, they tend to engage in two forms of aggression: scream fights and true fights (Kuester & Paul, 1992). In scream fights, males begin screaming at each other from a relatively close distance (1–10 meters). Scream fights may escalate into true fights, in which the males hit, thrash, and bite the competing males (Kuester & Paul, 1992). These competitive encounters are strongly focused on maximizing mating opportunities. The rate at which males inflict physical injuries in other males sharply increases during mating season (Kuester & Paul, 1992).

Similar phenomena are seen in Japanese macaques. Male macaques establish a social dominance ranking system based on physical aggression. Those who win fights become the dominant male and attempt to leverage their status for mating opportunities. Soltis and colleagues (1997) found that these dominant males are more likely to mate with a female during her fertile period; however, attractive males (those favored in female mate choice) sired more offspring regardless of their social dominance. Thus, physical aggression and social dominance may increase male macaques' reproductive success, but they are not the only influence.

The physical strength of male savannah baboons leads to social dominance. Displays of physical strength through successful fights with rival males increase social rank and thus lead to more mating opportunities with females (Alberts, Watts, & Altmann, 2003; Andersson, 1994). There is a very large positive correlation between male dominance rank and mating success (Alberts et al., 2003). Not only do the strongest, most dominant male baboons gain the most reproductive opportunities, but as the effectiveness of other males' competitive behaviors decreases, their reproductive chances decrease as well. Male yellow and anubis baboons form coalitions to fight a common male threat; however, chacma baboons do not form coalitions (Bulger, 1993). Male mating opportunities in chacma baboons strictly follow the dominance rank hierarchy, whereas male mating opportunities in baboons that do form certain social alliances are not as strictly tied to their rank in the dominance hierarchy (Bulger, 1993).

Male-male aggression manifested in physical displays of dominance, including physical violence and loud warning calls, is documented across the great apes. Male aggression is the result of extreme intrasexual competition for fecund females in orangutan societies (Mitani, 1990). As is the case with other primates, male orangutans physically compete with each other for reproductively viable females; however, it remains unclear whether physically dominant males actually produce more offspring (Schurmann & van Hooff, 1986).

Orangutans are also known to be a very asocial species. Male orangutans lead a solitary lifestyle that does not involve much interaction with fellow males (Galdikas, 1979). Dominant male orangutans also use "long calls," which humans can hear from 800 meters away, to keep lower ranking males from approaching their vicinity (Mitani, 1985). Although calls tend to keep lower ranking males at bay, they attracts fellow dominant males—presumably to displace the high-ranking male emitting the call. Thus, when male orangutans actually interact—which is rare—it consists of intense physical aggression over a desired mate and/or social ranking (Mitani, 1990).

Similar to the solitary male orangutan, mountain gorillas are classified as having one-male mating systems (Harcourt, 1981). Most male gorillas do not have to engage in male-male competition with other resident males for fecund females. Physical aggression comes in the form of competition with outgroup males and preventing the females of one's group from joining a different group (Sicotte, 1993). However, approximately 40% of mountain gorilla groups contain more than one male (Weber & Vedder, 1983). Multimale mating systems have benefits such as decreased rates of infanticide, increased potential to form coalitions against outgroup males, and thus overall increased rates of survival (Robbins, 1995), but they also create the potential for competitive behaviors among ingroup males. Robbins (1999) examined two multimale groups of mountain gorillas and found that a social dominance hierarchy formed. In these societies, 83% of the observed matings were performed by the dominant males. Many aggressive behaviors have been recorded between male mountain gorillas, including grunting, screaming, chest beating, hits, kicks, and bites (Harcourt, Stewart, & Hauser, 1993; Robbins, 1999).

Among our closer primate relatives, bonobos and chimpanzees, we see many parallels with human social behavior. Although chimpanzees are also observed as being a cooperative species (e.g., Crawford, 1937), there have been cases of both intergroup and intragroup aggression and killings among males (Boesch et al., 2007; Fawcett & Muhumuza, 2000). Common chimpanzees and humans both partake in coalitional aggression and warfare—conflicts between groups larger than four members (Tooby & Cosmides, 1988; Wrangham & Peterson, 1996). Boesch and colleagues (2007) found the body of an adult male in Loango

National Park, Gabon. The genetic evidence they collected—though not fully exonerating intragroup attackers—indicated that several chimpanzees from a neighboring society were responsible for the attack. Male coalitions of chimps systematically raid the territories of neighboring groups, killing neighboring males and expanding into their territories (Mitani, Watts, & Amsler, 2010). Both wild (Goodall, 1986; Hill et al., 2001; Nishida, 1990) and captive chimpanzee populations (Dyke et al., 1995) demonstrate higher mortality rates for males than females. When male chimpanzees engage in fatal aggression, specific actions are performed. For instance, although they attack the throat, they also attack the torso, thighs, and groin—in many cases removing the genitals from the body altogether (Boesch et al., 2007; Wilson & Wrangham, 2003).

Because chimpanzees form cooperative societies in order to protect themselves from outgroup members, intragroup killings are extremely rare and are hypothesized to occur in cases of extreme intrasexual competition among males (Wilson & Wrangham, 2003). Fawcett and Muhumuza (2000) documented the killing of a male chimpanzee from intragroup male members when the number of cycling females was extremely low. In this case, the lethal aggression may have been a product of intense competition for limited mating opportunities.

Bonobos are considered a peaceful species with very little violence and intrasexual competition (de Waal & Lantig, 1998). Bonobos have very strong female alliances, which may have led to this decrease in sexual coercion and violence (Wrangham, 1993). However, male bonobo chimps do sometimes exhibit high levels of aggression toward other males. This aggression seems to be used to decrease competitors' mating opportunities while simultaneously increasing one's own mating success. Hohmann and Fruth (2003) found that aggressive behaviors between males increase in frequency and intensity with the number of estrous females within a group as well as on mating days. In these instances, the aggressors mated more often than their victims.

The Functions of Social Friction: How Violence Promotes Survival and Reproduction

Theory in evolutionary psychology is not monolithic; there are sometimes multiple competing explanatory models. There is some divergence in accounting for the relationship between violent competition and homicide, even among those considered to be founders of the modern field. Some believe there are psychological adaptations facilitating homicide for specific strategic ends (Buss, 2005), whereas others believe that homicide is often the product of adaptations for sublethal motivations such as status competition combined with lethal modern technology (Daly & Wilson, 1988).

Buss (2005) gives eight separate possible forms of benefit from killing a male competitor: (1) preventing injury, rape, or death to oneself, spouse, or kin; (2) eliminating a crucial antagonist; (3) acquiring a rival's resources or territory; (4) securing access to a competitor's mate; (5) preventing cuckoldry for oneself; (6) cultivating a fierce reputation; (7) protecting resources needed for reproduction; and (8) eliminating an entire lineage of reproductive competitors.

Protecting Self and Kin

The motive of self-protection is enshrined in legal doctrine as the right to use deadly force to defend one's home and its inhabitants from violent attack or intrusions that might lead to violent attack (Merkt, McHose, & Chiappone, 2008). The common saying that "a man's home is his castle" not only reflects the rights of privacy and pursuit of happiness but also the notion that one must defend what is dear to him. Men have killed others who threatened themselves, their partner, and their children (Buss, 2005).

Eliminating Competitors

Sexual rivalry is a prominent theme in nearly all studies of homicide motives, and men are much more likely to kill their sexual rivals than are women (Daly & Wilson, 1988). Cross-culturally, men become upset when a male rival exceeds them in tasks related to financial prospects (indicating the ability to acquire more resources), career prospects (indicating higher social status), and physical strength (Buss, Shackelford, Chloe, Buunk, & Dijkstra, 2000). Data also show that when men compete, the winner's testosterone levels increase (Dabbs & Dabbs, 2000; Gladue, Boechler, & McCaul, 1989), and increased levels of testosterone have often been associated with aggressive behaviors (Dabbs & Dabbs, 2000). These aggressive behaviors often escalate into nonlethal and lethal violence. Several accounts of male intrasexual competition have led to physical altercations and even murder of a rival male (Ghiglieri, 1999).

Acquiring Resources or Territory

Disputes over property claims are a source of conflict in agricultural and pastoral societies. Homicide incidents resulting from disputes over land inheritance among brothers are a frequent theme in the anthropological record and the fictionalized stories told across cultures.

In contrast, there are no documented cases of fratricide in societies without land or livestock inheritance (Daly & Wilson, 1988). Men in technologically advanced societies also use violence to acquire more tangible material resources, and 92% of robberies and burglaries documented in the FBI Uniform Crime Report were committed by men (Daly & Wilson, 1988). Men who have the lowest access to resources, the young, unemployed, and unmarried, are most likely to commit homicides in the context of robberies (Daly & Wilson, 1988).

Raiding a Competitor's Mate

Ethnographic studies of several hunter-gather societies across the world have found that murder among men is usually caused by competition for mates (Daly & Wilson, 1988; Ghiglieri, 1999). Among the Inuit, young men were often killed by others who would kidnap their wives. In such dispersed populations, one is particularly vulnerable when allies are not easily accessible; men without formidable relatives nearby were more frequently targeted. The victim's relative would often form revenge parties, resembling war expeditions, seeking out the absconders (Balicki, 1970).

Preventing Cuckoldry

Evolutionary psychologists have argued that men typically are most threatened by their partner's sexual infidelity, and women typically are most threatened by their partner's emotional infidelity (Buss, Larsen, Westen, & Semmelroth, 1992). This difference in perceived threat stems from paternity uncertainty. Because men are not able to have complete paternal certainty, women's sexual infidelity can lead to cuckoldry, leaving the man to expend resources on another male's offspring (Buss, 1995; Shackelford & Buss, 1997). On the other hand, women generally perceive emotional infidelity as a greater threat than sexual infidelity because it could lead to the man deserting her for another woman. This would result in the loss of any protection and resources for her (and her offspring) that the man was providing (Buss, 1995; Shackelford & Buss, 1997).

Paternity uncertainty and the possibility of cuckoldry, sometimes with actual female infidelity, fuel male sexual jealousy and subsequently male-male competition and violence (Daly & Wilson, 1988; Ghiglieri, 1999). Women leaving their partner or being unfaithful are the two most prominent predictors of men's persistent homicidal thoughts (Buss, 1995). Adultery is a major motive category for the patrilineal Tiv farmers of central Nigeria (Daly & Wilson, 1988). Between 1920 and 1955, 22 homicides were recorded among the !Kung San of Botswana. Of these murders, 19 of the victims were men, and all of the 25 murderers were men (Lee, 1979). Almost all of the killings took place in the context of a woman accused of adultery. As a means of preserving one's social status/reputation and preventing the possibility of cuckoldry, the male mate of the adulterous woman would murder the new man with a poisoned arrow. This pattern is not solely existent in preindustrial societies. In Texas, until 1974 it was legal for a husband to murder his wife (along with her new male suitor) if he caught them committing adultery (Daly & Wilson, 1988).

Establishing Reputation

Men consistently display behaviors intended to elevate their social status to make them seem more appealing and powerful—increasing one's chances of being selected by a desired female. In tribal societies throughout the world, young men reach full adult status through homicide, and they gain honor with an increasing number of kills (Daly & Wilson, 1988). Men also exhibit these behaviors, along with other mate-retention tactics, to keep their mate from losing interest and mating with another male. In other words, displaying dominance over rival men and denigrating their social status increases one's chances of procuring and/or retaining a specific mate (Buss, 2006a; Buss & Shackelford, 1997). This constant competition often leads to negative emotions and aggressive actions toward other males.

Disputes escalating from status contests are overwhelmingly conducted by men (Daly & Wilson, 1988). In 2010, US President Obama held a "Beer Summit" to diffuse the aftermath of a personal conflict between two men that gained international attention. Both males, one a professor at Harvard and the other a Cambridge police sergeant, were likely accustomed to being treated as socially dominant. An esteemed panel of experts from across the nation convened and found that both men neglected opportunities to deescalate the situation. The panel specifically mentioned that both men failed to show respect for the other despite multiple opportunities, and they identified respect as the missing theme during the encounter (Valencia, 2010).

In the middle of the 20th century, altercations of relatively trivial origin were the most frequent (37%) cause of homicide in Philadelphia (Wolfgang, 1958) and subsequent studies replicated this pattern. Ethnographic work indicates that issues appearing trivial to those reading factual reports are of great concern to the individuals involved, and a man's social status is usually at stake (Katz, 1988). These conflicts follow a typical pattern, where one man perceives an insult to his status, demands a retraction from the other party, and threatens aggression if the other refuses to comply (Felson, 1982). Other individuals may attempt to intervene to end or fuel the conflict, but once someone issues a threat, it is difficult for him to back down because of the potential loss of status and respect (Felson, 1982).

Ensuring Reproduction

The Gebusi tribe of Papua New Guinea has an unusually high murder rate (Ghiglieri, 1999). The Gebusi practice an economic trade of females where two families each agree to provide a woman for marriage to a man from the other family. However, sometimes one family will not hold up their end of the deal, which has led to "sorcery homicides." Eighty percent of the Gebusi men murdered are killed because of their "sorcery," a term used to describe one (and/or one's kin) who owed the killer a woman (Knauft, 1985). Knauft hypothesized that this concept of sorcery homicides is a way of controlling reproductive opportunities by gaining a marriageable woman as well as redeeming one's social status—showing that one is not submissive and will not tolerate the loss of a reproductive opportunity.

Diminishing the Reproductive Success of Competitors

In addition to killing competitors directly, men may promote their relative reproductive success by debilitating or killing the offspring of other men. Adulterous conception is a basis for infanticide in some societies, such as the Yanomamo in the Amazonian rainforest and the Tikopia in Oceania. Men in these groups have demanded that the children their newly acquired wives had previously with other men be put to death. In other societies such as the Ojibwa (Dunning, 1959), women understood men's reluctance to invest in children fathered by another man, even when there was no direct male coercion. In modern nations, rates of child abuse are much higher for children in homes with stepparents than those living with two natural parents; stepparents are the single most powerful risk factor for child abuse that has yet been identified (Daly & Wilson, 1988). In the Paraguayan Ache, 43% of children raised by a mother and a stepfather died before age 15, compared to the 19% who grew up with two genetic parents (Hill & Hurtado, 1996). Duberman (1975) found that only 53% of stepfathers and 25% of stepmothers reported having "parental feeling" toward their stepchildren, and even fewer reported having "love" for them. Duberman's respondents were primarily middle-class individuals with no specifically identified distress or dysfunction.

Partner Violence and Homicide

Daly and Wilson (1988) view spousal homicide as an error in sexual conflict between partners because of the loss of investment and future reproductive value, as well as the strong likelihood of retribution by the victim's relatives and/or the legal system in modern societies. Men use violence and intimidation to monopolize the sexuality and reproductive output of women, and death is an extreme consequence of such tactics. Adultery, jealousy, and male sexual proprietariness are the themes most prevalent in violence against female partners (Carlson, 1984; Daly & Wilson, 1988). Men are most jealous with women having the highest reproductive value, as the risk of being killed by a spouse is highest for those under 20 years old. Buss (1995) noted that 43% of women murdered in North Carolina in 1991–1993 were killed after they left their mates, tried to leave their mates, or threatened to leave their mates. "Sexual matters" (affairs and refusals) were identified by convicted Canadian spouse killers as the cause of 85% of incidents, whereas financial problems were never identified as the primary source of marital conflict, even among those of lower socioeconomic status (Chimbos, 1978).

Human Life History and Violence

Behavioral and physiological strategies reflect trade-offs in the allocation of effort toward specific aspects of survival and reproduction across the life span. Life History Theory (LHT) is a powerful framework for understanding the allocation of biological resources for different purposes across stages of life and variation in behavioral and also physiological strategies as functional adaptations to environmental conditions. This framework may be extended to depict the ontogeny of violent behavior in an individual, how and why violence varies across the life of an individual, as well as why there are individual differences in tendencies for violence. LHT describes the allocation of effort toward specific aspects of survival and reproduction across the life span (Roff, 1992; Stearns, 1992). Time and resources are not infinite, so the total amount of effort is limited and organisms face trade-offs in allocations between different possible forms of investment.

The somatic effort of building and maintaining a body takes precedence over reproduction in the early stages of an organism's life. When an organism reaches sexual maturity, the organism's investments shift toward reproduction. For some species, reproductive effort is predominantly mating effort for securing reproductive partners; however, many animal species also exhibit parental care of offspring. Organisms must also make trade-offs between current and future reproduction, and between the quantity of offspring produced and the amount invested in each offspring. These inherent trade-offs in investment are influenced by the environmental conditions in which organisms live. Individual physiological and behavioral strategies generally reflect adaptations to developmental conditions (Roff, 1992; Stearns, 1992).

The developmental period is substantially longer in humans than in other primate species, and both maternal and paternal investments are higher among humans (Low, 1998). This extended developmental period is a result of the very large somatic investment in human brain development, which has been associated with the ecological dominance attained by our hominid ancestors and the reduction in pressures from predators and other external factors and the increased competition with other humans (Alexander, 1979). Although paternal investment has been relatively high, male mating effort remained substantial. The shift in the male allocation of effort from somatic to mating to parenting over the life course explains the pattern of risky and violent behavior, which peaks in young adulthood (Kruger & Nesse, 2006a). Gardner (1993, p. 67) notes that "the belief in the recklessness of youth is more than folk wisdom: It is a foundation of our social institutions." Young adult men form the front ranks of every nation's military, and "lacking the opportunity for warfare, some [young adult men] will find other ways to place their lives at risk."

Male Human Development and Tendencies for Violence Across the Life Course

The male reproductive neuroendocrine system (the HPT axis; hypothalamus, pituitary gland, and testes) regulates male gonadal function (Bribiescas, 2006). This self-regulating system acts like the thermostat for a furnace with a negative feedback loop. The thermostat is set very low in childhood; if the hypothalamus detects testosterone or estradiol in the bloodstream, it shuts off production of the gonadotropic releasing hormone to halt testosterone and estradiol production. The male HPT axis becomes more tolerant of male sex hormones around ages 12 and 13, as if the thermostat setting was being raised (Bribiescas, 2006). Adrenarche, associated with the steady rise in adrenal androgens, initiates the physical transition to adulthood. This marks the life history transition from predominantly somatic effort, building and maintaining the body, to include reproductive effort.

Childhood sex differences in behavior may reflect boys' preparation for the status contests of young adulthood (Campbell, 2005). By 13 months of age, boys are more assertive than girls (Goldberg & Lewis, 1969). Between the ages of 2 and 4, boys attack people, fight, and destroy things more often than do girls (Koot & Verhulst, 1991). Boys engage in rough-and-tumble play, involving chasing, capturing, wrestling, and restraining three to six times as frequently as girls (DiPietro, 1981). Boys consider establishing social dominance more important than girls, and rough-and-tumble play seems to be a mechanism for establishing social dominance (Jarvinen & Nicholls, 1996). Groups of boys exhibit dominance hierarchies from the age of 6 years, and a boy's relative status predicts his social rank 9 years later (Weisfeld, 1999).

Testosterone levels among men in Western industrialized countries peak shortly after age 20 and decline gradually until more rapid declines after age 40. Male testosterone levels decrease following marriage and increase following divorce (Mazur & Michalek, 1998), reflecting a life history shift in the allocation of effort from mating to parenting (and back toward mating after divorce), which also helps explain patterns of risky and violent behavior (Kruger & Nesse, 2006a). Testosterone levels appear related to male competition; they rise when males anticipate athletic competition and social status competition, possibly to prepare one's body and mind for engaging in competitive behaviors (e.g., Booth, Shelley, Mazur, Tharp, & Kittok,

1989; Cohen, Nisbett, Bowdle, & Schwarz, 1996; Gladue et al., 1989). In adolescent boys, testosterone levels are associated with social dominance (Schaal, Tremblay, Soussignan, & Susman, 1996). Men with high testosterone levels have increased rates of violence, infidelity, and divorce (Booth & Dabbs, 1993).

Production of testosterone is physiologically costly because of its detrimental impact on other somatic systems (Folstad & Karter, 1992), illustrating the trade-off between reproductive and somatic efforts. Male secondary sexual characteristics, including facial traits such as prominent brow ridges and large jaws, are dependent on testosterone levels. Because development of highly masculine features is physiologically costly and difficult to fake, these features signal a good match between the genotype and the developmental environment, as well as a stable developmental trajectory free of debilitating injury or disease. Such costly signals are used by females to evaluate prospective mates (Zahavi, 1975). Having these features is related to reproductive success across species (see Andersson, 1994).

People judge social dominance based on the degree of male facial masculinity (Berry & Brownlow, 1989; McArthur & Apatow, 1983), and these perceptions accurately reflect actual social status (Mazur, Mazur, & Keating, 1984; Mueller & Mazur, 1997). Both women and men associate highly masculine male faces with higher mating effort behavioral strategies, including greater tendencies for violence and lower parenting effort, in comparison with less masculine faces (Kruger, 2006). Higher degrees of male facial masculinity predict earlier ages of first sexual intercourse (Mazur, Halpern, & Udry, 1994). Although women prefer men with more masculine faces for sexual affairs (where genetic investment is predominant), they prefer men with more feminine faces for long-term relationships with expected paternal investment, such as marriage (Kruger, 2006). Men who have higher mate value because of social dominance or physiological quality may have a higher return on mating effort, and thus they may not allocate as much effort to parenting and long-term relationships. These men may pursue riskier mating strategies, including higher levels of violent conflict with their competitors. The overall relationship between testosterone and violence is likely mediated by relationships among social dominance, past aggression, and current contextual factors (Geary, 1998).

Male mating effort peaks in young adulthood, possibly in part because young men may not yet have partners or offspring to invest in, and they may be more attractive to females because they have not committed their resources (Hill & Kaplan, 1999). Young males who do not have substantial resources or status may be unable to establish enduring partnerships. Among Ache foragers, younger men were responsible for a greater proportion of offspring produced through extrapair copulations than older men, who produced most of their offspring within established, long-term relationships (Hill & Hurtado, 1996).

Patterns of violent behaviors converge with these trends: Homicide rates are negligible before age 14 and the highest rates for being both a perpetrator and victim of murder are during ages 20–29 (Daly & Wilson, 1988; Lester, 1991). Men between ages 20 and 34 are the modal demographic for offenders and victims in homicides (Daly & Wilson, 1988). The risky behavioral strategies of young males were selected for because they tended to promote social status and resource control as well as mating competition, ultimately enhancing reproductive success (Wilson & Daly, 1995). At least in ancestral times, men who controlled more resources married younger women, married more women, and produced offspring earlier (Low, 1998). Even in relatively egalitarian foraging societies there is some differentiation of status, and men with higher status have increased access to mates (Chagnon, 1992; Hill & Hurtado, 1996). Present-day hunter-gatherer women tend to mate and have offspring as soon as they become fertile, although initial reproduction for males is both later and more variable. The observed peak of risky behaviors in late adolescence and young adulthood corresponds with entrance into mating competition.

Some researchers note that steep discounting of the future by young people could be a rational response to uncertainty (e.g., Gardner, 1993; Wilson & Daly, 1997). This parallels the well-established prediction from evolutionary life history theory that individuals who develop in relatively uncertain environments will develop riskier behavioral strategies to take advantage of possibly fleeting opportunities (Chisholm, 1999; Roff, 1992; Stearns, 1992). The mechanism presumed to underlie this phenomenon is a convex-upward association between proximate outcomes of risk taking (e.g., social status) and reproductive success in unpredictable environments. The mean fitness benefit of risky strategies is more favorable than that of cautious strategies, even if the majority of those exhibiting risky strategies have detrimental outcomes (Wilson & Daly, 1997). Social norms may inflate or decrease behavioral tendencies that give rise to violent behavior. For instance, social forces encouraging risky male behavior (see Kraemer 2000) include social pressure for boys to be tough and discouraging emotions such as anxiety and shame (Kindlon & Thompson, 1999).

Nonindustrialized populations do not exhibit the same rate of testosterone decline in later adulthood (Ellison et al., 2002). This may reflect the different life history patterns occurring in industrialized and nonindustrialized societies. In Western industrialized countries, the male testosterone peak coincides with peaks in male mortality from behavioral causes, including intentional violence and accidents (Kruger & Nesse, 2004). Sex differences in mortality from behavioral causes peak in early adulthood and decline rapidly afterward. This gradual decline continues in later adulthood, although sex differences in suicide rates rise dramatically after age 65 (Kruger & Nesse, 2004).

In the forest-dwelling Ache of Paraguay, a flexible social system allowed for easy remarriage, and mating effort remained high throughout adulthood. Mating partnerships in the Ache were relatively short compared with those in the United States; most adult women had children by several different fathers, and partner desertion was common for both sexes. Adult men were expected to participate in perilous, organized club fighting among Ache bands, which gave women opportunities to evaluate men on mate-selection criteria such as strength, bravery, agility, and alliance connections. New relationships would often begin after club fights; mutual partner choice was common. Among the Ache, sex differences in mortality from behavioral causes remained high throughout adulthood (Kruger & Nesse, 2006a). In precontact Ache, homicide accounted for about half of all deaths. Cardiovascular disease, the leading cause of adult mortality in industrialized countries, was apparently absent (Hill & Hurtado, 1996).

Variation in Tendencies for Violence Across Individuals

Life history models were originally developed to describe variations in physiology and behavior across species. Species living in environments with unpredictable future events such as resource instability and high extrinsic mortality (death that cannot be prevented by investments) will tend to evolve clusters of traits associated with rapid reproduction, risky behavioral strategies, and relatively low investment in offspring (Roff, 1992; Stearns, 1992). These species are said to be "r-selected" (r is the growth rate of the population), or to have a fast life history. Species living in stable and predictable environments have a contrasting long-term strategy, investing more so in physiological maintenance as well as in their offspring (Roff, 1992; Stearns, 1992). These species are said to be "K-selected" (K is the carrying capacity of the population), or to have a slow life history.

Individual differences in life history within species are contingent on environmental conditions and thus LHT can be useful in understanding the causes of human individual differences in behavioral strategies and physiological functioning (Rushton, 1985). Although the heritability of life history strategies is evident, the degree to which these strategies are implemented in humans is likely shaped by environmental circumstances such as socioeconomic, cultural, and ecological conditions, and physical constraints (Heath & Hadley, 1998).

Theorists and previous research suggest that individuals developing in relatively less certain environments will exhibit riskier and more present-oriented behavioral strategies because of the low probability of reproductive success for more cautious approaches. For example, neighborhood homicide rates are predicted by neighborhood life expectancy (controlling for the impact of homicide) and neighborhood income inequality (Wilson & Daly, 1997). People who had shorter life-span estimates and higher estimates of the unpredictability of the future had a higher frequency of risk taking (Hill, Ross, & Low, 1997). Paternal investment in offspring is inversely related to pathogen load, as parental effort would be lower in environments where parenting cannot improve offspring survival (Quinlan, 2007). In these environments, male strategies shift toward relatively higher levels of mating effort with greater risk taking and violence.

Throughout human history, men who had few alternative strategies for acquiring status and resources became warriors in much higher proportions (as well as adventurers and explorers), and they also have committed disproportionate amounts of violence (Daly & Wilson, 1988, 2001). Our theoretical framework suggests that patterns of violence stemming from male mating competition may be related to male social status and economic power in modern industrial societies (Kruger & Nesse, 2006a, 2007). Within a society, men that need to compete more vigorously for social status and resources may show riskier behavioral strategies, including higher levels of violence. Male mating competition may be most intense among males of low status and with the fewest resources, because they have less to lose from the most dangerous competitive tactics such as physical violence and may also face the highest risk of reproductive failure (Daly & Wilson, 1988).

This notion is supported by data from population representative samples in the United States, where sex differences in mortality rates are higher for those in lower income groups and those with lower educational attainment (Kruger & Nesse, 2006a). In Scotland, men aged 20–59 in routine labor occupations died from assaults at a rate nearly 12 times that of men the same age in managerial and professional occupations (Leyland & Dundas, 2010). Men and women living in areas in the lowest 20% in socioeconomic status died from assaults at about 33 times the rate of those living in areas in the highest 20% in socioeconomic status.

Children growing up in impoverished neighborhoods are more frequently exposed to violence (Sampson & Lauritsen, 1994), and exposure is associated with one's own violent behaviors (Salzinger, Feldman, Stockhammer, & Hood, 2002). In one study, the extent of neighborhood poverty explained 71% of the variance in violent crime across Census Tracts (Coulton, Korbin, Su, & Chow, 1995). Physical discipline by parents partially mediates the relationship between neighborhood poverty and children's aggressive behavior, accounting for about half the effect (Dodge, Pettit, & Bates, 1994). Unmarried men also have higher mortality rates across the adult life span than married men (Kruger & Nesse, 2006a), also suggesting hazards associated with a life history centered on mating effort.

Steep socioeconomic gradients within populations may increase the riskiness of male strategies and promote violence. Large disparities in socioeconomic outcomes historically associated with male reproductive success may be associated with the intensity of male mating competition, including competition for resources and social status that make men desirable as reproductive partners. Across modern societies, those with greater degrees of economic inequality (as indicated by Gini coefficients) have disproportionately higher levels of male mortality (Kruger, 2010). Consistent with patterns observed across species, variation in human male mortality should also follow the degree of male reproductive inequality or polygyny. Economic inequality and male reproductive inequality each account for unique portions of the sex difference in mortality rates across countries, together explaining 53% of the variance (Kruger, 2010).

Riskier behavioral strategies may also emerge within societies across time following changes that increase economic uncertainty and variation and skew in social status and economic power. The naturalistic experiment of the economic transitions from state-planned to market economies in Central and Eastern Europe in the 1990s demonstrates this relationship. During the socialist period, centrally planned economics and industry lowered tendencies for aggressive competition because of the relatively low payoffs. Social status and material wealth variations were relatively small for most of the population, and employment was guaranteed during this time. The variance and skew in social status and resources increased tremendously during the rapid transition market economies (United Nations Development Program, 1998). Sex differences in mortality rates increased substantially for Eastern European nations during the years of economic transition, especially during early adulthood (Kruger & Nesse, 2007). This increase was due both to increases in risky and violent behavior and the impact of stress on physiological susceptibility. The minimal increases in Western European countries during this period provide contrasting trends.

The Croatian War of Independence in 1991–1995 provides another naturalistic experiment, enabling the analysis of systematic demographic data to gauge the impact of war and cultural disruption on violent behavior (see Kruger & Nesse, 2006b). The civilian population apparently shifted toward riskier behavioral strategies, induced by evolved facultative adaptations responding to adverse and unstable environments. As expected, Croatian men died at a much higher rate of war-related causes, nine times as high as for women. Although war-related mortality peaked in 1991, the peak in male non-war-related violence and accidents occurred 1 year later. The non-war-related homicide rate, especially for men, was considerably higher for several years following the conflict compared to levels before the war.

Conclusion

Aggression and violence are a part of human nature as are cooperation and child care. Our behavioral patterns are concordant with those of other species, despite our technologically advanced societies. Male mating competition is a strong factor in influencing patterns of human violence, including sex differences in violence and homicide, as it is in other species. Women have less to gain and more to lose from aggressive physical competition for partners. The greater the potential impact on reproductive success, the more to which violence and homicide will be evident. This pattern is seen within individuals over their life course, across individuals within societies, across human populations, and across species. Attempts to reduce levels of violence and homicide may greatly benefit from an explicit awareness of the evolved psychology related to reproductive competition and direct intervention on the proximal concerns that often lead to violent behavior.

Future Directions

Evolutionary theory offers a powerful framework for understanding patterns of human violence. Our behavioral tendencies arise from traits shaped by natural selection interacting with environmental and cultural variations, giving rise to complex patterns that would be difficult to explain with a non-evolutionary framework. Future efforts will likely extend our current insights into the proximate causes of violence, though there may be greater untapped potential in evolutionarily informed efforts to reduce the risks and consequences of violence. Interventions that take advantage of evolved psychological mechanisms may bear more fruit than punitive consequences after the events occur.

Relationship counseling programs would be wise to explicitly address the male and female concerns that often lead to violent behavior. These programs could be beneficial not just for couples who are visibly experiencing troubles but also as a generally available preventative program. Our ancestral environments may have left us with a penchant for future discounting, given their greater levels of unpredictability and mortality compared to current modern environments. Efforts to extend psychological time horizons may help reduce all forms of risky behaviors. Given the prominence of socioeconomic inequality among the influences for violent behavior, attempts to level the actual or perceived socioeconomic gradient could reduce injury and death from violent behavior. However, there will be resistance to redistributions of wealth or resources, especially from men. Men are both more sensitive to their position in the social hierarchy as well as to perceived threats to their relative status, so they may paradoxically resist efforts intended for their own benefit. Our solutions will fail unless they are within the possible range of human adaptation. This makes an evolutionary framework all the more useful and important for addressing violence and other pressing social issues.

References

Alberts, S. C., Watts, H. E., & Altmann, J. E. (2003). Queuing and queue-jumping: Long-term patters of reproductive skew in male savannah baboons, *papio cynocephalus*. *Animal Behaviour, 65*, 821–840.

Alexander, R. D. (1979). *Darwinism and human affairs*. Seattle: University of Washington Press.

Anderson, M. (1994). *Sexual selection*. Princeton, NJ: Princeton University Press.

Archer, J. (2000). Sex differences in aggression between heterosexual partners: A meta-analysis. *Psychological Bulletin, 126*, 651–680.

Balicki, A. (1970). *The Netsilik Eskimo*. Garden City, NY: The Natural History Press.

Bateman, A. J. (1948). Intra-sexual selection in *drosophila*. *Heredity, 2*, 349–368.

Bell, G. (1982). *The masterpiece of nature: The evolution and genetics of sexuality*. London: Croom Helm.

Berry, D. S., & Brownlow, S. (1989). Were the physiognomists right? Personality correlates of facial babyishness. *Personality and Social Psychology Bulletin, 15*, 266–279.

Betzig, L. (1986). *Despotism and differential reproduction: A Darwinian view of history*. Hawthorne, NY: Aldine de Gruyter.

Bjorkqvist, K., Lagerspetz, K., & Kaukianinen, A. (1992). Do girls manipulate and boys fight? Developmental trends in regard to direct and indirect aggression. *Aggressive Behavior, 18*, 117–127.

Boesch, C., Head, J., Tagg, N., Arandjelovic, M., Vigilant, L., & Robbins, M. M. (2007). Fatal chimpanzee attack in Loango National Park, Gabon. *International Journal of Primatology, 28*, 1025–1034.

Booth, A., & Dabbs, J. (1993). Testosterone and men's marriages. *Social Forces, 72*, 463–477.

Booth, A., Shelley, G., Mazur, A., Tharp, G., & Kittok, R. (1989). Testosterone, and winning and losing in human competition. *Hormones and Behavior, 23*, 556–571.

Bribiescas, R. G. (2006). *Men: Evolutionary and life history*. Cambridge, MA: Harvard University Press.

Brown, L. M. (1998). *Raising their voices: The politics of girl's anger*. Cambridge, MA: Harvard University Press.

Bulger, J. B. (1993). Dominance rank and access to estrous females in male savanna baboons. *Behaviour, 127*, 67–103.

Bulmer, M. G., & Parker, G. A. (2002). The evolution of anisogamy: A game-theoretic approach. *Proceedings of the Royal Society of London Series B, 269*, 2381–2388.

Buss, D. M. (1989). Sex difference in human mate preferences: Evolutionary hypotheses tested in 37 cultures. *Behavioural and Brain Sciences, 12*, 1–49.

Buss, D. M. (2006b). *The murderer next door: Why the mind is designed to kill*. New York: Penguin Press.

Buss, D. M. (2006a). Strategies of human mating. *Psychological Topics, 15*, 239–260.

Buss, D. M., Larsen R. J., Westen D., & Semmelroth J. (1992). Sex differences in jealousy: Evolution, physiology, and psychology. *Psychological Science, 3*, 251–255.

Buss, D. M., & Schmitt, D. P. (1993). Sexual strategies theory: An evolutionary perspective on human mating. *Psychological Review, 100*, 204–232.

Buss, D. M., & Shackelford, T. K. (1997). Human aggression in evolutionary psychological perspective. *Clinical Psychology Review, 17*, 605–619.

Buss, D. M., Shackelford, T. K., Choe, J., Buunk, B. P., & Dijkstra, P. (2000). Distress about mating rivals. *Personal Relationships, 7*, 235–243.

Campbell, A. (1993). *Men, women, and aggression.* New York: Basic Books.

Campbell, A. (1995). A few good men: Evolutionary psychology and female adolescent aggression. *Ethology and Sociobiology, 16*, 99–123.

Campbell, A. (1999). Staying alive: Evolution, culture, and women's intrasexual aggression. *Behavioural and Brain Sciences, 22*, 203–252.

Campbell, A. (2005). Aggression. In D. M. Buss (Ed.), *The handbook of evolutionary psychology* (pp. 628–675). Hoboken, NJ: Wiley.

Carlson, B. E. (1984). Children's observations of interparental violence. In A. R. Roberts (Ed.), *Battered women and their families* (pp. 147–167). New York: Springer.

Chagnon, N. A. (1988). Life histories, blood revenge, and warfare in a tribal population. *Science, 239*, 985–992.

Chagnon, N. A. (1992). *Yanomamo.* New York: Holt, Rinehart, & Winston.

Chimbos, P. D. (1978). *Marital violence: A study in interspouse homicide.* San Francisco: R & E Research Associates.

Chisholm, J. S. (1999). *Death, hope and sex: Steps to an evolutionary ecology of mind and morality.* Cambridge, England: Cambridge University Press.

Clutton-Brock, T. H. (1985) Size, sexual dimorphism and polygamy in primates. In W. L. Jungers (Ed.), *Size and scaling in primate biology* (pp. 211–237). New York: Plenum.

Clutton-Brock, T. H., & Isvaran, K. (2007). Sex differences in ageing in natural populations of vertebrates. *Proceedings of the Royal Society of London, Series B: Biological Sciences, 274*, 3097–3104.

Cohen, D., Nisbett, R. E., Bowdle, B. F., & Schwarz, N. (1996). Insult, aggression, and the southern culture of honor: An "experimental ethnography." *Journal of Personality and Social Psychology, 70*, 945–960.

Coulton, C., Korbin, J., Su, N., & Chow, J. (1995). Community level factors and child maltreatment rates. *Child Development, 66*, 1262–1276.

Crawford, M.P. (1937). The cooperative solving of problems by young chimpanzees. *Comparative Psychology Monographs, 14*, 1–88.

Cronin, H. (1991). *The ant and the peacock: Altruism and sexual selection from Darwin to today.* New York: Cambridge University Press.

Dabbs, J. M., & Dabbs, M. G. (2000). *Heroes, rogues, and lovers: Testosterone and behavior.* New York: McGraw-Hill.

Daly, M., & Wilson, M. (1978). *Sex, evolution, and behavior: Adaptations for reproduction.* North Scituate, MA: Duxbury Press.

Daly, M. & Wilson, M. (1988). *Homicide.* New York: Aldine de Gruyter.

Daly, M. & Wilson, M. (2001). Risk-taking, intrasexual competition, and homicide. *Nebraska Symposium on Motivation, 47*, 1–36.

Darwin, C. (1871). *The descent of man and selection in relation to sex.* London: Murray.

Dawkins, R. (1976). *The selfish gene.* New York: Oxford University Press.

DeMaris, A. (1992). Male versus female initiation of aggression: The case of courtship violence. In E. C. Viano (Ed.), *Intimate violence: Interdisciplinary perspectives* (pp. 111–120). Washington, DC: Hemisphere.

de Waal, F. B. M., & Lantig, F. (1998). *Bonobo: The forgotten ape.* Berkeley and Los Angeles: University of California Press.

De Weerth, C., & Kalma, A. (1993). Female aggression as a response to sexual jealousy: A sex role reversal? *Aggressive Behavior, 19*, 265–279.

DiPietro, J. A. (1981). Rough and tumble play: A function of gender. *Developmental Psychology, 17*, 50–58.

Dodge, K. A., Pettit, G. S., & Bates, J. (1994). Socialization mediators of the relation between socioeconomic status and child conduct problems. *Child Development, 65*, 649–665.

Duberman, L. (1975). *The reconstituted family: A study of remarried couples and their children.* Chicago: Nelson-Hall.

Dunning, R. W. (1959). *Social and economic change among the northern Ojibwa.* Toronto: University of Toronto Press.

Dyke, B., Gage, T. B., Alford, P. L., Swenson, S., & Williams-Blangero, S. (1995). Model life table for captive chimpanzees. *American Journal of Primatology, 37*, 25–37.

Eagly, A. E., & Steffen, V. (1986). Gender and aggressive behavior: A meta-analytic review of the social psychological literature. *Psychological Bulletin, 100*, 309–330.

Ellis, L., & Walsh, A. (2000). *Criminology: A global perspective.* Boston: Allyn & Bacon.

Ellison, P. T., Bribiescas, R. G., Bentley, G. R., Campbell, B. C., Lipson, S. F., Panter-Brick, C., & Hill, K. (2002). Population variation in age-related decline in male salivary testosterone. *Human Reproduction, 17*, 3251–3253.

Ember, C. R. (1978). Myths about hunter-gatherers. *Ethnology, 17*, 439–448.

Ember, M., Ember, C. R., & Low, B. S. (2007). Comparing explanations of polygyny. *Cross—Cultural Research, 41*, 428–440.

Fawcett, K., & Muhumuza, G. (2000). Death of a wild chimpanzee community member: Possible outcome of intense sexual competition. *American Journal of Primatology, 51*, 243–247.

Felson, R. B. (1982). Impression management and the escalation of aggression and violence. *Social Psychology Quarterly, 45*, 245–254.

Fisher, H. (1992). *Anatomy of love.* New York: Norton & Company.

Folstad, I., & Karter, A. J. (1992). Parasites, bright males, and the immunocompetence handicap. *American Naturalist, 139*, 603–622.

Frank, R. (1988). *Passions within reason: The strategic role of emotions.* New York: Norton.

Galdikas, B. (1979). Orangutan adaptation at Tanjung Puting Reserve: Mating and ecology. In D. Hamburg & E. McCown (Eds.), *The great apes* (pp. 194–233). Menlo Park, CA: Benjamin Cummings.

Gangestad, S. W., & Thornhill, R. (1997). Human sexual selection and developmental stability. In J. A. Simpson & D. T. Kenrick (Eds.), *Evolutionary social psychology* (pp. 169–195). Mahwah, NJ: Erlbaum.

Gardner, W. (1993). A life-span rational-choice theory of risk taking. In N. Bell & R. Bell (Eds.), *Adolescent risk taking* (pp. 66–83). Newbury Park, CA: Sage Publications.

Geary, D. C. (1998). *Male, female. The evolution of human sex differences.* Washington, DC: American Psychological Association.

Geary, D. C. (2005). Evolution of paternal investment. In D. Buss (Ed.), *The handbook of evolutionary psychology* (pp. 483–505). Hoboken, NJ: Wiley.

Geary, D. C., & Flinn, M. V. (2001). Evolution of human parental behavior and the human family. *Parenting: Science and Practice, 1*, 5–61.

Ghiglieri, M. P. (1999). *The dark side of man: Tracing the origins of male violence*. Reading, MA: Helix.

Gladue, B. A., Boechler, M., & McCaul, K. D. (1989). Hormonal responses to competition in human males. *Aggressive Behavior, 15*, 409–422.

Goldberg, S., & Lewis, M. (1969). Play behavior in the year-old infant: Early sex differences. *Child Development, 40*, 21–31.

Goodall, J. (1986). *The chimpanzees of Gombe*. Boston: Houghton Mifflin.

Harcourt, A. H. (1981). Intermale competition and the reproductive behavior of the great apes. In C. E. Graham (Ed.), *Reproductive biology of the great apes* (pp. 301–318). New York: Academic Press.

Harcourt, A. H., Stewart, K., & Hauser, M. (1993). Functions of wild gorilla "close" calls. I. Repertoire, context, and inter-specific comparison. *Behaviour, 124*, 91–122.

Harvey, P. H., & Clutton-Brock, T. H. (1985). Life history variation in primates. *Evolution, 39*, 559–581.

Hazzard, W. (1990). The sex differential in longevity. In W. Hazzard, R. Endres, E. Bierman, & J. Blass (Eds.), *Principles of geriatric medicine and gerontology* (2nd ed., pp. 37–47). New York: McGraw Hill.

Heath, K., & Hadley, C. (1998). *Dichotomous male reproductive strategies in a polygynous human society: Mating versus parental effort*. Current Anthropology, 39, 369–374.

Hill, E. M., Ross, L. T. & Low, B. S. (1997). The role of future unpredictability in human risk-taking. *Human Nature, 8*, 287–325.

Hill, K., Boesch, C., Goodall, J., Pusey, A., Williams, J., & Wrangham, R. (2001). Mortality rates among wild chimpanzees. *Journal of Human Evolution, 40*, 437–450.

Hill, K., & Hurtado, M. (1996). *Ache life history: The ecology and demography of a foraging people*. Hawthorne, NY: Aldine de Gruyter.

Hill, K., & Kaplan, H. (1999). Life history traits in humans: Theory and empirical studies. *Annual Review of Anthropology, 28*, 397–438.

Hohmann, G., & Fruth, B. (2003). Intra- and inter-sexual aggression by bonobos in the context of mating. *Behaviour, 140*, 1389–1413.

Hopcroft, R. L. (2006). Sex, status and reproductive success in the contemporary U.S. *Evolution and Human Behavior, 27*, 104–120.

Hrdy, S. B. (1977). *The langurs of Abu: Female and male strategies of reproduction*. Cambridge, MA: Harvard University Press.

Jarvinen, D. W., & Nicholls, J. G. (1996). Adolescents' social goals, beliefs about the causes of social success and dissatisfaction in peer relations. *Developmental Psychology, 32*, 435–441.

Kaplan, H., & Hill, K. (1985). Hunting ability and reproductive success among male Ache foragers. *Current Anthropology, 26*, 131–133.

Katz, D. (1988). *Seductions of crime: The moral and sensual attractions of doing evil*. New York: Basic Books.

Keeley, L. H. (1996). *War before civilization*. New York: Oxford University Press.

Kindlon, D., & Thompson, M. (1999). *Raising Cain: Protecting the emotional life of boys*. London: Michael Joseph.

Kirkwood, T. B., & Rose, M. R. (1991). Evolution of senescence: Late survival sacrificed for reproduction. *Philosophical Transactions of the Royal Society of London, Series B: Biological Sciences, 332*, 15–24.

Klindworth, H., & Voland, E. (1995). How did the Krummhörn elite males achieve above-average reproductive success? *Human Nature, 6*, 221–240.

Knauft, B. M. (1985). *Good company and violence: Sorcery and social action in a lowland New Guinea society*. Berkeley: University of California Press.

Koot, H. M., & Verhulst, F. C. (1991). Prevalence of problem behavior in Dutch children aged 2–3. *Acta Psychiatricia Scandinavica, 83*, 1–37.

Kraemer, S. (2000). The fragile male. *British Medical Journal, 321*, 1609–1612.

Kruger, D. J. (2006). Male facial masculinity influences attributions of personality and reproductive strategy. *Personal Relationships, 13*, 451–463.

Kruger, D. J. (2010). Socio-demographic factors intensifying male mating competition exacerbate male mortality rates. *Evolutionary Psychology, 8*, 194–204.

Kruger, D. J., & Nesse, R. M. (2004). Sexual selection and the Male:Female Mortality Ratio. *Evolutionary Psychology, 2*, 66–77.

Kruger, D. J., & Nesse, R. M. (2006a). An evolutionary life-history framework for understanding sex differences in human mortality rates. *Human Nature, 17*, 74–97.

Kruger, D. J., & Nesse, R. M. (2006b). Understanding sex differences in Croatian mortality with an evolutionary framework. *Psychological Topics, 15*, 351–364.

Kruger, D. J., & Nesse, R. M. (2007). Economic transition, male competition, and sex differences in mortality rates. *Evolutionary Psychology, 5*, 411–427.

Kuester, J., & Paul, A. (1992). Influence of mate competition and female choice on male mating success in Barbary macaques. *Behaviour, 120*, 192–217.

Lancaster, J. B. (1989). Evolutionary and cross-cultural perspectives on single-parenthood. In R. W. Bell & N. J. Bell (Eds.), *Interfaces in psychology* (pp. 63–72). Lubbock: Texas Tech University Press.

Lee, R. B. (1979). *The !Kung San: Men, women, and work in a foraging society*. New York: Cambridge University press.

Lees, S. (1993). *Sugar and spice: Sexuality and adolescent girls*. London: Penguin.

Lester, D. (1991). *Questions and answers about murder*. Philadelphia: Charles Press.

Leutenegger, W., & Kelly, J. T. (1977). Relationship of sexual dimorphism in canine size and body size to social, behavioral, and ecological correlates in anthropoid primates. *Primates, 18*, 117–136.

Leyland, A. H., & Dundas, R. (2010). The social patterning of deaths due to assault in Scotland, 1980–2005: Population-based study. *Journal of Epidemiology and Community Health, 64*, 432–439.

Low, B. (1998). The evolution of human life histories. In C. Crawford & D. Krebs (Eds.), *Handbook of evolutionary psychology: Ideas, issues, and applications* (pp. 131–161). Mahwah, NJ: Erlbaum.

Low, B. (2000). *Why sex matters: A Darwinian look at human behavior*. Princeton, NJ: Princeton University Press.

Low, B. (2003). Ecological and social complexities in monogamy. In U. Reichard & C. Boesch (Eds.), *Monogamy: Mating strategies and partnerships in birds, humans, and other mammals* (pp. 161–176). Cambridge, England: Cambridge University Press.

Low, B. (2007). Ecological and socio-cultural impacts on mating and marriage systems. In R. Dunbar and L. Barrett (Eds.), *The Oxford handbook of evolutionary psychology* (pp. 449–462). Oxford, UK: Oxford University Press.

Mazur, A., Halpern, C., & Udry, J. (1994). Dominant looking male teenagers copulate earlier. *Ethology and Sociobiology, 15*, 87–94.

Mazur, A., Mazur, J., & Keating, C. (1984). Military rank attainment of a West Point class: Effects of cadets' physical features. *American Journal of Sociology, 90*, 125–150.

Mazur, A., & Michalek, J. (1998). Marriage, divorce, and male testosterone. *Social Forces, 77*, 315–330.

McArthur, L. Z., & Apatow, K. (1983). Impressions of baby-faced adults. *Social Cognition, 2*, 315–342.

Merkt, R. A., McHose, A. L., & Chiappone, A. *The New Jersey self-defense law*. Stat. § 159 (2008).

Miller, G. F. (1998). How mate choice shaped human nature: A review of sexual selection and human evolution. In C. Crawford & D. Krebs (Eds.), *Handbook of evolutionary psychology: Ideas, issues, and applications* (pp. 87–129). Mahwah, NJ: Erlbaum.

Møller, A. P., Christe, P., & Lux, E. (1999). Parasitism, host immune function, and sexual selection. *Quarterly Review of Biology, 74*, 3–20.

Mueller, U., & Mazur, A. (1997). Facial dominance in Homo sapiens as honest signaling of male quality. *Behavioral Ecology, 8*, 569–579.

Mitani, J. C. (1985). Sexual selection and adult male orangutan long calls. *Animal Behaviour, 33*, 272–283.

Mitani, J. C. (1990). Experimental field studies of Asian ape social systems. *International Journal of Primatology, 11*, 103–126.

Mitani, J. C., Watts, D. P., & Amsler, S. J. (2010). Lethal intergroup aggression leads to territorial expansion in wild chimpanzees. *Current Biology, 20*, R507–R508.

Nishida, T. (1990). *The chimpanzees of the Mahale mountains*. Tokyo: University of Tokyo Press.

Palombit, R. A., Seyfarth, R. M., & Cheney, D. L. (1997). The adaptive value of "friendships" to female baboons: Experimental and observational evidence. *Animal Behavior, 54*, 599–614.

Plavcan, J. M. (2000). Inferring social behavior from sexual dimorphism in the fossil record. *Journal of Human Evolution, 39*, 327–344.

Plavcan, J. M., & van Schaik, C. P. (1997). Interpreting hominid behavior on the basis of sexual dimorphism. *Journal of Human Evolution, 32*, 345–374.

Plavcan, J. M., van Schaik, C. P., & Kappeler, P. M. (1995). Competition, coalitions and canine size in primates. *Journal of Human Evolution, 28*, 245–276.

Promislow, D. E. (1992). Costs of sexual selection in natural populations of mammals. *Proceedings of the Royal Society of London, Series B, 247*, 230–210.

Quinlan, R. J. (2007). Human parental effort and environmental risk. *Proceedings of the Royal Society of London, Series B, 274*, 121–125.

Reichard, U., & Boesch, C. (Eds.). (2003). *Monogamy: Mating strategies and partnerships in birds, humans, and other mammals*. Cambridge, England: Cambridge University Press.

Rice, W. R. (1996). Sexually antagonistic male adaptation triggered by experimental arrest of female evolution. *Nature, 381*, 232–234.

Roff, D. A. (1992). *The evolution of life histories: Theory and analysis*. Chicago: University of Chicago Press.

Robbins, M. M. (1995). A demographic analysis of male life history and social structure of mountain gorillas. *Behaviour, 132*, 21–47

Robbins, M. M. (1999). Male mating patterns in wild multimale mountain gorilla groups. *Animal Behaviour, 57*, 1013–1020.

Rushton, J. P. (1985). Differential K theory: The sociobiology of individual and group differences. *Personality and Individual Differences, 6*, 441–452.

Salzinger, S., Feldman, R. S., Stockhammer, T., & Hood, J. (2002). An ecological framework for understanding risk for exposure to community violence and the effects of exposure on children and adolescents. *Aggression and Violent Behavior, 7*, 423–451.

Sampson, R. J., & Lauritsen, J. (1994). Violent victimization and offending: Individual, situational and community-level risk factors. In A. J. Reiss & J. A. Roth (Eds.), *Understanding and preventing violence: Social influences* (Vol. 3, pp. 1–114). Washington, DC: National Academy Press.

Schaal, B., Tremblay, R. E., Soussignan, R., & Susman, E. J. (1996). Male testosterone linked to high social dominance but low physical aggression in early adolescence. *Journal of the American Academy of Child and Adolescent Psychiatry, 35*, 1322–1330.

Schurmann, C., & van Hooff, J. (1986). Reproductive strategies of the orangutan: New data and a reconsideration of existing socio-sexual models. *International Journal of Primatology, 7*, 265–287.

Shackelford, T. K., & Buss, D. M. (1997). Cues to infidelity. *Personality and Social Psychology Bulletin, 23*, 1034–1045.

Sicotte, P. (1993). Inter-group encounters and female transfer in mountain gorillas: Influence of group composition on male behavior. *American Journal of Primatology, 30*, 21–36.

Smuts, B. B. (1987). Gender, aggression, and influence. In B. B. Smuts, D. L. Cheny, R. M. Seyfarth, R. W. Wrangham, & T. T. Struhsaker (Eds.), *Primate societies* (pp. 400–412). Chicago: University of Chicago Press.

Smuts, B. B. (1995). The evolutionary origins of patriarchy. *Human Nature, 6*, 1–32.

Soltis, J., Mitsunaga, F., Shimizu, K., Nozaki, M., Yanagihara, Y., Domingo-Roura, X., & Takenaka, O. (1997). Sexual selection in Japanese macaques II: Female mate choice and male-male competition. *Animal Behaviour, 54*, 737–746.

Stearns, S. C. (1992). *The evolution of life histories*. Oxford, England: Oxford University Press.

Strassmann, B. I. (1981). Sexual selection, paternal care, and concealed ovulation in humans. *Ethology and Sociobiology, 2*, 31–40.

Strassmann, B. I. (1996). The evolution of endometrial cycles and menstruation. *Quarterly Review of Biology, 70*, 181–220.

Taylor, S. E., Klein, L. C., Lewis, B. P., Gruenewald, T. L., Gurung, R. A., & Updegraff, J. A. (2000). Biobehavioral responses to stress in females: Tend-and-befriend, not fight-or-flight. *Psychological Review, 107*, 411–429.

Tinbergen, N. (1963) On aims and methods in ethology. *Zeitschrift für Tierpsychologie, 20*, 410–433.

Tooby, J., & Cosmides, L. (1988). *The evolution of war and its cognitive foundations*. Technical report 88-1 for the Institute of Evolutionary Studies. Palo Alto, CA: Institute for Evolutionary Studies.

Trivers, R. L. (1971). The evolution of reciprocal altruism. *Quarterly Review of Biology, 46,* 35–56.

Trivers, R. (1972). Parental investment and sexual selection. In B. Campbell (Ed.), *Sexual selection and the descent of man: 1871–1971* (pp. 136–179). Chicago: Aldine.

United Nations Development Program, Regional Bureau for Europe and the CIS. (1998). *Poverty in transition?* New York: Author.

Valencia, M. J. (2010, July 1). Sergeant, Gates both to blame, report says. *The Boston Globe.* Available at: http://www.boston.com/news/local/massachusetts/articles/2010/07/01/sergeant_gates_both_to_blame_report_says/

Weber, A. W., & Vedder, A. (1983). Population dynamics of the Virunga gorillas: 1959–1978. *Biological Conservation, 26,* 341–366.

Weisfeld, G. E. (1999). *Evolutionary principles of human adolescence.* New York: Basic Books.

Williams, G. C. (1957). Pleiotropy, natural selection, and the evolution of senescence. *Evolution, 11,* 398–411.

Williams, G. C. (1966). *Adaptation and natural selection: A critique of some current evolutionary thought.* Princeton, NJ: Princeton University Press.

Williams, G. C. (1975). *Sex and evolution.* Princeton, NJ: Princeton University Press.

Wilson, M., & Daly, M. (1985). Competitiveness, risk taking, and violence: The young male syndrome. *Ethology and Sociobiology, 6,* 59–73.

Wilson, M., & Daly, M. (1997). Life expectancy, economic inequality, homicide, and reproductive timing in Chicago neighbourhoods. *British Medical Journal, 314,* 1271–1274.

Wilson, M. L., & Wrangham, R. W. (2003). Intergroup relations in chimpanzees. *Annual Review of Anthropology, 32,* 363–392.

Wolfgang, M. E. (1958). *Patterns in criminal homicide.* Philadelphia: University of Pennsylvania Press.

Wrangham, R. W. (1993). The evolution of sexuality in chimpanzees and bonobos. *Human Nature, 4,* 47–79.

Wrangham, R. W., & Peterson, D. (1996). *Demonic males.* Boston: Mariner Books.

Zahavi, A. (1975). Mate selection—a selection for a handicap. *Journal of Theoretical Biology, 53,* 205–214.

PART 3

Evolutionary Perspectives on Extrafamilial Violence and Homicide

CHAPTER
11

Evolutionary Psychological Perspectives on Sexual Offending: From Etiology to Intervention

Joseph A. Camilleri

Abstract

This chapter reviews the literature on evolutionary psychological explanations of sexual offending, which span nearly 30 years of research and scholarship. Other reviews have been published, but they have focused on particular areas of sexual offending or on specific hypotheses. Here, I review this diverse literature to give a general overview and commentary on evolutionary approaches to sexual offending etiology and intervention, and I conclude by proposing a typology of sexual offenders.

Key Words: rape, partner rape, pedophilia, incest, paraphilias, sexual disorders, developmentally disabled offenders, evolutionary psychology, individual differences

Introduction

This chapter reviews evolutionary explanations of sexual offending. This literature spans nearly 30 years of psychological, anthropological, and biological research and scholarship. Other reviews have been published, but they have focused on particular areas of sexual offending (Goetz, Shackelford, & Camilleri, 2008; Lalumière & Quinsey, 1998; McKibbin, Shackelford, Goetz, & Starratt, 2008; Quinsey, 2003; Quinsey & Lalumière, 1995) or on specific hypotheses (Archer & Vaughan, 2001), while other reviews have not been entirely accurate (e.g., Ellis, 1989; Emery Thompson, 2009; Stinson, Sales, & Becker, 2008; cf., Camilleri, 2010; Wilson & Daly, 1992a). Here, I review this diverse literature to give a general overview and commentary on evolutionary approaches to sexual offending. I conclude by synthesizing these approaches to propose a typology of sexual offenders.

Defining Sexual Offending

The term *sexual offending* is the broadest category of behaviors that involves any sexual act by one person that may cause unwanted physical or psychological harm to another person. *Sexual acts* include overt physical contact (or attempted contact) that targets erogenous zones or actions that are sexually motivated, and verbal statements that indicate these intentions. A person may be *offended* by these acts because they are unwanted, offensive, and lack consent. These behaviors vary in terms of the severity of physical and psychological injuries to the victim. *Sexual aggression*, though also a broad term, tends to focus more on severe forms of sexual offending, particularly acts that involve physical contact.

Terms subsumed under sexual offending typically address specific types of acts or are legally defined crimes. *Sexual coercion*, similar to sexual offending, is broad but implies use of force or manipulative tactics in order to obtain sex from someone who is reluctant (Camilleri, Quinsey, & Tapscott, 2009). Some sexual offenses may therefore not be coercive, such as voyeurism. Sexual aggression can either refer specifically to sexual offending behavior or to variations in sexual aggressiveness that are treated as individual difference characteristics.

In North America, *rape* (various US state laws), *sexual abuse* (US Code, 2010, Title 18, § 2242), and

173

sexual assault (Canada Criminal Code [CCC], 1985, § 271) are legal terms that refer to any assault of a sexual nature, though some US states define rape as requiring unwanted intercourse (e.g., Official Code of Georgia Annotated [OCGA], 2011, § 16-6-1). Other charges vary in terms of severity (e.g., *aggravated sexual assault* includes physical injury to victim; CCC, 1985, § 273) or in terms of relationship to the victim (e.g., child, kin, spouse). *Child molestation* and *sexual interference* refer to sexual acts with underage children (e.g., CCC, 1985, § 151). Spousal or marital rape refers to a conjugal sexual offense. Other terms describe sexual aggression in various types of existing sexual relationships, including *partner rape* or *partner sexual coercion* (i.e., any committed sexual relationship, ranging from steady dating relationships to marital rape; Camilleri & Quinsey, 2009a, 2012), *forced in-pair copulation* (Goetz & Shackelford, 2006), *date rape* (i.e., on a date), and *acquaintance rape* (i.e., in which the victim knows but is not romantically involved with the perpetrator), though sometimes date rape and partner rape have been included as types of acquaintance rape (Koss, Dinero, & Seibel, 1988). *Incest* refers to sexual intercourse between genetically related family members (e.g., CCC, 1985, § 155), though some US states and countries include nonkin family members or permit incest among consenting adults. Some paraphilias, if acted upon, meet the definition of sexual offenses, including *voyeurism, exhibitionism, pedophilia, frotteurism, zoophilia,* and *biastophilia*. *Sadism*, though sometimes considered a characteristic of rapists, is not criminal if it occurs between consenting adults. Understanding the differences between types of sexual offenses is important because their etiologies may be different.

Extent of the Problem

Considering the breadth of acts and definitions of sexual offending, victimization rates vary considerably. What is consistent across these definitions, however, is an inverse relationship between sexual offense severity and its frequency or prevalence. For instance, from a nationally representative sample of women, 9% reported ever experiencing unwanted sexual intercourse due to force or threatened force by a male, whereas 25% reported unwanted sexual touching from men who consistently pressured and argued for it (Koss, Gidycz, & Wisniewski, 1987). From cases reported to Canadian police in 2009, 122 were instances of *aggravated sexual assault* (i.e., sexual assault that "wounds, maims, disfigures or endangers the life of the complainant" [CCC, 1985, § 273:1]), whereas 20,460 were instances of *sexual assault* (Statistics Canada, 2009).

Although the frequency of sexual offending varies over time and location (Lalumière, Harris, Quinsey, & Rice, 2005), all documented periods and cultures have rules or laws against rape (Brown, 1991). Consequences to victims of sexual assault include physical injury, unwanted pregnancy, aggression, and sexually transmitted diseases (e.g., Gottschall & Gottschall, 2003; US Department of Justice, 2006). Understanding why these offenses occur, under what circumstances they take place, and knowing characteristics of who is most likely to commit them might position society to prevent or learn how to intervene more effectively.

Traditionally, explanations of sexual offending have been addressed by disciplines subsumed under the "Standard Social Sciences Model" (Tooby & Cosmides, 1992, 2005), including traditional approaches to psychology, sociology, criminology, and anthropology, in which the underlying assumption is that nurture is the root of all behavior. The trouble with this model is that it does not accurately represent the processes of development and the complex interactions between organisms and their environments in producing behaviors (Gaulin & McBurney, 2001). The benefit of an evolutionary psychological approach is that it provides a metatheory that links ultimate causes (i.e., why a mechanism has a particular function) and proximate causes (i.e., how the mechanism functions) and embeds psychology within the natural sciences. An evolutionary approach allows us to synthesize work on humans with biological advances being made on nonhuman animals, such as sexual coercion (e.g., Muller & Wrangham, 2009).

To address the diverse evolutionary literature on sexual offending, I divided the literature into the "early period," which includes the first set of publications that mostly address whether rape is something that could have evolved, followed by the "contemporary period," which addresses more complex hypotheses regarding the etiology of sexual offending.

Early Period
Costs and Benefits

Symons (1979) provided one of the earliest evolutionary accounts of human rape in his seminal book, *The Evolution of Human Sexuality*. He argued that rape occurs because men's default sexuality is to mate as often as possible, and so when men are faced with nonconsenting women, they use force when the costs of such behavior are low. The costs associated with female resistance to rape, listed by Symons, include male time, energy, and risk of injury. He cited the occurrence of rape during war as evidence for his analysis, because rape is rampant in these contexts, and the costs are exceedingly low (e.g., perpetrator has virtual anonymity).

Shields and Shields (1983) provided a more elaborate description of the evolution of rape by identifying conditions in which the fitness benefits might have outweighed the costs. First, they established how the sexes conflicted in their mating strategies—women, relative to men, prefer mate quality, whereas men, relative to women, prefer mate quantity. Second, because of these differences, traits among men that overcome female resistance may have been sexually selected. They argued that men facultatively use one of three mating strategies: (1) *cooperative bonding* by mating in a consenting monogamous relationship; (2) *deceitful or manipulative courtship* by using deceit for short-term mating; and (3) *forcible rape*, when women resist a nonpreferred male, and men use force to overcome resistance, even if the probability of fertilization is low.

The impact of costs and benefits on selection can be tested using mathematical models to identify whether a trait, given certain parameters, could have evolved (McElreath & Boyd, 2007). Shields and Shields (1983) were the first of only a few researchers to use mathematical modeling in the context of sexual coercion. The optimal strategy that emerged was a conditional one that included cooperative bonding, deceitful or manipulative courtship, and forcible rape. A concern with their model is that some of their parameters may be incorrect, such as assuming that seduction and forcible rape had a lower probability of fertilization than cooperative bonding. Recent evidence suggests that pregnancy is just as likely, if not more likely, to result from rape than from consensual sex (Gottschall & Gottshcall, 2003). This is not to say that someone who uses forcible rape has the same payoff as someone who employs cooperative bonding, but that interactions between benefits and costs are varied, complex, and need to be accounted for. Unfortunately, the only other model on humans (Smith, Borgerhoff Mulder, & Hill, 2001) had notable methodological problems (Kokko, 2001). Active work on mathematical modeling can be found in nonhuman research on conflict and coercion (e.g., Clarke, Pradhan, & van Schaik, 2009). The human literature would benefit from this methodology as well. Understanding the costs and benefits are important because it tells us (1) whether rape could have evolved; and (2) if it evolved, when it is likely to occur.

Adaptations and By-Products

One of the most widely discussed topics addressed in evolutionary explanations of rape is whether rape functions as an adaptation or is a by-product of other adaptations. To address this issue, I briefly review how evolutionary psychologists define and test for adaptations and by-products, then review the most widely cited hypotheses of rape in each case.

ADAPTATIONS

The crux of evolutionary psychological approaches to understanding human behavior is the adaptationist program—identifying how a psychological mechanism could have been naturally or sexually selected to overcome barriers to fitness (Buss, Haselton, Shackelford, Bleske, & Wakefield, 1998). By definition, an adaptation is an inherited trait that was naturally or sexually selected by conferring relative fitness benefits. An adaptation can be obligate, such that its expression is not dependent on the environment, or facultative, such that its expression is in response to environmental variations (Lalumière et al., 2005; Quinsey, 2002). Most psychological adaptations are thought to be facultative, though some psychological characteristics, such as personality, might be obligate (Gaulin & McBurney, 2001; Harpending & Sobus, 1987; Quinsey, 2002). Although adaptations are modifications of other phenotypes, and can therefore evolve to be quite complex, they must also be precise, efficient, reliable, and economical (Williams, 1966). Researchers have also provided evidentiary standards for psychological adaptations (see Andrews, Gangestad, & Matthews, 2002; Schmitt & Pilcher, 2004).

No single piece of evidence alone is sufficient for determining whether a trait is an adaptation. To do so requires ruling out alternative explanations while meeting the criteria for adaptations using multiple methodologies. Although adaptive explanations of rape have been proposed for over 20 years, researchers are still just scratching the surface. I review the most commonly cited evolutionary hypothesis for rape in light of these characteristics: the mate-deprivation hypothesis (Lalumière, Chalmers, Quinsey, & Seto, 1996).

MATE-DEPRIVATION HYPOTHESIS

While the cost-benefit approach toward explaining the evolution of rape assumed it was an adaptation, other approaches were more explicit about how rape functioned as an adaptation. An early and well-known ultimate explanation for rape is the mate-deprivation hypothesis—that rape is a facultative response among men who have a low probability of consensual mating opportunities. The earliest description of this hypothesis was provided by Alexander and Noonan (1979), who argued that as a result of concealed ovulation and women's selective receptivity toward mateships, males who were likely to be deprived of mating would have increased their fitness by using force.

Thornhill (1980) provided a more general hypothesis of rape as it relates to mate deprivation—that it should occur in species in which males control resources that improve female fitness. Competition for these resources means that some males end up with fewer or no resources, making them undesirable to the opposite sex. Because the accrual of tangible resources is difficult to fake, forced copulation becomes a viable conditional strategy under such dire reproductive circumstances.

Thornhill and Thornhill (1983) elaborated on this hypothesis as it applies to humans by suggesting that human mating was mostly characterized by polygyny, which would have favored facultative mating strategies. In polygynous mating systems, a small number of men monopolize a large number of mateships, leaving a significant number of men without mating opportunities. Selection would have therefore favored coercive mating among men who had "the greatest difficulty climbing the social ladder" and were thus unlikely to form a pair-bond (Thornhill & Thornhill, 1983, p. 141).

Several predictions derived from this hypothesis have been tested. First, Thornhill and Thornhill (1983) predicted that rape should occur when the competition for mateships is highest (i.e., prior to marriage). Thornhill and Thornhill found, based on population norms, that a greater proportion of younger men committed rape than what was expected by chance. Second, they predicted a correlation between the median age of rapists and the median age of married men—if men are getting married at a younger age, then competition is more intense at a younger age. They reported a significant correlation that disappeared after using a log transformation. Despite these inconsistent data that only included rapists whose median age ranged from 20 to 23 years, they observed moderate effect sizes with correlation coefficients greater than 0.4. Similarly, Starks and Blackie (2000) tested the prediction that divorce rates should be related to rape prevalence rates because serial monogamy increases men's variance in reproductive success (high divorce rates result in fewer available mating partners because divorced men typically remarry younger women). They expected, and found, higher rates of rape under these circumstances.

Third, Thornhill and Thornhill (1983) predicted that men who are least likely to attract a mate, such as poor men, are more likely to rape. They reported socioeconomic data among rapists that were consistent with this idea, but they lacked a nonoffender comparison group to test, for example, if the proportion of low socioeconomic rapists is different from the proportion of low socioeconomic nonrapists. Still, data from rape victimization studies also corroborate this prediction because rape victims are overrepresented in lower socioeconomic areas (Perkins & Klaus, 1996). Thornhill and Thornhill suggested the possibility that socioeconomic data are confounded by wealthy men's ability to either not get caught or to settle outside of court. Another issue is that socioeconomic status and age correlate with other crimes, and so any evolutionary account of mate deprivation needs to also account for these other criminal acts (Thornhill & Palmer, 2000).

Vaughan (2001) tried to integrate the cost-benefit approach with the mate-deprivation hypothesis by testing an alternative hypothesis that the costs and benefits are different for high-status men and for low-status men—high-status men have more to lose from raping a stranger. Because of this, low-status men are more likely to rape strangers, whereas high-status men are likely to rape acquaintances. Unfortunately, the validity of this cost is questionable because it is plausible that strangers represent the lowest cost due to being anonymous, regardless of social status. Not surprisingly, Vaughn did not find support for this hypothesis. Vaughn's results, however, were consistent with research on mate deprivation because she found that across victim–offender relationship types, there was a greater proportion of low-status than high-status men who raped. This was not a strong test of the hypotheses because many of the possible confounds mentioned earlier were not controlled.

Another prediction from this hypothesis is that men who are unsuccessful at obtaining mateships should be more sexually aggressive. Lalumière et al. (1996) provided a direct test of this prediction and found that men who were sexually coercive were not different from noncoercive men on self-perceived mating success, and they scored *higher* on reported number of sexual experiences—a result that was in the opposite direction than that predicted by the mate-deprivation hypothesis. Other data were consistent with this finding. For example, Malamuth, Sockloskie, Koss, and Tanaka (1991) found a significant relationship between promiscuity and sexual aggression, and Kanin (1985) also found that rapists had more consensual sexual experiences than did nonrapist controls. These data suggest sexually coercive men are not motivated from a lack of mating experiences. Lalumière et al. (1996) proposed an alternative hypothesis, which they called the *micro-mate-deprivation hypothesis*—men who adopt a short-term mating strategy require many mating partners to make up for the low probability of fertilization, so these men, when faced with refusal, are more likely to use sexually coercive tactics to obtain sex. Kanin's (1985) data are consistent with this alternative hypothesis because rapists were more sexually active than nonrapists in terms of coitus, fellatio, and masturbation.

The mate-deprivation hypothesis is not the only rape adaptation hypothesis. Thornhill and Palmer (2000) reviewed other possible rape adaptations, including the ability to assess victim vulnerability, choose victims based on sexual attractiveness, produce more sperm during rape than consenting sex, become sexually aroused to coercive sex, and commit rape under sperm competition. Some of these alternatives may be better understood as mechanisms of how a rape adaptation would function, rather than as adaptations per se (e.g., ability to assess victim vulnerability). With the exception of victim vulnerability and rape under sperm competition (reviewed below in the "Rape and Relationships" section), these additional explanations, in addition to having sparse evidence in support of them, also have particular theoretical setbacks. Though more rapists exhibit a sexual preference for coercive sex than nonrapists, it still begs the question as to why mostly rapists, not men in the general population, have such a preference (see "Paraphilias" section) or why sperm should be produced in greater abundance under rape scenarios.

BY-PRODUCTS

Behaviors might be unintentional outcomes of adaptations that serve no function—called by-products. To identify a by-product, researchers need to establish that the trait is not functional and need to identify what adaptations they are associated with and why (Buss et al., 1998; Tooby & Cosmides, 1992). A commonly cited example of this is the color of bones, which happens to be white because bones are made out of calcium. The color of bones is not an adaptation but is a by-product of an adaptation for strength.

Rape has been hypothesized to be a by-product of several adaptations, such as men's interest in impersonal sex when in low-risk situations (Symons, 1979). Thornhill and Thornhill (1983) rejected the hypothesis that rape is a by-product of men's persistence at copulating and women's refusal of sexual advances to select high-quality mates because men who adopted rape as a conditional strategy would have out-reproduced men who raped as a by-product. Still, even if rape were adaptive, it does not rule out the possibility that rape could also occur as a by-product in some cases.

Palmer (1991) drew from Symons' (1979) arguments to suggest that rape may be a by-product of men's greater arousal to visual stimuli, higher sex drive, lower ability to abstain from sex, greater desire for sexual variety, and lower discrimination among sexual partners. Palmer compared several evolutionary hypotheses about rape and concluded that the data are most consistent with the by-product hypothesis. Some of his points were validated, such as his criticism of the evidence that rapists are lower socioeconomic men who have a difficult time finding a partner, because a substantial proportion of rapists are not in a lower socioeconomic demographic and up to 60% of rapists had been married prior to committing their offense. Some points are not currently valid, however. For example, he suggested there is little evidence across species that rape is committed by subordinate males, but more recent reviews of the nonhuman animal literature indicate that this is the case in a number of species (Lalumière et al., 2005).

CONFUSING ADAPTATIONS AND BY-PRODUCTS

Researchers sometimes use the same data to support both adaptation and by-product explanations. A good example of this is the data on men's sexual arousal to rape scenarios when victims show signs of arousal (reviewed in Malamuth, 1981). These results were used to support the rape as an adaptation hypothesis because it is a condition where even nonrapists show arousal to rape (Thornhill & Thornhill, 1992), but were also used to support rape as a by-product of consenting sexual interactions (Palmer, 1991). These data likely support neither hypothesis because the stimuli are not ecologically valid. Though one study has shown that women exhibit genital arousal in response to depictions of rape, possibly as an adaptive response to minimize physical injury (Suschinsky & Lalumière, 2011), we do not know what proportion of rape victims show overt signs of sexual arousal, though reports indicate victim responses are mostly nonsexual, such as tonic immobility (i.e., motor inhibition from highly fearful situations), physical resistance (e.g., try to push away or hit), or verbal resistance (e.g., yell or plead) (Galliano, Noble, Travis, & Puechl, 1993; Ullman & Knight, 1995). Even when there are no signs of victim sexual arousal, some men exhibit sexual arousal to rape because the stimuli include sexual words, actions, and body parts. Allgeier and Wiederman (1992) found that 10% to 20% of words in phallometric stimuli described resistance or negative experiences, whereas most of the other words described what the man was doing, the man's arousal, and descriptions of the woman (percentages were not given for these categories). Having a rape victim show signs of enjoying the experience artificially signals consent and excludes aversive aspects of a rape that most men would not find arousing.

Thornhill and Thornhill (1992) also cited studies that showed rapists and nonrapists were sexually aroused, measured using penile tumescence, to rape scenarios to support their prediction that men's arousal and ability to copulate should not depend on a woman's consent. Again, these data are misleading because the arousal could have been due to the use of sexual words. More important, 90% of nonrapists show a preference for consenting sex, whereas 60% of rapists show a preference for rape scenarios, suggesting that not all men, even among rapists, show sexual preference for rape (Lalumière, Quinsey, Harris, Rice, & Trautrimas, 2003). Quinsey (1992) pointed out that difference scores between responses to rape versus consenting stimuli, rather than absolute arousal to either, do a better job at discriminating between rapists and nonrapists and at predicting the likelihood of future sexual offending. So any evolutionary explanations of rape need to account for these important individual differences (see section on "Individual Differences"). I expect that arousal to rape scenarios will covary with characteristics or conditions that cause rape. Men who are persistently deviant in terms of arousal should also be on a persistent path to sexual offending, such as psychopathy, whereas men who are on a facultative path to offending should exhibit a preference for rape only when conditions increase the likelihood of rape. In rare cases, a preference for coercive sex, known as biastophilia, is the only presenting condition that may have led to such offending.

What also complicates this discussion are unsupported assumptions. Thornhill and Thornhill (1992) introduced a premise that no dichotomy exists between coercive and noncoercive mating tactics because men use both when pursuing mateships. Palmer (1991) argued that if there is no distinction between coercive and noncoercive mating, there is no need to research "forced" copulation when it is not different from "unforced" copulation. This assumption confuses any discussion on rape as an adaptation because it lacks proper operationalization (Smuts, 1992). Also, a recent factor analysis of tactics people use to obtain sex in relationships found that these actions reliably cluster into two types, sexual coercion and sexual coaxing (Camilleri, Quinsey, & Tapscott, 2009). This factor structure was validated—the sexual coercion subscale correlated with attitude and behavioral measures of sexual coercion, not with measures of noncoercive sexual desire, whereas the opposite was true for sexual coaxing. It should also be noted that most instances of consenting sex only include noncoercive sexual acts, and that only some individuals, in response to refusal, start by using less severe tactics and proceed to more coercive ones. Byers and Lewis (1988) found that only 11% of their respondents, over a 4-week period, had a partner who physically continued unwanted sexual advances, whereas 61% had a partner who immediately stopped these advances and did not switch to more coercive behaviors. The rest had partners who were verbally coercive (7%), verbally angry (5%), or questioned the refusal (16%). So although men do exhibit both coercive and noncoercive behaviors, they are likely to be used under different contexts for different functions.

The trouble with much of the by-product literature is a focus on falsifying adaptive explanations instead of specifically testing predictions derived from a by-product hypothesis. In addition to identifying the adaptations of which rape might be a by-product, researchers need to test predictions that are falsifiable. For example, if the by-product hypothesis is true, we should expect the degree to which the sexes differ on sexually aggressive behavior to match the degree to which the sexes differ on characteristics of which rape is a by-product. As a brief example, the effect size difference between men and women on arrests for forcible rape is 15.2 (Cohen's *d* calculated using the FBI's Uniform Crime Reports average arrest rates from 1998–2009), which does not match effect size differences in mating psychology between the sexes, such as number of sexual partners desired, consenting to sex after knowing someone for 1 month, and seeking short-term mating, all of which ranges from 0.3 to 1.2 across 10 world regions (Schmitt et al., 2003). By-product explanations, if true, will need to account for this substantial discrepancy, such as the possibility of smaller differences in underlying factors having a cumulative effect on sex differences in rape.

Integrated Models
CONFLUENCE MODEL OF SEXUAL AGGRESSION

Another early approach for explaining rape included integrating evolutionary perspectives with other theories, particularly feminism. Malamuth's *confluence model of sexual aggression* is a prominent exemplar. I review the historical development of this model before commenting on its theoretical and methodological validity.

The first iteration of this model was conceived without an evolutionary framework in mind. Malamuth et al. (1991) studied a large nonforensic sample to test a proximal, developmental model on what they called "central factors" associated with sexual aggression, intended to provide a structure for explaining individual correlates, such as early experiences and personality. At the root of their model was early experiences, particularly parental violence and child abuse that influence delinquency (measured from having delinquent friends and running away from home). The delinquency factor splits into two separate paths. The first path is sexual promiscuity; the second path is attitudes toward violence, leading to hostile masculinity. These paths to sexual coercion against women are depicted as independent, even though the authors hypothesized an interaction between them. Also, the model does not account for why delinquency splits into two paths: that it sometimes causes sexual promiscuity, sometimes increases hostile masculinity, or sometimes causes both. Still, results of the study provided general support for the model.

Malamuth (1996) later endorsed this model as not just a confluence between variables, but between feminist and evolutionary paradigms. That is, he argued that feminists believe dominance and hostility mechanisms are associated with sexual violence, which is represented by the hostile masculinity path, whereas evolutionary psychologists believe that sexuality mechanisms, represented by the impersonal sex path, and dominance/hostility mechanisms are associated with sexual violence. The "evolutionary" part of this model is that sex differences in interest in impersonal sex stem from differences in minimal parental investment, and that men who are high on interest in impersonal sex may be sexually aroused even when faced with an unwilling partner, and it alludes to conditions that either increase or decrease costs of engaging in such acts. Dominance/hostility was explained as being part of a male psychology designed to control the reproductive interests of females through the use of coercion to overcome reproductive conflicts, such as paternity uncertainty. Although this explanation addresses overall sex differences in mating strategies and psychology, which are not depicted in the model, it does not explain how or why "delinquency" and "early experiences" precede hostile masculinity and interest in impersonal sex. To account for this, Malamuth, Heavey, and Linz (1993) described how experiencing abuse and having delinquent friends may trigger hostile attitudes toward women though this link is not found in subsequent models (Malamuth, Heavey, & Linz, 1996; Malamuth, Linz, Heavey, Barnes, & Acker, 1995). Malamuth (1998) also argued that early experiences may trigger later reproductive strategies—that males in harsher environments would benefit more from "quantity" of mates than from "quality," but an unanswered question is whether abuse and parental violence are indeed valid signs of competition for mateships.

The confluence model of sexual aggression is problematic for several reasons. Methodologically, it does not depict an interaction between interest in impersonal sex and hostile masculinity, as suggested by the original hypothesis. In some instances, paths were added to the model, not for theoretical reasons, but to force a model that would statistically fit the data (e.g., Malamuth et al., 1995), a process in structural equation modeling that is considered problematic (Kline, 2011). Also, constant changes to the model and its theory (e.g., Malamuth, 2003; Malamuth & Malamuth, 1999) make it difficult to identify conditions that are required to falsify it. Structural equation modeling is a tool meant to test hypotheses derived by theory—a good fit of the data does not mean the model is valid (Kline, 2011). A more thorough approach to structural equation modeling is to test alternative models (MacCallum & Austin, 2000) to thereby identify which one provides a better fit to the data.

Theoretically, the confluence model does not integrate evolutionary and feminist explanations of sexual coercion but uses both to explain different correlates of sexual offending depicted in the model. This does not mean evolutionary psychology should not be used to explain existing data. Many proximate mechanisms (i.e., correlates) have been identified by other disciplines but were later understood in light of their ultimate causes, leading to the development of new proximate hypotheses (e.g., partner rape; Goetz et al., 2008). Evolutionary approaches to psychology are domain specific—understanding that behaviors are not typically governed by general all-purpose mechanisms but by specialized ones. The confluence model is narrow in scope because of its assumption that all sexual offenses result from a simple interaction between two (or three, depending on the version) factors, one being a specific psychological construct, the other a behavioral one. This approach falls more within the purview of domain generality. Also, no evolutionary aspect of the model, or its iterations, was predicted a priori, and the model is not able to account for major correlates of sexual offending, such as age and sex. These issues, however, should not detract from important contributions of the model, such as linking early cues of harsh environments to mating strategies and recognizing the importance of using longitudinal studies, particularly by using structural equation modeling.

SYNTHESIZED THEORY OF RAPE

Similar integrated models have been proposed—such as Ellis's (1989) *synthesized theory of rape*, which combines feminist (i.e., power and control), evolutionary (i.e., sex differences in sexual drive), and behavioral (i.e., techniques on how to rape are learned through operant conditioning, imitation, and attitudes) theories of rape. Similar to the confluence model, aspects of this model are surely involved in sexual aggression (mating effort, hormones, mental algorithms that weigh benefits and costs), but it mostly describes rather than explains or synthesizes these disparate ideas. For example, although Ellis provides an ultimate explanation for why men are interested in controlling women's mating opportunities, he did not synthesize evolutionary and learning approaches; instead, he stated that both are important in accounting for rape (Wilson & Daly, 1992a). It is likely that because of these theoretical and methodological issues, integrated models, though developed 20 years ago, have not been successful at generating new hypotheses or research findings.

Contemporary Period

Rape is when a person uses force to overcome resistance for intercourse. In the early period, most evolutionary explanations looked at mostly one adaptive reason for why rape exists: mate deprivation. Treating rape as a homogeneous behavior with a singular cause is problematic, however (e.g., Jones & Goldsmith, 2005; Mealey, 1999). A consequence of advancing a single explanation is what Jones (1999) called "The Argument from Incomplete Explanation"—incorrectly falsifying one explanation of rape because it does not explain all types of sexual offending. Examples of this error abound (e.g., Stinson et al., 2008). In the contemporary period, researchers have moved beyond a singular "rape as an adaptation or by-product" explanation, and considered either specific design features of a possible rape adaptation (e.g., mating effort, risk taking, antisociality) or different contexts under which rape could have evolved (e.g., multiple rape adaptations or by-products, and disordered psychological mechanisms that may lead to rape). Many of these ideas, reviewed next, emerged in response to Thornhill and Thornhill's (1992) target article in *Behavioral and Brain Sciences* and are addressed in a series of articles published in a special issue of *Jurimetrics* (e.g., Lalumière & Quinsey, 1999) and in Lalumière et al.'s (2005) book *The Causes of Rape*.

Individual Differences

The concept of mate deprivation has been used differently across studies. Initially, Thornhill and colleagues treated it as an ultimate explanation—ancestral men who were mate deprived and had characteristics that motivated them to overcome female resistance outreproduced men in similar circumstances who did not use such a strategy. In other research, the effects of mate deprivation were treated more proximately by considering mating success. Support for the hypothesis came from aggregate data and indirect tests of mate deprivation, such as using age of perpetrator, age of marriage, or divorce rates, because each of these indicates more intense male-male-competition for mates. From individual-level data assessing mating frequency, either no relationship with sexual aggression was found, or the relationship was in the opposite direction (Lalumière et al., 1996; Malamuth et al., 1991). To reconcile these differences, rape in response to mate deprivation should not be thought of as a single adaptation but as a filter through which all hypothesized rape adaptations must have evolved. Thus, adaptive explanations need to identify *reliably occurring contexts* under which males would have been mate deprived and to which rape might have evolved as a solution. Lalumière et al. (2005) identified three such contexts, resulting in the development of individual difference characteristics that are associated with sexual coercion: (1) young men, (2) competitively disadvantaged men, and (3) psychopathic men.

THE YOUNG MALE SYNDROME

The young male syndrome refers to young males' willingness to tolerate risks, due to the intensity of competition for acquiring mateships (directly or indirectly through acquiring resources), as evidenced by men's greater reproductive variance (Wilson & Daly, 1985), and greater competition before establishing pair bonds. In other words, reproductive benefits were conferred on ancestral men who, during competition for mateships, were willing to take risks to acquire status, resources, and, ultimately, mates (Lalumière et al., 2005). Lalumière et al. hypothesized that this path accounts for a large proportion of sexual and nonsexual crimes. As they age, and have attained mates, men switch from risky mating effort to parental effort because taking such risks is no longer as beneficial (Lalumière et al., 2005). This path to offending can therefore be considered a *developmentally flexible facultative mechanism*, because certain conditions turn this behavior on and off (Camilleri & Quinsey, 2009b; Quinsey, Jones, Book, & Barr, 2006).

Moffit's (1993) "adolescent limited" offender category is consistent with the young male syndrome, because males start offending in adolescence, desist in early adulthood, and have a distinct etiology from other types of offenders. Most notably, this group appears to have normal or near-normal development (Moffitt, 2006). This path explains both the age and sex correlates that comprise the fundamental data of criminology (correlates are robust across time and locations; Hirschi & Gottfredson, 1983; Moffit, 1993).

There are also individual differences in the degree to which young male syndrome is expressed. According to Lalumière et al. (2005), there are men who have "more to gain—or less to lose—by using risky tactics of competition" (p. 89). Though most men increase risky behaviors and mating effort during this period, some men are more likely to do so if they are less successful or experience more competition. There is some evidence of higher homicide rates where competition, assayed by lower life expectancy, is high (Wilson & Daly, 1997). So not only does this path account for sex and age differences in criminal behavior, it is hypothesized to explain conditions that influence individual differences in committing sexual aggression, such as associating with antisocial peers, because such conditions elicit competitiveness (Lalumière et al., 2005). Further tests of this path would benefit by investigating how age and relationship status moderates the relationship between sexual offending and its correlates. For example, sexual arousal to coercive stimuli or attitudes supportive of sexual aggression should be more pronounced among single, young men than among other classes of men, and they should change when these conditions change.

THE COMPETITIVELY DISADVANTAGED

In addition to adolescent-limited offenders, Moffit (1993) identified a smaller group labeled "life-course persistent" offenders—those who performed antisocial behaviors in childhood and early adolescence, persisted in these behaviors throughout adulthood, and are characterized by early social and neurological adversity. Lalumière et al (2005) described this group as being competitively disadvantaged—men who, early in their development, faced either social adversity or neurological impairments resulting in lower embodied capital (i.e., attributes associated with health, gaining resources, mates) and, therefore, would have benefited from adopting a coercive mating strategy. This path represents one of the most commonly hypothesized predictors of sexual aggression by evolutionists and most closely resembles the mate-deprivation hypothesis. As I described earlier, the available data do not support the strong form of this mate-deprivation hypothesis but are consistent with the micro-mate-deprivation hypothesis.

Because neurological impairments endure and early experiences of social adversity cues the person to the environment under which mating competition will likely take place, this path appears to function as a *developmentally fixed facultative mechanism*—early experiences seem to permanently orient a person toward a coercive mating strategy. There is evidence to suggest that these men are, indeed, at a disadvantage when it comes to mateships. For example, if we use intelligence as a marker of embodied capital, men with lower intelligence have fewer dating and sexual experiences (Halpern, Joyner, Udry, & Suchindran, 2000; McCabe, 1999) and women prefer mates with higher intelligence (Buss, Shackelford, Kirkpatrick, & Larsen, 2001; Shackelford, Schmitt, & Buss, 2005; Singh, 1964). It is important here to consider intelligence as *relative* to that of rivals, because very low intelligence may represent a disordered path to sexual offending (see "Sexual Disorders" section).

This path accounts for an impressive list of neurological correlates of crime, including genetic vulnerabilities, labor and delivery problems, unhealthy pregnancy, head injuries, and malnutrition (Harris, Rice, & Lalumière, 2001; Quinsey, Skilling, Lalumière, & Craig, 2006). It also accounts for social development variables associated with sexual offending, such as being raised by a single parent, having lower socioeconomic status, physical abuse victimization, poor parenting and socialization, among others (see Lalumière et al., 2005).

So why are men more vulnerable than women to the effects of these variables? One explanation is that men are biologically more prone to neurodevelopmental insults than are women. This argument, however, does not apply to social adversity. The important consideration, therefore, is that the fitness consequences of low embodied capital, whether from neural or social sources, is higher for men, conferring fitness benefits to ancestral men who adopted a persistent mating strategy that involved risky coercive tactics. Although most sexual offenders desist with age, this path accounts for a small number of offenders who do not desist.

Future research on this path will need to establish a valid assessment of competitive disadvantage before identifying whether it is the intensity, frequency, or type of disadvantage that leads to a coercive strategy. Such an assessment would include various risk markers of competitive disadvantage that may cluster into two related factors: social and neurodevelopmental. At the moment, this path provides a hypothetical synthesis of a disconnected literature. More research is needed to determine whether these different cues measure a latent factor of competitive disadvantage. Also, if this path is independent from the young male syndrome, variables such as sexual arousal to coercive stimuli or attitudes supportive of sexual aggression should not be affected by age or relationship status among these men.

PSYCHOPATHY

The last path to sexual offending in this model is psychopathy—a personality construct that involves social cheating and exploiting, characterized by aggressive narcissism, a socially deviant lifestyle, and coercive/precocious sexuality (Harris, Rice, Hilton, Lalumière, & Quinsey, 2007). Like competitively disadvantaged men, these individuals show early signs of antisociality that persist throughout adulthood. Unlike competitively disadvantaged men, psychopaths do not appear to develop in response to environmental conditions. Psychopathy is thought to be an evolved "cheater" strategy—someone who takes advantage of cooperators for status, resources, and mates, and uses sexual coercion as way to achieve these means (Harpending & Sobus, 1987; Harris et al., 2007). This path is hypothesized to be an *alternative* (i.e., *obligate*) *strategy*. That is, these men may be genetically different from other offenders, and these genes are maintained in a population through frequency-dependent selection (Mealey, 1995). In support of this, there is some evidence to suggest psychopaths are a taxon (Harris, Rice, & Quinsey, 1994; Skilling, Quinsey, & Craig, 2001; Vasey, Kotov, Frick, & Loney, 2005), though some studies suggest psychopathy is on a continuum (Edens, Marcus, Lilienfeld, & Poythress, 2006; Marcus, John, & Edens, 2004). Why there is a discrepancy between these studies and how this might impact the hypothesis that psychopathy is an obligate social strategy remains unanswered. A possible confound in this research is the validity of currently available measures of psychopathy, because none include precocious and coercive sexuality, which are core diagnostic components of the construct (Harris et al., 2007).

Another prediction from this psychopathy hypothesis is that because it is not caused by developmental circumstances, it should not be related to variables associated with neurodevelopmental incidents or be comorbid with psychological disorders. Lalumière, Harris, and Rice (2001) found that psychopaths had fewer obstetrical problems than nonpsychopathic offenders. Although some research has linked lower IQ to psychopathy (Blackburn, Logan, Donnelly, & Renwick, 2003; Neumann & Hare, 2008), IQ appears to be negatively related to affective and behavioral factors of psychopathy (Farrington, 2006; Vitacco, Neumann, & Wodushek, 2008) but positively related to the interpersonal factor (Salekin, Neumann, Leistico, & Zalot, 2004; Vitacco et al., 2008). Studies on this topic are sometimes compromised or may include unknown confounds because they use psychiatric samples (e.g., Blackburn et al., 2003) or do not use full versions of either psychopathy or intelligence measures (Neumann & Hare, 2008). Studies that assess nonclinical samples and secure total psychopathy scores tend to find no relationship between IQ and psychopathy (e.g., Gladden, Figueredo, & Jacobs, 2009; Hart, Forth, & Hare, 1990; Kosson,

Smith, & Newman, 1990; Salekin et al., 2004). It is therefore possible that affective and behavioral factor scores evaluate variation in antisociality that are known to correlate with IQ, but when all factors are combined to measure psychopathy, the relationship with IQ weakens or disappears.

There are some neurological differences between psychopaths and nonpsychopaths, but these differences are not gross abnormalities (Harris, Skilling, & Rice, 2001; Lalumière, Mishra, & Harris, 2008). Likewise, psychopathy appears to be comorbid with disorders that share characteristics with psychopathy and are associated with risk taking, such as impulse control disorders and substance abuse, and personality disorders such as narcissistic and antisocial personality disorders (e.g., Hildebrand & de Ruiter, 2004; Pham & Saloppe, 2010). Though the presence of psychopathy may not increase or decrease the probability of variation in Axis I disorders, presence of both could interact to produce more violent behavior. For example, though IQ was unrelated to recidivism, low IQ psychopaths were most likely to recidivate (Beggs & Grace, 2008). Also, some of the highest risk offenders are psychopathic men who are sexually deviant (Harris et al., 2003).

Unlike the first two paths, we expect higher heritability coefficients for psychopathy. Unfortunately, much of the work has measured antisocial behavior more generally, and Lalumière et al. (2005) identified complications with interpreting heritability coefficients, such as the possibility of a psychopathy "hox" gene or genes that require environmental triggers. Other possible genetic explanations are genetic pleiotropy or psychopathy as a polygenic trait. Because characteristics of psychopathy present as exaggerated features of antisocial and competitively disadvantaged men, perhaps the only genetic difference among psychopaths is the presence of another gene or genetic "switches" (Carroll, 2005) that permanently turn on these characteristics early in development, unlike the young male syndrome, in which genes may be temporarily turned on through an influx of hormones during puberty. Thus, there may be no difference in genes associated with sexually coercive mating per se but in the conditions that evolved different switches that turn them on and off. Possible conditions that turn the genes off are cues to parental investment, such as forming a long-term pair bond.[1]

SUMMARY

This three-path model identifies three different conditions under which men, over many generations, would have faced reliably occurring barriers to sexual access. There is some evidence that supports the assumption that each of the paths represents a distinct etiology (Harris et al., 2001). Studying these paths requires assessment tools that can identify membership in one group. Similarly, using variables associated with mating effort, antisocial characteristics, or risk taking alone will not allow us to discriminate between offender types because they share these characteristics. Assessments are therefore required to include variables unique to each type, such as the conditions that lead to them.

Benefits of this three-path model are as follows: (1) the latent factors represent important differences between sexual offender types; (2) it links ultimate explanations to proximate ones; and (3) it accounts for a rather large proportion of sexual offending correlates. What is common to all three paths are barriers to status, resources, and mates that are overcome by engaging mating effort, risk taking, and antisociality. What is different are the ultimate sources of these barriers, leading to differences in their ontogeny. Future research in this area would benefit from longitudinal research to identify their onset and to determine what proportion of variance in sexual aggression is shared and not shared among them.

Rape and Relationships

PARTNER SEXUAL COERCION

Although Lalumière et al.'s (2005) individual difference paths to sexual offending accounts for a large proportion of such offenses, they may not account for other types, such as sexual offenses that take place in the context of relationships. Men in relationships are older than those who are not in relationships and were successful in competing for a mateship, and so explanations that involve youth or competitive disadvantage may not apply. Goetz and Shackelford (2006) also argued that partner rape is inconsistent with adaptive explanations that engaging in rape functions by increasing sexual partner number. Empirically, using both community and forensic samples, Camilleri and Quinsey (2009a) found that of the three paths, only psychopathy was significantly related to sexual coercion in committed relationships, but it accounted for only 7% of the variance in self-reported partner sexual coercion propensity.

Considering the low prevalence of psychopaths and relatively high prevalence of sexual coercion in relationships, an alternative explanation for the occurrence of partner rape is needed. An evolutionary-derived hypothesis given the most attention is the *cuckoldry risk hypothesis* (Camilleri & Quinsey, 2009b), that men are more likely to sexually coerce their partner when the risk of cuckoldry is high (Buss, 2003; Camilleri & Quinsey, 2012; Goetz & Shackelford, 2006; Lalumière et al., 2005; Thornhill & Palmer, 2000; Wilson & Daly, 1992b). Cuckoldry may have posed a serious barrier to reproduction for men in ancestral environments, resulting in the evolution of mechanisms designed to identify and reduce the risk, such as by use of sexual coercion.

Thus far, there have been three direct tests of this hypothesis. In the first study, Goetz and Shackelford (2006) found a correlation between self-reported partner infidelity and frequency of sexual coercion in both male perpetrator and female victim samples. Similarly, Starratt, Goetz, Shackelford, McKibbin, and Stewart-Williams (2008) found that men who insulted their partner regarding infidelity were more likely to use sexually coercive acts in that relationship. These studies demonstrated that an increase in the frequency of coercive acts is related to greater instances of infidelity risk, which is consistent with copulation frequency as a response to sperm competition found in other species (Birkhead, 2000). An alternative explanation of these data, however, is that these women were unfaithful because they were no longer interested in their coercive partner (Camilleri & Quinsey, 2012). Also, considering the costs associated with sexual coercion, an historical event such as infidelity should not increase a partner's sexual coerciveness indefinitely (though other behaviors, such as mate guarding, may be affected in the long term).

To investigate facultative mechanisms that may motivate sexual coercion in response to cuckoldry risk, Camilleri and Quinsey (2009b) hypothesized that it should function in response to *recent* and *direct* cues to partner infidelity. That is, because of the fitness costs associated with coercing a partner (e.g., possibility of relationship dissolution, victim injury that prevents pregnancy, family retribution), engaging in such behavior would maximize benefits by responding to current risk by engaging in sperm competition and using sexually coercive tactics to achieve these means. Unlike competitively disadvantaged men, for example, switching to a persistent coercive mating strategy as a result of cuckoldry risk would be costly, and waiting too long (or responding to infidelity that occurred before the most recent reproductive cycle) would fail to minimize any current risk. In a community sample, they found a positive relationship between the number of cuckoldry risk events and self-reported partner sexual coercion propensity only when the events took place recently. In a forensic sample of convicted partner rapists, they found that 70% experienced some degree of cuckoldry risk prior to their offense and experienced significantly more such events than non–sexually coercive partner assaulters. These data, taken together, are consistent with Williams's (1966) economy and precision criteria for an adaptation insofar as the mechanism motivating sexual coercion appears to be activated when there is substantial cuckoldry risk and when that risk is relatively recent. Future research will need to include larger samples of partner rapists to confirm these findings.

RAPE TO ESTABLISH RELATIONSHIPS

Another hypothesis addresses the use of sexual coercion not as a means to increase sexual partner number or to reduce cuckoldry risk but to establish a long-term sexual relationship. Ellis, Widmayer, and Palmer (2009) hypothesized that rape may be used to secure long-term mating partners,[2] as a result of the trauma or need for paternal investment if the offense leads to pregnancy. Not only have studies shown that some victims of sexual assault continue to date the perpetrator (reviewed in Ellis et al., 2009), Ellis et al. also found initial support for the trauma/insemination hypothesis because women were more likely to continue to have sexual intercourse with the perpetrator if the sexual assault was completed. A potential confound with Ellis et al.'s data, however, is that relationship status was not reported. It is therefore possible that cases of completed sexual assault happened in the context of a relationship, which might explain why intercourse continued. Still, this hypothesis remains interesting because it is consistent with the young male syndrome, in which men use coercive mating prior to establishing long-term relationships, and desistence seems to occur after acquiring a mate.

PATHOLOGICAL JEALOUSY

If jealousy is related to sexually coercive behaviors in relationships, men who are pathologically jealous should exhibit the most persistent and possibly the most severe forms of sexual coercion in relationships. Whether constructs such as the Othello syndrome, morbid jealousy, delusional disorder–jealous type, conjugal paranoia, and pathological jealousy are different names for the same pathology needs to be more clearly elucidated (American Psychiatric

Association, 2000; Buss, 2000; Easton, Schipper, & Sherman, 2007). Though men are hypothesized to overestimate partner's infidelities, explained as an adaptive false alarm (Haselton & Buss, 2000), it is possible that mechanisms that motivate sexual jealousy are unmitigated in men who are pathologically jealous. Some evidence indicates consistent sex differences in themes of jealousy in cases of pathological jealousy (Easton et al., 2007). Regardless of whether "pathological" jealousy represents the designed output of an evolved mechanism, suggesting it should not be called pathological, or an "overshooting" of adaptive errors in assuming partner infidelity, pathologically jealous men might be expected to display a host of cuckoldry prevention strategies. These acts would include persistent mate guarding and physical, verbal, and sexual abuse that does not necessarily vary with particular times or conditions, though they may be more easily elicited under times or conditions of real or perceived cuckoldry risk.

Sexual Disorders

Thus far, evolutionary explanations of sexual offending have focused on either adaptations or by-products. A third and sometimes overlooked consideration are sexual offenses as the product of disorders. Criteria for a disorder includes identifying which mechanism is not functioning in the way that it was designed to function, and identifying that the target behavior results in the person being harmed or deprived of benefit (Wakefield, 1992). Understanding disorders in this way provides explanations for offenses that (1) target victims or include behaviors that are not reproductively viable (i.e., some paraphilias and incest); or (2) are committed by offenders who lack the capacity to weigh the costs and benefits of coercive acts (i.e., intellectually disabled offenders).

PARAPHILIAS

Paraphilias are defined as abnormal sexual interests. I address paraphilias that are illegal if acted upon (e.g., voyeurism, exhibitionism, toucherism, frotteurism, pedophilia, biastophilia). Freund, Sher, and Hucker (1983) hypothesized that some paraphilias are disordered phases of the courtship process, leading to exaggerated or distorted displays of that phase. This closely resembles an evolutionary hypothesis because it identifies normal (perhaps evolved) courtship behaviors and suggests that certain paraphilias are disordered manifestations of these phases. According to Freund et al., voyeurism, a sexual interest in viewing people engaging in intimate behaviors, is a disorder of locating a potential partner. Exhibitionism, a sexual interest in exposing one's genitals or breasts, is a disorder of pretactile interaction (i.e., initiating verbal or nonverbal communication). Toucheurism, a sexual interest in touching a female stranger's breasts or genitals, and frotteurism, a sexual interest in pressing one's penis against the buttocks of a female stranger, is a disorder of tactile interaction (i.e., petting).

Freund et al.'s (1983) hypothesis, particularly its theoretical structure, has several problems, however. If each paraphilia results from a disordered phase of courtship, one might expect less comorbidity across them. But evidence of comorbidity was used to support Freund's hypothesis. What is therefore unclear is whether a courtship disorder is meant to account for similarities across certain paraphilias or for the differences between them. In other words, are courtship phases independent of one another, or are they controlled by a more general mechanism? Evidence for the latter possibility is that courtship-disorder paraphilias show greater comorbidity with each other than with paraphilias outside the courtship process (reviewed in Freund, Seto, & Kuban, 1997). In a sample of persistent exhibitionists, 71% were also voyeurs, 38% frotteurs, and 26% toucheurs (Lang, Langevin, Checkley, & Pugh, 1987), confirming earlier results (Freund et al., 1983). Freund et al. (1983) included preference for rape as part of the courtship disorders, suggesting it represents the absence of any courtship behaviors. In terms of sexual preference toward rape, the data are consistent with this hypothesis because nonrape paraphilics were similar to rapists in terms of their arousal to rape and violent rape stimuli (Seto & Kuban, 1996). However, in this same study, nonrape paraphilics and rapists were also not different from controls on arousal to rape, suggesting high variability in responding in this sample. What seems to be missing is a comparison of paraphilics on each type of paraphilia, both in terms of diagnosis and in assessing sexual preferences.

The courtship structure and attendant disorders need to be more clearly understood. Admittedly, despite the preponderance of evolutionary research on human mating behavior and preferences, very little has focused on the courtship *process*. Thus, demonstrating that courtship phases are produced by adaptations is required before drawing conclusions about their disordered consequences. Murphy and Page (2008) suggest that courtship disorder is the only theory that specifically addresses exhibitionism, which is problematic considering the theoretical and empirical gaps in this work.

One sexual preference that is clearly part of an evolved reproductive strategy is men's interest in reproductively viable women. Most men, measured phallometrically, exhibit greatest sexual arousal to images of young, sexually mature women (e.g., Harris, Rice, Quinsey, & Chaplin, 1996). Pedophilia, a sexual preference for children and a major cause of child molestation,[3] is thought to be a disorder of this preference.[4] Considering most men prefer young women as sexual partners, Quinsey and Lalumière (1995) hypothesized that pedophilia results from failed body shape detectors for sexual maturity, leaving mechanisms that detect youthfulness unconstrained. Though no direct tests of this hypothesis have been published, there is some indication that neurological impairments are related to pedophilia, such as a relationship between IQ and sexual arousal to prepubescents, and a fraternal birth order effect[5] on arousal to either children or coercive sex (Lalumière, Harris, Quinsey, & Rice, 1998). More directly, there are clear neurological impairments indicated in pedophiles, but the type and location differ across studies (Cantor et al., 2008; Joyal, Black, & Dassylva, 2007; Schiffer et al., 2007).

A possible exception to the paraphilia as a disorder hypothesis is coercive paraphilic disorder, also referred to as biastophilia, which is a sexual preference for coercive sex. Considering 60% of rapists (Lalumière et al., 2003), on average, exhibit a sexual preference for rape over consenting sex or do not distinguish between the two, this arousal pattern requires an explanation. Following Wakefield's definition of a disorder, Quinsey (2010; 2011) suggested that a sexual interest in coercive sex is not pathological but reflects variation in coercive sexuality that sometimes results in severe acts. So although a sexual preference for rape may characterize several sex offender groups, a persistent preference with no comorbid features might indicate another independent path to sexual offending.

DEVELOPMENTALLY DISABLED OFFENDERS

Developmentally disabled sexual offenders, defined as sexual offenders who are also diagnosed with mental retardation, have not been given sufficient attention from a Darwinian perspective, which is surprising given their high profile in clinical forensic psychology (e.g., Lindsay, Taylor, & Sturmey, 2004). Camilleri and Quinsey (2011) hypothesized that the relationship between developmental disabilities and sexual offending might result from two paths: either from a severe form of competitive disadvantage or from a disordered psychology. If sexual offending by developmentally disabled offenders is due to an evolved response to neurological impairments, then victims should primarily be young adult women. Victimizing same-sex adults and prepubescent boys or girls, on the other hand, would indicate a disorder. Not only do men with lower IQs tend to show a sexual preference for children,[6] developmentally delayed offenders display more deviant arousal to age and sex stimuli (Blanchard et al., 1999) and are more likely to have prepubertal and male victims (Rice, Harris, & Chaplin, 2008). Understanding this group as a disordered pathology might explain their higher recidivism rates, because having lower intelligence may prevent them from making treatment gains or may prevent them from learning protective skills. Isolating which mechanisms are disordered in this group, perhaps with attention to the perpetrator's ability to weigh costs and benefits of engaging in coercive sex, should be pursued.

INCEST OFFENDERS

A commonly cited example of psychological adaptation is incest avoidance, due to the deleterious effects of incest on progeny and universally found laws and taboos against incest (reviewed in Schmitt & Pilcher, 2004). To explain genetic father incest, Seto, Lalumière, and Kuban (1999) hypothesized that it might result from either a disorder of incest avoidance, of discriminative parental solicitude, or from pedophilic sexual interests. Westermarck (1891) suggested that people who spend time together while growing up are not likely to develop a sexual attraction to each other. If true, less solicitude and weaker incest avoidance should be exhibited by stepfathers, uncles, and grandfathers, whereas pedophilia should explain incest by genetic fathers because it overrides incest avoidance. Seto et al. (1999) found no relationship between genetic relatedness and pedophilic sexual interest, and the genetic incest group appeared to be the least deviant compared to those who offended against extended family, stepfathers, and extrafamilial child molesters. Their study ruled out pedophilia as a major explanation for incest and is consistent with other research that has shown intrafamilial child molesters are not as sexually deviant, are less psychopathic, are less likely to have intercourse with the victim, are less likely to have male victims, cause less injury, and have lower sexual and violence recidivism rates (Rice & Harris, 2002).

Still, incest offenders who targeted victims younger than 6 years of age exhibited greater substance abuse, greater degree of psychiatric disturbance, poorer sexual functioning, and greater likelihood of targeting a male victim (Firestone, Dixon, Nunes, & Bradford, 2005). Interestingly, these two groups showed no phallometric difference on the pedophilia index. This is consistent with another study that found that incestuous child molesters showed more normal sexual preferences than nonincestuous child molesters (Quinsey, Chaplin, & Carrigan, 1979). Langevin, Wortzman, Dickey, Wright, and Handy (1988) found that incest offenders against genetic relatives or stepchildren had lower IQ (but were in the normal range) than nonoffender controls. Taken together, pedophilia is an unlikely explanation for most incest offenders who do not target prepubescents, so perhaps it is a disorder of kin detection, not age detection. Seto (2007) hypothesized that incest may be more likely to occur in families where paternity uncertainty is higher. Studying kin detection deficiencies (other than processes derived from the Westermarck hypothesis) among incest offenders would be a fascinating way to investigate this topic.

An alternative to a disordered psychology hypothesis is considering incest toward reproductively viable kin as an evolved strategy that poses reproductive conflict to females (reviewed in Parker, 2006). Several mathematical models have been developed to explain the evolution of such behavior (Haig, 1999; Kokko & Ots, 2006; Welham, 1990) by identifying contexts that change the costs and benefits of incest, such as the amount of parental investment, and whether mating opportunities are presented simultaneously or sequentially. So although it may not be a preferred mating strategy, these models suggest that, in some species, under particular conditions, it could be an evolved reproductive strategy.

Future research will need to test these hypotheses by using experimental work on cognitive deficits associated with either kin recognition or incest avoidance, particularly after overcoming methodological problems by categorizing incest offenders based on age of victim (child, adolescent, adult, mixed) and relationship to victim (e.g., child, sibling, uncle).

Sexual Homicide

Sexual homicide has typically been explained as a by-product of paths to sexual offending. Although theoretical differences in the causes of sexual offending against strangers and partners suggest these cases should be categorized differently (Camilleri & Quinsey, 2009a, 2009b), historically they were treated similarly. Wilson, Daly, and Scheib (1997), interested in studying sexual uxoricide, recognized the difficulty in acquiring representative data, so they included data from mostly nonpartner sexual homicides to make possible inferences about sexual uxoricide. They hypothesized that several psychological mechanisms associated with sexuality and coerciveness are involved with lethal and nonlethal sexual assault—that "masculine coercive psychology and masculine sexual psychology are functionally and thus motivationally linked" (p. 453). So, for example, if violence is used to obtain sex, we should see the highest risk of harm among young females because men are most sexually attracted to this group. Wilson et al.'s sexual homicide data confirmed this: Sexual assault homicides are mostly committed against women 15–25 years of age. They ruled out "opportunity" as an explanation because theft homicide showed the opposite trend: The oldest women were at greatest risk, probably because they are least able to defend themselves. Shackelford (2002) replicated Wilson et al.'s results with a large national-level US database. Thus, femicide appears to occur as a by-product of coercive psychology associated with sexual assault.

As Shackelford (2002) pointed out, these data do not address why sexual assault sometimes results in homicide. If sexual assault functions to increase fitness, killing the victim poses an obvious barrier. Homicide could therefore either be an unintentional mistake (i.e., went too far) or an intentional act due to modern legal penalties that increase the costs, motivating the person to minimize chances of detection after committing the offense (Alexander & Noonan, 1979).

Another view of sexual homicide is to consider it as a by-product of other major paths to sexual offending. That is, sexual homicide is a rare outcome in each of the adaptive paths to sexual offending (young male syndrome, psychopathy, competitive disadvantage, cuckoldry risk). Consistent with this view, the likelihood of death or serious injury among rape victims is low (Quinsey & Upfold, 1985), and the risk of injury increases when perpetrated by individuals who score highest on antisociality, such as psychopathy (e.g., Harris et al., 2007).

Sexual Conflict Theory

I conclude the contemporary period with sexual conflict theory—possibly the most comprehensive theoretical framework on adaptive explanations of sexual offending. Sexual conflict occurs when reproductive interests between the sexes diverge. Genetically, the fitness benefit of a trait in one sex comes at a fitness cost to the other sex (Parker, 1979, 2006). There are two types of sexual conflict: intralocus (i.e., allele variation at one locus has different fitness consequences) and interlocus (i.e., different loci in each sex are in conflict). Interlocus is likely the type of conflict involved in coercion (Camilleri & Quinsey, 2012). Though sexual coercion was treated as a third mechanism of sexual selection, Watson-Capps (2009) argued that it emerged in the first place from conflict over who to mate with and when. This approach conceptualizes sexual coercion as both a cause of sexual conflict (negates female choice of optimal mating partner) and as a consequence of sexual conflict (e.g., female infidelity increases cuckoldry risk).

Sexual conflict theory accounts for the broad spectrum of coercive acts men use to obtain sex, either directly by using force, or indirectly by coercive mate guarding (Camilleri & Quinsey, 2012). Sexual conflict theory may clarify the conditions that lead to various types of coercion (Smuts, 1992; Wilson & Daly, 1992): *direct coercion*, which is the use of forceful tactics to overcome resistance, including forced copulation, harassment, intimidation, and punishment; *indirect coercion*, which includes herding, sequestration, and punishment; and *infanticide* (Muller, Kahlenberg, & Wrangham, 2009). This taxonomy has been elaborated in humans in the context of sexual coercion in relationships (Camilleri & Quinsey, 2012).

Applied Evolutionary Psychology and Sexual Offending

Evolutionary psychological approaches to sexual offending can be extended to applied topics. These topics include understanding laws that guide rape adjudication, developing assessments to evaluate rapists, informing treatment targets in order to prevent rape, and explaining variations in rape rates across time and location.

Jurisprudence

Some researchers have addressed the *psychology of law*, which is the study of the psychological causes and consequences of legal conventions (Haney, 1980), from a Darwinian framework. This body of work is mostly comprised of theoretical reviews, drawing from empirical work on morality. According to Alexander (1979), the "function of laws is to regulate and render finite the reproductive strivings of individuals and subgroups within societies, in the interest of preserving unity in the larger group" (p. 240). In the case of rape, many laws appear to protect a man's control of his spouse's or female family member's mating options. Historically, rape laws were written so that reparations for a rape are given to the victim's proprietor (e.g., father, husband)—consequences to the victim had little, if any, relevance. Also, if the victim was not married, the crime was viewed as relatively minor (Lalumière et al., 2005).

Other reviews have addressed the evolution of laws more generally (Cosmides & Tooby, 2006; Ellis & Walsh, 2000; Fiddick, 2004), have provided historical and ethnographic accounts of rape law (Lalumière et al., 2005), and have used evolutionary psychological research on the etiology of rape to inform legal policies and procedures (Jones & Goldsmith, 2005). Evolutionary psychology could be used to inform the criminal justice system by refining and updating legal models used to predict and manage behaviors and to guide our understanding of the costs and benefits of legal policies. For example, evolutionary psychologists may counter legal movements to consider rape a hate crime because it assumes rapists are motivated by misogyny, not by sexual desire (Jones & Goldsmith, 2005). Still, much more work needs to be done on the etiology side before we can confidently pursue these applications.

Variation in Rape Prevalence Across Time and Location

An interesting extension of evolutionary approaches to rape is to consider why its prevalence varies over time and location. Lalumière et al. (2005) proposed that risk acceptance, a psychological characteristic associated with many types of sexual offending, should increase when mating prospects are low. Population-wide characteristics that vary in these prospects should impact risk taking, in general, and sexual offending, in particular. To demonstrate how this might account for the drop in sexual assaults from the early 1990s, Lalumière et al. (2005) found declines in many variables associated with risk taking, such as other crimes, vehicle accidents, workplace injuries, students carrying weapon, and the proportion of students who wear seat belts.

Barber (2000) studied cross-national variation in rape rates and hypothesized that societies with lower sex ratios (fewer men to women) should exhibit higher degrees of conflict between the sexes because (1) such ratios give women less bargaining power in marriages; (2) as a result, conflict in relationships results in poor conditions for children; and (3) these poor conditions result in the development of antisocial behavior. Supporting this hypothesis, Barber found a significant negative relationship between sex ratio (number of men to number of women 15–64 years old) and rape rates, indicating higher rape rates when there are more women than men. This prediction, however, seems odd when considering how competition and risky coercive behaviors are related. One would think that more men relative to women would increase competitiveness among men because they have fewer mating opportunities. Also, sex ratio may not be a valid index of competition because lower sex ratios could be a consequence of high conflict between males (i.e., more men die younger if engaging in more risky competition), rather than a cause of it. Future research considering these issues and studying other variables associated with competition would be helpful.

Sexual Offender Assessment and Treatment

Using evolutionary approaches to understand the etiology of sexual offending may shed light on clinical areas of forensic psychology. For example, though mating effort is theoretically considered a core characteristic of psychopathy, its measurement would not improve the accuracy of diagnosing psychopathy because it also characterizes other offenders. Instead, Harris et al. (2007) hypothesized that aspects of mating effort, particularly precocious and coercive sexuality, are unique to psychopathy, and these items should be given more weight in the assessment of psychopathy. Factor analyses confirmed that these aspects of mating effort represent a third core component of psychopathy, challenging previously held beliefs that psychopathy is comprised of two factors (aggressive narcissism and a socially deviant lifestyle).

Camilleri and Quinsey (2011) provided recommendations on developing risk assessments of violent or sexual recidivism among developmentally disabled offenders. Because their offenses may result from disordered psychological mechanisms (such as those involved in sexual preferences) that result in targeting victims who are not reproductively viable, Camilleri and Quinsey predicted that risk assessments with this group may be more accurate when considering recidivism for child molestation than offenses against adult women. Also, because psychopathy appears to be a different etiological path to offending, its inclusion in risk assessments of developmentally disabled offenders may not be as useful (unless offenders who are comorbid present higher risk). These hypotheses have yet to be tested.

The final application of evolutionary forensic psychology to clinical issues is in using basic research and theory on the etiology of sexual offending to inform treatment targets. Valid assessments that can reliably diagnose the type of sex offender (see "Typology" section) would be helpful in determining treatment targets and in providing realistic expectations on the impact of treatment. The work I reviewed suggests that treatments that attempt to change psychological characteristics associated with sexual aggression (e.g., mating effort, antisociality, and risk tolerance) will be difficult without addressing the factors that triggered them in the first place. Offender types that should be most amenable to treatment are those whose function is not just facultative but also developmentally flexible. Treatment programs would then work on minimizing factors known to initiate the mechanism and introducing factors that are known to turn that mechanism off. Alternatively, the most effective means of dealing with developmentally fixed facultative paths would be primary prevention. Early identification and intervention are needed to prevent the onset of life-course-persistent traits associated with sexual aggression. Those whose sexual offenses are related to psychological disorders may require more intense, behavioral treatment if the disorder itself is not treatable. Obligate sexual offenders (i.e., possibly psychopaths) may benefit least from treatment, and so the focus should be on incapacitation and close management through highly controlled behavioral programs (Harris & Rice, 2006). The presence of obligate characteristics, though lacking in variation across natural environments, does not mean psychopaths are immune to the effects of *any* treatment, but only that identifying effective treatment targets is more difficult with this group.

The implication of this model is that the psychological mechanisms associated with sexual offending cannot be changed or are difficult to change without altering conditions that switched the mechanism on or introducing conditions that may switch the mechanism off. For example, there is surprisingly little research that demonstrates a change in antisocial attitudes from treatment results in a change of recidivism, despite extensive recidivism research being conducted for over 30 years.

Sexual Offender Typology

This review of the literature on evolutionary approaches to sexual offending not only identifies the complex etiology of this behavior but also implies an organizational framework that may guide future research. To conclude this chapter, I synthesize these various paths to sexual offending to propose a working typology of sexual offenders.

A number of people have argued against a singular path or explanation of rape (e.g., Mealey, 1999). Although rapist typologies tend to show some convergence (e.g., reviewed in Lalumière et al., 2005), I believe that a comprehensive and accurate typology of sexual offending can be based on etiological paths to such behavior, rather than treating a single trait or mechanism as a sex offender "type," as is found in many traditional and even evolutionary typologies (e.g., Knight, 1999; McKibbin et al., 2008). The concern with using a single trait or mechanism to differentiate between types of sexual offenders is that these traits or mechanisms may be involved in most sexual offenses despite having different ultimate causes. In this case, using these items may be helpful in describing characteristics of many rapists, but not in differentiating between them. An example of this is treating *mating effort* and *being opportunistic* (i.e., raping when benefits outweigh the costs) as separate rapist types (McKibbin et al., 2008). McKibbin et al. used psychopathy to exemplify high mating effort rapists, but there is evidence that people with psychopathic characteristics are also opportunistic, such as being better at evaluating victim vulnerability (Book, Quinsey, & Langford, 2007; Wheeler, Book, & Costello, 2009). Though it is possible that some rapists may fall into more than one category, there needs to be evidence of rapists who are high on mating effort but are not opportunistic, and opportunistic rapists who are not high on mating effort, and a theoretical explanation for why in some cases these characteristics should not covary.

To overcome these issues, I elaborate on Lalumière et al.'s (2005) use of facultative and obligate traits in categorizing forced copulation to create a typology of sexual offenders that is organized along two dimensions: adaptive-maladaptive (adaptation, by-product, disorder), and obligate-facultative (obligate, facultative—developmentally fixed, facultative—developmentally flexible) (see Table 11.1). Sexual offender types can be understood as falling into one of several categories based on combinations of these two dimensions (see Table 11.1). This typology can be modified by either adding or removing types, depending on the weight of empirical research or new theoretical developments.

Adaptations

In these cases, sexual offending was sexually selected under conditions of reduced mating opportunities. Adaptations can be obligate (men are genetically different and are not responsive to natural environmental variation) or facultative (men are not genetically different, and sexual offending results from interaction with the environment). Examples I reviewed are psychopathy (obligate), competitively disadvantaged (developmentally fixed facultative), young male syndrome, and cuckoldry risk (developmentally flexible facultative).

By-Products

In this case, researchers need to consider adaptations of which sexual offending is a by-product. By-products can result from adaptations that are either obligate or facultative. Sexual homicide was hypothesized to be an incidental by-product of adaptive paths to sexual offending, because sexual offending includes physical coercion, presenting some risk of unintentionally killing the victim.

Table 11.1 Evolutionary-Derived Typology of Sexual Offenders

	Adaptation	Byproduct	Disorder
Obligate	Psychopathy	Sexual homicide	Developmentally disabled; Incest; Paraphilias (gerontophilia, pedophilia, zoophilia)
Facultative—Developmentally Fixed	Competitively disadvantaged	Sexual homicide	
Facultative—Developmentally Flexible	Young male syndrome; Cuckoldry risk	Sexual homicide	Paraphilias (exhibitionism, frotteurism, toucherism, voyeurism); Pathological jealousy

Disorders

To identify disordered sexual offenders, researchers need to consider which adaptations may be disordered and why that particular disorder is related to sexual offending. The disorders I reviewed include incest offenders who may have a disorder associated with obligate kin detection. Also, paraphilias may be disorders of obligate mating preferences, such as age (pedophilia and gerontophilia) and species (zoophilia), though it is likely that some mating preferences are developmentally fixed because of the hormonal effects in utero in masculinizing the brain. Developmentally disabled offenders, due to their organic impairments, fall into the disordered category. It is possible that this disability affects psychological mechanisms associated with mating or impairs their ability to weigh costs and benefits of coercive sexuality. If some paraphilias, like exhibitionism and voyeurism, are courtship disorders, they should fall under the developmentally flexible facultative category, because courtship behaviors start and end at various points across the life span. It is possible that disorders permanently impair people in any of these domains, which is why deviant sexual preferences likely do not change over time.

Future Directions

In this chapter I reviewed the history of evolutionary perspectives on sexual offending in an attempt to identify the most promising ways forward. I also provided a critical review of contemporary research and theory and synthesized this literature to provide an organizational framework for future research. In addition to the future directions mentioned throughout the chapter, there are other areas that require more work. Identifying victim characteristics, elaborating on the role of resistance (Lalumière et al., 2005), studying the interactions between offender-victim dyads, and conducting developmental work on sexual bullies (Volk, Camilleri, Dane, & Marini, Chapter 16, this volume), particularly using longitudinal designs, will give a more complete picture on the causes of sexual offending. We have certainly progressed since Symons (1979) first explicitly addressed forcible rape from an evolutionary framework, but much more work has yet to be done.

Acknowledgments

I would like to thank Eric Bressler, Danny Krupp, Vern Quinsey, Martin Lalumière, Michael Seto, and the editors, Todd Shackelford and Viviana Weekes-Shackelford, for their helpful comments on an earlier draft of this chapter. This chapter was completed, in part, through Westfield State University's Semester Time Award for Research and Scholarship.

Notes

1. Testosterone, a hormone that may regulate mating effort and parental investment, is lower among married men, compared to single and divorced men (Gray, Kahlenberg, Barrett, Lipson, & Ellison, 2002; Mazur & Booth, 1998). This and other social cues need to be examined in terms of their effects on genes.

2. Similar hypotheses have been reviewed elsewhere (Emery Thompson, 2009).

3. Pedophilia is not synonymous with child molestation—pedophilia refers to a sexual preference for children, whereas child molestation refers to sexual behaviors toward prepubescent children (Camilleri & Quinsey, 2008). Though there is a strong correspondence between these two, there may be men who exhibit a preference for children but never act on those urges, and there may be men who molest children but sexually prefer adult women.

4. A Darwinian approach to defining pedophilia has also been proposed—Seto (1999, 2002) recommended using "prepubescence," instead of age, because age does not capture variation in rates of sexual development, and a preference for prepubescents indicates pathology. Also, choice of any particular age is arbitrary—laws on this vary across time and location.

5. See Blanchard (2001) for a review of the fraternal birth order effect on sexual differentiation of the fetal brain.

6. Even though IQ is used to gauge both competitive disadvantage and mental retardation, very low IQ indicates organic impairment, unlike men whose competitive disadvantage (and thus IQ) is *relative* to competitors. Lower IQ can therefore be in a nondisabled range yet still be detrimental toward acquiring mateships.

References

Alexander, R. D. (1979). *Darwinism and human affairs*. Seattle: University of Washington Press.

Alexander, R. D., & Noonan, K. M. (1979). Concealment of ovulation, parental care, and human social evolution. In N. A. Chagnon & W. Irons (Eds.), *Evolutionary biology and human social behavior* (pp. 436–453). North Scituate, MA: Duxbury Press.

Allgeier, E., & Wiederman, M. (1992). Evidence for an evolved adaptation to rape? Not yet. *Behavioral and Brain Sciences, 15*, 377–378.

American Psychiatric Association. (2000). *Diagnostic and statistical manual of mental disorders* (4th ed., Text rev.). Washington, DC: Author.

Andrews, P. W., Gangestad, S. W., & Matthews, D. (2002). Adaptationism—how to carry out an exaptationist program. *The Behavioral and Brain Sciences, 25*, 489–504.

Archer, J., & Vaughan, A. E. (2001). Evolutionary theories of rape. *Psychology, Evolution and Gender, 3*, 95–101.

Barber, N. (2000). The sex ratio as a predictor of cross-national variation in violent crime. *Cross-Cultural Research, 34*, 264.

Beggs, S. M., & Grace, R. C. (2008). Psychopathy, intelligence, and recidivism in child molesters: Evidence of an interaction effect. *Criminal Justice and Behavior, 35*, 683–695.

Birkhead, T. R. (2000). *Promiscuity: An evolutionary history of sperm competition*. Cambridge, MA: Harvard University Press.

Blackburn, R., Logan, C., Donnelly, J., & Renwick, S. (2003). Personality disorders, psychopathy and other mental disorders: Co-morbidity among patients at English and Scottish high-security hospitals. *Journal of Forensic Psychiatry and Psychology, 14*, 111–137.

Blanchard, R. (2001). Fraternal birth order and the maternal immune hypothesis of male homosexuality. *Hormones and Behavior, 40*, 105–114.

Blanchard, R., Watson, M. S., Choy, A., Dickey, R., Klassen, P., Kuban, M., & Ferren, D. J. (1999). Pedophiles: Mental retardation, maternal age, and sexual orientation. *Archives of Sexual Behavior, 28*, 111–127.

Book, A. S., Quinsey, V. L., & Langford, D. (2007). Psychopathy and the perception of affect and vulnerability. *Criminal Justice and Behavior, 34*, 531–544.

Brown, D. E. (1991). *Human universals*. Boston: McGraw-Hill.

Buss, D. M. (2000). *The dangerous passion*. New York: Free Press.

Buss, D. M. (2003). *The evolution of desire: Strategies of human mating* (2nd ed.). New York: Basic Books.

Buss, D. M., Haselton, M. G., Shackelford, T. K., Bleske, A. L., & Wakefield, J. C. (1998). Adaptations, exaptations, and spandrels. *American Psychologist, 53*, 533–548.

Buss, D. M., Shackelford, T. K., Kirkpatrick, L. A., & Larsen, R. J. (2001). A half century of mate preferences: The cultural evolution of values. *Journal of Marriage and Family, 63*, 491–503.

Byers, E., & Lewis, K. (1988). Dating couples' disagreements over the desired level of sexual intimacy. *Journal of Sex Research, 24*, 15–29.

Camilleri, J. (2010). Book review: Sexual coercion in primates and humans: An evolutionary perspective on male aggression against females. *American Journal of Human Biology, 22*, 224–230.

Camilleri, J. A., & Quinsey, V. L. (2008). Pedophilia: Assessment and treatment. In D. R. Laws & W. T. O'Donohue (Eds.), *Sexual deviance: Theory, assessment, and treatment* (2nd ed., pp. 183–212). New York: The Guilford Press.

Camilleri, J. A., & Quinsey, V. L. (2009a). Individual differences in the propensity for partner sexual coercion. *Sexual Abuse: A Journal of Research and Treatment, 21*, 111–129.

Camilleri, J. A., & Quinsey, V. L. (2009b). Testing the cuckoldry risk hypothesis of partner sexual coercion in community and forensic samples. *Evolutionary Psychology, 7*, 164–178.

Camilleri, J. A., & Quinsey, V. L. (2011). Appraising the risk of sexual and violent recidivism among intellectually disabled offenders. *Psychology, Crime and Law, 17*, 59–74.

Camilleri, J. A., & Quinsey, V. L. (2012). Sexual conflict and partner rape. In A. T. Goetz & T. K. Shackelford (Eds.), *Oxford handbook of sexual conflict in humans* (pp. 257–268). New York: Oxford University Press.

Camilleri, J. A., Quinsey, V. A., & Tapscott, J. L. (2009). Assessing the propensity for sexual coaxing and coercion in relationships: Factor structure, reliability, and validity of the tactics to obtain sex scale. *Archives of Sexual Behavior, 38*, 959–973.

Canada Criminal Code. (1985). Retrieved December 2011, from the Canadian Department of Justice website http://laws.justice.gc.ca/en/C-46/index.html

Cantor, J. M., Kabani, N., Christensen, B. K., Zipursky, R. B., Barbaree, H. E., Dickey, R.,...Blanchard, R. (2008). Cerebral white matter deficiencies in pedophilic men. *Journal of Psychiatric Research, 42*, 167–183.

Carroll, S. (2005). *Endless forms most beautiful*. New York: W.W. Norton.

Clarke, P., Pradhan, G., & van Schaik, C. (2009). Intersexual conflict in primates: Infanticide, paternity allocation, and the role of coercion. In M. N. Muller & R. W. Wrangham (Eds.), *Sexual coercion in primates and humans: An evolutionary perspective on male aggression against females* (pp. 42–77). Cambridge, MA: Harvard University Press.

Cosmides, L., & Tooby, J. (2006). Evolutionary psychology, moral heuristics, and the law. In G. Gigerenzer & C. Engel (Eds.), *Heuristics and the law* (pp. 181–212). Cambridge, MA: MIT Press.

Easton, J., Schipper, L., & Sherman, L. W. (2007). Morbid jealousy from an evolutionary psychological perspective. *Evolution and Human Behavior, 28*, 399–402.

Edens, J. F., Marcus, D. K., Lilienfeld, S. O., & Poythress, N. G. (2006). Psychopathic, not psychopath: Taxometric evidence for the dimensional structure of psychopathy. *Journal of Abnormal Psychology, 115*, 131–144.

Ellis, L. (1989). *Theories of rape*. Levittown, PA: Hemisphere.

Ellis, L., & Walsh, A. (2000). *Criminology: A global perspective*. Toronto: Allyn & Bacon.

Ellis, L., Widmayer, A., & Palmer, C. T. (2009). Perpetrators of sexual assault continuing to have sex with their victims following initial assault. *International Journal of Offender, 53*, 454–463.

Emery Thompson, M. (2009). Human rape: Revising evolutionary perspectives. In M. N. Muller & R. W. Wrangham (Eds.), *Sexual coercion in primates and humans: An evolutionary perspective on male aggression against females* (pp. 346–374). Cambridge, MA: Harvard University Press.

Farrington, D. P. (2006). Family background and psychopathy. In C. Patrick (Ed.), *Handbook of psychopathy* (pp. 229–250). New York: The Guilford Press.

Fiddick, L. (2004). Natural law and natural selection: Deontic reasoning as part of evolved human nature. In C. Crawford & C. Salmon (Eds.), *Evolutionary Psychology, Public Policy and Personal Decisions* (pp. 169-194). Mahwah, NJ: Lawrence Erlbaum Associates.

Firestone, P., Dixon, K. L., Nunes, K. L., & Bradford, J. M. (2005). A comparison of incest offenders based on victim age. *The Journal of the American Academy of Psychiatry and the Law, 33*, 223–232.

Freund, K., Scher, H., & Hucker, S. (1983). The courtship disorders. *Archives of Sexual Behavior, 12*, 369–379.

Freund, K., Seto, M. C., & Kuban, M. (1997). Frotteurism: The theory of courtship disorder. In D. R. Laws & W. T. O'Donohue (Eds.), *Sexual deviance: Theory, assessment, and treatment* (pp. 111–130). New York: Guilford Press.

Galliano, G., Noble, L. M., Travis, L. A., & Puechl, C. (1993). Victim reactions during rape/sexual assault: A preliminary study of the immobility response and its correlates. *Journal of Interpersonal Violence, 8*, 109–114.

Gaulin, S. J. C., & McBurney, D. H. (2001). *Psychology: An evolutionary approach*. Upper Saddle River, NJ: Prentice-Hall.

Gladden, P., Figueredo, A., & Jacobs, W. (2009). Life history strategy, psychopathic attitudes, personality, and general intelligence. *Personality and Individual Differences, 46*, 270–275.

Goetz, A. T., & Shackelford, T. K. (2006). Sexual coercion and forced in-pair copulation as sperm competition tactics in humans. *Human Nature, 17*(3), 265–282.

Goetz, A. T., Shackelford, T. K., & Camilleri, J. A. (2008). Proximate and ultimate explanations are required for a comprehensive understanding of partner rape. *Aggression and Violent Behavior, 13*, 119–123.

Gottschall, J. A., & Gottschall, T. A. (2003). Are per-incident rape-pregnancy rates higher than per-incident consensual pregnancy rates? *Human Nature, 14*, 1–20.

Gray, P. B., Kahlenberg, S. M., Barrett, E. S., Lipson, S. F., & Ellison, P. T. (2002). Marriage and fatherhood are associated with lower testosterone in males. *Evolution and Human Behavior, 23*, 193–201.

Haig, D. (1999). Asymmetric relations: Internal conflicts and the horror of incest. *Evolution and Human Behavior, 20*, 83–98.

Halpern, C. T., Joyner, K., Udry, J. R., & Suchindran, C. (2000). Smart teens don't have sex (or kiss much either). *Journal of Adolescent Health, 26*, 213–225.

Haney, C. (1980). Psychology and legal change: On the limits of a factual jurisprudence. *Law and Human Behavior, 4*, 147–199.

Harpending, H., & Sobus, J. (1987). Sociopathy as an adaptation. *Ethology and Sociobiology, 8*, 63S–72S.

Harris, G. T., & Rice, M. E. (2006). Treatment of psychopathy: A review of empirical findings. In C. Patrick (Ed.), *The handbook of psychopathy* (pp. 555–572). New York: The Guilford Press.

Harris, G. T., Rice, M. E., Hilton, N. Z., Lalumière, M. L., & Quinsey, V. L. (2007). Coercive and precocious sexuality as a fundamental aspect of psychopathy. *Journal of Personality Disorders, 21*(1), 1–27.

Harris, G. T., Rice, M. E., & Lalumière, M. L. (2001). Criminal violence: The roles of psychopathy, neurodevelopmental insults, and antisocial parenting. *Criminal Justice and Behavior, 28*, 402–426.

Harris, G. T., Rice, M. E., & Quinsey, V. L. (1994). Psychopathy as a taxon: Evidence that psychopaths are a discrete class. *Journal of consulting and clinical psychology, 62*, 387–397.

Harris, G. T., Rice, M. E., Quinsey, V. L., & Chaplin, T. C. (1996). Viewing time as a measure of sexual interest among child molesters and normal heterosexual men. *Behaviour Research and Therapy, 34*, 389–394.

Harris, G. T., Rice, M. E., Quinsey, V. L., Lalumière, M. L., Boer, D., & Lang, C. (2003). A multisite comparison of actuarial risk instruments for sex offenders. *Psychological Assessment, 15*, 413–425.

Harris, G. T., Skilling, T. A., & Rice, M. E. (2001). The construct of psychopathy. *Crime and Justice, 28*, 197–264.

Hart, S. D., Forth, A. E., & Hare, R. D. (1990). Performance of criminal psychopaths on selected neuropsychological tests. *Journal of Abnormal Psychology, 99*, 374–379.

Haselton, M. G., & Buss, D. M. (2000). Error management theory: A new perspective on biases in cross-sex mind reading. *Journal of Personality and Social Psychology, 78*, 81–91.

Hildebrand, M., & de Ruiter, C. (2004). PCL-R psychopathy and its relation to DSM-IV Axis I and II disorders in a sample of male forensic psychiatric patients in The Netherlands. *International Journal of Law and Psychiatry, 27*, 233–248.

Hirschi, T., & Gottfredson, M. (1983). Age and the explanation of crime. *American Journal of Sociology, 89*, 552–584.

Jones, O. D. (1999). Sex, culture, and the biology of rape: Toward explanation and prevention. *California Law Review, 87*, 827–942.

Jones, O. D., & Goldsmith, T. H. (2005). Law and behavioral biology. *Columbia Law Review, 105*, 405–502.

Joyal, C. C., Black, D. N., & Dassylva, B. (2007). The neuropsychology and neurology of sexual deviance: A review and pilot study. *Sexual Abuse: A Journal of Research and Treatment, 19*, 155–173.

Kanin, E. J. (1985). Date rapists: Differential sexual socialization and relative deprivation. *Archives of Sexual Behavior, 14*, 219–231.

Kline, R. (2011). *Principles and practice of structural equation modeling* (3rd ed.). New York: The Guilford Press.

Knight, R. A. (1999). Validation of a typology for rapists. *Journal of Interpersonal Violence, 14*, 303–330.

Kokko, H. (2001). Human rape—adaptive or not? *Trends in Ecology and Evolution, 16*, 488–489.

Kokko, H., & Ots, I. (2006). When not to avoid inbreeding. *Evolution, 60*, 467–475.

Koss, M., Dinero, T., & Seibel, C. (1988). Stranger and acquaintance rape: Are there differences in the victim's experience? *Psychology of Women Quarterly, 12*, 1–24.

Koss, M. P., Gidycz, C. A., & Wisniewski, N. (1987). The scope of rape: Incidence and prevalence of sexual aggression and victimization in a national sample of higher education students. *Journal of Consulting and Clinical Psychology, 55*, 162–170.

Kosson, D. S., Smith, S. S., & Newman, J. P. (1990). Evaluating the construct validity of psychopathy in black and white male inmates: Three preliminary studies. *Journal of Abnormal Psychology, 99*, 250–259.

Lalumière, M. L, Chalmers, L., Quinsey, V. L, & Seto, M. C. (1996). A test of the mate deprivation hypothesis of sexual coercion. *Ethology and Sociobiology, 17*, 299–318.

Lalumière, M. L., Harris, G. T., Quinsey, V. L., & Rice, M. E. (1998). Sexual deviance and number of older brothers among sexual offenders. *Sexual Abuse: A Journal of Research and Treatment, 10*, 5–15.

Lalumière, M. L., Harris, G. T., Quinsey, V. L., & Rice, M. E. (2005). *The causes of rape: Understanding individual differences in male propensity for sexual aggression*. Washington, DC: American Psychological Association.

Lalumière, M. L., Harris, G. T., & Rice, M. E. (2001). Psychopathy and developmental instability. *Evolution and Human Behavior, 22*, 75–92.

Lalumière, M. L., Mishra, S., & Harris, G. T. (2008). In cold blood: The evolution of psychopathy. In J. Duntley & T. K. Shackelford (Eds.), *Evolutionary forensic psychology: Darwinian foundations of crime and law* (pp. 139–159). New York: Oxford University Press.

Lalumière, M. L., & Quinsey, V. L. (1998). A Darwinian interpretation of individual differences in male propensity for sexual aggression. *Jurimetrics, 39*, 201–216.

Lalumière, M. L., Quinsey, V. L., Harris, G. T., Rice, M. E., & Trautrimas, C. (2003). Are rapists differentially aroused by coercive sex in phallometric assessments? *Annals of the New York Academy of Sciences, 989*, 211–224.

Lang, R. A., Langevin, R., Checkley, K. L., & Pugh, G. (1987). Genital exhibitionism: Courtship disorder or narcissism? *Canadian Journal of Behavioural Science/Revue Canadienne des Sciences du Comportement, 19*, 216–232.

Langevin, R., Wortzman, G., Dickey, R., Wright, P., & Handy, L. (1988). Neuropsychological impairment in incest offenders. *Sexual Abuse: A Journal of Research and Treatment, 1*, 401–415.

Lindsay, W. R., Taylor, J. L., & Sturmey, P. (2004). *Offenders with developmental disabilities*. Chichester, MA: Wiley.

MacCallum, R. C., & Austin, J. T. (2000). Applications of structural equation modeling in psychological research. *Annual Review of Psychology, 51*, 201–226.

Malamuth, N. M. (1981). Rape proclivity among males. *Journal of Social Issues, 37*, 138–157.

Malamuth, N. M. (1996). The confluence model of sexual aggression: feminist and evolutionary perspectives. In D. M. Buss & N. M. Malamuth (Eds.), *Sex, power, conflict: Evolutionary and feminist perspectives* (pp. 269–295). London: Oxford University Press.

Malamuth, N. M. (1998). An evolutionary-based model integrating research on the characteristics of sexually coercive men. In J. Adair, D. Belanger, & K. Dion (Eds.), *Advances in psychological science* (pp. 151–184). Hove, UK: Psychology Press.

Malamuth, N. M. (2003). Criminal and noncriminal sexual aggressors: Integrating psychopathy in a hierarchical-mediational confluence model. *Annals of the New York Academy of Sciences, 989*, 33–58.

Malamuth, N. M., Heavey, C. L., & Linz, D. (1993). Predicting men's antisocial behavior against women: The Interaction Model of sexual aggression. In G. C. N. Hall, R. Hirschman, J. R. Graham, & M. S. Zaragoza (Eds.), *Sexual aggression: Issues in etiology, assessment and treatment* (pp. 63–97). New York: Hemisphere.

Malamuth, N. M., Heavey, C. L., & Linz, D. (1996). The confluence model of sexual aggression: Combining hostile masculinity and impersonal sex. *Journal of Offender Rehabilitation, 23*, 13–37.

Malamuth, N. M., Linz, D., Heavey, C. L., Barnes, G., & Acker, M. (1995). Using the confluence model of sexual aggression to predict men's conflict with women: A 10-year follow-up study. *Journal of Personality and Social Psychology, 69*, 353–369.

Malamuth, N. M., & Malamuth, E. Z. (1999). Integrating multiple levels of scientific analysis and the confluence model of sexual coercers. *Jurimetrics, 39*, 157.

Malamuth, N., Sockloskie, R., Koss, M., & Tanaka, J. (1991). Characteristics of aggressors against women: Testing a model using a national sample of college students. *Journal of Consulting and Clinical Psychology, 59*, 670–681.

Marcus, D. K., John, S. L., & Edens, J. F. (2004). A taxometric analysis of psychopathic personality. *Journal of Abnormal Psychology, 113*, 626–635.

Mazur, A., & Booth, A. (1998). Testosterone and dominance in men. *Behavioral and Brain Sciences, 21*, 235–397.

McCabe, M. P. (1999). Sexual knowledge, experience and feelings among people with disability. *Sexuality and Disability, 17*, 157–170.

McElreath, R., & Boyd, R. (2007). *Mathematical models of social evolution*. Chicago: University of Chicago Press.

McKibbin, W. F., Shackelford, T. K., Goetz, A. T., & Starratt, V. G. (2008). Evolutionary psychological perspectives on rape. In J. D. Duntley & T. K. Shackelford (Eds.), *Evolutionary forensic psychology* (pp. 101–120). New York: Oxford University Press.

Mealey, L. (1995). The sociobiology of sociopathy: An integrated evolutionary model. *Behavioral and Brain Sciences, 18*, 523–599.

Mealey, L. (1999). The multiplicity of rape: From life histories to prevention strategies. *Jurimetrics, 39*, 217–226.

Moffit, T. E. (1993). Adolescence-limited and life-course-persistent antisocial behavior: A developmental taxonomy. *Psychological Bulletin, 100*, 674–701.

Moffitt, T. E. (2006). A review of research on the taxonomy of life-course persistent versus adolescent-limited antisocial behavior. In F. T. Cullen, J. P. Wright, & K. R. Blevins (Eds.), *Taking stock: The status of criminological theory* (pp. 277–312). New Brunswick, NJ: Transaction Publishers.

Muller, M. N., Kahlenberg, S. M., & Wrangham, R. W. (2009). Male aggression and sexual coercion of females in primates. In M. N. Muller & R. W. Wrangham (Eds.), *Sexual coercion in primates and humans: An evolutionary perspective on male aggression against females* (pp. 3–22). Cambridge, MA: Harvard University Press.

Muller, M. N., & Wrangham, R. W. (2009). *Sexual coercion in primates and humans: An evolutionary perspective on male aggression against females*. Cambridge, MA: Harvard University Press.

Murphy, W. D., & Page, I. J. (2008). Exhibitionism: Psychopathology and theory. In D. R. Laws & W. T. O'Donohue (Eds.), *Sexual deviance: Theory, assessment, and treatment* (pp. 61–75). New York: The Guilford Press.

Neumann, C. S., & Hare, R. D. (2008). Psychopathic traits in a large community sample: Links to violence, alcohol use, and intelligence. *Journal of Consulting and Clinical Psychology, 76*, 893–899.

Official Code of Georgia Annotated. (2011). Retrieved December 2011, from http://www.lexisnexis.com/hottopics/gacode/Default.asp

Palmer, C. (1991). Human rape: Adaptation or by-product? *Journal of Sex Research, 28*, 365–386.

Parker, G. (1979). Sexual selection and sexual conflict. In M. S. Blum & N. A. Blum (Eds.), *Sexual selection and reproductive competition in insects* (Vol. 123, pp. 123–166). New York: Academic Press.

Parker, G. (2006). Sexual conflict over mating and fertilization: An overview. *Philosophical Transactions of the Royal Society B: Biological Sciences, 361*, 235–259.

Perkins, C., & Klaus, P. (1996). *National crime victimization survey: Criminal victimization 1994*. Retrieved December 2011, from http://bjs.ojp.usdoj.gov/content/pub/pdf/Cv94.pdf

Pham, T. H., & Saloppe, X. (2010). PCL-R psychopathy and its relation to DSM Axis I and II Disorders in a sample of male forensic patients in a Belgian security hospital. *International Journal of Forensic Mental Health, 9*, 205–214.

Quinsey, V. L. (1992). Individual differences in the propensity to rape. *Behavioral and Brain Sciences, 15*, 400.

Quinsey, V. L. (2002). Evolutionary theory and criminal behaviour. *Legal and Criminological Psychology, 7*, 1–13.

Quinsey, V. L. (2003). The etiology of anomalous sexual preferences in men. *Annals of the New York Academy of Sciences, 989*, 105–117.

Quinsey, V. L. (2010). Coercive paraphilic disorder. *Archives of Sexual Behavior, 39*, 405–410.

Quinsey, V. L. (2011). Pragmatic and Darwinian views of the paraphilias. Archives of Sexual Behavior, 41, 217–220.

Quinsey, V. L., Chaplin, T., & Carrigan, W. (1979). Sexual preferences among incestuous and nonincestuous child molesters. *Behavior Therapy, 10*, 562–565.

Quinsey, V. L., Jones, G. B., Book, A. S., & Barr, K. N. (2006). The dynamic prediction of antisocial behavior among forensic psychiatric patients: A prospective field study. *Journal of Interpersonal Violence, 21*, 1539–1565.

Quinsey, V. L., & Lalumière, M. L. (1995). Evolutionary perspectives on sexual offending. *Sexual Abuse: A Journal of Research and Treatment, 7*, 301–315.

Quinsey, V. L., Skilling, T. A., Lalumière, M. L., & Craig, W. M. (2006). *Juvenile delinquency: Understanding the origins of individual differences*. Washington, DC: American Psychological Association.

Quinsey, V. L., & Upfold, D. (1985). Rape completion and victim injury as a function of female resistance strategy. *Canadian Journal of Behavioral Science, 17*, 40–50.

Rice, M. E., & Harris, G. T. (2002). Men who molest their sexually immature daughters: Is a special explanation required? *Journal of Abnormal Psychology, 111*, 329–339.

Rice, M. E., Harris, G. T., & Chaplin, T. C. (2008). Sexual preferences and recidivism of sex offenders with mental retardation. *Sexual Abuse: A Journal of Research and Treatment, 20*, 409–425.

Salekin, R. T., Neumann, C. S., Leistico, A. R., & Zalot, A. A. (2004). Psychopathy in youth and intelligence: An investigation of Cleckley's hypothesis. *Journal of clinical child and adolescent psychology, 33*, 731–742.

Schiffer, B., Peschel, T., Paul, T., Gizewski, E., Forsting, M., Leygraf, N., et al. (2007). Structural brain abnormalities in the frontostriatal system and cerebellum in pedophilia. *Journal of Psychiatric Research, 41*, 753–762.

Schmitt, D. P., & 118 Members of the International Sexuality Description Project. (2003). Universal sex differences in the desire for sexual variety: Tests from 52 nations, 6 continents, and 13 islands. *Journal of Personality and Social Psychology, 85*, 85–104.

Schmitt, D. P., & Pilcher, J. J. (2004). Evaluating evidence of psychological adaptation. *Psychological Science, 15*, 643–649.

Seto, M. C. (1999). Book review of *Paedophiles and sexual offenses against children*. *Archives of Sexual Behavior, 28*, 276–279.

Seto, M. C. (2002). Peer commentaries on Green (2002) and Schmidt (2002): Precisely defining pedophilia. *Archives of Sexual Behavior, 31*, 498–499.

Seto, M. C. (2007). *Pedophilia and sexual offending against children: Theory, assessment, and intervention*. Washington, DC: American Psychological Association.

Seto, M. C., & Kuban, M. (1996). Criterion-related validity of a phallometric test for paraphilic rape and sadism. *Behavior Research and Therapy, 34*, 175–183.

Seto, M. C., Lalumière, M. L., & Kuban, M. (1999). The sexual preferences of incest offenders. *Journal of Abnormal Psychology, 108*, 267–272.

Shackelford, T. K. (2002). Are young women the special targets of rape-murder? *Aggressive Behavior, 28*, 224–232.

Shackelford, T. K., Schmitt, D. P., & Buss, D. M. (2005). Universal dimensions of human mate preferences. *Personality and Individual Differences, 39*, 447–458.

Shields, W. M., & Shields, L. M. (1983). Forcible rape: An evolutionary perspective. *Ethology and Sociobiology, 4*, 115–136.

Singh, B. N. (1964). A study of certain personal qualities as preferred by college students in their marital partners. *Journal of Psychological Researches, 8*, 37–48.

Skilling, T. A., Quinsey, V. L., & Craig, W. M. (2001). Evidence of a taxon underlying serious antisocial behavior in boys. *Criminal Justice and Behavior, 28*, 450–470.

Smith, E. A., Borgerhoff Mulder, M., & Hill, K. (2001). Controversies in the evolutionary social sciences: A guide for the perplexed. *Trends in Ecology and Evolution, 16*, 128–135.

Smuts, B. (1992). Male aggression against women. *Human Nature, 3*, 1–44.

Starks, P. T., & Blackie, C. (2000). The relationship between serial monogamy and rape in the United States (1960–1995). *Proceedings of the Royal Society of London, 267*, 1259–1263.

Starratt, V. G., Goetz, A. T., Shackelford, T. K., McKibbin, W. F., & Stewart-Williams, S. (2008). Men's partner-directed insults and sexual coercion in intimate relationships. *Journal of Family Violence, 23*, 315–323.

Statistics Canada. (2009). *Police reported crime for selected offences*. Retrieved December 2011, from http://www.statcan.gc.ca/daily-quotidien/100720/t100720a1-eng.htm

Stinson, J. D., Sales, B. D., & Becker, J. V. (2008). *Sex offending: Causal theories to inform research, prevention, and treatment*. Washington, DC: American Psychological Association.

Suschinsky, K. D., & Lalumière, M. L. (2011). Prepared for anything? An investigation of female genital arousal in response to rape cues. *Psychological Science, 22*, 159–165.

Symons, D. (1979). *The evolution of human sexuality*. New York: Oxford University Press.

Thornhill, R. (1980). Rape in *Panorpa* scorpion flies and a general rape hypothesis. *Animal Behaviour, 28*, 52–59.

Thornhill, R., & Palmer, C. T. (2000). *A natural history of rape*. Cambridge, MA: MIT Press.

Thornhill, R., & Thornhill, N. W. (1983). Human rape: An evolutionary analysis. *Ethology and Sociobiology, 4*, 137–173.

Thornhill, R., & Thornhill, N. W. (1992). The evolutionary psychology of men's coercive sexuality. *Behavioral and Brain Sciences, 15*, 363–421.

Tooby, J., & Cosmides, L. (1992). The psychological foundations of culture. In J. H. Barkow, L. Cosmides, & J. Tooby (Eds.), *The adapted mind: Evolutionary psychology and the generation of culture* (pp. 19–136). New York: Oxford University Press.

Tooby, J., & Cosmides, L. (2005). Conceptual foundations of evolutionary psychology. In D. M. Buss (Ed.), *The handbook of evolutionary psychology* (pp. 5–67). Hoboken, NJ: Wiley.

Ullman, S. E., & Knight, R. A. (1995). Women's resistance strategies to different rapist types. *Criminal Justice and Behavior, 22*, 263–283.

US Department Of Justice. (2006). *Extent, nature, and consequences of rape victimization: Findings from the National Violence Against Women Survey*. Washington, DC: US Department of Justice, Office of Justice Programs, National Institute of Justice.

US Code. (2010). Title 18, § 2242.

Vasey, M. W., Kotov, R., Frick, P., & Loney, B. R. (2005). The latent structure of psychopathy in youth: A taxometric investigation. *Journal of Abnormal Child Psychology, 33*, 411–429.

Vaughan, A. (2001). The association between offender socioeconomic status and victim-offender relationship in rape offences. *Psychology, Evolution and Gender, 3*, 121–136.

Vitacco, M. J., Neumann, C. S., & Wodushek, T. (2008). Differential relationships between the dimensions of psychopathy and intelligence: Replication with adult jail inmates. *Criminal Justice and Behavior, 35*, 48–55.

Wakefield, J. C. (1992). The concept of mental disorder: On the boundary between biological facts and social values. *American Psychologist, 47*, 373–388.

Watson-Capps, J. J. (2009). Evolution of sexual coercion with respect to sexual selection and sexual conflict theory. In M. N. Muller & R. W. Wrangham (Eds.), *Sexual coercion in primates and humans: An evolutionary perspective on male aggression against females* (pp. 23-41). Cambridge, MA: Harvard niversity Press.

Welham, C. V. J. (1990). Incest: An evolutionary model. *Ethology and Sociobiology, 111*, 97–111.

Westermarck, E. A. (1891). *The history of human marriage*. London: MacMillan.

Wheeler, S., Book, A., & Costello, K. (2009). Psychopathic traits and perceptions of victim vulnerability. *Criminal Justice and Behavior, 36*, 635–648.

Williams, G. C. (1966). *Adaptation and natural selection* Princeton, NJ: Princeton University Press.

Wilson, M., & Daly, M. (1985). Competitiveness, risk taking, and violence: The young male syndrome. *Ethology and Sociobiology, 6*, 59–73.

Wilson, M., & Daly, M. (1992a). Book review: Theories of rape. *Archives of Sexual Behavior, 21*, 418–421.

Wilson, M., & Daly, M. (1992b). The man who mistook his wife for a chattel. In J. H. Barkow, L. Cosmides, & J. Tooby (Eds.), *The adapted mind: Evolutionary psychology and the generation of culture* (pp. 289–322). New York: Oxford University Press.

Wilson, M., & Daly, M. (1997). Life expectancy, economic inequality, homicide, and reproductive timing in Chicago neighbourhoods. *British Medical Journal, 314*, 1271–1274.

Wilson, M., Daly, M., & Scheib, J. E. (1997). Femicide: An evolutionary psychological perspective. In P. A. Gowaty (Ed.), *Feminism and evolutionary biology* (pp. 431–465). New York: Chapman & Hall.

CHAPTER 12

Women and Aggression

Anne Campbell *and* Catharine Cross

Abstract

Sex differences in aggression can be traced ultimately to sex differences in parental investment. Higher variance in reproductive success in men, resulting from lower parental investment, creates incentives for competition to achieve intrasexual dominance, while women's greater investment and role in caring for offspring creates costs for dangerous confrontations. Data suggest that, at a proximal psychological level, sex differences in fear, but not anger, mediate involvement in aggression. Although biparental care brings with it two-way sexual selection, female competition is chiefly conducted either intersexually (through the display of qualities attractive to men) or through indirect aggression (gossip and social exclusion), both of which are low-risk strategies. Under resource scarcity, competition between women can escalate to direct confrontation, but even then the severity of aggression is lower than that of men. Women and men are equal in the frequency of aggressive acts directed at intimate partners, which poses an explanatory problem for any theory of sex differences in aggression. We propose that the fear reduction in women necessary to permit sexual intimacy, possibly mediated by oxytocin, also diminishes women's normal restraint on aggressive behavior.

Key Words: women, intrasexual, intersexual, fear, anger, maternal, intimate partner, competition, jealousy

Introduction

The proposition that men are more aggressive than women is hardly a contentious one. Men represent the majority of violent criminals, prison inmates, war veterans, avenging Hollywood heroes, and rioting football fans. Until evolutionary theory was incorporated into psychologists' thinking, the reason for this was evident and wrong: We reward little boys for emulating and conforming to male adult stereotypes, which include aggressive behavior. It seemed that nobody wanted to confront the fact that this answer simply pushes the explanatory problem back one step to asking why such a male stereotype exists and why it is so ubiquitous. Male aggression crosses cultural boundaries and transcends historical periods. Moreover, as evolutionary biologists have noted, it is not confined to humans. Maybe the stereotype is rooted in reality. If so, perhaps the correlation between the masculine stereotype and men's behavior results from a causal connection precisely opposite to that proposed by social learning and social role theory: Rather than arbitrary stereotypes driving male conformity, stereotypes are the manifestation of our accurate appraisal of behavioral sex differences that we see around us. After all, males of other species do not, as far as we know, predicate their behavior on stereotypes. Why then are males more aggressive?

197

Evolutionary Biology: The Distal Origins of Sex Differences in Aggression

In about 90% of mammals, males make no contribution to the care of infants (Clutton-Brock, 1991). They limit their reproductive input to the supply of sperm and as Williams (1996, p. 118) succinctly put it: "A sperm is not a contribution to the next generation; it is a claim on contributions put into an egg by another individual." Eggs are costly, carrying as they do the nutrients needed to sustain the zygote (should one be formed) until it can embed itself in the uterine wall and sequester resources through the placenta directly from the mother's bloodstream. So the majority of parental care, beginning with anisogamy but continuing through gestation, lactation, and infant care, was firmly imposed on females in most mammalian species. This simple fact of differential parental investment had immense ramifications for the evolutionary bifurcation of male and female behavior (Trivers, 1972, but see Kokko & Jennions, 2008). Nowhere was this more true than in involvement in risky behavior, including aggression. In the currency of fitness, aggression is an advantageous strategy only if it has a net benefit (Parker, 1974). The rewards must exceed the costs (multiplied by the probability of obtaining them).

Let's look at the potential rewards. For males, inseminating multiple females became the holy grail of reproductive success. The more females a male could inseminate, the more offspring he could leave behind (Bateman, 1948). But, of course, this was also the optimal strategy for his similarly parentally unencumbered rivals, raising the levels of intermale competition. Male reproductive winners won big: In our own species, Moulay Ismail the Bloodthirsty (1672–1727) of Morocco fathered 888 children. Losers left no descendants. The greater human male variance in reproductive success continues today even under official monogamy (Jokela, Rotkirch, Rickard, Pettay, & Lummaa, 2010). This disparity between reproductive winners and losers made the stakes high and consequently increased male willingness to take risks in their pursuit (Wang, 2002). The benefits were sufficiently high to offset the costs.

Females were freed from the need to compete with one another for male insemination. This was the plus side to the heavy burden of parental investment females had assumed: Males were only too happy to oblige with a modest sperm deposit. Females did not benefit from superfluous copulations (though this finding has recently been challenged in insects; Jennions & Petrie, 2000; Simmons, 2005) and, indeed, once inseminated, why would a female risk the chance of disease, predation, physical injury, and possible coercive aggression from males that are associated with further copulations (Arnqvist & Rowe, 2005)?

So androcentric was our evolutionary thinking, however, that for many years it was assumed that because females did not fight for copulations there was nothing of consequence for them to fight about and therefore no reward for female aggression. But there is more to life than sex—such as the creation, care, and protection of new copies of our DNA. As Hrdy (1999, p. 81) more eloquently put it: "Unless mating results in the production of offspring who themselves survive infancy and the juvenile years and position themselves so as to reproduce, sex is only so much sound and undulation signifying nothing." Mothers need resources to successfully raise their offspring—surely these would be worth fighting for? Pregnant women need an extra 300 calories every day, and 500 more when they are lactating. Once on solid food, a toddler needs to consume 1,300 calories a day. Like most primates, humans are a group-living species, which means that food can be a contested resource and females must compete to feed themselves and their offspring. At the same time, they must supervise and protect their offspring from ecological dangers, potentially infanticidal males, and harassment by other females. These tasks could be achieved more easily by a dominant female because her status would elicit deference and compliance from lower ranking females. Surely then, females have as much to gain from forming and rising in a dominance hierarchy as males do, but with the female motivation being the ability to sequester resources and increase offspring number and survival, rather than copulations.

Paradoxically, the lower variance among females in reproductive success should fuel intense competition to achieve this dominance. Although the potential upper limit on the fitness rewards of male competition is higher, remember that females are not striving to out-reproduce males. Although at an individual level the most successful male will always out-reproduce the most successful female, every offspring has one father and one mother, so ultimately the two sexes are equal in their output. Females are in evolutionary competition with one another in the sense that a female who bears and raises more offspring to maturity leaves more of her genes in the next generation than her rivals do, including those that enhanced her successful mothering. The lower variance in female reproductive success means that women are more tightly bunched than men and the difference between winners and losers is much smaller. There should therefore be strong selection for any factor that bestows even a small advantage in bearing, raising, and protecting offspring. Wouldn't dominance confer such an advantage?

Dominant female primates typically have higher infant survival and more rapid production of offspring (Pusey, Williams, & Goodall, 1997). Yet dominance hierarchies are primarily restricted to female-bonded species where females are philopatric, remaining in their natal group while males disperse (Sterck, Watts, & van Schaik, 1997). In these species, dominance hierarchies are organized around matrilines. Dominance follows three clear rules. First, females inherit their mother's rank relative to other members of the group. Second, mothers dominate daughters for life. Daughters can rise to their mother's position in the matriline only upon her death. Third, as adults, younger sisters dominate older sisters. The point is that females, unlike males, rarely risk their lives to achieve dominance. They simply accept it happily when lineage and fate confer it on them. Among male chimpanzees (who also remain with their natal group), rank is strenuously, dangerously, and frequently contested, with alliance formations and surprise attacks that can be lethal. Females' reluctance to engage in direct attack is particularly puzzling because a successful challenge would not only immediately increase her food intake, freedom from harassment, and reproductive success, but all of these advantages would be passed down to her daughters. Unlike male chimps, her payoffs would not last merely months or years but through several generations. Yet matrilines remain remarkably stable over time. Walters (1980) found that a juvenile female's rank at the time of her birth correctly predicted her adult rank in 97% of cases. In a 400-day study of yellow baboons, Hausfater (1975) found not a single instance of an agonistically induced change of status among females. Chapais (1992) examined female rank challenge experimentally by setting up a number of female groupings to investigate the circumstances of such challenges and concluded that females pursue a "minimal risk strategy" of competition for dominance (Chapais, 1992, p. 44).

In non-female-bonded species, in which female group members emigrate from their natal group, dominance hierarchies are "weak or undiscernable, unstable, and non-linear" (Isbell & Young, 2002, p. 188; Van Hoof & van Schaik, 1992) and agonistic interactions are rare. When dominance has been reported, it is described in terms of broadband categories because "dominance behavior in stable groups or stable pairs of females is uncommon and is never observed among some dyads" (Pusey et al., 1997). The first report of a female linear dominance hierarchy was among chimpanzees at the Tai National Park in West Africa, where, significantly, the females show equally strong genetic relationships with group members as the males, despite male philopatry (Wittig & Boesch, 2003). The existence of strong kin support and evidence of "long-lasting friendships, including foodsharing and support" (p. 849) may mitigate the severity and danger of dominance contests. It seems then that dominance, while offering manifest rewards, was not strongly selected in females when it had to be fought for. This suggests that it was offset by higher costs.

The obvious cost of aggression is the possibility of injury or death, which surely must be equally bad news for males and females. At an experiential level, this is doubtless true—men do not welcome death any more than women. But from a long-term evolutionary viewpoint, costs are calculated in terms of reproductive success: the number of surviving descendants who themselves go on to reproduce. Here the costs differ by sex.

In a review of studies spanning 28 populations lacking access to contraception and medical care, Sear and Mace (2008) examined the impact of parental survival on offspring survival. The populations sampled ranged from 18th-century China to 20th-century Nepal; from Burkina Faso to New York State. In every case, a mother's survival increased the likelihood of her children surviving. The percentage of children surviving a mother's death ranged from 2% to 50%. The beneficial effects are more marked at younger ages, before children are weaned. In rural Gambia, a mother's death multiplies the odds of her child's death by 6.2 in infancy, 5.2 in toddlerhood, and 1.4 in childhood (Sear, Steele, McGregor, & Mace, 2002). Using data from 17th-century Quebec, Pavard, Gagnon, Desjardins, and Heyer (2005) cross-tabulated the age of the child when the mother died and the age at which the child itself died, controlling for a range of variables, including the possibility of transmitted infection and shared genetic vulnerability. If the mother died while the infant was still a neonate, the odds of the child dying in the neonatal period were multiplied by 5.52, dropping to 1.27 when the child was aged 5 to 15 years.

Despite the critical role of the mother, there has been a surge of interest in the idea of humans as "cooperative breeders," stressing the willingness of kin and others to contribute to the raising of children. But even those scholars advancing this communal view of childrearing acknowledge that "the consequences of losing a mother very early in life are catastrophic" (Sear & Mace, 2008, p. 5). Babies need mothers and mothers invest massively in each offspring. Pregnancy precipitates calcium loss, reduced immune function, oxidative stress, and cellular senescence (Penn & Smith, 2007). The repeated and cumulative effects of multiple pregnancies can result in maternal depletion syndrome. In the end, a woman's reproductive success will shorten her life, but, until that day comes, it is vital that she stays alive. If she dies, the offspring in whom she has already invested will likely die with her. It is the critical dependence of the young on her for their survival that means she must stay away from danger and the possibility of injury or death.

Women's childrearing obligations extend beyond her immediate offspring. The survival of her grandchildren will be enhanced if she can stay alive to assist them, especially those grandchildren with whom she can be sure that she shares a genetic link—her daughters' children. Sear and Mace (2008) found that a surviving maternal grandmother increased child survival in 69% of the populations they studied, especially around the time of weaning when solid foods bring the risk of pathogens and mothers are diverting their care and attention toward a younger sibling. The help offered by maternal grandmothers includes not just babysitting but sharing accumulated knowledge of where to find and dig out tubers, and how to crack nuts, for example (Hawkes, O'Connell, Blurton-Jones, Alvarez, & Charnov, 1998). Hrdy (2009) vividly describes the heroic interventions of ageing primate females, threatening and attacking infanticidal males to save the lives of their grandchildren. When their own reproductive career ends, it makes sense that grandmothers should become more willing to sacrifice themselves—and they are. Indeed, the fact that women survive for so long after becoming incapable of reproduction has been explained precisely in terms of the benefits they can deliver to the their daughters (Hamilton, 1966) and the next generation of their female kin (O'Connell, Hawkes, & Blurton-Jones, 1999)..

But what about fathers? In most mammalian species, females are already heavily committed by their higher parental investment and can be counted on to provide the necessary infant care. Males can move on—risking and sometimes losing their lascivious and combative lives. The costs of nonparticipation in this dangerous lifestyle are prohibitively high: celibacy and reproductive death. Reproductive death means that any genetic tendency to opt out of competition would be removed from the gene pool, resulting in sexual selection for increased intramale aggression over time. So fathers came to play a much less critical role in childrearing than mothers: In 68% of cases, across 22 populations, the death of a father has no effect on the survival of his children (Sear & Mace, 2008).

Evolutionary Psychology: The Proximal Mechanisms of Sex Differences in Aggression

Many hundreds of studies have examined sex differences in aggression using a range of techniques, including laboratory experiments, observation, personality assessment, and self- and peer-reported behavior. The results fit a clear pattern: the more dangerous and risky the form of aggression measured, the larger the sex difference. This appears to be true cross-culturally (Archer, 2009; Campbell, 2006). For physical acts such as hitting, punching, and kicking, the effect size lies between $d = 0.59$ and $d = 0.91$, while for verbal acts such as abuse and threats, the effect size is between $d = 0.28$ and $d = 0.46$ (Knight, Fabes, & Higgins, 1996; Knight, Guthrie, Page, & Fabes, 2002). Indirect aggression includes acts such as spreading stories, excluding, and stigmatizing when the aggressor can remain anonymous and the possibility of retaliation is consequently reduced. Here the sex difference is negligible and nonsignificant, $d = -0.02$ (Archer, 2004).

We have seen that the fitness rewards and costs of aggression (and other forms of risky behavior) differ for males and females. In net terms, aggression is more beneficial for males than females. But psychologists are interested in the ways that these long-haul sexual selection pressures are realized in the brain. Emotions run high in aggressive encounters and this suggests that its evolutionary roots are likely to be deeply buried in the brain structures governing emotion. For many years, economists and psychologists studied decision making in terms of expected utility theory, stressing its purely cognitive basis. Decisions resulted from some hypothetical expectation-based calculus, modeled in algebraic terms. If emotion played a role, it was in terms of anticipated emotions that might be evoked as a result of making one choice rather than another. The actual decision itself was treated as a purely cognitive activity. It is important to emphasize that when we speak of rewards and costs in relation to aggression, we do not mean to imply that individuals cognitively weigh up the pros, cons, and respective probabilities of different courses of actions, choosing the one with the highest positive net value. We argue that emotions, evolved over hundreds of thousands of years, act as "whisperings within" that guide our action (Barash, 1981). The role of emotion in decision making has been increasingly recognized in recent years (see Loewenstein, Weber, Hsee, & Welch, 2001). Emotions are designed to help people make approach-avoidance distinctions and these lie at the heart of aggressive behavior. This is not to imply that higher cortical processes are unimportant: Children do not have to learn how to aggress; rather, they learn how to inhibit their aggression (Tremblay & Nagin, 2005). As adults we do this on a daily basis and, without it, the dense social groups in which we live would implode.

Our task here is to understand why, as the aggressive confrontation becomes more dangerous, the disparity between men and women increases. This sex difference might be mediated by men's stronger attraction to rewards or by women's greater sensitivity to costs. Two basic emotions neatly align with these two processes. An appetite for reward implicates a strong *approach* motivation: The emotion of anger may form the accelerator pedal for aggression. Cost sensitivity implicates *avoidance* motivation: The emotion of fear could act as a braking mechanism. A difference in the threshold for experiencing one or both of these emotions might explain the sex difference in aggression.

The different effects of anger and fear on appraisals were investigated by Lerner and Keltner (2000, 2001). Anger triggers confidence and confrontation, whereas fear triggers avoidance. In situations where individuals have little certainty about or control over outcomes, fearful people make pessimistic risk estimates and risk-averse choices, whereas angry people show the reverse effect, reporting greater optimism and choosing risk-seeking options. Fear and anger have also been studied in the context of hypothetical aggressive conflicts. Winstok (2007) presented participants with vignettes in which they are approached by a male stranger in the street. The danger that he presents was varied simultaneously in terms of the stranger's demeanor (easily scared, not scared, ruthless) and the stranger's likelihood of reacting to the respondent's counteraggression (by backing off, escalating, trying to kill). Provocation by the stranger was also varied (verbal aggression, threatening with physical aggression, physical aggression). The highest levels of fear were reported in the high danger and high provocation condition and were associated with decreased probability of counteraggression. The highest levels of anger appeared in the low danger and high provocation condition. The study's conclusion is that "anger functions as aggression facilitator whereas fear functions as aggression inhibitor" (p. 131).

In situations of threat, anger and fear can and do co-occur. In some situations, the scales are tipped strongly in favor of anger so that fear barely registers as an emotion. In others, despite our fury, fear overpowers us and we retreat. We argue that men and women are capable of experiencing both emotions but that the relative balance between them is tipped more strongly in favor of overt aggression in men. But is this because men experience greater anger or lower fear?

Anger

The experience of anger is not a pleasant one, and our first task is to address how such a subjectively aversive experience might be associated with approach motivation. This is an alignment that has been hard for non–evolutionarily minded psychologists to accept because they have tended to reduce the subtle spectrum of human emotions to a simple dichotomy: nasty and nice. The fact that humans find some emotions pleasant and some unpleasant has formed the basis for a two-dimensional classification of emotion based on valence (Forgas, 1995). According to this view, emotions such as sadness and guilt are "negative" emotions that we seek to avoid, while others, such as joviality and serenity, are "positive" emotions that we enjoy. But natural selection is driven by functionality, not by our preferences. The route to understanding emotions is not through their valence—either hedonic (pleasant/unpleasant) or moral (right/wrong)—but through the behaviors they motivate. Emotions evolved to provide guidance about how to react to the world outside, and evolution is indifferent as to whether we happen to like the information we receive. For example, disgust warns us to avoid a stimulus and serves to put distance between us and pathogen-carrying substances such as decaying meat or human excrement. Pain tells us about bodily injury or malfunction, ensuring that we reduce our mobility and divert our energy resources to healing and immune system activity. Disgust and pain may be unpleasant experiences, but they do their job effectively.

The study of anger presents a particularly strong challenge to the view that our evaluations of emotional experiences provides a useful guide to their "natural" structure and function. It was thought that positively valenced emotions were associated with approach motivation and negative emotions with avoidance motivation (Davidson, 2000; Lang, Bradley, & Cuthbert, 1992; Watson, Wiese, Vaidya, & Tellegen, 1999). Anger is an unpleasant emotional state and by this logic should be associated with avoidance. However, there is much evidence that this is not the case (Carver & Harmon-Jones, 2009). Anger activates left frontal brain activity more strongly than right hemisphere activity, in common with other emotions associated with approach motivation (Murphy, Nimmo-Smith, & Lawrence, 2003). Anger correlates positively with psychometric scales measuring approach motivation and negatively with avoidance motivation scales (Harmon-Jones, 2003; Smits & Kuppens, 2005). In typically developing children, infant approach tendencies predict increased anger at later ages (Rothbart, Derryberry, & Hershey, 2000) and toddlers with externalizing problems, including aggression, show high levels of behavioral approach in laboratory tasks (Putnam & Stifter, 2005).

Anger increases muscle tension, heart rate, blood pressure, muscular blood flow, and body temperature. These are the familiar components of sympathetic nervous system activity preparing us for exertion and combat. The basic neurobiology of anger is well conserved across species and is organized hierarchically, running from the medial amygdala via the stria terminalis down to the medial hypothalamus, and then to the periaqueductal gray (Panksepp, 1998). In mammals the frontal cortex sits atop this system and can modulate its activity, especially the orbitofrontal region.

So anger represents the accelerator pedal for aggressive behavior. Is more frequent and severe aggression in males driven by their propensity to experience greater anger? It seems not. A narrative review by Kring (2000) concluded there was a marked absence of sex differences in anger, and this was confirmed by Archer (2004), who reported an effect size of $d = -0.004$ in his meta-analysis of data from 46 samples. In a poll of over 2,000 Americans, women reported more episodes of anger during the last 7 days than men, even after controlling for sex differences in emotional expressiveness (Mirowsky & Ross, 1995). Using national data from the US General Social Survey, Simon and Nath (2004) also found no difference in the frequency of anger, although women exceeded men significantly in the intensity and duration of the emotion, controlling for sociodemographic factors. If men do not exceed women in anger, do the sexes differ in fear?

Fear

The fear system is "designed to detect danger and produce responses that maximise the probability of surviving" (LeDoux, 1996, p. 128). The amygdala plays a central role in coordinating immediate responses to fear-provoking stimuli. Amygdala-cortical connections are bidirectional so that emotional states (such as fear) can direct information processing to threatening stimuli and, reciprocally, cortical representations of threat (even imaginary or vicarious ones) can activate an emotional response (Damasio, 1994; Derrybery & Reed, 1994). Once activated, the amygdala's connections to a variety of other brain structures stimulate the sympathetic nervous system and the hypothalamic pituitary axis. Extreme fear triggers behavioral freezing: Inhibitory connections allow the anticipatory activity in the fear system to suppress approach responses that might lead the organism into a harmful situation (Derryberry & Rothbart, 1997). Fear and anger systems follow very similar neural pathways: The fear system runs from the central and lateral amygdala through the ventral anterior and medial hypothalamus to the periaqueductal gray matter (Panksepp, 1998).

There is much evidence that the sexes differ in the frequency and intensity of fear (Else-Quest, Hyde, Goldsmith, & Van Hulle, 2006). Developmentally, girls express fear earlier than boys (Gartstein & Rotbart, 2003) and, in a large longitudinal study of personality development, more girls than boys were on a high fearfulness trajectory (Cote, Tremblay, Nagin, Zoccolillo, & Vitaro, 2002). Among adults, women experience fear more intensely than men (Brody & Hall, 1993; Fischer, 1993; Gullone, 2000). A 37-nation study found significant sex differences in the intensity, duration, and nonverbal expression of fear (Fischer & Manstead, 2000). Another international survey (Brebner, 2003) found a significant sex difference in the reported frequency ($d = -0.17$) and intensity ($d = -0.14$) of fear. Women express their fear more intensely, both verbally and nonverbally, than do men (see Madden, Feldman Barrett, & Pietromonaco, 2000). While women are superior to men in accurately identifying emotions, they show a greater accuracy for decoding fear than other emotions (Hall, Carter, & Horgan, 2000). Behaviorally, women show greater increases in skin conductance and a more marked startle reflex to physically threatening scenes (McManis, Bradley,

Berg, Cuthbert, & Lang, 2001). Testosterone seems to be an important mediator of this sex difference: A single dose of testosterone administered to women significantly reduces the potentiated startle response to anticipated electric shock (Hermans, Putman, Baas, Koppeschaar, & van Honk, 2006).

A sex difference in fear might explain why men make riskier decisions than women. This sex difference is especially marked when the risks are physical or life threatening and when actual risky behavior, rather than hypothetical choices, is examined (Hersch, 1997). It has been suggested that "fear responses may explain gender differences in risk taking more adequately than the cognitive processes involved in the reflective evaluation of options" (Byrnes, Miller, & Schafer, 1999, p. 378). In explaining the sex difference in risk taking, Loewenstein et al. (2001) also identify women's higher level of fear as particularly relevant. These consistent sex differences in fear, but not anger, strongly suggest that women's desistance from aggression, which becomes more marked as the degree of danger increases, results from their stronger fear responses.

Fear or Impulsivity?

Impulsivity has also been suggested as a mediator for sex differences in aggression (Campbell, 2006; Strüber, Luck, & Roth, 2008): Perhaps men are simply less successful in controlling their behavior than women and that includes, among other things, aggression. Impulsivity has proved a slippery concept in psychology, though most academics broadly agree that it refers to a "tendency to act spontaneously and without deliberation" (Carver, 2005, p. 313). We conducted a meta-analysis of sex differences from 277 studies of impulsivity and, in summarizing our results, there are two major distinctions that must be made (Cross, Copping, & Campbell, 2011).

The first is between lower order and higher order theories of impulsivity. Higher order theories see impulsivity as a failure of the cognitive control of behavior that a child develops with age (e.g., Rothbart & Bates, 2006). Researches who conceptualize impulsivity in this way often measure it as the inability to withhold a prepotent response or to plan for the future. Here, there are very few differences between men and women ($d = 0.08$). Lower order theories view impulsive actions as manifestations of basic affective and temperamental reactions, rather than the result of a cognitive deficit (e.g., Fowles, 1988; Gray & McNaughton, 2000). According to this view, impulsivity can arise either from overattraction to reward (e.g., "I want it so much I can't tolerate a delay") or from undersensitivity to punishment (e.g., "There may be a price to be paid for this decision, but I don't care about it"). Our analysis showed that men and women differ very little in their sensitivity to reward ($d = -0.02$, although effect sizes are strongly modulated by how sensitivity is measured), but women are consistently more sensitive than men to punishment ($d = -0.33$). This gels with the argument that women have evolved greater sensitivity to negative outcomes than men, including a lower threshold for fear. It also explains why women suffer higher rates of anxiety and depression than men at both a nonclinical and clinical level (Costa, Terracciano, & McCrae, 2001).

A second point relevant to understanding sex differences is the misleading inclusion of sensation seeking and risk taking as integral aspects of impulsivity. Zuckerman (1994, p. 27) defines sensation seeking as "the seeking of varied, novel, complex, and intense sensations and experiences and the willingness to take physical, social, legal, and financial risks for the sake of such experience." The central defining feature of impulsivity is acting without deliberation. This is absent in sensation-seeking activities. Parachute jumpers do not jump from planes on impulse; they plan carefully, checking their equipment, drop site, parachute, and timings. Questionnaires that measure sensation seeking ask about the respondent's preference for risky but exciting activities (e.g., parachute jumping) over safe but tedious ones. But the items make no reference to the failure of deliberation which is the hallmark of impulsive action. When we analyzed sensation seeking and risk taking separately from other forms of impulsivity, we found a marked sex difference in favor of men ($d = 0.41$). Men may not be more impulsive, but they certainly take greater risks with their lives.

In fact, men seem to seek risk out. Men's lower levels of punishment sensitivity and fear can help to explain this. Typically an inverted U-shaped function describes the relationship between the arousal (low—high) generated by an activity and its subjective hedonic valence to the actor (pleasant—unpleasant). If men have a higher fear threshold, their function will be displaced relative to women's. Hence, a higher degree of arousal will be necessary to generate the same degree of pleasure. Men will show a shift from enjoyment to excitement (and from apprehension to fear) at higher levels of arousal compared to women. Hence, a high-speed car ride that is unpleasant (aversive) to women could be exciting (attractive) to men.

In summary, impulsivity per se does not seem to show marked sex differences, but women are more punishment sensitive and risk averse than men. There is a potential area of overlap between impulsivity and sensation seeking. Some actions may be both impulsive and risky: running across a road, having sex with a stranger, or accepting an offer of drink or drugs, for example. The assessment of actions that are both risky and impulsive is an area in need of further research (Campbell & Muncer, 2009). Such "risky" impulsivity is likely to be of most relevance to understanding sex differences in aggressive behavior.

Monogamy, Two-Way Selection, and the Currency of Female Competition

In many species, notably birds, it is the males who display the gaudiest and most attractive phenotypes, as we would expect if males must charm the female into choosing them. A rather remarkable feature of humans is the fact that, in many societies, it is women more than men who take trouble with their appearance. Something changed that caused women, as well as men, to compete for mates. That something was the advent of monogamy. When males select a mate for life (or at least a considerable number of years), they become much choosier.

It is often pointed out that the majority of the world's cultures permit polygamy (Murdock, 1967), but it also true that most humans today marry or cohabit monogamously. Indeed, in Western nations, polygamy is against the law. But it seems that legal mandates and an extensive history of pair bonding have not completely eradicated men's eagerness for casual sex. There is abundant evidence that men fantasize about sex with different partners more than women, are the major consumers of pornography, masturbate more frequently, and have more positive experiences of casual sex (Campbell, 2008a; Oliver & Hyde, 1993). Worldwide, men score higher than women on the Sociosexual Orientation Inventory, designed to measure experiences with and attitudes toward unrestricted sexuality (Schmitt, 2005). Whenever men acquire extreme resources, power, or fame, many cannot resist the lure of "extra" women or the temptation to trade in their ageing wife for a newer model. Even today, men's reproductive success is increased more than women's by remarriage (Jokela et al., 2010). The weight of the evidence indicates that, although there is diversity in human mating patterns, humans are "socially monogamous" while retaining characteristics associated with polygynous species.

Monogamy, whenever it evolved, brought with it two-way sexual selection and meant that women as well as men had to compete for the best mates. This competition was enhanced when humans became agricultural and for the first time men could sequester, store, and barter resources rather than living hand to mouth. The variance between men in the resources they controlled became exaggerated, and women sought male partners who were in the best position to provide for their offspring. Darwin (1871/1998) identified two forms of sexual selection: intrasexual combat and intersexual choice. The first involved high risk and possible injury and, as we might expect, women took the latter route. The currency of female competition for a long-term partner are those qualities that men value. Men and women agree in placing their highest priority on kindness, intelligence, considerateness, and understanding. However, men value youth and physical attractiveness in a long-term mate more than women do. So the arena for women's competition was decided.

After a period of adolescent sterility, women become most fertile at the age of 25 at which point their fertility declines until it reaches zero by the age of about 50. When adult men are asked about age preference, they consistently choose someone who is younger than themselves and marriage patterns indicate that the typical age gap is about 3 years (Buss & Schmitt, 1993). As men age, they prefer ever-younger women, and by the age of 60, they prefer women who are on average 15 years younger than themselves (Kenrick & Keefe, 1992). Men's desire for physical attractiveness is closely bound up with women's age. Facial features that reflect youth include shiny hair, unwrinkled skin, large eyes, a small nose, and full lips (Etcoff, 1999). While men are more likely to compete with each other by exaggerating superiority, promiscuity, intensity, and popularity, women are more likely to compete with each other using alterations to their appearance, such as makeup, nail polish, fake tans, and tight clothing (Cashdan, 1998; Tooke & Camire, 1991; see also Buss, 1988a, 1988b).

Managing Female Competition

One way that women can compete without risking their safety or compromising their lives is through acts that ostracize, stigmatize, and otherwise exclude others from social interaction without risking direct physical confrontation. Such acts do not eliminate or physically injure the target, nor do they demonstrate the greater size, strength, or belligerence of the attacker. They do, however, inflict stress and diminish the opponents' reputation and social support. The target is attacked circuitously; therefore, the aggressor can remain unidentified and safe from retaliation, at least in the short term. This set of behaviors is referred to as *indirect or relational aggression* (Bjorkqvist, Lagerspetz, & Kaukiainen 1992; Crick & Grotpeter, 1995). These stigmatizing and excluding strategies can have devastating effects on the victim (Simmons, 2002). While early studies suggested that females exceeded males in their use of indirect aggression, Archer's (2004) meta-analysis finds a negligible sex difference ($d = -0.02$). Regardless of whether women exceed men in their use of indirect aggression or are simply equal to them, the basic argument remains intact: Sex differences are magnified for risky forms of aggression and minimized (even reversed) for less physically dangerous forms such as indirect aggression, where there is no face-to-face confrontation and the attacker can remain anonymous.

A key component of indirect aggression is the use of gossip to undermine an opponent's reputation and decrease his or her social capital. If physical attractiveness is especially important to men's choice of mates, women should not only compete with one another to meet men's preference criteria, but they should also use gossip as a way to derogate rivals. Physical appearance is the only topic of gossip to show a significant sex difference (Nevo, Nevo, & Derech-Zehavi, 1993) and is more often discussed in relation to female targets (Hall, 2002). When women evaluate their rivals, they attend particularly to their waist, hips, and legs (Dijkstra & Buunk, 2001). Of the 28 tactics which participants reported having used to make same-sex rivals undesirable to the opposite sex, Buss and Dedden (1990) found that "derogate competitor's appearance" was used significantly more often by women than men. Naturalistic studies concur that pejorative comments about other girls' appearance rank high in girls' topics of gossip (Brown, 1998; Duncan, 1999; Simmons, 2002).

Other traits that men find unattractive in a potential long-term partner are cues to likely infidelity (Buss & Schmitt, 1993). Paternity is never certain for a man and the costs of investing in another man's child are sufficiently great to alert men, at an emotional if not explicit level, to evaluate a woman's likely sexual fidelity. Because one of the best predictors of future behavior is past behavior, women might gain an advantage from undermining their rivals' sexual reputation while defending their own. That is why terms such as "slag," "tart," or "whore" are powerful sources of reputation challenge among women (Campbell, 1982, 1995; Duncan, 1999; Lees, 1993; Marsh & Patton, 1986). Indeed, girls themselves actively collude in enforcing the sexual double standard through gossip and rumor spreading (Baumeister & Twenge, 2002). Buss and Dedden (1990) found that young women were judged more likely than men to question a rival's fidelity and to draw attention to her promiscuity.

Escalation to Physical Aggression

Although women engage in physical confrontations with their own sex less frequently and less seriously than men, fights do occur. In a victimization survey of 1,455 British respondents, 7% of women reported an actual assault by another woman and a further 4% reported a threat of assault during the preceding 5 years (George, 1999). Data from self-report studies and from official crime statistics indicate that approximately 73% of adolescent girls' attacks are on other girls (Bureau of Justice Statistics, 1999; Campbell, 1986). In the United States and Britain, female assaults are most commonly directed at and committed by 15- to 24-year-olds and occur predominantly between friends and acquaintances. The most frequent forms of attack are pushing, shoving, grabbing, tripping, slapping, kicking, and punching (Campbell, 1986; Ness, 2004).

The reasons for fighting are often connected directly or indirectly to young men and fall broadly into three categories (Campbell, 1995). The first is defending a sexual reputation. Gossip about a girl's promiscuity gives rise to rumor that may find its way back to the target herself, acting as a trigger for attack as a means of reclaiming her threatened identity. A second source of provocation is competition for potential partners. Around the world, access to men and their resources is responsible for the majority of women's fights (Burbank, 1987; Ness, 2004; Schuster, 1985). Thirdly, jealousy about proprietary ownership of a current partner is a frequent source of conflict.

But the probability of escalating from indirect or verbal aggression to outright physical attack is not randomly distributed in women. There are ecological and demographic factors that concentrate it among the young in the poorest neighborhoods. Girls, like boys, show a marked age–violence relationship, rising in the early teenage years and falling away in the mid-20s. Male violence is far more prevalent than female violence, but the shape of the curve is very similar for both sexes—with one exception. Violence rises and peaks earlier in girls than boys by about 2 years, corresponding to girls' 2-year-earlier attainment of sexual maturity. For both sexes, postpubertal entry into the crucial arena of mate choice brings with it high stakes and increased competition.

The operational sex ratio is an index of the availability of prospective mates. Women are most likely to find a partner in the immediate neighborhood and to the extent that the local male-female ratio drops below unity, competition between women increases. A female-biased sex ratio not only means that women are forced to compete for available men, but that men find themselves in an excellent bargaining position. As in the market place generally, where demand is high the producers can charge higher prices. In this case, the currency is men's preferred mating strategy. As we have noted, men benefit from multiple partners, but usually only a very few well-resourced and highly desirable men are in a position to pursue such a polygynous strategy. When men are in short supply, many more of them can call the shots, effectively enforcing a "short-term only" mating strategy on women. Women might prefer men who commit and dream of finding a faithful long-term provider (Campbell, 1984; Joe Laidler & Hunt, 2001), but in a female-biased neighborhood men's commitment is optional, especially for those who have resources.

High variation in men's resources intensifies female competition. Among middle-class young women, the costs of escalating to direct competition are rarely worth it: The difference between marrying a doctor or an accountant is not sufficiently great (Campbell, 2011). But in deprived areas, the difference between the desperate poverty of "dope fiends" and the conspicuous consumption of "high rollers" is extreme. The desirability of access to material resources means that well-resourced men are worth fighting for. Antagonism can be heightened further after a young woman bears a man's child: Even after the relationship has ended, a "BM" (baby's mother) feels entitled to make claims on the father's income and to repel rival women who threaten to divert his resources (Ness, 2004). Young men's preference for sexual novelty is a constant threat to relationships, and young women are especially sensitive to girls whose appearance and demeanor suggest that they "think they're all that." Envy and jealousy often underlie what seems to be an inexplicable hostility to newly arrived or highly attractive girls: "It's like,

if another girl gets attention, she's taking it away from you. It's as if she's saying she's better than you. So you gonna knock her down a notch" (Ness, 2004, p. 40).

Despite these occasional eruptions of outright aggression, commentators and criminal statistics agree that female aggression is less frequent and less lethal than that of males. Weapons are rarely used, with fights confined overwhelmingly to fists and feet (Ness, 2004). Three-quarters of women's violent offences were limited to simple rather than aggravated assaults (Greenfeld & Snell, 1999).

Two Paradoxes: Maternal and Partner Aggression

We have argued that it is not usually in a female's best interests to risk her life and that fear confines female aggression to less confrontational forms. However, there are two notable exceptions to the usual finding of higher male aggression: women's aggression in defense of offspring and against intimate partners. We now consider whether our proposal can account for these reversals and, in both cases, we propose that fear reduction disinhibits female aggression.

Maternal Aggression

Saving the life of one's child's is a situation where the payoffs for aggression are much larger for a female than for a male. That young life has cost the mother dearly in terms of time, effort, vigilance, and protection. In polygynous species, that same young life has cost the father a few million easily replaceable sperm. Though animal mothers rarely go as far as sacrificing themselves, they are more willing to tolerate the risks of aggression for the sake of their offspring's survival than for any other reason. Maternal aggression has been documented in species from lemmings to lions, wherever male infanticide presents a serious threat. The mother's attack is ferocious and immediate. Among macaques, vervets, and baboons, females are extraordinarily vigilant to the presence of males near infants and, when an infant shows distress, a nearby male may be attacked even if he has displayed no overt aggression toward it (Smuts, 1987).

Maternal aggression has been most closely studied in rodents, where it begins during pregnancy and continues through lactation. Females discriminate between the danger posed by different intruders, reserving their most ferocious attacks for those males who are most likely to harm the young (sexually naive, newly arrived, and recently mated males) rather than paternal males or other females. The severity of maternal attack is directly related to the size of the litter that she is protecting. Maternal aggression corresponds to the period when the young are most vulnerable. It disappears when the pups are removed for 5 hours, but it is restored 5 minutes after the pups are returned. If the pups are attacked and killed, maternal aggression switches off immediately.

The nonapeptide oxytocin (OT) has been linked to a range of female reproductive events and is strongly implicated in maternal aggression (Campbell, 2008b). Peripherally, OT regulates uterine contractions during labor and milk ejection during lactation. Centrally, OT acts as a neuromodulator. Central OT release and neuronal activity can be elicited by sexual and reproductive stimuli (copulation, genital and breast stimulation, birth, olfactory stimuli, suckling) and nonsexual stimuli, including grooming, light massage, and exposure to offspring. In late pregnancy, in response to rising estrogen levels, OT receptors are upregulated in the uterus and the brain. Parturition triggers activation of OT neurons in the hypothalamus, stimulating release of OT in many brain areas that are critical for coordinated maternal behavior, including nest building, retrieving pups to the nest, licking them, and crouching to afford pups body heat and access to the nipple.

We can conceive of maternal aggression as the "other side of the coin" of mother–infant attachment. In rodents, OT simultaneously inhibits aggression directed toward the pups while enhancing attacks on intruders (Debiec, 2005). And, crucially for our proposed explanation of female aggression, *OT reduces fear* (Huber, Veinante, & Stoop, 2005). In rats, administering OT reduces amygdala activation, increases parasympathetic functioning, decreases corticosteroid release, and results in lower levels of fearful behavior (Windle et al., 2004). OT levels rise in the hypothalamic PVN in both the mother and a female intruder in the maternal defense test (Bosch, Kromer, Brunton, & Neumann, 2004), and this rise is correlated with aggressive behavior, especially for dams bred for high anxiety (Bosch, Meddle, Beiderbeck, Douglas, & Neumann, 2005). Infusion of OT into the central amygdala increases maternal aggression (Ferris et al., 1992) while lesions of the PVN decrease it (Consiglio & Lucion, 1996).

In humans, too, there is a rise in central OT during childbirth. Positive feelings and reduced anxiety postpartum are positively associated with OT levels (Takagi, Tanizawa, Otsuki, Haruta, & Yamaji, 1985). Prior to their first feeding, infants massage the mother's breast, resulting in peripheral OT release, which remains elevated during feeding (Matthiesen, Ransio-Arvidson, Nissen, & Uvnas-Moberg, 2001). Lactation is associated with lowered subjective stress, and there is a negative relationship between plasma OT and adrenocorticotropic hormone levels, which indicate stress activation (Chiodera et al., 1991). A pattern of increasing maternal OT during pregnancy has been found to be associated with stronger maternal–fetal bonding (Levine, Zagoory-Sharon, Feldman, & Weller, 2007). After the baby is born, attachment-related thoughts, gaze at the infant, affectionate touch, and frequent infant checking are predicted by OT levels in early pregnancy and immediately postpartum (Feldman, Weller, Zagoory-Sharon, & Levine, 2007). OT also facilitates mind reading (Domes, Heinrichs, Michel, Berger, & Herpetz, 2007), perhaps increasing emotional connectedness between mother and infant. Although human maternal behavior does not critically depend on OT as it may do in rodents, OT appears to play a supplementary role in enhancing bonding in the early weeks. This pattern of findings strongly suggests that OT may be involved in maternal aggression in our own species, either directly or indirectly via its bonding effects. Ethical issues make it all but impossible to investigate this directly, but there is some preliminary evidence that lactating mothers do show heightened aggression (Hahn-Holbrook, Holt-Lunstead, & Holbrook, 2009) and OT is involved in defensive and protective aggression in other contexts (De Dreu et al., 2010)

Partner Aggression

Most explanatory accounts of aggression between intimate partners have focused on male perpetration and female victimization. For many years it was widely held by feminist theorists that society's patriarchal nature positively fostered a culture of "wife beating"—unilateral violence suffered by women at the hands of men (Dobash & Dobash, 1979). Evolutionary accounts of partner aggression used this contention as their starting point (Dobash, Dobash, Wilson, & Daly, 1992) and therefore focused almost exclusively on explanations of male violence toward female partners. The evolutionary argument was based heavily on the role of male sexual jealousy: Because fertilization takes place inside the female body and women's ovulation is concealed, men can be deceived into investing in children who were sired by other males—at the expense of their own fitness. Ancestral men who reduced their risk of being cuckolded by "mate guarding"—controlling their partners' behavior, keeping track of their whereabouts, and restricting their movement so that they could not consort with other men—out-reproduced their less vigilant rivals. Partner aggression, therefore, is a tactic for ensuring paternity (Daly, Wilson, & Weghorst, 1982; Wilson & Daly, 1996). According to this argument, patriarchal societies condone male aggression, upholding the belief that a man has the right to control his own home. This leads to police and judicial reluctance to intervene in "domestic" disputes and allows male abuse of partners to go unchecked. Women's aggression toward male partners is rare and, in cases where it does occur, is "almost always... in response to cues of imminent assault" (Dobash et al., 1992, p. 80).

But does the evidence support this view? It is certainly true that the majority of people who are killed (Daly & Wilson, 1988) or injured (Archer, 2000; Whitaker, Haileyesus, Swahn, & Saltzman, 2007) at the hands of an intimate partner are women, and that the majority of cases of intimate partner violence that reach a criminal court involve a female victim and a male defendant (Smith & Farole, 2009). Women sustain serious injuries as a result of the markedly greater size and strength of men, and male-on-female violence represents a major public health concern. But does this mean that intimate partner aggression is chiefly a male-perpetrated form of aggression, and one that is predominantly motivated by sexual proprietariness? We consider evidence for the following claims: (1) that men's sexual jealousy is a greater cause of aggression than women's sexual jealousy; (2) that societal norms encourage (or at least tolerate) men's aggression toward female partners; and (3) that acts of intimate partner aggression are perpetrated predominantly by men.

SEXUAL JEALOUSY

The evolutionary hypothesis that men's sexual jealousy should be more intense than women's sparked a number of studies investigating the idea that men have evolved to be sensitive specifically to cues of sexual infidelity that threaten cuckoldry, while women's jealousy is focused more on emotional betrayal that threatens the loss of resource provision by their partner (Buss, Larsen, Westen, & Semmelroth, 1992). There has been debate as to the specific predictions arising from the evolutionary approach, the extent to which hypotheses have been empirically supported, and the appropriateness of measures employed (see Edlund & Sagarin, 2009; Harris 2003, 2005; Sagarin, 2005). Early studies mainly employed forced-choice paradigms in which men and women were asked to choose whether they found sexual or emotional infidelity more upsetting. These studies appeared to show a sex difference: Men, relative to women, were more likely to choose sexual infidelity as the more distressing form of betrayal (Harris, 2003). When men and women are offered a third option, however—that both forms of infidelity are equally distressing—the majority of both sexes endorse it (Lisher, Nguyen, Stocks, & Zilmer, 2008). And when men and women are asked to rate the distress associated with each kind of betrayal (rather than choose between them), results show no sex differences (DeSteno, Bartlett, Braverman, & Salovey, 2002). The data are therefore equivocal regarding sex differences in sexual jealousy.

While sex differences in sexual jealousy might or might not exist, there is little evidence to suggest that jealousy is more likely to motivate men's intimate partner aggression than women's. Although abandonment or infidelity by a partner matters to men and women for different reasons, both sexes have something to gain by controlling the behavior of their partners and preventing abandonment or infidelity (Buss et al., 1992). Recent research on controlling behavior in relationships reveals that men and women use controlling behaviors with equal frequency (Graham-Kevan & Archer, 2009), although the forms of controlling behavior may differ (Felson & Outlaw, 2007). Furthermore, controlling behavior predicts aggression equally well for both sexes (Graham-Kevan & Archer, 2009). The evidence therefore suggests that both sexes are motivated to control the behavior of a partner and aggression is a tactic used by both sexes.

Daly and Wilson (1988) argue that, because the majority of murders attributed to jealousy are committed by men, this is evidence for stronger jealousy in men than women. However, when the marked sex differences in base rates of homicide commission are taken into consideration, there is no evidence that men's killing of intimate partners is more likely to be motivated by jealousy than women's (Harris, 2003). Harris therefore suggests that men's greater absolute rates of partner killing might reflect not a sex difference in motivation but simply an advantage of size and strength.

SOCIAL NORMS

Do we live in a society that encourages or tolerates male aggression toward partners? The answer, at least in the West, appears to be no. Among the general population, men's aggression toward women is seen as more reprehensible than their aggression toward another man (Davidovic, Bell, Ferguson, Gorski, & Campbell, 2011; Felson & Feld, 2009). Within intimate partnerships, men's aggression toward a female partner is deemed more serious and more deserving of police intervention than women's aggression toward a male partner (Felson & Feld, 2009; Sorenson & Taylor, 2005). Men who assault their partners are more likely than their female counterparts to be convicted (Felson, 2008) or incarcerated (Smith & Farole, 2009). By contrast, women who assault male partners are disproportionately likely to avoid arrest (Felson & Pare, 2007) or criminal charges (Brown, 2004).

A review published in the early 1990s (Dobash et al., 1992) argued that male violence toward female partners is tolerated by society and unlikely to be punished by police. However, a more recent review (Felson & Pare, 2007) indicates that both sexes are less likely to be convicted for assaulting a known person than a stranger, regardless of whether they are a partner, a friend, or a family member. Furthermore, convictions for partner assault have been more stringently applied since the 1980s for assailants of both sexes. It might, therefore, be true that those who assault partners are less likely to be convicted than those who assault strangers but, importantly, this effect is diminishing over time, is not confined to partners, and is not confined to male assailants.

IS IT ONLY MEN WHO HIT?

The fact that women are more frequently injured than men might be taken to imply that aggressive acts are predominantly perpetrated by men. However, such an inference equates acts with outcomes. That acts and outcomes are distinct concepts is almost universally accepted, although there is considerable disagreement on how desirable it is to measure one or the other (Archer, 2000; Dobash et al., 1992). Researchers interested in the sequelae of partner aggression—intimate partner *violence*—will undoubtedly wish to focus more on outcomes than on acts: The same act (e.g., a punch) will have a different outcome depending on whether the perpetrator is male and the recipient female, or vice versa. However, researchers interested in the dynamics that precipitate aggression may well wish to focus more on acts than on outcomes: Ignoring a woman's aggressive act because it is less likely to cause serious injury than the same act committed by a man will result in major omissions in our explanatory accounts of intimate partner aggression.

The fact that women are more frequently injured by intimate partners than men therefore begs the question: Is it true that men use more aggressive acts toward partners than women do? In the West, once again, the answer appears to be no. Self- and partner-report studies conducted in community samples show that *women commit aggressive acts toward partners as often as men do, if not more often.* A large-scale meta-analysis of act-based measures of partner aggression (Archer, 2000) found an effect of $d = -0.05$, a very small but statistically significant effect in the female direction. To examine whether this might be a function of inflated self-reports by women or underreporting by men, partners' reports were also examined. Although the sex difference favoring women on self-reports became nonsignificant when partner reports were used, it did not reverse in favor of men. More recent studies have also found either gender symmetry in aggression (Robertson & Murachver, 2007; Straus & Ramirez, 2007) or greater use of aggression by women (Thornton, Graham-Kevan, & Archer, 2010). The most common pattern of aggression between partners is one of mutuality, and in at least half of cases of intimate partner violence where only one partner is aggressive, it is the woman (Langhinrichsen-Rohling, Neidig, & Thorn, 1995; Straus & Ramirez, 2007; Whitaker et al., 2007).

The argument that women's aggression is "almost always" motivated by self-defense (Dobash et al., 1992, p. 80) is not consistent with available data. In studies in which both partners are asked who initiated the attack, it is either more frequently the woman or there is no sex difference (Archer, 2002). Furthermore, Hettrich and O'Leary (2007) found that self-defense was one of the reasons most frequently cited by women as "*not* a cause" of their own aggression. Studies of college students have found no sex differences in the reporting of self-defense as a reason for aggression, although absolute rates vary widely between studies (Follingstad, Wright, Lloyd, & Sebastian, 1991; Harned, 2001).

Furthermore, the possibility that women's aggression toward their partners is confined to "minor" acts while men predominate in more severe acts was examined and found to be false in a second meta-analysis by Archer (2002): There was no sex difference in the use of guns or knives to threaten or to attack a partner. Furthermore, although men were more likely than women to report choking or strangling ($d = 0.13$), or beating up ($d = 0.07$) a partner, a substantial minority of those who committed these acts were women, and women were slightly more likely than men to report punching, biting, or kicking ($d = -0.12$), or slapping ($d = -0.18$) a partner. The sex differences in injury, therefore, are attributable to physical differences between the sexes such as men's greater upper-body strength rather than a sex difference in the use of aggressive acts more generally (Archer, 2009).

There are deplorable physical and psychological consequences of men's aggression to women, which we and others (e.g., Archer, 2006; Felson & Pare, 2007) acknowledge. Nevertheless, for researchers trying to gain a fuller understanding of female aggression, or indeed intimate partner aggression as a whole, women's equality with their male partners in the frequency of intimate aggression presents a real explanatory challenge. We attempt to begin addressing this challenge in the following sections.

WHAT EXPLAINS THE "TARGET PARADOX"?

We use the term "target paradox" to describe the disjunction between the very marked sex difference in same-sex aggression and its absence (or even reversal) in intimate partner violence. The sex-equal rates of aggressive behavior in intimate partnerships raise a number of questions. Do men lower their aggression in the context of an intimate partnership, or do women raise theirs?

We found that both of these shifts occur (Cross, Tee, & Campbell, 2011). Given the same provocation, men report being less likely to aggress toward a partner than toward a friend of the same sex. However, this effect is not specific to intimate partners: Men are unlikely to report using direct aggression toward a female target irrespective of whether she is a partner. This conclusion was confirmed in a further study that showed that men experience stronger inhibitory control and weaker impulsion to violence against women (whether partners or friends) than against men (Davidovic et al., 2011). In laboratory settings also, men inhibit their aggression to female targets relative to male targets (Taylor & Epstein, 1967), and in society at large men are more likely than women to be the victims of criminal assault (Hall & Innes, 2010). Men therefore appear to lower their aggression in the context of an intimate partnership not because they are interacting with a partner but because they are interacting with a woman.

Women, on the other hand, raise their aggression in the context of an intimate relationship (Cross et al., 2011). This poses a serious challenge to our explanation of sex differences in aggression predicated on women's lower threshold for experiencing fear. We have argued that women are adapted to place a premium on their own safety, but if this is so, why do they take the risk of attacking a male partner? Given the male advantage in size and strength, such an attack is even more dangerous than attacking a woman—and women rarely attack other women.

If our proposal that fear typically restrains women's aggression is correct, then women's characteristic fear of men must be reduced somehow in the context of an intimate relationship. But from where does this reduction come? Fiebert and Gonzalez (1997) argue that women who strike their partners believe that they are not in danger of being struck in retaliation. In support of this view, social norms in the United States proscribe male aggression toward women even in response to attack (Feld & Felson, 2008). This account, however, fails to explain why women do not raise their aggression levels toward men in general. Norms proscribing male aggression toward women apply to *all* women and not just intimate partners, yet women's aggression toward male acquaintances is lower than their aggression toward other women, as we would expect based upon women's fear of injury (Cross et al., 2011). There is something about intimate partners specifically that makes them the target of female aggression.

The peptide hormone oxytocin, as well as having a role in parturition and lactation, is also implicated in the formation of the pair bond (Young & Wang, 2004). As we have noted, mating is considerably more risky and costly for women than for men. In most species, the optimal mating rate for females is lower than that of males and "supernumerary" copulations increase a female's vulnerability to predation, disease transmission, and injury, as well as reducing her life expectancy (Chapman, Arnqvist, Bangham, & Rowe, 2003). Studies of sexually antagonistic coevolution show that males in many species have evolved tactics, detrimental to female interests, which function to overcome female reluctance to copulate. In human females also, mating brings risks of unwanted pregnancy, infection (sexually transmitted diseases pass more easily from male to female than the reverse; Devincenzi et al., 1992), and coercive male violence. One in six women is raped during her lifetime in the United States. The more partners a woman has, the greater are the chances that one of them will turn out to be sexually aggressive (Franklin, 2010), which has adverse consequences for a victim's fitness as well as being inherently traumatic (McKibbin, Shackelford, Goetz, & Starratt, 2008). Women are acutely sensitive to this threat: Over half of women said they would fear being harmed if they were left alone with someone they had just met in a bar, compared to fewer than 10% of men (Herold & Mewhinney, 1993). Furthermore, women experience greater disgust than men at the thought of "potentially fitness-reducing" sexual behaviors such as having sex with a stranger (Tybur, Lieberman, & Griskevicius, 2009). This suggests that, in order for a woman to enter a sexual relationship, a certain degree of fear or aversion must be overcome.

We suggest that the establishment of an intimate relationship entails a partner-specific reduction in a woman's fearfulness (Campbell, 2008b, 2010; Cross et al., 2011). Oxytocin reduces fear (Baumgartner, Heinrichs, Volanthen, Fischbacher, & Fehr, 2008). By reducing the normal apprehension associated with stranger interactions, it also enhances trusting behavior whether it be the transfer of money without guarantee of return (Kosfeld, Heinrichs, Zak, Fischbacher, & Fehr, 2005) or the sharing of confidential information about sexual activities (Mikolajczak, Pinon, Lane, de Timary, & Luminet, 2010). This decrease in fear and enhancement of trust early in a relationship may set the stage for sexual intercourse, which, like parturition in which oxytocin is also implicated, constitutes an intimate and potentially painful breach of a woman's bodily integrity. In rodents, for example, estrous females are typically wary of a strange male and the release of oxytocin facilitates lordosis (Debiec, 2007; Pedersen & Boccia, 2006). In humans, oxytocin is also released during copulation and orgasm (Carmichael et al., 1987): Oxytocin induces central dopamine release, and their coaction appears to be critical for partner preference in monogamous species.

The oxytocin-mediated reduction in fear may be responsible not only for the trust and intimacy of the pair bond relationship but—paradoxically—for women's greater aggression within it. A study by Ditzen and colleagues (2009) showed that administering a dose of oxytocin to couples prior to a discussion about a topic that caused conflict for them reduced their levels of the hormone cortisol, which is released as part of the body's stress response. Furthermore, this effect was slightly more pronounced in women than in men. Given that stress responses are negatively correlated with aggression in women (Verona & Kilmer, 2007), this suggests that oxytocin might facilitate women's aggression toward their partners.

Summary and Conclusions

Over time and nations, men exceed women in the frequency and level of their aggression, and the magnitude of this sex difference increases in line with the dangerousness of the act. Ultimate evolutionary explanations rest on sex differences in parental investment, which drive up male-male competition for dominance and its associated mating opportunities and drive down female aggression as a result of the importance of maternal care for offspring. Candidate psychological mediators include diminished anger or increased fear in women relative to men. Sex differences are not apparent in anger but are consistent and marked in fear. In addition to explaining sex differences in aggression, differences in fear underlie men's greater risk taking and women's greater vulnerability to anxiety and depression. Monogamy brings with it two-way sexual selection, and women's competition for long-term mates is generally intersexual and indirect, thus avoiding the dangers of intrasexual combat. However, in ecological niches where well-resourced men are scarce, competition between young women can intensify to direct attacks, although these events are rarer and less frequently lethal than those between young men. The usual sex difference in aggression is eliminated (or reversed) in intimate partner aggression. We propose that fear reduction and trust enhancement are important to women entering sexual relationships and that oxytocin, a hormone that is up-regulated by estrogen, may underlie both women's fear reduction and consequently their greater readiness to express aggression in this context.

Future Directions
Sex Differences in Fear

We have argued that young men's greater aggression is attributable to their lower levels of fear, while Daly and Wilson have emphasized their greater "taste for risk." Sensation seeking is a paradigm case of risk taking, and Zuckerman and Kuhlman (2000) have argued that it arises from a hyperactive dopamine system that mediates reward and strong appetitive motivation. This sensitivity to reward can be further augmented by an underfunctioning serotonin system, which is sensitive to punishment and underlies inhibition and withdrawal. Thus, the balance between the two systems determines risk taking. When we move into the area of aggression, which Wilson and Daly (1985) argue to be a specific form of risk taking, the balance is between the emotions of anger (an appetitive motivation) and fear (an inhibitory force). Here the weight of available evidence suggests that men and women do not differ in anger but differ markedly in fear. Further research focusing directly on the role of these two emotions in determining aggressive behavior is important, as is the balance between dopaminergic and serotonin systems. Neuroimaging technologies are important tools in addressing this issue, especially positron emission tomography, which can track neurotransmitter systems. They may also shed light on our ancillary proposal that men's apparent "appetite" for risk results from their higher threshold for experiencing fear. Men's lower fear may cause them to experience appetitive "excitement" in risky situations that would be aversively "frightening" to women. If the relationship between stimulation and pleasure in men is right-shifted relative to women, the result would be an active desire for risky activities. Correspondingly, at the other end of the continuum, we might expect women to be more tolerant of predictable or repetitive activities that men would find aversive.

Maternal and Partner Aggression

Maternal and partner-directed aggression offer unique insights for understanding women's aggression. Any comprehensive theory must be able to explain circumstances that heighten the expression of aggression by women, as well as their more usual desistance from it. Maternal aggression, although widely studied in nonhuman animals, presents serious ethical problems for research. Asking mothers to even contemplate a threat to their newborn is not only emotionally upsetting in the short term but carries the risk of longer term sensitization. We have suggested that partner-directed aggression may be facilitated by the reduction in fear that accompanies and permits sexual intimacy. Copulation and parturition are acts that at an evolutionary level are vital to continuance of the germ line. Yet for a woman these acts, which breech her body's physical boundary, have the potential to be painful, damaging, and even life threatening. The physiological and psychological trauma of rape is evident, and although childbirth may be a natural event, for any given women it can be pathological (Konner, 2010). Oxytocin, whose peripheral effects are associated with copulation and parturition, may function centrally to reduce fear and permit intimacy.

The corollary of the positive bonding mediated by oxytocin is that its anxiolytic effects may disinhibit maternal and partner-directed aggression. The rapid pace of research on neuropeptides may soon shed light on this possibility.

Culture

Although we have suggested that oxytocin underlies women's fear reduction in relation to their partners, culture also appears to play an important role in determining women's levels of intimate partner aggression. The relative disinhibition of women's aggression toward intimate partners may be specific to highly industrialized Western nations. Norms in the West—particularly in recent decades—have strongly proscribed men's aggression against their partners. This has accompanied greater equality for women. Cross culturally, women's victimization by their partners is inversely correlated with gender equality and positively correlated with sexist attitudes and approval of wife beating (Archer, 2006). This suggests that in patriarchal societies where a men's use of physical aggression toward partners is condoned, women's aggression may be constrained—to a greater extent than in the West—by a realistic fear of retaliation. Evolutionary psychologists tackling the dynamics of cultural transmission will, we hope, have much to say about the genesis and proliferation of normative beliefs about the nature, rights and responsibilities of the two sexes.

References

Archer, J. (2000). Sex differences in aggression between heterosexual partners: A meta-analytic review. *Psychological Bulletin, 126*, 651–680.

Archer, J. (2002). Sex differences in physically aggressive acts between heterosexual partners: A meta-analytic review. *Aggression and Violent Behavior, 7*, 313–351.

Archer, J. (2004). Sex differences in aggression in real world settings: A meta-analytic review. *Review of General Psychology, 8*, 291–322.

Archer, J. (2006). Cross-cultural differences in physical aggression between partners: A social role analysis. *Personality and Social Psychology Review, 10*, 133–153.

Archer, J. (2009). Does sexual selection explain human sex differences in aggression? *Behavioural and Brain Sciences, 32*, 249–311.

Arnqvist, G., & Rowe, L. (2005) *Sexual conflict*. Princeton, NJ: Princeton University Press.

Barash, D. P. (1981). *Whisperings within: Evolution and the origin of human nature*. London: Penguin.

Bateman, A. J. (1948). Intrasexual selection in *Drosophila*. *Heredity, 2*, 349–368.

Baumeister, R. F., & Twenge, J. M. (2002). Cultural suppression of female sexuality. *Review of General Psychology, 6*, 166–203.

Baumgartner, T., Heinrichs, M., Volanthen, A., Fischbacher, U., & Fehr, E. (2008). Oxytocin shapes the neural circuitry of trust and trust adaptation in humans. *Neuron, 58*, 639–650.

Bjorkqvist, K., Lagerspetz, K., & Kaukiainen, A. (1992). Do girls manipulate and boys fight? Developmental trends in regard to direct and indirect aggression. *Aggressive Behavior, 18*, 117–127.

Bosch, O. J., Kromer, S. A., Brunton, P., & Neumann, I. D. (2004). Release of oxytocin in the hypothalamic paraventricular nucleus but not central amygdala or lateral septum in lactating residents and virgin intruders. *Neuroscience, 124*, 439–448.

Bosch, O. J., Meddle, S. L., Beiderbeck, D. I., Douglas, A. J., & Neumann, I. D. (2005). Brain oxytocin correlates with maternal aggression: Link to anxiety. *Journal of Neuroscience, 25*, 6807–6815.

Brebner, J. (2003). Gender and emotions. *Personality and Individual Differences, 34*, 387–394.

Brody, L. R., & Hall, J. A. (1993). Gender and emotion. In M. Lewis & J. M. Haviland (Eds.), *Handbook of emotions* (pp. 447–460). New York: The Guildford Press.

Brown, G. A. (2004). Gender as a factor in the response of the law-enforcement system to violence against partners. *Sexuality and Culture, 8*, 3–139.

Brown, L. M. (1998). *Raising their voices: The politics of girls' anger*. Cambridge, MA: Harvard University Press.

Burbank, V. (1987). Female aggression in cross-cultural perspective. *Behavioral Science Research, 21*, 70–100.

Bureau of Justice Statistics. (1999). *Special report: Women offenders*. Retrieved January 2012, from http://bjs.ojp.usdoj.gov/index.cfm?ty=pbdetail&iid=568

Buss, D. M. (1988a). The evolution of human intrasexual competition: Tactics of mate attraction. *Journal of Personality and Social Psychology, 54*, 616–628.

Buss, D. M. (1988b) From vigilance to violence: Tactics of mate retention in American undergraduates. *Ethology and Sociobiology, 9*, 291–317.

Buss, D. M., & Dedden, L. A. (1990). Derogation of competitors. *Journal of Personal and Social Relationships, 7*, 395–422.

Buss, D. M., Larsen, R. J., Westen, D., & Semmelroth, J. (1992). Sex differences in jealousy: Evolution, physiology, and psychology. *Psychological Science, 3*, 251–255.

Buss, D. M., & Schmitt, D. (1993). Sexual strategies theory: An evolutionary perspective on human mating. *Psychological Review, 100*, 204–232.

Byrnes, J. P., Miller, D. C., & Schafer, W. D. (1999). Gender differences in risk taking: A meta-analysis. *Psychological Bulletin, 125*, 367–383.

Campbell, A. (1982). Female aggression. In P. Marsh & A. Campbell (Eds.), *Aggression and violence* (pp. 137–150). Oxford, England: Blackwell.

Campbell, A. (1984). *The girls in the gang*. Oxford, England: Blackwell.

Campbell, A. (1986). Self-report of fighting by females. *British Journal of Criminology, 26*, 28–46.

Campbell, A. (1995). A few good men: Evolutionary psychology and female adolescent aggression. *Ethology and Sociobiology, 16*, 99–123.

Campbell, A. (2006). Sex differences in direct aggression: What are the psychological mediators? *Aggression and Violent Behavior, 11*, 237–264.

Campbell, A. (2008a). The morning after the night before: Affective reactions to one night stands among mated and unmated women and men. *Human Nature, 19*, 157–173.

Campbell, A. (2008b). Attachment, aggression and affiliation: The role of oxytocin in female social behaviour. *Biological Psychology, 77*, 1–10.

Campbell, A. (2010). Oxytocin and human social behavior. *Personality and Social Psychology Review, 14*, 281–295.

Campbell, A. (2011). Ladies, choose your weapons. *The Evolutionary Review, 2*, 106–112. .

Campbell, A., & Muncer, S. (2009). Can "risky" impulsivity explain sex differences in aggression? *Personality and Individual Differences, 47*, 402–406.

Carmichael, M. S., Humbert, R., Dixen, J., Palmisano, G., Greenleaf, W., & Davidson, J. M. (1987). Plasma oxytocin increases in the human sexual response. *Journal of Clinical Endocrinology and Metabolism, 64*, 27–31.

Carver, C. S. (2005). Impulse and constraint: Perspectives from personality psychology, convergence with theory in other areas and potential for integration. *Personality and Social Psychology Review, 9*, 312–333.

Carver, C. S., & Harmon-Jones, E. (2009). Anger is an approach-related affect: Evidence and implications. *Psychological Bulletin, 135*, 183–204.

Cashdan, E. (1998). Are men more competitive than women? *British Journal of Social Psychology, 37*, 213–229.

Chapais, B. (1992) The role of alliances in social inheritance of rank among female primates. In A. Harcourt & F. B. M. de Waal (Eds.), *Coalitions and alliances in humans and other animals*. Oxford, England: Oxford University Press.

Chapman, T., Arnqvist, G., Bangham, J., & Rowe, L. (2003). Sexual conflict. *Trends in Ecology and Evolution, 18*, 41–47.

Chiodera, P., Salvarani, C., Bacchimodena, A., Spallanzani, R., Cigarini, C., Alboni, A., et al. (1991). Relationship between plasma profiles of oxytocin and adrenocorticotropic hormone during suckling or breast stimulation in women. *Hormone Research, 35*, 119–123.

Clutton-Brock, T. H. (1991). *The evolution of parental care*. Princeton, NJ: Princeton University Press.

Consiglio, A. R., & Lucion, A. B. (1996). Lesion of hypothalamic paraventricular nucleus and maternal aggressive behavior in female rats. *Physiology and Behavior, 59*, 591–596.

Costa, P. T., Jr., Terracciano, A., & McCrae, R. R. (2001). Gender differences in personality traits across cultures: Robust and surprising findings. *Journal of Personality and Social Psychology, 81*, 322–331.

Cote, S., Tremblay, R. E., Nagin, D., Zoccolillo, M., & Vitaro, F. (2002). The development of impulsivity, fearfulness and helpfulness during childhood: Patterns of consistency and change in the trajectories of boys and girls. *Journal of Child Psychology and Psychiatry and Allied Disciplines, 43*, 609–618.

Crick, N. R., & Grotpeter, J. K. (1995). Relational aggression, gender and social-psychological adjustment. *Child Development, 66*, 710–722.

Cross, C. P., Copping, L., & Campbell, A. (2011). Sex differences in impulsivity: A meta-analysis. *Psychological Bulletin, 137*, 97–130.

Cross, C. P., Tee, W., & Campbell, A. (2011). Symmetry in intimate aggression: An effect of intimacy or target sex? *Aggressive Behaviour, 37*, 268–277.

Daly, M., & Wilson, M. (1988). *Homicide.* New York: Aldine de Gruyter.

Daly, M., Wilson, M., & Weghorst, S. J. (1982). Male sexual jealousy. *Ethology and Sociobiology, 3,* 11–27.

Damasio, A. R. (1994). *Descartes' error: Emotion, reason and the human brain.* New York: Putnam.

Darwin, C. (1998). *The descent of man.* New York: Prometheus Books. (Original work published 1871).

Davidovic, A., Bell, K., Ferguson, C., Gorski, E., & Campbell, A. (2011). Impelling and inhibitory forces in aggression: Sex-of-target and relationship effects. *Journal of Interpersonal Violence, 26,* 3098–3126.

Davidson, R. J. (2000). Affective style, psychopathology, and resilience: Brain mechanisms and plasticity. *American Psychologist, 55,* 1196–1214.

De Dreu, C. K. W., Greer, L. L., Handgraaf, M. J. J., Shalvi, S., Van Kleef, G.A., Baas, M. et al. (2010). The neuropeptide oxytocin regulates parochial altruism in intergroup conflict among humans. *Science, 328,* 1408–1411.

Debiec, J., (2005). Peptides of love and fear: Vasopressin and oxytocin modulate the integration of information in the amygdala. *BioEssays 27,* 869–873.

Debiec, J. (2007). From affiliative behaviors to romantic feelings: A role of nanopeptides. *Febs Letters, 581,* 2580–2586.

Derrybery, D., & Reed, M. A. (1994). Temperament and attention: Orienting toward and away from positive and negative signals. *Journal of Personality and Social Psychology, 66,* 1128–1139.

Derryberry, D., & Rothbart, M. K. (1997). Reactive and effortful processes in the organization of temperament. *Development and Psychopathology, 9,* 633–652.

DeSteno, D., Bartlett, M. Y., Braverman, J., & Salovey, P. (2002). Sex differences in jealousy: Evolutionary mechanism or artifact of measurement? *Journal of Personality and Social Psychology, 83,* 1103–1116.

Devincenzi, I., Ancellepark, R. A., Brunet, J. B., Costigliola, P., Ricchi, E., Chiodo, F., et al. (1992). Comparison of female to male and male to female transmission of HIV in 563 stable couples. *British Medical Journal, 304,* 809–813.

Dijkstra, P., & Buunk, B. P. (2001). Sex differences in the jealousy-evoking nature of a rival's body build. *Evolution and Human Behavior, 22,* 335–341.

Ditzen, B., Schaer, M., Gabriel, B., Bodenmann, G., Ehlert, U., & Heinrichs, M. (2009). Intranasal oxytocin increases positive communication and reduces cortisol levels during couple conflict. *Biological Psychiatry, 65,* 728–731.

Dobash, R. E., & Dobash, R. P. (1979). *Violence against wives: A case against the patriarchy.* New York: Free Press.

Dobash, R. P., Dobash, R. E., Wilson, M., & Daly, M. (1992). The myth of sexual symmetry in marital violence. *Social Problems, 39,* 71–91.

Domes, G., Heinrichs, M., Michel, A., Berger, C., & Herpetz, S. C. (2007). Oxytocin improves "mind reading" in humans. *Biological Psychiatry, 61,* 731–733.

Duncan, N. (1999). *Sexual bullying: Gender conflict and pupil culture in secondary schools.* London: Routledge.

Edlund, J.E., & Sagarin, B.J. (2009). Sex differences in jealousy: Misinterpretation of nonsignificant results as refuting the theory. *Personal Relationships, 16,* 67–78.

Else-Quest, N. M., Hyde, J. S., Goldsmith, H. H., & Van Hulle, C. A. (2006). Gender differences in temperament: A meta-analysis. *Psychological Bulletin, 132,* 33–72.

Etcoff, N. (1999). *Survival of the prettiest.* London: Little, Brown and Company.

Feld, S. L., & Felson, R. B. (2008). Gender norms and retaliatory violence against spouses and acquaintances. *Journal of Family Issues, 29*(5), 692–703.

Feldman, R., Weller, A., Zagoory-Sharon, O., & Levine, A. (2007). Neuroendocrinological foundation of human affiliation: Plasma oxytocin levels across pregnancy and the postpartum period predict mother–infant bonding. *Psychological Science, 18,* 965–970.

Felson, R. B. (2008). The legal consequences of intimate partner violence for men and women. *Children and Youth Services Review, 30*(6), 639–646.

Felson, R. B., & Feld, S. L. (2009). When a man hits a woman: Moral evaluations and reporting violence to the police. *Aggressive Behavior, 35,* 477–488.

Felson, R. B., & Outlaw, M. C. (2007). The control motive and marital violence. *Violence and Victims, 22,* 387–407.

Felson, R. B., & Pare, P. P. (2007). Does the criminal justice system treat domestic violence and sexual assault offenders leniently? *Justice Quarterly, 24,* 435–459.

Ferris, C. F., Foote, K. B., Meltser, H. M., Plenby, M. G., Smith, K. L., & Insel, T. R. (1992). Oxytocin in the amygdala facilitates maternal aggression. *Annals of the New York Academy of Sciences, 652,* 456–457.

Fiebert, M. S., & Gonzalez, D. M. (1997). College women who initiate assaults on their male partners and the reasons offered for such behavior. *Psychological Reports, 80,* 583–590.

Fischer, A. H. (1993). Sex differences in emotionality: Fact or stereotype? *Feminism and Psychology, 3,* 303–318.

Fischer, A. H., & Manstead, A. S. R. (2000). Gender and emotions in different cultures. In A. H. Fischer (Ed.), *Gender and emotion: Social psychological perspectives* (pp. 71– 94). Cambridge, England: Cambridge University Press.

Follingstad, D. R., Wright, S., Lloyd, S., & Sebastian, J. A. (1991). Sex differences in motivations and effects in dating violence. *Family Relations, 40,* 51–57.

Forgas, J. P. (1995). Mood and judgment: The affect infusion model (AIM). *Psychological Bulletin, 117,* 39–66.

Fowles, D. C. (1988). Psychophysiology and psychopathology: A motivational approach. *Psychophysiology, 25,* 373–391.

Franklin, C. A. (2010). Physically forced, alcohol-induced, and verbally coerced sexual victimization: Assessing risk factors among university women. *Journal of Criminal Justice, 38,* 149–159.

Gartstein, M. A., & Rothbart, M. K. (2003). Studying infant temperament via the Revised Infant Behavior Questionnaire. *Infant Behavior and Development, 26,* 64–86.

George, M. J. (1999). A victimization survey of female-perpetrated assaults in the United Kingdom. *Aggressive Behavior, 25,* 67–79.

Graham-Kevan, N., & Archer, J. (2009). Control tactics and partner violence in heterosexual relationships. *Evolution and Human Behavior, 30,* 445–452.

Gray, J. A., & McNaughton, N. (2000). *The neuropsychology of anxiety: An enquiry into the functions of the septo-hippocampal system.*. Oxford, England: Oxford University Press.

Greenfeld, L. A., & Snell, T. L. (1999). *Bureau of Justice Statistics Special Report: Women offenders.* Washington, DC: US Department of Justice.

Gullone, E. (2000). The development of normal fear: A century of research. *Clinical Psychology Review, 20,* 429–451.

Hahn-Holbrook, J., Holt-Lunstead, J., & Holbrook, C. (2009, May). *New evidence for lactation aggression in humans*. Paper presented at the annual conference of the Human Behavior and Evolution Society, Fullerton, CA.

Hall, J. A., Carter, J. D., & Horgan, T. G. (2000). Gender differences in nonverbal communication of emotion. In A. H. Fischer (Ed.), *Gender and emotion: Social psychological perspectives* (pp. 97–117). Cambridge, England: Cambridge University Press.

Hall, K. (2002) *Who do men and women gossip about and what is discussed about them?* Unpublished Ph.D. dissertation, Durham University, Durham, England.

Hall, P., & Innes, J. (2010). Violent and sexual crime. In J. Flatley, C. Kershaw, K. Smith, R. Chaplin, & D. Moon (Eds.), *Crime in England and Wales 2009/10* Home Office Statistical Bulletin 12/10 (pp. 43–72). London: Home Office.

Hamilton, W. D. (1966). The moulding of senescence by natural selection. *Journal of Theoretical Biology, 12*, 12–45.

Harmon-Jones, E. (2003). Anger and the behavioural approach system. *Personality and Individual Differences, 35*, 995–1005.

Harned, M. S. (2001). Abused women or abused men? An examination of the context and outcomes of dating violence. *Violence and Victims, 16*, 269–285.

Harris, C. R. (2003). A review of sex differences in sexual jealousy, including self-report data, psychophysiological responses, interpersonal violence, and morbid jealousy. *Personality and Social Psychology Review, 7*, 102–128.

Harris, C.R. (2005). Male and female jealousy, still more similar than different: Reply to Sagarin (2005). *Personality and Social Psychology Review, 9*, 76–86.

Hausfater, G. (1975) Dominance and reproduction in baboons (Papio cynocephalus). *Contributions to Primatology, 7*, 1–150.

Hawkes, K., O'Connell, J. F., Blurton-Jones, N. G., Alvarez, H., & Charnov, E. L. (1998). Grandmothering, menopause, and the evolution of human life histories. *Proceedings of the National Academy of Sciences USA, 95*, 1336–1339.

Hermans, E. J., Putman, P., Baas, J. M., Koppeschaar, H. P., & van Honk, J. (2006). A single administration of testosterone reduces fear-potentiated startle in humans. *Biological Psychiatry, 59*, 872–874.

Herold, E. S., & Mewhinney, D. M. K. (1993). Gender differences in casual sex and aids prevention: A survey of dating bars. *Journal of Sex Research, 30*, 36–42.

Hersch, J. (1997). Smoking, seat belts and other risky consumer decisions: Differences by gender and race. *Managerial and Decision Economics, 11*, 241–256.

Hettrich, E. L., & O'Leary, K. D. (2007). Females' reasons for their physical aggression in dating relationships. *Journal of Interpersonal Violence, 22*, 1131–1143.

Hrdy, S.B. (1999) *Mother nature*. London: Chatto and Windus.

Hrdy, S. B. (2009). *Mothers and others*. Cambridge, MA: Harvard University Press.

Huber, D., Veinante, P., & Stoop, R. (2005). Vasopressin and oxytocin excite distinct neuronal populations in the central amygdala. *Science, 308*, 245–248.

Isbell, L. A., & Young, T. P. (2002). Ecological models of female social relationships in primates: Similarities, disparities and some directions for future clarity. *Behaviour, 139*, 177–202.

Jennions, M. D., & Petrie, M. (2000). Why do females mate multiply? A review of the genetic benefits. *Biological Review, 75*, 21–64.

Joe Laidler, K., & Hunt, G. (2001). Accomplishing femininity among the girls in the gang. *British Journal of Criminology, 41*, 656–678.

Jokela, M., Rotkirch, A., Rickard, I. J., Pettav, J., & Lummaa, V. (2010). Serial monogamy increases reproductive success in men but not in women. *Behavioral Ecology, 21*, 906–912.

Kenrick, D. T., & Keefe, R. C. (1992). Age preferences in mates reflect sex differences in human reproductive strategies. *Behavioral and Brain Sciences, 15*, 75–133.

Knight, G. P., Fabes, R. A., & Higgins, D. A. (1996). Concerns about drawing causal inferences from meta-analyses: An example in the study of gender differences in aggression. *Psychological Bulletin, 119*, 410–421.

Knight, G. P., Guthrie, I. L., Page, M. C., & Fabes, R. A. (2002). Emotional arousal and gender differences in aggression: A meta-analysis. *Aggressive Behaviour, 28*, 366–393.

Kokko, H., & Jennions, M. D. (2008). Parental investment, sexual selection and sex ratios. *Journal of Evolutionary Biology, 21*, 919–948.

Konner, M. (2010). *The evolution of childhood: Relationships, emotion, mind*. Cambridge, MA: Belknap Press.

Kosfeld, M., Heinrichs, M., Zak, P. J., Fischbacher, U., & Fehr, E.(2005). Oxytocin increases trust in humans. *Nature, 435*, 673–676.

Kring, A. M. (2000). Gender and anger. In A. H. Fischer (Ed.), *Gender and emotion: Social psychological perspectives* (pp. 211–231). Cambridge, England: Cambridge University Press.

Lang, P. J., Bradley, M. M., & Cuthbert, B. N. (1992). A motivational analysis of emotion: Reflex–cortex connections. *Psychological Science, 3*, 44–49.

Langhinrichsen-Rohling, J., Neidig, P., & Thorn, G. (1995). Violent marriages: Gender differences in levels of current violence and past abuse. *Journal of Family Violence, 10*, 159–176.

LeDoux, J. E. (1996). *The emotional brain*. New York: Simon and Schuster.

Lees, S. (1993). *Sugar and spice: Sexuality and adolescent girls*. London: Penguin

Lerner, J. S., & Keltner, D. (2000). Beyond valence: Toward a model of emotion-specific influences on judgement and choice. *Cognition and Emotion, 14*, 473–493.

Lerner, J. S., & Keltner, D. (2001). Fear, anger and risk. *Journal of Personality and Social Psychology, 81*, 146–159.

Levine, A., Zagoory-Sharon, O., Feldman, R., & Weller, A. (2007). Oxytocin during pregnancy and early postpartum: Individual patterns and maternal–fetal attachment. *Peptides, 28*, 1162–1169.

Lisher, D. A., Nguyen, S., Stocks, E. L., & Zilmer, E. J. (2008). Are sexual and emotional infidelity equally upsetting to men and women? Making sense of forced-choice responses. *Evolutionary Psychology, 6*, 667–675.

Loewenstein, G. F., Weber, E. U., Hsee, C. K., & Welch, N. (2001). Risk as feelings. *Psychological Bulletin, 127*, 267–286.

Madden, T. E., Feldman Barrett, L., & Pietromonaco, P. R. (2000). Sex differences in anxiety and depression. In A. H. Fischer (Ed.), *Gender and emotion: Social psychological perspectives* (pp. 277– 300). Cambridge, England: Cambridge University Press.

Marsh, P., & Paton, R. (1986). Gender, social class and conceptual schemas of aggression. In A. Campbell & J. Gibbs (Eds.),

Violent transactions: The limits of personality (pp. 59–85). Oxford, England: Blackwell.

Matthiesen, A.-S., Ransio-Arvidson, A.-B., Nissen, E., & Uvnas-Moberg, K. (2001). Postpartum maternal oxytocin release by newborns: Effects of infant hand massage and suckling. *Birth*, 28, 13–19.

McKibbin, W. F., Shackelford, T. K., Goetz, A. T., & Starratt, V. G. (2008). Why do men rape? An evolutionary psychological perspective. *Review of General Psychology*, 12, 86–97.

McManis, M. H., Bradley, M. M., Berg, W. K., Cuthbert, B. N., & Lang, P. J. (2001). Emotional reactions in children: Verbal, physiological and behavioural responses to affective pictures. *Psychophysiology*, 38, 222–231.

Mikolajczak, M., Pinon, N., Lane, A., de Timary, P., & Luminet, O. (2010).Oxytocin not only increases trust when money is at stake, but also when confidential information is in the balance. *Biological Psychology*, 85, 182–184

Mirowsky, J., & Ross, C. E. (1995). Sex differences in distress: Real or artifact? *American Sociological Review*, 60, 449–468.

Murdock, G. P. (1967). *Ethnographic atlas*. Pittsburgh, PA: University of Pittsburgh Press.

Murphy, F. C., Nimmo-Smith, I., & Lawrence, A. D. (2003). Functional neuroanatomy of emotion: A meta-analysis. *Cognitive, Affective, and Behavioral Neuroscience*, 3, 207–233.

Ness, C. D. (2004). Why girls fight: Female youth violence in the inner city. *Annals of the American Academy of Political and Social Science*, 595, 32–48.

Nevo, O., Nevo, B., & Derech-Zehavi, A. (1993). The development of the Tendency to Gossip Questionnaire: Construct and concurrent validity for a sample of Israeli college students. *Educational and Psychological Measurement*, 53, 973–981.

O'Connell, J. F., Hawkes, K., & Blurton-Jones, N. G. (1999). Grandmothering and the evolution of *Homo erectus*. *Journal of Human Evolution*, 36,461–485.

Oliver, M. B., & Hyde, J. S. (1993). Gender differences in sexuality: A meta-analysis. *Psychological Bulletin*, 114, 29–51.

Panksepp, J. (1998). *Affective neuroscience: The foundations of human and animal emotions*. Oxford, England: Oxford University Press.

Parker, G. A. (1974). Assessment strategy and the evolution of fighting behaviour. *Journal of Theoretical Biology*, 47, 223–243.

Pavard, S., Gagnon, A., Desjardins, B., & Heyer, E. (2005). Mother's death and child survival: The case of early Quebec. *Journal of Biosocial Science*, 37, 209-227.

Pedersen, C. A., & Boccia, M. L. (2006). Vasopressin interactions with oxytocin in the control of female sexual behavior. *Neuroscience*, 139, 843–851.

Penn, D. J., & Smith, K. R. (2007). Differential fitness costs of reproduction between the sexes. *Proceedings of the National Academy of Sciences USA*, 104, 553–558.

Pusey, A., Williams, J., & Goodall, J. (1997). The influence of dominance rank on the reproductive success of female chimpanzees. *Science*, 277, 828–831.

Putnam, S. P., & Stifter, C. A. (2005). Behavioral approach–inhibition in toddlers: Prediction from infancy, positive and negative affective components, and relations with behavior problems. *Child Development*, 76, 212–226.

Robertson, K., & Murachver, T. (2007). It takes two to tangle: Gender symmetry in intimate partner violence. *Basic and Applied Social Psychology*, 29, 109–118.

Rothbart, M. K., & Bates, J. E. (2006). Temperament. In W. Damon, R. Lerner, & N. Eisenberg (Eds.), *Handbook of child psychology. Vol. 3: Social, emotional, and personality development* (6th ed., pp. 99–166). New York: Wiley.

Rothbart, M. K., Derryberry, D., & Hershey, K. L. (2000). Stability of temperament in childhood: Laboratory infant assessment to parent report at 7 years. In V. J. Molfese & D. L. Molfese (Eds.), *Temperament and personality across the life span* (pp. 85–119). Mahwah, NJ: Erlbaum.

Sagarin, B.J. (2005). Reconsidering evolved sex differences in jealousy: Comment on Harris (2003). *Personality and Social Psychology Review*, 9, 62–75.

Schmitt, D. P. (2005). Sociosexuality from Argentina to Zimbabwe: A 48-nation study of sex, culture, and strategies of human mating. *Behavioral and Brain Sciences*, 28, 247–311.

Schuster, I. (1985). Female aggression and resource scarcity: A cross-cultural perspective. In M. Haug, D. Benton, P. Brain, B. Oliver, & J. Mos (Eds.), *The aggressive female* (pp. 185–208). Amsterdam: CIP-Gegevens Koninklijke Bibioteheek.

Sear, R., & Mace, R. (2008). Who keeps children alive? A review of the effects of kin on child survival. *Evolution and Human Behavior*, 29, 1–18

Sear, R., Steele, F., McGregor, I. A., & Mace, R. (2002) The effects of kin on child mortality in rural Gambia. *Demography* 39: 43–63.

Simmons, L. W. (2005). The evolution of polyandry: Sperm competition, sperm selection and offspring viability. *Annual Review of Ecology, Evolution and Systematics*, 36, 125–146.

Simmons, R. (2002). *Odd girl out: The hidden culture of aggression in girls*. London: Harcourt.

Simon, R. W., & Nath, L. E. (2004). Gender and emotion in the United States: Do men and women differ in self-reports of feelings and expressive behavior? *American Journal of Sociology*, 109, 1137–1176.

Smith, E. L., & Farole, D. J. (2009). *Profile of intimate partner violence cases in large urban counties*. Bureau of Justice Statistics Special Report NCJ 228193. Washington, DC: US Department of Justice.

Smits, D. J. M., & Kuppens, P. (2005). The relations between anger, coping with anger, and aggression, and the BIS/BAS system. *Personality and Individual Differences*, 39, 783–793.

Smuts, B. B. (1987) Gender, aggression and influence. In B. B. Smuts, D. L. Cheney, R. M. Seyfarth, R. W. Wrangham, & T. T. Struhsaker (Eds.), *Primate societies*. Chicago: University of Chicago Press.

Sorenson, S. B., & Taylor, C. A. (2005). Female aggression toward male intimate partners: An examination of social norms in a community-based sample. *Psychology of Women Quarterly*, 29, 78–96.

Sterck, E. H. M., Watts, D. P., & van Schaik, C. P. (1997). The evolution of female social relationships in nonhuman primates. *Behavioral Ecology and Sociobiology*, 41, 291–309.

Straus, M. A., & Ramirez, I. L. (2007). Gender symmetry in prevalence, severity, and chronicity of physical aggression against dating partners by university students in Mexico and USA. *Aggressive Behavior*, 33, 281–290.

Strüber, D., Luck, M., & Roth, G. (2008). Sex, aggression and impulse control: An integrative account. *Neurocase*, 14, 93–121.

Takagi, T., Tanizawa, O., Otsuki, Y., Haruta, M., & Yamaji, K. (1985). Oxytocin in the cerebrospinal fluid and plasma of pregnant and non-pregnant subjects. *Hormone and Metabolism Research, 17*, 308–310.

Taylor, S. P., & Epstein, S. (1967). Aggression as a function of interaction of sex of aggressor and sex of victim. *Journal of Personality, 35*, 474–486.

Thornton, A. J. V., Graham-Kevan, N., & Archer, J. (2010). Adaptive and maladaptive personality traits as predictors of violent and nonviolent offending behavior in men and women. *Aggressive Behavior, 36*, 177–186.

Tooke, W., & Camire, L. (1991). Patterns of deception in intersexual and intrasexual mating strategies. *Ethology and Sociobiology, 12*, 345–364.

Tremblay, R. E., & Nagin, D. S. (2005). The developmental origins of physical aggression in humans. In R. E. Tremblay, W. W. Hartup, & J. Archer (Eds.), *Developmental origins of aggression* (pp. 83–106). New York: The Guildford Press.

Trivers, R. L. (1972). Parental investment and sexual selection. In B. Campbell (Ed.), *Sexual selection and the descent of man 1871–1971* (pp. 136–179). Chicago: Aldine

Tybur, J. M., Lieberman, D., & Griskevicius, V. (2009). Microbes, mating, and morality: Individual differences in three functional domains of disgust. *Journal of Personality and Social Psychology, 97*, 103–122.

van Hoof, J.A., & van Schaik, C. P. (1992) Cooperation in competition: The ecology of primate bonds. In A. Harcourt & F.B.M. de Waal (Eds.), *Coalitions and alliances in humans and other animals*. Oxford, England: Oxford University Press.

Verona, E., & Kilmer, A. (2007). Stress exposure and affective modulation of aggressive behavior in men and women. *Journal of Abnormal Psychology, 116*, 410–421.

Walters, J. (1980) Interventions and the development of dominance relationships in female baboons. *Folia Primatologica, 34*, 61–89.

Wang, X. T. (2002). Risk as reproductive variance. *Evolution and Human Behavior, 23*, 35–57.

Watson, D., Wiese, D., Vaidya, J., & Tellegen, A. (1999). The two general activation systems of affect: Structural findings, evolutionary considerations, and psychobiological evidence. *Journal of Personality and Social Psychology, 76*, 820–838.

Whitaker, D. J., Haileyesus, T., Swahn, M., & Saltzman, L. S. (2007). Differences in frequency of violence and reported injury between relationships with reciprocal and nonreciprocal intimate partner violence. *American Journal of Public Health, 97*, 941–947.

Williams, G. C. (1996). *Adaptation and natural selection: A critique of some current evolutionary thought*. Princeton, NJ: Princeton University Press.

Wilson, M., & Daly, M. (1985) Competitiveness, risk-taking and violence: The young male syndrome. *Ethology and Sociobiology, 6*, 59–73.

Wilson, M. I., & Daly, M. (1996). Male sexual proprietariness and violence against wives. *Current Directions in Psychological Science, 5*, 2–7.

Windle, R. J., Kershaw, Y. M., Shanks, N., Wood, S. A., Lightman, S. L., & Ingram, C. D. (2004). Oxytocin attenuates stress-induced c-fos mRNA expression of forebrain regions associated with modulation of the hypothalamo–pituitary–adrenal activity. *Journal of Neuroscience, 24*, 2974–2982.

Winstok, Z. (2007). Perceptions, emotions, and behavioural decisions in conflicts that escalate to violence. *Motivation and Emotion, 31*, 125–136.

Wittig, R. M., & Boesch, C. (2003). Food competition and linear dominance hierarchy among female chimpanzees of the Tai National Park. *International Journal of Primatology, 24*, 847–867.

Young, L. J., & Wang, Z. (2004). The neurobiology of pair bonding. *Nature Neuroscience, 7*, 1048–1054.

Zuckerman, M. (1994). *Behavioral expressions and biosocial bases of sensation seeking*. New York: Cambridge University Press.

Zuckerman, M., & Kuhlman, D. M. (2000). Personality and risk-taking: Common biosocial factors. *Journal of Personality, 68*, 999–1029.

CHAPTER
13

Culture of Honor, Violence, and Homicide

Ryan P. Brown *and* Lindsey L. Osterman

Abstract

Culture promotes beliefs and values that help its constituents to address local and enduring problems. We propose that cultures that allow and encourage certain forms of violence do so in response to specific ecological problems, namely pervasive resource deprivation and unreliable law enforcement. The convergence of these problems over long periods of time, we argue, results in a social environment that requires vigilant and aggressive defense of reputation, person, and property as a means of deterrence. As an illustration of such a culture, we discuss the history of the Ulster Scots (or Scotch-Irish), who settled the southern and western United States in the 18th and 19th centuries—regions that are characterized even today as "cultures of honor." We review empirical evidence regarding behavioral patterns in these honor states, with a focus on evidence indicating that residents of these states are not more violent in general but tend to display behaviors related to the vigilant and aggressive defense of honor, at both the individual and collective levels. When such social adaptations become entrenched in a culture's schemas, scripts, and identity dynamics, they can be transmitted from one generation to the next, long after the ecological circumstances that encouraged them have dissipated.

Key Words: violence, aggression, culture of honor, lawlessness, resource deprivation

Introduction

"May you live in interesting times" is a well-known and somewhat tongue-in-cheek Chinese "curse" often invoked to acknowledge the inherent difficulties of navigating life when levels of uncertainty and complexity are high. It is probably true that people of every generation feel that this ancient curse applies to them, and that is no less true today. With the concept of "globalization" being one of the most recurrent themes of our language and our thinking, life today feels both uncertain and complicated. Alongside globalization has come a greater consciousness of and contact among different cultures, sometimes leading to enhanced levels of competition and conflict. One result of this increasing contact among different cultures has been the simultaneous awareness that cultures are more than just superficially variable. Indeed, the central struggle of the 21st century may well be the struggle to overcome cross-cultural barriers to coexistence in a world living in the shadow of weapons of mass destruction, which have substantially raised the costs of failure in this struggle.

This chapter will focus on a dimension of cross-cultural variability of particular relevance to the struggle to coexist—namely, cultural influences on aggression and violence. In a world full of jihadists and despots, this topic seems rather timely and contemporary. Even so, the approach we will take in this chapter will be one that falls back upon rather old ideas and historical issues, rather than merely contemporary ones. Specifically, we will attempt to ground our discussion of culture and violence on reasoning about selection forces that are argued to have shaped the human psyche over the history of our species, as people have struggled with the adaptive problems of survival and reproduction, problems largely involving intrasexual and, to a lesser extent, intersexual competition.

In our view, a cultural approach to violence can benefit from the insights offered by selectionist thinking, insofar as such thinking provides insights into the features of the human psyche upon which culture ultimately relies. Thus, to those who ask whether we believe that culture is evoked (i.e., predicated upon and derived from aspects of human nature that are themselves influenced by evolutionary forces) or is transmitted (i.e., passed on across generations through mechanisms of learning, imitation, and conformity), we would answer a resounding "yes." Culture is both evoked and transmitted, and recognition of this dual nature in culture will enhance our understanding of the human experience (Baumeister, Maner, & Dewall, 2006; Daly & Wilson, 1988; Gangestad, Haselton, & Buss, 2006; Konner, 2007; Tooby & Cosmides, 1992).

Our discussion of the role of culture in violence is also predicated on our definition and level of analysis of culture. Drawing upon previous theorists, we will define what we mean by "culture" as a dynamic set of beliefs, knowledge, skills, norms, meanings, and values shared by a group of people (Barkow, Cosmides, &Tooby, 1992; Cohen, 2001; Markus & Kitayama, 1991; Triandis, 1994, 2007). These shared beliefs, meanings, values, and so forth can be explicit or implicit, and they lead to commonly held schemas, scripts, and identity dynamics among those who share them. As indicated by the word "dynamic" in this definition, these elementary aspects of culture also change over time in response to ecological, technological, and social changes, even if the pace of change varies within and between groups. Although this definition of culture is somewhat generic, it allows us to think about culture at many levels, including the culture of a family; the culture of a corporation; the culture of a community; the culture of a state, province, or region; and the culture of a nation. When particular aspects of culture (e.g., beliefs about the legitimacy of governing authorities, the relative value of the individual vis-à-vis the collective, expected roles for men and women) are specified and become measureable, we can begin to investigate how these aspects of culture relate to other variables of interest, including aggression and violence, both cross-sectionally and longitudinally. To a limited extent, we might even create analogs of these elementary aspects of culture that we can then manipulate in controlled experiments to examine the causal role played by these aspects with regard to outcomes of interest.

In this chapter, we will focus our attention first on several low-level features of cultures that are associated with and seem to promote aggression and violence, with an eye toward understanding how these features relate to human solutions to adaptive problems. Our discussion of these features will coalesce on the subject of "cultures of honor," which we believe derive from the confluence of these lower level features over long periods of time. Furthermore, we will focus on data derived from US samples, supplemented where possible with data from around the world. The justification for this focus is two-fold. First, the quality of the US data is among the best in the world for testing notions related to cultures of honor (and violence), both because the United States collects such large amounts of relevant data and because social scientists have validated tools designed to assess features related to cultures of honor (most notably, a validated classification system for determining which regions reflect honor-based cultural systems and which do not) most prominently within the United States. Second, our focus on the culture of honor in the United States provides us with an opportunity to discuss both the evoked and transmitted features of culture because of certain historical dynamics related to the origination and transmission of the US culture of honor, and these dynamics are fairly well documented by cultural historians.

Basic Building Blocks of Violent Cultures

We argue that there are two prominent variables at work that can lead to cultural differences (as well as change within a culture over time) in violence: society-wide scarcity of resources, and the strength and reliability of the collective enforcement of social norms, especially those norms associated with justice and safety (often referred to as the rule of law). These two fundamental variables, we argue, lead to the formation of schemas, scripts, and identity dynamics that are the most proximal cultural precursors to aggression and violence.

Scarcity of Resources

The first major building block promoting the creation of a culture of violence is the scarcity of economic resources, or what is often referred to as economic deprivation. Sociologists interested in the social precursors to crime have long noted the role that economic deprivation seems to play in violent crime, including homicide, rape, and assault (e.g., Golden & Messner, 1987; Loftin & Parker, 1985). Indeed, when the unit of analysis is the city, state, or region, sociologists find that one of the most consistent predictors of variability in violent crime rates is poverty, the most commonly used index of economic deprivation (although median income and unemployment are also valuable indices). Well-documented racial differences in rates of violent crime in the United States have also been attributed in part to such economic factors (e.g., Sampson, 1987), although in some studies controlling for poverty does not eliminate the statistical significance of the race variable (e.g., Elliott & Ageton, 1980; Wolfgang, 1983).

The resource deprivation hypothesis of violent crime has recently been applied in a rather clever manner to understand changes in US violent crime rates over the past 40 years. Donohue and Levitt (2001, 2004) have argued that the legalization of abortion in the United States in the early 1970s (first in several states, such as New York and Alaska, and then nationally following *Roe v. Wade* in 1973) can account for as much as 50% of the drop in violent crime rates that occurred in the 1990s, a drop that has been variously attributed to factors such as community policing, declines in the crack cocaine trade, and increasingly tough sentencing by courts. Donohue and Levitt argued, however, that one important reason for the dramatic reduction in violent crime rates in the 1990s was that so many members of the demographic group that is typically responsible for such crimes in the United States (i.e., males aged 18–24 years born to poor, unwed mothers; Comanor & Phillips, 2002) were "missing" from the population starting in the early 1990s due to equally dramatic increases in abortion rates in the early 1970s. Thus, a demographic shift in the population that shrank the number of economically deprived individuals born to unwed mothers might help to account for reductions in rates of violence across the nation.

Although the evidence for this proposition is correlational, Donohue and Levitt showed that not only did the reduction in violent crime rates begin at the same time that the at-risk demographic group would have entered their teenage years, but these reductions in violence were also larger in states that exhibited the highest abortion rates and began earlier in the five states that legalized abortions prior to *Roe v. Wade*. In sum, the researchers demonstrated that a large demographic shift in a segment of the population that tends to be economically deprived can apparently result in a dramatic cultural shift in violent crime rates, offering something of a "naturalistic experiment" to support sociological contentions that resource deprivation can lead to violence.

Why might the scarcity of resources lead to increased levels of violence, rather than enhancing cooperation aimed at maximizing collective attainment of resources? One possible answer that social psychologists have offered derives from Sherif and colleagues' (1961) realistic group conflict theory. Sherif and colleagues argued that when resources are scarce, groups readily form coalitions in order to compete more effectively for those resources. Indeed, as Sherif and colleagues showed, only minimal influences are needed to facilitate the formation of competitive—even violent—coalitions under conditions of resource scarcity (such as when only one prize is available in a "friendly" sports game). Subsequent work by Tajfel and others support this contention, showing just how trivial an influence can be but still facilitate the formation of ingroup identities and intergroup hostilities (e.g., Tajfel, 1970; Tajfel, Billig, Bundy, & Flament, 1971). Thus, to a limited extent, resource scarcity does result in cooperative alliances, but these alliances seem designed to obtain and allocate scarce resources within only a limited subset of the local population—certainly not a "humanitarian" solution to the problem of scarce resources but arguably an adaptive one.

A complementary answer to the question of why scarcity of resources is often associated with increased levels of violence derives more directly from thinking about solutions to adaptive problems. Briefly, Trivers (1972) argued that in any sexually reproducing species, the sex that invests less in offspring (for the vast majority of such species, including humans, this is the male sex) exhibits greater variability in reproductive success than does the more investing, choosier sex. In other words, some members of the less investing sex enjoy high levels of reproductive success, and other members have extremely low levels of success. Because of this, the less investing sex must strive more vigorously to achieve success and avoid total failure. One consequence of this pattern, according to Trivers, is that the less investing sex tends to exhibit higher levels of aggressive, intrasexual competition and risk taking for the purposes of attaining higher social status, thus enhancing the opportunity to procure mates.

Applying this pattern to humans, it is not difficult to see how resource deprivation might lead to competition and violence, as individuals (particularly males) strive to avoid coming in last place in the competition for resources necessary for the ability to reproduce (a similar argument has been used to explain the positive association between birth order and risk taking more generally; Sulloway & Zweigenhaft, 2010). The intensity of intrasexual competition for scarce resources may become all the more intense, and ultimately violent, when both absolute deprivation (e.g., poverty) and relative deprivation (e.g., unequal distribution of economic resources) are high, and these forms of deprivation are, in fact, positively correlated. Indeed, not only do social scientists frequently find that absolute levels of resource deprivation are positively associated with societal levels of violence (such as homicide rates), but levels of social inequality in the distribution of economic resources are also sometimes found to relate to violence, controlling for absolute deprivation levels (e.g., Gurr, 1970; Henry, 2009; Walker & Smith, 2002).

The latter finding is noteworthy in part because of the strong statistical overlap between absolute and relative deprivation measures, and in part because studies examining these factors frequently focus on the United States, resulting in severe restrictions of range on both factors. In 1999, for instance, the range in income inequality (measured by the Gini index, which can vary from 0 to 1.0) across all 50 US states was only between 0.40 and 0.50, according to calculations by the US Census Bureau. A similarly narrow range of income inequality scores for US states appears 10 years earlier (from about 0.39 to about 0.48). In contrast, the United Nations Human Development Project reports that around the world—in countries where reliable data can be ascertained—the range in mean Gini scores (from 1992 to 2007) was from about 0.24 to about 0.74. Thus, investigations of the role of absolute and relative deprivation in the United States are statistically quite limited when these aspects of deprivation are examined simultaneously, simply due to restrictions in range and the typical overlap between these variables.[1]

Rule of Law

The second foundational variable leading to cultural differences in violence is pervasive lawlessness, or the absence of what is frequently called the rule of law. Lawlessness is a rather broad concept and can be conceptualized in a variety of ways, from the abstract and existential, to the concrete and behavioral. On the more existential end, Durkheim (1897) was the first social scientist to discuss the role of social cohesion and the strength of normative bonds in regulating social behavior. Although Durkheim's primary interest initially was in suicide, subsequent social control theorists have related his ideas about social cohesion and norm strength to crime and violent behavior more generally (e.g., Burgess, 1925; Kornhauser, 1978; Shaw & McKay, 1942). At a more concrete level, research on social deterrence has shown that the certainty of punishment for violent and nonviolent crimes is associated with lower crime rates, consistent with the broader notion of the importance of the rule of law within a cultural system (Averill, 1982; Colson, 1975, Daly & Wilson, 1988). In contrast, as experimental research on the "broken window effect" shows, physical displays of lawlessness within a social system can serve as signals that promote additional antisocial acts by people within that system (Keizer, Lindenberg, & Steg, 2008).

In one of the most important books on violent crime in the last quarter century, Daly and Wilson (1988) noted that the rise of the strong state coincides with dramatic historical reductions in violent behavior. Despite the near ubiquity across modern generations of the complaint about how violent the times are (implying that violence was less prevalent in the past), Eisner (2003) has shown convincingly that nothing could be further from the truth. Indeed, over the last 800 years, homicide rates have decreased at an exponential rate throughout Europe. So consistent is this reduction over time and across cultures that even the second half of the 20th century is demonstrably less violent (both in terms of individual homicides and warfare) than was the first half of the 20th century, and the last decade was less violent than the one before it. Eisner (2003) focuses on documenting this trend rather than explaining it, but one potential explanation (and one suggested by Eisner) is the rise of the strong state and a concomitant increase in the rule of law.

As Daly and Wilson (1988) note, throughout human history the restoration of social reputation (or honor) in response to perceived mistreatment has been one of the primary causes of human violence. With the historical development of stable patriclans among simple horticulturalists and pastoralists, in contrast to the even more primitive hunter-gatherers, the ability of wronged parties to muster the collective force of kinship networks exponentially enhanced the deadliness of corporate acts of vengeance. Personal affronts came to be seen as collective affronts, leading to tribal warfare and intergenerational blood feuds. With the rise of stable agricultural societies and the concomitant increase in wealth and social power, the state replaced the individual and the clan as the "aggrieved" party, and the king or local overlord took the responsibility of punishing crime. Given the large costs involved in seeking vengeance in response to personal or collective offenses, this shift in responsibility has generally been accepted throughout human history. However, if people lack confidence in the state's ability to enforce the law and punish wrongdoers, but the threat of attack is real and pervasive, then victims and their kin will typically feel the need to take the law into their own hands—in which case *lex talionis* becomes the ruling social principle (see also McCullough, 2008). The extent to which a given society exhibits the collective rule of law, rather than the rule of individual retaliation, is, thus, a strong predictor of cross-cultural differences in violence.

What Happened to Culture?

At this point, readers may well wonder what happened to the cultural element of our discussion. Indeed, neither resource deprivation nor lawlessness is typically thought of as a cultural dimension, even though societies might differ on both of these variables. How, then, do these factors fit within a cultural perspective on violence? We propose that although both resource deprivation (absolute and relative) and pervasive lawlessness can independently contribute to culture-wide increases in violence, the confluence of these two factors can lead, over long periods of time, to the formation of cultural schemas, scripts, and identity dynamics that reflect adaptive responses to these fundamental social problems. These schemas, scripts, and identity dynamics, furthermore, are capable of taking on a life of their own, persisting as cultural influences on aggression and violence even when the economic and social problems that produced them are no longer prevalent. The confluence of these two factors, we suggest, often leads to the genesis of what are known in the anthropological and social-psychological literatures as cultures of honor, the topic to which we now turn.

Historical Origins of a Culture of Honor

What kind of culture emerges in an ecology characterized by a long-standing lack of basic resources, and scarce or unreliable law enforcement despite the constant threat of attack from thieves and other enemies? What kinds of cultural characteristics would allow inhabitants of such a society to survive in the midst of such a perfect storm of hardships?

An illustrative example of just such a culture developed over the course of over 700 years in the border region between Northern England and the Scottish Highlands (see Fischer, 1989, for an extensive history). Between about 1000 AD and 1750, the southern Scottish Lowlands were fraught with constant violence, partly due to a long-standing dispute between Scotland and England regarding ownership of the area. For seven centuries, these two countries alternately invaded the border region in attempts to conquer and claim the land, and towns on both sides of the border were subjected to brutal destruction and looting by both of the warring armies. The constant destruction and rebuilding, combined with the medieval feudal system that remained in place in this region long after it had been abandoned by the rest of Europe, meant that the inhabitants of this border country subsisted in abject poverty, unable to pass land or other resources from one generation to the next, so that each generation essentially had to start with next to nothing (Leyburn, 1962). Economic and social progress was, thus, nearly nonexistent.

The border country was also a prime target for organized crime. Inhabitants were subject to routine "reiving" (burglary) and "rustling" (theft of livestock, itself a common form of livelihood in this area) by professional gangs. To add to the trouble, legal authorities could not be relied upon to bring thieves to justice, precisely because of the proprietary uncertainty of the land. This was a land with no king, no dominant authority capable of protecting the peace. Inhabitants were therefore required to ensure their own welfare. Thus, even during the brief intervals of peace in the border country, a climate of fear ruled the area.

The constant violence and devastation—perpetrated by common thieves and kings alike—along the border produced a culture that was distinct in several ways from both northern Scotland and the rest of England. First, the area accumulated a large body of capable warriors, who developed a reputation for strength and toughness. Second, the area was much more impoverished than the rest of Britain. The inhabitants of the border region were largely subsistence herders and primitive horticulturalists, never having adopted or developed advanced agricultural practices common to more stable environments. Third, the residents of the borderland became paranoid and xenophobic, and blood relationships became extremely important: Loyalty to kin was vastly more valued than loyalty to country. Fourth, border dwellers had no faith in legal institutions, as governments offered them little protection from thieves (and often perpetrated attacks themselves), so local disputes had to be settled personally. For people living in such conditions over such a long period of time, a man who developed a reputation for strength, resilience, and a readiness for violence was a man who *might* be left alone. Thus, it was natural for a culture that stressed the importance of creating and defending one's honor to grow over time.

Beginning in the 1600s, a political change transpired that, intuitively, might have precipitated positive change in the borderlands: The warring kingdoms to the north and south gradually united, beginning with the advancement of Scotland's own James VI to the English throne in 1603, and ending with the Act of Union in 1707, which officially united the kingdoms of England and Scotland into Great Britain. However, the process of unification was just as bloody as the violence it sought to end. Because the people of the borderlands had developed a reputation for being violent and unyielding, the government attempted to subdue them with similarly violent methods. Entire families (many of whom were known to be involved in organized crime or in violent, intergenerational feuding) were either executed or imprisoned. Some were exiled to Ireland, but the officials there were no better able to abide these unruly newcomers and, in turn, sometimes banished them to the American colonies. In a further attempt to subdue the Irish, who were no friends of the Protestant kings of England, King James also offered Irish lands in Ulster to Scots and Englishmen willing to move there, an offer that thousands of impoverished Lowland Scots could hardly refuse.

But the American colonies offered even greater promise to these poor immigrants, who found Northern Ireland to be less than hospitable. Consequently, a mass exodus ensued, primarily composed of poor farmers and herders, from both Northern Ireland and the Scottish Lowlands to the American continent. This group soon became known within the colonies as the "Ulster Scots" or "Scotch-Irish." The migration began slowly in the early 1600s and picked up speed in the early to mid-1700s. All told, nearly a quarter of a million Ulster Scots left the British Isles and headed for the New World, packing light but bringing their deeply ingrained cultural values with them.

Despite their low social and economic status, these transplanted Scots maintained a stubborn pride and unapologetically demanded respect from those who probably considered themselves to be their superiors. Their refusal to assume a submissive demeanor did little to endear these newcomers to the other American settlers, and the Ulster Scots were "encouraged" to move from coastal towns and cities into the American "backcountry," which was more sparsely settled (at least by Europeans). The Ulster Scots quickly dispersed toward the South, and they soon accounted for a majority of English-speaking inhabitants in many counties of the Carolinas, Georgia, Alabama, Tennessee, and Kentucky, eventually moving even farther westward, bringing the warrior mentality of the Lowland Scots' culture of honor with them.

The United States is currently a very different place than it was during its settlement. Rule of law is well established, and the uncertainty regarding land ownership is no longer the issue that it was in the 18th and 19th centuries. However, the honor-based culture of the Ulster Scots that took root in parts of the American South and West is still alive and well, according to the social-psychological literature. This literature defines a culture of honor as a system of socially transmitted norms, values, schemas, and scripts that emphasize the importance of upholding and defending one's reputation, particularly a man's reputation for strength and toughness—someone who is not to be taken lightly or trifled with (Nisbett & Cohen, 1996). Cultures of honor tend to have strictly prescribed gender roles for men and women, demanding both physical and emotional strength and resilience from men, and chastity and loyalty from women (e.g., Vandello & Cohen, 2003). Furthermore, the emphasis upon defense of self, property, and family results in an extreme sensitivity and reactivity to reputational threat. In other words, people from cultures of honor—particularly men—are more likely to perceive threats in ambiguous situations and to feel compelled to address those threats with aggression (Cohen, Nisbett, Bowdle, & Schwarz, 1996).

In the next sections, we will explore a potential psychological mechanism through which the culture of honor might affect violent outcomes. We will then review empirical evidence that has established consistent regional differences in violence in the United States as a function of culture-of-honor status, as well as experimental work demonstrating such cultural differences on an individual level.

Manhood in the Culture of Honor

Recently, Vandello, Bosson, Cohen, Burnaford, and Weaver (2008) proposed the "precarious manhood hypothesis," which states that manhood (as compared to womanhood) is a tenuous social status that must be constantly proven and affirmed. Whereas a girl "becomes a woman" via biological maturation and thus cannot fail to be a "real woman" thereafter, a boy "becomes a man" via feats of strength and courage. Thus, he can potentially fail to be a "real man," and because of this, threats to masculinity elicit behavioral displays designed to reaffirm one's identity as a man (e.g., Bosson, Vandello, Burnaford, Weaver, & Watsi, 2009; Vandello, Bosson, et al., 2008; Weaver, Vandello, Bosson, & Burnaford, 2010).

The precariousness of manhood, according to Vandello, Bosson, and their colleagues, is a universal phenomenon. After a threat to gender identity, men of all cultures feel compelled to reaffirm their masculinity. But cultures of honor appear to exacerbate the experience of this universal compulsion. There is evidence, for instance, that men from honor cultures have a much lower threshold for perceiving threats to masculinity: All else being equal, a man from a culture of honor is more likely to interpret an insult as a threat to masculinity than is a man who is not from such a culture (e.g., Cohen et al., 1996). This attention and reactivity to such threats makes a good deal of sense when viewed as a cultural adaptation to an ecology of uncertainty (due to poverty and lawlessness).

Thus, we argue that men living in honor cultures feel they must engage in masculinity-affirming displays more often and to more extreme degrees than do other men. Furthermore, because such displays are often violent and/or dangerous (e.g., Bosson et al., 2009), the precarious manhood hypothesis can help to explain the well-documented tendency for men living in honor cultures to be more aggressive and violent (e.g., Nisbett, Polly, & Lang, 1995; Nisbett & Cohen, 1996). We will review evidence in support of this idea next, including evidence that culture-of-honor regions manifest more *retaliatory* violence than nonhonor regions, rather than displaying more antisocial behavior in general, as well as evidence that men in cultures of honor exhibit unique affective, cognitive, and behavioral responses to threat and provocation compared to their non-culture-of-honor counterparts.

Field Studies of Violence in Cultures of Honor

In one of the seminal studies on the culture of honor in the United States, Nisbett, Polly, and Lang (1995) demonstrated that interstate variation in rates of argument-related homicide was partially attributable to the culture-of-honor status of each state. Specifically, states in the southern and western census regions of the United States (i.e., honor states) exhibited higher rates of argument-related homicide than did states in the North. Crucially, rates of other types of homicides did not vary significantly with honor status. In other words, other precipitants of fatal aggression (e.g., robbery) were *not* more prevalent in honor states, but homicides precipitated by insults and arguments *were*. The proposed inference was that residents of honor states are more likely to respond violently—even to the point of murder—to insults and threats than are residents of nonhonor states. This lends support to the idea that a culture of honor might promote violence as a method of maintaining and restoring masculine reputation. Subsequent studies have largely confirmed these findings and refined them, showing, for instance, that the proportion of a county's populace born in the US South is predictive of the argument-related homicide rate, but only among Whites living in rural areas and small towns (where one's reputation presumably would be of particular concern; Lee, Bankston, Hayes, & Thomas, 2007; Nisbett & Cohen, 1996). Furthermore, this proportion-Southern-born demographic variable is even predictive of White homicide rates in non-Southern counties (Lee et al., 2007), demonstrating that Southern Whites who migrate to other regions of the United States could potentially raise the violence quotient in their new communities, just as we have argued that the Ulster Scots did when they migrated to the United States in the 18th century.

Nisbett and colleagues (1995) focused upon adult violence in their study, as do most other studies on the culture of honor, but retaliatory violence is also higher among children and adolescents in honor states. Recently, Brown, Osterman, and Barnes (2009) found that school shootings in the United States are also more prevalent in honor states. Specifically, over a 20-year period (1988 to 2008), 108 prototypical school shootings occurred in the United States, according to archival research by Brown and colleagues, and of those, 75% occurred in honor states, despite the fact that these states account for less than 57% of the US population. Likewise, Brown et al. found that high school students living in honor states were more likely to report having brought a weapon to school (such as a gun or knife) in the last month compared to students living in nonhonor states. Furthermore, although not reported by Brown et al., it was subsequently found that school bombings (attempts and completions) were more frequent in honor states (Brown & Osterman, unpublished data). Of 208 school bombings (most of them only attempts that failed to detonate or that were stopped by law enforcement) that were reported to the US Bomb Arson Tracking System between 2005 and 2010, 147 (or 70.7%) occurred in honor states. Clearly, violence in honor states is not restricted to adults.

Past studies have suggested that school violence is often precipitated by rejection and bullying (e.g., Leary, Kowalski, Smith, & Phillips, 2003; Newman, Fox, Roth, Mehta, & Harding, 2005). Because social rejection and bullying are direct reputational threats, Brown and colleagues suggested that school shootings might represent extreme attempts to restore reputation in cultures of honor. Consistent with this idea, it is worth noting that culture-of-honor parents are more likely to endorse the belief that their children should *fight* bullies rather than reason with them (Cohen & Nisbett, 1994). This is not to suggest, of course, that these parents would endorse such extreme forms of school violence as mass shootings or bombings, but rather that the pervasive cultural scripts that endorse aggressive retaliation for honor threats might manifest in the behavior of children just as they do in the behavior of adults (Newman et al., 2005).

Another form of violence that seems to be both more common and more accepted in cultures of honor is domestic abuse. Vandello and Cohen (2003) compared residents of Brazil and the United States (the former, they argued, is a more prototypical culture of honor than the latter) regarding their perceptions of domestic abuse by husbands in the wake of female infidelity, and their evaluations of wives' reactions to being abused. The authors found that especially in Brazil, female infidelity damages a husband's reputation, and that retaliatory violence against an unfaithful wife can help to restore this reputation. Additionally, they found that women in Brazil are more respected when they remain with their husbands in the face of such violence. In short, domestic abuse, as with the other types of violence that we have explored thus far, seems related to the defense of masculine reputation in a culture of honor. Furthermore, the expectation that women will stay with abusive spouses not only underlines the importance of reputation for both men and women in cultures of honor but also makes clear that the reputational focus for women in a culture of honor is on sexual purity and loyalty. Thus, one of the interesting contributions of this study is that it demonstrates not only that retaliatory violence is more frequent in a culture of honor, but it is also culturally sanctioned and endorsed.

Indeed, laws regarding homicide are more permissive in cultures of honor, given certain situational constraints. When murder is defense or honor related, perpetrators are more likely to receive reduced sentences in honor states in the United States relative to nonhonor states (Nisbett & Cohen, 1996). Specifically, "hot-blooded" murders, such as the shooting of an intruder or a man found in bed with one's wife, are more likely to be acquitted or to result in milder sentences in cultures of honor. Tangentially, it has also been demonstrated that gun control legislation is also more permissive in honor states than in nonhonor states (Cohen, 1996), and this legal "liberality" coincides with the views of those living in honor states regarding the justifiability of lethal force in protecting one's family, one's property, and one's person. Attitudes toward such restricted forms of violence in cultures of honor reflect the same permissiveness as legal trends: Given the right circumstances (i.e., those involving the defense of one's person, family, property, or reputation), residents of honor states are more likely to say that violence is acceptable and appropriate (Cohen & Nisbett, 1994; Hayes & Lee, 2005). Furthermore, it seems that these permissive attitudes predict actual behavior toward perpetrators of violence, as employers in honor states are more sympathetic to job candidates who have criminal records compared to employers in nonhonor states, but only when the crime involved a defense of honor (Cohen & Nisbett, 1997). Legislative and attitudinal sympathy toward defense-related violence might reflect the cultural expectation that family patriarchs should be willing, able, and equipped to defend their own families, without heavy reliance upon legal authorities.

Cultures of honor not only promote retaliatory violence in one-on-one circumstances but also seem to promote such retaliation on a collective level. Barnes, Brown, and Osterman (in press) showed that after the terrorist attacks against the United States on 9/11, students from a university located in an honor state, compared to students at a university in a nonhonor state, more strongly endorsed lethal retaliation against the perpetrators of the attacks. Barnes and colleagues found further that in a nationally representative sample of adult respondents, individuals who personally endorsed honor-related beliefs and values expressed significantly more hostility and stronger desires for revenge in response to a hypothetical scenario in which the Statue of Liberty was blown up in a terrorist attack. These respondents went so far as to endorse a *nuclear* strike in retaliation for this attack, and they also exhibited heightened levels of suspicion and vigilance toward foreigners. Barnes et al. suggest that because terrorist attacks can be construed as collective insults, honor-related beliefs and values might promote a desire for retaliation and restoration of national honor/reputation in such situations, just as they do in one-on-one confrontations in which personal, rather than collective, honor has been threatened.

The culture of honor thus appears to promote a heightened readiness to aggress against those who threaten collective identities through acts of international terrorism. Ironically, though, honor norms and values might also promote *terrorist actions*, even at a domestic level. In a 2010 unpublished study, Brown and Barnes examined incidents of domestic terrorism—including both completed and prevented acts—reported by the US Federal Bureau of Investigation and the National Counter-Terrorism Center. Between 1996 and 2009, these federal agencies reported 107 such cases, excluding acts perpetrated by non-US citizens. Eighty-two of these acts of domestic terrorism (or 77%) occurred in honor states, a proportion that differs significantly from chance and that is remarkably consistent with the proportions of school shootings and bombings that have occurred in honor states in the United States over the last 20 years, as noted earlier. Why would people living in honor states be more indignant in response to external terrorist attacks but also more prone to instigate terrorist attacks themselves? One possible explanation for this apparent contradiction is that when individuals in a culture of honor feel as though their central values and beliefs are not being upheld in their community, they might be more prone to violent demonstrations of their discontent in order to affirm and assert their values, or at least temper the influence of competing values within their society, especially if they view these competing values to be imposed by illegitimate systems or authorities.

School shootings and acts of terrorism are examples of deliberative and complex behaviors, often involving cooperation among multiple agents. But as is often the case with argument-related homicides, not all instances of violence in culture of honor are so deliberative and planned. For instance, a recent study suggests that "accidental" deaths in the United States are more frequent in honor states than in nonhonor states, rather than being randomly distributed across the population (Barnes, Brown, & Tamborski, 2012). These accidental deaths included a wide variety of mechanisms, from automotive and boating accidents to electrocutions. The authors explained the systematic nature of these accidental deaths with reference to the precarious manhood hypothesis. Because, as previously discussed, culture-of-honor men feel that their masculine identity is under threat more often than do other men, displays of masculinity in an honor culture will tend to be more frequent as acts of "social proof." These displays often involve dangerous and aggressive behaviors (e.g., Bosson et al., 2009) because such displays are risky and overt, which makes them ideal forms of evidence: Only "real men" could carry them out. Thus, cultures of honor might be expected to facilitate dangerous, risk-taking behaviors as a form of masculine display, which might in turn explain the increased likelihood of people (both men and women, according to Barnes and colleagues) dying "accidentally" in honor states.

In summary, there is a wealth of diverse data at the level of the state, region, and (to a lesser extent) nation suggesting that cultures of honor promote specific types of violence. Legislation and personal attitudes regarding defense-related violence (at both the personal and national levels) are more permissive, and indeed defense-related violence is more prevalent in these areas. But it is worth emphasizing the qualification that we have, by now, made several times over: The types of violent behaviors and attitudes that are more prevalent in cultures of honor are related to *defense and reputation*. Only in response to physical or honor-related threats is violence explicitly endorsed by people living in honor cultures.

Laboratory Studies on Aggressiveness, Violence, and the Culture of Honor

In contrast to the region-level studies presented thus far, the laboratory studies on the culture of honor seek primarily to reveal more precise mechanisms through which the culture of honor facilitates violent retaliation. In a classic set of studies, Cohen, Nisbett, Bowdle, and Schwartz (1996) demonstrated differences between Southern- and Northern-born men in how they responded—affectively, cognitively, and behaviorally—to threat. In each of the three studies reported, unsuspecting male participants were insulted by a confederate who bumped into the participant in a narrow hallway and subsequently called them an "asshole." The researchers revealed four important findings that distinguished the Southern and Northern males' responses to the insult.

First, whereas Northern participants were more likely to find the incident strange, and even amusing, the Southern participants became angry and hostile. This was because Southern men were more likely than their Northern counterparts to interpret the incident as a threat to their masculinity, as demonstrated by participants' self-reports. This finding supports the argument we have made that manhood is an especially tenuous social status in cultures of honor, leading among other things to a hypervigilance to threat. Second, the Southern participants showed physiological signs of higher stress (increased cortisol levels) and readiness for aggression (higher testosterone levels). It should be noted that baseline cortisol and testosterone levels did *not* differ between the two groups of participants; it was only *after* the insult that this difference emerged. Thus, Southerners were more likely to be stressed by the insult (presumably because it threatened their masculinity) and were physiologically more prepared to respond aggressively (in order to restore their masculinity).

Third, the Southern males were more cognitively primed for aggression after the insult (but again, not at baseline), as revealed by projective measures. Specifically, Southern participants in the insult condition completed word stems with more aggressive words than did Northern participants (e.g., Southern participants completed "_ight" with "fight" rather than "light" and "gu_" with "gun" rather than "gum"), and similar results were obtained with a scenario-completion task in which participants completed the endings to stories involving a protagonist who was insulted. Fourth and finally, Southern participants were more likely to engage in actual behavioral displays that were aggressive or otherwise displayed masculinity or dominance. For example, in one study, participants encountered a large male (a confederate, but not the same one that delivered the earlier insult) walking toward them in a very narrow hallway. In order for the confederate and participant to pass each other, the participant had to give way to the other, much larger man. In the absence of an insult, the Southern men gave way to the confederate quite early (sooner, in fact, than did the Northern participants). However, after an insult, the Southern men waited significantly longer to give way to the confederate. Other behavioral outcomes were also assessed, including the firmness of the participant's handshake and the dominance of the participant's behavior during an interview. Time after time, Southern subjects were not especially aggressive or dominant in the absence of an insult, but they were extremely so *after* an insult.

There are a few findings from these studies that deserve to be highlighted. One is that culture-of-honor males are not *generally* more aggressive, hostile, or dominant than are other males. In the control conditions (the insult-absent conditions), Southern subjects were actually more polite than their Northern counterparts. However, Southern subjects were more likely to perceive the confederate's insult as a personal threat to their masculinity and were subsequently more inclined to restore their masculinity via aggressive and dominant displays. Thus, taken together, these findings reinforce the assertions that in cultures of honor, (1) the maintenance of masculine identity and reputation is a particularly salient concern, (2) threats to masculinity are perceived more readily, and (3) these threats evoke especially extreme reactions in service of restoring masculinity.

Another illuminating laboratory study investigated patterns of conflict escalation of Southern and Northern-born males (Cohen, Vandello, Puente, & Rantilla, 1999). In contrast to the Cohen et al. (1996) study, this investigation sought to compare culture-of-honor and non-culture-of-honor men regarding their reactions to minor social irritations, as well as differences in their styles of conflict resolution. Participants were informed that they were to take part in an "art therapy session," the intent of which was to examine the possible soothing effects of drawing. During the course of the study, a confederate (supposedly another participant) was instructed to deliver 11 "annoyances" to the participant, including throwing crumpled wads of paper at him and calling him a mildly demeaning nickname ("Slick"). The researchers anticipated that Southern men would become annoyed more quickly, and that they would be more confrontational, than would Northern men, but the extremity of the actual responses surprised them, as conveyed in this excerpt from the article:

> ... [I]t was believed that confederates sat far enough away from the subjects that they would have time to react if the subject did anything unexpected. The procedure, however, caused more aggression, and more sudden, unpredictable aggression, than was anticipated. In two cases, subjects—both southerners—made physical contact with our confederate
> (p. 263).

The general findings of the study were these: Northern participants expressed their irritation incrementally, giving fair warning to the confederate of their displeasure and increasing desire to retaliate—in lieu of *actual* retaliation, in most cases. After about the fifth annoyance, Northern participants' irritation and risk of confrontation leveled off and did not escalate further. The researchers inferred that the Northerners chose to ignore the confederate at this point, convinced that nothing they said or did would change his behavior. In stark contrast, Southerners initially withstood the repeated provocations with stoicism and gave no signs at all of their anger or their increasing desire to retaliate. However, after a threshold of disrespect was crossed (again, at around the fifth annoyance), Southerners showed sharp increases in displays of anger and aggressive behavior.

This study illustrates well how confrontations unfold in cultures of honor. Cohen et al. (1999) suggest that politeness norms can explain the initial stoicism of Southerners in their study, and this is no doubt part of the reason for this finding. Another part, however, might be that Northerners were *avoiding* an actual physical altercation by expressing anger and providing fair warning to the confederate, actions that would most likely discourage further provocation in a real-world setting, whereas the Southerners' behavior might have been *inviting* the escalation of the situation into a physical fight by suppressing warnings to the aggressor that an altercation was imminent. This initial concealment of negative affect not only deprived the confederate of a chance to cease his irritating behavior and avoid a fight (which would, it seems, also deprive the participant of a chance to affirm his masculinity), but it also made the surprising attack that typically ensued all the more effective and intimidating. In other words, the pairing of the initial nonresponsiveness with the subsequent hyperresponsiveness might be an especially strategic and potent combination, as the former both *justifies* and *magnifies* the latter, thus enhancing the effectiveness of the display for affirming the "victim's" masculinity.

Conclusion

From regional findings within the United States, we know that honor states have higher rates of retaliatory violence than do nonhonor states. Furthermore, members of honor states are not apologetic for this fact: Both legislation and attitude surveys indicate that people living in honor states actually sanction and endorse retaliatory violence. Laboratory studies suggest that this penchant for violence is rooted in notions about masculine identity, although in some contexts (e.g., romantic relationships) feminine identity is also relevant. Historically, it appears that this particular set of values and beliefs might have been an adaptive cultural response to living in dangerous, unstable, and poverty-stricken environments, such as the border region between Scotland and England and parts of the American frontier.

Indeed, it is worth returning to a point we made at the outset in our discussion of the origins of cross-cultural differences. We noted our agreement with other cultural theorists that cultural norms, schemas, scripts, and values do not arise out of nothing; rather, they represent evoked responses to adaptive problems faced by humans and experienced at both the individual and collective levels. When certain ecological factors, such as resource deprivation and lawlessness, persist for long enough and widely enough, individual response patterns (such as the aggressive defense of reputation, which reflects an individual-level psychological adaptation; Shackelford, 2005) become socially coordinated response patterns, and these social patterns eventually become ingrained deeply enough that they continue to be transmitted from one generation to the next long after the ecological factors that initially produced them have faded away. To be clear, we are not suggesting a form of group-level selection but rather are arguing that individual-level adaptations, which are sensitive to contextual inputs, can manifest themselves at a collective, cultural level when those contextual inputs are experienced pervasively, across a large group of people, over a long enough period of time.

The mechanisms involved in the intergenerational transmission of schemas, scripts, and identity dynamics are broad and varied, but cultural naming patterns provide a nice illustration of how a culture communicates and "teaches" its values and beliefs. For example, Kelly (1999) observed that honor states in the United States are significantly more likely to have town names that include violent words (e.g., gun, kill, murder) than are nonhonor states. A few illustrations are Cut and Shoot, Texas; Gun Point, Florida; War, West Virginia; Guntown, Mississippi; Cutthroat Gulch, California; and Gun Barrel City, Texas. Kelly also found that violent business names are also more common in honor states, excluding businesses directly related to violent activities, such as gun dealers. Examples reported by Kelly (1999) include Battle Ax Church and Outlaw Avionics in Texas, and Warrior Electronics and Gunsmoke Kennels in Alabama.

In addition to place names, honor cultures also manifest and transmit their beliefs and values through how people name their babies. Recently, an analysis of the most popular baby names across 24-year cycles in the United States by Brown and Carvallo (unpublished data) revealed that patronymic naming patterns (i.e., the use of a father's or grandfather's name, in whole or in part, in a child's name) were more pronounced in US honor states than in nonhonor states, although matronymic patterns were not. Furthermore, a state's patronym score, but not its matronym score, was significantly associated with its rate of "institutional violence" (i.e., state executions of convicted criminals) between 1930 and 2006.[2] Likewise, Brown and Carvallo found that following the threat to national honor of the terrorist attacks on 9/11, patronymic naming increased in honor states, but not in nonhonor states, thus providing another sort of "naturalistic experiment" to demonstrate the sometimes subtle role of identity dynamics in a culture of honor. Though perhaps humorous in the case of violent business names and curious in the case of baby names, these examples do illustrate the extent to which violence and masculine identity permeate cultures of honor, allowing for the transmission of cultural beliefs and values from one generation to the next in sometimes subtle ways. In much less subtle ways, these beliefs and values are also represented explicitly in laws related to retaliatory violence and gun control (Cohen, 1996), media accounts of interpersonal aggression and crime (Cohen & Nisbett, 1997), and *perceptions* of normative beliefs and behaviors associated with retaliatory violence (Vandello, Cohen, & Ransom, 2008).

Culture of Honor and Violence: Future Directions

Culture-of-honor research traditionally focuses upon how cultural norms impact *interpersonal* violence. But some new lines of research suggest that the valuing of traits like self-reliance, toughness, and strength in honor cultures might promote violence against the self—specifically, suicide—in the same way that they promote violence against others. Recently, we found that both suicide and depression rates are markedly higher, for both men and women, in honor states within the United States, controlling for a host of standard, statewide covariates (Osterman & Brown, 2011). In contrast, help-seeking tendencies (operationalized as the per-capita number of antidepressant prescriptions written in each state) were significantly lower in honor states compared to nonhonor states. Furthermore, we found that statewide levels of depression and suicide only exhibited a significant, positive relationship in honor states; the two variables were not significantly related in nonhonor states. This latter finding might indicate that, whereas depressed individuals in nonhonor states tend to seek help (as evidenced by the higher antidepressant prescription rates in these states), individuals in honor states are less likely to do so, and this stoic independence leaves them more vulnerable to suicidality. We suggest that the frequent and intense threats to gender identity experienced by members of honor cultures facilitate suicide, just as they do in the case of retaliatory interpersonal violence. Furthermore, we suggest that the potential reluctance to seek help (which could be seen as an admission of weakness) in cultures of honor might further exacerbate vulnerability to suicidality.

Considering other ways in which people living in cultures of honor might exhibit self-destructive behaviors in response to honor norms remains an interesting topic for future investigations. Likewise, unhealthy ways of thinking, feeling, and behaving in cultures of honor need not manifest themselves only in ways as dramatic or overt as suicide. Honor norms might also lead to subtle yet pervasive and powerful effects on help seeking in general, as well as institutional and legal impediments to help seeking. For instance, if people living in honor cultures value self-reliance and toughness, might they be less likely to create institutions for providing social services to the poor, the weak, and the elderly? Might people living in honor cultures be less likely to vote for laws that require health insurers to cover expenses related to certain kinds of health needs, such as mental health services? The common stigma associated with receiving mental health care seems likely to be especially pronounced in cultures of honor, and there could be a variety of ways that such a stigma could display itself, from the reticence of individuals to admit needing mental health care to the availability of mental health care providers. Thus, research on this topic, which has received no attention in the culture-of-honor literature to date, could bridge the domains of social and health psychology, with important potential ramifications for social policy.

In this chapter, we have focused our attention primarily on one example of a culture of honor and its historical precipitants, but this is certainly not the only case of an honor culture that has developed in the world. Other prominent examples include Japan, Brazil (as already noted) and many other countries in Latin and South America, the Middle East, and the Mediterranean (for a discussion of the latter, see Peristiany, 1966). Each instantiation of the culture of honor has its own distinct history, but others have written more extensively than we have in this chapter about what common factors might give rise to cultures of honor globally. For example, Nisbett and Cohen (1996) argue that the most important precipitant is the extent to which a society depends on resources that are easily stolen, such as livestock, an argument that is sometimes referred to as the "herding hypothesis" (see also Shackelford, 2005). The vulnerability of one's resources, then, gives rise to the defensiveness that characterizes cultures of honor (for a statistical critique of this herding hypothesis, see Chu, Rivera, & Loftin, 2000). Some historians have focused, as we have in this review, upon weak law enforcement and poverty as the primary environmental conditions that prompt the development of this particular set of cultural values (e.g., Fischer, 1989; Wyatt-Brown, 1982). This view is largely consistent with Nisbett and Cohen's (1996) argument about the importance of resource vulnerability, insofar as herding societies are typically both poor and spread out, leading to weaker law enforcement and resource vulnerability. When a society experiences widespread and long-term poverty, combined with the absence of a rule of law, the principle of *lex talionis* rules the land, and it is this principle, most fundamentally, that we think eventually morphs into the values and beliefs of the honor culture. Alternatively, Henry (2009) has argued that large power and status differentials in a society are the central social features that encourage the development of cultures of honor around the world, although we would hasten to add that such power differentials are most pronounced in impoverished and lawless societies.

Of course, there might be multiple paths that promote the development of cultures of honor, and it remains an ongoing pursuit for social scientists to propose and test theoretically based hypotheses about both the antecedents and consequences of honor-based cultures. To date, there exists no validated, quantitative measure of culture of honor status at the national level, although Henry's (2009) approach using national statistics related to pastoralism (i.e., the percentage of a country's total land area reserved for nonagricultural pastures) could prove useful in this regard. Creating and validating internationally appropriate measures of honor status remains an important challenge for researchers interested in testing hypotheses about honor cultures. Likewise, there is not a cross-culturally validated method for assessing degrees to which individuals embrace honor-related beliefs and values. Without the ability to examine honor dynamics at an individual level of analysis, rather than simply a regional level of analysis (e.g., the level of the state or country), research on cultures of honor will be seriously limited. Tools that enable researchers to examine more nuanced and fine-grained hypotheses about honor-related phenomena should enhance substantially our understanding of the complex associations between cultural and evolutionary influences that contribute to the aggressive and violent tendencies of human beings. Indeed, the understanding that could derive from such investigations could ultimately shape social policies and even guide international relations. This, at least, remains our hope, as we certainly live in interesting times, and we might benefit from some empirically and theoretically grounded enlightenment to guide us through them.

Notes

1. To investigate the value of examining these deprivation variables worldwide, we examined homicide data (2000–2004, log-transformed to reduce positive skew) supplied by the United Nations Crime Trends Survey for 92 nations, along with economic data computed by the United Nations, and other publically available information. We found that both income inequality (i.e., national Gini scores) and per-capita gross domestic product (GDP) (adjusted for purchasing power parity) were strong predictors of national homicide rates (β =.40 and –.51, respectively, $ps < .001$), despite the overlap between these indices of economic deprivation, and controlling for mean annual temperature, urbanicity, and literacy rates. Exchanging poverty rates (square-root transformed to reduce positive skew) for per-capita GDP did not reduce the association between income inequality and homicide, and this poverty model accounted for less variance overall (R^2 =.364) than did the model that included GDP (R^2 =.433).

2. Brown and Carvallo (unpublished data) also found that statewide patronym scores, but not matronym scores, were correlated with the percentage of the populace in each state reporting a Scotch-Irish heritage in the 2000 US Census, as well as with the US Army recruitment rates of youths from each state in 2008.

References

Averill, J. R. (1982). *Anger and aggression*. New York: Springer-Verlag.

Barkow, J., Cosmides, L., & Tooby, J. (Eds.). (1992). *The adapted mind: Evolutionary psychology and the generation of culture*. New York: Oxford University Press.

Barnes, C. D., Brown, R. P., & Tamborski, M. (2012). Living dangerously: Culture of honor, risk-taking, and the non-randomness of "accidental" deaths. *Social Psychological and Personality Science, 3*, 100–107.

Barnes, C. D., Brown, R. P., & Damphousse, K. (2010). "Them's fightin' words": The aggressive defense of personal honor and combative responses to the insult of terrorism. Poster presented at the annual meeting of the Society for Personality and Social Psychology (Political Psychology Preconference), Las Vegas, NV.

Baumeister, R. F., Maner, J. K., & DeWall, C. N. (2006). Evoked culture and evoked nature: Coevolution and the emergence of cultural animals. *Psychological Inquiry, 17,* 128–130.

Bosson, J. K., Vandello, J. A., Burnaford, R. M., Weaver, J. R., & Wasti, S. A. (2009). Precarious manhood and displays of physical aggression. *Personality and Social Psychology Bulletin, 35,* 623–634.

Brown, R. P., Osterman, L. L., & Barnes, C. D. (2009). School violence and the culture of honor. *Psychological Science, 20*(11), 1400–1405.

Burgess, E. (1925). Can neighborhood work have a scientific basis? In R. Park & E. Burgess (Eds.), *The city* (pp. 142–155). Chicago: University of Chicago Press.

Chu, R., Rivera, C., & Loftin, C. (2000). Herding and homicide: An examination of the Nisbett-Reaves hypothesis. *Social Forces, 78*(3), 971–987.

Cohen, D. (1996). Law, social policy, and violence: The impact of regional cultures. *Journal of Personality and Social Psychology, 70,* 961–978.

Cohen, D. (2001). Cultural variation: Considerations and implications. *Psychological Bulletin, 127*(4), 451–471.

Cohen, D., & Nisbett, R. E. (1994). Self-protection and the culture of honor: Explaining southern violence. *Personality and Social Psychology Bulletin, 20,* 551–567.

Cohen, D., & Nisbett, R. E. (1997). Field experiments examining the culture of honor: The role of institutions in perpetuating norms about violence. *Personality and Social Psychology Bulletin, 23*(11), 1188–1199.

Cohen, D., Nisbett, R. E., Bowdle, B. F., & Schwarz, N. (1996). Insult, aggression, and the southern culture of honor: An "experimental ethnography." *Journal of Personality and Social Psychology, 70,* 945–960.

Cohen, D., Vandello, J. A., Puente, S., & Rantilla, A. K. (1999). "When you call me that, smile!" How norms for politeness, interaction styles, and aggression work together in Southern culture. *Social Psychology Quarterly, 62,* 257–275.

Colson, E. (1975). *Tradition and contract: The problem of order.* Chicago: Aldine.

Comanor, W. S., & Phillips, L. (2002) The impact of income and family structure on delinquency. *Journal of Applied Economics, 5*(2), 209–232.

Daly, M., & Wilson, M. (1988). *Homicide.* New York: Aldine de Gruyter.

Donohue, J. J., & Levitt, S. D. (2001). The impact of legalized abortion on crime. *The Quarterly Journal of Economics, 116*(2), 379–420.

Donohue, J. J., & Levitt, S. D. (2004). Further evidence that legalized abortion lowered crime: A reply to Joyce. *The Journal of Human Resources, 39*(1), 29–49.

Durkheim, E. (1897). *Le suicide: Etude de socologie.* Paris, France: F. Alcan.

Eisner, M. (2003). Long-term historical trends in violent crime. *Crime and Justice, 30,* 83–142.

Elliott, D., & Ageton, S. (1980). Reconciling race and class differences in self-reported and official estimates of delinquency. *American Sociological Review, 45,* 95–110.

Fischer, D. H. (1989). *Albion's seed: Four British folkways in America.* New York: Oxford University Press.

Gangestad, S. W., Haselton, M. G., & Buss, D. M. (2006). Evolutionary foundations of cultural variation: Evoked culture and mate preference. *Psychological Inquiry, 17*(2), 75–95.

Golden, R. M., & Messner, S. F. (1987). Dimensions of racial inequality and rates of violent crime. *Criminology, 25,* 525–541.

Gurr, T. R. (1970). *Why men rebel.* Princeton, NJ: Princeton University Press.

Hayes, T. C., & Lee, M.R. (2005). The Southern culture of honor and violent attitudes. *Sociological Spectrum, 25,* 593–617.

Henry, P. J. (2009). Low-status compensation: A theory for understanding the role of status in cultures of honor. *Journal of Personality and Social Psychology, 97*(3), 451–466.

Keizer, K., Lindenberg, S., & Steg, L. (2008). The spreading of disorder. *Science, 322,* 1681–1685.

Kelly, M. H. (1999). Regional naming patterns and the culture of honor. *Names, 47,* 3–20.

Konner, M. (2007). Evolutionary foundations of cultural psychology. In S. Kitayama & D. Cohen (Eds.), *Handbook of cultural psychology* (pp. 77–108). New York: The Guildford Press.

Kornhauser, R. R. (1978). *Social sources of delinquency: An appraisal of analytic models.* Chicago: University of Chicago Press.

Leary, M.R., Kowalski, R.M., Smith, L., & Phillips, S. (2003). Teasing, rejection, and violence: Case studies of the school shootings. *Aggressive Behavior, 29,* 202–214.

Lee, M. R., Bankston, W. B., Hayes, T. C., & Thomas, S. A. (2007). Revisiting the Southern culture of violence. *The Sociological Quarterly, 48,* 253–275.

Leyburn, J. G. (1962). *The Scotch-Irish: A social history.* Chapel Hill: The University of North Carolina Press.

Loftin, C., & Parker, R. N. (1985). An errors-in-variable model of the effect of poverty on urban homicide rates. *Criminology, 23,* 269–287.

Markus, H. R., & Kitayama, S. (1991). Culture and the self: Implications for cognition, emotion, and motivation. *Psychological Review, 98,* 224–253.

McCullough, M. E. (2008). *Beyond revenge: The evolution of the forgiveness instinct.* San Francisco: Jossey-Bass.

Newman, K.S., Fox, C., Roth, W., Mehta, J., & Harding, D. (2005). *Rampage: The social roots of school shootings.* New York: Basic Books.

Nisbett, R. E., & Cohen, D. (1996). *Culture of honor: The psychology of violence in the South.* Boulder, CO: Westview Press.

Nisbett, R. E., Polly, G., & Lang, S. (1995). Homicide and U. S. regional culture. In B. Ruback & N. Weiner (Eds.), *Interpersonal violent behavior: Social and cultural aspects* (pp. 135–151). New York: Springer.

Osterman, L. L., & Brown, R. P. (2011). Culture of honor and violence against the self. *Personality and Social Psychology Bulletin, 37,* 1611–1623.

Peristiany, J. G. (1966). *Honour and shame: The values of Mediterranean society.* London: Weidenfeld and Nicholson.

Sampson, R. J. (1987). Urban Black violence: The effect of male joblessness and family disruption. *The American Journal of Sociology, 93*(2), 348–382.

Shackelford, T. K. (2005). An evolutionary psychological analysis of cultures of honor. *Evolutionary Psychology, 3,* 381–391.

Shaw, C. R., & McKay, H. D. (1942). *Juvenile delinquency in urban areas.* Chicago: University of Chicago Press.

Sherif, M., Harvey, O. J., White, B. J., Hood, W. R., & Sherif, C. W. (1961). *Intergroup conflict and cooperation: The robber's cave experiment*. Norman: University of Oklahoma Book Exchange.

Sulloway, F. J., & Zweigenhaft, R. L. (2010). Birth order and risk taking in athletics: A meta-analysis and study of major league baseball. *Personality and Social Psychology Review, 14*(4), 402–416.

Tajfel, H. (1970). Experiments in intergroup discrimination. *Scientific American, 223*(2), 96–102.

Tajfel, H., Billig, M., Bundy, R., & Flament, C. (1971). Social categorization and intergroup behavior. *European Journal of Social Psychology, 1*, 149–178.

Tooby, J., & Cosmides, L. (1992). The psychological foundations of culture. In J. Barkow, L. Cosmides, & J. Tooby (Eds.), *The adapted mind: Evolutionary psychology and the generation of culture* (pp. 19–136). New York: Oxford University Press.

Triandis, H. C. (1994). *Culture and social behavior*. New York: McGraw-Hill.

Triandis, H. C. (2007). Culture and psychology: A history of the study of their relationships. In S. Kitayama & D. Cohen (Eds.), *Handbook of cultural psychology* (pp. 59–76). New York: The Guilford Press.

Trivers, R. L. (1972). Parental investment and sexual selection. In B. Campbell (Ed.), *Sexual selection and the descent of man* (pp. 136–179). Chicago: Aldine-Atherton.

Vandello, J. A., Bosson, J. K., Cohen, D., Burnaford, R. M., & Weaver, J. R. (2008). Precarious manhood. *Journal of Personality and Social Psychology, 95*, 1325–1339.

Vandello, J. A., & Cohen, D. (2003). Male honor and female fidelity: Implicit cultural scripts that perpetuate domestic violence. *Journal of Personality and Social Psychology, 84*, 997–1010.

Vandello, J. A., Cohen, D., & Ransom, S. (2008). U.S. southern and northern differences in perceptions of norms about aggression: Mechanisms for the perpetuation of a culture of honor. *Journal of Cross-Cultural Psychology, 39*, 162–177.

Walker, I., & Smith, H. (2002). *Relative deprivation: Specification, development, and integration*. Cambridge, England: Cambridge University Press.

Weaver, J. R., Vandello, J. A., Bosson, J. K., & Burnaford, R. M. (2010). The proof is in the punch: Gender differences in perceptions of action and aggression as components of manhood. *Sex Roles, 62*, 241–251.

Wolfgang, M. (1983). Delinquency in two birth cohorts. *American Behavioral Scientist, 27*, 75–86.

Wyatt-Brown, B. (1982). *Southern honor: Ethics and behavior in the Old South*. New York: Oxford University Press.

CHAPTER 14

Sacrifice and Sacred Values: Evolutionary Perspectives on Religious Terrorism

Richard Sosis, Erika J. Phillips, *and* Candace S. Alcorta

Abstract

Evolutionary theories of religion and sacred values are essential for understanding current trends in terrorist activity. We clarify religion's role in facilitating terror and outline recent theoretical developments that focus on four cross-culturally recurrent features of religion: communal participation in costly ritual, belief in supernatural agents and counterintuitive concepts, separation of the sacred and the profane, and adolescence as the critical life phase for the transmission of religious beliefs and values. These four characteristics constitute an adaptive complex that evolved to solve problems of group cooperation and commitment, problems faced by all terrorist organizations. We examine how terrorists employ these features of religion to achieve their goals and describe how terrorists utilize costly rituals to conditionally associate emotions with sanctified symbols and signal group commitments. These sanctified symbols are emotionally evocative and motivationally powerful, fostering ingroup solidarity, trust, and cooperation. Religious beliefs, including promised rewards in the afterlife, further serve to facilitate cooperation by altering the perceived payoffs of costly actions, including suicide terrorism. Patterns of brain development unique to adolescence render this the ideal developmental stage to attract recruits, inculcate sacred beliefs, and enlist them in high-risk behaviors. We conclude by offering insights, based on our evolutionary analysis, concerning conflict resolution when sacred values are in dispute.

Key Words: cooperation, religion, ritual, sacred values, terrorism

Introduction

In recent years there has been a rise in the proportion of terrorists motivated by religious concerns. This trend is particularly troubling because there is a significant correlation between religious motivation and the lethality of terrorist attacks (Benjamin & Simon, 2002; Hoffman, 2003). Data collected by the US State Department on 3,932 terrorist attacks between 1968 and 2007 indicate that attacks by religious groups were four times as lethal as attacks by secular groups (Berman, 2009). One reason religious terrorism is so deadly is the increased use of suicide attacks, which have risen from an average of 4.7 per year from 1981 to 1990, to 16 per year from 1991 to 2000, to an average of 180 per year from 2001 to 2005 (Atran, 2006). At least 70% of suicide attacks from 2000 to 2003 were religiously motivated (Atran, 2004). From 1980 to 2003 suicide attacks accounted for only 3% of all terrorist incidents, but (excluding 9/11) they inflicted 48% of the fatalities, and 73% if 9/11 is included (Pape, 2005).

Some scholars have argued that secular state-sponsored terrorism is somewhat constrained because states do not want to undercut their claims of legitimacy and alienate potential supporters who would revile indiscriminate violence against civilians (Richardson, 2006). In contrast, "religious terrorists often seek the elimination of broadly defined categories of enemies and accordingly regard such large-scale violence not only as morally justified but as a necessary expedient for the attainment of their goals" (Hoffman, 2006, pp. 88–89). Religiously motivated terrorists "want a lot of people watching and a lot of people dead" (Simon & Benjamin, 2000, p. 71). Why would religious terrorists not feel as constrained as secular political actors? Why would they want more people watching? Why is religiously motivated terrorism becoming more common? Why would anyone become a suicide bomber? And what governmental policies can stem religiously motivated violence?

In this chapter we explore how the evolutionary sciences can inform us about religious terrorism. The dominant approach to the study of terrorism, by academic, intelligence, and military researchers, is grounded in rational choice models. We argue, however, that rational actor approaches cannot explain why individuals sacrifice their lives for lands lacking material wealth, abstract ideological causes, insults to intangible values such as honor, and other seemingly irrational motivations. We believe evolutionary research on religion and sacred values can explain such sacrifices.

This chapter will proceed as follows. We begin by defining religious terrorism. Then we clarify religion's role in causing, motivating, and facilitating terror. Next we examine how recent work on the evolution of religion and sacred values can help us address the questions posed earlier. We conclude with a discussion about the adaptability of religion and how our approach can inform conflict resolution.

What Is Religious Terrorism?

Religious terrorism is a concept not without controversy. The controversy concerns whether religious terrorism exists at all. Some argue that terrorism is never religious per se because political motives are always the root cause of terrorist activity (Bloom, 2005; Pape, 2005). Moreover, it is unclear how to distinguish between secular and religious terrorism (Nardin, 2001). Others, such as terrorist expert Bruce Hoffman, maintain that the "radically different value systems, mechanisms of legitimation and justification, concepts of morality, and worldview" (2006, p. 88) explain why religiously motivated terrorism is so lethal, and thus it justifies distinguishing religious terrorism as a distinct category. While Hoffman is likely correct, those who emphasize that it is difficult to distinguish religious terrorism from other types of terrorism are also justified in their concern; religious terrorism is an ambiguous category, consisting of two words that are both notoriously difficult to define. To demarcate the scope of our inquiry into religious terrorism, we begin by clarifying what these concepts, religion and terrorism, mean. We believe that our definitions, derived from an evolutionary approach, can help distinguish religious terrorism from other forms of violence and cast light on specific elements of religion that render it particularly efficacious for achieving terrorists' objectives.

Defining Terrorism

What constitutes terrorism is not straightforward and may depend on one's vantage point; there is truth to the adage "one person's terrorist is another's freedom fighter." Not surprisingly, many definitions of terrorism have been offered. The US Department of State defines terrorism as "Premeditated, politically motivated violence perpetrated against noncombatant targets by subnational groups or clandestine agents" (http://www.state.gov/s/ct/). The Federal Research Division of the Library of Congress considers terrorism to be "the calculated use of unexpected, shocking, and unlawful violence against noncombatants (including, in addition to civilians, off-duty military and security personnel in peaceful situations) and other symbolic targets perpetrated by a clandestine member(s) of a subnational group or a clandestine agent for the psychological purpose of publicizing a political or religious cause and/or intimidating or coercing a government(s) or civilian population into accepting demands on behalf of the cause" (Hudson, 1999, p. 164).

There are four prominent features that recur in most definitions of terrorism (Jongman & Schmid, 1983). First, terrorism involves violence and/or destruction. Second, the attack has a political motive. Third, there is an intention to strike widespread fear in the attacked community. Fourth, the victims of the attack are civilians. We will consider terrorism to be attacks that exhibit these four features.

Defining Religion

Similar to "terrorism," there are likely as many definitions of "religion" as those who study it. Even the Latin origins of the English word remain obscure and do not provide guidance. According to the *Oxford English Dictionary*, "religion" is either derived from *relegere* (to read over again) or *religare* (to bind), but even if the latter as some scholars contend, it is unclear whether the binding is to the gods, community, or both. James Frazer, in his classic study *The Golden Bough*, defined religion as "a propitiation or conciliation of powers superior to man which are believed to direct and control the course of nature and of human life" (1915/2010, p. 53). In the most influential sociological examination of religion in the 20th century, Emile Durkheim wrote that "a religion is a unified system of beliefs and practices relative to sacred things, that is to say, things set apart and forbidden—beliefs and practices which unite into one single moral community called a Church, all those who adhere to them" (1912/1995, p. 44).

These definitions, and the hundreds of others that have been offered by scholars, either fail to incorporate some aspects of what others believe to constitute religion, or they are unable to distinguish religion from other cultural institutions. If religion is anything at all, it is an inherently fuzzy category with unclear boundaries. Therefore, rather than offer a descriptive definition of religion, many scholars have concluded that religion can be best defined and studied by considering its constituent parts (Alcorta & Sosis, 2005; Atran & Norenzayan, 2004; Bering, 2005; Bulbulia, 2005; Molloy, 2008; Whitehouse, 2008).

Essentialist definitions of religion, which break religion down into its more easily definable core elements, have two particular advantages for the study of religious terrorism. First, essentialist definitions avoid endless debates concerning whether Marxism, patriotism, atheism, and so on are religions. It is clear that religion shares some core elements with other cultural institutions, and indeed, this approach clarifies that most of religion's core elements are not unique to religion. Ritual, myth, music, and taboo, to consider a few examples, are also manifest in other cultural institutions, including politics and sports. Not surprisingly, as we will discuss, so-called secular terrorism shares many features with religious terrorism. Second, by breaking religion down into its core elements it becomes obvious that these elements did not evolve together. Ritual, for example, has antecedents in many other species (Alcorta & Sosis, 2005, 2007; D'Aquili, Laughlin, & McManus, 1979) and presumably has a much deeper evolutionary history in our lineage than many other core elements, such as myth. Religion, therefore, did not simply appear in the human lineage; its evolution consisted of uniting cognitive processes and behaviors that for the most part already existed. Although these elements evolved separately, they coalesce in similar ways across all cultures and at some point in human evolution they began to regularly coalesce.

Examining how the elements of religion interrelate is important for understanding how terrorists effectively employ religion to further their political goals.

We have previously argued that religion may best be understood as an evolved complex of traits incorporating cognitive, affective, behavioral, and developmental elements (Alcorta & Sosis, 2005). Central to this complex are four cross-culturally recurrent features of religion:

- Communal participation in costly ritual
- Belief in supernatural agents and counterintuitive concepts
- Separation of the sacred and the profane
- Adolescence as the critical life phase for the transmission of religious beliefs and values

Later we examine these features of religion and show how terrorists use each of these features to solve inherent problems they face in achieving their objectives.

Defining Religious Terrorism

We consider religious terrorism to be politically motivated violent and/or destructive attacks aimed at civilians that seek to strike fear in the victims' communities and that employ an ideology usually transmitted during adolescence that encompasses costly ritual behavior, beliefs in supernatural agents, and separation of the sacred and profane.

Notice that in contemporary societies, our four core elements of religion co-occur within secular contexts as well. For example, the adoption of communal rituals and initiation rites by nominally secular terrorist groups, such as the Liberation Tigers of Tamil Eelam (LTTE), and their quasi-deification of Marxist-Leninist ideals, blurs the line between what is secular and what is religious (Roberts, 2005). These groups engage important elements of the previously described religious adaptive complex and reap many of the adaptive benefits achieved by religion. Thus, despite avowing secular ideals, their behavior falls within our definition, and indeed, we can gain a much better understanding of their success by examining them through the lens of religious terrorism.

It is also worth emphasizing that religious terrorism is never exclusively religiously motivated; there is always some political motivation as well (Juergensmeyer, 2004b; Pape, 2005). The balance between religious and political motivation differs between terrorist groups; some groups rely on religious motivation more than others. For example,

Judge Zvi Cohen, who presided over the trial of members of the Jewish Underground, a terrorist network that sought to blow up mosques on the Temple Mount (see Gorenberg, 2000), described three motivations for these convicted terrorists: "The first motive, at the heart of the Temple Mount conspiracy, is religious. The second motive—the security of settlers in the West Bank...A less prominent motive is that of relations among friends" (Pedahzur & Perliger, 2009, p. 46). Not only will the balance between religious and political motivations differ between terrorist groups, but as Judge Cohen noted for the Jewish Underground, motivations will vary within a single operation. Moreover, some religious terrorists act alone, but as we will discuss later, relations and commitments among friends are also a powerful motivator for many terrorists.

The Landscape of Contemporary Religious Terrorism

It has been claimed that terrorism is probably as old as *Homo sapiens* (Atran, 2010, p. 91), but the story of contemporary terrorism, especially the religious variety that we will explore here, begins with the forces of globalization. Globalization is often lauded for bringing people together and increasing the knowledge we have of one another. But for many, globalization is perceived as the uncontrollable spread of Western norms and values—norms and values that are believed to be at odds with their own (Ruthven, 2004). While some view globalization as a means to bring about peace and understanding, at times globalization may fuel cultural conflict (Schneider et al., 2003). In addition to conflicting cultural values, those living in underdeveloped regions of the world can witness via mass media technologies, particularly the Internet, the extraordinary economic disparity between themselves and the West.

Immigrants to Western societies and their descendants, who seek to maintain their traditional cultural ways, can find themselves being pulled in two divergent directions. For those in such a situation, intercultural contact can result in "social ambiguity, role conflicts, and status inconsistencies and incongruities" (Alcorta, 2010), fostering cognitive dissonance, feelings of powerlessness, and a sense of anomie. Even ambitious men from immigrant communities, who are well educated and financially secure, often find limits to what they can achieve in Western society. Such experiences of anonymity, devaluation, and powerlessness can have very real and severe psychological and physical affects.

Intercultural contact is certainly not new; social and cultural changes initiated by such contact constitute a dominant theme throughout human history (Wolf, 1982). What is new about the advent of global industrialization, however, is the scope and rate of change it has initiated. Social change introduced by industrial urbanization has been identified as a major factor in the global health transition (World Health Organization [WHO], 2001). Increased blood pressure, elevated cortisol levels and changes in cortisol profiles, as well as escalated EBV antibody levels, have been documented in populations worldwide as they are integrated into a global industrial economy (Dressler & Bindon, 2000; Flinn & England, 1995; McDade, 2002; McDade, Stallings, & Worthman, 2000). These markers all indicate activation of the body's "stress system." Although adaptive as a short-term response to immediate environmental threats, long-term activation of this system can be deadly (Sapolsky, 1996). Escalating rates of depression, schizophrenia, and other psychoses (Krabbendam & van Os, 2005; McGrath et al., 2004; Sundquist, Frank, & Sundquist, 2004; van Os, 2004), as well as an unprecedented incidence of suicide, particularly among adolescents, have all accompanied the urban industrial transition (Desjarlais et al., 1995). The World Health Organization (2001) reports that mental and neurological disorders make up 11% of the global disease burden and are expected to rise to 14.6% by 2020. Depression, a precursor for 80%–90% of all suicides, is currently among the top 10 causes of death in most countries that report rates, and it is among the top three causes of death in the population aged 15–34 years (WHO, 2001). These escalating rates of depression, schizophrenia, and suicide within urban environments are particularly pronounced among adolescent males (see Alcorta, 2010).

The stress and anxiety of rapid cultural change has not gone unnoticed by religious commentators. Sayyid Qutb, leader of the Egyptian Muslim Brotherhood in the 1950s and 1960s, described the "hideous schizophrenia" of modern life. He argued that this schizophrenia was a product of the Christian West's separation of religion from the physical world, the distinct compartmentalizing of religion and science (Qutb, 2007). In a discussion on Qutb's writings, Paul Berman insightfully observes that Qutb "put his finger on precisely the inner experience that Salman Rushdie described in *The Satanic Verses* many years later—the schizophrenia or alienation, the feeling of being two instead of one, the pain of living in two worlds at once, the experience that Muhammad Atta and suicide soldiers of 9/11 must surely have felt in their everyday existences in the West" (2004, p. 76).

Muslim Jihad

Terrorism is a political tool that has been employed, with varying success, by all the world religions (Hoffman, 2006). Because of its geopolitical impact, considerable media and scholarly attention has focused on Islamic terrorism with the unfortunate consequence that in the West terrorism is often implicitly (and sometimes explicitly) associated with Islam. There is no inherent relationship, however, between Islam and terror. The causal factors behind the rise of terrorism in the Islamic world are varied but include perceptions of injustice, colonization, and the disparity in economic and technological development (Lewis, 2003). The Islamic world in the Middle Ages was philosophically and scientifically more advanced than the Christian world; only China was comparable among civilizations (Lewis, 2002). And the military power of the Islamic world was unparalleled (Karsh, 2007). The contrast in the Islamic world between then and now, however, could not be more striking. The annual Arab Development Reports (http://www.arab-hdr.org/), which do not include data on the considerable Muslim populations throughout South East Asia, describe a remarkable gap between the West and the Arab world in literacy, book translations, scientific research productivity, Internet use, and other indicators of human development. The reports further highlight the significant economic gap between the Arab world and the West. While the glory of Islamic civilization has passed and been supplanted by Western civilization and imperialism, this history has not been forgotten in the Islamic world and often serves as a source of animosity toward the West.

In this context it is not surprising that many Muslims have turned toward their faith for answers, comfort, and stability. Yet, as globalization expands Western cultural and economic influence, Muslim hegemony and sacred values are perceived to be threatened. Western values, including democracy, are viewed by some as inferior to Muslim values that, it is believed, derive from Allah. Muslim law, *sharia*, must be protected and prevented from being subjugated to human law. Accordingly, democracy is viewed as inherently flawed because humans are limited in their wisdom and may not willingly choose to live by *sharia*. Therefore, these laws must be imposed on populations, even by force, for their own good (Atran, 2010).

Marc Sageman (2008) has shown that global jihad terrorism has occurred in three major waves. The first wave consisted of those who fought against the Soviets in the 1980s. They were upper- and middle-class college-educated Egyptian professionals, and most were married. The second wave spanned the 1990s and ended with the US-led military invasion of Afghanistan after 9/11. The second-wave jihadis were mostly middle-class Europeans and Saudis. Many of them held advanced degrees in science or medicine, and overall they were materially and educationally better off than their populations of origin. The third wave began after the United States and British invasion of Iraq in 2003. Many of these jihadis were either second-generation or infant immigrants from the West, and they were primarily lower or middle class. Atran (2010) has found these jihadis, in contrast to previous waves, to be more marginalized, underemployed, and have a history of prior criminal activity unrelated to jihad. They often find religion in their early 20s and are more likely to be single.

Why has the profile of jihadis changed from educated, economically well-off men to petty criminals who are newly religious? Atran argues that US counterterrorism efforts forced "would-be terrorists to rely on local, low-cost, underground, and informal methods of financing. In addition, the elimination of Al Qaeda's training facilities in Afghanistan and the disruption of its networks for supplying expertise in logistics, bomb making, and so forth, meant that jihadis would have to find new means for executing terrorist operations" (2010, pp. 207–208). Petty criminals, who live at the edge of cultural contact and personally experience the impacts of anomie and devaluation discussed earlier, have been well situated to fill that niche. Moreover, because they are disenfranchised and looking for a moral cause to take up, they are "even more altruistically prone than others are to give up their lives for their comrades and a cause" (Atran, 2010, pp. 207–208).

The Relationship Between Religion and Terror

The media may be responsible for the popular belief that religion, especially Islam, and terror are strongly associated (on the US State Department's list of foreign terrorist organizations, less than half are religious). Suicide terrorists in particular are often depicted in the media as delusional religious fundamentalists, hopelessly brainwashed and out of touch with reality. This characterization, however, is inaccurate. The terrorist career itself is extraordinary, but individuals who eventually become terrorists are otherwise quite ordinary. As Atran observes, "Anthropologically and psychologically, terrorists usually are not remarkably different from the rest of the population" (2010, p. 36). Berrebi (2007), for example, has shown that Palestinian suicide bombers have above average education and are economically better off than the general population. Krueger (2007) also demonstrates that poverty is not a predictor of participation in political violence or support for terrorism. Moreover, Sageman (2004) found no evidence of psychopathology in an international sample of Muslim terrorists. Leaders of terrorist organizations are clear that recruits may not be depressed or suicidal. As one spokesman for the Palestinian Islamic Jihad explains, "In order to be a martyr bomber you have to want to live" (Richardson, 2006, p. 117). Terrorists themselves point out that even suicide bombers have plenty of hope; otherwise there would be no point in killing themselves (Atran, 2003).

If terrorists in general, and suicide bombers in particular, are not crazed religious zealots, what then is the relationship between religion and terrorism? Various researchers, as noted earlier, have argued that terrorists have political, not religious goals (Berman, 2009; Bloom, 2005; Juergensmeyer, 2003; Pape, 2005). Former US Ambassador Michael Sheehan commented, "A number of terrorist groups have portrayed their causes in religious and cultural terms. This is often a transparent tactic designed to conceal political goals, generate popular support and silence opposition" (http://www.brookings.edu/events/2000/0210terrorism.aspx). Thus, religion may not be the root cause of conflicts, but it is rather a tool used by terrorists to achieve their goals. Recast in evolutionary terms, religious beliefs, rituals, and institutions are proximate mechanisms that facilitate otherwise improbable behavioral outcomes. But why would religion be an effective tool for terrorists? Here we review six main reasons.

Framing the Conflict

Juergensmeyer (2003) argues that while religion is not the cause of most conflicts involving terror, religion is the means by which terrorists translate a local political struggle into a cosmic war. In other words, terrorists often frame their disputes in religious rather than political terms. This has various advantages, most significantly in motivating others to sacrifice themselves for the cause. This transformation from political to religious struggle encourages actors to perceive that they are participating in something of divine significance that transcends individual self-interest. Among Sikh militants in the Punjab, Juergensmeyer describes joining the struggle as "motivated by the heady sense of spiritual fulfillment and the passion of holy war" (2004a, p. 2). Atran (2010) describes how many of the men responsible for the Madrid train bombings wanted to belong to, or lead, something bigger than themselves to feel important and influential on a cosmic scale. Fighting for Islam, or at least their understanding of it, provided them with the feeling of personal importance they had been seeking. The stress of social ambiguity and status inconsistencies, as mentioned earlier, can be alleviated by aligning oneself with a cosmic cause, releasing the person from the social and economic pressures of the material world.

It is remarkable how successful contemporary terrorists have been in shaping worldviews so that they are consistent with their own views. Bin Laden, for instance, was particularly successful in transforming his local grievance (i.e., getting US troops off "Muslim" soil) into a cosmic clash between civilizations. The use of religion to transform local power struggles into cosmic conflicts benefits terrorist groups who may otherwise be viewed as economically and politically self-serving. In an age of instantaneous electronic communications, such religious framing of essentially local conflicts serves to broaden both the ideological and geographic base of terrorism. A second consequence of the religious framing of political conflicts is the extension of the horizon for victory. Terrorists perceive that they are fighting a cosmic war in divine time, thus eliminating incentives to "win" within one's own lifetime. Commenting on an interview with Hamas leader Abdul Aziz Rantisi, Juergensmeyer observes that "[i]n his calculation, the struggles of God can endure for eons" (2004b, p. 35).

Moral Justification

Religion also facilitates terrorists' goals by providing moral legitimacy to their cause (Hoffman, 2006; Juergensmeyer, 2004c). All contemporary world religions impose a moral framework upon their adherents, thereby enabling terrorists to present their conflicts in morally absolute dichotomies, such as good versus bad or righteous versus evil. While legitimizing ones' own cause, religions are particularly effective at demonizing those with opposing views. The history of religion is replete with examples in which ingroup passions are aroused and outgroup hatreds are dangerously ignited. One consistent predictor of suicide terrorism is a religious difference between the perpetrator and victim (Pape, 2005). This occurs even when the terrorist group appears to have secular motivations, such as the LTTE, who were Hindus fighting a Buddhist majority. In Berman and Laitin's (2008) extensive sample of suicide terrorism, almost 90% of the attacks were aimed at victims of a different religion. Data from the ongoing situation in Iraq would undoubtedly lower this percentage, as Muslim suicide bombers are killing other Muslims, but that conflict also highlights that categories such as Muslim, Buddhist, or Hindu are too broad. Enemy "outgroups" can exist within these broad categorical labels. Indeed, religious extremism typically emerges concomitantly with secularism and begins with intrareligious conflict, such as the rise of the Muslim Brotherhood in Egypt and ultimate incarceration and execution of many of its members and leaders, including aforementioned Sayyid Qutb (Armstrong, 2000).

Spiritual and Eternal Rewards

Religion not only provides a divine dimension and moral legitimacy to terrorist activity; it also defines the rewards that combatants can attain. After considering the benefits that Sikh militants attain, Juergensmeyer concluded that "[t]he reward for these young men was the religious experience in the struggle itself: the sense that they were participating in something greater than themselves" (2004a, p. 2). In addition to such spiritual rewards of transcendence, religion may also explicitly offer benefits in the afterlife that can rarely be matched in this world. The 9/11 hijackers all believed that they "would meet in the highest heaven" (Lincoln, 2003, p. 98), which we can assume helped them rationalize their actions.

Adaptability

While religions are often viewed as a conservative social force, they are in fact highly responsive to social, political, and economic conditions. We return to the misconception of religion as inflexible later; here we simply emphasize that the vast sacred writings and mythical traditions of contemporary religions play an important role in religion's flexibility, a quality that makes religion an effective tool for terrorists. Religious texts that endure do so because they are open to multiple interpretations. Extensive use of metaphor and poetry in religious texts and oral traditions engages subconscious processes of personal significance to create contextual meaning (Belanger, Baum, & Titone, 2009; Sidtis, 2006). As a result, each new generation reinterprets religious texts in relation to their own meaningful experiences, thereby keeping them living, relevant, and fresh. Past interpretations are not necessarily rejected per se, but they are transformed or ignored by the community. They remain available, however, should cultural change make their message relevant again.

The sacred writings of contemporary religious traditions are vast repositories that leaders draw upon at various points in history, emphasizing aspects that are socially and politically expedient, and disregarding those that are not. Terrorists often rely on these repositories, including alternative interpretations of sacred texts that have been largely forgotten by mainstream adherents. Consider, for example, the Jewish Underground, mentioned earlier. They sought rabbinical sanction for their operation, as is common among religious terrorists (Hoffman, 2006, p. 89), but no prominent rabbis would endorse their plans. Since they were unable to gain approval from living rabbis, "they sought justification for attacking the Temple Mount mosques in the teachings and adjudications of rabbis who were no longer living. For example, Dan Be'eri scoured the writings of Rabbi Zvi Yehuda Kook for some reference to a possible endorsement of the plan for exploding the mosques" (Pedahzur & Perliger, 2009, pp. 60–61).

Extended Communities of Support

As we discuss later, terrorist networks exploit religion's ability, typically through intense ritual and shared counterintuitive beliefs, to create tight social bonds. But many religions, especially contemporary world religions, also create extended communities. Whitehouse (2004) argues that repetitive rituals provide a cognitive foundation for abstract communities. Infrequently performed rituals that are highly evocative and emotionally arousing create strong bonds among performers. Whitehouse claims that these experiences are stored in episodic memory and have long-term neurological effects. In contrast, the memories of low-arousal repetitive rituals, such as daily prayer, are stored in semantic memory. While performers of a painful initiation rite will recall who participated in the ritual, regular churchgoers would be unable to recall who attended church on any particular Sunday, unless there was a notable event to help recall. However, regular churchgoers would be able to describe in detail what happened on any particular Sunday because the same rituals are performed in the same manner every week. Whitehouse argues that the storing of ritual knowledge in semantic, rather than episodic, memory leads to anonymous religious communities. What makes someone a Christian, for example, are abstract properties of belief and performance that do not need to be witnessed by the entire population for one to be considered a member of the religious community.

Terrorists rely on extended anonymous communities, which are created by frequent ritual performance, for political and material support. Those willing to take the risk of a terrorist operation are generally few in number; it is the support of the extended community that is vital for terrorists to achieve their political aims (Merari, 1993). Thus, it is the larger public rather than the victims who are the real targets of terrorist activity. It is the publicity of spectacular terrorist attacks that serves as the oxygen that feeds the fire of modern terrorism (Ginges, Hansen, & Norenzayan, 2009). And increasing media technologies, of course, have only added fuel to this fire. Menachem Livni of the Jewish Underground, for example, "was so preoccupied with public support for the underground that he followed the public opinion polls in the newspapers measuring the support for their terrorist attacks" (Pedahzur & Perliger, 2009, p. 56). Attacks do not have to successfully injure or kill anyone to be successful in the eyes of the perpetrators. As Atran notes, "With publicity, even failed terrorist acts succeed in terrorizing; without publicity, terrorism would fade away" (2010, p. 278).

Religious Symbols, Myths, and Rituals

Religion's most significant role in terrorism may be its incorporation of emotionally evocative and highly memorable symbols, myths, and rituals that serve to individually motivate and collectively unify diverse individuals under a common banner. All terrorist groups face the challenge of creating group commitment and individual devotion to a common cause. Anthropologists have long noted that fundamental "faith-based" elements of religion, that is, symbols, myths, and rituals, foster this ingroup commitment better than any other social institution. Not surprisingly, secular and religious terrorists alike maintain communal rituals and initiation rites that communicate an individual's level of commitment to the group (Atran, 2003; Dingley & Kirk-Smith, 2002; Roberts, 2005). For religious terrorists, cohesiveness is further fostered through powerful religious symbols, which "often become focal points in occupations involving a religious difference" (Pape, 2005, p. 89). And of course, martyrdom itself means to sacrifice one's life for one's faith. Religion provides the rituals and symbols to both motivate and memorialize these local heroes, thereby affording them an otherwise unattainable status that is also eternal. Pape observes that "[s]uicide terrorist organizations commonly cultivate 'sacrificial myths' that include elaborate sets of symbols and rituals to mark an individual attacker's death as a contribution to the nation" (2005, p. 29).

The bonding that occurs through religion does not always have to be strong to be effective for terrorists. As Atran (2010) shows in numerous contexts, terrorism often begins on the football pitch; friends are simply recruiting friends and the commitments are ones that have been built by growing up and playing together. On the other hand, some terrorist networks are loosely organized collectives of virtual strangers. For example, most members of the Jewish Underground did not even know each other and most people involved simply did one aspect of an operation, such as driving somewhere or fixing something, without knowledge of the plans for the entire operation (Pedahzur & Perliger, 2009). Although members did not have strong bonds, they did share similar religious commitments, which facilitated being drawn into various activities at the requests of friends. Indeed, given the loose connections in the social network of the Jewish Underground, it is unclear how they could have accomplished any of their goals (they murdered three Arab mayors) without their shared religious identity and commitment. As Berman remarks on the Jewish Underground's failure to carry out their primary attack, bombing the Temple Mount, "Their strong theological commitment to their cause must have been necessary for the Underground's members to attempt such dangerous and severe acts of destruction, yet it was not sufficient for their conspiracy to succeed" (2009, p. 9).

Terrorism and the Core Elements of Religion

We defined religious terrorism earlier to include four cross-culturally recurrent features of religion. We have previously argued (Alcorta & Sosis, 2005) that these elements of religion derive from ritual systems selected for in early hominin populations because they contributed to the ability of individuals to overcome ever-present ecological challenges. By fostering cooperation and extending the communication and coordination of social relations across time and space, these traits served to maximize the potential resource base for early human populations, thereby benefiting individual fitness. Here we explore how these four characteristics make religion an effective tool for terrorists.

Communal Participation in Costly Ritual

Among the most significant challenges terrorists face is ensuring that fellow insurgents are trustworthy and will not defect on the cause (Berman, 2009). How can a prospective terrorist guarantee that he will not reveal the locations of hidden conspirators, secret codes of communication, and that he will not turn aside when asked to carry out a risky or suicidal attack? At first glance, evolutionary theories of religion would appear to hold little promise for answering these questions or understanding terrorism at all. Natural selection favors genes that get themselves into the next generation, yet terrorists often take great risks with their lives and some of course intentionally sacrifice themselves for their ideological beliefs. Such actions seem to contradict evolutionary expectations. The solution to this puzzle lies in understanding religion as an evolved system of communication, which offers mechanisms that can promote ingroup trust and overcome commitment problems (Alcorta & Sosis, 2005; Atran & Norenzayan, 2004; Bulbulia, 2004a; Henrich, 2009; Irons, 2001; Rappaport, 1999; Sosis, 2003). Irons (2001), for example, posits that the primary adaptive benefit of religion is its ability to foster cooperation and overcome problems of collective action that humans have faced throughout their evolutionary history. The costliness of religious activities, or specifically what Sosis (2006) refers to as the four "B's"—religious belief, behavior (rituals), badges (such as religious attire), and bans (taboos)—enables them to serve as reliable and honest signals of group commitment. Only those who are committed to the group will be willing to incur the energetic, time, and opportunity costs of religious belief and performance. In other words, adherents pay the costs of religious adherence, but by doing so they demonstrate their commitment and loyalty to the group and can thus achieve a net benefit from successful collective action and other status benefits available to trusted signalers (see Bulbulia, 2004b; Sosis, 2003; Sosis & Alcorta, 2003).

The increased commitment and trust resulting from religious signaling provides strategic advantages for religious terrorists over other militant groups, enabling them to reduce the threat of defection. Signaling models also offer insight into a curious feature of religious terrorist organizations, such as Hamas and Hizbollah; in addition to their violent operations, these terrorist organizations serve as mutual aid societies, providing resources and services that weak and ineffective governments are unable to supply. In an insightful analysis employing economic signaling models, Berman argues that the cooperation needed to produce these collective services benefit terrorist actions by reducing the likelihood of defection: "Having already weeded the cheaters and shirkers out of their mutual aid operations, they can be confident that the remaining members are loyal" (2009, p. 17).

Surprising to many observers, costly religious demands are today increasing in many communities throughout the world. Indeed, the global rise in religious terrorism has been paralleled by a worldwide growth in religious fundamentalism. Fundamentalism typically refers to a religious ideology that embraces scriptural literalism and traditional religious values. Current fundamentalist trends, however, have placed *higher* demands on their practitioners than the traditional practices that they claim to emulate. For example, the standards of *kashrut* (laws pertaining to edible food) among Ultra-Orthodox Jews are more stringent now than at any time in Jewish history (Sosis, 2009). Signaling theory suggests three factors that may be motivating the fundamentalist trend toward increasing ritual requirements. First, the rising costs of membership may be a direct response to increases in perceived risk of apostasy faced by religious groups; a risk generated by the rapid improvement in mass media technologies, which expose wide audiences to Western secular values and culture. Second, and somewhat paradoxically, the multicultural openness of Western societies may also contribute to fundamentalist trends. While the celebration of multiculturalism has yet to embrace aggressive fundamentalism, in societies where group differences are tolerated and even encouraged, maintenance of ingroup cohesion requires that groups increase their distinctiveness in order to preserve the relative costliness of the group's previous bans and badges. Thus, multiculturalism may actually initiate movements toward fundamentalism, even while vehemently rejecting fundamentalism's message of possessing life's only true path. Notably, Juergensmeyer (2002) observes that one of the universal features of religious terrorists is a strong rejection of Western multiculturalism. Third, signaling theory predicts an increase in signal costs as resource competition escalates. In highly competitive modern multicultural nation-states, the higher costs incurred by religious fundamentalism are likely to be offset by the economic and political gains achievable through religious consolidation and organization of group membership.

The evolutionary signaling theory of religion assumes an inverted-U-shaped relationship between the costliness of religious activity and ingroup cooperation. Since imposing costly requirements upon group members is challenging and greater-than-optimum costs are expected to negatively impact group cohesion, most groups are predicted to impose less than their optimal level of costly requirements and thus be observed on the increasing side of the U-shaped distribution. Experimental, cross-cultural, and ethnohistorical research evaluating this prediction has been largely supportive (Ginges et al., 2009; Ruffle & Sosis, 2007; Soler, 2008; Sosis & Bressler, 2003; Sosis, Kress, & Boster, 2007; Sosis & Ruffle, 2003, 2004). Religious terrorists of course employ religiously defined costly requirements to signal commitment, resulting in high levels of ingroup cohesiveness and trust that are essential for carrying out their clandestine activities (e.g., Hassan, 2001). As Pape describes, terrorists have "a close bond of loyalty to comrades and devotion to leaders; and they have a system of initiation and rituals signifying an individual's level of commitment to the community" (2005, p. 8). Interestingly, among many terrorist cells these rituals also include the recording of a video testament prior to an attack (Atran, 2003). Such video testaments not only serve to immortalize the suicide terrorist and his cause among followers; they also create undeniable contracts. Defecting on a mission after declaring and documenting one's intentions would result in severe psychological, social, and presumably spiritual costs.

Evolutionary signaling theory assumes that the short-term costs of displaying a signal are repaid through individual gains. This creates a particular challenge for understanding suicide terrorism from a signaling theory perspective since individuals are obviously not around to reap any benefits from their actions. How can suicide terrorism possibly constitute an adaptive response? There would appear to be four noncompeting alternative explanations.

First, while the individual faces the ultimate sacrifice, suicide terrorism is likely to benefit the group, and Pape's (2005) analysis showing that groups deploying suicide terrorists tend to achieve their goals supports this interpretation. Suicide terrorism may offer the most promising example of strong selective pressures operating at the group level (Villarreal, 2008). Atran, for example, maintains that Hamas benefits from sacrificing its high-quality youth: "[t]hrough spectacular displays involving the sacrifice of their precious 'human capital' (educated youth with better-than-average prospects), they also signal a costly commitment to their community, which the community honors by providing new volunteers and added funding" (2010, p. 363). Second, it is possible that suicide bombers recoup their losses through benefits to their kin (Qirko, 2009). For example, the families of Palestinian suicide terrorists receive financial payments (up to US $10,000) for their martyred sons and daughters. However, Israel's policy of destroying suicide bombers' homes would appear to counterbalance these indirect fitness gains and be a strong negative incentive to sacrifice oneself for one's family. Noting research that Hezbollah suicide bombers attained above-average education, Azam (2005) argues that suicide bombers may be investing in future kin generations (their higher education makes them appreciate the importance of investing in the future). However, this poses a significant collective action problem, and it would appear that under most conditions one would be better off letting someone else make the investment (i.e., sacrifice one's life for future generations). Third, life history theory predicts that risk aversion decreases when life expectancy is low, particularly among adolescents, and there is considerable empirical work supporting this prediction (e.g., Bulled & Sosis, 2010; Hill & Hurtado, 1996; Wilson & Daly, 1997). High-risk responses to dangerous and uncertain environments are often adaptive, although it is unclear how suicide bombers could individually benefit from their actions. A fourth possibility is that the payoffs motivating suicide bombers are not material but rather otherworldly. Indeed, when applying evolutionary signaling theory to religious activity, both Sosis (2003) and Bulbulia (2004b) incorporate *perceived* gains into their models, which include payoffs attained in the afterlife. They independently found that afterlife payoffs can dramatically alter the dynamic of the game and favor costly religious activity. Moreover, we suspect that not only do martyrs expect to reap their heavenly rewards, but that they also include the reputational benefits they expect to receive as a martyr into their calculations (e.g., Richardson, 2006, p. 124), even though they will of course not be around to enjoy their newly attained status. If afterlife rewards and concerns of postmortem reputation are motivating suicide bombers, such beliefs are likely to be maladaptive, unless kin significantly benefit from being related to a martyr.

Not only are costly rituals effective for creating the trust and close bonds needed for successful suicide missions, but they are also effective at instilling the individual motivation and building the coalitional support necessary for terrorists to achieve their political aims. Ginges et al. (2009) argued that religion's relationship to suicide attacks may derive from religion's ability to enhance individual commitment to coalitional identities via collective ritual. In a series of experimental and survey studies, Ginges et al. showed that support for suicide attacks was related to attendance at worship services. Their findings were consistent among Palestinian and Israeli samples, as well as a cross-cultural sample of six religions in six countries. In their studies, support for suicide attacks were unrelated to religious beliefs or prayer frequency, but attending community services at a house of worship was a highly significant predictor of support for martyrdom and measures of outgroup hostility. Attending worship services is likely to reinforce individual emotional commitment to group symbols, including beliefs, while signaling coalitional commitments and generating the popular support terrorists need to thrive.

Belief in Supernatural Agents and Counterintuitive Concepts

The second feature of the adaptive religious complex that Alcorta and Sosis (2005) describe concerns supernatural agents and counterintuitive concepts. Evolutionary cognitive scientists have shown that the supernatural agents of religious belief systems are "full access strategic agents" (Boyer, 2001). They are "envisioned as possessing knowledge of socially strategic information, having unlimited perceptual access to socially maligned behaviors that occur in private and therefore outside the perceptual boundaries of everyday human agents" (Bering, 2005, p. 418). Furthermore, accumulating research indicates that humans exhibit a developmental predisposition to believe in such socially omniscient supernatural agents, appearing in early childhood and diminishing in adulthood. Cross-cultural studies conducted with children between the ages of 3 and 12 years indicate that young children possess an "intuitive theism" that differentiates the social omniscience of supernatural agents from the fallible knowledge of natural social agents, such as parents (Kelemen, 2004). By late childhood, supernatural agents are not only socially omniscient, they are regarded as agents capable of using such knowledge to reward and punish deeds that are now viewed within a moral framework. Several evolutionary researchers have emphasized the role that supernatural punishment plays in promoting community-defined moral behavior, and specifically ingroup cooperation (Atkinson & Bourrat, 2010; Bulbulia, 2004b; Johnson, 2005; Schloss & Murray, 2011; Sosis, 2005). Recent experimental evidence indicates that "even subtle unconscious exposure to religious ideas can dramatically encourage prosocial over selfish behavior" in theists and atheists alike (Shariff & Norenzayan, 2007).

Evolutionary cognitive scientists have further noted that the counterintuitive concepts that characterize religious beliefs, such as bleeding statues and virgin births, are both attention arresting and memorable (Atran, 2002; Boyer, 2001). These features make them particularly effective for both vertical (across generations) and horizontal (within generations) transmission and can help explain why religious ideologies, including those of terrorists, often spread quickly through populations. In addition to their mnemonic efficacy, they comprise almost unbreakable "codes" for the uninitiated. Counterintuitive concepts are not readily generated on the basis of intuitive concepts; thus, the chances of spontaneously re-creating a preexistent counterintuitive concept are exceedingly low. By incorporating counterintuitive concepts within belief systems, religion creates reliable costly signals that are difficult to "fake." Sosis (2003) has argued that repeated ritual performance fosters and internalizes these counterintuitive beliefs, which typically include a nonmaterial system of reward and punishment, including expectations about afterlife activities.

Although afterlife rewards are rarely a prime motivator of suicide terrorism (Atran, 2010; Berman, 2009), they are a critical feature of successful ideologies that enable terrorist organizations to motivate recruits to carry out their missions. As a Hamas member describes, "We focus his attention on Paradise, on being in the presence of Allah, on meeting the Prophet Muhammad, on interceding for his loved ones so that they, too, can be saved from the agonies of Hell, on the *houris* [virgins], and on fighting the Israeli occupation and removing it from the Islamic trust that is Palestine" (Hassan, 2001, p. 39). Female martyrs are promised to be the chief of the virgins and exceed their beauty (Richardson, 2006, p. 122). Even kamikaze pilots were assured that they would be "transcending life and death" (Atran, 2003, p. 1535). Experimental studies demonstrate that humans have a natural inclination to believe that some element, typically a soul, survives death (Bek & Lock, 2011; Bering, 2006). Indeed, most of us, including atheists, have difficulty conceiving of a complete cessation of mental and social activity following death. Nobody knows what it is like to be dead, so people attribute to dead agents the mental traits that they cannot imagine being without. Religious and other cultural beliefs serve to enrich or degrade beliefs in the afterlife, but Bering's work suggests that appeals to rational arguments about the irrationality of afterlife beliefs are likely to face strong resistance. If it is strategically important to alter terrorists' beliefs about the afterlife, the greatest success can be achieved by exposing children and adolescents to alternative belief schemas *before* they are exposed to the afterlife rewards promised by terrorists.

Separation of the Sacred and the Profane

The separation of the sacred and profane and the emotional power of sanctified symbols are critical for understanding how terrorists utilize religion for their benefit. Religious ritual is universally used to define the sacred and to separate it from the profane (Durkheim, 1912/1995; Eliade, 1959). As noted by Rappaport (1999), ritual does not merely identify that which is sacred; it *creates* the sacred. Holy water is not simply water that has been discovered to be holy or water that has been rationally demonstrated to have special qualities. It is, rather, water that has been *transformed* through ritual. For adherents who have participated in sanctifying rituals, the cognitive schema associated with that which has been sanctified differs from that of the profane. Of greater importance from a behavioral perspective, the emotional significance of holy and profane water is quite distinct. Not only is it inappropriate to treat holy water as one treats profane water; it is emotionally repugnant. While sacred and profane things are cognitively distinguished by adherents, the critical distinction between the sacred and the profane is the emotional charging associated with sacred things (Alcorta & Sosis, 2005).

It is the emotional significance of the sacred that underlies "faith," and it is ritual participation that invests the sacred with emotional meaning. Extensive research indicates that emotions constitute evolved adaptations that weight decisions and influence actions (Damasio, 1994). The ability of religious ritual to elicit both positive and negative emotional responses in participants provides the substrate for the creation of motivational communal symbols. Through processes of incentive learning, as well as classical and contextual conditioning, the objects, places, and beliefs of religious ritual are invested with emotional significance. The use of communal ritual to invest previously neutral stimuli with deep emotional significance creates a shared symbolic system that subsequently weights individual choices and motivates behavior.

It is noteworthy that the sacred may most commonly be encountered as physical space (Eliade, 1959). Pape (2005) argues that at the root of each suicide terror campaign is a dispute over land—an occupying power that must be removed from the homeland. Such conditions are ripe for religious symbolism and, indeed, homelands in these conflicts are almost always publicly perceived as sacred. Sosis (2011) argues that the sacralization of land is an adaptive strategy aimed at increasing coalitional commitment. Pape (2005, p. 85) comments that "[a]lthough boundaries may be ambiguous and history may be contested, the homeland is imbued with memories, meanings, and emotions." Religious rituals sustain memories, shape meanings, and foster these emotions. Religion's reliance on such emotionally evocative symbols also explains why religious terrorist groups are more successful than secular ones in mobilizing their forces (Bloom, 2005). Religious terrorists do not appeal to rational political arguments to win public approval; they rely on sacred symbols imbued with emotional power to enlist followers in their cause.

Once recruits are secured, group solidarity can be further enhanced through negative affect rituals. Neuropsychological research has shown that negatively valenced stimuli are both more memorable and have greater motivational power than positive stimuli (Cacioppo, Gardner, & Berntson, 2002). As a result of this "negativity bias," negatively valenced elements of religion provide a more reliable emotionally anchored mechanism for the subordination of immediate individual interests to cooperative group goals (Alcorta & Sosis, 2005). Research on the rituals that terrorist cells employ is scant, but apparently deprivation, such as lengthy fasts, is not uncommon (Friedland, 1992; Hassan, 2001).

One of the most productive areas of evolutionary analyses of terror is the work by Ginges, Atran, and colleagues on sacred values. Psychologists have shown that people find it insulting when monetary prices are placed on their sacred values (e.g., McGraw, Tetlock, & Kristel, 2003; Tetlock, McGraw, & Kristel, 2003). Tetlock (2003) argues that some categories of mental operations are off limits because they require the assignment of finite appraisals to values that our moral communities treat as unquestionable and absolute commitments. To mix the sacred with the profane and consider sacred values in finite terms is to commit a taboo, and those who do so generally feel impure and desire to morally cleanse themselves. A belief that martyrdom is a means of symbolic moral cleansing leads some down the path toward suicide terrorism (Bodansky, 2007).

Commitments to a sacred and higher cause enable terrorists to achieve greater sacrifice than is typically possible with traditional reward structures that are based on material incentives. As Atran keenly observes, the "jihad fights with the most primitive and elementary forms of human cooperation, tribal kinship and friendship, in the cause of the most advanced and sophisticated form of cultural cooperation ever created: the moral salvation of humanity" (2010, p. 35). In a survey of Palestinian support for suicide bombings, support was not based on a belief that Jews or Israelis are inherently bad or evil; it was a perceived sense of injustice that predicted a belief that Islam sanctions martyrs (Atran, 2010), an injustice committed against the group. Another survey (Atran, 2010) found that people are distrustful of polls showing that the other side wants an "open society" or peace; sacred values are preserved and protected even in the face of empirical evidence.

In a study on reactions to compromises aimed at ending the Israeli-Palestinian conflict, Ginges et al. (2007) found that there was some anger and disgust, as well as some propensity for violence, when respondents were asked to compromise over a sacred value. These responses actually increased for individuals deemed "moral absolutists" when the compromises included an additional instrumental incentive, such as money. As a guest of the Pashtun tribes in Afghanistan, Osama bin Laden was the beneficiary of sacred values associated with hospitality. These sacred values, based on group identity and forms of cooperation, override the rational choice of receiving the millions of dollars that were offered for the capture of bin Laden. Atran argues that the "[d]evotion to some core values may represent universal responses to long-term evolutionary strategies that go beyond short-term individual calculations of self-interest but that advance individual interests in the aggregate and long run" (2010, p. 345). Sacred values can surface for issues with comparatively little importance or historical background when they become tangled up with conflicts over collective identity. The fusion of sacred values and group identity can mean that "[m]atters of principle, or 'sacred honor,' are enforced to a degree far out of proportion to any individual or immediate material payoff when they are seen as defining 'who we are'" (Atran, 2010, p. 345).

Group identities can be firmly established early in life. Psychologist Brian Barber, who studies youth experiences with violence and war, explains that personal experiences with violence shape how youths respond to the conflict in which they are raised. According to Barber, "much of identity can be sourced externally, in that political conflict can literally divide and define who one is (ethnically, religiously, politically, culturally, etc.)" (2008, p. 306). Collective identity can be critical for youths, and living through an intense conflict can bind a population together. For Palestinian youth, for example, the "extensive engagement in the struggle, and their willingness to sacrifice for it—even their childhood—was thoroughly informed by a realm of meaning that comprehensively detailed for them their identity and justified and legitimized the goals and tactics of their fight" (Barber, 2008, p. 307).

Adolescence as the Critical Life Phase for the Transmission of Religious Beliefs and Values

The human brain demonstrates great plasticity during development. Infancy, childhood, adolescence, and adulthood are marked by differentiated growth patterns in various brain cortices and nuclei (Alcorta, 2006). The differential patterns of brain growth across the life course create sensitive periods for particular types of learning. The unique changes occurring in the adolescent brain render this a particularly sensitive developmental period in relation to social, emotional, and symbolic stimuli. Social stimuli assume increased importance as the adolescent enters into sexual, competitive, and coalitional nonkin relationships. Risk taking and novelty seeking escalate, particularly in males, and human sensation-seeking scores peak (Steinberg, 2007). At the same time, mental processing speeds increase, the ability to focus on task-relevant information improves, and abstract, symbolic reasoning develops (Dahl, 2004; Kwon & Lawson, 2000). The brain changes that occur during adolescent development drive the social and sexual behaviors of the teen years (Dahl, 2004; Steinberg, 2007). The higher impulsivity, increased risk taking, and enhanced novelty seeking of adolescent males are related to the changes occurring in the dopaminergic pathways of the brain. The resultant behaviors motivate adolescent males to move from the security of their kin networks to the less predictable and more competitive arena of nonkin interactions (Alcorta, 2010).

In addition to the heightened sociality and emotional responsivity of adolescence, this developmental period is also marked by the ongoing maturation of both the social processing region of the brain, the temporal cortex, and the abstract, "executive" processing region, the prefrontal cortex. A shift in the brain's reward circuitry to greater prefrontal dominance occurs concomitantly with the ongoing maturation of this region. These simultaneous changes in the adolescent brain provide a unique window of opportunity for the creation of emotionally weighted and socially meaningful symbolic schemata, and for integrating these schemata into the brain's reward circuitry (Alcorta, 2006; Blakemore, 2008). As a result, adolescence is a time when communal ritual performance is likely to be particularly influential (Alcorta & Sosis, 2005).

Adolescent rites of passage comprise one of the most consistent features of religions across cultures (Lutkehaus & Roscoe, 1995). Rites of passage not only teach initiates the social and cultural mores of the group as embodied in unfalsifiable beliefs; they also imbue these beliefs with emotional significance and motivational force. Participation in rites of passage engages unconscious emotional processes, as well as conscious cognitive mechanisms. Such rites frequently evoke intense emotions of love, anger, fear, and awe and associate these emotions with socially significant symbols and beliefs. Because such symbols are deeply associated with emotions engendered through ritual, they take on motivational force. The use of communal ritual to evoke emotions and conditionally associate them with socially salient symbols can be expected to be particularly effective during adolescence as a result of the brain changes occurring during this time. Abstract social mores are thus not only cognitively instantiated; they are also imbued with motivational salience through sanctification. When such rites are simultaneously experienced by groups of individuals, the conditioned association of evoked emotions with socially relevant cognitive schema creates a cultural community bound in motivation, as well as belief.

It is therefore not surprising that most terrorists begin their militant life during adolescence. Victoroff suggests that the "typical development of terrorist sympathies perhaps follows an arc: young adolescents are plastic in their political orientation and open to indoctrination. Positions harden later in adolescence... [and] many retired 'terrorists' reveal a mellowing of attitude" (2005, p. 28). Of course, by the time those raised in a culture of martyrdom reach adolescence they are already prepared to sacrifice themselves without further indoctrination (Atran, 2003; Brooks, 2002). Bloom observes that by the age of 6, Palestinian boys and girls report that they wish to grow up and become *isitshhadis* (martyrs). "By the age of 12, they are fully committed and appreciate what becoming a martyr entails" (2005, p. 88). As a senior member of the Palestinian group al-Qassam declares, "it is easy to sweep the streets for boys who want to do a martyrdom operation" (Hassan, 2001, p. 39). Nonetheless, the profile of those who actually carry out suicide attacks may be somewhat older (Hassan [2001] reports a range of 18–38 years among Palestinians), suggesting that the enthusiasm of youth must be balanced with training and the development of trust to carry out such a mission. Indeed, Benmelech and Berrebi (2007) found that older and more educated Palestinian suicide bombers were assigned more important targets, caused more casualties in their attacks, and were less likely to fail.

Secular Terrorism

While some have questioned whether religious terrorism exists (e.g., Nardin, 2001), it might be more appropriate to ask whether secular terrorism exists. One advantage of the evolutionary approach we offer here is that by delineating the core adaptive features of religion that facilitate cooperation we can avoid definitional quagmires concerning what constitutes religion. This is important because we suspect that similar to their religious counterparts, successful secular terrorists employ some of these core features, such as emotionally evocative symbols, rituals, and myths. For example, although it is claimed that the LTTE movement is "secular and is eager to maintain its secular status" (Schalk, 2003, p. 395), there is considerable evidence that they employ the same features of religion that religious terrorists use to achieve their aims. The LTTE, for instance, use Hindu symbols for purposes of recruitment and rely on the language of religious martyrdom to justify and reward the sacrifice. And similar to the function of video testaments, prior to suicide missions Tamil Tigers partake in a "ritual dinner" with their leader, obviously sealing their commitment to carry out the attack (Gambetta, 2005). Furthermore, the annual "Heroes' Day" ritual celebration, commemorating the LTTE martyrs, inspires the masses and mobilizes support (Roberts, 2005). In a detailed ethnographic study, Roberts shows that these rites for martyrs "parallel the manner in which they approach the deities [and] enables those Tamils who are so inclined to appeal to the divine forces and convince themselves that their actions, and those of the LTTE, are in harmony with the cosmological arrangements" (2005, p. 83). Therefore, the secular-religious distinction made by Western societies with institutionalized religious systems may not be a useful paradigm for examining the determinants of terrorist activity. Rather, analyses would be better served by concentrating on how terrorist organizations use the particular characteristics of the human religious adaptive complex we have outlined here to inspire group commitment and individual action.

Religion as an Adaptive System

Aside from the four core features of religion discussed earlier, another aspect of religion that makes it a valuable tool for terrorists is its adaptability. This may seem surprising. Terrorists who profess strong religious commitments are viewed as inflexible and resistant to change. Because of their religious commitments, it is believed, there is no possibility of the compromise necessary for successful negotiation. Their own statements would seem to attest to inflexibility. For example, Osama bin Laden's mentor, Abdullah Yusuf Azzam, regularly repeated his trademark slogan, "Jihad and the rifle alone: no negotiations, no conferences, and no dialogues" (Rubin & Rubin, 2002).

Religious sanctity is often conceived by insiders and outsiders to be permanent and eternal. But this is simply incorrect, and the error has been made by scholars and laypeople alike. Pioneering scholars of religion, such as Durkheim, repeatedly asserted that "there is something eternal in religion" (1912/1995, pp. 429 and 432) and modern commentators have made similar claims (e.g., Berman, 2010, p. 205). In describing the sacralization of space, Hassner (2003, p. 6) states, "Once a religious presence, a hierophany, has been identified in a place, it grants the place permanent sanctity." But religions are not eternal and sanctity is not permanent; religions are flexible, malleable, and often respond adaptively to changing environmental conditions, and Hassner is fully aware of this. For example, in other work Hassner (2006) carefully describes how mosques in Iraq were targeted and recklessly destroyed when US troops were inside, suggesting a temporary suspension of their sanctity. Also during the first Gulf War, despite laws preventing Jews from entering Saudi Arabia because their presence would defile the sacred land, Jewish-American soldiers were reluctantly permitted to enter Saudi Arabia. To replace their Jewish dog tags, Jewish soldiers were given dog tags labeled "Protestant B" (Darvick, 2003). Pragmatism trumped sacred values. And since 1972, successive Israeli governments have consistently proclaimed Gaza as eternally united with Israel (Lustick, 1993); nonetheless, governance was transferred to the PLO in 1993 and in 2005 Israeli settlements were dismantled and the remaining settlers relocated to Israel.

Religion is not inflexible, and sacred values are not eternal. But why does religion appear to be resistant to change? One of the remarkable features of religion is its ability to adapt to local environmental conditions while adherents experience partaking in an eternally consistent and changeless tradition. Rappaport (1999) argues that religion achieves this through a hierarchy of religious discourse. He claims there is an inverse relationship between the material specificity of a religious claim and the durability of the claim. Religious ideas are hierarchically organized within communities and at the apex of a community's conceptual hierarchy is what Rappaport refers to as ultimate sacred postulates, such as the *Shahada*, *Shema*, or *Vandana Ti-sarana* for Muslim, Jewish, and Buddhist communities, respectively. These ultimate sacred postulates lack material specificity and are highly resistant to change. However, below ultimate sacred postulates in the religious hierarchy are various cosmological axioms, ritual proscriptions, commandments, directives, social rules, and other religious assertions that do experience varying levels of change, depending on their material specificity.

Religious norms and practices change all the time, but it is understood by those who experience such changes as an intensification of acceptance (Purzycki & Sosis, 2009; Rappaport, 1999). Religions rarely invalidate the old completely; change occurs by adding to previous practices and beliefs and elaborating upon them, while other beliefs and practices slip away unnoticed. Once sacralization is internalized, it is indeed very difficult to convince adherents that something consecrated is no longer holy. Hence, when undergoing change, religions often retain the most sacralized elements and augment them. Missionaries often retain the dates of pagan celebrations, Jewish prayers appear in the Catholic Mass, and many indigenous populations have held onto their pantheon of gods and ancestral spirits by incorporating them into the Biblical myths that are now prominent in their lives.

Two other misconceptions about the inflexibility of religion are worth mentioning. First, religious communities, even fundamentalist communities, are not homogeneous in their beliefs. In interviews one of us (R. S.) conducted among Israeli Ultra-Orthodox Jews, some have confided that they are agnostics or atheists, but they remain in their communities despite their lack of belief because they view the Ultra-Orthodox way of life positively, or at least better than the alternatives. Other researchers have reported similar experiences (e.g., Margolese, 2005; Winston, 2005). Goody (1996) has shown that doubt is widespread in world and indigenous religions and he argues that doubt is an inherent part of religious belief; theologians have made similar claims (Lamm, 1985). Second, outsiders expect religious actors who have articulated and ritually displayed their priorities—typically implying that their religious commitments are their ultimate concern—to behave in ways that directly reflect this ordering of priorities. Religious cognition, however, appears to be strongly encapsulated, preventing most religious actors from pursuing fitness-destroying behaviors (Bulbulia, 2005). Thus, while many may express extreme commitments to their sacred values, even martyrdom, the actions of most who articulate such views do not match the enthusiasm of their rhetoric.

To summarize, viewing religion as inflexible is not only inaccurate, but it impedes productive conflict resolution (Gopin, 2002). Religions are complex adaptive systems that respond effectively to changing socioeconomic and ecological conditions (Alcorta & Sosis, 2005; Purzycki & Sosis, 2009; Sosis, 2009). One of religion's vital adaptive features is its ability to appear timeless and unchanging to adherents yet be responsive to varying circumstances (Rappaport, 1999). Religions achieve this slight of hand by retaining core religious elements while readjusting social rules to accommodate new realities. Music, metaphors, poetry, and unfalsifiable postulates all contribute to this adaptability. Change for adherents is not experienced as something radically new; it is experienced as increased acceptance of eternal and personally relevant truths that have always been part of their religious tradition.

Conclusions

Dingley and Kirk-Smith suggest that "positing a rational and causal 'means-end' calculation may not be a sufficient explanation for all terrorist acts by themselves. An understanding of how terrorists think on a subjective and culturally determined level is also required, where visions, images, emotional states and experiences overlap and induce each other and find their representation in symbols" (2002, pp. 103–104). By and large we agree, but we would add that describing how terrorists think at a cultural level is not sufficient either. We maintain that an evolutionary analysis, at the proximate and ultimate levels, that explains why symbolic images and sacred values are such effective motivators is also needed. Evolutionary explanations of terrorist actions can address shortcomings of the rational choice models, particularly in analyzing sacred values, and provide us with a powerful approach to understand, and ultimately combat, terrorism.

While sacred values are used by terrorists to secure coalitional support, they also hold the key for resolving difficult conflicts that have been framed in religious terms (Sosis & Alcorta, 2008). For example, Ginges et al. (2007) have shown how symbolic concessions with little economic value, such as apologies, carry significant weight among conflicting parties. Using an evolutionarily stable strategies (ESS) approach, Sosis (2007) has shown how in territorial conflicts, sacralizing land can outperform other strategies; it appears that strategies that sacralize land can only be defeated by other sacred strategies. He has argued that to solve sacred land conflicts, the hierarchy of sacred values needs to be reordered. Fortunately, life is sacred in all the world religions (e.g., Deuteronomy 30:19, Koran 4:29), providing the possibility of a sacred life strategy outcompeting a sacred land strategy. Although it is difficult for the sacred life strategy to emerge when embraced by only a few within a population, it can stabilize if it is able to achieve high frequency. The key is convincing disputants that life has greater sanctity than land. Such debates are ongoing among theologians. In Judaism, for example, the sanctity of life is captured by the concept *pikuach nefesh*, and some prominent Orthodox rabbis, such as Joseph Soloveitchik, have argued that saving human lives has greater sanctity than the Land of Israel. Ovadia Yosef, former Sephardi Chief Rabbi of Israel and spiritual mentor of the Ultra-Orthodox Shas political party, used this argument in 1979 to justify returning the Sinai to Egypt, and regarding the conflict with the Palestinians he stated:

> If the heads of the army with the members of the government declare that lives will be endangered unless territories in the Land of Israel are relinquished, and there is the danger of an immediate declaration of war by the neighboring Arab [states]...and if

territories are relinquished the danger of war will be removed, and that there are realistic chances of lasting peace, then it appears, according to all the opinions, that it is permissible to relinquish territories of the Land of Israel...[according to the principle of] *pikuach nefesh*.
(Rosenfeld & Tabory, 1990)

It is clear that successful conflict resolution will need to operate in the currency of sacred values. Tragically, however, sacred values are rarely taken seriously by negotiators and policy makers. Representatives of religious communities, for example, have been left out of the majority of negotiations between Israelis and Palestinians. As conflict specialist Marc Gopin remarks, "Religious figures are generally considered part of the problem, but not part of creative solutions by most people in the public policy arena. Religion itself is seen as so explosive politically that to even touch upon it lays the president and high officials vulnerable to intense attack" (2002, p. 46). Ironically, although evolutionary science is often viewed as an enemy of religion, our analyses suggest that religious and sacred values must be taken seriously for conflicts to be resolved and peace sustained.

We have focused our discussion on how evolutionary theories of religion and sacred values can inform us about terrorism, but there are numerous ways in which evolutionary analyses can be productively applied to the problem of terrorism (see Sagarin & Taylor, 2008). Some scholars, for example, have posited that humans have been able to extend social relations beyond kin through an "imagined kinship" (Qirko, 2009). Political scientist Gary Johnson (1987) has explored the usage of kinship terminology as a means to inspire self-sacrifice. He posits that the purpose of employing kin terms is to elicit altruistic behavior among nonkin. Poets, orators, and writers use kin terms when they seek to evoke or create an emotional bond with a human group to which an individual is not otherwise naturally bonded. Examples include American patriotic speeches of "brotherhood," the 1970s feminist movement's usage of the word "sisters," and frequent use of kinship terminology in Christianity. Atran suggests that friends in terror networks often use familial terms and act as substitute families, while many real families are unaware that their children or siblings are involved in terrorist activities until it is too late. Islam, he argues, is a potent ideology for terrorist recruiters because "[n]early all major ideological movements, political or religious, require the subordination or assimilation of the real family (genetic kinship) to the larger imagined community of 'brothers and sisters.' Indeed, the complete subordination of biological loyalty to loyalty for the cultural cause of the Ikhwan, the 'Brotherhood' of the Prophet, is the original meaning of the word *Islam*, 'submission'" (Atran, 2010, p. 13).

There are some scholars, including prominent evolutionary scientists such as Dawkins, who have attacked religion because of its alleged association with violence (see Purzycki & Gibson, 2011). It is argued that a humanistic science should replace religion or at least that a proper scientific education could eliminate dangerous religious thinking. But as Atran points out, "An underlying reason for religion's endurance is that science treats humans and intentions only as incidental elements in the universe, whereas for religion they are central" (2010, p. 429–430). And as mentioned earlier, many terrorists have degrees in science, so it is not clear that a scientific education would necessarily reduce levels of terrorism. What is needed, however, is a scientific understanding of how terrorists employ and manipulate religion and sacred values for their benefit. Only through such understanding can we begin to identify effective strategies for combating religious terrorism.

Future Directions for Research

Our review of evolutionary perspectives on religious terrorism leaves many questions unanswered and points to the need for considerable research. We consider a few areas that we believe deserve particular attention.

1. There is some debate among evolutionary researchers regarding the role of religious beliefs in motivating and supporting terrorist attacks. Ginges et al.'s (2009) study on support for suicide attacks, for example, has been criticized by Liddle et al. (2010) for prematurely rejecting the religious-belief hypothesis. Liddle et al. argue that Ginges et al. failed to measure religious beliefs per se but rather used measures of devotion as proxies for religious beliefs. We agree with Liddle et al. that it is important to examine the genesis of motivationally salient religious beliefs in relation to suicide terrorism. The approach we have presented here, however, suggests that such religious beliefs represent proximate mechanisms derived from and reinforced through group ritual. Ritual is a vital mechanism that terrorists employ to instill beliefs and secure commitment, but detailed studies on the ritual lives of terrorists

are limited. Comparative research that examines the relationship between group ritual, religious beliefs, and suicide terrorism is needed to productively advance discussions on the role of religious belief in motivating and supporting terror. Testing for a direct effect of religious belief on terrorist activity or support for terrorist activity, however, is not straightforward. As Ginges et al. note, "To retest the belief hypothesis empirically one needs to do so in a manner that does not measure independent and dependent variables that are so close in meaning as to make relationships between these variables entirely unsurprising—or tautological" (2010, p. 347). Evidence of post hoc religious justifications by terrorists, public testimonials of religious belief, and support for violence in sacred texts do not provide adequate data for testing the religious-belief hypothesis; sophisticated research methods that disentangle casual effects will be required.

2. The study of sacred values is in its infancy. Future work must address how sacred values arise, become internalized, and spread. Among religious communities, myths that support claims to sacred lands, for example, are often quickly embraced (Sosis, 2011), but we are not aware of any studies that systematically examine the spread of sacred values in any population. Most important, research is needed to understand the flexibility of sacred values and the social conditions under which sacred values can ignite violence and bloodshed.

3. Our analyses suggest that adolescence is the critical development phase during which terrorists are created, and thus adolescents should be the focus of considerable terror-related research.

4. Rigorous experimental and ethnographic studies that examine the determinants of religious change, especially among extremist forms of religion, are urgently needed.

5. Selectionist logic suggests that high-risk behaviors, such as terrorism, are more common in high-fertility populations (e.g., Wilson & Daly, 1997). Recent studies by economists indicate a link between terrorism, religiosity, and fertility decisions (Berman, 2009). Such investigations are important because if there is a positive relationship between terror and fertility, encouraging demographic transitions through such means as expanded female educational and economic opportunities may be one means of reducing terror activity. We suspect that the predictive power of the models that have been employed by economists would be enhanced if informed by life history theory. We currently lack evolutionary models of fertility decisions that integrate evolutionary signaling theory and life history theory, but such integrated models are likely to be important for understanding the relationship between fertility, religion, and terrorist activity.

Acknowledgments

We thank Todd Shackelford and Viviana Weekes-Shackelford for helpful comments on an earlier draft of this manuscript, and Sosis thanks the Templeton Foundation for generous funding of this research.

References

Alcorta, C. S. (2006). Religion and the life course: Is adolescence an "experience expectant" period for religious transmission? In Patrick McNamara (Ed.), *Where God and science meet. Vol. 2: The neurology of religious experience* (pp. 55–80). Westport, CT: Praeger Publishers.

Alcorta, C. S. (2010). Biology, culture, and religiously motivated suicide terrorism: An evolutionary perspective. *Politics and Culture*. Retrieve January 2012, from http://www.politicsandculture.org/2010/04/29/biology-culture-and-religiously-motivated-suicide-terrorism-an-evolutionary-perspective/

Alcorta, C. S., & Sosis, R. (2005). Ritual, emotion, and sacred symbols: The evolution of religion as an adaptive complex. *Human Nature, 16*, 323–359.

Alcorta, C. S., & Sosis, R. (2007). Rituals of humans and animals. In M. Bekoff (Ed.), *Encyclopedia of human-animal relationships* (Vol. 2, pp. 599–605). Westport, CT: Greenwood Publishers.

Armstrong, K. (2000). *The battle for God*. New York: Random House.

Atkinson, Q. D., & Bourrat, P. (2010). Beliefs about God, the afterlife and morality support the role of supernatural policing in human cooperation. *Evolution and Human Behavior, 32*, 41–49.

Atran, S. (2002). *In gods we trust: The evolutionary landscape of religion*. Oxford, England: Oxford University Press.

Atran, S. (2003). Genesis of suicide terrorism. *Science, 299*, 1534–1539.

Atran, S. (2004). Mishandling suicide terrorism. *Washington Quarterly, 27*, 67–90.

Atran, S. (2006). The moral logic and growth of suicide terrorism. *Washington Quarterly, 29*, 127–147.

Atran, S. (2010). *Talking to the enemy: Faith, brotherhood, and the (un)making of terrorists*. New York: HarperCollins.

Atran, S., & Norenzayan, A. (2004). Religion's evolutionary landscape: Counterintuition, commitment, compassion, communion. *Behavioral and Brain Sciences, 27*, 713–730.

Azam, J-P. (2005). Suicide-bombing as intergenerational investment. *Public Choice, 122*, 177–198.

Barber, B. K. (2008). Contrasting portraits of war: Youths' varied experiences with political violence in Bosnia and Palestine. *International Journal of Behavioral Development, 32*, 298–309.

Bek, J., & Lock, S. (2011). Afterlife beliefs: Category specificity and sensitivity to biological priming. *Religion, Brain & Behavior, 1*, 5–17.

Belanger, N., Baum, S. R., & Titone, D. (2009). Use of prosodic cues in the production of idiomatic and literal sentences by individuals with right- and left-hemisphere damage. *Brain and Language, 110,* 38–42.

Benjamin, D., & Simon, S. (2002). *The age of sacred terror.* New York: Random House.

Benmelech, E., & Berrebi, C. (2007). Human capital and the productivity of suicide bombers. *Journal of Economic Perspectives, 21,* 223–238.

Bering, J. (2005). The evolutionary history of an illusion: Religious causal beliefs in children and adults. In B. Ellis & D. Bjorklund (Eds.), *Origins of the social mind: Evolutionary psychology and child development* (pp. 411–437). New York: The Guilford Press.

Bering, J. (2006). The folk psychology of souls. *Behavioral and Brain Sciences, 29,* 453–498

Berman, E. (2009). *Radical, religious and violent: The new economics of terrorism.* Cambridge, MA: MIT Press.

Berman, E., & Laitin, D. (2008). Religion, terrorism and public goods: Testing the club model. *Journal of Public Economics, 92,* 1942–1967.

Berman, P. (2004). *Terror and liberalism.* New York: Norton.

Berman, P. (2010). *The flight of the intellectuals.* New York: Melville House Publishing.

Berrebi, C. (2007). Evidence about the link between education, poverty, and terrorism among Palestinians. *Peace Economics, Peace Science and Public Policy, 13*(1), Article 2.

Blakemore, S-J. (2008). The social brain in adolescence. *Nature Reviews Neuroscience, 9*(4), 267–277.

Bloom, M. (2005). *Dying to kill: The global phenomenon of suicide terror.* New York: Columbia University Press.

Bodansky, Y. (2007). *Chechen jihad: Al Qaeda's training ground and the next wave of terror.* New York: HarperCollins.

Boyer, P. (2001). *Religion explained: The evolutionary origins of religious thought.* New York: Basic Books.

Brooks, D. (2002). The culture of martyrdom. *Atlantic Monthly, 289,* 18–20.

Bulbulia, J. (2004a). Religious costs as adaptations that signal altruistic intention. *Evolution and Cognition, 10,* 19–38.

Bulbulia, J. (2004b). Area review: The cognitive and evolutionary psychology of religion. *Biology and Philosophy, 18,* 655–686.

Bulbulia, J. (2005). Are there any religions? An evolutionary exploration. *Method and Theory in the Study of Religion, 17,* 71–100.

Bulled, N., & Sosis, R. (2010). Examining the influence of life expectancy on reproductive timing, total fertility, and educational attainment. *Human Nature, 21,* 269–289.

Cacioppo, J. T., Gardner, W. L., & Berntson, G. G. (2002). The affect system has parallel and integrative processing components: Form follows function. In J. T. Cacioppo, G. G. Berntson, R. Adolphs, C. S. Carter, R. J. Davidson, M. K. McClintock,...S. E. Taylor (Eds.), *Foundations in social neuroscience* (pp. 493–522). Cambridge, MA: MIT Press.

Dahl, R. E. (2004). Adolescent brain development: A period of vulnerabilities and opportunities. In R. E. Dahl & L. P. Spear (Eds.), *Adolescent brain development: Vulnerabilities and opportunities* (pp. 1–22). New York: New York Academy of Sciences.

Damasio, A. (1994). *Descartes' error: Emotion, reason, and the human brain.* New York: Avon Books.

D'Aquili, E. G., Laughlin, C. D., & McManus, J. (1979). *The spectrum of ritual.* New York: Columbia University Press.

Darvick, D. B. (2003). *This Jewish life.* New York: Eakin Press.

Desjarlais, R., Eisenberg, L., Good, B., & Kleinman, A. (1995). *World mental health.* New York: Oxford University Press.

Dingley, J., & Kirk-Smith, M. (2002). Symbolism and sacrifice in terrorism. *Small Wars and Insurgencies, 13,* 102–128.

Dressler, W. W., & Bindon, J.R. (2000). The health consequences of cultural consonance: Cultural dimensions of lifestyle, social support and arterial blood pressure in an African American community. *American Anthropologist, 102*(2), 244–260.

Durkheim, E. (1995). *The elementary forms of religious life.* New York: The Free Press. (Original work published 1912).

Eliade, M. (1959). *The sacred and the profane: The nature of religion.* New York: Harcourt Brace Jovanovich.

Flinn, M. V., & England, B. G. (1995). Childhood stress and family environment. *Current Anthropology, 36,* 854–866.

Frazer, J. G. (2010). *The golden bough.* Old Saybrook, CT: Konecky & Konecky. (Original work published 1915).

Friedland, N. (1992). Becoming a terrorist: Social and individual antecedents. In L. Howard (Ed.) *Terrorism: Roots, impact, responses* (pp. 81–93). New York: Praeger.

Gambetta, D. (2005). *Making sense of suicide missions.* Oxford, England: Oxford University Press.

Ginges, J., Atran, S., Medin, D., & Shikaki, D. (2007). Sacred bounds on rational resolution of violent conflict. *Proceedings of the National Academy of Sciences USA, 104,* 7357–7360.

Ginges, J., Hansen, I., & Norenzayan, A. (2009). Religion and support for suicide attacks. *Psychological Science, 20*(2), 224–230.

Ginges, J., Hansen, I., & Norenzayan, A. (2010). Religious belief, coalitional commitment, and support for suicide attacks. *Evolutionary Psychology, 8,* 346–349.

Goody, J. (1996). A kernel of doubt. *The Journal of the Royal Anthropological Institute, 2,* 667–681.

Gopin, M. (2002). *Holy war, holy peace: How religion can bring peace to the Middle East.* Oxford, England: Oxford University Press.

Gorenberg, G. (2000). *The end of days: Fundamentalism and the struggle for the temple mount.* New York: Free Press.

Hassan, N. (2001, November). An arsenal of believers: Talking to the "human bombs." *The New Yorker, 19,* 36–41.

Hassner, R. (2003). "To halve and to hold": Conflicts over sacred space and the problem of indivisibility. *Security Studies, 12,* 1–33.

Hassner, R. (2006). Fighting insurgency on sacred ground. *The Washington Quarterly, 29,* 149–166.

Henrich, J. (2009). The evolution of costly displays, cooperation and religion: Credibility enhancing displays and their implications for cultural evolution. *Evolution and Human Behavior, 30,* 244–260.

Hill, K., & Hurtado, A. M. (1996). *Ache life history: The ecology and demography of a foraging people.* New York: Aldine de Gruyter.

Hoffman, B. (2003). The logic of suicide terrorism. *The Atlantic Monthly, 291,* 40–47.

Hoffman, B. (2006). *Inside terrorism.* New York: Columbia University Press.

Hudson, R. A. (1999). *The sociology and psychology of terrorism: Who becomes a terrorist and why?* A report prepared under an interagency agreement by the Federal Research Division, Library of Congress, September 1999. Retrieved December 2011, from http://www.loc.gov/rr/frd/pdf-files/Soc_Psych_of_Terrorism.pdf

Irons, W. (2001). Religion as a hard-to-fake sign of commitment. In R. Nesse (Ed.), *Evolution and the capacity for commitment* (pp. 292–309). New York: Russell Sage Foundation.

Johnson, D. (2005). God's punishment and public goods: A test of the supernatural punishment hypothesis in 186 world cultures. *Human Nature, 16*, 410–446.

Johnson, G. R. (1987). In the name of the fatherland: An analysis of kin term usage in patriotic speech and literature. *International Political Science Review, 8*(2), 165–174.

Jongman, A., & Schmid, A. P. (1983). *Political terrorism.* Amsterdam: North Holland.

Juergensmeyer, M. (2002). *Religious terror and global war.* Global and International Studies Program, Paper 2. Retrieved December 2011, from http://repositories.cdlib.org/gis/2

Juergensmeyer, M. (2003). *Terror in the mind of god: The global rise in religious violence.* Berkeley: University of California Press.

Juergensmeyer, M. (2004a, October 14–15). *From Bhindranwale to bin Laden: The rise of religious violence.* Presentation at Arizona State University, Tempe, AZ.

Juergensmeyer, M. (2004b). Holy orders: Opposition to modern states. *Harvard International Review, 25*, 34–38.

Juergensmeyer, M. (2004c). Is religion the problem? *Hedgehog Review, 6*, 21–33.

Karsh, E. (2007). *Islamic imperialism: A history.* New Haven, CT: Yale University Press.

Kelemen, D. (2004). Are children "intuitive theists"? Reasoning about purpose and design in nature. *Psychological Science, 15*, 295–301.

Krabbendam, L., & van Os, J. (2005). Schizophrenia and urbanicity: A major environmental influence—conditional on genetic risk. *Schizophrenia Bulletin, 31*, 795–799.

Krueger, A. B. (2007). *What makes a terrorist: Economics and the roots of terrorism.* Princeton, NJ: Princeton University Press.

Kwon, Y. J., & Lawson, A. E. (2000). Linking brain growth with the development of scientific reasoning ability and conceptual change during adolescence. *Journal of Research in Science Teaching, 37*(1), 44–62.

Lamm, N. (1985). *Faith and doubt: Studies in traditional Jewish thought.* New York: Ktav.

Lewis, B. (2002). *What went wrong? Western impact and Middle Eastern response.* London: Phoenix.

Lewis, B. (2003). *The crisis of Islam: Holy war and unholy terror.* New York: Random House.

Lincoln, B. (2003). *Holy terrors: Thinking about religion after September 11.* Chicago: University of Chicago Press.

Liddle, J. R., Machluf, K., Shakelford, T. K. (2010). Understanding suicide terrorism: Premature dismissal of the religious-belief hypothesis. *Evolutionary Psychology, 8*, 343–345.

Lustick, I. S. (1993). Reinventing Jerusalem. *Foreign Policy, 93*, 41–60.

Lutkehaus, N. C., & Roscoe, P. B. (Eds.). (1995). *Gender rituals: Female initiation in Melanesia.* New York: Routledge.

Margolese, F. (2005). *Off the derech: How to respond to the challenge.* Jerusalem: Devora Publishing.

McDade, T. W. (2002). Status incongruity in Samoan youth: A biocultural analysis of culture change, stress, and immune function. *Medical Anthropology Quarterly, 16*(2), 123–150.

McDade, T. W., Stallings, J. F., & Worthman, C. M. (2000). Culture change and stress in western Samoan youth: Methodological issues in the cross-cultural study of stress and immune function. *American Journal of Human Biology, 12*, 792–802.McGrath, J., Saha, S., Welham, J., El Saadi, E., MacCauley, C., & Chant, D. (2004). A systematic review of the incidence of schizophrenia: The distribution of rates and the influence of sex, urbanicity, migrant status and methodology. *BMC Medicine, 2*, 13.

McGraw, A. P., Tetlock, P. E., & Kristel, O. V. (2003). The limits of fungibility: Relational schemata and the value of things, *Journal of Consumer Research, 30*, 219–229.

Merari, A. (1993). Terrorism as a strategy in insurgency. *Terrorism and Political Violence, 5*, 213–251.

Molloy, M. (2008). *Experiencing the world's religions: Tradition, culture, and change.* Boston: McGraw-Hill.

Nardin, T. (2001). Review: Terror in the mind of God. *The Journal of Politics, 64*, 683–684.

Pape, R. (2005). *Dying to win: The strategic logic of suicide terrorism.* New York: Random House.

Pedahzur, A., & Perliger, A. (2009). *Jewish terrorism in Israel.* New York: Columbia University Press.

Purzycki, B. G., & Gibson, K. (2011). Religion and violence: An anthropological study on religious belief and violent behavior. *Skeptic, 16*, 24–29.

Purzycki, B. G., & Sosis, R. (2009). The religious system as adaptive: Cognitive flexibility, public displays, and acceptance. In E. Voland & W. Schiefenhövel (Eds.), *The biological evolution of religious mind and behavior* (pp. 243–256). New York: Springer Publishers.

Qirko, H. N. (2009). Altruism in suicide terror organizations. *Zygon: Journal of Religion and Science, 44*, 289–322.

Qutb, S. (2007). *Islam: Religion of the future.* New Dehli, India: Markazi Maktaba Islami.

Rappaport, R. A. (1999). *Ritual and religion in the making of humanity.* London: Cambridge University Press.

Richardson, L. (2006). *What terrorists want.* New York: Random House.

Roberts, M. (2005). Saivite symbols, sacrifice, and Tamil Tiger rites. *Social Analysis, 49*, 67–93.

Rosenfeld, E., & Tabory, B. (1990). *Crossroads: Halacha & the modern world.* Jerusalem: Urim.

Rubin, B., & Rubin, J.C. (2002). *Anti-American terrorism and the Middle East.* New York: Oxford University Press.

Ruffle, B., & Sosis, R. (2007). Does it pay to pray? Costly rituals and cooperation. *The BE Press of Economic Policy and Analysis (Contributions), 7*, 1–35(Article 18).

Ruthven, M. (2004). *Fundamentalism: The search for meaning.* New York: Oxford University Press.

Sageman, M. (2004). *Understanding terror networks.* Philadelphia: University of Pennsylvania Press.

Sageman, M. (2008). *Leaderless jihad: Terror networks in the twenty-first century.* Philadelphia: University of Pennsylvania Press.

Sagarin, R., & Taylor, T. (Eds.). (2008). *Natural security: A Darwinian approach to dangerous world.* Berkeley: University of California Press.

Sapolsky, R. M. (1996). Why stress is bad for your brain. *Science, 273*, 749–750.

Schalk, P. (2003). Beyond Hindu festivals: The celebration of Great Heroes' Day by the Liberation Tigers of Tamil Eelam (LTTE) in Europe. In M. Baumann, B. Luchesi, & A. Wilke (Eds.), *Tempel und Tamilien in zweiter Heimat* (pp. 391–411). Wurzburg, Germany: Ergon Verlag.

Schloss, J., & Murray, M. (2011). Evolutionary accounts of belief in supernatural punishment: A critical review. *Religion, Brain & Behavior, 1*, 46–99.

Schneider, G., K. Barbieri, K., & Gleditsch, N.P. (Eds.). (2003). *Globalization and armed conflict.* Lanham, MD: Rowman and Littlefield.

Shariff, A., & Norenzayan, A. (2007). God is watching you: Supernatural agent concepts increase prosocial behavior in an anonymous economic game. *Psychological Science, 18,* 803–809.

Sidtis, D. V. (2006). Where in the brain is nonliteral language? *Metaphor and Symbol, 21,* 213–244.

Simon, S., & Benjamin, D. (2000). America and the new terrorism. *Survival, 42,* 59–75.

Soler, M. (2008). Commitment costs and cooperation: evidence from Cadomble, an Afro-Brazilian religion. In J. Bulbulia, R. Sosis, E. Harris, C. Genet, R. Genet, & K. Wyman (Eds.), *The evolution of religion: Studies, theories, and critiques* (pp. 167–173). Santa Margarita, CA: Collins Foundation Press.

Sosis, R. (2003). Why aren't we all Hutterites? Costly signaling theory and religion. *Human Nature, 14,* 91–127.

Sosis, R. (2005). Does religion promote trust? The role of signaling, reputation, and punishment. *Interdisciplinary Journal of Research on Religion, 1,* 1–30 (Article 7).

Sosis, R. (2006). Religious behaviors, badges, and bans: Signaling theory and the evolution of religion. In P. McNamara (Ed.), *Where God and science meet: How brain and evolutionary studies alter our understanding of religion. Vol. 1: Evolution, genes, and the religious brain* (pp. 61–86). Westport, CT: Praeger Publishers.

Sosis, R. (2007, October 11–13). *The evolutionary logic of sacred land*. Paper presented at the Religion and Violence Symposium: Evolutionary and Political Perspectives, St. Louis, MO.

Sosis, R. (2009). Why are synagogue services so long? An evolutionary examination of Jewish ritual signals. In R. Goldberg (Ed.) *Judaism and biological perspective: Biblical lore and Judaic practices* (pp. 199–233). Boulder, CO: Paradigm Publishers.

Sosis, R. (2011). Why sacred lands are not indivisible: The cognitive foundations of sacralizing land. *Journal of Terrorism Research, 2,* 17–44.

Sosis, R., & Alcorta, C. S. (2003). Signaling, solidarity and the sacred: The evolution of religious behavior. *Evolutionary Anthropology, 12,* 264–274.

Sosis, R., & Alcorta, C.S. (2008). Militants and martyrs: Evolutionary perspectives on religion and terrorism. In R. Sagarin & T. Taylor (Eds.), *Natural security: A Darwinian approach to a dangerous world* (pp. 105–124). Berkeley: University of California Press.

Sosis, R., & Bressler, E. (2003). Cooperation and commune longevity: A test of the costly signaling theory of religion. *Cross-Cultural Research, 37,* 211–239.

Sosis, R., Kress, H., & Boster, J. (2007). Scars for war: Evaluating alternative signaling explanations for cross-cultural variance in ritual costs. *Evolution and Human Behavior, 28,* 234–247.

Sosis, R., & Ruffle, B. (2003). Religious ritual and cooperation: Testing for a relationship on Israeli religious and secular kibbutzim. *Current Anthropology, 44,* 713–722.

Sosis, R., & Ruffle, B. (2004). Ideology, religion, and the evolution of cooperation: Field tests on Israeli kibbutzim. *Research in Economic Anthropology, 23,* 89–117.

Steinberg, L. (2007). Cognitive and affective development in adolescence. *Trends in Cognitive Sciences, 9,* 69–74.

Sundquist, K., Frank, G., & Sundquist, J. (2004). Urbanisation and incidence of psychosis and depression. *British Journal of Psychiatry, 184,* 293–298.

Tetlock, P. E. (2003). Thinking the unthinkable: Sacred values and taboo cognitions. *Trends in Cognitive Sciences, 7,* 320–324.

Tetlock, P. E., McGraw, A. P., & Kristel, O. (2003). Proscribed forms of social cognition: Taboo trade-offs, blocked exchanges, forbidden base rates, and heretical counterfactuals. In N. Haslam (Ed.), *Relational models theory: A contemporary overview* (pp. 247–262xx). Mahwah, NJ: Erlbaum.

van Os, J. (2004). Does the urban environment cause psychosis? *British Journal of Psychiatry, 184,* 287–288.

Victoroff, J. (2005). The mind of the terrorist: A review and critique of psychological approaches. *Journal of Conflict Resolution, 49,* 3–42.

Villarreal, L. P. (2008). From bacteria to belief: Immunity and security. In R. Sagarin & T. Taylor (Eds.), *Natural security: A Darwinian approach to a dangerous world* (pp. 42–68). Berkeley: University of California Press.

Whitehouse, H. (2004). *Modes of religiosity: A cognitive theory of religious transmission*. New York: Alta Mira Press.

Whitehouse, H. (2008). Cognitive evolution and religion; cognition and religious evolution In J. Bulbulia, R. Sosis, E. Harris, C. Genet, R. Genet, & K. Wyman (Eds.), *The evolution of religion: Studies, theories, and critiques* (pp. 31–41). Santa Margarita, CA: Collins Foundation Press.

Wilson, M., & Daly, M. (1997). Life expectancy, economic inequality, homicide, and reproductive timing in Chicago neighbourhoods. *British Medical Journal, 314,* 1271–1274.

Winston, H. (2005). *Unchosen: The hidden lives of Hasidic rebels*. Boston: Beacon Press.

Wolf, E. (1982). *Europe and the people without history*. Berkeley: University of California Press.

World Health Organization. (2001). Burden of mental and behavioural disorders. In *World Health Organization report 2001* (pp. 19–45). New York: Author.

CHAPTER 15

Animal Abuse and Cruelty

Emily G. Patterson-Kane *and* Heather Piper

Abstract

This chapter addresses animal abuse and animal cruelty, along with some of the explanations that a range of disciplines have proffered when seeking to understand and predict such behaviors, with a focus on evolutionary biology. While providing yet another theory from which to explain violence and cruelty is not the main endeavor of this chapter, nevertheless some suggestions are made that may help future consideration of cruelty and violence. In particular, the need for inter/multidisciplinary research on animal abuse and cruelty is highlighted. Also, it is suggested that the study of morally weighted behavior benefits from moving between paradigms to distinguish issues of causality and consequence from issues of social approbation and political agendas.

Key Words: aggression, animal abuse, animal cruelty, evolutionary biology, violence

Introduction

Many disciplines and professions address social issues such as animal abuse and cruelty. These include psychology, anthropology, sociology, psychiatry, and a growing number of cognate fields of study. They employ an array of philosophical and scientific theories and/or paradigms, attempting to explain and in some contexts predict and influence the occurrence of these undesirable behaviors. Evolutionary biology (including sociobiology and evolutionary psychology) is one complementary strand of this endeavor. An evolutionary perspective promotes understanding of the innate biological factors that might contribute to the occurrence of animal abuse either through biological predisposition, repurposing or distortion of natural motivational systems, or the breakdown of normal function due to a biology/environment dissonance. Conscious of the extended timescales required for anything classified as evolution to take place, such terms as "historic," "traditional," or "ancestral" are recognized here as sometimes being used in a relatively flexible but heuristic way.

Definitions

"Aggression" is typically defined as causing pain or harm, most frequently to a member of one's own species. Socially unacceptable forms of aggression, and those with lasting effect, are referred to as "violence." One of the most persistent difficulties of this term is that categorizing together a broad class of behaviors in a single category can lead to the assumption that these behaviors share a single cause, motivation, or goal. And equally, separating out violence/aggression from other antisocial behaviors, such as substance abuse, damaging property, or swearing, makes it less likely that any real understanding based on social and economic factors will be reached. Many researchers have encouraged the development of a scheme for recognizing fundamentally different motivations for different violent acts, and more recently a similar approach is being applied to the different kinds of violence against animals (e.g., Arluke & Lockwood, 1997; Hensley & Tallichet, 2005).

When it comes to discussing animals as victims, animal abuse and animal cruelty do not enjoy standardized definitions (Vermeulen & Odendaal, 1993); however, these terms are in common and academic usage, distinguishing two broad types of human behavior. Conduct that causes an animal to suffer is generally referred to as animal abuse—this is a broad category including willful, ignorant, and negligent acts (Cazaux, 1999). Cruelty is a more narrowly defined category relating to the deliberate infliction of pain (Nell, 2006). It includes, but is not always limited to, situations where causing pain is the main or only motivation of the action and where the perpetrator enjoys inflicting and observing pain (e.g., Kurt-Swanger & Patcosky, 2003; Rowan, 1993).

Many animal uses sanctioned by mainstream society are typically not categorized as cruelty even when they do result in pain or other forms of suffering (Rowan, 1993, c.f. Kochi, 2009). The ethical implications of many of these practices, for example, traditional and commercial meat production and fishing, and even particular approaches to dog breeding, are contested topics. This discussion is for the most part focused on instances that would commonly be judged to involve violence and cruelty per se and cannot deal substantially with the arguably distinct issue of nonviolent causes of animal suffering such as neglect, incorrect care, abandonment, or close confinement (Henry, 2009; Mason, 1998; Novek, 2005). However, it is impossible to consider this topic without making reference to the complex and ambiguous manner in which humans have always dealt (conceptually, mentally, and physically) with nonhuman animals.

Even given the tight focus on acts of violence and cruelty per se, and while avoiding issues such as changing farming practices, disputes over commercial fishing and hunting, and the rise of ethically motivated vegetarianism, in a discussion of evolutionary approaches, there are necessary and relevant self-limiting historical and cultural points to be made. In Europe only a few hundred years ago, public bear baiting and dog or cock fighting were unexceptional spectacles. The sight of extreme violence being visited on a tired or unwilling "beast of burden" would cause no comment. Over time, attitudes and regulations have changed. Specialized police units seek out those humans responsible for clandestine dogfights, and aged or injured racing greyhounds that once would have been dispatched as a matter of routine are now made available for "rescue," to save the "industry" from prosecution or bad publicity. In Turkey and its region, the dancing bears that were once common are now fewer and increasingly anachronistic. In Spain the ubiquity and nobility of the *corrida*, long a national signature tradition, is now being questioned.

In the longer term, while some religions have, in effect, permitted a relatively careless approach to animal well-being, for instance, by giving humans dominion over them, others (particularly linked to Buddhism) have conceived of the protection of all life forms as an absolute human priority. These changes and variations are mentioned because all are observable within a much shorter time frame than is needed for the imperatives of evolutionary biology to apply or be effective. They indicate the extensive changes and variations that occur, notwithstanding any biologically evolutionary influences, and suggest the power of change at the level of human ideas and values, as well as the developing economic and social context in which this takes place. While these realities cannot be the focus of the present discussion, they remain relevant.

The issue of animal cruelty is most frequently addressed by a consideration of three questions: the first being why aggression is shown toward animals; the second why some individuals are violent toward animals when this is not socially acceptable; and finally, how social acceptability is established and enforced.

Animal cruelty appears to be universally present in human societies and human history as far as it is possible to ascertain, and it is relatively common in young children (although some commentators treat it as evidence of an exceptional and individual pathology). On this basis it is argued by some that animal cruelty and other "immoral" behavior must in some way reflect species-wide evolutionary processes (e.g., Lieberman, Tooby, & Cosmides, 2003). It would appear also that animal cruelty is more common than is widely realized. Surveys show that around 37% of males report having committed at least one act of animal cruelty (Patterson-Kane & Piper, 2009) and while the incidence in females is less clear it may be that lower reported rates result in part from the greater difficulty that females may have in admitting to such typically "masculine"/aggressive behavior (Piper, 2003).

Animal Cruelty as an Expression of Adaptive Drives

Several accounts of human aggression suggest that aggression is a generally adaptive behavior that promotes learning, often occurring in situations that evoke feelings of curiosity or frustration. Under these circumstances the identity of the victim, for example, as an animal, is not necessarily functionally important. The animal is implicated in the broader conditions that facilitate a behavior with a cruel outcome—without that outcome being the primary object of the behavior. In other words, the victim could just as likely be a young child, or a peer, or a stranger, or in fact anyone who happens to be available.

DIRTY PLAY

In individuals characterized by incomplete cognitive development, such as young children, cruel play may be entered into and enjoyed because of a lack of understanding or full consideration of (rather than a disregard of) the fact that the animal being manipulated is being harmed or is suffering. The same may be observed when children harm themselves or others when learning more about cause and effect (e.g., by poking a finger in someone's eye or pinching someone). The investigation of novelty and the practice of operant behaviors are generally adaptive, leading to improved future competence. Play, in general, is practice for life and coping with surprises (Spinka, Newberry, & Bekoff, 2001) and animals are uniquely suited to produce unexpected outcomes because they are complex and unpredictably reactive. In these cases it can be argued that the cruelty is an extension of instrumental and normative impulses that are to be expected, but they should be redirected for humane reasons.

Many traditional societies had complex and subtle conceptual and practical relationships with nonhuman animals, exemplified, in fiction, for instance, by "the last of the Mohicans" eulogizing and thanking the deer that he had just killed for its meat (Fenimore Cooper, 1826/1998). Casual cruelty or "dirty play" would probably have been directed largely toward low-status wild or feral animals without the knowledge or intervention of society—currently instanced by infelicitous but not infrequent youthful practices such as firing BB guns at birds, bursting frogs by inflating them with straws, or removing the wings from flies. As industrialized nations become more affluent and more urbanized, the animals available for explorative cruelty have become predominantly domesticated companion animals (as some children living in cities rarely or never see farm or wild animals). The abuse of pets is far more likely to be discovered and condemned due to a pet's status as an owned animal and companion.

As individuals come to realize that animals are sentient and to recognize the realities of cause and effect, and notions of responsibility, they may strike a balance between how exciting the play is and how severe or irreparable the harm to the animal is. For example, they may limit the cruel play to teasing and tormenting an animal but not physically hurting it, or by limiting cruelty to wild animals or insects (Arluke, 2002). Where dirty play clearly results in socially unacceptable cruelty (due to severity or target choice), this requires further explanation, such as the existence of stronger motivation for the performance of cruelty, cruelty to the animal acquiring specific rewards value, and/or the absence of mechanisms to inhibit cruelty.

FRUSTRATION AND ANGER

Emphatic and uninhibited behavior has been observed in many species in response to frustration. Dollard et al. (1939) proposed that frustration was the primary source of motivation for aggressive behavior (referred to as the "frustration-aggression hypothesis"). When a previously successful course of behavior is thwarted, an animal will often show increased behavioral variability and intensity—and so increase the chance of happening upon a new productive (rewarded) course of action. As such, frustration-aggression and learning are analogous to random mutation and natural selection, and the nature and effects of frustration-aggression tend to be relatively indiscriminate. This characteristic of aggression may explain why studies often find correlations of similar strength between "deviant" acts against animals, people, and property rather than, for example, there being a particularly high correlation between crimes with sentient victims (i.e., humans and animals) (Arluke, 2000).

In a more generalized sense, a suboptimal environment may cause more long-term states such as hunger, stress, discomfort, and fear, which may change general levels and types of behavioral reactivity so that outbursts of frustration become more frequent, severe, or aberrant (Grinde, 2000). However, critics of the frustration-aggression hypothesis point out that although frustration produces arousal, in most people acts of actual violence are inhibited by the knowledge that the victim is sentient (or that the act is socially unacceptable). As a consequence, outbursts take other forms such as thoughts, verbal behavior, or actions against inanimate objects. Thus, even in situations that elicit frustration the degree of violence in an outburst, and particularly the choice of a target animal, appear to require further explanation (e.g., Bandura, 1973; Gordon, Kinlock, & Battjes, 2004).

FITNESS INCREASING MALE AGGRESSION

Biological science, in general, and ethology in particular, have been dogged by a naturalist or essentialist approach to sex (i.e., male, female; see Cadwallader, 2005). For example, there is a perception (contrary to modern studies of many species such as lions and wolves) that males are exclusively the hunters of the animal kingdom (c.f. Singh, 2001). This is extended across species, resulting in the view that women are not "naturally" hunters and, therefore, should not be the providers and breadwinners even in modern society. As a corollary, women who contravene this assumption are seen as somehow unnatural and acting in a way that is counter to the good of society.

Similarly, over the last half century a powerful discourse has developed around sociobiology and evolutionary psychology. It is argued that the male role is partly determined by evolutionary imperatives and impulses from our past, which required the male to be dominant or to assert control (Demarrest & LaTorre, 1998), which is to say, to be aggressive. As such, aggression is often studied and explicated as predominantly or even exclusively a male activity, and behaviors such as war and rape are explained as either natural or aberrant expressions of masculinity (c.f. humanity, see Schell, 2007).

The predominance of young adult men as the perpetrators of most severe, overt violence is widely apparent (e.g., Baldry, 2003, 2005; Desnoyers, 2009; Flynn, 1999, 2002; Henry, 2004; Lea, 2008; Pagani, Robustelli, & Ascione, 2007). However, the interaction between gender and the motivations behind different types of violence (rather than incidence and severity alone) is rarely examined. For example, the near-equivalent rates of domestic violence, initiated by women and by men, reported by several surveys released from the mid-1970s up to recent years, remains controversial and poorly explained (e.g., Kelly, 2003; Mhaka-Mutefa, 2009; Plumridge & Fielding, 2009; Stets & Straus, 1990). The disproportionate involvement of females in nonviolent animal abuse (starvation, hoarding, neglect; see Desnoyers, 2009; Herzog, 2007) may also be underexamined in proportion of the amount of animal suffering it causes.

One study of a group of psychology students found that attitudes toward animal cruelty were related to different emotional experiences in men versus women, suggesting some difference in underlying motivations (men: hostility and need for power; women: serenity, Oleson & Henry, 2009, c.f. Felthous & Yudowitz, 1977). As such female perpetrators of animal abuse may require different types of intervention from those developed for male offenders.

That said, the predominance of males as perpetrators of overt violence can be seen across species, where the evolutionarily functional violence of young males is expressed through attacks on members of their own or other species. For example, incidents of dolphins attacking and killing porpoises have been described. The most plausible explanation for this behavior, shown by groups of juvenile male dolphins, is that they are acting out of frustration while free from normal social constraints, or practicing for infanticide by isolating and killing juveniles to make females available for breeding (Stewart, 1999).

This general masculine motivation is seen by some as the basis for the use of violence as a means of entertainment and as a mechanism for obtaining social power and control (Wilson & Daly, 1985). For example, the threat of violence against pet animals may be used as a method to intimidate or control a spouse or child. However, actual violence to pets may result from the hierarchy of unacceptability impacting on the choice of victim on whom to vent frustration in the domestic situation (e.g., the weakest member of the family ends up kicking the dog). In fact, common approaches to all kinds of domestic violence tend to be framed implicitly on this understanding of the gendered function of cruelty with the abuser described as "the dominant male" (Zilney, 2007). Common forms of animal abuse demonstrated by young men, particularly when in groups, are also seen as an assertion to their peers of their personal power and/or masculinity.

The majority of extreme, physically violent acts of animal cruelty are committed by boys or men. However, while sex (male, female) is part of the context in which animal cruelty may occur, it is neither a necessary nor a sufficient cause or predictor of such behavior in general (George, 1997). It is possible, and indeed appears likely (Desnoyers, 2009), that acts of animal cruelty carried out by women may be seriously underreported, due to their unexpected nature and more covert character (e.g., more often relating to psychological rather than physical suffering, their occurrence within the home, and the relative taboo against female admission to violent acts, or indeed against men wanting to admit to being the subject of a woman's violence; see Herzog, 2007).

It is also the case that the majority of young men do not carry out violent crimes, and also that cruelty correlates with certain "styles" of masculinity (e.g., "macho" attitude; Grandin, 1988) not just biological sex. One major area where social acceptability is in flux is the nature of "manliness" and diverse "masculinities" and how this relates to aggressive and violent behavior, including animal abuse (Boddice, 2008).

It has also been recognized that the suppression of violence is as much a part of the role of males as is the commission of violence (e.g., Huizinga, Schumann, Ehret, & Elliott, 2004). There have been observations in many animal species, including a wide range of primates in both free and captive environments, that the presence of a senior male reduces the levels of aggression shown between individuals in a group. In the absence of a senior male, two types of aggression increase: "acting out" by young males, and violence between females (e.g., Hoff, Nadler, & Maple, 1982). The behavior of interfering and breaking up fights is shown not only by the alpha male but by most mature males and females. Males typically intervene by confronting aggressively the instigator of a conflict until the instigator desists. In particular, they are defensive of family members (Petit & Thierry, 1994). Equally important, they demonstrate effective reconciliation skills to normalize relationships once the aggressive episode ends (De Waal, 2004), and this reconciliation ability is an important acquired social skill motivated by the need to maintain valuable relationships. Mature females are naturally aggressive in the defense of juveniles, even when they are normally less dominant or of lower status than the instigator of the aggression (Kaplan, 2005). The presence of fathers, other mature males, or even patrilineal females, is associated with reduction of community violence in humans (Huizinga et al., 2004) and other species (e.g., elephants: Slotow & Van Dyk, 2001).

Thus, any simplistic picture of males as a source of violence fails to give emphasis to the role of mature individuals in suppressing violence and defending vulnerable members of their social group. On this basis, one potential intervention is to provide supervision by dominant individuals to suppress violence by juveniles and young adults, and to promote the development of a mature sex role where authority is gained through social skills, including appeasement and reconciliation (Bernstein, 1976).

The typically dichotomized treatment and conflation of sex (male, female), aggression, and abuse fails to address the situational legitimacy of aggressive defense of self and/or vulnerable others (see Saunders, 1986). It seems to be less important that aggression be minimized per se, but rather that it is employed only functionally, constructively, and defensively by both males and females of a species (e.g., Albert, Walsh, Zalys, & Dyson, 1987), which would most likely lead to a lower level of violence and abuse overall. Returning to earlier points, we may consider domesticated animals to be particularly vulnerable community members who are not "persons" with a legal right to defend themselves aggressively (Srivastava, 2007). Therefore, a person (male or female) who abuses a defenseless companion animal, and a person (male or female) who does not act to protect his or her animals from abuse, can be seen as having malfunctions in his or her aggressive behavior in relation to the functional biological role of aggression.

Animal Suffering and Reward Value
EXPRESSION OF PREDATORY INSTINCTS

One of the principal benefits of aggression in the human ancestral environment was success in hunting, which was necessary for survival and reproduction (see Mysterud & Poleszynski, 2003; Smil, 2002). Success in hunting requires the twin skills of understanding and predicting animal behavior, in order to encounter and kill the animal. Thus, the effective human hunter is characterized both by empathy and the capacity to neutralize such empathy when the time is right (Serpell, 1989). This suggests the existence of psychological mechanisms to dissociate humans from animals that are perceived as prey (as examined in Martens, Kosloff, Greenberg, Landau, & Schmader, 2007). Interestingly, parallel research into serial killers suggests that they do not lack empathy per se but categorize people so that some deserve empathy and respect, and others do not. Similarly, when questioned, some who will admit to harming cats report that they would "kill anyone who harms my dog" (Piper, 2004).

The root cause of abuse is often suggested to be predatory, such that the targeted animal fills the role of a prey animal, for whom[1] compassion is neutralized. Others argue that activities victimizing any animal (e.g., hunting, slaughterhouse work) are destructive to overall character and compassion (c.f. studies finding no connection, Carlisle-Frank, Frank, & Nielsen, 2004; Flynn, 2002). However, the context in which such judgments of moral value are made is variable, since the categories of animals determined to be "fair game" are a matter of mutual incomprehension and dispute in and between modern societies (e.g., Anadu, Elamah, & Oates, 1988; Kochi, 2009; Rollin, 2001). Other distinctions are also far from absolute, including the particular status of pet animals. Of course, like humans many pet species have predatory impulses that may be elicited under specific circumstances. Young children are at risk of prompting chasing and attack behavior from dogs, making them the highest-risk group for serious dog bites (Avner & Baker, 1991; Sacks, Kresnow, & Houston, 1996). Also, under extreme circumstances pets will eat humans and humans will eat pets, just as (exceptionally) humans will eat humans.

DELIBERATE DEVIANCE

Animal cruelty may be attractive to some people because it is socially unacceptable. For example, known boundaries may be challenged and crossed during the developmental phase of adolescent rebellion (Arluke, 2002). Also in the purposive category is "shock art," which aims to destabilize assumptions and evoke feelings of outrage or disgust, as it sometimes employs real or hoax animal cruelty. For example, Marco Evaristti created an art exhibit of goldfish displayed in fully operational food blenders, allowing members of the public to destroy the fish on a whim. In a display of 10 fish, 5 were killed and 5 were rescued and removed before the museum was ordered to cut power to the blenders (Wienberg, 2000). Presumably the artist made an assessment, playing on common ambiguities and confusions and seeking to optimize the balance between artistic, animal, moral, and financial hierarchies. House flies or mosquitoes in the blenders may have provoked insufficient empathy and response from the public, while to introduce kittens for the role might have led the museum to terminate his commission. This artistic and regulatory event also shows, in microcosm, the ability for some to be actively and unnecessarily cruel, and others to be actively protective. But the question of identifying the basis of these differences remains.

Animal Cruelty as a Failure of Inhibition
LOSS OF QUASI-HUMAN/FAMILY STATUS

Many researchers have concluded that working and/or companion animals often enjoy protection from harmful use (e.g., as a food source) and abuse as a result of being accepted within the human social circle (e.g., Bonas, McNicholas, & Collis, 2000; Cohen, 2002). Most people consider their pet a member of the family, yet it must be acknowledged that pets are frequently abandoned, with a large number ultimately entering shelters and/or being euthanized for reasons of convenience rather than necessity (yet interestingly, in the United Kingdom at least, a charity appealing for funding for animals will often do better than one appealing for funding for children; see Glendinning, 2008). Perpetrators of violence who target pets tend to be those who previously showed less affection to the pet and view them as property and not family members (Carlisle-Frank et al., 2004). The presence of some kind of human-animal bond is considered to help protect animals from abuse, including not only pets but also livestock (Anthony, 2003).

Beyond this protective relationship, status is sometimes dependent on utility, so that old or impaired animals are dispatched, with or without regret. Furthermore, the privileging of an animal as equal to or more than a human is widely condemned, and in some social contexts the responsibility of pet keeping is criticized as wasteful or extravagant on an economic or environmental basis (Hadley & O'Sullivan, 2009; Vale & Vale, 2009).

Thus, the level of privilege and protection that should be accorded to companion animals is far from a settled matter even within a particular society. Across a wide range of cultures, animals are widely seen as of greater value than nonprecious inanimate objects, but of less value than humans (e.g., Roscoe, Haney, & Peterson, 1986). (However, the value of a specific animal can be found anywhere in and beyond this range from prized pet to vermin; Beatson, Loughnan, & Halloran, 2009). Animal inferiority is the basis for most languages possessing a wide range of insults based on referring to a human by an animal name (Leach, 1964) (These insults often are targeted at women—although some animal descriptors are less clear in their intention, e.g., foxy, kittenish, and leonino/e). And it is often assumed that if animals are given essentially the same status as humans (e.g., eliminating speciesism), this would drastically improve their treatment. However, even as quasi-humans, animals would remain vulnerable and unequal citizens within human culture, and in these circumstances the relationship between inequality and abuse appears likely to remain significant, if variable.

Chisholm and Burbank (2001) argue that humans generally react poorly to inequality. They posit that hunter-gatherer societies are relatively egalitarian and individuals have limited opportunities to treat other humans disrespectfully without personally experiencing negative repercussions. If this is the kind of environment in which the human mind evolved, it may lack a behavioral module to restrain individuals from abusing power over vulnerable individuals through self-restraint alone. They argue also that humans are not well adapted to experiencing inequality and that the main result of being in a disadvantaged group, subject to risk and adversity, is to reproduce earlier and more often in the hope of having offspring who are able to survive under these difficult circumstances, with resulting negative effects on health and welfare. Humans whose experience of life is brutish and short, and whose priorities are focused accordingly, appear less likely to demonstrate cross-species empathy and the recognition of intrinsic (rather than utility) value in other animals, or indeed, in other humans.

ABERRANT HUMAN/FAMILY STANDING

It must also be recognized that animals can be abused because of family or quasi-human standing. Pets may be subject to jealousy from aspiring or actual romantic partners, or children (see Hellman & Blackman, 1966; MacDonald, 1963; e.g., Jordan, 2010). They may be seen as adversaries by neighbors (e.g., Barcott, 2007; Sutschek, 2010). Cats seem to be subject to particularly sadistic abuse due to their symbolic association with human femininity, in general, and witchcraft in particular (Lockwood, 2005).

It has been suggested that children may see a pet as a rival. "The Triad" (also called "The MacDonald Triad") is a theory that three types of deviant behavior—fire setting, bed wetting, and animal abuse—are likely to occur together (c.f. Sendi & Blomgren, 1975). However, this account has subsequently been challenged (Prentky & Carter, 1984; Ryan & Skrapec, 2008), as has the idea of the "links" (i.e., that violence leads to violence), which, although subject to critique, gained some precedence, as many have sought to identify children harming animals as a distinct deviant act. It is also argued that children may abuse pets because they receive (human) parental love of which the child feels he or she is deprived (Hellman & Blackman, 1966; MacDonald, 1963).

Humane Concern for Animals

A tension may be identified, between on one hand the idea that cruelty and compassion are both "normal" (Kraemer, 1996) (which is to say, may be performed by individuals with fully developed and uncompromised physical and psychological systems) and, on the other hand, the assertion that one of these states is normal and the other exists only as an aberration. On this basis it is worth considering the support for kindness as a basic evolutionary trait just as we have considered cruelty. All existing cultures show voluntary affinity with animals in the form of pet keeping (Beck & Meyers, 1996). In human society, humane concern for the well-being of (at least some) animals seems to have a history just as broad and extensive as animal abuse and cruelty (Ascione & Lockwood, 2001), and thus it may also have a biological basis.

BIOPHILIA

Wilson (1984) suggested that humans have an innate tendency to orient to and pay attention to life and lifelike processes. It has been suggested that the tension between this biophilia and nature-impoverished modern environments (Gullone, 2000) and nutritionally impoverished modern diets (Mysterud & Poleszynski, 2003) might lead to mental pathology potentially including abusive behavior. And, indeed, there is some evidence that residents of urban areas who commit animal abuse are more likely to do so for "fun" and without remorse (Hensley & Tallichet, 2005).

The Biophilia Hypothesis is often interpreted in an aspirational way to suggest that people have an innate respect for nature, wildlife, and animals, in general. However, given the diverse roles of animals and the varied relationships with them experienced by our ancestral hunter-gatherers, there is unlikely to have been an adaptive benefit to protecting the welfare of all animals (Beck & Katcher, 2003). Some were food sources, some competitors, some beneficial, and some predatory or venomous. People are, in fact, predisposed to be phobic of animals such as snakes and spiders rather than be attracted to them. Thus, the notion of general biophilia is increasingly being broken down into a concept of various modules of biophilia and phobia (Herzog, 2002) that are triggered by the characteristics of the animal and the circumstances of the interaction.

EVOLUTIONARY CONTINUITY

Bandura posits that, for humans, compassion is the norm, and cruelty requires that the perpetrator become morally disengaged from the group he or she victimizes (Bandura, 2006; see also Costello & Hodson, 2009). Generally, from a range of perspectives, cruelty is seen as an abnormality or defect in normal function (Ines de Aguirre, 2006), potentially a result of exposure to abuse or general stress that prevents the development of normal attachments (Endenburg, 1995). Evolutionary theory, from its advent, emphasized continuity between species, which appears contrary to human moral disengagement from animals. It seems likely that similarities between humans and other animal species were promoted within the spiritual belief systems of other (sub)cultures and historical time periods (Mason, 1995; Winkelman, 2002).

Charles Darwin made many explicit arguments for the continuity of morally significant characteristics between species, including (with some prevarication) between humans and nonhuman animals (Romanes & Darwin, 1884). He was particularly convinced that dogs exhibited intellect and emotion (Darwin, 1896), and as a result he was prominently embroiled in the vivisection controversies surrounding the use of dogs in the United Kingdom in the late 19th century, as the dog was a key physiological model of the time. He was also heavily involved in the regulation of research using any animal, to curtail practices considered cruel and unnecessary (Feller, 2009). While causal links are hard to trace, recent data suggest that there is a correlation between belief in evolution and support for animal rights (DeLeeuw, Galen, Aebrsold, & Stanton, 2007). And reminders of this species continuity cause people to express more positive attitudes toward animals (Beatson, Loughnan, & Halloran, 2009) and even other marginalized types of humans such as immigrants (Costello & Hodson, 2009).

Modern arguments of continuity between humans and other animals tend to rest upon an evolutionary understanding, and the identification of various capacities shared between species as a basis for moral consideration (including sentience, ability to suffer, and being "subject of a life"; Regan, 1983). Conscious awareness of evolutionary continuity is not in itself an evolutionary force except in that it has become a "meme" in modern culture. Dawkins (1976) proposed that ideas of this type can become the cultural equivalent of a gene that are replicated in the human mind and passed on to other human minds. The idea that animal sentience is fundamentally comparable to human sentience has become such a meme, picked up and slightly modified and passed on to wide audiences by prominent writers and speakers such as Tom Regan (1983) and Peter Singer (1976), and some have suggested that a child harming an animal is equivalent to self-harm in some children (e.g., Piper, 2003). However, claimed evidence of humanlike emotions in animals continues to be a hotly contested topic (Appleton, 2006; Guldberg, 2001).

Evolutionary Benefits of the Human-Animal Bond

PET KEEPING IMPROVES FITNESS

Evolutionary theories of care or altruism tend to rest upon shared genes (not applicable to other species), reciprocity, group selection, or cultural influences (i.e., "nonevolutionary" mechanisms) (Nesse, 2009a). As an example of reciprocity, a wide range of evidence supports the idea that pet keeping has benefits for psychological and physical health. This suggests that there may be immediate health benefits that arise from possession of the motivation to acquire and humanely care for pet animals. Specifically, pet owners seem to cope better with stress, and the more attached they are to their pet, the greater the benefit (e.g., Allen, 2003; Knight & Edwards, 2008). Others have suggested that the presence of an animal in a care home (e.g., for elderly people) creates happiness and a feeling of calm, some even reporting that a cat sitting on someone's knee or someone stroking a dog can lower blood pressure (e.g., Allen, Blascovich, & Mendes, 2002). It has also been suggested that, in some societies, keeping pets has other tangible benefits such as education relevant to hunting; however, animals kept for this purpose are not necessarily kept long or cared for well (Serpell, 1989).

Most companion animals fill a need for affectionate relationships and lifelong companionship that was, perhaps, more commonly available from fellow humans in our evolutionary past than it is in many modern societies (Grinde, 2000). However, it may be simplistic to see animal relationships as replacing human relationships, as the form of attachment is different and in at least one aspect (i.e., security) superior (Beck & Madresh, 2008). Instead human, animal, and other attachments may represent "mix and match" options for satisfying social and other needs (see House, Landis & Umberson, 1988; Johnson, 2009).

THE ANCIENT CONTRACT

Reciprocality on a species scale that encompasses companion, agriculture, and other domains of use and interaction is described variously as "The Ancient Contract" (Blackwell & Rollin, 2008) or "The Animal Connection" (Stacey, 2010). It has been debated whether animal domestication/

husbandry and pet keeping preceded agriculture or whether these practices developed simultaneously. Large-scale domestication is often seen as a simple human exploitation of nonhuman animals, but it has also been seen as a coevolution based on mutual benefit (Lund & Olsson, 2006). Farmers with positive relationships with their livestock, for example, who spend time with time animals, name them, and handle them gently, benefit in tangible ways such as higher milk production from dairy cows (Bertenshaw & Rowlinson, 2009).

While it is generally considered that widespread domestication occurred around 13,000 years ago, the divergence of some species such as dogs from their wild ancestors can be traced as far back as 100,000 years ago (Vila et al., 1997). Furthermore, coevolution may have begun significantly prior to noticeable domestication of these canids (Brantingham, 1998), such that animal domestication could be considered an extensive period of coevolutionary negotiation.

It is widely accepted that the sociability toward humans shown by domesticated animals results from artificial selection over generations (Albert et al., 2009; Trut, 1999). It may likewise be suggested that the virtue of kindness, and specifically kindness to animals, would lead to increased success in early communities that depended upon domesticated animals (Schleidt & Shalter, 2003). Thus, domestication may be seen as a process in which both human and nonhuman animals developed a capacity for docility and nonviolence to sustain intensive, multispecies communities and households (see Nesse, 2009b.) That is, it would do the dog no good to evolve a greater tendency to orient toward and serve people, if people did not equally develop a tendency to feel affection toward and to, more literally, "care" for dogs (c.f. Keith, 1946).

In this context, abuse may be more likely to emerge when one partner to a contract becomes powerless (e.g., Renzetti, 1992; Smith & Brain, 2000). For example, gentle handling of a horned bull in open pasture is necessary to avoid being chased and gored, but a dehorned and castrated steer in a metal crush is wholly dependent on its keeper's compassion. In extreme cases the animal's viable responses may be limited to whether it lives and produces the product for which it is kept.

THE CUTE FACTOR

In contrast, if it is accepted that large-scale domestication has existed only for 13,000 years or so, practices such as pet keeping must be viewed as a modification/repurposing of preexisting evolutionary relations and motivations. For example, even after millennia of herding, sheep do not move away from the sheepdog because it is perceived as an extension of the shepherd's will, but rather because they have an innate aversion to predatory species.

Another basic evolutionarily based motivation seems to be what is referred to as "the cute factor" (see Serpell, 2003). Across many species, babies and juveniles are able to conduct themselves with relative impunity because most adults are attracted to and will not behave aggressively toward them (e.g., Silk, 1999; Taylor, 1982). The infantile features of a large head and eyes, small size, and uncoordinated movement exist across many species and may underlie the initial desire to acquire "pets," which is found across all human cultures. In most cases pet animals are acquired early in their life when they still possess infantile features; many domesticated species seem to preserve these features to some extent throughout their lives (a.k.a. "neotony"), and in any case many owners are prone to use "baby talk" in their company (see Johnson, 2009). Under this framework pet ownership becomes a kind of quasi-parental care and shares the same failures as child abuse and neglect, which, like animal abuse, also occur in apparently otherwise unlikely perpetrators (Daly & Wilson, 1980, 1996; Herzog, 2002). Pets occupy a role similar to children in that their principal caregivers are more often female, and many owners would agree with the statement that their pets are "like children" to them. However, there are some observable variations on these themes that deserve mention, including the desire of some humans (more often male) to possess dogs that are the opposite of cute (for protective and aggressive purposes), and of others to breed pets of such particular physical characteristics that cuteness must be in the eye of the beholder (again, probably for status-related reasons, even if less dangerous to others).

An adult pet receives greatly reduced protection because it becomes less cute (Staats, Miller, Carnot, Rada, & Turnes, 1996), which may explain the relatively high desertion rate of pets even in relatively affluent cultures such as the United States, where approximately one-third of dogs will eventually find themselves in a shelter for unwanted animals. Thus, abuse of animals may be seen as a failure of the animal's quasi-infantile protection mechanism. Ideally, while under the protection of the disarming "cute" mechanism, the pet will become party to an enduring human-animal bond or acquire its working function, and so achieve the benefit of transition to an individualized protection from a specific human or human group.

Under situations of strain, characteristics that render a dependent infant or young person more likely to be abused include being a nonbiological child of one or both parents. As Daly and Wilson summarized: "the risk of abuse and neglect is likely to be exacerbated where substitute individuals fill the role of biological parents" (p. 282). A nonhuman pet may represent an extreme category of vulnerability under this principle. Humans appear to have an innate "empathy bias" toward humans versus nonhuman animals in distress (Delgado, Rodriguez-Perez, Vaes, Leyens, & Betencourt, 2009; Westbury & Neumann, 2008). This is reflected in the general public response when asked to rate the importance of animal issues relative to those that concern people, although some individuals of course do not share this prioritization (e.g., Hills, 1993; Paul, 1995).

Social Acceptability

One difficulty in judging who is cruel to animals is that the social acceptability of practices that cause animal suffering varies geographically, culturally, generationally, across time, and individually. It encompasses what is done, to whom, by whom, and why (Boddice, 2008). As noted previously, the full range of these variations, which relate to diverse social, cultural, ethical, religious, and pragmatic effect, is beyond the scope of the current discussion, although a number of examples have been presented. Suffice it to say that, while most people in most societies may be expected to react in similar ways to a given example of extreme violence or cruelty to an animal, across societies there are particular differences in this area that lead people to doubt the humanity and civilization of their neighbors. In some places, killing and eating dogs, bears, and guinea pigs is considered wholly normal, as is the clubbing of infant seals. Placed in an historical frame, these variations are multiplied. Although it could be argued that a key international characteristic of "social development" and rising levels of "civilization" (both concepts that may provoke many raised eyebrows) is increased levels of care and concern for others, humans or animals, in the case of animals, this idea is subject to serious variations of interpretation (as evidenced by international responses to seal and whale hunting, or bull fighting).

Resolving Competing Theories

There is a long-standing tension between the notions that the human species is innately cruel or that we are innately kind (Longo & Malone, 2006). Putting aside the "Naturalistic Fallacy" (i.e., that which is predominant in nature is good—see Abed, 2000; Nesse, 2009a; Ruse, 1986), the more practical question may be not which trait predominates in an absolute or universal sense, but rather, when, why, and in whom.

One approach to individual difference in the area of animal cruelty has been to try to identify subtypes that take cruel versus compassionate strategies. Also within cruelty there may be types based upon intensity of behavior, whether the target is a cosseted pet or random stray (Tallichet & Hensley, 2005), or whether the cruelty stems from a lack of empathy, occurs early in life, has causing pain as an explicit goal (see Beattie & Wake, 1964; Mayes, 2009), is biologically based, or resistant to treatment (Pitchford, 2001). Some consider the more treatment-resistant "psychopathic" offender to be relatively uncommon (Herbert, 1982), but it is difficult to assess the type or its prevalence with accuracy (see Arluke & Lockwood, 1997). Animal cruelty, like other types of abuse, certainly has distinct subtypes that will need to be addressed separately rather than as an amorphous mass (Arluke & Lockwood, 1997; Hensley & Tallichet, 2005; Oleson & Henry, 2009).

In fact, types of abuser may be defined, based on personality, compartmentalization (justifying abuse of carefully defined victim types), life stage (e.g., "rampaging bachelors"), and early/ongoing environment (e.g., early trauma, toxic parenting)—especially the social environment. It is often suggested that animal abuse is a symptom of a form of mental illness or personality disorder (Ascione, 1993; Gleyzer, Felthous, & Holzer, 2002), but it should not be assumed that that these conditions are congenital or irreversible (see Patterson-Kane & Piper, 2009). Psychiatric categories are general and merely descriptive in nature and as such they identify, rather than explain, specific subgroups in the human population. On the fuzzy culture/biology boundary, it is easy to make the mistake of defining animal abuse as deviant, and including it without a priori empirical justification (Gleyzer et al., 2002) as the equivalent of a psychiatric diagnosis (i.e., antisocial personality), and from there assuming that the underlying problem is "congenital" and evolutionary/immutable in origin.

That said, Mealey (1995) suggested that persistent delinquent behavior, not limited to adolescence when reproductive imperatives are at their peak, occurs in a distinct subtype in the population. Thus, hyperaggressive behaviors that would be pathological in the majority would be essentially normal in members of this group who are born strongly predisposed to antisocial conduct, exploiting a parasitic niche present only in predominantly peaceful societies. While it would be tempting to equate this idea to the small subgroup of severe and repeat animal abusers, no empirical data to date support the existence of this suggested biological subtype or its association with performance of animal abuse.

From an evolutionary perspective, a child raised in a nonnurturing and risky environment might be expected to switch from a compassionate, relationship-based approach to an aggressive and exploitative/competitive approach to interactions in order to maximize his or her own survival and fitness in a hostile environment. Indeed, theories such as "General Strain" (focused on risk factors; Agnew, 1985), the Desensitization Thesis (based on the intermediate mechanism of empathy and empathy impairment; Taylor & Signal, 2008), and "General Deviance" (focused on behavioral outcomes; Osgood, Johnston, O'Malley, & Bachman, 1988) all posit that the more stress a person is under, the more he or she will show socially unacceptable behaviors of all types ranging from substance abuse and self-abuse to all types of crime, including animal abuse, and less serious forms of dishonesty. Such arguments would appear to justify anxiety for the future of human relationships with each other and with animals, given the widening inequality and heightened economic stress levels characteristic of many Western societies in the aftermath of the 2008 financial crisis.

Conclusion

A fundamental tension in the research into animal cruelty is between the tendency to explain cruelty as an adaptive behavior or as an aberration. The truth may well be somewhere in between. Lieberman et al. (2003) suggest that "...our universal architecture plays a part in generating the cultural baseline and...individuals will exhibit lawful departures from the baseline given by ambient culture" (p. 819). This is particularly relevant to concepts such as animal cruelty, which are explicitly defined as the cause of animal suffering in a manner that is not deemed necessary or justifiable by the wider community. The common ambiguity between adaptation and aberration may account for the apparent absence of accounts that encompass both positive and negative interactions between people and nonhuman animals.

Kotchoubey writes that there have been thousands of myths written about human aggression "from Homer to Lorenz" (1996, p. 232). Theories surrounding animal cruelty fit within this vexed discussion, which combines a subject difficult to study directly and the pernicious influences of moral, religious, and political imperatives; moral panics; and armchair philosophizing. A broad view of all evolutionary perspectives offered suggests that aggression and even some forms of violence have a biological function in acquiring food, competition, maintaining social harmony, and defending vulnerable community members.

Socially unacceptable violent behavior may initially fall within these functions, especially for an individual who has not matured and integrated into a healthy, harmonious immediate "tribe" and wider community. It may also indicate an individual who has malfunctioned in response to social or economic pressures, mental illness, or personality disorder. Such a person may act as an economic criminal, a rampaging bachelor, or turn his or her aggression toward vulnerable individuals such as animals (which offer the additional advantage of being ineffective reporters of what has been done to them). To understand what is happening, in general terms or with any individual, a purely evolutionary approach has limitations in not bringing into focus the role of ontology and the immediate environment. But it does suggest the existence of broad strategies of temperament and behavior, some of which have negative outcomes for the individual and society.

To explain how a person arrives at his or her approach to life requires reference to multiple social, psychological, and economic factors; to understand why some act in significantly different ways from the majority requires additional complexity, including recourse to evidence of physiological or medical difference but also to key notions of human agency and choice. Evolutionary theory could be an important tool in integrating these diverse strands of information (Ayton, 2000; Mysterud & Poleszynski, 2003).

Animal abuse and cruelty is a social phenomenon, and attempts to discuss the nature and characteristics of society in evolutionary terms have become less frequent than they were during the hegemony of functionalism in the mid-20th century. Human beings may well be subject to the constraints of their genes, physiology, traditions, religions, and also the availability of resources, but in the end they can make choices about the way they treat nonhuman animals, and much else, too.

The study of violence is not purely observation; it is done with the goal of prevention, prediction, and intervention. And this perspective is necessary to escape the tautologies of which evolutionary theory is accused (Schlinger, 1996). For example, it is less significant that men are violent because they are men than that the culture of masculinity may be an effective arena for "immunizing" boys against becoming animal abusers, and an avenue to influence and correct them when they are. By integrating phylogeny/ontogeny and theory/practice, we can move from "just so" to social and psychological "adjustment" of our stone-age hardware to our modern communities (Flynn, 2001; Kennair, 2003). Also, the success or failure of evolutionarily informed strategies has the potential to validate, challenge, or refine those developing and often contradictory theories.

Finally, an evolutionary perspective draws our attention to the importance of accepting the functional role of aggression and the importance of nurturing and guidance by mature community members, to sanction unacceptable behavior and to foster something better. It also draws attention to the need to understand the factors causing a person to abuse animals because, like other forms of violence, there is not a single root cause, and so no single corrective measure will apply in all cases. In relation to cruelty toward animals, human culture is the bridge between what biology predisposes us—collectively—to do, and what ethics and morality lead us to want to do. Currently we seem to be attempting to build this bridge while standing in the middle of the river, rather than by thoroughly surveying either shore.

Future Directions

1. Can evolutionary understandings alone answer questions about the incidence of violence?

2. Is it useful to treat animal abuse and cruelty as discrete phenomena in evolutionary (or any other) terms?

3. From an evolutionary perspective, how may the variations in the treatment of animals between different societies be accounted for?

4. The evolutionary contribution to the violent behavior of nonhuman animals is taken for granted, but what is the significance of the way that humans clearly modify such behavior within nonevolutionary time frames?

Note

1. Interestingly, the "grammar check" on the software used to type this text wants us to delete "whom" and replace it with "which." The capacity to neutralize feelings of affinity with non-human animals seems to extend beyond hunters.

References

Abed, R. T. (2000). Letter. *British Journal of Psychiatry, 177,* 370.

Agnew, R. A. (1985). A revised strain theory of delinquency. *Social Forces, 64,* 151–167.

Albert, F. W., Carlborg, O., Plyusnina, I., Besnier, F., Hedwig, D., Lautenschlager, S., et al. (2009). Genetic architecture of tameness in a rat model of animal domestication. *Genetics, 182,* 541–554.

Albert D. J., Walsha M. L., Zalysa C., & Dysona E. M. (1987). Maternal aggression and intermale social aggression: A behavioral comparison. *Behavioural Processes, 14,* 267–276.

Allen, K. (2003). Are pets a healthy pleasure? The influence of pets on blood pressure. *Current Directions in Psychological Science, 12,* 236–239.

Allen, K., Blascovich J., & Mendes, W. (2002). Cardiovascular reactivity and the presence of pets, friends, and spouses: The truth about cats and dogs. *Psychosomatic Medicine, 64,* 727–739.

Anadu, P. A., Elamah, P. O., & Oates, J. F. (1988) The bushmeat trade in southwestern Nigeria: A case study. *Human Ecology, 16,* 199–208.

Anthony, R. (2003). The ethical implications of the human-animal bond on the farm. *Animal Welfare, 12,* 505–512.

Appleton, J. (2006) A great aping of human's rights. *Spiked.* Retrieved July 2010, from http://www.spiked-online.com/index.php?/site/article/384/

Arluke, A. (2000). The web of cruelty: what animal abuse tells us about humans. *AV Magazine,* Winter, 4, 27.Arluke, A. (2002). Animal abuse as dirty play. *Symbolic Interaction, 25,* 405–430.

Arluke, A., & Lockwood, R. (1997). Understanding cruelty to animals. *Society and Animals, 5,* 183–193.

Ascione, F. (1993). Children who are cruel to animals: A review of research and implications for developmental psychopathology. *Anthrozoos, 5,* 226–247.

Ascione, F. R., & Lockwood, R. (2001). Cruelty to animals: Changing psychological, social, and legislative perspectives. In D. J. Salem & A. N. Rowan (Eds.), *State of the animals 2000* (pp.39–53). Washington, DC: Humane Society Press.

Avner, J. R., & Baker, M. D. (1991). Dog bites in urban children. *Pediatrics, 88,* 55–57.

Ayton, A. (2000). Letter. *British Journal of Psychiatry, 177,* 370.

Baldry, A. C. (2003). Animal abuse and exposure to interparental violence in Italian youth. *Journal of Interpersonal Violence, 18,* 258–281.

Baldry, A. C. (2005). Animal abuse among preadolescents directly and indirectly victimized at school and home. *Criminal Behaviour and Mental Health, 15,* 97–109.

Bandura, A. (1973). Aggression: A social learning analysis. Englewood Cliffs, NJ: Prentice-Hall.

Bandura, A. (2006). A murky portrait of human cruelty. *Behavioral and Brain Sciences, 29,* 225–226.

Barcott, B. (2007, December 2). Kill the cat that kills the bird? *New York Times.* Retrieved November 2010, from http://www.nytimes.com/2007/12/02/magazine/02cats-v--birds-t.html

Beatson, R., Loughnan, S., & Halloran, M. (2009) Attitudes toward animals: The effect of priming thoughts of human-animal similarities and moral salience on the evaluation of companion animals. *Society and Animals, 7,* 72–89.

Beattie, K., & Wake, F. R. (1964). Physical cruelty: A review of the literature. *Canadian Psychologist, 5*, 233–244.

Beck, A. M., & Katcher, A. H. (2003). Future directions in human-animal bond research. *American Behavioral Scientist, 47*, 79–93.

Beck, L., & Madresh, E. A. (2008) Romantic partners and four-legged friends: An extension of attachment theory to relationships with pets. *Anthrozoös, 21*, 43–56.

Beck, A. M., & Meyers, N. M. (1996). Health enhancement and companion animal ownership. *Annual Review of Public Health, 17*, 247–257.

Bernstein, I. (1976). Dominance, aggression and reproduction in primate societies. Journal of *Theoretical Biology, 60*, 459–472.

Bertenshaw, C., & Rowlinson, P. (2009). Exploring stock managers' perceptions of the human-animal relationship on dairy farms and an association with mild production. *Anthrozoos, 22*, 59–69.

Blackwell, T. E., & Rollin, B. E. (2008). Leading discussions on animal rights. *Journal of the American Veterinary Medical Association, 233*, 868–871.

Boddice, R. (2008). Manliness and the morality of field sports: EA Freeman and Anthony Trollope 1869–71. *The Historian, 70*, 1–29.

Bonas, S., McNicholas, J., & Collis, G. (2000). Pets in the network of family relationships: An empirical study. In A. L. Podberscek, E. S. Paul, & J. A. Serpell (Eds.), *Companion animals & us* (pp. 209–236). Cambridge, England: Cambridge University Press.

Brantingham, P. J. (1998) Hominid-carnivore coevolution and invasion of the predatory guild. *Journal of Anthropological Archeology, 17*, 327–353.

Cadwallader, A. H. (2005). When a woman is a dog: Ancient and modern ethology meet the Syropoenician women. *The Bible and Critical Theory, 1*, 1–17.

Carlisle-Frank, P., Frank, J. M., & Nielsen, L. (2004). Selective battering of the family pet. *Anthrozoös, 17*, 26–41.

Cazaux, G. (1999). Beauty and the beast: Animal abuse from a nonspeciesist criminological perspective. *Crime, Law and Social Change, 31*, 105–126.

Chisholm, J. S., & Burbank, V. K. (2001). Evolution and inequality. *International Journal of Epidemiology, 30*, 206–211.

Cohen, S. P. (2002). Can pets function as family members? *Western Journal of Nursing Research, 24*, 621–638.

Costello, K., & Hodson, G. (2009) Exploring the roots of dehumanisation: The role of animal-human similarity in promoting immigrant humanization. *Group Processes and Intergroup Relations, 13*, 3–22.

Daly, M., & Wilson, M. (1980). Discriminative parental solicitude: A biological perspective. *Journal of Marriage and Family, 42*, 277–288.

Daly, M., & Wilson, M. (1996). Evolutionary psychology and marital conflict: the relevance of stepchildren. In D. M. Buss & N. Malamuth (Eds.), *Sex, power, conflict: Feminist and evolutionary perspectives* (pp. 9–28). New York: Oxford University Press.

Darwin, C. R. (1896). *The expression of emotions in man and animals*. New York: Philosophical Library.

Dawkins, R. (1976). *The selfish gene*. New York: Oxford University Press.

DeLeeuw, J. L., Galen, L. W., Aebrsold, C., & Stanton, V. (2007). Support for animals rights as a function of belief in evolution, religious fundamentalism, and religious denomination. *Society and Animals, 15*, 353–363.

Delgado, N., Rodriguez-Perez, A., Vaes, J., Leyens, J-P., & Betancor, V. (2009). Priming effects of violence on infrahumanization. *Group Processes and Intergroup Relation, 12*, 699–714.

Demarrest, J., & LaTorre, E. M. (1998, July 12). *Animal abuse: An evolutionary perspective*. Poster presentation at the International Society for Research on Aggression XIII World Meeting, Ramapo College, Mahwah, New Jersey

Desnoyers, R. C. (2009). What we can learn about animal cruelty cases from Rhode Island: Research and perspective. *Animal Law Newsletter, Spring, 1*, 3–8.

De Waal, F. B. M. (2004). Evolutionary ethics, aggression, and violence: lessons from primate research. *Journal of Law, Medicine, and Ethics, 32*, 18–23.

Dollard, J., Doob, L., Miller, N., Mowrer, O., & Sears, R. (1939). *Frustration and aggression*. New Haven, CT: Yale University Press.

Endenburg, N. (1995). The attachment of people to companion animals. *Anthrozoös, 7*, 83–89.

Feller, D. A. (2009). Dog fight: Darwin as animal advocate in the antivivisection controversy of 1875. *Studies in History and Philosophy of Biological and Biomedical Sciences, 40*, 265–271.

Felthous, A. R., & Yudowitz, B. (1977). Approaching a comparative typology of assaultive female offenders. *Psychiatry, 40*, 270–276.

Fenimore Cooper, J. (1998). *The last of the Mohicans*. Oxford, England: Oxford University Press. (Original work published 1826).

Flynn, C. P. (1999). Exploring the link between corporal punishment and children's cruelty to animals. *Journal of Marriage and the Family, 61*, 971–981.

Flynn. C.P. (2001). Acknowledging the "zoological connection": A sociological analysis of animal cruelty. *Society and Animals, 9*, 71–87.

Flynn, C. P. (2002). Hunting and illegal violence against human and other animals: Exploring the relationship. *Society and Animals, 10*, 37–154.

George, M. J. (1997). Into the eyes of Medusa: Beyond testosterone, men, and violence. *The Journal of Men's Studies, 5*, 295–313.

Glendinning, L. (2008, April 26). Donkeys in clover—but charity leaders call for a rethink. *The Guardian.* http://www.guardian.co.uk/society/2008/apr/26/voluntarysector.animalwelfare

Gleyzer, R., Felthous, A. R., & Holzer, C. E. (2002). Animal cruelty and psychiatric disorders. *The Journal of the American Academy of Psychiatry and the Law, 30*, 257–265.

Gordon, M. S., Kinlock, T. W., & Battjes, R. J. B. (2004). Correlates of early substance use and crime among adolescents entering outpatient substance abuse treatment. *American Journal of Drug and Alcohol Abuse, 30*, 39–59.

Grandin, T. (1988). Behavior of slaughter plant and auction employees toward the animals. *Anthrozoös, 1*, 205–213.

Grinde, B. (2000). Social behavior: making the best of the human condition. *Mankind Quarterly, 41*, 193–210.

Guldberg, H. (2001) The great ape debate. *Spiked*. Retrieved July 2010, from http://www.spiked-online.com/articles/000000005549.htm

Gullone, E. (2000). The biophilia hypothesis and life in the 21st century: Increasing mental health or increasing pathology. *Journal of Happiness Studies, 1*, 293–321.

Hadley, J., & O'Sullivan, S. (2009). World poverty, animal minds and the ethics of veterinary expenditure. *Environmental Values, 18*, 361–378.

Hellman, D. S., & Blackman, N. (1966). Enuresis, firesetting and cruelty to animals: A triad predictive of adult crime. *American Journal of Psychiatry, 122*, 1431–1435.

Henry, B. C. (2004). The relationship between animal cruelty, delinquency, and attitudes toward the treatment of animals. *Society and Animals, 122*, 185–207.

Henry, B. C. (2009). Can attitudes about animal neglect be differentiated from attitudes about animal abuse? *Society and Animals, 17*, 21–37.

Hensley, C., & Tallichet, S. E. (2005). Animal cruelty motivations: Assessing demographic and situational influences. *Journal of Interpersonal Violence, 20*, 1429–1443.

Herbert, W. (1982). The evolution of child abuse. *Science News, 122*, 24–26.

Herzog, H. (2002). Darwinism and the study of human-animal interactions. *Society and Animals, 10*, 361–367.

Herzog, H. A. (2007). Gender differences in human-animal interactions: A review. *Anthrozoos, 20*, 7–21.

Hills, A. M. (1993). The motivational bases of attitudes toward animals. *Society and Animals, 1*, 111–128.

Hoff, M. P., Nadler, R. D., & Maple T. L. (1982). Control role of an adult male in a captive group of lowland gorillas. *Folia Primatologica, 38*, 72–85.

House, J. S, Landis, K. R., & Umberson, D. (1988). Social relationships and health. *Science, 214*, 540–545.

Huizinga, D., Schumann, K., Ehret, B., & Elliott, A. (2004). *The effect of juvenile justice system processing on subsequent delinquent and criminal behavior: A cross-national study*. Final Report to The National Institute of Justice Grant Number: 1999IJCX0037. https://www.ncjrs.gov/pdffiles1/nij/grants/205001.pdf

Ines de Aguirre, M. (2006). Neurobiological bases of aggression, violence and cruelty. *Behavioral and Brain Sciences, 29*, 228–229.

Johnson, J. (2009). Dogs, cats, and their people: The place of the family pet and attitudes about pet keeping. University of Waterloo, Waterloo, Ontario, Canada. http://uwspace.uwaterloo.ca/bitstream/10012/4379/1/Johnson_Jill.pdf

Jordan, J. (2010, November 14). Family says son killed dog out of jealousy. *NewsOn6.com*. Retrieved November 2010, from http://www.newson6.com/Global/story.asp?S=13501182

Kaplan, J. R. (2005). Patterns of fight interference in free-ranging rhesus monkeys. *American Journal of Physical Anthropology, 47*, 279–287.

Keith, A. (1946). *Evolution and ethics*. New York: G.P. Putnam's Sons.

Kelly, L. (2003). Disabusing the definition of domestic violence: How women batter men and the role of the feminist state. *Florida State University Law Review, 30*, 791–855.

Kennair, L. E. O (2003). Evolutionary psychology and psychopathology. *Current Opinion in Psychiatry, 16*, 691–699.

Knight, S., & Edwards. V. (2008). In the company of wolves—The physical, social, and psychological benefits of dog ownership. *Journal of Aging and Health, 20*, 437–455.

Kochi, T. (2009). Species war: Law, violence and animals. *Law, Culture and the Humanities, 5*, 353–369.

Kotchoubey, B. (1996). Signifying nothing? Myth and science of cruelty. *Behavioral and Brain Sciences, 29*, 232–233.

Kraemer, S. (1996). The cruelty of older infants and toddlers. *Behavioral and Brain Sciences, 29*, 233–234.

Kurt-Swanger, K., & Patcosky, J. L. (2003). *Violence in the home: Multidisciplinary perspectives*. New York: Oxford University Press.

Lea, S. R. G. (2008). *Delinquency and animal cruelty: Myths and realities about social pathology*. New York: LFB Scholarly Publishing.

Leach, E. (1964). Anthropological aspects of language: Animal categories and verbal abuse. In E. H. Lenneberg (Ed.), *New directions in the study of language* (pp. 151–165). Cambridge, MA: MIT Press.

Lieberman, D., Tooby, J., & Cosmides, L. (2003). Does morality have a biological basis? An empirical test of the factors governing moral sentiments relating to incest. *Proceedings of the Royal Society of London B, 270*, 819–826.

Lockwood, R. (2005). Cruelty toward cats: Changing perspectives. In D. J. Salem & A. N. Rowan (Eds.), *The state of animals* (3rd ed., pp 15–26). Washington, DC: Humane Society Press..

Longo, S. B., & Malone, N. (2006). Meat, medicine, and materialism: A dialectic analysis of Human relationships to nonhuman animals and nature. *Human Ecology Review, 13*, 111–121.

Lund, V., & Olsson, A.A.S. (2006). Animal agriculture: Symbiosis, culture, or ethical conflict. *Journal of Agricultural and Environmental Ethics, 19*, 47–56.

MacDonald, J. M. (1963). The threat to kill. *American Journal of Psychiatry, 120*, 125–130.

Martens, A., Kosloff, S., Greenberg, J., Landau, M. J., & Schmader, T. (2007). Killing begets killing: Evidence from a bug-killing paradigm that initial killing fuels subsequent killing. *Personality and Social Psychology Bulletin, 33*, 1251–1264.

Mason, J. (1995). The beast within. *E Magazine, 6*, 38–41.

Mason, W. A. (1998). Words, deeds, and motivations: Comments on Maestripieri and Carroll (1998). *Psychological Bulletin, 123*, 231–233.

Mayes, G. R. (2009) Naturalizing cruelty. *Biology and Philosophy, 24*, 21–34.

Mealey, L. (1995). Sociopathy. *Behavioral and Brain Sciences, 18*, 523–599.

Mhaka-Mutepfa, M. (2009). Spousal abuse in Zimbabwe: Nature and extent across socio-economic class, gender and religiosity. *Interpersona, 3*, 75–88.

Mysterud, I., & Poleszynski, D.V. (2003). Expanding evolutionary psychology: Toward a better understanding of violence and aggression. *Social Science Information, 42*, 5–50.

Nell, V. (2006). Cruelty's rewards: The gratifications of perpetrators and spectators. *Behavioral and Brain Sciences, 29*, 211–224.

Nesse, R. M. (2009a). How can evolution and neuroscience help us understand moral capacities? J. Verplaetse, J. de Schrijver, S. Vanneste, & J. Braeckman (Eds.), *The moral brain* (pp. 201–209). New York: Springer Science and Business Media.

Nesse, R. M. (2009b). Runaway social selection for displays of partner value and altruism. J. Verplaetse, J. de Schrijver, S. Vanneste, & J. Braeckman (Eds.), *The moral brain* (pp. 143–155). New York: Springer Science and Business Media.

Novek, J. (2005). The pigs and people: Sociological perspectives on the discipline of nonhuman animals in intensive confinement. *Society and Animals, 13*, 221–244.

Oleson, J. C., & Henry, B. C. (2009). Relations among need for power, affect and attitudes toward animal cruelty. *Anthrozoos, 22*, 255–265.

Osgood, D. W., Johnston, L. D., O'Malley, P. M., & Bachman, J. G. (1988). The generality of deviance in late adolescence and early adulthood. *American Sociological Review, 53,* 81–93.

Pagani, C., Robustelli, F., & Ascione, F. R. (2007). Italian youths' attitudes toward, and concern for, animals. *Anthrozoos, 20,* 275–293.

Patterson-Kane, E. G., & Piper, H. (2009). Animal abuse as a sentinel for human violence: A critique. *Journal of Social Issues, 65,* 589–614.

Paul, E. (1995). Us and them: Scientists' and animal rights campaigners' views of the animal experimentation debate. *Society and Animals, 3,* 1–21.

Petit, O., & Thierry, B. (1994). Aggressive and peaceful interventions in conflicts in Tonkean macaques. *Animal Behaviour, 48,* 1427–1436.

Piper, H. (2003). Children and young people harming animals: Intervention through PSHE? *Research Papers in Education, 18*(2), 197–213.

Piper, H. (2004). The linkage of animal abuse with interpersonal violence: A sheep in wolf's clothing? *Journal of Social Work, 3*(2), 161–177.

Pitchford, I. (2001). The origins of violence: Is it psychopathy or adaptation? *The Human Nature Review, 1,* 28–36.

Plumridge, S. J., & Fielding, W. J. (2009). Domestic violence in the homes of college students, New Providence, the Bahamas. *The College of the Bahamas Research Journal, 15,* 45–55.

Prentky, R. A., & Carter, D. L. (1984). The predictive value of the triad for sex offenders. *Behavioral Sciences and the Law, 2,* 341–354.

Regan, T. (1983). *The case for animal rights.* Berkeley: University of California Press

Renzetti, C. M. (1992). *Violent betrayal: Partner abuse in lesbian relationships.* Thousand Oaks, CA: Sage.

Rollin, B. E. (2001). An ethicist's commentary on shooting farmed deer. *Canadian Veterinary Journal, 42,* 598.

Romanes, G. J., & Darwin, C. (1884). *Mental evolution in animals.* London: Kegan Paul Trench.

Roscoe, B., Haney, S., & Patterson, K. L. (1986). Child/pet maltreatment: Adolescents' ratings of parent and owner behaviors. *Adolescence, 21,* 807–814.

Rowan, A. N. (1993). Animal well-being: Key philosophical, ethical, political, and public issues affecting food animal agriculture. In *Food animal well-being 1993 conference proceedings and deliberations* (pp. 23–36). West Lafayette, IN: USDA and Purdue University Office of Agricultural Research Programs.

Ruse, M. (1986). Evolutionary ethics: A phoenix arisen. *Zygon, 21,* 95–112.

Ryan, K., & Skrapec, C. (November, 2008). *The Macdonald Triad: Predictor of violence or urban myth?* Paper presented at the annual meeting of the ASC Annual Meeting, St. Louis Adam's Mark, St. Louis, MO.

Sacks, J. J., Kresnow, M., & Houston, B. (1996). Dog bites: how big a problem? *Injury Prevention, 2,* 52–54.

Saunders, D. G. (1986). When battered women use violence: Husband-abuse or self-defense? *Victims and Violence, 1,* 47–60.

Schell, H. (2007). The big bad wolf: Masculinity and genetics in popular culture. *Literature and Medicine, 26,* 109–125.

Schleidt, W. M., & Shalter, M. D. (2003). Co-evolution of humans and canids. *Evolution and Cognition, 9,* 57–72.

Schlinger, H. D. (1996). How the human got its spots. *Skeptic, 4,* 68–76.

Sendi, I. B., & Blomgren, P. G. (1975). A comparative study of predictive criteria in the predisposition of homicidal adolescents. *American Journal of Psychiatry, 132,* 423–427.

Serpell, J. A. (1989). Pet-keeping and animal domestication: A reappraisal. In J. Clutton-Brock (Ed.), *The walking larder: Patterns of domestication, pastoralism and predation* (pp. 10–21). London: Unwin Hyman.

Serpell, J. A. (2003). Anthropomorphism and anthropomorphic selection—beyond the "cute response." *Society and Animals, 11,* 83–100.

Silk, J. B. (1999). Why are infants so attractive to others? The form and function of infant handling in bonnet macaques. *Animal Behavior, 57,* 1021–1032.

Singer, P. (1976). *Animal liberation.* London: Cape.

Singh, K. S. (2001). Gender roles in history: Women as hunters. *Gender, Technology and Development, 5,* 113–124.

Slotow, R., & Van Dyk, G. (2008). Role of delinquent young "orphan" male elephants in high mortality of white rhinoceros. Pilanesberg National Park, South Africa. *Koedoe—African Protected Area Conservation And Science, 44,* 85–94.

Smil, V. (2002). Eating meat: Evolution, patterns and consequences. *Population and Development Review, 28,* 599–639.

Smith, P. K., & Brain, P. (2000), Bullying in schools: Lessons from two decades of research. *Aggressive Behavior, 26,* 1–9.

Spinka, M., Newberry, R. C., & Bekoff, M. (2001). Mammalian play: Training for the unexpected. *Quarterly Review of Biology, 76,* 141–168.

Srivastava, A. (2007). "Mean, dangerous, and uncontrollable beasts": Mediaeval animal trials. *Mosaic, 40,* 127–144.

Staats, S., Miller, D., Carnot, M. J., Rada, K., & Turnes, J. (1996). The Miller-Rada commitment to pets scale. *Anthrozoos, 9,* 88–94.

Stacey, K. (2010). Animal connection: New hypothesis for human evolution and human nature. *ScienceDaily.* Retrieved July 2010, from http://www.sciencedaily.com/releases/2010/07/100720123639.htm

Stets, J. E., & Straus, M. A. (1990). Gender differences in reporting marital violence and its medical and psychological consequences. In M. A. Straus & R. J. Gelles (Eds.), *Physical violence in American families: Risk factors and adaptations to violence in 8,145 families* (pp. 227–244). New Brunswick, NJ: Transaction Publishing.

Stewart, M. (1999, October 18). Dolphins: Flipper or killer? *Science World.* Retrieved December 2010, from http://findarticles.com/p/articles/mi_m1590/is_4_56/ai_57041274/

Sutschek, S. (2010, November 24). *Huntley man shoots, kills dog attacking his chickens.* Retrieved December 2010, from the tribLocal.com website http://triblocal.com/huntley/2010/11/24/huntley-man-shoots-kills-dog-attacking-his-chickens/

Tallichet, S. E., & Hensley, C. (2005). Rural and urban differences in the commission of animal cruelty. *International Journal of Offender Therapy and Comparative Criminology, 49,* 711–726.

Taylor, G. (1982). Urinary odors and size protect juvenile laboratory mice from adult male attack. *Developmental Psychobiology, 15,* 171–186.

Taylor, N., & Signal, T. (2008). Throwing the baby out with the bathwater: Towards a sociology of the human-animal-abuse "link"? *Sociological Research Online.* Retrieved http://www.socresonline.org.uk/13/1/2.html

Trut, L. N. (1999). Early canid domestication: The farm-fox experiment. *American Scientist, 87,* 160–169.

Vale, R., & Vale, B. (2009). *Time to eat the dog: The real guide to sustainable living.* London: Thames & Hudson.

Vermeulen, H., & Odendaal, J. (1993). Proposed typology of companion animal abuse. *Anthrozoos, 6,* 248–257.

Vila, C., Savolainene, P., Maldonada, J. E., Amorim, I. R., Rice, J. E., Honeycutt, R. L., et al. (1997). Multiple and ancient origins of the domestic dog. *Science, 276,* 1687–1689.

Wienberg, C. (2000, February 14). Goldfish in blenders cause outrage. *The Independent.* http://web.archive.org/web/20081218134532/http://www.independent.co.uk/news/world/europe/goldfish-in-blenders-cause-outrage-724729.html

Wilson, E. O. (1984). *Biophilia.* Cambridge, MA: Harvard University Press

Wilson, M., & Daly, M. (1985). Competitiveness, risk taking, and violence: The young male syndrome. *Ethology and Sociobiology, 6,* 59–73.

Winkelman, M. (2002). Shamanism as neurotheology and evolutionary psychology. *American Behavioral Scientist, 45,* 1873–1885.

Westbury, H. R., & Neumann, D. L. (2008). Empathy-related responses to moving film stimuli depicting human and non-human animal targets in negative circumstances. *Biological Psychology, 78,* 66–74.

Zilney, M. (2007). Preface. In L. A. Zilney (Ed.), *Linking animal cruelty and family violence* (pp. xix–xxiii). London: Cambria Press.

CHAPTER
16
If, When, and Why Adolescent Bullying Is Adaptive

Anthony Volk, Joseph A. Camilleri, Andrew Dane, *and* Zopito Marini

Abstract

Adolescent bullying appears to be a cross-cultural, worldwide phenomenon. A substantial literature has addressed this phenomenon due to the important implications bullying presents for adolescents. The ubiquity of bullying, along with its heritability, suggests the possibility that some bullying may be the result of evolved adaptations. Unfortunately, the bullying literature has failed to formally examine this possibility in depth. The current chapter is an effort to redress this situation as we look at if, when, and why adolescent bullying is adaptive. We find significant evidence for the functionality of modern bullying and the absence of psychopathologies typically associated with maladaptive development, supporting the claim that bullying may be an evolved adaptation. Evidence from hunter-gatherers and historical data further support this claim. We examine the individual differences, contextual factors, and developmental pathways that may lead to bullying being an important, functional, adaptive behavior among adolescents. We end the chapter with a discussion of the implications an adaptive view of bullying has for intervention, research, and adolescents.

Key Words: bullying, evolution, evolution of bullying, adolescents, aggression

Introduction

Bullying is a specific form of aggression that can be defined as a relationship problem characterized by an imbalance of power whereby a more powerful individual repeatedly causes harm to a weaker individual (Olweus, 1993; Pepler, Jiang, Craig, & Connolly, 2008). While bullying behavior is seen in both sexes and in children (and adults) of virtually all ages (Pellegrini, 1998), it is more common in boys and appears to peak at around age 14 years in both sexes (Volk, Craig, Boyce, & King, 2006). Bullying is an international issue (Nabuzoka, 2003; Pepler & Craig, 2008), involving an estimated 100–600 million youth across the globe each year (Volk et al., 2006). The ubiquity of bullying across different cultures, ages, and sexes brings to mind the possibility that there may be a biological predisposition toward bullying. The goal of the current chapter is to explain how bullying may represent one or more evolutionary adaptations for adolescents.

For a behavior to be an evolutionary adaptation, it must have a genetic component that natural and/or sexual selection could have operated on in the past (Dawkins, 1989). This does not mean that the behavior is innate or genetically predetermined, or that there is a single gene that completely controls the expression of the behavior. In practice, when speaking about complex behaviors, this generally means that there are multiple genes whose combined effects probabilistically relate to the developmental expression of the adaptive behavior (e.g., bullying), and that these genes can be probabilistically selected, individually or as a group, by natural or sexual selection (Symons, 1990). Put simply, this means that there is the opportunity for natural or sexual selection to alter the frequency of genes related to the behavior (bullying) in ancestral populations. Without such a genetic link to bullying, there would be no "traction" for evolution to act upon, and thus no opportunity for evolution to influence bullying. So a crucial question is whether there is any such evidence for genes related to bullying.

Currently the evidence for the heritability of bullying is limited. Ball and colleagues (2008) used the Child Behavior Checklist (Achenbach, 1991) to examine the heritability of bullying and victimization. Unfortunately, this checklist did not directly measure bullying as it is traditionally defined (Olweus, 1993), so some caution should be applied with respect to the following heritability coefficients. That said, Ball et al. (2008) found that in a cohort of over 1,000 10-year-old twins, differences in genes accounted for 73% of the variation in victimization and 61% of the variation in bullying, with differences in environmental factors accounting for the rest of the variation. It should be noted that these heritability estimates do not mean, for example, that 73% of all bullying behavior is due solely to the influence of genes. Rather, we use this information to demonstrate that it appears very likely that there is some degree of genetic linkage with bullying and victimization. This in turns means that it was very likely for evolutionary selection to occur with respect to bullying (Symons, 1990). Further support for this conclusion comes from the larger body of literature on general aggression. General aggression shows a similar degree of heritability as bullying (DiLalla, 2002), leaving us confident in concluding that there existed enough genetic traction for natural and/or sexual selection to operate on in past environments with respect to ancestral bullying and victimization behaviors. Thus, bullying appears to have met the first necessary, but not sufficient, criterion for an evolutionary adaptation—it has some degree of heritability.

Yet to be an evolutionary adaptation, a second criterion must be met, which is that the behavior has to show evidence of functional design compatible with the environment of evolutionary adaptation (Alcock, 2001; Irons, 1998; Symons, 1990). That is, the behavior has to appear to have a specific function that achieved a specific goal in its evolutionary past. Applying the human definition of bullying to animal aggression (a stronger individual repeatedly causing harm to a weaker individual) reveals that bullying is widespread among animals (Archer, 1988; Lorenz, 1966). Dominance and resource control are important social motivations for a wide range of animals' bullying behavior.

For example, chickens will repeatedly harass weaker individuals to establish a literal pecking order for access to resources (Masure & Allee, 1934), wolf and wild dog females will systematically harass subordinate females over the right to breed (Mech, 1970; Scott, 1991), and male chimpanzees will individually, or as a coalition, bully other males in order to achieve the dominance status that is associated with access to both females and food resources (Goodall, 1986). Thus, there is a strong comparative basis from which to expect human bullying to serve similar adaptive purposes. With respect to human bullying, this means it had to have served one or more reliable, functional purposes. Naturally, collecting direct data on past human behaviors is difficult, if not impossible. We therefore propose to use three widely accepted substitute forms of evidence that, when combined, offer a strong substitution for comprehensive, direct, past data on human behavior. The first form of evidence is that bullying serves one or more reliable, functional purposes for modern adolescents in modernized societies. The second is that bullying serves one or more reliable, functional purposes for modern adolescents living in isolated hunter-gatherer communities that are believed to approximate ancestral populations and environments. Finally, one can look for the limited but direct evidence that bullying served one or more reliable functions for adolescents from historical populations.

Modern Bullying
Bullying as an Adolescent Adaptation for Dominance and Resource Control—Intrasexual Bullying

Repeatedly picking on weaker individuals (bullying) may offer adolescents some benefits in intrasexual competition over status, resources, and/or mating opportunities (all important evolutionary goals). According to some researchers, threats or acts of physical aggression are adaptive for male humans because they facilitate access to short-term sexual partners and long-term marital partners, and they afford protection from potential aggressors (e.g., Benenson, 2009). In addition, Hawley (2007) proposed that coercive strategies, which can include theft, threatening, and bullying, may be effective resource control strategies that enhance social status and increase influence over peers. A number of studies suggest that bullying affords similar benefits. In particular, bullying has often been positively associated with peer nominations and teacher ratings of perceived popularity (Caravita, Di Blasio, & Salmivalli,

2009, 2010; Juvonen, Graham, & Schuster, 2003; Rodkin & Berger, 2008; Vaillancourt, Hymel, & McDougall, 2003) that indicate which children are popular without reference to whether they are liked or disliked. These are seen by investigators as measures of social impact, visibility, reputation, and of being socially well connected. Perceived popular youth have also been described in studies as athletic, cool, and good leaders, though they are also perceived as unkind, untrustworthy, and antisocial (Cillessen & Mayeux, 2007). In addition, perceived popularity is strongly correlated with peer-nominated power ($r = .67$; Vaillancourt et al., 2003), which was operationalized as being able to pressure others into doing things. Other findings indicated significant links between bullying and peer nominations of being powerful (Vaillancourt et al., 2003), teacher ratings of dominance (Pellegrini, Bartini, & Brooks, 1999; Pellegrini & Long, 2002), and peer nominations of being leaders of social network groups (Estell, Farmer, & Cairns, 2007). Thus, bullying appears to offer the possibility of controlling social resources and/or power.

Bullying may also be used to open up dating opportunities. To begin with, students in grades 5 through 8 who bullied were found to date at a younger age, to engage in more dating activities, and to be more likely to have a current boyfriend or girlfriend than students who had not bullied (Connolly, Pepler, Craig, & Taradash, 2000). In addition, dominance, which is positively associated with bullying, was also related to peer nominations of dating popularity (Pellegrini & Long, 2003). Finally, boys' bullying of boys was specifically related to greater acceptance by girls in grades 5 to 8 (Veenstra, Lindenberg, Munniksma, & Dijkstra, 2010). Given that boys' bullying in this age group is linked with increases in being liked by female peers, this outcome may be seen as laying the groundwork for future dating opportunities.

According to Benenson (2009), adolescent and young adult human females use a different form of aggression to achieve adaptive outcomes in the realm of intrasexual competition. Specifically, relationally aggressive strategies, such as social exclusion and the denigration of competitors, may be used to help attract higher quality marital partners. These theoretical propositions have received some support empirically, with Pellegrini and Long (2003) reporting that increases in relational aggression by females from grade 6 to grade 7 were associated with increases in dating popularity over the same period. Results that pertain specifically to female bullying do not address dating outcomes per se, but they do suggest that it may enhance their social status more generally, particularly with male peers, which in turn may create dating opportunities. In particular, female bullies were found to be prominent members of highly visible social networks (Estell et al., 2007). Furthermore, girls' bullying (of unspecified form) was positively associated with acceptance by boys ages 11 and 12 (Dijkstra, Lindenberg, & Veenstra, 2007), and girls' bullying was positively associated with desired acceptance from boys in grades 6 to 8, whereas it was negatively associated with acceptance actually received from girls, especially other girls involved in bullying, with whom they might be engaged in intrasexual competition (Olthoff & Goosens, 2008). Support for the proposition that relational forms of bullying play an adaptive role in female intrasexual competition is provided by the finding that physically attractive adolescent females were at increased risk of being targeted with relationally aggressive attacks (Leenars, Dane, & Marini, 2008). As theoretical and empirical research suggests that enhancing one's attractiveness is a common female strategy for boosting attractiveness to potential sexual or marital partners (Benenson, 2009; Buss, 1988a), Leenars et al.'s research is consistent with the hypothesis that bullying of a relationally aggressive nature facilitates female intrasexual competition for sexual partners. It is further supported by qualitative evidence from the bullying literature suggesting that adolescent girls target each other's physical appearance. When Owens, Shute, and Slee (2000a) interviewed female students about their experiences with intrasexual bullying, they found that most accounts came in the form of verbal insults of physical or sexual characteristics.

But not all female bullying is covert or indirect. In both sexes, insulting a victim in terms of his or her sexuality and sexual behavior often also takes place in public, supporting the idea that bullying may also be used to visibly raise one's status at the expense of another's (Timmerman, 2003). Examples of this sort of bullying are verbal statements that insult a person's sexual inadequacy or lack of masculinity if directed at males or indiscriminate sexual proclivity if directed at females (e.g., Renold, 2002). While this type of bullying involves sexual gestures and motions, it may not be sexual per se. Instead, it is meant to publicly humiliate someone in order to reduce his or her status relative to one's own, and it is an example of the potential benefits of bullying to both sexes in intrasexual competition.

Despite these apparent advantages for bullying, not all social outcomes related to bullying are positive. A well-established finding is that whereas bullying is connected to perceived popularity, it is also inversely associated with peer nominations of social preference (liking minus disliking) and acceptance, and positively linked with rejection (Caravita et al., 2009, 2010; Dijkstra et al., 2007; Estell et al., 2007; Lee, 2009; Pellegrini et al., 1999; Rodkin & Berger, 2008, Vaillancourt et al., 2003). Although they are perceived as popular, socially prominent, well-connected, and highly visible members of the peer group, it seems that bullies are not liked by many of their classmates. It would stand to reason that bullies are disliked by peers they have victimized. Another factor that may contribute to peer disliking is the negative perceptions that children and adolescents attach to perceived popular individuals (which is correlated with bullying), specifically that they are unkind, untrustworthy, and have more hostile intentions (Cillessen & Mayeux, 2007; Lafontana & Cillessen, 1998). Interestingly, qualities such as trustworthiness and kindness are associated with sociometric popularity, that is, being liked by one's peers (Newcomb, Bukowski, & Pattee, 1993; Parkhurst & Hopmeyer, 1998). This may explain, in part, why not all adolescents engage in bullying. Bullying may offer benefits, but it may also impose costs on the bully. Whether an adolescent chooses to engage in bullying likely depends on a host of individual and environmental factors that will be discussed throughout this chapter.

Possible Mechanisms by Which Bullying Produces Adaptive Social Outcomes

Given some of the negative social outcomes and peer perceptions linked with bullying, how do we explain its evolutionary adaptiveness with regard to intrasexual competition and social dominance? Tying together several strands of theory and evidence regarding overt forms of bullying, it seems that the perceived popularity and high social status of male bullies with male peers may be related at least in part to its protective function. One way that bullying may help to establish and maintain social dominance is by cultivating a reputation for toughness, which in turn can afford protection from aggressive challenges. The protective benefit of a reputation for toughness is illustrated in a recent study in which older adolescents indicated they would be less likely to physically aggress against an individual who was known to be tough, even when that individual had provoked them with an insult (Archer & Benson, 2008). The desire of male peers to make friends with a bully with a tough reputation may partly account for the social prominence of bullies within male social circles. Given that forming alliances with male nonkin is a key strategy that males may use to gain protection from potential aggressors, it may be particularly beneficial for children to form friendships with bullies in view of their reputation for toughness and the protective shield that this provides against peer aggressors (Benenson, 2009). Also, from the standpoint of group dynamics, the popularity of some youth who bully may stem from the powerful psychological desire of adolescents to be part of the ingroup (Sherif & Sherif, 1970) and to avoid being a member of the outgroup, who are more likely to be the targets of bullying (Cillessen & Mayeux, 2007). Maccoby (2004) notes that boys' aggression is often (but not always) directed to members outside of boys' groups, while girls' aggression is most often directed toward members within girls' groups. In other words, groups of boys tend to band together to attack outsiders *and* members of their own group, whereas groups of girls tend to mainly attack *only* members of their own group.

Beyond its role in attaining social dominance, bullying also appears to play a role in male intrasexual competition for sexual partners. Research has shown that men are more likely than women to display strength and athleticism as a means to attract a mate (Buss, 1988a), and thus male bullying may play a role in competing with other males for access to sexual partners. Female adolescents, for their part, may be attracted to youth who bully and/or are socially dominant, because given the greater investment of women relative to men in rearing offspring, it is important for them to select high-status mates who can provision and protect their children (Buss, 1988a, 1988b; Trivers, 1972).

Female adolescents' intrasexual competition seems to rely more on relational rather than direct forms of bullying to enhance their prospects for marital partners, presumably because it is less risky and seems particularly well suited to undermining aspects of a rival's reputation that affect male perceptions of a female's attractiveness as a sexual or marital partner. In light of the high level of investment that women make in rearing offspring, physical aggression is often too risky given the likelihood of physical injury (Vaillancourt, 2005). Therefore, they use relationally aggressive bullying, which involves tactics like social exclusion and rumor spreading—strategies that female adolescents use to increase their attractiveness to potential mates relative to their competitors (Benenson, 2009). Furthermore, the likelihood of attracting an acceptable potential marital partner may be higher for female adolescents who are socially prominent and perceived as popular because they may have more opportunities to meet high-quality mates. Several studies have shown that relational aggression and female bullying are adaptive in this respect, being shown to enhance the social prominence and perceived popularity of perpetrators (Estell et al., 2007; Rose, Swenson, & Waller, 2004; Zimmer-Gembeck, Geiger, & Crick, 2005). In addition, bullying of a relationally aggressive form may simultaneously lower the social standing of a rival. For example, social exclusion may lessen an adversary's opportunities for meeting a potential mate, whereas rumor spreading may denigrate a competitor's reputation and therefore lessen her attractiveness. This would especially be the case if the rumors suggest that the rival female is sexually promiscuous (Renold, 2002), as research has shown that women try to enhance their attractiveness by "playing hard to get," which may signal to men that they will be faithful and that they are desirable enough that they can afford to be choosy (Buss, 1988b). Finally, female adolescents may wish to form alliances with relationally aggressive girls who bully in order to gain priority access to high-status potential mates, given that relationally aggressive youth, with their high social status, can better dictate social agendas and may be gatekeepers to social events where sexual relationships may be formed. For example, when Owens, Shute, and Slee (2000b) interviewed 15- to 16-year-old female students about their experiences with intrasexual bullying, the participants reported observing social exclusion and rumor spreading being used to compete over potential sexual partners. Specifically, the girls and their teachers reported that relational aggression was used to attain popularity and determine membership in the ingroup, which in turn provided opportunities to invite or exclude classmates from parties where there would be opportunities to meet potential sexual partners. Additionally, girls mentioned that "when two girls…want one guy…what they do to each other to get to these guys [is] telling guys, like this one has a really bad reputation" (p. 36).

Adaptiveness of Bullying Moderated by Characteristics of the Bully, Victim, and Social Context

Despite evidence that bullying, in both physical and relational forms, can yield adaptive outcomes, research also shows that the functionality of bullying depends on the characteristics of the bully, the victim, and the context in which the bullying occurs. For example, bullying performed by bully-victims, individuals who both bully and are bullied, is not linked to positive outcomes in the areas of social dominance and intrasexual competition. Like bullies, they were lower in social preference and peer liking, and higher in peer disliking (Estell et al., 2007; Pellegrini et al., 1999; Rodkin et al., 2008). However, in contrast to bullies, they scored lower than uninvolved participants, bullies or victims, in teacher-rated popularity and peer nominations of perceived popularity (Estell et al., 2007; Rodkin et al., 2008). Furthermore, bully-victim status was nonsignificantly correlated with dominance, associated with fewer reciprocated friendship nominations, and these individuals had more peer relationship problems than did bullies, victims, or uninvolved peers (Marini, Dane, & Bosacki, 2006; Pellegrini et al., 1999). Notably, the peer relationship problem measure used by Marini and colleagues made reference to a lack of both friendships and dating opportunities.

Resource control theory (Hawley, 2007) suggests a reason why the bullying of "pure" bullies may be more adaptive than that of bully-victims. Its central tenet is that aggressive behavior in general is likely to achieve desirable outcomes only when it is performed by children who are also skilled in the use of prosocial behavior (Hawley, 2007). According to resource control theory, aggression is a coercive strategy that may be used to control resources such as social status and access to sexual partners. Prosocial strategies, including reciprocation, cooperation, being nice, and promising friendship, are alternative means to obtain the same ends. The research of Hawley and colleagues (e.g., Hawley, Little, & Card, 2007) has shown that bistrategic controllers, who frequently employ both prosocial and coercive strategies to control resources, fare better in this regard than coercive controllers, who rely mostly on aggression alone to advance their aims. Although bistrategic controllers are high in both overt and relational aggression (Hawley, 2003), they score higher than coercive controllers on several measures of social dominance and social centrality, including peer-nominated resource control (e.g., who is best at getting what he or she wants), measures of peer liking, perceived popularity, and desired affiliation (Hawley, Little, & Card, 2008). Additional research has shown that bistrategic controllers also surpass their coercive counterparts in social skills; have friendships with more positive qualities such as closeness, fun, and companionship; and are more agreeable, extroverted, and open to experience (Hawley, 2003; Hawley, Little, & Pasupathi, 2002; Hawley et al., 2007). In contrast, coercive controllers have been likened to children who lack social skills and are socially rejected (Hawley, 2007). Relative to bistrategic or prosocial controllers, they lack the ability to influence others through prosocial means, have a lower sense of well-being, are more hostile, and their behavior is undercontrolled (Hawley, 2002, 2007).

In line with research on resource-control groups or on subtypes of aggression, the bullying literature suggests that bullying is also a heterogeneous behavior (Volk et al., 2006), and that the type of bullying involvement would likely affect its adaptiveness. Specifically, an important theoretical and empirical distinction has been made between bullies and bully-victims, who are involved in high levels of both bullying and victimization. Similar to coercive controllers, research has shown that bully-victims are less adept at prosocial behavior, less athletic and attractive, lower in social competence and self-control, and higher in activity level than bullies, victims, or uninvolved children (Estell et al., 2007; Haynie et al., 2001; Marini et al., 2006; Rodkin & Berger, 2008). These attributes fit well with both popular stereotypes of bullying as well as the general psychopathological view that bullying is the result of individual and/or environmental developmental insults.

In contrast, bullying has been positively linked in some studies with theory of mind ability, cognitive empathy, leadership, social competence, and self-efficacy (Caravita et al., 2009, 2010; Vaillancourt et al., 2003), although some studies point to bullies having a deficit in prosocial behavior relative to victims or uninvolved youth (Estell et al., 2007; Rodkin & Berger, 2008). Furthermore, and contrary to popular stereotypes, pure bullies (i.e., excluding bully-victims) do not report increased mental health problems and problems with peers. Instead, they report equal or better mental health and peer popularity than average adolescents (e.g., Berger, 2007; Ireland, 2005; Juvonen et al., 2003; Volk et al., 2006; Wolke, Woods, Bloomfield, & Karstadt, 2001). This evidence is difficult to reconcile with the traditional psychopathological view of bullies, but it does fit well with an evolutionary view of bullies and bullying. Thus, in accord with previous writings suggesting that some bullies may use social skills toward antisocial ends (Sutton, Smith, & Swettenham, 1999), bullies may be better able than bully-victims to adaptively employ both coercive and prosocial resource control strategies. Thus, bullying may be more adaptive for some adolescents (pure bullies) than others (bully-victims) and consequently may result in the former group's higher social status and better access to social resources, including dating opportunities.

Another reason why the bullying of "pure" bullies may be more functional than that of bully-victims is that the former may be more selective in choosing victims and the context for their aggressive attacks, consistent with Action-Control theory. Action-Control theory states that individuals modify their aggressive behavior with respect to timing, severity, context, and selected targets, in order to maximize rewards and minimize costs (Card & Little, 2007). For example, recent research has shown that bullies appear to select victims who are rejected and less accepted by their peers, presumably to ensure that the gains with respect to dominance are not outweighed by disapproval from the peer group (Veenstra et al., 2010). The sex of the victim is also important because boys who bullied mostly girls had lower perceived popularity than boys who bullied mostly boys (Rodkin & Berger, 2008). In addition, classroom context is another consideration, with bullying having a greater negative relation with acceptance and higher positive association with rejection in classrooms in which fewer popular adolescents were involved in bullying (Dijkstra et al., 2008). Taken together, these results highlight that bullying can be adaptive when it is used selectively and judiciously.

Several lines of research suggest that the bullying practiced by bully-victims is less likely than that of "pure" bullies to be selective with respect to potential targets and to the social context, which would likely reduce its adaptiveness. First, as indicated, bully-victims are characterized by a lack of social competence and self-control, and their bullying is seen as a product of emotional dysregulation (Estell et al., 2007; Haynie et al., 2001; Marini et al., 2006; Rodkin & Berger, 2008; Schwartz, Proctor, & Chien, 2001). In addition, bully-victims are more apt than bullies to engage in reactive aggression (Salmivalli, & Nieminen, 2002), a subtype of aggression that is retaliatory, emotional, and impulsive in nature, and less planned, goal-directed, and calculated than proactive aggression (Hubbard, McAuliffe, Morrow, & Romano, 2010). Given their impulsivity, emotional volatility, and predilection for uncontrolled, unplanned, emotional acts of aggression, bully-victims may be more likely than "pure" bullies to direct their acts of bullying toward ill-advised targets (e.g., popular children; boys' bullying girls) without taking social context into consideration, and to thereby experience more sanctions and social disapproval from their peers. It then follows that the bullying of bully-victims would be ineffective and/or maladaptive in regard to achieving social dominance or competing for sexual partners. Again, this points to two different pathways to bullying. The first is the likely adaptive behavior of pure bullies that is characterized by selective behavioral choices and relatively positive outcomes. The second pathway is more similar to the traditional psychopathological view of bullying wherein bully-victims employ bullying strategies ineffectively as a result of poor inhibition and social skills.

A final consideration regarding individual differences in propensity to bully are personality factors. Bullies appear to possess personality traits that facilitate the development of bullying behaviors. In a study of the relationship of the "Big Five" personality traits with bullying, Tani and colleagues (2003) found that Italian children who bullied tended to show a similar pattern of low friendliness (agreeableness) and higher emotional instability (neuroticism). A study among American children again found a negative correlation with agreeableness, but no relationship with neuroticism and a significant negative relationship with conscientiousness (Bollmer, Harris, & Milich, 2006). Scholte and colleagues (2005) found that undercontrollers (characterized by moderate to high scores on extraversion, and low scores on agreeableness and conscientiousness) were more likely to bully other children. A study of callous-unemotional traits and bullying reported a modest positive correlation between callous-unemotional traits and bullying (Viding, Simmonds, Petrides, & Frederickson, 2009). Thus, bullying as an adaptation is likely to be influenced by personality traits (Book, Volk, & Hosker, 2012), which have been argued to be evolutionary adaptations (Ashton & Lee, 2001).

The data addressing callous-unemotional traits suggest yet another developmental path, possibly the most destructive pathway to all forms of bullying: psychopathy. Psychopathy is a personality construct that includes aggressive narcissism, a socially deviant lifestyle, and coercive/precocious sexuality (Camilleri & Quinsey, 2009a; Hare, 1998; Harris, Rice, Hilton, Lalumière, & Quinsey, 2007). While some debate still exists, there is mounting evidence that psychopathy begins to emerge in childhood (Forth & Book, 2007; Salekin, 2006) in the absence of developmental instabilities or insults (Lalumière, Harris, & Rice, 2001). The absence of detectable environmental causes (e.g., poor parenting) for psychopathy, the results of heritability studies, and the unique social skills associated with psychopathy have led some to suggest that psychopathy may be a suite of adaptive, evolved personality traits (Mealey, 1995). If so, psychopathic children may present an extreme personality that is adapted to being callous, impulsive, fearless, and manipulative, allowing them to become the consummate bullies. We would not be surprised that a proportion of bullies who commit the most persistent and violent examples of sexual bullying start at a young age and continue into adulthood because they are psychopaths (for further discussion on the role of psychopathy in bullying, in general, see the section on "Bullying as an Adaptation for Adolescents Through History").

Adolescent Bullying in Sexual Relationships—Intersexual Bullying

Moving beyond intrasexual competition, bullying may also serve an adaptive role in some social relationships between the sexes. Sexual bullying is a more recent topic for theory development and research, but it has been hampered by a lack of consistent definitions. Sometimes researchers include sexually aggressive behaviors as a type of bullying tactic (e.g., Cavendish & Solomone, 2001), or they refer to the act of sexual harassment as bullying or conceptualize these behaviors as the interface between sexual harassment and bullying (Fredland, 2008). The trouble with this latter approach is the assumption that sexual bullying is simply the overlap between two possibly unrelated constructs. Sexual harassment itself has been a difficult construct to define, though most seem to agree on a general definition that all cases involve unwanted sexual attention (McMaster, Connolly, Pepler, & Craig, 2002).

Rather than assume the composition of sexual bullies in our definition, we focus on classifying the presence and absence of specific acts. We therefore extend the definition of bullying described earlier to classify sexual bullying as a relationship problem that has a power imbalance where *sexual* acts are repeatedly and intentionally used by a more powerful individual, causing harm to a weaker individual. Using the same criteria for bullying, but focusing only on acts that are sexual, allows for more consistent language when studying theoretical similarities and differences between the bullying types.

We therefore consider three contexts under which sexual bullying could have evolved: (1) during courtship either to pursue mateships or to establish dominance; (2) in sexual relationships as proprietary and/or anticuckoldry risk management; and (3) in platonic relationships where a power imbalance exists and men use the imbalance to pursue short-term mating. Lastly, we again explore possible individual difference characteristics related to sexual bullying. Due to the novelty of this area of research, we sometimes draw upon the adult sexual bullying literature to help elucidate possible aspects of adolescent sexual bullying.

Courtship

Adolescence is an time during which sexual interest in the opposite sex emerges in earnest and where courtship behaviors begin. It is not surprising that the number of adolescents involved in a dating relationship increases as they age and sexually mature (Collins, 2003; Dornbusch et al., 1981) and that coercive sexual behaviors also emerge at this age (McMaster et al., 2002). In a nationally representative sample of American students from grades 6 to 10, using a broad definition of bullying that included sexual comments or gestures, Nansel et al. (2001) found that 47% of males reported ever being victimized (17.5% were victimized weekly), whereas 57.2% of females reported ever being victimized (20.5% were victimized weekly). When considering sexual bullying alone, the general trend is that boys mostly commit this behavior (Nansel et al., 2001). For example, across 10 types of sexual harassment acts, boys were more likely to be perpetrators on five of the acts and showed similar trends on the other acts (McMaster et al., 2002). Unlike nonsexual bullying, sexual bullying does not desist as adolescents age (AAUW, 2001; Volk et al., 2006). McMaster et al. (2002) also found an increase in the probability of cross-sex sexual harassment over grades 6 through 8, with no change in the amount of male-male sexual harassment, probably because the latter was already at an elevated level. To explain some of these sexual bullying trends in adolescence, we suggest that there are two paths to sexual bullying during courtship: derogatory bullying to establish dominance (the intrasexual competition discussed earlier) and coercive bullying to establish sexual relationships (intersexual competition).

With regard to the latter, we expect that coercive sexual bullying as a reproductive tactic takes place in two contexts: (1) in private, where more direct tactics are used to obtain sex access, or (2) in either public or private, where indirect tactics, sometimes referred to as *pushing and poking courtship behavior*, are used to gauge sexual interest while minimizing the probability of public rejection (Pellegrini, 2001) and avoiding the costs of publicly coercing someone, such as familial, social, or legal sanctions. In support of this, some research has shown that physical sexual bullying by boys against girls is rare in public (Shute et al., 2008). When physical sexual bullying does take place, it usually takes the form of "playful hitting, pushing, grabbing, and teasing an opposite sex peer" (Pellegrini, 2001, p. 121). Private behaviors could range from verbal or physical hints of sexual interest that might make someone uncomfortable, to physically coercing someone into sex, whereas public coercion is more likely to be verbal or less severe than physical behaviors used in private. In any of these cases, the function is to increase the probability of mating with that person.

Coercive sexual bullying may be a type of reproductive behavior because bullying by males against females emerges with sexual maturity. McMaster et al. (2002) found that sexual harassment was related to the onset of puberty for cross-sex harassment, not for same-sex harassment, even after controlling for age. Not only is sexual maturity a factor associated with perpetration of sexual aggression, it is also associated with sexual victimization. Craig et al. (2001), for example, found that adolescents who were sexually victimized also had early onset of puberty. In other words, perpetrators of sexual aggression tend to target reproductively viable victims.

An important assumption of this functional hypothesis that requires further investigation is that sexual bullying should eventually lead to successful mateships. There are two lines of evidence for this. First, there is some indication that the acts used by adult sexual offenders against the same victim progresses to more invasive acts. Walker (1997) found that over multiple coercive acts with the same victim, offenders often used more severe and invasive acts until copulation was achieved (Lalumière, Harris, Quinsey, & Rice, 2005). The behaviors did not escalate to more violence after this, suggesting that sex, not more severe abuse, was the goal of many perpetrators.

Similarly, there is some evidence that victims of severe sexual aggression continue to have sexual relations with their aggressor. Ellis, Widmayer, and Palmer (2009) found that 23% of rape victims continued to have intercourse with the perpetrator on subsequent occasions. It is unclear whether these cases were in the context of abusive relationships, but it has interesting (if disturbing) implications for outcomes of sexual bullying during courtship. The prevalence of sexually aggressive courtship behaviors may depend on environmental variables related to the availability of mates. Wood, Mafora, and Jewkes (1998), for example, found that in South Africa, a nation with one of the lowest life expectancies, sexual aggression in relationship formation and duration was perceived to be the norm as males aggressively pursued any available opportunities rather than engaging in lengthier, less hostile courtships. Adolescent sexually coercive bullying may serve the same functions as these more severe adult forms of sexual bullying—that is, obtaining copulation opportunities.

It is also possible that coercive sexual bullying might not have an adaptive function. An alternative hypothesis is that coercive sexual bullying may be a by-product of youthful exuberance combined with the onset of sexual maturity. The influx of sex hormones, combined with an underdeveloped frontal lobe, may provide an alternative explanation for the prevalence of inappropriate sexual acts perpetrated by adolescent boys. In this scenario, adolescent boys' eagerness for a partner overrides their social inhibitions, result in bullying behaviors. This may be particularly salient among bullies who already lack impulse control (e.g., bully-victims), and it may result in poorer outcomes than better regulated and more selective instances of bullying.

Bullying Within Sexual Relationships

Persistent sexual coercion in relationships meets the definition of sexual bullying because the perpetrator is in a position of power (e.g., physically stronger), the interaction causes physical or emotional harm, and it occurs more than once. We consider two possible paths to this type of sexual bullying: bullies outside of relationships who become bullies in relationships, and men (and thus presumably male adolescents) in relationships who exhibit or develop coercive behaviors as a facultative response to cuckoldry risk.

BULLIES TURN INTO RELATIONSHIP BULLIES

There are some "playground bullies" who continue their miscreant acts when they sexually mature and form sexual relationships. Connolly et al. (2000) found that individuals identified as bullies reported more instances of verbal and physical aggression with girlfriends or boyfriends than individuals not identified as bullies. Although the acts were nonsexual, they showed that aggressive behavior outside relationships could be generalized to relationships. More directly, in a longitudinal study, Pellegrini (2001) found a strong relationship between bullying in grade 6 and committing sexual harassment at the end of grade 7. There is also some evidence to suggest that variables more generally associated with sexual aggression are also related to sexual aggression in relationships (Camilleri & Quinsey, 2009a). Considering that relationship formation reduces the probability of men's antisocial behavior (Hanson & Bussiere, 1998), it appears as though some men are immune to the protective effects of relationships, as witnessed by their continuing high levels of bullying, whereas most men lower their antisocial activity when in a relationship. A subset of these bullies may present generalized antisocial characteristics that include sexual bullying throughout the life span. We review the research on men with these characteristics in the "Individual Differences" section.

CUCKOLDRY RISK MANAGEMENT

Sexual conflict theory has been proposed to explain a variety of antisocial acts by men in relationships, including verbal, physical, and sexual aggression (Camilleri & Quinsey, 2012). Sexual conflict occurs when the mating strategies of one sex inflict costs on the other sex, which leads to adaptations to overcome the conflict and may lead to the evolution of counteradaptations (Parker, 2006). A relevant source of conflict is cuckoldry risk, which is when an unfaithful partner increases the risk of wrongful paternity. Camilleri and Quinsey (2012) suggested that sexual coercion may (1) prevent opportunities that promote cuckoldry risk or (2) reduce cuckoldry risk once infidelity has occurred. Sexual bullying is more likely to occur under direct risk of cuckoldry because it is a strategy that increases the probability of successful fertilization without injuring the victim to the extent that it would make pregnancy unlikely. For example, there is preliminary evidence that sexual aggression in relationships is preceded by more signs of infidelity than is physical aggression (Camilleri & Quinsey, 2009b). Shields and Hanneke (1983) also found that 47% of women who were raped by their husband also reported being sexually unfaithful, whereas 23% of women who were beaten and 10% who were not victimized reported infidelity.

An interesting related topic is sexually motivated bullying by women of men. Although prevalence rates indicate that males commit most of this behavior, we also need to explain why it is sometimes perpetrated by females against males. Adolescent girls do engage in intersexual aggression in the context of relationships, often as a means of controlling their partner's behavior (Capaldi, Kim, & Shortt, 2004). For these girls, aggression (and often bullying) toward their partner helps ensure both their partner's fidelity as well as the girl's desired level of investment of resources (time, money, effort) from her male partner (Capaldi et al., 2004). This relates to the popular stereotype of the "hen-pecked husband" that alludes to both bullying and intersexual dominance. Women's intersexual aggression differs from men's in that their aggression is generally of a lower intensity (reflecting women's lower tolerance for physical violence and the associated risks; Wilson & Daly, 1985) and frequently in the context of mutual partner aggression (reflecting perhaps suboptimal relationships; Capaldi, Kim, & Shortt, 2007). Clearly, this is an area of research that requires greater study, but it is currently hampered by the social stigma of men/adolescent boys admitting to being victimized by their female partner(s).

Pathways to Intersexual Bullying

The domains of sexual bullying we have described thus far identify conditions that may increase the probability of sexual bullying. Yet as with intrasexual bullying, most adolescents who are in the aforementioned conditions do not engage in sexual bullying. We refer readers to the previous section on individual differences with regard to intrasexual bullying as a simultaneous explanation of individual differences with regard to intersexual bullying. One possible pathway worth expanding on in the specific context of intersexual aggression is life-course-persistent antisocial behavior, which includes both competitively disadvantaged and psychopathic men who typically show early onset of puberty, begin performing antisocial acts at a young age, and are characterized by being high in mating effort (Lalumière et al., 2005)—these characteristics are consistent with some data on bullies (e.g., Connolly et al., 2000). Indeed, a number of researchers also contend that bullies generalize their oppressive acts to their relationships (Connolly et al., 2000; Pellegrini, 2001), suggesting that upon reaching puberty, with the onset of sexual interest in mating, bullies might use these behaviors to obtain mateships. A potentially productive line of research would be to focus on assessments that might distinguish between these types of bullies.

Bullying Among Hunter-Gatherer Adolescents

So far, we have focused on modern evidence supporting the assertion that bullying is an adaptive behavior. However, as mentioned earlier, evolution works in a forward direction, so today's adaptations are a response to yesterday's selective pressures. This requires us to look backward for evidence of adaptation. Unfortunately, behavioral evidence from the human environments of evolutionary adaptation (including bullying) is extremely scarce. We deal with this limited evidence in the next, final section on adaptiveness of bullying (historical bullying). The current section of the chapter uses data from modern hunter-gatherer lifestyles that may be useful in understanding, if not approximating, the behavior of our Pleistocene ancestors (Konigsberg & Frankenberg, 1994; Miller & Kanazawa, 2007; Milner, Wood, & Boldsen, 2000).

A critical demographic trend that impacted the social environment adolescents faced in ancestral environments was childhood mortality—roughly 50% of children in hunter-gatherer groups fail to survive to adulthood (Volk & Atkinson, 2008). This means that if resources became scarce, the specter of child death could have exerted a tremendous evolutionary pressure on children to obtain the resources necessary for survival, whatever the means—including bullying. Among the displaced Ik hunter-gatherers, starvation was a constant threat, and their children engaged in high levels of direct bullying, particularly over food resources (Turnbull, 1972). We wish to emphasize that this function of bullying is all but absent in modern Western bullying. Given the extremely high mortality rates associated with hunter-gatherer childhood, bullying presumably occasionally served the immediate purpose of survival by ensuring immediate access to resources required for day-to-day survival. This would entail a life-or-death hunter-gatherer variation of the familiar "bullying for milk money" theme, in which the goal of the bully is to obtain immediate economic/survival rewards regardless of longer term consequences such as alienating a potential future ally from an already small pool of allies. Given the potential long-term costs, these short-term bullying strategies were most likely employed in difficult environments and/or during difficult times of drought or famine that may have frequently plagued hunter-gatherers (Lee & Daly, 1999).

This conditional use of a strategy is known as facultative adaptation whereby the adaptation is expressed under certain specific environmental conditions (Underwood, 1954; Williams, 1957). Indeed, modern studies suggest that facultative adaptations may be more ubiquitous than previously thought (e.g., Meaney, 2001). Environmentally induced flexibility is an important theme in evolutionary developmental psychology, where the environment helps dictate when, which, and how genes are expressed in child development (Bjorklund & Pellegrini, 2000; Weaver et al., 2004). When mortality rates are higher than normal, children may have employed behaviors that discounted future investments (that are less valuable in the face of higher odds of dying) in favor of present investments (that may immediately help to mitigate those increased odds of dying; Del Giudice & Belsky, 2010; Williams, 1957). Again, this appears to have been the case among the Ik, who over the course of less than two generations, are believed to have changed from a typical, egalitarian, family-oriented hunter-gatherer society (Lee, 1979) to the very model of a selfishly amoral society. Turnbull (1972) suggested that this change was due to the dramatic drop in food production caused by a forced resettlement from a freely mobile hunter-gathering lifestyle to a fixed agricultural lifestyle in a territory poorly suited for agriculture. The most antisocial among the Ik were the children/adolescents, and then their parents. Meanwhile, the grandparents, who still remembered the earlier, better times, retained a stronger degree of prosociality until their deaths (which occurred earlier due to severe bullying from their own children and grandchildren).

Besides scarcity, there are at least three other important environmental-cultural factors that likely influenced the evolution of bullying among hunter-gatherer adolescents. First, adult hunter-gatherers have a generally low tolerance for violence and overt aggression (Briggs, 1970). For instance, avoidance and/or group chastising (rather than overt reactive aggression) are the two typical responses to adult-adult aggression (Lee, 1979; Turnbull, 1961). Second, dominance is typically established through relationships and altruistic contributions (e.g., shared meat) rather than intimidation. Indeed, many hunter-gatherer groups explicitly encourage egalitarianism and discourage overt displays of aggression, dominance, and/or status (e.g., Briggs, 1972; Ingold, 2004; Lee, 1979; Thomas, 1989; Turnbull, 1961). Finally, high levels of individual and group mobility and flexibility allow for the dissipation of latent conflicts and constantly shift the locus of authority, which promotes egalitarianism (Marlowe, 2010; Turnbull, 1972). Combined, these three social factors likely reduced the prevalence and effectiveness of overt/direct bullying for dominance in adults as well as adolescents. Indeed, in the rare instances in which it has been studied (excluding the Ik), hunter-gatherer children's play is generally noted for its remarkable absence of direct aggression, except toward nonhuman animals (Kamei, 2005; Marlowe, 2010).

However, this does not mean that there is no aggression—particularly indirect social aggression. Spreading rumors, sabotaging peer networks, vandalism, and social exclusion can all be forms of indirect bullying. While not widely observed among hunter-gatherer children (Kamei, 2005), the nature of indirect bullying dictates that it is difficult for nonparticipants, particularly adults, to observe (Craig & Pepler, 1998). Indeed, if adults typically negatively sanctioned children or adolescents who were aggressive or bullies (Briggs, 1970), indirect bullying may have evolved as a discreet form of aggression that adolescents could employ with impunity from adults' sanctions. While some forms of indirect aggression may be seen in chimpanzees (Goodall, 1986), true indirect bullying requires a degree of sophistication that is largely beyond other apes' cognitive abilities. The novel human capacity for highly sophisticated theory of mind judgments (Wellman, 1992) suggests that hunter-gatherers are well equipped for using more subtle forms of bullying that might have been more effective than direct, overt aggression because indirect bullies would be less vulnerable to both adult sanctions and costly, direct confrontations with the victim. For example, among hunter-gatherer adults, boasting, physical coercion, and other obvious attempts at social dominance are typically met with indirect aggression such as social ridicule (Turnbull, 1961). But manipulation of social networks, the use of gossip, and controlling access to social groups are generally condoned, if not encouraged (Briggs, 1972; Ingold, 2004; Marlowe, 2010; Thomas, 1989; Turnbull, 1961). So even if overall hunter-gatherer childhood aggression and bullying are low, indirect forms of bullying are likely to be of increasing importance to some hunter-gatherer adolescents. We thus propose that the roots of indirect bullying may lie in hunter-gatherer adolescents who were able to use indirect aggression as a more effective and subtle form of bullying that avoided adult or cultural sanctions, risky physical conflicts, and overt within-group conflict, while still allowing these adolescents to use aggression to increase their access to desired resources (particularly for longer term reproductive goals). The idea that indirect aggression is a successful adaptation may be supported by modern data showing that indirect aggression is typically associated with less negative immediate, environmental, and developmental outcomes (Card, Stucky, Sawalani, & Little, 2008).

Thus, hunter-gatherer bullying may at times serve an immediate function. It may also serve the longer term, developmental purpose of gaining social dominance and/or access to social resources. In this second, longer term perspective, hunter-gatherer adolescent bullying may serve to accumulate social and physical capital that could be later used to facilitate adult survival and reproductive success (e.g., Geary, 1999; Leenaars et al., 2008). This means that hunter-gatherer children have at least two types of reasons for bullying other children: a short-term, facultative response to acute environmental stress, and a long-term developmental trajectory aimed at improving adult reproductive success similar to what we described for modern children (e.g., Campbell, 1999; Hrdy, 2009; Ingold, 2004; Lee, 1979; Low, 1989).

A final note on hunter-gatherer bullying is that many of the children in any particular hunter-gatherer group are likely to be related to each other (Hewlett & Lamb, 2005). The presence of shared genes in other children may have promoted increased altruism through kin selection. In kin selection, altruism helps copies of one's genes that are shared with those in a relative's body (Hamilton, 1965). This may have led to lower levels of bullying as (all else equal) aggression against a relative hurts copies of one's own genes at the same time as it benefits one's own genes. The fact that (other than identical twins) genetic relatedness between children was no greater than 50% (for full siblings) left plenty of room for aggression and bullying. But compared to modern, or even postagricultural populations, where the average genetic relatedness of children is likely to be closer to 0%, we would expect lower levels of bullying between the more closely related hunter-gather children than we would expect between the nonkin relationships of modern children.

Bullying as an Adaptation for Adolescents Through History

Our final source of evidence for bullying as an adaptation comes from historical data, typically drawn from within the last few thousand years. A potential argument against the impact of this relatively recent (from an evolutionary perspective) data is that there has not been sufficient time for complex adaptations to evolve in response to evolutionary pressures that occurred in the past 10,000 years (Cochran & Harpending, 2009). This could pose a problem for any theory that posited the appearance of a novel form of bullying due solely to evolution within the past 10,000 years because there may not have been enough time for random mutations to occur, be selected for, and develop toward a new complex behavioral adaptation (Miller & Kanazawa, 2007). Fortunately, there is a simple answer to this argument: No complex, novel adaptations had to occur for children to become genetically predisposed toward engaging in higher levels or different forms of bullying. Evolution simply had to increase the already present, low levels of physical aggression among hunter-gatherer adolescents to result in higher levels of physical bullying for agriculturalist adolescents. This would require something along the order of adjusting the expression of existing genotypes rather than creating entirely new adaptations (Carroll, 2005; Cochran & Harpending, 2009; Irons, 1998). Temperament, personality, and traits that we have previously discussed are (for the most part) genetically influenced attributes that appear to operate in this flexible manner and that could easily account for differences in adolescents' aggression over a relatively short evolutionary time period (Bollmer, Harris, & Milich, 2006; Plomin, Defries, Craig, & McGuffin, 2002).

The advent of civilization did not immediately usher major changes from the previous periods. Child mortality remained very high, with half of all children again failing to survive past puberty (Volk & Atkinson, 2008). From an evolutionary perspective, these mortality rates would continue to offer crucial reproductive variation for natural selection to work with (Cochran & Harpending, 2009). As civilized history progressed, at least two important factors arose that may have seriously influenced the purpose and prevalence of bullying: psychopathy and formal schooling.

Psychopathy

The first factor may have been the appearance of true psychopathy. While psychopaths are capable of reading and imitating normal human emotions, they lack the typical empathic response toward the emotions of others (Hare, 1998). This makes psychopaths superb social cheaters and exploiters (Book &

Quinsey, 2004). However, a psychopathic hunter-gatherer would be very likely to cause significant intragroup conflict, toward which hunter-gatherers are generally intolerant (Thomas, 1989). Indeed, the usual responses toward extreme antisociality among the !Kung bushmen is group execution of the offender (Lee, 1979; Thomas, 1989). Psychopaths' strategies of manipulation, deception, and exploitation generally rely on a degree of anonymity and mobility (Hare, 1998) that simply was rare (e.g., Turnbull, 1972), if not absent, among ancestral hunter-gatherers. Any potential benefits from psychopathic group members (e.g., against rival groups) would almost certainly have been more than offset by the tremendous cost these individuals impose on a group (Colman & Wilson, 1997). But the advent of large, stable, civilized populations connected by trade may have allowed psychopaths to distribute these costs among numerous groups thanks to the increased mobility and anonymity associated with civilized life. If psychopathy operates along a personality trait continuum (Guay, Ruscio, Knight, & Hare, 2007), this could make the evolution of psychopathic bullies over the last 10,000 years as simple as dialing up or down existing personality attributes such as empathy, impulsivity, extraversion, narcissism, and sensation seeking once the environmental and cultural penalties for the disorder were offset by changes in civilized environments and cultures. As previously discussed (Bollmer et al., 2006; Plomin et al., 2002), personality traits in general appear to operate along just such a genetically scalable continuum.

With regard to bullying, this would lead to a new category of bullies: bullies who lacked two important impediments toward bullying—the ability to engage in bullying without paying any internal emotional penalty, and immunity to internal empathic, and external altruistic, social influences. While the specific motives for psychopathic bullying may not differ from traditional bullying (e.g., dominance, sexual access, economic resources, etc.), psychopathic bullies presumably have different propensities toward engaging in bullying because they are essentially adapted toward an antisocial lifestyle (Mealey, 1995). Beyond the importance of different motives, if psychopathic bullies are like psychopathic adult offenders (Hare, 1998), they are likely to commit a disproportionate amount of bullying in terms of frequency, severity, and versatility. Thus, the evolution of juvenile psychopaths may have had an important influence on the prevalence, if not the functions, of bullying.

This brings us to a critical part of any evolutionary theory: What are the possible developmental mechanisms and trajectories that could enable the hypothesized adaptation to be expressed? Psychopathic bullies may be an excellent example of how a similar behavior (bullying) might entail multiple independent developmental trajectories (Moffitt, 1993). Bullying can thus be the result of a normal adaptation (e.g., bullying to promote long-term reproductive success), a facultative adaptation (e.g., bullying to gain economic resources under periods of intense scarcity), or an alternate lifestyle (e.g., bullying resulting from a psychopathic lifestyle). This highlights the complexity of evolutionary adaptations. They are quite often not fixed, universal programs of behavior that are insensitive to environmental inputs (Bjorklund & Pellegrini, 2000; Del Giudice & Belsky, 2010). Instead, an evolutionarily informed examination of bullying requires a detailed knowledge of the environmental influences (past and present), as well as genetic influences and gene–environment interactions (Scarr & McCartney, 1983). Again though, we emphasize that there are also likely to be developmental pathways toward bullying that were potentially maladaptive in the past (e.g., a psychopathic lifestyle among hunter-gatherers) and/or the present (e.g., reactive aggression amongst modern bully-victims; Little, Jones, Henrich, & Hawley, 2003; Marini et al., 2006). What we are arguing is that for some bullies, antisocial behavior may not be the result of an impoverished, maladaptive, or misguided development, but rather the result of adaptive, evolutionary, alternative development.

Formal Schooling

Another major change to occur in historical civilizations was the advent of formal schools, job/military training, and/or apprenticeships (Cunningham, 2005; Golden, 1990; Hsiung, 2005; Rawson, 2003). All of these activities require children to explicitly compete against other children, not just for survival or dominance (as had previously been the case) but for explicit new surrogate goals such as marks, prestige, literacy, rank, and/or salary (Stearns, 2006). This competition no doubt increased the prevalence of bullying, particularly among boys for whom these goals were most salient (girls, for the most part, were expected to lead domestic lives; Golden, 1990; Hsiung, 2005). Furthermore, the severity of this increased bullying was also likely to increase for three other concurrent social factors: (a) few of the children were related to each other, removing an important evolutionary constraint on bullying (i.e., harming the shared genes of kin; Hamilton, 1965); (b) fewer of the children would grow up to rely on each other, reducing the motive for reciprocal altruism and group cohesivity (another former evolutionary constraint; Trivers, 1971); and (c) more children of the same age were grouped together. Evidence shows that children of the same age are more likely to engage in conflict with each other than the mixed age groups more characteristic of earlier environments (Feldman & Gray, 1999). Presumably, this is due to the more ambiguous dominance hierarchies that are present in children of similar ages and capacities. An 8-year-old represents a greater threat to another 8-year-old than to a 16-year-old. When combined with the increased competitiveness explicitly thrust upon civilized children, these three factors may have increased the level of bullying among civilized children. Furthermore, an ancient form of bullying began to become more common as a result of an increasing number of novel, fixed hierarchies: hazing (Nuwer, 1999). Hazing is a potent driving force behind severe bullying in a wide range of settings and occupations (Nuwer, 1999).

Culturally, in the West, these increases in aggression may have been tolerated due to the increased general levels of aggression associated within Western cultures (Orme, 1995, 2002). The picture from other cultures is not as clear, although there is evidence that ancient Chinese children did engage in high levels of at least verbal and social bullying (Hsiung, 2005). So an increase in the competitiveness of childhood, combined with the removal of previous restraints on bullying, may have increased the amount and/or severity of bullying experienced by civilized children. New social arenas for bullying, combined with an increase in associated hazing rituals, may have further magnified the problem. When combined with the appearance of psychopathic traits in children, bullying was likely to have taken a turn for the worse during civilized times. This means that contextual and environmental changes associated with civilization may have played an important role in continuing, and even amplifying, the biological and cultural evolution of bullying.

Future Directions

In summary, we have presented evidence for both the heritability of bullying as well as its adaptive functions in modern, hunter-gatherer, and historical populations. Thus, we believe adolescent bullying may be an evolutionary adaptation. Adolescents may be predisposed to engage in bullying, a conclusion that has many important implications. While we cannot address all of these implications here, we outline four that are most urgent and/or in need of further research.

1. Bullying is an adaptation, but it may not always be adaptive. We have argued that bullying is an evolutionary adaptation. Despite this, or indeed because of this, it is crucial to point out that this does not mean that all bullying is adaptive. Clearly, bullying is not likely to be adaptive to the victim, and this is reason enough to want to develop antibullying interventions. But bullying may also not always be adaptive for the bully. While bully-victims appear to illustrate this most clearly, even successful bullies suffer from losses in peer nominations of liking and acceptance (e.g., Bachini et al., 2008; Caravita et al., 2009, 2010; Dijkstra et al., 2007), face potentially severe costs from retaliating victims or punishing adults, and often engage in corelated antisocial behaviors that are harmful to the bully (Volk et al., 2006). Thus, while some bullying may be a way of obtaining social status, social or physical resources, and/or sexual access, it does not come without (sometimes significant) costs. Our claim that bullying is adaptive is therefore in no way a justification for its continued existence or a denial of its potential costs. The cautions about naturalistic and deterministic fallacies hold for bullying just as they do for other human behaviors. These cautions refer to, respectively, that bullying is neither naturally moral nor irreversibly genetically determined. Given that bullying is associated with severe costs for victims, bully-victims, and sometimes bullies, it is clearly desirable to continue searching for ways of reducing both bullying and its negative impacts. This leads to our next point.

2. Implications for intervention. If bullying is adaptive, this suggests that some adolescents may gain more benefits than costs from its use. This raises a significant challenge for intervention programs that ask adolescents to freely do away with a beneficial (to them) behavior. As we have discussed, not all bullying appears to be caused by social or emotional ignorance. Indeed, some bullies show greater levels of Machiavellian thinking (Sutton & Keogh, 2000) than most adolescents. This means that successful antibullying interventions will have to address the loss of a beneficial behavior to the bully and offer appropriate substitutions or benefits. We recommend two parallel directions for future antibullying interventions. First, interventions can increase the costs of bullying by increasing social sanctions/ attitudes by peers (e.g., turning bystanders into defenders), parents, and educators for bullying; increasing adult awareness/punishment of bullying; and encouraging peers to withdraw their support of bullying activities. Second, we suggest that interventions should consider bullies as skilled, intelligent, and motivated adolescents who are effective at using a behavioral tool (i.e., bullying) to obtain their goals without incurring undue costs. Interventions should offer these adolescents specific, novel, social alternatives that capitalize on bullies' natural strengths and traits. For example, bullies' tendency to use aggressive tactics to obtain dominance could be directed toward competing for status via prosocial acts of charity (e.g., who can give the most?). These kinds of "forced" acts of charity and prosociality appear to be common mechanisms thought to reduce aggression in many hunter-gatherer societies and may be helpful in reducing modern bullying.

3. *Bullying in children and adults.* Our chapter has largely focused on bullying in adolescents, both because that is where the majority of research has been conducted and because mid-adolescence appears to be a peak period for bullying. That does not mean that bullying is absent prior to, or following, adolescence. Indeed, bullying is present in both age contexts. In younger children, bullying appears to serve many of the same dominance and social resource control functions. Naturally, the sexual functions for bullying are generally absent for younger children. The importance of early intervention suggests that further research into the adaptiveness of bullying for children is warranted. Among adults, bullying serves essentially the same functions as it does for adolescents. Two important distinctions are that adults generally engage in lower levels of bullying and that a new motive for bullying, parental solicitude, may emerge during adulthood. With regard to the former, adults generally find more prosocial and less risky methods of gaining social status, but the difference is not as large as one might hope (Randall, 1997). With regard to the latter, parents screaming at, taunting, and even assaulting child athletes competing against their own child reveal that parental care can sometimes have a dark side (Docheff & Conn, 2004). The competition to provide for one's offspring can be intense, and it can lead adults to engage in serious incidents of bullying directed at both other parents as well as children who are viewed as potential competitors to the parents' child(ren).

4. *Bullying is not an aberration.* All too often, bullies are simply dismissed as being ill raised, of low intelligence, socially awkward, and developmentally challenged. The idea is that these are children who have somehow slipped through the cracks and are now displaying inappropriate behaviors. For some bullies, this may be the case. However, for many other bullies, nothing could be further from the truth. Some bullies are clever, accomplished, socially skilled, and come from decent (or better) homes. It is troubling to think that these conditions can lead to a behavior as patently antisocial and harmful as bullying, but this appears to be the case. As with aggression in general, bullying has proven to be advantageous to many adolescents over the entire course of human history, and it has thus "won" a spot as an evolutionary adaptation for adolescents. While this does not mean that bullying is impossible to eliminate, it does mean that it is unlikely that bullying will go away on its own. The seductive misbelief that bullying is an aberration may not only hide the truth from researchers trying to develop effective intervention strategies, but it may also weaken the resolve of the public to tackle what is an important, and currently intrinsic, aspect of adolescence.

References

Achenbach, T. M. (1991). *Manual for the Child Behavior Checklist/4-18 and 1991 Profile.* Burlington: University of Vermont, Department of Psychiatry.

Alcock, J. (2001). *The triumph of sociobiology.* Toronto: Oxford University Press.

American Association of University Women (AAUW). (2001). *Hostile hallways.* New York: AAUW Educational Foundation.

Archer, J. (1988). *The behavioral biology of aggression.* Cambridge, England: Cambridge University Press.

Archer, J., & Benson, D. (2008). Physical aggression as a function of perceived fighting ability and provocation: An experimental investigation. *Aggressive Behavior, 34,* 9–24.

Ashton, M., & Lee, K. (2001). A theoretical basis for the dimensions of personality. *European Journal of Personality, 15,* 327–353.

Ball, H. A., Arsenault, L., Taylor, A., Maughan, B., Caspi, A., & Moffitt, T. E. (2008). Genetic influences on victims, bullies, and bully-victims in childhood. *The Journal of Child Psychology and Psychiatry, 49,* 104–112.

Benenson, J. F. (2009). Sex differences in aggression from an adaptive perspective. In M. J. Harris (Ed.), *Bullying, rejection, and peer victimization: A social cognitive neuroscience perspective* (pp. 171–198). New York: Springer.

Berger, K. S. (2007). Update on bullying at school: Science forgotten? *Developmental Review, 27,* 90–126.

Bjorklund, D. F., & Pellegrini, A. D. (2000). Child development and evolutionary psychology. *Child Development, 71,* 1687–1708.

Bollmer, J. M., Harris, M. J., & Milich, R. (2006). Reactions to bullying and peer victimization: Narratives, physiological arousal, and personality. *Journal of Research in Personality, 40,* 803–828.

Book, A. S., & Quinsey, V. L. (2004). Psychopaths: Cheaters or warrior-hawks? *Personality and Individual Differences, 36,* 33–45.

Book, A. S., Volk, A. A., & Hosker, A. (2012). Adolescent bullying and personality: An adaptive approach. *Personality and Individual Differences, 52,* 218–223.

Briggs, J. L. (1970). *Never in anger.* Cambridge, MA: Harvard University Press.

Buss, D. M. (1988a). The evolution of human intrasexual competition: Tactics of mate attraction. *Journal of Personality and Social Psychology, 54,* 616–628.

Buss, D. M. (1988b). From vigilance to violence: Tactics of mate retention in American undergraduates. *Ethology and Sociobiology, 9,* 291–317.

Camilleri, J. A., & Quinsey, V. L. (2009a). Individual differences in the propensity for partner sexual coercion. *Sexual abuse: A journal of research and treatment, 21,* 111–129.

Camilleri, J. A., & Quinsey, V. L. (2009b). Testing the cuckoldry risk hypothesis of partner sexual coercion in community and forensic samples. *Evolutionary Psychology, 7,* 164–178.

Camilleri, J. A. & Quinsey, V. L. (2012). Sexual conflict and partner rape. In A. T. Goetz, & T. K. Shackelford (Eds.), *Oxford Handbook of Sexual Conflict in Humans* (pp. 257–268). New York: Oxford University Press.

Campbell, A. (1999). Staying alive: Evolution, culture, and women's intrasexual aggression. *Behavioral and Brain Sciences, 22,* 203–252.

Capaldi, D. M., Kim, H. K., & Shortt, J. W. (2004). Women's involvement in aggression in young adult romantic relationships: A developmental systems model. In M. Putallaz & K. L. Bierman (Eds.), *Aggression, antisocial behavior, and violence among girls* (pp. 223–241). New York: The Guilford Press.

Capaldi, D. M., Kim, H. K., & Short, J. W. (2007). Observed initiation and reciprocity of physical aggression in young, at-risk couples. *Journal of Family Violence, 22,* 101–111.

Caravita, S. C. S., Di Blasio, P., & Salmivalli, C. (2009). Unique and interactive effects of empathy and social status on involvement in bullying. *Social Development, 18,* 140–163.

Caravita, S. C. S., Di Blasio, P., & Salmivalli, C. (2010). Early adolescents' participation in bullying: Is ToM involved? *The Journal of Early Adolescence, 30,* 138–170.

Card, N. A., & Little, T. D. (2007). Differential relations of instrumental and reactive aggression with maladjustment: Does adaptivity depend on function? In P. Hawley, T. Little, & P. Rodkin (Eds.), *Aggression and adaptation: The bright side to bad behavior* (pp. 107–134). Mahwah, NJ: Erlbaum.

Card, N. A., Stucky, B. D., Sawalani, G. M., & Little, T. D. (2008). Direct and indirect aggression during childhood and adolescence: A meta-analytic review of gender differences, intercorrelations, and relations to maladjustment. *Child Development, 79,* 1185–1229.

Carroll, S. (2005). *Endless forms most beautiful.* New York: W.W. Norton & Company.

Cavendish, R., & Salomone, C. (2001). Bullying and sexual harassment in the school setting. *The Journal of School Nursing, 17,* 25–31.

Cillessen, A. H. N., & Mayeux, L. (2007). Developmental changes in the association between aggression and status in the peer system. In P. Hawley, T. Little, & P. Rodkin (Eds.), *Aggression and adaptation: The bright side to bad behavior* (pp. 135–156). Mahwah, NJ: Erlbaum.

Cochran, G., & Harpending, H. (2009). *The 10,000 year explosion.* New York: Basic Books.

Collins, W. A. (2003). More than myth: The developmental significance of romantic relationships during adolescence. *Journal of Research on Adolescence, 13,* 1–24.

Colman, A. M., & Wilson, J. C. (1997). Antisocial personality disorder: An evolutionary game theory analysis. *Legal and Criminological Psychology, 2,* 23–34.

Connolly, J., Pepler, D., Craig, W., & Taradash, A. (2000). Dating experiences of bullies in early adolescence. *Child Maltreatment, 5,* 299–310.

Craig, W. M., & Pepler, D. J. (1998). Observations of bullying and victimization in the school yard. *Canadian Journal of School Psychology, 13,* 41–59.

Craig, W., Pepler, D., Connolly, J., & Henderson, K. (2001). Developmental context of peer harassment in early adolescence: The role of puberty and the peer group. In S. Graham & J. Juvonen (Eds.), *Peer harassment in school: The plight of the vulnerable and victimized* (pp. 242–262). New York: The Guilford Press.

Cunningham, H. (2005) *Children and childhood in Western society since 1500* (2nd ed.). Toronto: Pearson-Longman Press.

Dawkins, R. (1989). *The selfish gene.* New York: Oxford University Press.

Del Giudice, M., & Belsky, J. (2010). Sex differences in attachment emerge in middle adolescence: An evolutionary hypothesis. *Child Development Perspectives, 4,* 97–105.

Dijkstra, J. K., Lindenberg, S., & Veenstra, R. (2007). Same-gender and cross-gender peer acceptance and peer rejection and their relation to bullying and helping among preadolescents: Comparing predictions from gender-homophily and goal-framing approaches. *Developmental Psychology, 43,* 1377–1389.

Dijkstra, J. K., Lindenberg, S., & Veenstra, R. (2008). Beyond the class norm: Bullying behavior of popular adolescents and its relation to peer acceptance and rejection. *Journal of Abnormal Child Psychology, 36,* 1289–1299.

DiLalla, E. F. (2002). Behavior genetics of aggression in children: Review and future directions. *Developmental Review, 22,* 593–622.

Docheff, D. M., & Conn, J. H. (2004). It's no longer a spectator sport—eight ways to get involved and help fight parental violence in youth sports. *Parks and Recreation, 39,* 62–70.

Dornbusch, S. M., Carlsmith, J. M., Gross, R. T., Martin, J. A., Jennings, D., Rosenberg, A., & Duke, P. (1981). Sexual development, age, and dating: A comparison of biological and social influences upon one set of behaviors. *Child Development, 52,* 179–185.

Ellis, L., Widmayer, A., & Palmer, C. (2009). Perpetrators of sexual assault continuing to have sex with their victims following initial assault. *International Journal of Offender, 53,* 454–463.

Estell, D. B., Farmer, T. W., & Cairns, B. D. (2007). Bullies and victims in rural African American youth: Behavioral characteristics and social network placement. *Aggressive Behavior, 33,* 145–159.

Feldman J., & Gray, P. (1999). Some educational benefits of freely chosen age mixing among children and adolescents. *Phi Delta Kappan, 80,* 507–512.

Forth, A. E., & Book, A. S. (2007). Psychopathy in youth: A valid construct? In H. Herve & J. C. Yuille (Eds.), *The psychopath: Theory, research, and practice* (pp. 369–387). Mahwah, NJ: Erlbaum.

Fredland, N. M. (2008). Sexual bullying: Addressing the gap between bullying and dating violence. *Advances in Nursing Science, 31*, 95–105.

Geary, D. C. (1999). Evolution and developmental sex differences. *Current Directions in Psychological Science, 8*, 115–120.

Golden, M. (1990). *Children and childhood in classical Athens.* New York: The John Hopkins University Press.

Goodall, J. (1986). *The chimpanzees of Gombe: Patterns of behavior.* Cambridge, MA: Harvard University Press.

Guay, J., Ruscio, J., Knight, R. A., & Hare, B. (2007). A taxometric analysis of the latent structure of psychopathy: Evidence for dimensionality. *Journal of Abnormal Psychology, 116*, 701–716.

Hamilton, W. (1965). The genetical evolution of social behavior. I. *Journal of Theoretical Biology, 7*, 1–16.

Hanson, R. K., & Bussiere, M. T. (1998). Predicting relapse: A meta-analysis of sexual offender recidivism studies. *Journal of Consulting and Clinical Psychology, 66*, 348.

Hare, R. D. (1998). *Without conscience.* New York: The Guilford Press.

Harris, G. T., Rice, M. E., Hilton, N. Z., Lalumière, M. L., & Quinsey, V. L. (2007). Coercive and precocious sexuality as a fundamental aspect of psychopathy. *Journal of Personality Disorders, 21*, 1–27.

Hawley, P. H. (2002). Social dominance and prosocial and coercive strategies of resource control in preschoolers. *International Journal of Behavioral Development, 26*, 167–176.

Hawley, P. H. (2003). Strategies of control, aggression and morality in preschoolers: An evolutionary perspectives. *Journal of Experimental Child Psychology, 85*, 213–235.

Hawley, P. H. (2007). Social dominance in childhood and adolescence: Why social competence and aggression may go hand in hand. In P. H. Hawley, T. D. Little, & P. C. Rodkin (Eds.), *Aggression and adaptation: The bright side to bad behavior* (pp. 1–29). Mahwah, NJ: Erlbaum.

Hawley, P. H., Little, T. D., & Card, N. A. (2007). The allure of a mean friend: Relationship quality and processes of aggressive adolescents with prosocial skills. *International Journal of Behavioral Development, 31*, 170–180.

Hawley, P. H., Little, T. D., & Card, N. A. (2008). The myth of the alpha male: A new look at dominance-related beliefs and behaviors among adolescent males and females. *International Journal of Behavioral Development, 32*, 76–88.

Hawley, P. H., Little, T. D., & Pasupathi, M. (2002). Winning friends and influencing peers: Strategies of peer influence in late childhood. *International Journal of Behavioral Development, 26*, 466–474.

Haynie, D. L., Nansel, T., Eitel, P., Crump, A. D., Saylor, K., Yu, K., & Simons-Morton, B. (2001). Bullies, victims, and bully/victims: Distinct groups of at-risk youth. *Journal of Early Adolescence, 21*, 29–49.

Hewlett, B. S., & Lamb, M. E. (Eds.). (2005). *Hunter-gatherer childhoods.* London: Transaction.

Hrdy, S. B. (2009). *Mothers and others.* Cambridge, MA: Harvard University Press.

Hsiung, P. C. (2005). *A tender voyage: Children and childhood in late imperial China.* Stanford, CA: Stanford University Press.

Hubbard, J. A., McAuliffe, M. D., Morrow, M. T., & Romano, L. J. (2010). Reactive and proactive aggression in childhood and adolescence: Precursors, outcomes, processes, experiences, and measurement. *Journal of Personality, 78(1)*, 95–118.

Ingold, T. (2004). On the social relations of the hunter-gatherer band. In R. B. Lee & R. Daly (Eds.), *Hunters and gatherers* (pp. 309–330). New York: Cambridge University Press.

Ireland, J. L. (2005). Psychological health and bullying behavior among adolescent prisoners: A study of young and juvenile offenders. *Journal of Adolescent, 36*, 236–243.

Irons, W. (1998). Adaptively relevant environments versus the environment of evolutionary adaptedness. *Evolutionary Anthropology, 6*, 194–204.

Juvonen, J., Graham, S., & Schuster, M. A. (2003). Bullying among young adolescents: The strong, the weak, and the troubled. *Pediatrics, 112*, 1231–1237.

Kamei, N. (2005). Play among Baka children in Cameroon. In B. S. Hewlett & M. E. Lamb (Eds.), *Hunter-Gatherer childhoods* (pp. 343–359). New Brunswick, NJ: Aldine Transaction.

Konigsberg, L. W., & Frankenberg, S. R. (1994). Paleodemography: "Not quite dead." *Evolutionary Anthropology, 3*, 92–105.

LaFontana, K. M., & Cillessen, A. H. N. (1998). The nature of children's stereotypes of popularity. *Social Development, 7*, 301–320.

Lalumière, M. L., Harris, G. T., & Rice, M. E. (2001). Psychopathy and developmental instability. *Evolution and Human Behavior, 22*, 75–92.

Lalumière, M. L., Harris, G. T., Quinsey, V. L., & Rice, M. E. (2005). *The causes of rape: Understanding individual differences in male propensity for sexual aggression.* Washington, DC: American Psychological Association.

Lee, E. (2009). The relationship of aggression and bullying to social preference: Differences in gender and types of aggression. *International Journal of Behavioral Development, 33*, 323–330.

Lee, R. B. (1979). *The!Kung San.* Cambridge, England: Cambridge University Press.

Lee, R. B., & Daly, R. (Eds). (1999). *The Cambridge encyclopedia of hunter-gatherers.* Cambridge, England: Cambridge University Press.

Leenaars, L. S., Dane, A., V., & Marini, Z. A. (2008). Evolutionary perspective on indirect victimization in adolescence: The role of attractiveness, dating and sexual behavior. *Aggressive Behavior, 34*, 404–415.

Little, T. D., Jones, S., M., Henrich, C., C., & Hawley, P. H. (2003). Disentangling the "whys" from the "whats" of aggressive behavior. *International Journal of Behavioral Development, 27*, 122–133.

Lorenz, K. (1966). *On aggression.* Toronto: Bantam.

Low, B. S. (1989). Cross-cultural patterns in the training of children: An evolutionary perspective. *Journal of Comparative Psychology, 103*, 311–319.

Maccoby, E. (2004). Aggression in the context of gender development. In M. Putallaz & K. L. Bierman (Eds.), *Aggression, antisocial behavior, and violence among girls* (pp. 3–22). New York: The Guilford Press.

Marini, Z. A., Dane, A., Bosacki, S., & YLC-CURA. (2006). Direct and indirect bully-victims: Differential psychosocial risk factors associated with adolescents involved in bullying and victimization. *Aggressive Behavior, 32*, 551–569.

Marlowe, F. W. (2000). Paternal investment and the human mating system. *Behavioural Processes, 51*, 45–61.

Marlowe, F. W. (2010). *The Hadza hunter-gatherers of Tanzania.* Los Angeles: University of California Press.

Masure, R. H., & Allee, W. C. (1934). The social order in flocks of the common chicken and the pigeon. *The Auk, 51*, 306–327.

McMaster, L. E., Connolly, J., Pepler, D., & Craig, W. M. (2002). Peer to peer sexual harassment in early adolescence: A developmental perspective. *Development and Psychopathology, 14*, 91–105.

Mealey, L. (1995). The sociobiology of sociopathy: An integrated evolutionary model. *Behavioral and Brain Sciences, 18*, 523–599.

Meaney, M. (2001). Maternal care, gene expression, and the transmission of individual differences in stress reactivity across generations. *Annual Review of Neuroscience, 24*, 1161–1192.

Mech, D. L. (1970). *The wolf: The ecology and behavior of an endangered species.* New York: Natural History Press.

Miller, A., & Kanazawa, S. (2007) *Why beautiful people have more daughters.* New York: Perigee.

Milner, G. R., Wood, J. W., & Boldsen, J. L. (2000). Paleodemography. In M. A. Katzenberg & S. R. Saunders (Eds.), *Biological anthropology of the human skeleton* (pp. 467–497). New York: Wiley-Liss Press.

Moffitt, T. E. (1993). Adolescence-limited and life-course-persistent antisocial behavior: A developmental taxonomy. *Psychological Review, 100*, 674–701.

Nabuzoka, D. (2003). Experiences of bullying-related behaviours by English and Zambian pupils: A comparative study. *Educational Research, 45*, 95–109.

Nansel, T. R., Overpeck, M., Pilla, R. S., Ruan, W., Simons-Morton, B., & Scheidt, P. (2001). Bullying behaviors among US youth: Prevalence and association with psychosocial adjustment. *Journal of the American Medical Association, 285*, 2094.

Newcomb, A. F., Bukowski, W. M., & Pattee, L. (1993). Children's peer relations: A meta-analytic review of popular, rejected, neglected, controversial, and average sociometric status. *Psychological Bulletin, 113*, 99–128.

Nuwer, H. (1999). *Wrongs of passage.* Bloomington: Indiana University Press.

Olthof, T., & Goossens, F.A. (2008). Bullying and the need to belong: Early adolescents' bullying-related behavior and the acceptance they desire and receive from particular classmates. *Social Development, 17*, 24–46.

Olweus, D. (1993). *Bullying at school: What we know and what we can do.* New York: Wiley-Blackwell.

Orme, N. (1995). The culture of children in medieval England. *Oxford Journal: Past and Present, 148*, 107–112.

Orme, N. (2002). *Medieval children.* New Haven, CT: Yale University Press.

Owens, L., Shute, R., & Slee, P. (2000a). "Guess what I just heard": Indirect aggression among teenage girls in Australia. *Aggressive Behavior, 26*, 67–83.

Owens, L., Shute, R., & Slee, P. (2000b). "I'm in and you're out…" Explanations for teenage girls' indirect aggression. *Psychology, Evolution and Gender, 2*(1), 19–46.

Parker, G. (2006). Sexual conflict over mating and fertilization: An overview. *Philosophical Transactions of the Royal Society B: Biological Sciences, 361*, 235–259.

Parkhurst, J. T., & Hopmeyer, A. (1998). Sociometric popularity and peer-perceived popularity: Two distinct dimensions of peer status. *The Journal of Early Adolescence, 18*, 125–144.

Pellegrini, A. D. (1998). Bullies and victims in school: A review and a call for research. *Journal of Applied Developmental Psychology, 19*, 165–176.

Pellegrini, A. D. (2001). A longitudinal study of heterosexual relationships, aggression, and sexual harassment during the transition from primary school through middle school. *Journal of Applied Developmental Psychology, 22*, 119–133.

Pellegrini, A. D., Bartini, M., & Brooks, F. (1999). School bullies, victims, and aggressive victims: Factors relating to group affiliation and victimization in early adolescence. *Journal of Educational Psychology, 91*, 216–224.

Pellegrini, A. D., & Long, J. D. (2002). A longitudinal study of bullying, dominance, and victimization during the transition from primary school through secondary school. *British Journal of Developmental Psychology, 20*, 259–280.

Pellegrini, A. D., & Long, J. D. (2003). A sexual selection theory longitudinal analysis of sexual segregation and integration in early adolescence. *Journal of Experimental Child Psychology, 85*, 257–278.

Pepler, D., & Craig, W. (Eds.). (2008). *Understanding and addressing bullying: An international perspective.* Bloomington, IN: Author House.

Pepler, D., Jiang, D., Craig, W., & Connolly, J. (2008). Developmental trajectories of bullying and associated factors. *Child Development, 79*(2), 325–338.

Plomin, R., Defries, J. C., Craig, I. W., & McGuffin, P. (Eds.). (2002). *Behavioral genetics in the postgenomic era.* Washington, DC: American Psychological Association.

Randall, P. (1997). *Adult bullying.* New York: Routledge.

Rawson, B. (2003). *Children and childhood in Roman Italy.* Toronto: Oxford University Press.

Renold, E. (2002). Presumed innocence: (Hetero)Sexual, heterosexist, and homophobic harassment among primary school girls and boys. *Childhood, 9*, 415–434.

Rodkin, P. C., & Berger, C. (2008). Who bullies whom? Social status asymmetries by victim gender. *International Journal of Behavioral Development, 32*, 473–485.

Rose, A. J., Swenson, L. P., & Waller, E. M. (2004). Overt and relational aggression and perceived popularity: Developmental differences in concurrent and prospective relations. *Developmental Psychology, 40*, 378–387.

Salekin, R. T. (2006). Psychopathy in children and adolescents. In C. J. Patrick (Ed.), *Handbook of psychopathy* (pp. 389–414). New York: Guilford Press.

Salmivalli, C., & Nieminen, E. (2002). Proactive and reactive aggression among school bullies, victims, and bully-victims. *Aggressive Behavior, 28*, 30–44.

Scarr, S., & McCartney, K. (1983). How people make their own environments: A theory of genotype-environment effects. *Child Development, 54*, 424–435.

Scholte, R. H., van Lieshout, C. F., de Wit, C. A., & van Aken, M. A. (2005). Adolescent personality types and subtypes and their psychosocial adjustment. *Merrill-Palmer Quarterly, 51*, 258–286.

Schwartz, D., Proctor, L. J., & Chien, D. H. (2001). The aggressive victim of bullying: Emotional and behavioral dysregulation as a pathway to victimization by peers. In J. Juvonen & S. Graham (Eds.), *Peer harassment in schools: The plight of the vulnerable and victimized* (pp. 147–174). New York: The Guilford Press.

Scott, J. (1991). *Painted wolves.* Toronto: Penguin Books.

Sherif, M., & Sherif, C. W. (1970). Motivation and intergroup aggression: A persistent problem in levels of analysis. In L. A. Aronson, E. Tobash, D. S. Lehrman, & J. S. Rosenblatt (Eds.), *Development and evolution of behavior: Essays in memory of TS. Schneirla* (Vol. 1, pp. 563–579). San Francisco: W. H. Freeman.

Shields, N. M., & Hanneke, C. R. (1983). Battered wives' reactions to marital rape. In D. Finkelhor, R. J. Gelles, G. T. Hotaling & M. A. Straus (Eds.), *The dark side of families* (pp. 131–148). Beverly Hills, CA: Sage.

Shute, R., Owens, L., & Slee, P. (2008). Everyday victimization of adolescent girls by boys: Sexual harassment, bullying or aggression? *Sex Roles, 58,* 477–489.

Stearns, P. N. (2006) *Childhood in world history.* New York: Routledge.

Sutton, J., & Keogh, E. (2000). Social competition in school: Relationships with bullying, Machiavellianism and personality. *British Journal of Educational Psychology, 70,* 443–456.

Sutton, J., Smith, P. K., & Swettenham, J. (1999). Bullying and theory of mind: A critique of the social skills deficit view of anti-social behaviour. *Social Development, 8,* 117–127.

Symons, D. (1990). Adaptiveness and adaptation. *Ethology and Sociobiology, 11,* 427–444.

Tani, F., Greenman, P. S., Schneider, B. H., & Fregoso, M. (2003). Bullying and the Big Five: A study of childhood personality and participant roles in bullying incidents. *School Psychology International, 24,* 131–146.

Thomas, E. M. (1989). *The harmless people* (2nd ed.). Toronto: Random House.

Timmerman, G. (2003). Sexual harassment of adolescents perpetrated by teachers and peers: An exploration of the dynamics of power, culture, and gender in secondary schools. *Sex Roles, 48,* 231–244.

Trivers, R. L. (1971). Parental investment and sexual selection. In B. Campbell (Ed.), *Sexual selection and the descent of man* (pp. 136–179). London: Heinemann.

Trivers, R. L. (1972). Parental investment and sexual selection. In B. Campbell (Ed.), *Sexual selection and the descent of man, 1871–1971* (pp. 136–179). Chicago: Aldine.

Turnbull, C. M. (1961). *The forest people.* Toronto: Touchstone.

Turnbull, C. M. (1972). *The mountain people.* New York: Touchstone.

Underwood, G. (1954). Categories of adaptation. *Evolution, 8,* 356–377.

Vaillancourt, T. (2005). Indirect aggression among humans: Social construct or evolutionary adaptation? In R. E. Tremblay, W. H. Hartup, & J. Archer (Eds.), *Developmental origins of aggression* (pp. 158–177). New York: The Guilford Press.

Vaillancourt, T., Hymel, S., & McDougall, P. (2003). Bullying is power: Implications for school-based intervention strategies. *Journal of Applied School Psychology, 19,* 157–176.

Veenstra, R., Lindenberg, S., Munniksma, A., & Dijkstra, J. K. (2010). The complex relation between bullying, victimization, acceptance, and rejection: Giving special attention to status, affection, and sex differences. *Child Development, 81,* 480–486.

Viding, E., Simmonds, E., Petrides, K. V., & Frederickson, N. (2009). The contribution of callous-unemotional traits and conduct problems to bullying in early adolescence. *Journal of Child Psychology and Psychiatry, 50,* 471–481.

Volk, A. A., & Atkinson, J. (2008). Is child death the crucible of human evolution? *Journal of Social and Cultural Evolutionary Psychology, 2,* 103–116.

Volk, A., Craig, W., Boyce, W., & King, M. (2006). Adolescent risk correlates of bullying and different types of victimization. *International Journal of Adolescent Medicine and Health, 18,* 375–386.

Walker, W. D. (1997). *Patterns in sexual offending.* Unpublished Ph.D. dissertation, Queen's University, Kingston, ON, Canada.

Weaver, I. C., Cervoni, N., Champagne, F. A., D'Alessio, A. C., Sharma, S., Seckl, J. R., et al. (2004). Epigenetic programming by maternal behavior. *Nature Neuroscience, 7,* 847–854.

Wellman, H. M. (1992). *The child's theory of mind.* Cambridge, MA: MIT Press.

Williams, G. C. (1957). Pleiotropy, natural selection, and the evolution of senescence. *Evolution, 11,* 398–411.

Wilson, M., & Daly, M. (1985). Competitiveness, risk taking, and violence: The young male syndrome. *Ethology and Sociobiology, 6,* 59–73.

Wolke, D., Woods, S., Bloomfield, L., & Karstadt, L. (2001). Bullying involvement in primary school and common health problems. *Archives of Disease in Childhood, 85,* 197–201.

Wood, K., Maforah, F., & Jewkes, R. (1998). "He forced me to love him": Putting violence on adolescent sexual health agendas. *Social Science and Medicine, 47,* 233–242.

Zimmer-Gembeck, M. J., Geiger, T. C., & Crick, N. R. (2005). Relational and physical aggression, prosocial behavior, and peer relations: Gender moderation and bidirectional associations. *The Journal of Early Adolescence, 25,* 421–452.

PART 4

Evolutionary Perspectives on War

CHAPTER
17

The Male Warrior Hypothesis: The Evolutionary Psychology of Intergroup Conflict, Tribal Aggression, and Warfare

Mark Van Vugt

Abstract

Social science literature abounds with examples of human tribalism, which is the tendency to categorize individuals on the basis of their group membership and to treat ingroup members benevolently and outgroup members malevolently. I argue that this tribal inclination is an evolved response to the threat of coalitional aggression and intergroup violence that were endemic in ancestral human environments (and are still common today). Here I hypothesize that intergroup conflict has profoundly affected the psychology of men, in particular—the male warrior hypothesis—and present evidence consistent with this hypothesis. I also discuss implications of this hypothesis for managing intergroup relations in our society.

Key Words: warfare, intergroup relations, sex differences, social identity, coalitional aggression

Introduction

Alien biologists collecting data about different life forms on Planet Earth would no doubt come up with contradictory claims about human nature. They would witness the human capacity to help complete strangers in sometimes large groups, yet they would also observe many incidents of extreme violence, especially between groups of males. To make sense of the data, the alien researchers would probably conclude that humans are a fiercely tribal social species. Some time ago, Charles Darwin speculated about the origins of human tribal nature: "A tribe including many members who, from possessing in a high degree the spirit of patriotism, fidelity, obedience, courage, and sympathy, were always ready to aid one another, and to sacrifice themselves for the common good, would be victorious over most other tribes; and this would be natural selection" (1871, p. 132). Unfortunately, Darwin's brilliant insight was ignored for more than a century by fellow scientists, but it is now gaining attention. Here I offer an evolutionary perspective on the social psychology of intergroup conflict, offering new insights and evidence about the origins and manifestation of coalitional and intergroup aggression.[1]

Social scientists are increasingly adopting an evolutionary approach to develop novel hypotheses and integrate data on various aspects of human social behavior (Buss, 2005; Van Vugt & Schaller, 2008). An evolutionary approach is based on the premise that the human brain is a product of evolution through natural selection in the same way as our physiology has been selected for. Evolutionarily minded psychologists further propose that the human brain is essentially social, comprising many functionalized mechanisms—or adaptations—to cope with the various challenges of group living (Van Vugt & Schaller, 2008). One such specialized mechanism is coalition formation. Forming alliances with other individuals confers considerable advantages in procuring and protecting reproductively relevant resources—such as food, territories, mates, or offspring—especially in large and diverse social groups. Coalitional pressures may have led in evolution to the emergence of some rather ... human traits such as language, theory of ...nd, culture, and warfare. It has been argued that ultimately the need to form ever-larger coalitions spurred the increase in human social network size and led to a concomitant brain size increase in order to hold these networks together and deal effectively with an intensified competition for resources—this has been dubbed the Machiavellian Intelligence hypothesis, the Social Brain hypothesis, or the Social Glue hypothesis (Byrne & Whiten, 1988; Hart, 1993; Van Vugt & Hart, 2004). According to these hypotheses, our social brain is therefore essentially a tribal brain.

In searching for the origins of the human tribal brain, it is useful to make a distinction between *proximate* and *ultimate* causes. An act of intergroup aggression such as war, terrorism, gang-related violence, or hooliganism could be explained at two different levels at least. First, why did this particular group decide to attack the other? This proximate question interests mostly sociologists, political scientists, historians, and social psychologists studying social conflict. Second, one could ask why humans have evolved the capacity to engage in intergroup aggression; this ultimate question interests mostly evolutionary-minded psychologists and anthropologists. Addressing questions at different levels produces a more complete picture, but these levels should not be confused (Buss, 2005; Van Vugt & Van Lange, 2006).

In terms of ultimate causes of intergroup aggression, there are three classes of explanations generally invoked (Kurzban & Neuberg, 2005; McDonald, Navarrete, & Van Vugt, 2012; Van Vugt, 2009). The first treats it as a by-product of an adaptive ingroup psychology. Being a highly social and cooperative species, humans likely possess tendencies to favor helping members of ingroups (Brewer, 1979; Brewer & Caporael, 2006; Tajfel & Turner, 1979). As a by-product of this ingroup favoritism, people show either indifference or (perhaps worse) a dislike for members of outgroups. An alternative by-product hypothesis views intergroup aggression as an extension of interpersonal aggression. The argument is that humans have evolved specialized mechanisms to engage in aggression against conspecifics, and these mechanisms have been co-opted to cope with a relatively novel evolutionary threat, namely aggression between groups (Buss, 2005). The third class focuses explicitly on an adaptive intergroup psychology. The argument is that humans likely evolved specific psychological mechanisms to interact with members of outgroups because such situations posed significant reproductive challenges for ancestral humans. This latter hypothesis accounts for the highly textured social psychology of intergroup relations and is therefore more persuasive. For instance, people do not have some hazy negative feeling toward an outgroup; in some instances, outgroups motivate a desire to approach or avoid and, in other instances, to fight, dominate, exploit, or exterminate.

Recent work on prejudice and intergroup relations recognizes this textured nature of intergroup psychology and has generated many new insights and empirical findings consistent with this view (Cottrell & Neuberg, 2005; Kurzban & Leary, 2001; Schaller, Park, & Mueller, 2003; Sidanius & Pratto, 1999; Van Vugt, De Cremer, & Janssen, 2007; Van Vugt, 2009). Given the complexity of intergroup relations, there are probably many different adaptive responses pertaining to the nature and type of intergroup challenge. From an evolutionary perspective, not all intergroup situations are equal because not all outgroups are equal. For instance, not all outgroups consist of coalitions of individuals who engage in coordinated action—think of the homeless, the elderly, or people with blue eyes. Humans are likely to have evolved coalition-detection mechanisms that are responsive to various indicators of tribal alliances (Kurzban, Tooby, & Cosmides, 2001). As Kurzban and Leary (2001) note, "membership in a potentially cooperative group should activate a psychology of conflict and exploitation of outgroup members—a feature that distinguishes adaptations for coalitional psychology from other cognitive systems" (p. 195). In modern environments, heuristic cues such as skin color, speech patterns, and linguistic labels—regardless of whether they actually signal tribal alliances—may engage these mechanisms (Kurzban et al., 2001; SchallerPark & Mueller, 2003). Perhaps equally important, many other salient cues—gender, age, eye color—may be far less likely to engage this tribal psychology. We should note that although this tribal psychology likely evolved in an evolutionary context of competition for resources (such as territories, food, and mates), this does not imply that it is contemporarily activated only within contexts involving actual intergroup conflict as proposed, for instance, by realistic conflict theory (Campbell, 1965).

The specific psychological reactions of individuals in intergroup contexts should further depend on whether one's group is the aggressor. For the aggressors, desires to dominate and exploit—and the associated psychological tendencies—would be functional. For the defending party, desires to yield, avoid, or make peace—and the associated psychological tendencies—would be functional. Of course, in many situations, a group's position as being the dominant or subordinate party is transient or ambiguous, so it is likely that the two psychological tendencies are activated in similar situations by similar cues and moderated by similar variables (social dominance theory; Sidanius & Pratto, 1999).

The Male Warrior Hypothesis

An implication of this evolutionary tribal brain hypothesis is that intergroup conflict may have affected the psychologies of men and women differently. Intergroup conflict has historically involved rival coalitions of males fighting over scarce reproductive resources, and this is true for early humans as well as chimpanzees, one of our closest genetic relatives (Chagnon, 1988; De Waal, 2006; Goodall, 1986). Men are by far the most likely perpetrators and victims of intergroup aggression, now and in the past. As a consequence, this aspect of coalitional psychology is likely to be more pronounced among men, which we dubbed the *male warrior hypothesis* (MWH; McDonald et al., 2012; Van Vugt et al., 2007; Van Vugt, 2009). This hypothesis posits that due to a long history of male-to-male coalitional conflict men have evolved specialized cognitive mechanisms that enable them to form alliances with other men to plan, initiate, execute, and emerge victorious in intergroup conflicts with the aim of acquiring or protecting reproductively relevant resources.

Evolutionary Models

The MWH fits into a tradition of evolutionary hypotheses about sex differences in social behavior. There is already considerable evidence for sex differences in morphology, psychology, and behavior that are functionally related to different selection pressures operating on men and women throughout human, primate, and mammal evolution (Campbell, 1999; Eagly & Wood, 1999; Geary, 1998; Taylor, Klein, Lewis, & Gruenewald, 2000). Due to a combination of differences in parental investment and parental certainty, men and women pursue somewhat different mating strategies (Buss & Schmitt, 1993; Trivers, 1972). In humans—as in all mammals—mothers invest more heavily in their offspring and, as a consequence, it will be physiologically and genetically costlier for women to be openly aggressive (Archer, 2000; Campbell, 1999;

Taylor et al., 2000). Yet, as the less investing sex and under the right conditions, it can be attractive for men to form aggressive coalitions with the aim of acquiring and protecting valuable reproductive resources.

Tooby and Cosmides's (1988) risk contract hypothesis specifies four conditions for the evolution of a psychology of coalitional aggression, which underscores the evolutionary logic of the hypothesized sex differences in warrior psychology. First, the average long-term gains in reproductive success (i.e., mating opportunities) must be sufficiently large to outweigh the average costs (i.e., injury or death). Second, members of warfare coalitions must believe that their group is likely to emerge victorious in battle. Third, the risk that each member takes and the importance of each member's contribution to victory must translate into a corresponding share of benefits (cf. the free-rider problem). Fourth, when individuals go into battle, they must be cloaked in a "veil of ignorance" about who will live or die. Thus, if an intergroup victory produces, on average, a 20% increase in reproductive success, then as long as the risk of death for any individual coalition member is less than 20% (say 1 in 10 die) such warrior traits could be selected for. This model assumes that the spoils of an intergroup victory are paid out in mating opportunities for the individual males involved, and thus it is essentially an individual selection model based on sexual selection.

Alternatively, a specific male warrior psychology could have evolved via group-level selection. Multilevel selection theory holds that if there is substantial variance in the reproductive success among groups, then group selection becomes a genuine possibility (Wilson, Van Vugt, & O'Gorman, 2008). As Darwin noted (see earlier quote), groups of selfless individuals do better than groups of selfish individuals. Although participating in intergroup conflict is personally costly—because of the risk of death or injury—genes underlying propensity to serve the group can be propagated if group-serving acts contribute to group survival. In a recent empirical test of this model, Choi and Bowles (2007) showed via computer simulations that altruistic traits can spread in populations as long as there is competition between groups and altruistic acts benefit ingroup members and harm outgroup members (parochial altruism). It is not clear yet whether intergroup pressures were sufficiently strong in our ancestral environment to kick-start genetic group selection, so this remains an empirical question requiring further examination.

One condition conducive to group-level selection occurs when the genetic interests of group members are aligned, such as in kin groups. In kin-bonded groups, individuals benefit not just from their own reproductive success but also from the success of their family members (inclusive fitness; Hamilton, 1964). Ancestral human groups are likely to have been based around male kin members, with females moving between groups to avoid inbreeding (so-called patrilocal groups). This offers a complementary reason for the evolution of male coalitional aggression because the men are more heavily invested in their group and, hence, they have more to lose when the group ceases to exist. In addition, the collective action problem underlying coalitional aggression is less pronounced when group members' genetic interests are aligned. Incidentally (but perhaps not coincidentally), the same patrilocal structure is found in chimpanzees, and male chimpanzees also engage in coalitional aggression (Goodall, 1986; Wrangham & Peterson, 1996).

These evolutionary models do not preclude the possibility that cultural processes may be at work that could exacerbate or undermine male warrior instincts (Richerson & Boyd, 2005). In fact, many of the evolved propensities for coalitional aggression are likely to be translated into actual psychological and behavioral tendencies by socialization practices and cultural norms. Thus, it is possible that in certain environments it could be advantageous for societies to suppress male warrior tendencies—so-called peaceful societies—or turn females into dedicated warriors. A modern-day example of the latter is the state of Israel, which is involved in a continuous war with its Arab neighbors. To increase its military strength, Israel has a conscription army of both men and women, and it currently has the most liberal rules regarding the participation of women in actual warfare, although women are not involved in front-line combat (Goldstein, 2003). We would expect the socialization practices among Israeli girls to match those of boys, potentially attenuating any innate psychological differences.

Evidence for the Male Warrior Hypothesis From the Behavioral Sciences

Evidence for various aspects of this male warrior phenomenon can be found throughout the behavioral science literature, for instance, in anthropology, history, sociology, political science, biology, psychology, and primatology. As stated, across all cultures, almost any act of intergroup aggression is perpetrated by coalitions of males, for instance, in situations of warfare, genocide, rebellion, terrorism, street gangs, and hooligan violence (Goldstein, 2003; Livingstone Smith, 2007). Evidence of male-to-male coalitional aggression goes back as far as 200,000 years ago (e.g., mass graves containing mostly male skeletons with evidence of blunt force trauma; Keeley, 1996). Men are also the most likely victims of intergroup aggression. On average, male death rates due to warfare among hunter-gatherers are 13% (according to archaeological data) and 15% (according to ethnographic data; Bowles 2006), suggesting a relatively strong selection pressure on male warrior traits. The figure is sometimes even higher. Among the Yanomamö in the Amazon Basin an estimated 20%–30% of adult males die through tribal violence (Chagnon, 1988). (This compares to less than 1% of the US and European adult male populations in the 20th century.) Finally, the primate literature reveals that among chimpanzees adult males form coalitions to engage in violence against members of neighboring troops. This suggests that there is phylogenetic consistency between humans and our closest related genetic relatives (Wilson & Wrangham, 2003).

Male warriors in traditional societies have higher status, more sexual partners, and more children (Chagnon, 1988), suggesting a direct reproductive benefit; Dawkins labeled this the "Duke of Marlborough" effect (1976). The sexual attractiveness of the male warrior might still be operative in modern society. A US study revealed that male youth street gang members have more sexual partners than ordinary young males (Palmer & Tilley, 1995). We recently found that military men have greater sex appeal, especially if they have shown bravery in combat (Leunissen & Van Vugt, unpublished data). Thus, there may be reputational benefits associated with "warrior" behaviors in men (cf. competitive altruism; Hardy & Van Vugt, 2006).

In light of the support for the MWH, it is noteworthy that many published intergroup studies in social psychology do not report the results for men and women separately and some only use male samples. One of the classic social psychological studies, the Stanford prison experiment (Zimbardo, 1971), which highlighted some disturbing aspects of human coalitional aggression, used an all-male sample. Team game experiments also often use all-male groups (e.g., Bornstein, 2003). In a personal communication, one of the authors of this study (Bornstein, personal communication) suggested that pilot research showed that female groups were less competitive.

Psychological Mechanisms Underlying Male Warrior Phenomena

The MWH offers an integrative, conceptual framework in which findings from diverse literatures can be woven into a coherent story. If men have a more pronounced warrior psychology, we should expect them to think and feel differently about intergroup conflict and be more likely to plan, support, and commit acts of intergroup aggression (McDonald et al., 2012; Van Vugt, 2009). In addition, men in groups should make adaptive intergroup choices depending upon information about the sex, size, and formidability of the outgroup. For instance, they should respond with anger and aggression toward a weaker outgroup and with fear and avoidance to a stronger outgroup (especially an all-male group). Finally, these reactions are likely to be produced automatically and spontaneously.

To assess several aspects of the MWH (including predicted sex differences in relevant evolved psychological mechanisms), I will present some research findings pertaining to several domains, such as (1) frequency and likelihood of aggression toward outgroups; (2) protection of ingroup against external threats; (3) likelihood of political support for intergroup aggression; and (4) tribal social identifications. These studies provide preliminary support for the MWH, yet much work still remains to be done (see Table 17.1).

Propensity for Intergroup Aggression

A first prediction from the MWH is that men should, on average, have a lower threshold to engage in acts of intergroup aggression when given the opportunity. We tested this in various ways. First, we examined how men and women make decisions in war games simulated in the laboratory. Upon being told that they are the leader of a fictitious country interacting with leaders of other countries, a study by Johnson et al. (2006) found that men are significantly more likely to attack another country without provocation (a so-called preemptive strike).

Table 17.1 The Male Warrior Hypothesis: Domains of Evidence, Hypothesized Mechanisms, Predictions, and Support for Gender Differences

Domain of Evidence	Hypothesized Mechanism	Prediction About Gender Difference	Supported
1. Intergroup aggression	Propensity to engage in intergroup aggression	Men are more likely to make unprovoked outgroup attacks	Yes
		Men report having more (competitive) intergroup experiences	Yes
2. Intergroup prejudice	Infra/dehumanization of members of antagonistic outgroups	Men are more likely to infrahumanize members of outgroups	Yes
3. Intragroup dynamics	Ingroup cooperation in response to outgroup threat	Men contribute more to group during intergroup competition	Yes
	Ingroup loyalty during intergroup conflict	Men show more ingroup loyalty during intergroup conflict	
	Male leadership bias in intergroup conflict	Groups show stronger preference for male leaders during intergroup competition	
4. Tribal politics	Political support for intergroup aggression	Men show stronger political support for warfare in opinion polls	Yes
	Preferences for social dominance hierarchies	Men score higher on social dominance orientation scale	Yes
5. Tribal social identity	Affiliation to tribal groups	Men are more likely to make spontaneous tribal associations when defining themselves	Yes

Moreover, warfare is most intense when men are playing against other men despite not knowing the sex of their rivals. The lower threshold for intergroup aggression may be due to expectations of success. Indeed, men held more positive illusions about winning these simulated intergroup conflicts, a belief that increased the probability that they would attack their opponent (Johnson et al., 2006). Another study analyzing the same data set found that more male-typical 2D:4D digit ratios, which index prenatal testosterone exposure, predicted aggression in the war-game experiments over and above sex. These sex differences also emerge when individuals play economic games between groups: All-male groups tend to be more competitive than all-female groups or mixed-sex groups (Wildschut, Pinter, Vevea, Insko, & Schopler, 2003).

Second, there is evidence that men and women differ in their involvement in acts of intergroup aggression outside the laboratory (Pemberton, Insko, & Schopler, 1996). When asked to indicate the frequency with which they performed various categories of social interactions over the past month, men reported more group-to-group interactions ($M = 18.47$, $SD = 73.48$) than women ($M = 12.77$, $SD = 59.68$). Furthermore, men rated these interactions as more competitive (Ms male vs. female = 3.17 vs. 2.31, SDs = 2.50 and 2.22; scale is 1 = *very cooperative*, 5 = *very competitive*). Thus, consistent with the MWH, men experience intergroup competition more often, they have a lower threshold to start an intergroup conflict, and they are more optimistic about winning such conflicts.

Intergroup Prejudice and Stereotyping

The MWH further predicts that men are more likely to be prejudiced and openly discriminate against members of outgroups, especially outgroups that can be viewed as coalitional threats. One manifestation of outgroup prejudice is infrahumanization, the tendency to consider members of outgroups subhuman or animal-like, which is often a precursor of intergroup violence (Haslam, 2006; Leyens et al., 2001). The evolutionary logic is that by considering outgroups as inferior it will be psychologically easier to treat them badly. In a recent study (Van Vugt, 2009), men and women—all Christians—were asked to describe a Christian or Muslim target using either human-typical (e.g., civil) or animal-typical (e.g., feral) words. Christian men were more likely to describe the Muslim target in animal-typical ways, thus showing evidence of infrahumanization. The MWH also predicts that infrahumanization strategies are most likely in male-to-male intergroup contests, but this remains to be tested.

Men also show other intergroup biases such as racism and xenophobia more readily and especially in threatening situations Several experiments yield a greater sensitivity of outgroup stereotypes for ingroup men, especially under conditions of intergroup conflict (Gerard & Hoyt, 1974; Sidanius, Cling, & Pratto, 1991). Schaller, Park, and Mueller (2003) have shown that men use danger-relevant stereotypes toward outgroup members more when influenced by cues of ambient darkness. Finally, the notorious outgroup homogeneity effect disappears when ingroup members are shown angry faces of outgroup males but not females (Ackerman et al., 2006), which is consistent with the idea that outgroup males pose a heightened threat. These findings support the MWH in that men are more likely to be prejudiced against members of outgroups especially when these constitute a coalitional threat and, in addition, outgroup men are more likely to be discriminated against.

Protecting the Group Against External Threats

The MWH also expects the presence of psychological mechanisms that enable men to protect their ingroup against external threats. To defend the group requires that people bond together and help the ingroup (Brewer & Brown, 1998; Van Vugt et al., 2007). Based on the MWH, we predicted that during intergroup conflict particularly men will increase their efforts to help the ingroup. Consistent with this prediction, in public-good games we found that men raised their group contributions, but only when we activated competition between groups (Van Vugt et al., 2007). In Experiment 1, Van Vugt et al. found that during intergroup competition 92% of men contributed to the public good, but only 53% of women did. In addition, men showed greater ingroup loyalty by sticking with the group even if it was more (financially) attractive to leave (Van Vugt et al., 2007). As a proxy for ingroup cohesion, men were also more likely to increase their identification with the group under conditions of intergroup conflict. It remains to be seen whether men are also more likely to be altruistic punishers of free-riding group members during intergroup conflict, as the MWH would predict.

Males are also more likely to be chosen as group leaders during intergroup conflict. Van Vugt and Spisak (2008) found that when two equally suitable candidates of different sexes, Sarah and John, vied for the position of leader in an intergroup conflict, groups preferred the male leader (78%). The male leader was also more effective in eliciting followers' group contributions during intergroup threat. (When the problem shifted toward conflict within the ingroup, virtually all groups preferred the female leader.)

Preference for Hierarchies

There is some evidence that male groups have different dynamics that make them more suitable to engage in coalitional aggression. Whereas female groups are more egalitarian, groups of males form more hierarchical groups and these hierarchies tend to be more stable over time. The difference in group structure corresponds with sex differences in leadership style (Eagly & Johnson, 1990; Van Vugt, 2006). Military specialists assume that hierarchy formation is an effective response in dealing with intergroup conflict that requires an urgent, coordinated response.

Research on developmental differences in social play reflects male warrior tendencies. Boys play in larger groups than girls and more often play complex competitive team games, which sometimes involve the use of weapons such as toy guns and swords (Geary, 1998). Boys also put greater social pressure on team members to conform to group norms during play activities (Sherif, Harvey, White, Hood, & Sherif, 1961), and they have more transient friendships with a larger number of peers than girls (Geary, 1998). Thus, consistent with the MWH, males have psychological mechanisms that enable them to work in and function better in larger and more hierarchically structured groups, and the primary function of such group structures is to compete with other groups.

Support for Tribal Politics

The MWH further predicts sex differences in political attitudes toward intergroup conflict. We predicted that men would show relatively stronger political support for warfare as a solution to international conflict because they have more to gain potentially (at least in ancestral times) from intergroup conflict. We tested this prediction using data from a random selection of 10 recent national and international opinion polls that we were able to find on the Internet and found consistent sex differences (sometimes large, other times small, but always in the same direction). For instance, a *Washington Post* poll in 2003 (n = 1,030) asked the question, "Do you support the US having gone to war in Iraq?" to which 82% of men agreed versus 72% of women. As another example, a recent poll by Gallup (n = 7,074) found that 46% of men (vs. 37% women) answered "no" to the question: "Do you think the Iraq War was a mistake?"

The MWH also predicts men to have a stronger preference for between-group dominance hierarchies. An intergroup dominance hierarchy is the inevitable outcome when groups compete with each other. To test this prediction, we asked an international survey of people to complete the short 10-item Social Dominance Orientation scale (Pratto, Sidanius, Stallworth, & Malle, 1994). This scale contains items such as "Some groups of people are simply inferior than others," "We should do what we can to equalize conditions for different groups," and "To get ahead in life, it is sometimes necessary to step on other groups." Consistent with other results (Pratto et al., 1994), we found that men were significantly more socially dominant (M = 2.56, SD = 1.13) than women (M = 2.28, SD = 1.0). Thus, in agreement with the MWH, men are generally more belligerent in their tribal politics.

Tribal Social Identity

A final prediction from the MWH is that men's personal self-concept should be affected more strongly by their affiliations to tribal groups. In contrast, women's self-concept should be influenced primarily by having meaningful connections with close others. Men have indeed a more collective sense of self that is more strongly derived from their group memberships and affiliations (Baumeister & Sommer, 1997). Gabriel and Gardner (1999) asked students to describe themselves by completing the statement "I am…" They found that male students were twice as likely to make statements referring to a tribal association (e.g., "I am a member of a fraternity").

In a recent study (McDonald et al., 2012; Van Vugt, 2009), we asked 100 people around the University of Kent campus to indicate their favorite color and to explain why they picked this particular color. Among men, almost 30% mentioned a tribal association (e.g., their favorite football team, the colors of the flag of their country of origin); none of the women did so. Thus, men's social identity seems to be more strongly based on their tribal affiliations than women's, which is consistent with the MWH.

Implications for Intergroup Relations

In this chapter, I have presented a framework for studying the psychology of intergroup aggression from an evolutionary perspective. This analysis suggests that not all intergroup relations are alike because not all outgroups are alike. How groups interact with each other is determined by the specific contextual threats and opportunities. When such challenges correspond to evolutionarily relevant threats—threats that were significant enough in ancestral social environments that humans have evolved to deal with them—they activate a specific tribal psychology. I have argued that a history of coalitional aggression has produced a distinct human tribal brain, including an interrelated set of functional cognitive and behavioral reactions to attack and defend against members of outgroups. Furthermore, as the most likely perpetrators and victims, I hypothesized that male psychology has been particularly affected by intergroup conflict episodes, and I dubbed this the male warrior hypothesis, or MWH. I reviewed the literature on sex differences in intergroup psychology in light of predictions from the MWH and found the results of this literature to be generally supportive of the MWH.

In addition to intergroup conflict, there might be other significant ancestral challenges involving groups, which I do not address further in this chapter. Disease is one such threat and we would expect a different set of functional responses to a contagion threat rather than physical threat from an outgroup, for instance, behavioral avoidance rather than aggression. When a disease threat is salient, perhaps women respond more strongly. There is some evidence that women are more prejudiced toward strangers when in their most fertile menstrual phase (McDonald et al., 2012; Navarrete, Fessler, & Eng, 2007). In general, we know little about the intergroup psychology of females. In addition, the neuroscience underpinning sex differences in intergroup psychology ought to be examined—for instance, which hormonal differences might drive these sex differences in tribal psychology?

An evolutionary framework can be used to generate suggestions for interventions to improve intergroup relations. When outgroups pose a coalitional threat, interventions might be targeted specifically at male-to-male interactions because males are the most likely perpetrators and victims of intergroup aggression. In terms of their objectives, interventions may be particularly successful when they eliminate the sense of threat associated with a particular outgroup. Attempts must be made to individuate members of such outgroups, for instance, by accentuating their personal achievements rather than the achievements of their group. A second aim of interventions might be to alter the perceptual cues that elicit threat responses toward particular outgroups such as new immigrant groups. For instance, language, dress code, and particular rituals or customs serve as tribal markers, and the less noticeable they are the more these outgroups will receive positive treatment. Thus, for the sake of attenuating the effects of coalitional psychology, it may be important for societies to make it easier for new immigrant groups to adopt the language and customs of the ingroup. Third, interventions might be focused on changing the specific cognitive and affective responses toward outgroups. However, if it is true that these responses are evolved, then the link between threat and response might be difficult to inhibit or extinguish (cf. fear of snakes and spiders; Ohman & Mineka, 2001). Nevertheless, we suspect that frequent positive interactions with members of outgroups may over time reduce initial aversion or hostility. For instance, the Jigsaw class room experiments (Aronson & Bridgeman, 1979) demonstrate that cooperative relations between members of different ethnic groups can be a successful means of reducing prejudice.

Future Directions

There are various interesting lines of research inspired by the MWH that are worth pursuing. A first question concerns the neurobiological mechanisms underlying the MWH. One possibility, suggested by recent research (De Dreu et al., 2010), is that the neuropeptide oxytocin plays a role in male bonding during warfare.

Functional magnetic resonance imaging techniques (fMRI) could help in detecting possible sex differences in brain activity when individuals are involved in intergroup conflict. Behavioral geneticists are investigating the genetic underpinnings of male aggression, and it may well be that there are specific markers for male warrior tendencies (MAO-A has been suggested as a candidate).

A third line of research is to examine cross-species variability in warrior tendencies. For example, coalitional aggression is found in a number of species such as chimpanzees, lions, and hyenas, but it may not always be conducted by males (among lemurs it is the females). Such comparisons could reveal the phylogenetic origins of the MWH as well as the selection pressures favoring coalitional aggression in either the males or females of a particular species.

More research is needed into women's intergroup psychology. A history of warfare has perhaps also selected for specific female intergroup adaptations.

It may be that women respond to intergroup threats not by fighting (or fleeing) but by tending (of children) and befriending (of victorious outgroup males; Taylor et al., 2000).

Finally, it may be profitable to consider that there may be different psychological adaptations for different kinds of intergroup relations. For instance, humans may have evolved a specific peace psychology as well as warfare psychology. In addition, some outgroups pose a coalitional threat, yet others may pose a disease threat, and this requires a different functional response (i.e., avoidance rather than approach). Many different predictions can be derived from the MWH and many still require careful examination.

Note

1. I will use the terms "coalitional aggression" and "intergroup aggression" interchangeably throughout this chapter. Although there is a difference in the scale of these activities both types of aggression involve individuals who as members of groups commit acts of aggression against members of other groups (Brewer & Brown, 1998).

References

Ackerman, J. M., Shapiro, J. R., Neuberg, S. L., Kenrick, D. T., Becker, D. V., & Griskevicius, V. (2006). They all look the same to me (unless they're angry). *Psychological Science, 17*, 836–840.

Archer, J. (2000). Sex differences in aggression between heterosexual partners: A meta-analytic review. *Psychological Bulletin, 126*, 651–680.

Aronson, E., & Bridgeman, D. (1979). Jigsaw groups and the desegregated classroom: In pursuit of common goals. *Personality and Social Psychology Bulletin, 5*, 438–446.

Baumeister, R. F., & Sommer, K. L. (1997). What do men want? Gender differences and two spheres of belongingness: Comment on Cross and Madson (1997). *Psychological Bulletin, 122*, 38–44.

Bornstein, G. (2003). Individual, group, and collective interests. *Personality and Social Psychology Review, 7*, 129–145.

Bowles, S. (2006). Group competition, reproductive levelling, and the evolution of human altruism. *Science, 314*, 1569–1572.

Brewer, M. B. (1979). In-group bias in the minimal intergroup situation: A cognitive–motivational analysis. *Psychological Bulletin, 86*, 307–324.

Brewer, M. B., & Brown, R. J. (1998). Intergroup relations. In D. T. Gilbert, S. T. Fiske, & G. Lindzey (Eds.), *The handbook of social psychology* (4th ed., pp. 554–594). New York: McGraw-Hill.

Brewer, M. B., & Caporael, L. (2006). An evolutionary perspective on social identity: Revisiting groups. In M. Schaller, J. A. Simpson, & D. T. Kenrick (Eds.), *Evolution and social psychology* (pp. 143–161). New York: Psychology Press.

Buss, D. M. (2005). *Handbook of evolutionary psychology*. Hoboken, NJ: Wiley.

Buss, D. M., & Schmitt, D. P. (1993). Sexual strategies theory: An evolutionary perspective on human mating. *Psychological Review, 100*, 204–232.

Byrne, D. & Whiten, A. (1988). *Machiavellian intelligence: Social expertise and the evolution of intellect in monkeys, apes, and humans*. New York: Oxford University Press.

Campbell A. (1999). Staying alive: Evolution, culture and intra-female aggression. *Behavioural and Brain Sciences, 22*, 203–252.

Campbell, A. (1999). Staying alive: Evolution, culture, and women's intrasexual aggression. *Behavioral and Brain Sciences, 22*, 203–252.

Campbell, D.T. (1965). Ethnocentric and other altruistic motives. In D. Levine (Ed.), *Nebraska symposium on motivation* (pp. 283–311). Lincoln: University of Nebraska Press.

Choi, J-K. & Bowles, S. (2007). The coevolution of parochial altruism and war. *Science, 318*(5850), 636–640.

Chagnon, N. A. (1988). Life histories, blood revenge, and warfare in a tribal population. *Science, 239*, 985–992.

Cottrell, C. A., & Neuberg, S. L. (2005). Different emotional reactions to different groups: A sociofunctional threat-based approach to "prejudice." *Journal of Personality and Social Psychology, 88*, 770–789.

Darwin, C. (1871). *The descent of man, and selection in relation to sex*. London: Murray.

Dawkins, R. (1976). *The selfish gene*. Oxford, England: Oxford University Press.

De Dreu, C. K. W., Greer, L. L., Handgraaf, M. J. J., Shalvi, S., Van Kleef, G. A., et al. (2010). The neuropeptide oxytocin regulates parochial altruism in intergroup conflict among humans. *Science, 328*, 1408–1411.

De Waal, F. (2006). *Our inner ape*. London: Granta Books.

Dunbar, R. (1993). Co-evolution of neocortical size, group size and language in humans. *Behavioral and Brain Sciences, 16*, 681–735.

Eagly, A. H., & Johnson, B. T. (1990). Gender and leadership style: A meta-analysis. *Psychological Bulletin, 108*, 233–256.

Eagly, A. H., & Wood, W. (1999). The origins of sex differences in human behavior: Evolved dispositions versus social roles. *American Psychologist, 54*, 408–423.

Gabriel, S., & Gardner, W. L. (1999). Are there his and hers types of interdependence? The implications of gender differences in collective versus relational interdependence for affect, behavior and cognition. *Journal of Personality and Social Psychology, 77*, 642–655.

Geary, D. C. (1998). *Male, female: The evolution of human sex differences*. Washington, DC: American Psychological Association.

Gerard, H. B., & Hoyt, M. F. (1974). Distinctiveness of social categorization and attitude toward ingroup members. *Journal of Personality and Social Psychology, 29*, 836–842.

Goldstein, J. (2003). *War and gender*. Cambridge, England: Cambridge University Press.

Goodall, J. (1986). *The chimpanzees of Gombe: Patterns of behavior*. Cambridge, MA: Harvard University Press.

Hamilton, W. D. (1964). The genetical evolution of social behaviour. *Journal of Theoretical Biology, 7*, 1–52.

Hardy, C. L., & Van Vugt, M. (2006). Nice guys finish first: The competitive altruism hypothesis. *Personality and Social Psychology Bulletin, 32*, 1402–1413.

Haslam, N. (2006). Dehumanization: An integrative review. *Personality and Social Psychology Review, 10*, 252–264.

Johnson, D. D. P., McDermott, R., Barrett, E. S., Crowden, J., Wrangham, R., McIntyre, M. H., & Rosen, S. P. (2006). Overconfidence in war games: Experimental evidence on expectations, aggression, gender and testosterone. *Proceedings of the Royal Society B, 273*, 2513–2520.

Keeley, L. (1996). *War before civilization.* New York: Oxford University Press.

Kurzban, R., & Leary, M. R. (2001). Evolutionary origins of stigmatization: The functions of social exclusion. *Psychological Bulletin, 127,* 187–208.

Kurzban, R., & Neuberg, S. (2005). Managing ingroup and outgroup relationships. In D. M. Buss (Ed.), *The handbook of evolutionary psychology* (pp. 653–675). Hoboken, NJ: Wiley.

Kurzban, R., Tooby, J., & Cosmides, L. (2001). Can race be erased? Coalitional computation and social categorization. *Proceedings of the National Academy of Sciences USA, 98,* 15387–15392.

Leyens, J. P., Rodriquez-Perez, A., Rodriguez-Torres, R., Gaunt, R., Paladino, M., Vaes, J., & Demoulin, S. (2001). Psychological essentialism and the differential attribution of uniquely human emotions to ingroups and outgroups. *European Journal of Social Psychology, 31,* 395–411.

Livingstone Smith, D. (2007). *The most dangerous animal in the world: Human nature and the origins of war.* New York: St. Martin's Press.

McDonald, M. M., Navarrete, C. D., & Van Vugt, M. (2012). Evolution and the psychology of intergroup conflict: The male warrior hypothesis. *Philosophical Transactions of the Royal Society-Biological Sciences.* doi: 10.1098/rstb.2011.0301

Navarrete, C., Fessler, D., & Eng, S. (2007). Elevated ethnocentrism in the first trimester of pregnancy. *Evolution and Human Behavior, 28,* 60–65.

Öhman, A., & Mineka, S. (2001). Fear, phobia, and preparedness: Toward an evolved module of fear and fear learning. *Psychological Review, 108,* 483–522.

Palmer, C. T., & Tilley, C. F. (1995). Sexual access to females as a motivation for joining gangs: An evolutionary approach. *Journal of Sex Research. 32,* 213–217.

Pemberton, M. B., Insko, C. A., & Schopler, J. (1996). Memory for and experience of differential competitive behavior of individuals and groups. *Journal of Personality and Social Psychology, 71,* 953–966.

Pratto, F., Sidanius, J., Stallworth, L. M., & Malle, B. F. (1994). Social dominance orientation: A personality variable predicting social and political attitudes. *Journal of Personality and Social Psychology, 67,* 741–763.

Richerson, P., & Boyd, R. (2005). *Not by genes alone: How culture transformed human evolution.* Chicago: University of Chicago Press.

Schaller, M. (2003). Ancestral environments and motivated social perception: Goal-like blasts from the evolutionary past. In S. J. Spencer, S. Fein, M. P. Zanna, & J. M. Olson (Eds.), *Motivated social perception: The Ontario Symposium* (pp. 215–231). Mahwah, NJ: Erlbaum.

Schaller, M., Park, J. H., & Faulkner, J. (2003). Prehistoric dangers and contemporary prejudices. *European Review of Social Psychology, 14,* 105–137.

Schaller, M., Park, J. H., & Mueller, A. (2003). Fear of the dark: Interactive effects of beliefs about danger and ambient darkness on ethnic stereotypes. *Personality and Social Psychology Bulletin, 29,* 637–649.

Sherif, M., Harvey, O. J., White, B. J., Hood, W. R., & Sherif, C. W. (1961). *Intergroup conflict and cooperation: The Robbers Cave experiment.* Norman, OK: University Book Exchange.

Sidanius, J., Cling, B. J., & Pratto, F. (1991). Ranking and linking as a function of sex and gender role attitudes. *Journal of Social Issues, 47,* 131–149.

Sidanius, J., & Pratto, F. (1999). *Social dominance: An intergroup theory of social hierarchy and oppression.* New York: Cambridge University Press.

Tajfel, H., & Turner, J. C. (1979). An integrative theory of intergroup conflict. In W. G. Austin & S. Worchel (Eds.), *The social psychology of intergroup relations* (pp. 33–47). Monterey, CA: Brooks/Cole.

Taylor, S. E., Klein, L. C., Lewis, B. P., & Gruenewald, R. A. R. (2000). Biobehavioral responses to stress in females: Tend-and-befriend not fight-or-flight. *Psychological Review, 107,* 413–429.

Tooby, J., & Cosmides, L. (1988). *The evolution of war and its cognitive foundations.* Institute for Evolutionary Studies Tech. Rep. No. 88-1. Palo Alto, CA: Institute for Evolutionary Studies.

Trivers, R. L. (1972). Parental investment and sexual selection. In B. Campbell (Ed.), *Sexual selection and the descent of man* (pp. 136–179). Chicago: Aldine

Van Vugt, M. (2006). The evolutionary origins of leadership and followership. *Personality and Social Psychology Review, 10,* 354–372.

Van Vugt, M. (2009). Sex differences in intergroup competition, agression, and warfare. *Annals of the New York Academy of Sciences, 1167,* 124–134.

Van Vugt, M., De Cremer, D., & Janssen, D. P. (2007). Gender differences in cooperation and competition: The male-warrior hypothesis. *Psychological Science, 18,* 19–23.

Van Vugt, M., & Hart, C. M. (2004). Social identity as social glue: The origins of group loyalty. *Journal of Personality and Social Psychology, 86,* 585–598.

Van Vugt, M., & Schaller, M. (2008). Evolutionary perspectives on group dynamics: An introduction. *Group Dynamics, 12,* 1–6.

Van Vugt, M., & Spisak, B. (2008). Sex differences in leadership emergence during competitions within and between groups. *Psychological Science, 19,* 854–858.

Van Vugt, M., & Van Lange, P. A. M. (2006). Psychological adaptations for prosocial behavior: The altruism puzzle. In M. Schaller, J. A. Simpson, & D. T. Kenrick (Eds.), *Evolution and social psychology* (pp. 237–261). New York: Psychology Press.

Wildschut, T., Pinter, B., Vevea, J. L., Insko, C. A., & Schopler, J. (2003). Beyond the group mind: A quantitative review of the interindividual–intergroup discontinuity effect. *Psychological Bulletin, 129,* 698–722.

Wilson, D. S., Van Vugt, M., & O'Gorman, R. (2008). Multilevel selection theory and its implications for psychological science. *Current Directions in Psychological Science, 17,* 6–9.

Wilson, M. & Wrangham, R. (2003). Intergroup relations in chimpanzees. *Annual Review of Anthropology, 32,* 363–392.

Wrangham, R. W., & Peterson, D. (1996). *Demonic males: Apes and the origins of human violence.* Boston: Houghton Mifflin Co.

Zimbardo, P. (1971). The power and pathology of imprisonment. *Congressional Records, 15,* 10–25.

CHAPTER 18

A Feminist Evolutionary Analysis of the Relationship Between Violence Against and Inequitable Treatment Women, and Conflict Within and Between Human Collectives, Including Nation-States

Valerie M. Hudson *and* Andrea M. den Boer

Abstract

In this chapter we examine the theoretical linkage between the security of women and the security of states, drawing insights from evolutionary biology and psychology, political sociology, and psychology. A feminist evolutionary approach demonstrates the way in which male reproductive interests can and often do lead to strategies of sexual coercion of females, including violence. That violence can be directed at other males and other groups as male dominance hierarchies develop a parasitical approach to resource accumulation, involving coalitional aggression against outgroups in order to strip such groups of their resources. The mitigation of male dominance hierarchies is thus, we argue, key to the mitigation of dysfunctional, conflictual intergroup relations. We illustrate the effects of male dominance and structural patriarchy through an examination of polygyny and through historical cases before finally discussing strategies for mitigating male dominance hierarchies.

Key Words: gender, women, evolution, violence, war, family law, patriarchy

Introduction

In the fields of International Relations and Security Studies, the study of conflict, war, and aggression within and between states takes center stage. Many theories and conceptual frameworks have been adumbrated to address these topics, most centering around explanatory variables having to do with power relationships between states, ethno-nationalistic forces, and regime type, among others (Brainard & Chollet, 2007; Doyle, 1983; Homer-Dixon, 2001; Huntington, 1996; Ray, 1995). Recently, some researchers have suggested that the situation of women within a society might provide important clues concerning state predisposition toward conflict (Caprioli, 2000; Caprioli & Boyer, 2001; Hudson, Caprioli, Ballif-Spanvill, McDermott, Emmett, 2008/2009; Marshall & Ramsey, 1999; Melander, 2005). These scholars argue that sexual differentiation represents the "first difference" between human beings, and that "[i]t is always the difference of the sexes that serves as a model for all other differences, and the male/female hierarchy that is taken as a metaphor for all inter-ethnic hierarchies" (Agacinski, 2001, p. 14).

A long tradition in social psychology has found three basic differences that individuals notice immediately when they encounter a new person almost from infancy: age, gender, and race (Brewer & Lui, 1989; Fiske & Neuberg, 1990; Messick & Mackie, 1989). Although there is some preliminary evidence that recognition of racial differences can be "erased" when such differences are crossed with coalitional status, no one has shown a similar disabling of sexual recognition (Kurzban, Tooby, & Cosmides,

Indeed, the psychologist Alice Eagley asserts, "...nder stereotypes trump race stereotypes in every ...ial science test" (Stephen, 2008). In this way, sex, like age, becomes a basic category of identification and a profound marker of difference (Derrida, 1978).

Sex and age categorizations play variant roles in society. Everyone will someday move into another age group; in general, however, this cannot be said of sex groupings. Sexual difference is arguably the primary formative fixed difference experienced in human society,[1] and sex serves as a critical model for the societal treatment of difference between and among individuals and collectives. We argue that societally based differences in gender status beliefs, reflected in practices, customs, and law, have important political consequences, including consequences for nation-state security policy and conflict and cooperation within and between nation-states.

If the treatment of sexual difference does affect the characteristics and behavior of human collectives, including nation-states, then evolutionary theory should add valuable insights to any conceptual framework proposing to explain conflict, war, and aggression. After all, sexual reproduction is the strongest evolutionary driver of human social arrangements (Lopreato, 1984; Wrangham & Peterson, 1996). How societies organize sexual reproduction will have cascading effects on many social phenomena, even those that seem at first glance to be quite removed from the topic. As Alexander puts it, "culture [can be seen] as a gigantic metaphorical extension of the reproductive system" (Alexander, Hoogland, Howard, Noon, & Sherman, 1979, p. 77). Since human sexual reproduction is (currently) impossible without a relationship between the sexes, the nature of that relationship should be a foundational element in any attempt to apply evolutionary theory to conceptualize and explain conflict, war, and aggression within and between human collectives.

Feminist Evolutionary Theory and Patriarchy

> What is natural need not be passively accepted. Rain is natural, but I have enough sense to get out of it.
> —*Irwin S. Bernstein* (1997, p. 580)

One of the most important contributions of feminist evolutionary analysis (FEA) is an explication of patriarchy and its prevalence in human societies in terms of ultimate causes. Such an explication is not a rival to other types of explanation, such as sociological, psychological, or historical; these explanations are mutually nonexclusive. Nevertheless, an FEA approach to patriarchy supplements theories of more proximate causes with a theory of ultimate cause. While some have argued that "Terminology, politics, and ignorance are, in retrospect, major barriers to the dialectic of feminism and evolutionary biology" (Waage & Gowaty, 1997, p. 585), we agree with Hannagan that "a Darwinian feminist approach can serve as a kind of meta-feminism because it provides footing for explanations involving the ultimate causes of power relations" (Hannagan, 2008, p. 467), and also with Tang-Martinez that by "understanding the evolutionary origins of male dominance, we will be able to formulate more effective responses to counteract female oppression" (Tang-Martinez, 1997, p. 118).

In using evolutionary theory for an account of ultimate cause in human affairs, it is important to remember, as Gat suggests, that "evolutionary theory does not compete in explaining motivation with scholarly constructs such as psychoanalytic theories or the realist approach in IR; rather, evolutionary theory may encompass some of their main insights within a comprehensive interpretative framework" (Gat, 2009, p. 583). It is also important to keep in mind that (1) evolutionary forces are not deterministic; rather, they are significantly influential but can be mitigated, and (2) evolutionary theory does not posit an essentialist account of male-female differences but rather suggests that evolutionary forces may predispose males and females toward particular behaviors in the absence of countervailing forces. Evolutionary forces may make certain behaviors more likely, but unless these are maintained through the processes of social learning and social diffusion, they may not persist.[2] And any equation of evolutionary theory with simplistic essentialist accounts of male-female behavior, such as presuming women are pacifist angels, is completely unwarranted. With these caveats and cautions in mind, an evolutionary explanation for persistent patterns of patriarchy throughout human history may be sought.

In this section, we will highlight the work of anthropologist Barbara Smuts on the evolutionary origins of patriarchy (Smuts, 1992, 1995). Smuts asserts that "Humans exhibit more extensive male dominance and male control of female sexuality than is shown by most other primates" (Smuts, 1995, p. 1). Furthermore, she (somewhat controversially[3]) argues that patriarchy's beginnings are to be found long before the development of agriculture.

Male reproductive success centers on control of female sexuality; without the intensive labor provided by females in gestation, lactation, and nurture of the young, males cannot reproduce. Trivers's 1972 theory argues that the more competitive (or in Darwin's language, the more "eager") sex is usually the sex that invests less in reproduction, in terms of both gamete production and parental investment in offspring survival (Archer, 2009; Trivers, 1972). As Archer explains, "the sex showing higher parental investment becomes a limiting resource, the other sex competing for reproductive access" (Archer, 2009, p. 250). In a similar manner, differences in the reproductive success of males and females further drive competitive processes of sexual selection. Whereas females are not able to mate again immediately after producing offspring, males do not experience any interruption and can therefore move on to mate with other females to increase their reproductive success.

While there are a wide variety of male-female interactions that result in reproduction, one of the most common in nonhuman primates is sexual coercion by the male of the female, according to Smuts (1995). Such coercion lowers the costs to males of reproduction, compared to strategies such as assisting females in the care of the young. Such sexually coercive strategies involve not only forced copulation (usually on pain of physical violence) but also infanticide by males of nonrelated offspring of the woman with whom he seeks copulation. Smuts explains that the females typically do mate with the males who have killed their infants, thereby reducing the females' reproductive success, in order to receive protection for their future offspring. They may also have little choice in resisting mating with a violent male who could potentially kill the female as well as her infants. Sexual coercion, then, can be effective as a male mating strategy.

Indeed, Gowaty suggests that even sexual dimorphism can be better explained if we place relations between the sexes as the most influential factor in its development: "Female-male competition over control of female reproduction is an untested, viable alternative to the male-male competition explanation for 'males larger' in sexually dimorphic species" (Gowaty, 1997, p. 378). Interestingly, Gowaty's own research (2003) demonstrates that in contrast to the typical "coy" behavior of females in a typical group setting, when males and females have been reared separately (and thus females have never witnessed male-on-female violence), females do not exhibit "coyness" or choosiness when introduced to the males, suggesting that they had not to fear male aggression.

An FEA approach, then, asserts that conflict among humans was the clash of tive interests between males and females. Rosser to assert, "Women's oppression is most widespread, and deepest oppression" (1997, p. 32) and Gowaty to opine, "[S]exist oppression is fundamental to—is 'the root' of—all other systems of oppression" (Gowaty, 1992, p. 219). This is why Smuts argues that patriarchy predates agriculture. Smuts concludes that "men use aggression to try to control women, and particularly to try to control female sexuality, not because men are inherently aggressive and women inherently submissive, but because men find aggression to be a useful political tool in their struggle to dominate and control women and thereby enhance their reproductive opportunities" (1992, p. 30). Smuts adds that "male use of aggression as a tool is not inevitable but conditional; that is, under some circumstances coercive control of women pays off, whereas under other circumstances it does not" (1992, p. 30).

Why is human male dominance so much more pervasive and elaborate than male dominance in other primate species, then? Smuts theorizes the differences have to do with how effective or ineffective female resistance to control by males is within a given collective. The more ineffective that resistance, the deeper and wider will be male dominance—and social structures and processes that systematically decrease the effectiveness of female resistance will, in general, be chosen by males for just such purposes.

Smuts hypothesizes that several near-universal social structures and processes in traditional human societies preclude effective female resistance: Patrilocality (female movement from their natal group to another group when sexually mature; also present in chimpanzees) is first and foremost, a practice that deprives a woman of female kin networks that could potentially prohibit sexual coercion. Anne Campbell (2006) claims that hunter-gatherer societies adopted patrilocal mating patterns in which women left their natal families to mate with males outside their kinship system, thereby weakening natal bonds. This is the first example Smuts offers of how "male aggression has influenced not only female behavior but also the form of the social system itself" (Smuts, 1992, p. 8).[4]

The second strategic development is the formation of male-male alliances, which aid males in the primary conflict with females. Because of patrilocality, most males in a particular area are

, which provides a natural foundation for alliances. Smuts notes, "male reproductive strategies came to rely increasingly upon alliances with other males... Male reliance on alliances with other males in competition for status, resources, and females is a universal feature of human societies" (Smuts, 1995, p. 13; Smuts, 1992, p. 15). Again, male reproductive advantage appears to be the root. Chagnon's research into hunter-gatherer societies demonstrates that individual men who are aggressive have higher status in the village and greater reproductive success (1988). Simply put, "Better fighters tend to have more babies. That's the simple, stupid, selfish logic of sexual selection" (Wrangham & Peterson, 1996, p. 173).

As such, fraternal alliances developed, the male dominance hierarchy structure was increasingly selected as a way to dampen male-male competition within the group. Indeed, pair-bonding in human societies may have developed as a social structure to that very end; that is, to produce "male respect of the mating privileges of their allies" (Smuts, 1992, p. 11). With amelioration of ingroup conflict among males, such male dominance hierarchies were more effective in coercing women, as well as in facing threats from outgroup male coalitions. These male coalitions also formed the foundation for male control of economic resources important for female reproduction. Male hunting parties would control division of game; male raiding parties would control division of spoils. Smuts notes, "men may use their alliances with other men to prevent actions that may benefit the women, but at a cost to the men" (Smuts, 1992, p. 19).

Male dominance hierarchies can, however, become extremely hierarchical, with some men controlling a vastly disproportionate share of the resources and power. Smuts hypothesizes that in such inegalitarian contexts, women will be subject to the most extreme forms of coercion, as the fear of powerful men over "the problem of imperfect monopolization of the mate" increases (Wilson, Daly, & Scheib, 1997, p. 457). Powerful men with greater resources have much more to lose than poor men if their control over women is ineffective, and so they will use their resources and power to ensure they will not be losers. Smuts suggests, "the degree to which men dominate women and control their sexuality is inextricably intertwined with the degree to which some men dominate others" (Smuts, 1995, p. 18).

In environments in which resources are distributed more equitably, males will exhibit less aggressive behavior toward one another. This holds in contemporary studies of violence: "evidence indicates that relative deprivation (as indexed by income inequality) is typically a more powerful predictor of variation in male violence than other socioeconomic measures such as percent below the poverty line or average income" (Pound, Daly, & Wilson, 2009, p. 286).

This increasing male monopoly over the economic resources needed by females for reproduction is not mirrored in nonhuman primates, where females collect their own food. It is in human societies where, especially after the development of agriculture and animal husbandry in which land and animals belonged exclusively to men, that the complete economic dependence of females could be effected (Mies, 1988). As Smuts notes in a survey of empirical results, the lower the share of female contribution to subsistence, the higher the level of wife beating and rape within the society (Smuts, 1995). In such a state of relative prostration of women, more effective and less costly means of sexual coercion were developed that did not require constant one-on-one violence. Indeed, Smuts argues that "gender ideology" was the first product of human speech (Smuts, 1992). Men created codes of conduct for women, including marriage patterns, which would favor their control interests over female autonomy interests. Furthermore, they can easily coerce women to adopt and enforce such codes: "women's adoption of cultural values that appear to go against their own interests may in fact be necessary for survival" (Smuts, 1992, p. 26).

Male aggression is, then, in the first place, a strategy in the battle of the sexes, as are male alliances and other social structures and practices. Smuts suggests, "in many primates, hardly an aspect of female existence is not constrained in some way by the presence of aggressive males" (Smuts, 1992, p. 6). Furthermore, she asserts, "Evolutionary analysis suggests that whenever we consider any aspect of gender inequality, we need to ask how it affects female sexuality and reproduction in ways that benefit some men at the expense of women (and of other men)" (Smuts, 1995, p. 22).

This is not to say that all men are aggressive, or that all men coerce females, or that such oppressive social systems are inevitable or biologically determined. Far from it. While selected, these phenomena are not genetically determined: "[C]ulture affects phenotype, and the phenotypes of individuals in any one generation can, in turn, affect the culture encountered by the subsequent generation. Thus, an individual's phenotype is the result of dynamic interactions among an individual's genotype (genetic makeup) and the biotic, abiotic, social, and historical environment in which the individual develops and lives" (Gowaty, 1997, p. 12). We are seeing a complex and varying interplay between genetic, epigenetic, and extragenic influences, and the result thereof is subject to change by, among other things, altered cultural values. Nevertheless, we would be remiss if we did not notice that FEA tells us that there is a strong evolutionary component to violence and that its origin is male-female conflict over reproduction.

That such general male-female conflict resulting in gender inequality exists in our world today is difficult to dispute. Indeed, some scholars have opined that gender inequality is one of the most visible system structure elements of the current international system (Sjoberg, 2009). Using the information and scales of the WomanStats Database (http://www.womanstats.org), we find that an examination of a scale of the Physical Security of Women (a 5-point scale from 0 to 4, with 0 being a situation of security for women) yields the insight that, sadly, no country achieved the highest ranking (0), which would indicate women are physically secure.[5] To obtain such a ranking, the country would have laws against not only murder but also domestic violence, rape, and marital rape; those laws would be enforced; and there would be no taboos or norms against reporting these crimes, which would be rare.

At the next scale point of 1, women have comparatively high levels of physical security. All 10 of the countries at this scale point are Western European. Noteworthy is that the United States and Canada are coded at scale point 2, indicating that while their laws are exemplary, levels of violence against women remain relatively high. The two categories in which women are relatively physically insecure, in which women have limited or no physical security, are clustered primarily across the Middle East, Africa, South Asia, the former Communist bloc, and most of Latin America. Tunisia and Djibouti do appear to have higher levels of physical security for women than other Arab countries of the Middle East and North Africa. Regional patterns obviously exist, but there are also glaring regional exceptions, where some countries appear quite discrepant given their regional location.

The average Physical Security of Women score for all states in 2006 was 3.02 on a scale of 0–4—a score that highlights the widespread and persistent violence perpetrated against women worldwide. The majority of women live in countries where laws prohibiting violence against women are either nonexistent or unenforced and where social norms do not define domestic violence, rape, and even murder as serious, accurately reported crimes. In addition, many of these women live in ostensibly democratic states, which is a counterintuitive finding. Generally speaking, women's rights are disproportionately either ignored by state laws, as for example by the lack of marital rape or domestic violence laws, or the state subjects women to laws that may increase the level of violence against them, as was the case with the infamous *zina* laws in Pakistan, which were thankfully modified in 2006, but now those reforms are under attack in 2010 (Asian Human Rights Commission, 2010). It is difficult to fathom the global extent of violence that women experience daily—a gendered violence that permeates the personal, cultural, and state environments for the majority of the world's population.

If one turned to an examination of the relative valuation of male versus female offspring in a measure of Son Preference and Sex Ratio, one finds the average Son Preference/Sex Ratio for all states in 2006 is 2.07 on a 0–4 scale in the WomanStats Database, indicating a general, globalized son preference. This in itself is an important characteristic of our current world system that often goes unremarked. Globally, male offspring are valued more highly than female offspring. However, since the average is 2.07, this generalized son preference appears not to necessarily result in female infanticide or sex-selective abortion in most states. Nevertheless, the comparatively low value ascribed to female life penetrates every aspect of women's daily lives, thus both perpetuating the cycle of gendered violence and resulting in their own diminished sense of self (Caprioli, 2005).

An examination of several other scales in the WomanStats Database yields similar results. For example, a scale of the degree of Inequity in Family Law yields a global average of 2.01, meaning that, in general, laws are not equitable for women, or if they are, they are not enforced; for Educational Attainment, the global average is 1.63, with an average gap of 4.85% between male and female rates; for Government Participation of Women, the global average is 2.74, meaning that women are in a significant minority within governments, with a global average of less than 20% representation. It is hard not to come to the conclusion that our 21st-century world is deeply structured by a generally high level of violence against and inequitable treatment of women. Whatever the diversity of gender relations in hunter-gatherer societies in the past (and the very few that remain in the present), gender hierarchy is a general and global feature of our world today.

The Women and Peace Thesis: A Feminist Evolutionary Approach to International Relations

To establish the theoretical linkage between the security of women and the security of states, we synthesize insights from several disciplines, including evolutionary biology and psychology, which provide an account of ultimate causes of human behavior in terms of natural selection; political sociology, which offers an account of the social diffusion of both naturally selected and culturally selected traits; and psychology, which provides an account of more proximate causal mechanisms of diffusion in terms of cultural selection through social learning.

Evolutionary Biology and Psychology

Evolutionary biology and psychology have been underutilized by social scientists, leading Thayer to comment that "this leads to an artificially limited social science" using assumptions about human behavior that may be "problematic, or fundamentally flawed" (2004, pp. 8–9). Evolutionary theory provides explanations in terms of ultimate cause, not proximate cause, framing the context within which individual creatures strive to increase their fitness (survival and reproductive success). As we have seen in the previous section, feminist evolutionary theory, in particular, has made a significant contribution to our understanding of the origins of male dominance and oppression of women, drawing attention to the "peculiarly lopsided power relations seen in our own species" (Campbell, 2006, p. 70). As Barbara Smuts explains, evolutionary theory is particularly important for research into gendered behavior because it attempts to explain male power over women: "evolutionary theory not only considers how men exercise power over women, as feminist theory does, but also investigates the deeper question of why males want power over females in the first place, which feminists tend to take as a given" (1995, p. 2).

More About Male Dominance Hierarchies

While an FEA approach posits that male alliances arose first and foremost as a male reproductive strategy, the social form of the male dominance hierarchy provides the crucial theoretical linkage between what is happening between men and women in a society, and what is happening between societal collectives. Therefore, a more in-depth look of male dominance hierarchies and their characteristics is warranted.

Sex differences across animal species produce a dazzling diversity of male-female interaction, and evolutionary perspectives attempt to demonstrate that selective mechanisms work in conjunction with the environment and culture to produce broad variation in human action and traits. Richard Wrangham and Dale Peterson note, however, that out of "4,000 mammals and 10 million or more other animal species" only two species (humans and chimpanzees) live in "patrilineal, male-bonded communities wherein females routinely reduce risks of inbreeding by moving to neighboring groups [to mate within these communities].... with [these communities having] a system of intense, male-initiated territorial aggression, including lethal raiding into neighboring communities in search of vulnerable enemies to attack and kill.... The system of communities defended by related men is a human universal that crosses space and time" (1996, pp. 24–25). While noting this universality in human systems, they also note that "we quickly discover how odd that system really is, [making] humans appear as members of a funny little group that chose a strange little path" (Wrangham & Peterson, 1996, p. 231).

As we have noted, male dominance hierarchies are a system wherein a subgroup of superordinate (or "alpha") males dominate subordinate males, and alpha males generally control sexual access to females. In contemporary terms, male dominance hierarchies are the foundation of patriarchy. Wrangham and Peterson write, "Patriarchy is worldwide and history-wide, and its origins are detectable in the social lives of chimpanzees. It serves the reproductive purposes of the men who maintain the system. Patriarchy comes from biology in the sense that it emerges from men's temperaments, out of their evolutionarily derived efforts to control women and at the same time have solidarity with fellow men in competition against outsiders.... Patriarchy has its ultimate origins in male violence" (Wrangham & Peterson, 1996, p. 125).

In the first place, as we have seen, this violence is directed against women. Unfortunately, given sexual dimorphism in humans, coercion is an effective male mating strategy. Women accede to dominance hierarchies because of "the one terrible threat that never goes away" (Wrangham & Peterson, 1996, p. 159)—the need of females to have protection from killer males, who will injure or kill not only females but also the children that females guard. The battering that women suffer from the males they live with is the price paid for such protection, and it occurs "in species where females have few allies, or where males have bonds with each other" (Wrangham & Peterson, 1996, p. 146). Indeed, among humans, sex differences trump the blood ties associated with natural selection for inclusive fitness. As anthropologist Barbara D. Miller notes, "Human gender hierarchies are one of the most persistent, pervasive, and pernicious forms of inequality in the world. Gender is used as the basis for systems of discrimination which can, even within the same household, provide that those designated 'male' receive more food and live longer, while those designated 'female' receive less food to the point that their survival is drastically impaired" (Miller 1993, p. 22).

The entrenchment of patriarchy also leads to aggression against outgroups. Males in dominance hierarchies quickly discover that resources may be gained with little cost and risk through coalitional violence; and these resources include women. The form of exogamy practiced among humans and chimpanzees (where daughters leave the group to mate) means that males of the group are kin. As a result, blood ties provide the necessary trust to engage in such violence as male-bonded gangs. Coercion of outgroups becomes relatively inexpensive in this context, with potentially great payoff. Dominant males in coalition with male kin are able to adopt a parasitical lifestyle based on physical force: With very little effort, but with a willingness to harm, kill, and enslave others, they can be provided with every resource that natural selection predisposes them to desire: food, women, territory, resources, status, political power, pride. As Kemper puts it, "The dominant are not dependent for their sense of well-being on the voluntary responses of others. The dominant simply take what they want" (1990, p. 109).

Contemporary human societies do not inhabit the evolutionary landscape of hundreds of thousands of years ago. We would be remiss, however, if we did not note how primal male coalitionary violence and resulting patriarchy are, and what influence those forces still have today. Thayer (2004) notes that humans are only about 400 generations removed from that landscape, and only eight generations have passed since the Industrial Revolution: The past still bears heavily on our behavioral proclivities. The men among us have certain behavioral proclivities induced by the "strange path" our ancestors took: Wrangham and Peterson argue "Men have a vastly long history of violence [which] implies that they have been temperamentally shaped to use violence effectively, and that they will therefore to stop. It is startling, perhaps, to r absurdity of the system: one that wo our genes rather than our conscious s inadvertently jeopardizes the fate of dants" (1996, p. 249). In other wor policy of human groups, including modern states, more dangerous because of the human male evolutionary legacy: "Unfortunately, there appears something special about foreign policy in the hands of males. Among humans and chimpanzees at least, male coalitionary groups often go beyond defense [typical of monkey matriarchies] to include unprovoked aggression, which suggests that our own intercommunity conflicts might be less terrible if they were conducted on behalf of women's rather than men's interests. Primate communities organized around male interests naturally tend to follow male strategies and, thanks to sexual selection, tend to seek power with an almost unbounded enthusiasm" (Wrangham & Peterson, 1996, p. 233).

Thayer concurs, noting that "war evolved in humans because it is an effective way to gain and defend resources" (2004, p. 13). Moreover, because the evolutionary environment produced egoism, domination, and the ingroup/outgroup distinction, "these specific traits are sufficient to explain why state leaders will maximize their power over others and their environment, even if they must hurt others or risk injury to themselves" (Thayer, 2004, p. 76). Indeed, the title of Thayer's book speaks to the point: *Darwin and International Relations*. He finds ultimate cause for such observable modern state-level phenomena as offensive realism and ethnic conflict in natural selection, which supports recent research by other scholars (Potts & Hayden, 2008).

Patriarchy and its attendant violence among human collectives are not inevitable, however; and this is not simply a politically correct view—it is the view of evolutionary theorists. As Wrangham and Peterson note, "Patriarchy is not inevitable... Patriarchy emerged not as a direct mapping of genes onto behavior, but out of the particular strategies that men [and women] invent for achieving their emotional goals. And the strategies are highly flexible, as every different culture shows" (1996, p. 125).

Political Psychology and Social Diffusion Theory

Theories of political sociology underscore the view of evolutionary theorists that the legacy of violent patriarchy comes to permeate all levels of social course. The primal character of violent patriarchy ensures that it becomes a template for broad classes of social behavior—specifically, those that concern social difference. Because human males, generally speaking, code the primal difference between male and female as a hierarchy in which the naturally selected goal is control and domination of the subordinate female, all those coded as "different" will be treated in accordance with that template of control and domination: outgroup males, outgroup females, and even in certain circumstances ingroup males. Thus, the ultimate causes posited by evolutionary theory are supplemented by more proximate causal mechanisms in the diffusion of these templates of domination and control.

Theories of social diffusion are not alien to security studies. Scholars in the field have investigated the relationship between the spread of new forms of social relations, such as democracy, and resulting observable differences in state security and behavior (Maoz & Russett, 1993). Interestingly, several theorists believe that the rise of democracy is rooted in the amelioration of violent patriarchy. For example, some have posited that the social imposition of monogamy and later marriage for women (leading to a lessening of gender inequality) were necessary, though not sufficient, conditions for the rise of democracy and capitalism in the West (Alexander, 1981; Greene & Pole, 1983; Hartman, 2004). Breaking key elements of male dominance hierarchies—polygamy, patrilocality, early to mid-teen marriage for females—may have been the first, critical steps to eventually breaking the political power of such hierarchies. Although in the initial stages the rise of democracy did not facilitate women's political power, without an adjustment in the fundamental character of male-female relations, these scholars assert that democracy may never have been a historical possibility for humans. And as norms of democracy arose, the stage was set for women to achieve political power. If these theorists are correct, then levels of violence against women should be more predictive of state security and peacefulness than levels of procedural democracy. In other words, in states where democracy arose from within through amelioration of gender inequality, we should find greater state security; but where democracy was imposed or veneered over systems where male-female relations did not undergo fundamental transformation, we should not find as significant differences in state security and peacefulness.

Just as a proclivity toward international peace in democratic societies is based, in part, "on tolerance and a respect for the rights of opponents" (Raymond, 2000, p. 290), so scholars might also contemplate that norms of gender-based violence have an inflammatory impact on domestic and international behavior. For example, studies have shown that if domestic violence is normal in family conflict resolution in a society, then that society is more likely to rely on violent conflict resolution and to be involved in militarism and war than are societies with lower levels of family violence (Cockburn, 2001; Erchak, 1997; Erchak & Rosenfeld, 1994; Levinson, 1989). A vicious circle may result, where such state violence may in turn lead to higher levels of gender violence (Brownmiller, 1975; Elshtain, 1987; Reardon, 1985; Ruddick, 1995). Indeed, lower levels of gender inequality hinder the ability of societies to mobilize for aggression through demoralizing women (Caprioli, 2005).

Johan Galtung, a political scientist specializing in political sociology, offers two concepts that help explain how a generalized ideological justification for violence is formed and diffuses throughout society: structural violence and cultural violence (1975, 1990). Galtung's conceptualization of structural violence paints a picture of pervasive and systematic exploitation that makes open violence in the public sphere unnecessary—"The amateur who wants to dominate uses guns, the professional uses social structure" (1990, p. 80). According to Galtung, structural violence has at least four manifestations: exploitation based on a division of labor wherein benefits are asymmetrically distributed; control by the exploiters over the consciousness of the exploited, resulting in the acquiescence of the oppressed; fragmentation, meaning that the exploited are separated from each other; and marginalization, with the exploiters as a privileged class with their own rules and forms of interaction (1990, pp. 264–265).

The concordance between this list and the means by which gender inequality is typically maintained in human societies is clear. Gender roles lead to highly differential possibilities for personal security, development, and prosperity, even in today's world. An example of this kind of exploitation occurs when women "naturally" receive less pay than men for equal work, or when domestic violence is considered "normal." The second component, manipulation of consciousness to ensure acquiescence, is maintained through socialization, gender stereotyping, and a constant threat of domestic violence—all of which insidiously identify women as inferior. The perpetrators of female infanticide, for example, are virtually all female. The third component, fragmentation, is easily effected from women's circumstances of patrilocality and greater family responsibilities (and, in some cases, a physical *purdah* may be used), thus minimizing social access that could otherwise be used to build networks with other women. And finally, marginalization serves to clearly distinguish men and women, with no doubt as to the relative status of each sex.

Galtung posits that structural violence arises from cultural violence; the day-to-day use of overt or implicit force to obtain one's ends in social relations. Thus, while structural violence may obviate the need for open violence in the public sphere, it is based on open or implicit violence in the private sphere of the home. Norms of cultural violence diffuse within religion, ideology, language, and art, among other aspects of culture. "Cultural violence makes direct and structural violence look, even feel, right—or at least not wrong," writes Galtung (1990, p. 291). Violent patriarchy is the primary basis of cultural violence in human collectives: Although women have become active agents with notable success in the struggle for equality in many states, violence remains an enduring component of relations between men and women in the private sphere the world over, providing a natural wellspring for social diffusion (Caprioli et al., 2009).

Gendered hierarchies also help explain the violence associated with nationalism, for the hierarchical difference between men and women that is at the root of structural inequality and violence diffuses to become an integral aspect of nationalism. Evolutionary theory tells us that clan or national identity is almost exclusively male defined, for in the evolutionary landscape, it was males who defined who was a member of the ingroup and who belonged to outgroups, based on male reproductive concerns. "Gender relations are a crucial, not peripheral, dimension of the dynamics of group identities and intergroup conflicts" (Peterson, 1998, pp. 42–43), thus helping to explain the inherent nationalist antipathy toward feminist goals. Given this linkage between violent patriarchy and nationalism, any reforms of the cultural distribution of power between men and women will be viewed as a threat to nationalist efforts to protect or unify the community (Caprioli, 2005; Papanek, 1990; Tessler & Warriner, 1997; Tickner, 1992, 2001). Legitimized by gendered structural and cultural violence, patriarchal nationalism provides justification for advancing state interests through the use of force. In that light, we expect that neither a meaningful decrease in societal violence nor a sustainable peace among nations is possible in human society without a decrease in gender inequality (Hunt & Posa, 2001; Tickner, 1992). But is that possible?

Social Learning Theory From Psychology

As we have shown, even evolutionary theorists assert that violent patriarchy is not inevitable in human society. Psychologists strongly agree, and their findings are pertinent here as more proximate causes of cultural heritage, as well as more sites of action for a change in that heritage. First, social-learning psychologists argue that biology does increase the likelihood that a child will engage in aggressive or violent behavior, but it does not guarantee it. For example, twin and adoption studies find genes make a small contribution to various forms of antisocial behavior compared to environmental factors. For example, while finding that having a biological parent who was antisocial increased the risk for antisocial behavior to be seen in an adopted child, these same studies also demonstrated that having a disrupted home environment contributed more significantly to the risk for a child to engage in antisocial behavior (Bohman, 1996; Cadoret, Cain, & Crowe, 1983; Cadoret, Leve, & Devor, 1997; Ge et al., 1996).

Social-learning psychologists elaborate that violence is heavily influenced by a sequence of long-term training of the individual: Children who learn aggressive behaviors very early develop serious deficits in prosocial skills (Patterson, 2008). Violent individuals are inadvertently trained by siblings and parents through their reinforcement of coercive behavior with little positive reinforcement for prosocial behavior, and these parenting practices are handed down from one generation to the next. In concordance with evolutionary theory, psychologists argue that the key to training an individual to become violent, both within the family and in peer groups, is the functionality of violence. Violence and coercion must "work" for these to be perpetuated, or in the parlance of evolutionary theory, "selected for." The reactions of parents, siblings, and peers teach individuals to select actions that work and to ignore those that do not. True to evolutionary theory, individuals repeat responses that are functional and drop those that are nonfunctional; for example, Thayer notes, "Culture allows warfare to be either suppressed or exacerbated ... it is difficult to overstate the significance of educational systems, popular culture, and the media, among many [proximate] causal mechanisms" (2004, pp. 151–152). It is the environment that determines the nature of the fittest response (Patterson, 2008). Here we glimpse the proximate causes of cultural selection in the very act.

Indeed, findings in psychology demonstrate that very young boys do not display more violence toward girls than girls display toward boys. Although many studies have concluded that among preschool age children, boys are more physically aggressive than girls (Baillargeon et al., 2007; Ostrov & Keating, 2004), when the stimulus of gender is removed (Hyde, 2007) there is no difference between the amount of aggression boys display against girls and girls display against boys (Ballif-Spanvill, Clayton, Nicols, & Kramer, unpublished manuscript). Rather, three factors are likely to play prominent roles in training individuals to become more violent against women: modeling, immediate reinforcement, and male-bonded groups.

Modeling

The first adults that children observe regularly interacting are their parents. In homes where interparental violence occurs, children who witness such violence are susceptible to adopting the aggressive behavior patterns they observe (Cummings, Goeke-Morey, Papp, 2004; Edleson, 1999; Graham-Bermann, 1998; Margolin & Gordis, 2000). Such child witnesses of violence between their parents are more likely to be violent with their peers and with their partners in future relationships. Those children found to be most violent are sons of abusers following in their fathers' footsteps by becoming violent in the same types of conflicts that trigger their fathers' violence (Ballif-Spanvill, Clayton, & Hendrix, 2007). Sons' imitation of their fathers' aggression toward their mothers may be the first step in perpetuating patterns of violence against women across generations.

Immediate Reinforcement

Violence committed against women in the home is almost always related to fulfilling emotional needs or physical needs of men (Bornstein, 2006). Such violence provides almost immediate gratification. The selfish satisfaction inherent in male domination is often justified by cultural and religious traditions that are themselves results of social diffusion, and that in turn offer additional social rewards for the perpetrator's aggression. Although individual differences clearly exist (Ballif-Spanvill, Clayton, & Hendrix, 2003), male children who imitate the violence they observe against women in the home are likely to perpetuate it as long as it gets them what they want. Unless aggression toward women becomes less rewarding to men, and prosocial skills become more functional within families, communities, and societies, violence against women will continue.

Male-Bonded Groups

In concert with findings of evolutionary biology concerning male coalitions, studies of children have repeatedly found evidence that boys prefer to play with boys (Fabes, Martin, & Hanish, 2003; Munroe & Romney, 2006). Bonnie Ballif-Spanvill and her coauthors found that when 3-year-old boys play with other 3-year-old boys, the amount of prosocial behavior between them significantly increases (Ballif-Spanvill et al., unpublished manuscript). Such positive interactions were not found among girls or in mixed-gender dyads. This male camaraderie may not only be the basis for the same-gender preferences observed in children at play but everyday anecdotal observations of athletic teams and male-only clubs as well. Same-sex groupings of men may also accentuate their views of women as different, a view reinforced when men do not feel the positive interactions with women they experience when they are in the presence of other men. These dynamics may also be interpreted by some men as evidence of the inferiority of women and serve as a justification for objectifying and dehumanizing them.

Female children or women do not appear to have comparable positive same-sex compatibility. This finding, coupled with the fact that in most societies women are structurally organized in patrilocal families under the direction of men, could explain why even when women associate with other women, their allegiance is primarily to the male heads of their households. As previously discussed, this may also be a tragic by-product of human evolution as it pertains to female choice.

Extrapolating from the aforementioned findings, young male children who see that violence against women rewards their fathers are likely to perpetuate violence in their own relationships with women, and perhaps even generalize their violent responses to all women. Couple these acquired behaviors in boys with the findings of camaraderie among groups of boys, and the foundation for emerging groups of men treating women poorly begins to take shape. As aggressive boys gravitate toward each other, they acquire more social and political power. The group identity of such male collectives is often strengthened by various initiations and rituals that often dehumanize nonmembers and enhance willingness to use violence against them (Clayton, Barlow, & Ballif-Spanvill, 1999). Furthermore, these characteristic group behaviors are used to train new recruits to carry on in the dynamics of the group across generations.

In cultures where violence against women is allowed to persist, individuals (particularly male individuals) are committing continual, possibly daily, acts of aggression and violence. Extrapolating from Patterson's model (2008), the relative rate of reinforcement is a significant predictor for the relative rate of aggressive behavior, and the rate of reinforcement for violence against women is extremely high, resulting in overlearned violent acts that become automatic. Furthermore, Patterson also states that boys who engage in high frequencies of antisocial behavior are at a significantly greater risk to commit violent acts within their communities. This strongly suggests that violence at different levels of analysis is connected, in that states that allow violence against women to persist are allowing men—that half of society that holds both physical and political power—to engage in frequent antisocial acts, perhaps even on a daily basis. This increases the likelihood that they will experience low barriers to engaging in violence on an even larger scale, up to and including intrasocietal and interstate conflict. Societal expectations of benefits from violence at every level of analysis will almost certainly be higher if men—who are dominant in political power in virtually every human society—have received many rewards from committing high frequencies of aggressive acts toward women.

The special contribution of psychology to the women and peace thesis is the identification of the discrete proximate causes that can be manipulated to counteract and even undermine violent patriarchy. Very young boys are not demonstrably prone to aggression against girls, and it takes active modeling, reinforcement, and rewarding of gendered violence to make it appear functional to boys. If it is not modeled, if it is not reinforced, if it is actively punished, its incidence can be severely limited. These are proximate causes that humans can consciously control. If gendered violence can be undermined at its taproot—domestic violence within the home—the effects, as we have shown with violent patriarchy, should cascade outward to affect many social phenomena, including state security and behavior. Furthermore, if institutions can be created that depersonalize political power, thus severing its connection to physical power in which men have an advantage, then legal systems and political institutions that allow female of relational violence from males, and to form countervailing female alliance male violence and dominance, will a found effect on state security and b extent that the security of women i ority, the security and peacefulness of the state w... be significantly enhanced. State security rests, in the first place, on the security of women.

Structural Patriarchy and Its Legacy

In their work analyzing responses from the World Value Survey, Ronald Inglehart and Pippa Norris (2003) uncovered an unusual finding: There was little cross-national variation in the degree to which survey respondents valued democracy and democratic institutions. "With the exception of Pakistan, most of the Muslim countries surveyed think highly of democracy: In Albania, Egypt, Bangladesh, Azerbaijan, Indonesia, Morocco, and Turkey, 92 to 99% of the public endorsed democratic institutions—a higher proportion than in the United States (89%)" (Norris & Inglehart, 2003, p. 1). Rather, the most extreme differences in attitudes that they found concerned the role and place of women in society:

> Huntington is mistaken in assuming that the core clash between the West and Islam is over political values. At this point in history, societies throughout the world (Muslim and Judeo-Christian alike) see democracy as the best form of government. Instead, the real fault line between the West and Islam, which Huntington's theory completely overlooks, concerns gender equality and sexual liberalization. In other words, the values separating the two cultures have much more to do with *eros* than *demos*.
> (Norris & Inglehart, 2003, p. 1)

While *eros* may be the root, the blossoms of patriarchy are both varied and ubiquitous. One place to see the continued legacy of patriarchy is in the *structural control* offered men by family law systems. As Miller notes, "[H]uman gender hierarchies are one of the most persistent, pervasive, and pernicious forms of inequality in the world" (1993, pp. 3, 22).

According to evolutionary theory, higher ranked males made family law *in the image of their own reproductive interests*. Consider the remarkable convergence of family law throughout both time and space in human history: Adultery as a much greater crime for women than for men; female infanticide as an historically sanctioned practice in virtually all human cultures; polygyny legal but polyandry proscribed; divorce easy for men and almost impossible for women; male-on-female domestic violence and marital rape not recognized as crimes; a common legal sequel to rape being the marriage of the victim to the rapist; the legal age of consent and of marriage years younger for females than for males; and inheritance of resources preferentially allocated to males. Still other practices that are an expression of physical and sexual dominance of men over women, such as infibulation, chastity belts, *droit de seigneur*, and gender-based dress codes that inhibit the mobility of women, are also understandable in this light. The convergence in family law systems, expansively defined, through time and space leads us to the conclusion that the formation of family law is at least in part due to higher ranked men in all cultures having originally created family law through their political power, and having created it in the image of male reproductive interests as shaped by our evolutionary heritage. Control over females by males, baldly put, is at the foundation of historical family law because of our common evolutionary legacy.[6]

While it is possible to find full "patriarchal family law," as described earlier, prevalent still in many areas of the world, in other regions there have been sustained and consistent departures from this template. In many areas of the world, there is no longer any significant level of female infanticide, or of polygyny. In many societies, it is as straightforward for a woman to obtain a divorce or to inherit from her parents as it is for a man.

What we find, then, in the early 21st century of recorded human history, is a broad spectrum of family law along a putative continuum between full evolutionary family law that encodes male dominance over females, and relatively equitable family law that encodes a meaningful degree of parity between men and women. If we were to examine the resulting range of law (and practice) across the globe, some societies would appear much closer to our evolutionary heritage than others in the area of family law, while other societies would be seen to have successfully and proactively mitigated the male bias of evolutionary family law.

Why would the examination of nation-state location on such a spectrum of family law be useful or interesting to scholars of international relations? As Inglehart and Norris have argued (from survey results), so we argue (from an evolutionary lens) that the key cultural differences between human societies may have less to do with ethnic and religious differences and more to do with whether the society has chosen to continue the evolutionary and cultural heritage of male dominance over women or purposefully acts to mitigate that heritage. Family law offers a particularly insightful view of which path a society has taken to this point.

In other words, in cultures more closely tied to our evolutionary heritage, male dominance over females certainly takes a physical form but also involves the creation of structural conditions facilitating control of females by males. Overt physical dominance is buttressed by the creation of structural means to more easily ensure male control over females and thus over families. Thus, we should expect that inequitable family law systems and high levels of violence against women would be highly correlated, and indeed, that is what we find (Hudson, Bowen, & Nielsen, 2011).

What structural means ensure male control over females and families? As we have seen, these structures include, in the first place, marriage arrangements. Thus, in human clan-based societies across time and space, we see a preponderant convergence on patrilocal marriage of pubescent brides:

> While particular marriage structures have varied widely, couples in southern and eastern Europe, India, the Middle East, China, and parts of Africa typically married early, with brides being seven to ten years younger than grooms. Families ordinarily arranged their children's marriages, and few persons remained single throughout their lifetimes.... Newlyweds most often moved into the existing residence of the groom's family, carrying on multifamily or joint households of two or more married couples.
> (*Hartman*, 2004, p. 22)[7]

The historian Mary Hartman goes on to note that in societies with this form of marriage, sex ratios typically favor males, polygyny is often sanctioned, and there is a general devaluation of female life and female abilities (Hartman, 2004). With brides typically married at ages 14–16 years (and often without their genuine consent), and grooms being on average in their late 20s or older, marriages are not companionate but hierarchical. The pervasiveness of inequitable family law, then, is a sign that male dominance hierarchies form the template for a society's organization. As Potts and Hayden note, "Speaking very broadly, one of the themes through much of human history is men laboring to keep women under control, and benefiting from their success in achieving this" (2008, p. 310).

Male Dominance Hierarchies and Their Effect on the State

How does male dominance with its attendant physical and structural control of women affect state-level behavior? The most illustrative example is that of polygyny (Divale & Harris, 1976; Gat, 2006). Polygyny produces especially unstable societies, because it means that certain males in the clan will have several mates, and others may have none, undermining the solidarity necessary among the males of the group. As Robert Wright puts it, "Extreme polygyny often goes hand in hand with extreme political hierarchy, and reaches its zenith under the most despotic regimes" (Wright, 1995, p. 98). Laura Betzig, in an intriguing empirical study of 186 societies, found the correlation between polygyny and despotism to be statistically significant (Betzig, 1986). Anthropologists have found significant correlation between polygyny and the amount of warfare in which societies engage (Harris, 1993); Kanazawa suggests that "polygyny may be the first law of intergroup conflict (civil wars)" (2009, p. 32); and Boone (1983) even suggests that polygynous societies are more likely to engage in expansionist warfare as a means of distracting low-status males who may be left without mates. Richard Alexander et al. have posited that the first evidence of transition from a clan-based foundation of society is the prohibition of polygyny:

> Because of the importance of mate competition, socially imposed monogamy exemplifies the essence of societal laws—the restricting of the ability of societal members to exercise fully their different capacities for reproductive competition and success, and enhancing the security and potential reproductive success of the individuals who collaborate to conceive and enforce the laws.... There can be no doubt that there is strong correlation between nations' becoming very large and the imposition of monogamy on their citizens. It is almost as if no nation can become both quite large and quite unified except under socially imposed monogamy. This is not to say that large polygynous polities have not existed (e.g., under Islam, the Ottoman Empire) but that their numbers, sizes, unity, and durability have been less than those of large nations with socially imposed monogamy. Socially imposed monogamy inhibits the rise of the kind of disproportionately large and powerful lineages of close relative shown by Chagnon to be involved in the fissioning of Yanomamo groups, and responsible for the development of their own set of laws and the avenging of kin. One of the correlates of the rise of nations, and a function of systems of law, is to suppress the right of responsibility to avenge wrongs done to kin, and to prevent subgroups and clans from attaining undue power.
>
> (*Alexander* et al., 1979, pp. 423, 432–433)

But polygyny is but an extreme example. Speaking more broadly, we would expect that states in which the structural control of women by men is allowed to persist will exhibit not only higher levels of violence against women but higher levels of authoritarianism, higher levels of violence within society, and enjoy lower levels of state peacefulness both at home and abroad. Gat notes, "Students of war scarcely think of sexuality as a motive for fighting. The underlying links that connect the various elements of the human motivational system have largely been lost sight of" (Gat, 2009, p. 586). Wrangham and Peterson elaborate:

> Male coalitionary violence is primal... We are a part of a group within the apes where the males hold sway by combining into powerful, unpredictable, status-driven and manipulative coalitions, operating in persistent rivalry with other such coalitions... This helps explain why humans are cursed with males given to vicious, lethal aggression. Thinking only of war, putting aside for the moment rape and battering and murder, the curse stems from our species' own special party-gang traits: coalitionary bonds among males, male dominion over an expandable territory, and variable party size. The combination of these traits means that killing a neighboring male is usually worthwhile, and can often be done safely... Species with coalitionary bonds and variable party size—let us call them party-gang species—are wont to kill adult neighbors.
>
> (1996, pp. 231, 233, 167–168, 165)

What evolution has produced in men, generally speaking, is a tendency "to seek power with an almost unbounded enthusiasm" and to engage in "unprovoked aggression," according to Wrangham and Peterson (1996, p. 233). Potts and Hayden note, "[M]ale Homo sapiens...have an inherited predisposition to team up with kin—or *perceived kin*—and try to kill their neighbors (Potts & Hayden, 2008, p. 96, emphasis ours). It is important to note, then, that nationalist identity can substitute for biological kin ties, as "shared cultural traits functio[n] as cues for kinship" (Gat, 2009, p. 591).

It is Stephen Rosen who postulates a concrete explanatory linkage between the logic of small clan aggression and the logic of state aggression. He notes that particular societal arrangements and cultural beliefs will bring clan-minded men to positions of highest authority:

> [S]ome societies do embody values that reward strong responses to perceived challenges. This means not only that men with a higher predisposition to react strongly to challenges will be rewarded, but also that, as these men interact with each other, a cycle of reinforcing behavior would emerge that could explain...high levels of aggression that are provoked and sustained by perceived affronts among habitually interacting males...Once established, the culture might survive its...origins because of institutions that inculcated and reinforced those patterns of behavior. The biological argument suggests that, in addition to those cultural factors, the ways in which members of such cultures would tend to interact with each other would produce elevated testosterone levels that would also create a self-sustaining cycle, producing individuals who are prone to [dominance behaviors]...[A]re there societies and institutions that we would expect to select for and reinforce the behavior of high testosterone males? The answer, in theory and empirically, is that there are and have been societies and political structures that do just that.
> (*Rosen*, 2005, pp. 89–90, 95)

Rosen is explicit in his predictions for such states: "[A] population of states run by groups of men who are prone to react to perceived challenges by punishing the challenger should see more conflict. Such systems will be prone to war..." (Rosen, 2005, p. 96). When we step back, we cannot help but notice the dysfunctionality of a state system influenced by evolutionary male behavior. Potts and Hayden put it best:

> [W]arfare, terrorism, and their attendant horrors are based on just this sort of inherited predisposition for team aggression which, whatever its origins, has become a horribly costly and counterproductive behavior in the modern world...The original survival advantage enjoyed by individual males with a predisposition for team aggression has long since been replaced by a major, verging on suicidal, disadvantage for our species as a whole...[T]o a very large extent...the natural tendencies of men are not consistent with the survival and well-being of their sexual partners, their children, and future generations to come.
> (*Potts & Hayden*, 2008, pp. 25–26, 197, 301)

The Mitigation of Male Dominance and Its Effects on the State: The Hajnal-Hartman Thesis

Despite the bleak picture painted earlier, human beings and their resulting collectives are not powerless in the face of evolutionary legacy. As Wrangham and Peterson note,

> Patriarchy is not inevitable...Patriarchy emerged not as a direct mapping of genes onto behavior, but out of the particular strategies that men [and women] invent for achieving their emotional goals. And the strategies are highly flexible, as every different culture shows...People have long known such things intuitively and so have built civilizations with laws and justice, diplomacy and mediation, ideally keeping always a step ahead of the old demonic principles.
> (*Wrangham & Peterson*, 1996, pp. 125, 198–199)

It is at the conceptual level of social learning and social diffusion that the mitigation of these evolutionary norms must take place—and psychologists tell us the odds of mitigation are high if societies are proactive on this score. Very young boys are not more violent than girls: Although many studies have concluded that among preschool age children, boys are more physically aggressive than girls (e.g., Baillargeon et al., 2007; Ostrov & Keating, 2004), when the stimulus of gender is removed (see Hyde, 2007), there is no difference between the amount of aggression boys display against girls and girls display against boys (Ballif-Spanvill, Clayton, Nicols, & Kramer, unpublished data). It takes active modeling, reinforcement, and rewarding of gendered violence to make it appear functional to boys. If it is not modeled, if it is not reinforced, if it is actively punished, its incidence can be severely limited. These are proximate causes that humans can consciously control. If gendered violence and structural control of females by males can be undermined, the effects, as we have seen with violent patriarchy, should cascade outward to affect many social phenomena, including state peacefulness and forms of state government.

Is there any evidence that the mitigation of evolutionary forces by states affects state attributes and behavior? The answer is yes. Human collectives that have undermined the evolutionary legacy of structural control of females by males—defined here as minimally the prohibition of polygyny and the elimination of early marriage for girls with its attendant patrilocality—are simply different entities than collectives that embrace the full evolutionary heritage.

In addition to Alexander's aforementioned insight on the greater levels of cooperation and lower levels of violence to be found in nonpolygynous cultures (Alexander, 1981), the most significant theory in this regard is the Hajnal-Hartman thesis. While confining themselves to the case of Europe, their research points to a more general relationship between the mitigation of male dominance hierarchies and changes in states characteristics. Before examining the more general thesis, let us begin with an overview of their European case.

The work of John Hajnal, a demographer, and Mary Hartman, an historian, identifies a remarkable "global anomaly" that has heretofore gone overlooked by scholars in their quest for understanding the immense changes that originated in northwestern Europe from the 1500s to the 1800s (Hartman, 2004, p. 8). The anomaly was that, starting around the 1200s, families in northwestern Europe began to marry their daughters "late," meaning on average around age 24 years, to grooms that were on average age 27 years.

Lest the reader not understand the magnitude of that change, since such marriage is fairly common now, Hajnal notes that this late marriage system "presumably *arose only once in human history*" (Hajnal, 1982, p. 476; italics added). What Hajnal means is that never before in human history prior to the 1200s in one corner of Europe were women married in their mid-20s to men of approximately the same age.

Late marriage for women created a completely new form of marriage from "evolutionary" marriage. And it is important to note that this late marriage system began first among the masses, not among the elite. Let us consider the many differences involved. First, men and women chose their own spouses, for by their mid-20s, young people of both sexes were usually employed in households or occupations that necessitated their removal from their natal household. Not only were the young men economic actors, but the young women also had experience in negotiating their employment and maintaining control over their wages, and thus were on much more equal footing as they approached marriage. Furthermore, in most cases, marriage did not involve patrilocality, but rather the establishment of a household independent from the parents or siblings of either party. This household arrangement had a significant impact on the family power structure and a profound effect on the personality formation of the children born within such homes. As Hajnal notes, "The emotional content of marriage, the relation between the couple and other relatives, the methods of choosing or allocating marriage partners—all this and many other things cannot be the same in a society where a bride is usually a girl of 16 and one in which she is typically a woman of 24" (Hajnal, 1965, p. 132). Indeed, in some areas of England up until the 17th century, in particular, the average age of first marriage for women was recorded as being close to 30 (Potts & Hayden, 2008, p. 309).

The late marriage relationship, then, becomes one of significantly mitigated male structural control over females in this historically unusual context. As Hartman puts it,

> Within households, men came to depend less on their own male blood relatives and more on their wives for livelihood and support, whereas outside households they came increasingly to rely on unrelated men rather than on kin networks. Women, for their part, emerged as more active if not equal partners with their husbands in decision making within households and also within their local communities... Husbands requiring responsible partners were obliged, however reluctantly, to abandon the image of the irrational and unruly female, and to refashion women's image more closely to their own.... [t]he whole society was becoming less, not more, patriarchal, starting at the basic level of the household... the unity of kin and property that for thousands of years had been the central focus of most men's worlds began to dissolve.
> (*Hartman*, 2004, pp. 179, 206, 215, 192)

As we have seen with selection for violence in more fully evolutionary societies, late marriage societies also culturally select for particular capabilities and proclivities—in this case, wholly different ones. First, because these nonpatrilocal companionate marriages were more economically vulnerable than multigeneration patrilocal estates, Hartman argues that the persons in late marriage households had to develop skills of "long-range planning, risk-taking, personal responsibility, and independence" (Hartman, 2004, p. 270). She notes that these virtues have "been held up as evidence of a peculiar European genius," when in reality, "maintaining unstable households, let alone enhancing their assets, quite literally depended on these qualities, [and so] it is hardly surprising that they turned up with some regularity in the humblest households, and in the behavior of women as well as men" (Hartman, 2004, p. 270). In other words, Hartman argues that mass-based entrepreneurial capitalism developed first in this region because a new form of marriage system encouraged the psychological predisposition for it.

But capitalism is not the only consequence of the breaking of evolutionary marriage patterns and structural control of females by males. Hartman feels that the development of democracy is also directly traceable to the anomalous late marriage pattern of northwestern Europe, for state power structures are grounded in household power structures: When the latter changes, the former will, too:

> Long before the contingent nature of the marital contract was recognized in law, marriages were conducted in northwestern Europe as joint enterprises by the two adult members, each of whom had recognized reciprocal duties and obligations. In circumstances that required both members of an alliance to work and postpone marriage until there was a sufficient economic base to establish a household, individual self-reliance was a requirement long before individualism itself became an abstract social and political ideal. A sense of equality of rights was further promoted by such arrangements long before notions of egalitarianism became the popular coin of political movements. These later marriages, forged now through consent by the adult principals, offered themselves as implicit models to the sensibilities of political and religious reformers grappling with questions of authority. Experience in families, which were miniature contract societies unique to northwestern Europe, offers a plausible explanation for popular receptivity to the suggestion that the state itself rests upon a prior and breakable contract with all its members. And if this is so, the influence of family organization on the ways people were coming to conceive and shape the world at large can hardly be exaggerated. The lingering mystery about the origins of a movement of equal rights and individual freedom can be explained. Contrary to notions that these were imported items, it appears that they, along with charity, began at home.
> (*Hartman*, 2004, p. 229)

In a sense, then, the companionate marriages of the late marriage system were a training ground for participatory democracy. To live domestic parity day in and day out, year after year, allowed the majority of individuals in society to appreciate the virtues of voluntary association in larger collectives, including the state. As Hartman puts it, "More important than [class and religious divisions] for the appearance of equality as a popular political ideal was the shared domestic governance most people

has experienced from the Middle Ages" (Hartman, 2004, p. 221).

While Hajnal and Hartman confine themselves to the historical case of Europe, their findings point to a more general thesis of how the mitigation of male dominance hierarchies and structural control of females by males affects important state characteristics. In general, then, according to the Hajnal-Hartman thesis, we expect that in societies that have traveled the path of mitigating structural control over females by males, we will find greater levels of democracy, greater generalized prosperity, greater innovation, and lower levels of violence not only toward women but also toward subnational groups and toward outgroups sharing the same values (Kanazawa, unpublished manuscript). The latter hypothesis has already been corroborated in the field of International Relations, in its empirical confirmation of "democratic peace theory"; however, the Hajnal-Hartman thesis walks the cat back from democracy as the root cause of the democratic peace to its prior precondition, which is the mitigation of the human evolutionary legacy in gender relations (Doyle, 1983; Huth & Allee, 2003; Maoz & Russett, 1993; Ray, 1995). Potts and Hayden note, "Empowered women tend to counterbalance the most chaotic and violent aspects of men's predisposition for brutal territoriality and team aggression... [I]n the human species, the empowerment of women and the possibility of peace and freedom... are united in important and genuine ways" (Potts & Hayden, 2008, p. 329). In the first place, according to the Hajnal-Hartman thesis, that empowerment can only arise with the development of more equitable family law systems. Thus, the family law system adopted by a state should empirically tell us much about its possibilities for freedom, peace, and stability.[8]

Summary of the "Women and Peace" Thesis

To recap our theoretical journey, an FEA approach leads us to the conclusion that the first conflict of interest is that between men and women over reproduction. Male reproductive interests can and often do lead to strategies of sexual coercion of females, including the use of violence. Where female resistance is less effective, for example, when patrilocality deprives women of female kin networks, such strategies will become paramount. Male fraternal alliances offer significant advantages in the sexual coercion strategy, and these may lead to the development of male dominance hierarchies and male monopolization of the economic resources women need to reproduce. Less direct but still effective means of structural control of females will emerge, in the first place regulating female reproduction in the realm of family and personal status law.

Male dominance hierarchies secondarily develop a parasitical approach to resource accumulation, involving, among other things, coalitional aggression against outgroups in order to strip such groups of their resources. Using the functionality of violence in the battle between the sexes as a template, male coalitions extend that strategy to other "others." The coalitions will select for leaders that use violence most effectively. Conflict and warfare with outgroups become endemic.

The mitigation of male dominance hierarchies is thus, we argue, key to the mitigation of dysfunctional, conflictual intergroup relations. Lifting the control and coercion of females attacks the taproot of the dysfunction, and where such amelioration in the security and situation of women has occurred historically, it has been accompanied by a movement toward greater egalitarianism (reflected, for example, in more democratic governance) and a lessening of group initiation of intergroup conflict with others. This is so because the first "other" is always woman, and if one can make peace with the first other without resorting to coercion, one will have templates in place to know how to do so with other "others." The clearest barometer, then, of a collective's predisposition toward peaceful behavior is the security and situation of women within that collective. Such collectives include states.

Empirical Support for the Women and Peace Thesis

What empirical support exists for the "women and peace" thesis? We have already noted the work of Hajnal and Hartman, who show through careful historical process-tracing that a significant diminution of structural control over women in northwestern Europe during the Middle Ages provided the groundwork for the development of a robust participatory democracy in that area, leading eventually to greater peace between nations that international relations scholars term "the democratic peace."

Historical process-tracing is also capable of showing us the reverse. That is, when a society profoundly compromises the security of its women over time, one can see a concomitant decrease in societal stability and state security. An excellent case is point is that of the "bare branches" of China, India, and other Asian nations (Hudson & den Boer, 2004; the following discussion and statistics draw from that source).

Normal birth sex ratios are between 105–107 male babies born for every 100 female babies. Given the advent of ultrasound and other fetal sex identification technologies, demographers have noted sharp upticks in the birth sex ratios of these nations since these technologies became available in the mid-1980s. China, for example, now has a birth sex ratio of approximately 122; in some areas, such as Hainan Island, the birth sex ratio is as high as 136. In India, the birth sex ratio hovers between 133 and 114, again with areas of extremely high birth sex ratios in the north and northwest provinces (in one area, birth sex ratios as high as 156 have been reported). Other nations, such as Vietnam, have birth sex ratios as high as China. Some nations, such as Taiwan and Bangladesh, have birth sex ratios that are abnormal but still below those of India.

The reasons for this phenomenon are a mixture of old and new forces. In all of these areas, we find the historical practice of female infanticide stretching back a millennium or more. Furthermore, whether we speak of Confucian or Vedic texts, the life of a female is explicitly deemed inferior to the life of a male in the normative ideology of the surrounding cultures. The usual structural elements of male reproductive control are also firmly in place in these cultures. Patrilocality and patrilineal inheritance have been the general rule, and chastity of females until very recently has been deemed much more important than their life or death. Neither society has common pension schemes to offset poverty in old age, thereby increasing the value of sons, who, due to patrilineal inheritance, are tasked with the maintenance of elderly parents. In India, though dowry is illegal, dowry costs to marry off a daughter can cripple a family's finances; in China, the one-child policy creates a strong incentive to make sure that offspring are male.

But for every girl child culled from these populations, society is also creating a "bare branch"—a young man who is "surplus" to the number of females in his generational cohort. Current estimates suggest that between 12% and 15% of the young adult male population in China and India are "bare branches." The Chinese government is predicting that there will be 40 million "bare branches" by the year 2020, and with each year's births, the total number of present and future bare branches grows significantly.

The important question from our perspective in this chapter is, What happens in a society where 12%–15% of its young adult males cannot undergo the social and hormonal transition to head of household, having a stake in a system of law that protects his own interests better than he can by his own physical strength?

In our process-tracing effort, we found there were two levels of analysis from which to answer this question. At the level of the bare branches themselves, we find that hypergyny sets in, where young men with advantages will be able to become heads of households, but where poor, low-skilled, undereducated males will not. These young men are already at substantial risk for sociopathic behavior, such as substance abuse and violent crime, and the lack of male social transition predisposes them to take by force what society has denied them otherwise. These young men tend to congregate both on and off their job sites, leading to the formation of young male coalitionary bands, often a source of crime and instability within the society.

As such crime and instability increase, we found that governments are not in the dark about who the perpetrators are. Historically, governments figure out fairly quickly that their bare branches are the source of much of the disruption within their societies. Governments at various times and in various locations have tried a diversity of strategies designed to keep bare branches from threatening government rule. Some of the strategies bring little blowback, such as efforts to promote emigration of young men. Other strategies are associated with increased risks. For example, some governments felt the best way to handle their bare branch problem was to recruit these young men into the military, bloating the size of their armed forces. Unfortunately, these governments soon discovered they were arming and training the very individuals who would use these resources in the most destabilizing fashion. Some chronicles tell how these bare branches were soldiers by day and criminal gang members (or leaders) by night. At times, governments, realizing the risks, would purposefully send their militaries on assignment far from the society's metropoles. Indeed, in more than one case, governments either provoked or exacerbated existing subnational or international conflicts in order to produce simmering wars of attrition that would thin the ranks. Similarly, governments, recognizing they needed to keep the respect of their bare branches, would often use more bellicose rhetoric in foreign policy, becoming ever so sensitive to any perceived slight to the honor of the nation.

In these ways, then, culling girl babies from the population set off a chain of unforeseen and unwanted consequences that undermined the stability of the nation due to increased levels of crime and violence with the society, as well as the potential for increased military conflict and bellicose foreign policy. Decreasing the security of females did in fact decrease the stability and security of nation-states.

While some may treat process-tracing skeptically, viewing it as anecdotal evidence, there are many new aggregate statistical findings that underscore the conclusions of these process-tracing efforts. Marshall and Ramsey (1999) find a relationship between gender empowerment and state willingness to use force. Caprioli (2000; see also 2003, 2004) finds that greater domestic gender equality is correlated with less emphasis by the state on using military force to resolve international disputes. Caprioli and Boyer (2001) find that severity of violence used in an international conflict decreases with greater levels of domestic gender equality. Regan and Paskeviciute (2003) find that the degree of women's access to political power in a society is predictive of the likelihood of that state engaging in interstate disputes and war. Caprioli and Trumbore (2006) find that states with lower levels of gender equality are more likely to be the aggressors and to initiate the use of force in interstate disputes (confirmed by Sobek, Abouharb, & Ingram, 2006). Caprioli and Trumbore (2003) and Melander (2005) find that states with lower levels of domestic gender equality are more likely to be involved in intrastate conflict. Hudson, Caprioli, Ballif-Spanvill, McDermott, and Emmett (2008/2009) find that states with higher levels of violence against women are also less peaceful internationally, less compliant with international norms, and less likely to have good relations with neighboring states and that violence against women is a better predictor of these outcomes than level of democracy, level of wealth, or presence of Islamic civilization. Betzig (1986) and Fish (2002) find authoritarian rule more likely in those states where levels of gender inequality are high.

New analysis, not yet published, is poised to add to what has been already found. Hudson, Bowen, and Nielsen (unpublished data) find that the degree of inequity in family law systems correlates tightly with levels of violence against women. Hudson, den Boer, McDermott, Thayer, and others are investigating the linkage between prevalence of polygyny and measures of state instability, including the emergence of violent extremist groups (see, for example, Thayer and Hudson, 2010). A future project will examine the relationship between the treatment of women and the treatment of ethnic minorities within human societies.

Furthermore, some scholars have also been performing experimental research examining sex differences in negotiating style, strategic choice, and use of force in simulations. Given that nearly all leaders of nation-states are men, this is another way of asking questions about the relationship between sex and national security. Rose McDermott and Jonathan Cowden (2002) examined sex differences in aggression within the context of a simulated crisis game. In these experiments, all-female pairs were significantly less likely than all-male pairs to spend money on weapons procurement or to go to war in the face of a crisis. In further research, McDermott and her coauthors find that in simulation, males are more likely to display overconfidence prior to gaming and are more likely to use unprovoked violence as a tactic (Johnson et al., 2006; see also Boyer et al., 2009).

Much of this research has been aided by new data infrastructure regarding the security and situation of women cross-culturally. For example, the WomanStats Database, begun in 2001, codes for over 300 variables in this regard, making it the most comprehensive compilation of information on women available anywhere in the world today. The database covers 174 nations (those with at least 200,000 population) and has well over 110,000 data points. New information is added every day on the practices, laws, and prevalences of pertinent phenomena across these nations. Innovative scalings and mappings are freely available as well, to anyone with an Internet connection (http://womanstats.org). In other words, in terms of data availability, it's a good time to be asking these types of questions about the relationship between the security of women and the security of states, between violence against women and violence within and between human collectives.

When the First Difference is construed as a battle, men, women, and children all suffer. But it does not have to be that way. We can, indeed, come in out of the rain, no matter how lengthy and "natural" the evolutionary and cultural genealogy of coercion of women has been in human history. By examining the ultimate causal theories of evolution, plus the proximate causal theories of sociology and psychology, we can see how to uproot male dominance hierarchies. The Baha'i say that humanity is like a bird that cannot fly because one of its two wings—women—has been crippled and hurt. It is time to *see* the relationship between the security of women and the security of states, and by seeing, we will know what it is that we must do to ensure a more peaceful world.

In other work, we have argued that the three most important policy issues in the mitigation of male dominance hierarchies are (1) action to prevent violence against women from being functional to men, including attention to socialization and social diffusion forces; (2) reformation of family law to remove persistent elements of structural control of women; and (3) parity in the councils of human decision making at all levels, from the household to the international system (Hudson et al., 2011). These three policy foci represent a counterevolutionary turn in human societies, a purposeful cultural selection for values that cannot be realized within the structural confines of male dominance hierarchies. While an evolutionary approach can give us theoretical insight into the linkages between the security of women and the security of states, it is only by human effort to overcome our common evolutionary legacy that peace may be obtained. Human peace, in the first place, can only be built upon the foundation of peace between the sexes.

Future Directions

There are many possibilities for future research into these key themes of male dominance, aggression, violence against women, and state-level violence. Further exploration of the evolutionary biology literature may offer additional insight into the emergence of male dominance hierarchies and patriarchal structures as well as the mechanisms for mitigating their effects. There is also considerable scope for more empirical research into male dominance, gender-based violence, and state violence through large comparative analyses as well as case studies, and into the consequences of adopting policies that aim to reduce structural control of women.

Notes

1. We recognize that persons in nearly every society, modern and historical, have found ways to modify their assigned gender. However, this involves a very small minority of persons, with gender assignment being otherwise immutable for the overwhelming majority of society (Mahalingam, Haritatos, & Jackson, 2007).

2. Likewise, the actual behavior of specific human beings often defies evolutionary analysis; for example, particular men have been effective spokespersons for better treatment of women.

3. When one turns to evolutionary theory's account of male-female relations formative evolutionary environment (FEE) of tens of thousands of years, one quickly finds two apparently contradictory viewpoints in the theoretical literature. One major

school of thought, exemplified by the work of Wrangham and Peterson (1996), suggests that the FEE produced a generalized social system of male dominance hierarchies, encoding a deep hierarchical relationship between men and women whose long duration surely and profoundly shaped natural selection. However, another school of thought, exemplified by the work of Leacock (1983) suggests that in the hunter-gatherer societies representative of the FEE, there was no generalized male dominance over females, and thus human beings and the collectives they form have not been subject to more than ten millennia of male dominance. Both schools concur that once agriculture and animal husbandry became mainstays of human food systems approximately 10,000 years ago, generalized male dominance did arise globally across human societies (Mies, 1988).

4. Very different social systems can emerge where female networks are in place. Rebecca Hannagan (2008) supports the theory of the cooperative female, arguing that women made a significant contribution toward the development of cooperative groups in hunter-gatherer societies. Women, she argues, may have been supportive of cooperative behavior in order to protect their offspring. Pregnant women, in particular, stood to benefit from food sharing in times of scarcity. "Maintaining certainty in their position in the lunch line, so to speak, is of greater concern to females than males due to the fundamental trade-off between somatic effort and reproductive effort" (2008, p. 469). Female hunter-gatherers are believed to have cooperated with one another for gathering, hunting, and child-rearing, but Hannagan argues that their role as facilitators may have extended to the males and the group as a whole: "in foraging societies women are as likely as men to curb the deviant behavior of 'upstarts'—those who attempt to disrupt the social balance by violating group norms" (2008, p. 469). The sexual freedom and independence of females, Campbell argues, changed with the onset of agriculture 10,000 years ago when women began to be confined to smaller spaces of home and land, and men, who became the suppliers of food and other resources, were able to exercise greater control over women and achieve parental certainty (2006). While male dominance hierarchies may have become entrenched at this time, male aggression and patriarchal practices are argued to have been one of the dominant strategies used in sexual selection during hunter-gatherer periods of human history (Smuts, 1995).

5. We thank *International Security* for permission to reprint here excerpts from the article by Hudson, Caprioli, Ballif-Spanvill, McDermott, & Emmett (2008/2009). We also thank the David M. Kennedy Center for International Studies;, the Department of Political Science;, the College of Family, Home, and Social Sciences;, the Office of Research and Creative Activities;, and all of Brigham Young University, as well as Hunt Alternatives, for their support of the WomanStats Database.

6. Some scholars believe that intense control of females by males only arose after agriculture and animal husbandry developed (see, for example, Mies, 1988), while other scholars, such as Wrangham and Peterson (1996), believe such control stretched unbroken from prehistoric times.

7. It is noteworthy that in some areas of the world, especially in the parts of the Middle East and Sub-Saharan Africa, girls are married as young as 8 even today, in the 21st century. This is a real marriage, not a betrothal of children, and the girl moves to her husband's household, where she is forced to engage in sexual relations with her husband.

8. In a fascinating analysis, Ann Towns demonstrates that European nations systematically stripped women of previously granted rights in the late 18th and 19th centuries, and these events presaged some of the bloodiest wars in the conflict-ridden history of Europe (Towns, 2010).

References

Agacinski, S. (2001). *Parity of the sexes*. New York: Columbia University Press.

Alexander, R. D. (1981). Evolution, culture, and human behavior: Some general considerations. In R. D. Alexander & D. W. Tinkle (Eds.), *Natural selection and social behavior* (pp. 509–520). New York: Chiron Press.

Alexander, R. D., Hoogland, J. L., Howard, R. D., Noonan, K. M., & Sherman, P. W. (1979). Sexual dimorphisms and breeding systems in pinnipeds, ungulates, primates, and humans. In N. A. Chagnon & W. Irons (Eds.), *Evolutionary biology and human behavior* (pp. 402–435). North Scituate, MA: Duxbury Press.

Archer, J. (2009). Does sexual selection explain sex differences in aggression? *Behavioral and Brain Sciences, 32*, 249–311.

Asian Human Rights Commission. (2010). *Pakistan: Sharia court launches major challenge to protection of women act*. Retrieved December 2011, from http://www.ahrchk.net/statements/mainfile.php/2010statements/3010/

Baillargeon, R. H., & Zoccolillo, M., Keenan, K., Cote, S., Perusse, D., Wu, H., et al. (2007). Gender differences in physical aggression: A prospective population-based survey of children before and after 2 years of age. *Developmental Psychology, 43*(1), 13–26.

Ballif-Spanvill, B., Clayton, C., & Hendrix, S. (2003). Gender types of conflict, and individual differences in the use of violent and peaceful strategies among children who have and have not witnessed interparental violence. *American Journal of Orthopsychiatry, 73*(2), 141–153.

Ballif-Spanvill, B., Clayton, C. J., & Hendrix, S. B. (2007). Witness and nonwitness children's violent and peaceful behavior in different types of simulated conflict with peers. *American Journal of Orthopsychiatry, 77*(2), 206–215.

Bernstein, I. S. (1997). Females and feminists, science and politics, evolution and change: An essay. In P. A. Gowaty (Ed.), *Feminism and evolutionary biology: Boundaries, intersections, and frontiers* (pp. 575–582). New York: Chapman and Hall.

Betzig, L. (1986). *Despotism and differential reproduction: A Darwinian view of history*. New York: Aldine de Gruyter.

Bohman, M. (1996). Predisposition to criminality: Swedish adoption studies in retrospect. In G. R. Bock & J. A. Goode (Eds.), *Genetics of criminal and antisocial behavior* (pp. 99–114). West Sussex, England: Wiley.

Boone, J. L. (1983). Noble family structure and expansionist warfare in the late middle ages: A socioecological approach. In R. Dyson-Hudson & M. A. Little (Eds.), *Rethinking human adaptation: Biological and cultural models* (pp. 79–96). Boulder, CO: Westview Press.

Bornstein, R. F. (2006). The complex relationship between dependency and domestic violence: Converging psychological factors and social forces. *American Psychologist, 31*(6), 595–606.

Boyer, M. A., Urlacher, B., Hudson, N. B., Niv-Solomon, A., Janik, L., Butler, M. J., et al. (2009). Gender and negotiations: Some experimental findings from an international negotiation simulation. *International Studies Quarterly, 53*, 23–47.

Brainard, L., & Chollet, D. (Eds.). (2007). *Too poor for peace? Global poverty, conflict, and security in the 21st century*. Washington, DC: The Brookings Institution.

Brewer, M., & Lui, L. (1989). Primacy of age and sex in the structure of person categories. *Social Cognition, 7*(3), 262–274.

Brownmiller, S. (1975). *Against our will: Men, women and rape.* New York: Simon & Schuster.

Cadoret, R. J., Cain, C. A., & Crowe, R. R. (1983). Evidence for gene-environment interaction in the development of adolescent antisocial behavior. *Behavior Genetics, 13*, 301–310.

Cadoret, R. J., Leve, L. D., & Devor, E. (1997). Genetics of aggressive and violent behavior. *Anger, Aggression, and Violence, 20*, 2, 301–322.

Campbell, A. (2006). Sex differences in direct aggression: What are the psychological mediators? *Aggression and Violent Behavior, 11*(3), 237–264.

Caprioli, M. (2000). Gendered conflict. *Journal of Peace Research, 37*, 51–68.

Caprioli, M. (2003). Gender equality and state aggression: The impact of domestic gender equality on state first use of force. *International Interactions, 29*, 195–214.

Caprioli, M. (2004). Democracy and human rights versus women's security: A contradiction? *Security Dialogue: Special Issue Gender and Security, 35*(4), 411–428.

Caprioli, M. (2005). Primed for violence: The role of gender inequality in predicting internal conflict. *International Studies Quarterly, 49*, 161–178

Caprioli, M., & Boyer, M. A. (2001). Gender, violence, and international crisis. *Journal of Conflict Resolution, 45*, 503–518.

Caprioli, M., Hudson, V. M., McDermott, R., Ballif-Spanvill, B., Emmett, C. F., & Stearmer, S. M. (2009). The WomanStats project database: Advancing an empirical research agenda. *Journal of Peace Research, 46*, 6, 1–13.

Caprioli, M., & Trumbore, P. F. (2003). Identifying 'rogue' states and testing their interstate conoict behavior. *European Journal of International Relations, 9*, 3, 377–406.

Caprioli, M., & Trumbore, P. F. (2006). Human rights rogues in interstate disputes, 1980–2001. *Journal of Peace Research, 43*(2), 131–148;

Chagnon, N. A. (1988). Life histories, blood revenge, and warfare in a tribal population. *Science, 239*, 985–992.

Clayton, C. J., Barlow, S. H., & Ballif-Spanvill, B. (1999). Principles of group violence with a focus on terrorism. In H. V. Hall & L. C. Whitaker (Eds.), *Collective violence: Effective strategies for assessing and interviewing in fatal group and institutional aggression* (pp. 277–311). Boca Raton, FL: CRC Press.

Cockburn, C. (2001). The gendered dynamics of armed conflict and political violence. In C.O. N. Moser & F. C. Clark (Eds.), *Victims, perpetrators or actors?: Gender, armed conflict, and political violence* (pp. 13–29). New York: Zed Books.

Cummings, E. M., Goeke-Morey, M. C., & Papp, L. M. (2004). Everyday marital conflict and child aggression. *Journal of Abnormal Child Psychology, 32*, 191–202.

Derrida, J. (1978). *Writing and difference.* London: Routledge.

Divale, W., & Harris, M. (1976). Population, warfare, and the male supremacist complex. *American Anthropologist, 78*, 521–538.

Doyle, M. W. (1983). Kant, liberal legacies, and foreign affairs. *Philosophy and Public Affairs, 12*(3), 205–235.

Edleson, J. L. (1999). Children's witnessing of adult domestic violence. *Journal of Interpersonal Violence, 14*, 849–870.

Elshtain, J. B. (1987). *Women and war.* New York: Basic Books.

Erchak, G. M. (1997). Family violence. In C. R. Ember & M. Ember (Eds.), *Research frontiers in anthropology. Vol. 4: Ethnology, linguistic anthropology, the study of social problems* (pp. 95–112). Englewood Cliffs, NJ: Prentice Hall.

Erchak, G. M., & R. Rosenfeld. (1994). Societal isolations, violent norms, and gender relations: a re-examination and extension of Levinson's model of wife beating. *Cross-Cultural Research, 28*(2), 111–133.

Fabes, R. A., Martin, C. L., & Hanish, L. D. (2003). Young children's play qualities in the same-other and mixed-sex peer groups. *Child Development, 74*(3), 921–932.

Fish, S. M. (2002). Islam and authoritarianism. *World Politics, 55*(1), 4–37.

Fiske, S., & Neuberg S. (1990). A continuum of impression formation, from category—based to individuating processes: Influences of information and motivation on attention and interpretation. *Advances in Experimental Social Psychology, 23*, 1–74.

Galtung, J. (1975). *Peace: Research, education, action: Essays in peace research, volume one.* Bucuresti, Romania: CIPEXIM.

Galtung, J. (1990). Cultural violence. *Journal of Peace Research, 27*(3), 291–305.

Gat, A. (2006). *War in human civilization.* Oxford, England: Oxford University Press.

Gat, A. (2009). So why do people fight? Evolutionary theory and the causes of war. *European Journal of International Relations, 15*(4), 571–600.

Ge, X., Conger, R. D., Cadoret, R. J., Neiderhiser, J. M., Yates, W., Troughton, E., & Stewart, M. A. (1996). The developmental interface between nature and nurture: A mutual influence model of child antisocial behavior and parent behaviors. *Developmental Psychology, 33*, 2, 574–589.

Gowaty, P. A. (1992). Evolutionary biology and feminism. *Human Nature, 3*(3), 217–249.

Gowaty, P. A. (Ed.). (1997). *Feminism and evolutionary biology.* New York: Chapman.

Gowaty, P. A. (2003). Sexual natures: How feminism changed evolutionary biology. *Signs: Journal of Women in Culture and Society, 28*(3), 901–921.

Graham-Bermann, S. A. (1998). The impact of woman abuse on children's social development: Research and theoretical perspectives. In G. W. Holden & R. Geffner (Eds.), *Children exposed to marital violence: Theory, research, and applied issues* (pp. 21–54). Washington, DC: American Psychological Association.

Greene, J. P., & Pole J. R. (Eds.). (1983). *Colonial British America: Essays in the new history of the early modern era.* Baltimore: The Johns Hopkins University Press.

Hajnal, J. (1965). European marriage patterns in perspective. In D. V. Glass & D. E. C. Eversley (Eds.), *Population in History: Essays in Historical Demography* (pp. 101–143). London: Arnold.

Hajnal, J. (1982). Two kinds of preindustrial household formation systems. *Population and Development Review, 8*, 470–482.

Hannagan, R. J. (2008). Gendered political behavior: A Darwinian feminist approach. *Sex Roles, 59*, 465–475.

Harris, M. (1993). The evolution of human gender hierarchies. In B. D. Miller (Ed.), *Sex and gender hierarchies* (pp. 57–79). Cambridge, England: Cambridge University Press.

Hartman, M. (2004). *The household and the making of history: A subversive view of the Western past.* Cambridge, England: Cambridge University Press.

Homer-Dixon, T. (2001). *Environment, scarcity, and violence.* Princeton, NJ: Princeton University Press.

Hudson, V. M., Ballif-Spanvill, B., Caprioli, M., & Emmett, C. (2011). *Sex and world peace: Roots and wings of international relations.* New York: Columbia University Press.

Hudson, V. M., Caprioli, M., Ballif-Spanvill, B., McDermott, R., & Emmett, C. F. (2008/2009). The heart of the matter: The security of women and the security of states. *International Security, 33*(3), 7–45.

Hudson, V.M., Bowen, D.L., & Nielsen, P.L. (2011). What is the relationship between inequity in family law and violence against women? Approaching the issue of legal enclaves. *Politics & Gender, 7*(4), 453–492.

Hudson, V., & den Boer, A. (2004). *Bare branches: The security implications of Asia's surplus male population*. Cambridge, MA: MIT Press.

Hunt, S., & Posa, C. (2001, May/June). Women waging peace. *Foreign Policy*, p. 38–47.

Huntington, S. P. (1996). *The clash of civilizations and the remaking of world order*. New York: Simon & Schuster.

Huth, P., & Allee, T. (2003). *The democratic peace and territorial conflict in the twentieth century*. Cambridge, England: Cambridge University Press.

Hyde, J. S. (2007). New directions in the study of gender similarities and differences. *Current Directions in Psychological Science, 16*(5), 259–263.

Johnson, D., McDermott, R., Barrett, E., Cowden, J., Wrangham, R., McIntyre, M., & Rosen, S. (2006). Overconfidence in wargames: Experimental evidence on expectations, aggression, gender, and testosterone. *Proceedings of the Royal Society of London B: Biological Sciences, 273*, 2513–2520.

Kanazawa, S. (2009). Evolutionary psychological foundations of civil wars. *The Journal of Politics, 71*(1), 25–34.

Kemper, T. D. (1990). *Social structure and testosterone*. New Brunswick, NJ: Rutgers University Press.

Kurzban, R., Tooby, J., & Cosmides, L. (2001). Can race be "erased"? Coalitional computation and social categorization. *Proceedings of the National Academy of Sciences USA, 98*(22), 15387–15392.

Leacock, E. (1983). Interpreting the origins of gender inequality: Conceptual and historical problems. *Dialectical Anthropology, 7*(4), 263–284.

Levinson, D. (1989). *Family violence in cross-cultural perspective*. Newbury Park, CA: Sage Publications.

Lopreato, J. (1984). *Human nature and biocultural evolution*. Boston: Allen & Unwin.

Mahalingam, R., Haritatos, J., & Jackson, B. (2007), Essentialism and the cultural psychology of gender in extreme son preference communities in India. *The American Journal of Orthopsychiatry, 77*(4), 598–609.

Maoz, Z., & Russett, B. (1993). Normative and structural causes of democratic peace, 1946–1986. *American Political Science Review, 87*, 624–638.

Margolin, G., & Gordis, E. B. (2000). The effects of family and community violence on children. *Annual Review of Psychology, 51*, 445–479.

Marshall, M. G., & Ramsey, D. (1999). *Gender empowerment and the willingness of states to use force*. Unpublished research paper, Center for Systemic Peace. Retrieved December 2011, from http://www.systemicpeace.org/CSPpaper2.pdf

McDermott, R., & Cowden, J. (2002). The effects of uncertainty and sex in a crisis simulation game. *International Interactions, 27*(4), 353–380.

Melander, E. (2005). Gender equality and interstate armed conflict. *International Studies Quarterly, 49*(4), 95–714.

Messick, S., & Mackie, D. (1989). Intergroup relations. *Annual Review of Psychology, 40*, 45–81.

Mies, M. (1988). Social origins of the sexual division of labor. In M. Mies, V. Bennholdt-Thomsen, & C. Von Werlhof (Eds.), *Women: The last colony* (pp. 67–95). London: Zed Books.

Miller, B. D. (1993). The anthropology of sex and gender hierarchies. In B. D. Miller (Ed.), *Sex and gender hierarchies* (pp. 3–31). Cambridge, England: Cambridge University Press.

Munroe, R. L., & Romney, A. K. (2006). Gender and age differences in the same-sex aggregation and social behaviors: A four-culture study. *Journal of Cross-Cultural Psychology, 37*(1), 3–19.

Norris, P., & Inglehart, R. (2003, March/April). The true clash of civilizations. *Foreign Policy*, p. 62–70.

Ostrov, J. M., & Keating, C. F. (2004). Gender differences in preschool aggression during free play and structured interaction: An observational study. *Social Development, 13*(2), 255–277.

Papanek, H. (1990). To each less than she needs, from each more than she can do: Allocations, entitlements, and value. In I. Tinker (Ed.), *Persistent inequalities: Women and world development* (pp. 162–181). New York and Oxford, England: Oxford University Press.

Patterson, G. R. (2008). A comparison of models for interstate war and for individual violence. *Perspectives on Psychological Science, 3*(3), 203–223.

Peterson, V. S. (1998). Gendered national: Reproducing "us" versus "them." In L. A. Lorentzen & J. Turpin (Eds.), *The women and war reader* (pp. 41–49). New York: New York University Press.

Potts, M., & Hayden, T. (2008). *Sex and war*. Dallas, TX: Benbella Books.

Pound, N., Daly M., & Wilson, M. (2009). There's no contest: Human sex differences are sexually selected. *Behavioral and Brain Sciences, 32*(3/4), 286–287.

Ray, J. L. (1995). *Democracy and international conflict: An evaluation of the democratic peace proposition*. Columbia: University of South Carolina Press.

Raymond, G. A. (2000). International norms: Normative orders and peace. In J. A. Vasquez (Ed.), *What do we know about war* (pp. 281–297). New York: Rowman & Littlefield.

Reardon, B. (1985). *Sexism and the war system*. New York: Teachers College Press.

Regan, P. M., & Paskeviciute, A. (2003). Women's access to politics and peaceful states. *Journal of Peace Research, 40*, 287–302.

Rosen, S. (2005). *War and human nature*. Princeton, NJ: Princeton University Press

Rosser, S. V. (1997). Possible implications of feminist theories for the study of evolution. In P. A. Gowaty (Ed.), *Feminism and evolutionary biology: Boundaries, intersections, and frontiers* (pp. 21–41). New York: Chapman & Hall.

Ruddick, S. (1995). *Maternal thinking: Towards a politics of peace*. New York: Beacon Press.

Sjoberg, L. (2009). *Gender and international security: Feminist perspectives*. New York: Routledge.

Smuts, B. (1992). Male aggression against women: An evolutionary perspective. *Human Nature, 3*(1), 1–44.

Smuts, B. (1995). The evolutionary origins of patriarchy. *Human Nature, 6*(1), 1–32.

Sobek, D., Abouharb, M. R., & Ingram, C. G. (2006). The human rights peace: How the respect for human rights at home leads to peace abroad. *The Journal of Politics, 68*(3), 519–529.

Stephen, A. (2008, May 22). Hating Hillary. *The New Statesman.* http://www.newstatesman.com/north-america/2008/05/obama-clinton-vote-usa-media

Tang-Martinez, Z. (1997). The curious courtship of sociobiology and feminism: A case of irreconcilable difference. In P. A. Gowaty (Ed.), *Feminism and evolutionary biology: Boundaries, intersections, and frontiers* (pp. 116–150). New York: Chapman & Hall.

Tessler, M., & Warriner, I. (1997). Gender, feminism, and attitudes toward international conflict. *World Politics, 49,* 250–281.

Thayer, B. (2004). *Darwin and international relations: On the evolutionary origins of war and ethnic conflict.* Lexington: University of Kentucky Press.

Thayer, B. A., & Hudson, V. M. (2010). Sex and the Shaheed: Insights from the life sciences of Islamic suicide terrorism. *International Security, 34*(4), 37–62.

Tickner, J. A. (1992). *Gender in international relations: Feminist perspectives on achieving global security.* New York: Columbia University Press.

Tickner, J. A. (2001). *Gendering world politics.* New York: Columbia University Press.

Trivers, R. L. (1972). Parental investment and sexual selection. In B. Campbell (Ed.), *Sexual selection and the descent of man, 1871–1971* (pp. 136–179). Chicago: Aldine.

Towns, A. (2010). *Women and states: Norms and hierarchies in international society.* Cambridge, England: Cambridge University Press.

Waage, J. K., & Gowaty, P. A. (1997). Myths of genetic determinism. In P. A. Gowaty (Ed.), *Feminism and evolutionary biology: Boundaries, intersections, and frontiers* (pp. 585–614). New York: Chapman & Hall.

Wilson, M., Daly, M., & Scheib, J. (1997). Femicide: An evolutionary psychological perspective. In P. A. Gowaty (Ed.), *Feminism and evolutionary biology: Boundaries, intersections, and frontiers* (pp. 431–465). New York: Chapman & Hall.

Wrangham, R., & Peterson, D. (1996). *Demonic males: Apes and the origins of human violence,* New York: Mariner Books

Wright, R. (1995). *The moral animal.* New York: Vintage.

CHAPTER 19

War Histories in Evolutionary Perspective: Insights From Prehistoric North America

Patricia M. Lambert

Abstract

This chapter takes an evolutionary perspective on the causes of violence and warfare in prehistoric North America. Three culture areas of western North America—the Santa Barbara Channel Area of southern California, the Four Corners region of the American Southwest, and the northeastern Great Plains—provide geographic foci for exploring the relationship between environmental variables and levels and types of violence as indicated by archaeological settlement data and injuries in human skeletal remains. All three regions reveal an association between unpredictable, drought-prone conditions and the escalation of serious warfare during the Late Prehistoric period (ca. AD 1000–1500). In all three areas males emerge as the primary, though not exclusive, targets in violent conflict and to the extent ascertainable, also its primary participants. These data shed light on environmental contexts that may be conducive to war, and they support a multitiered explanatory model of warfare causation ultimately rooted in the evolutionary history of our ancestors.

Key Words: archaeology, bioarchaeology, California, Great Plains, human skeletal remains, North America, prehistoric warfare, projectile injuries, Southwest, violence

Introduction

This chapter uses archaeological data from three regions of western North America to explore the utility of a multilevel theoretical approach to the study of warfare. This research addresses two fundamental problems with the application of evolutionary theory to the study of recent and modern warfare: the lack of time depth and the deviation of modern environments from those characterizing the environment of evolutionary adaptation. While there is no dearth of war stories emerging from global newsrooms, and though historical documents may extend this record of human conflict back several centuries, these records nonetheless pertain to a social landscape very different in some important respects from that occupied by humans over most of our evolutionary history. Technological advancements and the development of state-level political systems have depersonalized warfare, making it more difficult to study causation from the perspective of the individuals on whom natural selection acts. Given the nature of modern military organization, the motivations of those actually engaged in field combat may be quite distinct from the motivations of decision makers in control of military engagements, raising important questions about the extent to which the causes of modern warfare have roots in our evolutionary past.

This is one advantage of the archaeological record, which can provide a broad window on human behavior before the ages of exploration, discovery, and industry—back to a time when warfare was more intimate and the causal links less complicated by modern technology and state-level bureaucracy. Archaeology can provide a longitudinal perspective on human behavior across political and economic transitions and in relation to environmental stimuli such as climate change and population-resource imbalances. This record presents an opportunity to step back from the complex causal narratives that surround our understanding of recent and modern wars to look instead for diachronic and cross-cultural patterns in the data. This is the perspective pursued in this chapter, focusing in particular on the archaeological record of western North America.

Not all scholars agree on the definition of warfare, so it is essential to begin with a working definition for this inquiry. Here warfare is defined as "a state or period of armed hostility existing between politically autonomous communities" (Meggitt, 1977, p. 10). This definition includes small-scale forms of engagement, such as raiding and ambush, that tend to characterize band and tribal warfare (e.g., Boehm, 1984; Chagnon, 1992; Fadiman, 1982; Keeley, 1996; Meggitt, 1977; Rice & LeBlanc, 2001), as well as the battles and other forms of open engagement more typical of larger, more complex polities (e.g., Keegan, 1993; Keeley, 1996; Keen, 1999)—although surprise attacks such as the 9/11 air raids are evidence that military strategies are not necessarily defined by the size or political power of aggressors or targets. Raids and other forms of surprise attack can be further differentiated from open battles according to the relative importance of power imbalances (fundamental in raiding) and the willingness of both sides to engage in fighting (more characteristic of battles) (Wrangham, 1999, 2004). Based on studies of warfare in modern prestate societies (e.g., Chagnon, 1992; Keeley, 1996; Radcliffe-Brown, 1948; Wrangham, 2004), raiding and other strategies of limited engagement would likely have predominated in the prestate political landscape of prehistoric North America, the geographic focus of this chapter, so it is critical to have a working definition of war in keeping with its expected expression in the archaeological record of this region.

A cursory review of the warfare literature reveals widely varying perspectives on its causes that range from those seeking larger and more inclusive explanations (e.g., LeBlanc, 1999; Wrangham, 2004) to those focusing on the cause of a specific battle or war (e.g., McPherson, 1997). In part, this reflects different interests and goals of individual scholars and disciplines. A military scientist, for example, is likely to focus on strategies and outcomes, whereas a historian might emphasize the importance of a sequence of events. These divergent perspectives are not mutually exclusively or even conflicting, however. Instead, they suggest that warfare causation may be best understood as a nested series of increasingly specific causes that span the spectrum from proximate events that trigger a violent response to the ultimate evolutionary forces that underlie human aggression. A trigger might be an incident as singular as the discharge of a firearm, a rebellion such as the Boston Tea Party, the suspicious death of a leader, or a lethal raid such as the 9/11 attacks. The immediate response to the incident could be fight, flight, or negotiation. Which of these is selected and what follows relate at least in part to the history of relationships between groups involved in the incident: whether these are generally amicable, mutually dependent, or hostile, and if there have been previous incidents. The broader history of relations might be such that there is long-standing enmity between groups, perhaps an ongoing cycle of feuding, long-standing inequities, or a history of previous wars.

These broader historical patterns of interaction may in turn be related to conditions in the physical and/or social environment that impact access to critical resources essential for survival. Environmental stressors such as drought and resource depletion are powerful selective forces that act on individuals, populations, and species, and they would have played an important role in the evolution of human behavior. Therefore, these stressors might be expected to stimulate powerful responses, such as increased territoriality and aggressive defense, which have been successful in the history of our species.

Ultimately, there must reside in the human behavioral suite the capacity and bio-behavioral triggering mechanisms for an aggressive response, and this response is likely to have much deeper evolutionary roots (c.f., Archer, 2009). A historical and global view of warfare reveals one particularly pertinent observation in regard to the evolutionary underpinnings of violent aggression: War is a predominantly male activity (c.f., Keegan, 1993; Keeley, 1996; Keen, 1999; Lambert, 1994; Wrangham, 2004). This is also true of violent assault and homicide (e.g., Daly & Wilson, 1988), although females certainly can be aggressive—particularly in mating contexts (e.g., Lienard, 2011) and do sometimes participate in these violent activities (Daly & Wilson, 1990). This male-centered pattern of violent aggression is not surprising given that human males have a greater biological capacity for an aggressive response in terms of both anatomy and behavior (Archer, 2009; Puts, 2010; see also Johnson et al., 2006). A review of aggressive behavior in primate species suggests that male aggression is strongly linked to intrasexual mating competition (e.g., Archer, 2009; Hohmann & Fruth, 2003; Puts, 2010; Wolovich, Evans, & Green, 2010; Wrangham & Peterson,

1996) and thus to Darwinian fitness. In chimpanzees, the primate species with the closest phylogenetic relationship to humans, intrasexual aggression most commonly finds sublethal expression in competitions among males within a social group (de Waal, 1982, 1989) and lethal expression in territorial competitions between groups of allied males (Nishida & Hiraiwa-Hasegawa, 1987; Wrangham, 2004; Wrangham & Peterson, 1996). From this perspective, human aggression may be viewed as a primitive behavior shaped by natural selection to enhance reproductive outcomes through increased survivorship and access to mating opportunities essential to long-term reproductive success. It is a behavioral strategy that, while potentially costly, can be very successful for individuals and their kin (Lambert, 1994; Puts, 2010; Wrangham, 2004).

Archaeology is not a particularly useful approach to the study of the more proximate causes of war as outlined earlier, due to the palimpsest nature of the archaeological record. Seldom is a specific event identifiable, unless it is tied to historic accounts. For example, cranial trauma and scalp marks in 11 European males buried at Fort Laurens, Ohio, provide tangible evidence of an 18th-century ambush by local Native Americans described in historic accounts (e.g., Williamson, Johnston, Symes, & Schultz, 2003), but in the absence of historic records the ambush and the historical sequence of events that led to it would not be identifiable. The archaeological record is more amenable to the study of midlevel causation—that related to conditions (or preconditions) in the physical and social environment in which warfare tends to occur. These can be good proxies for economic conditions and thus for examining materialist aspects of war of relevance to evolutionary models. The significance of environmental conditions is often missed in the study of modern warfare because the focus tends to be on traumatic triggering events such as the 9/11 attacks, rather than on the economic and social conditions that may have encouraged young men to participate in those attacks. The archaeological record can also provide information about the age and sex of victims and participants in war, and thus potentially expand our understanding of the fundamental biobehavioral aspects of human aggression and thus of foundational evolutionary causation.

Reconstructing War in the Archaeological Record

Four categories of evidence figure prominently in the archaeological investigation of warfare: settlement data, injuries in human skeletal remains, war weaponry, and iconography (Lambert, 2002, 2007; LeBlanc, 1999; Rice & LeBlanc, 2001; Vencl, 1984). The first two form the focus of this chapter. Settlement data pertain to where people live and how they manipulate their landscape, and they are used to identify concern with defense. Defensive behavior visible in the archaeological record includes shifts in village locations from valley floors with ready access to water and agricultural fields to steep slopes, inaccessible rock shelters, mesa tops, islets, and other refuges requiring greater energy expenditure for day-to-day living (e.g., Haas & Creamer, 1993; Moss & Erlandson, 1992). Population aggregation in larger, more compact settlements also may signal increased concern with defense (e.g., Haas & Creamer, 1993), particularly where economic benefit is not evident, because aggregation has similar energy costs as well as health risks associated with disease exposure and social tensions. Walls, forts, towers, moats, and other defensive structures are costly to build and maintain, so their appearance should also correlate with a perceived need for defense sufficient to warrant reallocation of resources (Lambert, 2002; LeBlanc, 1999). The burning of structures, on the other hand, is a common consequence of war (e.g., Hoig, 1993; Holliman & Owsley, 1994; Rice & LeBlanc, 2001; Willey, 1990), and evidence of burned structures can therefore help document actual attacks, although other possible causes of burning (e.g., accidental fires, intentional clearing) must also be considered (e.g., Kuckelman, 2010).

Injuries in human skeletal remains provide more direct evidence of the impact of war on individuals and groups. Though archaeological population samples are generally quite small in comparison to those used in modern studies, relative proportions can provide an empirical basis for establishing the frequency and prevalence of different types of violence. Several types of injuries tend to occur in the context of physical conflict and thus serve as proxies for violence and warring behavior, including projectile injuries, depressed cranial vault fractures from clubbing implements, cut marks and other signs of trophy taking, and body mutilation. The most definitive of these are injuries from a projectile weapon such as a spear, atlatl & dart, bow & arrow or gun, particularly where projectiles (e.g., arrow tips, bullets) remain embedded in bone or are discovered between skeletal elements or within body cavities. The lethal capacity of these weapons implies intent to kill, and indeed these weapons are those most commonly employed by modern hunter-gatherers and tribal peoples in warring contexts (e.g., Chagnon, 1992; Fadiman, 1982; Koch, 1974; Meggitt, 1977). Studies of warfare practices and the impacts of weapons on the human body in modern groups provide a basis for reconstructing warfare from the skeletal remains of its victims (e.g., Lambert, 1994). For example, using medical data from the American Indian Wars (Bill, 1862; Haines, 1994), Milner (2005) discovered that on average only one in three arrows actually strikes bone in bow and arrow warfare, a figure suggesting that for every projectile wound observed in bone, two others were sustained. Clubbing injuries to the skull, face, ribs, and forearms can be used to identify close-range, hand-to-hand engagements that may be associated with warfare (c.f. Ames & Maschner, 1999), but they may also occur in other types of conflict (c.f., Chagnon, 1992; Lambert, 1994, 1999, 2002; Walker, 1989). Among the Yanomamö, horticulturalists of the Amazon Basin, most head injuries are incurred by men in the context of nonlethal club fights that serve as a mechanism for dispute resolution—often involving women (Chagnon, 1992). In other contexts, such as several noted later in this chapter, clubbing implements may be used for highly lethal conflict; the size, location, and healing status of cranial injuries can be used to differentiate sublethal from lethal intent (c.f., Lambert, 1994). Trophy taking sometimes occurs in war and can be identified in the archaeological record through evidence of decapitation, scalps, scalping cut marks, missing limbs, and human bone artifacts (Andrushkov, Schwitalla, & Walker, 2010; Chacon & Dye, 2007; Owsley & Jantz, 1994). Corpse mutilation and cannibalism, as indicated by extensive perimortem bone breakage, cut marks, anvil abrasions, and burning (Lambert, Billman, & Leonard, 2000; Turner & Turner, 1999; White, 1992), have also been associated with warfare in some contexts (e.g., Billman, Lambert, & Leonard, 2000; Kuckelman, Lightfoot, & Martin, 2002) and may signal intergroup aggression as well as attitudes toward enemy groups.

There are a number of other types of skeletal evidence that may also be used to identify and reconstruct patterns of violence. Carnivore tooth marks and other signs of corpse exposure provide evidence that a body was not protected from the elements, as usually occurs when people die of illness or accidental injury, and therefore may signal violent death (e.g., Milner, Anderson, & Smith, 1991; Lambert, 1999; Willey, 1990). Victim profiles can identify those at risk and help sort out the nature of violence (e.g., Lambert, 1994; Milner, 1999; Milner et al., 1991). Population profiles derived from skeletal series may reveal population-level impacts of war, such as the loss of young males killed in battle or young women captured by enemies (e.g., Hurst & Turner, 1993; Willey, 1990). The archaeological context in which skeletons are found may also provide evidence as to the nature of the death: whether in a flexed position with accompanying burial goods, for example, or sprawled on a house floor.

All of these lines of evidence are used to reconstruct patterns of violence in the past. In combination, they can provide compelling evidence for the existence, prevalence, and conduct of war in the absence of written records.

The Archaeological Record of Warfare in North America

The archaeological record of North America reveals a long history of violent conflict and war dating back thousands of years and involving human groups from the arctic regions of Alaska in the far north to the highland civilizations of tropical Mexico (Ames & Maschner, 1999; Bridges, Jacobi, & Powell, 2000; Hassig, 1992; Lambert, 2002; LeBlanc, 1999; Melbye & Fairgrieve, 1994; Milner, 1999; Moss & Erlandson, 1992). One of the earliest known victims of violence (although not necessarily warfare) is Kennewick Man, a Paleoamerican from the Columbia Plateau who survived a projectile wound to the hip approximately 9,500 years ago (Preston, 1997; Slayman, 1997). While it would be erroneous to suggest that violence and warfare were ubiquitous in prehistoric North America from the time of the Paleoamericans, and though the evidence in earlier time periods in particular is at times sporadic, it is nonetheless difficult to identify a region that did not have warfare at some point in the prehistoric past. In recent years, a number of literature reviews have sought to synthesize the evidence of prehistoric violence and warfare in various North American culture areas (e.g., Bridges et al., 2000; Chacon & Mendoza, 2007; Lambert, 2002; LeBlanc, 1999; Milner, 1999; Rice & LeBlanc, 2001). These have revealed substantial evidence for intergroup violence across the North American landscape but also considerable temporal and geographic variability in levels and types of violence (Lambert, 2002, 2007). This variability supports the hypothesis that the human propensity for war may be linked to conditions in the physical and/or social environment that invoke or predispose people to a violent response, a relationship that is explored in greater detail later in this chapter.

This survey is not meant to provide a comprehensive review of the North American evidence, or even of the three culture areas discussed later (for that see Bridges et al., 2000; Lambert, 2002, 2007; LeBlanc, 1999; Milner, 1999). Rather, each section addresses the nature and extent of violence, the evidence for a relationship between environmental stressors and war, and the demographics of participants and victims in each region with the goal of addressing causal factors in North American warfare and of violent conflict in humans more generally.

Santa Barbara Channel Area, California

One region where warfare history has been well studied from both chronological and environmental perspectives is the Santa Barbara Channel area of coastal southern California, comprising the Northern Channel Islands and the adjacent mainland coast from Gaviota in the west to Point Magu in the east (Kennett, 1998; Kennett & Kennett, 2000; Lambert, 1994, 1997; Lambert & Walker, 1991; Walker, 1989; Walker & Lambert, 1989). The hunter-gatherers of this region lived in semisedentary villages; exploited a range of marine and wild terrestrial resources; built ocean-going plank canoes for fishing, transport, and trade; manufactured shell beads and bead money (Arnold, 1991, 1992, 1993; Kennett, 1998); and buried their dead in cemeteries. The act of interment, as well as natural conditions conductive to preservation, has resulted in a skeletal record of health and injury spanning over 7,500 years that can be used to reconstruct levels, types, and contexts of violence (and peace) over the millennia (Lambert, 1994, 1997; Lambert & Walker, 1991; Walker, 1989; Walker & Lambert, 1989). Settlement systems are also well preserved on the (largely) undisturbed islands of Santa Cruz and Santa Rosa, so it has been possible through survey and excavation to reconstruct changing land use and social relations (e.g., Arnold, 1990; Kennett, 1998; Kennett & Kennett, 2000). In addition, paleoclimatic data from tree rings and sea cores obtained for the region provide a proxy record of precipitation and temperature that can be used to identify time periods that would have been conducive (high precipitation) or detrimental (drought) to the resource base of this semiarid region (Kennett, 1998; Kennett & Kennett, 2000; Lambert, 1994; Raab & Larsen, 1997). In combination, these data sources make it possible to address the goals of this chapter in determining when, how, and why people went to war in the region prehistorically.

In the early 1990s, the author conducted a study of health and violent injury in a sample of 1,744 individuals from 30 archaeological sites spanning a 7,500-year period from this region (Lambert, 1994, 1997). Patterns of violence were reconstructed using data on cranial vault fractures and projectile injuries. The goal of the study was to document both sublethal and lethal forms of violence as indicated by injuries in human skeletal remains to test several models of warfare causation. Foremost among these was a materialist model positing a relationship between resource stress and increased violence and warfare (as per Ferguson, 1989; Harris, 1984; see also Wrangham, 2004, pp. 32–33).

The most common form of intentional injury identified in the Santa Barbara Channel area skeletal remains is healed depression fractures to the cranial vault from some sort of clubbing implement (see also Walker, 1989). Most are small and round, suggesting the use of rounded, possibly wooden clubs. Overall, healed cranial fractures are present in about 17% of individuals with relatively complete (scorable) skulls (128/753). Of those affected, 95% are adult—although some of their injuries may have been sustained in adolescence (Lambert 1997). Though affecting individuals from all time periods, healed cranial injuries are not equally distributed across time. In adults, they are least common (12.3%) in the earliest inhabitants (5500–1600 BC[1]), most prevalent (24.1%) in those of the Middle period (ca. 1600 BC–AD 1350[1])—particularly in males (31.5%), and less common (15.8%) again in skeletons dating to the final centuries before European contact (Lambert, 1994, 1997). Males are almost twice as likely (23.8%) as females (13.5%) to have sustained this type of cranial fracture, with most incurred between the ages of 10 and 26 years (Lambert, 1994). These findings indicate that adolescent and young adult males were the primary participants in activities leading to depressed cranial vault fractures. Injuries in males tend to concentrate on the forehead, a pattern reminiscent of injuries sustained in the ritualized club fights of Yanomamö men (Chagnon, 1992; Lambert, 1994; Walker, 1989), which suggests that males engaged in a face-to-face form of sublethal conflict resolution that involved delivering or trading blows to the head. The increase in the frequency of these injuries in the Middle period further implies that disputes leading to these encounters became more common after 1600 BC. This shift corresponds to an increase in the size of the population and a concomitant shift to more intensive subsistence strategies (Kennett,

1998; Lambert, 1994), socioeconomic conditions that would be predicted to cause an increase in social tensions. Female injury frequencies follow a similar temporal pattern but their injuries are more equally distributed about the head than in males, suggesting a distinct and possibly more domestic context for sustaining these injuries (Lambert, 1994, 1997).

A few lethal (blunt force) cranial fractures are also present in these remains (1.7% of 753 crania). Most date to the time period when healed cranial injuries peak and affect a similar ratio of males to females (2:1). However, there are some notable differences. Lethal cranial fractures are generally larger than healed injuries and tend to be located on the side and back of the skull, a distribution that contrasts with the frontal location of many healed cranial fractures. In at least 7 of 10 recorded cases, individuals with a perimortem (occurring around the time of death) cranial vault fracture also have one or more projectile injuries, indicating that the intent (and thus context) of these blows was distinct from that associated with healed cranial injuries (Lambert, 1994) and more strongly aligned with that described later in this chapter.

There is considerable evidence for a more common form of lethal violence in this region involving the use of projectile weapons (Lambert, 1994). The type of weaponry used for this purpose varied through time, from spears and possibly atlatls before about AD 800–900[1] to the bow and arrow thereafter—some 200 years after its apparent initial introduction into the region.[1] This shift in the technology of warfare changed the nature of lethal conflict by increasing both range and killing capacity (Blitz, 1988; Lambert, 1994). A total of 118 projectile injuries in 58 victims (3.3%) was identified in the sample of 1,744 individuals for which skeletal remains and/or burial excavation records were available for analysis. While not all were fatal, as indicated by the healing status of individual wounds, most victims (>72%) appear to have died from their injuries, an unsurprising finding given the nature of the sample (i.e., a death assemblage). Of those individuals for whom age could be determined, 4 were adolescents (1.2% of 345 subadults) and 54 were adults (5.1% of 1,060 adults). Sex-based patterning was even stronger in these injuries than for healed skull fractures, with a total of 42 males (9.6% of 436) showing evidence of projectile wounds as compared to 14 females (3.7% of 381)—most between the ages of 18 and 40 years (Lambert, 1997). Sex differences were also evident in the location of these injuries, with 60% of male injuries sustained while facing the shooter as compared to only 38% of female injuries. In combination with archaeological evidence for a strong male bias in grave-associated (nonwound) projectile weapons—found with 18% of male and 6% of female burials—these sex biases suggest that males were the primary participants in this form of lethal conflict (Lambert, 1994; see also Keeley, 1996; Puts, 2010).

What is particularly notable about the distribution of projectile injuries beyond sex patterning is the distinct increase in their frequency between ca. AD 600 and 1350[1] (during the Late Middle period) conservatively estimated at 9.7% affected (39/402). For adult males, the rate is 21.9% (28/128). This contrasts with population rates varying between 0.8% and 1.8% for other millennia before (the earliest injury victim dates to 3500–3000 BC) and after this period. Although not all people died of these wounds, more than 72% did, and as noted earlier, reported rates likely underestimate the actual frequency of these injuries. To give some perspective on these rates, warfare constituted cause of death in 3% of all deaths in 19th-century France and less than 1% of male deaths in the 20th-century United States and Europe (Keeley, 1996: Table 6.2), so even the "low" rates reported for other time periods do not imply an absence of serious violence. Rather, they serve to highlight the lethality of violence during the Late Middle period. Notably, this is the only time period with evidence of adolescent (10–18 years) victims (4.2% affected), as well as a more substantial proportion of female victims (10.7%, 9/84). It may be that some of these were opportunistic kills of women and young people out performing daily tasks, as Milner and colleagues (1991) argue may have occurred at Norris Farms, a 14th-century Oneota settlement in west-central Illinois, where 16% (43/264) of the inhabitants died from violence. The inclusion of more women as well as younger victims suggests that "enemies" were more broadly defined during this time period to include any vulnerable group member. Victims from the Late Middle period were also more likely to have multiple projectile injuries—one had 16 points in his body (Lambert, 1994, 1997). Drawing an analogy with modern tribal peoples such as the Yanomamö of Venezuela (Chagnon, 1992) and the Jalé of New Guinea (Koch, 1974), some of these cases may reflect a pattern of revenge warfare in which related males collectively kill one or more individuals (usually males) from another group to avenge the death of a kinsman (see also Otterbein, 1985). Although it is possible that whole villages were attacked, as described later, the lack of mass graves suggests instead that these high death rates were the result of small-scale raids and ambushes, the highly lethal nature of which has been documented for a number of modern tribal societies (Chagnon, 1992; Keeley, 1996; Meggitt, 1977; Wrangham, 2004).

Settlement data from the Northern Channel Islands shed light on the social environment in which this escalation in lethal violence occurred. Using archaeological survey data in a geographic information system to evaluate settlement systems on the Northern Channel Islands over an 11,000-year period, Kennett (1998) documented an increased tendency toward the establishment of permanent villages on headlands and sea cliffs after AD 700. Settlements appear to have been situated to maximize views of the coast and sea, while minimizing visual contact with adjacent coastal villages, suggesting increasing concern with political autonomy, territoriality, and defense—and potentially identifying "enemy" groups as those occupying the an adjacent bluff.

The paleoclimate record from this semiarid region strongly suggests that conditions in the physical environment played an important role in escalating violence during the Late Middle period. Tree ring data provide a 1,600-year record of precipitation in the Santa Barbara Channel beginning in AD 400 (Raab & Larson, 1997). These data record highly unstable, drought-prone conditions between AD 650 and 1250. Notable droughts occurred between AD 750 and 770 and AD 1120 and 1150, with a sustained low level of precipitation evident from AD 1100 to 1250. The latter drought appears to have led to the partial abandonment of both Santa Cruz Island and Santa Rosa Island during the years AD 1150–1300 (Arnold, 1991; Kennett, 1998). Although this record cannot speak to conditions before AD 400, it does provide clear evidence that the Late Middle period was the most unpredictable and drought-prone period of this 1,600-year record. Drought would have seriously impacted terrestrial plant resources such as berries, seeds, and nuts, and perhaps more important, sources of potable water, a hypothesis supported by evidence of unprecedented health stress in human remains dating to this time period (Lambert, 1993, 1994; Walker & Lambert, 1989). The unpredictable nature of these droughts would have exacerbated competition for prime resource zones and fostered mistrust among neighboring groups—even in years when climatic conditions improved (as per Ember & Ember, 1992). Although such conditions must have occurred in earlier time periods, the human population had been steadily increasing through time (Lambert, 1994) and may have reached a critical threshold (as per Haas, 1999) for the existing economy. By the Late Middle period, the population was fairly sedentary and territorial (Kennett, 1998; Kennett & Kennett, 2000) and could not readily respond through settlement shifts and other nonviolent mechanisms for alleviating resource shortages, as may have been feasible in previous millennia.

The shift in weapon technology during the Late Middle period may have contributed to the observed increase in number of war dead, but it did not cause the initial escalation in warfare. Increasing lethal violence began in the first half of the Late Middle period when spears were still the primary weapon of war (Lambert, 1994). It is therefore more likely that the bow and arrow was adopted because it enhanced killing capacity in a time of war than that its introduction caused the escalation in warfare.

According to the osteological record, both lethal and sublethal conflict declined after AD 1350[1] in concert with cooler, wetter conditions (Raab & Larson, 1997) that would have been advantageous for the resource base of this region. This is not to say that climate played an exclusive role in its decline. Craft specialization, an elaboration of trade networks, and more complex political systems are among the cultural developments that emerged out of the Late Middle period, and these would have provided alternative opportunities for competition, conflict resolution, and resource acquisition/redistribution (Arnold, 1992, 1993; Kennett & Kennett, 2000; Lambert, 1994, 1997; Lambert & Walker, 1991). Therefore, it is likely that these uniquely human cultural responses also played an important role in the shift to less violent times that characterized the last few centuries of the prehistoric period here.

Four Corners Region of the Southwest

The Four Corners region of the American Southwest is another culture area of North America with a growing body of evidence for prehistoric warfare (e.g., Dean & Van West, 2002; Haas & Creamer, 1993; LeBlanc, 1999; Rice & LeBlanc, 2001; Turner & Turner, 1999; Wilcox & Haas, 1994). This landscape is even more arid than the Santa Barbara Channel area, but it has a similar history, albeit more episodic, of population growth, consolidation, territoriality, and an escalation of warfare in association with drought (Billman et al., 2000; Dean, Doelle, & Orcutt, 1994; Dean & Van

West, 2002; Larson, Neff, Graybill, Michaelsen, & Ambos, 1996; LeBlanc, 1999; Varien, Lipe, Adler, Thompson, & Bradley, 1996). The Puebloan peoples of this region practiced floodwater farming; built their villages of wood and mortar, and stone and adobe; constructed subterranean ceremonial structures; domesticated turkeys; grew storable crops of maize, beans, and squash; foraged for wild foods—and, at times, fought each other.

Several different lines of evidence have been important in reconstructing warfare in the Southwest, including osteological and settlement data but also weaponry and iconography (LeBlanc, 1999; Rice & LeBlanc, 2001). The archaeological record of the Southwest is particularly amenable to the study of warfare due to a natural environment conducive to the preservation of human remains and the cultural practice of burial among the Anasazi of the northern region (e.g., Lambert, 1999). In addition, nonperishable materials such as stone and adobe were used to construct residential buildings, walls, towers, tunnels, and other defensive architectural features (e.g., Haas & Creamer, 1993; LeBlanc, 1999; Rice & LeBlanc, 2001)—and these preserve a much more revealing picture of intergroup relations than the shell midden deposits of coastal California.

The osteological record of violence and warfare in the Southwest extends back at least 2,000 years (LeBlanc, 1999; Turner & Turner, 1999) and includes cranial fractures, projectile wounds, unburied bodies, corpse mutilation, scalping cut marks, scalps, and other trophies (e.g., Billman et al., 2000; Kuckelman, 2010; Kuckelman et al., 2002; LeBlanc, 1999; Turner & Turner, 1999; White, 1992). Unlike the cemetery record from the Santa Barbara Channel area, where victims occur in small numbers, here there are also sites with mass graves or signs of attack on a scale that suggests the involvement of larger numbers of people in intervillage warfare (Kuckelman, 2010; LeBlanc, 1999).

In his extensive review of the archaeological evidence for war in the prehistoric Southwest, Steven LeBlanc (1999) identified 32 sites from the period AD 1–900 with unburied bodies, skulls, fragmented skeletons, and/or scalps. At most of these sites the remains were limited to one or two individuals, findings suggestive of small-scale conflict. However, two of these early sites contained the unburied remains of larger numbers of individuals, many showing signs of lethal trauma. The most notable is Grand Gulch Cave 7 in southeastern Utah (ca. AD 1–400). As reported by the original excavators, the cave deposit contained the remains of as many as 92 individuals (though this estimate may be high; see LeBlanc, 1999). Nine skeletons were found with projectile points lodged in bones or between ribs, and a number of others had points in association (Turner & Turner, 1999). Many skulls showed massive trauma to the head and face, and a few had cut marks suggestive of scalping (verified by the author in 2009). Of 61 individuals subsequently studied by physical anthropologists (Hurst & Turner, 1993; Turner & Turner, 1999), 52 were determined to be adult and 40 (of 55 for which sex could be determined) were identified as male (73%). This ratio suggests that the attack targeted men, and that women and children were spared or more likely taken prisoner (c.f., Chagnon, 1992; Fadiman, 1982; Keeley, 1996; Otterbein, 2000). A possible massacre ca. 250 BC–AD 400 is also suggested by human remains recovered from a cist at Battle Cave in northeastern Arizona (LeBlanc, 1999; Turner & Turner, 1999). Of 11 individuals recovered from this deposit, ten have been identified as follows: six adult males, one older adult female, and three young children—a pattern again suggesting the targeting of men and sparing of women. As at Cave 7, a number of crania exhibit severe trauma from bludgeoning (as observed by the author in 2009; see also Turner & Turner, 1999).

The environmental context of these apparent massacres is not well as well understood as that for later episodes of violence in the region. However, a recently published tree ring record from southern Colorado indicates that the period A.D. 1–400 was characterized by unusually dry conditions. Notably, two of the longest droughts (A.D. 77–282 and A.D. 301–400) in the 2276-year tree ring sequence (B.C. 268–A.D. 2009) fall within this 400-year period (Routson et al., 2011). Although the resolution of dates for the human remains from Cave 7 and Battle Cave is at present insufficient to directly correlate these episodes of violence with particular periods of drought, a correspondence between extreme violence and resource stress is suggested. Beyond this finding, both cases also document serious, male-oriented violence in the northern Southwest long before events of the Late Prehistoric period described later in this chapter.

As in prehistoric southern California, the climate record of the northern Southwest shows highly variable climatic conditions from AD 900 to AD 1300 that vacillated between periods of wet, or moderately wet conditions, and episodes of drought. Although climatic conditions were variable in this broad geographic region, climatic reconstructions from tree ring data in both the Black Mesa (Arizona) and Mesa Verde (Colorado) regions show strong correspondence in major drought episodes—most notably between AD 1130 and 1180 and AD 1276 and 1299 (Dean & Van West, 2002; Larson et al., 1996; see also Routson et al., 2011). Both time periods were marked by low alluvial groundwater levels and soil erosion, two conditions particularly detrimental to agriculture (Dean & Van West, 2002; Haas & Creamer, 1993). The latter drought also corresponds to cooling temperatures and shortened growing seasons associated with the onset of the Little Ice Age (Petersen, 1992; see also LeBlanc, 1999). Although demographic and environmental trends are far from uniform across the region, archaeological data indicate that in general this 400-year period was a time of increasing population size, density, and village size (Dean, 1996; Haas & Creamer, 1993; Larson et al., 1996; Varien et al., 1996), as well as growing dependence on stored agricultural produce (maize and beans). These circumstances would have made the population increasingly vulnerable to climatic perturbations impacting food production (Billman et al., 2000; Dean et al., 1994; Kuckelman, 2010; Larson et al., 1996).

Settlement systems dating from AD 900 to 1150, a time period marked by conditions favorable to dry farming for all but the last two decades (Dean & Van West, 2002), are generally lacking in evidence for defensive behavior, leading some scholars to dub this time period *Pax* Chaco, a period of peace associated with cultural developments centered in Chaco Canyon, New Mexico (e.g., Lekson, 1999). However, a growing number (>40) of sites with collections of unburied broken, butchered, and frequently burned human remains representing 1 to 35 people (Baker, 1990; Billman et al., 2000; LeBlanc, 1999; Turner & Turner, 1999; White, 1992), many of which date to this time period, are difficult to reconcile with this peaceful depiction. Although there has been considerable debate concerning the fate of people (and corpses) in these assemblages (Bullock, 1998; Darling, 1998; Dongoske, Martin, & Ferguson, 2000; Lambert, Leonard et al., 2000), systematic study of the remains has led most osteological researchers to conclude that the bodies were cannibalized (Baker, 1990; Billman et al., 2000; Lambert, Billman, & Leonard 2000; Turner & Turner, 1999; White, 1992). This outcome has been verified at a small, 12th-century village along Cowboy Wash in southwestern Colorado, where the disarticulated and broken remains of seven people (three adult males, one adult female, and three subadults) were recovered from floors and features of two residential pithouses (Billman et al., 2000). Biochemical analysis of a human coprolite (feces) deposited in the hearth and residues on a ceramic cooking pot from the floor of a third pithouse document both the consumption and cooking of human flesh (Marlar, Leonard, Billman, Lambert, & Marlar, 2000). Steven LeBlanc (1999) and Christy and Jaqueline Turner (1999) have argued that cannibalism was a strategy used by an expansionist polity centered at Chaco Canyon in northwestern New Mexico to intimidate and control its populace. However, at Cowboy Wash violent bodily injury (e.g., the bludgeoning of the face of a 7-year-old child), cannibalism, and subsequent community abandonment around AD 1150 occur in the middle of a 50-year period of fluvial degradation and drought (AD 1130–1180; Dean & Van West, 2002), suggesting a less symbolic association—one linking serious intergroup violence with drought-induced resource stress (Billman et al., 2000; Lambert, Leonard, et al., 2000).

Some of the strongest settlement evidence for full-scale warfare postdates AD 1150 and comes from the canyons and valleys of the Kayenta Anasazi region of northern Arizona (Haas & Creamer, 1993, 1996). Tracking settlement behavior ca. AD 1000–1300 through archaeological survey work in this region, archaeologists Jonathan Haas and Winifred Creamer found that the resident population lived in small settlements scattered throughout valley floors from about AD 1000 to 1150. The population shifted to better watered sections of valleys during the period AD 1150–1250, remaining in small but more clustered settlements, a move that increasingly isolated once-interactive populations and may have set the stage for intervalley warfare. In the period AD 1250–1300, major changes occurred in human settlement in the region, marked by shifts in settlement from valley floors to highly inaccessible and defensible natural land forms, the creation of no-man's lands, the construction of defensive features such as walls, towers, and moats, the aggregation of people within or around a defensible pueblo, the protection of potable water sources, the establishment of line-of-sight visibility between allied settlements, and the burning of houses and other structures (Haas & Creamer, 1993, 1996; Wilcox & Haas, 1994). The shift to a defensive landscape occurred here and throughout the northern Southwest in association with high populations, environmental degradation, and severe drought between A.D. 1276 and

1299 (Dean and Van West 2002; LeBlanc, 1999; Lightfoot & Kuckelman, 2001; Varien et al., 1996). Collectively, these settlement data provide compelling evidence that the whole northern region was embroiled in warfare during the latter half of the 13th century.

In recent years an increasing number of human skeletal remains with evidence of violent death have come to light, providing more direct evidence for the nature of violence during this time period (Billman et al., 2000; Kuckelman, 2010; Kuckelman et al., 2002; Lambert, 1999; LeBlanc, 1999). At a small village (5MT9943) on the southern piedmont of Sleeping Ute Mountain in southwestern Colorado, a women and three children appear to have been killed in a violent attack around A.D. 1250 (Lambert, 1999; Billman, 2003). The woman was found sprawled on her back on the floor of a residential pithouse, a lethal cranial fracture attesting to the nature of her death. The bodies of the children, aged 3 to 12 years, had been dumped into a large roasting pit (Billman 2003; Lambert 1999). One of the skeletons had carnivore chew marks and another had a perimortem club injury and cut marks from scalping on the back of the skull (Lambert, 1999). Just to the north of Sleeping Ute Mountain at Castle Rock Pueblo, a fortified village on McElmo Creek occupied from circa AD 1256 to 1285, the skeletal remains of at least 41 people were recovered from kivas, towers, and open areas. The bodies were mostly disarticulated and some showed signs of perimortem fracturing, crushing, cut and chop marks, and burning suggestive of cannibalism. A few others had carnivore damage. All of the human remains appear to have been deposited in a single warfare event around AD 1280–1285 that may have resulted in the death of as many as 75 people of all ages and both sexes, after which the village was abandoned (Kuckelman et al., 2002). At nearby Sand Canyon Pueblo, a contemporaneous fortified pueblo, the remains of 35 men, women, and children were recovered from nonburial contexts dating to the time of site abandonment sometime shortly after AD 1277. Twenty-three of these individuals were found in abandonment context, sprawled on floors and other surfaces, and the other 12 were represented by scattered bones; all appear to have been killed in a devastating attack. A dramatic decline in maize kernels and turkey bones in deposits dating to the final occupation of Sand Canyon pueblo support the interpretation that the attack occurred during a period of food shortage associated with the "Great Drought" of AD 1276–1299 (Kuckelman, 2010; Kuckelman et al., 2002).

These cases document the severity of warfare during the late 13th century and help to explain the extreme defensive measures that people began to take throughout the northern Southwest after AD 1250. As in coastal southern California, this highly lethal period of violence corresponds to a period of highly unstable, drought-prone conditions that impacted the resource base of a sedentary population unable to readily respond through dispersal. In both areas this appears to have been internecine warfare, rather than conflict borne of border disputes among culturally distinct groups (Kennett, 1998; Kuckelman, 2010; Lambert, 1994). Unlike the maritime hunter-gatherers of the Santa Barbara Channel area who continued to occupy the region into the historic period, however, Puebloan farmers abandoned the northern San Juan Basin after events of the 13th century and did not return. Warfare continued into the historic period in the greater Southwest, but improved climatic conditions, defensive construction, and depopulation may explain why it did not again reach the magnitude characterizing the late 13th century (Haas, 1999; LeBlanc, 1999).

Northern Great Plains

The Great Plains culture area lies just to the east of the Southwest region and, like coastal southern California and the northern Southwest, has a long but uneven history of violence and warfare (Bamforth, 1994, 2006; Lambert, 2002; Owsley & Jantz, 1994; Willey, 1990). The seminomadic peoples of this region are probably better known than the others for warfare during the historic period (Bamforth, 2006; Hoig, 1993, 1994; Newcomb, 1950; see also various in Owsley & Jantz, 1994), including notorious events during the American Indian Wars such as the Battle of Little Bighorn (Montana) and the massacres at Wounded Knee (South Dakota) and Sand Creek (Colorado). The prehistoric peoples of this region were also at times embroiled in warfare (Bamforth, 2006; Owsley & Jantz, 1994) and at levels that may have sometimes exceeded those reported for the post-European contact period (c.f., Willey, 1990; Zimmerman & Bradley, 1993).

As in the regions described earlier, there is some archaeological evidence for violence and limited warfare before AD 1000, but once again it is much more prominent in terms of both settlement and osteological data in the Late Prehistoric period (AD 1000–1650), particularly among settled farmers of the northern Plains. Two notable sites dating to this time period are the Fay Tolten site (AD 950–1250) and Crow Creek (ca. AD 1325) in central South Dakota. At Fay Tolten, a fortified Initial Middle Missouri village on the Missouri River, limited excavation of 6% of the identified houses revealed the remains of five unburied bodies on house floors or in features; two were burned while fleshed and another had a lethal projectile injury (Holliman & Owsley, 1994). If the rest of the houses in village contain similar numbers of bodies, this extrapolates to a massacre ca. AD 1157–1214 (Bamforth, 2006) of approximately 83 people.

At the large Initial Coalescent village of Crow Creek, a massacre ca. AD 1325 is clearly indicated by the mass burial of 486 bodies discovered in a fortification ditch. Evidence of violent death includes unhealed cranial vault fractures from clubbing implements in 41% of skulls that could be scored for this injury ($n = 101$), scalping cut marks on 89% of identified frontal bones ($n = 415$), other signs of trophy taking, and tooth marks from scavenging carnivores (Willey, 1990; Willey & Emerson, 1993). Of those individuals that could be sexed ($n = 181$), 99 are male and 82 are female. As at Cave 7 and Battle Cave in the Southwest, this ratio suggests that men were differentially targeted in the killing. This was particularly true for young men between the ages of 15 and 29 ($n = 64$, or 65% of male victims). Young women of this age comprised a much smaller proportion of total female victims ($n = 29$, or 35%), though older women (45+ years) do not appear to have been spared ($n = 39$, or 48%), a pattern suggesting that young women of childbearing age were taken prisoner in the attack (Willey, 1990). With one possible exception (Casas Grandes, Chihuahua, northern Mexico; see LeBlanc, 1999), the Crow Creek massacre is the largest known massacre in prehistoric North America. To give some perspective on its size and potential social impact, deaths in this single event exceeded the combined deaths incurred in the historic massacres at Wounded Knee (Richardson, 2010) and Sand Creek (Hoig, 1974).

There is some debate concerning the cause(s) of the escalation in late prehistoric warfare on the northern Plains, including the possible role of climate change. Paleoclimatic reconstructions have documented a climatic episode (Pacific I climatic episode; see Bamforth, 2006; Bryson, Baerreis, & Wendland, 1970) that overlaps with those discussed earlier, and brought lower temperatures and decreased precipitation to the region circa AD 1250–1450. It has been argued that this episode may have been the stimulus for population migration and consequent warfare among peoples of different cultural traditions during this period (Bamforth, 1994, 2006; see various in Owsley & Jantz, 1994; Willey, 1990)—an uneasy mix that may explain the annihilative nature of the Crow Creek massacre.

To test this climate-based model of warfare causation, Douglas Bamforth (2006) conducted a study of the relationship between defensive behavior and drought during the period AD 1050–1650 among the dry-land horticulturalists of the Middle Missouri region. Twenty archaeological sites were included in the study. Defensive behavior was documented by ditch and palisade fortifications as well as the use of naturally defensible locations: 9 sites were characterized as fortified and 11 as unfortified on this basis. Bamforth found a strong correlation between fortified villages/village attacks and periods of drought, a relationship supported by archaeological evidence of food shortages at some of these sites. The pattern was not quite as clear for the 10 unfortified villages, though half of these appear to have been built during nondrought years and another 3 have ambiguous dates. Overall, however, the data support the hypothesis that drought was a powerful stimulus for warfare during the Late Prehistoric period in the Middle Missouri region of the northern Great Plains (Bamforth, 2006), a pattern in keeping with that observed in the Santa Barbara Channel area of coastal California and in the Four Corners region of the Southwest. In this region, however, at least for the period AD 1300–1650, enemies were not closely related groups but were instead people of distinct cultural traditions brought into close proximity and competition by periods of drought (Bamforth, 2006).

Conclusions

The data presented in this chapter illustrate the nature of the archaeological record of violence and warfare in prehistoric North America. Several observations of relevance to evolutionary perspectives on human violence and warfare can be made regarding patterning in these data. First, there is abundant evidence for violence and warfare in all three regions prehistorically, findings that clearly indicate violent conflict is not a product of recent political, technological, or demographic developments. Second, some of the most serious violence recorded in the archaeological record of these regions corresponds with unstable, drought-prone climatic conditions. This correlation supports the assertion that people are more likely to go to war when the resource base they have relied on is negatively impacted or becomes increasingly unpredictable and thus potentially threatened (Ember & Ember, 1992). Third, in all contexts where sufficient numbers of identifiable victims were available for analysis, males emerged as the primary targets of lethal violence, especially in relation to women of child-bearing age. This sex bias has also been documented for prehistoric farmers of the Eastern Woodlands region (where males constitute 80% of 140 identified projectile-wound victims; Milner, 1999) and is a pattern in keeping with the overwhelming majority of casualties in historic and modern warfare, where men are both the primary participants and victims of lethal aggression (Keegan, 1993; Keeley, 1996). These findings are evidence for a long history of male-oriented aggression in prehistoric North America in contexts that would be predicted by an evolutionary model of warfare causation.

It is important to note that the prehistoric inhabitants of these western regions may not have recognized resource stress as a cause of their escalating war or consciously fought over food, fishing grounds, water, or farm lands. Their acknowledged reasons likely were far more proximate—akin to the kind of triggering events and particularistic histories described at the beginning of this chapter. In addition, it may not have been those struggling with inadequate resources that instigated war. Given the variable impact that climate change can have on a region, it may be that groups who found themselves in more advantageous positions relative to others took advantage of an imbalance of power to raid weakened enemies for supplies or women, to extend their territory, or to eliminate potential competitors in anticipation of future shortfalls (Chagnon, 1988, l992; Ember & Ember, 1992; Puts, 2010; Wrangham, 2004). Whatever the details, however, the correlation between escalating warfare and climatic perturbations strongly suggests that environmental conditions can be a powerful stimulus for war. Furthermore, the identity of the majority of victims as males (or the targeting of prime age males in the case of Crow Creek; Willey, 1990) ultimately places this violence in the broader evolutionary framework of intrasexual competition where men target for elimination unrelated men over women and children because it is ultimately in their reproductive interest to do so.

Future Directions

It has taken over a century of archaeological work in North America to accumulate the data necessary to begin to reconstruct detailed regional prehistories that can enable researchers to address major theoretical questions concerning the origins and causes of human violence and warfare (c.f. Bamforth, 2006; Chacon & Mendoza, 2007; Lambert, 1994, 2002; LeBlanc, 1999; Turner & Turner, 1999). It is only at this level of analysis that larger demographic, geographic, and diachronic patterning in the data of relevance to theoretical inquiries such as that pursued in this chapter can be elucidated. There are many regions for which integrative regional studies have yet to be completed, or even initiated, and the research questions in these cases must first and foremost be concerned with presence, prevalence, and chronology. In regard to the particular research questions addressed in this chapter, more work is needed to refine existing chronologies and to bridge chronologic sequences between and among different regions so that the impact of larger evolutionary forces such as population pressure and climate change can be identified. Paleoclimatic data need similar attention, as these tend to be localized and vary by type and level of resolution. Only when high-resolution dates and climate records are combined with thorough settlement survey and human osteological data can we empirically test models of warfare causation linked to climate change.

The science of paleopathology and in particular the identification and interpretation of violent injuries in human skeletal remains has improved substantially in the last 20 years, leading to a reassessment and more realistic accounting of violent injury in the past. Bioarchaeologists reconstruct violence and warfare from its victims, so even the most subtle signs of violent injury are crucial for accurately estimating its frequency and demographics. Many extant collections of human skeletal remains, as well as the excavation records that report on body position, grave associations, and so forth, could use another look in this regard. At the other end of the equation, Milner's (2005) study of arrow injuries in recent and modern human populations is a good example of the kinds of bridging work needed to facilitate the interpretation of injuries in archaeological human skeletal remains (see also Lambert, 1994). Reconstructions will only be as good as our understanding of the behavior that leads to a particular type of injury or the likelihood that a skeleton will record this injury, and answers to these methodological questions must come from clinical, experimental, historic, and ethnographic studies where the link can be documented. From an evolutionary perspective, one of the biggest questions to be asked of the archaeological record in terms of human violence is its role in the history of our species. The bodies of ancient people have important stories to tell in this regard and their collective experiences as recorded in archaeological human skeletal remains can help us answer this fundamental question. For this we need more and better data, and perhaps also, greater emphasis in bioarchaeology on the potential evolutionary significance of our data.

Note

1. Based on recent AMS dates on burial-associated shell beads obtained and calibrated by the author (National Science Foundation grant 0623356).

References

Ames, K. M., & Maschner, H. D. G. (1999). *Peoples of the Northwest coast: Their archaeology and prehistory*. London: Thames & Hudson.

Andrushko, V. A., Schwitalla, A. W., & Walker, P. L. (2010). Trophy-taking and dismemberment as warfare strategies in prehistoric Central California. *American Journal of Physical Anthropology, 141*, 83–96.

Archer, J. (2009). Does sexual selection explain human sex differences in aggression. *Behavioral and Brain Sciences, 32*, 249–311.

Arnold, J. E. (1990). An archaeological perspective on the historic settlement pattern on Santa Cruz Island. *Journal of California and Great Basin Anthropology, 12*, 112–127.

Arnold, J. E. (1991). Transformation of a regional economy: sociopolitical evolution and the production of valuables in southern California. *Antiquity, 65*, 953–962.

Arnold, J. E. (1992). Complex hunter-gatherer-fishers of prehistoric California: Chiefs, specialists, and maritime adaptations of the Channel Islands. *American Antiquity, 57*, 60–84.

Arnold, J. E. (1993). Labor and the rise of complex hunter-gatherers. *Journal of Anthropological Archaeology, 12*, 75–119.

Baker, S. A. (1990). *Rattlesnake Ruin (42Sal8434): A case of violent death and perimortem mutilation in the Anasazi culture of San Juan County, Utah*. Master's thesis, Department of Anthropology, Brigham Young University, Provo, UT.

Bamforth, D. B. (1994). Indigenous people, indigenous violence: Precontact warfare on the North American Great Plains. *Man, 29*, 95–115.

Bamforth, D. B. (2006). Climate, chronology and the course of war in the middle Missouri region of the North American Great Plains. In E. N. Arkush & M. W. Allen (Eds.), *The archaeology of warfare: Prehistories of raiding and conquest* (pp. 66–100). Gainesville: University Press of Florida.

Bill, J. H. (1862). Notes on arrow wounds. *American Journal of the Medical Sciences, 88*, 365–387.

Billman, B. R. (2003). *The Puebloan occupation of the Ute Mountain piedmont, Vol. 7: Synthesis and conclusions*. Soil Systems Publications in Archaeology, No. 22, Vol. 7. Phoenix, AZ: Soil Systems, Inc.

Billman, B. R., Lambert, P. M., & Leonard, B. L. (2000). Cannibalism, warfare, and drought in the Mesa Verde region during the 12th century A.D. *American Antiquity, 65*, 145–178.

Blitz, J. H. (1988). Adoption of the bow in prehistoric North America. *North American Archaeologist, 9*, 123–145.

Boehm, C. (1984). *Blood revenge: The enactment and management of conflict in Montenegro and other tribal societies*. Philadelphia: University of Pennsylvania Press.

Bridges, P. S., Jacobi, K. P., & Powell, M. L. (2000). Warfare-related trauma in the late prehistory of Alabama. In P. M. Lambert (Ed.), *Bioarchaeological studies of life in the age of agriculture: A view from the Southeast* (pp. 35–62). Tuscaloosa: University of Alabama Press.

Bryson, R., Baerreis, D., & Wendland, W. (1970). The character of late-glacial and post-glacial climatic changes. In W. Dort & J. Jones (Eds.), *Pleistocene and recent environments of the Great Plains* (pp. 53–74). Lawrence: University of Kansas Press.

Bullock, P. Y. (1998). Does the reality of Anasazi violence prove the myth of Anasazi cannibalism? In P. Y. Bullock (Ed.), *Deciphering Anasazi violence* (pp. 35–51). Santa Fe, NM: HRM Books.

Chacon, R. J., & Dye, D. H. (Eds.). (2007). *The taking and displaying of human body parts as trophies by Amerindians*. New York: Springer.

Chacon, R. J., & Mendoza, R. G. (2007). *North American indigenous warfare and ritual violence*. Tucson: The University of Arizona Press.

Chagnon, N. A. (1988). Life histories, blood revenge, and warfare in a tribal population. *Science, 239*, 985–992.

Chagnon, N. A. (1992). *Yanomamö* (4th ed.). Fort Worth, TX: Harcourt Brace Jovanovich College Publishers.

Daly, M., & Wilson, M. (1988). *Homicide*. New York: Aldine de Gruyter.

Daly, M., & Wilson, M. (1990). Killing the competition: Female/female and male/male homicide. *Human Nature, 1*, 81–107.

Darling, J. A. (1998). Mass inhumation and the execution of witches in the American Southwest. *American Anthropologist, 100*, 732–752.

de Waal, F. (1982). *Chimpanzee politics: Power and sex among apes*. New York: Harper & Row.

de Waal, F. (1989). *Peacemaking among primates*. Cambridge, MA: Harvard University Press.

Dean, J. S. (1996). Kayenta Anasazi settlement transformations in northeastern Arizona: A.D. 1150–1350. In M. A. Adler (Ed.), *The prehistoric Pueblo world, A.D. 1150–1350* (pp. 29–47). Tucson: University of Arizona Press.

Dean, J. S., Doelle, W. H., & Orcutt, J. D. (1994). Adaptive stress: Environment and demography. In G. J. Gumerman (Ed.), *Themes in Southwest prehistory* (pp. 53–86). Santa Fe, NM: School of American Research Press.

Dean, J. S., & Van West, C. R. (2002). Environment-behavior relationships in southwestern Colorado. In M. D. Varien & R. H. Wilshusen (Eds.), *Seeking the center place: Archaeology and ancient communities in the Mesa Verde region* (pp. 81–100). Salt Lake City: University of Utah Press.

Dongoske, K. E., Martin, D. L., & Ferguson, T. J. (2000). Critique of the claim of cannibalism at Cowboy Wash. *American Antiquity, 65*, 179–190.

Ember, C., & Ember, M. (1992). Resource unpredictability, mistrust, and war. *Journal of Conflict Resolution, 36*, 242–262.

Fadiman, J. A. (1982). *An oral history of tribal warfare: The Meru of Mt. Kenya*. Athens: Ohio University Press.

Ferguson, R. B. (1989). Ecological consequences of Amazonian warfare. *Ethnology, 28,* 249–264.

Haas, J. (1999). The origins of war and ethnic violence. In J. Carman & A. Harding (Eds.), *Ancient warfare: Archaeological perspectives* (pp. 11–24). Stroud, England: Sutton Publishing.

Haas, J., & Creamer, W. (1993). *Stress and warfare among the Kayenta Anasazi of the 13th century A.D.* Fieldiana, Anthropology, New Series, No. 21, Publication 1450. Chicago: Field Museum of Natural History.

Haas, J., & Creamer, W. (1996). The role of warfare in the Pueblo III period. In M. Adler (Ed.), *Pueblo cultures in transition* (pp. 205–213). Tucson: University of Arizona Press.

Haines, J. D. (1994). Treatment of arrow wounds in the American Indian-fighting army: The technique of Brevet Lt. Col. Joseph H. Bill. *Journal of the Oklahoma State Medical Association, 87,* 64–68.

Harris, J. M. (1984). A cultural materialist theory of band and village warfare: The Yanomamo test. In R. B. Ferguson (Ed.), *Warfare, culture, and environment* (pp. 111–140). New York: Academic Press.

Hassig, R. (1992). *War and society in ancient Mesoamerica.* Berkeley: University of California Press.

Hohmann, G., & Fruth, B. (2003). Intra- and intersexual aggression by bonobos in the context of mating. *Behavior, 140,* 1389–1413.

Hoig, S. (1974). *Sand Creek massacre.* Norman: University of Oklahoma Press.

Hoig, S. (1993). *Tribal wars of the Southern Plains.* Norman: University of Oklahoma Press.

Holliman, S. E., & Owsley, D. W. (1994). Osteology of the Fay Tolton site: Implications for warfare during the initial middle Missouri variant. In D. W. Owsley & R. L. Jantz (Eds.), *Skeletal biology in the Great Plains: Migration, warfare, health, and subsistence* (pp. 344–354). Washington, DC: Smithsonian Institution Press.

Hurst, W. B., & Turner, C. G., II. (1993). Rediscovering the "great discovery": Wetherill's First Cave 7 and its record of Basketmaker violence. In V. M. Atkins (Ed.), *Anasazi Basketmaker: Papers from the 1990 Wetherill-Gulch Symposium* (pp. 143–191). Salt Lake City, UT: Bureau of Land Management.

Johnson, D. D. P., McDermott, R., Barret, E. S., Cowden, J., Wrangham, R. McIntyre, M. H., & Rosen, S. P. (2006). Overconfidence in wargames: Experimental evidence on expectations, aggression, gender, and testosterone. *Proceedings of the Royal Society of London B, 273,* 2513–2520.

Keegan, J. (1993). *A history of warfare.* New York: Alfred A. Knopf.

Keeley, L. H. (1996). *War before civilization.* Oxford, England: Oxford University Press.

Keen, M. (Ed.). (1999). *Medieval warfare: A history.* Oxford, England: Oxford University Press.

Kennett, D. (1998). *Behavioral ecology and the evolution of hunter–gatherer societies on the Northern Channel Islands, California.* Unpublished Ph.D. dissertation, Department of Anthropology, University of California, Santa Barbara.

Kennett, D., & Kennett, J. P. (2000). Competitive and cooperative responses to climatic instability in coastal southern California. *American Antiquity, 65,* 379–396.

Koch, K. (1974). *War and peace in Jalemo.* Cambridge, MA: Harvard University Press.

Kuckelman, K. (2010). The depopulation of Sand Canyon Pueblo, a large ancestral Pueblo village in southwestern Colorado. *American Antiquity, 75,* 497–525.

Kuckelman, K., Lightfoot, R. R., & Martin, D. L. (2002). The bioarchaeology and taphonomy of violence at Castle Rock and Sand Canyon Pueblos, southwestern Colorado. *American Antiquity, 67,* 486–513.

Lambert, P. M. (1993). Health in prehistoric populations of the Santa Barbara Channel Islands. *American Antiquity, 58,* 509–521.

Lambert, P. M. (1994). *War and peace on the Western front: A study of violent conflict and its correlates in prehistoric hunter–gatherer societies of coastal Southern California.* Ph.D. dissertation, Department of Anthropology, University of California, Santa Barbara.

Lambert, P. M. (1997). Patterns of violence in prehistoric hunter–gatherer societies of coastal southern California. In D. L. Martin & D. W. Frayer (Eds.), *Troubled times: Violence and warfare in the past* (pp. 77–109). Amsterdam: Gordon and Breach Publishers.

Lambert, P. M. (1999). Human remains. In B. R. Billman (Ed.), *The Puebloan occupation of the Ute Mountain piedmont. Vol. 5: Environmental and bioarchaeological studies* (pp. 111–161, 203–236). Phoenix, AZ: Soil Systems Publications in Archaeology No. 22.

Lambert, P. M. (2002). The archaeology of war: A North American perspective. *Journal of Archaeological Research, 10,* 207–241.

Lambert, P. M. (2007). The osteological evidence for North American warfare. In R. J. Chacon & R. G. Mendoza (Eds.), *North American indigenous warfare and ritual violence* (pp. 202–221). Tucson: The University of Arizona Press.

Lambert, P. M., Billman, B. R., & Leonard, B. L. (2000). Explaining variability in mutilated human bone assemblages from the American Southwest: A case study from the southern piedmont of Sleeping Ute Mountain, Colorado. *International Journal of Osteoarchaeology, 10,* 49–64.

Lambert, P. M., Leonard, B. L., Billman, B. R., Marlar, R. A., Newman, M. E., & Reinhard, K. J. (2000). Response to critique of the claim of cannibalism at Cowboy Wash. *American Antiquity, 65,* 397–406.

Lambert, P. M., & Walker, P. L. (1991). The physical anthropological evidence for the evolution of social complexity in coastal southern California. *Antiquity, 65,* 963–973.

Larson, D. O., Neff, H., Graybill, D. A., Michaelsen, J., & Ambos, E. (1996). Risk, climatic variability, and the study of Southwestern prehistory: An evolutionary perspective. *American Antiquity, 61,* 217–241.

LeBlanc, S. A. (1999). *Prehistoric warfare in the American Southwest.* Salt Lake City: University of Utah Press.

Lekson, S. H. (1999). *The Chaco meridian: Centers of political power in the ancient Southwest.* Walnut Creek, CA: Alta Mira Press.

Lienard, P. (2011). Life stages and risk-avoidance: Status- and context-sensitivity in precaution systems. *Neuroscience and Biobehavioral Reviews, 35,* 1067–1074.

Lightfoot, R. R., & Kuckelman, K. A. (2001). A case of warfare in the Mesa Verde region. In G. E. Rice & S. A. LeBlanc (Eds.), *Deadly landscapes: Case studies in prehistoric Southwestern warfare* (pp. 51–64). Salt Lake City: University of Utah Press.

Marlar, R. A., Leonard, B. L., Billman B. R., Lambert, P. M., & Marlar, J. E. (2000). Biochemical evidence of cannibalism at a prehistoric Puebloan site in southwestern Colorado. *Nature, 407,* 74–78.

McPherson, J. M. (1997). *For cause and comrades: Why men fought in the Civil War.* New York: Oxford University Press.

Meggitt, M. (1977). *Blood is their argument: Warfare among the Mae Enga tribesmen of the New Guinea highlands.* Palo Alto, CA: Mayfield Publishing Company.

Melbye, J., & Fairgrieve, S. I. (1994). A massacre and possible cannibalism in the Canadian Arctic: New evidence from the Saunaktuk site (NgTn-1). *Arctic Anthropology, 31,* 57–77.

Milner, G. R. (1999). Warfare in prehistoric and early historic eastern North America. *Journal of Archaeological Research, 7,* 105–151.

Milner, G. R. (2005). Nineteenth-century arrow wounds and perceptions of prehistoric warfare. *American Antiquity, 70,* 144–156.

Milner, G. R., Anderson, E., & Smith, V. G. (1991). Warfare in late prehistoric west-central Illinois. *American Antiquity, 56,* 581–603.

Moss, M., & Erlandson, J. (1992). Forts, refuge rocks, and defensive sites: The antiquity of warfare along the north Pacific coast of North America. *Arctic Anthropology, 29,* 73–90.

Newcomb, W. W. (1950). A re-examination of the causes of Plains warfare. *American Anthropologist, 52,* 317–330.

Nishida, T., & Hiraiwa-Hasegawa, M. (1987). Chimpanzee and bonobos: Cooperative relationships among males. In B. B. Smuts, D. L. Cheney, R. M. Seyfarth, R. W. Wrangham, & T. T. Struhsaker (Eds.), *Primate societies* (pp. 165–177). Chicago: University of Chicago Press.

Otterbein, K. (1985). Feuding: Dispute resolution or dispute continuation? *Reviews in Anthropology, 122,* 73–83.

Otterbein, K. (2000). Killing of captured enemies: A cross-cultural study. *Current Anthropology, 41,* 439–442.

Owsley, D. W., & Jantz, R. L. (Eds.). (1994). *Skeletal biology in the Great Plains: Migration, warfare, health, and subsistence.* Washington, DC: Smithsonian Institution Press.

Petersen, K. L. (1992). *A warm and wet Little Climatic Optimum and a cold and dry Little Ice Age in the Southern Rocky Mountains, U.S.A.* Paper prepared for the US Department of Energy, Office of Environmental Restoration and Waste Management. Richland, WA: Westinghouse Hanford Company.

Preston, D. (1997, June 16). A reporter at large: The lost man. *The New Yorker,* pp. 70.

Puts, D. A. (2010). Beauty and the beast: mechanisms of sexual selection in humans. *Evolution and Human Behavior, 31,* 157–175.

Raab, L. M., & Larson, D. O. (1997). Medieval climatic anomaly and punctuated cultural evolution in coastal southern California. *American Antiquity, 62,* 319–336.

Radcliff-Brown, A. R. (1948). *The Andaman Islanders: A study in social anthropology.* Cambridge, England: Cambridge University Press.

Rice, G. E., & LeBlanc, S. A. (Eds.) (2001). *Deadly landscapes: Case studies in prehistoric Southwestern warfare.* Salt Lake City: University of Utah Press.

Richardson, H. C. (2010). *Wounded Knee: Party politics and the road to an American massacre.* New York: Basic Books.

Routson, C. C., Woodhouse, C. A., & Overpeck, J. T. (2011). Second century megadrought in the Rio Grande headwaters, Colorado: How unusual was medieval drought? *Geophysical Research Letters, 38:* L22703.

Slayman, A. L. (1997, Jan/Feb). A battle over bones. *Archaeology,* p. 16–23.

Turner, C. G., & Turner, J. A. (1999). *Man corn: Cannibalism and violence in the prehistoric American Southwest.* Salt Lake City: University of Utah Press.

Varien, M. D., Lipe, W. D., Adler, M. A., Thompson, I. M., & Bradley, B. A. (1996). Southwestern Colorado and southeastern Utah settlement patterns: A.D. 1100–1300. In M. A. Adler (Ed.), *The prehistoric Pueblo world A.D. 1150–1350* (pp. 86–113). Tucson: The University of Arizona Press.

Vencl, S. (1984). War and warfare in archaeology. *Journal of Anthropological Archaeology, 3,* 116–132.

Walker, P. L. (1989). Cranial injuries as evidence of violence in prehistoric southern California. *American Journal of Physical Anthropology, 80,* 313–323.

Walker, P. L., & Lambert, P. M. (1989). Skeletal evidence for stress during a period of cultural change in prehistoric California. In L. Capasso (Ed.), *Advances in paleopathology. Journal of Paleopathology: Monographic Publication 1* (pp. 207–212). Chieti, Italy: Marino Solfanelli.

White, T. D. (1992). *Prehistoric cannibalism at Mancos 5MTUMR-2346.* Princeton, NJ: Princeton University Press.

Wilcox, D., & Haas, J. (1994). The scream of the butterfly: Competition and conflict in the prehistoric Southwest. In G. J. Gummerman (Ed.), *Themes in Southwest prehistory* (pp. 211–238). Santa Fe, NM: School of American Research Press.

Willey, P. (1990). *Prehistoric warfare on the Great Plains.* New York: Garland.

Willey, P., & Emerson, T. E. (1993). The osteology and archaeology of the Crow Creek massacre. *Plains Anthropologist, 38,* 227–269.

Williamson, M. A., Johnston, C. A., Symes, S. A., & Schultz, J. J. (2003). Interpersonal violence between 18th century Native Americans and Europeans in Ohio. *American Journal of Physical Anthropology, 122,* 113–122

Wolovich, C. K., Evans, S., & Green S. M. (2010). Mated pairs of owl monkeys (*Aotus nancymaae*) exhibit sex differences in response to unfamiliar male and female conspecifics. *American Journal of Primatology, 72,* 942–950.

Wrangham, R. (1999). Is military incompetence adaptive? *Evolution and Human Behavior, 20,* 3–17.

Wrangham, R. (2004). Killer species. *Daedalus, 133*(4), 25–35.

Wrangham, R., & Peterson, D. (1996). *Demonic males: Apes and the origins of human violence.* Boston: Houghton Mifflin.

Zimmerman, L. J., & Bradley, L. E. (1993). The Crow Creek massacre: Initial coalescent warfare and speculations about the genesis of extended coalescent. *Plains Anthropologist, 38,* 215–226.

CHAPTER 20

War, Evolution, and the Nature of Human Nature

David Livingstone Smith

Abstract

This chapter aims to arrive at a credible account of the relations between evolution, human nature, and the propensity for war. Virtually nothing is known about war during prehistory. The conclusions of anthropologists, archaeologists, and primatologists are underdetermined by evidence; therefore, claims about the antiquity of war cannot be used to support the thesis that war is rooted in human nature. To examine the connection between war and human nature, one needs an explicit theory of human nature. Equating human nature with a human essence is unacceptable. The nomological theory of human nature holds that human nature consists of evolved psychological traits that are widespread and not dimorphic. The nomological theory is used to distinguish components of human nature from expressions of human nature. The disposition to war is an expression of human nature rather than a component of it.

Key Words: war, human nature, essentialism, nomological theory, ethnocentrism

> The study of the basic philosophies or ideologies of scientists is very difficult because they are rarely articulated. They largely consist of silent assumptions that are taken so completely for granted that they are never mentioned...[but] anyone who attempts to question these "eternal truths" encounters formidable resistance.
> —Ernst Mayr (1982, p. 835)

Introduction

For centuries, scholars have pondered the question of why human beings wage war. The idea that war is rooted in human nature is not recent, but it is one that emerged with renewed vigor in the wake of Darwin. From the 19th century to the present, scholars have attempted to harness the power of evolutionary theory to explain the puzzle of war (Crook, 1998). A plausible argument in support of the claim that war is rooted in human nature begins with the premise that war "has been endemic to every form of society, from hunter-gatherer bands to industrial states" (Wilson, 1978, p. 101). The pervasiveness of war is taken as evidence that there is something in human nature that disposes us to war—something best explained by our species' evolution. Those who argue for a biological explanation of war often additionally assert that war evolved "by selective retention of traits that increase the selective fitness of human beings" (Wilson, 1978, p. 115). In other words, the features of human nature that are responsible for war are biological adaptations.

This argument bristles with ambiguities. The key theoretical terms to which it appeals—"war," "human nature," and "product of evolution"—allow for multiple readings, and these yield a range of assertions, some of which are clearly false and others of which are quite plausible. My aim in this chapter is to evaluate some of these options with a view to arriving at a credible account of the connection between evolution, human nature, and the propensity for war. I will begin by considering the claim that war was widespread during prehistory, and I will argue that the combined resources of comparative primatology, anthropology, and prehistoric archaeology do not allow for a determination of whether war was common, or whether it existed at all, during most of prehistory. It follows that prehistoric war cannot be recruited as support for the thesis that war is rooted in human nature. I next consider two conceptions of the nature of human nature. After assessing and rejecting the essentialist approach, I endorse a modified version of Machery's (2008) nomological account as an attractive alternative. Finally, I consider whether the proposition that war is rooted in human nature is consistent with the nomological account of human nature. I conclude that a disposition to war cannot reasonably be regarded as a component of human nature, but that it may be an *expression* of certain features of human nature or of human male nature.

War in Prehistory

It is a truism to note that history is, to a great extent, a narrative of atrocities perpetrated by human communities against one another. However, strange as it may seem, nobody knows how frequent war has been over the broad sweep of human history. The figures that sometimes creep into the literature—for example, the claim that there have been only 292 years of peace since 3600 BC—are usually baseless fabrications (see Jongman & van der Dennen, 1988, for an engaging account of the proliferation of these fictions). Even sober, empirically based studies turn provide wildly disparate estimates of its true extent. For example, Wright (1965) gives a minimum of 284 wars from the beginning of the 16th century to 1940, while Luard (1986) reports that over 1,000 wars have occurred in the past 600 years.

As uncertain as they are, judgments about the frequency of wars undertaken by complex societies during relatively recent history at least have some sound basis. In contrast, claims about the incidence of war during prehistory are based almost entirely on speculation. The question of whether our Stone Age ancestors regularly made war upon one another has acquired an ideological significance that often outstrips reasonable assessment of the evidence. Consequently, the literature is peppered with unwarranted claims about the absence of war or, alternatively, its omnipresence, prior to the Neolithic revolution. The reason why the issue of prehistoric warfare matters so much mainly concerns the light that it is supposed to throw on the link—or lack of one—between war and human nature. If it is a fact that primal human communities lived in peace with one another, this purportedly lends credence to the view that war is a perversion of the human condition instead of a natural feature of it. If, on the other hand, our remote ancestors existed in a condition of ongoing bloody strife, this is believed to show that *Homo sapiens* (or at least *Homo sapien* males) are natural-born killers.

The question of whether and to what extent prestate societies engage in warfare is given great weight in discussions of the origins of war. This is because anthropologists consider contemporary hunter-gatherer bands to be good models for prehistoric human societies. It is almost certainly true that humans were nomadic foragers during most of prehistory. As such, ancestral humans were therefore subject to ecological pressures that were comparable to those affecting hunter-gatherer groups in recent times. This suggests that the lifeways of recent and present-day hunter-gatherers may yield insights into the lifeways of their prehistoric counterparts.

It is at this point that confusion sets in. Some researchers claim that war is a regular feature of hunter-gatherer life, while others claim that it is infrequent or nonexistent (van der Dennen, 1995). One explanation for such diametrically opposed conclusions lies in the failure of some scholars to consistently discriminate between simple, complex, and equestrian hunter-gatherer societies. Simple hunter-gatherers are probably most representative of prehistoric social organization. They are nomadic or seminomadic people who lack domesticated animals and do not employ social class distinctions. Complex hunter-gatherer societies may be sedentary and may have class distinctions. Equestrian hunter-gatherers rely on horses for hunting, and they did not exist prior to the domestication of horses less than 6,000 years ago. Ethnographic data indicate that all of the complex and equestrian hunter-gatherer societies that have been studied engage in war, while nearly two-thirds of the simple hunter-gatherer societies do not engage in war at all, and war is far less frequent, less intense, and less protracted among the remaining one-third than it is among complex and equestrian hunter-gatherers (Fry, 2006, 2007; Kelly, 2000; Sponsel, 1996). In fact, almost two-thirds of the simple hunter-gatherer groups surveyed do not appear to engage in war at all. This is not to say that simple hunter-gatherer societies are necessarily peaceful; it is only to say that a certain form of collective, organized violence is muted or absent (Kelly, 2000). Murder, revenge killings, lethal feuding, and execution are all known to occur in simple hunter-gatherer societies (Fry, 2006; Kelly, 2000).

Using data about present-day hunter-gatherers to arrive at the conclusion that our prehistoric ancestors did not wage war is a dubious inference. It is true that these groups exemplify a way of life that was once universal. The proliferation of complex societies have, over thousands of years, driven the vast majority of hunter-gatherers to extinction and pushed the rest into remote, inhospitable environments, and it may be that this has left us with a misleading impression of prehistoric hunter-gatherer societies. Suppose that Paleolithic groups were predominantly warlike, and that only a minority of them were peaceful. It seems reasonable to assume that the more warlike groups would have responded aggressively to the complex societies that encroached upon them. Given the numerical, organizational, and technological superiority of the latter, it also seems reasonable to think that any hunter-gatherer groups that attempted to wage war against intruders would have been defeated and either absorbed into the conquering civilization or obliterated. In contrast, hunter-gatherer groups that were less bellicose would have been more likely to flee than to resist, and they would therefore have been more likely to survive and remain intact. If something like this occurred, then the typically unwarlike character of simple hunter-gatherers may be a result of a comparatively recent historical process rather than a reflection of prehistoric social conditions.

Archaeology provides another window for peering into the lives of our distant ancestors. Because archaeologists have access to the artifacts and remains of prehistoric people, one would expect their conclusions to be more soundly based than the more speculative inferences made by anthropologists. The evidence from archaeology is consistent with the ethnographic picture described earlier. The first unambiguous archaeological evidence of war comes from a cemetery at Jebel Sahaba in northern Sudan, which contains the bodies of 59 individuals, 24 of whom were killed with weapons around 13,000 years ago (Wendorf, 1968). Some take this to indicate that war did not exist prior to this date. However, one should not overestimate the significance of the dearth of evidence from earlier periods. There is good reason to think that if war occurred prior to the development of permanent agricultural settlements, it would have been unlikely to have left any traces that are detectable by archaeologists.

Small-scale raiding is the paradigmatic form of war in prestate societies, so if prehistoric people practiced war they would probably have done so in this form. In a typical raid, a small group of men ambush a single individual and then retreat to their home territory. If raiding was widely practiced during prehistory, archaeological evidence of it would be thin to nonexistent. The suggestion that raiding was the characteristic form of prehistoric war embroils us in yet another controversy, this time about whether raiding is a form of war. There are obvious differences between raiding, as I have described it, and more paradigmatic forms of war. It is not clear whether it is legitimate to include both forms of coalitional violence under the single heading of war. If feuding is included as a form of war, then the number of nonwarring hunter-gatherer societies decreases considerably (Fry, 2006), and our picture of prehistoric hunter-gatherers undergoes a corresponding alteration. As van der Dennen perceptively remarks,

> The problem of the definition of "war," including "primitive war," is not merely a topic of sterile academic debate or trivial casuistry. On the contrary, it is of paramount importance within a general theoretical framework concerning the problem of whether war existed at the dawn of mankind's evolution.
> (1995, p. 92)

The question boils down to this: Are raiding and paradigmatic war two forms of one thing, or are they two distinct things? There is something to be said in favor of both options. If we consider war to be organized violence between communities, then raiding looks like a type of war, but if war must involve combat between *groups*, then raiding does not look much like war at all. They are also distinguished by significant motivational differences. War, in the usual sense of the term, is undertaken at a leader's behest and waged against an enemy whom the warrior has little or no reason to harm. As

Mark Twain so aptly put it, man "is the only animal that for sordid wages will march out... and help to slaughter strangers of his own species who have done him no harm and with whom he has no quarrel" (1973, pp. 84–85). Soldiers kill out of duty, or under duress, or in expectation of material rewards. Conventional war is also extremely dangerous. An ancient soldier confronting an Assyrian phalanx, or a medieval French knight trapped beneath a deluge of arrows from English longbows, was faced with the likelihood of imminent death. In contrast, raids are low-risk operations in which the killers typically have a strong *personal desire* to extract retribution for a real or imagined harm. It is not clear whether these differences warrant the exclusion of raiding from the category of war. In the present chapter, I will treat raiding as a form of war, more for the sake of expository simplicity than for any deep theoretical reason.

There is both forensic and artistic support for the contention that war was practiced during the upper Paleolithic period in southern Europe. On the forensic side, archaeologists have discovered skeletons with projectile points imbedded in them as well as skeletal trauma indicative of death by clubbing. However, this is not necessarily evidence of war. It might equally attest to the occurrence of homicide, execution, or human sacrifice (Ferguson, 1997). Moving on to rupestrian art, there are cave paintings and stone etchings from southern Europe (and also Arnhem Land in Australia) that portray acts of deadly violence. For example, a rock etching at Cosquer Cave in Provence, thought to be around 22,000 years old, shows a human figure falling backward with a number of projectiles penetrating his body (Guillaine & Zammit, 2005), and other works of art depict similarly gruesome scenes.

> A loose pebble from Paglicci cave in the southeast of Italy... shows a human-like figure which has been struck with several spears from the head down to the pelvis.... In Cougnac (Lot, France), a decapitated body is shown, struck in the back by three projectiles, whilst another individual has been struck by seven spears all over his body. In the Pech-Merle cave in Cabrerets (Lot, France), one individual is shown to have been hit by arrows all over his body, both from the front and from behind. In Combel, part of the same network of caves, a human-like figure with an animal-shaped posterior... can be seen collapsing, after having sustained several injuries. A carving upon a bone in Gourdan (France), showing only the pelvis and legs of a human figure..., shows several arrows penetrating the victim's legs and rear. Also of interest is a rock engraving discovered in the cave at Sous-Grand-Lac (France)... [which]... shows a figure injured in both the neck and back by a number of projectiles. Arrows also appear to have struck this individual's posterior and penis.
> (*Guillaine & Zammit*, 2005, pp. 55–56)

This is all very suggestive, and it is certainly consistent with the hypothesis that war was common during prehistory. However, it is also consistent with the rarity or even the absence of war. Prehistoric artists might have portrayed war precisely because it was unusual, or it might be that these are illustrations of murders, executions, human sacrifice, or even mythological motifs.

Anyone wishing to use the archaeological record to draw conclusions about prehistoric war is faced with a dilemma about how to interpret the data. Should one go only as far as the evidence warrants, or is it more sensible to make an inferential leap? If one hugs the scientific coastline, one must conclude that war was either infrequent or entirely absent during most of prehistory (Guillaine & Zammit, 2005). The bolder strategy is attractive if there is reason to believe that the available evidence is misleading if taken at face value and if there are compelling theoretical reasons for stepping beyond it.

Some scholars believe that comparative primatology provides one such theoretical rationale and lends heft to the claim that our Paleolithic ancestors were more warlike than not. The argument from primatology trades on some striking behavioral similarities between humans and chimpanzees. Small groups of male chimpanzees have been observed to periodically patrol areas of forest adjacent to their territory, and they occasionally make deep incursions into areas controlled by neighboring troops of chimpanzees. The chimps' behavior during these forays suggests that their aim is to find and kill isolated individuals. That this type of violence has been observed in geographically far-flung communities suggests that it is instinctive (Amsler, 2010; Mitani, Watts, & Amsler, 2010; Wrangham, 1999). Wrangham (1999) proposes that these behaviors were selected for because they have the power to erode neighboring troops' resource-holding capacity, and he conjectures that the selection pressures responsible for this form of aggression may also account for certain manifestations of human violence.

One way to account for the similarities between chimpanzee violence and human violence is to suppose that they were both inherited from the common ancestor of the two species. As Wrangham (1999) points out, this suggests that "there has been selection for a male psyche that, in certain circumstances, seeks opportunities to carry out low-cost attacks on unsuspecting neighbors" (p. 22). The claim that human raiding is part of our primate legacy supports the idea that raiding was a fixture of prehistoric life. However, the behavioral ecology of chimpanzees tells us even less about prehistory than anthropology and archaeology do. One source of uncertainty concerns the question of whether the common chimpanzee is the best living representative of the progenitor of the human and chimpanzee lineages. *Homo sapiens* are just as closely related to the bonobo as they are to the common chimpanzee, and as far as we know, bonobos do not engage in lethal coalitionary violence. It may be that the bonobo is a better model for the common ancestor than the common chimpanzee is (de Waal, 2002). But even if that is not the case, why assume that the patterns of aggression found in today's chimpanzees were present from the beginning of their lineage? Although suggestive, conjectures about the social behavior of extinct primates do not provide a scientific platform firm enough to support claims about the place of violence in human nature.

There is also another more pressing reason for questioning the hypothesis that chimpanzees and humans inherited their violent proclivities from a common ancestor. Let us suppose that the similarities between chimpanzee violence and human war have an evolutionary explanation. This might be either because they are homologous (inherited from a common ancestor) or because they are analogous (similar solutions to similar adaptive challenges). The Wrangham-style approach assumes that chimpanzee raiding and human raiding are behavioral homologies. But observations of intercommunity violence among spider monkeys, the form of which is remarkably similar to that of chimpanzees, indicates that it may be more accurate to think of them as behavioral homologies. Aureli et al. point out that:

> Coalitionary intergroup killing in humans and chimpanzees could be interpreted as a result of homology derived from a common ancestor...but this interpretation is weakened by the apparent lack of such lethal attacks in the closely related bonobo.... The similarity of spider monkey raids with those of chimpanzees and humans advocates that the basis of coalitionary intergroup killing is a matter of convergent response to similar socio-ecological conditions, such as fission-fusion social dynamics and male-male bonding.
> (2006, p. 494)

Of course, the hypothesis that human and chimpanzee violence are analogous supports the thesis that war was prevalent during deep prehistory just as much as the hypothesis that they are homologs does. However, these two options do not exhaust the explanatory possibilities, because it is also possible that there is no *straightforwardly* biological relation between human war and coalitionary killing among chimpanzees at all. It is true that there is an uncanny likeness between chimpanzee violence and primitive war, but there are also profound differences between them. The most salient divergence between them has to do with the cultural character of war. As Ferguson (2001) observes, humans "conceptualize, and so act out, war through complex cultural constructions involving classifications of social and moral distance, ideas about physical and supernatural aggression, and a pattern of symbolic and ritual exchanges" (p. 106). It is more than plausible that an elaborate cultural apparatus is *necessary* for war, and that the transition from coalitional killing *simpliciter*, which is found in a variety of nonhuman organisms (van der Dennen, 1995), to even the most rudimentary form of human war, is far more dramatic than is usually recognized by those who emphasize the continuity between them. To bring this qualitative distinction into sharper focus, it is informative to compare Wrangham and Peterson's description of how chimpanzees initiate a patrol with Chagnon's report of how the Yanomamö prepare for a raid.[1] Wrangham and Peterson (1997) tell us that:

> A raid could begin deep in the home area, with several small parties and individuals of the community calling to each other. Sometimes the most dominant male—the alpha male—charged between the small parties dragging branches, clearly excited. Others would watch and soon catch his mood. After a few minutes they would join him. The alpha male would only have to check back over his shoulder a few times.
> (p. 14)

Contrast the unsophisticated chimpanzee scenario with the sequence of events set out in Chagnon's (1996) detailed narrative, which involves a plethora of ritualistic and symbolic activities. First, a ceremonial feast was held on the day before the raid was to be launched. After the warriors finished eating, a grass dummy representing the enemy was set up in the village center. The men painted themselves black, pretended to search for their enemy's tracks, fired a volley of arrows into the dummy, screamed, and ran out of the village. After night fell, the warriors filed into the center of the village, clacking their arrows against their bows and making animalistic sounds.

> When the last one was in line, the murmurs among the women and children died down and all was quiet in the village once again.... Then the silence was broken when a single man began singing in a deep baritone voice: "I am meat hungry! I am meat hungry! Like the carrion-eating buzzard I hunger for flesh!" When he completed the last line, the rest of the raiders repeated his song, ending in an ear-piercing, high-pitched scream.... A second chorus led by the same man followed the scream. (p. 130)

After several more choruses, during which the warriors worked themselves into a rage, they moved into a tight formation, holding their weapons held in the air.

> They shouted three times, beginning modestly and then increasing their volume until they reached a climax at the end of the third shout: "Whaaa! Whaaa! WHAAA!" They listened as the jungle echoed back their last shout, identified by them as the spirit of the enemy. They noted the direction from which the echo came. On hearing it, they pranced about frantically, hissed and groaned, waving their weapons...and the shouting was repeated three more times. At the end of the third shout of the third repetition, the formation broke, and the men ran back to the respective houses, each making a noise—"Bubububububububu!"—as he ran. When they reached their hammocks, they all simulated vomiting, passing out of their mouths the rotten flesh of the enemy they had symbolically devoured in the line-up. (p. 130)

It would be perverse to deny that a *vast* gulf extends between the practices of the Yanomamö and the practices of chimpanzees. Acknowledging this does not render one a traitor to the Darwinian cause, for one can accept with Darwin that "There can be no doubt that the difference between the mind of the lowest man and the highest animal is immense" (1981, p. 106) without diminishing the explanatory significance of evolution for human behavior or ignoring the parallels between human and chimpanzee violence. To see how, we must identify the contours of an acceptable notion of human nature.

The Nature of Human Nature

At least one thing is certain among all of the uncertainties that I have surveyed: There are no grounds for making confident assertions about the presence or the absence of war during prehistory, and we should therefore refrain from making them. Exercising this sort of restraint does not entail abandoning the project of trying to understand the relation between war and human nature. It is undoubtedly true that if we knew more about our prehistoric forbears, this would enhance our understanding of human nature, but understanding human nature does not *depend* on having this sort of knowledge.

Human nature is often invoked, but it is seldom reflected upon. Pronouncements that such and such is a feature of human nature roll easily off the tongue, but we do not often pause to consider what such claims boil down to. Clearly, saying that some trait is part of human nature is supposed to convey something more substantial than saying that the trait is a human characteristic. Human nature does not encompass the *whole* of what we are, as this would render it otiose. To a first approximation, human nature is supposed to consist of those attributes that are, in some unspecified sense, fundamental or deeply imbedded in us—not just in a single individual or subpopulation but in human beings generally.

Putting the matter in this way already begs the question of what sort of beings come under the heading of "human." It is easy to lose sight of the fact that the category "human" belongs to a folk taxonomy rather than a scientific one. In practice, calling someone human is a way of saying that he or she is a member of one's own kind, a characterization that is so elastic that it is easily contracted to exclude certain members of our species, as when the Nazis described Jews and others as *Untermenschen* (subhumans), or expanded to include other species (see Corbey, 2005; Smith, 2011; Willermet & Clark, 1997). I will ignore these intricacies, as they are not directly relevant to the task at hand, and treat "human" as synonymous with "*Homo sapien*." "Nature" is even more slippery than "human." It comes in many flavors. Sometimes what is natural is contrasted with what is supernatural or miraculous, as when we search for a "perfectly natural" explanation for a seemingly anomalous phenomenon.

Anything that accords with the laws of nature is natural in this sense of the word, and this is plainly too broad a notion to put to work in a theory of human nature. On other occasions "natural" is employed as a normative stamp of approval. What is natural in this sense of the word is uncorrupted by human intervention (think of the "natural" environment and "natural" food). This conception of natural cannot serve our purposes either, because "human nature" refers to what we are, not what we ought to be. The concept of naturalness required for a theory of human nature is something like *that which is typical of a kind in virtue of the way things of that kind are typically constituted*. We will shortly be in a position to clarify and tighten up this proposal, but we must first attend to a couple of broader conceptual issues.

Any theory of human nature that equates being human with being a member of our species needs to cohere with a broader theory of the species' nature, of which it is a special case. One such theory identifies the nature of a species with its *essence*: the properties that are individually necessary and jointly sufficient for species' membership. Philosophers often illustrate essences using the example of chemical elements. This is partially for historical reasons, but it is mainly because chemistry is one of the few domains in which essentialism unquestionably pays its way. Consider the element gold. Anything that is gold possesses the property of having atomic number 79 (its constituent atoms each have 79 protons), and nothing that is not gold has atomic number 79. Having atomic number 79 thus corresponds to the essence of gold. If species have essences, it must be the case that there are properties that every member of a species necessarily possesses and which, necessarily, no member of any other species possesses. But no such properties exist. From a Darwinian perspective, there is only one characteristic that every member of a species necessarily has in common: descent from a common ancestor. Species membership is based on relational and historical facts about the position occupied by organisms in biological lineages rather than facts about their intrinsic properties. In this respect, biological categories are markedly different from chemical ones. Considerations of descent are irrelevant to chemical classification; anything that has atomic number 79 is gold and anything that is gold has atomic number 79, irrespective of its causal history.

Members of a species have numerous characteristics in common. But the fact that they are members of the same species is not explained by their having these characteristics. Rather, it is explained by *why* they have them in common. Consider the following analogy. Vivaldi's concertos have certain characteristics that make them recognizable to the trained ear as Vivaldi concertos, but it would be foolish to think that possessing these characteristics is what *makes* them Vivaldi concertos. They are Vivaldi concertos in virtue of their common authorship—their membership in the reproductively established family of Vivaldi concertos.[2]

If you are not yet convinced that species essences are historical essences, perhaps the following thought experiment will persuade you. Suppose that at some future date, scientists develop the technological expertise to produce organisms out of materials synthesized artificially in the lab. One day, they use this method to create an animal that is indistinguishable from a North American porcupine (*Erethizon dorsatum*). What species would the creature belong to? When trying to decide, there are two sets of considerations that pull in opposite directions. Since it possesses all of the morphological, physiological, and behavioral characteristics of North American porcupines, right down to its quill tips, one might propose that the animal *is* a North American porcupine on the time-honored principle that anything that walks like a duck and quacks like a duck is a duck. But looking at the situation from a cladistic perspective drives one to the opposite conclusion. Since the creature does not share an ancestor with any porcupine, living or dead, classifying it as a specimen of *Erethizon dorsatum* would be a blunder. Perhaps it is best considered as a counterfeit porcupine, on the analogy with counterfeit money. What makes money counterfeit has nothing to do with its substance or morphology, and everything to do with its lineage. A counterfeit gold coin might be physically indistinguishable from a genuine one. It might look exactly the same, and even be made out of real gold of exactly the same quality as the genuine article. What makes the coin-like object counterfeit is solely a matter of how it came into being. Similar considerations apply in the case of the artificially engineered pseudo-porcupine.

On the other side of the coin, real North American porcupines do not always have the full complement of attributes that are typical of their species. Although porcupines normally have four legs, a single tail, and an abundant supply of quills, an animal could have three legs, two tails, or no quills, without thereby being disqualified from porcupinehood. Injury, disease, developmental peculiarities, and genetic mutations can all produce atypical individuals that are nonetheless members of the same species as standard exemplars of their kind. As Griffiths (1999) remarks,

> Cladistic taxa...have historical essences. Nothing that does not share the historical origin of the kind can be a member of the kind. Although Lilith might not have been a domestic cat she is necessarily a member of the genealogical nexus between the speciation event in which the taxon originated and the speciation or extinction event at which it will cease to exist. It is not possible to be a domestic cat without being in that genealogical nexus. (p. 219)

If common descent is the only thing that *must* be unique to a species and shared by all of its members, and if the nature of a species consists of the characteristics that are typical of it, then the essence of a species and its nature come apart. It is possible for an animal to be a member of species S_1 while lacking morphological, physiological, or behavioral characteristics that are typical of S_1. These cases are deviations from the norm, and they are relatively infrequent, thanks to phylogenetic inertia (Brooks & McLennan, 1991), but the fact that they are possible demonstrates the logical independence of the concepts of species nature and species essence.

Some philosophers of biology (notably Buller, 2005; Ghiselin, 1997; Hull, 1986; Mayr, 1959/1976; Sober, 1980) have rejected the notion of human nature on the grounds that it is essentialist and therefore inconsistent with an evolutionary point of view, but this makes sense only if there are no plausible nonessentialist conceptions of human nature. The outline of one such alternative, which I have sketched in the preceding paragraphs, is a version of what Machery (2008) calls the *nomological* theory of human nature. The nomological theory states that human nature consists of the properties that *Homo sapiens* typically possess in consequence of the evolution of their species. It is not an essentialist criterion that *defines* what it is to be human. The nomological theory does not demand that the all humans share every feature of human nature, for "Although the capacity to speak is part of human nature, not all humans are able to speak, because the development of this capacity requires exposure to language.... What is required of the properties that are part of human nature is that they be shared by *most* humans" (2008, p. 323). Unlike essentialist accounts, the nomological approach allows that nonhuman animals can possess traits that belong to human nature (for example, startle reactions) as well as allowing that human nature can change over time. Finally, it is important that, although the nomological approach ties human nature to evolution, it does not limit human nature to adaptations. The traits that constitute human nature can also be "by-products of adaptations, outcomes of developmental constraints, or neutral traits that have come to fixation by drift" (Machery, 2008, p. 324). All that matters is that they were produced by evolution.

I think that there are some respects in which Machery's version of the nomological theory needs some fine-tuning. One concerns his claim that for a trait to count as a feature of human nature, *most* humans must possess it. I do not think this goes far enough, because it is consistent with a trait being part of human nature even though it predominates by only a very slender margin. It seems wrong to say that a trait that is possessed by only 51% of human beings is part of human nature. To me, it makes more sense to require that the overwhelming majority of humans possess the traits ascribed to human nature. This is underwritten by phylogenetic inertia: Shared ancestry is overwhelmingly likely to give rise to shared morphology, physiology, and behavior. Machery also excludes dimorphic traits on the grounds that the job of the concept of human nature is to capture species-wide similarities rather that differences between subpopulations. I agree with him on this point but also think that it is useful to supplement the notion of human nature with more restricted categories of "human male nature" and "human female nature." One final point: Machery apparently includes *any* unimodal, evolutionarily based trait that is possessed by most human beings under the umbrella of human nature. This seems too broad, and it leads to some odd results—for instance, the conclusion that bones are part of human nature. I submit that human nature should include only psychological and behavioral traits.

War and Human Nature

Having clarified the nature of human nature, we can resume our investigation of the relation between war and human nature. On my slightly modified version of the nomological theory, a psychological disposition is part of human nature just in case (a) it is a product of evolution, (b) it is overwhelmingly prevalent among human beings, and (d) it is not dimorphic. Our next and final task is to determine whether the claim that a disposition to war is part of human nature satisfies these criteria.

The first criterion concerns the biological pedigree of the traits comprising human nature. There is a trivial sense in which *every* trait can be seen as a product of evolution in virtue of belonging to an organism that is a member of a biological lineage. However, it would be vapid to assert that (for example) the fondness for cupcakes is a product of evolution. To be a product of evolution in a *meaningful* sense, a trait must have been acted upon by evolutionary processes such as drift and natural selection, and for this to occur, the trait must be genetically transmittable. A preference for cupcakes is not that sort of trait. Cupcakes are cultural artifacts, and cultural artifacts are not genetically encoded (there is no gene for *fondness for cupcakes*). However, there is obviously *some* connection between fondness for cupcakes and evolved human preferences. The preference for sugary and buttery tastes is genetically transmittable, and this probably explains why most people enjoy eating cupcakes. If most people have a preference for buttery and sugary tastes and if this is explicable with reference to the evolution of our species, then fondness for buttery and sugary tastes qualifies as a component of human nature.

Let us describe the preference for these tastes as a *component* of human nature, and the fondness for consuming cupcakes as an *expression* of this component. Components of human nature are traits that satisfy the conditions spelled out in the nomological theory, and their expressions are means by which they are realized. It is evident from the cupcake example that components of human nature are sometimes realized by means of cultural artifacts. In such cases, expressions of human nature are contingent upon the availability of certain nonbiological items. In a nutshell, it is impossible to have a preference of cupcakes in a culture without cupcakes. I have already suggested that war is a cultural artifact—a form of collective aggression that is contingent upon a cultural apparatus. The culture dependence of war rules out the possibility that it is a component of human nature, but it leaves open the possibility that it is an expression of human nature. For that to be the case, there have to be features of human nature the realization of which *in the form of war* depends upon the presence of certain social practices, institutions, hierarchical structures, symbolic frameworks, and so on. Wilson offers a prima facie plausible hypothesis about one of these components. "The force behind most warlike policies," he writes, "is ethnocentrism, the irrationally exaggerated allegiance of individuals to their kin and fellow tribesmen" (Wilson, 1978, p. 111).

The term "ethnocentrism" was coined in 1907 by a Yale University sociologist named William Graham Sumner. Sumner defined it as the belief that "one's own group is the center of everything, and all others are scaled and rated with reference to it... Each group nourishes its own pride and vanity, boasts itself superior, exalts its own divinities, and looks with contempt on outsiders" (Sumner, 2002, p. 13). The most extreme manifestation of ethnocentrism is the belief that only the members of one's own group are human beings—the phenomenon known as dehumanization. According to Sumner,

> When the Caribs were asked whence they came, they answered "We alone are people." The meaning of the name Kiowa is "real or principal people." The Lapps call themselves "men" or "human beings".... The Tunguses call themselves "men." As a rule, it is found that native peoples call themselves "men." Others are something else—perhaps not defined—but not real men. In myths, the origin of their own tribe is that of the real human race. They do not account for the others.
> (*Sumner*, 2002, p. 14)

As the ethnographic database expanded, Sumner's insight was abundantly corroborated by observations gleaned from cultures all over the globe. Three decades after Sumner, Franz Boas commented that "Among many primitive people, the only individuals dignified by the term human beings are members of the tribe. It even happens in some cases that language will designate only tribal members as 'he' or 'she', while all foreigners are 'it' like animals" (Boas, 1943, p. 161). There is a great deal of evidence that extreme ethnocentrism is a normal feature of war, genocide, and other forms of collective violence, and that it is rooted in a set of all-but-universal cognitive biases (Smith, 2011).

Treating the disposition to war as an expression of human nature rather than a component of it also disposes of the objection that the attraction to warfare is a sexually dimorphic trait characteristic only of males. It is true that, historically, only a tiny minority of warriors have been female. Two sorts of explanations have been proposed for this. One is that for biological reasons the majority of women lack both enthusiasm and ability for warfare (Browne, 2007). The other is that women have been actively excluded by males, who have relegated them to menial support roles such as cooking and tending the wounded. An argument can be made that the disposition to war is partially an expression of a sexually dimorphic trait and that this trait combines with the ethnocentrism that men and women share to make men, but not women, natural-born warriors. But this argument is ill considered. There is no credible evidence that men are *naturally* attracted to combat. Of course, both boys and men indulge in pleasurable fantasies about war —fantasies fed by the highly idealized representations of it found in literature, film, and other media. But such fantasies are remote from the gruesome realities of combat. One of the first people to acknowledge this was the picaresque US army historian S. L. A. Marshall, who wrote in his influential book *Men Against Fire* that "the average and normally healthy individual—the man who can endure the mental and physical stresses of combat—still has such an inner and usually unrealized resistance towards killing a fellow man that he will not of his own volition take life if it is possible to turn away from that responsibility" (Marshall, 2000, p. 79). William Manchester's graphic description of killing a Japanese sniper at close range on Okinawa strikingly confirms Marshall's contention. Manchester recounts catching the man off guard and shooting him through the heart. "He dipped a hand in it and listlessly smeared his cheek red.... Almost immediately a fly landed on his left eyeball" as the young Marine pumped more bullets into the corpse. He then paused, and stared.

> I don't know how long I stood there staring. A feeling of disgust and self-hatred clotted darkly in my throat, gagging me. Jerking my head to shake off the stupor, I slipped a new fully loaded magazine into the butt of my .45. Then I began to tremble, and next to shake, all over. I sobbed, in a voice still grainy with fear: "I'm sorry." Then I threw up all over myself.
> I recognized the half-digested C-ration beans dribbling down my front, smelled the vomit above the cordite. At the same time I noticed another odor; I had urinated in my skivvies.... I knew I had become a thing of tears and twitching and dirtied pants. I remember wondering dumbly: Is that what they mean by conspicuous gallantry?
> (*Manchester*, 1980, pp. 17–18)

The trauma attendant upon killing may also account for some of the psychiatric impairments suffered by veterans. A recent study of almost 3,000 soldiers by Maguen et al. (2009) found that those who reported having killed in combat were significantly more likely to have psychological problems than those who had not killed. The experience of killing was found to be strongly correlated with severity of posttraumatic stress disorder, dissociation, violent behavior, and general psychological impairment. The horror of killing is apparently not restricted to the developed world. Turney-High raises this point in his classic *Primitive War*, where he notes that "War and killing push men into some kind of marginality which is at least uncomfortable, for there seems to be a basic fear of blood-contamination, an essential dread of human murder" (Turney-High, 1991, p. 225).[3]

Conclusion

Assessing the connections between war, evolution, and human nature requires one to attend to a whole range of empirical, theoretical, and philosophical matter, as well as interrelations between several scholarly disciplines. I have attempted to clarify some of the basic issues and extract some modest conclusions from them. I hope that I have succeeded in avoiding the kind of the sweeping and unwarranted pronouncements that all too often deface investigations into this important subject.

At the most abstract level, I have set out three core issues that scholars who are interested in the evolutionary roots of war would benefit from addressing. The first concerns evidence: Why should anyone think that war is rooted in human nature and that this has an evolutionary basis? How and to what degree are claims of this nature justified? The second concerns human nature. What exactly are we talking about when we talk about human nature? What does it mean for a trait to belong to human nature? Can traits belong to human nature in disparate ways? The third concerns the question of whether or to what degree one's perspective on the evolution of war fits with one's conception of human nature. I think that this three-pronged approach may provide a model for future discussion and research.

I began this chapter secure in the conviction that the impulse to war is a part of human nature. By the time I finished, I had abandoned this belief. It was close attention to *conceptual* issues that facilitated this change of heart. Investigations into the wellsprings of human nature have a profoundly philosophical caste, and approaching them in this spirit, while wielding the intellectual tools of the trade, can be immensely rewarding. Questions about human nature are among the most momentous ones that we can address, in part because, as David Hume pointed out almost 300 years ago, "'Tis evident, that all the sciences have a relation, greater or less, to human nature; and that however wide any of them may seem to run from it, they still return back by one passage or another" (1985, p. 42).

Future Directions

1. Are there plausible alternatives to the essentialist and nomological theories of human nature?

2. By what means can the question of whether raiding and conventional war are two forms of the same thing or two different things be settled?

3. What components of human nature does war express?

Notes

1. Although the Yanomamö are horticulturalists rather than hunter-gatherers, I use them here because they are so frequently held up as a model of prehistoric society.

2. See Millikan (1984) for a detailed discussion of the concept of reproductively established families.

3. See also van der Dennen (1998) and Eibl-Eibesfeldt (1989).

References

Amsler, S. J. (2010). Energetic costs of territorial boundary patrols by wild chimpanzees. *American Journal of Primatology, 72,* 93–103.

Aureli, F., Schaffner, C. M., Verpooten, J., Slater, K., & Ramos-Fernandez, G. (2006). Raiding parties of male spider monkeys: Insights into human warfare? *American Journal of Physical Anthropology, 131,* 486–497.

Boas, F. (1943). Individual, family, nation and race. *Proceedings of the American Philosophical Society, 87,* 161–164.

Brooks, D. R., & McLennan, D. A. (1991). *Phylogeny, ecology and behavior.* Chicago: Chicago University Press.

Browne, K. (2007). *Co-ed combat: New evidence that women shouldn't fight the nation's wars.* New York: Sentinel.

Buller, D. J. (2005). *Adapting minds.* Cambridge, MA: MIT Press.

Chagnon, N. (1996). *Yanomamö.* New York: Harcourt Brace.

Corbey, R. H. A. (2005). *The metaphysics of apes: Negotiating the human-animal boundary.* Cambridge, England: Cambridge University Press.

Crook, P. (1998). Human pugnacity and war: Some anticipations of sociobiology. *Biology and Philosophy, 13,* 263–288.

Darwin, C. (1981). *The descent of man and selection in relation to sex.* Princeton, NJ: Princeton University Press.

de Waal, F. B. M. (2002). Apes from Venus: Bonobos and human social evolution. In F. B. M. de Waal (Ed.), *The tree of origin: What primate behavior can tell us about human social evolution.* (pp. 39–68) Cambridge, MA: Harvard University Press.

Eibl-Eibesfeldt, I. (1989). *Human ethology.* New York: Aldine de Gruyter.

Ferguson, R. B. (1997). Violence and war in prehistory. In D. L. Martin & D. W. Frayer, (Eds.), *Troubled times: Violence and war in the past. War and society* (Vol. 3, pp. 321–356). Amsterdam: Gordon Breach.

Ferguson, R. B. (2001). Materialist, cultural and biological theories on why Yanomami make war. *Anthropological Theory, 1,* 99–116.

Fry, D. P. (2006). *The human potential for peace.* New York: Oxford University Press.

Fry, D. P. (2007). *Beyond war.* New York: Oxford University Press.

Ghiselin, M. T. (1997). *Metaphysics and the origin of species.* Albany, NY: SUNY Press.

Griffiths, P. E. (1999). Squaring the circle: Natural kinds with historical essences. In R. A. Wilson (Ed.), *Species: New interdisciplinary essays* (209–228). Cambridge, MA: MIT Press.

Guillaine, J., & Zammit, J. (2005). *The origins of war: Violence in prehistory.* New York: Blackwell.

Hull, D. L. (1986) On human nature. *PSA: Proceedings of the Biennial Meeting of the Philosophy of Science Association, 2,* 3–13.

Hume, D. (1985). *A treatise of human nature.* New York: Penguin.

Jongman, B., & van der Dennen, J. (1988). The great "war figures" hoax: An investigation in polemomythology. *Security Dialogue, 19,* 197–202

Kelly, R. C. (2000). *Warless societies and the origin of war.* Ann Arbor: University of Michigan Press.

Luard, E. (1986). *War in international society: A study of international sociology.* London: I. B. Tauris.

Machery, E. (2008). A plea for human nature. *Philosophical Psychology, 21,* 321–329.

Maguen, S., Metzler, T. J., Litz, B. T., Seal, K. H., Knight, S. J., & Marmar, C. R. (2009). The impact of killing in war on mental health symptoms and related functioning. *Journal of Traumatic Stress, 22,* 435–443.

Manchester, W. (1980). *Goodby darkness: A memoir of the Pacific war.* New York: Dell.

Marshall, S. L. A. (2000). *Men against fire: The problem of battle command.* Norman: University of Oklahoma Press.

Mayr, E. (1976). Typological versus population thinking. In E. Mayr (Ed.), *Evolution and the diversity of life* (pp. 26–29). Cambridge, MA: Harvard University Press. (Original work published 1959).

Mayr, E. (1982). *The growth of biological thought.* Cambridge, MA: Harvard University Press.

Millikan, R. G. (1984). *Language, thought, and other biological categories.* Cambridge, MA: MIT Press.

Mitani, J. C., Watts, D. P., & Amsler, S. J. (2010). Lethal intergroup aggression leads to territorial expansion in wild chimpanzees. *Current Biology, 20,* R507–R508.

Smith, D. L. (2011). *Less than human: Why we demean, enslave, and exterminate others.* New York: St. Martin's Press.

Sober, E. (1980). Evolution, population thinking, and essentialism. *Philosophy of Science, 47,* 350–383.

Sponsel, L. (1996). The natural history of peace: A positive view of human nature and its potential. In T. A. Gregor (Ed.), *The natural history of peace* (pp. 95–125) Nashville, TN: Vanderbilt University Press.

Sumner, W. G. (2002). *Folkways: The study of mores, manners, customs and morals.* Mineola, NY: Dover.

Turney-High, H. H. (1991). *Primitive war: Its practices and concepts.* Charleston: University of South Carolina Press.

Twain, M. (1973). *What is man? and other philosophical writings.* Berkeley: University of California Press.

van der Dennen, J. M. G. (1995). *The origin of war: The evolution of a male-coalitional reproductive strategy.* San Rafael, CA: Origin.

van der Dennen, J. M. G. (1998). The politics of peace in primitive societies: The adaptive rationale behind corroboree and calumet. In I. Eibl-Eibesfeldt & F. K. Salter (Eds.), *Ethnic conflict and indoctrination: Altruism and identity in evolutionary perspective* (pp. 151–188). New York: Berghahn Books.

Wendorf, F. (1968). Site 117: A Nubian final Paleolithic graveyard near Jebel Sahaba, Sudan. In F. Wendorf (Ed.), *The prehistory of Nubia* (pp. 954–987). Dallas, TX: Southern Methodist University.

Wilson, E. O. (1978). *On human nature*. Cambridge, MA: Harvard University Press.

Willermet, C., & Clark, G. (1997). *Conceptual issues in modern human origins research*. New York: Aldine Transaction.

Wrangham, R. W. (1999) "Evolution of coalitionary killing." *Yearbook of Physical Anthropology, 42*(1), 1–30.

Wrangham, R. W., & Peterson, D. (1997). *Demonic males: Apes and the origins of human violence*. New York: Hughton Mifflin.

Wright, Q. (1965). The escalation of international conflicts. *Journal of Conflict Resolution, 9*, 434–449.

CHAPTER
21

Parasite Stress, Collectivism, and Human Warfare

Kenneth Letendre, Corey L. Fincher, *and* Randy Thornhill

Abstract

We recently proposed a new model to explain cross-national variation in the frequency of intrastate conflict based on the parasite-stress theory of sociality. In regions of high pathogen severity, cultures are characterized by xenophobia and ethnocentrism, which function in the avoidance and management of infectious disease. The xenophobia expressed in environments with high pathogen severity creates barriers to intergroup cooperation. These barriers cause greater poverty in environments with increased pathogen severity, in addition to the direct effects of disease on the human capital that is essential to economic growth. Xenophobic groups in competition for resources are unwilling to resolve this competition through cooperative means, and they are more likely to resort to violent conflict. Here, we extend our findings to other categories of conflict. We discuss the implications of our model to the understanding of human warfare in evolutionary context and to foreign aid directed at reducing poverty and conflict.

Key Words: armed conflict, collectivism-individualism, coups, infectious disease, peace, revolutions

Introduction

According to the parasite-stress model of sociality, temporal and spatial variation in parasite stresses generated past Darwinian selection that built species-typical, conditional psychological adaptations functionally designed for assessing local parasite stress. These adaptations guide the adoption and use of values (morals) pertaining to ingroup and outgroup behaviors that manage the risk and cost of exposure to infectious diseases. Hence, parasite stresses generated the selection that caused the evolution of this conditional psychology (ultimate causation); such stresses are ancestral cues that cause that psychology's behavioral manifestations within the lifetime of the individual (proximate causation). Host–parasite antagonistic coevolutionary races are variable and localized spatially across the range of a single human culture, yielding local coadaptation between hosts and their local parasites (see Fincher & Thornhill, 2008a; Thompson, 2005). This creates a situation in which contact and interaction with nongroup members (outgroups) is costly, because outgroup members, relative to ingroup members, carry parasites to which ingroup members are not adapted immunologically. This can involve different parasite species or different variants of single parasite species. Xenophobia—the avoidance of and antagonism toward outgroups—appears to be an evolved solution to the problem of maladaptation to the infectious diseases parasitizing outgroups (Faulkner, Schaller, Park, & Duncan, 2004). Ethnocentrism is a complementary, evolved solution to the fitness challenge imposed by parasite stress: loyalty toward, assistance of, and interdependence with ingroup members insures against the mortality and morbidity caused by local parasites (Navarrete & Fessler, 2006; Sugiyama, 2004; Sugiyama & Sugiyama, 2005). This ethnocentrism is comprised

351

two parts: (a) nuclear- and extended-family nepotism; and (b) cooperation with ingroup, nonfamily members with shared values and immunology. The greater the parasite stress in a region, the greater the ethnocentrism and xenophobia; likewise, the lower the pathogen prevalence, the lower the ethnocentrism and xenophobia. Low ethnocentrism is the value of prioritizing nuclear-family-focused nepotism and with limited extended-family interactions and other ingroup allegiance. Low xenophobia (= high xenophilia) is the value of attractiveness of outgroup interactions and relations. Outgroup interactions provide benefits to individuals of broader social networks and intergroup alliances, but such benefits will exceed costs only when parasite stresses are low. Consequently, the model proposes that parasites causally influence human values/morals, a major category of human preferences, pertaining to family life and to ingroup and outgroup feelings, motivations, and behavior in general (Fincher & Thornhill, 2008a, 2008b; Fincher, Thornhill, Murray, & Schaller, 2008; Schaller & Duncan, 2007; Thornhill, Fincher, & Aran, 2009).

Moreover, the model asserts that high parasite intensity leads to individuals with collectivist values/behaviors and, thus, emergent collectivist cultures, and that low levels of infectious diseases lead to individuals with individualistic values/behaviors and emergent individualistic cultures. The cross-national relationship between a country's location on the collectivism–individualism value unidimension and parasite prevalence in the country provides strong support for this aspect of the model: Across many countries of the world, high parasite stress corresponds to high collectivism, whereas low parasite stress corresponds to low collectivism, that is, high individualism (Fincher et al., 2008). Collectivism (as opposed to individualism) is a value system of outgroup devaluation; ingroup support; conformity to ingroup norms; closed-ness to new ideas and ways; and allegiance to traditional values, hierarchy, and authority. The collectivist understands self as immersed in and interdependent with the ingroup and places emphasis on distinguishing ingroup from outgroup members. In contrast, the ideology of individualism recognizes the validity and value of interactions with outgroups who have different norms and beliefs, and it prioritizes openness to novelty, thus placing less importance on tradition and authority. The individualist understands self as relatively independent of the ingroup, and ingroup and outgroup boundaries are dynamic and blurred (Fincher et al., 2008; Gelfand, Bhawuk, Nishii, & Bechtold, 2004; Thornhill et al., 2009).

Furthermore, parasite stress and collectivism negatively relate to democratization across the countries of the world: High parasite stress and associated high collectivism correspond to low levels of democratization, that is, high autocracy (Thornhill et al., 2009; Thornhill, Fincher, Murray, & Schaller, 2010). The interrelationship among parasites, collectivism, and democracy across countries is supportive of the parasite-stress model. Compared to individualistic countries, collectivist countries exhibit greater and more widespread poverty, inequality, morbidity, and mortality as a result of the reduced investment in public welfare, health, infrastructure, education, and other public goods and services by the state. This reduced investment by elites stems from the collectivist ideology of devaluing outgroup members, valuing ingroup members, and general endorsement of human inequality (Thornhill et al., 2009, 2010).

Intrastate Armed Conflict

In a cross-national study of intrastate armed conflicts, a category of within-state conflict that includes civil wars (Letendre, Fincher, & Thornhill, 2010), we proposed that in nations with relatively high intensity of infectious disease, the combination of increased resource competition (due to widespread economic dearth and inequality) and the ethnocentrism and xenophobia characteristic of collectivist societies cause increased frequency of intrastate armed conflict. In addition to the direct, negative effect of the mortality and morbidity of infectious disease on the human capital that is necessary for the generation of wealth (Bonds, Keenan, Rohani, & Sachs, 2010; Price-Smith, 2001, 2009), xenophobic groups are less willing to invest in public goods—such as infrastructure, education, and economic development—that will be shared across many groups within a nation (Letendre et al., 2010; Thornhill et al., 2009). In such countries, conflicts for resources are more likely to arise, and these conflicts are more likely to be resolved through armed conflict or to escalate to civil war. In contrast, nations with relatively low intensity of infectious disease experience less severe resource competition (higher gross domestic product [GDP] per capita and more equitable resource distribution) and decreased ethnocentrism and xenophobia. Hence, conflicts for resources are less likely to arise in these nations; and, when they do arise, they are more likely to be reconciled through cooperative means instead of through war. This view is consistent with

Hofstede's characterization of a "high risk of domestic intergroup conflict" in collectivist societies as a key difference from individualist societies (Hofstede, 2001, p. 251; see also Price-Smith, 2009; Schaller & Neuberg, 2008).

The ideology of collectivism promotes within-state fractionation based on strong and localized preferences for ingroup values and behaviors. As predicted, parasite stress positively corresponds with both language and religion diversity across the countries of the world (Fincher & Thornhill, 2008a, 2008b). High parasite stress leads to ideological and linguistic boundaries that cause cultural diversity within regions and within political boundaries. The within-state fractionation generated by collectivist values likely contributes to civil conflict.

Letendre et al. (2010) analyzed two data sets on outbreaks of intrastate armed conflicts across nations of the world: Fearon and Laitin's (2003) data on outbreaks in 157 states in the years 1945–1999, and Strand's (2006) data on outbreaks in 177 states in the years 1946–2004. Strand's (2006) data included small-scale intrastate armed conflict wars resulting in at least 25 battle deaths in 1 year, as well as large-scale civil wars. Fearon and Laitin's (2003) data, based on the Correlates of War Intrastate War data set (Singer & Small, 1994), tallied major civil wars—those killing at least 1,000, with a minimum yearly average of 100 dead, and at least 100 killed on both sides. Hence, data were analyzed for intrastate armed conflicts across a range of magnitude in terms of mortality.

The parasite-stress model of sociality applied to civil war was supported (Letendre et al., 2010). The statistical analyses and their empirical results indicated that pathogen severity positively predicted the frequency of civil-war outbreaks across the globe, and this was found in separate analyses for small-scale conflicts with relatively low mortality, as well in large-scale civil wars with high mortality. Letendre et al. (2010) reviewed prior literature advocating theories of civil war based on environmental variables and the distribution and competition for resources. That review shows that the parasite-stress model of sociality integrates many diverse findings and hypotheses reported in the political-science literature on the incidence of civil war (see also "Discussion and Conclusions").

Other Intergroup Conflicts

Intrastate armed conflict is a specific category of domestic/intrastate conflict, according to standard definitions employed by political scientists (see "Methods"). However, these are not the only type of such conflicts. There are additional types of these conflicts that are expected to be illuminated by the parasite-stress model. Herein, we explore extensions of the model to frequencies of (1) nonstate-government wars, hereafter nonstate wars, that is, intergroup, within-state conflicts in which the state government is not a combatant; (2) political coups and revolutions; and (3) within-state terrorist events. As does civil war, all three of these additional intrastate conflicts derive from major differences in ideological preferences among groups within a nation. In nonstate wars, organized groups war against one another, and the national government is not a combatant. A coup (also called a coup d'état) occurs when a national government is suddenly usurped and replaced by a faction (often the military) of the same government. Revolutions, like coups, involve regime changes, but over longer periods of time and involving social transformation of the old government by a considerable segment of the society. Within-state terrorism is the destruction of outgroup's noncombatant civilians and/or their property because of conflicting political preferences. We hypothesize that all three types of intrastate conflicts arise, at least in part, from elevated outgroup intolerance and devaluation, and ingroup alliance and cooperation, and hence will be most frequent in nations with high pathogen severity and related high collectivism. Specifically, for each of these three types of conflict, the parasite-stress model predicts that measures of parasite prevalence and of collectivism will each correlate positively with the incidence of these events across countries, and that individualism will correlate negatively with the incidence of each of the three categories of conflicts. We also reanalyze the small-scale intrastate armed conflicts we studied in Letendre et al. (2010), in order to test the robustness of our results when applying an additional control (see later discussion).

Finally, we examine the application of the parasite-stress model to a measure of peace across countries. The measure combines information about the presence or absence of internal and external war across many nations. This analysis allows the extension of the parasite-stress model to international warfare, as well as to internal conflict. From the parasite-stress model, it is expected that, across nations, as parasite stress and collectivism decrease, peace will be more prevalent.

Methods

In all cases, our analyses were of geopolitical regions (mostly countries, but some autonomous territories) that maintain a separate government—hereafter referred to as countries. Due to noncorrespondence in the original data sources, sample sizes of countries vary across the analyses. We used Cohen's (1988) guidelines that an effect size of 0.1 is a small effect, 0.3 is an intermediate/moderate effect, and 0.5 is a large/strong effect.

Later, we introduce five independent variables we will analyze. The first four of these are variables indicate the incidence of four different categories of within-state conflict. These four variables are zero inflated: Many countries experienced zero conflicts, while others experienced several. These zero-inflated variables cannot be normalized by transformation. We therefore collapsed each to a dummy variable coded "0" for countries that experienced no conflicts, or "1" for countries that experienced one or more. This dummy coding allows us to analyze these data using binary logistic regression, as in Letendre et al. (2010). The last independent variable we will introduce is a composite variable indicating the overall degree of peace versus conflict within nations. As a composite of a variety of indicators of peace versus conflict, this variable is continuous and can be normalized by log-transformation. Therefore, this variable lends itself to analysis with least-squares regression and path analysis, which we describe later in this chapter.

Intrastate Armed Conflicts

We took data on the occurrence of intrastate armed conflicts from Strand's (2006) data set of conflict onsets in 177 independent countries over the period 1946 to 2004, based on the Uppsala/PRIO Armed Conflict Dataset (ACD). The ACD defines intrastate armed conflict as "a contested incompatibility that concerns government or territory or both where the use of armed force between two parties results in at least 25 battle-related deaths. Of these two parties, at least one is the government of a state" (Gleditsch, Wallensteen, Eriksson, Sollenberg, & Strand, 2002, pp. 618–619).

Here, we focus on intrastate armed conflicts that occur between the state government and another internal opposition group(s), which do not reach the threshold of 1,000 battle deaths in 1 year to meet the definition of a civil war (Gleditsch et al., 2002). These are the small-scale intrastate conflicts analyzed by Letendre et al. (2010), and which we reanalyze here to test the robustness of our results while including a control for world culture region (see "Control Variables").

These data contain 119 countries that experienced zero conflicts over the period 1964 to 2004, while 58 experienced one or more.

Nonstate Wars

Data on nonstate war occurrences were taken from the Uppsala Conflict Data Program (UCDP) Web site. We used UCDP Non-State Conflict Dataset V.1.1, 2002–2005, accessible at http://www.pcr.uu.se/research/UCDP/index.htm. This is a cross-national (255 countries) data set with information about armed conflict onset between two organized groups within a country, neither of which is the government of the country, resulting in at least 25 battle-related deaths in a calendar year; both military and civilian deaths are counted as battle-related deaths. Hence, these nonstate wars are a different type of conflict than intrastate armed conflicts, as the latter always involve the government of a state versus an organized warring group(s) within that state. These wars are escalated interethnic or clan wars; examples are in Uganda, the Pokot clan versus the Sabiny clan; Syria, Arabs versus Kurds; and Somalia, the Jareer subclan of the Hawiye clan versus the Jiddo subclan of the Digil clan. This data set lists 231 countries that experienced zero nonstate war onsets, and 24 countries with one or more over the period of 2002–2005.

Revolutions and Coups

We used the Barro-Lee Dataset for a panel of 138 countries (Barro & Lee, 1994). The Barro-Lee variable used was REVCOUP, which they define as "[T]he number of revolutions and coups per year, averaged over the period 1960–1984." The source for these data is Banks (1979, updated). This variable was used in a recent cross-national analysis of political instability by Nettle et al. (2007). The events appear to reflect the standard definitions of revolutions and coups as used in political science (see earlier discussion).

Terrorism

We used all terrorist incidents listed in the Worldwide Incidents Tracking System (WITS), the National Counterterrorism Center's (NCTC) database for the period 2005–2007 (http://www.nctc.gov). In all of the years in this period, the same definitions of terrorism and methodology were employed. Prior to 2005, a "limited methodology" was used that focused on international terrorism (NCTC, 2007 Report on Terrorism, April 30, 2008,

p. 2; http://www.nctc.gov/witsbanner/docs/2007_report_on_terrorism.pdf). International terrorism involves citizens or property of more than one country. The data set 2005–2007 contains both international and domestic incidents, primarily the latter. Only a very small fraction of total terrorism is international (see Abadie, 2006). The country attributed to the terrorism event is the one in which it occurred. The 2005–2007 data consistently used the following definition:

> [T]errorism occurs when groups or individuals acting on political motivation deliberately or recklessly attack civilians/non-combatants or their property and the attack does not fall into another special category of political violence, such as crime, rioting or…tribal violence.
> (NCTC, 2007)

Terms in this definition (e.g., political motivation, noncombatants, and so on) are defined in the NCTC 2007 Report.

Peace

We used the Global Peace Index for 2008, collated and calculated by the Economist Intelligence Unit. The Index is available for 140 countries and is comprised of 24 qualitative and quantitative indicators, which combine factors pertaining to countries' relative peace status. Peace here prioritizes measures of an absence of violent conflicts with neighboring countries and of internal wars. The 24 indicators include the following: the level of distrust in other citizens; political instability; relations with neighboring countries; the number of external and internal conflicts fought between 2000–2005; the number of deaths from both external and internal conflict; military expenditures; potential for terrorist acts; and homicide rate.

The Index ranges from 1 to 5, where 1 is the most peaceful and 5 the least peaceful. Iceland is the most peaceful, with a score of 1.176; Iraq is the least peaceful, with a score of 3.514. Data and descriptions of ranking methods used are at http://www.visionofhumanity.org/gpi/results/rankings.php. For clarity in interpreting the relationships between the Global Peace Index and other variables we examine, we reversed the coding of the Global Peace Index so that high values correspond to greatest peace, and low values correspond to least peace. Thus, for example, we predict that pathogen severity correlates negatively with the Global Peace Index after reverse coding. We log-transformed the Global Peace Index in order to obtain a normally distributed variable.

We also Z-score standardized this variable for ease of comparison of results between our regression and path analyses. It is this reverse-coded, normalized, log-transformed index that we will use throughout.

Parasite Stress

As our measure of the variation in parasite stress across countries, we used the Contemporary Pathogen Severity Index assembled by Fincher and Thornhill (2008b). This is an index of a subset of infectious diseases for each country using data extracted from the Global Infectious Disease and Epidemiology Network (GIDEON; http://www.gideononline.com). We used a set of parasites similar to those used in prior research (e.g., Gangestad, Haselton, & Buss, 2006; Low, 1990), using the seven classes of important human infectious disease identified by Low (1990) but expanded to include all entries in GIDEON for each class (a total of 22 human parasites). We classified the country-wide disease level of seven groups of parasites: leishmaniasis, trypanosomes, malaria, schistosomes, the filariae, spirochetes, and leprosy.

We used GIDEON's three-point scale of parasite prevalence (3 = endemic, 2 = sporadic, 1 = not endemic) based on distribution maps and coding provided in GIDEON. Leprosy was handled differently, because GIDEON does not map the precise distribution; rather the infection rates are presented. Thus, we coded infection rates per capita of 0–0.01/100,000 as 1, 0.01–1/100,000 as 2, and > 1/100,000 as 3. Trypanosomiasis–African was given in GIDEON in a similar way. We coded infection rate "not endemic" as 1, >0 to 0.25/100,000 as 2, and >0.25/100,000 as 3. The values for the different parasites were summed and provide our index of contemporary pathogen severity (mean = 31.5 ± 6.8, n = 225, range = 23–48). These data were collected from April to August 2007 and are in Fincher and Thornhill (2008b).

The validity of this index is supported by its strong, positive correlation with other cross-national measures of the intensity of infectious disease (Fincher et al., 2008; Letendre et al., 2010), including the World Health Organization's Disability Adjusted Life Years for infectious disease, which is an index of years of life lost due to the mortality and morbidity caused by infectious disease (World Health Organization, 2004). The Contemporary Pathogen Severity Index also correlates strongly and positively with Gangestad and Buss's (1993) historical pathogen severity index (r = .819, n = 27, p < .001). This index is based on prevalence of pathogens and parasites in the same seven groups identified by Low (1990) as recorded in world distribution maps dating as far back as the early 1900s. This strong correlation indicates the stability of cross-national variation in infectious disease over time. The Contemporary Pathogen Severity Index also strongly correlates with the three major measures of collectivism–individualism across countries of the world (with collectivism, positively; with individualism, negatively) (see Fincher et al., 2008).

Collectivism–Individualism

For the purposes of path analysis, we selected family ties as our measure of collectivism-individualism. Alesina and Giuliano (2007) reported that "family ties"—a composite variable of several values from the World Values Survey (http://www.worldvaluessurvey.org/)—was correlated positively with collectivism (and negatively with individualism) across the many countries in the World Values Survey. Family ties is a measure of allegiance to and importance of the extended family—a major part of collectivist values (Fincher et al., 2008; Gelfand et al., 2004).

Family ties shows moderate to high correlations with other measures of collectivism–individualism: Hofstede individualism (Hofstede, 2001), $r = -.481$, $n = 57$; ingroup collectivism practices (IGCP; Gelfand et al., 2004), $r = .688$, $n = 44$; Suh individualism (Suh, Diener, Oishi, & Triandis, 1998), $r = -.383$, $n = 52$. The highest scores on family ties correspond to high collectivism, and the lowest scores correspond to high individualism. We selected family ties as our measure of collectivism because of its relatively large sample size, $n = 81$ countries (cf. Hofstede: $n = 72$; IGCP: $n = 62$; Suh: $n = 61$). Because path analysis is particularly demanding of sample size (Streiner, 2005) and because the available measures of collectivism are limited relative to the other variables we will include in our analysis, we selected the measure with the largest available sample size among these.

Control Variables

As in Letendre et al. (2010) we include in our regression analyses an exhaustive battery of variables identified in a sensitivity analysis by Hegre and Sambanis (2006) as robust predictors of the onset of intrastate armed conflict. We include all categories of predictors that were found to be robust, significant (two-tailed $p < .05$) predictors of both small- and large-scale intrastate armed conflict: GDP per capita, population size, democratization, political instability, and economic growth.

GROSS DOMESTIC PRODUCT PER CAPITA

GDP per capita is relevant to the incidence of conflict, as a measure of the resources available to the people of a country. Ultimately all conflict is over reproductive resources (Low, 2000; Manson & Wrangham, 1991), and GDP per capita is an empirically relevant measure of the availability of such resources (Letendre et al., 2010). We predict that GDP per capita will correlate negatively with the frequency of the various categories of conflict, but positively with peace.

As in Letendre et al. (2010), we used GDP per capita values derived from a series covering the period 1945 to 1999 published by Fearon and Laitin (2003). We collapsed GDP per capita values from this series to a single value for each country for analysis at the level of the country by taking the mean over the time period.

POPULATION SIZE

Population size is a standard control in the political science literature on the occurrence of intergroup conflict (Hegre & Sambanis, 2006). Many definitions for various categories of conflict include some minimum threshold for number of death (see earlier), and so it is to be expected that as population size increases, there is increasing potential for events that meet those definitions. We predict that population size will correlate positively with conflict, and negatively with peace, as among the indicators that comprise the composite Global Peace Index is the frequency of internal conflicts. We took population size from the series by Fearon and Laitin (2003) over the period 1945 to 1999, with values collapsed to a single value for each country, as earlier.

DEMOCRATIZATION

Degree of democratization has been hypothesized to relate to the frequency of intrastate conflicts in two ways. First, democratic institutions may reduce the motivation to engage in violence against the government or other groups within the state, as democratic institutions allow greater possibility for citizens or groups to address grievances without resorting to violence than do autocratic institutions (Gleditsch, Hegre, & Strand, 2009). Second, democratic institutions may increase the opportunity to engage in violence to address grievances relative to autocratic societies in which liberties are strictly curtailed (Gleditsch et al., 2009).

These two factors have been hypothesized to produce a U-shaped relationship between intergroup conflict and democratization. However, Hegre and

Sambanis (2006) report only a robust effect for the linear component of democratization on the frequency of intrastate armed conflict and civil war, and therefore we include only this linear component as a control here. Degree of democratization relates to the parasite stress theory of sociality in that democratization and associated liberal values negatively vary cross-nationally with parasite stress (Thornhill et al., 2009, 2010).

We take our measure of democratization from the Polity IV Project's Polity 2 Index (Marshall & Jaggers, 2009). Polity 2 is an index of countries democratic versus autocratic institutions, including the existence of procedures by which citizens can express political preferences, constraints on executive power, and guarantees on the civil liberties of citizens. Higher scores indicate greater degree of democratization. Polity 2 is a yearly series, and thus as in Letendre et al. (2010) and as described earlier, we collapsed values to a single mean value for each country in our analysis.

POLITICAL INSTABILITY

Hegre and Sambanis (2006) found political instability to be a robust, positive predictor of small-scale intrastate armed conflict and civil war. As in Letendre et al. (2010), we take our indicator of political instability from the series covering the years 1945–1999 by Fearon and Laitin (2003), based on countries' change in score on the Polity 2 index over time. Fearon and Laitin (2003) coded their political instability series "1" for years in which countries experienced a change in Polity score, or "0" for years in which countries experienced no change. We calculated average number of changes per year from this series, in order to obtain a single value for each country.

GROSS DOMESTIC PRODUCT PER CAPITA GROWTH

Finally we include GDP per capita growth, which is relevant to the analysis of intrastate conflict as a measure of resource unpredictability. Low GDP per capita growth may increase the frequency of violent conflict by producing times of scarcity (Ember & Ember, 1992; Zhang, Brecke, Lee, He, & Zhang, 2007) and anxiety about future shortages (Ember & Ember, 1992). Following Fearon and Laitin (2003), we calculated GDP per capita growth as percent change in countries' GDP per capita. We obtained a single value for each country based on Fearon and Laitin's (2003) yearly GDP per capita series.

WORLD REGION

Although Hegre and Sambanis (2006) did not find variables encoding geographic regions per se to be robust predictors of intrastate armed conflict or civil war, critics of the research program supporting the parasite stress theory of sociality (e.g., Nettle, 2009) have questioned the validity of analyses that do not account for dependence among cultures within regions. In addition, there are other possible confounds that may vary with geographic region, such as Africa and South America's history of colonization by European nations (see later discussion). Therefore, to control for such possible confounds, we include a categorical variable coding each country's membership in one of Murdock's (1949) six world culture areas.

Regression Analyses

We collapsed intrastate armed conflicts, revolutions and coups, nonstate wars, and terrorism into binary dummy variables, coded "0" for countries that experienced no conflict, or "1" for countries that experienced one or more. We examined each of these using binary logistic regression analysis, with all predictors and control variables entered simultaneously.

The Global Peace Index is normally distributed when log-transformed to correct for skew. Therefore, we used least-squares regression to analyze this variable, with all predictors and control variables entered simultaneously.

We performed regression analyses using Systat version 11 (http://www.systat.com). We report one-tailed p values for all regression analyses, as we have unambiguous directional predictions based on the parasite-stress theory and the results in Letendre et al. (2010). We report standardized βs throughout.

Path Analysis

The model we propose has its causal basis in the influence of parasite stress on human behavior and cultural values, and it links parasite stress to intergroup conflict via the ethnocentrism and xenophobia of collectivist cultures, and further via indirect effects such as national wealth and degree of democratization. Path analysis allows us to investigate the relative effects of all these variables in a comprehensive fashion.

For the purposes of path analysis, we chose the Global Peace Index as our measure of conflict, for two reasons. First, the Global Peace Index is a composite index that includes in its scores a diversity of factors that contribute to overall peace versus conflict within a country. These measures include the number of internal conflicts and potential for terrorist acts; the Global Peace Index reflects a number of the other direct measures of conflict described earlier, and it is therefore a useful summary variable for the general association between parasite stress and conflict that our model seeks to explain. Second, unlike the measures of civil war analyzed in Letendre et al. (2010) and the nonstate wars, revolutions, coups, and terrorism described earlier—which, because they include many countries that experience none of these events and a few that experience many, are zero inflated and not possible to normalize—the Global Peace Index has better fit to a normal distribution and therefore lends itself to path analysis.

Because the sample size of our total model was limited by the relatively small samples available for measures of collectivism (family ties: $n = 81$), we limited our path analysis to a relatively simple model, including a small number of relevant variables. As mediators of the relationship between parasites and collectivism and their effect on peace, we included measures of GDP per capita and democratization. As mentioned earlier, these variables are theoretically relevant to the model presented here (see also "Discussion and Conclusions"). These variables' correlations with intrastate conflict are robust and widely recognized, and they are commonly regarded as important control variables in models of intrastate conflict (Hegre & Sambanis, 2006).

Finally, we included population size as a control variable in our model. Population size is a standard control variable in models of the incidence of intrastate conflict (Hegre & Sambanis, 2006) because of the reasoning that with increasing population size there is more opportunity for the occurrence of conflict. Population size is a relevant control variable here because in our model, conflict results upon the emergence of group boundaries and intergroup hostilities; and with increasing population size there are likely to be more of these conflicting subgroups within the political boundaries of a country. We performed path analyses with PROC CALIS, using SAS version 9.1 (http://www.sas.com/).

Results
Intrastate Armed Conflicts

As predicted by the parasite-stress model, pathogen severity was the strongest, positive predictor of the incidence of intrastate armed conflict ($\beta = 0.71$, $p = .032$, $n = 148$ countries). Intrastate armed conflict was also positively predicted by population size ($\beta = 0.38$, $p = .044$). There was a marginally significant, negative effect of GDP per capita growth ($\beta = -0.33$, $p = .056$). World area did not significantly predict intrastate armed conflict, nor did GDP per capita, democracy, nor political instability. See Table 21.1 for a summary of these results.

Table 21.1 Regression Analyses of Conflict by Country

	Intrastate Armed Conflict	Nonstate Wars	Revolutions and Coups	Terrorism	Global Peace Index
Log GDP per capita	0.05	−0.92*	−0.08	−0.59*	0.19*
Log population size	0.38*	1.17**	0.09	0.95***	−0.04
Democracy	0.08	0.21	−0.56†	0.22	0.12
Political instability	0.02	0.28	1.85**	0.34	0.0
GDP per capita growth	−0.33†	−0.02	−0.92†	0.27	0.19**
World area	n.s.	n.s.	n.s.	n.s.	n.s.
Pathogen severity	0.71*	1.16*	1.09*	0.20	−0.48***
N	148	148	117	148	129

Note. Standardized parameter estimates for predictors of conflict. Analyses of intrastate armed conflict, revolutions and coups, nonstate wars, and terrorism are binary logistic fits. Analysis of the Global Peace Index is a least-squares fit.
†$p < 0.10$; *$p < 0.05$; **$p < 0.01$; ***$p < 0.001$. Significance values are one-tailed probabilities.
GDP, gross domestic product; n.s., not significant.

Nonstate Wars

As predicted by the parasite-stress model, the incidence of nonstate wars was positively predicted by pathogen severity (β = 1.16, p = .021, n = 148 countries). Population size was also a positive predictor (β = 1.17, p = .001), while GDP per capita was a negative predictor (β = –0.92, p = .042). World area did not significantly predict nonstate wars, nor did democracy, political instability, nor GDP per capita growth. See Table 22.1.

Revolutions and Coups

As predicted, revolutions and coups were positively predicted by pathogen severity (β = 1.09, p = .044, n = 117 countries). The incidence of revolutions and coups was also positively predicted by political instability (β = 1.85, p = .001). (The large magnitude of the effect of political instability on revolutions and coups may in part be due to endogeneity. The definition of both of these variables includes some change in the makeup or behavior of the government; thus, while political instability may play a causal role in the incidence of revolutions and coups, the converse may simultaneously be true. While this may exaggerate the strength of this relationship in these results, nevertheless we found similar results with respect to the other variables included here whether political instability was included or excluded as an independent variable.) There were also marginally significant, negative effects of democratization (β = –0.56, p = .071) and GDP per capita growth (β = –0.92, p = .082). World area was not a significant predictor of revolutions and coups, nor was GDP per capita or population size. See Table 21.1.

Terrorism

When controlling for the other independent variables included here, terrorism is not significantly predicted by pathogen severity (p > .10). The incidence of terrorism was positively predicted by population size (β = 0.95, p < .001, n = 148 countries), and negatively by GDP per capita (β = –0.59, p = .047). World area was not a significant predictor, nor was democracy, political instability, nor GDP per capita growth. See Table 21.1.

As in our analysis of civil wars in Letendre et al. (2010), we investigated a possible indirect role of pathogen severity on the incidence of terrorism via pathogen severity's negative effect on GDP per capita (e.g., Price-Smith, 2001). To test GDP per capita as a mediator of a relationship between pathogen severity and terrorism (Baron & Kenny, 1986), we repeated the aforementioned regression analysis with GDP per capita excluded from the model. Still, we found that pathogen severity is not a significant predictor (p > .10). We will discuss this contrary finding further later in this chapter.

Peace

Our least-squares fit of the Global Peace Index revealed that, as predicted by the parasite-stress model, pathogen severity is the strongest, negative predictor of peace across countries of the world (β = –0.48, p < .001, n = 129 countries). GDP per capita (β = 0.19, p = .043) and GDP per capita growth (β = 0.19, p = .007) were significant, positive predictors of peace. World area did not significantly predict peace, nor did population size, democracy, or political instability.

Path Analysis

The hypothesized model is illustrated in Figure 21.1. Rectangles represent measured variables. Straight lines represent hypothesized causal pathways, with plus (+) and minus (–) signs indicating the hypothesized positive or negative direction of the relationship; the curved line indicates a covariance relationship between the two exogenous variables, pathogen severity and population size.

We hypothesized that peace is predicted positively by GDP per capita, negatively by family ties, positively by polity (democratization), and negatively by population size. We hypothesized that GDP per capita is negatively predicted by pathogen severity and family ties. We hypothesized that democratization (polity) is negatively predicted by family ties. Finally, we hypothesized that family ties are positively predicted by pathogen severity. This analysis thus includes ten variables: six observed and four unobserved variables. (The four unobserved variables are error terms associated with each of the four endogenous variables. These unobserved variables must be estimated by the model, and therefore they must be taken into consideration when evaluating sample size; Streiner, 2005.)

We included in our analysis only cases for which we had complete data for all six observed variables included in our model (n = 66 countries). Per the method described by Tabachnick and Fidell (2007), we evaluated the multivariate normality of our data by examining pairwise correlations of each pair of variables. We found that relationships among our variables are linear where relationships exist. However, the residuals of some of these relationships showed evidence of nonnormality; therefore,

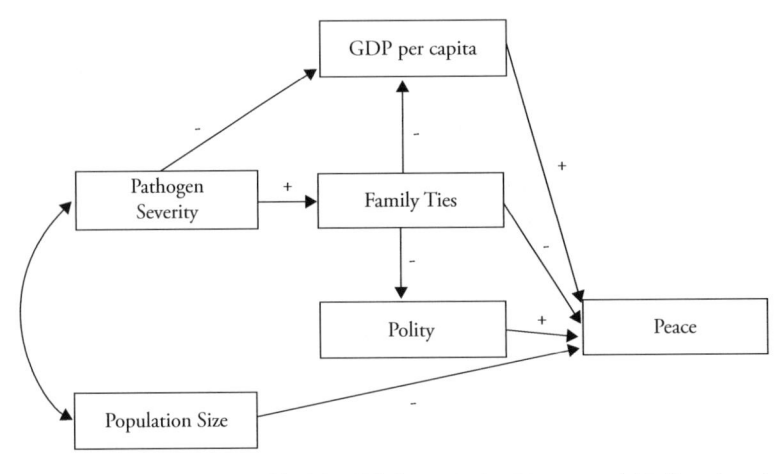

Figure 21.1 Hypothesized structural equation model of the Global Peace Index. Minus signs (–) indicate hypothesized negative relationships. Plus signs (+) indicate hypothesized positive relationships. GDP, gross domestic product.

we used the maximum likelihood method of estimation in our analyses. Among the n = 66 countries, we found two outliers with respect to population size (China and India) and one outlier with respect to the relationship between GDP per capita and democratization (Saudi Arabia). We therefore excluded these from our analysis (see Tabachnick & Fidell, 2007), leaving a final sample size of n = 63 countries.

We found poor support for the hypothesized model as originally specified: χ^2 p = .0078; RMSEA = 0.1725; NFI = 0.8910 (χ^2 p > .10, RMSEA < 0.06, and NFI > 0.95 indicate a good fitting model; Tabachnick & Fidell, 2007). We therefore performed post hoc model modifications to identify a better fitting model. The largest Lagrange multiplier suggested the fit of the model improves with the addition of a direct relation between pathogen severity and peace (p = .0068); this addition makes theoretical sense in that the model we proposed seeks to account for cross-national variation in conflict as the result of variation in the intensity of infectious disease. The Wald test suggested that the removal of the relation between democratization and peace would not decrease the fit of the model (p = .6743), and we therefore removed this relation.

We subsequently found that once the model takes into account a direct relationship between pathogen severity and peace, the relationships of population size and family ties with peace are no longer significant, and unnecessary for the fit of the model (Wald tests p = .2459 and p = .2424, respectively). Finally, because democratization and population size no longer play a causal role in our model of peace, and in order to produce a simpler

model better served by our limited sample size, we eliminated these two variables from the final model.

Our final model fits the data well: χ^2 p = .3794; RMSEA < 0.0001; NFI = 0.9969. It contains seven variables: four observed, and three unobserved error terms. The ratio of sample size to variables is thus 9:1. The final model is illustrated in Figure 21.2. Peace was predicted negatively by pathogen severity (standardized coefficient β = –0.5394, p < .0001) and positively by GDP per capita (β = 0.2321, p = .0404). GDP per capita was predicted negatively by pathogen severity (β = –0.3290, p = .0174) and family ties (β = –0.3707, p =.0074). Family ties was predicted positively by pathogen severity (β = 0.7151, p < .0001). This model accounts for 49.66% of the variation in peace across our sample.

Discussion and Conclusions

The major empirical findings are that the predictions of the parasite-stress model, when applied to

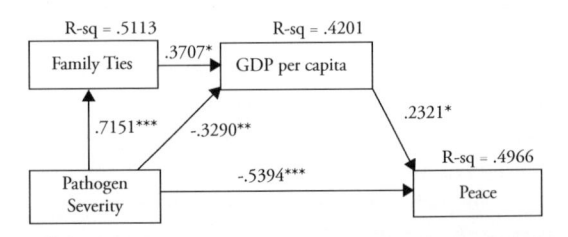

Figure 21.2 Final structural equation model of the Global Peace Index. Model fit statistics: χ^2 p = .3794; RMSEA < 0.0001; NFI = 0.9969. Path weights are standardized coefficients. R-sq indicates proportion of variation accounted for by the model for each endogenous variable. *p < .05; **p < .01; ***p < .001. GDP, gross domestic product.

political conflicts across the countries of the world, were largely satisfied. As predicted, the incidence of intrastate armed conflict, nonstate wars, and revolutions and coups was predicted by parasite stress; the predicted relationships also were seen with a measure of peacefulness, the absence of internal and external conflict. As parasite stress and its associated collectivism increase, and GDP per capita decreases across countries, so does the incidence of intrastate armed conflict, nonstate war, and revolutions and coups. Peacefulness increases as parasite stress and collectivism decline across countries and GDP per capita increases. These results are robust across a variety of categories of conflict, even when controlling for a battery of demographic, economic, and political indicators.

The one category of conflict that did not satisfy the prediction of the parasite-stress theory was terrorist incidents. We failed to find support for either a direct or indirect effect of pathogen severity on the incidence of terrorism. This analysis should be viewed as preliminary, due to limitations of the available data. We could not discern confidently international from domestic terrorism events, although we are confident that the vast majority of events in the data set we used (WITS) are domestic. We could not find the data set used by Abadie (2006), the World Market Research Center's Global Terrorism Index. We did not use the Global Terrorism Database of the US Department of Homeland Security, because it is stated on the Web site that its methods involve "no set definition...covering several definitions of terrorism" (http://www.start.umd.edu/data/gtd/gtd1-and-gtd2.asp). Given that, in some regions of the world, propaganda about terrorism and its threat are used in political competitions, it may be difficult to obtain data free from political manipulation of terrorist reports.

Another consideration is the fact that terrorism, and especially modern suicide terrorism, is extremely asymmetric: Attackers can inflict damage on a multitude of undefended, civilian targets, using cheap and readily available materials that are difficult to detect (Atran, 2003). Therefore, it may be that it is generally collectivist elements within a country that are responsible for terrorist events, as we hypothesize; however, if only a few collectivist individuals can carry out terrorist attacks in countries otherwise characterized by relatively individualist cultures (e.g., the Oklahoma City bombing, carried out by right-wing extremist Timothy McVeigh in the United States in 1995; Blee & Creasap, 2010), then the regression analyses performed here at the cross-national level will not reveal this relationship. Our hypothesis with respect to terrorism is suggested by Sosis and Alcorta's (2008) finding that terrorism is tied strongly to ethnocentric convictions about the truth of ingroup religious beliefs and the falsity of outgroup religious beliefs. Even secular terrorism, they suggest, is the result of strong ideological preference differences between groups. MacNeill (2004) posited that religion is an evolutionary adaptation for warfare in general—an adaptation likely to be implicated even in a relatively novel expression of intergroup violence such as terrorism. The positive association of parasite stress and religiosity has been described, tested, and supported by Fincher and Thornhill (in press); thus, our approach places these diverse findings in the context of a general model based fundamentally on parasite stress. We hope that given relevant data, this theory may yet shed light on the causes of terrorism.

Throughout our regression analyses, we included a control for world cultural region, in order to address the issue of cultural dependence among cultures within a region that share characteristics as a result of recent common cultural descent (e.g., Nettle, 2009), and also possible confounds such as European nations' history of colonialism of African, South American, and Asian nations. In each of our analyses, we found no significant effect of world region on the incidence of conflict, or on peace. Other researchers have concluded that the high frequency of civil wars in Africa, for example, is explicable as the result of common predictors of civil war across the world, such as Africa's high levels of poverty and the characteristics of its political institutions (Collier & Hoeffler, 2002; Elbadawi & Sambanis, 2000). Likewise, we find that variation in the frequency of conflict and degree of peace within cultural regions is explained by the economic and political variables included in our analyses; and we add variation in the intensity of infectious disease as an important causal factor in the economic performance (Letendre, 2010) and political makeup (Thornhill et al., 2009) of nations. Rather than the history of cultures in different regions of the world driving the association between infectious disease and conflict, we argue that ecologically determined variation in the intensity of infectious disease has caused different histories of poverty and wealth (Price-Smith, 2001), democracy and autocracy (Thornhill et al., 2009), conflict and peace, imperialism and colonialism, and technological development in different regions and nations across the world (Letendre et al., 2010).

These findings, combined with the detailed, longitudinal and cross-sectional analyses of civil wars and small-scale intrastate conflict by Letendre et al. (2010), support the application of the parasite-stress model of sociality to political conflict. Our analyses of the Global Peace Index across countries allow an initial examination of the parasite-stress model in relation to international political conflicts. Although path analysis of our model of the Global Peace Index was not supported as originally specified, we found support for a revised model that agrees with the overall argument that infectious disease plays an important causal role in variation in peace across countries. These results indicate that the parasite-stress model may be an important way to understand many major types of political conflicts.

Fundamentally, the parasite-stress model of political conflicts rests on earlier scientific findings that human behavior and its associated psychological foundations have been crafted ultimately by past biological evolutionary processes. This conclusion is based on a huge empirical base in biology and related areas of scholarship generated over the last 150 years. The parasite-stress model proceeds from this scientific conclusion—that every aspect of the human phenotype was caused ultimately by evolutionary historical processes—to a specific model of the human behavioral, emotional, motivational, and deductive phenotypes that are manifested in the context of political conflicts.

In our theoretical approach to the functional organization of human political conflicts, we have focused on evolved adaptations of individuals rather than upon group-related adaptation that may hypothetically arise from group selection, because it is at the level of genes and individuals that Darwinian selection causes the evolutionary changes that create psychological adaptations (e.g., West, Griffin, & Gardner, 2007; Williams, 1966). This selection favors traits of individuals that provide the bearers with the highest relative inclusive fitness—that is, traits that allow their bearer to produce the greatest number of reproductively successful genetic relatives (descendant and/or nondescendant). The behavior of groups emerges from the behavior of individuals, who are designed by evolution to maximize inclusive fitness in ancestral environments.

The parasite-stress model proposes that political conflicts can be understood as follows. They are caused by behavioral and psychological features functionally designed for (i.e., directly selected in the context of) the xenophobia that functions in the avoidance of novel pathogens that may be carried by outgroup members. This outgroup avoidance brings competitive interactions to the forefront of humans' relations with outgroup members. In relatively xenophilic cultures, cooperative and positive social interactions may dominate; but when the increasing cost of social contact and risk of disease exposure, and the xenophobia these costs evoke, make these positive social interactions impossible, then, in humans as much as in any species, competitive intraspecific interactions dominate (Letendre et al., 2010). Given the demonstrated, robust association between pathogen severity and intergroup conflict, it is not surprising that xenophobia manifests not only as fear of contagion but also as general outgroup mistrust (Ember & Ember, 1992). For any human group expressing the degree of xenophobia that is optimal given the local disease ecology, neighboring groups are experiencing similar disease stresses, and members of those groups likely express similar degrees of xenophobia and outgroup hostility. Thus, one's own degree of outgroup hostility is predictive of the degree of outgroup hostility and proclivity to violent intergroup conflict expressed by local outgroup members.

The ethnocentrism associated with collectivist cultures functions in part in the management of the morbidity and mortality of infectious disease (Navarrete & Fessler, 2006; Sugiyama, 2004; Sugiyama & Sugiyama, 2005). Additionally, given the association between pathogen severity and intergroup conflict, the ethnocentrism associated with collectivism may serve an adaptive function in within-group cohesion in defense against coercion and aggression by outgroups, and in offensive coercion and aggression against outgroups (Navarrete, Kurzban, Fessler, & Kirkpatrick, 2004). Thus, the robust association between xenophobia and conflict may account, in part, for the reliable association between xenophobia and ethnocentrism that makes up the cultural dimension of collectivism-individualism.

In this regard, the psychology of collectivism is causal, because to an important extent it is designed for (a) distinguishing group boundaries through adherence to shared ingroup values and behaviors and, hence, for identifying outgroups, and (b) producing negative feelings (dislike, disgust) toward them. The other relevant part of collectivist emotions and behavior is designed for investment in, support of, and loyalty toward ingroup members comprised of extended family and other group members with the same values/morals. Collectivism is interdependency on and high valuation of ingroup members with simultaneous devaluation of outgroup members. Collectivism is appropriately cast as ingroup cooperation. Therefore, collectivism is the basis of success in both defensive and offensive outgroup hostility. The degree of cooperation achieved among members of a warring group—whether a raiding party of egalitarian hunter–gatherers or a highly hierarchical, modern army—is recognized widely as critical for effectiveness in warring (e.g., see Buss's [2004] discussion of warfare). Apparently, coalitional aggression against outgroups is pursued exclusively by men (Alexander, 1979; Wrangham & Peterson, 1996). However, the people (including women) not participating directly in warring participate by providing moral support and associated assistance, which, like the amity among members of the warring coalition, is promoted by collectivist ideology.

There is increasing evidence of psychological adaptation of men that is functionally designed for war. Its information-processing capacities include an assessment of benefits from war in the form of access to women and other resources, as well as an assessment of coalitional support and strength of own versus enemy group (Duntley & Buss, 2009). This adaptation may have been directly sexually selected in the context of men's competition for status, women, and related resources (Buss, 2004; Low, 1993; Manson & Wrangham, 1991; Wrangham & Peterson, 1996). In the parasite-stress model, the war adaptation interacts with the psychological adaptations that function in adopting and using human values, such that xenophobia and ingroup allegiance (collectivism) affect the decision that war is the appropriate means for dealing with intergroup conflict. Hence, warfare is caused partly by war adaptation in men and partly by collectivist values.

At first glance, it may seem contradictory that warfare is partially caused by the need to avoid the risks and costs of exposure to novel pathogens, given men's motivation to participate in warfare because of the opportunity to gain sexual access to outgroup women through wife capture (Chagnon, 1997; Low, 2000; Manson & Wrangham, 1991) and the ubiquity of wartime rape (e.g. Gotschall, 2004; Thornhill & Palmer, 2000). Schaller and Murray (2008) and Thornhill et al. (2009) found a strong, negative correlation between infectious disease prevalence and desire for sexual variety and number of sex partners (using the Sociosexual Orientation Inventory; Simpson & Gangestad, 1991) among women cross-culturally but a weak to nonexistent relationship among men. Thus, for men, it may be that the fitness benefits of gaining sexual access to women outweigh the risk of exposure to novel diseases even in environments in which high intensity of infectious disease favors outgroup avoidance. Furthermore, in environments with high pathogen prevalence, people prioritize physical attractiveness as a marker of health in their mate choices (Gangestad & Buss, 1993; Gangestad et al., 2006). Thus, the women targeted for wife capture or rape during wartime in environments with high intensity of infectious disease are predicted to be younger, more physically attractive, and healthier; and that this is a strategy on the part of men to take advantage of the fitness benefits of acquiring new mates while minimizing the cost of exposure to novel infectious diseases. In environments with reduced intensity of infectious disease, women may be targeted for wife capture and wartime rape with less discrimination.

The parasite-stress model proposes that the psychology of collectivism and of war gives rise to political conflict when perceived benefits of intergroup conflict exceed its high costs. One benefit of pursuit of the conflict is decreased competition and greater access to resources in the event of victory over the outgroup. Another benefit is the exclusion of the outgroup from the region, and in some cases, outgroup extermination. Although warfare may expose warriors to the risk of contracting new diseases from the enemy during combat, warfare may importantly reduce future intergroup contact and interaction relative to the degree of intergroup contact and contagion risk that would result from sharing territory or a resource in the long term (Letendre et al., 2010). According to the parasite-stress model, during human evolutionary history, this future reduction of intergroup contact and interaction provides inclusive fitness benefits greater than the risk and cost of contracting infectious diseases during combat. In this view, the xenophobia that motivated intergroup aggression had as its net effect avoidance of problems resulting from infectious diseases.

Thus, fundamentally, the model rests on the ultimate cause of direct selection resulting from mortality and morbidity from infectious diseases. This parasite-based selection built collectivist psychology and its capacity for evaluating, adopting, and using collectivist values and behavior, which function in avoidance of novel infectious disease (xenophobia), and management of the mortality and morbidity of disease, and resulting intergroup conflict (ethnocentrism).

The parasite-stress model also rests on the existence of moral psychological adaptation with *condition-dependent* expression ranging from high collectivism to high individualism (Thornhill et al., 2009). Condition dependence is the design of moral psychology, because in human evolutionary history, there was spatial and temporal variation in the risks and costs of infectious diseases. Accordingly, moral psychology's function is to adopt the set of values appropriate for the local ecology of human parasite prevalence. Individualism emerges in ecological settings with low infectious disease stress and has the important benefits of intergroup trade, barter, exchange of ideas and technology, and expansion of one's pool of participants for reciprocity and mating. Its benefit-to-cost ratio increases as infectious disease problems decrease. Empirically, as predicted, there is an increase in the degree of widespread individualism as parasite stress declines across the countries of the world. Similarly, as predicted, the degree of widespread collectivism increases as parasite stress increases across countries (Fincher et al., 2008).

In the context of infectious disease, past selection created a condition-dependent moral psychology: the psychological adaptations that manifest in human cognitions and behavior as collectivism and associated xenophobia and ethnocentrism, or as individualism. The moral psychology is designed to incorporate values during development (ontogeny) by learning socially those values well suited to local parasite stress. Separately, some possible ontogenetic ancestral cues that may guide historically adaptive construction of individuals' moral repertoires have been proposed (Fincher et al., 2008; Thornhill et al., 2009). High parasite stress proximately causes a willingness to accept the costs of political conflict, whereas low parasite stress proximately builds pacifism and other positivism toward outgroups. The model, then, may explain much of the variation in the values affecting domestic and interstate conflicts across the globe.

In the model, the following are proximate causes of political conflict, as well as its antipole, pacifism/absence of such conflict: the war psychological adaptation, the moral psychological adaptation, the psychology of collectivism–individualism, the psychology that assesses local parasite stress, the ontogenetic events involved in the production of all this phenotypic machinery, and local parasite stress. Of course, the ontogenetic events mentioned include the important role of the evocation of values as well as the social learning of values within and across generations, which give rise to what many researchers call "cultural evolution," referring to changes in the frequencies of ideas, values, and related behavior (Richerson & Boyd, 2006). The ontogeny of the social-learning machinery, like the ontogeny of all phenotypic features, is causally dependent on genes as a partial proximate cause.

We use "cause" here in its typical, scientific interpretation: that, without which, an effect will not occur. Each proximate cause listed earlier is necessary, but insufficient alone, to generate political conflict, the effect of focal interest here. Each is a partial cause; again, using the standard conception of cause in science.

By definition, proximate biological causes are those that act to generate an effect within the lifetime of the organism. Each piece of machinery in the aforementioned list of proximate causes is the product of evolutionary historical causation, that is, ultimate causation. We have treated only the selection history of this machinery and ignored phylogenetic ultimate causation, a distinct and complementary causal framework that addresses the location on the Tree of Life where traits first appeared in the history of life. According to the parasite-stress model, the selection that built all the proximate machinery (listed earlier) was direct selection in the context of parasite stress, or in the case of the war adaptation, direct sexual selection for condition-dependent warring behavior.

The parasite-stress model of political conflicts predicts (i.e., requires for its support) that the frequency of political conflicts across countries will show a positive correlation with parasite stress and collectivism (and a negative correlation with individualism). If these patterns are not seen, the model is false; the findings to date reported herein and in Letendre et al. (2010) support the model.

The parasite-stress model is about the causes of values and their effects. A given cause–effect model specifies the predicted effects, and those effects are sought empirically to determine whether the model is supported. The civil-conflict literature is voluminous, especially with regard to civil war (partial reviews in Hegre & Sambanis, 2006 and Nettle et al., 2007 [civil war and interethnic conflict]; Alesina, Ozler, Roubini, & Swagel, 1996 [coups]; Abadie & Gardeazabal, 2008; Sosis & Alcorta, 2008 [terrorism]). This literature proposes various causal models for these conflicts, as well as numerous tests of the models. Often, the factors of population size, GDP per capita, Gini (a measure of wealth inequality), time since last conflict (in the case of civil war), inconsistent democratic institutions, political instability, war-prone and undemocratic neighboring countries, ethnic diversity, and a low rate of economic growth are considered to be basic causes of such conflicts. Often in research looking at one or a few of these variables that predict conflict, other variables are considered confounds and, hence, are statistically controlled.

In the parasite-stress model, however, these variables are effects of the same underlying proximate and ultimate causation: parasite stress and its effects on values. Even increased population size, which is positively correlated with the frequency of within-country conflicts (e.g., Hegre & Sombanis, 2006), may be an effect of parasite stress in many parts of the globe, because infectious disease is correlated positively with birth rate cross-nationally, as expected from life-history theory (Guégan, Thomas, Hochberg, de Meeûs, & Renaud, 2001). Separately, treated in detail, is how GDP/capita, economic growth, and democratization are predicted consequences of the parasite-stress model. In short, upon relative emancipation from infectious diseases, peoples' values become more individualistic or liberalized, which results in greater investment in public goods and services and the welfare of outgroups, in general (Fincher et al., 2008; Thornhill et al., 2009). The relationships between ethnic or cultural diversity and parasite stress are treated by Fincher and Thornhill (2008a, 2008b). Furthermore, it has been proposed that the spatial autocorrelation in domestic conflict events among countries within a geographical region results from regional differences in the ecological conditions (e.g., rainfall and temperature) affecting parasite stress (see Fincher & Thornhill 2008a, 2008b). We propose, too, that the variable "time since last civil conflict" is an effect of the parasite-stress model. Hence, the parasite-stress model cannot be tested appropriately by controlling statistically these variables. For example, to control for GDP per capita and/or democratization in an analysis of, say, parasite stress and nonstate wars would reduce the ability to detect the predicted relationships, because GDP per capita and democratization are consequences of parasite stress: Low GDP per capita and low democracy derive from high parasite stress (and associated collectivist values), and high GDP per capita and high democracy from low parasite stress (and associated individualistic values). Thus, it is noteworthy that we found a significant effect of pathogen severity on all indicators of conflict, except terrorism, even when controlling other economic and political indicators that are themselves causally dependent on the intensity of infectious disease.

Because of the aforementioned considerations, aspects of the parasite model of civil conflict do not lend themselves to analysis by multiple regression analysis, controlling for the variety of known correlates that are standard controls (which we propose are mediating variables in the causal relationship between infectious disease and conflict) in such analyses. Path analysis therefore seems to be a more appropriate method. Path analysis did not support our hypothesized model as originally specified. However, with minor post hoc modification of the model, adding and removing paths according to the Lagrange multiplier and Wald test, we arrived at a model that fits our data well and supports the theory we propose here.

Our hypothesized model did not include a direct relation between pathogen severity and the Global Peace Index, but instead it linked these two indirectly via some of the intermediary effects we have discussed: family ties (collectivism), GDP per capita, and democratization. Analysis of our hypothesized model suggested that the model would be strongly improved by the inclusion of a direct relation of pathogen severity to peace (Lagrange multiplier: p = .0068). This addition agrees with our theory because, in order to restrict our analysis to relatively simple models, we did not include a number of other known correlates of conflict that we argue are intermediary to the relationship of infectious disease to peace (e.g., wealth disparity, political instability, etc.).

We found that the Wald test suggested that removal of the relation of democratization to peace would not decrease the fit of the model. This suggests that, while democratization is a known correlate of conflict, its relationship with conflict is spurious and is accounted for by both variables' association with infectious disease and collectivism. We also found that removal of the direct relation of family ties to peace did not decrease the fit of the model. This may be because the family ties variable, although it correlates highly with other measures of collectivism, measures allegiance to the extended family and may therefore be primarily a measure of ethnocentrism. While ethnocentrism is an important component of the cultural unidimension of collectivism-individualism, it does not correlate perfectly with the other component of collectivism, xenophobia (e.g., Cashdan, 2001). Thus, there is the possibility that xenophobia and ethnocentrism play distinct roles in our path model. There may be a mediating role of xenophobia between pathogen severity and peace, which is not explicit in our model because we do not have a corresponding measure of xenophobia in the analysis. Alternatively, it may be, as our final model suggests, that collectivism leads to increased conflict (decreased peace) entirely through other intermediary effects, such as collectivism's negative impact on GDP per capita.

The results of our path analysis support the model we propose. Our final model fits very well to our data (e.g., RMSEA < 0.0001; models with RMSEA < 0.06 are regarded as having good fit, while RMSEA = 0.0 indicates perfect fit; Tabachnick & Fidell, 2007). Nevertheless, the results of this analysis should be regarded as preliminary. The sample size of our data set was limited by the sample sizes for the available measures of collectivism. We selected family ties for its large sample size relative to other measures and restricted our analysis to as simple models as possible; still, its sample size is fairly small for the purposes of path analysis, and the samples with complete overlap with our other variables were even smaller. Our final 9:1 ratio of $n = 63$ sample size to seven variables (four observed and three unobserved) is somewhat less than the desired ratio in path analysis (Klein, 1998, recommends ten samples per variable, whereas five is too few). Furthermore, although we removed univariate and multivariate outliers from our data set, we did see evidence of multivariate nonnormality in the pairwise correlations of our variables. This suggests further caution in the interpretation of these results. We hope that in the future measures of collectivism may become available for more countries of the world, perhaps in future waves of the World Values Survey, which will enable a more conclusive analysis. Nevertheless, we report that path analysis of the data available provides preliminary support for the infectious disease model of civil conflict.

Hegre and Sambanis (2006) point out that published analyses of civil conflicts across countries are highly variable in model components and specifications of relevant statistical-control variables, and they propose that this is because "[W]e do not know the true model" (p. 513). The models of human activity that are most general and useful for scientific discovery are those based in the evolutionary science of human functional design (examples are the empirical cornucopia from Hamilton's [1964a, 1964b] model of nepotism; Trivers's [1971] model of direct reciprocal altruism; Alexander's [1987] model of indirect reciprocity and reputation). Hence, the most general and useful models of human political conflict will be those based in human psychological functional design, and models ignoring evolved psychological adaptations are of relatively limited scientific value. In the long tradition of political conflict research, there is no generally accepted model, because the research has not been inspired by evolutionary theory. This chapter is an attempt to identify a general model of political conflict that is inclusive of all the relevant values and their effects—for example, the value of outgroup dislike brings about the effect of disfranchisement of much of the citizenry of a country—that arise under high parasite stress as well as under emancipation from parasite stress. These values interact with men's psychological war adaptation.

The parasite-stress model does not suggest that there is adaptation(s) that functions specifically in the context of the various types of political conflicts we have addressed (nonstate war, revolutions and coups, terrorism, international war). Hence, there is no adaptation functionally designed for nonstate war per se or for coups. Rather, the model implies that these conflicts are manifestations of moral psychological adaptation designed for historically adaptive ingroup and outgroup relations.

Moreover, the model does not imply or require that these conflicts are adaptive currently. For example, it does not predict that intrastate conflict, on average, has a net benefit in promoting inclusive fitness of combatants in modern, large-scale civil war. In the model, the adaptive value is in terms of the moral psychological adaptation, and solely in evolutionary historical environmental settings that caused its evolution by direct selection. Modern human environments often differ greatly from the evolutionary historical settings that were responsible ultimately for the effective selection of human adaptations. Each of the types of conflicts we have treated may be currently adaptive or maladaptive at the individual level, depending on the circumstances.

Certainly, ours is not the first proposal that people have psychological adaptation that is designed to select the most relevant values for dealing with the Darwinian hostile forces in their local environment. This hypothesis is seen in the earlier writing of Alexander (1987), Wright (1994), Thornhill (1998), Hauser (2006), and others. The present chapter differs from these earlier works in proposing that important components of moral psychology are designed by selection in the context of parasite stress and function in adopting values conditionally based on local parasite stress levels.

As mentioned earlier, the parasite-stress model of conflict is compatible with the proposals in the scientific literature that men's sexually selected pursuit of high mate number affects positively men's decisions to engage in coalitional aggression (e.g., Buss, 2004; Kanazawa, 2009; Low, 1993; Wrangham & Peterson, 1996). Low (1990) reported that, across traditional societies, polygynous marriage systems are more frequent in geographical regions of high parasite stress than in regions of low parasite stress. She also found that, in traditional societies, wife capture from neighboring groups by warring men is most frequent under high parasite stress. This finding supports Low's hypothesis that high parasite stress intensifies sexual selection on males (i.e., increases the variance among men in access to mates with whom children are produced). In this case, the sexual selection intensity stems from parasites generating high phenotypic and associated genetic variance in male quality that is visible to females during mate choice. Hence, parasite stress, through its effect of enhancing polygyny and associated limitations on men's access to mates, may contribute to a net benefit of intergroup aggression to obtain outgroup mates (Kanazawa, 2009).

We emphasize that the parasite-stress model of conflict is consistent with an important role for nepotistic coalitions in warring decisions (e.g., Low, 1993). Nepotistic adaptation is central to collectivism and hence, as we have explained, to cooperation in warring. Also, as we have discussed earlier, collectivism is more than nepotism: It includes assortative, ingroup favoritism toward others who are not genetic relatives. Both of these aspects of collectivism, according to the model and its empirical tests, are related causally and positively to parasite stress.

We close by considering the implications of our findings for international aid directed at reducing the cycle of poverty and conflict in regions such as Africa, equatorial South America, and Southeast Asia. We (Letendre et al., 2010) and Bonds et al. (2010) proposed a disease trap, by which nations in regions with high levels of infectious disease become trapped in self-reinforcing poverty. Infectious disease depresses economic development through its negative effect on human capital, and this is reinforced as poverty prevents efforts at disease reduction (Bonds et al., 2010). Additionally, the xenophobia evoked by high intensity of infectious disease further diminishes the willingness of people to invest in public goods that will be shared across groups, such as economic and health infrastructure, and public goods such as municipal water sources and sanitation systems; and diminishes the willingness to engage in trade with neighboring groups for goods and technologies. Finally, the violent conflict that erupts among impoverished groups who are unwilling to seek cooperative solutions when intergroup competition arises further compounds the infectious disease problem as violent conflict causes death, disability, and disease beyond those killed directly in conflict (Ghobarah, Huth, & Russett, 2003).

Other researchers who have found that the incidence of violent conflict in war-torn regions such as Africa results from the same economic factors that predict conflict in any other region (e.g., Elbadawi & Sambanis, 2000) have recommended international aid targeted at building economic institutions in those regions. Considering the effects infectious diseases have on societies, Hotez and Thomson (2009) and we (Letendre et al., 2010) instead recommended international aid targeted at control and elimination of tropical diseases. Based on our findings here and in Letendre et al. (2010), we advocate that this sort of targeted aid has the greatest potential to get directly to the root cause of poverty and conflict, and to disrupt the infectious disease trap that locks billions of people into poverty and conflict. Dunn et al. (2010) found that investment in public health can significantly negatively affect the prevalence of human pathogens; thus, there is evidence that such directed investment in public health can be effective.

Furthermore, we point out that it is in countries with high intensity of infectious disease that foreign aid directed at economic development may most frequently be misappropriated for the personal benefit of corrupt government officials. In previously unpublished analyses, we find that pathogen severity correlates strongly and positively with government corruption cross-nationally. Transparency International's Corruption Perception Index (http://www.transparency.org/policy_research/surveys_indices/cpi/) scores countries of the world based on expert assessment and opinion polls, and it is scored with highest values corresponding to least corruption. Mean values for this index from 2005 to 2009 correlate strongly and negative with pathogen severity ($n = 178$ countries; $r = -.60$; $p < .001$), indicating that greater corruption is predicted by higher pathogen severity. It is widely recognized that foreign aid directed to corrupt governments is largely wasted (e.g., Burnside & Dollar, 2004; Easterly & Pfutze, 2008); yet because the intensity of infectious disease causes both poverty and the establishment of autocratic (Thornhill et al., 2009) and corrupt regimes, foreign aid directed at alleviating this poverty is necessarily directed toward countries where it is most likely to be misappropriated or otherwise squandered by corrupt officials. We suggest that direct economic aid may more readily be misappropriated, whereas aid directed at diminishing the intensity of infectious disease, such as delivery of vaccines or the construction of sewage and municipal water systems, may be more likely to provide the intended benefit to the people of these countries.

Future Directions

Given the asymmetry of terrorist acts, the logistic regression analysis that we used here may not be a valid test of the applicability of the parasite stress theory to the incidence of terrorism. The quality of available data is also a limiting factor. In the future, better quality data that more thoroughly distinguish domestic from international terrorist incidents may facilitate the appropriate analyses. Such a data set likely will be zero inflated, like the other conflict data sets we examined here, and thus it may be necessary to find appropriate nonparametric methods to analyze the number of terrorist events experienced by countries. It may also be fruitful to develop a data set that catalogs only domestic terrorist events that are supported by a terrorist organization, and which excludes events committed by individuals acting alone. Such a data set may be more indicative of acts carried out by groups of people who share values (i.e., collectivist values) and motivations.

More generally, it may be useful to obtain temporal indicators of the intensity of infectious disease in countries of the world, to allow more thorough longitudinal analysis of the predictive power of infectious disease on conflict. The Contemporary Pathogen Severity Index used here assigns a single value to each country. We used this index in the longitudinal analyses in Letendre et al. (2010) based on the justification that the high correlation between this index and Gangestad and Buss's (1993) historical pathogen severity index ($r = .819$, $n = 27$, $p < .001$) indicates stability in the prevalence of infectious disease over time. Nevertheless, there is some temporal variation in the prevalence of infectious disease, with periodic outbreaks and epidemics.

According to the model we have proposed, temporal variation in the prevalence of infectious disease may temporally predict the onset of conflicts. Such a data set of the timing of epidemics within countries of the world could be used to predict conflict onsets some number of years later. This longitudinal analysis may help tease apart the causal influence of disease on conflict from the endogenous effect of conflict increasing the severity of disease, such as with cholera outbreaks among refugee populations following civil war (although our longitudinal analyses controlled these effects to some extent; Letendre et al., 2010). Additionally, such a temporal analysis may help reveal the mechanism by which infectious disease produces the associated changes in human values that cause increased frequency of conflict. Does an epidemic predict increased likelihood of conflict 1 or 2 years later? Or does an epidemic predict increased likelihood of conflict a generation later, as would be suggested by the hypothesis that prevalence of disease during childhood establishes the intergroup values that will be expressed throughout life (Fincher et al., 2008; Thornhill et al., 2009)?

Finally, we hope that in the future, larger cross-national samples of collectivism-individualism may become available. We selected the variable family ties for use in path analysis, because of its large sample size relative to other measures of collectivism. Even so, our sample size in our final model was marginal given the number of parameters estimated. Additionally, it appears that family ties may be primarily a measure of the ethnocentrism component of collectivism, and our final model suggests that ethnocentrism and xenophobia may play somewhat distinct roles in the relationship between infectious disease and conflict. Thus, we also hope that in the future, a cross-national measure of xenophobia will become available, corresponding to the ethnocentrism represented by family ties. These variables in combination may facilitate further path analyses that will clarify the mechanisms by which infectious disease leads ultimately to conflict.

Acknowledgments

For help with data collection and processing, we thank John Branch, Phuong-Dung Le, Brandon Rice, Pooneh Soltani, Devaraj Aran, and Mary Walker. We thank Barb Brumbach for help with path analysis. We thank Anne Rice for her help in preparing the chapter. Thanks to Chris Eppig, Angela Hung, Astrid Kodric-Brown, and Rhiannon West for comments on the manuscript. K. Letendre gratefully acknowledges support from Sandia National Labs under graduate research fellowship LDRD 09-1292.

References

Abadie, A. (2006). Poverty, political freedom, and the roots of terrorism. *American Economic Review, 96*, 50–56

Abadie, A., & Gardeazabal, J. (2008). Terrorism and the world economy. *European Economic Review, 52*, 1–27.

Alesina, A., & Giuliano, P. (2007). *The power of the family.* Discussion paper No. 2132. Cambridge, MA: Harvard Institute of Economic Research, Harvard University.

Alesina, A., Ozler, S., Roubini, N., & Swagel, P. (1996). Political instability and economic growth. *Journal of Economic Growth, 1*, 189–211.

Alexander, R. D. (1979). *Darwinism and human affairs.* Seattle: University of Washington Press.

Alexander, R. D. (1987). *The biology of moral systems.* New York: Aldine de Gruyter.

Atran, S. (2003). Genesis of suicide terrorism. *Science, 299*, 1534–1539.

Banks, A. S. (1979). *Cross-national time series data archive.* Binghamton: Center for Social Analysis, SUNY Binghamton. September, 1979, updated.

Barro, R. J., & Lee, J. W. (1994). *Data set for a panel of 138 countries.* Retrieved December 2011, from http://www.nber.org/pub/barro.lee/readme.txt

Baron, R. M., & Kenny, D. A. (1986). The moderator-mediator variable distinction in social psychological research: Conceptual, strategic, and statistical considerations. *Journal of Personality and Social Psychology, 51*, 1173–1182.

Blee, K. M., & Creasap, K. A. (2010). Conservative and right-wing movements. *Annual Review of Sociology, 36*, 269–286.

Bonds, M. H., Keenan, D. C., Rohani, P., & Sachs, J. D. (2010). Poverty trap formed by the ecology of infectious diseases. *Proceedings of the Royal Society of London B, 277*, 1185–1192.

Burnside, A. C., & Dollar, D. (2004). *Aid, policies, and growth: Revisiting the evidence.* Working Paper No. 3251. Geneva, Switzerland: World Bank Policy Research. Retrieved January 2011, from http://ideas.repec.org/p/wbk/wbrwps/3251.html

Buss, D. M. (2004). *Evolutionary psychology: The new science of the mind* (2nd ed.). Boston: Allyn & Bacon.

Cashdan, E. (2001). Ethnocentrism and xenophobia: A cross-cultural study. *Current Anthropology, 42*, 760–765.

Chagnon, N. A. (1997). *Yanomamö* (5th ed.). Fort Worth, TX: Harcourt Brace.

Cohen, J. (1988). *Statistical power analysis for the behavioral sciences* (2nd ed.). Hillsdale, NJ: Erlbaum.

Collier, P., & Hoeffler, A. (2002). On the incidence of civil war in Africa. *Journal of Conflict Resolution, 1*, 13–28.

Dunn, R. R., Harris, N. C., Davies, T. J., & Gavin, M. C. (2010). Global drivers of human pathogen richness and prevalence. *Proceedings of the Royal Society of London B, 277*, 2587–2595.

Duntley, J. H., & Buss, D. M. (2009, June 16–20). *The psychology of warfare.* Paper presented at the Human Behavior and Evolution Society Conference, Fullerton, CA.

Easterly, W., & Pfutze, T. (2008). Where does the money go? Best and worst practices in foreign aid. *Journal of Economic Perspectives, 22*, 29–52.

Elbadawi, I., & Sambanis, N. (2000). Why are there so many civil wars in Africa? Understanding and preventing violent conflict. *Journal of African Economies, 9*, 244–269.

Ember, C. R., & Ember, M. (1992). Resource unpredictability, mistrust, and war. *Journal of Conflict Resolution, 36*, 242–262.

Faulkner, J., Schaller, M., Park, J. H., & Duncan, L. A. (2004). Evolved disease-avoidance mechanisms and contemporary xenophobic attitudes. *Group Processes and Intergroup Relations, 7*, 333–353.

Fearon, J. D., & Laitin, D. D. (2003). Ethnicity, insurgency, and civil war. *The American Political Science Review, 97*, 75–90.

Fincher, C. L., & Thornhill, R. (2008a). A parasite-driven wedge: Infectious diseases may explain language and other biodiversity. *Oikos, 117*, 1289–1297.

Fincher, C. L., & Thornhill, R. (2008b). Assortative sociality, limited dispersal, infectious disease, and the genesis of the global pattern of religion diversity. *Proceedings of the Royal Society of London B, 275*, 2587–2594.

Fincher, C. L., & Thornhill, R. (in press.) Parasite stress promotes ingroup assortative sociality: The cases of strong family ties and heightened religiosity. *Behavioral and Brain Sciences.*

Fincher, C. L., Thornhill, R., Murray, D. R., & Schaller, M. (2008). Pathogen prevalence predicts human cross-cultural variability in individualism/collectivism. *Proceedings of the Royal Society of London B, 275*, 1279–1285.

Gangestad, S. W., & Buss, D. M. (1993). Pathogen prevalence and human mate preferences. *Ethology and Sociobiology, 14*, 89–96.

Gangestad, S. W., Haselton, M. G., & Buss, D. M. (2006). Evolutionary foundations of cultural variation: Evoked cultural and mate preferences. *Psychological Inquiry, 17*, 75–95.

Gelfand, M. J., Bhawuk, D. P. S., Nishii, L. H., & Bechtold, D. J. (2004). Individualism and collectivism. In R. J. House, P. J. Hanges, M. Javidan, P. W. Dorfman, & V. Gupta (Eds.), *Culture, leadership, and organizations: The GLOBE study of 62 societies* (pp. 437–512). Thousand Oaks, CA: Sage Publications.

Ghobarah, H. A., Huth, P., & Russett, B. (2003). Civil wars maim and kill people—long after the shooting stops. *American Political Science Review, 97*, 189–202.

Gleditsch, N. P., Hegre, H., & Strand, H. (2009). Democracy and civil war. In M. I. Midlarsky (Ed.), *Handbook of war studies* (Vol. 3, pp. 155–192). Ann Arbor: University of Michigan Press.

Gleditsch, N. P., Wallensteen, P., Eriksson, M., Sollenberg, M., & Strand, H. (2002). Armed conflict 1946–2001: A new dataset. *Journal of Peace Research, 39*, 615–637.

Gotschall, J. (2004). Explaining wartime rape. *The Journal of Sex Research, 41*, 129–136.

Guégan, J-F., Thomas, F., Hochberg, M. E., de Meeûs, T., & Renaud, F. (2001). Disease diversity and human fertility. *Evolution, 55*, 1308–1314.

Hamilton, W. D. (1964a). The genetical evolution of social behaviour. I. *Journal of Theoretical Biology, 7*, 1–16.

Hamilton, W. D. (1964b). The genetical evolution of social behaviour. II. *Journal of Theoretical Biology, 7*, 17–52.

Hauser, M. D. (2006). *Moral minds: How nature designed our universal sense of right and wrong.* New York: Harper Collins.

Hegre, H., & Sambanis, N. (2006). Sensitivity analysis of empirical results on civil war onset. *Journal of Conflict Resolution, 50*, 508–535.

Hofstede, G. (2001). *Culture's consequences: Comparing values, behaviors, institutions, and organizations across nations* (2nd ed.). Thousand Oaks, CA: Sage Publications.

Hotez, P. J., & Thompson, T. G. (2009). Waging peace through neglected tropical disease control: A US foreign policy for the bottom billion. *PloS Neglected Tropical Diseases, 3,* 1–4.

Klein, R. B. (1998). *Principles and practice of structural equation modeling.* New York: The Guilford Press.

Kanazawa, S. (2009). Evolutionary psychological foundations of civil wars. *The Journal of Politics, 71,* 25–34.

Letendre, K., Fincher, C. L., & Thornhill, R. (2010). Does infectious disease cause global variation in the frequency of intrastate armed conflict and civil war? *Biological Reviews, 85,* 669–683.

Low, B. S. (1990). Marriage systems and pathogen stress in human societies. *American Zoologist, 30,* 325–339.

Low, B. S. (1993). An evolutionary perspective on war. In W. Zimmerman & H. K. Jacobson (Eds.), *Behavior, culture and conflict in world politics* (pp. 13–55). Ann Arbor: University of Michigan Press.

Low, B. S. (2000). *Why sex matters: A Darwinian look at human behavior.* Princeton, NJ: Princeton University Press.

MacNeill, A. D. (2004). The capacity for religious experience is an evolutionary adaptation to warfare. *Evolution and Cognition, 10,* 43–60.

Manson, J. H., & Wrangham, R. W. (1991). Intergroup aggression in chimpanzees and humans. *Current Anthropology, 32,* 369–390.

Marshall, M., & Jaggers, K. (2009). *Polity IV project: Political regime characteristics and transitions, 1800–2007.* Retrieved December 2011, from http://www.systemicpeace.org/polity/polity4.htm

Murdock, G. P. (1949). *Social structure.* New York: Macmillan.

Navarrete, C. D., & Fessler, D. M. T. (2006). Disease avoidance and ethnocentrism: The effects of disease vulnerability and disgust sensitivity on intergroup attitudes. *Evolution and Human Behaviour, 27,* 270–282.

Navarrete, C. D., Kurzban, R., Fessler, D. M. T., & Kirkpatrick, L. (2004). Anxiety and intergroup bias: Terror-management or coalitional psychology? *Group Processes and Intergroup Relations, 7,* 370–397.

NCTC, National Counterterrorism Center. (2007). About the worldwide incidents tracking system. Retrieved January 2012, from http://www.nctc.gov/witsbanner/wits_subpage_about.html

Nettle, D. (2009). Ecological influences on human behavioural diversity: A review of recent findings. *Trends in Ecology and Evolution, 24,* 618–624.

Nettle, D., Grace, J. B., Choisy, M., Cornell, H. V., Guegan, J., & Hochberg, M. E. (2007). Cultural diversity, economic development and societal instability. *PLoS, 9,* 1–5.

Price-Smith, A. T. (2001). *The health of nations: Infectious disease, environmental change, and their effect on national security and development.* Cambridge, MA: MIT Press.

Price-Smith, A. T. (2009). *Contagion and chaos: Disease, ecology, and national security in the era of globalization.* Cambridge, MA: MIT Press.

Richerson, P. J., & Boyd, R. (2006). *Not by genes alone: How culture transformed human evolution.* Chicago: University of Chicago Press.

Schaller, M., & Duncan, L. A. (2007). The behavioral immune system: Its evolution and social psychological implications. In J. P. Forgas, M. G. Haselton, & W. von Hippel (Eds.), *Evolution and the social mind* (pp. 293–307). New York: Psychology Press.

Schaller, M., & Murray, D. R. (2008). Pathogens, personality, and culture: Disease prevalence predicts worldwide variability in sociosexuality, extraversion, and openness to experience. *Journal of Personality and Social Psychology, 95,* 212–221.

Schaller, M., & Neuberg, S. L. (2008). Intergroup prejudices and intergroup conflicts. In C. Crawford & D. L. Krebs (Eds.), *Foundations of evolutionary psychology* (pp. 399–412). Mahwah, NJ: Erlbaum.

Simpson, J. A., & Gangestad, S. W. (1991). Individual differences in sociosexuality: Evidence for convergent and discriminant validity. *Journal of Personality and Social Psychology, 60,* 870–883.

Singer, D. J., & Small, M. (1994). *Correlates of war project: International and civil war data, 1816–1992.* Data file, Inter-University Consortium for Political and Social Research, Ann Arbor, MI.

Sosis, R., & Alcorta, C. (2008). Militants and martyrs: Evolutionary perspectives on religion and terrorism. In R. Sagarin & T. Taylor (Eds.), *Natural security: A Darwinian approach to a dangerous world* (pp. 105–124). Berkley: University of California Press.

Strand, H. (2006). *Reassessing the civil democratic peace.* Ph.D. dissertation, Department of Political Science, University of Oslo and Centre of the Study of Civil War, PRIO.

Streiner, D. L. (2005). Finding our way: An introduction to path analysis. *Research Methods in Psychiatry, 50,* 115–122.

Suh, E., Diener, E., Oishi, S., & Triandis, H. C. (1998). The shifting basis of life satisfaction judgments across cultures: Emotions versus norms. *Journal of Personality and Social Psychology, 74,* 482–493.

Sugiyama, L. S. (2004). Illness, injury, and disability among Shiwiar forager–horticulturalists: Implications of human life history. *American Journal of Physical Anthropology, 123,* 371–389.

Sugiyama, L. S., & Sugiyama, M. S. (2005). Social roles, prestige, and health risk: Social niche specialization as a risk-buffering strategy. *Human Nature, 14,* 165–190.

Tabachnick, B. G., & Fidell, L. S. (2007). *Using multivariate statistics* (5th ed.). New York: Pearson Education.

Thompson, J. N. (2005.) *The geographic mosaic of coevolution.* Chicago: The University of Chicago Press.

Thornhill, R. (1998). Darwinian aesthetics. In C. Crawford & D. L. Krebs (Eds.), *Handbook of evolutionary psychology: Ideas, issues, and applications* (pp. 543–572). Mahwah: Erlbaum.

Thornhill, R., & Palmer, C. (2000). *A natural history of rape: Biological bases of sexual coercion.* Cambridge, MA: MIT Press.

Thornhill, R., Fincher, C. L., & Aran, D. (2009). Parasites, democratization, and the liberalization of values across contemporary countries. *Biological Reviews, 184,* 113–131.

Thornhill, R., Fincher, C. L., Murray, D. R., & Schaller, M. (2010). Zoonotic and non-zoonotic diseases in relation to human personality and societal values: Support for the parasite-stress model. *Evolutionary Psychology, 8,* 151–169.

Trivers, R. L. (1971). The evolution of reciprocal altruism. *Quarterly Review of Biology, 46,* 35–57.

West, S. A., Griffin, A. S., & Gardner, A. (2007). Social semantics: Altruism, cooperation, mutualism, strong reciprocity and group selection. *Journal of Evolutionary Biology, 20,* 415–432.

Williams, G. C. (1966). *Adaptation and natural selection.* Princeton, NJ: Princeton University Press.

World Health Organization. (2004.) Disease and injury country estimates. Retrieved January 2012, from http://www.who.int/healthinfo/global_burden_disease/estimates_country/en/index.html

Wrangham, R., & Peterson, D. (1996). *Demonic males.* Boston: Houghton Mifflin.

Wright, R. (1994). *The moral animal.* New York: Vintage.

Zhang, D. D., Brecke, P., Lee, H. F., He, Y., & Zhang, J. (2007). Global climate change, war, and population decline in recent human history. *Proceedings of the National Academy of Sciences USA, 104,* 19214–19219.

CHAPTER 22

Band of Brothers or Band of Siblings?: An Evolutionary Perspective on Sexual Integration of Combat Forces

Kingsley R. Browne

Abstract

Sexual integration of combat forces presents underappreciated challenges. Sex differences in physical capacity remain important in modern warfare, and the sexes also differ in combat-relevant psychological traits, including risk taking and aggressiveness. Moreover, group dynamics have consequences for unit cohesion and combat performance. Men more easily participate in coalitions organized to mete out violence, a tendency enhanced in the presence of intergroup competition. Men's coalitions require lower levels of investment and can persist for longer in the face of within-group conflict than women's coalitions. Combat units rely on cohesion to enable performance, and introduction of women tends to reduce cohesion because, among other reasons, men often find it difficult to trust women. The attributes that soldiers value in comrades are ones that would have been important for primitive warriors, including strength, physical courage, and other aspects of masculinity, which may mean that women cannot evoke trust in their male comrades the way other men can.

Key Words: coalitions, sex differences, women in combat, military, risk taking, physical aggressiveness, cohesion, trust, combat motivation

Introduction

Throughout the ages, participation in violent intergroup conflict has been overwhelmingly the province of men. No modern society significantly relies, and virtually no premodern society relied, on women as combat soldiers. Not only is warfare a male occupation, in many ways it has been viewed as the quintessential "manly" pursuit. Unlike, say, the manufacture of musical instruments—a task that also tends cross-culturally to be performed by men (D'Andrade, 1966)—warfare has often been the defining feature of masculinity for a culture. In many primitive societies, for example, a male was not entitled to full status as a man until he distinguished himself in warfare, usually by killing an enemy (Turney-High, 1971, p. 161). Moreover, women were often among the "spoils" of primitive warfare and sometimes one of its primary goals (Chagnon, 1988).

Just as warfare has been associated with men, peace has been associated with women. Although the Shoshone girl Sacagawea is often erroneously referred to as Lewis and Clark's "guide," her most significant contribution to that epic journey was that her presence, in William Clark's words, "reconciles all the Indians, as to our friendly intentions [because] a woman with a party of men is a token of peace" (Lewis & Clark, 1814/1904, entry of Oct. 13, 1805, p. 111). Similarly, Australian prospector Michael Leahy recalled the relief he felt when first contacting the highlanders of New Guinea in the early 1920s, when it appeared that the armed men were accompanied by women, leading his lowland native guide to assure him that there would be no fight (Connolly & Anderson, 1987, p. 24). Thus, it is not only a consistent pattern that men engage in warfare but also that women do not (Brightman, 1996). This pattern parallels the exclusion of women from big-game hunting, as exemplified by the !Kung, who "believe that femaleness weakens the hunters' prowess and endangers his chance of success" (Marshall, 1976, p. 96).

Many modern nations are now adopting policies that attempt to overturn the long-standing link between men and warfare. Some countries, such as Canada, Norway, and the Netherlands, have eliminated all bars to women serving in combat, though there have been few takers in those volunteer militaries (Browne, 2007a, p. 268). Others, such as the United States and Britain, have opened many formerly closed combat positions to women, while maintaining a ban on women in offensive ground combat, although even this exclusion has been subjected to heavy criticism (e.g., Solaro, 2006). The question is not, as some would have it, whether women can be good *soldiers*; they clearly can be and have been in large numbers. The real question is whether in the contemporary military they can be effective *warriors*, that is, people who possess "a strong individual existential commitment to combat" (Henriksen, 2007, p. 206) and enhance the effectiveness of their units.

A variety of assumptions underlie initiatives to expand women's combat opportunities. One is that exclusion of women really never made sense; it was based on the assumption that because *many* women lacked the physical and emotional wherewithal to engage in combat, *all* women should be excluded. Underlying this view is the notion that there is really nothing inherently "masculine" about war—that the association between men and warfare is mere happenstance—and that warfare neither calls for nor rewards masculinity. One feminist professor, for example, has found it difficult "to pinpoint why it is that the army is more male than the university" (Addis, 1994, p. 17). Another perception is that although the historic reliance on men in combat may have made sense in the past, changes in the nature of warfare have transformed warfare from a contest of brawn into one of brains, rendering the sexes interchangeable in combat (Addis, Russo, & Sebesta, 1994, p. xv; De Groot, 1995, p. 259). Under this view, the primary obstacle to integration today is outdated sexist attitudes that cause men to resist inclusion of women into the "band of brothers." These attitudes, it is argued, can be overcome by proper leadership and training (Harrell & Miller, 1997, p. 99).

The primary purpose of this chapter is to show that these assumptions are flawed. First, the sexes differ on an array of combat-related physical and psychological dimensions. The most obvious, and least controversial, differences are physical. Despite claims to the contrary, these differences remain relevant, because modern combat continues to impose serious physical challenges (Browne, 2007a, pp. 59–72). Second, the assumption that men and women are largely identical in combat-relevant traits other than physical strength overlooks a vast literature on psychological sex differences. Many traits in which the sexes differ are critical to combat personnel, including physical aggressiveness, willingness to kill strangers at close range, and willingness to expose oneself to physical risk. On the other hand, nurturance and empathy, which are more characteristic of women, can interfere with combat performance. Some of these traits are difficult to measure meaningfully in advance of actual combat, and although there is overlap between the sexes on all of them, there is a serious question about whether there is enough to justify inclusion of women.

Finally, and more important, however, is the fact that irrespective of the characteristics of an individual woman, she is still a woman, and the fact of her sex by itself can have an array of effects on her unit's performance. Effective combat units are cohesive, and introduction of women can interfere with cohesion even if individual women possess the traditional warrior attributes. Moreover, men seem less inclined to trust women in dangerous situations. Although beyond the scope of this chapter, inclusion of women can also have adverse effects as a consequence of sexual competition and other sexual tensions, in addition to factors such as men's tendency to protect women, potential rape of captured women, and effects of women's reproductive role, such as pregnancy, menstruation, and motherhood (especially single motherhood) (Browne, 2007a).

Combat-Related Physical and Psychological Sex Differences

The first set of sex differences consists of individually measurable traits. Some of these differences are important in their own right, and they can also affect group dynamics in a number of ways described later. Although some can be effectively measured in advance, others cannot.

Physical Differences

The most obvious, and least controversial, differences are in physical capacity, including strength, speed, throwing speed and accuracy, aerobic and anaerobic capacity, endurance, and pain tolerance, not to mention height, weight, and bone mass (Browne, 2007a, pp. 19–27). Although the magnitude of the sex difference varies from trait to trait, there is very little overlap between the sexes on some of them, such as upper-body strength (Pheasant, 1983). The probability that a man selected at random from the population will have greater upper-body strength than a randomly selected woman typically ranges between 95% and 99%, depending upon the sample and the measure employed. Many of these differences are observable in children and increase with puberty (Thomas & French, 1985). This male physical advantage reflects a common primate, even mammalian, pattern. In most such species, sexual dimorphism in size and strength is an evolutionary consequence of male-male competition (Plavcan & Van Schaik, 1997), and as will be seen later, this dimorphism is coupled with psychological adaptations facilitating intrasexual competition.

The need for strength and endurance in modern combat has not disappeared. In fact, the infantry soldier of today carries more gear than his World War II counterpart (Scales, 2005). Although most soldiers will not engage in hand-to-hand combat, which relies primarily on upper-body strength, some still do, and such combat is the last resort of all warriors—whether infantry riflemen, tank drivers, or downed fighter pilots attempting to resist capture or to escape (McConnell, 1985)—and even of those occupying support positions. Many other combat tasks require strength, as well, including lifting of heavy artillery shells, damage-control tasks on a warship, carrying a machine gun, or digging fighting holes. Because combat is physically arduous and must be sustained in adverse conditions, knowing how to perform a task and being able to perform it in training are not enough. Although Israeli women serve as tank instructors, for example, they are not eligible for combat assignments in the Armored Corps because they lack the endurance to load heavy shells for extended periods (Schechter, 2004). Even if one's assigned job is not physically demanding, combat may render it so. If a ship is struck by a missile, all hands may have to turn to the tasks of damage control, such as fire fighting, flood limitation, and evacuation of the wounded. The difference between a ship's sinking and staying afloat may turn on the crew's ability to sustain such intense physical activity (Peniston, 2006, pp. 150–151, 156).

Women who would serve in combat would not be randomly selected, and self-selection would ensure that women who volunteered would be more male-like than average. Self-selection has only limited effects, however. A 2002 British Ministry of Defence study found that only about one-tenth of 1% of female recruits and 1% of trained female soldiers could satisfy the physical standards for infantry and armor (Ministry of Defence, 2002, p. B-5). Similarly, a study by the US Navy found that although virtually all male sailors could meet the standards for critical damage-control tasks, most women could not (Presidential Commission, 1992, p. 74). The very different physical-fitness standards that the military sets for the two sexes reflect its recognition of these large sex differences. For example, 18-year-old females in the US Army are required to do only about one-third the number of push-ups as 18-year-old males and are allowed more time to run 2 miles than 41-year-old men (Vanden Brook, 2006).

Finally, the sexes differ in their tolerance for pain. A major review of pain studies found average effect sizes of between 0.5 and 0.6 for both pain threshold (the level at which a stimulus is perceived as painful) and pain tolerance (the level at which pain is no longer bearable) (Riley, Robinson, Wise, Myers, & Fillingim, 1998). The importance of a soldier's ability to endure physical pain scarcely requires mention. A wounded soldier must sometimes continue to fight despite his wounds, and the more pain he is experiencing, the less able he is to fight.

In some respects, physical sex differences present the easiest challenge for sexual integration, because sex-neutral physical tests could, in principle, be used to screen applicants, although rigorous standards would exclude most women. As we will see later, however, psychological sex differences create more difficult issues.

Psychological Sex Differences

The sexes differ on average in a variety of psychological attributes, including risk taking, physical aggression, fear, and empathy. Many of these differences are observable early in childhood and increase substantially at the time of puberty. Like physical sex differences, these psychological differences may have substantial impact on combat performance.

RISK TAKING

One of the largest sex differences is in risk-taking behavior, especially with respect to physical risks, with the difference peaking in young adulthood (Wilson & Daly, 1985). Although in most laboratory studies, sex differences are only moderate (Byrnes, Miller, & Schafer, 1999), in naturalistic settings, the differences are stark, whether in high-risk employment, recreation, or simply "lifestyle." In the workplace, for example, men are overwhelmingly represented in risky employment, with well over 90% of workplaces deaths in the United States being males (Bureau of Labor Statistics, 2003). In a meta-analysis of sex differences in risk taking, Byrnes, Miller, and Schafer (1999) concluded that "males took risks even when it was clear that it was a bad idea," while females seemed "disinclined to take risks even in fairly innocuous situations or when it was a good idea to take a risk" (p. 378). This finding is significant for military risk taking, because many militarily appropriate risks are, from a personal perspective, a "bad idea," even if they are a good idea from an institutional perspective. The sexes also differ in the effect of emotions on their risk-taking behavior, as anger increases risk taking among men but does not do so for women, while disgust inhibits risk taking among women, but it does not for men (Fessler, Pillsworth, & Flamson, 2004), effects that would be predicted to influence combat behavior.

FEAR

Risk taking and fear are intimately related, as the latter tends to inhibit the former. Females from childhood through adulthood experience higher levels of fear than males (McLean & Anderson, 2009). Indeed, sex differences in expression of fear are observable even in infancy (Nagy et al., 2001), and they increase into adulthood (Gullone & King, 1997). Sex differences in fear and risk perception have two components. Women are more likely than men to perceive risk, and even when they perceive the same level of risk as men, they have higher levels of fear about the risk. For example, notwithstanding the fact that women are less frequently victimized by violent crime, they are more fearful of it than men (Smith & Torstensson, 1997), with women's fear being highest among those of peak reproductive age. Women's heightened fear of crime does not appear to be just a function of their special vulnerability to rape, as it extends to other crimes as well, such as murder—even though women are substantially less likely to be murdered than men—and to property crimes. When two snipers were terrorizing the Washington, D.C., area in 2002, women reported being substantially more likely than men to modify their behaviors, even though objectively there was a very low risk of harm and men made up more than two-thirds of the sniping victims (Zivotofsky & Koslowsky, 2005). A study of male and female soldiers serving in support positions during the Gulf War, none of whom had seen combat, found that women reported experiencing significantly more psychological stress than men, especially stress related to anticipation of combat (Rosen, Wright, Marlowe, Bartone, & Gifford, 1999). Women also suffer more from posttraumatic stress disorder (PTSD), a sex difference that is not entirely attributable to sex differences in sexual assault (Pratchett, Pelcovitz, & Yehuda, 2010). Similarly, Israeli girls suffer more from PTSD than boys after terror attacks, a difference that is largely a result of their greater fear levels (Laufer & Solomon, 2009).

PHYSICAL AGGRESSION

The sexes also differ in their attitudes toward, and willingness to engage in, physical aggression. Like risk taking, sex differences in physical aggression appear early in development, being present from about 2 years of age. Fights among school children, for example, are overwhelmingly between boys (Boulton, 1993). A meta-analysis of aggression studies found that the age group showing the largest sex difference is 18–21-year-olds ($d = 0.66$), followed closely by 22–30-year-olds ($d = 0.60$) (Archer, 2009), the prime demographics for combat soldiers. As aggressive behavior becomes more dangerous, the sex difference in aggression increases. Thus, when criminal behavior is considered, which is typically not done in psychological studies of aggression, the sex difference is even more compelling. Between 1976 and 2004, almost 90% of convicted murderers in the United States were male (as were over three-quarters of their victims) (Fox & Zawitz, 2006). In 2000, state and federal prisons held approximately 1.3 million inmates (US Department of Justice, 2003, p. v), of whom 93% were male (and a greater proportion of male prisoners than female prisoners were serving time for violent offenses). Men not only engage in more physical forms of attack, they also have more positive attitudes toward aggression, being more likely to view it as an acceptable way of achieving one's ends and experiencing less guilt and anxiety about engaging in aggression than women do (Campbell & Muncer, 1994).

EMPATHY AND NURTURANCE

Although perhaps not as obvious as the case with traits such as risk taking and aggression, sex differences in empathy and nurturance are also relevant to combat service. The psychological process of "pseudo-speciation" (Eibl-Eibesfeldt, 1979, pp. 122–125), which allows—or even encourages—soldiers to kill, is the antithesis of compassion and sensitivity. Indeed, it is a mechanism that precludes empathy, for only by categorizing the enemy as someone not entitled to a full measure of compassion is it possible for most people to kill without experiencing the guilt that usually follows the killing of another human being. A high degree of empathy not only engenders a reluctance to kill, it also increases the psychological cost of killing if that reluctance is overcome. Having engaged in conduct inconsistent with their personal natures, many soldiers have a difficult time living with what they have done and in extreme cases suffering from PTSD (Kilner, 2002).

From childhood, girls engage in more nurturing behavior than boys, and in all societies, women engage in overwhelmingly more parental care than men (Hewlett, 1988). Women also score higher on most measures of empathy (Baron-Cohen & Wheelwright, 2004), which may be responsible for the heightened guilt and anxiety that women feel about acting aggressively (Archer, 2004). The sexes also differ in the circumstances that attenuate empathy. A study comparing empathic responses of men and women using functional magnetic resonance imaging (fMRI) of the brain found that although both sexes showed activation in areas of the brain that respond to their own pain and to observation of pain in others when "innocent" people were electrically shocked, when someone who "deserved" harm (in the study, someone who had played a game unfairly) was shocked, the empathic response of men, but not of women, was substantially reduced (Singer et al., 2006). On the other hand, areas of the brain associated with reward processing showed enhanced activation in men, but not women, when the "deserving" player was shocked. These findings suggest that men's empathy may be more easily "switched off" than women's and that men may derive greater satisfaction from at least some sorts of physical revenge.

The fact that women are likely to feel greater empathy for the enemy (and more fear) than men is consistent with reports from Iraq suggesting that women are suffering PTSD at a substantially higher rate and of a more serious nature than men (Scharnberg, 2005), despite the fact that they are exposed to substantially less combat danger. Thus, women may be less likely than men to kill and more likely to pay a heavy psychological cost for it when they do.

Studies May Underestimate the Magnitude of Sex Differences

Sex differences in individual traits such as risk taking, fear, aggressiveness, dominance, and empathy are substantial, but there is significant overlap between the sexes in many of these traits. Psychological studies may underestimate the magnitude of the relevant sex differences, however. One reason is that the traits, though often correlated, are not perfectly so, meaning that the sex imbalance among those possessing substantial amounts of all of the relevant traits would be greater than for any one trait. As Del Giudice (2009) has shown, simultaneous measurement of multidimensional constructs will often yield effects much larger than the average of the unidimensional separate effects.

Another reason that the magnitude of sex effects may be underestimated is that the relevant emotions may not have been activated. It is one thing to ask city dwellers whether they would be willing to spend a night in the woods in grizzly-bear country; it is quite another thing to put them in a bear-filled forest and observe their physiological, emotional, and behavioral responses, or to determine whether they have voluntarily placed themselves in such positions. Thus, measures of observed behaviors tend to reveal larger effects than paper-and-pencil trait measures or even self-reports (Archer, 2004; Byrnes et al., 1999). Moreover, some sex differences, such as those in risk taking, are enhanced in group settings (Ronay & Kim, 2006), despite usually being measured in individual settings.

Examining people's actual physically risky behavior is likely to provide a more accurate view of relevant sex differences than laboratory studies. One real-world demonstration of men's greater risk-taking propensity comes from the Carnegie Hero Fund Commission, which bestows awards for heroism. Johnson (1996) found that 92% of the recognized acts of heroism from 1989 through 1995 were performed by men. There was also a significant difference in the beneficiaries of the heroism: Over half of those rescued by women were known to the rescuer, while over two-thirds of those rescued by men were strangers. Similar results were obtained in a study of rescues in the United Kingdom, with over 94% of rescuers being male, and a majority of those rescued by men being strangers compared to less than 20% for women (Lyons, 2005). The same pattern is exhibited in the awarding of the United States Lifesaving Association's (USLA) Medal of Valor, which is presented to professional lifeguards who have risked their lives to an extraordinary degree, with all 35 of the medals bestowed through 2008 having been awarded to men (USLA, n.d.). The USLA also bestows its Heroic Act Award on non-lifeguards who have risked their lives to an extraordinary degree in a rescue or attempted rescue of an unrelated person, with 38 of 48 such awards having been given to men (and 7 of the women given awards were among 16 collegiate sailors in 2002 who had engaged in a single rescue, with the awards being granted for their collective efforts rather than for individual actions) (USLA, n.d.; International Sailing Federation, 2002).

A subset of the Carnegie awards may be even more telling on the subject of sex differences. Most of the Carnegie awards examined by Johnson involved nonaggressive actions, such as rescuing a victim from fire or drowning. More relevant to the combat question are situations in which there is not only a substantial risk of death or serious injury but also a need to confront physically violent people. So, who are the people who foil robberies, chase down purse snatchers and carjackers, and rescue others from criminal assaults? The Carnegie awards suggest that it is men who are the principal protectors of crime victims. Between 1998 and July 2006, over 90% of the almost 800 awards went to males (Browne, 2007a, pp. 35–36). Eighty-two of the awards went to people responding to an assault, and the pattern there is revealing. First, men were much more likely to engage the assailant physically. Of the 47 rescuers responding to an assailant armed with a gun, 5 were women, but none of these women physically engaged the assailant, whereas 35 of the 42 male rescuers did. Second, men were much more likely to sustain fatal injuries in the process. Ten rescuers were killed while aiding assault victims, all of them men. Third, men were much more likely to intervene to protect a stranger. Only 40% of the women were rescuing strangers, compared to 90% of the men. Another study specifically focusing on individuals who intervened to thwart violent crimes, such as muggings, armed robberies, and bank holdups, found that only 1 of 32 rescuers in the sample was female (Huston, Ruggiero, Conner, & Geis, 1981).

Becker and Eagly (2004) have argued that the Carnegie awards provide a skewed view of the true sex distribution of heroes. They argue that the association of heroic behavior with men reflects a failure to appreciate women's heroic behavior. Heroic behavior, they say, has two components: It is both risky and prosocial. They acknowledge that men are generally more inclined to engage in risky behaviors, but they argue that women are more likely to engage in prosocial behaviors, so these two tendencies might be expected to cancel each other out in producing the sex distribution of heroes. The heroic acts of Carnegie medal recipients count as heroic, they argue, but so, too, do a number of other behaviors that women are as likely—or even more likely—to engage in. They examined data from the "Righteous Among the Nations," which recognizes non-Jews who risked their lives to save Jews during the Holocaust. They found that in Poland, the Netherlands, and France, men and women were roughly equally likely to be listed, although if married couples were excluded—because of uncertainty about whether the husband and wife were equally involved in the activity—women predominated.

It is unclear whether the Holocaust study taps into behaviors that are strongly implicated in daring physical exploits, such as combat service. Certainly, assisting Jews was risky business, although the point of the activity was avoiding detection rather than engaging in violent confrontation. It is also difficult to draw any inferences about global sex differences in heroic behaviors (or the lack thereof) from this sample without knowing what the men were doing while the women were aiding Jews. In all three countries studied, there was an active resistance against the Nazis. Members of the resistance—who were predominantly male—engaged in a variety of behaviors, including attacks on the enemy, sabotage, acquisition and transmission of intelligence, distribution of underground newspapers, organizing strikes, as well as providing shelter not only to Jews but also to Allied soldiers and downed airmen. Moreover, presumably many of the husbands of the women who were listed were serving in the military (or dead). When all of these activities are cumulated, it is likely that there was a strong disproportion of men involved. Thus, Becker and Eagly's conclusion (p. 173) that "women made heroic choices at least as often as men" is possible only by carving out one particular facet of resistance to the Nazis, notably one that was carried on surreptitiously and primarily in the home. Although Becker and Eagly express hope that their research will produce a "cultural shift whereby heroism will be viewed as more androgynous" (p. 175), their data do not establish that such a shift is warranted.

Individual Sex Differences and Combat Motivation

The aforementioned traits—risk taking, fear, physical aggressiveness, and empathy—all show substantial sex differences, and all are related in one way or another to combat motivation. Obviously, combat demands risk taking, willingness to engage in physical aggression, and sufficient depersonalization of the enemy to allow his killing. Empathy may affect combat motivation by inhibiting the willingness to kill, and men's diminished empathy for those who "deserve" punishment may enhance their willingness to kill the enemy. Moreover, the strength of the mother–infant bond seems to make the long deployments sometimes required by military service more difficult for mothers than for fathers (Browne, 2007a, pp. 255–256). In addition to causing greater psychological pain for women, this may also undermine their performance.

The fear that is ever present on the battlefield also affects combat performance, but its impact is complex, because soldiers face an array of fears in battle. The most obvious of these fears are of death and serious injury. Such fears are negatively motivating, and women's greater fear of physical harm predictably would result in a greater reduction in motivation to fight. As Campbell (1999) has shown, women have evolved to act as though they see less potential gain and more potential loss than men do from exposing themselves to physical risks.

Perhaps surprisingly, however, fear of death and injury are not necessarily the greatest fears that men face in combat. Rather, men's greatest fear going into battle, especially men going into battle for the first time, is that they will show themselves to be cowards (Dollard, 1944, pp. 18–19). Commenting on the American soldier in World War II, Stouffer and colleagues noted that combat is a "dare," and "one never knew for sure that he could take it until he had demonstrated that he could" (Stouffer et al., 1949, pp. 131–132). Showing cowardice in battle brought not just censure for cowardice itself; even more powerfully, "to fail to measure up as a soldier in courage and endurance was to risk the charge of not being a man."

Why do so many men fear cowardice even more than their own deaths? Primarily because of the "desire to appear a man amongst men," and battle is the "acid test." As Holmes (1985, pp. 142–143) puts it, "there are occasions when this desire to preserve status is quite literally stronger than the fear of death." The "status" that the soldier seeks is not a hierarchical status—in fact, it is unrelated to formal military rank—but rather a kind of "membership" status. Unlike other situations in which men compete against each other for top positions, as in tribal or corporate politics (see Browne, 2002), men in combat units seek acceptance into the "band of brothers"; they seek acknowledgment of other men that they are valuable coalition partners. As Keegan (1993, p. 226) observed of the soldier, "It is the admiration of other soldiers that satisfies him—if he can win it."

Fear of not measuring up as a man, unlike fear of death or injury, is positively motivating, because it causes men to engage in behaviors that might hasten their death. Because women do not feel a man's need to be considered a "man among men," they are likely to be less inclined to expose themselves to the risk of death to achieve that respect. They may be motivated by a desire not to be labeled cowards, but that probably tends to be a relatively weak motivation for women, since to label a woman a "coward" is far less insulting than labeling a man one. Indeed, one seldom hears that label being attached to a woman. The dictionary defines "coward" as "one who shows disgraceful fear or timidity" (Merriam-Webster, 2005). We do not decline to label women cowards because they do not display fear or timidity but rather because we do not find women's fear or timidity disgraceful. Thus, the reluctance to label women cowards arises not because women are physically braver than men but because they are not and are not expected to be, a phenomenon captured by Aristotle's observation that "a man would be thought a coward if he had no more courage than a courageous woman" (Aristotle, 2000, p. 109). The reduced expectation of women's courage raises an additional problem, which is that because of the strong equality norms in combat units, the failure to expect much courage from female soldiers may have the effect of defining bravery down for all (Browne, 2007a, pp. 108–111).

In theory, average sex differences could be dealt with through improvements in personnel selection. As discussed previously, the physical disparity between men and women could be rendered largely irrelevant by the imposition of rigorous sex-neutral physical standards. Selection criteria might also be identified that would, on a wholesale basis, attempt to distinguish individuals who would also possess the requisite combination of risk taking, physical aggressiveness, and courage that would allow them to be lions in combat. Thus could a small cohort of women be created who were as physically and psychologically suited to ground combat as their male comrades.

Reality is different from theory, however. One of the truisms of combat is that it is never known before the shooting starts who will perform well and who will not (Marshall, 1947, p. 61; Richardson, 1978, p. 95). Good performance in training often does not translate to good performance in combat, and people who perform poorly in training may turn out to be masters of the battlefield. Moreover, no matter how accurate individual selection criteria might be made, there is another, more difficult problem: No matter what the individual attributes of a female warrior, she is still a woman, and her femaleness may affect a unit's effectiveness in a variety of ways, a problem obscured by an atomistic focus on individual traits. As we will see later, these group dynamics raise serious doubts about whether women can be fully integrated into male combat groups.

Differences in Single-Sex and Mixed-Sex Groups

Group dynamics are critical in combat, as a vast literature on combat motivation shows. Men fight for many reasons, but if any reason could be labeled primary, it is that they fight for their comrades with whom they have bonded. This bond—often characterized as "male bonding (Tiger, 1969)—is a powerful one. In addition to the "horizontal cohesion" that connects the "band of brothers" is the "vertical cohesion" between leaders and subordinates. The prospect of integration raises a number of questions that are critical to combat effectiveness. Do men have an innate predisposition to resist introduction of women into certain all-male groups even if the women possess as much strength, aggressiveness, and inclination to take risks as many men? Or, if men lack an inclination to actively resist their introduction, do they also lack the psychological mechanisms that will affirmatively facilitate inclusion of women in combat groups? Moreover, if women are eligible to be combat soldiers, they will also be eligible to be combat leaders, leading to the question of whether men are as inclined to follow a woman into battle as they are another man. It may be that for very fundamental reasons women do not evoke in men the same feelings of comradeship and "followership" that men do. Although the Standard Social Science Model (SSSM) view is that men and women, and male, female, and mixed-sex groups, are different only because of social learning, there is substantial reason to believe that something more fundamental is at play.

Male Coalitionary Psychology: The "Male Warrior Hypothesis"

All-male groups are common throughout the world—whether secret societies, warrior groups, street gangs, sports teams, or college fraternities. They are often involved with the use of force, which is virtually a male monopoly. Intergroup hostility and competition in humans occurs primarily between groups of men and can be activated (among men but not women) by even subtle cues of intergroup conflict (Yuki & Yokota, 2009), and in public-goods games, men, but not women, increase their group contribution when intergroup competition is activated (Van Vugt, De Cremer, & Janssen, 2007). Whereas women tend to form their identity based upon their relationships with other individuals, men are more likely to form their identity based upon the group (sports team, fraternity, etc.) to which they belong and are more likely to engage in costly sacrifice for their group (Gabriel & Gardner, 1999).

Where does this tendency of men to band together in circumstances of intergroup competition come from? It seems likely that our species' history of "frequent and violent intergroup conflict has shaped the social psychology and behavior of men in general" (Van Vugt et al., 2007). The "male-warrior hypothesis" of Van Vugt and colleagues posits that men possess a psychology that makes them more likely to engage in coalitionary behavior and intergroup rivalry than women, because of the reproductive benefits that coalition membership brought to ancestral males involved in conflicts with outgroups.

Sex differences in group behavior are observable even in children and suggest a phylogenetic history of such differences. A principal function of play in both humans and nonhumans is to prepare the individual for the challenges of adulthood (Parker, 1984). The spontaneous aggregation of boys into all-male groups, as well as the play hunting and fighting that these groups engage in—even when discouraged by adults—performs such a function in boys, just as play child care seems to for girls. By age 6, boys, but not girls, spontaneously form multichild groups, and much of their play takes place in such groups (Benenson, Apostoleris, & Parnass, 1997). Boys obtain substantial emotional rewards from this group play, despite its rough and dominance-oriented nature (Martin & Fabes, 2001), and the thrill-motivated risky play that children, especially boys, engage in seems to function to reduce anxiety associated with hazardous activities and allow them to master dangerous situations (Sandseter & Kennair, 2011).

The tendency of boys to form coalitions in which they struggle for dominance is likely the result of an "evolved motivational disposition associated with coalitionary male-male competition" that prepares them for their traditional role (Geary, Byrd-Craven, Hoard, Vigil, & Numtee, 2003, p. 457). Moreover, many of the specific behaviors involved in boys' play—running, throwing, and tracking projectiles—mirror skills important in primitive warfare. Thus, rough-and-tumble play in boys, including play fighting, serves the twin functions of providing experience in negotiation of dominance hierarchies and also in practicing specific behaviors useful in adulthood for engaging in intergroup competition. Most organized male sports also involve the strength (especially upper-body strength), speed, and throwing ability that would have been important in hunting and warfare (Lombardo, 2012), and the greater sport "fandom" displayed by males is probably a by-product of male coalitional psychology (Winegard & Deaner, 2010).

The banding together of males into all-male groups is not simply a consequence of a "formalized hostility" to women but in large part due to a "positive valence" between men (Tiger, 1969, p. xii). Consistent with the male warrior hypothesis, Tiger argued that men tend to bond most strongly in situations involving power, force, and dangerous work, and that they consciously and emotionally exclude females from these groups. These interpersonal effects are visible in a variety of male groups, including soldiers, police, and firefighters, and appear to be related to characteristic sex differences in group dynamics.

Sex Differences in Group Formation and Attachment

Males and females tend to self-organize into—and be most comfortable in—different kinds of groups. Men's relationships tend to be broad, shallow, and activity centered, while women's tend to be narrow, deep, and emotion centered. Accordingly, despite the stereotype of greater female sociality, men report significantly more close friends than women do (Vigil, 2007), they are more tolerant of same-sex peers than women (Benenson et al., 2009), and their friendships are more resistant to termination because of conflict than female friendships (Benenson & Alavi, 2004). Men have a lower threshold for creating large cooperative groups and can maintain them with lower levels of investment.

The flip side of that tendency explains the lack of persistence of the groups after their members physically separate, as male friendship tends to be "proximity and activity dependent" rather than "talk dependent," as female friendships are (Gurian, 1999, pp. 48–49). This activity dependence led Gurian to characterize men's friendships as "fragile," yet it may be this very dynamic that allows the group bonding to occur in the first place, and it may contribute to the widely held belief that the "bonding" that cements soldiers is in fact "male bonding." Male comradeship is sustained by proximity and shared tasks and experiences, and it is made stronger if the experience is a difficult and dangerous one (Gray, 1959, pp. 89–90). A man's ability to work in a common endeavor with his comrades is not dependent upon his affection toward individual unit members, and male groups can be sustained even in the presence of internal conflict. What is required among the members is not affection but trust.

Female relationships are fragile in a different way from men's, as they are emotionally deeper but at the same time more subject to disruption by conflicts. As Geary and Flinn (2002) have observed, if male coalitions required the same level of investment as female groups, they could not be sustained at their often large size. Women have a lower threshold for conflict and interpersonal slight (Vigil, 2007), and they are more likely to form exclusionary alliances and ostracize members of the group (Benenson, Antonellis, Cotton, Noddin, & Campbell, 2008; Benenson, Hodgson, Heath, & Welch, 2008), facts that are likely related to the greater difficulty that women have in cooperating with people (especially other women) they do not like (Fisher, 1999, pp. 43–44). In contrast, ostracism by males would be detrimental to the effectiveness of their large coalitions organized for warfare or big-game hunting. Female relationships are more egalitarian than those of males, and females are less comfortable with hierarchy than males are (Benenson & Schinazi, 2004), a tendency that seems to hold true even among military women (Browne, 2007a, pp. 165, 212–213). Although women value group membership, that is largely because it provides an opportunity to develop and maintain relational attachments, whereas men are more likely to value membership for the collective identity that it provides in addition to the individual relationships that it facilitates (Seeley, Gardner, Pennington, & Gabriel, 2003). Consistent with the notion that males may be more tightly bound to their groups, men have been found to be less likely than women to defect from a group in the presence of intergroup competition in circumstances in which it is more individually beneficial to leave (Van Vugt & Park, 2010).

These differences in group structure and attachment may have substantial combat implications. The military is heavily dependent upon the cohesiveness of combat groups, and fostering the bond among soldiers is one of the primary objects of military training. The military structure deemphasizes individualism, and the soldier is "constantly reminded of his responsibilities to his buddies, to his leaders, to the squad, to the platoon, and ultimately to the people and the nation or party through the structure of his immediate unit" (Henderson, 1985, p. 18). Men's greater valuing of collective identity would tend to strengthen the bonding of the group, thereby enhancing combat performance.

Cohesion and Combat Groups

It is common today to emphasize the quantitative and technological aspects of war, but it is wrong to think that material factors necessarily determine the outcome of a battle. The importance of the "moral factor" in combat has long been recognized. Xenophon observed two and a half millennia ago that "not numbers or strength brings victory in war; but whichever army goes into battle stronger in soul, their enemies generally cannot withstand them" (Xenophon, 1947, p. 64). Over 2,000 years later, Napoleon gave voice to the same thought in his famous observation that "in war the moral is to the material as three to one" (Heinl, 1966, p. 196).

Although a variety of influences can be important in motivating men to fight, there is a relatively broad consensus among those who have observed and studied the behavior of men in combat—and among those who have been in battle—that they fight primarily for their survival, for their immediate comrades, and for their standing in the eyes of those comrades. As Henderson (1985) has noted, "the only force strong enough to make the soldier willing to advance under fire is his loyalty to the small group and that group's expectations that he will advance" (p. 107). The bond that cements this loyalty and holds groups of fighting men together is widely viewed by students of the military as critical to combat effectiveness. This bond, a combination of trust and reciprocal obligation (Ingraham & Manning, 1981), leads individuals to value the group more than they value themselves and inclines them to further group objectives at substantial peril to themselves. When men lack connection to a bonded group, they are substantially less likely to persevere in the face of adversity (Shils & Janowitz, 1948).

A striking feature of men's wartime memoirs is the deep emotional connection they had with their comrades, a connection often compared favorably in strength to the male-female bond. Caputo (1977, p. xvii) observed that "the communion between men is as profound as any between lovers." Indeed, it is more so, he says, as "it does not demand for its sustenance the reciprocity, the pledges of affection, the endless reassurances required by the love of men and women." This bond is paradoxical in that it is simultaneously intense and ephemeral. Unlike the male–female bond, which can endure—though not always easily—long periods of separation, the bond among fighting men is transitory, usually lasting only as long as the group is together. Moskos (1970) found, for example, that once a squad member left Vietnam to return home, he seldom contacted those remaining behind and they seldom contacted him (pp. 145–146). Thus, it may be wrong to characterize the bond that cements a cohesive group as "friendship," as some do (MacCoun, Kier, & Belkin, 2006); indeed, it is not necessary that all members of the group even like each other.

Despite the US military's current emphasis on diversity, one of the leading contributors to group cohesion is a set of "common attitudes, values, and beliefs" (Henderson, 1985, p. 75). Thus, psychological homogeneity within a squad is associated with greater combat effectiveness (Watson, 1978, pp. 116–117). Traditionally, part of the shared values for combat troops has been the bond of masculinity (Marlowe, 1983), a bond that women simply cannot share.

High levels of cohesion are associated with substantial benefits both to the individual and the group. Members of cohesive groups express less anxiety about physical dangers (Kellett, 1982, p. 45), and individuals who have strong group identification can withstand more physical pain (Buss & Portnoy, 1967). Group cohesion also seems to enhance psychological resilience and protect against PTSD (Brailey, Vasterling, Proctor, Constans, & Friedman, 2007), and it allows units to cope better with extended periods of sleeplessness in operations (Noy, 1991). Acts of heroism are also more likely to emerge from highly cohesive units than from less cohesive units (Gal & Gabriel, 1982). Squads exhibiting high cohesion have also been found to perform at a higher level than other squads (Goodacre, 1953), though the arrow of causation no doubt points in both directions.

Although the importance of cohesion to military performance has been "a staple of military doctrine for 2500 years" (Manning, 1991, p. 456), the evidence from social science remains equivocal (Kier, 1998). As one leading researcher on military cohesion put it, "There is little consensus concerning the who, what, where, when, how, and why of cohesion" (Siebold, 1999, p. 6). Discussions of cohesion in the literature tend to fall into one of two categories: descriptions of an almost mystical force that is of central importance in combat, and descriptions of a dry sociological construct that is difficult to understand, let alone measure, and not obviously related to any particular outcome.

Most sociological and psychological studies on cohesion have been conducted in settings that do not closely mimic the combat environment. Many studies are performed on civilians (often college students), and those that have been conducted on military subjects have concentrated primarily on peacetime tasks. These studies have generally found that "social cohesion"—which is sometimes described as "interpersonal attraction"—is not positively correlated with group performance, while "task cohesion"—shared commitment to achieving goals—is correlated, albeit moderately, with performance (Mullen & Copper, 1994; Rostker, 1993, pp. 291–294). Though no doubt ignorant of these studies, soldiers appear to be aware of the difference between these forms of interpersonal relationship, as soldiers in effective units often choose different colleagues for combat tasks than they select to accompany on leave (Watson, 1978, p. 114). However, given the tendency of females to select their friends when picking teams for sports—rather than choosing the best player, as boys do (Evans, 1986)—that same behavior might not be true for women.

One problem with laboratory measures of cohesion is that they may not be capturing the relevant phenomenon (Manning & Fullerton, 1988). Cohesion is viewed by the military as a "performance enabler" rather than a "performance enhancer" (Griffith, 2007). Rather than enhancing technical performance, it correlates with military performance "by maintaining the organized group at its tasks in the face of severe stresses of battle" (Marlowe, 1979, as cited in Griffith, 2007). Because sociological studies of cohesion generally do not take place in particularly stressful conditions, their results may substantially underestimate the importance of cohesion in the primary circumstances in which it really matters.

As the technology of war develops, cohesion becomes more critical but also more difficult to achieve. In Napoleon's day, soldiers acted under the close watch of their superiors, standing shoulder to shoulder with their comrades and drawing strength from their presence (Henderson, 1985, p. 107). Today, however, direct control of troops has become more difficult and soldiers operate more independently. Urban warfare, such as that conducted in Iraq, negates some of the technological edge of modern armies and requires dispersal into small groups, magnifying the importance of the individual soldier and his small group. Indeed, according to Scales (2005), "the isolation inherent in urban fighting...requires a degree of small-unit cohesion never before seen in the American military" (p. 16).

If men and women are socially interchangeable, then inclusion of women in combat groups should not change this fundamental dynamic. There is strong reason to believe, however, that inclusion of women in groups of men actually does alter group dynamics and quite likely in the direction of reduced cohesion and therefore lesser combat effectiveness.

Sexual Integration and Cohesion

Studies of performance of sexually integrated non–combat units suggest that inclusion of women in combat units may disrupt unit cohesion. Rosen et al. (1996), for example, found a significant negative correlation between cohesion and the percentage of women in a group of junior enlisted personnel, although a subsequent study disclosed no such relationship (Rosen & Martin, 1997). A review of five separate studies—three on deployments (in the Persian Gulf, Somalia, and Haiti) and two garrison studies—found in four of the five studies that the more women in the unit, the lower the cohesion (Rosen et al., 1999). In the deployment studies, the negative impact of women correlated with the extent of physical danger, being most pronounced in Somalia, where the risk of coming under fire was greatest; only moderate in the Persian Gulf, where the risk was somewhat less; and neutral to mildly positive in Haiti, where the risk was virtually nil.

The dynamics of cohesion differ between the field and garrison, calling into question the generalizability of many of the military cohesion studies to integration of combat units. Increased time in the field tends to be positively correlated with "group hypermasculinity"—defined as "expressions of extreme, exaggerated, or stereotypic masculine attributes and behaviors"—in both all-male groups and mixed-sex groups (Rosen, Knudson, & Fancher, 2003, p. 326). In mixed-sex groups, field duty time is associated with decreased acceptance of women, probably because the field environment tends "to emphasize 'warrior' values of toughness, independence, and aggression" (p. 343). In male-only groups, hypermasculinity is associated with both increased vertical and horizontal cohesion and readiness. Rosen and colleagues have concluded that military effectiveness is positively associated with a culture of hypermasculinity and that "ungendered professionalism," which has positive effects in the garrison environment, "may be difficult to maintain in the field where a warrior culture is likely to develop, a culture that may be necessary for the successful accomplishment of the mission" (p. 345).

Substantial numbers of military men (and women) share the view that inclusion of women impairs cohesion (Presidential Commission, 1992, pp. 29, 66). Even in the Air Force, the service with the most women, a third of male pilots expressed the view that women should not fly in combat, their primary concerns being that women would destroy unit cohesion, that they are more emotional and less aggressive than men, and that they are a distraction to male aircrew members (Voge & King, 1997). A survey at the Air Force Academy almost three decades after its sexual integration found that 40% of cadets, both male and female, believed that physical and psychological differences between the sexes mean that women will never be completely accepted in the military, and 20% of male cadets believed that women should not be at the Academy at all (Gray, Smith, & Luedtke, 2004).

If women tend to decrease the cohesion of combat groups, it is important to understand the mechanism by which this occurs. One major contributor seems to be that it is difficult for men to trust women in dangerous circumstances.

Cohesion and Trust

Trust is central to cohesive combat units (Ingraham & Manning, 1981), as it is to all sorts of relationships. Cottrell, Neuberg, and Li (2007) found that across group types, "trustworthiness" is of paramount value, more important, in fact, than cooperativeness. Interpersonal trust, they suggest, "may be foundational to the development and maintenance of all close relationships" (p. 227). Application of the theory of reciprocal altruism to warfare suggests that "the cohesion of war-making coalitions composed of distantly or unrelated kin will be based on the perceived likelihood or trust that support in conflicts will be reciprocated in the future" (Patton, 2000, p. 421).

Assessment of the value of peers focuses on both the capacity to provide desirable resources and the likelihood that they will make those resources available (Vigil, 2007). Thus, combat compatriots must have trust in both their comrades' willingness and their ability to satisfy their obligations. The earnest assurance "I've got your back" is a cheap signal that is worth little in the absence of the courage, toughness, and skill to deliver on the promise. Conversely, all the courage and strength in the world are worth little to a soldier's comrades if he lacks the disposition to risk death in support of them. Trust among soldiers "is characterized by the willingness to put oneself at risk because of confidence that the other person will do what is expected of him or her" (Ruark, Orvis, Horn, & Langkamer, 2009, p. 1925). Thus, the concern of military men about sexual integration involves both aspects of trust, as many are concerned that a woman will not have the physical wherewithal to support the mission or her comrades, while others are concerned that a woman would be insufficiently aggressive and thus fail to provide the support that a man would (Browne, 2007a).

The need for trust increases with danger, as individuals become increasingly interdependent. This tendency may explain the increasing strength of the same-sex preference among boys as their groups roam farther from home (Maccoby, 1998), as well as male soldiers' preference for male comrades. A soldier's trust in his commander and comrades has been described as "the most important factor for security" (Noy, 1991, p. 518). The especially negative attitudes to sexual integration expressed by soldiers in combat specialties is explainable by this tendency (Browne, 2007a, pp. 148–149), as may be the cool reception of women in dangerous civilian occupations, such as in police work and firefighting (Browne, 2007a, pp. 284–285).

Assessment of trustworthiness involves more than passive evaluation. Hazing of new members is common in groups facing danger, and an individual's reaction to hazing affects the extent to which he is accepted by the group (Josefowitz & Gadon, 1989). Women, even military women, are less likely to view hazing as a permissible method of encouraging group cohesion (Pershing, 2006) and, consistent with a pattern that begins in childhood, are more likely to complain to authority figures. This reaction is typically perceived as disloyal to the group and interferes with the development of trust.

There is reason to believe that men's lack of trust in female comrades has evolutionary roots. The decision whether to trust a potential combat compatriot—or a comrade in other dangerous cooperative enterprises, such as big-game hunting—is a consequential one that would have recurred over evolutionary time. Just as indicators of prowess as a warrior and hunter—dominance, strength, and courage—are attractive to women seeking mates (Buss, 1994, pp. 38–40; Farthing, 2007), they would also be attractive to men seeking coalition partners (Sugiyama, 2005, p. 305). Men who were as willing to stand shoulder to shoulder in battle or on the hunt with weak and cowardly men—or with women—as they were with strong and brave men would probably have found themselves at a substantial disadvantage.

Haselton and Funder (2006) have suggested that "an evolved propensity for accurate personality judgment" would likely have arisen for traits important to survival and reproduction (p. 31). Even many nonhuman species exhibit specific biases in partner preferences. According to Dugatkin and Sih (1995, p. 273), "we expect partner choice to be more likely to occur in situations where the identity of one's partner has a great effect on fitness." Indeed, they show that in a number of fish species, for example, individuals prefer to associate with others who have shown themselves trustworthy in foraging or antipredator behavior, a pattern also observed in chimpanzees (Melis, Hare, & Tomasello, 2006).

In formation of the bonds of cohesion in our evolutionary past, males and females were not interchangeable. Most females would be pregnant, nursing, or caring for children most of the time and therefore would be unable to participate effectively in big-game hunting or warfare (Tiger, 1969, pp. 44–45). Those who did would risk the loss of their offspring, born or unborn (Campbell, 1999). Moreover, men who permitted women to join their ventures would also be at a disadvantage, because women would be less valuable contributors and their presence could disrupt the cooperative nature of the enterprise by engendering competition among the men for sexual access to the women.

The cause of men's trust or lack thereof may not be consciously accessible to them. Trust decisions are "fast, shallow, and context-sensitive" (Messick and Kramer, 2001, p. 98); that is, they are not the product of systematic processing but instead derive from rules of thumb of which we are largely unaware. Thus, men would be expected to make judgments, even if at a less than conscious level, about whom to trust in combat based on the extent to which the potential comrade displays attributes associated with effective warriors in the past, just as men make similarly intuitive assessments of potential mates without making conscious judgments about fertility. In assessing trustworthiness, whether consciously or not, men are likely to be particularly attentive to attributes of potential comrades that pose a threat to the combat unit, including their membership in groups that are perceived as posing such threats, such as women, for whom well-known stereotypes involve weakness and timidity.

Negative feelings about the prospect of female combat comrades do not necessarily reflect generalized hostility toward women. Cottrell and Neuberg (2005) have shown that rather than being an undifferentiated negative attitude toward a group, prejudice is a more nuanced phenomenon. The negative emotion that a particular group elicits turns on the nature of the perceived threat. They suggest that people who are highly dependent upon their groups (as combat soldiers are) are "especially attuned to potential threats to reciprocity," and their vigilance "must be accompanied by psychological responses that function to minimize—or even eliminate—recognized threats and their detrimental effects" (p. 771). These results are consistent with the fact that men may simultaneously have positive views of women in noncombat military positions and strongly negative views about their service in combat, as it is in the latter case that women may pose the greatest risk to the group's well-being. Perhaps significantly, female soldiers are even less likely than male soldiers to want to work with women (Rosen et al., 1996; Sion, 2001).

The uncertainty involved in making judgments about whom to trust—decisions that are more intuitive than cognitive—means that these judgments are prone to error, and, according to error management theory (Haselton & Buss, 2000), these errors are not likely to be random. The decision of whom to trust in coalitions organized to mete out violence is one that is fraught with serious fitness consequences. Moreover, it is a judgment that likely carries with it asymmetric costs of error. Declining to trust a potential comrade who in fact would have performed well would probably tend, on average, to be less costly than trusting a comrade who performs poorly. One would suppose, then, that the default position is not to trust potential combat comrades. That is one of the central reasons that units train together—to develop trust—and an initial disposition to distrust is probably the primary reason that it takes time and experience for new members of units to gain the trust of their comrades.

Attributes of Individuals Whom Men Identify as Effective Soldiers

As would be predicted, combat soldiers do have strong preferences concerning their comrades, and they do not trust other soldiers, even male ones, indiscriminately. It seems that soldiers somehow pick up on signals from other men indicating their combat capability even if they have not witnessed their combat performance. Immediately after combat in Korea ended in 1953, about 300 men were classified as either "fighters" or "nonfighters" by their peers, judgments that were validated through independent verifications of the combat incidents that served as the basis for the classification (Berkun & Meeland, 1958). These men were placed in groups of 15 to 18 men each, such that no group member knew any other member of his group. Those designated "fighters" and "nonfighters" were mixed together, but nobody knew about these designations or the purpose of the study. Each group then lived together for a week of psychological testing. At the end of that week, they were asked to identify the two men they would most and least like to have next to them in combat or leading them in combat. Fighters overwhelmingly chose other fighters as most suitable, both as combat comrades and leaders, and nonfighters chose fighters as the most suitable combat leaders. Fighters and nonfighters alike identified nonfighters as least suitable as comrades and leaders. The researchers concluded, "Obviously some observable manifestation correlated with fighter status served as the basis for these judgments" (p. 148).

More masculine men are judged by their peers to be more effective fighters than less masculine men. A study of combat performance in the Korean War found that the five main factors distinguishing good fighters were, in decreasing order of importance, leadership, masculinity, intelligence, sense of humor, and emotional stability (Egbert et al., 1957, as cited in Binkin, 1993, p. 39). The attributes of effective fighters ranged from calmness under fire to "the highest kind of daring and bravery," while the attributes of ineffective fighters included firing at imaginary objects, failing to fire, and running away under fire (Egbert, 1954).

Supporting the existence of a male preference for comrades who would have been effective hunters or fighters is the finding that even civilian men have a preference for same-sex friends who are physical risk takers (Farthing, 2005), as both hunting and warfare often reward the bold (although not necessarily the "overly bold" or reckless) and penalize the timid. Both men and women have a preference for same-sex friends who are willing to take "heroic" physical risks—such as rescuing someone endangered by fire—although men's preference for such friends is much higher than women's. Even with respect to "nonheroic" risks—such as dangerous sports—men have a preference for risk takers, in contrast to women's preference for same-sex friends who avoid such risks. These tendencies are consistent with the finding of Lewis et al. (2011, p. 554) that "friend selection in male-male dyads—even in modern conditions—revolved around characteristics that would have facilitated hunting and warfare in ancestral environments."

The long-standing link between warfare and masculinity appears to have hormonal correlates. Gimbel and Booth (1996) found, long after the Vietnam War, a positive correlation between testosterone levels and extent of combat exposure among Vietnam veterans. They found that testosterone had a positive effect on assignment to the combat arms, and that among those in the combat arms, it had a positive effect on the extent of combat exposure they experienced. These findings suggest that Army assignment policies somehow tended to select more masculine soldiers for combat duty.

Leadership

Beyond the question of women as combat comrades is the question of women combat leaders. Women leading men in combat (or in any other dangerous endeavor) would have been unusual in our evolutionary past, and it is unlikely that male and female psychologies have evolved in ways that make the vertical cohesion between female leader and male follower any more likely—and perhaps it is even less likely—than the horizontal cohesion that occurs within groups of soldiers. Men's desire for a "man of steel" as a leader (Henderson, 1985, p. 114) would have been adaptive in a time when most combat was face to face and at close range, and it probably remains so today. Men have never faced any adaptive pressure to follow women into battle, so it would not be surprising if male psychology is not designed to make that an easy behavior to evoke.

There is, in fact, good reason to believe that in at least some contexts women may not evoke followership behavior (in either men or women) to the same extent that men do (Eagly, Karau, & Makhijani, 1995; Eagly, Makhijani, & Klonsky, 1992; Rice, Bender, & Vitters, 1980). Even in early childhood, girls find it difficult to influence boys, and frustration with that lack of influence may be a major contributor to the tendency of boys and girls to separate into single-sex groups (Maccoby, 1990). In the civilian sector, women supervisors are usually trusted less by both men and women, and men and women often prefer male supervisors to female supervisors, with women's preference for a male supervisor often being stronger than men's (Jeanquart-Barone & Sekaran, 1994; Eagly & Karau, 2002), although the magnitude of the preference for a male boss has diminished somewhat over the last few decades (Eagly, 2007). Both male and female subordinates have a more negative reaction to the imposition of discipline by female superiors than by male superiors (Atwater, Carey, & Waldman, 2001).

Studies of leadership emergence and preferences have found substantial sex differences, especially in areas that would be relevant to combat leadership. Men tend to emerge more frequently in initially leaderless groups when leadership is defined by contribution to the group's task, while women tended to emerge more frequently as "social leaders," although the preference for male task leadership is reduced to the extent that the task is considered "feminine" (Eagly & Karau, 1991). Even though military groups tend to be the diametric opposite of leaderless given the clearly understood hierarchy of formal rank, leadership can emerge in combat independent of rank when the designated leader is weak (Stouffer et al., 1949, p. 117). Leadership preferences are condition dependent, with there being a strong preference for male leaders under conditions of intergroup competition (Van Vugt & Spisak, 2008).

Men and women also often exhibit different leadership styles, a fact that also has implications for combat leadership. Men are more likely to adopt an autocratic or directive style and women to adopt a democratic or participatory style (Eagly & Johnson, 1990). Yet, in combat groups, democratic leadership may destroy group solidarity (Shils, 1951). Although women's tendency to adopt a democratic leadership style is weakened in settings that are highly male dominated, Eagly and Johnson (1990) found that women who adopt an authoritarian style of leadership tend to be devalued as leaders. Although the bulk of studies evaluating the effectiveness of leaders have found men and women to be equivalent in their effectiveness, military studies (which have been limited to noncombat activities) "deviated strongly from all other classes of studies" (Eagly et al., 1995, p. 135). These peacetime studies, it should be noted, almost certainly understate the size of sex differences related to combat-leadership effectiveness.

Both men and women in military training associate male cadets more with leader-like qualities, such as leadership, self-confidence, dedication, and physical fitness (Boldry, Wood, & Kashy, 2001). Even men who hold—or at least profess—egalitarian views, often display visible signs of negative feelings toward female leaders (Rice et al., 1980). Although experience with being led by female commanders might be supposed to reduce men's sexual stereotyping of military leadership, in fact the opposite seems to occur. A study at the Air Force Academy found that male cadets' seniority and experience with women increased, rather than decreased, masculine stereotyping (Boyce & Herd, 2003). Peer perceptions of women's lack of military leadership potential have led the service academies to eliminate peer ratings of leadership—despite the fact that peers are often better judges of leadership ability than superiors (Watson, 1978, pp. 160–161)—because women consistently received lower ratings than men (Mitchell, 1998, p. 63; Rice, Yoder, Adams, Priest, & Prince, 1984). Because combat leaders must evoke followership under conditions that may result in the death of the follower, the stakes of leadership effectiveness are at their peak, and less than full confidence in the leader can have fatal consequences.

Men's Distrust of Female Comrades May Be Resistant to Change

If the proximate triggers that lead to trust among comrades and in leaders are ones that are associated with men and masculinity, it may be difficult to overcome the hurdle of initial distrust of female comrades. That is, if men's aversion to women in combat units reflects an evolved biological predisposition rather than merely being a product of social learning, it may be more resistant to modification than proponents of integration have assumed. This would likely be true even if the reasons that selection favored the aversion have disappeared. That is, even if it were true that changes in the nature of warfare have made women equally competent comrades and even if women displayed the same leadership behaviors as men, the factors that trigger trust are ones that evolved over the course of evolutionary history, not necessarily ones that are predictive of competence today.

Decision-making processes are designed to be attentive to the kinds of information that were available in the environment in which the mind evolved (Haselton & Funder, 2006). In considering men's resistance to female comrades, an analogy to mate preferences may be instructive. We have no difficulty understanding that a man's sexual attraction to a beautiful 25-year-old known to be infertile is likely to be substantially greater than to a 45-year-old who, with the assistance of modern medicine, possesses the fertility of a 25-year-old notwithstanding her age-appropriate appearance. It is not actual fertility that is the proximate trigger of sexual attraction, but rather possession of visible attributes that have been markers of fertility over evolutionary time. Similarly, good grades at a military academy or impressive performance on a paper-and-pencil personality test—even if they were truly valid predictors of combat capability—are likely to carry far less weight with potential comrades than the indicia of masculinity that have been important over our evolutionary history, such as courage, dominance, and physical capacity. So, even if there is a logical reason for men to trust women, women may not embody the proximal triggers of that trust, meaning that they may not be trusted despite their fitness for combat.

Men's disinclination to trust female comrades may be easily reinforced by a small amount of adverse experience but not easily extinguished by a lot of good experience. "Biologically prepared" emotions are not only easier to acquire but also harder to extinguish, as experience with biologically prepared fears has shown (Öhman & Mineka, 2001). Sworn statements from a hundred health inspectors that a taco stand's food is wholesome may not be sufficient to outweigh the negative experience of food poisoning from one bad taco.

In sum, men seem to be psychologically predisposed not to welcome women into combat groups, and the expectation that they will accommodate may be overly optimistic. Military training, which already presents so many challenges, may face the ultimate challenge if it attempts to undo this tendency, which seemingly has origins deep within men.

Conclusion

Sexual integration of combat forces presents obstacles that may not be obvious to those steeped in the SSSM view of human psychology. The assumption that military discipline will overcome all impediments to inclusion of women in combat units may be naive. The US military has been plagued by a succession of sex scandals, for example, even when women were not included in most, or any, combat units (Browne, 2007b). The assumption that integration will succeed because "combatants follow orders" (Shields, Curry, & Nichols, 1990, p. 24) neglects the fact that although the military can compel or forbid certain behaviors, it is far more limited in its ability to coerce changes in feelings of its personnel. As one Marine Corps officer has noted, "units cannot be ordered to 'be cohesive'" (McBreen, 2002, p. 11). Similarly, the military cannot force men to trust women or ignore the physical and psychological differences between the sexes.

Even if it is accepted that women may undermine combat effectiveness, it does not necessarily follow that they should be excluded from combat. Some argue that excluding women from combat on the rationale that they would weaken the military inappropriately elevates the common good of national defense over individual rights (Addis, 1994, pp. 3–4; Peach, 1996, p. 165). That is an argument that science cannot resolve, as it revolves around contestable values. What science can do, however, is provide insights about difficulties that particular policies may create and, potentially, help guide decision makers in their formulation and implementation of policies, whatever they might be.

Future Directions

A number of issues covered in this chapter could be illuminated with better data:

• Laboratory studies of such traits as risk taking, aggression, and fear tend to reveal smaller sex differences than revealed by real-world observations of actual behavior. Ethical constraints on treatment of research subjects obviously preclude too much realism, but it appears that laboratory measures have far to go in capturing phenomena of real-world interest.

• Although combat soldiers seem to have definite preferences concerning desirable comrades and are moved to trust some comrades more than others, there is relatively little data on the subject, and much of it dates back to the Korean War or before. The large pool of experienced combat soldiers created by the wars in Iraq and Afghanistan provides an opportunity for further study.

- Better data on the effect of cohesion on military performance are needed. Most existing research is aimed at measuring whether cohesion enhances performance outside of the combat arena. Yet, if the function of cohesion is not to act as a global performance enhancer, but rather to enable performance under severe combat stress, the current literature on cohesion does not measure the cohesion–performance relationship where it really matters.

- Although women in the US military are not assigned to ground combat positions, they have recently been exposed to combat, providing an experience base from which some conclusions might be reached. Unfortunately, however, the military has been relatively steadfast in not releasing—and in many cases not even collecting—data that might reflect on women's performance (Browne, 2007a, pp. 216–217, 220–222). Despite the fact that large numbers of female military personnel in Iraq were shipped home because of pregnancy, for example, the Army has announced that it was "not tracking" that data (Browne, 2007a, p. 245). If systematic and objective data on women's performance in combat situations exist, they might shed light on the effects of women's integration into combat units.

References

Addis, E. (1994). Women and the economic consequences of being a soldier. In E. Addis, V. E. Russo, & L. Sebesta (Eds.), *Women soldiers: Images and realities* (pp. 3–27). New York: St. Martin's Press.

Addis, E., Russo, V. E., & Sebesta, L. (1994). Introduction. In E. Addis, V. E. Russo, & L. Sebesta (Eds.), *Women soldiers: Images and realities* (pp. xi–xxiv). New York: St. Martin's Press.

Archer, J. (2004). Sex differences in aggression in real-world settings: A meta-analytic review. *Review of General Psychology, 8*, 291–322.

Archer, J. (2009). Does sexual selection explain human sex differences in aggression? *Behavioral and Brain Sciences, 32*, 249–311.

Aristotle. (2000). *Politics* (B. Jowett, Trans.). New York: Dover.

Atwater, L. E., Carey, J. A., & Waldman, D. A. (2001). Gender and discipline in the workplace: Wait until your father gets home. *Journal of Management, 27*, 537–561.

Baron-Cohen, S., & Wheelwright, S. (2004). The empathy quotient: An investigation of adults with Asperger Syndrome or high functioning autism, and normal sex differences. *Journal of Autism and Developmental Disorders, 34*, 163–175.

Becker, S. W., & Eagly, A. H. (2004). The heroism of women and men. *American Psychologist, 59*, 163–178.

Benenson, J. F., & Alavi, K. (2004). Sex differences in children's investment in same-sex peers. *Evolution and Human Behavior, 25*, 258–266.

Benenson, J. F., Antonellis, T. J., Cotton, B. J., Noddin, K. E., & Campbell, K. A. (2008). Sex differences in children's formation of exclusionary alliances under scarce resource conditions. *Animal Behaviour, 76*, 497–505.

Benenson, J. F., Apostoleris, N. H., & Parnass, J. (1997). Age and sex differences in dyadic and group interaction. *Developmental Psychology, 33*, 538–543.

Benenson, J. F., Hodgson, L., Heath, S., & Welch, P. J. (2008). Human sexual differences in the use of social ostracism as a competitive tactic. *International Journal of Primatology, 29*, 1019–1035.

Benenson, J. F., Markovits, H., Fitzgerald, C., Geoffroy, D., Flemming, J., Kahlenberg, S. M., & Wrangham, R. W. (2009). Males' greater tolerance of same-sex peers. *Psychological Science, 20*, 184–190.

Benenson, J. F., & Schinazi, J. (2004). Sex differences in reactions to outperforming same-sex friends. *British Journal of Developmental Psychology, 22*, 317–333.

Berkun, M., & Meeland, T. (1958). Sociometric effects of race and of combat performance. *Sociometry, 21*, 145–149.

Binkin, M. (1993). *Who will fight the next war? The changing face of the American military*. Washington, DC: Brookings Institution.

Boldry, J., Wood, W., & Kashy, D. A. (2001). Gender stereotypes and the evaluation of men and women in military training. *Journal of Social Issues, 57*, 689–705.

Boulton, M. J. (1993). Aggressive fighting in British middle school children. *Educational Studies, 19*, 19–39.

Boulton, M. J. (1996). A comparison of 8- and 11-year-old girls' and boys' participation in specific types of rough-and-tumble play and aggressive fighting: Implications for functional hypotheses. *Aggressive Behavior, 22*, 271–287.

Boyce, L. A., & Herd, A. M. (2003). The relationship between gender role stereotypes and requisite military leadership characteristics. *Sex Roles, 49*, 365–378.

Brailey, K., Vasterling, J. J., Proctor, S. P., Constans, J. I., & Friedman, M. J. (2007). PTSD symptoms, life events, and unit cohesion in U.S. soldiers: Baseline findings from the Neurocognition Deployment Health Study. *Journal of Traumatic Stress, 20*, 495–503.

Brightman, R. (1996). The sexual division of foraging labor: Biology, taboo, and gender politics. *Comparative Studies in Society and History, 38*, 687–729.

Browne, K. (2002). *Biology at work: Rethinking sexual equality*. New Brunswick, NJ: Rutgers University Press.

Browne, K. (2007a). *Co-ed combat: The new evidence that women shouldn't fight the nation's wars*. New York: Sentinel.

Browne, K. (2007b). Military sex scandals from Tailhook to the present: The cure can be worse than the disease. *Duke Journal of Gender Law and Policy, 14*, 749–789.

Bureau of Labor Statistics. (2003). *Fatal occupational injuries by worker characteristics and event of exposure, all United States, 2002*. Retrieved December 2011, from http://www.bls.gov/iif/oshwc/cfoi/cftb0161.pdf

Buss, A. H., & Portnoy, N. W. (1967). Pain tolerance and group identification. *Journal of Personality and Social Psychology, 6*, 106–108.

Buss, D. M. (1994). *The evolution of desire: Strategies of human mating*. New York: Basic Books.

Byrnes, J. P., Miller, D. C., & Schafer, W. D. (1999). Gender differences in risk taking: A meta-analysis. *Psychological Bulletin, 125*, 367–383.

Campbell, A. (1999). Staying alive: Evolution, culture, and women's intrasexual aggression. *Behavioral and Brain Sciences, 22*, 203–252.

Campbell, A., & Muncer, S. (1994). Sex differences in aggression: Social representation and social roles. *British Journal of Social Psychology, 33,* 233–240.

Caputo, P. (1977). *A rumor of war.* New York: Henry Holt.

Chagnon, N. A. (1988). Life histories, blood revenge, and warfare in a tribal population. *Science, 239,* 985–992.

Connolly, B., & Anderson, R. (1987). *First contact: New Guinea's highlanders encounter the outside world.* New York: Viking.

Cottrell, C. A., & Neuberg, S. L. (2005). Different emotional reactions to different groups: A sociofunctional threat-based approach to "prejudice." *Journal of Personality and Social Psychology, 88,* 770–789.

Cottrell, C. A., Neuberg, S. L., & Li, N. P. (2007). What do people desire in others? A sociofunctional perspective on the importance of different valued characteristics. *Journal of Personality and Social Psychology, 92,* 208–231.

D'Andrade, R. G. (1966). Sex differences and cultural institutions. In E. E. Maccoby (Ed.), *The development of sex differences* (pp. 174–204). Stanford, CA: Stanford University Press.

De Groot, G. J. (1995). Women warriors. *Contemporary Review, 266,* 257–260.

Del Giudice, M. (2009). On the real magnitude of psychological sex differences. *Evolutionary Psychology, 7,* 264–279.

Dollard, J. (1944). *Fear in battle.* New York: AMS Press.

Dugatkin, L. A., & Sih, A. (1995). Behavioral ecology and the study of partner choice. *Ethology, 99,* 265–277.

Eagly, A. H. (2007). Female leadership advantage and disadvantage: Resolving the contradictions. *Psychology of Women Quarterly, 31,* 1–12.

Eagly, A. H., & Johnson, B. T. (1990). Gender and leadership style: A meta-analysis. *Psychological Bulletin, 108,* 233–256.

Eagly, A. H., & Karau, S. J. (1991). Gender and the emergence of leaders: A meta-analysis. *Journal of Personality and Social Psychology, 60,* 685–710.

Eagly, A. H., & Karau, S. J. (2002). Role congruity theory of prejudice toward female leaders. *Psychological Review, 109,* 573–598.

Eagly, A. H., Karau, S. J., & Makhijani, M. G. (1995). Gender and the effectiveness of leaders: A meta-analysis. *Psychological Bulletin, 117,* 125–145.

Eagly, A. H., Makhijani, M. G., & Klonsky, B. G. (1992). Gender and the evaluation of leaders: A meta-analysis. *Psychological Bulletin, 111,* 3–22.

Egbert, R. L. (1954, October). Profile of a fighter. *Infantry School Quarterly, 44:* 46–51.

Egbert, R. L., Meeland, T., Cline, V. B., Forgy, E. W., Spickler, M. W., & Brown, C. (1957). *Fighter I: An analysis of combat fighters and non-fighters.* Technical Report 44. Presidio of Monterey, CA: U.S. Army Leadership Human Research Unit.

Eibl-Eibesfeldt, I. (1979). *The biology of peace and war: Men, animals, and aggression.* New York: Viking Press.

Evans, J. (1986). Gender differences in children's games: A look at the team selection process. *CAHPER Journal, 52*(5), 4–9.

Farthing, G. W. (2005). Attitudes toward heroic and nonheroic physical risk takers as mates and as friends. *Evolution and Human Behavior, 26,* 171–185.

Farthing, G. W. (2007). Neither daredevils nor wimps: Attitudes toward physical risk takers as mates. *Evolutionary Psychology, 5,* 754–777.

Fessler, D. M. T., Pillsworth, E. G., & Flamson, T. J. (2004). Angry men and disgusted women: An evolutionary approach to the influence of emotions on risk taking. *Organizational Behavior and Human Decision Processes, 95,* 107–123.

Fisher, H. (1999). *The first sex: The natural talents of women and how they are changing the world.* New York: Random House.

Fox, J. A., & Zawitz, M. W. (2006). *Homicide trends in the United States.* Washington, DC: US Department of Justice, Office of Justice Programs, Bureau of Justice Statistics.

Gabriel, S., & Gardner, W. L. (1999). Are there "his" and "hers" types of interdependence? The implications of gender differences in collective versus relational interdependence for affect, behavior, and cognition. *Journal of Personality and Social Psychology, 77,* 642–655.

Gal, R., & Gabriel, R. A. (1982). Battlefield heroism in the Israeli Defense Force. *International Social Science Review, 57,* 232–235.

Geary, D. C., Byrd-Craven, J., Hoard, M. K., Vigil, J., & Numtee, C. (2003). Evolution and development of boys' social behavior. *Developmental Review, 23,* 444–470.

Geary, D. C., & Flinn, M. V. (2002). Sex differences in behavioral and hormonal response to social threat: Commentary on Taylor et al. (2000). *Psychological Review, 109,* 745–750.

Gimbel, C., & Booth, A. (1996). Who fought in Vietnam? *Social Forces, 74,* 1137–1157.

Goodacre, D. M., III. (1953). Group characteristics of good and poor performing combat units. *Sociometry, 16,* 168–179.

Gray, D., Smith, H., & Luedtke, C. (2004). *Fall 2004 Cadet Climate Survey.* Colorado Springs, CO: US Air Force Academy. Retrieved December 2011, from http://www.usafa.edu/superintendent/pa/Fall2004CadetClimateSurvey12-oct-04.pdf

Gray, J. G. (1959). *The warriors: Reflections on men in battle.* New York: Harper & Row.

Griffith, J. (2007). Further considerations concerning the cohesion-performance relation in military settings. *Armed Forces & Society, 34,* 138–147.

Gullone, E., & King, N. J. (1997). Three-year follow-up of normal fear in children and adolescents aged 7 to 18 years. *British Journal of Developmental Psychology, 15,* 97–111.

Gurian, M. (1999). *A fine young man: What parents, mentors, and educators can do to shape adolescent boys into exceptional men.* New York: Putnam.

Harrell, M. C., & Miller, L. L. (1997). *New opportunities for military women: Effects upon readiness, cohesion, and morale.* Santa Monica, CA: RAND.

Haselton, M. G., & Buss, D. M. (2000). Error management theory: A new perspective on biases in cross-sex mind reading. *Journal of Personality and Social Psychology, 78,* 81–91.

Haselton, M. G., & Funder, D. C. (2006). The evolution of accuracy and bias in social judgment. In M. Schaller, J. A. Simpson, & D. T. Kenrick (Eds.), *Evolution and social psychology* (pp. 15–37). New York: Psychology Press.

Heinl, R. D., Jr. (1966). *Dictionary of military and naval quotations.* Annapolis, MD: Naval Institute Press.

Henderson, W. D. (1985). *Cohesion: The human element in combat.* Washington, DC: National Defense University Press.

Henriksen, R. (2007). Warriors in combat—What makes people actively fight in combat? *Journal of Strategic Studies, 30,* 187–223.

Hewlett, B. S. (1988). Sexual selection and paternal investment among Aka pygmies. In L. Betzig, M. Borgerhoff Mulder, & P. Turke (Eds.), *Human reproductive behaviour: A Darwinian perspective* (pp. 263–276). Cambridge, England: Cambridge University Press.

Holmes, R. (1985). *Acts of war: The behavior of men in battle.* New York: Free Press.

Huston, T. L., Ruggiero, M., Conner, R., & Geis, G. (1981). Bystander intervention into crime: A study based on naturally-occurring episodes. *Social Psychology Quarterly, 44,* 14–23.

Ingraham, L. H., & Manning, F. J. (1981). Cohesion: Who needs it, what is it, and how do we get it to them? *Military Review, 59*(6), 2–12.

International Sailing Federation (2002, May 8). US sailing to present rescue award at university graduation ceremony. Retrieved January 2012, from http://www2.sailing.org/default.asp?ID=j/2F9tzC&format=popup

Jeanquart-Barone, S., & Sekaran, U. (1994). Effects of supervisor's gender on American women's trust. *Journal of Social Psychology, 134,* 253–255.

Johnson, R. C. (1996). Attributes of Carnegie medalists performing acts of heroism and of the recipients of these acts. *Ethology and Sociobiology, 17,* 355–362.

Josefowitz, N., & Gadon, H. (1989, May). Hazing: Uncovering one of the best-kept secrets of the workplace. *Business Horizons,* pp. 22–26.

Keegan, J. (1993). *A history of warfare.* New York: Alfred Knopf.

Kellett, A. (1982). *Combat motivation: The behavior of soldiers in battle.* Boston: Kluwer Nijhoff.

Kier, E. (1998). Homosexuals in the U.S. military: Open integration and combat effectiveness. *International Security, 23*(2), 5–39.

Kilner, P. (2002). Military leaders' obligation to justify killing in war. *Military Review, 82*(2), 24–31.

Laufer, A., & Solomon, Z. (2009). Gender differences in PTSD in Israeli youth exposed to terror attacks. *Journal of Interpersonal Violence, 24,* 959–976.

Lewis, D. M. G., Conroy-Beam, D., Al-Shawaf, L., Raja, A., DeKay, T., & Buss, D. M. (2011). Friends with benefits: The evolved psychology of same- and opposite-sex friendship. *Evolutionary Psychology, 9,* 543–563.

Lewis, M., & Clark, W. (1904). *Original journals of the Lewis and Clark expedition* (Vol. 3, R. G. Thwaites, Ed.). New York: Dodd, Mead. (Original work published 1814).

Lombardo, M. P. (2012). On the evolution of sport. *Evolutionary Psychology, 10,* 1–28.

Lyons, M. T. (2005). Who are the heroes? Characteristics of people who rescue others. *Journal of Cultural and Evolutionary Psychology, 3,* 245–254.

Maccoby, E. E. (1990). Gender and relationships: A developmental account. *American Psychologist, 45,* 513–520.

Maccoby, E. E. (1998). *The two sexes: Growing up apart, coming together.* Cambridge, MA: The Belknap Press of Harvard University.

MacCoun, R. J., Kier, E., & Belkin, A. (2006). Does social cohesion determine motivation in combat? An old question with an old answer. *Armed Forces & Society, 32,* 646-654.

Manning, F. J. (1991). Morale, cohesion, and esprit de corps. In R. Gal & A. D. Mangelsdorff (Eds.), *Handbook of military psychology* (pp. 453–470). New York: Wiley.

Manning, F. J., & Fullerton, T. D. (1988). Health and well-being in highly cohesive units of the U.S. Army. *Journal of Applied Social Psychology, 18,* 503–519.

Marlowe, D. H. (1979). *Cohesion, anticipated breakdown, and endurance in battle: Consideration for severe and high intensity combat.* Walter Reed Army Institute of Research, Neuropsychiatry Division. Washington, DC.

Marlowe, D. H. (1983). The manning of the force and the structure of battle: Part 2—men and women. In R. K. Fullinwider (Ed.), *Conscripts and volunteers: Military requirements, social justice, and the all-volunteer force.* Totowa, NJ: Rowman & Allanheld.

Marshall, L. (1976). *The !Kung of Nyae Nyae.* Cambridge, MA: Harvard University Press.

Marshall, S. L. A. (1947). *Men against fire: The problem of battle command in future war.* New York: William Morrow.

Martin, C. L., & Fabes, R. A. (2001). The stability and consequences of young children's same-sex peer interactions. *Developmental Psychology, 37,* 431–446.

McBreen, B. B. (2002). *Improving unit cohesion: The first step in improving Marine Corps infantry battalion capabilities.* Commandant of the Marine Corps National Fellowship Program. Retrieved December 2011, from http://www.2ndbn5thmar.com/coh/mcbreen2002.pdf

McConnell, M. (1985). *Into the mouth of the cat: The story of Lance Sijan, hero of Vietnam.* New York: W. W. Norton.

McLean, C. P., & Anderson E. R. (2009). Brave men and timid women? A review of the gender differences in fear and anxiety. *Clinical Psychology Review, 29,* 496–505.

Melis, A. P., Hare, B., & Tomasello, M. (2006). Chimpanzees recruit the best collaborators. *Science, 311,* 1297–1300.

Merriam-Webster. (2005). *Merriam-Webster's collegiate dictionary* (11th ed.). Springfield, MA: Merriam-Webster.

Messick, D. M., & Kramer, R. M. (2001). Trust as a form of shallow morality. In K. S. Cook (Ed.), *Trust in society* (pp. 89–117). New York: Russell Sage Foundation.

Ministry of Defence (United Kingdom). (2002). *Women in the armed forces.* Report by the Employment of Women in the Armed Forces Steering Group. Retrieved December 2011, from http://www.mod.uk/NR/rdonlyres/A9925990-82C2-420F-AB04-7003768CEC02/0/womenaf_fullreport.pdf

Mitchell, B. (1998). *Women in the military: Flirting with disaster.* Washington, DC: Regnery.

Moskos, C. C. (1970). *The American enlisted man: The rank and file in today's military.* New York: Russell Sage Foundation.

Mullen, B., & Copper, C. (1994). The relation between group cohesiveness and performance: An integration. *Psychological Bulletin, 115,* 210–227.

Nagy, E., Loveland, K. A., Kopp, M., Orvos, H., Pal, A., & Molnar, P. (2001). Different emergence of fear expressions in infant boys and girls. *Infant Behavior and Development, 24,* 189–194.

Noy, S. (1991). Combat stress reactions. In R. Gal & A. D. Mangelsdorff (Eds.), *Handbook of military psychology* (pp. 507–530). New York: Wiley.

Öhman, A., & Mineka, S. (2001). Fears, phobias, and preparedness: Toward an evolved module of fear and fear learning. *Psychological Review, 108,* 483–522.

Parker, S. T. (1984). Playing for keeps: An evolutionary perspective on human games. In P. K. Smith (Ed.), *Play in animals and humans* (pp. 271–293). London: Blackwell.

Patton, J. Q. (2000). Reciprocal altruism and warfare: A case from the Ecuadorian Amazon. In L. Cronk, N. Chagnon, & W. Irons (Eds.), *Adaptation and human behavior: An anthropological perspective* (pp. 417–436). Hawthorne, NY: Aldine de Gruyter.

Peach, L. J. (1996). Gender ideology in the ethics of women in combat. In J. H. Stiehm (Ed.), *It's our military, too!: Women and the U.S. military* (pp.156–194). Philadelphia: Temple University Press.

Peniston, B. (2006). *No higher honor: Saving the USS Samuel B. Roberts in the Persian Gulf*. Annapolis, MD: Naval Institute Press.

Pershing, J. L. (2006). Men and women's experiences with hazing in a male-dominated elite military institution. *Men and Masculinities, 8*, 470–492.

Pheasant, S. T. (1983). Sex differences in strength: Some observations on their variability. *Applied Ergonomics, 14*, 205–211.

Plavcan, J. M., & Van Schaik, C. P. (1997). Intrasexual competition and body weight dimorphism in anthropoid primates. *American Journal of Physical Anthropology, 103*, 37–68.

Pratchett, L. C., Pelcovitz, M. R., & Yehuda, R. (2010). Trauma and violence: Are women the weaker sex? *Psychiatric Clinics of North America, 33*, 465–474.

Presidential Commission on the Assignment of Women in the Armed Forces. (1992). *Women in combat: Report to the President*. McLean, VA: Brassey's.

Rice, R. W., Bender, L. R., & Vitters, A. G. (1980). Leader sex, follower attitudes toward women, and leadership effectiveness: A laboratory experiment. *Organizational Behavior and Human Performance, 25*, 46–56.

Rice, R. W., Yoder, J. D., Adams, J., Priest, R. F., & Prince, H. T. (1984). Leadership ratings for male and female military cadets. *Sex Roles, 10*, 885–901.

Richardson, F. M. (1978). *Fighting spirit: A study of psychological factors in war*. London: Leo Cooper.

Riley, J. L., Robinson, M. E., Wise, E. A., Myers, C. D., & Fillingim, R. B. (1998). Sex differences in the perception of noxious experimental stimuli: A meta-analysis. *Pain, 74*, 181–187.

Ronay, R., & Kim, D-Y. (2006). Gender differences in explicit and implicit risk attitudes: A socially facilitated phenomenon. *British Journal of Social Psychology, 45*, 397–419.

Rosen, L. N., Durand, D. B., Bliese, P. D., Halverson, R. R., Rothberg, J. M., & Harrison, N. L. (1996). Cohesion and readiness in gender-integrated combat service support units: The impact of acceptance of women and gender ratio. *Armed Forces & Society, 22*, 537–553.

Rosen, L. N., Knudson, K. H., & Fancher, P. (2003). Cohesion and the culture of hypermasculinity in U.S. Army units. *Armed Forces & Society, 29*, 325–351.

Rosen, L. N., & Martin, L. (1997). Sexual harassment, cohesion, and combat readiness in U.S. Army support units. *Armed Forces & Society, 24*, 221–244.

Rosen, L. N., Wright, K., Marlowe, D., Bartone, P., & Gifford, R. K. (1999). Gender differences in subjective distress attributable to anticipation of combat among U.S. Army soldiers deployed to the Persian Gulf during Operation Desert Storm. *Military Medicine, 164*, 753–757.

Rostker, B. D. (1993). *Sexual orientation and U.S. military personnel policy: Options and assessment*. Santa Monica, CA: RAND

Ruark, G. A., Orvis, K. L., Horn, Z., & Langkamer, K. L. (2009). Trust as defined by U.S. Army soldiers. In *Proceedings of the Human Factors and Ergonomics Society, 53rd Annual Meeting* (pp. 1924–1928). Santa Monica, CA: Human Factors and Ergonomics Society.

Sandseter, E. B. H., & Kennair, L. E. O. (2011). Children's risky play from an evolutionary perspective: The anti-phobic effects of thrilling experiences. *Evolutionary Psychology, 9*, 257–284.

Scales, R. H. (2005). Urban warfare: A soldier's view. *Military Review, 85*(1), 9–18.

Scharnberg, K. (2005, March 22). Stresses of battle hit female GIs hard: VA study hopes to find treatment for disorder. *Chicago Tribune*, p. C1.

Schechter, E. (2004, January 29). Anything boys can do. *Jerusalem Post*, p. 29.

Seeley, E. A., Gardner, W. L., Pennington, G., & Gabriel, S. (2003). Circle of friends or members of a group? Sex differences in relational and collective attachment to groups. *Group Processes and Intergroup Relations, 6*, 251–263.

Shields, P. M., Curry, L., & Nichols, J. (1990). Women pilots in combat: Attitudes of male and female pilots. *Minerva Quarterly, 8*, 21–35.

Shils, E. A. (1951). The study of the primary group. In D. Lerner & H. D. Lasswell (Eds.), *The policy sciences* (pp. 44–69). Stanford, CA: Stanford University Press.

Shils, E. A., & Janowitz, M. (1948). Cohesion and disintegration in the Wehrmacht in World War II. *Public Opinion Quarterly, 12*, 280–315.

Siebold, G. L. (1999). The evolution of the measurement of cohesion. *Military Psychology, 11*(1), 5–26.

Singer, T., Seymour, B., O'Doherty, J. P., Stephan, K. E., Dolan, R. J., & Frith, C. D. (2006). Empathic neural responses are modulated by the perceived fairness of others. *Nature, 439*(7075), 466–469.

Sion, L. (2001). "The weakest link": Women in two Dutch peacekeeping units. *Minerva: Quarterly Report on Women and the Military, 19*(3/4), 3–26.

Smith, W. R., & Torstensson, M. (1997). Gender differences in risk perception and neutralizing fear of crime: Toward resolving the paradoxes. *British Journal of Criminology, 37*, 608–634.

Solaro, E. (2006). *Women in the line of fire: What you should know about women in the military*. Emeryville, CA: Seal Press.

Stouffer, S. A., Lumsdaine, A. A., Lumsdaine, M. H., Williams, R. M., Jr., Smith, M. B., Janis, I. L.,…Cottrell, L. S., Jr. (1949). *The American soldier: Combat and its aftermath* (Vol. 2). Princeton, NJ: Princeton University Press.

Sugiyama, L. S. (2005). Physical attractiveness in adaptationist perspective. In D. M. Buss (Ed.), *The handbook of evolutionary psychology* (pp. 292–343). Hoboken, NJ: Wiley.

Thomas, J. R., & French, K. E. (1985). Gender differences across age in motor performance: A meta-analysis. *Psychological Bulletin, 98*, 260–282.

Tiger, L. (1969). *Men in groups*. New York: Random House.

Turney-High, H. H. (1971). *Primitive war: Its practice and concepts* (2d ed.). Columbia: University of South Carolina Press.

US Department of Justice. (2003). *Census of state and federal correctional facilities, 2000*. Washington, DC: Office of Justice Programs, Bureau of Justice Statistics.

United States Lifesaving Association. (n.d.). *USLA Heroic Acts in Aquatic Lifesaving*. Retrieved January 2012, from http://www.usla.org/?page=HEROIC

Vanden Brook, T. (2006, August 1). Army makes way for older soldiers. *USA Today*, p. 1A.

Van Vugt, M., De Cremer, D., & Janssen, D. P. (2007). Gender differences in cooperation and competition: The male-warrior hypothesis. *Psychological Science, 18*, 19–23.

Van Vugt, M., & Park, J. H. (2010). The tribal instinct hypothesis: Evolution and the social psychology of intergroup relations. In S. Stürmer & M. Snyder (Eds.), *The psychology of prosocial behavior: Group processes, intergroup relations, and helping* (pp. 13–32). Malden, MA: Wiley-Blackwell.

Van Vugt, M., & Spisak, B. R. (2008). Sex differences in the emergence of leadership during competitions within and between groups. *Psychological Science, 19*, 854–858.

Vigil, J. M. (2007). Asymmetries in the friendship preferences and social styles of men and women. *Human Nature, 18*, 143–161.

Voge, V. M., & King, R. E. (1997). Women in combat: Concerns of U.S. Air Force and U.S. Army rated male and female aircrew. *Military Medicine, 162*, 79–81.

Watson, P. (1978). *War on the mind: The military uses and abuses of psychology.* New York: Basic Books.

Wilson, M., & Daly, M. (1985). Competitiveness, risk taking, and violence: The young male syndrome. *Ethology and Sociobiology, 6*, 59–73.

Winegard, B., & Deaner, R. O. (2010). The evolutionary significance of Red Sox nation: Sport fandom as a by-product of coalitional psychology. *Evolutionary Psychology, 8*, 432–446.

Xenophon. (1947). *Anabasis: March up country.* (W. H. D. Rouse, Trans.). Ann Arbor: University of Michigan Press.

Yuki, M., & Yokota, K. (2009). The primal warrior: Outgroup threat priming enhances intergroup discrimination in men but not women. *Journal of Experimental Social Psychology, 45*, 271–274.

Zivotofsky, A. Z., & Koslowsky, M. (2005). Gender differences in coping with the major external stress of the Washington, D.C. sniper. *Stress and Health, 21*, 27–31.

CHAPTER 23

An Evolutionary Perspective on Child Development in the Context of War and Political Violence

Jay Belsky

Abstract

Lethal intergroup conflict has been part of the human experience ever since our species emerged on the African savannah. Modern evolutionary thinking suggests that children's development could have evolved a variety of responses to it, some of which are highlighted upon considering, from the field of behavioral ecology, life-history theory, and, derived from it, Belsky, Steinberg, and Draper's (1991) evolutionary theory of socialization. This speculative chapter examines the implications of such thinking, specifically with regard to insecure attachment, anxiety, depression, aggression, pubertal and sexual development, and mating and parenting. Considered, too, are issues of intergenerational transmission and variation in developmental reactivity to exposure to deadly political violence of the ethnic-cleansing variety in childhood.

Key Words: attachment, evolution, life history, puberty, reproductive strategy

Introduction

Almost 15 years ago now, the distinguished developmental journal *Child Development* devoted a special section to research examining the effects of ethnic and political violence on children's psychological and behavioral development (Cairns & Dawes, 1996; Ladd & Cairns, 1996), with empirical studies of race riots in Los Angeles (Farver & Frosch, 1996); political violence in the Palestinian territories (Garbarino & Kostelny, 1996), South African townships (Straker, Mendelsohn, Moosa, & Tudin, 1996), and in Israel (Punamäki, 1996); and war in Lebanon (Macksoud & Aber, 1996) and Cambodia (Sack, Clarke, & Seeley, 1996). This work was important for several reasons, including calling attention to millions of children exposed to political violence of one sort or another around the globe and developmentalists' limited understanding of these formative experiences, especially understanding that could inform intervention. Noteworthy variation was noted in how exposure to politically inspired violence affects children (Cairns & Dawes, 1996; see also Barber, Schluterman, Denny, & McCouch, 2005; Barenbaum, Ruchkin, & Schwab-Stone, 2004). Also highlighted were the potentially protective effects of ideological commitment (Dawes & de Villiers, 1987; Protacio-Marcelino, 1989; Punamäki, 1996; Punamäki, Quota, & El Sarraj, 1997) and the mediating and moderating role of family support in the face of political conflict (Garbarino & Kostelny, 1996; Smith, Perrin, Ule, & Rabe-Hesketh, 2001), as well as the need to consider the nature and dosage of exposure to conflict (Garbarino & Kostelny, 1996; Ladd & Cairns, 1996; Macksoud & Aber, 1996).

The scientific contribution of this groundbreaking work was clearly evident in Kerestes's (2006) subsequent research on the functioning of elementary-school children in grades 6–8 from two Croatian towns that varied in terms of exposure to the most recent war in the Balkans. Not only did this research build upon and extend previous inquiry by focusing on positive and negative consequences of war exposure (i.e., prosocial and aggressive behavior; see also Garbarino, 1990; Jensen & Shaw, 1993; Macksoud & Aber, 1996; Ressler, Boothby, & Steinbeck, 1988), but it did so using a longitudinal design, following children whose 5-year exposure to war began when they were 5–8 years of age, while relying on multiple informants to assess child development (peers, parents, teachers, self-report) and examining the protective effect of positive parenting. Most of the work preceding this investigation, including that cited earlier, was in no position to do many of these things, and none could do them all. Even still, Kerestes (2006) acknowledged how limited research in this field remains. Relatedly, Barber et al. (2005, p. 171) observed that "not enough is yet known about human functioning (of any age group) in the face of political violence to permit solid conclusions or predictions as to how an individual or homogeneous groups of persons will process, participate in and/or adapt to conditions of war."

Given the nature of the subject matter and its psychological (or psychiatric) focus, it is not surprising that all the aforementioned research, like most other war-related inquiry pertaining to children, including very recent work (Cummings et al., 2010; Montgomery, 2010), has been guided by what might be referred to generally as "mental health theory" (MHT). Central to MHT is the implicit if not explicit assumption that war, political violence, and the like adversely affect children's well-being, promoting disturbances in development, even if not clinical disorders per se. Indeed, as Barber et al. (2005, p. 171) observe upon noting "the relatively narrow focus" of work to date, "the predominant focus of the existing research on the effects of political violence has been to test its association with individual-level psychopathology, which some theory has predicted is the natural, near-inevitable consequence of exposure to or participation in violence, particularly to those types and levels of violence that often characterize political conflict" (e.g., Shaw, 2003). The disproportionate focus on posttraumatic stress disorder (PTSD) symptoms in assessments of the functioning of children exposed to political violence attests to this perhaps more than anything else (Barenbaum et al., 2004; Kuterovac-Jagodic, 2003; Macksoud & Aber, 1996; Sack et al., 1996; Smith et al., 2001). Clearly, the question guiding most, even if not all, inquiry has been, not unreasonably, how and to what extent does exposure to war and political conflict harm children?

The core assumption underlying the speculative analysis presented in this chapter of effects of war and political violence on children is that a mental health orientation is not the only way to approach the complexity of children's short-term and longer term responses to war exposure (see also Barber, 2008a). Indeed, the central premise of this chapter is that a modern evolutionary perspective on war, political violence, and child development may provide additional insights into the phenomena while highlighting new avenues of inquiry. While not denying the indisputable pain and suffering that children, as well as adults, surely experience in the face of war and political conflict, it will be argued that many responses to such deadly violence (and the threat of it) may reflect adaptations in the evolutionary—not just psychological—sense of the term rather than simply disturbances in, or deviations from, "optimal" development. More specifically, because, as will be argued shortly, murderous conflict between genetically unrelated peoples probably has characterized the human experience since our species emerged on the African savannah, developmental response(s) to it may well have been selected by Darwinian processes over the course of human (if not preceding primate) evolution. Thus, what might be regarded routinely as "negative" consequences of war exposure today may represent, in part, naturally selected adaptations that once promoted the survival and reproduction of the self and descendants—and may even still to this day.

Survival and reproduction of self and descendants figure centrally in this chapter because from an evolutionary point of view, a perspective relevant to understanding all living things, humans included, the fundamental goal of life is to disperse genes into future generations. This can be achieved directly, by surviving to reproductive age and bearing offspring, or indirectly, via the survival and reproduction of kin (e.g., siblings, cousins) and their descendants (e.g., nieces, nephews). Thus, evolutionists make reference to "inclusive fitness." Even though all living things have been shaped by natural selection to maximize inclusive fitness, it is important to appreciate that this does not necessarily or simply translate into bearing more offspring, having more nieces and nephews, and so forth. Sometimes having fewer immediate and collateral descendants proves more successful in maximizing fitness in the long run than having more, if only because resources for supporting and raising more descendants who would themselves be reproductively successful may be limited. Ultimately, then, all living things, in all their complexity (or even simplicity), can be regarded as devices shaped by natural selection to pass genes on from one generation to the next. Indeed, natural selection is the Darwinian process that modifies organisms over time and across generations in ways that make them more reproductively fit given the ecological circumstances that they have encountered over long (or even short) periods of history.

With this foundation established, the remainder of this chapter will explore some of its implications for thinking about children's exposure to deadly conflict, especially conflict experienced early in life of the ethnic-cleansing variety (see Barber et al., 2005, 2008a for in-depth and informative summaries and analyses of research on adolescents and political violence). I begin by developing the aforementioned working assumption that human history, from its inception, has involved deadly conflict between genetically unrelated peoples. I next call attention to life-history theory, a branch of evolutionary theory that is considered of central importance to understanding human development because of the role it attributes to developmental experiences in shaping the life course. Thereafter and before drawing some brief conclusions, I consider aspects of development, mostly even if not exclusively "negative" in character, that are conceivably affected by exposure to deadly conflict during childhood, some of which have not yet been investigated. To be noted is that important topics which have been widely and thoughtfully considered in many other writings on children's exposure to political conflict are purposefully not considered here to any great extent, if at all; these include assessment of war events (e.g., Barenbaum et al., 2004; Macksoud & Aber, 1996), duration of war effects (e.g., Ajdukovic & Ajdukovic, 1998; Elbedour, ten Bensel, & Bastien, 1993), age differences in reactivity to conflict (e.g., Garbarino & Kostelny, 1996; Punamäki, 2002), cultural variation in the manifestation of sequelae (e.g., Labor & Wolmar, 2002), and the role of meaning in attenuating would-be adverse effects (Barber, 2008b; Punamäki et al., 1997; Slone, 2005).

Human Ancestral Conditions

Evolutionary theory stipulates that developmental processes and outcomes that have, over the course of human (and prehuman) history, fostered survival and reproduction, thereby enhancing (reproductive) fitness, have been selected via Darwinian processes. Thus, one way of gaining insight into human development from an evolutionary perspective is to entertain the kinds of ecological challenges that the species might have faced, especially repeatedly, early in its history and which thereby contributed, at least conceivably, to making us who we are, or at least seem to be, today (Buss, 1999; Cosmides & Tooby, 1987; Tooby & Cosmides, 1990). This should not be read to imply that human development is exclusively a function of selection pressures experienced while the species was evolving on the African savannah, as it is now appreciated that selection can operate over shorter periods of time than once considered possible (Cochrane & Harpending, 2009; Grant & Grant, 1995; Laland & Brown, 2006; Thompson, 1998).

A fundamental assumption on which this chapter is based is that political conflicts and especially those of the ethnic-cleansing variety are something that humans have probably experienced since they emerged on the savannahs of Africa. One may even wonder whether these played some role in the exodus of *Homo sapiens* out of Africa, resulting in the eventual peopling of the planet (Oppenheimer, 2003). Although some may regard ethnic cleansing as a relatively modern phenomenon, it seems more likely that it has been a feature of our species' behavior since families, tribes, or larger groups of genetically related people—who share more genes with one another than with others—found themselves in competition for what were regarded, accurately or inaccurately, as limited—or even just desired—resources. Those resources probably took any of a variety of forms, but they surely included land, water, shelter, and food, as well as anything else that contributed to survival and reproduction, either directly or indirectly, including breeding-age females. It seems unlikely that much effort would have been expended, at least for very long, trying to eliminate entirely a set of genetically unrelated competitors (i.e., genocide), especially if their numbers were reasonably large, if only because of the great energy and risk entailed, which is not to say that such a goal was never pursued or achieved. Rather, the argument advanced here is that if what was desired were resources to promote survival and reproduction, which it is assumed was not uncommonly the case, then murderous actions to terrify resource competitors may have been a particularly effective and efficient means of convincing them, over the short term or longer term, to abandon what they otherwise regarded as their own, thereby leaving it to their adversaries.

Notable in this regard is what Buss (1999, p. 279) referred to as Wrangham and Peterson's (1996) "remarkable observation" that of the more than 10 million animal species that exist, including 4,000 mammals, only two show intense male-initiated territorial aggression, including coordinated coalitions that raid neighboring territories and result in lethal attacks on members of their own species—chimpanzees and humans. In all cultures men have bonded together routinely to attack other groups or to defend their own. And this is not just a modern phenomenon. Rates of homicide are commonly high among many aboriginal peoples who still inhabit the earth, including the Yanomamö of Venezuela (Chagnon, 1988), the Ache of Paraguay (Hill & Hurtado, 1996), the Tiwi of northern Australia (Hart & Pilling, 1960), and the putatively peaceful !Kung San of Botswana, whose rate of homicide exceeds that of Detroit (Daly & Wilson, 1988). Moreover, human recorded history, in line with many ethnographies of tribal cultures, reveals male coalitional warfare to be a worldwide phenomenon (Chagnon, 1988; Tooby & Cosmides, 1988). To the extent that the frightening murder of some of one's neighbors succeeded in securing their resources and, thereby, promoting the aggressors' reproductive fitness, there is every reason to suspect that such ways of thinking about and dealing with others who have things one covets would have themselves been selected by Darwinian processes (Buss, 1999).

It seems likely, moreover, that when competitors were frightened sufficiently into believing that they were in mortal danger and might not or could not prevail in an open conflict, that they made the decision, or at least some of them did, to give up their livelihoods in favor of their lives. Others, either in larger or smaller numbers, probably decided to remain and fight to the death for what was theirs. And still others probably would have liked to escape but found they could not and lacked the will or capability to fight to the death against their adversaries. Unlike contemporary times when, due to modern communication technology and complex geopolitical considerations, such ethnic cleansing may (eventually) elicit assistance from outsiders, it seems likely that losers in these ancient conflicts suffered greatly and for long periods of time, especially if they could not reclaim the very resources they had been forced to abandon, if they survived. More specifically, it seems unlikely that other neighbors whose land, water, and other resources they were perhaps forced to encroach upon would have welcomed these refugees with open arms, especially if resources were regarded as limited and the dislocated interlopers were not kin. Giveing the reproductive value of breeding-age (or soon-to-be breeding-age) females (Buss, 1999; Chagnon, 1988; Tooby & Cosmides, 1988) and the economic value of able-bodied youth, however, exceptions would surely have been made to this central tendency. This discussion highlighting the potentially additive and sequential nature of traumas often inflicted on survivors of ethnic cleaning is notable vis-à-vis selection pressures on children's psychological and behavioral responses to war and political conflict because it is particularly when adversities accumulate—such as death, loss of a home, and continued threats from old enemies, new neighbors, or ecological conditions (e.g., limited shelter, lack of food), or what Weine and associates (2008) refer to as "the trauma bundle"—that adverse effects (e.g., PTSD) are most likely to occasion (Barenbaum et al., 2004; Garbarino & Kostelny, 1996; Husain et al., 1998).

It seems indisputable that people living hundreds if not thousands of miles away would not have come to the aid of the endangered, dislocated, and/or dispossessed, as they often do today, if only because they could not have known about the plight of those subjected to ethnic cleansing. Besides, what would have motivated them to risk their own lives and livelihoods for others not genetically related to them—and thus whose fitness interests they shared virtually not at all? From this perspective, then, the very existence of a state like Israel must be regarded as a uniquely modern event, probably never before occasioned in the history of humankind. After all, what is the likelihood that a people not simply subject to ethnic cleansing on a grand scale, but to genocide on an industrial scale, would have been saved by genetically unrelated others and given resources and land with which to build a new life, a new community, indeed, a new society? The fact, however, that such humanitarian action occurred in recent history, and surely transpired on much smaller scales throughout human history—as altruism, not just murderous aggression, also carries fitness benefits—does not obviate the fact that biological forces may incline some to treat terribly those who share few of their genes and are regarded as competitors for valued resources.

If the preceding suppositions are even partially correct, and specifically if being evicted from one's resource base after one or more terrifying, life-threatening, and murderous encounters was a not uncommon experience of ancestral humans, it stands to reason that Darwinian processes would have selected human responses to such fitness-threatening events. That is, response tendencies of individuals to the threats under consideration that proved successful in promoting survival and, thereby, reproduction would have evolved, in contrast especially to responses that would have reduced the likelihood of such outcomes. Behavioral ecologists refer to such fitness-enhancing responses as "facultative," meaning that such response potentials exist within the evolved behavioral repertoire of the organism but only manifest when stimulated by appropriate contextual conditions, because it is under these conditions that they prove biologically valuable. To develop the argument that, in all likelihood, response tendencies to ethnic-cleansing type experiences have evolved, attention is turned to the structure of the human life course.

Life-History Theory and the Plasticity of Human Development

Students of human development, especially those working from traditional psychological perspectives, generally take for granted the biological structure of the life course, typically failing to appreciate that our relatively helpless status at birth, our extended juvenile period, our very delayed reproductive maturation and, in the case of females, a rather long postreproductive life (i.e., menopause) represents a life-history pattern that itself remains to be explained. (For competing accounts, see Hawkes, 2003; Hawkes, O'Connell, Blurton-Jones, Alvares, & Charnov, 2000; Kaplan, Lancaster, & Hurtado, 2000.) Moreover, even though existence of diverse developmental trajectories stimulates great interest among developmentalists (e.g., Broidy et al., 2003; NICHD Early Child Care Research Network, 2004), rarely is this variation considered from the perspective of evolutionary biology. Yet an entire subfield of evolutionary inquiry, that of behavioral ecology, is guided by life-history theory (LHT), which regards the structure of the life course as a phenotype that has been shaped by natural selection, including its capacity to change facultatively, that is, in response to environmental conditions in the service of fitness goals.

More specifically, LHT is the metatheoretical framework within more general evolutionary theory that seeks to account for the timing of reproductive and life-span developments in terms of evolved strategies for distributing metabolic resources between the competing demands of growth, maintenance, and reproduction (Charnov, 1993; Ellis, 2004; Kuzawa, 2005; McArthur & Wilson, 1967; Stearns, 1992). LHT describes an individual's total bioenergetic and material resources as allocated between somatic effort (i.e., resources devoted to the continued survival) and reproductive effort (i.e., resources devoted to producing-supporting offspring). Reproductive effort can be further divided into mating effort (i.e., resources devoted to obtaining-retaining sexual partners) and parental effort (i.e., resources devoted to enhancing offspring survival and quality). Life-history traits are the basic units of analysis in LHT and include, for example, age at weaning, age at sexual maturity, adult body size, time to first reproduction, and litter size.

LHT provides a useful means of organizing life-history traits in a manner that highlights costs, benefits, and trade-offs of different patterns of development. Such trade-offs are inevitable because time and energy used for one purpose cannot be used for another. In a determinant growing species like humans (i.e., cease growing at reproductive maturity), the decision of when to switch from investing energy in growth to investing in reproduction is a classic example of such an adaptive trade-off. So, too, is that between number and fitness of offspring. Even though there are benefits, reproductively speaking, of large adult size, risks are associated nevertheless with delaying maturity in order to grow large; this is because there is always the chance of dying—due to war, political violence, or ethnic cleansing, for example—before the reproductive benefits of large size are realized (Williams, 1966). At the age when mortality risk associated with delaying maturity outweighs the reproductive benefits of growing larger, as it may be in wartime, LHT predicts that the organism will cease growth and direct energy otherwise devoted to growth into supporting reproduction. These assumptions about the costs and benefits of delaying maturity have been used to predict the timing of reproductive maturity across species (Charnov, 1993).

The notion of life-history variation and trade-offs applies not only to between-species comparisons but is also relevant to within-species variation. Indeed, Belsky, Steinberg, and Draper (BSD) (1991) sought to recast much of human socialization theory and research in evolutionary perspective two decades ago now, linking childhood experience, interpersonal orientation, and reproductive strategy. Central to BSD theory was the thesis that stressful and supportive extrafamilial environments influence family dynamics, most especially parent–child and marital/pair-bond relations, thereby shaping children's early emotional and behavioral development and, through it, subsequent social and emotional development, including sexual/mating behavior, pair bonding, and parenting. Moreover, BSD argued, this complex and environmentally sensitive developmental system evolved as a means of fitting the organism to its environment in the service of promoting reproductive fitness (i.e., not psychological well-being).

Of central importance to BSD theory was the view that parenting, the parent–child relationship, and, in particular, the attachment relationship mediated the influence of stressors and supports external to the parent–child relationship on the child's general trustful–mistrustful outlook on the world and opportunistic/advantage taking versus mutually beneficial orientation toward others, as well as his or her behavior. But what fundamentally distinguished BSD from all other theories of, or perspectives on, early experience and human development was the explicitly labeled "uncanny" prediction that these developmental experiences and psychological orientations would influence somatic development by affecting the timing of puberty; and that this cascade of developments shaped, in adolescence and adulthood, sexual behavior, pair-bond orientation, and parenting.

More specifically, BSD posited two distinctive developmental trajectories for purposes of presentation—after noting that it remained unclear whether environmental processes and the development of reproductive strategies should be conceptualized dimensionally or typologically (i.e., continuous vs. discrete phenotypic plasticity). A quantity-oriented reproductive strategy was most likely to arise, BSD argued, in the context of a variety of stressors that would undermine parental well-being and family relationships, including general stress, marital discord, and/or inadequate financial resources. These forces would, probabilistically, give rise to harsh, rejecting, insensitive, and/or inconsistent parenting, which would foster insecure attachment, a mistrustful internal working model, and an opportunistic, advantage-taking interpersonal orientation. These developments would accelerate pubertal development (within the organism's range of reaction) and the onset of sexual activity, fostering short-term and unstable pair bonds and limited parental investment. This was because the adverse developmental experiences under consideration would have reduced individuals' chances of living long enough to have any or many offspring and compromised their capacity to attract and maintain high-quality mates and skillfully rear offspring, developmental sequelae that would have limited grandchildren's development in similar ways. Better, then, to mature fast, breed early and repeatedly, and not invest too heavily in offspring, given the fundamental goal of maximizing descendants in the long run. After all, delaying maturation, deferring mating, and investing heavily in offspring could prove a fool's errand should life prove short, should high-quality mates prove unavailable or inaccessible, or should one's capacity to protect one's offspring, to say nothing of enhance their life prospects, prove limited.

The alternative, quality-oriented developmental trajectory would be fostered by exposure to a safe and secure extrafamilial environment, which would itself give rise to a supportive rearing milieu, characterized by spousal harmony and adequate financial resources. These ecological foundations would themselves promote, again probabilistically, sensitive, supportive, responsive, and positively affectionate styles of mothering and fathering and, thereby, secure attachments, a trusting internal working model and a mutually beneficial and reciprocally rewarding interpersonal orientation. Collectively, these developments would delay pubertal maturation (within the range of reaction) and defer the onset of sexual activity, thereby fostering enduring pair bonds and elevated levels of parental investment. This was because under the development-facilitating circumstances in question, children would have a longer time to grow, thereby literally embodying psychological and materially resources available in their environment, ones that would enhance their ability to attract and maintain high-quality mates and to skillfully care for offspring. Because these sequelae would themselves increase the prospect that offspring would survive to reproductive age, attract and maintain high-quality mates, and care skillfully for their own progeny (i.e., grandchildren), there would be less need to bear more offspring in order to increase the chances of having descendants in future generations.

As BSD made clear at the time, a great deal of traditional developmental research provided evidence that stressful rearing milieus, whether conceptualized in demographic terms (e.g., low income, lone parenthood), relationships terms (e.g., harsh/neglecting parenting; marital conflict, divorce), or psychological terms (e.g., depressed mother, insecure attachment), predict developmental "outcomes" that are regarded by mainstream child developmentalists—and many others—as "unfavorable" and certainly not "optimal." These included, among other things, precocious and promiscuous sexual behavior, aggressive/antisocial behavior, depression, relationship instability, and unsupportive, if not harsh, parenting. The opposite tends to be true of rearing environments that are well resourced and emotionally and relationally supportive (e.g., Bradley, Caldwell, & Rock, 1988; Cicchetti & Carlson, 1989; Emery, 1988; McLoyd, 1990; Patterson, 1986; Pettit & Bates, 1989). In the time since BSD advanced their theory, the publication of evidence highlighting such environmental effects has continued unabated (e.g., Amato, 2001; Belsky & Fearon, 2002; Buehler & Gerard, 2002; Parke et al., 2004; Seccombe, 2000).

As already noted, what made BSD distinctive was the hypothesis that social-developmental experiences within the family would influence the timing of sexual maturation (i.e., puberty) (Belsky, 2007). Because this is a core life-history trait and because it is a feature of development that no other theory of, or perspective on, human development suggests would be affected by social-developmental experiences in the family, BSD theory highlighted the potential "added value" of an evolutionary approach to human development. A good deal of evidence has emerged consistent with BSD's theoretically derived prediction that less supportive home environments would be associated with (somewhat) earlier onset of puberty, at least in the case of females, leading Ellis (2004, pp. 935–936) to conclude in his elegant and comprehensive review of research on the determinants of pubertal timing in girls that "empirical research has provided reasonable, though incomplete" support for BSD theory. In the shrt time since these words were written, Ellis, among others, has provided additional evidence consistent with BSD theorizing (Belsky et al., 2007; Belsky, Houts, & Fearon, 2010; Ellis & Essex, 2007; Tither & Ellis, 2008).

Although BSD had nothing to say about war, political violence, or ethnic conflict, especially of the ethnic-cleansing kind that is the principal focus of this chapter, their theoretical ideas can easily incorporate these extrafamilial stressors, as BSD conceptualized intrafamily processes as the means by which information about the extrafamilial world pertinent to future reproductive success was transmitted to the child, thereby enabling the developing person to adjust his or her developmental trajectory to optimize fitness. Indeed, it would seem rather likely that ancestors exposed to ethnic cleansing would have been more likely to rear reproductively successful offspring if information about deadly enemies had been passed on to them, consciously or unconsciously, and if offspring adjusted their development accordingly. It therefore seems reasonable to hypothesize that natural selection not only shaped adult minds to pass on such information but also shaped children's bodies and minds to monitor and respond to such information. In fact, Chisholm (1993, 1996, 1999), in extending BSD theorizing, has argued that local mortality rates—which would certainly be elevated in times of war and political violence—are one of the critical environmental cues that direct individuals down different developmental and reproductive pathways.

Developmental Sequelae of War and Political Conflict

In the remainder of this chapter, I explore the implications of LHT and BSD thinking with respect to the effects of war, political violence, and ethnic cleansing on child development. Insecure attachment is considered first, moving on to consider thereafter anxiety, depression, and aggression, before focusing explicitly on reproductive functioning, including pubertal development, sexual behavior, pair bonding, and parental investment. In what follows, there is no presumption that commonly conceived "negative" sequelae are the only derivatives of exposure to war and conflict, even if these are the focus of much of what follows, nor is there any presumption that the kinds of sequelae under consideration are inevitable (Barber, 2008a). What is presumed, instead, is that many putatively "negative" sequelae may have been—and may still be—functional with respect to survival and reproduction (i.e., evolutionarily adaptive).

Insecure Attachment

Even though no studies have examined the effects of war or ethnic cleansing on child–parent attachment, there are strong theoretical grounds for expecting attachment security to be undermined by exposure to deadly conflict. To begin with, it is well established that all kinds of stressors can foster intrusive, overcontrolling, and hostile parenting or detached, disengaged, and neglectful rearing, or even both patterns of insensitive care known to contribute to insecure attachment (for reviews, see Belsky & Fearon, 2002, 2008; Belsky & Jaffee, 2006; De Wolff & van IJzendoorn, 1997). In addition, some war-related research strongly suggests that parenting is "adversely" affected by the stress of deadly conflict (Cairns, 1996; Dybdahl, 2001; Kalantari, Yule, & Gardner, 1993) and that such consequences mediate and moderate war effects on children (e.g., Barber, 2001; Punamäki, Qota, & El Sarraj, 2001). Just as notable, though, may be convincing evidence that frightening maternal behavior promotes disorganized attachment (e.g., Abrams, Rifkin, & Hesse, 2006; Goldberg, Benoit, Blokland, & Madigan, 2003; Madigan, Moran, & Pederson, 2006), the pattern most consistently linked to clinical disturbances in development (Carlson, 1998; Cicchetti, Rogosch, & Toth, 2006); and it is not difficult to imagine how in the extremely dangerous circumstances associated with deadly conflict that the very young child could come to regard some maternal behavior as frightening (e.g., intrusively grabbing the child with no warning to move him out of harm's way, acting frightened when in danger).

Moreover, there is every reason to expect that the general conditions which often coincide with ethnic cleansing or deadly political violence, such as being cold, hungry, or relocated repeatedly in search of safer places, not just ones involving unsupportive parenting, would themselves foster insecurity. There would seem to be a need, then, to extend Davies and Cummings's (1994) "emotional-security hypothesis" beyond sources of influence known to operate within the microsystem of the family (i.e., parenting, marital relations). From both an evolutionary and commonsense standpoint, feeling insecure would seem eminently appropriate and adaptive in an insecure world, reflecting perhaps "optimal" rather than compromised development. Not only should it encourage hypervigilance to signs of threat (Rieder & Cicchetti, 1989), fostering physical closeness to those most (biologically) invested in preserving the child's safety (i.e., close kin), but in so doing it would likely have increased the probability of survival in ancestral times, thereby becoming a target for natural selection. This argument was, of course, central to Bowlby's (1969) original formulation of the evolutionary function of the attachment behavioral system. As it turns out, Cummings and associates (2010) recently reported a study carried out in strife-torn Northern Ireland showing that a history of political violence in the community predicts greater concurrent sectarian violence and, thereby, a sense of "insecurity in the community," that is, feelings of lack of safety and heightened threat regarding the community.

Also worth highlighting is a remarkable study of the long-term effects of the Holocaust carried out by Sagi-Schwartz and associates (2003)—requiring more than 30,000 telephone interviews in Israel to identify appropriate cases—which documented adverse effects on attachment among aged child survivors. Comparison of 48 female Holocaust survivors who resided in Europe before and during World War II, lost their parents, and immigrated to Israel as orphans after the war, with 50 carefully matched counterparts, also born in Europe but who immigrated to Israel with their parents prior to the onset of hostilities, showed that the former manifest more unresolved loss on the Adult Attachment Interview; they also displayed more anxious and traumatic stress on other measurements, with effects sizes qualifying as strong.

From an intergenerational perspective, there is further reason to suspect that exposure to war, political violence, and ethnic cleansing could foster insecure attachment. Central to attachment theory is the notion, substantiated by evidence (Belsky, 2005a; van IJzendoorn, 1995), that attachment security is intergenerationally transmitted, with parents whose state of mind regarding attachment is dismissing or preoccupied being more likely to rear offspring who develop insecure attachments to them than parents whose state of mind is autonomous secure. This observation raises the prospect that insecurity-inducing political conflict, including ethnic cleansing, in one generation could be transmitted to the next, even in the absence of direct exposure to life-threatening danger. If this is the case, then a most intriguing developmental question arises: For how many generations must threats of deadly violence be absent before the psychological legacy of such is no longer transmitted from one generation to the next, especially when a people's history is one of multigenerational victimization?

This question calls attention to a concept recently introduced to the study of a distinctly different intergenerational process that may be relevant to those pertaining to adverse effects of ethnic cleansing, war, and political violence. "Phenotypic inertia" is the term Kuzawa (2005) coined to characterize a phenomenon whereby the in utero experience of a grandmother growing under resource-limited conditions exerts a growth-limiting effect on her grandchild whose intrauterine experience is substantially different. Despite encountering sufficient nourishment, the grandchild develops smaller than would be expected. Why should this be? According to Kuzawa (2005), developing in a manner consistent with a legacy established two generations earlier would be developmentally strategic and naturally selected if, over the course of history, it proved to forecast more accurately the resource conditions that the (grand) child would likely face, even if this meant, on occasion, that a child's growth failed to reflect the rich resources encountered during his or her own lifetime (in utero and thereafter). If it proved to be the case, as probability and the prevailing ecology might have it, that times of plenty prove to be the exception and times of scarcity the rule, the child seemingly lucky enough to be conceived and born during times of plenty would be placed at severe risk if he or she grew large because of intrauterine experience, only to encounter thereafter a resource-limited environment that could not sustain so large a body. Better, it would seem, to err on the side of caution: grow small so as to match the historically probable limited resource base rather than risk overshooting it, with all the adverse consequences that could then occasion (e.g., illness, death). The term "phenotypic inertia," then, describes the tendency of the grandmother's phenotype to be maintained even when a child's own ecological circumstances would seem to afford a rather contrasting one.

Might it be the case that psychological and behavioral development operates similarly, especially with respect to populations exposed repeatedly to ethnic-cleansing-type experiences? Would a single—or even a few adjacent—generation(s) of relative safety and security be sufficient to offset an established multigenerational legacy of life-threatening danger, fear, and uncertainty? Do intergenerationally recurrent threats to survival and reproduction operate in a manner similar to intermittent reinforcement, making extinction—in this case of fear, anxiety, insecurity, and mistrust—extremely difficult, with these sentiments ever so easily evoked even after extended periods of seeming safety and security? Have humans, in fact, evolved a psychology to resist such extinction to threats that can eliminate an entire people, not just an individual life, because individuals and groups that developed a sense of safety and security prematurely—and mistakenly—simply did not prove sufficiently successful to leave descendants who would inherit any such genetically mediated inclinations?

From this perspective one can even wonder whether, or to what extent, it is wise for a repeatedly persecuted people to succumb to the wishes and entreaties of outsiders to forgive their once deadly neighbors or even just to live in relative peace with them. Whose true biological interest, one can further wonder, is ultimately served by such potentially temporary interethnic harmony? Could it actually be more in the (biological) self-interest of outsiders pushing for peace rather than the self-interest of those who have historical grounds for doubting that a peace will remain secure? From this perspective, there may even be grounds for questioning the (bio) ethics of well-intentioned interventions designed to ameliorate intergroup hostilities and promote intergroup understanding and cooperation following bouts of ethnic cleansing and the like. What happens if these succeed in the short run but fail in the longer, intergenerational run? One might surmise that some Rwandans already know the answer to this question.

Anxiety

Common sense and MHT lead to the expectation that anxiety would be a psychological response to life-threatening exposure to war, political violence, and ethnic conflict—and that this would be so in the case of those inclined to flee in the face of threats of danger, those who would prefer to flee but prove unable to do so, and even those inclined to fight their enemies rather than escape them. This is no doubt why so much attention has been paid to PTSD in studies of the psychological sequelae of exposure to deadly conflict (e.g., Dawes, Tredoux, & Feinstein, 1989; Dickason, Him, & Sack, 1999; Yule, 2000). To the extent, however, that anxiety fostered vigilance to danger and, in so doing, served to increase the chances of child survival and, thereby, reproduction over the course of human history, there would seem to be a need to consider evolutionary processes.

The first such consideration may be especially pertinent to those inclined to flee life-threatening danger and can be illuminated by a seemingly straightforward question whose answer would seem to carry intriguing implications: Who in the ancestral—or even recent—past would have been most likely to survive the murderous intentions of deadly neighbors, thereby affording them the opportunity to mate and procreate sometime in the future, thus positioning them to rear reproductively successful descendants? Quite conceivably, it would have been those most susceptible to anxiety in the first place and thus most likely to fear the heinous acts of genetically unrelated enemies who coveted their resources, motivating flight from danger. To the extent this observation is valid, it carries implications for population genetics: Is it the case that alleles associated with anxiety occur in greater frequency in populations that have been subjected, over history, to repeated bouts of ethnic cleansing?

Even if it proves to be the case that repeatedly persecuted peoples have high-anxiety genotypes resulting from their differential survival and reproduction relative to less anxious kin who perhaps failed to flee their enemies before being victimized, this would not eliminate or even undermine the prospect of a facultative—meaning environmentally induced and naturally selected—response to deadly violence (or the threat of it) involving anxiety. It is not hard to imagine, given the process of natural selection, that individuals genotypically predisposed to react anxiously to deadly threats (i.e., not just have high levels of generalized anxiety) would have been more likely to relocate (if at all possible), survive, and thus pass on their anxiously reactive genetic dispositions to their offspring. Furthermore, in view of the fact that contemporary research indicates that maternal anxiety affects parenting (for review, see Belsky & Jaffee, 2006), an additional and nongenetic means of transmitting (potentially life-saving) anxiety to offspring must be acknowledged. Such exclusively environmentally mediated transmission could have proven especially valuable in the case of offspring not genetically predisposed to high levels of (generalized or reactive) anxiety.

In light of the preceding discussion of attachment insecurity and these observations pertaining to the survival value of anxiety, one empirical discovery regarding a repeatedly persecuted people and a type of insecurity seems noteworthy: In Israel, and perhaps in Jewish populations elsewhere, an insecure attachment pattern involving high manifest anxiety, insecure ambivalence, uniquely occurs to the virtual exclusion of the other organized insecure attachment pattern, insecure avoidance, that is routinely found to predominate in all other populations studied to date (Van IJzendoorn & Sagi, 1999; Van IJzendoorn & Sagi-Schwartz, 2008). Given recent behavioral genetic evidence indicating that attachment patterns are not heritable (Bokhorst et al., 2003), this finding pertaining to Israeli Jews, coupled with the history of the Jewish people, invites the hypothesis that insecure ambivalence may itself represent a facultative response to generationally recurrent exposure to deadly enemies. This proposition, of course, returns us to the issue raised earlier regarding the intergenerational transmission of attachment insecurity.

Developmentally and functionally, what insecure-ambivalence seems to be very much about is the promotion in the child, by the caregiver, of dependency, an effect that should (a) not only promote distrust of others but (b) keep the child physically and psychologically close to the parent and hyperanxious when it comes to separating from her. If history teaches a people that others pose deadly threats to them, or at least have done so in the past, then the psychological costs of inducing what mainstream mental health and developmental thinking regards as "nonoptimal" may actually have carried great fitness benefits, especially if successful escape from these potential adversaries was not possible. Indeed, such reasoning leads to the testable prediction that insecure-ambivalent attachment should be disproportionately evident in any population that has been subject to repeated persecution and ethnic cleansing, not just among Israeli Jews.

As it turns out, when this issue was addressed by assessing patterns of attachment in the grandchildren of the aged child survivors of the Holocaust whom Sagi-Schwartz et al. (2003) studied, no evidence emerged to substantiate the proposition just advanced (Sagi-Schwartz, van IJzendoorn, & Bakermans-Kranenburg, 2008). Whether this null result in a study with decent statistical power to detect only an effect size in excess of .5 would be replicated in related research remains to be seen. Not to be discounted, of course, is the unique Israeli experience referred to earlier, one of survivors of genocide being granted a homeland following their horrific persecution. Thus, it is not unreasonable to wonder whether a similar absence of intergeneration transmission would characterize people who succeed in escaping murderous enemies but still must confront "the trauma bundle" also mentioned earlier. Given general views on cumulative stress, this seems less than likely. In fact, upon finding no evidence of "secondary traumatization" in children—not just grandchildren—of Holocaust survivors in their meta-analysis of 32 samples involving almost 4,500 participants, van IJzendoorn, Bakermans-Kranenburg, and Sagi-Scwhartz (2003) cautioned against overinterpreting such seemingly heartening findings. Indeed, they invoked a stress-diathesis model in light of other research, including work showing that Israeli soldiers who grew up in families with one or two Holocaust survivors as parents manifested significantly more evidence of PTSD upon encountering combat in the Lebanon war in the 1980s than compatriots without this family background (Solomon, Kotler, & Mikulincer, 1988). Once again, then, one must wonder about intergenerational effects under conditions in which survival does not translate into security and protection, but rather fear and uncertainty.

Depression

MHT, as well as common sense, calls attention to depression as another plausible consequence of exposure to political violence, as does research on the effects of war (e.g., Dickason et al., 1999;

Elbedour, 1998; Zivcic, 1993). Certainly a learned-helplessness framework (Abramson, Seligman, & Teasdale, 1978) suggests that the inability to control truly life-threatening conditions or effectively regulate the anxiety that invariably accompanies them would engender depression. Not inconsistent with this view, perhaps, are Cummings and associates' (2010) recent findings showing that internalizing problems among 7–17-year-olds in Belfast, Northern Ireland proved to be indirectly related to sectarian violence in the community, whose effect was mediated via elevated levels of marital conflict and a child's insecurity about the marital relationship (according to mother).

Returning to the topic of ethnic cleansing, it is not unimaginable that a depressive response to such violence might itself represent a facultative response, especially among those not capable of escaping deadly enemies. Consider the possibility that it might effectively serve to inhibit an enemy's murderous hostility, functioning more or less as a submissive gesture, particularly in the case of females of childbearing age and of girls approaching reproductive maturity. At least one evolutionary psychologist has argued that as a result of the critical role that maternal care plays in offspring survival, "staying alive" is the biological imperative of women (Campbell, 1999). Thus, even if depression undermined sensitive, supportive maternal care, it could still represent a sound trade-off for offspring exposed to "nonoptimal" parenting by reducing the probability of maternal death or even one's own death.

But even if it failed to do so, as was probably often the case given the lack of reproductive interest a male engaged in ethnic cleansing would have in someone else's children, depression that even just sometimes effectively inhibited a girl's or a woman's murder still could have evolved. Such selection would seem especially likely if the depressed response increased the chances of the female in question surviving to realize her biological ambition of bearing and rearing to reproductive maturity (replacement?) children. Not to be forgotten in this context is that ethnic cleansing routinely involves rape and that nonmurderous behavior (Shields & Shields, 1983), including rape, could itself have evolved due to the biological benefits it afforded males engaged in ethnic cleansing upon encountering a depressed (and passive) female victim (Thornhill & Palmer, 2000). In all likelihood, the securing of breeding-age (or soon-to-be-breeding-age) females was one of the primary motivations of raiders in ancestral times (Buss, 1999), as there are few resources more valuable, at least from an evolutionary perspective, than reproductively mature women. These considerations lead to the perhaps unsurprising prediction that it will be girls approaching reproductive maturity (and women still capable of bearing offspring) who will be most likely to respond to deadly ethnic conflict by becoming depressed. Might consideration of the possible evolutionary legacy under discussion even shed some light on the mystery of why, around puberty but not before, girls become so much more susceptible to depression than do boys (Hankin et al., 1998)?

Aggression

Another response to war, political violence and especially ethnic cleansing that could have been selected by Darwinian processes, is most obviously, aggression. If there is a chance that resources taken could be reclaimed, and especially if the alternative is to have one's fitness severely compromised, then it would certainly make evolutionary sense for children to develop aggressive tendencies in response to deadly political conflict. This would seem to be especially the case with respect to boys, as unlike girls they would probably not be regarded by deadly enemies as reproductive resources to be exploited. Arguing along similar lines, but one focused on mediating parenting processes, Hinde (1986) speculated that if maternal rejection is induced by harsh environments in which competition for limited resources is intense (perhaps like ones that foster war), offspring who are aggressive and noncooperative as a result of such maternal behavior might have higher reproductive fitness as adults than those who do not display such attributes.

Of course, one does not require an evolutionary mindset to consider aggression a likely consequence of war exposure. Not only have psychoanalytic thinkers called attention to such a linkage between experience and development (Freud & Burlingham, 1944), but as Kerestes (2006) recently observed, such effects of war on children are also derivable from other theoretical perspectives, including social-learning (e.g., Bandura, 1977; Berkowitz, 1993) and information-processing ones (e.g., Dodge, 1980, 2006; Huesmann, 1988). Indeed, it was this very (nonevolutionary) theoretical foundation that led Kerestes (2006) to predict—and discover—that Bosnian children growing up in a war-exposed town would be more aggressive 3 years after the Balkan wars ended than age mates who resided in a comparable town much further from the front lines (see also Farver & Frosch, 1996). One interesting developmental question that arises in the face of such results, which only longitudinal study—and future history—can answer, is whether such affected children will themselves prove disproportionately susceptible to inducements to ethnic conflict and perhaps even ethnic cleansing in the future. To the extent that they would, this would raise the issue of whether psychological-behavioral responses to certain developmental experiences have been selected as part of a strategy to "prepare" the organism for fitness-enhancing functioning in the future. It is certainly not hard to view Israeli assertions of "never again" from this perspective.

Despite the arguments advanced through this point, it is undoubtedly mistaken to presume, even in the case of males, that aggression—or any other developmental sequelae under consideration—is an inevitable developmental response to exposure to deadly political and ethnic conflict. Indeed, as Barber et al. (2008a) make clear, there is an abundance of evidence indicating that many anticipated adverse effects of war and political violence on children are by no means inevitable. Consider in this regard aggression-related findings from the aforementioned Northern Ireland research. Cummings et al. (2010) observed that for sectarian violence to be related to increased externalizing problems, it first needed to undermine parental monitoring and/or promote a child's sense of insecurity in the community (Cummings et al., 2010).

But it is not just evidence like this—or even common sense—that should alert us to the fact that putatively adverse effects on children of war, ethnic cleansing, and community violence are not inevitable. Evolutionary considerations also suggest this to be so; and, more specifically, that children should vary in terms of their susceptibility to such developmental experiences. As I have pointed out elsewhere (Belsky, 1997, 2000, 2005b Belsky, Bakermans-Kranenburg, & van IJzendoorn, 2007; Belsky et al., 2009; Belsky & Pluess, 2009a, 2009b), because the future is uncertain, and thus because the future is not guaranteed to conform to expectations derived from developmental experience, it seems unlikely that natural selection would have shaped human development to always track earlier experience. Doing so would certainly have proved misguided some of the time, thereby undermining fitness. Bet-hedging logic (Horn & Rubenstein, 1984; Promislow & Harvey, 1990) thus leads to the prediction that, especially within a family, greater fitness benefits would accrue to parents and children if children varied in their susceptibility to rearing or other developmental experiences, including deadly political conflict of the ethnic-cleansing variety (see Boyce & Ellis, 2008, for related argument). This is because some children would be protected should developmental experiences shape siblings in ways that ultimately proved to undermine survival and reproduction, as they would not be so influenced and affected, whereas other offspring shaped by experience would be protected if being resistant to developmental influences proved reproductively costly.

The fact that (full) siblings share 50% of their genes, just as parents do with their offspring, means that even if a particular child's reproductive success was compromised by being susceptible—or unsusceptible—to developmental experiences, he or she could still benefit, fitness-wise, from the reproductive success of siblings who differed from him or her in terms of susceptibility to developmental experiences. Thus, whereas some offspring should be more or less "plastic" strategists whose future development is guided by their prior experience, including exposure to deadly violence, others should be "fixed" strategists following a developmental trajectory more or less impervious to developmental experiences. Over the course of history, each of these developmental strategies would likely have "paid off" fitness-wise—because sometimes being susceptible would have carried benefits vis-à-vis survival and reproduction, whereas at other times the opposite would have been true (i.e., being unsusceptible).

One might even wonder, given the preceding analysis, if some populations include more plastic or more fixed strategists than do others as a result of their selection histories. One might speculate, for example, that fixed strategists inclined toward high levels of aggression irrespective of their developmental experiences would characterize a disproportionate percentage of males in a population with a history of more or less continuous exposure to deadly political conflict, whereas plastic strategists capable of becoming highly aggressive in response to deadly violence would characterize more males in a population exposed to only intermittent bouts of ethnic cleansing throughout its history. The most important conclusion to draw from these observations, pertinent to all potential effects of exposure to war, political violence, and ethnic conflict considered through this point, as well as throughout the remainder of this chapter, is that the developmental sequelae of these experiences should vary both within and across populations. This may indeed account for why the pertinent research literature has not yielded entirely consistent findings (Barber et al., 2005).

Reproductive Functioning: Pubertal Timing, Sexual Behavior, Pair Bonding, and Parenting

As previously noted, evolutionary theorizing (Belsky et al., 1991; Belsky, 2007), like so much general developmental theory, leads to the expectation that exposure to political violence, war, and ethnic conflict will undermine sensitive, supportive parenting, a finding that emerges in some relevant investigations (Barber, 2001; Cairns, 1996; Dybdahl, 2001; Kalantari et al., 1993; Punamäki et al., 2001), if only by inducing fear, anxiety, and exhaustion in parents, thereby increasing rates of insecure attachment and elevated levels of anxiety, depression, and/or aggression in progeny. One recent cross-cultural analysis, showing that parental investment in the form of maternal care is inversely related to a society's experience of warfare (i.e., the more war, the less parental investment), was premised on a somewhat different argument, however. Quinlan (2006) contended, again drawing on LHT, that parental investment will be reduced when parental effort simply cannot improve offspring survival.

But it is not just parenting and, as already discussed, its psychological and behavioral sequelae that evolutionary theorizing suggests should be affected by exposure to political conflict. It further—and uniquely—predicts that pubertal development could be accelerated (i.e., earlier age of menarche)—unless, of course, stressors are so great, as in the case of starvation, that survival needs override reproductive goals (Belsky et al., 1991). In light of evolutionary bet-hedging analysis (Horn & Rubenstein, 1984; Promislow & Harvey, 1990) and for reasons already outlined, when mortality rates are high in a local area, as one would expect them to be in the context of political violence, the "optimal" reproductive strategy should entail early mating so current fertility is maximized (Chisholm, 1993, 1999). Thus, it further might be expected, in line with BSD theorizing, that in the face of contextual circumstances characterized by deadly threats, the onset of sexual activity would be accelerated, which would be part and parcel of a reproductive strategy involving unstable pair bonding and frequent childbearing coupled with relatively low levels of parental investment. Pesonen and associates (2008) endeavored to address aspects of such thinking by studying the life-course development of 899 members of the 1934–1944 Helsinki Birth Cohort, 396 of whom, during World War II, had been sent unaccompanied by their parents to temporary foster families in Sweden and Denmark and 503 who had no separation experiences. Former evacuees, it turned out, had earlier menarche than the other female study members; in fact, they also had more children by late adulthood. More specifically, evacuated girls were, relative to nonevacuees, twice as likely to have their first period before or at the age of 12 years than after age 13 years and they were more than twice as likely to have three or more children than a single child.

Chisholm's (1999) analysis of time preference calls attention to a psychological process that may be related to, indeed part and parcel of, a developmentally accelerated, quantity-oriented reproductive strategy, one that would seem to merit investigation with respect to the sequelae of exposure to deadly political conflict. Time preference, which is associated with delay of gratification tendencies, reflects the degree to which individuals prefer to—or believe they will achieve—their desires now (immediately) versus later (in the future). Individuals raised in dangerous or uncertain environments in which waiting for rewards might result in leaving no descendants should prefer immediate payoffs, even if delayed ones might be superior (Wilson & Daly, 2005). Several notable findings appear consistent with Chisholm's (1999) theorizing, though the research in question was not carried out in direct response to it. First, Daly and Wilson (1988) found that as life expectancy declined across Chicago neighborhoods, often due to community violence, the probability of a woman reproducing by age 30 increased. Similarly, Johns (2003) discovered that teen mothers in Gloucestershire, England expected to die at younger ages than did women who became mothers after their teenage years. Such results not only accord with Geronimus's (1996) qualitative interviews with poor, African American teen mothers, which reveal their awareness of their risks for an early death, but also with her "weathering hypothesis" suggesting that early birth is a strategic response to the rapid decline in health of these women in their third and fourth decade of life. Considered together, these illustrative results, none having to do with war or political violence per se, suggest ways in which such life-threatening experiences can shape the process of human development and, in particular, developing reproductive strategies and their associated psychological mechanisms.

Conclusion

Despite the focus in most of this chapter on adverse effects of children's exposure to war and political violence, it is important to not lose sight of Barber's (2008a) astute analysis of adolescent development in the context of such danger: If negative sequelae are presumed to be automatic, the coping and adaptational capacities of adolescents will not be fully appreciated and even the prospect of positive consequences under some conditions of even deadly conflict will be neglected. These ideas tie directly to ones advanced in the speculative analysis offered in this chapter. Even effects that, on their face, seem negative from the standpoint of MHT may represent evolutionary adaptations, that is, outcomes that have been selected by evolutionary forces to enhance reproductive fitness. Whether they still do so in the modern era, however, remains completely unknown. But even if they do, there seems little reason to presume that they always have or will and thus that there will be across-the-board effects of conflict exposure on children's development. As noted already, because the future is uncertain, evolution shapes probabilistically successful behavioral and psychological development, not certainly successful, in a reproductive fitness sense, outcomes.

From a probabilistic standpoint, multiple sequelae, including none whatsoever, can be fitness enhancing. Anxious response can prove life saving, especially among those able to escape, by encouraging flight in the face of anticipated danger. Depression may make good sense if safe escape is unlikely and one is a potential reproductive resource that an enemy can exploit (i.e., young females). And, of course, aggression through tactics of self-defense and/or hostile offense (i.e., attacking the would-be enemy before he attacks you) may be adaptive, especially among those who cannot successfully flee and who will not be regarded as reproductive resources to be exploited (i.e., males). But if exposure to conflict is likely to be, more or less, rare and not repeated, even no response to it may be an evolved, fitness-enhancing response.

However accurate any of the observations and speculations offered here prove to be, there is no need to lose sight of the fact that children's exposure to war, deadly violence, and political conflict is dangerous and potentially seriously harmful. An evolutionary analysis, in other words, should not be read as giving a "green light" to life-threatening danger or desensitize us toward it. It may, nevertheless, alert us to sequelae that might not otherwise be considered (e.g., pubertal timing, sexual behavior, mating, procreating) or provide insights into why expectations of developmental responses are not always substantiated empirically. Ideally, it might even provide some insight into strategies for dealing with sequelae, but that certainly remains to be seen.

Future Directions

One way to close this chapter is to consider directions for future research. Most important will be to move beyond outcomes like PTSD to which MHT calls attention and consider some of the reproductive-strategy-related outcomes to which this chapter has called attention. Thus, future work should consider developmental outcomes like orientation toward others—advantage taking versus mutually beneficial—pubertal timing, sexual behavior, pair bonding, and eventual parenting to determine whether exposure to political violence does, in fact, regulate the development of reproductive strategy. But such efforts should also take into account the differential-susceptibility hypothesis and thus the prospect that not all individuals will be equally susceptible to such anticipated effects of exposure to conflict (Belsky, 1997, 2005b; Belsky et al., 2009; Belsky & Pluess, 2009a). Thus, it will also be important for investigators to endeavor to secure data on potential moderators of environmental effects, be they measures of temperament, physiology, or genetics.

References

Abrams, K.Y., Rifkin, A., & Hesse, E. (2006). Examining the role of parental fright-ened/frightening subtypes in predicting disorganized attachment within a brief observational procedure. *Development and Psychopathology, 18*, 345–361.

Abramson, L.Y., Seligman, M.E., & Teasdale, J.D. (1978). Learned helplessness in humans. *Journal of Abnormal Psychology, 87*, 49–74.

Ajdukovic, M., & Ajdukovic, D. (1998). Impact of displacement on psychological well-being of refugee children. *International Review of Psychiatry, 10*, 186–195.

Amato, P. (2001). Children of divorce in the 1990s. *Journal of Family Psychology, 15*, 355–370.

Bandura, A. (1977). *Social learning theory*. Englewood Cliffs, NJ: Prentice-Hall.

Barber, B. K. (2001). Political violence, social integration and youth functioning. *Journal of Community Psychology, 29*, 259–280.

Barber, B. K. (2008a). Glimpsing the complexity of youth and political violence. In B. K. Barber (Ed.), *Adolescents and war: How youth deal with political violence* (pp. 3–32). New York: Oxford University Press.

Barber, B. K. (2008b). Making sense and no sense of war: Issues of identity and meaning in adolescents' experience with political conflict. In B. K. Barber (Ed.), *Adolescents and war: How youth deal with political violence* (pp. 281–311). New York: Oxford University Press.

Barber, B. K., Schluterman, J. M., Denny, E. S., & McCouch, R. M. (2005). Adolescents and political violence. In M. Fitzduff & C. Stout (Eds.), *The psychology global conflicts: From war to peace. Volume 2: Group and social factors* (pp. 168–190). Westport, CT: Praeger Press.

Barenbaum, J., Ruchkin, V., & Schwab-Stone, M. (2004). The psychosocial aspects of children exposed to war. *Journal of Child Psychology and Psychiatry, 45,* 41–62.

Belsky, J. (1997). Variation in susceptibility to environmental influences: An evolutionary argument. *Psychological Inquiry, 8,* 182–186.

Belsky, J. (2000). Conditional and alternative reproductive strategies: Individual differences in susceptibility to rearing experience. In J. Rodgers, D. Rowe, & W. Miller (Eds.), *Genetic influences on human fertility and sexuality: Theoretical and empirical contributions from the biological and behavioral sciences* (pp. 127–146). Boston: Kluwer.

Belsky, J. (2005a). The developmental and evolutionary psychology of intergenerational transmission of attachment. In C. S. Carter, L. Ahnert, K. Grossman, S. Hrdy, M. Lamb, S. Porges & N. Sascher (Eds.), *Attachment and bonding: A new synthesis* (pp. 169–198). Cambridge, MA: MIT Press.

Belsky, J. (2005b). Differential susceptibility to rearing influence: An evolutionary hypothesis and some evidence. In B. Ellis & D. Bjorklund (Eds.), *Origins of the social mind: Evolutionary psychology and child development* (pp. 139–163). New York: The Guilford Press.

Belsky, J. (2007). Childhood experiences and reproductive strategies. In R. Dunbar & L. Barrett (Eds.), *Oxford handbook of evolutionary psychology* (pp. 237–254) Oxford, England: Oxford University Press.

Belsky, J., Bakermans-Kranenburg, M., & van IJzendoorn, M. (2007). For better *and* for worse: Differential susceptibility to environmental influences. *Current Directions in Psychological Science, 16,* 305–309.

Belsky, J., & Fearon, R. M. P. (2002). Early attachment security, subsequent maternal sensitivity, and later child development: Does continuity in development depend upon continuity of caregiving? *Attachment and Human Development, 3,* 361–387.

Belsky, J., & Fearon, R. M. P. (2008). Precursors of attachment security. In J. Cassidy & P. Shaver (Eds.), *Handbook of attachment theory and research* (2nd ed., pp. 295–316). New York: The Guilford Press.

Belsky, J., Houts, R. M., & Fearon, R. M. P. (2010). Infant attachment security and timing of puberty: Testing an evolutionary hypothesis. *Psychological Science, 21,* 1195–1201.

Belsky, J., & Jaffee, S. (2006). The multiple determinants of parenting. In D. Cicchetti & D. Cohen (Eds.), *Developmental psychopathology, Vol. 3: Risk, disorder and adaptation* (2nd ed., pp. 38–85). New York: Wiley.

Belsky, J., Jonassaint, C., Pluess, M., Stanton, M., Brummet, B., & Williams, R. (2009). Vulnerability genes or plasticity genes? *Molecular Psychiatry, 14,* 746–754.

Belsky, J., & Pluess, M. (2009a). Beyond diathesis-stress: Differential susceptibility to environmental influences. *Psychological Bulletin, 135,* 885–908.

Belsky, J., & Pluess, M. (2009b). The nature (and nurture?) of plasticity in early human development. *Perspectives in Psychological Science, 4,* 345–351.

Belsky, J., Steinberg, L., & Draper, P. (1991). Childhood experience, interpersonal development, and reproductive strategy: An evolutionary theory of socialization. *Child Development, 62,* 647–670.

Belsky, J., Steinberg, L., Houts, R., Friedman, S. L., DeHart, G., Cauffman, E., . . . The NICHD Early Child Care Research Network. (2007). Family rearing antecedents of pubertal timing. *Child Development, 78,* 1302–1321.

Berkowitz, L. (1993). *Aggression: Its causes and consequences.* New York: McGraw-Hill.

Bokhorst, C. L., Bakermans Kranenburg, M. J., Fearon, R. M. P., van IJzendoorn, M. H., Fonagy, P., & Schuengel, C. (2003). The importance of shared environment in mother–infant attachment security: A behavioral genetic study. *Child Development, 74,* 1769–1782.

Bowlby, J. (1969). *Attachment and loss, Vol. 1: Attachment* (2nd ed.). New York: Basic Books.

Boyce, T., & Ellis, B. (2008). Biological sensitivity to context. *Development and Psychopathology, 17,* 271–301.

Bradley, R. H., Caldwell, B. M., & Rock, S. L. (1988). Home environment and school performance. *Child Development, 59,* 852–867.

Broidy, L. M., Nagin, D. S., Tremblay, R. E., Bates, J. E., Brame, B., Dodge, K. A., . . . Vitaro, F. (2003). Developmental trajectories of childhood disruptive behavior and adolescent delinquency: A six-cite, cross-national study. *Developmental Psychology, 39,* 222–245.

Buehler, C., & Gerard, J. (2002). Marital conflict, ineffective parenting, and children's and adolescent's maladjustment. *Journal of Marriage and the Family, 64,* 78–92.

Buss, D. (1999). *Evolutionary psychology: A new science of the mind.* Boston: Allyn & Bacon.

Cairns, E. (1996). *Children and political violence.* Oxford, England: Blackwell.

Cairns, E., & Dawes, A. (1996). Children: Ethnic and political violence—a commentary. *Child Development, 67,* 120–139.

Campbell, A. (1999). Staying alive: Evolution, culture, and women's intrasexual aggression. *Behavioral and Brain Science, 22,* 203–252.

Carlson, E. A. (1998). A prospective longitudinal study of attachment disorganization/disorientation. *Child Development, 69,* 1107–1128.

Chagnon, N. A. (1988). Life histories, blood revenge and warfare in a tribal population. *Science, 239,* 985–992.

Charnov, E. L. (1993). *Life history invariants.* Oxford, England: Oxford University Press.

Chisholm, J. S. (1993). Death, hope, and sex. *Current Anthropology, 34,* 1–24.

Chisholm, J. S. (1996). The evolutionary ecology of attachment organization. *Human Nature, 7,* 1–38.

Chisholm, J. S. (1999). *Death, hope and sex.* New York: Cambridge University Press.

Cicchetti, D., & Carlson, V. (Eds.). (1989). *Child maltreatment.* New York: Cambridge University Press.

Cicchetti, D., Rogosch, F. A., & Toth, S. L. (2006). Fostering secure attachment in infants in maltreating families through preventive interventions. *Development and Psychopathology, 18,* 623–649.

Cochrane, G., & Harpending, H. (2009). *The 10,000 year explosion.* New York: Basic Books.

Cosmides, L., & Tooby, J. (1987). From evolution to behavior. In J. Dupre (Ed.), *The latest on the best: Essays on evolution and optimality* (pp. 124–147). Cambridge, MA: MIT Press.

Cummings, E. M., Merrilees, C. E., Schermerhorn, A. C., Goeke-Morey, M. C., Shirlow, P., & Cairns, E. (2010). Testing a social ecological model for relations between political violence and child adjustment in Northern Ireland. *Development and Psychopathology, 22*, 405–418.

Daly, M., & Wilson, M. (1988). *Homicide.* New York: Aldine de Gruyter.

Davies, P., & Cummings, E. M. (1994). Marital conflict and child adjustment: An emotional security hypothesis. *Psychological Bulletin, 116*, 387–411.

Dawes, A., & de Villiers, C. (1987) Preparing children and their parents for prison. In D. Hanson (Ed.), *Mental health in transition.* Cape Town, South Africa: OASSA Second National Conference Proceedings.

Dawes, A., Tredoux, C., & Feinstein, A. (1989). Political violence in South Africa: Some effects on children of the violent destruction of their community. *International Journal of Mental Health, 18*, 16–43.

De Wolff, M. S., & Van IJzendoorn, M. H. (1997). Sensitivity and attachment. *Child Development, 68*, 571–591.

Dickason, D., Him, C., & Sack, W. (1999). Twelve-year follow-up study of Khmer youths who suffered massive war trauma as children. *Journal of the American Academy of Child and Adolescent Psychiatry, 38*, 1173–1179.

Dodge, K. (1980). Social cognition and children's aggressive behavior. *Child Development, 51*, 162–170.

Dodge, K. (2006). Translational science in action: Hostile attributional style and the development of aggressive behavior problems. *Development and Psychopathology, 18*, 791–814.

Dybdahl, R. (2001). Children and mothers in war: An outcome study of a psychological intervention program. *Child Development, 72*, 1214–1230.

Elbedour, S. (1998). Youth in crisis: The well-being of Middle Eastern youth and adolescents during war and peace. *Journal of Youth and Adolescence, 27*, 539–556.

Elbedour, S., ten Bensel R., & Bastien, D. T. (1993). Ecological integrated model of children of war: Individual and social psychology. *Child Abuse and Neglect, 17*, 805–819.

Ellis, B. J. (2004). Timing of pubertal maturation in girls. *Psychological Bulletin, 130*, 920–958.

Ellis, B. J., & Essex, M. J. (2007). Family environments, adrenarche, and sexual maturation: A longitudinal test of a life history model. *Child Development, 78*, 1799–1817.

Emery, R. (1988). *Marriage, divorce and children's adjustment.* Beverly Hills, CA: Sage Publications.

Farver, J. M., & Frosch, D. L. (1996). L. A. Stories: Aggression in preschoolers' spontaneous narratives after the riots of 1992. *Child Development, 67*, 19–32.

Freud, A., & Burlingham, D. (1944). *Infants without families: The case against residential nurseries.* London: International University Press.

Garbarino, J. (1990). *Children and youth in war zones: Coping with consequences.* Testimony prepared for the U.S. Senate Committee on Human Resources.

Garbarino, J., & Kostelny, K. (1996). The effects of political violence on Palestinian children's behavior problems: A risk accumulating model. *Child Development, 67*, 33–45.

Geronimus, A. T. (1996). What teen mothers know. *Human Nature, 7*, 323–352.

Goldberg, S., Benoit, D., Blokland, K., & Madigan, S. (2003). Atypical maternal behavior, maternal representations, and infant disorganized attachment. *Development and Psychopathology, 15*, 239–257.

Grant, P. R., & Grant, B. R. (1995). Predicting microevolutionary responses to directional selection on heritable variation. *Evolution, 49*, 241–251.

Hankin, B. L., Abramson, L. Y., Moffitt, T. E., Silva, P. A., McGee, R., & Angell, K. E. (1998). Development of depression from preadolescence to young adult-hood: Emerging gender differences in a 10-year longitudinal study. *Journal of Abnormal Psychology, 107*, 128–140.

Hart, C. W., & Pilling, A. R. (1960). *The Tiwi of North Australia.* New York: Hart, Rinehart & Winston.

Hawkes, K. (2003). Grandmothers and the evolution of human longevity. *American Journal of Human Biology, 15*, 380–400.

Hawkes, K., O'Connell, J. F., Blurton Jones, N. G., Alvarez, H., & Charnov, E. L. (2000). The grandmother hypothesis and human evolution. In L. Cronk, N. Chagnon, & W. Irons (Eds.), *Adaptation and human behavior: An anthropological perspective* (pp. 231–252). New York: Aldine de Gruyter.

Hill, K., & Hurtado, A. M. (1996). *Ache life history.* New York: Aldine de Gruyter.

Hinde, R. A. (1986). Some implications of evolutionary theory and comparative data for the study of human prosocial and aggressive behavior. In D. Olweus, J. Block, & M. Radke-Yarrow (Eds.), *Development of anti-social and prosocial behavior* (pp. 13–32). Orlando, FL: Academic Press.

Horn, H. S., & Rubenstein, D. I. (1984). Behavioural adaptations and life history. In J. R. Krebs & N. B. Davies (Eds.), *Behavioural ecology: An evolutionary approach* (2nd ed., pp. 279–29). Oxford, England: Blackwell Scientific Publications.

Huesmann, L. R. (1988). An information processing model for the development of aggression. *Aggressive Behavior, 14*, 13–44.

Husain, A. S., Nair, J., Holcomb, W., Reid, J., Vargas, V., & Nair, S. S. (1998). Stress reactions of children and adolescents in war and siege conditions. *American Journal of Psychiatry, 155*, 1718–1719.

Jensen, P. S., & Shaw, J. (1993). Children as victims of war: Current knowledge and future research needs. *Journal of the American Academy of Child and Adolescent Psychiatry, 32*, 697–708.

Johns, S. E. (2003). *Environmental risk and the evolutionary psychology of teenage motherhood.* Unpublished Ph.D. dissertation, University of Bristol, England.

Kalantari, M., Yule, W., & Gardner, F. (1993). Protective factors and behavioral adjustment in preschool children of Iranian martyrs. *Journal of Child and Family Studies, 2*, 97–108.

Kaplan, H. S., Lancaster, J., & Hurtado, A. M. (2000). A theory of human life history evolution. *Evolutionary Anthropology, 9*, 156–185.

Kerestes, G. (2006). Children's aggressive and prosocial behavior in relation to war exposure. *International Journal of Behavioral Development, 30*, 227–239.

Kuterovac-Jagodic, G. (2003). Posttraumatic stress symptoms in Croatian children exposed to war: A prospective study. *Journal of Clinical Psychology, 59*, 9–25.

Kuzawa, C. W. (2005). Fetal origins of developmental plasticity: Are fetal cues reliable predictors of future nutritional environments? *American Journal of Human Biology, 17*, 5–21.

Ladd, G. W., & Cairns, E. (1996). Introduction—children: Ethnic and political violence. *Child Development, 67*, 14–19.

Laland, K. N., & Brown, G. R. (2006). Niche construction, human behavior, and the adaptive-lag hypothesis. *Evolutionary Anthropology, 15*, 95–104.

Labor, N., & Wolmar, L. (2002). Children exposed to disaster: The role of the mental health professional. In M. Lewis (Ed.), *Child and adolescent psychiatry: A comprehensive* (pp. 925–937). Philadelphia: Lippincott Williams & Wilkins.

Macksoud, M. S., & Aber, J. L. (1996). The war experiences and psychosocial development of children in Lebanon. *Child Development, 67*, 70–88.

Madigan, S., Moran, G., & Pederson, D. R. (2006). Unresolved states of mind, disorganized attachment relationships, and disrupted interactions of adolescent mothers and their infants. *Developmental Psychology, 42*, 293–304.

McArthur, R. H., & Wilson, E. O. (1967). *The theory of island biogeography*. Princeton, NJ: Princeton University Press.

McLoyd, V. C. (1990). The impact of economic hardship on black families and children. *Child Development, 61*, 311–346.

Montgomery, E. (2010) Trauma and resilience in young refugees: A 9-year follow-up study. *Development and Psychopathology, 22*, 477–489.

NICHD Early Child Care Research Network. (2004). Trajectories of physical aggression from toddlerhood to middle childhood. *Monographs of the Society for Research in Child Development, 69*(4), Serial No. 278.

Oppenheimer, S. (2003). *Out of Eden: The peopling of the world*. New York: Constable & Robinson.

Parke, R., Coltrane, S., Duffy, S., Buriel, R., Dennis, J., Powers, J.,...Widaman, K. (2004). Economic stress, parenting, and child adjustment in Mexican American and European families. *Child Development, 75*, 1613–1909.

Patterson, G. R. (1986). Performance models for antisocial boys. *American Psychologist, 41*, 432–444.

Pesonen, A., Raikkonen, K., Heinonen, K., Kajantie, E., Forsen, T., & Eriksson, J. G. (2008). Reproductive traits following a parent-child separation trauma during childhood: A natural experiment during World War II. *American Journal of Human Biology, 20*, 345–351.

Pettit, G. S., & Bates, J. W. (1989). Family interaction patterns and children's behavior problems from infancy to four years. *Developmental Psychology, 25*, 413–420.

Promislow, D. E. L., & Harvey, D. H. (1990). Living fast and dying young: A comparative analysis of life-history variation among mammals. *Journal of Zoology, 220*, 417–437.

Protacio-Marcelino, E. (1989). Children of political detainees in the Philippines: Sources of stress and coping patterns. *International Journal of Mental Health, 18*, 712–726.

Punamäki, R-L. (1996). Can ideological commitment protect children's psychosocial well-being in situations of political violence. *Child Development, 67*, 55–69.

Punamäki, R-L. (2002). The uninvited guest of war enters childhood: Developmental and personality aspects of war and military violence. *Traumatology, 8*, 45–63.

Punamäki, R-L., Quota, S., & El Sarraj, E. (1997). Models of traumatic experiences and children's psychological adjustment. The roles of perceived parenting and the children's own resources and activity. *Child Development, 68*, 718–728.

Punamäki, R-L., Quota, S., & El Sarraj, E. (2001). Resiliency factors predicting psychological adjustment after political violence among Palestinian children. *International Journal of Behavioral Development, 25*, 256–267.

Quinlan, R. J. (2006). Human parental effort and environmental risk. *Proceedings of the Royal Society of London B, 10*, 1–6.

Ressler, E. M., Boothyby, N., & Steinbeck, D. J. (1988). *Unaccompanied children: Care and protection in wars, natural disasters and refugee movements*. New York: Oxford University Press.

Rieder, C., & Cicchetti, D. (1989). Organizational perspective on cognitive control functioning and cognitive-affective balance in maltreated children. *Developmental Psychology, 25*, 382–393.

Sack, W. H., Clarke, G. N., & Seeley, J. (1996). Multiple forms of stress in Cambodian adolescent refugees. *Child Development, 67*, 107–116.

Sagi-Schwartz, A., van IJzendoorn, M.H, & Bakermans-Kranenburg, M. (2008). Does intergenerational transmission of trauma skip a generation: No meta-analtyic evidence for tertiary traumatization with third generation of Holocaust survivors. *Attachment and Human Development, 10*, 105–121.

Sagi-Schwartz, A., van IJzendoorn, M. H., Grossmann, K. E., Joels, T., Grossmann, K., Scharf, M., ... Alkalay, S. (2003). Attachment and traumatic stress in female Holocaust child survivors and their daughters. *American Journal of Psychiatry, 160*, 1086–1092.

Seccombe, K. (2000). Families in poverty in the 1990s. *Journal of Marriage and the Family, 62*, 1094–1113.

Shaw, J. A. (2003). Children exposed to war/terrorism. *Clinical Child and Family Psychology Review, 6*, 237–246.

Shields, W. M., & Shields, L. M. (1983). Forcible rape: An evolutionary analysis. *Ethology and Sociobiology, 4*, 115–136.

Slone, M. (2005). Growing up in Israel: Lessons on understanding the effects of political violence to children. In B. K. Barber (Ed.), *Adolescents and war: How youth deal with political violence* (pp. 139–156). New York: Oxford University Press.

Smith, P., Perrin, S., Yule, W., & Rabe-Hesketh, S. (2001). War exposure and maternal reactions in the psychological adjustment of Children from Bosnia-Hercegovina. *Journal of Child Psychology and Psychiatry, 42*, 395–404.

Solomon, Z., Kotler, M., & Mikulincer, M. (1988). Combat-related posttraumatic stress disorder among 2nd-generation Holocaust survivors—preliminary findings. *American Journal of Psychiatry, 145*, 865–868.

Stearns, S. (1992). *The evolution of life histories*. Oxford, England: Oxford University Press.

Straker, G., Mendelsohn, M., Moosa, F., & Tudin, P. (1996). Violent political contexts and the emotional concerns of township youth. *Child Development, 67*, 46–54.

Thompson, J. N. (1998). Rapid evolution as ecological process. *Trends in Ecology and Evolution, 13*, 329–332.

Thornhill, R., & Palmer, B. C. (2000) *A natural history of rape: Biological bases of sexual coercion*. Cambridge, MA: MIT Press.

Tither, J. M., & Ellis, B. J. (2008). Impact of fathers on daughters' age at menarche: A genetically and environmentally controlled sibling study. *Developmental Psychology, 44*, 1409–1420.

Tooby, J., & Cosmides, L. (1988). *The evolution of war and its cognitive foundations*. Institute for Evolutionary Studies, Technical Report #88 1–45.

Tooby, J., & Cosmides, L. (1990).The past explains the present: emotional adaptations and the structure of ancestral environments. *Ethology and Sociobiology, 11*, 375–324.

Van IJzendoorn, M. H. (1995). Associations between adult attachment representations and parent–child attachment, parental responsiveness and clinical status: A meta-analysis on the predictive validity of the Adult Attachment Interview. *Psychological Bulletin, 117*, 387–403.

Van IJzendoorn, M. H., Bakermans-Kranenburg, M. J., & Sagi-Schwartz, A. (2003). Are children of Holocaust survivors less well-adapted? A meta-analytic investigation of secondary traumatization. *Journal of Traumatic Stress, 16*, 459–469.

Van IJzendoorn, M., & Sagi, A. (1999). Cross-cultural patterns of attachment: Universal and contextual dimensions. In J. Cassidy & P. Shaver (Eds.), *Handbook of attachment* (pp. 713–735). New York: The Guilford Press.

Van IJzendoorn, M., & Sagi-Schwartz, A. (2008). Cross-cultural patterns of attachment: Universal and contextual dimensions. In J. Cassidy & P. Shaver (Eds.), *Handbook of attachment* (2nd ed., pp. 880–905). New York: The Guilford Press.

Weine, S., Lecik, K., Celik, A., Bicic, M., Bambur, N., & Salcin, M. (2008). Tasting the world. Life after wartime for Bosnian teens in Chicago. In B. K. Barber (Ed.), *Adolescents and war: How youth deal with political violence* (pp. 255–280). New York: Oxford University Press.

Williams, G. C. (1966). *Adaptation and natural selection: A critique of some current evolutionary thought*. Princeton, NJ: Princeton University Press.

Wilson, M., & Daly, M. (2005). Carpe diem: Adaptation and devaluing the future. *Quarterly Review of Biology, 80*, 55–60.

Wrangham, R., & Peterson, D. (1996). *Demonic males*. Boston: Houghton Mifflin.

Yule, W. (2000). Emanuel Miller Lecture. From pogroms to "ethnic cleansing": Meeting the needs of war affected children. *Journal of Child Psychology and Psychiatry, 41*, 695–702.

Zivcic, I. (1993). Emotional reactions of children to war stress in Croatia. *Journal of the American Academy of Child and Adolescent Psychiatry, 32*, 709–713.

PART 5

Conclusions and Future Directions for Evolutionary Perspectives on Violence, Homicide, and War

CHAPTER 24

The Extremes of Conflict in Literature: Violence, Homicide, and War

Joseph Carroll

Abstract

Literature depicts emotions arising from conflict and makes them available to readers, who experience them vicariously. Literary meaning lodges itself not in depicted events alone but also, and more importantly, in the interpretation of depicted events: in the author's treatment of the depicted events; the reader's response to both the depicted events and the author's treatment; and the author's anticipation of the reader's responses. This chapter outlines possible stances toward violence, makes an argument for the decisive structural significance of violence in both life and literature, and then presents a representative sampling of violent acts in literature. The examples from literature are organized into the main kinds of human relationships: one's relation to oneself (suicide); sexual rivals, lovers, and marital partners; family members (parents, children, siblings, aunts, uncles, and cousins); communities (violence within social groups); and warfare (violence between social groups).

Key Words: literature, emotions, interpretation, author, reader, suicide, lovers, family, community, war

Introduction

What a book a devil's chaplain might write on the clumsy, wasteful, blundering, low, and horribly cruel works of nature!
—*Darwin*, 1903; 1: 94; letter to Joseph Hooker of July 13, 1856

The world is a violent place. More are born, in every generation, than can survive. Natural selection filters out weaker organisms. Among creatures with nervous systems, those that do not survive seldom go quietly into that good night. They struggle and often suffer horribly before they die. Many become food for other animals. All compete for scarce resources against other creatures, including members of their own species. Human beings, despite all their technological and cultural contrivances, have not escaped this universal struggle. Conflict and struggle are integral to the evolved and adapted characteristics of human nature. Literature arises out of and depicts human nature, so conflict is integral to literature, too.

Literary works sometimes depict hostile encounters between alien groups, but more frequently, the emotional interest of literary works arises out of conflicts among people who are intimately related to one another. Such conflicts are a natural product of inclusive fitness. Like other animals, human beings share fitness interests with their mates and offspring. Except for identical twins, though, the fitness interests of even the most closely related kin are not identical. Inclusive fitness produces a perpetual drama in which intimacy and opposition, cooperation and conflict, are closely intertwined.

The evolved reproductive strategies of men include both paternal investment, which requires mate guarding, and low-investment short-term mating, which often requires eluding the vigilance of other men. Men form coalitions for cooperative endeavor but also compete for mates (Geary & Flinn, 2001). Women have evolved strategies for securing a bonded attachment with men willing to commit resources, but they have also evolved strategies for taking advantage of short-term mating opportunities with other men, especially men who have higher genetic quality than their own mates (Buss, 2000, 2003; Geary, 1998). The pleasurable feelings associated with sexual relations are thus necessarily tinged with suspicion, jealousy, frustration, and resentment. Much of the time, men and women manage workable compromises, but sexual relations sometimes break down in rejection, violent emotional struggle, and physical abuse, including murder (Buss, 2000; Daly & Wilson, 1988).

A parent and child both have a fitness interest in the child surviving and reproducing, but a child has a 100% genetic investment in itself; each parent has only a 50% genetic investment in a child. Mother–child conflict begins in the mother's womb, with the embryo struggling to acquire more resources from the mother than the mother is willing to give. Siblings share fitness interests but also compete for resources. Parents must often distribute resources across multiple offspring, all of whom want more than an equal share. Parents often prefer some children to others, and they must also make choices between effort devoted to parenting and effort devoted to mating. Such tensions can and do erupt into homicidal violence, in both life and literature.

The conflicts generated from differing fitness interests manifest at the proximal level as motives that are driven by emotions: desire, love, jealousy, guilt, shame, frustration, resentment, rage, and hatred (Cosmides & Tooby, 2000; Ekman, 2003; Plutchik, 2003). Literature depicts such emotions, evokes them, and makes them available to readers, who experience them vicariously (Oatley, 1999, 2002, 2003; Tan, 2000). An author and a reader inhabit an imagined world created by the author, who chooses a subject, adopts a stance toward that subject, organizes the presentation of the subject, and modulates style and tone to affect the reader's responses. Readers can passively register the images and sensations thus evoked, but they can also stand apart from them, situating them in their own analytic and evaluative frameworks. Literary criticism is only the most explicit and highly developed form of readers' reflections on the imagined worlds created by authors.

Literary meaning lodges itself not in depicted events alone but also, and more importantly, in the interpretation of depicted events: in the author's treatment of the depicted events; the reader's response to both the depicted events and the author's treatment; and the author's anticipation of the reader's responses. It is worth pausing to emphasize the fundamentally social and psychological character of literature. Meaning in literature cannot be reduced to plot. Meaning consists in an imaginative experience at least partially shared between an author and a reader. When we analyze narrative/mimetic literature (stories, plays, and novels, as opposed to lyric poems), we have to consider the interplay of perspectives among characters, authors, and readers: how characters regard one another, what they think about one another, what the author thinks of them, what the author anticipates readers will think, and what readers actually do think about the characters and also about the author's responses to the characters. Consequently, in this chapter, the literary examples do not consist only in plot summaries. The chapter also takes account of authorial stances and readers' responses. Authorial stance and reader response are the substance of literary experience; they are, accordingly, the proper subject matter of literary criticism.

After outlining a range of stances toward psychopathic violence, this chapter makes an argument for the decisive structural significance of violence in both life and literature. The chapter then presents a representative sampling of violent acts in literature. The examples from literature are organized into the main kinds of human relationships: one's relation to oneself (suicide); sexual rivals, lovers, and marital partners; family members (parents, children, siblings, aunts, uncles, and cousins); communities (violence within social groups); and warfare (violence between social groups).

Stances Toward Cruelty

Psychopathic cruelty is relatively rare (Baumeister, 1996; Grossman, 2009). Even in genocidal warfare, people seldom regard their own behavior as intentional harm inflicted for pleasure. Instead they rationalize violence as self-defense or as a means toward a greater good. They also minimize or turn a blind eye toward the suffering of victims and instead magnify threats to themselves (Baumeister, 1996; Smith, 2007). Studies of soldiers in warfare support the contention that most people in postagricultural societies are on the whole reluctant to harm others. Even after heavy conditioning, and even when they are themselves in danger, many soldiers never fire their weapons, or they fire to miss (Grossman,

2009; Marshall, 1947). (Wade [2006] and Cochran and Harpending [2009] argue that sedentism, a prerequisite to agricultural and industrial economies, has selected for personalities less prone to violence.) Psychopaths, people who actively enjoy killing and feel no remorse, evidently constitute only about 2% of modern male populations (Swank & Marchand, 1946; cited in Grossman, 2009, p. 44). A similar percentage would probably prevail among male literary authors, and a still smaller percentage among female authors. Only a very few literary authors clearly invite readers to participate vicariously in sadistic pleasure. The Marquis de Sade, whose name is the source for the term "sadism," is one such author. (See for instance *One Hundred Days of Sodom*.) In the final chapter of Anthony Burgess's *A Clockwork Orange*, the first-person narrator unconvincingly disavows the gleeful psychopathic violence in the main body of the novel. In contemporary fiction, the most prominent overtly psychopathic novel is Bret Easton Ellis's *American Psycho*. Film directors attracted to sadistic cruelty include Stanley Kubrick and Brian de Palma. Kubrick produced a film version of *A Clockwork Orange*; and both Kubrick and de Palma produced film versions of Stephen King novels, eliminating, in both cases, the compassion that gives emotional depth to King's explorations of horror (Kubrick, *The Shining*; de Palma, *Carrie*). In most literary works that depict psychopathic cruelty, the author's stance registers revulsion against cruelty.

Baumeister (1996) defines "evil" most simply as "the adversary of good" (p. 67). We tend to regard ourselves and our associates as good people, and our enemies as bad people. Our enemies, who have their own distinct points of view, reverse the nomenclature. In fiction, the "good" is typically embodied in protagonists—agents with whom readers are invited to sympathize—and evil is embodied in their adversaries, that is, in antagonists (Carroll, Gottschall, Johnson, & Kruger, 2008; Carroll, Gottschall, Johnson, Kruger, & Georgiades, 2010; Johnson, Carroll, Gottschall, & Kruger, 2008, 2011). Among literary characters, most psychopaths are antagonists, for instance: Iago in Shakespeare's *Othello*; the malignant dwarf Daniel Quilp in Charles Dickens's *The Old Curiosity Shop*; Mr. Hyde in Robert Louis Stevenson's *Dr. Jekyll and Mr. Hyde*; the Catholic priest who tortures Dr. Monygham in Joseph Conrad's *Nostromo*; the renegade Blue Duck in Larry McMurtry's western *Lonesome Dove*; and the serial killer Arnold Friend (based on a real person) in Joyce Carol Oates's frequently anthologized story "Where Are You Going, Where Have You Been?"

A few narratives adopt a structurally ironic stance, taking psychopaths as ostensible protagonists but treating them with implicit contempt and anger. Instances include Henry Fielding's caustic 18th-century narrative about a professional criminal, *Jonathan Wilde*, and William Makepeace Thackeray's depiction of Barry Lyndon, a heartless rogue who leaves a trail of wreckage behind him. (Kubrick's filmed version of *Barry Lyndon* eliminates Thackeray's satiric stance and turns the story into a prettily filmed picaresque adventure.)

Some writers are hard to locate clearly on either side of the divide between psychopathic and sympathetic perspectives. Flannery O'Connor, for instance, a Catholic American writer from the middle of the 20th century, envisions homicidal violence as a means of transcending ordinary social life, which she regards as hypocritical and spiritually shallow. Her story, "A Good Man Is Hard To Find"—one of the most widely anthologized of all short stories—depicts a psychopathic killer, The Misfit, as a religious skeptic. The protagonist of the story is an old woman who achieves, in terror for her life, a moment of Christian charity toward her killer. The protagonists of O'Connor's novels *The Violent Bear It Away* and *Wise Blood* both achieve spiritual metamorphosis through acts of homicidal violence.

Among contemporary writers held in high esteem, Cormac McCarthy gives an exceptionally prominent place to graphic violence. Throughout McCarthy's novels, gaining a tough-minded, realistic perspective means accepting the ultimate, decisive reality of homicidal violence. The dead do not get to establish moral norms. In *All the Pretty Horses*, McCarthy's protagonist is a young man who gets thrown into a brutal Mexican prison. To survive, he has to accept that lethal violence takes priority over all moral considerations, but his struggle to come to terms with the necessity of his situation tacitly locates his homicidal behavior in a moral context. The protagonist of *No Country for Old Men* is humane and warm hearted. He ultimately falls victim to a psychopath who tempts readers to identify with his stance of cool command. A similar kind of temptation for the reader is at work in Shakespeare's depiction of Richard III. Like the protagonist of *A Clockwork Orange*, Richard is witty and droll, though vicious. Even when dominant characters are purely destructive, they naturally tempt readers to identify with them, but Shakespeare and McCarthy also include characters who offer alternative perspectives. Both authors leave it to the reader's own strength of mind to decide how to feel about the characters. In *Blood Meridian*, based on a historical event from the middle of the 19th century, McCarthy depicts a band of psychopathic killers who cut a swath of random violence through Mexico and the American Southwest. The protagonist is a boy who had been traumatized by violence from the time of his earliest memories. Though tagging along with the band, in a psychologically numbed condition, he is not ultimately absorbed into mindless and heartless brutality. In *The Road*, a futuristic novel situated in an American landscape devastated by an ecological holocaust, possibly nuclear, the moral lines are more clearly demarcated. The protagonists, a father and his son, are struggling to survive in an environment dominated by cannibalistic bands. The emotional focal point of the story is the father's devotion to his son. Though McCarthy is preoccupied with violence and often noncommittal in his own emotional responses, it seems safe to say that he is not ultimately a sadist along the lines of Burgess, Ellis, de Palma, and Kubrick. He just pushes the reader harder, in morally challenging ways, than most writers do.

How Important Is Violence in Literature?

Within social groups, the exercise of power tends heavily toward containing and deflecting lethal violence (Boehm, 1999). In virtually all social groups, the amount of time spent in violent encounters is small relative to the time spent in peaceful interaction. Nonetheless, because violence is the ultimate sanction against behavior that violates group norms, the potential for violence has a powerful organizing influence on behavior within a group. A similar point can be made with respect to interactions between social groups. One possible way to look at collective violence is to suppose that history consists in periods of peace and stability occasionally disturbed by military conflict. It would be more accurate to say that periods of peace and stability are contained and organized by periods of mass violence (Potts & Hayden, 2008, pp. 12, 268). Consider American history. Americans have not had a war within their territorial boundaries since the Civil War, 150 years ago, but the country was founded on aggressive acts of territorial acquisition from the natives; the natives the first colonists encountered were just the survivors of about 15,000 years of savage tribal warfare; the nation came to birth, as a nation, in an act of collective, organized violence (The War of Independence); the South had an economy heavily dependent on slaves held in place by coercive force; the regional political conflict between the North and South was finally suppressed only in a bloody civil war; and during the last century America participated in the two largest wars in history, thus consolidating, for half a century, its now rapidly fading position as the dominant military and economic power in the world.

The picturesque landscapes of Europe—crumbling castles, walled towns overgrown with moss and ivy—are the quaint relics of a history of mass violence that shaped the demographic and political landscape. On the largest scale, world history consists in migrations and invasions: huge masses of armed people descending on other peoples, killing many of them, enslaving others, and gradually merging with the survivors. Instances on a continental scale include the barbarian hordes that inundated the Roman Empire; the Mongol invasions of China and Europe; the European invasions of North and South America; the Bantu expansion south and east in Africa; and the English colonization of Australia and New Zealand (Gibbon, 1776–1789/1994; Roberts, 2003; Turchin, 2007; Wells, 1921). Great Britain is the product of multiple genocidal events: the Germanic invasions that overwhelmed the Romanized Celts, who had themselves pushed aside the Picts; the Danish incursions into Anglo-Saxon lands; the brutal Norman conquest that subjugated the Anglo-Saxons and Danes; and the English conquests of Scotland and Ireland, especially Ireland (Davies, 1999; Johnson, 1980). World War II was initiated chiefly by German and Japanese efforts once again to change the shape of populations over whole continents (Davies, 2006; Gilbert, 1989; Keegan, 1990; Snyder, 2010; Spector, 1984). Both before and during the war, the Soviets reshaped and redistributed their vast population by starving, shooting, or deporting millions of their own citizens (Snyder, 2010). The period of relative geopolitical stability produced by World War II will not last forever. Expanding global population is placing increasing pressure on scarce resources, and that kind of pressure has always been a chief cause for the mass movement of populations. Sometime within the present century, the geopolitical landscape will perhaps be once again transformed by cataclysmic upheavals (Friedman, 2009; Wilson, 1998, ch. 12).

The case for the organizing power of violence on a world-historical scale has a bearing on even the most domestic and polite form of literature: the "novel of manners." Novels by authors such as Jane Austen and Anthony Trollope (both British writers of the 19th century) contain very little overt violence. *Pride and Prejudice* and *Barchester Towers*, for instance, chiefly concern themselves with conflicts over mate choice and social status. But these domestic dramas take place within a sociopolitical landscape that is the stabilized result of acts of domination: the domination of whole populations over others, in fashioning the British nation; the domination of the whole population by an elite class living off the proceeds of agricultural labor; and the political and religious upheavals, culminating in the English Civil War, that created a national church and associated it with the elite political class descended from military barons who had domineered over a population of serfs. Austen's novels take place during the era of the Napoleonic Wars. No battles are depicted, but officers of the army and navy figure very largely among the casts of characters. In *Persuasion*, the male protagonist, Captain Wentworth, has become rich off the spoils of the French vessels he has defeated in battle. The polite manners and well-regulated social hierarchies in domestic novels are like the rock formations produced by molten lava once it has cooled. The exercise of social power in such novels has stabilized, so that violence is no longer often necessary, but violence helped create the stabilized social order and still sustains it through foreign wars.

The novel of manners is built on a foundation of cooled and congealed violence. The action in much canonical literature is violence still hot and liquid. ("Canonical" literature is literature that has had a seminal, creative force that makes itself felt in subsequent literature.) For the literature of the West—Europe, the Americas, Australia, and those portions of Asia, especially Japan, that have come under the cultural sway of the West—canonical literature has two chief wellsprings: ancient Greece and the Bible. Both sources offer abundant entertainment for readers with a taste for what the protagonist of *A Clockwork Orange* fondly describes as "ultraviolence."

The Old Testament consists largely in chronicling the wars, conquests, defeats, and enslavements of an ancient pastoral people who commonly practiced genocide against their neighbors (Headlam Wells, 2011). In the story of Noah's Flood, God goes the Hebrews one better, wiping out not just a few neighboring tribes but the whole human race, all but Noah and his family. The first family drama in the Bible, after Adam and Eve are cast out of paradise, is the murder of one brother by another. That theme is taken up again in Shakespeare's *Hamlet*, probably the single most widely known work of modern Western literature. Contemplating his crime, Claudius, Hamlet's uncle, laments, "O, my offence is rank, it smells to heaven; / It hath the primal eldest curse upon't, / A brother's murder" (3.3.36–38; for an evolutionary interpretation of *Hamlet*, see Carroll, 2011b, pp. 123–147).

So also with the Greeks. The oldest classic that has come down to us is Homer's *Iliad*. Much of the *Iliad* consists in graphic depictions of the grisly forms of death produced by barbarian warriors wielding edged and pointed weapons (Gottschall, 2008b). Before the Greeks could set sail to rape, murder, and pillage among the Trojans, the Greek leader, Agamemnon, had to placate the Gods by sacrificing his daughter Iphigenia. And thereon hangs a tale, or series of tales: the *Oresteia*, three plays by Aeschylus (*Agamemnon*, *The Libation Bearers*, and *The Eumenides*). The act of child sacrifice sets off a chain reaction: Agamemnon is murdered by his wife, Clytemnestra, and her lover, Aegisthus; and Clytemnestra and Aegisthus are murdered by Clytemnestra's son Orestes. In addition to being Clytemnestra's lover, Aegisthus had a second motive for murdering Agamemnon: Agamemnon and Aegisthus are cousins; Agamemnon's father Atreus had murdered Aegisthus's brothers, who, like Aegisthus, were Atreus's nephews. (The murderous conflict between Atreus and his brother Thyestes is the subject of a play, *Thyestes*, by the Roman playwright Seneca the Younger.)

If we fast forward to the Christian Middle Ages, skipping past the derivative drama of Rome and the illiterate centuries of barbarian chaos, the most prominent landmark is Dante's *Inferno*, which consists largely of graphic, gruesome descriptions of physical torture, varied with monstrous ingenuity, in the nine circles of hell. Fast forward once again, and the next major landmark in Western literature is Shakespeare. Shakespeare's Roman history plays *Julius Caesar* and *Antony and Cleopatra* hinge on assassination and war. The English history plays chronicle the Wars of the Roses, a drawn-out sequence of intrigues, betrayals, assassinations, and bloody battles. The major tragedies (*Othello*, *Macbeth*, *Hamlet*, and *King Lear*) turn on murder, war, torture, or all three. Move up to the 19th century, a period in which representational/mimetic literature is dominated by the novel, and ask: What is widely regarded as the greatest of all novels? *War and Peace*, many would say. The central subject in *War and Peace* is Napoleon's invasion of Russia and the retreat in which most of his army perished. Tolstoy's chief competitor for title of greatest Russian novelist is Dostoevsky. *Crime and Punishment* is about a young man who uses an axe to murder two old women; *The Brothers Karamazov* is about a malignant old man who is murdered by his illegitimate, psychopathic son. And in our own time, the last major canonical American novel that formed a shaping imaginative experience for a whole generation, many people feel, is Joseph Heller's *Catch-22*, a war novel full of violent deaths.

In answer then, to the question, How important is violence to literature? we can say that violence is as important in literature as it is in life. Like sex, even when it does not take much time, proportionally, it can have a decisive impact on subsequent events. Gloucester in *King Lear* jokes that there was "good sport" at the making of his illegitimate son Edmund, but then Edmund betrays Gloucester to his enemies, who gouge out Gloucester's eyes. McMurtry's *Lonesome Dove* offers an illustration of the same point. The protagonists are two middle-aged cowboys, former Texas Rangers, on a cattle drive. At one point, they must fulfill the unpleasant task of hanging one of their old friends. The friend is good natured but morally lax and had inadvertently become involved with a band of psychopathic killers. Over the years, the amount of time the three friends had spent in genial exchange was much more extensive than the few minutes required to perform the hanging, but the hanging is more important, practically, than anything that had preceded it; moreover, it sets the moral quality of the relationship into stark relief, revealing that the executioners, unlike their condemned friend, have a severe commitment to a moral code.

The emotional intensity and decisive practical character of homicidal violence invest it with special significance as evidence for underlying force in human mental and emotional life. Hence the very large role violence plays in literature.

Literary Depictions of Violence in the Phases of Human Life History: A Sampling

Beneath all variation in the details of organization, the life history of every species forms a reproductive cycle. In the case of human beings, successful parental care produces children capable, when grown, of forming adult pair bonds, becoming functional members of a community, and caring for children of their own. Survival, mating, parenting, and social life thus form natural categories in the organization of human life. They are common topics in textbooks of evolutionary psychology and also common themes in literature. In this section, these categories are used to organize a sampling of depictions of violence in literature.

Violence Against Oneself
UNDERSTANDING SUICIDE FROM AN EVOLUTIONARY PERSPECTIVE

People seem to have a natural inhibition against harming their own kind and a much greater inhibition against harming themselves. They often overcome both inhibitions, but not without a psychological cost. When we speak of "violence," the connotations of that word do not limit themselves to actions. "Violence" suggests high stress: intense passion and conflict, including inner conflict. Popular "action" movies are imaginatively uninteresting because they falsely depict violence as easy; they are emotionally shallow. Literary depictions of violence are most interesting when they evoke the greatest degree of inner struggle. No form of inner struggle is more intense than that which culminates in taking one's own life.

Most forms of violence can plausibly be described as extensions of adaptive behavior—sexual jealousy, struggles for dominance or resources. Not suicide. Efforts to explain self-inflicted death as a strategy for propagating one's genes have a strained look about them (deCatanzaro, 1981). From an evolutionary standpoint, not all significant features of human physiology and behavior need be regarded as adaptive. Illnesses such as stroke, cancer, heart attack, and diabetes are not adaptations; they are breakdowns in complex adaptive systems. That does not mean that evolutionary explanations are irrelevant. To understand how and why a system breaks down, one must understand the function for which it was designed. Adaptation by means of natural selection is the default explanation for complex functional organization (Pinker, 1997; Tooby & Cosmides, 1992). It also provides the necessary explanatory context for dysfunctional behavior.

Humans have a uniquely developed sense of self-awareness that derives from the evolution of the neocortex. Individual persons have a sense of personal identity continuously developing over time, and they consciously locate themselves as individuals within social networks and within nature. Self-awareness facilitates planning and actions that require shared images of collective purpose (Hawkins & Blakeslee, 2004; Lane, 2009, ch. 9; Tomasello, Carpenter, Call, Behne, & Moll, 2005). Self-awareness is evidently functional; it is complex, expensive, universal, and reliably developing. It is also fragile. Human beings are peculiarly vulnerable to conceptions of their own existence that cause them intolerable mental pain. Grief, guilt, self-loathing, and the feeling of being trapped in impossible social situations or incurable mental illness can drive people to escape from their own minds in the only way possible: escaping from life itself.

GUILT

Literary suicides arising from simple grief are relatively rare. They do not reveal complex inner conflicts and thus offer little insight into inner life. Romeo kills himself because he mistakenly thinks Juliet is dead; Juliet kills herself because Romeo has killed himself. Lyrically moving, yes; psychologically interesting, no. Guilt is a more complex emotion than simple sorrow and a more common motive for literary suicide. In the best known of all ancient plays, Sophocles's *Oedipus Rex*, Oedipus stops short of suicide, but when he discovers that he has murdered his father and married his mother, even though he had acted inadvertently, he gouges out his own eyes. Oedipus's incestuous marriage produced a daughter, Antigone. In Sophocles's *Antigone*, the autocrat Creon is Antigone's uncle but has Antigone walled up alive for defying his orders. She hangs herself. Creon's son, who is in love with Antigone, kills himself when she dies. His mother then kills herself. *Antigone* does not reach an emotional climax in Antigone's despair, her lover's grief, or the grief of his mother. It reaches emotional climax in the tragic anguish of Creon, humbled, shattered, chastened, riven by guilt, with his vision of himself and the world fundamentally and permanently changed. Shakespeare's Othello murders Desdemona out of sexual jealousy. When he realizes that he has been duped and that she was innocent, he first mortally wounds the man who deceived him and then kills himself, turning his sense of justice against himself. In Jean Racine's 17th-century version of the Phaedra story (*Phèdre*), a stepmother succumbs to a guilty passion for her stepson; when her husband, Theseus, brings down a fatal curse on his son, unable to endure the commingled grief and guilt, she poisons herself. In Conrad's novel *Victory*, the protagonist Axel Heyst loses faith in the woman he loves. Too late he realizes that while he had been cynically repudiating her, she had been giving her life for him. He builds a funeral pyre for her and uses it also to immolate himself. In Émile Zola's *Thérèse Raquin*, Thérèse has a passionate affair with her husband's closest friend. She and her lover murder her husband, but the guilt torments them until they take poison to escape from themselves and from each other.

In most readers' perceptions, Thérèse and her lover undergo a transition in role: from being objects of horror—merely villains—to being objects of tragic pity. They learn about the moral magnitude of their crime only by committing it, but they do learn. As moral agents, they are thus radically distinct from characters such as Richard III, who commit horrible atrocities—Richard murders children—without ever feeling a shiver of guilt. On the scale of guilt, Shakespeare's Macbeth falls somewhere between Othello and Richard III. Macbeth and his wife are both tormented by guilt at the murders they have committed; she kills herself, but Macbeth, like Richard III, fights on to the end. Such a death leaves most readers suspended between a feeling of tragic pathos and a feeling of satisfaction at a just retribution. That ambivalent feeling can be contrasted to the simple emotions of grief and horror readers feel when Macbeth's henchmen murder Macduff's wife and children. (For convenience, responses to drama are designated as responses of "readers," though of course drama is in the first instance intended to be watched and listened to, not read.)

Oscar Wilde's *The Picture of Dorian Gray* has a fantastic plot device: Dorian remains perpetually young and beautiful, but his portrait becomes ever older and more hideously ugly, revealing the depravity of his soul, which has been corrupted by cruelty, drugs, and sexual excess. The portrait is an externalized image of his conscience. Riven by unresolvable conflicts between irrepressible desires and guilty self-loathing, he stabs the portrait in the heart; the portrait returns to its original state, and he himself lies dead, old and vile. Self-loathing is also the motive for suicide in Thomas Hardy's *The Mayor of Casterbridge*. In middle age, the title character finds himself bereft of everything he had ever wanted or achieved; he is an outcast, without social standing, without friends, without family. He feels himself despised and also despises himself. He starves himself to death and leaves behind a will demanding that no man remember him. He has not lived a good or wise life, but having passed such severe judgment on himself, he leaves none for the reader to exercise in vindictive satisfaction.

SOCIAL FAILURE

People are social animals. Even their most intimate feelings about their own identities reflect their sense of their place in a social network. Some of the best-known literary suicides find themselves caught in a socially intolerable situation—entangled in forbidden or hopeless passions, pushed against the wall for lack of money, or trapped in an ideological or political impasse.

In *Hippolytus*, Euripides's version of the Phaedra story, Phaedra is caught out in an illicit passion for her stepson, realizes she is socially lost, and hangs herself. Virgil's *Aeneid*, the most prestigious and influential literary work of the Roman world, contains a long episode in which Aeneas, fleeing from the havoc at Troy, lingers with the Carthaginian Queen Dido. When he abandons her to pursue his destiny, she builds her own funeral pyre and dies on it. (Christopher Marlowe produced a dramatic version of the story, and Purcell an operatic version.) Dido dies not merely from sorrow but from the recognition that she has hopelessly compromised her position as queen. Anna Karenina leaves her husband for the man she loves. Discovering that passion alone, outside the system of accepted social roles, cannot sustain her, she throws herself under a train. Winnie Verloc, in Conrad's *The Secret Agent*, murders her husband, flings herself at another man, and when he abandons her, throws herself overboard from a ship. Lily Bart, the protagonist in Edith Wharton's *The House of Mirth*, cannot bring herself to marry for money without love, or for love without money. She loses her place in the social world and poisons herself. In George Gissing's *New Grub Street*, Harold Biffen, an impoverished author, realizes he has no hope of winning a worldly woman's love. He poisons himself. In George Orwell's *Burmese Days*, John Flory, a colonial administrator, is publicly humiliated and then rejected by the woman he loves. He shoots himself and his dog.

In Gustav Flaubert's *Madame Bovary*, Emma Bovary takes arsenic because she has secretly gone into debt. The protagonist of Willa Cather's story "Paul's Case" is a sensitive adolescent aesthete, unfit for the world of middle-class squalor into which he is born. He steals money, lives a few days in luxury, and then throws himself in front of a train. In Dickens's *Little Dorrit*, the charlatan financier Mr. Merdle—a Bernie Madoff of the Victorian period—creates a speculative bubble and then cuts his throat before the bubble bursts. In Anthony Trollope's *The Prime Minister*, Ferdinand Lopez plays a high-stakes game for money and social position, loses, and throws himself in front of a train.

Cleopatra in Shakespeare's *Antony and Cleopatra*, and Cassius and Brutus in *Julius Caesar*, are all political people; their inner sense of self is bound up in their political identity. When they come to the end of their political ropes, they all take their own lives. Cleopatra uses an adder to poison herself; Cassius and Brutus fall on their swords. Hyacinth Robinson, in Henry James's *The Princess Casamassima*, takes an oath to perform a political assassination. He loses confidence in the righteousness of his cause but still feels bound by his oath; he resolves his dilemma by shooting himself. In Kate Chopin's *The Awakening*, Edna Pontellier feels stifled by the sociosexual roles open to her in turn-of-the-century New Orleans; she swims out to sea and drowns. In Chinua Achebe's *Things Fall Apart*, the protagonists Okonkwo attempts to lead the people of his tribe in a revolt against White domination; when the rebellion fails to take fire, he hangs himself.

Meaning in fiction depends heavily on the degree to which an author's perspective corresponds to that of any given character. Gissing's perspective in *New Grub Street* is morose and self-pitying; he identifies closely with Biffen, and even more closely with Biffen's friend, Edward Reardon, who dies of illness brought on by hunger and exposure. Tolstoy's stance toward Anna Karenina remains clinically detached, registering the vacuity of the social conventions against which Anna rebels, but registering also the self-destructive character of her emotional impulsiveness. Cather evokes Paul's aestheticism in a sensitive way, but she looks with cold irony at the delusions with which he sustains his fragile arrogance. Emma Bovary, too, lives in flattering delusions. Flaubert sustains a stance of cool contempt for her, as he does for most of his bourgeois characters, in all of his fiction. (His stance toward his protagonists in *Salammbô*, in contrast, is almost tender. The protagonists are barbarian warriors leading a slave revolt in the ancient Near East. *Salammbô* luxuriates in a voluptuous welter of vengeful cruelty on a massive scale.) Emma's death is particularly painful and ugly. Flaubert dwells on the physically repulsive details of death by arsenic.

An author's moral and ideological views often strongly influence how he or she responds emotionally to characters. Euripides evidently expects readers to disapprove of Phaedra's willingness to sacrifice fidelity to a guilty passion. Her death seems right and necessary. Virgil regards Dido as a tragic victim of historical forces larger and more important than individual passion. He sympathizes with her, but his sympathy is tinged with contempt. Trollope regards Lopez as both an outsider and a psychopathic adventurer. Lopez's self-destruction reestablishes social equilibrium and thus serves as a form of resolution. For Dickens, Merdle virtually embodies fraudulent social pretense; Dickens exults in vindictive glee over Merdle's death. Chopin seems to regard Edna Pontellier as a victim of a stifling social order—hence Edna's current status as an icon of resistance to patriarchy. James elicits pity for the death of Hyacinth Robinson and indignation against the maliciously manipulative anarchist who has placed him in an untenable position. Orwell's John Flory is intelligently appreciative of Burmese culture; he serves Orwell as a foil for the unintelligent arrogance of the British Raj. Nonetheless, Orwell registers the weakness of Flory's ego with pitying contempt. For Conrad, Winnie Verloc's passionate though "morbid" devotion to her retarded brother serves as a counterweight to the moral vacuity of the anarchists who surround her. Conrad treats Winnie's death with a combination of overstrained pathos and ironic distaste.

Tragedy requires an element of grandeur or nobility lacking in most cases of suicide for reasons of social failure, but Achebe's Okonkwo and Shakespeare's Roman protagonists are tragic figures. Okonkwo is a strong but flawed man, victimized both by circumstances and by the limitations in his own perspective. In the deaths of Cleopatra, Cassius, and Brutus, Shakespeare evokes a Roman ethos in which suicide is the only honorable conclusion to a failed political intrigue.

MENTAL ILLNESS

Mental illness is a neurophysiological dysfunction that produces mental anguish (Oakley, 2007). Virginia Woolf suffered recurrent bouts of mental illness; rather than go through it one more time, she drowned herself. Some sense of the horror she must have experienced is captured in one of her novels, *Mrs. Dalloway*. Over the course of a single day, Woolf counterpoints Mrs. Dalloway's placid ruminations with the hallucinatory terror of a battle-shocked veteran suffering from schizophrenia. At the end of the story, as Mrs. Dalloway is enjoying herself at a party, he kills himself by jumping out of a window. In *Maid in Waiting*, John Galsworthy gets readers close to the suicidal anguish of uncontrolled bipolar disorder, before that disorder had a clinical name. Edward Ashburnham, in Ford Madox Ford's *The Good Soldier*, is a slave to recurrent and irresistible romantic passions. He finally escapes by cutting his own throat. Severe clinical depression gets canonical expression in Hardy's last novel, *Jude the Obscure*. Jude is a disappointed man, morose and fearful. His oldest child, a virtual personification of clinical depression, hangs himself and his siblings. Jude eventually stays out in the rain long enough to get pneumonia, thus bringing his own misery to an end. Chief White Halfoat, in *Catch-22*, uses the same strategy for ending his life.

EXISTENTIAL DESPAIR

Human beings are the only species with a brain so highly developed that they can locate themselves in a cosmic scheme of things. Humans are susceptible to religious fantasies and supernatural terrors. They often need to feel that their existence has some "meaning" within the larger scheme of things. Shakespeare's Hamlet, caught somewhere in between medieval supernaturalism and modern metaphysical nihilism, yearns to destroy himself but fears the afterlife. In his closet drama, *Empedocles on Etna*, Matthew Arnold captures the mid-Victorian mood of metaphysical despair, translocating his own metaphysical gloom into the voice of an early Greek philosopher. After discoursing eloquently about the futility of human life, Empedocles flings himself into a volcanic crater. In the later 19th century, with the widespread loss of religious belief among educated people, the sense of existential despair became a predominating theme in literature. Conrad is particularly effective in giving voice to that theme. In Conrad's epic novel *Nostromo*, Decoud, a Gallicized South American patrician, is trapped in solitude on a small boat for several days. Losing all sense of purpose or meaning in life, he shoots himself and falls over the side of the boat. Conrad speaks of this death with mocking contempt, but the contempt is directed as much at himself as at his character. Decoud's perspective is a close approximation to one main aspect of Conrad's own point of view; and, indeed, Decoud kills himself by shooting himself in the chest, the same method that in his youth Conrad had adopted for attempting suicide. Aldous Huxley's futuristic utopia/dystopia *Brave New World* depicts a society in which life is perfectly regulated by genetic engineering and behavioral conditioning. The protagonist, a "Savage" who had grown up on an Indian reservation and has thus escaped conditioning, cannot fully articulate what he feels is intolerable about such a society, but he ends up hanging himself in despair. The existential problems explored by writers like Shakespeare, Arnold, Conrad, and Huxley have not been solved; they are part of our active cultural heritage.

All in the Family

Next to one's relation to one's self, one's closest relations, genetically, are to parents, offspring, and siblings. The "ultimate" causal force, inclusive fitness, creates "proximal" feelings of psychological closeness. Blood is thicker than water, but in family dramas blood sometimes runs like water, producing in readers peculiarly intense sensations of shock and horror. Not surprisingly, in Dante's *Inferno*, people who commit crimes against kin are placed in the ninth circle of hell, the lowest circle.

Family violence is sometimes complex and sequential. The cycle of family violence that motivates Aeschylus's trilogy about the house of Atreus has already been mentioned: Agamemnon murders Iphigenia, is murdered in turn by his wife, Clytemnestra, who in turn is murdered by her son Orestes. Sophocles's depiction of Oedipus has also been mentioned: Oedipus murdered his father and married his mother, then in remorse gouges out his own eyes; Oedipus's daughter Antigone defies her uncle Creon and is executed by him; Creon's son, who loves Antigone, kills himself, and his mother then kills herself. In both Euripides's and Racine's versions of Phaedra's story, Theseus's wife, Phaedra, betrays her stepson; Theseus invokes the power of a god to destroy his son; and Phaedra commits suicide. In *King Lear*, Edmund betrays both his father and his brother Edgar. Lear's two oldest daughters, Goneril and Regan, collude in humiliating their father but then fall out over a sexual rivalry, each competing for Edmund's favor. Goneril poisons Regan, and then, when she is exposed and trapped, stabs herself to death. Edgar kills Edmund in combat, but Edmund has already ordered the execution of Lear's youngest daughter, Cordelia. After she dies, Lear dies from grief. In Dostoevsky's *The Brothers Karamazov*, Fyodor Karamazov's illegitimate son Smerdyakov, inspired by the atheistic writings of his brother Ivan, murders his father. Then, feeling betrayed by Ivan, Smerdyakov kills himself, leaving another brother, Dmitry, to take the blame for the patricide.

Murdering one's own children has a peculiarly horrific effect, since it combines the revulsion against murdering kin with the revulsion against murdering children. In Flaubert's *Salammbô*, the worshippers of Baal are fighting off a genocidal revolt of slaves, and the war is going badly. To propitiate Baal, they burn alive all the infants in the city, flinging them one by one into the glowing belly of the great brass god. Medea, in a play by Euripides, abandons her homeland for Jason's sake; when he later abandons her, she murders their two sons for revenge. In George Eliot's novel *Adam Bede*, an unmarried woman, Hetty Sorrel, leaves her newborn infant to die in the woods. In William Styron's *Sophie's Choice*, Sophie has to choose which of her two children to sacrifice to the gas chambers at Auschwitz. Later, tormented by guilt, she commits suicide. The protagonist of Toni Morrison's *Beloved* chooses to murder her children rather than have them returned to slavery. In King's *The Shining*, Jack Torrance is gradually possessed by evil spirits in an isolated hotel; under their influence, he almost succeeds in murdering his wife and child.

In fiction, murdering members of one's own family almost always has an evil cast, but evil can be contextualized in many different ways, depending on the total worldview of the writer. Greek tragedies tend to adopt a stance that hovers ambiguously between moralism and fatalism, that is, between emphasizing the consequences of behavioral choices and counseling resignation to the caprice of the gods. In *Salammbô*, Flaubert seems to be aiming at a purely aesthetic goal: evoking the ferocity of a barbarian culture, without judging it from a moral stance. George Eliot, in contrast, dwells on a moral theme: the opposition between egoism and empathy. She sets up a clear moral dichotomy between the vain and shallow nature of Hetty Sorrel, who abandons her newborn child, and the loving nature of the female protagonist, Dinah Morris. The three main characters in Styron's *Sophie's Choice*—a Polish Catholic woman victimized by the Nazis, a Jewish schizophrenic, and a descendant of Southern slave owners—offer an occasion for meditations on problematic racial and ethnic relationships. Morrison's *Beloved* is designed as an indictment of slavery in the American South. Dostoevsky situates Smerdyakov's patricide within the context of a philosophical debate over morality and religion. Jack Torrance in King's *The Shining* is a recovering alcoholic and a failed writer. His demonic possession is cast in terms of an inner struggle between egoistic vanity, fueled by alcohol, and his devotion to his wife and child. *The Shining* is essentially a moral drama, like *Adam Bede*. *King Lear*, too, is a moral drama. Goneril and Regan are faithless and wantonly cruel; they provide a foil for the idea of family bonds personified in their sister Cordelia.

Violence and Sex
SEXUAL RIVALS

The biblical story of David and Bathsheba exemplifies homicide prompted by sexual desire. Greek myth is replete with instances of Hera, queen of Olympus, punishing Zeus's mortal lovers or their offspring. Lethal jealousy is a major theme also in the three great epics of the Greco-Roman world—the *Iliad*, the *Odyssey*, and the *Aeneid*. The Trojan War, the subject of the *Iliad*, takes place, ostensibly, because the Trojan prince Paris runs off with Helen, the wife of the Greek leader Agamemnon. Gottschall (2008b) makes a compelling argument that this specific motive was merely the symbolic tip of the iceberg. All of Greek tribal culture in this historical period was organized around raiding for women. (Gottschall draws inspiration from Napoleon Chagnon's [1979] studies of the Yanomamö.) The *Odyssey*, recounting Odysseus's efforts to return home after the Trojan War, culminates with Odysseus slaughtering the suitors who had gathered around his wife, Penelope. The last half of the *Aeneid* occupies itself with Aeneas's war in Italy against Turnus. The ostensible occasion for the war is rivalry over the hand of the princess Lavinia. The first story in Chaucer's *Canterbury Tales*, "The Knight's Tale," turns on the jealous rivalry of two former friends, who fight in knightly combat until one eventually dies. In Guy de Maupassant's *Une Vie*, a husband discovers his wife in a tryst inside a covered cart, which he rolls off a cliff, killing both his wife and her lover. Bradley Headstone in Dickens's *Our Mutual Friend* tries to drown Eugene Wrayburn in jealousy over Lizzie Hexam. William Boldwood, in Hardy's *Far From the Madding Crowd*, has a wedding party that is spoiled when his fiancée's husband, erroneously supposed dead, shows up at the party. Boldwood shoots and kills the husband. In Cather's *O Pioneers!*, the protagonist's brother is murdered by a jealous husband. Jean Toomer's "Blood-Burning Moon" depicts homicidal violence animated by both sexual jealousy and racial hatred; both rivals die, one with his throat slit, and the other burned at the stake by a lynch mob. Zora Neale Hurston's "Spunk" depicts a hapless wronged husband pitted against a cocky, dominant rival, Spunk, who shoots him. On the surface, Spunk seems unrepentant, but he is haunted by the murdered man's ghost, who pushes him into a buzz saw.

Sexual jealousy leading to violence, and especially male jealousy of rival males, is a human universal (Buss, 2003; Daly & Wilson, 1988; Geary, 1998). However, differences in cultural attitudes make a large difference in the stance authors take toward this universal disposition. From the perspective of Greeks in the barbarian period, Odysseus is wholly within his rights to murder his rivals, and along with them the serving maids with whom the suitors had had sex. In modern literature, men who resort to violence in response to sexual jealousy are seldom if ever treated as epic heroes. More often, they seem self-destructively obsessed with passions they cannot control. There are no modern literary heroes, like Odysseus, who are celebrated for murdering hordes of their rivals. Odysseus is a chief in a polygynous warrior culture. Modern heroes have to conform to the ethos of a monogamous bourgeois culture (Gottschall, 2008b; Jobling, 2001).

LOVERS' QUARRELS

Jealous hatred of a rival, like grief, is a simple passion. Jealousy of a lover or spouse is more likely to put intense emotions into conflict with one another. After murdering Desdemona, Othello describes himself as a man who "loved not wisely but too well" (5.2.44). In Racine's version of the Phaedra story, Phèdre is torn between jealous rage and shame; she colludes in a false accusation that results in her stepson's death, and then guilt, grief, and shame drive her to suicide. In Robert Browning's dramatic monologue "Porphyria's Lover," the speaker has been driven insane by jealousy. After strangling his lover with her own hair, he tells himself that he has fulfilled her own wish, since she can now "give herself to me forever." In William Faulkner's frequently anthologized story "A Rose for Emily," Miss Emily has an affair with a man disinclined to marriage. Like the speaker in "Porphyria's Lover," she kills him in order to keep him with her. Many years later, after her death, the town's folk find the lover's skeleton in a bed in her house, with a strand of her gray hair on a pillow next to it. In Honoré de Balzac's novel *Cousine Bette*, the fickle and opportunistic siren Valérie strings along several men at once, exploiting all of them, and is finally poisoned, along with her new husband, by one of her deceived lovers. Tolstoy, in his own life, was tormented by obsessive jealousy, a theme that figures prominently in both *War and Peace* and *Anna Karenina*. In "The Kreutzer Sonata," the first-person narrator explains that he murdered his wife because he was enraged both by ordinary sexual jealousy and by his own enslavement to sensual passion. In Zola's *La Bête Humaine*, Jacques Lantier is driving a train on which his mistress is a passenger; another woman, prompted by jealous rage, derails the train, killing many people, but not the two she was intending to kill. Remorse drives her to suicide. Lantier himself, afflicted with a mental disease that couples sexual passion with homicidal fury, eventually murders his mistress. D. H. Lawrence's *Women in Love* pits two egoistic and dominating personalities, Gerald and Gudrun, against one another. After nearly strangling Gudrun to death, Gerald wanders away, yearning for a release from passion, and falls off a cliff.

Murder/suicide is as common in the crime section of the newspaper as it is in works of fiction. The commingling of love and hatred in works such as those just described gives readers imaginative access to the states of mind that animate such real-life behavior. Literary depictions also give us access to a range of possible attitudes toward this behavior. Racine's play is a neoclassical tragedy; it elicits responses that mingle emotions of horror and compassion. Browning's monologue creates a sensation of horror like that in some of the works of Edgar Allen Poe ("The Tell-Tale Heart," for instance)—horror both at homicidal violence and at mental derangement. Insanity precludes the dignity and grandeur that are typical of tragic emotion, but most readers' revulsion against Browning's lunatic is nonetheless tinged with pity. Commenting on "A Rose for Emily," Faulkner (1965) declared that his own attitude toward the story was essentially one of compassion for Emily's wasted life. Balzac's attitude toward Valérie and her lovers has an air of moral disapproval tinged with sensationalistic fascination. The first-person narrator in Tolstoy's story evokes little compassion for the wife he murdered; he wishes instead to mitigate his guilt by treating sexuality itself as a mental disease. In this story, Tolstoy not only depicts a deranged state of mind but also exemplifies it. Zola adopts a naturalistic stance—clinical, detached, empirical, fascinated by the spectacle of power out of control. At the end of *La Bête Humaine*, Lantier is driving a train full of drunken soldiers toward the front in the Franco-Prussian War. He gets into a fight with his stoker, with whose wife he is having an affair, and both fall overboard, leaving the train without a driver, hurtling toward disaster. Lawrence's stance in *Women in Love* is essentially moralistic; Gerald and Gudrun are used as foils for another couple, Birkin and Ursula, who represent, for Lawrence, a more wholesome form of sexual passion.

Killing a lover, like killing oneself or one's kin, limits opportunities to propagate one's genes. So in what way can an evolutionary perspective illuminate this kind of homicide? Two explanations seem most plausible. One is that a known disposition for uncontrollable violence can have a powerful deterrent effect (Frank, 1988; Schelling, 1960, cited in Wright, 1994, p. 278). Some people decrease their fitness by killing a mate; but many mates avoid infidelity at least in part because spurned or cuckolded lovers can be dangerous. The other explanation is that human passions are not necessarily optimized for inclusive fitness in every possible combination of circumstances. All adaptations have costs; all adaptive benefits involve trade-offs against other possible adaptive benefits; and some adaptations conflict with others. Male bears have adaptations for having sex and also for eating small animals; they sometimes eat their own offspring. Humans have adaptations for erotic fixation and also for punishing cheaters; they sometimes kill their lovers. In "Ballad of Reading Gaol," Oscar Wilde meditates on a man condemned to hang for murdering his lover. Protesting against singling this man out for punishment, Wilde declares that "all men kill the thing they love." The generalization stretches the point further than it will quite bear, but many people do indeed kill the thing they love; they thus also sometimes destroy themselves.

Violence Within the Social Group
INSTRUMENTAL VIOLENCE

Much of the violence outside the family circle, in literature as in life, is largely instrumental in character. People harm or kill others to defend themselves or their family and friends, to obtain money or other resources, or to remove an obstacle to social ambition. Odysseus jams a burning pole into the Cyclops's eye because the Cyclops is eating his companions. Robinson Crusoe, in Daniel Defoe's novel, also kills cannibals. In Dickens's *A Tale of Two Cities*, the elderly and very proper Miss Pross shoots Mme. Defarge in order to protect Lucie Manette's family from the guillotine. In Haruki Murakami's *Kafka on the Shore*, Nakata, a gentle old man, stabs Johnny Walker to death to stop him from torturing cats. In *Crime and Punishment*, Raskolnikov murders a pawnbroker because he needs money; and he murders her sister to cover up the deed. In Frank Norris's *McTeague*, McTeague beats his wife to death over the money she is hoarding. Macbeth murders Duncan because Macbeth wants to be king, and Duncan is in the way. Claudius murders Hamlet's father for the same reason; and the future Richard III murders several people to eliminate the obstacles between himself and the throne. In Eliot's *Middlemarch*, Bulstrode murders Raffles because Raffles is threatening to expose his shady past and thus ruin his social standing. In Theodore Dreiser's *An American Tragedy*, Clyde Griffiths murders his pregnant girlfriend, Roberta, because she is threatening to spoil his chances of social advancement. In cases such as these, though violence might be fueled by rage or hatred, harming someone else is not the ultimate purpose of violence; harming someone else is merely a means to an end.

The value attached to instrumental violence, like the value attached to all depicted behavior, depends on the state of mind of the character, the author's stance toward the character, and the reader's response to both. The stance of the author and the reader's response are in most cases heavily conditioned by the cultural ethos of the character, the author, and the reader, but any given cultural ethos is itself only a particular organization of the elements of human nature.

Odysseus exults over defeating his monstrous enemy, and most readers rejoice with him. Miss Pross is permanently shaken by the enormity of the deed required of her, but Dickens clearly regards her as a hero and as a symbol of British moral courage. Nakata is deeply disturbed to discover his own capacity for violence but recognizes, dimly, that violence is sometimes necessary to sustain humane conditions of life. Raskolnikov, finding he cannot rationalize murder, ultimately turns himself in; remorse and redemption are the central themes of *Crime and Punishment*. McTeague, in contrast, does not have a moral consciousness sufficiently developed to experience remorse. *McTeague* is a "naturalist" novel, a genre that typically depicts characters operating at a level of mindless animal brutality. Richard III, unlike McTeague, is not a mindless brute, but he is a psychopath, and he delights in his cunning manipulations. Readers are simultaneously lured into his perspective and repelled at his viciousness. Claudius and Macbeth are more like Raskolnikov than like Richard III; they are unable to reconcile themselves to the murders they have committed. Richard III requires readers to establish their own independent moral perspective; *Hamlet* and *Macbeth* provide an internal moral monitor in the conscience of the characters. *An American Tragedy*, like *McTeague*, is naturalistic. Clyde Griffiths has a social imagination more refined than McTeague's, but he seems morally helpless before the lure of social glamour. Though planning and executing a murder, much of the time he seems baffled, frightened, and wistful. One central implication of a naturalist vision is that people are ultimately driven by forces outside their control—a conclusion that converges with the fatalistic stance in much Greek drama. The polar opposite to that stance can be located in highly moralistic writers such as George Eliot. Bulstrode in *Middlemarch* serves Eliot as an exemplar of a morally ambiguous nature: a man with high ideals, low ambitions, and intellectual integrity too weak to acknowledge the discrepancy between them. For Eliot, Bulstrode's morally underdeveloped mind serves as a foil for the protagonistic characters who exemplify the power of directing one's own behavior in morally conscious ways.

DOMINANCE AND RECIPROCATION

In addition to association by kinship, there are two basic principles in human social organization: dominance and reciprocation (Boehm, 1999; de Waal, 1982; Trivers, 1971; Wilson, 1993). In social groups not related by kinship, if violence does not serve a primarily instrumental function, it usually serves either to assert social dominance, to suppress dominance in others, or to punish transgressions against equitable behavior. Shakespeare's *Julius Caesar* offers a straightforward instance of dominance as a central theme. Caesar seizes dictatorial power, overthrowing the collective power of the senatorial class. In assassinating him, the senators exemplify the social dynamic delineated by Boehm (1996): collective force aimed at suppressing dominance in individuals. Suppressing dominance in individuals blends into punishing transgressions against equity. Individuals typically assert dominance by harming others; they thus violate an implicit social contract to treat others equitably.

In chimpanzee societies, sheer physical power establishes dominance. Even when weaker males form coalitions to overpower stronger males, physical strength ultimately determines hierarchical status. Two relatively weak males working together can be physically stronger than a single male who is stronger than either individually (de Waal, 1982). Physical power also undergirds human social relations, but human social relations are heavily regulated by norms and laws that prescribe obligations according to social roles (Hill, 2007). Civil society leaves little scope for individuals to assert dominance through sheer brute strength. Humans must instead use accumulated resources and acquired skills, including social skills, to establish their place in a social hierarchy. Sports constitute a partial exception. In Shakespeare's *As You Like It* and Achebe's *Things Fall Apart*, the protagonists gain prestige through victory in wrestling matches. But, then, sports are not means for dominating a social hierarchy through raw physical strength; they are forms of regulated social activity.

In most literary traditions, domestic violence—asserting individual dominance through physical force—falls outside the range of acceptable behavior. The most famous character in medieval English literature, Chaucer's Wife of Bath, takes as her chief theme the moral norm that prohibits violence against wives. In the prologue to her tale, she describes her relationship with her fourth husband, a scholar and misogynist. They quarreled; she ripped pages out of his favorite antifemale tract, and in a rage he struck her, knocking her senseless. His remorse was so severe that he conceded complete interpersonal dominance to her. She says they were very happy together after that. Her actual tale, as distinct from her prologue, is a fable illustrating the idea that men should yield domestic dominance to women.

In literature as in life, alcoholic derangement often plays a precipitating role in domestic violence. In *The Dram Shop*, Zola depicts the moral squalor of the alcoholic underclass in Paris. A father who gradually beats his prepubescent daughter to death is only the most poignant instance of pervasive, gratuitous violence. McTeague is drunk when he beats his wife to death. In King's *The Shining*, Jack Torrance reverts to alcoholism, beats his wife nearly to death, and tries to murder his son. At the time, he is under the influence of "evil spirits" in both senses of the word. The supernaturalism of the novel serves as a symbolic vehicle for depicting Torrance's losing struggle to resist his own inner demons.

Individuals in literature seldom assert dominance through sheer force, but groups often do. Racial or ethnic domination forms the theme of works such as Sir Walter Scott's *Ivanhoe*, Harriet Beecher Stowe's *Uncle Tom's Cabin*, Faulkner's *Light in August*, Richard Wright's *Native Son*, Tadeusz Borowski's *This Way for the Gas, Ladies and Gentlemen*, Art Spiegelman's *Maus*, William Styron's *Sophie's Choice* and *The Confessions of Nat Turner*, and J. M. Coetzee's *Disgrace*. Class conflicts culminating in riots with fatal consequences appear in Scott's *The Heart of Midlothian*, Benjamin Disraeli's *Sybil*, and Eliot's *Felix Holt*. Dickens's *Barnaby Rudge* climaxes in a deadly riot animated by religious strife. In *A Tale of Two Cities*, Dickens depicts the Terror that followed the French Revolution. In most representations of collective violence, authors sympathize with protests against racial oppression, class injustice, or political tyranny. At the same time, few literary authors give an approving depiction of mob violence.

REVENGE

Individuals who assert dominance through sheer physical force belong to a despised fringe in both life and literature. Using violence to gain revenge for injuries or insults is a different matter. Bullies are held in contempt, but characters who seek revenge through violence often elicit readers' respect, if not their conscious approval.

Personal injury motivates many instances of murderous revenge. Samson is tricked, blinded, and shackled for public display. When his strength returns along with his hair, he crushes the Philistines, along with himself, under the stones of their temple. In *One Thousand and One Nights*, a medieval Islamic collection of stories, Sharyar, a Persian king, discovers that his wife is unfaithful. He has her executed, and then, extending his revenge to womankind in general, marries a new woman every night, executing each the next morning. (Scheherazade avoids this fate by telling Sharyar a new story each night, but leaving each unfinished until the following night.) In Mary Shelley's *Frankenstein*, Frankenstein's monster develops a grudge against his creator and eventually kills everyone in Frankenstein's family. In Dickens's *Oliver Twist*, the criminal psychopath Bill Sikes beats his girlfriend to death because he thinks, mistakenly, that she has informed against him. The protagonist of Hardy's *Tess of the d'Urbervilles* is raped and her hopes of happiness ruined by Alex d'Urberville. She stabs him with a carving knife. In Conrad's *The Secret Agent*, the anarchist *agent provocateur* Mr. Verloc lures his wife's retarded younger brother into trying to blow up the Greenwich Conservatory. The brother stumbles en route and is himself blown to smithereens. Like Tess, Verloc's wife uses the instrument nearest to hand, a carving knife, to take her revenge. In John Steinbeck's *The Grapes of Wrath*, Tom Joad kills a policeman who has just smashed in the skull of his friend preacher Casy. In Vladimir Nabokov's *Lolita*, Clare Quilty helps Lolita escape from Humbert Humbert; in return, Humbert tracks Quilty down and shoots him multiple times. In King's *Carrie*, the town outcast, a teenage girl, is humiliated at the senior prom; she uses her telekinetic powers to slaughter the whole graduating class of the high school, trapping them inside a burning building.

Indignation at personal injury is a close cousin to offended pride. The protagonist of Shakespeare's *Coriolanus* is driven into traitorous homicidal fury by outraged pride. Iago destroys Othello because Othello has passed him over for promotion. In Edgar Allen Poe's "The Cask of Amontillado," the narrator protagonist Montresor says his acquaintance Fortunato has casually insulted him, so he shackles Fortunato to a wall deep underground and bricks up the niche. The Duke in Browning's monologue "My Last Duchess" has his wife murdered because she shows too little regard for the dignity of his rank. In Dickens's *Bleak House*, the French maid Hortense murders the lawyer Tulkinghorn because he has insulted her.

Harm to kin or lovers is a common motive for revenge. Aeschylus's *Oresteia* consists in a sequence of vengeful murders within a single family. In Shakespeare's first tragedy, *Titus Andronicus*, Lavinia is raped, and her rapists, to prevent her from identifying them, cut out her tongue and cut off her hands. (The source story, the myth of Philomela, appears in Ovid's *Metamorphoses*.) Lavinia nonetheless succeeds in identifying her assailants. In the subsequent cascade of vengeful acts, the two rapists are killed, cooked in a pie, and fed to their unsuspecting mother. (The same kind of revenge appears in Seneca the Younger's play *Thyestes*.) Laertes in *Hamlet* stabs Hamlet with a poisoned rapier because Hamlet has murdered Laertes's father, Polonius. Hamlet murders Claudius, his uncle, because Claudius murdered his own brother, Hamlet's father. In one of the earliest English novels, Samuel Richardson's *Clarissa*, Clarissa is abducted, drugged, and raped. After she dies from grief, her uncle kills her assailant in a duel. In F. Scott Fitzgerald's *The Great Gatsby*, Gatsby is murdered because a man mistakenly believes that Gatsby killed the man's wife. In Denis Lehaene's *Mystic River*, a father murders a childhood friend because he believes, mistakenly, that the friend murdered his daughter.

Though often moralistic on other themes, many literary authors display a strikingly tolerant attitude toward revenge as a motive. Revenge looks like a basic form of justice and often gives a feeling of emotional satisfaction to readers. If that were not the case, "poetic justice" would not be so widely used as a plot device. Poetic justice occurs when "good" characters are rewarded and "bad" characters made to suffer. Judging by the relative frequency of plot structures, we could reasonably infer that readers can more easily tolerate a plot in which a "good" character comes to a sad end than a plot in which a "bad" character lives happily ever after.

Blood feuds are a special case. One murder leads to another, but the whole sequence proceeds in a senselessly mechanical way. The deaths of Romeo and Juliet result in an agreement to end the blood feud between the Capulets and the Montagues. The darkest moments in Mark Twain's *Huckleberry Finn* involve the murderous feud between the Sheperdsons and the Grangerfords. When Huck asks his Grangerford friend what started the feud, the boy cannot provide an answer, but he nonetheless falls victim to the feud. Twain clearly expects readers to register the sad futility in killing of this kind.

DEATH BY LAW

Legal execution is partly instrumental—it aims at deterrence—and partly a form of collective revenge. When it serves the purposes of "poetic justice," legal execution can be neatly folded into the emotional satisfaction with which a story concludes. Even Billy Budd's hanging, in Herman Melville's *Billy Budd*, is presented as a tragic sacrifice to the necessities of naval discipline. At other times, though, legal execution is presented as the medium of a malign fate, an unjust social order, or both. At the end of Stendhal's *The Red and the Black*, Julien Sorel is guillotined for shooting his former mistress. He and Stendhal both seem to regard his fate as an indictment against an aristocratic social order that provides no career open to talent. When Tess of the d'Urbervilles is hanged for stabbing her rapist to death, Hardy explicitly protests against some cosmic principle of injustice. In Steinbeck's *Of Mice and Men*, the retarded giant, Lenny, accidentally kills a woman. His friend and protector, George, shoots him before he can be lynched. In *The Grapes of Wrath,* Steinbeck explicitly protests against social injustice. In *Of Mice and Men*, he seems less interested in protesting against injustice than in stimulating the reader's compassion for the plight of an itinerant male underclass. In Ambrose Bierce's "Incident at Owl Creek Bridge," a Southern civilian is hanged by Federal troops. The bulk of the story consists in depicting his fantasized escape, as the rope breaks and he falls into the water under the bridge. At the end of the story, he is snapped back to reality, with a broken neck, swinging beneath the bridge. The story focuses emotional attention not on retributive satisfaction, social protest, or simple compassion. Instead, it evokes the love of life and the horror of death. It also captures the sharp contrast between the victim as a mere object, for his executioners, and his own intense inner consciousness, frantic with terror and yearning.

HUMAN SACRIFICES

Along with "A Good Man Is Hard To Find" and "A Rose for Emily," Shirley Ann Jackson's "The Lottery" is one of the most frequently anthologized short stories. In a quiet farming village, somewhere in mid-century America, the local people gather for the annual lottery, selecting slips of paper from a box. The "winner," Tessie Hutcheson, is stoned to death. Her own family members, including her toddler, take part in the stoning. Stories do not become canonical merely because they are shocking and bizarre. "The Lottery" has a deep symbolic resonance; it suggests that even within civil society, in a time of peace, there is a force that subjugates individuals and family relationships to the collective identity of the social group. The coercive power of the social group is given symbolic form also in William Golding's *Lord of the Flies*. A group of English school boys, stranded on an island by a plane crash, quickly revert to savagery. The three boys who retain civilized values—Piggy, Simon, and Ralph—are sacrificed to the cohesion of the savage band. In *1984*, George Orwell locates coercive social force in a totalitarian regime. At the end of the novel, the protagonist Winston Smith is being tortured by an agent of the government. To end the torture, he must betray the woman he loves, begging his torturer to hurt her rather than him. During the torture, he is required to guess the right answer to a question about what motivates the totalitarian government. The right answer, as it turns out, is a desire for power, as an end in itself. The final stage in Winston Smith's subjugation is to come to feel, sincerely, that he loves the totalitarian regime that will soon, as he knows, murder him.

The totalitarian regime in *1984* is essentially psychopathic. Its practices are a collective equivalent of the psychopathic cruelty that animates novels such as *A Clockwork Orange* and *American Psycho*. Unlike Burgess and Ellis, Orwell does not invite readers to participate vicariously in the enjoyment of cruelty. *1984* is designed to create a sense of angry outrage in its readers. It is a symbolic indictment of totalitarianism, not a peep show. In that respect, it adopts a stance similar to Alexandr Solzhenitsyn's realistic depiction of the Gulag in *One Day in the Life of Ivan Denisovich*. A tacit indictment of the psychopathic political culture of Stalinist Russia also informs Vasily Grossman's *Life and Fate*.

War

There are only two primate species in which coalitions of males band together for the express purpose of making lethal raids on neighboring bands of conspecifics: chimpanzees and human beings (Jünger, 2010; Potts & Hayden, 2008; Wrangham, 1999). This behavior has evidently been conserved from the last common ancestor shared by humans and chimpanzees some 7 million years ago, and specifically human forms of evolutionary development gave an extra impetus to coalitional violence. Early in their evolutionary history, humans gained "ecological dominance" (Alexander, 1989; Flinn, Geary, & Ward, 2005); that is, they became the dominant predator in their environments. The most dangerous creatures they faced were members of other human bands. Male coalitional violence thus became a primary selective force in human evolution. Highly organized modern warfare is an extension of the coalitional aggression that characterizes most bands and tribes in preliterate cultures.

War has figured as a main subject of literature for every phase of history, from the ancient world, the medieval period, the Renaissance and Enlightenment, to the 19th and 20th centuries. War forms the subject matter of verse epics, plays, prose fiction, and lyric poetry. Much war literature blends closely with autobiography and history: lightly fictionalized memoir and accurate historical reconstruction that includes many actual historical persons.

We have no surviving narratives from prehistory, but William Golding's *The Inheritors* offers a powerful reconstruction of lethal interaction between Neanderthals and Cro-Magnons. The *Iliad* and the Bible evoke the warrior ethos of barbarian cultures; and Flaubert's *Salammbô*, like Golding's *The Inheritors*, raises historical reconstruction to the level of high literary art. Steven Pressfield's *Gates of Fire* reconstructs the Battle of Thermopylae.

The oldest surviving classic of French literature, the *Song of Roland*, describes an 8th-century battle in which the protagonists, like the Greek warriors at Thermopylae, are all killed. Scott's *The Talisman* locates its action in the Crusades. In the classic Japanese medieval epic, *The Tale of the Heiki*, two clans struggle to dominate Japan. A 14th-century Chinese novel, Luo Guanzhong's *Romance of the Three Kingdoms*, also focuses on dynastic struggles. Shakespeare dramatizes the English Wars of the 15th century. The Thirty Years' War—the religious war that devastated Germany in the 17th century—provides the setting for Hans von Grimmelshausen's semiautobiographical tale *Simplicissimus*. The protagonist in Friedrich Schiller's dramatic trilogy *Wallenstein* is a general in the Thirty Years' War.

Eighteenth-century wars include the first and second Jacobite uprisings (rebellions aimed at restoring the Stuarts to the throne of England), the Seven Years War (the struggle among the main European powers that spread into the American continent in *The French and Indian War*), and the American War of Independence. Thackeray's protagonist in *Henry Esmond* joins the first Jacobite uprising, and Scott's protagonist in *Waverly* joins the second. Henry Fielding's protagonist in *Tom Jones* sets off to fight in that same military venture, though he never arrives. Thackeray's Barry Lyndon fights in the Seven Years War, which also forms the background to Major von Tellheim's plight in G. E. Lessing's play *Minna von Barnhelm*. James Fennimore Cooper's *Last of the Mohicans* is set in the French and Indian War. In Thackeray's *The Virginians*, two brothers, grandsons of Henry Esmond, fight on different sides in the American War of Independence. Children's novels about that war include Esther Forbes's *Johnny Tremain* and James Collier's *My Brother Sam Is Dead*.

The Napoleonic Wars dominated European politics in the first 15 years of the 19th century. Different phases of that war figure prominently in *War and Peace* and Thackeray's *Vanity Fair*. Bernard Cornwell's Sharpe series of novels and Patrick O'Brian's Aubrey-Maturin series chronicle this period with gritty military and naval detail. Cornwell's *Waterloo* offers a brilliant fictional reconstruction of the Battle of Waterloo. Thackeray gives a short but rhetorically powerful description of the same battle in *Vanity Fair*. The protagonist in Stendhal's *Charterhouse of Parma* witnesses Waterloo from the fringes, though without understanding the course of the action.

European wars between 1815 and 1914—from the Battle of Waterloo to the beginning of World War I—include the Crimean War, the Franco-Prussian War, various Balkan conflicts, and the small imperial wars on the fringes of the British Empire, including the Boer War. Tennyson's poem "Charge of the Light Brigade" chronicles an episode in the Crimean War. Several of Maupassant's short stories are set in the period of the Franco-Prussian War. The protagonist of G. B. Shaw's play *Arms and the Man* is a mercenary Swiss soldier serving in the Serbo-Bulgarian War. Several of Kipling's early stories depict British military actions in India, what is now Pakistan, and Afghanistan. Kenneth Ross's play *Breaker Morant*, which provides the basis for the Bruce Beresford film of that name, is set in the Boer War.

Conrad's *Nostromo* depicts a South American revolution that transforms the lives of the characters, including English and Italian expatriates. Gabriel Garcia Marquez's *100 Years of Solitude* takes up similar themes from a South American perspective.

The major American war of the 19th century was of course the Civil War, which produced a crop of contemporary novels and a steady flow of historical reconstructions, including Stephen Crane's *The Red Badge of Courage*, Michael Shaara's *The Killer Angels*, Shelby Foote's *Shiloh*, and Charles Frazier's *Cold Mountain*. Children's novels about the American Civil War include Harold Keith's *Rifles for Watie* and Irene Hunt's *Across Five Aprils*.

Among the many novels about World War I, Erich Maria Remarque's *All Quiet on the Western Front* holds a special place as one of the greatest of all war novels. The last scene of Thomas Mann's *The Magic Mountain* presents its philosophical protagonist charging across a battlefield in World War I, with limited prospects for survival. Henri Barbusse's *Under Fire* gives a French perspective on the war. American novels about World War I include Hemingway's *A Farewell to Arms*, William March's *Company K*, John Dos Passos's *Three Soldiers*, and Dalton Trumbo's *Johnny Got His Gun*. British novels include Ford's *Parade's End*, Jennifer Johnston's *How Many Miles to Babylon*, and Pat Barker's *Regeneration Trilogy*. Some of Faulkner's and Kipling's best short stories are set in World War I. Charles Harrison's *Generals Die in Bed* gives a Canadian perspective on the war. For Russians, World War I merges into the Bolshevik Revolution and the Russian Civil War. That period forms the background for Michail Sholokhov's *And Quiet Flows the Don*, Boris Pasternak's *Doctor Zhivago*, and Aleksandr Solzhenitsyn's series of novels included in *The Red Wheel*. In addition to novels and short stories, the war generated a large body of fine lyric poetry by poet-soldiers such as Wilfred Owen, Siegfried Sassoon, and Edmund Blunden.

World War II produced major novels in several national literatures. American novels include Heller's *Catch-22*, Norman Mailer's *The Naked and the Dead*, James Jones's *The Thin Red Line*, Kurt Vonnegut's *Slaughterhouse 5*, and James Dickey's *To the White Sea*. *Everybody Comes to Rick's*, an unpublished play by Murray Burnett and Joan Alison, was the basis for the film *Casablanca*. The Spanish Civil War, a prelude to World War II, is the setting for Ernest Hemingway's *For Whom the Bell Tolls*. Colin McDougall's *The Execution* is the most important Canadian novel about World War II. German experience in the war forms the subject of Günter Grass's *The Tin Drum*, Willi Heinrich's *Cross of Iron*, Russ Schneider's *Siege*, Heinrich Gerlach's *The Forsaken Army*, and Theodor Plievier's *Stalingrad*. The greatest Russian novel of the war, Vasily Grossman's *Life and Fate*, is designed to cover multiple theaters of the war and to interweave politics, combat, the Holocaust, and civilian terror in the Soviet Union. Curzio Malaparte's *Kaputt* gives an Italian perspective on the war. British involvement in the war forms the background for Evelyn Waugh's *Sword of Honour* trilogy and J. G. Ballard's *Empire of the Sun*. Ian McEwan's *Atonement* reconstructs the British retreat to Dunkirk. Japanese novels about the war include Ashihei Hino's *Wheat and Soldiers*, Tatsuzō Ishikawa's *Soldiers Alive*, and Ooka Shohei's *Fires on the Plain*. The international order in Orwell's *1984* includes a perpetual world war.

Novels of Vietnam include Larry Heinemann's *Close Quarters*, James Webb's *Fields of Fire*, John del Vecchio's *The Thirteenth Valley*, and Tim O'Brien's *The Things They Carried*. Báo Ninh's novel *The Sorrow of War* offers a Vietnamese perspective. Francis Ford Coppola's film *Apocalypse Now* takes the core of its plot from Conrad's *The Heart of Darkness*, which is set in the Belgian Congo, and transposes the plot to Vietnam. The script writer, Michael Herr, incorporates episodes from *Dispatches*, his own journalistic memoir about his experiences as a reporter in Vietnam.

In science fiction, war is often projected into a fictional future and extended to conflicts between humans and other species. H. G. Wells's *War of the Worlds* provides a prototype for this genre. More recent examples include Robert Heinlein's *Starship Troopers*, Joe Haldeman's *The Forever War*, and Orson Scott Card's *Ender's Game*.

Fantasy worlds are as likely to be riven by war as actual worlds. John Milton's *Paradise Lost* depicts the war in heaven between the good and bad angels. (They use cannons with gunpowder, as in the English Civil War, but to little effect, since they are immaterial beings.) J. R. R. Tolkien's *Lord of the Rings* trilogy culminates in an epic conflict among the inhabitants of Middle Earth. Though written in the interwar period, Tolkien's account of this war looks like an eerie forecast of World War II. C. S. Lewis's *The Lion, the Witch, and The Wardrobe* chronicles a war in Narnia between the forces of good and evil—and indeed most fantasy wars, compared with real wars, are more easily reducible to ethical binaries. J. K. Rowling's *Harry Potter* series culminates in a bloody battle between the protagonists, practitioners of benign magic, and the minions of Voldemort, the Dark Lord.

Though deeply ingrained in genetically transmitted human dispositions, war puts exceptional stress on men's minds. Combat elicits instinctive fight-or-flight responses but channels them into highly disciplined patterns of behavior regulated by rigidly hierarchical social structures. Shared danger creates a bond among soldiers that many describe as the most intense and intimate they have known. At the same time, war systematically dehumanizes the enemy in ways that make it easier to breach the psychological inhibition most people feel against doing violent bodily harm to other people (Baumeister, 1996; Grossman, 2009; Smith, 2007). Some fictional treatments of war, and some lyric poetry inspired by war, adopt emotionally simple stances: heroism and patriotism, or protest and revulsion. Most evoke an ambivalent swirl of emotions that include terror, rage, exultation, resentment, pride, horror, guilt, and self-pity. Authors seldom stand wholly outside the emotions they evoke. Readers can easily enough adopt ideological principles that either justify war or condemn it, but the conscious formulation of explicit ideological principles is not the same thing as an imaginative poise that reflects genuine emotional mastery. Psychopaths have the least difficulty accommodating themselves to the emotional challenges of war (Baumeister, 1996; Grossman, 2009). For most people, war remains a troubling and sometimes traumatic experience. The quality of that experience varies from individual to individual and from war to war. The perspectives of authors and characters are often heavily conditioned by the nature and outcome of the war. Most novels about World War I and about Vietnam register a dreary sensation of futility mingled with horror and revulsion. Novels about the Napoleonic Wars, the American Civil War, and World War II have a much wider emotional range. The total emotional trajectory of World War II was very different for Americans, British, Russians, Germans, and Japanese. Such differences necessarily enter into authorial perspectives on the emotional significance of the violence they depict.

Conclusion

When we think of literature, we tend to think of quiet, civilized activity: writers sitting at a desk, pen in hand; readers sitting in poised contemplation over the pages of a book; the solemn hush of a library; the mellow leisure of a bookstore. At first glance, then, literature would seem to have little to do with violence—with men beating or raping women; people stabbing or shooting each other; individuals poisoning, shooting, drowning, or hanging themselves, cutting their own throats, or throwing themselves out of windows; or with large masses of men caught up in the frenzy of mutual slaughter. And yet, as this survey suggests, violence is pervasive in literary representation. William Wordsworth defines poetry as emotion recollected in tranquility (1800/1957). Is literary violence, then, just a form of sensationalistic emotional self-indulgence? No. Freud (1907/1959) made a great error in supposing that literature consists in wish-fulfillment fantasies. Most of the instances of violence cited in this essay are ugly and painful. Very few people have ever enjoyed watching as Cornwall gouges out Gloucester's eyes, or have felt pleasure listening to Lear's howls of grief after Cordelia is hanged. Most depictions of murder and suicide produce discomfort, at the mildest, in readers' minds. The satisfaction of revenge and the lust of battle offer partial exceptions, but such pleasures are hardly pure. Revenge is at best a bitter satisfaction (Baumeister, 1996). The warriors of the *Iliad* who exult in a momentary victory also have a despairing consciousness that they will probably die a similar death, and soon (Gottschall, 2008b).

The painful character of violence in literature points us toward what is, in the present author's view, the central adaptive function of the arts. We do not read stories primarily because they produce vicarious sensations of pleasure; we read them because they give us a deeper, more complete sense of the forces that motivate human life (Carroll, 2011b). Humans do not operate by instinct alone. They have a uniquely developed capacity for envisioning their lives as a continuously developing sequence of actions within larger social and natural contexts. Affective neuroscientists have shown that human decision making depends crucially on emotions; we are not simply "rational" creatures (Damasio, 1994; Linden, 2007; Panksepp, 1998). Literature and other emotionally charged imaginative constructs—the other arts, religions, and ideologies—inform our emotional understanding of human behavior. The arts expand our feeling for why other people act as they do, help us to anticipate how they are likely to respond to our behavior, and offer suggestions about what kind of value we should attach to alternative courses of action.

Fictional violence delineates extreme limits in human experience. We do not necessarily enjoy reading about violent acts, but we do enjoy finding out about the extreme limits of experience. That is a kind of information for which we have evolved an adaptively functional need.

Future Directions

For many scholars and scientists, in both the humanities and the social sciences, literary experience seems hopelessly outside the reach of empirical scientific knowledge. Such scholars and scientists might acknowledge that biographical information about authors and facts about plots can be determined in a reasonably objective way. They might also acknowledge that the demographics of literacy can be assessed with the statistical methods of the social sciences. But the heart of the matter—the meaning authors build into plots and the effects such meanings have on the minds and emotions of readers—all of that, many scholars and scientists feel, must always remain a matter of vague speculation, subjective at best, fanciful or absurd at worst, in any case not accessible to scientific inquiry.

I am confident that this set of assumptions is mistaken. Outside the now obsolete behaviorist school, mental events—images, thoughts, and feelings—are the standard subject matter of psychology. Pen-and-paper tests, experimental designs with live subjects, and neuroimaging give access to mental events. Mental events also form the substance of literary experience. Mental events in the responses of readers are as accessible to empirical inquiry as any other mental events, and the responses of readers provide an opening to the intentions of authors and the psychosocial functions of literary works (Carroll et al., 2008, 2010).

To make major advances in empirical knowledge about literary experience, two main changes in attitude need to occur. Social scientists need to recognize how large and important a place every kind of imaginative experience holds in human life; and literary scholars need to recognize that incorporating empirical research into scholarly study will give their research a kind of epistemological legitimacy it desperately needs. Integrating humanistic and empirical methods of inquiry will also vastly expand the scope of literary inquiry, making it possible to locate literary study in relation to multiple contiguous disciplines.

Literary meanings and effects like those described in this chapter are complex phenomena. To make them accessible to objective scientific knowledge, we have to break them down into components and devise empirical methods for analyzing each component. We should start with recognizing that literary meaning is a form of communication, an intentional meaning created by an author who anticipates responses of readers. At the base of empirical literary research, then, we need to tease apart the relations between mirror neurons, empathy, emotional circuits, and mental images (Baron-Cohen, 2005; Decety, 2011a, 2011b; Rizzolatti & Fogassi, 2007).

We also have to work out the relations between responses to actual events and "offline" responses to fiction—that is, emotional responses "decoupled" from immediate action (Tooby & Cosmides, 2001). Neurocognitive research on the way people process emotionally charged information will make it possible to produce empirical knowledge about the formal aspects of fiction: narrative structure, syntax and prose rhythm, word choice, modulations of tone, and symbolic imagery.

To locate neurocognitive findings within comprehensive explanatory sequences, we have to link the highest level of causal explanation—inclusive fitness, the ultimate regulative principle of evolution—to particular features of human nature and to particular structures and effects in specific works of art. Human life history theory offers the best available framework for analyzing the components of human nature (Kaplan, Hill Lancaster, & Hurtado, 2000; Low, 2000; MacDonald, 1997; Wrangham, 2009). Gene-culture coevolution offers the best available framework for understanding how specifically human mental capabilities interact with basic motives and emotions (Carroll, 2011a). Gene-culture coevolution also provides a framework for analyzing the way specific cultures organize the elements of human nature.

A comprehensively adequate explanation of a given work of art would stipulate the character and causes of its phenomenal effects (tone, style, theme, formal organization); locate the work in a cultural context; explain that cultural context as a particular organization of the elements of human nature within a specific set of environmental conditions (including cultural traditions); register the responses of readers; identify the sociocultural, political, and psychological functions the work fulfills for specific audiences (perhaps different functions for different audiences); locate those functions in relation to the evolved needs of human nature; and link the work comparatively with other artistic works, using a taxonomy of themes, formal elements, affective elements, and functions derived from a comprehensive model of human nature.

In addition to locating individual works in evolutionary explanatory contexts, scholars and scientists must also deal with groups of works, organized by period, national literature, and features of formal organization and style (genre). These are standard categories in traditional literary research, and for a good reason: They constitute conventions within which authors encode meanings and readers decode those meanings. All such traditional categories of literary scholarship should now be studied with an eye toward generating explanations integrated with principles of human life history and gene-culture coevolution.

Evolutionary study tends toward an emphasis on human universals. That is an indispensable starting point. It gives access to basic motives and basic emotions. Identifying cross-cultural regularities makes it possible to isolate the elements that enter into complex cultural configurations. But the particular character of those cultural configurations does in fact substantially alter the quality of lived and imagined experience. We are only just beginning to understand gene-culture coevolution at a rudimentary theoretical level (Carroll, 2011a). To advance in our understanding, we need highly particularized studies of specific cultural moments focusing both on macro-structures of social dynamics (Turchin, 2007) and also on the neurophysiological character of experience within given ecologies (Smail, 2008). Cultural analysis is a necessary middle level in literary research.

The study of individual identity is yet another level at which literary scholars need to work. They have to understand individual differences in personality as those differences apply to authors, characters, and readers. Evolutionary psychology took a wrong turn, early on, in deprecating the adaptive significance of individual differences (Tooby & Cosmides, 1990). That wrong turn is now being corrected (Figueredo et al., 2005; Nettle, 2007a, 2007b). That correction will make the evolutionary standpoint much more valuable both to psychologists studying live subjects and to literary critics studying fictional subjects (Johnson et al., 2011; McCrae, in press).

Substantial progress has already been made in many of the research areas recommended here (Boyd, 2009; Boyd, Carroll, & Gottschall, 2010; Carroll, 2011a, 2011b; Gottschall, 2008a, 2008b). But in truth, we have only just begun. In physics, "dreams of a final theory" involve integrating the weak nuclear force, the strong nuclear force, electromagnetism, and gravity (Weinberg, 1992). In all areas that concern human behavior, integrating the humanities and the social sciences presents a similarly fundamental challenge. The opportunities are immense. Violence is only one topic within the broad field of evolutionary literary research, but it is such an important topic that advances in understanding literary violence will almost certainly open out into generalizable principles across the whole range of human behavior.

References

Most of the literary works mentioned in this chapter are available in multiple editions, and many are available in multiple translations. Literary works are not included in the following list of references.

Alexander, R. D. (1989). Evolution of the human psyche. In P. Mellars & C. Stringer (Eds.), *The human revolution: Behavioral and biological perspectives in the origins of modern humans* (pp. 455–513). Princeton, NJ: Princeton University Press.

Baron-Cohen, S. (2005). The empathizing system: A revision of the 1994 model of the mindreading system. In B. J. Ellis & D. F. Bjorklund (Eds.), *Origins of the social mind: Evolutionary psychology and child development* (pp. 468–92). New York: The Guilford Press.

Baumeister, R. F. (1996). *Evil: Inside human cruelty and violence.* New York: W. H. Freeman.

Boehm, C. (1999). *Hierarchy in the forest: The evolution of egalitarian behavior.* Cambridge, MA: Harvard University Press.

Boyd, B. (2009). *On the origin of stories: Evolution, cognition, and fiction.* Cambridge, MA: Harvard University Press.

Boyd, B., Carroll, J., & Gottschall, J. (2010). *Evolution, literature, and film: A reader.* New York: Columbia University Press.

Buss, D. M. (2000). *The dangerous passion: Why jealousy is as necessary as love and sex.* New York: Free Press.

Buss, D. M. (2003). *The evolution of desire: Strategies of human mating* (Rev. ed.). New York: Basic Books.

Carroll, J. (2011a). Human life history and gene-culture co-evolution: An emerging paradigm. *The Evolutionary Review: Art, Science, Culture, 2,* 23–37.

Carroll, J. (2011b). *Reading human nature: Literary Darwinism in theory and practice.* Albany, NY: SUNY Press.

Carroll, J., Gottschall, J., Johnson, J. A., & Kruger, D. J. (2008). Human nature in nineteenth-century British novels: Doing the math. *Philosophy and Literature, 33,* 50–72.

Carroll, J., Gottschall, J., Johnson, J. A., Kruger, D. J., & Georgiades, S. (2010). Quantifying tonal analysis in *The Mayor of Casterbridge. Style, 44,* 164–188.

Chagnon, N. A. (1979). *Yanomamö: The fierce people* (3rd ed.). New York: Holt, Rinehart, & Winston.

Cochran, G., & Harpending, H. (2009). *The 10,000 year explosion: How civilization accelerated human evolution.* New York: Basic Books.

Cosmides, L., & Tooby, J. (2000). Evolutionary psychology and the emotions. In M. Lewis & J. M. Haviland-Jones (Eds.), *Handbook of emotions* (2nd ed., pp. 91–115). New York: The Guilford Press.

de Waal, F. (1982). *Chimpanzee politics: Power and sex among apes.* New York: Harper & Row.

Daly, M., & Wilson, M. (1988). *Homicide.* Hawthorne, NY: Aldine de Gruyter.

Damasio, A. (1994). *Descartes' error: Emotion, reason, and the human brain.* New York: G. P. Putnam.

Darwin, C. (1903). *More letters of Charles Darwin. A record of his work in a series of hitherto unpublished letters* (F. Darwin & A. C. Seward, Eds., 2 Vols.) London: Murray.

Davies, N. (1999). *The isles: A history.* New York: Oxford University Press.

Davies, S. (2006). *No simple victory: World War II in Europe, 1939–45.* New York: Penguin.

deCatanzaro, D. (1981). *Suicide and self-damaging behavior: A sociobiological perspective.* New York: Academic Press.

Decety, J. (2011a). Dissecting the neural mechanisms mediating empathy. *Emotion Review, 3,* 92–108.

Decety, J. (2011b). Promises and challenges of the neurobiological approach to empathy. *Emotion Review, 3,* 115–116.

Ekman, P. (2003). *Emotions revealed: Recognizing faces and feelings to improve communication and emotional life.* New York: Henry Holt.

Faulkner, W. (1965). *Faulkner in the university: Class conferences at the University of Virginia, 1957–58* (F. L. Gwynn & J. L. Blotner, Eds.). New York: Vintage.

Figueredo, A. J., Sefcek, J. A., Vasquez, G., Brumback, B. H., King, J. E., & Jacobs, W. J. (2005). Evolutionary personality psychology. In D. M. Buss (Ed.), *The handbook of evolutionary psychology* (pp. 851–877). Hoboken, NJ: Wiley.

Flinn, M. V., Geary, D. C., & Ward, C. V. (2005). Ecological dominance, social competition, and coalitionary arms races: Why humans evolved extraordinary intelligence. *Evolution and Human Behavior, 26,* 10–46.

Frank, R. (1988). *Passions within reason: The strategic role of the emotions.* New York: Norton.

Friedman, T. L. (2009). *Hot, flat, and crowded: Why we need a green revolution—and how it can renew America.* New York: Picador.

Freud, S. (1959). Creative writers and daydreaming. In J. Strachey (Ed. & Trans.), *The standard edition of the complete psychological works of Sigmund Freud* (Vol. 9, pp. 142–153). London: Hogarth. (Original work published 1907).

Geary, D. C. (1998). *Male, female: The evolution of human sex differences.* Washington, DC: American Psychological Association.

Geary, D. C., & Flinn, M. V. (2001). Evolution of human parental behavior and the human family. *Parenting: Science and Practice, 1,* 5–61.

Gibbon, E. (1994). *The history of the decline and fall of the Roman Empire* (D. Wormsley, Ed., 3 Vols.). New York: Penguin. (Original work published 1776–1789).

Gilbert, M. (1989). *The Second World War: A complete history* (Rev. ed.). New York: Henry Holt.

Gottschall, J. (2008a). *Literature, science, and a new humanities.* New York: Palgrave Macmillan.

Gottschall, J. (2008b). *The rape of Troy: Evolution, violence, and the world of Homer.* Cambridge, England: Cambridge University Press.

Grossman, D. (2009). *On killing: The psychological cost of learning to kill in war and society* (Rev. ed.). New York: Little, Brown.

Hawkins, J., & Blakeslee, S. (2004). *On intelligence.* New York: Henry Holt.

Headlam Wells, R. (2011). Why we should read the Bible: Sacred texts, human nature, and the just society. *The Evolutionary Review: Art, Science, Culture, 2,* 82–93.

Hill, K. (2007). Evolutionary biology, cognitive adaptations, and human culture. In S. W. Gangestad & J. A. Simpson (Eds.), *The evolution of mind: Fundamental questions and controversies* (pp. 348–356). New York: The Guilford Press.

Jobling, I. (2001). Personal justice and homicide in Scott's *Ivanhoe*: An evolutionary psychological perspective. *Interdisciplinary Literary Studies, 2,* 29–43.

Johnson, J. A., Carroll, J., Gottschall, J., & Kruger, D. J. (2008). Hierarchy in the library: Egalitarian dynamics in Victorian novels. *Evolutionary Psychology, 6,* 715–738.

Johnson, J. A., Carroll, J., Gottschall, J., & Kruger, D. J. (2011). Portrayal of personality in Victorian novels reflects modern research findings but amplifies the significance of agreeableness. *Journal of Research in Personality, 45,* 50–58.

Johnson, P. (1980). *Ireland, land of troubles*. London: Eyre Methuen.

Jünger, S. (2010). *War*. New York: Hachette Book Group.

Kaplan, H. S., Hill, K., Lancaster, J., & Hurtado, A. M. (2000). A theory of human life history evolution: Diet, intelligence, and longevity. *Evolutionary Anthropology, 9*, 156–185.

Keegan, J. (1990). *The Second World War*. New York: Penguin.

Lane, N. (2009). *Life ascending: The ten great inventions of evolution*. New York: Norton.

Linden, D. J. (2007). *The accidental mind*. Cambridge, MA: Harvard University Press.

Low, B. S. (2000). *Why sex matters: A Darwinian look at human behavior*. Princeton, NJ: Princeton University Press.

McCrae, R. R. (in press). The five-factor model in fact and fiction. In H. A. Tennen & J. M. Suls (Eds.), *Handbook of psychology, Vol. 5: Personality and social psychology*. Hoboken, NJ: Wiley.

MacDonald, K. B. (1997). Life history theory and human reproductive behavior: Environmental/contextual influences and heritable variation. *Human Nature, 8*, 327–359.

Marshall, S. L. A. (1947). *Men against fire: The problem of battle command*. New York: William Morrow.

Nettle, D. (2007a). Individual differences. In R. Dunbar & L. Barrett (Eds.), *The Oxford handbook of evolutionary psychology* (pp. 479–490). Oxford, England: Oxford University Press.

Nettle, D. (2007b). *Personality: What makes you the way you are*. Oxford, England: Oxford University Press.

Oakley, B. (2007). *Evil genes: Why Rome fell, Hitler rose, Enron failed, and my sister stole my mother's boyfriend*. Amherst, NY: Prometheus Books.

Oatley, K. (1999). Why fiction may be twice as true as fact: Fiction as cognitive and emotional simulation. *Review of General Psychology, 3*, 101–117.

Oatley, K. (2002). Emotions and the story worlds of fiction. In M. C. Green, J. J. Strange, & T. C. Brock (Eds.), *Narrative impact: Social and cognitive foundation* (pp. 36–69). Mahwah, NJ: Erlbaum.

Oatley, K. (2003). Emotional expression and experience in the visual and narrative arts. In R. J. Davidson, K. R. Scherer, & H. H. Goldsmith (Eds.), *Handbook of the affective sciences* (pp. 481–502). New York: Oxford University Press.

Panksepp, J. (1998). *Affective neuroscience: The foundations of human and animal emotions*. New York: Oxford University Press.

Pinker, S. (1997). *How the mind works*. New York: Norton.

Plutchik, R. (2003). *Emotions and life: Perspectives from psychology, biology, and evolution*. Washington, DC: American Psychological Association.

Potts, M., & Hayden, T. (2008). *Sex and war: How biology explains warfare and terrorism and offers a path to a safer world*. Dallas, TX: Benbella Books.

Rizzolatti, G., & Fogassi, L. (2007). Mirror neurons and social cognition. In R. Dunbar & L. Barrett (Eds.), *The Oxford handbook of evolutionary psychology* (pp. 179–195). Oxford, England: Oxford University Press.

Roberts, J. M. (2003). *The new history of the world* (4th ed.). Oxford, England: Oxford University Press.

Schelling, T. (1960). *The strategy of conflict*. Cambridge, MA: Harvard University Press.

Smail, D. L. (2008). *On deep history and the brain*. Berkeley: University of California Press.

Smith, D. L. (2007). *The most dangerous animal: Human nature and the origins of war*. New York: St. Martin's Press.

Snyder, T. (2010). *Bloodlands: Europe between Hitler and Stalin*. New York: Basic Books, 2010.

Spector, R. H. (1984). *Eagle against the sun: The American war with Japan*. New York: Macmillan.

Swank, R. L., & Marchand, W. E. (1946). Combat neuroses: Development of combat exhaustion. *Archives of Neurology and Psychology, 55*, 236–247.

Tan, E. S. (2000). Emotion, art, and the humanities. In M. Lewis & J. M. Haviland-Jones (Eds.), *Handbook of emotions* (2nd ed., pp. 116–134). New York: The Guilford Press.

Tomasello, M., Carpenter, M., Call, J., Behne, T., & Moll, H. (2005). Understanding and sharing intentions: The origins of cultural cognition. *Behavioral and Brain Sciences, 28*, 675–691.

Tooby, J., & Cosmides, L. (1990). On the universality of human nature and the uniqueness of the individual: The role of genetics and adaptation. *Journal of Personality, 58*, 17–67.

Tooby, J., & Cosmides, L. (1992). The psychological foundations of culture. In J. H. Barkow, L. Cosmides, & J. Tooby (Eds.), *The adapted mind: Evolutionary psychology and the generation of culture* (pp. 19–136). New York: Oxford University Press.

Tooby, J., & Cosmides, L. (2001). Does beauty build adapted minds? Toward an evolutionary theory of aesthetics, fiction, and the arts. *SubStance, 30*, 6–27.

Trivers, R. L. (1971). The evolution of reciprocal altruism. *The Quarterly Review of Biology, 46*, 35–57.

Turchin, P. (2007). *War and peace and war: The rise and fall of empires*. New York: Plume.

Wade, N. (2006). *Before the dawn: Recovering the lost history of our ancestors*. New York: Penguin.

Weinberg, S. (1992). *Dreams of a final theory: The search for the fundamental laws of nature*. New York: Pantheon.

Wells, H. G. (1921). *The outline of history: Being a plain history of life and mankind*. New York: Macmillan.

Wilson, E. O. (1998). *Consilience: The unity of knowledge*. New York: Knopf.

Wilson, J. Q. (1993). *The moral sense*. New York: Macmillan.

Wordsworth, W. (1957). *Preface to* Lyrical Ballads, *edited and with an introduction by W. J. B. Owen*. Copenhagen, Denmark: Rosenkilde & Bagger. (Original work published 1800).

Wrangham, R. (1999). Evolution of coalitionary killing. *Yearbook of Physical Anthropology, 42*, 1–30.

Wrangham, R. (2009). *Catching fire: How cooking made us human*. New York: Basic Books.

Wright, R. (1994). *The moral animal: The new science of evolutionary psychology*. New York: Pantheon Books.

CHAPTER 25

Why Religion Is Unable to Minimize Lethal and Nonlethal Societal Dysfunction Within and Between Nations

Gregory S. Paul

Abstract

The widely held premise that godly religion is important if not critical to maximizing the socioeconomic success of societies while suppressing criminal violence and war is undergoing growing historical and scientific scrutiny. Research indicates that theism is not reliably efficacious even when moderate or progressive, and often contributes to societal dysfunction and war when it is conservative or reactionary in nature. Theism cannot be part of the solution because theism is popular only when socioeconomic conditions are sufficiently defective to compel the majority to relieve their chronic anxiety by petitioning supernatural forces for aid and protection. The most successful and pacific societies in history have been the most nontheistic modern democracies, in part because a high level of secure prosperity always suppresses mass religion. So rather than being universal and integral to human psychology, religious supernaturalism is superficial and elective, and it is poorly developed even in some hunter-gatherers. The best human option is atheistic liberal democracy.

Key Words: religion, secularism, atheism, violence, war, societal dysfunction, societal success

Introduction: The Big "Is Religion Good or Bad" Question

On one hand, religion has experienced a historically unprecedented implosion in the most advanced prosperous democracies, dramatically reducing its social impact in much of Europe and North America, Australia and New Zealand, and Japan. At the same time, the opinion that at least one supernatural deity exists and plays a crucial role in human affairs continues to play an enormous role in most of the world at the individual, community, national, and international levels, including in civil and military strife and terrorism. Large numbers are obsessed with supernaturalistic religion, some to the extent that they are inspired to engage in lethal violence. It is therefore necessary to assess, on a scientific basis, whether religion and nonreligion are positive or negative influences on humanity, a test that is made possible by the wide variation and popularity of religion and associated societal conditions in modern nations.

The need for such an examination is reinforced because one of the most popular opinions over time and between differing peoples—the godly-religion socioeconomic hypothesis—has been that it is at best difficult if not impossible for societies to be successful and nonviolent internally and externally, unless the great majority of the population is supernaturalistically religious in that they believe that at least one moral deity exists and must be worshipped. At the same time, the presence of a strong religious component in most of the strife that is afflicting the world, and the aggressive stance of harsh fundamentalist doctrines, is raising concerns about the corrosive influence of religion.

The Great War[1] of 1914–1918 played a pivotal role in the growing social struggle between advocates of theism and nontheism because many theoconservatives interpreted the extreme death toll of the European war as exposing the perils of nations being insufficiently godly and under the undue influence of Darwinian thinking. William Jennings Bryan became a dedicated creationist for this reason, leading the notorious Scopes Monkey Trial and the ensuing and ongoing battle between creationism and evolutionary science in the United States (Numbers, 2005). Others argue that the Great War was yet another in a long series of wars in which Eurochristians fought Eurochristians, and that the scale of the conflict was the result of technological advances exploited by strongly religious societies. World War II and the Jewish Holocaust have become an issue because many theoconservatives vehemently contend that the primary cause of the war and genocide, Hitlerian Nazism, was an expression of Darwinistic atheism (Brooks, 2006; Coulter, 2006; D'Souza, 2007; O'Reilly, 2006), while others have presented the historical evidence that Nazism was profoundly theistic in origins and nature, and that the racism often associated with early Darwinism was a pseudoscientific contamination inherited from Christian civilization (Hastings, 2010; Paul, 2003, 2004; Phayer, 2000, 2008; Scholder, 1988; Steigman-Gall, 2003). In the latter view, World War II was a religious conflict in which godly Fascists with the aid of major Christian elements attempted to extinguish irreligious communism as well as Jews.

How religion and the lack of it impacts daily lives in national societies not directly experiencing war had been insufficiently investigated (Bloom, 2007; Dennett, 2006; Paul, 2005), but it is seeing a rapid expansion of research (Barber, 2011; Gill & Lundsgaarde, 2004; Norris & Inglehart, 2004; Paul, 2005, 2009a, 2010a, 2010b; Rees, 2009; Ruiter & Tubergen, 2009; Verweij, Ester, & Nauta, 1997; Zuckerman, 2008, 2009; Pinker, 2011). The history of the extensive support for the general godly-religion socioeconomic hypothesis is presented in Paul (2005, 2009a) and Zuckerman (2008, 2009). Many variants of the general theory are extant, so its complexity is high. The most widely held single subset is the moral-creator socioeconomic hypothesis that more specifically posits that mass worship of the one and only purposeful creator of the universe is necessary for societies to function properly and pacifically (Paul, 2009a, 2010b), and this is a vital tenant of the monotheistic Abrahamism that half the global population adheres to.

Contained within the moral-creator socioeconomic hypothesis are further important subvariants.

Of course, many contend that a particular sect within the Abrahamist tradition produces the best results, the sect usually being the one that a given Jew, Christian, or Muslim belongs to. Some conservative and all moderate and liberal theists deny that mass acceptance of bioevolution contributes to social ills even if they think the moral-creator socioeconomic hypothesis as a whole is operative. Conservative adherents to the moral-creator socioeconomic hypothesis often contend that popular approval of Darwinian science is societally disadvantageous for two proposed reasons. Mass acceptance of evolution tends to suppress levels of belief in a supernatural creator that is necessary for properly functional societies, and the process of biological evolution is a purposeless, amoral struggle for survival that leads to ungodly brutal social Darwinism and individual immorality.

Especially in the contemporary United States, the moral-creator socioeconomic hypothesis is a core, driving belief among much of the political Right, who propose that the mix of laissez faire capitalism, minimal government, and low taxes of economic libertarianism combined with faith-based charity is the godly version of socioeconomics best suited for producing a beneficent "opportunity" society (Boyle, 2005; Coulter, 2006; D'Souza, 2007; O'Reilly, 2006; Palin, 2010; Stark, 2008; Warren, 2002). The American majority agrees that "God has granted America a special role in human history" (PRRI, 2010). In the theoconservative worldview, the American Way is the best possible earthly arrangement, blessed by God. American Exceptionalism accordingly stands as the Reaganian "Shining City on the Hill" to the rest of the world. This contradictory belief—contradictory in that the unrestrained free markets the religious Right largely supports and promotes constitute the very Spencerian socioeconomic survival of the fittest, the materialistic socioeconomic "Darwinism," that the same religious Right professes to oppose so strongly that they reject Darwinian evolution—is most common among Protestant economic libertarians and is most extreme within Prosperity Christianity. However, the hypercapitalistic version of the moral-creator socioeconomic hypothesis is rejected by some Protestant traditionalists who fear the secularization effect of the corporate consumer culture (including Warren, 2002 to a certain extent). It is also less accepted within the Catholic Right because church doctrine opposes free-wheeling capital (Benedict XVI, 2009). Many moderate and liberal Christians similarly dismiss the muscular capitalist expression of the moral-creator socioeconomic hypothesis. The rejection of capitalism by some Christians is properly scriptural because the Christian Testaments do not detail the free markets or property rights that theoconservatives contend are biblical, but instead describe the ideal Christian community as entirely socialistic. The general view that religion is a vital social positive is so strongly held in America (Public Religion Research Institute, 2010; Putman & Campbell, 2010) that atheists are the victims of a degree of bigotry as "others" outside the consensus norm so high that they are largely excluded from politics and marriage with theists, as well as the Boy Scouts (Edgell, Gertel, & Hartmann, 2006; Gervais, Shariff, & Norenzayan, 2011; Paul & Zuckerman, 2011; Zuckerman, 2009).

Liberal theists and even some who doubt the existence of deities have often accepted that supernaturalistic religion among the masses can be helpful to keeping those masses in societal line (Armstrong, 2009; Wright, 2008). And some denounce both fundamentalism and assertive atheism as opposing yet equivalent extremes that each augment societal problems, unlike what they consider more benign mainline faiths (Egginton, 2011; Hedges, 2009). However, there are dissenters to the godly-religion socioeconomic hypothesis. This includes some theists who deny that large-scale nonreligiosity is automatically dangerous to societies, but it has become prominent in recent years as a wave of popular antireligious and/or proatheist works have appeared (Bloom, 2008; Dawkins, 2006; Dennett, 2006; Epstein, 2009; Harris, 2006, 2010; Hitchens, 2007; Paul, 2010c; Paul & Zuckerman, 2007, 2011; Shermer, 2006). It is also notable that the populations of some modern first-world countries express substantial skepticism about the beneficial effect of religion upon national societies (International Social Survey Program, 2001; Paul, 2005), and Euroatheists are accepted to the degree that they often openly participate in politics at the highest levels, while overtly religious figures are viewed with skepticism. It has been proposed that highly religious nations are inherently unable to achieve the level of overall societal success, including low levels of lethal violence, enjoyed by the most secular democracies, leading to the secular-democratic socioeconomic hypothesis (Paul, 2009a). The secular-democratic socioeconomic hypothesis generally presumes that a progressive mix of regulated capitalism and government assistance is associated with the best cumulative societal conditions in modern nations on an empirical and theoretical basis, although a few propose that libertarian policies can achieve the same results. With the failure of irreligious communism, the noncapitalistic, nondemocratic version of the secular socioeconomic hypothesis no longer enjoys substantial support.

The question of whether religious faith and practice are good, bad, or neither for national societies should have important implications for international violence. This is because the plausible hypothesis that well-run, pacific countries are less likely to engage in serious violence against one another than are more dysfunctional societies is empirically supported by the absence of major military conflict within and between the relatively well-run first-world democracies compared to the numerous wars ongoing in many second- and third-world countries. It follows that it is important for societies to better understand whether it is mass religion or irreligion that is more likely to produce superior democratic societies. Until recently all sides of the grand debate on these issues and questions were relying largely on anecdote and speculative opinion due to the scarcity of scientific analysis on the problem. Fortunately, this is changing as the technical research discovers how and why differing levels of organized supernaturalism and societal conditions interact with and influence one another. It is therefore becoming increasingly feasible for bodies politic to be sufficiently informed to make decisions concerning the future course of their societies based on sophisticated psychosociological analysis.

It Is All Connected

Although examining the relationships between the societal conditions and religiosity is intrinsically important as well as interesting, it does not occur in a vacuum. A happy scientific and educational side effect of the research is that the information is proving critical to finally answering a number of long-standing, major questions about the psychology, origin, and popularity of religious belief and its absence.

The questions include the following. Is religion always sufficiently popular that it is essentially universal, as is often contended? Is religious supernaturalism deeply set in the human psyche, perhaps through a "God gene" or programmed "God module," like language skills and materialism? Or is it usually a superficial opinion, in which case it cannot be strongly genetically programmed in response to selective forces? Are any of a host of popular proposals centered on internal workings of the human mind—fear of death and eternal torment, fear of societal chaos, the desire for social community and support, the euphoria of worship, memes, or the actual existence of the gods—primary causes of religion? Do higher levels of religious freedom and plurality create a Darwinian competition that boosts overall religiosity? Or is the quality of the human environment the most important factor driving the popularity of theism versus atheism? Specifically, the socioeconomic dysfunctionality hypothesis (a more specific version of the uncertainty hypothesis) states that religion is popular when societies are seriously dysfunctional (presuming that the government is not enforcing antitheist policies). The complementary socioeconomic security hypothesis (a more specific version of the existential security hypothesis) states that the development of a middle-class majority that is sufficiently financially and socially secure due to progressive secular socioeconomic policies results in a serious and measurable decline in religiosity. Also necessary to know is the way the mechanisms, if they exist, by which the level of popular non/religiosity effect societal conditions and vice versa operate—if, for example, lower levels of religiosity are correlated with better societal circumstances, is it because religion contributes to societal ills, or because good conditions suppress the popularity of faith, or both? And how do these factors influence one another? Conversely, determining how and why belief and disbelief in gods effects societal success and vice versa in modern times requires examining the nature, beginnings, and popularity of religious opinion from its remote beginnings up to the present. This, in turn, entails assessing and comparing the popularity of religious opinion and practice over time. Also required is a comprehensive comparison of social and economic conditions in successful democracies. Comparing the popularity of religion to national conditions not only helps answer the question of whether secular or religious societies tend to be more successful, but it reveals whether it is possible for a faith-based or a strongly nontheistic nation to be successful.

Defining and Grading Religiosity

A defect of a number of past analyses is to treat religion too simplistically and without sufficient definition. For example, claims that religion is as universal among humans as language (as per Bloom, 2007) are usually not testable because, while nonwritten language (including signing among the deaf) is well developed in all mentally healthy mature humans, religion can be extremely variable in characteristics and especially in intensity among individuals and societies. If all the world's people were head over heels, God-believing Christians who prayed hourly to their personal God and spent most of each Sabbath in church while avoiding leisure activities, then the globe would be far more religious than if all the world's people were equally convinced God-believing Deists who never prayed to the remote deity and never attended religious services. Actual differences in religious orientation and intensity have real effects. For example, Americans' level of belief in ghosts and haunted houses is nearly as widespread as fundamentalist creationism (Gallup, 2005, 2006a), but the former is not a major cultural ideology and movement that has the profound impact on national politics enjoyed by the creationist cause. Nor is the degree of belief in ghosts commonly cited as a potential causal factor in the level of national societal dysfunction either in academic studies or best-selling popular books, and it is rarely raised in electoral contests. Likewise, Gallup (2005) observes that Americans' belief in paranormal phenomena is almost as high as is the level of belief in god(s),[2] yet the latter has a much greater effect on the culture war. The sociopolitical influence of organized religion compared to other supernaturalistic belief systems is due in part to its organization, combined with the claim that the deity of worship is an all-important moral agent.

For particular research purposes, insufficient attention has, therefore, been paid to the important differences that distinguish the type, depth, and universality of spirituality and religious belief and activity. In this chapter and in my own research, a spiritual person who believes in and worships a god with moral attributes and regularly attends religious services is rated more religious than one who equally believes in a moral god but does not participate in organized worship, who in turn is more religious than a person who does not believe in or worship a god but does have a spiritual belief in amoral ghosts or astrology, and so forth. A set of measures of religious and nonreligious belief and practice are used to compare absolute and relative levels of opinion, as discussed later (and further detailed in Paul, 2009a). In general, religion is defined for the purposes of this chapter and my research to include a supernaturalistic element. Because the emphasis is on popular trends, terms such as "religious" and "secular" are used to characterize and contrast the views of national populations, rather than the configuration of governments. For example, the United States is labeled as religious compared to secular Britain because the population of the latter is less theistic than that of the former, even though the British government is officially Anglican and the American Constitution is secular.

The terminology for disbelievers is often mishandled. All persons are either theists who believe in at least one god, or atheists who lack belief in a god, there is no gap between them. Agnosticism is a philosophical methodology rather than a conclusion, and can apply to both theists and atheists. Because agonistic is not, therefore, a demographic measure of a person's degree of nontheistic belief that sits between atheist and theist, the term cannot be used to describe survey respondents that supposedly lie outside of theism or atheism. Basic atheists are simply all who at least lack belief in a god, core atheists are the subcohort that also reject higher powers, universal spirits, etc.

War, Homicide, Socioeconomic Conditions, and Religion From Prehistory to the Present
Hunter-Gatherers

It is widely assumed that prehistoric hunter-gatherers were and are consistently highly religious in that they are shamanistic animists (Boyer, 2001, 2008; Dennett, 2006; Norenzayan & Shariff, 2008). This assumption is problematic because some hunter-gatherers exhibit minimal religion. The Hadza of east Africa are among the last true hunter-gatherers extant, and their lineage extends back into the Pleistocene (Marlowe, 2002, 2004, 2010; Paul, 2010a). Although they fear death, they do not believe in an afterlife. In Hadza cosmology, the sun is a supernatural entity, but they do not actively worship it or try to influence its actions in their favor. Pre- and posthunting rituals are absent, and other rituals are limited in scope. Shamans are absent, and the tribe proved highly resistant to Christian recruitment. Also unconvertible, Everett (2008) found the Amazonian Piraha to be markedly less religious than devout Christians, especially in their absence of god figures that provide moral guidance.

Although shamanism is widespread in most recent and extant low-technology cultures (Boyer, 2001, 2008; Dennett, 2006; Epson, 2009; Norenzayan & Shariff, 2008), the minimal spirituality of some current examples creates a serious data problem because it cannot be automatically assumed that most prehistoric cultures were highly spiritual, much less religious with a corresponding moral ideology. Perhaps the Hazda are a rare or unique exception to the norm, but it is possible that they are a remnant of what was once a broader or even predominant pattern of low or absent theism. An absence of serious spiritualism may help explain the scarcity of art in many Paleolithic cultures. The existence of prehistoric artifacts, including art and other preserved behaviors such as burials, may be of limited value in assessing ancient spirituality due to the difficulty of interpreting what was actually intended in a given case (Narr, 2008; Pfeiffer, 1985)—that may have varied between individuals as well as cultures—or of demonstrating that the messages being illustrated represented the majority or minority opinion at the time they were created. Assume that the modest majority of persons living circa 40,000 years before present were not highly spiritual, and as a result they had low rates of production of artifacts and preservable behaviors that might record their supernatural thinking. Also, some of their artifacts and behaviors are subject to incorrect interpretation as evidence of supernaturalism. Meanwhile, a large spiritual minority generates numerous artifacts and actions that record their supernaturalism. The paleoarchaeological record could seem to support a much higher level of protoreligion than was actually present. Perhaps in a given region supernaturalism ranged from very high in some groups to low in others living at the same time and general location—perhaps the hill people were one and the valley folks the other, or perhaps some hill people were nonspiritual while others in the same highlands were believers. The data needed to properly assess the level of supernaturalism prior to 10,000 BP may be permanently lost, precluding acquiring the degree of knowledge needed to determine the relationship between the beginnings of religion and violence in prehistoric peoples. What we do know is that the popularity and depth of religiosity in low-technology, nonfarming peoples is highly variable and can be minimal.

Socioeconomic conditions among prehistoric, preagricultural humans included short average life spans of about two decades, with juvenile mortality rates of one half or more (Paul, 2008, 2009b). Medical care was minimal and nonexpert (as it is among modern hunter-gatherers; Marlowe, 2004). Nutrition levels may have been fairly good in many cases due to a varied diet, and prehistoric humans generally had larger brains and bodies than the more domesticated modern humans (Ruff, Trinkaus, & Holliday, 1997). Economic levels were severely impoverished by modern standards, but there were no examples of wealthier cultures, and any elites were not much better off than the rest, so envy levels were probably absent or modest. Lacking long-term food storage capacity, and vulnerable to severe periodic declines in food sources, early human clans may have been under substantial pressure to acquire and protect their resource bases with violent actions when necessary.

Levels of intraspecific violence vary widely among animals and can be quite high. The two primates most closely related to human, bonobos and chimpanzees, exhibit large differences in intraspecific violence. The latter are often violent within a clan and practice what may qualify as low-grade wars between neighboring clans for meat and territory (Goodall, 1986). Direct affirmation of intraspecific violence in early *Homo* species is so far lacking, perhaps because population densities were too low and new territory too abundant for chronic interclan conflicts. There is evidence for cannibalism in *H. neanderthalensis* that seems to represent aggressive violence (Rosas et al., 2006; White, 2001). That only one species of what was once a diverse array of hominins is extant may be because *H. sapiens* wiped out the competition, but nonviolent forms of competition and evolutionary chance may have been more important. Evidence for low-grade warfare in prehistoric *H. sapiens* increases as population density rises and may have included cannibalism (Keeley, 1996; Kelly, 2000; LeBlanc & Register, 2004; Otterbein, 2004; Pinker, 2011; White, 2001). That protohumans and prehistoric humans were well armed with stone, wood, and bone weapons at least in part for hunting purposes may have facilitated intraspecific aggression both within and between cohesive groups (Otterbein, 2004). It cannot be presumed that all nonagricultural groups practiced aggressive warfare, because some modern groups do not, including the Hadza and !Kung bushmen (Keeley, 1996; Marlowe, 2010).

Ancient Agriculture and Civilization

The evidence concerning popular religiosity and violence improves immensely with the advent of agriculture and civilization. Data sources include stone, brick, and concrete religious structures and written records. Organized religion involving extensive priesthoods—generally patriarchal—was often well developed in preindustrial civilizations, but substantial variation in popularity and depth also occurs, to the degree that some societies have had little in the way of theism. The oldest and largest civilization, the Chinese, never developed a major indigenous supernaturalistic faith—there is no great Chinese god figure comparable to Vishnu, Quetzalcotal, Jesus, Allah, Zeus/Jupiter, Thor—or adopted a major foreign deity (Yang, 1970). Although minor deity and ancestor worship was widespread among the masses, a powerful priesthood did not develop, and philosophy has been emphasized over organized supernaturalism, largely nontheistic Confucianism being dominant over recent millennia.[3] Even though China has not been strongly atheistic over most of its history, its level of paranormal faith appears to have been well below that of comparable civilizations more steeped in religion, such as neighboring Hindu India or old Christian Europe. Core Buddhism, Jainism, and Carvakism qualify as atheistic (Geertz & Markussan, 2010; Thrower, 1980), to the extent that the religious nature of the first is often debated.

Also highly inconsistent have been speculations concerning the nature of an afterlife. Relatively few religions have proposed the existence of a blissful paradise for the masses, Christianity and Islam being the major exceptions. Early religions were polytheistic and correspondingly usually tolerant of other religions, although often prone to claiming a degree of superiority. Some polytheistic religions imposed forms of faith-based terror, the Aztecs perhaps being the best example. Starting out small, Abrahamism became increasingly monotheistic and intolerant of other forms of supernaturalism, gained substantial numbers during the later stages of the Roman Empire, and made up nearly half the global population by the industrial era. The inability to survey past civilizations scientifically makes it somewhat difficult to quantify and compare their degree of religious supernaturalism, leading some to question the level of actual devotion of the masses (Stark & Finke, 2000) while others have emphasized how religion pervaded many societies (Summerville, 2002); the level of intensity appears to have varied considerably.

The advent of agriculture and even civilization initially did remarkably little to improve some basic aspects of human lives. Natural juvenile and adult mortality rates did not drop dramatically, and nutrition levels may have declined somewhat due to overreliance on a few agricultural staples in a given society. Famines resulted from mass crop failure, while high population densities facilitated mass mortalities from disease. Most persons continued to live impoverished lives, but income disparity soared as a small elite acquired the extensive wealth made possible by mass organized societies, producing significant envy among the lower class majority. Wealth provided only minor advantages in regard to health and mortality because general medical knowledge remained primitive. Ancients often exhibited prejudice toward other peoples, and practiced primitive forms of eugenics, including extensive infanticide. Slavery was widespread and was made more pernicious still in that a slave state is automatically a terror state because the slaves will leave unless they are kept in perpetual fear of the consequences of seeking their freedom. Slaves are also vulnerable to routine abuse because of their lack of legal and social status. An opportunity was missed during the Roman era, perhaps due to the ready availability of slave labor: Water-driven industries were well developed (Wilson, 2002), and steam power was known but not exploited, precluding the possible early development of modern economics and politics, albeit with considerable cost to the environment and the risk of a mass nuclear conflict.[4]

The ability to assemble large armies and equip them with abundant weaponry facilitated large-scale conflict, and the global tally of wars since the advent of civilization numbers somewhere in the thousands. Some old wars killed off people in numbers similar to those of the worst modern conflicts. Three Chinese rebellions probably dispatched about 30 million each; the Mongol conquests contributed to perhaps half that total.[5] The pagan Greeks invented democracy and the Romans the republic for nonreligious purposes, but both experiments failed without either adopting nonaggressive military policies. According to the Bible, God told the Israelites to wage an optional unprovoked war of conquest involving ethnic cleansing via terror and genocide, although the historical accuracy of these accounts is dubious (Bright, 2000). The Diaspora imposed by the Romans on the Jews has been disastrous in that allowing for normal population growth through reproduction, Jews should be 20 times more numerous than they are (Carroll, 2001). Christians established an exceptionally intolerant theocracy that threatened and used terror and violence to enforce religious conformity for a millennium and a half. This eventually evolved into the Inquisitions that threatened and sometimes employed torture[6] and death by fire against alleged and real dissidents, while practicing violent anti-Semitism. The latter led to the "First Holocaust" associated with the beginning of the First Crusade in which large Jewish populations were exterminated, and soon after that Catholicism dispatched the entire Gnostic Cathar religion with another crusade plus the first stage of the Inquisition. Murphy (2012) explains that the Catholic Inquisition was perversely ground breaking because it was a new, modern systematic institution for gathering intelligence including by violent means on civilians and dispensing punishment. It set the precedent for the modern form of bureaucratic state terror later adopted by more secular governments. The culture of the warrior Christian Knight developed among the elites, their propensity toward violence supposedly being moderated by virtuous chivalry. Christian Europe was afflicted by a long series of wars between Christians of differing sects as well as the effort to oust Muslims from the continent and the Middle East. The latter effort revived the cannibalism that appears to have been fairly common among "less" civilized peoples (Rubenstein, 2008; White, 2001).

Also targeted, largely by Protestants, were women accused of practicing witchcraft. Starting in the 1500s, Catholic and then Protestant nations used various forms of violence to defraud native peoples of their territory and/or resources as they colonized large parts of the planet in the first wave of globalization. The American end of the effort was bolstered by the ideology of Manifest Destiny, which proposed that the seemingly mysterious dying off of Amerindians (actually due to disease, Paul 2009b) was God clearing the way for European conquests, combined with the need to convert the heathens. During and following the religious wars that racked Europe in the 1500s and 1600s, zealous Protestants decamped to northern European colonies in North America in the hope of establishing godly utopias, and apparently priming the future United States for being more religious than the old countries, where the religious strife may have degraded mass interest in religion (Ruiter & Tubergen, 2009). Large-scale violence remained a largely male affair.

Late medieval Christian Europe provides some early sociological data. The people were well armed with blunt and edged weapons; brigands roamed about city, town, and country; disrespect of a man's honor required extreme retribution; and "murderous brawls were.... everyday events" anticipated by ordinary folk as ready sporting events (Beeghley, 2003); one observer noted that "few self respecting gentleman passed through the hot season of youth without having perpetrated a homicide or two." Yearly homicide rates were around 20 to 30 deaths per 100,000, comparable to America's most dangerous inner cities; in some cities, it was around 50. Beeghley (2003) characterizes the Europeans of the time as a "wild bunch." Legal punishments were increasingly draconian and often lethal for relatively minor offenses. When secularization associated with the Renaissance began to take hold, lethal crime began to decline. By Shakespeare's time the homicide rate was down to 15 per 100,000; it was 10 in the 1600s, 5 in the 1700s, and by the 1800s less than 2. There is some evidence that the United States was more religious than western Europe at this time (De Tocqueville, 1835), and that it also suffered from higher levels of homicide.[7] The rise of Western secularism and democracy degraded the position of the churches sufficiently that the Catholic Inquisition had to be abandoned. The initial stages of Western secularization were not associated with a concomitant decline in warfare, which remained frequent, and reached a new height with the first actual world war, the Seven Years' War (aka the French and Indian War).

Modern Times

Early Western secularization was associated with, and may have been encouraged by, the development of scientific methodology that at the time was widely perceived as supporting the existence of a creator (Paley, 1802). The first influences of Deism and then atheism began to be felt in the later 1700s. Deists were instrumental to the American Revolution, which rejected the divine authority of the Anglican British crown. Deists were also an important factor in the French Revolution against the Catholic crown, including The Terror, Robespierre being an ardent Deist. Atheists were also involved in the revolt against the French crown. Matching the death toll of The Terror, the suppression of the Paris Commune was a battle between secularists and Catholics. In the mid-1800s, the advent of evolutionary science (Darwin, 1859) posed the most direct threat to traditional religion yet seen, and some theorized on how the biological system applies to human affairs (Spencer, 1884).[8]

Because mass slavery is incompatible with industrial, corporate-consumer capitalism (Smith, 1776), the scheme rapidly disappeared after the appearance of modern economics. The primary opposition to ending slavery came from southern American Protestants who rejected modern capitalism (Catton, 1960; Freehling, 2007) in favor of a more primitive scheme that continued to concentrate wealth in the hands of slave exploiting elites to the detriment of free laborers and the overall regional economy. The result was the first mass industrial war—in other words, the first modern war pitted secular capitalism against slave-exploiting theism. Because the southern attempt failed, the United States remained large enough to become a superpower.[9] The subsequent southern American development of a brutal apartheid terror state that featured regular, public lynchings (Blackman, 2008; Budiansky 2008; Dray, 2003) was the product of the same Protestant society. In the late 1800s in Germany, extreme wings of Catholicism and Protestantism developed ideologies that combined eugenics, a view of Germans as uber-Aryans, eliminationist anti-Semitism, and extreme nationalism (Hastings, 2010). In some German colonies genocidal acts against African populations presaged those of the 1900s.

Many Christians presumed that the dramatic improvements in literacy and in communication and travel technologies in the 1800s that had contributed to a great expansion of Christianity until it made up a third of the global population in 1900 would continue into the 20th century, inspiring the Watchword movement (Barrett, Kurian, & Johnson, 2001). A contrary prediction based on the appearance of the science-based atheism in the 1800s postulated that religion would suffer serious losses in an age of rationalism.

In the 20th century, the Great War was triggered by Catholic versus Orthodox strife in the Balkans. With Europe still a significantly religious continent, the war was Christian versus Christian, with the monarchs of most of the combatants each claiming divine justification. The beginning of the war was greeted with tremendous enthusiasm by the bulk of religious citizens. In the Ottoman Empire Muslim action against Christians was another major genocide early in the century.

Toward the end of the war, communists seized control of the Russian empire that had already overturned the Orthodox autocracy. Atheistic Soviet governments would pursue policies that resulted in the deaths of tens of millions of citizens while preventing the empire from becoming a capitalist player and power on the global stage, to the benefit of the rising and still theistic United States. A long-term effort to remove the atheistic regime was mounted, led by fascism. The most extreme expression of fascism, Nazism, was established largely by hard-right Catholics as a direct outgrowth of prewar developments (Hastings, 2010). The Party was later predominantly Protestant with significant neopagan/occult influences (Hastings, 2010; Paul, 2003, 2004). In the Balkans Catholic Fascists committed exceptionally brutal genocide against Orthodox Christians (Phayer, 2000, 2008). Whether the Nazis or Soviets killed more civilians in eastern Europe remains unsettled (Snyder, 2010). During the world wars, both sides targeted civilians via artillery and especially bombing. Germany initiated these attacks in Europe during the two wars on a modest scale. The superior industrial capacity of the United Kingdom and the United States allowed them to upscale mass terror bombing to kill about a million civilians; area bombing of cities continued even after this did not force Germany to surrender before an invasion became necessary (Dower, 2010; Friedrich, 2006). America's unique scientific and industrial abilities allowed it to target cities with nuclear weapons just before the war ended. When the Nazi war of conquest proved as impractical as it was, and the right wing attempt to extinguish communism by mass war failed, Soviet Communism took advantage of the power vacuum and occupied east central Europe—albeit without the large-scale genocide practiced by the Nazis and Croat Catholics. Although the nuclear arms race got out of hand to the extent that the existence of much or all of civilization was threatened, the uberweapons made further mass war impractical, so it was replaced by the lower grade Cold War containment strategy. The result was a series of mini-wars, including Korea and Vietnam. The Cold War was theologically intriguing in that both sides experienced significant secularization, complicating attempts to characterize it as a simple atheist versus theist confrontation. Until 1900, the number of basic atheists may have numbered only in the low millions; the new century saw an explosion of this cohort to a billion by 2000 (Fig. 25.1; Barrett et al., 2001; Paul & Zuckerman, 2007). In the Communist Bloc, antitheist policies and indoctrination were operative. In the Western Bloc, the aftereffects of the two most lethal wars of history may have contributed to the greatest spontaneous secularizing of societies in history as the dozen and a half democracies enjoyed unprecedented prosperity from the 1950s to the present (Bruce, 2002; Norris & Inglehart, 2004; Paul, 2009a; Paul & Zuckerman, 2007). The only Western nation to retain a strongly religious position was the United States, where the concept of American Exceptionalism, also known as the American Way, boasted that the combination of popular Christianity and libertarian capitalism is the best possible socioeconomic arrangement. Soviet suppressions of anticommunist movements in neighboring countries occurred until the last and most violent in Afghanistan contributed to the collapse of the economically nonviable Soviet empire. Mao reunited China, but his obtuse policies liquidated tens of millions as they held back economic development by 30 years, preventing the colossal country from becoming the largest economy by the end of the 1900s—Mao's Sinofailure enormously boosted the fortunes of the United States from the 1970s to today. Having adopted autocratic capitalism circa 1980, China has become a fast-growing economic power, as has democratic and very theistic India after abandoning overly socialistic policies. Cambodian Communism proved to be genocidal; the North Korean variant—which includes considerable supernaturalism—is incompetent to the point of being lethal on a mass basis. The Marxist Tamil Tiger rebels initiated suicide bombing as an anticivilian terror tactic on a regional basis, although this may have involved some level of theism.[10] Currently neither Fascism nor Communism is a major contributor to global violence, although they cause local problems in some places.

Also developing in the Cold War era was the faith-based strife in the Middle East between Muslims and Jews along with their Western allies. With the socioeconomic failure of communism, the Cold War terminated, dramatically reducing but not eliminating the possibility of a nuclear catastrophe. The end of the Cold War contradicted President

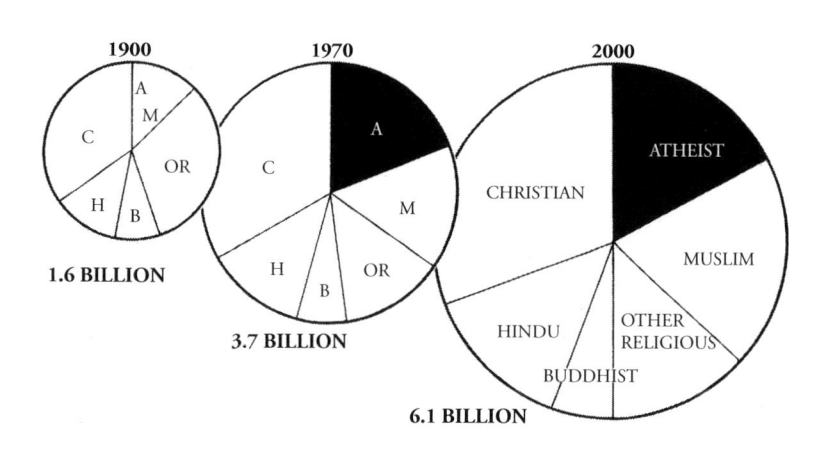

Figure 25.1 Changing distribution of religions and irreligion within the global population. (Data from Barrett et al., 2001.)

Reagan's contention that the ungodly Communist bloc was the focus of evil in the world, or that its elimination would result in a Fukuyama (1992) end of history in favor of liberal democracy and capitalism. The decline of de facto empires, and the rise of India and especially China which lack a grand global mission, has and is facilitating global unrest (Kaplan, 2010), most of it in the form of religious conflicts. An early bout was the Balkans conflict of the 1990s. The 21st-century War on Terror involves Western Christians, Jews, and seculars along with moderate Muslims against militant Islam, which has developed suicide terrorism into a global institution, while parts of Africa are wracked by a regional conflict between Christians, Muslims, and animists. In the United States the greatest militant threat stems from right-wing theists, most of Christian influence, who see progressivism as against the will of their creator.

A notable and analytically important feature of the largely secular prosperous democracies is their friendly relations and corresponding lack of tendency to engage in war among themselves.[11] Of these countries, the relatively religious United States is the most prone to go to war with less developed nations, including when not immediately threatened. However, even the advanced democracies have not been able to eliminate organized crime, which is expanding in much of the underdeveloped world.

From a psychosociological perspective, the later 20th and now the 21st centuries are data goldmines in terms of examining levels of religiosity and their relationship to socioeconomic conditions, because of the unprecedented survey and statistical information that is being gathered and recorded, especially in the more developed nations. For example, Google statistics show that the frequency of the use of the word "God" in books declined precipitously after the early 1800s and has held steady at a small fraction of the peak in recent decades (Jean-Baptiste et al., 2010). Until the Great War, the religious Right dominated mainstream Western culture, imposing strict social rules based on conservative doctrines. But Barrett et al. (2001) observe that after 1900:

> massive defections from Christianity...subsequently took place in Western Europe due to secularism..., & in the Americas due to materialism...The number of nonreligionists...throughout the 20th century has skyrocketed from 3.2 million in 1900, to 697 million in 1970, and on to 918 million in AD 2000...Equally startling has been the meteoric growth of secularism....Two immense quasi-religious systems have emerged at the expense of the world's religions: agnosticism...., & atheism...From a miniscule presence in 1900, a mere 0.2% of the globe, these systems...are today expanding at the extraordinary rate of 8.5 million new converts each year, and are likely to reach one billion adherents soon. A large percentage of their members are the children, grandchildren or the great-great-grandchildren of persons who in their lifetimes were practicing Christians.

No religious philosophy has enjoyed similar expansion. Buddhism has suffered serious losses, as have a host of traditional polytheistic sects. Despite the rapid population growth of India, Hinduism has barely edged up and remains largely limited to the subcontinent. Assorted New Age movements are enjoying limited success. Christianity has been fixed at a third of the global population since 1900. Islam has made some major gains and now stands at nearly a quarter of the world, but the growth has mainly been via rapid reproduction, and despite significant migration it is predominantly a belief of an eastern hemisphere zone lying above the equator. Irreligion alone has proven able to make big gains by spontaneous conversion, despite the low fecundity of nontheists.

The countries in which religion has lost the greatest ground due to spontaneous conversion are first-world democracies. In quantitative terms, the extent of the losses has been well documented (see Bruce, 2002; Norris & Inglehart, 2004; Paul, 2009a, 2010b; Paul & Zuckerman, 2007; Zuckerman, 2008, 2009; contrary to Stark & Finke, 2000 and Stark, 2008); basic atheists constitute large minorities to strong majorities, and core atheists range up to a third of the population (Times/Harris, 2006), while levels of religious practice are very low in the same countries (Fig. 25.2a,b). In some Western nations, active Christians are now small minorities, and the religious Right is usually a fringe movement. The failure of alternative forms of supernaturalism to replace more than a fraction of the losses in Christian devotion in Europe (Bruce, 2002), and the reduction in popular religion in Japan, show that the first-world religious decline is general rather than specific to Christianity. The loss of supernaturalistic belief, including the existence of an afterlife, and activity has often proceeded swiftly (see Fig. 4.3 in Norris & Inglehart, 2004). Spain was

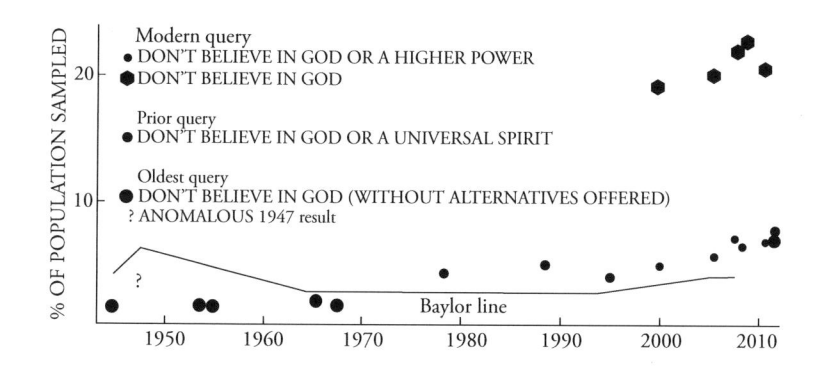

Figure 25.2 Relationships of socio-economic factors relative to overall religiosity in first-world nations. (Plots from Paul, 2009a.)

Modern query
● DON'T BELIEVE IN GOD OR A HIGHER POWER
● DON'T BELIEVE IN GOD

Prior query
● DON'T BELIEVE IN GOD OR A UNIVERSAL SPIRIT

Oldest query
● DON'T BELIEVE IN GOD (WITHOUT ALTERNATIVES OFFERED)
? ANOMALOUS 1947 result

still a Catholic-dominated Fascistic state the same year that the then-new *Saturday Night Live* parodied the death of Franco. Spain is now a secularized democracy so low in religiosity that most churches are centuries old and have reduced levels of attendance, and homosexuals can marry and divorce. Ireland saw a similarly dramatic shift from Catholic dominance to considerable secularization over the same period. Christians are in danger of becoming smaller minorities than Muslims in a few western European countries. Currently Muslims make up only a few percent of the population of the region (Pew Research, 2011). Substantial majorities, up to 8 in 10, support evolutionary science in first-world countries, aside from the United States. It is sociologically significant that the rapid loss of western European, Canadian, and Australian piety occurred without a major culture war in which atheistic and theistic organizations contended with one another for the adherence of the population. Secularization occurred with remarkably little sociopolitical fuss.

Even though the United States remains the most theistic Western democracy, and the most theoconservative with creationism remaining popular, it is not nearly as pious as it used to be—or seems to many to be. Presumably because of the previously noted high levels of bigotry directed against nontheists, Americans significantly overreport their religiosity while understating their lack of belief and worship (Brenner, 2011; Marler & Hadaway, 1999; Taylor, 2003). Even without taking this phenomenon into account, America scores as only half as religious as the most pious nations (Pew Research, 2002; Putman & Campbell, 2010; World Values Survey, 2007), and just half of Americans claim to believe absolutely in a personal God (Pew Research, 2008); these figures may require some adjustment downward. Nominal Christians have slipped from nearly 95% of the population to 75% (Smith & Kim, 2004). But only two-thirds of those are absolute believers when the Pew (2008) calculation on absolute believers is factored in, and only half of those are regular church goers, so about a quarter of Americans are dedicated church-going Christians, if that. Native Catholics are becoming a smaller portion of the population, only Hispanic immigration keeps the overall church percentage steady (Kosmin & Keysar, 2009; Smith & Kim, 2004). Protestants are about to lose their historic majority status (Kosmin & Keysar, 2009; Smith & Kim, 2004). Rigorous analysis finds that only a fifth to a quarter of Americans attend Sunday services on a frequent basis (Brenner, 2011; Marler & Hadaway, 1999), and church attendance has persistently declined (Gruber & Hungerman, 2006; Smith & Kim, 2004; contrary to Stark & Finke, 2000) with congregation size shrinking by a fifth in the last decade according to Rozen (2011) as the age of attendees rises; so the growth of megachurches represents a consolidation of less than a tenth of church goers, rather than a major expansion of religious activity. A large body of data refutes the common impression that the religious Right is thriving as the mainline churches shrink (Paul & Zuckerman, 2007; Putman & Campbell, 2010; Rozen, 2011). Fast-reproducing Bible literalists have decreased from 40% to 30% since 1980 (Gallup, 2006a), undermining the foundation of Genesis creationism, which may be starting to slip in popularity (Gallup, 2011). Fecund Southern Baptists are in gradual decline because they are baptizing new members no faster than in the 1950s when the nation's population was half its current size (Rainer, 2005); the church is especially losing ground among youth. Only a few percent of Americans live strict Bible-based lifestyles, and the broader religious Right has been driven into a large minority parallel culture perpetually unable to redominate the mainstream society, despite vigorous efforts to do so.

The increasing irreligiosity of American youth is especially informative. Commonly disregarding their elder's intolerance against nontheists, the number of nonreligious has doubled among 18–29-year-olds over just 20 years (Putman & Campbell, 2010). A new Lifeway Christian Research poll finds that just two-thirds of the twenty-something generation considers themselves Christian; and even that is inflated because only 15% qualify as deeply committed to the creed, and the majority are "Christian-light" who have little interest in the actual doctrines or practices. The decreased piety of succeeding generations via conversion has been overcoming the more rapid reproduction of religious couples. As a given generation ages, its level of religious practice rises, but that succeeding generations are less faith focused than the previous one indicates that America is rapidly secularizing (contrary to Stark, 2008), and the progressive generational increase in secularism is being recorded in the general population statistics. Multiple surveys agree that the nonreligious have been rapidly expanding in recent decades, and the "no response" to Gallup questions on God belief shows that nonbelievers have quadrupled since the 1960s, easily outpacing the rise of the fast-breeding Mormons (Fig. 25.3). Gallup and Harris (Taylor, 2003; Times/Harris, 2006) polls indicate that a fifth of Americans qualify as basic atheists, core atheists are in the high single digits.[12] The slow breeders who think evolution and not God created humans have been edging up (Gallup, 2011). Thirty years ago outnumbered by Bible literalists four to one, skeptics of the Bible have risen so rapidly that the two categories are now nearly equal, with the doubters on a trajectory to become the larger group (Gallup, 2006a). America is currently following the other prosperous democracies as it rapidly secularizes. This is occurring in the context of an intense culture war in which the theoconservative minority has mounted an intense theopolitical countercampaign in reaction to secularization. To do so, the religious Right has formed an alliance with corporate interests, although as noted later this has proved to be a double-edged sword. Who has been dominating the culture in America and the rest of the West is measured by the rise of tolerance for nontraditional lifestyles, from the acceptance of sexual activity outside of marriage (Finer, 2007) to dramatic improvement in the social status of gays.

Although the data from less developed nations are of somewhat lesser quality than for most prosperous democracies, all these data are informative (Paul & Zuckerman, 2007). The most religious nations are Islamic, with some Christian nations and Hindu also scoring as highly religious (Pew Research, 2002). Some Catholic countries of the Americas have seen serious losses in religiosity, including acceptance of contraception to the degree that fertility rates have lowered dramatically. Claims of major gains in religiosity in formerly or less Communist nations are exaggerated, and in some cases interest in the gods remains low or has declined. Largely Islamic Turkey is moderately religious, although fundamentalism may be on the rise. The same may be true for Christianity in South Korea, which has a large irreligious population. The one area in which religion has made recent gains is in the area of reactionary fundamentalism (Kaufmann, 2010; Longman, 2006; Paul & Zuckerman, 2007; Putman & Campbell 2010; Shah & Toft, 2006). This is true among all three primary sects of Abrahamism as well as Hinduism. It is especially true in a number of underdeveloped regions, and in Israel.

The data for societal and economic conditions in first-world nations range from excellent to good; for less developed countries these data vary from excellent to not available. For example, nonlethal crime statistics are not sufficiently reliable for cross-national comparisons even between the prosperous democracies because of inconsistencies in reporting, recording, and definition (Barclay & Taveres, 2002; Beeghley, 2003; Paul, 2005, 2009a, 2010b). Only homicide is sufficiently reliably recorded because it is not self-reported and involves the counting of bodies after forensic investigation. Even in developed nations, levels of sexually transmitted diseases are only approximately known; in underdeveloped countries such statistics are less reliable, if they exist at all.

The most comprehensive comparison to date of socioeconomic conditions in the most successful prosperous democracies is the Successful Societies Scale (SSS; Fig. 25.2a,c) presented by Paul (2009a, 2010b, which include an extended justification and sourcing of the over two dozen factors used to construct the SSS, data tables and plots, plus a description of the method of scoring the results; at the same time, Wilkinson and Picket [2009] presented the second most comprehensive comparison up to that time). Factors compared between first-world countries include homicide, incarceration, juvenile mortality, life span, adolescent and all-age gonorrhea

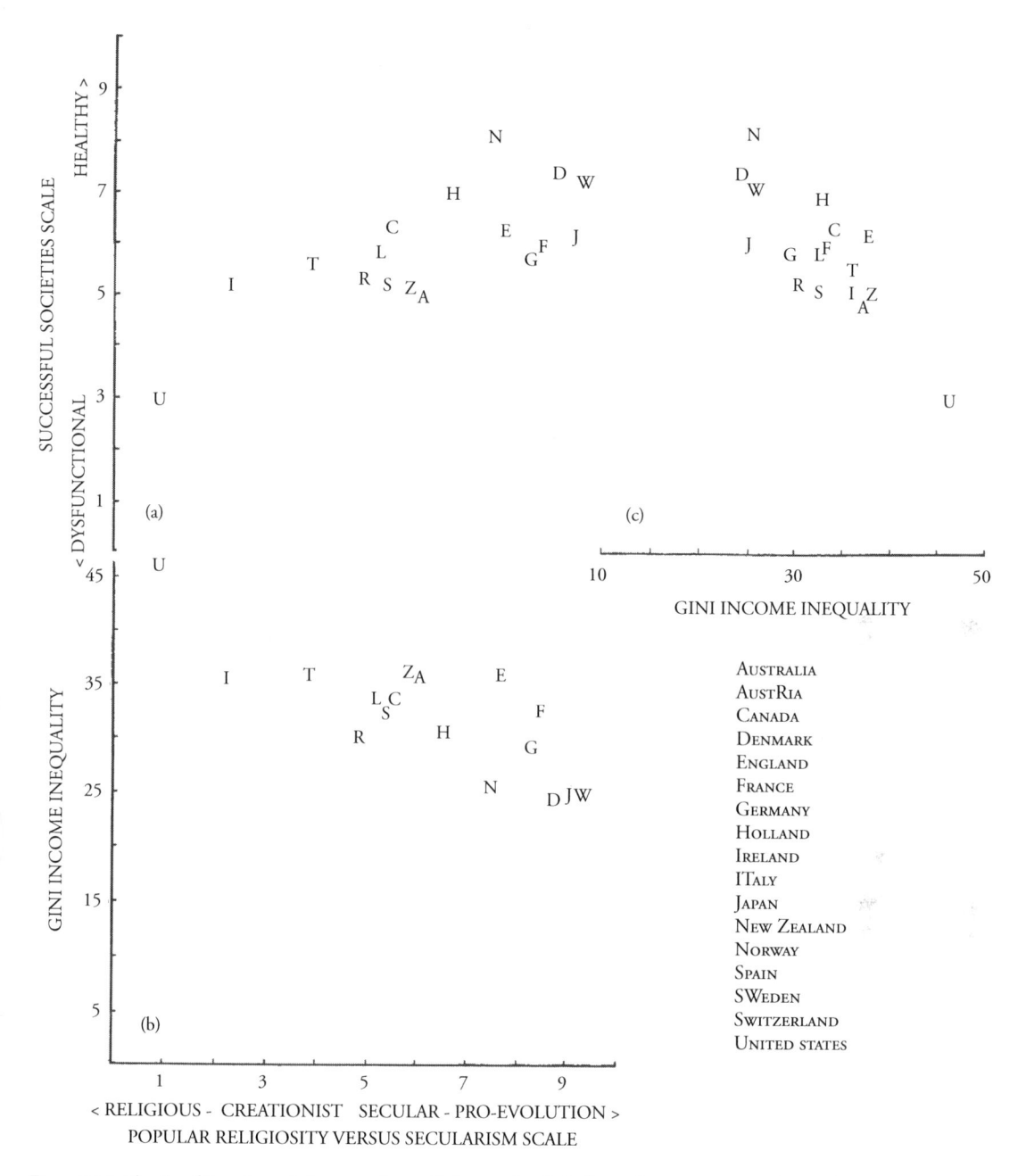

Figure 25.3 The rise of American atheism according to Gallup results. Only the modern query captures basic atheists who at least lack belief in any god. Although the two older queries captured only core atheists who also lack belief in higher powers, universal spirits, etc., they provide the best longitudinal tracking data that is available for the U.S. Baylor line is from Stark (2008) in which initial two Gallup values are inflated by including nonrespondents.

and syphilis infections, adolescent abortion, adolescent births, youth and all-age suicide, fertility, child well-being, marriage, marriage duration, divorce, life satisfaction, mental illness, alcohol and illicit drug consumption, corruption, trust, education performance, per capita income, income disparity, poverty, employment, social mobility, work hours, and resource exploitation base. These factors individually and collectively are correlated with levels of mass opinion on non/religiosity as measured by absolute belief in a supernatural creator deity (a superior measure of religious devotion than general belief in God because the latter includes partial doubters), Bible literalism (a proxy for the conservatism of mass faith), frequency of attendance at religious services and frequency of prayer as assessments

PAUL | 447

of religious activity, belief in an afterlife, percentage of atheists, and acceptance of human descent from animals—a converse measure of creationist opinion (Fig. 25.2a,b). Also compared are levels of immigration and ethnic diversity.

Homicide rates remain far lower in the more secular prosperous democracies than the United States, which is an outlier in this regard, despite a significant decline in the last two decades. Lethal violence is especially prevalent in urban America, particularly among minorities, and is also higher in more religious regions of the nation. With 1 in 500 deaths attributable to murder, the lowest homicides rates seen in the secular democracies may represent the minimal levels achievable in human societies. The available data indicate that nonlethal crime is often common in the nations examined, with America being a high crime nation. Zuckerman (2008) notes that the modest crime rates in some secular democracies are achieved with minimal police presence, and recent declines in American murder appear to be more dependent upon the application of effective secular methods of addressing the problem (Kennedy, 2011; Pinker, 2011) than upon the popularity of theism. Incarceration has soared in the United States to the degree that no other country, even China, has more prisoners in absolute terms, and America is about a dozen times higher than the Western norm in proportional rates. The United States is again a statistical outlier, including in its draconian punishments (Zuckerman, 2008). The US prisoner population is strongly skewed toward minorities, to the degree that the male population of inner cities has been seriously impacted. Although all first-world countries have low juvenile mortality compared to historical norms, an almost two-fold variation remains, with higher rates correlating strongly with greater popular religiosity, the lowest losses being in the most secular nations sampled, while they are the highest in the most religious sections of the United States. All advanced nations enjoy long cumulative life spans, but America now has the shortest within the group and performs even worse in time lived in good health (Muenning & Glied, 2010). The correlation between lower religiosity and longer life span is significant but not tight. The United States is losing ground in regard to this factor, and life spans are actually decreasing in regions of the Bible Belt, where lives are already on the short side. No other advanced nation is experiencing regional reductions in life span (Ezzati et al., 2008). Americans used to be exceptionally tall, but they have lost substantial ground relative to other prosperous democracies and are now below the secular maximum as health levels slip relative to the other countries (Komlos & Lauderdale, 2007). Suicide rates are disturbingly high in all nations examined; correlations with religiosity are not highly significant, and the United States and Scandinavian countries are not atypical.

Regarding alcohol consumption, marriages, fertility, life satisfaction, and employment, large correlations between lesser religiosity and better conditions do not exist, and/or the United States performs typically or well. The United States used to score typically in corruption, but revelations of the massive financial manipulations that are primarily responsible for the Great Recession have lowered its ranking to near the bottom of Western nations (Transparency International, 2010), and the nation is mediocre when it comes to trust (Uslaner, 2002). Moderate to large correlations between lesser religiosity and better conditions do exist regarding abortion, sexually transmitted disease (STD) infections, teen pregnancy outside of marriage, and resource exploitation. The United States performs poorly in the just-listed factors, often being the worst off, sometimes by very large degrees. America is also seriously dysfunctional in high work hours, mental illness (Bijl et al., 2003; Friedli, 2009), illicit drug use (Degenhardt et al., 2008), child well-being (Pickett & Wilkinson, 2007), overall education performance (United Nations [UN], 2008), and gender equality (UN, 2009).

In the cumulative SSS, 0 is the lowest possible score among the nations sampled, 10 the highest (Paul, 2009a, 2010b). The observed variation is from below 3 to 8, with a very strong statistical correlation between greater atheism and superior socioeconomic conditions (Fig. 25.2a,c; Paul, 2009a). The highest scoring countries are all among the most secular; the United States has the lowest overall score. Fundamentalist (including creationist), moderate and liberal theism all correlate similarly with inferior circumstances, atheism (including acceptance of evolution) with better environments (Fig. 25.4; Paul, 2009a, 2012). Other cross-national comparisons—including the Happy Planet Index and Human Development Report—have produced broadly similar rankings of socioeconomic dysfunction, with the United States not scoring particularly well (Barber, 2011; Gill & Lundsgaarde 2004; Marks, Abdallah, Sims, & Thompson, 2006; Norris & Inglehart, 2004; Rees, 2009; UN, 2008, Verweij et al., 1997; Wilkinson & Picket, 2009; Zuckerman, 2008). The United States is the most second-world-like nation of the first-world countries

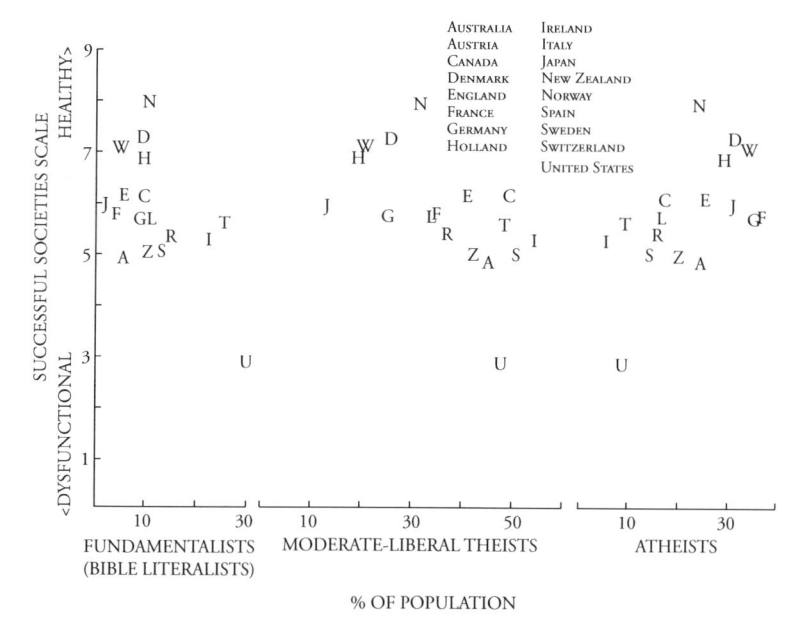

Figure 25.4 Relationships of fundamentalism (as measured by Bible literalism, moderate-liberal theism (as measured by belief in god less Bible literalism), and atheism relative to Successful Societies Scale in first-world nations. (Plots in part from Paul, 2009a.)

socioeconomically and religiously, to the degree that its first-world status is marginal in many regards and may be at risk. In recent years, the World Economic Forum has downgraded the United States from its long-standing first-place status in global economic competitiveness, , ranking some other democracies, including Sweden, Finland and Switzerland, as more competitive (World Economic Forum, 2012), and Germany's economy appears to be the strongest overall (Geoghegan, 2010); America is no longer the leading "opportunity society" because it is below average in upward income mobility, is no longer the leading generator of small businesses or innovation, is investing an unusually small portion of its wealth in infrastructure, has lost more of its industrial base than most other prosperous democracies, and has higher national debt and a lower credit rating than a number of more fiscally disciplined secular nations (Blanden, Gregg, & Machin, 2005; Geoghegan, 2010; Vastag, 2011). Levels of lethal and nonlethal crime have generally improved as the United States secularizes. So have STD rates and youth pregnancy rates, but not to the same extent as the more secular democracies. Immigration levels and population diversity do not correlate significantly with levels of socioeconomic dysfunction, including lethal crime, in part because the United States is no longer exceptional regarding these factors (Fearon, 2003; Geoghegan, 2010; Paul, 2009a).[13] Nor is there a significant correlation between per capita income and religiosity in the most prosperous countries, although the United States ranks high in this factor. Lower income disparity and lower poverty intensity correlate strongly with both lesser religiosity and with superior societal conditions, including deadly malfeasance (Fig. 25.2c). Levels of media violence are not a critical factor because the American model has spread across the prosperous democracies (Tomlinson, 1991). Muenning and Glied (2010) found that higher rates of homicide, accidents, obesity, and smoking do not adequately account for the inferior health outcomes of Americans. The relatively poor health of Americans is all the more perturbing since the nation spends much more per person on health care (Anderson, Frogner, Johns, & Reinhardt, 2006; Banks, Marmot, & Smith, 2006; Kawachi & Kennedy, 2002; Muenning & Gleid, 2010; Paul, 2009c; Reid, 2009; Schoen et al., 2005).

The first-world pattern also applies within the United States. Social pathologies tend to be elevated to a lesser or greater degree within those regions and populations—such as the Bible Belt and inner cities—of the United States that exhibit higher levels of theism (Aral & Holmes, 1996; Barna, 2004; Beeghley, 2003; Delamontagne, 2010; Doyle, 2000, 2002; Edelman, 2009; Paul, 2005; Zuckerman, 2008; Kennedy, 2011).

The good conditions enjoyed by the citizens of irreligious first-world countries appear contrary to the widespread hypothesis that individuals within a given first-world nation benefit from participating in religious worship and/or activities (as per Powell, Shahabi, & Thoresen, 2003; Brooks, 2006; Inzlicht, McGregor, Hirsh, & Nash, 2009; Norenzayan & Shariff, 2008; Norris & Inglehart, 2004), leading to an apparent sociological paradox (Bloom, 2008; Shermer, 2006). But the paradox may not be real. Galen and Kloet's (2011) statistical reanalysis indicates that committed atheists and theists share similar levels of quality of life—it is theistic fence sitters that appear to be doing less well—and other studies cast doubt on the hypothesis that the less religious are less well off (Blumenthal et al., 2007; Chida, Steptoe, & Powell, 2009; Keister, 2008; Paul, 2008; Powell et al., 2003; Putman & Campbell, 2010)[14]; this is compatible with the tendency of religiosity to decline with increasing financial and educational status (Gallup, 2006b).[15]

The Total Toll

The total human population has amounted to some 100 billion (Haub, 1995/2004). About half of those born have died as infants and children, and the vast majority of premature natural deaths are attributable to disease (Paul, 2009b). Domestic infanticide may have resulted in the culling of about one tenth of the population (Pinker, 2011), in which case it is by far the most widespread form of human death via human action. Post infant homicide is responsible for perhaps half a percent of all deaths, or some half a billion over history. The basic death toll from wars and genocides over human existence is in the area of 400 million,[16] so about one-third of a percent of deaths are attributable to war and genocide. Of the historical total, about a third, perhaps 150 million (at least two thirds in the two super wars) occurred in the 1900s, a century in which 10 billion lived, resulting in a war-induced mortality rate of about 1.5%. Losses due to famines resulting from political repression or ideology probably exceed 50 million, and deaths attributable to colonization are perhaps 100 million. The total number of deaths due to war and especially homicide is therefore in the area of 10 billion, almost all of that figure being newborns. Older humans lost to human action are about 1 billion, or 1 in 100. The figures, especially the latter, are too low to seriously impact the global population over time—war is therefore not a form of population control—although the wastage can effect more local populations. To dramatically increase the percentage of deaths stemming from deliberate human action requires a large-scale nuclear war or the intentional release of an easily transmitted pathogen with a high mortality level and no ready means of medical defense. Pinker (2011) details how relative rates of lethal violence have tended to decline over history.

The Male Factor

Overt physical violence has been predominantly a male activity, and noncombatant victims of violence have often been women, including via rape. Whether this strong trend is largely cultural or genetic-hormonal in nature remains a matter of controversy, and some matriarchal societies, including Polynesian and Amerindian, have been militaristic (Buss, 2005; Coie & Stucky, 1997; Goldstein, 2001). The major exception to the trend is infanticide, which often involves the actions of the mother, albeit in some but not all cases under the pressure of males.

Analysis
The Godly American Way: Not All It's Cracked Up To Be

The evidence indicates that at the first-world level, mixed economies that modulate capitalism with progressive socialistic policies are producing superior overall national circumstances compared to the more laissez faire capitalism and private charity favored in the United States (Delamontagne, 2010; Geoghegan, 2010; Harris, 2006, 2010; Kawachi & Kennedy, 2002; Marmot, 2004; Reid, 2004, 2009; Sapolsky, 2005; Wilkinson & Picket, 2009; Zuckerman, 2008). America is performing so poorly in many regards despite its immense wealth that it should be a matter of grave national concern—rather than the overglorification of the American Way by its promoters.

Because highly secular democracies are significantly and regularly outperforming the more theistic ones, all versions of the godly-religion socioeconomic hypothesis are refuted, while the secular-democratic socioeconomic hypothesis is strongly supported. These conclusions are in general accord with an expanding body of research (Barber, 2011; Gill & Lundsgaarde, 2004; Norris & Inglehart, 2004; Paul, 2005, 2009a, 2010b; Rees, 2009; Ruiter & Tubergen, 2009; Verweij et al., 1997; Zuckerman, 2008, 2009). The examinations of a broad range of first-, second-, and third-world nations in some of the aforementioned studies generally falsify the godly-religion socioeconomic hypothesis. A study to the contrary that utilizes a broad range of socioeconomic factors has yet to emerge, despite the widespread promulgation of the godly-religion socioeconomic hypothesis. The next task is to uncover the factors that are producing the real world results.

The Nonuniversality and Noninternal Nature of Popular Religiosity

A remarkable facet of investigating the origins and evolution of human violence and religion is that critical data are, it turns out, found among the least supernaturalistic of both the least and most advanced current societies. The failure of strong supernaturalism to appear among some hunter-gatherers, and the broad and rapid loss of popular religiosity among a number of highly developed democracies in the absence of a concerted antitheist campaign, disproves the thesis that religion is universal among humans. So does the significant variation of religious intensity in preindustrial civilizations. Far more universal is basic materialism in terms of the interest in material goods and services. Materialism is not consistently developed among individuals and groups, but it is always significant.[17] The specialized opposable thumbs of humans, dedication of large areas of the brain to manipulating the environment, and the inability of humans to survive and thrive without tools indicate that materialism is strongly genetically programmed and inherent to humans (Paul, 2009a). Language is truly universal in that all mentally capable adults have excellent, complex speaking or signing skills, the language of all peoples being roughly comparable in sophistication. The uniquely configured human vocal tract, dedication of large areas of the brain to language, the rapid ease with which it is learned by children, and the inability to run any level of human society without well-developed language abilities indicate that language is strongly genetically programmed and correspondingly integral to the human brain and condition (Deacon, 1998; Pinker, 1994; although Prinze [2010] disagrees). Writing, in contrast, is non-universal, being totally absent until a few millennia ago and still lacking among a significant number of individuals and groups. Nor is art entirely universal, being minimal in some individuals and variable in its presence across societies. The ability of societies to exist without art or especially writing indicates they are not genetically programmed but instead that they are secondary effects of the presence of opposable thumbs and high-level mental capacity, including imagination.

Because religion is highly variable, in the manner of art and writing, and is not necessary for the existence of human societies, religiosity is correspondingly optional, like writing and art. Because supernaturalism is variable and elective rather than universal, there cannot be a "God gene" in that religiosity cannot be strongly genetically programmed—religion is therefore no more genetically programmed than writing and art. So there cannot be a specialized "God module" in the brain, and religion is not inherent to the human psyche. The lack of a strong genetic component means that selective pressures could not have been a primary force behind the appearance and development of religion—in other words, religiosity did not evolve in order to improve social cohesion in a manner that imparted a reproductive advantage to group members (contra the position taken in Voland and Schiefenhovel, 2009). This conclusion is reinforced by the absence of strong spirituality in the Hadza, who have survived for a tremendous stretch of time apparently without social cohesion via religion, and whose low religiosity may have been more widespread among Paleolithic peoples. It follows that religious devotion is a by-product of the imaginative human mind, broadly similar to writing and art.

The nonuniversality of religion also rules out other factors as primary causes. Fear of death and hell in preference for a pleasant afterlife is not a critical motivator in most persons (contra Becker, 1998) in view of the lack of belief in an afterlife in the Hadza and hundreds of millions of first worlders (Paul, 2009a; Zuckerman, 2008).[18,19] The same principle applies to a desire for social community and support, a fear of societal chaos sans a godly population, a means to acquire greater power, childhood gullibility continuing into adulthood, memes that spread religious ideas like viruses, and so forth. At most these can be secondary causes of religiosity or play roles in the Darwinian societal competition between sects to recruit and retain those who are already religious largely for other reasons. The perfect afterlife promised to all adherents by Christianity and Islam may help explain their massive displacement of other faiths. Nor is the theistic speculation that people believe in the transcendent because the latter is real and it is therefore normal to connect with the transcendent supported by the nonuniversality of religion, so religion is natural in origin (as per Bloom, 2007) rather than supernatural. An additional implication of the nonuniversality, and frequently easy loss, of religiosity is that in most persons it is not a deeply set worldview but is a more superficial opinion subject to rapid change. This does not mean that all persons whose religiosity is superficial will admit it; they may ardently defend their faith-based opinions. But humans are prone to overdefending their commitment to a given opinion even if it is fundamentally superficial; consider how a sports fan can be fanatical about a local team until the fan relocates and supports another with equal ardor. So although religious opinion is frequently obstinate, it is also often fragile in the same persons.

Why Western Religion Is on Life Support
THE SOCIOECONOMIC SECURITY FACTOR

The absence of a fundamental internal mental root of serious religious supernaturalism indicates that the essential cause must be environmental. The relatively low religiosity present in some hunter-gatherers and some preindustrial civilizations establishes that dysfunctional socioeconomic conditions do not necessarily result in high levels of supernaturalism (Paul, 2010a; contra Paul, 2009a). However, a growing body of research is supporting the uncertainty hypothesis (Malinowski, 1954) that the insecurity that stems from a seriously defective social and especially economic environment is necessary for religion to be highly popular on empirical and theoretical grounds (Barber, 2011; Gill & Lundsgaarde, 2004; Norris & Inglehart, 2004; Paul, 2009a, 2010b; Rees, 2009; Verweij et al., 1997; Zuckerman, 2008). Higher levels of prosperity tend to be associated with lower levels of religiosity on both an individual and national basis (Gallup, 2006b; Norris & Inglehart, 2004; Pew Research, 2002), but matters cannot be so simple since the United States is a partial outlier due to its unusual combination of wealth and religiosity. The strong correlation between religiosity on the one hand and income disparity and the cumulative societal conditions measured by the SSS (Fig. 25.2a-c) suggests these factors are influencing one another. All the more so since the most religious and dysfunctional first-world country has the most socioeconomically Darwinistic arrangement, including the unique absence of universal health care. The discussion in the subsequent three paragraphs stems from the information and analysis found in the following works (American Academy of Pediatrics, 1998, 2000; Anderson et al., 2006; Banks et al., 2006; Barber, 2011; Beeghley, 2003; Delamontagne, 2010; Finer, 2007; Geoghegan, 2010; Gill & Lundsgaarde, 2004; Himmelstein, Warren, Thorne, & Wollhander, 2005; Kawachi & Kennedy, 2002; Lane, 1997; Marmot, 2004; Muenning & Gleid, 2010; Neapolitan, 1997; Norris & Inglehart, 2004; Paul, 2009a, 2009c, 2010b; Paul & Zuckerman, 2007; Pratt & Godsey, 2003; Rees, 2009; Reid, 2004, 2009; Rosenbaum, 2009; Ruiter & Tubergen, 2009; Sapolsky, 2005; Schoen et al., 2005; Trenholm, 2007; Verweij et al., 1997; Wellings et al., 2006; Wilkinson & Picket, 2009; Winkleby, Cubbin, & Ahn, 2006; Zimring & Hawkins, 1999; Zuckerman, 2008).

The socioeconomic security hypothesis explains that national societies that provide a prosperous middle-class majority with a high level of social and especially economic security encourage the propensity of increasing numbers of individuals to lose interest in the gods with increasing personal security and wealth. In all but one first-world countries, the great majority of a population enjoys the modern comforts and advantages of life typical of advanced democracies, and their middle class status is strongly protected by government policies that minimize the possibility that a given person or family will suffer financial ruin and physical endangerment. The latter threat is also alleviated by anticorporal punishment policies, antibullying policies, handgun control policies, and rehabilitative incarceration on a modest scale. Workers' leisure and family time are protected, and child care support is extensive. Universal health care ensures all given citizen that they and their loved ones will receive adequate medical care regardless of their personal finances, while protecting the latter. As a result of the high level of earthly comfort and security, a large portion or majority of the population no longer has sufficient interest in seeking the aid and protection of supernatural deities in their daily lives to continue to worship or believe in them. The reduction in interest in religion reduces attendance at religious ceremonies, further reducing the influence of the religious industry upon individuals, resulting in additional decreases in religious activity and opinion. The partial replacement of faith-based charitable institutions with government agencies further reduces the outreach of religious organizations into the general public.

Because religious opinion is usually casual rather than deeply set in most minds, the consistent outcome is a downward spiral, often rapid, of theism. This superficiality of opinion means that the loss and absence of religious opinion is in itself typically superficial, in that most do not drop supernaturalistic thinking because they have carefully considered and weighed the options, but because the circumstances of their daily lives have improved to the degree that they no longer have much interest in theism. The process therefore does not require significant promotion by evangelically antitheistic organizations that have remained very small—much smaller than organized religion—even in the most atheistic democracies. That there are no major first-world exceptions to this pattern, that the process is often rapid, and that a significant religious revival has yet to occur in a secular democracy indicate that the socioeconomic security process of democratic secularization is a highly effective side effect of progressive economic policies. The universality of the effect is further supported by pagan Japan experiencing the same basic secularization process as the EuroChristian secular democracies.

The United States is the most religiously aberrant prosperous nation because it is the most socioeconomically aberrant member of the group, the country standing as an example of the socioeconomic dysfunctionality hypothesis that predicts that insecure life circumstances favor religiosity. Provided with comparatively low levels of government support and protection in favor of less restrained "cowboy" capitalism, members of the middle class are at serious risk of financial and personal ruin if they lose their job or private health insurance; around a million go bankrupt in a year, about half due in part to often overwhelming medical bills. The need to acquire wealth as a protective buffer encourages an intense competitive race to the top, made worse by the "Reaganomics" that have made the nation's economy the most efficient at transferring large funds from the middle class to the small wealthy elite through a number of devices. The corporate effort to move into debt people in the middle and bottom (see later discussion) results in the latter paying massive interest to the top. Lower wages and benefits, including retirement funds associated with deunionization, reduce costs for capital while increasing worker debt and interest loads. Poorly regulated high finance regularly devolves into legal but unsustainable pyramid schemes that defraud middle-class investors of enormous sums before the ploys collapse. Lowering taxes on all classes serves the upper tier most by increasing the amount of lower and middle level money that can be shifted up the class scale, and then allowing the upper class to keep more of their gains. The result of this Darwinian economy has been growing income inequality that leaves a large cohort mired in poverty while stagnating the financial growth of the middle class, forcing a large portion into debt, reducing or eliminating medical and retirement security, and raising habitual anxiety levels. Gun control policies are weak, and incarceration is retributive and abusive on a mass scale that discriminates against minorities, especially urban. Not surprisingly, levels of societal pathology, including lethal crime, are high. The majority of Americans are left feeling sufficiently economically and physically insecure that they think they must seek the aid and protection of a supernatural creator, boosting levels of religious opinion and participation. The nation's high ratings in life satisfaction and happiness are compatible with a large segment of the population using religion to psychologically compensate for high levels of apprehension. The ultimate expression of this phenomenon is the large minority who adhere to the evangelical Prosperity Christianity and Rapture cultures (which are highly Pentecostal), whose Bible-based worldview favors belief in the Genesis creation story, as well as Mormonism, which is not young earth creationist.

THE CORPORATE-CONSUMER FACTOR

In view of the absence of the hybrid capitalist-socialist economy that drives secularization in the rest of the West, why is religion losing ground in the United States—including the religious Right, which, despite being well organized, is persistently unable to break out of the parallel minority culture it has been driven into? An important, if not the leading, factor driving American secularization appears to the corporate-consumer culture. It is in the interest of profit-focused capitalism to exploit the strong human genetic propensity toward materialism in order to radically alter society by converting pious, "square" traditionalist citizens who contribute time and money to religious organizations into materialistic, individualist "hip" consumers who center their lives and resources around goods and entertainment to the point that they go into interest-generating debt. To a fair extent, commerce is in competition with religion. Corporations began to displace churches as the dominant feature of American culture in the 1920s as new technologies further facilitated mass production and mass advertising, contributing to the "flapper" culture that overturned long-standing traditional mores. The historically revolutionary counterculture of the 1960s began as a grassroots anticorporate movement, but it was quickly captured and exploited by the corporations to further radicalize Western societies. A major portion of the profit-based secularization project has centered on the transformative power of the mass entertainment media that attracts enormous audiences. American mercantile interests also backed the repeal of the puritanical "Blue Laws" intended to boost church attendance at the expense of retail traffic, helping lower the rates of church attendance (Gruber & Hungerman, 2006). The financial resources that capitalism can call upon to materialize societies dwarf those that churches can deploy in resistance.[20] Although led by capitalists, the corporate-consumer culture is not imposed on the majority against their will; despite persistent complaints, the Western public has largely gone along with the extreme materialization of their societies. Overtly religious programming is scarce on the commercial networks because it garners insufficient viewers.[21] The hip factor of the corporate-consumer society gives it a particular advantage among younger generations because it is difficult for religious cults to shed their square image even when they adopt aspects of modernity.[22] It is all the more ironic that the recent commercialization of Christianity that has been heralded as evidence of a national revival may be contributing to the decline of religiosity in youth who find it cynical (Boorstein, 2010).

THE SCIENCE AND TECHNOLOGY FACTOR

The third factor helping secularize western societies, especially western cultures, is the combination of modern science and advanced technology. Had science verified the existence of a supernatural creator,[23] then atheistic secularization would have been aborted in favor of some form of fact-based (rather than faith-based) theism. Instead, science has effectively removed the need for persons to believe in any form of supernaturalism, both allowing and encouraging the rise of nontheism (Dawkins, 2006; Hawkings & Mlodinow, 2010; Paul, 2010b). It is probably not a coincidence that the frequency of the use of the word "God" has dropped, while usage of "evolution" has soared (Jean-Baptiste et al., 2010), and it follows that irreligion is widespread among the well educated, especially scientists (Gallup, 2006b; Larson & Witham, 1999; Preston & Epley, 2009). The god-like achievements of modern science and technology are lowering the awe factor that has facilitated religion (Paul & Cox, 1996). The chronic use of various technologies by ordinary middle-class citizens can degrade mass religiosity simply by absorbing time that could otherwise be dedicated to godly pursuits. As Putman (2000) argued, air conditioning, television, and, more recently, digital media have been suppressing membership in social clubs. Because religion is a time-consuming social club, it is vulnerable to such sociotechnological temporal pressures. The advent of digital personal electronics may be posing a particular threat to the religiosity of younger generations because of an exceptional diversionary impact—one that helps explain the dramatic decline in youth faith.

THE TRIPLE THREAT TO WESTERN FAITH

The combination of secure middle-class prosperity, the corporate-consumer culture, and advanced science and technology constitute the triple threat to Western faith (Paul, 2010b). The three dynamics work synergistically in that they blend together and reinforce one another—the first two factors, in particular, would not be possible without the existence of the latter. In most advanced democracies, the first factor is the most important, and when combined with the other two it has produced the most potent secularization effect. In the United States, the first component is not sufficiently operative because of the "Wild West" economy to produce a secular progressive majority, but the second dynamic is prevalent and has proved effective enough to terminate Karl Rove's grand project to establish a permanent theoconservative Republican majority. As effective as these secularization forces can be, they are largely accidental side effects rather than calculated efforts to destroy popular supernaturalism. Putman and Campbell (2010) attribute much or all of American secularization to yet another—and ironic—theosociological accident. They contend that the rise of the religious Right intended to return the nation to the churches in reaction to large-scale secularization is instead causing its own reactionary backlash as the younger generations reject its intolerant stridence. This effect may well be a fourth component to American secularization, but it does not explain Western de-Christianization in general, ignores that it is the moderate denominations that have suffered the largest losses, and it neglects the effect that digital personal technologies are probably having on youth (the last is an especially surprising failure for Putman; Paul, 2010c). Based on a statistical analysis, Ruiter and Tubergen (2009) conclude that, in addition to socioeconomic conditions, the religious heritage of a nation plays a role in its long-term religiosity, including the degree of religious regulation; however, the hypothesis that a free market of religion is a major factor behind high levels of religiosity has been falsified, as per Norris and Inglehart (2004).

More on the Superficiality of Religion—and Popular Nontheism

The ease and rapidity with which religion has lost much or most of its popularity in the advanced democracies despite the absence of a potent atheistic movement, and often in the face of organized religion, indicates that religious belief and practice are a common but usually superficial psychological coping mechanism for alleviating the high level of anxiety associated with living in a sufficiently dysfunctional socioeconomic environment, and that religious opinion is readily abandoned in many or most people if their daily lives become sufficiently secure and prosperous. This not only refutes the hypothesis (as per Barrett, 2004) that most people must deliberately strive to overcome a supposedly strong natural human propensity to be religious if they are to become irreligious, but also it means that nontheism is similarly superficial in the hundreds of millions who have casually lost their faith without thinking about it all that much. That the great Western secularization has established that religious opinion is inconsistent and often casual in turn allows us to better examine the beginning and evolution of religiosity and its relationship to individual and mass violence; in particular, we can avoid errant conclusions that stem from assuming religion is universal and deeply set in the species.

It follows that the fact that the great majority of humans have and continue to be religious is not evidence for religiosity being the human default mode, because the great majority of humans have and continue to live in the dysfunctional circumstances that promote religiosity. To better discover the actual propensity of people to be pious or not would require running the entire planet so that every person enjoyed the level of secure middle class or higher prosperity and peace now prevalent only in the most successful democracies for a sustained period of time. Presumably, popular religiosity would sink to the low levels currently extant in such nations—whether nontheism would continue to grow to even higher or consensus levels is unknown and open to question. Also questionable is whether this pacific prosperity experiment will ever be run.

The Interactions Between Theism, Nontheism, and Violence

Because intraspecies violence and war are not human inventions, being present in nonhumans, including some apes, they are not the result of religion. Increasingly complex language and materialism probably evolved due to selective pressures before the evolution of advanced *Homo sapiens* and involve a strong genetic component. The nongenetic and nontranscendent nature of religion indicated by its usual superficiality, along with the minimal religiosity of some societies, including some living hunter-gatherers, plus the difficulty of assessing the presence and degree of supernaturalism in prehistory, means it cannot be presumed that intense shamanistic supernaturalism appeared before or among early *Homo sapiens*, and it was widespread before the advent of agriculture. But it may well have appeared early and been common. The development of basal religion is likely to have been primarily a side effect of the human imagination that evolved as a means of inventing a variety of mental concepts and can diverge into less functional areas. The process is likely to have been facilitated by dreams, which can seem to represent a connection to spiritual realms, and the use of mind-altering drugs that can produce the same impression. The propensity of humans to be obstinate in their opinions regardless of whether they are justified further facilitates supernaturalism. Considering the strength of these effects, it is the minimal religiosity of some hunter-gatherers—rather than the emergence of religion—that is rather surprising, and it verifies that religious devotion is not the human default mode. Because it cannot be presumed that all prehistoric peoples were religious and believed in an afterlife, and because the actual distribution of religiosity and violence among them cannot be assessed and correlated, it is not now and is unlikely to ever be practical to determine the relationship between religion, homicide, and war prior to 10,000 BP. It cannot be determined whether supernaturalistic thinking encouraged or discouraged prehistoric strife, or if it conferred an advantage or disadvantage in combat. Studies that come to strong conclusions on these matters probably go beyond the recoverable data. Because religion lacks a strong genetic component, its evolution as a powerful force of social cohesion in a survival, including military, context is improbable at best and studies that conclude otherwise are probably errant. The nonuniversality of war in human cultures and the rarity of homicide indicate they too are not genetically programmed (Kelly, 2000) and are more similar to art and writing than to language and materialism. It remains possible that the higher propensity for males to engage in violence involves a genetic component.

As history comes onto the modern human scene, assessing and correlating faith and violence becomes more practical. The combination of widespread religiosity in early agricultural and civilized peoples with substantial levels of homicide and war leaves no doubt that mass polytheism did not come close to solving the violence and brutality problem, to the detriment of the godly-religion socioeconomic hypothesis. This was true even though most polytheistic cults were relatively tolerant of other sects. Most of the wars appear to have been struggles over territory, resources, and slaves. Polytheistic doctrines did not promote nonviolent worldviews to the degree necessary to dramatically suppress or prevent these wars and murder, and the tendency of a given people to believe that their gods are better than the other's gods can facilitate conflict. The development of the Roman Empire is an interesting case because not only did the Romans not wage aggressive war on religious grounds, but also they even adopted the gods of one of the peoples they conquered. An example of a polytheistic religion leading directly to wars occurred in middle America, where doctrines required the capture and sacrifice of enemy persons for what were considered urgent theistic purposes. The Aztecs developed this system to such an extreme degree that surrounding client states were maintained as targets for annual campaigns purely to capture thousands of victims each year (Hassig, 1988). Khan was a devout animist (Weatherford, 2004), and his conquests were driven in part by a feeling of religious unity and perhaps superiority.[24] The many tens of millions killed by the Mongol conquests demonstrates the potential lethality of polytheistic wars. The even greater numbers lost in the Chinese civil wars in the 700s, 1600s, and 1800s shows the same for their less supernaturalistic culture. The most recent expression of mass war caused by polytheistic racism was the attempt by Japan to conquer China and the rest of Asia that cost 40 million lives; such a strategic impossibility seemed doable only if the Japanese were divinely special and protected. Many polytheistic societies were tolerant of or required torture, draconian punishments, and human sacrifice, including sacrificing children, in some cases.

Buddhism is interesting because in its original and most basic form it is a nonsupernaturalistic philosophy. It and some Hindu sects have developed pacifist philosophies. On the other hand, Hindu doctrine centers around the extremely discriminatory caste system, and the Indian polytheists have engaged in intense strife with Muslims, peaking with the mass atrocities sparked by the independence of India and Pakistan.

Abrahamic monotheism did not seriously improve the human situation concerning homicide, war, torture, and slavery, but its helping suppress most infanticide or human sacrifice that may stand as the greatest antiviolence successes of the ideology.[26] Assessing the early stages of the evolution of Hebrew monotheism is complicated because the anthropological data contradict the wars of extreme genocidal aggression and ethnic cleansing during the unprovoked conquest of the Promised Land described in scripture (Bright, 2000). Jews were the victims of Roman aggression, but although their rebellions were justifiable, the terror tactics invented by Hebrew religious zealots were not. Nor were the repeated revolts, driven by religious ideology rather than strategic assessment, a sound proposition because they were bound to fail and led to the permanent destruction of the temple, and the disastrous Diaspora. Upon being elevated to the top religion of the Roman Empire, Christianity failed to promote democracy, tolerance, and political individual freedom. It did the opposite by imposing a terror state, where torture, agonizing execution, slavery, and anti-Semitism were legal and normal. Actions against Jews included ghettoization, economic restrictions, wearing of badges of identification, and forced conversion (Carroll, 2001). The tradition of anti-Semitism was continued by Protestants (as per Luther, 1543). The very poor socioeconomic performance of Europe when it was at its most Christian seriously undermined the Christian version of the moral-creator socioeconomic hypothesis. Matters began to change when the growth of mercantile capitalism in parts of northern Europe, the Netherlands especially, pressured entrepreneurial Protestants to adopt tolerance for other sects and began to elevate general living conditions. The degree to which Christianity suppressed and/or encouraged the development of modern economics and science is controversial (Diamond, 2005; Stark, 2006); for example, it has been proposed that the cultural and political diversity resulting from the complex geographic topography of the European peninsula was the crucial factor behind the development of modernity. In the end, the confession at least allowed or was unable to prevent the advances; the absence of a scriptural requirement for a theocracy may have facilitated this result.

Nor did Christianity adopt nonaggressive military policies upon becoming the dominant cult of Europe. The Catholic nation invented the concept of "just war," and then used the theory to justify a series of unethical wars. Wars between Catholics did not involve a religious dispute, but they did establish the inability of the faith to suppress warfare, further damaging the moral-creator socioeconomic hypothesis. The war against the Cathars was pure, unprovoked religious genocide facilitated by mass theft (Pegg, 2008). The eastern Crusades were religion driven on multiple levels that were interlinked. Aside from the desire to push back the aggressive Islam that was threatening Christendom and regain the Holy Lands, the operation was so strategically untenable in the long term that it could be justified only on the premise that the creator of the universe favored the Christian cause. At the beginning of the Crusades, the Pope promised eternal rewards for combatants and declared that Muslims were heathens outside the protections of the Decalogue (Asbridge, 2004, 2010).[27] The first encouraged participation, and the latter allowed the use of the terror tactics that were necessary for the Crusaders to achieve their initial victories. This included the murder of the inhabitants of the Muslim and Jewish citizens of some of the cities seized and the practice of cannibalism on non-Christians during some sieges (Asbridge, 2004, 2010; Peters, 1971; Rubenstein, 2008).[28] At first, eating Muslims was compelled by hunger, but it appears to have evolved into a prominent means of inspiring terror as a military tactic. Occasional assaults upon Orthodox Christians during the Crusades, including the sacking of Constantinople, were largely opportunistic.

The expansion of Islam was largely through military conquest, that of India alone probably cost 80 million (Lal, 1973). A major exception was Indonesia, which is predominantly Sufi. The latter is more pacific than the Sunni and Shiite sects. The notorious Hashshashin proved that the faith was capable of generating extreme terror, setting an unfortunate precedent. Islam was markedly more tolerant of Judaism and Christianity than the last was of other forms of Abrahamism,[29] but it has been just as bigoted against polytheists, apostates, and nontheists.

Significant pacifist Christian sects have evolved, Quakers and Mennonites among them, but these have been minority movements that have not precluded the frequent involvement of Christians in a long series of conflicts. The European wars of the 1500s and 1600s were largely religious, with Catholicism attempting and failing to destroy the new sects. In the theologically diverse English American colonies, religious strife, sometimes lethal, between assorted Protestants, Catholics, Jews, and Deists contributed to the new democracy being officially secular. Because the distance between the American colonies and the English crown gave the American colonists substantial experience with local democratic practices and removed the need to directly attack the monarchy, the revolution did not descend into outright terror—although atrocities did occur on both sides, especially in the southern colonies, where the conflict devolved into an often ruthless civil war. The high level of societal violence in the early American republic when it was more pious than less homicidal Europe offers further contradiction of the moral-creator socioeconomic hypothesis. In France the need to outright destroy the monarchy to prevent its return, and a lack of democratic experience, led the Deistic regime to employ extreme terror. Counterattacks by Christian elements against French secularism proved equally ruthless. As the fortunes of the Papal States waned in the face of secular modernity, the Holy See continued to employ military forces in an ultimately futile effort to prevent being reduced to a normal church (Pollard, 2005).

Had industrial-consumer capitalism rather than Christianity appeared in Roman times, slavery very probably would have become too uneconomical to remain legal two millennia ago. Had the Gospels strictly prohibited slavery, then major portions of Christianity would not have defended slavery for two millennia, leading to a theological civil war between Christians in the late 1700s and 1800s— the Southern Baptists formed in 1845 specifically to defend the peculiar institution—and the actual civil war might have been avoided. The Vatican still defended slavery after the American Civil War (Maxwell, 1975). That slavery finally and quickly became illegal at the same time that modern economics was developing, and long after the advent of the Abrahamic faiths, strongly indicates that finances had much more to do with the end of the system than did religious abolitionists. Conversely, if not for the advent of Smithian capitalism, it is likely that slavery would still be legal and common. Ergo, even taking into account religious abolitionists, religion slowed down, making slavery illegal. The Jim Crow lynching culture enabled by Southern and Midwestern Protestants after the war was so out of control that most of the killings were public spectacles, held every few weeks, in which the victim was brutalized to death, often in an obscene manner (see Dray, 2003). There was no significant involvement of atheists in this terror; indeed, a person who publicly proclaimed his or her atheism or proevolution stance at that time and place was at risk. The termination of the American apartheid terror state involved center-left religious and atheist elements,[30] but the system was unsustainable in a prosperous democracy in which television was exposing the brutality and hatred of racist Christians.[31] Afrikaner apartheid was based on biblical Protestantism, and it was defeated by an atheistic liberation movement headed by nonbeliever Nelson Mandela allied with liberal Christian elements.

Catholics initiated the transatlantic slave trade in the Caribbean (Maxwell, 1975). As North American Protestants took over the African traffic while wishing to avoid being enslaved themselves, they elevated the theory that only lesser races were suitable for human bondage (as per Jefferson, 1783) to a new level. Christians then perpetuated this deception in modified form in the apartheid era, contending that those of African heritage were not suitable for participating in democratic politics, and that Black males posed a sexual threat to virtuous White women (Dray, 2003).[32] By the 1800s, Christians had developed a broad array of prejudices against others both within and outside the faith. As late as World War II, democratic Western and other societies that were still religious remained racist to a degree that is difficult to comprehend today. They largely excluded Black Africans from combat duties in part due to theories of mental inferiority; African Americans who did serve were unable to utilize public facilities in the southern states that German prisoners of war could enjoy, while Japanese families were interned. Because the scientists of the era were steeped in a heritage of Christian bigotry, the latter inevitably contaminated the new science of human biology (Paul, 2003, 2004). It is therefore not surprising that the new pseudoscientific version of eugenics was widely adopted by Protestants, as well as some Catholics (Hastings, 2010).[33] A majority of American states adopted eugenics laws—some of those states also banned teaching evolution.

Theology-grounded racism and forced eugenics backed by pseudoscientific theories were developed to their most extreme in Germany by rightist Christians and neopagans (Paul, 2003, 2004; Hastings, 2010). The Nazi opinion that Jews were the creations of Satan (Hitler, 1925) ultimately led to the tremendous effort to exterminate the Hebrew "race."[34] The retention of anti-Semitic attitudes by the Catholic Church and many Protestant sects abetted the Nazi version (Carroll, 2001; Gellately, 2001; Paul, 2003, 2004; Phayer, 2008; Scholder, 1988; Steigman-Gall, 2003). Nazi ideology presumed that the supernatural superiority of Aryans who alone among humans had been created by the creator gave Germans the capacity to achieve enormous conquests that would have otherwise been understood as strategically impractical for a modest-sized population (Hitler, 1925; Paul, 2003, 2004).[35] A Vatican panel commissioned to assess the relative dangers of Communism and Nazism recognized that the latter was theistic and concluded that it posed the greater threat due to its aggressive racism (Phayer, 2008)—far from being atheistic in origin, Nazism was the most deadly form of theism yet seen.[36] The Holy See decided otherwise, so the church directly aided the assent of Hitler to power and backed the Fascist powers in their war against Communism to the degree that American and British aid to the Soviet Union was denounced, criticism of Fascist atrocities and mass genocides was minimal while the lesser crimes of leftist forces were emphasized, and Fascist war criminals were protected after the war (Phayer, 2008). Protestant elements were often virulently anti-Semitic, and both Christian confessions exploited slave labor in Germany (Gellately, 2001; Legg, 2008).[37] Since the war, the Vatican has engaged in a periodically bizarre series of collaborations with organized crime that has destabilized the Italian democracy and led to murders, as well as the better known scandals involving the abuse of children.[38] Anti-choice Christians are putting far more effort into making women who have abortions legally guilty of murder than opposing the growth of international organized crime.

The secular Left used to be a leading source of terror acts, and it still produces some of the latter as well as substantial street protest violence against the forces of capital. In the United States, right-wing militants tend to be Christians.[39] The ongoing strife in Africa includes extremist Christian elements such as the Lord's Resistance Army and The Army of the Ten Commandments that have engaged in radical atrocities and rape against other Christians, Muslims, pagans, and "witches" as a standard course of action (Griswold, 2008; Lester, 2002). Genocidal leaders such as Charles Taylor and Joseph Kony regularly use Christian rhetoric (Vick, 2003), and Rwanda and Congo are majority Christian (Barrett et al., 2001). Muslims have also engaged in atrocities in these conflicts (Griswold, 2008). On the global stage, the Islamic world is too economically and militarily weak to directly engage the Western powers if it wished to do so. Although the oil-rich Saudi Arabian monarchy itself is not hard line, their funding of the strict Wahabbi sect, and Western backing of militant Muslims fighting atheist forces in Afghanistan, has encouraged the global development of extremist Islamic elements that reject socioeconomic modernity and have copied and greatly expanded upon the comparatively secular Tamil Tigers suicide terror tactics[40]; but to date, modern Islamic terror has far from matched the scale of anticivilian terror achieved in World War II.[41] It is notable that Muslims have recently revived the use of nonmurderous suicide in the form of self-immolation—in the 1900s first used to oppose governmental corruption in Southeast Asia—as part of a more secular and democratic movement against corrupt autocracies whose future prospects are uncertain in the face of reactionary Islam. In Israel, the growth of the Orthodox through fast reproduction and immigration from the United States has increased strife with secular Jews and complicated achieving peace with Muslims. Fundamentalism in the modern second- and third-world countries is proving so dysfunctional and sufficiently popular that it is raising concerns among those who predict a recovery of mass religiosity in coming decades (Kaufmann, 2010; Longman, 2006; Shah & Toft, 2006).

That Abrahamism has failed to produce sufficiently pacific results over the millennia up to current times makes it necessary to examine the ideologies that about half of the world has been following. The basic monotheistic doctrine that a single omnipotent deity created the world is highly problematic. The planet is so defective in construction that it is a death trap for immature humans, most of whom die before reaching adulthood, aborting the ability to express free will that is supposed to justify the creator's failure to control earthly events (Paul, 2008, 2009b). The scale of this disaster is so maximal—higher juvenile losses would crash the population—that it refutes the core premise that the creator is a pro-life source of sound moral guidance,[42] and the premise that one should not kill humans primarily because of the instructions of a God that has overseen the death of many billions of children; this is a classic example of doing what the authority figure says, not what the authority figure does. Note that the absence of a benign creator also applies to monotheistic Deism and to pacific Bahaism.

Written by ancient peoples who lacked advanced ethics, the Hebrew, Christian, and Islamic scriptures are similarly defective.[43] Note that whether the events described in the texts actually occurred is not as critical as the fact that many adherents think the texts represent the word of a deity that cannot be disobeyed. The Decalogue did not ban war, homicide, or slavery on a universal basis or torture on any basis. The commandments were an exclusive covenant between God and observant Hebrews, and they left the Jews free to kill the nonobservant. So when Moses was about to present the commandments, he was justified in having the Israelites who had returned to worshipping a pagan deity slaughtered for doing nothing more than expressing their religious preference. Genocidal wars of conquest against and enslavement of gentiles were justifiable for the same reason, and the Decalogue does not mention torture or promote democracy and freedom of speech, religion, and sexuality—deficits that characterize the rest of the monotheistic scriptures. According to some interpretations, the commandments apply to observant Christians, but they do not pertain to heathens. The curse of Ham is potentially racist because his descendants are supposedly the Africans. Not only is slavery not banned in either the Hebrew testaments or the Gospels, but slaves are warned not to seek their freedom in the latter, and abuse and death are described as legitimate punishments in the former and by Jesus. The Old Testament deity either kills enormous numbers of humans preborn, immature, and adult directly or orders his loyal followers to do so. Jesus specifically denies that he has come to Earth to bring peace, cites the death of the opponents of kings as a warning against disbelievers, allows his entourage to purchase swords,[44] and instead of employing peaceful protest methods as per Gandhi or King criminally uses a whip without prior warning against nonviolent fellow civilians in the temple. In Revelations, Jesus is a warrior deity who slaughters humans. The Quran does not describe genocide to the same extreme, but it does not condemn slavery, and it does discuss the use of discriminatory policies, including violence against nonbelievers, polytheists and atheists especially, the latter requirements stemming from the need for the state to be an Islamic theocracy. Abrahamic scripture is archpatriarchal to the point of misogyny, and it is antihomosexual. The socialism described in the Gospels is contaminated because it is enforced by the death of Christians who fail to comply. Almost all the tenets proffered in Abrahamic scriptures are one way or another enforced by threats of violence and death, with the ultimate expression of abusive retribution being unrelenting torture in hell. The Bible's chronic fear factor stems from being composed in antiquated societies in which intolerance and violence up to death were a regular means of dealing with perceived difficulties, so the volume is not able to provide the formula for peaceful national societies.

Not being universal, the peace offered by the Bible and Quran is the impractically ideological peace of extreme conformity in which strife will cease only when all agree with the one correct creed. The mixed moral messages—ranging from forgiveness, turning the other cheek, and love for one's neighbor and enemy, on one hand, to extreme retribution and violence, on the other—contained within the archaic Abrahamic scriptures is a psychological recipe for moral confusion and conflict that has only been partly cured by the liberalizing effect of the Enlightenment upon Judeo-Christianity, which did not moderate more theocratic Islam to the same extent. It follows that Wright (2008) and Armstrong (2009) are overly optimistic concerning the pacific foundations and positive evolution of religion. Abrahamic patriarchy overempowers men at the expense of women, leaving the latter more vulnerable to oppression and worse from the former. The absence of support for democracy and individual liberties aborted their adoption in the Christian world for millennia and has facilitated draconian inquisitional policies. According to doctrinal ideology, in order to obtain rewards a follower of God must obey all his orders, including instructions to kill or otherwise abuse innocent persons as occurs in scriptures; so those who believe they have received such instructions are vulnerable to concluding that they have no choice, and the aspiration for a heavenly reward promised by Christianity and Islam precludes true altruism.[45]

Because the biblical commandment against killing does not apply to nonbelievers, the Pope felt justified in declaring Muslims outside its protection, increasing the rapaciousness of the Crusades to the point of cannibalism. The story of Ham and discriminatory policies in the Bible and Quran have contributed to bigotry on racial, ethnic, and religious grounds, to the degree that some contemporary creationists describe the races on blatantly prejudiced grounds. The scriptural support for slavery allowed and encouraged its retention among Jews, Christians, and Muslims to the beginning of modern times, resulting in a massive war. The charge by Jesus in the Gospels that Jews are the children of Satan, the Gospel portrayal of Jews as his killers, and the violent side of the Jesus story were integral to the development of the Aryan Deutsch Christianity that evolved into Nazism. In this interpretation of scripture, Christ was an Aryan warrior sent by God to combat the Jews.[46] Even mainstream Bible scholars cite the whipping delivered by Jesus as an example of why violence is sometimes necessary (as per the commentary in Shelley et al., 1994), despite the lack of sufficient provocation in the Gospel story. The militant, anti-infidel, theocratic aspects of the Quran, exacerbated by the absence of an Islamic Enlightenment, form the basis of suicidally extremist Islam.

Turning to the daily lives of contemporary ordinary citizens, the extreme death toll of immature humans undermines the thesis that the creator is truly opposed to murder, and God-ordained violence in the Bible is so intense and extensive that experimental exposure appears to elevate levels of aggression in the manner of violent media (Bushman et al., 2007). The repeated use of extreme personal and mass violence to address various problems in the scriptures may have enabled "honor cultures" that demand extreme retribution for even trivial slights (Dray, 2003; Ehrman, 2008; Ellison, Burr, & McCall, 2003; Grasmick, Davenport, Chamblin, & Bursick, 1992; Messner & Zevenbergen, 2005; Neapolitan, 1997; Niditch, 1993; Nisbett & Cohen, 1999). The results of Jensen (2006) support the hypothesis that populations that follow a conservative "malevolent" theology centered on battling Satanic forces are prone toward higher levels of homicide than are followers of less fear-based, more "benevolent" doctrines. Bible-based juvenile corporal punishment (Dobson, 2007a, 2007b) appears to contribute to a tendency toward violence in adult years (American Academy of Pediatrics, 1998, 2000). The warrior nature of God's followers in the Bible is used to oppose gun control in murderous America (Paul, 2009c).[47] Hood et al. (1986), Scheepers et al. (2002), and Hall et al. (2010) find that higher levels of conservative religious practice are associated with elevated levels of racial and ethnic prejudice. The concept that there is but one god of salvation compels insufficiently enlightened Islam to impose harsh punishments on alleged critics of the faith via antiblasphemy laws, and to direct threats and attacks upon those who fail to exhibit demanded respect. Scriptural injunctions against homosexuality fuel homophobia, sometimes violent; this is resulting in massive and increasing oppression of gays by evangelicals and Muslims in Africa.[48] Hard-line Islamic patriarchy justifies extreme of oppression of women. Although less harsh, the patriarchal nature of traditional evangelical marriage may contribute to high levels of violence and instability (Bennett, 2007), and conservative religious values do not appear to suppress uses of pornography that sometimes is violently misogynist to levels as low as those with more liberal views (Edelman, 2009; "Evangelicals are addicted…", 2006). Extensive research indicates that the biblically inspired abstinence-only sex education programs are not as efficacious in reducing adverse consequences of sexual activity as the less traditionalist, more pragmatic, protection-emphasizing programs directed toward European youth (Finer, 2007; Panchaud, Singh, Darroch, & Darroch, 2000; Paul, 2009c; Rosenbaum, 2009; Singh & Darroch, 2000; Trenholm, 2007; Wellings et al., 2006), and Strayhorn and Strayhorn (2009) explicitly demonstrate a link between high levels of theoconservativism and unintended pregnancy. Not scriptural, however, is the religious project to stop abortions by making it murder subject to harsh punishments[49] because the procedure is not banned in the Bible, and it is impractical because abortion is common regardless of whether it is legal (Sedgh, Henshaw, Singh, Ahman, & Shah, 2007; Shah & Ahman, 2009).

Powerful elements of the American religious Right have strategically focused on promoting a series of what they claim are scripturally based wedge issues rather than addressing social ills (Phillips, 2006; Putman & Campbell, 2010; Weisman & Cooperman, 2006). The ideology of these conservative forces favors the deregulated, reduced taxation (especially for the wealthy), free market economy that raises personal risk. As a result, the incoherent religious Right that is the main opponent to Darwinian science and to socialism has become a leading proponent of socioeconomic Darwinism despite the promotion of socialism in the Gospels. As an adjunct to privatization, religious conservatives are promoting the displacement of government services with faith-based charities that increase outreach into the general population, even though data showing that faith-based charities are more effective than government alternatives have not been produced (Johnson, Tompkins, & Webb, 2002), and charities lack the enormous financial resources and infrastructure needed to provide the comprehensive assistance that the government can offer (contra Brooks, 2006). America's high levels of adult and especially juvenile mortality are largely due to the lack of a comprehensive, cost-efficient medical system that is opposed by most elements of the religious Right because of opposition to socialistic policies in favor of more faith-based treatments (Anderson et al., 2006; Banks et al., 2006; Kawachi & Kennedy, 2002; Muenning & Glied, 2010; Paul, 2008, Reid, 2009; Schoen et al., 2005; Wilkinson & Pickett, 2009; Winkleby et al., 2006).

Not only can the tragedy of Nazism not be attributed to nontheism, but the socioeconomic component of both nationalist socialism as well as Communist doctrine is not atheistic since the concept of socialism enforced by the fear of lethal retribution first appeared in the Gospels as the ideal form of Christian community, or Christocommunism. Even so, irreligious dictatorships have proven capable of committing mass violence comparable to the record of theist powers. This is not surprising in that both atheism and theism are morally neutral—gods or the one God can be as bad as they can be good. Although the absence of belief in a moral deity can allow depravity, the ideological belief in a "purposeful" deity that is perceived to be moral even though it cannot be so can be even more dangerous because of the supernaturalistic justification, requirements, and rewards the latter imparts.[50] The absence of absolutist supernatural justification may help explain why mass Communism has faded with remarkably little trouble and considerable speed.[51,52] Conversely, the perception of godly compulsion and an eternal paradise in exchange for ardor is probably reinforcing the hard-line stance of fundamentalists whose religiosity would be less intense or absent if not for dysfunctional circumstances.[53]

The greater danger posed by theism may be reflected in the numbers. To date, the number killed by the nonsupernaturalists is somewhere between 50 and 100 million,[54] a significant but minor fraction of the order of magnitude larger casualties attributable to supernaturalists. The latter have had a much longer time over which to dispatch fellow human beings, but wrongdoing nonreligious people have had modern technology and a larger population base to work with, and Pinker (2011) shows that the lethal violence rate of the 1900s was not exceptional on a per capita basis. Attacking and killing fellow humans on a group scale is always driven to at least some extent by the desire to steal land or resources. But some conflicts and genocides are unlikely to have occurred if not for religious motivation or cover of other motives (the Holocausts, the Aztec wars of sacrifice, the anti-Cathar/Muslim Crusades, some of the European conflicts of the 1500–1600s, the Inquisitions, and the war on witches fall into this category) or ill-advised strategic thinking due to the illusion of divine superiority (the Middle Eastern Crusades, the German and Japanese assaults of Russia and China, respectively, in World War II). Many conflicts predominantly over territory and assets have been exacerbated by supernaturalistic disputes (currently the Jewish-Muslim conflicts and much of the strife in Africa) or belief of divine favor for the aggressors (the conquest of the Americas). In even more cases religion has not been a primary cause or exacerbation of violence from the largest scale to the smallest, but it has proven impotent to stop conflicts between peoples of faith, often the same faith (as per the Great War, and homicide in general). And although it is true that infanticide was ended by theists, it was also largely practiced by theists.

The telling truth is that the general reduction in human violence (Pinker, 2011) has occurred at the same time that atheism has been waxing at the expense of theism.

Conclusion

Dictatorships, religious or atheistic, are dangerous, and none has produced a highly successful society. Neither was democracy created for religious purposes; it arose out of political pragmatism among pagans. There is no evidence that patriarchal fundamentalism can produce successful societies. Only democratic cultures that maximize women's rights can provide socioeconomic success in the context of human freedom, so the question is whether it is better to be highly supernaturalistic or nonsupernaturalistic. No strongly monotheistic or polytheistic democracy has been as successful at providing its citizens with the degree of secure middle-class prosperity and safety as have the most irreligious and progressive examples. Although the latter are not utopias, which probably cannot exist, the most atheistic democratic societies are the most successful in history. They are also the least likely to engage in unprovoked war. If, as it seems, the best cumulative socioeconomic environments invariably suppresses popular religiosity across the left-right spectrum, then it is not possible for a highly successful, pacific nation to be highly religious contrary to what appear to be the psychosociologically naïve hopes of theomoderates (like Egginton, 2011; Hedges, 2008). That even a progressively religious country cannot succeed in that the very achievement of success will repress the religiosity no matter how enlightened and pacific it may be explains why mainline theism is as statistically tied to poor national conditions as is dysfunctional fundamentalism; the latter being somewhat more resistant to the secularization process because its reactionary nature garners adherents who resist secular modernity.

The psychoideological reasons for the exceptional social success and nonlethal nature of the least religious democracies have yet to be properly researched (Zuckerman [2008] being an early effort); it is not attributable to atheist or secular ideology, of which there is none, nor to active popular adherence to secular humanist doctrine because the movement is too limited in scale and popularity to be a major influence. The reduction of the popularity of the more dysfunctional aspects of religious ideologies may contribute to the posttheism success. The most important component may be the mere presence of benign conditions that, while suppressing mass religiosity, alleviate anxiety (Sapolsky, 2005). Simple salutary lifestyle practices, such as family dinners, may be as or more effective than grand ideologies to improve individual and societal function (Center on Addiction and Substance Abuse, 2003; Eisenberg, Olson, Neumark-Sztainer, Story, & Bearinger, 2004). The promotion of the rights and participation of women in the public sphere, both private (see Adler, 2001; Stephenson, 2004) and political is vital in view of women's ability to suppress reckless and aggressive behavior—this requirement is not religion friendly because the major sects are patriarchal. The nonreligious, pragmatic moral justifications for treating fellow humans well and fairly that work in the more secular democracies are practical reciprocity and the altruism of being good for the sake of goodness (Epstein, 2009).

The fact that progressive socioeconomic policies damage popular faith helps explain why the American religious Right is opposed to such policies (Gill & Lundsgaarde, 2004) and why American conservatives regularly denounce other first-world societies, despite their obviously superior conditions (Boyle, 2005; Brooks, 2006; Coulter, 2006; D'Souza, 2007; Murray, 2009; O'Reilly, 2006; Palin, 2010; Stark, 2008), while proclaiming the American Way as superior, despite its equally evident flaws. The best hopes for theism to remain as prevalent as possible are for most of human society to remain mired in the dysfunctional environment that popular religion requires, and for the reactionary fundamentalists that are most likely to spawn dangerous militants to reproduce as fast as their anticontraceptive doctrine allows them to. Ergo, religion cannot be the solution.[55] The ability of religion to suppress secularism is dubious. The alliance of Western theoconservatives with capitalism is the unavoidable deal with the corporate devil that continues to secularize cultures, especially those of the most developed nations, while digital technologies promise to further divert youth from organized supernaturalism at a rate that threatens to overwhelm the rapid reproduction of fundamentalists.[56] Conversely, if humanity succeeds in further and greatly enhancing the safety and prosperity of the peoples of the world, then religion will further fade from the scene;[57] if the US health complex becomes more universal then the nation's religiosity should decline.

Perhaps that would be for the best. With the secular superpower nuclear contest over, the most likely way that the numbers of humans killed by fellow humans can be driven to much higher levels than already seen—by hundreds of millions or billions—is via biowarfare involving the release of virulent pathogens.[58] The persons likely to execute such an act are religious extremists who see all outside their narrow cult (presumably protected by a vaccine) as warranting death, and/or who wish to initiate an apocalypse. Assuming that mass bioterror is technologically practical, religion constitutes the greatest human threat to humanity.[59]

Although eliminating theism will not necessarily solve the world's troubles because atheism can also decline into depravity on an individual to national basis, only the later in a liberal democratic context has proven able to thrive in the most successful societies. That is the atheist advantage.

Future Directions

The general need is for extensive scientific investigation of the relationship between theism, nontheism, and societies. To do so requires overcoming deeply set theopolitical correctness, which has suppressed research by implying that such work is offensive to the sensibilities of the religious or contradicts the demands of one or more gods. Also required is an end to the common evasion and denial of the morally flawed nature of religious dogmas, as well as scientific investigation of the potential dangers posed by scriptures (initiated by Bushman, Ridge, Das, Key, & Busath, 2007). There is an urgent technical need to conduct extensive research on how nontheistic inhabitants of the highly secularized democracies are living lives and running societies successful or not in the absence of popular organized religion, a neglected project initiated by Zuckerman (2008). Hypotheses on the origin and popularity of religion based on the errant premise that religion is universal and deeply set in the human mind need revision in view of the low level of supernaturalism in some hunter-gatherers and more developed cultures. How differing levels of theism and nontheism impact the life quality of individuals needs deeper investigation. On a cross-regional and cross-national basis, comparisons of socioeconomic conditions as a function of religiosity and other factors will become increasingly comprehensive. As per the challenge by Paul (2005, 2009a), those who continue to defend the godly-religion socioeconomic hypothesis must produce comprehensive data showing that deity worship actually does produce superior results on a national scale, as well as at the level of the individual, in view of the questions raised by Galen and Kloet (2011).

Notes

1. It is the "Great War" in that the conflict was concentrated in Europe, and the earlier Seven Years' War was a true world war.

2. Similar comprehensive data on rates of paranormalism appear to not be available for other prosperous democracies.

3. The scarcity of ardent faith in China may help explain the lack of greater resistance to communist atheism.

4. Another downside to the early development of advanced technologies would have been the defrauding on the aboriginal peoples of the Americas of their lands and freedoms, and mass mortality due to exposure to Old World diseases (Paul, 2009b).

5. A compilation of death statistics due to wars and other anthropogenic catastrophes is at http://en.wikipedia.org/wiki/List_of_wars_and_anthropogenic_disasters_by_death_toll.

6. Among the tortures developed during the Inquisition was water boarding (Scott, 2004; Murphy, 2012).

7. American homicide was exacerbated by long-term, honor-driven clan feuds in the southern states, which are bitterly exposed by Twain (1884).

8. Spencer's application of Darwinian biology to socioeconomics was misapplied in that the former did not fully understand the latter's science, but the basic concept that free-wheeling capitalism resembles bioevolution in many regards is valid.

9. The potential for recurring wars between North and South following a successful splitting of the United States has been portrayed in the speculative "Southern Victory" series by H. Turtledove.

10. The actual nature of the non/theism among the Tamil Tigers and how it related to persuading or compelling persons to kill themselves for political persons has been little researched, and it may remain so considering the situation. It is possible that the leaders and suicide terrorists were influenced by Hindu beliefs.

11. The last major military contest between the Western democracies was the naval arms race between Great Britain and the United States in the 1920s, although it was partly driven by competition with an increasingly autocratic and militaristic Japan. The expensive competition was aborted by treaties.

12. Additional evidence that Americans are not as religious as they pretend is found in the study of atheistic clerics by Dennett and LaScola (2010).

13. Nor is the United States exceptional in having a frontier past because this also applies to Canada and Australia.

14. Putman and Campbell (2010) show that the higher level of charitable giving reported among religious Americans is attributable to their greater social networking vis-à-vis the less organized nonreligious.

15. In recent decades, nonreligion has been rising among less educated Westerners (Putman & Campbell, 2010), perhaps because of the breakdown of social organizations and networking.

16. See note 5.

17. Materialism is well developed, even among many who deny its extreme modern expression. The Mennonites, for

example, are proud of their properties and the goods they produce. True rejection of material items, as among some religious ascetics, is very rare.

18. Interviews of Danes by Zuckerman (2008) reveals their common casual lack of concern about death and an afterlife, and ISSP (2001) found a majority of Danes do not believe there is life after death.

19. The absence of an eternal paradise in the doctrine of many religions further undermines the thesis that death is a leading cause of religion.

20. For example, with revenues in the hundreds of billions, Wal-Mart, whose stores directly compete for attendance with churches on Sundays, enjoys about 10 times the annual income of the global Catholic Church.

21. Rupert Murdoch is an example of how even theoconservative capitalists can damage religion. Although his popular FoxNews is a strong opponent of secular progressivism, his Fox entertainment empire is a leader in presenting antitraditionalist, edgy programming that is helping secularize the culture.

22. Such as Christian rock and hip-hop, which rarely breaks into the mainstream.

23. For example, if organisms appeared in the fossil record in a random manner that precluded evolution, and/or genetic systems in different organisms were too radically divergent, then natural evolution would be precluded in favor of some form of supernatural creation. If the geological record showed that the Earth was only a few thousand years old and a global flood had occurred, then the Abrahamic deity would be technically verified. The existence of a benign creator who granted all humans free will would be indicated if children possessed such remarkably effective immune systems that they were not vulnerable to death by disease.

24. The polytheistic Khan was religiously and intellectually tolerant.

25. The seemingly miraculous destruction of the otherwise unstoppable Mongol invasion fleet in the 1200s by the "divine kamikaze wind" produced by a typhoon facilitated the belief of divine favor. The involvement of religion in the motivation of the Japanese kamikaze attacks is uncertain because many if not the great majority of the pilots were forced to commit suicide (Ohnuki-Tierney, 2006).

26. However, the story of the Israelite King Jephthah involves his sacrifice of his daughter to God. The general Abrahamic ban on these actions is based on the premise that human lives are owned by their creator and cannot be taken without just cause by humans, a premise undermined by the Holocaust of the Children (Paul, 2009b).

27. In his moral defense of the crusades, Stark (2009).

28. Again, apologist Stark (2009) downplays these events.

29. However, this tolerance was limited, with non-Muslims being second-class citizens periodically subject to abuse.

30. Two of the men murdered by Klansmen during the 1964 "Summer of Freedom," Michael Schwerner and Andrew Goodman, were nonbelievers (Schwarz, 2006). Their deaths along with Christian James Chaney contributed to the passage of the Voting Rights Act.

31. This exposure would force conservative Catholic W. Buckley (1957) to abandon his prosegregationist stance.

32. The truth was that it was White men who posed a persistent threat to Black women.

33. The Vatican was not entirely opposed to eugenics (Gerrard, 1914).

34. That Jews were the creations of Satan supposedly explained how they could be subhumans, yet so intelligent that they posed a grave danger to the Aryans created by God. That Hitler actually believed this explains why so much exertion that would have been better used against the allies went into eliminating Jews.

35. The ability of Nordic Aryan Finns to resist the onslaught of the huge but Slavic Soviet army in 1940 probably contributed to this opinion.

36. Sections of Hitler (1925) read as a religious tract.

37. Further evidence of the involvement of religion in the Nazi regime is presented in Scholder (1988) and Steigman-Gall (2003).

38. The collaborations between Paul VI and John Paul II with organized crime elements is detailed in Martin (1982), Fonzo (1983), Dionne (1986), Colby (1987), and Raw (1992). Vatican involvement in the largest-ever American insurance fraud is covered by Behar (1999), and current Vatican banking troubles are detailed in Donadio (2010).

39. Timothy McVey appears to have been an idiosyncratic theist when he committed the Oklahoma bombing (Cole, 1996).

40. The opinion that it is inherently difficult to recruit suicide terrorists is psychologically naïve in that suicide is fairly common. A large portion of Muslim suicide-murderers appear to be mentally and physically afflicted persons that terrorist elites appear to be searching for and exploiting by providing an "honorable" path to suicide in a culture in which the latter is otherwise strictly taboo (Lankford, 2010; Merari, 2010).

41. Whether the use of conventional and nuclear bombs to destroy cities and many of their inhabitants shortened the war is doubtful (Dower, 2010; Friedrich, 2006; Hasegawa, 2005), and the operations over Europe resulted in extremely high Allied aircrew casualties.

42. See last observation in note 23.

43. Ehrman (2008) provides a seminal analysis of the moral flaws of the Bible. Asbridge (2004) applies the defects to the specific issue of the Crusades.

44. An example of how such biblical passages directly influence current thinking occurred during competing rallies for and against gun control following the 2011 Tucson massacre: A reverend cited the passage in which Jesus approves the purchase of swords as justification for his carrying both the New Testament and a semi-automatic (Kunkle & Helderman, 2011).

45. The anti-Christian Twain (2010) exposed this critical moral defect when the God-fearing character Finn commits true altruism by declining the reward of heaven in order to do the right thing for his friend Jim (Twain, 1884). Actual altruism cannot occur in the presence of a reward.

46. Early in his political career, Hitler carried a whip to honor Christ's assault upon the Jews in their Temple.

47. As per note 44. A lesser but also telling example of how theoconservative ideology can automatically oppose attempts to alleviate societal dysfunction is how Sarah Palin rejected a campaign led by Michelle Obama to improve childhood nutrition as interfering with the God-given right of parents to feed their offspring as they see fit.

48. The bigotry has been abetted by American evangelicals and includes an attempt to make homosexuality a potentially capital crime in Uganda (Raghavan, 2010); the most gay-friendly nation on the continent is relatively secular South Africa.

49. In El Salvador, women who are caught after performing an abortion on themselves are imprisoned for murder.

50. For example, because a nontheist is a moral free agent, he or she is free to pledge to obey all laws banning the murder

of children and refuse instructions from a higher authority to the contrary. Because a monotheist derives all his or her moral authority from his or her proposed creator and is depending upon the deity for boons, he or she cannot refuse his or her god's instructions to harm innocents as per the Israelites killing the children of the people's they were ethnically cleansing.

51. Christianity did not play the fundamental part in defeating Communism; the role of churches was important only in Poland and Romania. East Germany was and is one of the most atheistic regions on the planet, and the Russian Orthodox Church was too compromised by its collaboration with the Czarist regimes and, to a lesser extent, the Communists, and does not have a large membership. Most critical were inferior economic performance and suppression of cultural freedom, especially among youth.

52. The Soviet dissident most responsible for defeating communism, Andrei Sakharov, was an atheist. The leading opponent of the nominally communist Burmese regime, San Suu Kyi, is a nontheist Buddhist.

53. This does not mean that Islamic terrorists directly derive from impoverished circumstances; instead, for historical and theological reasons the Islamic world is sufficiently dysfunctional in a number of regards to promote violence against civilians.

54. The broad range of this figure is due to the uncertainty of the numbers killed by the Stalin and Mao regimes; see note 5.

55. It follows that predominantly Islamic countries that overturn autocratic regimes will enjoy greater socioeconomic success if they adopt a democratic secular government as per booming Indonesia rather than a theocratic state as per stagnant Iran. Which of these alternatives occurs will further test how well Islam can accommodate enlightened modernity, an important question because rapid reproduction means the religion will be the fastest growing in coming decades (Kaufmann, 2010; Pew Research, 2011), although the latter show the demographic gains should not be overemphasized because Euromuslims fertility rates are dropping, also only a small minority are highly observant much less militant.

56. That younger Americans are more progressive than the boomers also favors long-term secularization (Paul, 2010b; Putman & Campbell, 2010; Zogby, 2008). The Tea Party movement is predominantly boomer in demographic nature (Przybyla, 2010)—their propensity to invoke such historical nostalgia as tricorner hats has limited appeal among generations X and Y.

57. The development of a rapidly expanding population of super intelligent, cognitive machines has the potential to further complicate and degrade the future status of religion in multiple respects (Paul & Cox, 1996).

58. The disease agent may be a modified microbe, or a form of replicative nanotechnology (Paul & Cox, 1996).

59. The Aum Shinrikyo terrorists who tried to deploy anthrax were religious, via an amalgam of Christianity and Buddhism (Kaplan & Marshall, 1996).

References

Adler, R. (2001). Women in the executive suite: Correlate to higher profits. *Harvard Business Review, 79*(10), 30.

American Academy of Pediatrics. (1998). Policy statement: Guidance for effective discipline. *Pediatrics, 101*, 723–728.

American Academy of Pediatrics. (2000). Policy statement: Corporal punishment in schools. *Pediatrics, 106*, 343.

Anderson, G., Frogner, B., Johns, R., & Reinhardt, U. (2006). Health care spending and use of information technology in OECD countries. *Health Affairs, 25*, 819–831.

Aral, S., & Holmes, K. (1996). Social and behavioral determinants of the epidemiology of STDs: Industrialized and developing countries. In S. Morse, R. Ballard, K. Holmes, & A. Moreland (Eds.), *Sexually transmitted diseases* (3rd ed., pp. 39–76). New York: McGraw-Hill.

Armstrong, K. (2009). *The case for God*. New York: Knopf.

Asbridge, T. (2004). *The first crusade: A new history*. Oxford, England: Oxford University Press.

Asbridge, T. (2010). *The crusades: An authoritative history*. New York: Harper Collins.

Banks, J., Marmot, M., & Smith, J. (2006). Disease and disadvantage in the United States and in England. *Journal of the American Medical Association, 295*, 2037–2045.

Barber, N. (2011). A cross-national test of the uncertainty hypothesis of religious belief. *Cross-Cultural Research, 45*, 318–333.

Barclay, G., & Taveres, C. (2002). International comparisons of criminal justice statistics 2000. *Research Development and Statistics Publications*. Retrieved December 2011, from http://www.homeoffice.gov.uk/rds/pdfs2/hosb502.pdf

Barna, G. (2004). Born again Christians just as likely to divorce as are non-Christians. *Barna Research Online*. Retrieved April 2012, fhttp://www.barna.org/barna-update/article/5-barna-update/194-born-again-christians-just-as-likely-to-divorce-as-are-non-christians.

Barrett, D., Kurian, G., & Johnson, T. (Eds.). (2001). *World Christian encyclopedia*. Oxford, England: Oxford University Press.

Barrett, J. (2004). *Why would anyone believe in God?* Walnut Creek, CA: Altamira.

Becker, E. (1998). *Denial of death*. New York: Free Press.

Beeghley, L. (2003). *Homicide: A sociological explanation*. Lanham, MD: Rowman & Littlefield.

Behar, R. (1999, August 16). Washing money in the Holy See: What do Martin Frankel, several senior Vatican figures, and a bigwig Reaganite lawyer have in common? It may take years to tell all. *Fortune*, pp. 128–137.

Benedict XVI. (2009). *Caritas in veritate*. http://www.vatican.va/holy_father/benedict_xvi/encyclicals/documents/hf_ben-xvi_enc_20090629_caritas-in-veritate_en.html.

Bennett, L. (2007). *The feminine mistake*. New York: Voice.

Bijl, R., de Graaf, R., Hiripi, E., Kessler, R. C., Kohn, R., ... Wittchen, H. U. (2003). Prevalence of treated and untreated mental disorders in five countries. *Health Affairs, 22*, 122–133.

Blackman, D. (2008). *Slavery by another name: The reenslavement of Black Americans from the Civil War to World War II*. New York: Doubleday.

Blanden, J., Gregg, P., & Machin, S. (2005). Intergenerational mobility in Europe and North America. *Centre for Economic Performance, London School of Economics*. Retrieved December 2011, from http://cep.lse.ac.uk/about/news/IntergenerationalMobility.pdf

Bloom, P. (2007). Religion is natural. *Developmental Science, 10*, 147–151.

Bloom, P. (2008). Does religion make you nice? Does atheism make you mean? *Slate*. Retrieved December 2011, from http://www.slate.com/articles/life/faithbased/2008/11/does_religion_make_you_nice.html

Blumenthal, J., Babyak, M. A., Ironson, G., Thoresen, C., Powell, L., Czajkowski, S., ... The ENRICHD Investigators.. (2007).

Spirituality, religion, and clinical outcomes in patients recovering from an acute myocardial infarction. *Psychosomatic Medicine, 69,* 501–508.

Boorstein, M. (2010, December 22). Soul-searching among the shelves. *The Washington Post,* p. B1, B6.

Boyer, P. (2001). *Religion explained.* New York: Basic Books.

Boyer, P. (2008). Religion: Bound to believe? *Nature, 455,* 1038–1039.

Boyle, D. (2005). *Vile France.* New York: Encounter Books.

Brenner, P. (2011). Exceptional behavior or exceptional identity? Over reporting of church attendance in the US. *Public Opinion Quarterly, 75,* 19–41.

Bright, J. (2000). *A history of Israel.* Louisville, KY: Westminster John Knox Press.

Brooks, A. (2006). *Who really cares?* New York: Basic Books.

Bruce, S. (2002). *God is dead: Secularization in the West.* Oxford, England: Blackwell.

Buckley, W. (1957, August 24). Editorial. *National Review,* p. 148–149.

Budiansky, S. (2008). *The bloody shirt: Terror after appomattox.* New York: Viking.

Bushman, B., Ridge, R., Das, E., Key, C., & Busath, G. (2007). When God sanctions killing: Effect of scriptural violence on aggression. *Psychological Science, 18,* 204–207.

Buss, D. (2005). *The murderer next door: Why the mind is designed to kill.* New York: Penguin Press.

Carroll, J. (2001). *Constantine's sword: The church and the Jews: A History.* New York: Houghton Mifflin.

Catton, B. (1960). *The Civil War.* New York: American Heritage.

Center on Addiction and Substance Abuse. (2003). The importance of family dinners. *National Center for Addiction and Substance Abuse at Columbia University.* Retrieved July 2004, from http://www.Casacolumbia.org/pdshopprov/shop/item.asp?itemid=35

Chida, Y., Steptoe, A., & Powell, C. (2009). Religiosity/spirituality and mortality. *Psychotherapy and Psychosomatics, 78,* 81–90.

Coie, J., & Stucky, B. (1997). Aggression and antisocial behavior. In W. Damon & N. Eisenberg (Eds.), *Handbook of child psychology* (Vol. 3, pp. 777–862). New York: Wiley.

Colby, L. (1987, May 27). Italian imbroglio: Vatican bank played a central role in fall of Banco Ambrosiano. *The Wall Street Journal,* p. 1,15

Cole, P. (1996, March 30). A look back in time: Interview with Timothy McVeigh. *Time,* p. 30.

Coulter, A. (2006). *Godless: The church of liberalism.* New York: Crown Forum.

Darwin, C. (1859). *On the origin of species.* London: Murray.

Dawkins, R. (2006). *The God delusion.* New York: Houghton Mifflin.

Deacon, T. (1998). *The symbolic species: The co-evolution of language and the brain.* New York: W. W. Norton.

Degenhardt, L., Chiu, W. T., Sampson, N., Kessler, R. C., Anthony, J. C., Angermeyer, M.,... Wells, J. E. (2008). Toward a global view of alcohol, tobacco, cannabis, and cocaine use: Findings from the WHO World Mental Health Surveys. *PloS Medicine, 5,* 1053–1067.

Delamontagne, R. (2010). High religiosity and societal dysfunction in the United States during the first decade of the twenty-first century. *Evolutionary Psychology, 8,* 617–657.

Dennett, D. (2006). *Breaking the spell: Religion as a natural phenomenon.* New York: Viking.

Dennett, D., & LaScola, L. (2010). Preachers who are not believers. *Evolutionary Psychology, 8,* 122–150.

de Tocqueville, A. (1835). *Democracy in America London:* Saunders and Ofley.

Diamond, J. (2005). *Guns, germs and steel: The fates of human societies.* London: Vintage.

Dionne, E. (1986, March 22). Italy says it found cyanide in Sindona. *The New York Times,* p. A3.

Dobson, J. (2007a). Does spanking work for all kids? *Focus on the Family* Retrieved June 2008, from http://www.family.org/parenting/A000001547.cfm

Dobson, J. (2007b). To spank or not to spank. *Focus on the Family.* Retrieved July 2008, from http://www.family.org/parenting/A000001548.cfm

Donadio, R. (2010, September 21). Money-laundering inquiry touches Vatican bank. *The New York Times.* Retrieved December 2011, from http://www.nytimes.com/2010/09/22/world/europe/22vatican.html

Dower, J. (2010). *Cultures of war.* New York: W. W. Norton.

Doyle, R. (2000) The roots of homicide. *Scientific American, 283*(3), 22.

Doyle, R. (2002) Quality of life. *Scientific American, 286*(4), 32.

Dray, P. (2003). *At the hands of persons unknown: The lynching of Black America.* New York: Random House.

D'Souza, D. (2007). *What's so great about christianity.* Washington, DC: Regenery.

Edelman, B. (2009). Red light states: Who buys online adult entertainment? *Journal of Economic Perspectives, 23,* 209–220.

Edgell, P., Gertels, J., & Hartmann, D. (2006). Atheists as 'other': Moral boundaries and cultural membership in American society. *American Sociological Review, 71,* 211–234.

Egginton, W. (2011). *In defense of religious moderation.* Baltimore: The Johns Hopkins University Press.

Ehrman, B. (2008). *God's problem.* New York: Harper One.

Eisenberg, M., Olson, R. E., Neumark-Sztainer, D., Story, M., & Bearinger, L. H. (2004). Correlations between family meals and psychological well-being among adolescents. *Archives of Pediatrics and Adolescent Medicine, 158,* 792–796.

Ellison, C., Burr, J., & McCall, P. (2003). The enduring puzzle of Southern homicide: Is regional religious culture the missing piece? *Homicide Studies, 7,* 326–352.

Epson, G. (2009). *Shammanism: A cross-cultural study of beliefs and practices.* Jefferson, NC: McFarland.

Epstein, G. (2009). *Good without God: What a billion nonreligious people do believe.* New York: Crown.

Everett, D. (2008). *Don't sleep. There are snakes: Life and language in the Amazonian jungle.* New York: Pantheon.

"Evangelicals are addicted to porn." (2006). *ChristiaNet: The Worldwide Christian Community.* Retrieved December 2011, from http://christiannews.christianet.com/1154951956.htm

Ezzati, M., Friedman, A. B., Kulkarni, S. C., & Murray, C. J. L. (2008). The reversal of fortunes: Trends in county mortality and cross-country mortality disparities in the United States. *PLoS Medicine, 5,* e66.

Fearon, J. (2003). Ethnic and cultural diversity by country. *Journal of Economic Growth, 8,* 195–222.

Finer, L. (2007). Trends in premarital sex in the United States, 1954–2003. *Public Health Reports, 122,* 73–78.

Fonzo, L. (1983). *St. Peter's banker: Michele Sindona.* New York: Franklin Watts.

Freehling, W. (2007). *The road to disunion, Vol. 2. Secessionists triumphant 1854–1861.* Oxford, England: Oxford University Press.

Friedli, L. (2009). Mental health, resilience and inequalities: How individuals and communities are affected. *World Health*

Organization. Retrieved December 2011, from http://www.euro.who.int/__data/assets/pdf_file/0012/100821/E92227.pdf

Friedrich, J. (2006). *The fire: The bombing of Germany, 1940–1945*. New York: Columbia University Press.

Fukuyama, F. (1992). *End of history and the last man*. New York: Free Press.

Galen, L., & Kloet, J. (2011). Mental well-being in the religious and nonreligious: Evidence for a curvilinear relationship. *Mental Health, Religion and Culture, 14*, 673–689.

Gallup. (2005). Three in four Americans believe in the paranormal. *Gallup Brain*.

Gallup. (2006a). Twenty-eight percent believe Bible is actual word of God. *Gallup Brain*.

Gallup. (2006b). Who believes in God and who doesn't? *Gallup Brain*.

Gallup. (2011). Four in 10 Americans Believe in Strict Creationism, from http://www.gallup.com/poll/145286/four-americans-believe-strict-creationism.aspx.

Geertz, A., & Markusson, G. (2010). Religion is natural, atheism is not: On why everybody is both right and wrong. *Religion, 40*, 152–165.

Gellately, R. (2001). *Backing Hitler: Consent and coercion in Nazi Germany*. Oxford, England: Oxford University Press.

Geoghegan, T. (2010). *Were you born on the wrong continent?* New York: New Press.

Gerrard, T. (1914). The church and eugenics. *New Advent*. Retrieved December 2011, from http://www.newadvent.org/cathen/16038b.htm

Gervais, W., Shariff, A., & Norenzayan, A. (2011). Do you believe in atheists? Distrust is central to anti-atheist prejudice. *Journal of Personality and Social Psychology, 101*, 1189–1206.

Gill, A., & Lundsgaarde, E. (2004). State welfare spending and religiosity. *Rationality and Society, 16*, 399–436.

Goldstein, J. (2001). *War and gender: How gender shapes the war system and vice versa*. Cambridge, England: Cambridge University Press.

Goodall, J. (1986). *The chimpanzees of Gombe: Patterns of behavior*. Cambridge, MA: Harvard University Press.

Grasmick, H., Davenport, G., Chamblin, M., & Bursick, R. (1992). Protestant fundamentalism and the retributive doctrine of punishment. *Criminology, 30*, 21–45.

Griswold, E. (2008). God's country. *The Atlantic Monthly, 301*(2), 40–55.

Gruber, J., & Hungerman, D. (2006). The church vs. the mall: What happens when religion faces increased secular competition? *National Bureau of Economic Research*. Retrieved December 2011, from http://papers.nber.org/papers/w12410.pdf

Hall, D., Matz, D., & Wood, W. (2010). Why don't we practice what we preach? A meta-analytic review of religious racism. *Personality and Social Psychology Review, 14*, 126–139.

Harris, S. (2006). *Letter to a Christian nation*. New York: Knopf.

Harris, S. (2010). *The moral landscape: How science can determine human values*. New York: Free Press.

Hasegawa, T. (2005). *Racing the enemy: Stalin, Truman and the surrender of Japan*. Cambridge, MA: The Belknap Press of Harvard University.

Hassig, R. (1988). *Aztec warfare: Imperial expansion and political control*. Norman: University of Oklahoma Press.

Hastings, D. (2010). *Catholicism and the roots of Nazism*. Oxford, England: Oxford University Press.

Haub, C. (1995/2004). How many people have ever lived on Earth? *Population Reference Bureau*. Retrieved December 2011, from http://www.prb.org/Articles/2002/HowManyPeoplehaveEverLivedonEarth.aspx

Hawkings, S., & Mlodinow, L. (2010). *The grand design*. New York: Bantam Books.

Hedges, C. (2009). *When atheism becomes religion: America's new fundamentalists*. New York: Free Press.

Himmelstein, D., Warren, E., Thorne, D., & Wollhander, S. (2005). Illness and injury as contributors to bankruptcy. *Health Affairs*. Retrieved April 2005, from http://pnhp.org/PDF_files/MedicalBankruptcy.pdf

Hitchens, C. (2007). *God is not great: How religion poisons everything*. New York: Twelve Books.

Hitler, A. (1925). *Mein kampf* (R. Manheim, Trans.). Boston: Haughton Mifflin.

Hood, R., Bernard, S., Hunsberger, B., & Gorsuch, R. (1986). *The psychology of religion, an empirical approach*. New York: The Guilford Press.

Inzlicht, M., McGregor, I., Hirsh, J., & Nash, K. (2009). Neural markers of religious conviction. *Psychological Science, 20*, 385–392.

International Social Survey Program. (2001)., *Religion II*.

Jean-Baptiste, M., Shen, Y. K., Aiden, A. P., Veres, A., Gray, M. K., Google Books Team, . . . Aiden, E. L. (2010). Quantitative analysis of culture using millions of digitized books. *Science*. Retrieved December 2011, from http://www.sciencemag.org/content/331/6014/176

Jefferson, T. (1787). *Notes on the state of Virginia* London: John Stockdale.

Jensen, G. (2006). Religious cosmologies and homicide rates among nations: A closer look. *Journal of Religion and Society, 8*. 1–14.

Johnson, B., Tompkins, R., & Webb, D. (2002). Objective hope: Assessing the effectiveness of faith-based organizations: A review of the literature. *Manhattan Institute for Policy Research*. Retrieved December 2011, from http://www.manhattan-institute.org/html/crrucs-obj_hope.htm

Kaplan, D., & Marshall, A. (1996). *The cult at the end of the world*. New York: Crown.

Kaplan, R. (2010, December 5). A world with no one in charge. *The Washington Post*, p. B1, B4.

Kaufmann, E. (2010). *Shall the religious inherit the Earth?* London: Profile Books.

Kawachi, I., & Kennedy, B. (2002). *The health of nations: Why inequality is harmful to your health*. New York: New Press.

Keeley, L. (1996). *War before civilization: The myth of the peaceful savage*. Oxford, England: Oxford University Press.

Keister, L. (2008). Conservative protestants and wealth: How religion perpetuates asset poverty. *American Journal of Sociology, 113*, 1237–1271.

Kelly, R. (2000). *Warless societies and the origin of war*. Ann Arbor: University of Michigan Press.

Kennedy, D. (2011). *Don't shoot: One man, a street fellowship, and the end of violence in inner-city America*. New York: Bloomsbury.

Komlos, J., & Lauderdale, B. (2007). Underperformance in affluence: The remarkable relative decline in U.S. heights in the second half of the 20th century. *Social Science Quarterly, 88*, 283–305.

Kosmin, B., & Keysar, A. (2009). *American Religious Identification Survey (ARIS) 2008*. Retrieved December 2011, from http://b27.cc.trincoll.edu/weblogs/AmericanReligionSurvey-ARIS/reports/ARIS_Report_2008.pdf

Kunkle, F., & Helderman, R. (2011, January 18). Sticking to their guns, pro or con. *The Washington Post*, p. B1, B4.

Lal, K. (1973). Growth of Muslim Population in Medieval India. Dlhi: Research Publications in Social Sciences.

Lane, R. (1997). *Murder in America: A history*. Columbus: Ohio State University Press.

Lankford, A. (2010). Do suicide terrorists exhibit clinically suicidal risk factors? *Aggression and Violent Behavior. 15*, 334–340.

Larson, E., & Witham, L. (1999). Scientists and religion in America. *Scientific American, 281*(3), 88–93.

LeBlanc, S., & Register, K. (2004). *Constant battles: The myth of the peaceful, noble savage*. New York: St. Martin's Griffin.

Legg, P. (2008). German church admits aiding Nazis. *BBC News*. Retrieved December 2011, from http://news.bbc.co.uk/2/hi/7337748.stm

Lester, T. (2002). Oh, Gods! *Atlantic Monthly, 289*(3), 37–45.

Longman, P. (2006, July/August). The return of patriarchy. *Foreign Policy*, p. 56–65.

Luther, M. (1543). *On the Jews and their lies* Wittenberg: H. Lufft.

Malinowski, B. (1954). *Magic, science and religion, and other essays*. Garden City, NY: Doubleday.

Marks, N., Abdallah, S., Sims, A., & Thompson, S. (2006). The happy planet index. *New Economics Foundation* Retrieved December 2011, from http://www.happyplanetindex.org

Marler, P., & Hadaway, C. (1999). Testing the attendance gap in a conservative church. *Sociology of Religion, 60*, 175–186.

Marlowe, F. (2002). Why the Hadza are still hunter-gatherers. In S. Kent (Ed.), *Ethnicity, hunter-gatherers, and the other* (pp. 247–281). Washington, DC: Smithsonian Institution Press.

Marlowe, F. (2004). The Hadza. In C. Ember & M. Ember (Eds.), *Encyclopedia of medical anthropology II* (pp. 689–696). New York: Plenum Publishers.

Marlowe, F. (2010). *The Hadza: Hunter-gatherers of Tanzania*. Berkeley: University of California Press.

Marmot, M. (2004). *The status syndrome*. London: Bloomsbury.

Martin, M. (1982, July 18). Checks and imbalances at the Vatican bank. *The New York Times*, p. E3.

Maxwell, J. (1975). *The Catholic Church and slavery*. Chichester, England: Barry Rose.

Merari, A. (2010). *Driven to death: Psychological and social aspects of suicide terrorism*. Oxford, England: Oxford University Press.

Messner, S., & Zevenbergen, M. (2005). The legacy of lynching and Southern homicide. *American Sociological Review, 70*, 633–655.

Muenning, P., & Glied, S. (2010). What changes in survival rates tell us about US health care. *Health Affairs, 29*, 2105–2113.

Murphy, C. (2012). *God's jury: The Inquisition and the making of the modern world*. New York: Houghton Mifflin Harcourt.

Murry, C. (2009, March 20). Thank God America isn't like Europe – yet. The Washington Post, www.washingtonpost.com/wp=dyn/content/article.2009/03/20/AR2009032001779.html.

Narr, K. (2008). Prehistoric religion. *Britannica Online Encyclopedia*. Retrieved December 2011, from http://concise.britannica.com/oscar/print?articleId=109434&fullArticle=true&tocId=52333

Neapolitan, J. (1997). *Cross-national crime*. Westport, CT: Greenwood Press.

Niditch, S. (1993). *War in the Hebrew Bible: A study in the ethics of violence*. Oxford, England: Oxford University Press.

Nisbett, R., & Cohen, D. (1999). *Culture of honor: The psychology of violence in the South*. Boulder, CO: West View Press.

Norenzayan, A., & Shariff, A. (2008). The origin and evolution of religious prosociality. *Science, 322*, 58–62.

Norris, P., & Inglehart, R. (2004). *Sacred and secular*. Cambridge, England: Cambridge University Press.

Numbers, R. (2005). *The creationists: From scientific creationism to intelligent design*. Cambridge, MA: Harvard University Press.

Ohnuki-Tierney, E. (2006). *Kamikaze diaries: Reflections of Japanese student soldiers*. Chicago: University of Chicago Press.

O'Reilly, B. (2006). *Culture warrior*. New York: Broadway.

Otterbein, K. (2004). *How war began*. College Station: Texas A&M University Press.

Paley, W. (1802). *Natural theology*. Bridgewater Treatises, Faulder.

Palin, S. (2010). *America by heart: Reflections on family, faith and flag*. New York: Harper.

Panchaud, C., Singh, S., Darroch, D., & Darroch, J. (2000). Sexually transmitted diseases among adolescents in developed countries. *Family Planning Perspectives, 32*, 24–32.

Paul, G. (2003). The great scandal: Christianity's role in the rise of the Nazis, 1. *Free Inquiry, 23*(4), 20–29.

Paul, G. (2004). The great scandal: Christianity's role in the rise of the Nazis, 2. *Free Inquiry, 24*(1), 28–33.

Paul, G. (2005). Cross-national correlations of quantifiable societal health with popular religiosity and secularism in the prosperous democracies. *Journal of Religion and Society, 7*, http://moses.creighton.edu/JRS/2005/2005-11.html

Paul, G. (2008). The remote prayer delusion: Clinical trials that attempt to detect supernatural intervention are as futile as they are unethical. *Journal of Medical Ethics, 34*, e18.

Paul, G. (2009a). The chronic dependence of popular religiosity upon dysfunctional psychosociological conditions. *Evolutionary Psychology, 7*, 398–441.

Paul, G. (2009b). Theodicy's problem: A statistical look at the holocaust of the children and the implications of natural evil for the free will and best of all possible worlds hypotheses. *Philosophy and Theology, 19*, 125–149.

Paul, G. (2009c). How are other first-world nations suppressing the adverse consequences of violence and youth sex in the modern media environment? *Pediatrics, 123*, e364.

Paul, G. (2010a). Religiosity tied to socioeconomic conditions. *Science, 327*, 642.

Paul, G. (2010b). The evolution of popular religiosity and secularism: How 1st world statistics reveal why religion exists, why it has been popular, and why the most successful democracies are the most secular. In P. Zuckerman (Ed.), *Atheism and secularity* (pp. 49–209). Santa Barbara, CA: Praeger.

Paul, G. (2010c, October 27). What's really hurting Christianity in America. *Los Angeles Times*. Retrieved December 2011, from http://articles.latimes.com/2010/oct/27/opinion/la-oew-paul-religion-secularism-20101027

Paul, G. (2012). Moderate Religion is Not Good for Societies. The Secular Web, http://www.infidels.org/kiosk/article847.html

Paul, G., & Cox, E. (1996). *Beyond humanity: Cyber evolution and future minds*. Rockland, MA: Charles River Media.

Paul, G., & Zuckerman, P. (2007). Why the gods are not winning. *Edge*. Retrieved December 2011, from http://www.edge.org/3rd_culture/paul07/paul07_index.html

Paul, G., & Zuckerman, P. (2011, April 30). Don't Dump on Atheists. *The Washington Post*, A15, from http://www.washingtonpost.com/opinions/why-do-americans-still-dislike-atheists/2011/02/18/AFqgnwGF_story.html

Pegg, M. (2008). *Most holy war: The Albigensian crusade and the battle for Christendom*. Oxford, England: Oxford University Press.

Peters, E. (1971). *The first crusade*. Philadelphia: University of Pennsylvania Press.

Pew Research. (2002). Among wealthy nations US stands alone in its embrace of religion. *Pew Global Attitudes Project*. Retrieved December 2002, from http://pewglobal.org/reports/display.php?reported=167

Pew Research. (2008). U.S. religious landscape survey. Retrieved June 2008, from http://religions.pewforum.org/pdf/report2 religious-landscape-study-full.pdf

Pew Research. (2011). The future of the global Muslim population. *Pew Forum on Religion & Public Life*. Retrieved December 2011, http://www.pewforum.org/future-of-the-global-muslim-population-regional-europe.aspx

Pfeiffer, J. (1985). *The creative explosion: An inquiry into the origins of art and religion*. Ithaca, NY: Cornell University Press.

Phayer, M. (2000). *The Catholic church and the Holocaust, 1930–1965*. Bloomington: Indiana University Press.

Phayer, M. (2008). *Pious XII, the Holocaust, and the Cold War*. Bloomington: Indiana University Press.

Phillips, K. (2006). *American theocracy*. New York: Viking.

Pickett, K., & Wilkinson, R. (2007). Child wellbeing and income inequality in rich societies: Ecological cross sectional study. *British Medical Journal, 335*, 1080–1086.

Pinker, S. (1994). *The language instinct: How the mind creates language*. New York: Perennial.

Pinker, S. (2011). *The better nature of our angels: Why violence has declined*. New York: Viking.

Pollard, J. (2005). *Money and the rise of the modern papacy*. Cambridge, England: Cambridge University Press.

Powell, L., Shahabi, L., & Thoresen, C. (2003). Religion and spirituality: Linkages to physical health. *American Psychologist, 58*, 36–52.

Pratt, T., & Godsey, T. (2003). Social support, inequality and homicide: A cross-national test of an integrated theoretical model. *Criminology, 41*, 611–643.

Preston, J., & Epley, N. (2009). Science and God: An automatic opposition between ultimate explanations. *Journal of Experimental Social Psychology, 4*, 238–241.

Prinz, J. (2012). *Beyond human nature: How culture and experience shape our lives*. New York, Allen Lane.

Przybyla, H. (2010). Tea Party advocates who scorn socialism want a government job. *Bloomberg News*. Retrieved March 2010, from http://www.bloomberg.com/apps/news?pid=newsarchive&sid=aLBZwxqgYgwl

Public Religion Research Institute. (2010). American values post-election survey 2010. Retrieved December 2010, from http://www.publicreligion.org/objects/uploads/fck/filo/AUS%202010%20Post-Election%20Topline%20Final.pdf

Putman, R. (2000). *Bowling alone: The collapse and revival of American community*. New York: Simon & Schuster.

Putman, R., & Campbell, D. (2010). *American grace*. New York: Simon & Schuster.

Raghavan, S. (2010, December 12). Gays in Africa face growing persecution. *The Washington Post*, p. A12.

Rainer, T. (2005). A resurgence not yet realized: Evangelistic effectiveness in the Southern Baptist Convention since 1979. *The Southern Baptist Journal of Theology, 9*, 54–69.

Raw, C. (1992). *The Moneychangers*. London: Harper Collins.

Rees, T. (2009). Is personal insecurity a cause of cross-national differences in the intensity of religious belief? *Journal of Religion and Society*, 11, from http://moses.creighton.edu/JRS/2009/2009-17.html

Reid, T. (2004). *The United States of Europe*. New York: Penguin Press.

Reid, T. (2009). *The healing of America*. New York: Penguin Press.

Rosas, A., Martínez-Maza, C., Bastir, M., García-Tabernero, A., Lalueza-Fox, C., Huguet, R ... Fortea, J. (2006). Paleobiology and comparative morphology of a Neandertal group from El Sidon, Asturia, Spain. *Proceedings of the National Academy of Sciences USA, 103*, 19266–19271.

Rosenbaum, E. (2009). Patient teenagers? A comparison of the sexual behavior of virginity pledgers and matched nonpledgers. *Pediatrics, 123*, e110–e120.

Rozen, D. (2011). A decade of change in American congregations. Faith Community Today, from http://faithcommunitiestoday.org/sites/faithcommunitiestoday.org/files/Decade%20of%20Change%20Final_0.pdf

Rubenstein, J. (2008). Cannibals and crusaders. *French Historical Studies, 31*, 525–552.

Ruff, C., Trinkaus, E., & Holliday, T. (1997). Body mass and encephalization in Pleistocene *Homo*. *Nature, 387*, 173–176.

Ruiter, S., & Tubergen, F. (2009). Religious attendance in cross-national perspective: A multilevel analyis of 60 countries. *American Journal of Sociology, 115*, 863–895.

Sampson, R., Raudenbush, S., & Earls, F. (1997) Neighborhoods and violent crime: A multilevel study of collective efficacy. *Science, 277*, 918–924.

Sapolsky, R. (2005). Sick of poverty. *Scientific American, 293*(6), 92–99.

Scheepers, P., Gijsberts, M., & Hello, E. (2002). Religiosity and prejudice against ethnic minorities in Europe: Cross-national tests on a controversial relationship. *Review of Religious Research, 43*, 242–265.

Schoen, C., Osborn, R., Huynh, P. T., Doty, M., Zapert, K., Peugh, J., & Davis, K. (2005). Taking the pulse of health care systems: Experience of patients with health problems in six countries. *Health Affairs*. Retrieved December 2011, from http://www.commonwealthfund.org/Publications/In-the-Literature/2005/Nov/Taking-the-Pulse-of-Health-Care-Systems--Experiences-of-Patients-with-Health-Problems-in-Six-Countri.aspx

Scholder, K. (1988). *The churches and the Third Reich, Vols 1 & 2*. Philadelphia: Fortress Press.

Schwarz, S. (2006). *Judaism and justice: The Jewish passion to repair the world*. Woodstock, NY: Long Mill Partners.

Scott, R. (2004). *The history of torture throughout the ages*. London: Kegan Paul.

Sedgh, G., Henshaw, S., Singh, S., Ahman, E., & Shah, I. H. (2007). Induced abortion: Estimated rates and trends worldwide. *The Lancet, 37*, 1338–1345.

Shah, I., & Ahman, E. (2009). Unsafe abortion: Global and regional incidence, trends, consequences, and challenges. *Journal of Obstetrics and Gynaecology Canada, 12*, 1149–1158.

Shah, T., & Toft, M. (2006, March/April). Why God is winning. *Foreign Policy*, p. 38–43.

Shelley, M., Doebler, R., Woods, P., Gunden, J., Gardner, J., Goetz, D.... Wilde, G. (1994). *The Quest Study Bible*. Grand Rapids, MI: Zondervan Publishing House.

Shermer, M. (2006). Bowling for God. *Scientific American, 295*(6), 44.

Singh, S., & Darroch, J. (2000). Adolescent pregnancy and childbearing: Levels and trends in developed countries. *Family Planning Perspectives, 32*, 14–23.

Smith, A. (1776). *An inquiry into the nature and cause of the wealth of nations* London: W. Strahan and T. Cadell.

Smith, T., & Kim, S. (2004). The vanishing protestant majority. *GSS Social Change Report, 14*, 1–22.

Snyder, T. (2010). *Bloodlands: Europe between Hitler and Stalin*. New York: Basic Books.

Spencer, H. (1884). *The man versus the state* London: William and Norgate.

Stark, R. (2006). *The victory of reason: How Christianity led to freedom, capitalism and Western societies*. New York: Random House.

Stark, R. (2008*). What American really believes*. Waco, TX: Baylor University Press.

Stark, R. (2009). *God's battalions: The case for the crusades*. New York: Harper One.

Stark, R., & Finke, R. (2000). *Acts of faith*. Berkeley: University of California Press.

Steigman-Gall, R. (2003). *The holy Reich*. Cambridge, England: Cambridge University Press.

Stephenson, C. (2004). Leveraging diversity to maximum advantage: The business case for appointing more women to boards. *Ivery Business Journal, 69*(1), 1–5.

Strayhorn, J., & Strayhorn, J. (2009). Religiosity and teen birth rate in the United States. *Reproductive Health, 6*, 14.

Summerville, S. (2002). Stark's age of faith argument and the secularization of things: A commentary. *Sociology of Religion, 63*, 361–372

Taylor, H. (2003). While most Americans believe in God, only 36% attend a religious service once a month or more often. *Harris Interactive*. Retrieved December 2011, from http://www.harrisinteractive.com/harris_poll/index.asp?PID=408

Thrower, J. (1980). *The alternative tradition: Religion and the rejection of religion in the ancient world*. The Hague, The Netherlands: Mouton.

Times/Harris. (2006). Religious views and beliefs vary greatly by country, according to the latest Financial Times/Harris poll. *Harris Interactive*. Retrieved December 2011, from http://www.harrisinteractive.com/NEWS/allnewsbydate.asp?NewsID=1130

Tomlinson, J. (1991) *Cultural imperialism: A critical introduction*. Baltimore: Johns Hopkins University Press.

Transparency International. (2010). *Corruption perceptions index*. Retrieved December 2011, from http://www.transparency.org/policy_research/surveys_indices/cpi/2010/results

Trenholm, B., Devaney, B., Fortson, K., Quay, L., Wheeler, J., & Clark, M. (2007). Impacts of four Title V section 510 abstinence education programs. Report to Congress. Retrieved February 2008, from http://aspe.hhs.gov/hsp/abstinence07

Twain, M. (1884). *Adventures of Huckleberry Finn*. New York: Charles L. Webster.

Twain, M. (2010). *The Autobiography of Mark Twain, Vol. 1*. Berkeley: University of California Press.

Uslaner, E. (2002). *The moral foundations of trust*. Cambridge, England: Cambridge University Press.

United Nations. (2008). *Human development report 2007/2008*. Retrieved December 2008, from http://hdrstats.undp.org/en/indicators/1.html

United Nations. (2009). *Human development report 2009: Gender empowerment measure and its components*. Retrieved December 2011, from http://hdr.undp.org/en/media/HDR_2009_EN_Table_K.pdf

Vastag, B. (2011, January 28). Obama's call for innovation follows slump in most sectors. *The Washington Post*, p. A4.

Verweij, J., Ester, P., & Nauta, R. (1997). Secularization as an economic and cultural phenomenon. *Journal for the Scientific Study of Religion, 36*, 309–324.

Vick, K. (2003, August 12). Taylor resigns, leaves Liberia. *The Washington Post*, p. A1.

Voland, E., & Schiefenhovel, W. (Eds.). (2009). *The biological evolution of religious mind and behavior*. New York: Springer.

Warren, R. (2002). *The purpose driven life*. Grand Rapids, MI: Zondervan Publishing House.

Weatherford, J. (2004). *Genghis Khan and the making of the modern world*. New York: Crown.

Weisman, J., & Cooperman, A. (2006, December 14). A religious protest largely from the left: Conservative Christians say fighting cuts in poverty programs is not a priority. *Washington Post*, http://www.washingtonpost.com/wp-dyn/content/article/2005/12/13/AR2005121301764.html

Wellings, K., Collumbien, M., Slaymaker, E., Singh, S., Hodges, Z., Patel, D., & Bajos, N. (2006). Sexual behavior in context: A global perspective. *Lancet, 368*, 1706–1728.

White, T. (2001). Once were cannibals. *Scientific American, 285*(8), 58–65.

Wilkinson, R., & Pickett, K. (2009). *The spirit level: Why more equal societies almost always do better*. London: Allen Lane.

Wilson, A. (2002). Machines, power, and the ancient economy. *The Journal of Roman Studies, 92*, 1–32.

Winkleby, M., Cubbin, C., & Ahn, D. (2006). Individual socioeconomic status, neighborhood socioeconomic status, and adult mortality. *American Journal of Public Health, 96*, 2145–2153.

World Economic Forum. (2012). The Global competitiveness report 2011-2012. Retrieved April 2012, from http://www.weforum.org/reports/global-competitiveness-report-2011-2012.

Wright, R. (2008). *The evolution of God*. New York: Little, Brown.

World Values Survey. (2007). *World values survey 2005–2007*.

Yang, C. (1970). *Religion in Chinese society*. Berkeley: University of California Press.

Zimring, F., & Hawkins. G. (1999) *Crime is not the problem: Lethal violence in America*. Oxford, England: Oxford University Press.

Zogby, J. (2008). *The way we'll be: The Zogby report on the transformation of the American dream*. New York: Random House.

Zuckerman, P. (2008). *A society without God: What the least religious nations can tell us about contentment*. New York: New York University Press.

Zuckerman, P. (2009, March 6). Atheism, secularity, and well-being: How the findings of social science counter negative stereotypes and assumptions. *Sociology Compass*, p. 949–971.

CHAPTER
26

Peace and the Human Animal: Toward Integration of Comparative Evolutionary Psychology and Peace Studies

Nancy K. Dess

Abstract

Peace is arguably the problem of the 21st century. Peacefulness is not uniquely human, but a dearth of it among humans disproportionately threatens people and other animals around the globe. The urgent need for peace—if not immediately, everywhere, at any cost, then soon, as a pervasive norm—coincides with unprecedented scholarly attention to peace and to the implications of evolution for psychological functioning in the context of complex sociality. The time is ripe to integrate evolutionary perspectives into peace studies. Toward that end, this chapter describes potential impediments to an evolutionary peace project, provides a basic lexical and conceptual tool kit, and identifies some promising research directions.

Key Words: peace, evolution, prosocial, embodiment, comparative psychology, nonhuman animals

Introduction

On a beautiful spring day in 2010, two young primates—one a female western lowland gorilla, the other a boy in striped overalls—seal their encounter at the Los Angeles Zoo with a kiss (see Fig. 26.1). How are their relatives engaged? Plans proceed in earnest across town in Highland Park for the 2010 Peace in the Northeast march and, across the Atlantic, for Africa Day 2010, on which the 50+ nations of the African Union will advance the twin themes of peace and security. Not far away—havoc. By the end of the month, dozens of people from infants to the elderly are shot, stabbed, strangled, or beaten to death in Los Angeles County. A Human Rights Watch (2010) report documents the massacre of children, women, and men in Makombo, Democratic Republic of Congo (DRC); they join the millions of people dead so far due to the war between DRC and its neighbors, during which whole families of western lowland gorillas have succumbed to poaching, disease, and habitat destruction. Snapshots of other continents similarly would reveal a montage of peace and violence.

Moving through time also reveals sharp contrasts between peace and mayhem. Historians studying why peace gives way to war and vice versa scan backward and forward through tens, hundreds, or a few thousands of years. From the 20th-century sociopolitical landscape, for example, they glean reasons that relatively friendly relations between Japan and the United States yielded to the bombing of Pearl Harbor, Nagasaki, and Hiroshima, then later were restored. How might turning the clock back further—back 10,000, 100,000, or millions of years—enhance that understanding? What would an account of peace rooted in deep time look like?

This chapter peers at peace through an evolutionary lens. The need is great: Nuclear proliferation stimulated by the Cold War doctrine of Mutual Assured Destruction threatens the Korean peninsula, the fragile relationship between Pakistan and India and between Iran, its neighbors, and NATO,

471

Figure 26.1 An encounter between a young boy and a young gorilla at the Los Angeles Zoo, March 2010.

and anyone anywhere a "dirty bomb" can reach. Ethnic, gang, and domestic violence pervade many societies. Concern about the viability of human life on Earth has spread beyond doomsday cults. Peace is arguably the problem of the 21st century. The need is as great as the opportunity. Globally, peace activism and scholarship have grown to unprecedented levels and are key components of the interdisciplinary project of sustainability. Evolutionary psychological approaches have burgeoned, matured, and entered the mainstream of scholarly discourse. The time is ripe to merge these streams of intellectual energy by applying evolution in new ways to the massively complex problem of peace. Doing so requires realistic appraisal of challenges and a plan for facilitating the future efforts of diverse scholars. The sections that follow deal with impediments, lexical and conceptual issues, and key research directions in an evolutionarily informed study of peace.

Perceiving Threat: Impediments to an Evolutionary Peace Project

Differences of perspective that generate healthy, spirited exchange are usefully distinguished from differences with the potential to impede constructive exchange. The latter are dealt with here. Persistent sources of resistance to evolutionary psychology have been addressed elsewhere (e.g., Confer et al., 2010; Dess, 2003; Hagen, 2005; Pinker, 2002). Their brief treatment here is tailored to create a realistic, if sobering, context for peace scholarship.

Peace-Relevant Ideology and Identity

People believe and feel passionately about peace and war. Even people who share a desire for peace can harbor beliefs about when, how, and with whom to be peaceable that are not easily reconciled. Dwight Eisenhower and Albert Einstein both expressed a yearning for peace. Eisenhower famously warned of the "military-industrial complex" in his presidential farewell—but, a warrior, he meant only to set a boundary condition on militarism, asserting, "A vital element in keeping the peace is our military establishment. Our arms must be mighty, ready for instant action." In contrast, Einstein insisted that "Striving for peace and preparing for war are incompatible with each other" (as cited by Nathan & Norden, 1981, p. 528). If beliefs such as these simply reflected ideas about the most sensible way of achieving peace, rational discussion and evidence might settle the matter. However, *militarism* and *pacificism* signify ideologies (value systems) and identities (e.g., hawk/dove, conservative/liberal) and thus are deeply bound up with people's views of themselves in relation to others, the nature of human being, and the way things ought to be (e.g., D'Agostino, 1995; Graham, Haidt, & Nosek, 2009; Malka & Lelkes, 2010). People on either side of a national divide can, for instance, view compatriots as "peace loving" and people on the other side as "war mongering" (Haque, 1973; Rath & Das, 1958).

It would be naïve to assume that shared interest in peace will ensure equanimity among psychologists. Critiques of psychologists by psychologists sometimes mirror broader discourses on war and peace. Consider, for instance, *Psychology's War on Religion* (Cummings, O'Donohue, & Cummings, 2009). A favorably impressed reviewer contends that "Psychology has literally declared war on religion," a war prosecuted by the leftist-controlled American Psychological Association (APA; Magee-Egan, 2009). From the postmodern edge comes a call for an *unscientific psychology* revolution to overthrow, by such subversive tactics as "infiltrating" the APA convention, the "myth/hoax" of a psychology that "[d]isguises itself as a science" and is "harmful to most of the world's people" (Newman & Holzman, 2006, pp. 61, 134, 3, and 67, respectively).

Not all challenges to an evolutionary account of peace, then, will hinge on attitudes toward evolution. Some will be rooted in broader ideologies and identities relevant to peace that will make some conversations difficult or unproductive. Strategies will have to be devised for identifying worthwhile conversations and overcoming bridgeable differences.

Animus Toward Evolution

Growing enthusiasm for evolutionary scholarship notwithstanding, "implacable hostility" (Dawkins, 2005) toward it remains a potent force in public and academic discourse. Repudiation of evolution has become a brand for national leaders on the political far Right (see Lavender, 2011). In 1999, then-Majority Whip Tom DeLay (R-TX) linked the Columbine school massacre to teaching children that "they are nothing but glorified apes who have evolutionized out of some primordial soup of mud" (106th Congressional Record, June 16, 1999). At a 2009 congressional hearing, John Shimkus (R-IL), chair of the House Subcommittee on Environment and Economy in the 112th Congress, invoked the "the infallible word of God" to downplay climate change, saying "that's the way it's going to be for His creation… The Earth will end only when God declares it's time to be over. Man [*sic*] will not destroy this Earth" (WorldNews, 2009). Though the latest Gallup poll on origins indicates majority endorsement of some version of evolution (54%), a majority of Republicans (52%) endorse the position that "God created present humans pretty much in their present form within the last 10,000 years" (Newport, 2010). The wind blowing behind rightwing leadership does not bode well for teaching and research in evolution in the coming decade.

With respect to peace, evolutionary scholarship likely will be seen from the far Right as propaganda from peaceniks, atheists, and "wusses" who imperil the nation (Christie, Tint, Wagner, & Winter, 2008). Consider the video series, *Resisting the Green Dragon*, which warns that the "multi-faceted environmentalist movement"—to which sustainable peace is inextricably tied (see section on "Thinking Ahead")—is "without doubt one of the greatest threats to society and the church today" (http://www.resistingthegreendragon.com). The series was produced by the Cornwall Alliance for the Stewardship of Creation, whose founder, E. Calvin Beisner, explains:

> [B]ecause environmentalism—the word coming from French meaning "surroundings," that is, "everything," and so meaning literally "everythingism"—because environmentalism is inherently totalitarian, demanding to define and control every aspect of life, it aims to take control of our entire political and legal structure, and indeed has already advanced far in that direction over the last three decades. You, as an individual, have a tremendously important role to play in the church's battle against this impostor, with its alternative world view, its substitute doctrines of God, creation, man [*sic*], sin, and salvation, and its lethal mix of bogus science and Marxist economics that threaten to fulfill the radical environmentalists' and deep ecologists' dream of ending industrial society and forcing humanity back into a primitive lifestyle—in which, as Thomas Hobbes put it, life was solitary, poor, nasty, brutish, and short.
> (*Beisner*, n.d.)

The one world government Beisner invokes is a sign of the apocalypse in rapture theology, the basis of the *Left Behind* novel series featuring as Antichrist a peace-promoting Romanian who becomes secretary-general of the United Nations. That Antichrist is not unlike the Jewish one recruited by Satan while serving in the Peace Corps in former presidential candidate Pat Robertson's novel *The End of the Age* (2002), or the one who becomes a peace-promoting European Union President in John Hagee and Andre van Heerden's (1998) movie *Vanished in the Twinkling of an Eye*.

Do rapture theology and associated fiction have anything to do with evolutionary psychology or peace studies? They do. The fiction popularizes an indigenous American ideology that fuels a political machine hostile to evolution and secular peace efforts. The back matter to Robertson's novel states that it "captures how today's headlines may be foreshadowing the imminent approach of the last days." *Vanished* movie maker and televangelist

Hagee's latest book, *Can America Survive?* (2010), includes, says the jacket, a "spellbinding description of Armaggedon" in 2012. Hagee, whose endorsement was (initially) welcomed by 2008 presidential candidate John McCain, wrote, "We also know the Antichrist will enter the world stage with a reputation of being a powerful man of peace. Perhaps he will be a Nobel Peace Prize winner" (Hagee, 2003). The *Left Behind* Web site proclaims, "It's happening now"; the more than 65 million books sold are part of a multimedia franchise that includes movies and video games. *Left Behind* coauthor and Moral Majority cofounder Tim LaHaye said in a televised 2010 interview with Mike Huckabee—former governor and presidential candidate—that President Barack Obama promotes "government control and government domination of everything…It's going to work against our country and bringing us closer to the apocalypse." When Huckabee asked, "Are we now living in the end times, from your perspective?" LaHaye answered, "Very definitely, Governor." Even before that interview aired, one in four Republicans believed that Obama—a Nobel Peace Prize winner—may be the Antichrist (Harris Poll Interactive, 2010). Beisner's Cornwall Alliance coordinates politically active fundamentalist clergy, academics, media moguls, and organizations. He testified before the same 2009 climate change hearing at which John Shimkus provided scriptural assurance against devastating floods.

As journalist Bill Moyers notes in *Welcome to Doomsday* (2006), "the delusional is no longer marginal but has come in from the fringe to influence the seats of power" (p. 3). In *America Right or Wrong* (2004), Anatol Lieven, then with the Carnegie Endowment for International Peace, articulated the connection between rapture theology, antienvironmentalism, and support for all-out war in the Middle East. There is no mistaking rapture adherents' sinister view of secular peace efforts and its comportment with the policy positions of far-Right politicians. Evolutionary psychologists everywhere who are interested in peace need to be aware that in the United States, this network enjoys a solid base of support and has a science policy agenda. Engaging zealous creationists on evolution might not be productive, but searching for common ground, understanding their appeal, and engaging advocacy processes responsibly will be.

Evolutionary psychology continues to be an object of scorn for the academic Left. Misguided critiques remain in vogue, such as *Love of Shopping Is Not a Gene: Problems With Darwinian Psychology* (Dagg, 2004), the premise of which is:

> …although Darwinian psychology for animals has been a fruitful topic for biology, Darwinian psychology for human beings has not… The view that human social behaviors are correlated with our human genes is largely held by people who are right wing politically.
>
> (p. ix, xii)

Even many more scholarly works are better designed to alienate than to open a conversation. In *Neo-Liberal Genetics* (2006), McKinnon claims to have uncovered the free-market values that energize evolutionary psychologists, who "reduce social relations to a reflex of genetic self-maximization"; this, combined with stunning cultural blindness, yields prescriptive, universalist, "astonishingly reductive myths" that are "complete fiction" (pp. 1, 2, 4). In *Pure Society: From Darwin to Hitler* (2009), Pichot takes Darwin to task for "scientistic stupidity" (p. 63), and sociobiology for being "idiotic" (p. 76) and "totally ridiculous" (p. 78). For him, intervention in "the political-social order" based on "genetics or Darwinism" (p. 341)—ineluctably, to achieve "a supposedly natural order"—is "unacceptable." The implication is clear: When it comes to peace, evolutionary psychologists are personae non grata.

This genre perpetuates the thesis that evolutionary psychologists are a cadre of pseudoscientific genetic determinists who are party to a vast right-wing conspiracy. Current critiques are the same, at base, as those formulated in the 1970s by biologists Gould and Lewontin and popularized through journalistic sneering at "evo-psychos" (Angier, 1999). The imperviousness of the thesis to empirical (Tybur, Miller, & Gangestad, 2007) and conceptual rebuttal (e.g., Confer et al., 2010; Geher, 2006; Kenrick, Trost, & Sundie, 2004) tempts dismissal of the genre. Dismissal would be a mistake, for two main reasons. First, many critics charge specifically that by "naturalizing" war and all manner of violence, an evolutionary account justifies them and props up patriarchal structures that perpetuate them (e.g., Marecek, Crawford, & Popp, 2004; Moran, 2005; Zur, 1987). The historical underrepresentation of women and minorities in academe—particularly in science, higher ranks, and leadership roles (American Association for the Advancement of Science, 2001; Glass & Minnotte, 2010; National Academies of Science, 2010)—has lent credence to claims of sexism and racism. Academe's "ivory ceiling," along with some tone deafness to early cultural critiques of science, exacerbated polarization of the academic community. Psychology has been more attentive to structural inequality than some sciences and, as in most fields, women are now earning more degrees than men—yet disparities persist. For instance, in the United States, proportionately fewer women and people of color earn PhDs in cognitive, experimental, and neuroscience subfields than in "hierarchy-attenuating" (Sidanius & Pratto, 2004) subfields such as counseling, school, and developmental psychology (National Science Foundation [NSF], 2009). Of the 26 biology subfields identified by NSF, in only 5 do women earn fewer of the PhDs than in evolutionary biology. Reasons for these disparities are complex (e.g., Halpern et al., 2007), and it is unfair to lay what ails academe at the feet of evolutionary scholars; they are not exempt, however, from the structural and interpersonal dynamics that sometimes put them on the defensive. Taking on peace is another way for evolutionary psychologists to unsettle claims of contentment with the status quo, not just symbolically but by helping to reshape the scholarly community.

Second, evolutionary scholars' manifest interest in aggression has exceeded interest in peace (Sponsel, 1996). A PsycInfo search on *evolutionary* yields five times more hits when crossed with *war* than with *peace*, and hundreds of hits when crossed with, respectively, *aggression* and *violence* compared to a total of fewer than a dozen when crossed with *nonaggressive*, *nonviolent*, or *nonviolence*. Those results partially reflect a historical negative bias in psychology—that is, toward stress, illness, fear, prejudice, and so on—that is being balanced by increased attention to "positive psychology" (resilience, health, happiness, prosociality). Even the peace psychology movement took shape partly as a reaction to the threat of nuclear annihilation. Nonetheless, the larger accumulated literature on aggression than on peace abets charges of androcentrism (Crane-Seeber & Crane, 2010; Liesen, 2007; Lloyd, 2005).

The stereotyping of evolutionary psychology as conservative, militaristic, and androcentric should be understood and belied, not dismissed. Some worries on the academic Left about what evolutionary scholars are up to are understandable. There is healing to do. The topic of peace creates an excellent opportunity for it because it pulls for cooperation. Being effective means being civil and authentic. It means understanding the sociopolitical situatedness of the field. It means being clear that an evolutionary peace project is not a search for a "war gene" or "peace gene" that distinguishes groups. It means being clear that it does not make the slightest bit of sense from an evolutionary point of view to think about some humans as "more like animals" than others (see section on "Lexical Issues"). It means being clear that the peace project concerns the evolution and developmentally, socially, and environmentally contingent expression of humans' species-wide capacity for peace.

Siren Songs of Simplicity

Credit satirist H. L. Mencken with saying "For every complex problem, there is a solution that is simple, neat, and wrong." Peace is complex, and accounting for it requires negotiating simplicity. The impediment addressed here is not evolutionary scholars' foreclosure on a simple explanation; few would expect or respect one. The challenge will be threefold. First, generating a novel, impactful account of peace will not happen fast. Evolutionary psychology and peace psychology still are emerging fields. For example, neither is yet a fixture in the psychology curriculum. Moreover, their constituencies do not overlap much with each other or with other crucial (sub)disciplines—including, surprisingly, comparative psychology (Vonk & Shackelford, 2012). The task, then, is to undertake a multifaceted project that includes research and development of infrastructure for long-term efforts. Academic business as usual would be simpler, but it will not do.

Second, to have an impact, evolutionary peace scholars may have to tolerate more simplicity than is comfortable. They will need to leave their comfort zone and enter the fray of policy before having a fully satisfactory account of peace. Doing so runs against the grain of respect for the partial, tentative nature of scientific knowledge, not to mention against the will of those who warn them to keep out. It can feel recklessly close to a rocky shoal. But while worrying about the imperfection of an account that surely is too simple, policies will be developed, wars waged, and opportunities for peace lost, sometimes by people who balk at having been evolutionized from mud soup or otherwise lack compunction about rejecting science. Surely evolutionary psychologists can participate at least as competently, even while they keep working at the science. Irrelevance and inaction can be reckless, too.

The third challenge of simplicity concerns communication between people who have traveled a long way down separate institutional and intellectual paths. Where a common lexicon and trust ideally exist, simplifying heuristics and derivative understandings often exist instead. Take, for instance, *human nature*. Evolutionary psychologists concern themselves with it. What do they mean by it? Certainly not the essentialist bugaboo of "genetic selection, divine mandate [!], or historical inevitability" that lurks "under the broad heading of 'evolutionary psychology'" (Crane-Seeber & Crane, 2010, p. 218; see also DeLamater & Hyde, 1998; Dusek, 1999; Marecek et al., 2004; Zur, 1987). Nonetheless, the nature/nurture dichotomy is alive and well in academic and public discourse (David & DiGiuseppe, 2010). Dichotomizing nature and nurture and picking a side are socially situated, motivated processes (Horowitz, 1995). More bad news: Biological constructs (*nature*) are heuristically linked to immutable essences and are congenial to politically conservative attitudes and media (Brescoll & LaFrance, 2004; Dambrun, Kamiejski, Haddadi, & Duarte, 2009; Dupré, 2003). Essentialism is a simple, compelling ontology that can persist beyond childhood (Dar-Nimrod & Heine, 2010; Keller & Bless, 2004; Racine, Waldman, Rosenberg, & Illes, 2010; Shtulman & Schulz, 2008), offering stiff competition to the alternative compelled by contemporary science—variation constrained probabilistically at multiple levels of organization on timescales ranging from epochal to developmental to instantaneous.

Another problematic dichotomy manifests in depictions of human nature as pacific *or* violent. "Rousseauan" and "Hobbesian" humans in their "natural condition" serve as foils in dead-end debates over whether peacefulness or aggressiveness is more normal, pathological, or quintessentially human (Karlberg & Buell, 2005; Robarchek, 1989). The "natural persons" of 17th- and 18th-century philosophy are hard to recognize in most contemporary explications. Not only did Rousseau never use the phrase *noble savage*, it and the *peaceable kingdom* trope are inapplicable to his view of humans' precivil existence. Rousseau reasoned that the centrality of self-preservation in such existence would warrant aggression (in the *Second Discourse*, 1754/1997, p. 127). Indeed, he imagined a *state of war* prior to language and moral convention, elaborated in *Languages* as follows:

> Knowing nothing they feared everything, they attacked in order to defend themselves. A man abandoned on the face of the earth at the mercy of mankind [*sic*] had to be a ferocious animal. He was ready to inflict on others all the harm he feared from them. Fear and weakness are the sources of cruelty... These times of barbarism were the golden age; not because men were united, but because they were separated... Men may have attacked one another upon meeting, but they rarely met. Everywhere the state of war prevailed, yet the whole earth was at peace.
> (pp. 267–269)

According to Rousseau, peace prevailed not because people were essentially peaceful but because they didn't bump into each other often. "Natural goodness" included pity but was "emphatically not beneficence," and "[n]othing in Rousseau's account of men [*sic*] in the pre-political state of nature justifies calling them 'noble savages'" (Gourevitch, in Rousseau, p. xxi).

Likewise, the state of nature that Hobbes described in *Leviathan* (1651/1996) is only partly the nasty, brutish existence to which, warns the Cornwall Coalition's Beisner, environmentalists would return us. Hobbes did conjecture that humans in precivil condition would have been in competition—a "war of all against all." But he also believed "it was never generally so" and deduced from that state of war "passions that incline men [*sic*] to peace":

> [I]t is a precept, or general rule of reason, *that every man [sic], ought to endeavor peace, as far as he has hope of obtaining it...* The first branch of which rule, containeth the first, and fundamental law of nature; which is *to seek peace*, and *follow it.*
> (pp. 85–87)

Peace seeking is so seldom mentioned as foundational to his view of human nature that the term "Hobbesian" is, in practice, synonymous with Tennyson's "nature red in tooth and claw." Leaving aside problems with Rousseau's and Hobbes's unsavory assumptions about "savage peoples" and the political philosophies deduced from their theories of human nature, those theories have been unhelpful in psychology less because of their substance than because the two have been distilled into a dichotomy.

Confusion is compounded by the habit of projecting the Rousseau/Hobbes dichotomy onto others. A comment in *10 Books That Screwed Up the World* (Wiker, 2008) illustrates:

> [Rousseau's speculation] proves to be a pattern for many modern intellectuals... They fashion a utopia in the distance, either in the mists of the distant past or the sunlit slopes of the distant future. By the

power of their words, they drive otherwise sane and healthy men and women to waste their own lives and the lives of countless others, sometimes to the ruination of their countries.

If we might be a bit glib, whereas Hobbes's men in the state of nature were gorillas—nasty, brutish, and curiously short—Rousseau's primitive men were suave, peaceful, innocent, carefree, and cheerfully libidinous bonobos. Rousseau therefore gave us a new Adam, a carefree, make-love-not-war ancestral archetype who became the societal ideal of the "free love" movement.

(pp. 44–45)

Wiker is a senior fellow at the creationist Discovery Institute—he also deems Darwin's *Descent of Man* a world-screwing book—and his allusion to "modern intellectuals" dwelling in the "distant past" was not lost on an intelligent-design blogger who commented: "The modern 'evolutionary psychology' movement is largely dedicated to giving Hobbes's and Rousseau's imaginings the veneer of science" (O'Leary, 2009). Wiker's peculiar dichotomy—Hobbes's vicious gorilla versus Rousseau's fun-loving bonobo—thus serves to mock evolutionary psychologists. Rousseau and Hobbes are invoked less often to romanticize peace or to valorize violence than to accuse others of doing so. Going forward, evolutionary scholars (including this chapter's author; Dess, 2003) should avoid indulging the dichotomy because, no matter how its use is qualified (e.g., Barash & Webel, 2008; Duntley & Shackleford, 2008; Pinker, 2002), its meaning has been hopelessly compromised. Developing sound, accessible alternatives to unhelpful dichotomies and other seductive shoals of simplicity remains an important task.

The Way Forward

In such a fraught context, should evolutionary psychologists forge ahead with peace studies? Absolutely. For one thing, they are. It is fair to say that the evolutionary study of aggression has been aimed at mitigating it and/or its adverse impacts. Peace is, of course, more than the absence or suppression of aggression (see section on "Making and Using Tools"); a kiss is more than the absence of a slap. Recognizing this distinction, the "natural history" of peace has emerged as a field of study (e.g., de Waal, 1989; Fry, 2007; Gregor, 1996; Hand, 2003; Sapolsky, 2006; Silk, 1998; Silverberg & Gray, 1992). A current introductory textbook for peace and conflict studies was coauthored by an evolutionary psychologist (Barash & Webel, 2008). A great deal of evolutionarily informed research has been done on "peace bits"—elements, at different levels of organization, of a comprehensive peace studies. It is a good start.

Also, wholesale condemnation of evolution in psychology is a specialty of subgroups within larger, heterogeneous groups. While underestimating the threat posed by committed antagonists would be a mistake, so would stereotyping as friendly or hostile as everyone who leans Left or Right, conservative or liberal, secular or religious. Attitudes to evolutionary psychological metatheory are underdetermined by ideology and identity. Advocacy for evolution can even be found in theological communities; witness two 2008 volumes, Dowd's (2007) *Thank God for Evolution* and Giberson's (2008) *Saving Darwin*. On the academic Left, calls to "stir up conflict" (Derksen, 2010) resonate with a shrinking audience, as scholars eschew insularity in favor of blending insights from postmodernism with other approaches. An emerging literature integrates discursive and prediscursive constructs, qualitative and quantitative methods, and cultural, feminist, psychodynamic, literary, and evolutionary theory (e.g., Carroll, 2004; Hegarty & Pratto, 2004; Mallon & Stich, 2000; Pratto, Sidanius, & Levin, 2006; Solomon, Greenberg, & Pyszczynzki, 2004; Vandermassen, 2005; Wilson, 2005). In *Darwin and Derrida*, Spolsky (2002) articulates the commensurability of the evolutionary principles of facultative adaptation and "permanently unstable ontological categories" (p. 43), cognitive neuroscience, and the postmodern concepts of performativity, fluidity, and destabilized meaning. A remarkable reservoir of complementary expertise and openness to evolutionary psychology exists in diverse areas of psychology.

With respect to peace, many psychologists active in peace studies are interested in evolutionary perspectives. Consider the leadership of the American Psychological Association's Peace Psychology Division (Division 48, Society for the Study of Peace, Conflict, & Violence). Morton Deutsch, inaugural president, wrote near the time of the Division's founding of the contributions to research on conflict resolution of three "intellectual giants"—Freud, Marx, and Darwin—saying "[a]ll three theorists appeared—on a *superficial* reading—to emphasize the competitive, destructive aspects of conflict"; he defends Darwinism against charges of racism, sexism, and militarism by referring to its "vulgarization" and "*mis*application" (emphases his; 1990, p. 237).

President for 2010–2011 Joseph de Rivera is director of Peace Studies at Clark University, a concentration affiliated with a social psychology program in which "[t]he cultural psychology perspective also builds bridges with evolutionary theorizing in contemporary social sciences" (Clark University, n.d.); his scholarship reflects this integrative approach (e.g., de Rivera, 2003). Between these bookends, in 2004, Ethel Tobach (American Museum of Natural History), served as Division president; trained as a comparative psychologist, she is a former president of the Division for Physiological & Comparative Psychology and tireless advocate for peace projects, including social justice, the internationalization of psychology, and conservation. These leaders and others have built bridges between psychology and allied disciplines, have created an infrastructure for international collaboration, and have generated a rich literature. Impediments ought not deter any evolutionary psychologist from joining this vibrant scholarly enterprise, in pursuit of a peace studies agenda ranging from cells to society.

Making and Using Tools: Lexical and Conceptual Issues

A working vocabulary and conceptual scaffolds for an evolutionary study of peace must be both conventional—to enable communication—and dynamic—to accommodate new findings and negotiated meanings. In that dialectical spirit, what follows is a provisional tool kit that draws on others' work, especially Christie, Wagner, and Winter (2008), Kalayjian and Paloutzian (2009), Mayton (2009), and Aureli and de Waal (2000).

Lexical Issues

For *Natural Conflict Resolution* (Aureli & de Waal, 2000), which encompasses multispecies, interdisciplinary, and international research, the editors tasked a diverse group of scholars with producing a concise lexicon to which contributors were asked to conform. Using such a model to develop a lexicon for an even more ambitious peace studies agenda would be worthwhile. In the meantime, the following basic vocabulary is proposed.

Just as health is more than the absence of illness, peace is more than the absence of aggression and *can* be defined without reference to it (Mayton, 2009). Yet the two lexicons are bound up with each other. One reason is that most social animals inhabit a world in which peace and aggression are mutually constitutive. For example, in contradiction of a stereotype of peaceful societies as idyllic, Bonta (1997) points out that some groups socialize peacefulness in part through contradictory messages—of love and cruelty, of trust and mistrust—to teach children not to take for granted others' peaceful intent, and to be vigilant to and proactive about threats to peace. A parent may, for instance, teasingly tell a boy to kill his baby brother, or allow children to care for a small animal then encourage them to kill it.

The lexicons also are conflated because greater emphasis on aggression has privileged the development of "aggression language" (see Fuentes, 2004, on framing). As a result, calling a behavior *aggressive* seems meaningful enough with respect to its form, intent, and operationalization that adding *unpeaceful* or *nonpeaceful* seems superfluous. In contrast, calling a behavior *peaceful* seems about as meaningful as calling it *nonaggressive*, even though it reduces peace and aggression to a binary and makes them methodologically circular. Consistent with this conjecture, a disjunctive search on *nonaggressive, nonaggression,* or *unaggressive* yields over 1,200 hits in PsycInfo, whereas *non*(or *un*)*peaceful*(or *able*) yields none. Thus, *aggression* functions as a norm, or default: The absence of aggressiveness warrants its own term, but the absence of peacefulness does not. Ways in which the peace lexicon has been developed by peace psychologists can promote discussion of how to scale up *prosocial* constructs—which are common in evolutionary and comparative research and tend to refer to focal individuals—and scale down peace constructs, which tend to be relational, to interface with them. It should be possible to leverage the rich literature on prosociality into rich discourse about peace inclusive of comparative evolutionary psychology. Vocabularies related to both aggression and peace are considered here, with attention to implications for multispecies research.

CONFLICT AND ASSOCIATED CONSTRUCTS

Conflict refers to real or perceived incompatibility of goals. Conflict may arise from attitudes, interests, or needs, to the extent that they are linked to incompatible goals. *Conflict resolution* refers to processes that align goals, thus creating *concord*. It can be distinguished from *conflict management*, which mitigates conflict without ending it; examples include ritualized fighting and submission. In social life, conflict is inevitable, but conflict, even unresolved, does not inevitably lead to aggression. That this is so is uncontroversial.

Competition refers to a situation in which demands on a resource by multiple entities exceed resource availability. Evolutionary usage does not assume that psychological mechanisms are engaged. Sperm competition, for instance, does not impute to sperm motive or intent, only differential success in fertilizing ova. Psychological mechanisms are engaged at higher levels of organization, when individuals or groups compete. Such competition may, but does not necessarily, involve *aggression*, that is, behavior marked by an intent to harm another physically, psychologically, or socially (*relational aggression*). Although intentionality is a thorny construct, a conservative meaning ("goal-directed action") is broadly applicable to humans and nonhuman animals (Allen, 1995; Pezzulo & Castelfranchi, 2009). Games may be marked by "friendly competition," in the sense that only the most liberal definition of "harm" includes a deft drop shot in an unscored tennis rally. Nonetheless, conflict and inequitable outcomes are at the heart of even ritualized competition, coalitional biases are readily invoked (Winegard & Deaner, 2010), and unusually peaceful societies are marked by low levels of competition (Fry, Bonta, & Baszarkiewicz, 2009). The "aggressive competitor" in hockey, business, or partisan politics illustrates how fine the line between competition and aggression can be.

The World Health Organization defines *violence* as "the intentional use of physical force or power, threatened or actual, against oneself, another person, or against a group or community that either results in or has a high likelihood of injury, death, psychological harm, mal-development or deprivation" (Krug, Mercy, Dahlberg, & Zwi, 2002). This definition captures the connotative difference between *violence* and *aggression* based on severity. Application to multispecies work deserves consideration. *Aggression* is used more frequently than *violence* in reference to laboratory rodents, whose *aggression* may be used to model human *violence* (e.g., Melloni & Ricci, 2010; Tulogdi et al., 2010). Such usage could connote *violence* as immoral and/or illegal, which would tend to invoke humans more than other animals (e.g., *domestic violence* rather than *domestic aggression*, independently of intensity). This explanation is unsatisfying because *violence* is commonly used in reference to nonhuman primates (e.g., Howell et al., 2007; Wrangham, Wilson, & Muller, 2006). A more parsimonious explanation focuses on a qualitative dimension—proximate social regulation. In selectively bred rodent lines, high-aggression lines' attacks are faster, less ritualized, directed at more vulnerable body parts, less sensitive to context, and less inhibited by submission signaling (de Boer, Caramaschi, Ntarajan, & Kolhaas, 2009; Natarajan & Caramaschi, 2010); these attributes warrant the term *violent*. The severity of their aggression results largely from absence of control by social signals of appeasement or submission that typically deescalate intragroup aggression. This distinction between aggression and violence provides a vocabulary for patterns that seem paradoxical when aggression and violence are arranged on a continuum—for example, more frequent physical aggression but less violence in some macaque species (e.g., stumptail, Tonkean) compared to others (e.g., rhesus, Japanese; de Waal & Luttrell, 1989; Thierry, 2007) and, in intimate heterosexual human relationships, more frequent physical aggression by women but more violence by men (Archer, 2009).

Peace psychologists refer less frequently to *aggression* than to *violence*. *Aggression* appears only a few times in Christie, Wagner, and Winter's (2008) authoritative volume, and in PsycInfo, *peace psychology* cross-references with *violence* eight times more frequently than with *aggression*. Discussion of how the comparative/evolutionary and peace psychology lexicons differ with respect to distinguishing aggression from violence would be worthwhile. A crucial distinction is made in peace psychology between *direct violence* and *structural violence*, to which peace constructs are differently connected (see Table 26.1). Evolutionary research connects transparently to the former—violence with direct, episodic, and fast effects. Direct violence can occur at many levels of organization, from self-mutilation and suicide at the individual level to *war*. The definition of *war* has a great deal to do with whether it is regarded as uniquely human. The level of organization at which war is defined shapes analyses of war and the design of potential interventions. Level is unavoidably confounded with species—for instance, all social animals distinguish ingroups from outgroups, but only humans name, talk about, and institutionalize the distinction. This confounding is important to recognize, because simplicity combined with anthropocentrism can pull explanations to the highest levels of organization for humans and leave them at the lowest levels for other species, leading to neglect of what they might share.

A useful definition of *war* for comparative purposes is *collective violence carried out by one group against members of another group* (adapted from Livingstone Smith, 2007). This definition captures the collective intergroup nature of war fundamental to most sociopolitical, evolutionary, and

Table 26.1 A Four-Way Framework for Violence and Peace

		FAST		SLOW
VIOLENCE				
	Direct Violence	Kills directly	**Structural Violence**	Kills indirectly
		Kills quickly		Kills slowly
		Somatic harm		Somatic deprivation
		Acute insult to well-being		Chronic insult to well-being
		Dramatic		Mundane
		Intermittent		Continuous
		Subject-action-object observable		Subject-action-object unobservable
PEACE				
	Peacemaking	Reduces direct violence	**Peacebuilding**	Reduces structural violence
		Emphasis on nonviolent means		Emphasis on socially just ends
		Reactive		Proactive
		Limited in time and space		Ubiquitous
		Prevention of violent episodes		Promotion of social justice
		Largely compatible with status quo		Threatens status quo

Source: Adapted from Christie et al. (2008).

comparative analyses. It does not limit war to killing or to certain motives or means. It also does not imply involvement of a moral community, as does inclusion of "sanctioned" (Livingstone Smith, 2007, p. 16). This definition can serve as a heuristic in the analytic strategy of applying increasingly stringent criteria to the comparative study of war. Sanctioning, arguably, limits war to humans and chimpanzees. How is *war* in those species different from, for instance, war between wolf packs, male dolphin coalitions, or lions and hyenas? Is collective hierarchy-based violence—what Sidanius and Pratto (2004) call *systematic terror*—usefully distinguished from *war* in some, or all, of those species? Empirical comparison of collective intergroup violence that meets various criteria, such as sanctioning, ritualization, or institutionalization, will clarify how such constraints matter, and why.

Structural violence—social domination, political oppression, economic exploitation, environmental racism—is indirect and chronic. Because the term *violence* so strongly connotes *direct violence*, *structural violence* may seem abstract or metaphorical, a term that likens the moral or aesthetic offensiveness of the *idea* of social injustice to physical harm. Structural violence, however, kills "just as surely as direct violence" (Christie et al., 2008, p. 8). A global body of evidence shows that income inequality predicts poorer population health status and higher mortality (Wilkinson & Pickett, 2006). Structural violence can kill slowly by material means—for example, malnutrition, inadequate shelter, untreated disease, environmental degradation. However, psychosocial processes, such as the chronic stress of *microaggressions*, lack of control, and negative emotions, also contribute to the long-term effects of structural violence (e.g., Brondolo, ver Halen, Libby, & Pencille, 2011; Gallo & Matthews, 2003; Kaikkonen, Rahkonen, Lallukka, & Lahelma, 2009; Sue, 2010). Indeed, *subjective* socioeconomic status predicts health independently of *objective* status (e.g., Cohen et al., 2008; Sakurai, Kawakami, Yamaoka,

Ishikawa, & Hashimoto, 2010). Thus, material conditions do not account fully for the chronic effects of status inequalities. Moreover, structural violence can kill quickly via its relationship with direct violence (Wilkinson, 2004; Winter, Pilisuk, Houck, & Lee, 2008). For instance, women's lack of economic, political, and ideological power makes them more vulnerable to rape and other forms of direct violence (Pratto & Walker, 2004), and damage to infrastructure or the environment in war often disproportionately impacts marginalized groups, increasing social inequality. Thus, structural and direct violence together comprise a *system of violence*.

Though *structural violence* is not part of the comparative psychology lexicon, core aspects have counterparts there—such as despotic social organization and social dominance and subordination—that are associated with delivering, receiving, and witnessing aggression. Coupling the study of structural violence in humans with the study of despotism, intolerance, harassment, and other features of intragroup aggression in other species will be valuable. Studying other animals can reveal something about how social structure is related to aggression through mechanisms other than language and institutions. In addition, studies of nonhuman animals in laboratories, zoos, or semi-free-ranging settings, when practicable, allow more experimental control with its attendant analytic advantages.

Social structure, status, aggression, and well-being are intertwined in humans and other social animals (e.g., Adler et al., 2008; McClintock, Conzen, Gehlert, Masi, & Olopade, 2005; Sapolsky, 2004). However, they are not linked in a simple, invariant way within or across species; even the seemingly simple question of how social status relates to stress hormone levels has a complex answer (e.g., Abbott et al., 2003; Cohen, Doyle, & Baum, 2006; Creel & Sands, 2003). Further study of how other species' socially patterned aggression compares to humans' will complement in an important way the literature on structural violence. Conversely, recognizing correspondences between structural violence in humans and chronic costs of social stress in nonhuman animals means that a comparative evolutionary psychology of aggression should be integrated with research on how animals perceive, respond to, and are affected in the long term by social inequity (Brosnan, 2006; Brosnan et al., 2010; Wilkinson, 2004).

CONCORD AND ASSOCIATED CONCEPTS

If *conflict* refers to incompatibility of goals, another term should signify when goals are compatible and linked, to distinguish that circumstance from when conflict is absent because the actors' goals are simply irrelevant to each other. *Concord* seems appropriate, defined in the *American Heritage Dictionary* as "agreement between persons, groups, nations, etc.; concurrence in attitudes, feelings, etc.; unanimity; accord." In politics, *concord* refers to peace treaties and to harmonious relations—not merely an easing of tensions (*détente*), or ceasefire. Man and Bond (2005) used factor analysis to study dyadic relationship quality and found only one factor that emerged consistently across different kinds of age/sex dyads. They named it *concord*. Items with positive factor loadings included "harmonious," "agree without planning," and "mutual assistance for mutual success." Concord scales up to higher order relationships, can shift over time and contexts, and applies to diverse species, attributes desirable for a construct in the integrative study of peace. It also can be operationalized, as Man and Bond suggest, in terms of "number or length of interactions between the relationship members, the nature of role activity involved, and the hierarchy or complexity of the dyadic role" (p. 113), a methodology de rigueur in comparative psychology that usefully supplements self-report by humans. Unlike dispersal or annihilation, *concord* is an affirmative outcome of conflict resolution that provides a pathway to peace.

Concord is neither necessary nor sufficient for *cooperation* to occur. The most general definition of cooperation requires only that one actor assist another. In an evolutionary framework, *cooperation* refers to social interaction in which an actor accrues a cost that benefits another actor; the apparent adaptive problem of cooperation—that is, an actor pays a price without recouping any immediate material, emotional, or reputational benefit from the interaction (*altruism*)—may be resolved with concepts such as *inclusive fitness*, *reciprocal altruism*, and *bounded rationality* (Kappeler & van Schaik, 2006). Cooperation can be defined practically and proximately as two or more individuals acting together to achieve a common goal (Boesch, 2003). In this case, concord is prerequisite to and facilitates cooperation. *Cooperation* can be unpacked along lines suggested by Boesch and Boesch (1989), with *similarity*, *synchrony*, *coordination*, and *collaboration* signifying increasing degrees of social integration (see also Knoblich & Sebanz, 2009). All involve a common goal but differ in their cognitive, behavioral, and emotional components and thus will be sensitive to variables such as physical context, species, age, gender, and the individuals' interactional history. Quick leaps from the prosocial connotation of *cooperation* to peacefulness or egalitarianism are risky: Although cooperation can quell violence and spread social benefits, it also can be used to mount bloody coups or raids (Boesch, 2003), and *cooperative breeders* with high reproductive skew can have cruel, intolerant dominants (Clutton-Brock, 2006) or be peaceable in part due to the reproductive inhibition of most group members (Schaffner & Caine, 2000).

Nonviolence is not just the absence of violence (Mayton, 2009). The term can refer to a philosophy based on love, commitment to truth, and sacrifice, or to a specific strategy for resolving conflict or reducing violence that may or may not be deeply principled. Mayton offers as a definition of nonviolence that is amenable to a comparative approach, "an action that uses power and influence to reach one's goal without direct injury or violence to the [individuals] working to thwart one's goal achievement" (p. 8). Nonviolence would include, for instance, persuasion, boycott, and noncooperation. It is not incompatible with aggression of any kind; nonviolence can intentionally harm its targets (e.g., economic loss, loss of face or power). Philosophy might elude nonhuman animals, but the comparative literature provides ample evidence that other animals use cost-effective alternatives to violence to achieve goals, to an extent that likely has been underestimated given how social interaction has been measured (Bearzi & Stanford, 2010; Cheney & Seyfarth, 2007; Croft, James, & Krause, 2008). How these alternatives mitigate aggression belongs in peace studies.

Distinguishing *direct violence* from *structural violence* leads to important distinctions among peace constructs (Christie, Wagner, & Winter, 2008). Blocking or mitigating direct violence leaves in its place *negative peace*, so called to distinguish mitigation of direct violence from the justice and its benefits that characterize *positive peace*. Several processes generate negative peace. *Peacemaking* refers to processes that reduce violence by reducing the conflict from which it stems; *mediation* is an example. *Peacekeeping* prevents short-term exacerbation or recurrence of the violence; the underlying conflict may remain, as when combatants are separated for a "cooling off" period. *Postviolence peacebuilding* involves providing structural support for recovery from violence by, for instance, restoring basic services and monitoring elections. *Positive peace* processes, on the other hand, transform social, political, and economic institutions to promote justice and equity, thus reducing structural violence. They are proactive rather than reactive or restorative of a status quo ante and, like postviolence peacebuilding, involve changes at higher (community, nation) rather than lower (dyadic, family) levels of organization. Examples include changes in health care access and delivery systems, institutionalization of peace education (Salomon & Cairns, 2010), and a congressional proposal to create a cabinet-level US Department of Peace and Nonviolence (HR-808) equal to the Department of Defense (formerly the Department of War).

A *system of peace* comprised of shorter term peacemaking and longer term peacebuilding supports descriptive and injunctive norms comprising a *culture of peace*. *Peaceful societies* are characterized not by a complete absence of aggression but by the presence of nonviolence norms that result in little direct violence within the society and between it and others and that minimize structural violence: interpersonal harmony, negative sanctioning of violence and positive sanctioning of refraining from it, effective nonviolent strategies for managing and resolving conflict, and valuing of women and nurturance (Fry et al., 2009; Staub, 1997). *Peaceful individuals* have attributes—for example, agreeableness, anger control, and empathy—that make peaceful interactions more likely (Mayton, 2009). Attributes such as these vary among individuals from early in life, but they are not immutable; they and their behavioral expressions develop in dynamic relation to social interactions. Hill, Allemand, and Burrow (2010) explain that over the course of adaptive identity development, personality traits that promote social well-being increase. For example, the "Big Five" personality attribute *agreeableness* mediates the emergence of a tendency toward forgiveness, which plays a key role in reconciliation (Kalayjian & Paloutzian, 2009). Importantly, agreeableness (Weiss, King, & Figueredo, 2000), anger control (Suomi, 2003), and empathy (de Waal, 2010) are measurable in diverse species. The comparative evolutionary study of temperament and personality (Figueredo, Gladden, Vasquez, Wolf, & Jones, 2009; Roulin, Dreiss, & Kölliker, 2010) can contribute importantly to elucidation of how peacefulness emerges from the intersection of individual-, dyadic-, and group-level processes.

UTILITY OF THE LEXICON

Exploration of evolutionary affordances and constraints on peace processes within this lexical framework is a promising avenue for future research.

Discursive accounts of contemporary human history, such as the modern feminist movement to unsettle Western-style patriarchy, can be integrated with examination of its prehominid roots; neither males' attempts to limit females' power and reproductive prerogative nor females' resistance to coercion and abuse is original to genus *Homo*, much less Western civilization (Hrdy, 1997). Moreover, social change occurs in other species. Sapolsky and Share (2004) describe a remarkable cultural transformation in a baboon community: Ten years after tuberculosis killed all of the most aggressive males in the Forest Troop, the remaining males had dispersed and had been replaced by immigrants. Despite the initial aggressiveness of the immigrants, the newly constituted troop developed a society pacific by baboon standards, characterized by increased proximity to females of all ages by males and by other females, less male aggression toward females, more male grooming of and by females, more tolerant dominant males, and less stress among subordinate males.

Whereas baboons, even in the transformed Forest Troop, live under more or less despotic regimes, the structure of human societies seems to be bistable, with despotic and egalitarian equilibria. Drawing on anthropological and primatological literatures, Boehm (1999) suggests that this "political ambivalence" is "grounded in highly contradictory behavioral tendencies, which we share with many other primates" (p. 3). Status seeking and affiliation, and tensions between those tendencies, are not uniquely human but, according to Boehm, the nature of egalitarianism is. Egalitarian social structure is a "reverse" hierarchy in which subordinates collectively prevent domination. Despots are replaced, upstarts controlled, and egalitarianism maintained by virtue of a uniquely human form of moral community:

> [T]he collective weapon of the rank and file has been their ability to define their own social life in moral terms, and to back up their thoughts about political parity with pointed actions in the form of collectivized social sanctioning.
> (p. viii)

The justice orientation of peacebuilding and the occasional effectiveness of nonviolent revolution against seemingly intransigent despotism are consistent with this evolutionary framing of human social change.

The disease outbreak that resulted in a majority-female Forest Troop was in some ways a freak occurrence. However, demographic shifts have occurred throughout evolutionary time, and continue to occur, in nonhuman animal as well as human populations, and the social status quo ante is not always restored. War is one reason for dramatic shifts. After the 1994 genocide in Rwanda, 70% of the population was female. Women now hold over half of the parliamentary seats, the only female-majority legislature in the world (cf. the United States, at 26%, ranks 70th, and over 40 countries have less than 10%). The government has launched reforms aimed at gender-based violence, reproductive and sexual rights, and environmental protection. Early signs that a more just society is emerging (Hughes, 2009; Wallace, Haerpfer, & Abbott, 2008) are consistent with evidence that females' collective clout reduces structural inequality and violence (e.g., Caprioli, 2005; Caprioli et al., 2009; Parish & de Waal, 2000). Longer term effects are not assured; the extent and impacts of women's power in Rwanda are not uncomplicated (Hogg, 2009). Here, the example makes the point that demographic shifts—whether due to disease, war, famine, gender-selective infanticide, or immigration—are one reason that societies shift at many levels of organization in many species, with consequences for their equanimity (Mesquida & Weiner, 1996). The dynamics favoring peace will be understood sooner if a comparative evolutionary approach is used.

History and events to come provide means of testing predictions grounded in that approach. Using lexicons that overlap will help researchers working in different peace-relevant paradigms find each other. That is, linguistically marking peace-relevant research *as* relevant to peace would help diverse researchers connect. For instance, Oishi and Schimmack (2010) refer to societies characterized by material security, a sense of trust and freedom, and close relationships as "psychologically wealthy"; such societies might tend to be peaceful, but they do not use the term. If they had, it would come up in key word searches. In comparative terms, honest, low-cost signals—"cheap talk"—can promote communication even when the social partners have conflicting interests, "as long as the interest in achieving coordination is sufficiently great" (Silk, Kaldor, & Boyd, 2000, p. 423). More cheap talk about peace could help.

A flow chart incorporating terms from this lexicon and a few others, with illustrative pathways, is shown in Figure 26.2. Conditions favoring conflict or concord, shown on the left, include all relevant features of the social and other-than-human ecology. Those conditions probabilistically and

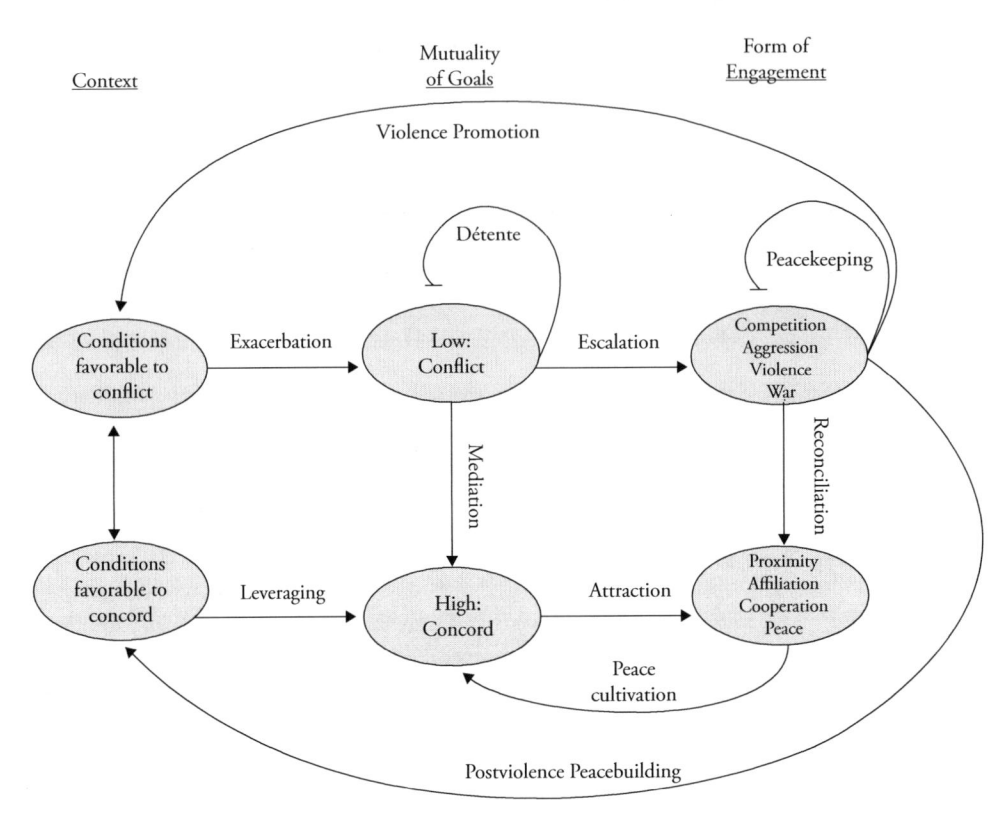

Figure 26.2 Schematic depiction of relations among some terms in a peace lexicon.

conditionally generate *conflict* or *concord*, which in turn probabilistically and conditionally leads to forms of aggressive or peaceful engagement, shown on the right. Moving through the schematic illustrates some basic relationships and distinctions. For example, *détente* limits conflict and thus mitigates direct violence but does not transform conflict into concord. In contrast, peacemaking mitigates direct violence by creating concord, either directly (through *mediation*) or indirectly (through *reconciliation*). Unlike peacemaking, *peacebuilding* is aimed at transforming the conditions conducive to conflict to conditions favoring concord, such as a culture of peace.

An alternative path from aggression—*violence promotion*—indicates a "cycle of violence" in which aggression enhances conditions that perpetuate it. For instance, gun sales in the United States skyrocketed within days of killing sprees in 2007 at Virginia Tech and in the 2011 assassination attempt on Congresswoman Gabrielle Giffords (D-AZ). Stockpiling weapons in response to violence reflects and reinforces a "gun culture" rooted in history and maintained structurally by, for example, a powerful gun lobby and broad interpretation of the Second Amendment by the Supreme Court. The US population is the most heavily armed in the world (The Graduate Institute, 2007). These conditions make gun use more likely (e.g., Azrael & Hemenway, 2000), and conflict involving guns will on average be more lethal than, say, fist fights. Indeed, the United States has more gun deaths per capita than any other developed nation.

Finally, the schematic indicates that the relationship between conditions favoring conflict and concord is bidirectional. Concord between some individuals or groups, for instance, may increase when a prized resource becomes available to them yet also generate conflict between them and others who seek access to it (Ali, 2007). Also, conditions favorable to positive peace and postviolence peacebuilding can set the stage for conflict with those who benefit from the structural status quo. More hopefully, war can create conditions that motivate peace processes.

The schematic is a template. Line weights can be varied to indicate the probability, frequency, or importance of path activation in different contexts, dyads, groups, or species. Terms can be moved, added, replaced, or modified. For instance, the *concord* node could be disaggregated to distinguish goal alignments that are strategic ("cool") rather than intimate ("warm"), a distinction that may be associated with different antecedents and with the probability and depth of subsequent peaceable interactions (see "Levels of Organization"). Also, many empirically justifiable or hypothetically interesting pathways are not included. Consider peaceful postaggression interaction, observed in primates, ungulates, canids, equines, hyenas, and dolphins (Silk, 2002). The term *reconciliation* in the schematic implies that the participants in the aggressive encounter are social partners whose peaceful interaction functions to *re*-concile them. However, a close relationship is neither necessary nor sufficient for peaceful postaggression interaction to occur: It can occur when the actors did not have an especially friendly relationship (e.g., in young children; Butovskaya, Verbeek, Ljungberg, & Lunardini, 2000), and some highly social animals (e.g., meerkats, Kutsukake & Clutton-Brock, 2008, and tamarins, Schaffner, Aureli, & Caine, 2005) do not appear to reconcile. Moreover, peaceful postaggression interaction has many social and individual-level effects, stimulating productive debate about its adaptive functions (de Waal, 2000; Silk, 2002). Thus, a simple direct *reconciliation* path does not adequately represent social partners' interactions after a fight. Other paths could include nodes for mediators at the individual (e.g., uncertainty, information seeking, anxiety) or dyadic (relationship value, security, compatibility) level, which predict peaceful postaggression interactions differently in different dyads, contexts, and species (e.g., Colmenares & Silveira, 2008; Fraser, Stahl, & Aureli, 2010; Koski, Koops, & Sterck, 2007; Majolo, Ventura, & Koyama, 2009). For highly valued, insecure, symmetrical relationships, relationship disruption may inherently generate concord—the shared goal of reconciling—in which case a new pathway from aggression is warranted to indicate that concord mediates the reconciliation. Peaceful postaggression interactions also have sequelae beyond the dyad's relationship, at the individual (e.g., stress reduction, access to resources) and social (e.g., observation by others in the group) level; these could be depicted as paths leaving the *peace* node.

These are examples of how the schematic might be fruitfully elaborated. It provides a starting point for lexical integration of diverse literatures with humans and other species. Where consensus is reached and data exist, parameterized paths can be established. Where consensus or data are lacking, conversations and collaboration might ensue. Whether the schematic is used conceptually or for formal path analysis, new answers and questions could emerge.

OTHER LEXICAL ISSUES

Language implying a binary distinction between humans and other species—for example, "humans and animals"—undermines evolutionary reasoning (Dess & Chapman, 1998). "Humans and other animals," "nonhuman animals," or more specific terms (e.g., nonhuman primates, rodents, dogs) should be used. Consistent use of nondichotomizing constructions will make it clearer that when humans are compared to other species, the underlying assumption is that all humans are animals. In light of troubled discourse around evolution and aggressiveness, preempting the charge that particular comparisons dehumanize some groups of people is prudent. (For discussion of de/infrahumanization and intergroup hostility, see Castano & Kofta, 2009; Motyl, Hart, & Pyszczynski, 2010) Humans-are-animals language also can help transform the word *peace* from a term tightly bound to uniquely human constructs into one that is comparatively meaningful, encompassing evolutionarily old and more recent adaptations to group living that increase proximity, tolerance, cohesion, and health.

Fastidious use of gender-neutral language also is advisable. Great progress has been made in this direction, thanks to feminist consciousness raising and adoption of gender-neutral style in the APA *Publication Guide* in the 1970s. Even occasional usage of "mankind" to refer to humans, "she" to refer to nature, and so on undercuts claims that patriarchy and sexism do not inform the work. *Humans, people*, or, if a flourish seems necessary, *humankind* should be used. Nature has no gender. Inappropriately gendered language in quotations should be followed by "[sic]," to flag its deviation from gender neutrality. Changing up common phrases—"women and men" instead of "men and women," "female and male" instead of "male and female" (the male-first constructions get 10–20 times more Google hits)—is a good idea, as conventional ordering subtly privileges male forms. For similar reasons, limiting aggression/war metaphors in scholarly debate and referring to "peace and war" instead of "war and peace" are advisable.

The term *natural* poses problems. *Natural* (or *life*) *sciences* are often contrasted with *social sciences*, an institutional distinction troublesome for psychology and academe generally. *Natural* often contrasts with *cultural* (e.g., *natural history* versus *cultural history*). These constructions equate the human with the social or cultural, and separate these from the rest of the world. Contrasting *natural* with *artificial* or *unnatural* also is problematic. Connotations of *good/moral* and *bad/immoral* can scuttle conversations. Moreover, the natural/artificial dichotomy can be used to invalidate research in laboratories or zoos, on grounds that they are *artificial* and, thus, the behavior observed is "not natural." A laboratory is not a zoo is not a savanna, and animals are sensitive to context. Evolutionary psychology is all about contexts—the contexts in which psychological processes evolved and the contemporary contexts that shape their expression. Treating contexts as structured, and therefore as differentially affording and constraining expression of behavioral repertoires, makes sense—but treating them as "natural" or "artificial" does not. The *natural* problem needs to be solved with new conventions.

Language is a tool. Using it to represent and construct *Homo*'s social world likely played a key role in its evolution (Dunbar, 2003), functions that have been conserved. Language that comports with evolution and facilitates civil discourse with diverse others will move work on peace forward faster.

Time and Levels of Organization: From Reality to Practicality

Life unfolds on time scales ranging from billions of years to nanoseconds and on levels of organization ranging from subcellular to interstellar. Little of it is irrelevant to peace. Identification of self versus other and cooperation appear to be rooted in virus/host evolution, in which case the peace story begins with the last universal common ancestor—that is, at the cellular-molecular level around 3.5 billion years ago (López-Larrea, 2011; Villareal, 2008). This is no trivia tidbit: Bannert and Kurth (2004) observed, "Almost half of the mammalian genome is derived from ancient transposable elements" (i.e., endogenous retroviruses; p. 14572). Retroviruses have been linked to the evolution of the placenta (Dunlap et al., 2006) and diversification of primates (Johnson & Coffin, 1999). In a real sense, all of mammalian evolution "went viral." Moreover, viruses remain a part of the lives and, probably, the ongoing evolution of humans and other animals. If the story of peace began with viruses, our task is daunting: How do we get from back then to the present, meanwhile scaling up from cells to dyads—like a boy and gorilla kissing at the zoo—and up further still, to their relatives working in multinational coalitions to save the gorilla's conspecifics from extinction,

end internecine warfare, and promote sustainable development and peace (Nellemann, Redmond, & Refisch, 2010)?

Grappling with the ontological complexity of peace is complicated by the fact that scholars do not examine life from the outside: Human researchers live life on time and organizational scales different from many of the species they study (Alyushin, 2010; McClamrock, 2008). They differ from each other with respect to the nature and scales of events to which their scholarly gaze is drawn. Finally, there is the problem of how levels of *organization* in the world map on to levels of *analysis* in scholarship.

Integrating comparative evolutionary psychology into peace studies thus presents an enormous challenge. Luckily, integration is "in." Witness cultural primatology, Darwinian psychopharmacology, evolutionary health psychology, evolutionary cognitive neuroscience, neuroeconomics, and developmental social cognitive neuroscience, and books such as *The Sapient Mind: Archeology Meets Neuroscience* (Renfrew, Frith, & Malafouris, 2009), *The Social Neuroscience of Empathy* (Decety & Ickes, 2009), and *Behavioral Evolutionary Ecology* (Westneat & Fox, 2010). Dynamical systems models are being developed in peace studies and psychology to formally handle complexity of this order (MacLennan, 2002; Musallam, Coleman, & Nowak, 2010; Wiese, Vallacher, & Strawinska, 2010). Kenrick et al. (2002) describe how such models can simulate interactions between evolved, domain-relevant psychological processes and developmental and situational/momentary changes at levels of organization from genes to ecosystems to iteratively predict, for instance, aggressive or peaceful relations with neighbors. These models avoid the incompleteness of bottom-heavy (reductionist) or top-heavy (holistic) conceptualizations. Importantly, they do not obviate the need for research focused on limited time and organizational scales. To the contrary, they, like the carnivorous plant in *The Little Shop of Horrors*, demand, "Feed me!" Diverse theoretical and empirical work is needed to "educate the decision rules built into those models and to explore the validity of model outcomes" (Kenrick et al., 2002, p. 23). This valuable interplay, however, will never entirely comprise peace studies. Only some scholars will be inclined to take up computer simulation, and it does not provide a friendly entry point. More accessible conceptual models remain important. Toward that end, a time scale and scheme for levels of organization are suggested here.

TIME SCALES

A comparative evolutionary analysis of peace will attend to critical transitions in peaceful sociality, to locate adaptations and other processes that account for its varied expression in diverse species. Obviously, everything in the evolutionary past makes every contemporary expression of peacefulness possible. Evolution made it possible for a boy and a gorilla to share a kiss: Is the apparent intimacy a Clever Hans illusion, the result of zookeeper or visitor operant conditioning, noise? Or might the moment attest to the adaptive value of kissing and similarly socialized, age-appropriate behaviors to one or both species? If so, has it been conserved from a common ancestor, or did the separate hominoid lines converge on it later as a solution to a common problem—starting from a shared exaptation, or not? Is the kiss evidence of selective pressure on interspecies intimacy—seems far fetched, but which possibilities should be dismissed out of hand and which pursued (Patterson, Richter, Gnerre, Lander, & Reich, 2006)? If kissing is functionally linked to a constellation of peaceful behaviors that solved an adaptive problem, how ought that problem be conceptualized?

Humans clearly can live peacefully even if they don't all the time. An important question concerns the extent to which humans are adapted to peaceful living. Answering it will require thinking through how peace by design differs from other reasons that most social animals, most of the time, do not attack each other. Adaptations for peace will reveal themselves as easy to cultivate, efficient, and relatively cheap; exaptations will have provided a scaffold that made adaptations to peace possible. Stories about two ubiquitous human behaviors in the domain of eating—predation and cooking—illustrate how exploration of peace might unfold in different ways in different time frames. The common ancestor of all primates looked forward. Forward-looking convergent eyes are characteristic of predators, and evidence favors a critical role for binocular vision, along with prehensile hands, in primate evolution (Egi, 2004). Forward-looking eyes transformed primate sociality into a face-to-face affair. From birth to death, faces, eyes, and mouths comprised critical features of the social world. Neonatal imitation and reciprocated intimacy involving mouth-mouth contact and lip smacking coincident with mutual gaze mediated the first peaceful relationship—infant–caregiver attachment (Ferrari, Paukner, Ionica, & Suomi, 2009). That relationship served as a working model for peaceful relationships later in life (Music, 2011). In a few primate species (humans, bonnet and rhesus macaques), a secure primary attachment promoted good peer relations in offspring otherwise prone to socially dysregulated (impulsive) aggression and low agreeableness by virtue of a serotonin transporter polymorphism that apes and most macaques lack (Canli & Lesch, 2007; Herman, Winslow, & Suomi, 2010). Unlike monomorphic cousins, species with the polymorphism enjoyed spectacular success in exploiting diverse habitats, perhaps explaining the persistence of an allele that, in the absence of competent rearing, put offspring at risk of peer rejection and other social liabilities (Suomi, 2006).

A sophisticated visual system also enabled slowly developing young in complex societies to recognize individuals and social signals (Nakata, 2008; Parr, Winslow, Hopkins, & de Waal, 2000; van Schaik & Deaner, 2003). The mouth remained vital: Laughing (relaxed open mouth displays) and smiling (ritualized in species-typical ways from fear grimacing) emerged to signal benign intent and facilitate affiliation (van Hooff & Preuschoft, 2003). Intense appetitive motivation and coalition formation that enhanced predation—the thrill of the collective hunt—was co-opted for intraspecies competition (Carver & Harmon-Jones, 2009; Corning, 2007; Elbert, Weierstall, & Schauer, 2010; Nell, 2006); this, in turn, heightened the adaptive value of appeasement, consolation, reconciliation, and perception of others' intent.

In this scenario, forward-looking eyes belong in the peace story, but they are not an adaptation for peace. The original selection pressures were rooted in the food domain early in primate evolution, and some of the morphological, neurohormonal, and behavioral consequences of that adaptation were co-opted in the regulation of social behavior. Only some would have manifested as peace, and only some of those would have been subjected to selective pressure in some primate lineages. Cooking provides a useful contrast. By the time human ancestors started cooking—probably *Homo erectus*—they already had a sophisticated peace repertoire, as did all hominins, along with some cetaceans and canids. In *Catching Fire*, Wrangham (2009) hypothesizes that cooking catalyzed a brain-body-behavior revolution: Eating cooked food was so energetically advantageous that it became the main driver of *Homo* evolution; anything that increased reliable access to or utilization of cooked food likely promoted fitness, perhaps including attraction to fire (Fessler, 2006). Tradeoffs mattered: Barging in on someone else's cooked meal and beating the person up to get the food would have quelled hunger. Cooking was costly, however, so in a communal setting, retaliation would undermine brute-force strategies. The advantages of sharing cooked food with family and allies would have constituted selective pressure on peace:

> Among the eaters of cooked food who were attracted to a fireside meal, the calmer individuals would have more comfortably accepted others' presence and would have been less likely to irritate their companions. They would have been chased away less often, would have had more access to cooked food, and would have passed on more genes to succeeding generations than the wild-eyed and intemperate bullies who disturbed the peace to the point that they were ostracized by a coalition of the calm... If the intense attractions of a cooking fire selected for individuals who were more tolerant of one another, an accompanying result should have been a rise in their ability to stay calm as they looked at one another, so they could better assess, understand, and trust one another. Thus the temperamental journey toward relaxed face-to-face communication should have taken an important step forward with *Homo erectus*.
> (pp. 184–185)

Here, then, is an example of argument for a turning point in human evolution at which selective pressure exerted on the facultative expression of individual-level temperamental and cognitive attributes and coalitional processes, in certain social contexts, yielded adaptations for peace. Lest this sound halcyon, on Wrangham's logic, females became vastly more dependent than before on males for provisions and protection: "Cooking created and perpetuated a novel system of male cultural superiority. It is not a pretty picture" (p. 177). Thus, a change that increased peace among men and reduced direct violence against women ratcheted up structural violence.

A truncated, punctuated chronology of human evolution is shown in Table 26.2, beginning arbitrarily with the emergence of placental mammals and ending with a time frame during which further species-defining changes in the genome become controversial. The chronology highlights moments

Table 26.2 Punctuated Human Evolution Time Scale, With Possible Turning Points for Peace

Time Frame	Years Before Present	Transitions Relevant to Evolution of Peace
Placental mammals	ca. 125 mya	Play fighting, social grooming, empathy, consolation
Primates	ca. 55 mya	Forward-looking eyes, dextrous prehensile hands, slowly developing young, increased social complexity; cerebral/affective asymmetry (Corballis, 2008; Dimond & Harries, 1984)
Hominoids	ca. 8 mya	Gestural communication to solicit help or other actions by social partners (Pika, 2008); (proto)cultural transmission (McGrew, 2003); moral appraisal and inequity complaints (Brosnan et al., 2010).
Australopithecines	ca. 4 mya	Dedicated bipedalism (Carrier & Janis, 2007), concealed ovulation (Gangestad et al., 2005), throwing (Cantalupo & Hopkins, 2010)
Homo erectus	ca. 2 mya	Moral communities (Boehm, 1999); cooking (Wrangham, 2009); theory of mind, negotiated sharing (Rochat & Ferreira, 2008); cooperative rearing (Hrdy, 2009)
Spoken language	ca. 100–700,000 ybp	Referential symbols for absent or abstract referents (e.g., future/past, peace, fairness; Tse, 2008); consonant-parsing of vowels (MacNeilage, 1998)
Homo sapiens	ca. 100,000 ybp	Autobiographical and cultural narratives (Cupchik & Hilscher, 2004; Oatley & Mar, 2005) and instruction (Tomasello, 2009), enhanced in/outgroup marking, group identification; religion; art
Permanent settlement	ca. 15,000 ybp	Accumulation of wealth and social stratification; trade; group identities become purely symbolic as size of social groups exceeds peripersonal space

at which some transitions important to human peace might appear if it were reverse engineered into deep time (also see Mithen, 2007; Zihlman & Bolter, 2004). Examples are given of peace-relevant capacities that emerged either de novo or, more often, in altered forms or with new contingencies. For instance, play and grooming are phylogenetically older than placental mammals—even cockroach larvae groom socially (Seelinger & Seelinger, 1983)—but they assumed new forms and functions in different lineages and time frames. Among mammals, touch is central to both grooming and social play, and play-fighting is the most typical play form; these features are well suited to behavioral regulation in intimate mammalian relationships (Pellis & Pellis, 2010). Earlier transitions scaffold later ones, and additional peace-relevant transitions in grooming and play occurred as primates emerged (Fagen, 2002). Antonacci, Norscia, and Palagi (2010), for example, reported that when male resident lemurs encounter a strange male during mating season, residents—not surprisingly—groom other residents more than they do strangers, with ingroup grooming appearing to reinforce and signal ingroup solidarity. However, residents *play* more with strangers than with other residents, which reduces subsequent aggression. Mitigation of xenophobia by play resonates with the delicate balance between aggression and peace through wrestling contests between relatively peaceful societies in Brazil's Xingu River basin (Fry et al., 2009) and the promotion of peace through the Olympics and regional programs such as Football for Peace (Sugden, 2006). Palagi (2009) observed that tail play is a common form when lemurs are less familiar with each other and play is therefore riskier; tail play works for lemurs but not so much in apes. Play, then, has gone in varied directions in primate evolution.

Nested within those time frames are life span development and shorter term influences. Developmental research with a variety of species and across human (sub)cultures will be important in the study of peace, more so than 25 years ago due to the progress under the rubrics of evo devo (Carroll, 2005) and *social epigenesis* (Thierry, 2004; see also Konner, 2010). The time is ripe for comparative examination of peace from these points of view—that is, with consideration of how variation between species, within species, and over the life span results from the speeding up, slowing down, or direction of the ontogenetic or momentary expression of heritable characteristics. Not only is epigenesis supplanting models in which genes or the environment have direct effects, the observation of *heritable*, reversible modifications to DNA (e.g., methylation caused by diet or stress) is opening a whole new, interesting can of worms (Morgan & Whitelaw, 2008; Szyf, McGowan, Turecki, & Meaney, 2010). How, for instance, might experiences of peace transgenerationally modify social interactions such that peace becomes more likely? How the evolutionary research community can be more inclusive of, but not subsumed by, developmental perspectives (or vice versa) will have to be resolved (e.g., Bjorklund & Ellis, 2005; Krebs & Hemingway, 2008; Lickliter & Schneider, 2006).

For animals growing up in complex societies, the legacy of evolution is not immutable social behavior. Situational plasticity reflects, in part, evolved biases in real-time attentional, perceptual, decision-making, associative, memory, and emotional responses. Some literatures in this vein—on mate selection, taste aversion, and fear conditioning—are well developed. Existing literature can be mined and new data produced to yield understanding of how biases in multiple, interacting systems influence peace. For example, empathy and trust enable peaceful interaction—consolation, cooperation, helping, sharing, and so on—but prosocial emotions and behaviors are not elicited or deployed unconditionally. Even rodents and ants deploy them differentially depending on whether the individual in distress is a cagemate or relative rather than a stranger, a response also moderated by dispositional sociability (Ben-Ami Bartal, Decety, & Mason, 2011; Chen, Panksepp, & Lahvis, 2009; Langford et al., 2006; Nowbahari, Scohier, Durand, & Hollis, 2009). And chimpanzees, like humans, for all their empathic capacity and sensitivity to inequity, can be spectacularly unhelpful, even when helping has no material cost (Silk et al., 2005). Elicitation and deployment of trust also are contingent on, for instance, social vulnerability (Stirrat & Perrett, 2010) and cues as to the reliability of a social partner (Fetchenhauer & Dunning, 2010), even when trustingness is experimentally boosted with oxytocin (Mikolajczak et al., 2010). Appraisal of, memories about, and behavior toward social partners pass through filters derived in dynamic fashion from evolution, socially situated life histories, and immediate conditions, and we need to better understand when the result is an inclination toward peace. A schematic helpful to visualizing iterative processes on multiple time scales, from Li (2003), is shown in Figure 26.3.

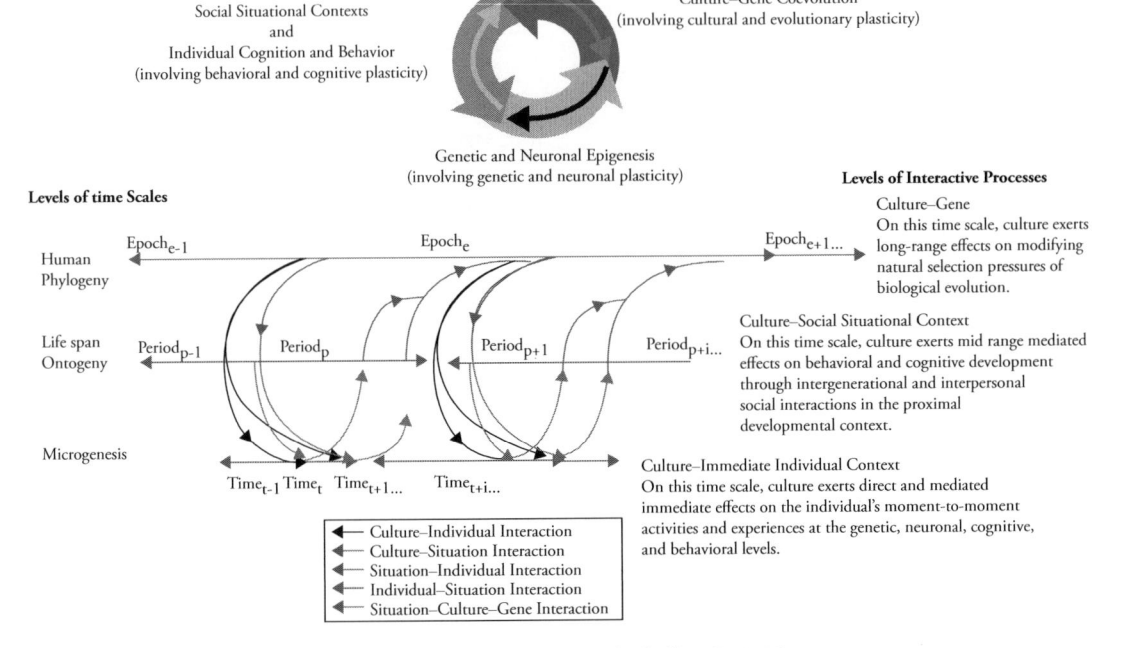

Figure 26.3 Biocultural orchestration of developmental plasticity across levels (from Li, 2003).

LEVELS OF ORGANIZATION

The far left column of Table 26.3 shows a typical scale for levels at which life is organized, next to illustrative distinctions among levels of organization emphasized in published works. Scholars tend to work in ranges of smaller or larger units of analysis—a sensible strategy. There is a place, though, for comprehensive conceptual frameworks. They can help scholars locate their research program in the larger scheme of things and can help research communities set longer term goals and move from a "cacophony of opinions" (Preston & de Waal, 2002) to synthesis. Levels touched on in Kenrick et al.'s (2002) dynamical systems approach, in the far right column, closely approximate the full scope of life. A schematic spanning those levels is shown in Figure 26.4, with some peace-relevant variables shown at each level. In light of the foregoing, it should be largely self-explanatory, so only two points warrant comment. First, nesting is used to avoid the implication that larger scale levels are "layered on" to smaller levels, as hierarchical representations can imply. Some processes may be consonant across levels of organization; for example, severe corporal punishment as a parenting strategy and an injunctive norm is contrary to a culture of peace at several levels (Skinner, 1985). Even so, processes emerging on larger scales are not just aggregates of individual attributes. With respect to gender differences in peacefulness, for instance, the gender typicality of children's behavior varies across social situations, such that individual-level attributes, such as gender identity or aggressiveness, leave much variance unaccounted for (Maccoby, 2002). Group-level attributes—group size, for example—constrain and shape social interaction. Smaller groups are characterized by more collaborative discourse, responsiveness to others' needs, and perspective taking and less conflict and competition. Relational attributes of boys' dyads can account for as much variance in aggressiveness as do individual-level (actor, target) attributes (Coie et al., 1999). From childhood, due to self-selection, asymmetrical exclusion (girls' groups exclude boys less than the other way around), and contexts arranged for them by adults, girls typically spend more time in small groups and boys in larger ones, creating peer cultures that shape the future development of individuals and cohorts in directions differentially conducive to peace. Thus, group processes neither trump nor reduce to individual-level processes. Attention to both yields a more complete understanding.

The idea of multilevel analysis is popular. What, then, accounts for ongoing acrimony around evolution, violence, gender, and race? A factor is the absence of shared scholarly discourse about complexity that

Table 26.3 Examples of Distinctions Among Levels of Organization[†]

Life	Lesch (2007)	Shaver & Mikulincer (2011)	Mayton (2009)	Bronfenbrenner (1992)	Galtung (2010)	Kenrick et al. (2003)
(sub)atomic						
molecular						
(sub)cellular	genes	genes				genes
	proteins					
	neurons	brain				
organ (system)	circuits					
organism	behavior	individual	intrapersonal	Individual	Individual	organism
		interpersonal	interpersonal	Intimates (micro)	Interpersonal (micro)	interpersonal
population		intergroup	cultural and societal	micro interactions (meso) institutional structures (exo) cultural context (macro)	within country (meso)	intergroup
					between nations (macro)	cultures
		regional			between regions (mega)	
species						species
community						community
ecosystem						ecosystem
biosphere						

[†] Terms for elements in this table are spatially distributed to graphically depict, in a crude way, conceptual distances among levels of organization.

avoids excesses, real and perceived, of reductionism and holism. Its development is impeded by the privileging in academe of study of smaller units (Fox, 1999). In a quantitative analysis of the science status hierarchy, Simonton (2004) found that "disciplines could be reliably ranked in the following order: physics, chemistry, biology, psychology, and sociology" (p. 59; see Fig. 26.5). The higher the status, the lower the proportion of women, American Indians, Latinos/as, and African Americans who earn PhDs in those disciplines in the United States (NSF, 2009). That politically disenfranchised groups disproportionately work at larger, less prestigious levels of organization adds status differences to other forms of segregation that make new collaborations more challenging and more important.

Cultivation of a shared conceptualization of complexity and the value of integrating across levels is critical to progress in understanding peace and aggression. Those shared understandings would not preclude scholarship focused at one level or another. They would unsettle assumptions that study at different levels is a contest or necessarily enacts social inequalities, instead reinforcing the truism that any person's scholarly output is a small part of a complex puzzle that will require many minds and a long time to solve. Where tension would otherwise be a wedge, collegial discussion might ensue.

Second, two important discontinuities are depicted in the figure. The first separates shaded from unshaded areas. Shading encompasses the individual and the *peripersonal space* within hands' reach; the unshaded areas comprise *extrapersonal space* beyond hands' reach (Malafouris, 2009, p. 97). Near spaces are intimate, and social interactions in near space will differ from those at a distance. Near

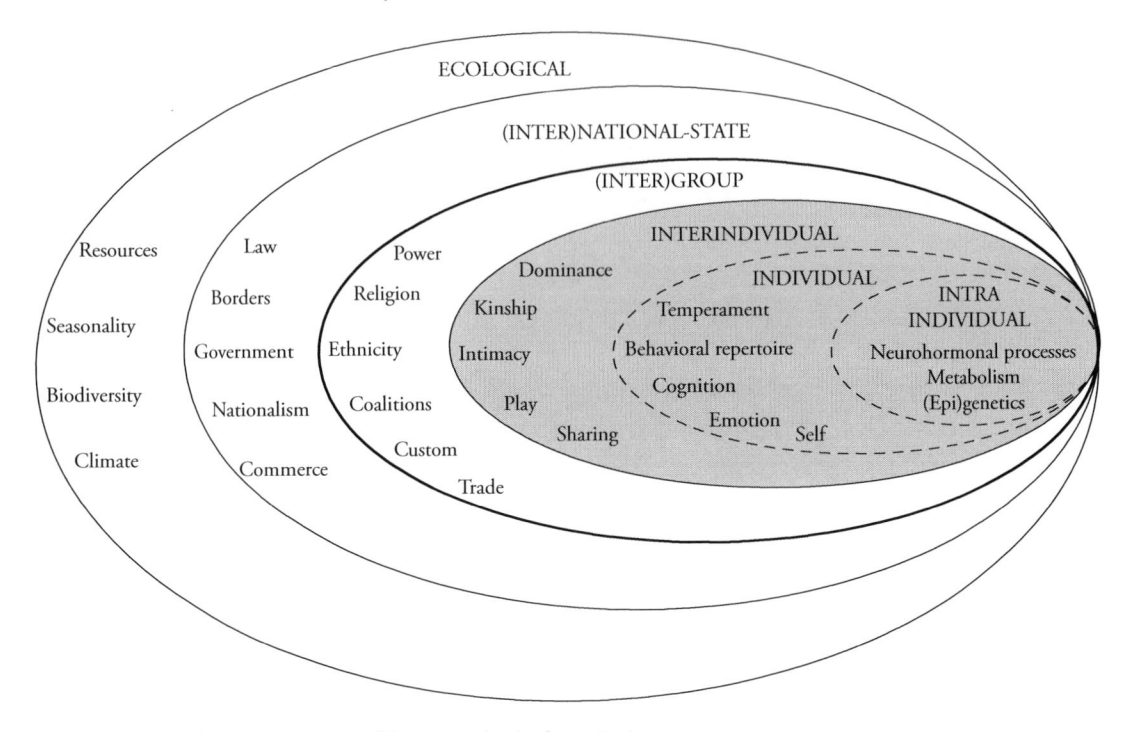

Figure 26.4 Some elements in a peace model at various levels of organization.

events compel a response more reliably than do far events. Sensuous and body senses—smell, taste, skin senses, haptic touch, kinesthesia, balance—are critical within peripersonal space; they are phylogenetically older, are represented differently in the brain, and are more affective than are the means by which extrapersonal space is engaged. Humans can communicate anger, fear, disgust, love, gratitude, and sympathy tactilely (Hertenstein et al., 2006). Interacting in peripersonal space involves more vulnerability, requires more trust, and allows subtler real-time emotional synchrony than does interacting at a distance, something Tinbergen argued was vital to peace in his classic 1968 paper, *On War and Peace in Man [sic] and Animals*.

Peripersonal and extrapersonal spaces are bridgeable. For example, Berti and Frassinetti (2000) showed that using a hand tool to manipulate objects in extrapersonal space resulted in a neural remapping of "far" to "near" (see also Wilson, 1998).

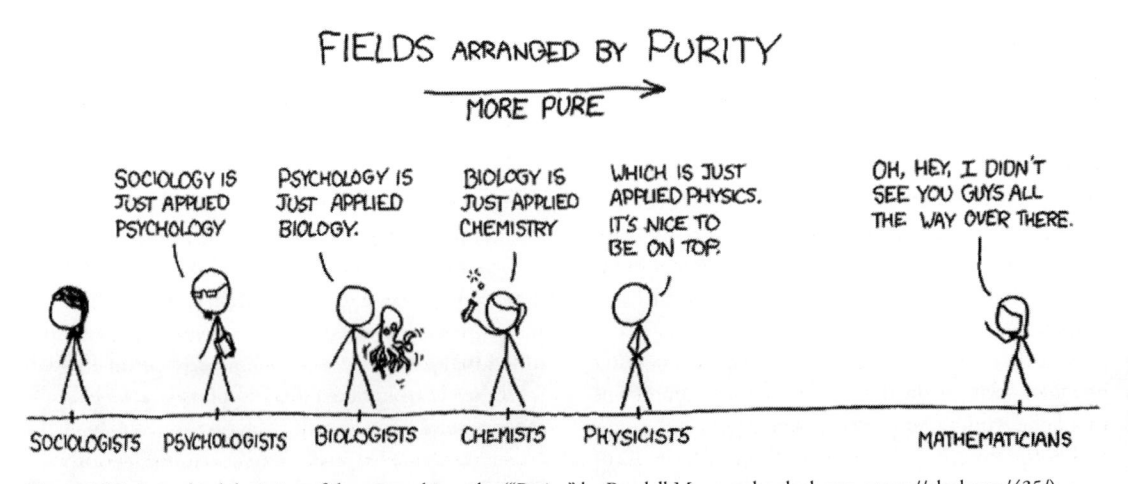

Figure 26.5 A graphical depiction of the science hierarchy ("Purity," by Randall Munroe aka xkcd.com, at ttp://xkcd.com/435/).

492 | PEACE AND THE HUMAN ANIMAL

Their finding is consistent with craft objects being viewed as extensions of the self and thus being used in trade to generate and test trust (Fry et al., 2009). The limits of this remapping through material culture—music (Kirschner & Tomasello, 2010), or virtual life technology (Bailenson & Yee, 2008), for instance—bear exploration. The peripersonal/extrapersonal distinction also may help explain the development of *relational* and *collective* forms of interdependence, which (re)produce different contexts for peaceful and aggressive interactions within and between social units. "In-fighting" at the dyadic or coalitional level, for instance, can turn to solidarity in the face of external threat. The forms emerge differentially among females and males (Eblen, Stout Rohrbauck, & Lori, 2009; Gardner & Gabriel, 2004), and examining their relation to socially patterned responses to threat, such as tend and befriend (Taylor, 2006) and tend and defend (De Dreu et al., 2010; Yamagishi & Mifune, 2009; Yuki & Yokota, 2009), may suggest ways of leveraging peacefulness across levels of organization and genders.

The second discontinuity is shown as a heavy line between (inter)group and (inter)national-state levels of organization. The latter emerged over the last 15,000 years or so as nomadic lifestyles gave way to settlement, transforming social relations within and between groups (Bickerton, 2007; Fishbein & Dess, 2003; Renfrew, 2009; Thayer, 2009). Groups grew larger and more heterogeneous. Cognitive and emotional processes that had evolved in the context of troops or bands began to play out in entirely new ways. Group identification at this new level—citizenship—was not based on kinship and interactional history, the basic mechanisms of which emerge in infancy and early childhood. It was based on place and maintained largely through symbolic abstractions, such as allegiance to rulers, worldviews, and institutions. Eventually, most compatriots existed only as an idea. Power became more centralized, society more stratified. Classes formed on the basis of arbitrary set distinctions, and a new kind of "outside"—and outsider—came into being. Larger scale social-structural abstractions were more cognitively demanding, creating more developmental desynchrony of children's capabilities vis á vis adult roles.

Peace and war existed before settlement, and they existed afterward. But their nature and that of *friends* and *enemies* was dramatically altered in this new, ultimately global paradigm for human niche construction (Boehm & Flack, 2010; Eibl-Eibesfeldt & Salter, 1998). Disputes, for instance, ended in court rather than intimate acts of reconciliation (Yarn, 2000). Differences between communities and nation-states suggest a framework for understanding why resolution of civil/intergroup conflict has "warm," affective components characteristic of primate reconciliation (empathy, forgiveness) more often than does resolution of international/state conflict, which conform better to a "cool," rational choice model (Long & Brecke, 2003), a difference to which the truth-and-reconciliation movement is responsive (Hamber, 2009). Promoting peace at different levels of organization will require many strategies, for psychological as well as practical reasons.

Thinking Ahead: Key Directions for an Evolutionary Peace Project

More than 40 years after Tinbergen's *On War and Peace*, the "crying need for a crash program" (p. 1417) on peace remains. His exhortation to scientists—to redirect their and the public's upset about the interrelated problems of violence, overpopulation, and environmental destruction into solution-oriented research—sounds fresh. Hopefully, the overview and tools presented here suggest some new avenues to integrative peace studies. Three contemporary themes in psychological research seem tailor-made for comparative evolutionary psychologists seeking to make contributions to peace. First, after decades of a largely "disembodied" psychology, the body is back. Humans have big bodies that, brain and all, evolved and develop and move in a complex environment. Hands matter in myriad ways (Goldin-Meadow, 2005; Petitto & Marentette, 1991; Wilson, 1998). Hand shaking is a "close salutation" (Kendon, 1990) in a pancultural repertoire of ritualized gestures involving touch, taste, and smell (Mallery, 1891, as cited by Arendsen, 2008). It is not uniquely human; wild and captive chimpanzees use group-specific hand clasps (Bonnie & de Waal, 2006; McGrew, Marchant, Scott, & Tutin, 2001). Viewing the 1993 handshake between Itzhak Rabin and Yasir Arafat through the lens of primate evolution—that is, peripersonal interactions, third-party mediation, reconciliation, social voyeurism—is irresistible:

> But the audience in attendance, and perhaps the millions more watching back in the Middle East, *seemed less interested in the formal signing than in the visual moment that would somehow make this tentative peace real*: the handshake between the two old warriors who personified the conflict between their peoples. Moments after the documents were

signed, Mr. Clinton took Mr. Arafat in his left arm and Mr. Rabin in his right arm and gently coaxed them together, needing to give Mr. Rabin just a little extra nudge in the back. Mr. Arafat reached out his hand first, and then Mr. Rabin, after a split second of hesitation and with a wan smile on his face, received Mr. Arafat's hand. The audience let out a simultaneous sigh of relief and peal of joy, as a misty-eyed Mr. Clinton beamed away. Two hands that had written the battle orders for so many young men, two fists that had been raised in anger at one another so many times in the past, locked together for a fleeting moment of reconciliation.

(emphasis added; *New York Times*, Friedman, 1993)

Discursive analysis (e.g., Milstein & Manusov, 2009) is appropriate, but interpreting the handshake as symbolic in a totally disembodied way does not seem reasonable in a comparative light. President Clinton said, in prelude, "The peace of the brave is *within our reach*" (emphasis added). That might literally be true sometimes, even if a fleeting handshake seldom will be sufficient to grasp it firmly and for all time.

Moving a large body through trees placed heavy kinesthetic demands on the brain, an idea at the core of one theory of the evolution of self (Barth, Povinelli, & Cant, 2004). Leaning that big body to the left in the here and now liberalizes political attitudes (Oppenheimer & Trail, 2010). Righthanders implicitly associate honesty with rightward space, lefthanders with leftward space (Casasanto, 2009). Making a fist enhances power-related self-construals among men, but not women (Schubert & Koole, 2009). Aggression against self and others appears to increase with "touch deprivation" and decrease with affectionate touch or massage (Field, Diego, & Hernandez-Reif, 2007). Eating is quintessentially corporeal; feeding behaviors (e.g., food sharing, co-feeding) mark and regulate relationships in diverse taxa and human cultures (Jones, 2007; Kaplan & Gurven, 2005; McGrew & Feistner, 1992; Scheid, Schmidt, & Koole, 2008), and tasting something sweet or bitter can, respectively, decrease or increase the harshness with which outgroups are dealt (Eskine, Kasinic, & Prinz, 2011; Hirschberger & Ein-Dor, 2005). Perhaps peace is as peace does: Peace from dyadic to intercultural levels might be facilitated by choreographing corporeal interactions to heighten peace-affirming affect and cognition.

Embodied cognition is not far afield from *intersubjectivity*. Today's intersubjectivity is an edgy blend of Husserl's phenomenology and Jung's collective unconscious with cutting-edge empirical research. Intersubjectivity is decentralized, distributed experience that mediates "the effect of the ecology on individuals' responses and adaptations" (Chiu, Gelfand, Yamagishi, Shteynberg, & Wan, 2010). Neural mirroring "solves the 'problem of other minds'... and makes intersubjectivity possible, thus facilitating social behavior" (Iacoboni, 2009, p. 653)—a critical example of which, for humans, may have been the cooperative rearing of children (Hrdy, 2009). Mind reading does not ensure peaceful interaction. However, intersubjectivity blurs ego boundaries, extending the self into and through others and the more-than-human environment. In a recent neuroimaging study, Anders et al. (2011) report that "during ongoing facial communication a 'shared space' of affect is successively built up between senders and perceivers of affective facial signals" (p. 439). Intersubjectivity renders violence against others self-destructive and peace self-protective.

Corporeality means death, something that humans might be uniquely aware pertains to the self. Fear of death increases ingroup bias (Landau, Solomon, Pyszczynski, & Greenberg, 2007); it also is associated with conceptual rigidity (conservatism, Jost, Nosick, & Gosling, 2008; low integrative complexity, Suedfeld, 2010). Importantly for peace studies, mortality fear effects can be mitigated developmentally and situationally. Hence, Hirschberger and Pyszczynski (2011) propose that "better understanding of the role played by mortality concerns in political reasoning provides insight into ways to move beyond violence and to promote peace" (p. 297).

Second, that gender matters to peace and war is not news, but the potential for truly transdisciplinary study of the relationship is. Males do more killing in war than do females, and more dying (Goldstein, 2001; Livingstone Smith, 2007; even prenatally, Catalano, Bruckner, Marks, & Eskenazi, 2006; Zorn, Sucur, Stare, & Meden-Vrtovec, 2002), and more females are sexually violated and humiliated (Lindner, 2010; Potts & Hayden, 2008). Women are less dominance oriented and more politically liberal than men (Norrander & Wilcox, 2008; Sidanius & Pratto, 2004) and have founded more peace organizations—Code Pink, International Women's Peace Service, PeaceWomen, and others (Cachola, Kirk, Natividad, & Pumarejo, 2010). These cross-cultural consistencies and, at some levels of organization, multispecies counterparts (Geary, 2010) are hard to explain without some appeal to classic evolutionary concepts such as anisogamy, intrasexual competition, and reciprocal altruism. Global peace efforts commonly involve reproductive and sexual rights, a pattern whose roots in evolution and corporeal existence would be dismissed only in absurdly bourgeois argument. As Potts and Hayden conclude in *Sex and War* (2008):

> [E]volutionary psychology also suggests new perspectives on waging peace…unless women can achieve greater equality and are also enabled to have control over their own childbearing, then efforts to address the many other sources of conflict and terrorism will be much less likely to succeed.
> (p. 331)[1]

Yet the relationship of gender to peace and violence clearly cannot be explained in terms of binary sex. Participation in killing, sexual violation, and resistance to being made into a warrior, while gendered, are not uniquely female or male (e.g., Bourke, 1999; Cunningham, 2009; Fry et al., 2009; Jones, 2009; Pusey et al., 2008). No sound evolutionary account presumes that women are destined for peace and men violence by dint of the distant past. In fact, from a comparative evolutionary point of view, gender and sexuality are more like Swiss army knives than cookie cutters, with multiform plasticity across species and life histories (e.g., Bryant & Schofield, 2007; Crews, 1998; Diamond, 2004; Thornhill & Gangestad, 2008; Wunsch, 2010). The confluence of contemporary research from evolutionary and developmental biology to political science and critical theory makes clear that, as mammals go, humans are modestly dimorphic, play with gender, and engage in far more nonprocreative sex than most, with myriad proximate functions—bonding, reconciliatory, erotic, palliative, instrumental, aggressive. An important direction for peace scholarship is reconciliation of binary and dimensional views of gender, of aspects that are relatively discrete (e.g., sex chromosomes, childbearing) and those that are more fluid (e.g., social identities, social roles). Recursiveness between meaning-making, culture, and evolutionary older processes can be explored in models that incorporate evolved legacies and the open-loop processes and social structures that produce bodies, behavior, and lived experience. Comparative evolutionary research on gender similarities and differences in hierarchy attenuation, cooperation, morality, metacognition, and social emotions can be integrated with research on the social construction of gender (Harness & Hall, 2010; Winter et al., 2001), multiple-identity intersectionality (Cole, 2009; Navarrete, McDonald, Molina, & Sidanius, 2010), biopolitics (Foucaldian, Inhorn, 2007, and non-Foucaldian, Falger, 1992), and state feminism (Lovenduski, 2005) to say something new and useful about gender and peace.[2]

Finally, sustainability matters. Risks to life everywhere are, taken together, sufficient to render all other challenges moot within a few human generations. Sustainability is receiving intense scrutiny in diverse disciplines, and peace and conservation psychologists have become key players (Abdel-Hadi, Tolba, & Soliman, 2010; Clayton & Myers, 2009; Kroger & Winter, 2010). New models capture how the environment is affected by and affects peacefulness: Ecological and sociocultural determinism are both being abandoned in favor of neo-socioecological models that incorporate co-construction of the biosphere, niches, and sociality (Janson, 2000; Mysterud & Polezynski, 2003; Winter & Cava, 2006). Comparative evolutionary psychologists working at various levels of organization clearly belong in this movement. Access to resources is at the center of evolutionary reasoning and of ethology and thus constitutes rich common ground for collaboration with scholars of political, economic, and cultural systems. A deep, unromantic understanding of how animals, including humans, peacefully resolve conflicts over resources, and what gets in the way, is critically needed. For instance, transnational protected areas, or "peace parks," are a promising way of promoting peace while conserving precious resources (Ali, 2007). Can an evolutionary perspective help policy makers in identifying targets of opportunity for, proposing, negotiating, utilizing, and monitoring peace parks, to boost the chances of success? Can individual-level motives for conservation of other animals and the inanimate environment—for example, restorative effects of experiencing nature (Kjellgren & Buhrkall, 2010), biophilia (Kellert, 2002; Simaika & Samways, 2010), or the quest for immortality (Dickinson, 2009)—be leveraged into significant support for peace? Questions such as these present challenges and opportunities that evolutionarily aware scholars should embrace.

Acknowledgments

During World War II, William J. Dess (Lt. Col, USAF Ret.) was a B-29 pilot in the Pacific. On the home front, Mary E. (Proctor) Dess (years later, MA in English and published writer) waited after every mission—as did all loved ones of the crew of The City of Vincennes ("Many Happy Returns") and other crews in the 39th Bomb Group—to learn who had survived. Unlike many on all sides of the war, he every time. Thus, I exist. Writing a chapter on peace in a way immune to my parents' experiences and perspectives would have been simpler—but inconceivable. I am grateful to them for so much, including the ways they informed and complicated this work. Thanks also to Dale Chapman, Jacki Rodríguez, and Deborah Du Nann Winter for inspiration and to Marie Krawchuk for superb technical assistance.

Notes

1. To childbearing should be added caregiving, because social obligations are a critical and nonfungible basis of power that is panculturally gendered (Pratto & Walker, 2004).

2. See de Magalhaes (2010) for an example of an explicit call for this sort of integration based on recent developments in diverse literatures. Only the abstract is in English and thus accessible to this chapter's author.

References

106th Cong. Rec, H4364-H4414 (1999, June 16) (statement of Representative DeLay).

Abbott, D. H., Keverne, E. B., Bercovitch, F. B., Shively, C. A., Mendoza, S. P., Saltzman, W., … Sapolsky, R. M. (2003). Are subordinates always stressed? A comparative analysis of rank differences in cortisol levels among primates. *Hormones and Behavior, 43*(1), 67–82.

Abdel-Hadi, A., Tolba, M. K., & Soliman, S. (Eds.). (2010). *Environment, health, and sustainable development.* Cambridge, MA: Hogrefe Publishing.

Adler, N., Singh-Manoux, A., Schwartz, J., Stewart, J., Matthews, K., & Marmot, M. (2008). Social status and health: A comparison of British civil servants in Whitehall-II with European- and African-Americans in CARDIA. *Social Science and Medicine, 66*(5), 1034–1045.

Ali, S. (Ed.). (2007). *Peace parks: Conservation and conflict resolution.* Cambridge, MA: MIT Press.

Allen, C. (1995). Intentionality: Natural and artificial. In H. L. Roitblat & J. Meyer (Eds.), *Comparative approaches to cognitive science* (pp. 93–110). Cambridge, MA: MIT Press.

Alyushin, A. (2010). Time scales of observation and ontological levels of reality. *Axiomathes, 20*(4), 439–460.

American Association for the Advancement of Science. (2001). *In pursuit of a diverse science, technology, engineering, and mathematics workforce.* Retrieved February 2011, from http://ehrweb.aaas.org/mge/Reports/Report1/AGEP/

Anders, S., Heinzle, J., Weiskopf, N., Ethofer, T., & Haynes, J. (2011). Flow of affective information between communicating brains. *NeuroImage, 54*(1), 439–446.

Angier, N. (1999, February 21) Men, women, sex and Darwin. *New York Times Magazine.* Retrieved January 2012, from http://www.nytimes.com/1999/02/21/magazine/men-women-sex-and-darwin.html?pagewanted=all&src=pm.

Antonacci, D., Norscia, I., & Palagi, E. (2010). Stranger to familiar: Wild strepsirhines manage xenophobia by playing. *PLoS ONE, 5*(0).

Archer, J. (2009). Does sexual selection explain human sex differences in aggression? *Behavioral and Brain Sciences, 32*(3–4), 249–266.

Arendsen, J. (2008). *Garrick Mallery (1891): Greeting by gesture. Gesture, 8*(3), 386–390.

Aureli, F., & de Waal, F. B. M. (Eds.). (2000). *Natural conflict resolution.* Berkeley: University of California Press.

Azrael, D., & Hemenway, D. (2000). "In the safety of your own home": Results from a national survey on gun use at home. *Social Science and Medicine, 50*(2), 285–291.

Bailenson, J. N., & Yee, N. (2008). Virtual interpersonal touch: Haptic interaction and copresence in collaborative virtual environments. *Multimedia Tools and Applications, 37,* 5–14.

Bannert, N., & Kurth, R. (2004). Retroelements and the human genome: New perspectives on an old relation. *Proceedings of the National Academy of Sciences USA, 101,* 14572–14579.

Barash, D. P., & Webel, C. P. (2008). *Peace and conflict studies* (2nd ed.). Thousand Oaks, CA: Sage.

Barth, J., Povinelli, D. J., & Cant, J. G. H. (2004). Bodily origins of SELF. In D. R. Beike, J. M. Lampinen, & D. A. Behrend (Eds.), *The self and memory* (pp. 11–43). New York: Psychology Press.

Bearzi, M., & Stanford, C. B. (2010). *Beautiful minds: The parallel lives of great apes and dolphins.* Cambridge, MA: Harvard University Press.

Beisner, C. E. (n.d.). The competing world views of environmentalism and Christianity. *Cornwall Alliance.* Retrieved January 2012, from http://www.cornwallalliance.org/articles/read/the-competing-world-views-of-environmentalism-and-christianity/

Ben-Ami Bartal, I., Decety, J., & Mason, P. (2011). Empathy and pro-social behavior in rats. *Science 334*(6061), 1427–1430.

Berti, A., & Frassinetti, F. (2000). When far becomes near: Remapping of space by tool use. *Journal of Cognitive Neuroscience, 12*(3), 415–420.

Bickerton, D. (2007). The ape in the anthill. In O. Vilarroya & F. Forn i Argimon (Eds.), *Social brain matters: Stances on the neurobiology of social cognition* (pp. 243–247). Atlanta, GA: Editions Rodopi.

Bjorklund, D. F., & Ellis, B. J. (2005). Evolutionary psychology and child development: An emerging synthesis. In B. J. Ellis & D. F. Bjorklund (Eds.), *Origins of the social mind: Evolutionary psychology and child development* (pp. 3–18). New York: The Guilford Press.

Boehm, C. (1999). *Hierarchy in the forest: The evolution of egalitarian behavior.* Cambridge, MA: Harvard University Press.

Boehm, C., & Flack, J. C. (2010). The emergence of simple and complex power structures through social niche construction. In A. Guinote & T. K. Vescio (Eds.), *The social psychology of power* (pp. 46–86). New York: The Guilford Press.

Boesch, C. (2003). Complex cooperation among Taï chimpanzees. In F. B. M. de Waal & P. L. Tyack (Eds.), *Animal social complexity: Intelligence, culture, and individualized societies* (pp. 93–110). Cambridge, MA: Harvard University Press.

Boesch, C., & Boesch, H. (1989). Hunting behavior of wild chimpanzees in the Tai National Park. *American Journal of Physical Anthropology, 78,* 547–573.

Bonnie, K. E., & de Waal, F. B. M. (2006). Affiliation promotes the transmission of a social custom: Handclasp grooming among captive chimpanzees. *Primates, 47*(1), 27–34.

Bonta, B. D. (1997). Cooperation and competition in peaceful societies. *Psychological Bulletin, 121*(2), 299–320.

Bourke, J. (1999). *An intimate history of killing: Face-to-face killing in 20th-century warfare.* New York: Basic Books.

Bryant, J., & Schofield, T. (2007). Feminine sexual subjectivities: Bodies, agency and life history. *Sexualities, 10*(3), 321–340.

Brescoll, V., & LaFrance, M. (2004). The correlates and consequences of newspaper reports of research on sex differences. *Psychological Science, 15*(8), 515–520.

Brondolo, E., ver Halen, N. B., Libby, D., & Pencille, M. (2011). Racism as a psychosocial stressor. In R. J. Contrada & A. Baum (Eds.), *The handbook of stress science: Biology, psychology, and health* (pp. 167–184). New York: Springer.

Bronfenbrenner, U. (1992). Ecological systems theory. In R. Vasta (Ed.), *Six theories of child development: Revised formulations and current issues* (pp. 187–250). Philadelphia: Jessica Kingsley.

Brosnan, S. F. (2006). Nonhuman species' reactions to inequity and their implications for fairness. *Social Justice Research, 19*(2), 153–185.

Brosnan, S. F., Houser, D., Leimgruber, K., Xiao, E., Chen, T., & de Waal, F. B. M. (2010). Competing demands of prosociality and equity in monkeys. *Evolution and Human Behavior, 31*(4), 279–288.

Butovskaya, M., Verbeek, P., Ljungberg, T., & Lunardini, A. (2000) A multicultural view of peacemaking among young children. In F. Aureli & F. B. M. De Waal (Eds.), *Natural conflict resolution* (pp. 243–258). Berkeley: University of California Press.

Cachola, E., Kirk, G., Natividad, L., & Pumarejo, M. R. (2010). Women working across borders for peace and genuine security. *Peace Review, 22*(2), 164–170.

Canli, T., & Lesch, K. (2007). Long story short: The serotonin transporter in emotion regulation and social cognition. *Nature Neuroscience, 10*(9), 1103–1109.

Cantalupo, C., & Hopkins, W. (2010). The cerebellum and its contribution to complex tasks in higher primates: A comparative perspective. *Cortex: A Journal Devoted to the Study of the Nervous System and Behavior, 46*(7), 821–830.

Caprioli, M. (2005). Primed for violence: The role of gender inequality in predicting internal conflict. *International Studies Quarterly, 49*(2), 161–178.

Caprioli, M., Hudson, V. A., McDermott, R., Ballif-Spanvill, B., Emmett, C. F., & Stearmer, M. (2009). The WomanStats Project Database: Advancing an empirical research agenda. *Journal of Peace Research, 46*(6), 1–13.

Carrier, D., & Janis, C. (2007). The short legs of great apes: Evidence for aggressive behavior in australopiths. *Evolution, 61*(3), 596–605.

Carroll, J. (2004). *Literary Darwinism: Evolution, human nature, and literature*. New York: Routledge.

Carroll, S. B. (2005). *Endless forms most beautiful: The new science of evo devo and the making of the animal kingdom*. New York. W. W. Norton & Company.

Carver, C. S., & Harmon-Jones, E. (2009). Anger is an approach-related affect: Evidence and implications. *Psychological Bulletin, 135*(2), 183–204.

Casasanto, D. (2009). Embodiment of abstract concepts: Good and bad in right- and left-handers. *Journal of Experimental Psychology: General, 138*(3), 351–367.

Castano, E., & Kofta, M. (2009). Dehumanization: Humanity and its denial. *Group Processes and Intergroup Relations, 12*(6), 695–697.

Catalano, R., Bruckner, T., Marks, A. R., & Eskenazi, B. (2006). Exogenous shocks to the human sex ratio: The case of September 11, 2001 in New York City. *Human Reproduction, 21*(12), 3127–3131.

Chen, Q., Panksepp, J. B., & Lahvis, G. P. (2009). Empathy is moderated by genetic background in mice. *PloS One, 4*(2), e4387–e4387.

Cheney, D. L., & Seyfarth, R. M. (2007). *Baboon metaphysics: The evolution of a social mind*. Chicago: University of Chicago Press.

Chiu, C., Gelfand, M. J., Yamagishi, T., Shteynberg, G., & Wan, C. (2010). Intersubjective culture: The role of intersubjective perceptions in cross-cultural research. *Perspectives on Psychological Science, 5*(4), 482–493.

Christie, D. J., Tint, B. S., Wagner, R. V., & Winter, D. D. (2008). Peace psychology for a peaceful world. *American Psychologist, 63*(6), 540–552.

Christie, D. J., Wagner, R. V., & Winter, D. D. (Eds.). (2008). *Peace, conflict, and violence: Peace psychology for the 21st century*. Los Altos, CA: Indo American Books.

Clark University Social-Evolutionary-Cultural Psychology Program. (n.d.). Retrieved January 2012, from Clark University, Worcester, MA, Psychology Department website http://www.clarku.edu/departments/psychology/grad/social/index.cfm .

Clayton, S., & Myers, G. (2009). *Conservation psychology: Understanding and promoting human care for nature*. West Sussex, UK: Wiley-Blackwell.

Clutton-Brock, T. H. (2006). Cooperative breeding in mammals. In P. M. Kappeler & C. P. van Schaik (Eds.), *Cooperation in primates and humans: Mechanisms and evolution* (pp. 173–190). New York: Springer.

Cohen, S., Alper, C. M., Doyle, W. J., Adler, N., Treanor, J. J., & Turner, R. B. (2008). Objective and subjective socioeconomic status and susceptibility to the common cold. *Health Psychology, 27*(2), 268–274.

Cohen, S., Doyle, W. J., & Baum, A. (2006). Socioeconomic status is associated with stress hormones. *Psychosomatic Medicine, 68*(3), 414–420.

Coie, J. D., Cillessen, A. H. N., Dodge, K. A., Hubbard, J. A., Schwartz, D., Lemerise, E. A., & Bateman, H. (1999). It takes two to fight: A test of relational factors and a method for assessing aggressive dyads. *Developmental Psychology, 35*(5), 1179–1188.

Cole, E. R. (2009). Intersectionality and research in psychology. *American Psychologist, 64*(3), 170–180.

Colmenares, F., & Silveira, F. (2008). Post-conflict non-aggressive behaviours may be neither friendly nor conciliatory: Conflict management of male hamadryas baboons. *Ethology, 114*(11), 1101–1112.

Confer, J. C., Easton, J. A., Fleischman, D. S., Goetz, C. D., Lewis, D. M. G., Perilloux, C., & Buss, D. M. (2010). Evolutionary psychology: Controversies, questions, prospects, and limitations. *American Psychologist, 65*(2), 110–126.

Corballis, M. C. (2008) Of mice and men—and lopsided birds. Cortex 44:3–7.

Corning, P. A. (2007). Synergy goes to war: A bioeconomic theory of collective violence. *Journal of Bioeconomics, 9*(2), 109–144.

Crane-Seeber, J., & Crane, B. (2010). Contesting essentialist theories of patriarchal relations: Evolutionary psychology and the denial of history. *The Journal of Men's Studies, 18*(3), 218–237.

Creel, S., & Sands, J. L. (2003). Is social stress a consequence of subordination or a cost of dominance? In F. B. M. de Waal & P. L. Tyack (Eds.), *Animal social complexity: Intelligence, culture, and individualized societies* (pp. 153–168). Cambridge, MA: Harvard University Press.

Crews, D. (1998). The evolutionary antecedents to love. *Psychoneuroendocrinology, 23*(8), 751–764.

Croft, D. P., James, R., & Krause, J. (2008). *Exploring animal social networks*. Princeton, NJ: Princeton University Press.

Cummings, N., O'Donohue, W., & Cummings, J. (Eds.). (2009). *Psychology's war on religion*. Phoenix, AZ: Zeig, Tucker & Theisen.

Cunningham, K. J. (2009). Female survival calculations in politically violent settings: How political violence and terrorism are viewed as pathways to life. *Studies in Conflict and Terrorism, 32*(7), 561–575.

Cupchik, G. C., & Hilscher, M. C. (2004). Personal life-narratives in an evolutionary context. *Journal of Cultural and Evolutionary Psychology, 2*(3–4), 321–336.

Dagg, A. I. (2004). *"Love of shopping" is not a gene: Problems with Darwinian psychology*. Tonawanda, NY: Black Rose Books.

D'Agostino, B. (1995). Self-images of hawks and doves: A control systems model of militarism. *Political Psychology, 16*(2), 259–295.

Dambrun, M., Kamiejski, R., Haddadi, N., & Duarte, S. (2009). Why does social dominance orientation decrease with university exposure to the social sciences? The impact of institutional socialization and the mediating role of geneticism. *European Journal of Social Psychology, 39*(1), 88–100.

Dar-Nimrod, I., & Heine, S. J. (2010). Genetic essentialism: On the deceptive determinism of DNA. *Psychological Bulletin, 137*, 800–818.

David, D., & DiGiuseppe, R. (2010). Social and cultural aspects of rational and irrational beliefs: A brief reconceptualization. In D. David, S. J. Lynn, & A. Ellis (Eds.), *Rational and irrational beliefs: Research, theory, and clinical practice* (pp. 49–61). New York: Oxford University Press.

Dawkins, R. (2005). Afterword. In D. M. Buss (Ed.), *The handbook of evolutionary psychology* (pp. 975–979). Hoboken, NJ: Wiley.

de Boer, S. F., Caramaschi, D., Natarajan, D., & Koolhaas, J. M. (2009). The vicious cycle towards violence: Focus on the negative feedback mechanisms of brain serotonin neurotransmission. *Frontiers in Behavioral Neuroscience, 3*(20), 52.

De Dreu, C. K. W., Greer, L. L., Handgra, M. J. J., Shalvi, S., Van Kleef, G. A., Baas, M., . . . Feith, S. W. (2010). The neuropeptide oxytocin regulates parochial altruism in intergroup conflict among humans. *Science, 328*(5984), 1408–1411.

de Magalhaes, I. A. (2010). A instancia corporea do humano: Sexualidades e subjectividades, mulheres e etica. [The bodily nature of the human: Sexualities and subjectivities, women and ethics] *Revista Critica De Ciencias Sociais, 89*, 111–125.

de Rivera, J. (2003). Aggression, violence, evil, and peace. In T. Millon & M. J. Lerner (Eds.), *Handbook of psychology: Personality and social psychology* (Vol. 5, pp. 569–598). Hoboken, NJ: Wiley.

de Waal, F. (1989). *Peacemaking among primates*. Cambridge, MA: Harvard University Press.

de Waal, F. B. M. (2000). The first kiss: Foundations of conflict resolution research in animals. In F. Aureli & F. B. M. de Waal (Eds.), *Natural conflict resolution* (pp. 15–33). Berkeley: University of California Press.

de Waal, F. B. M. (2010). *The age of empathy: Nature's lessons for a kinder society*. New York: Three Rivers Press.

de Waal, F. B., & Luttrell, L. (1989). Toward a comparative socioecology of the genus *Macaca*: Different dominance styles in rhesus and stumptail monkeys. *American Journal of Primatology, 19*(2), 83–109.

Decety, J., & Ickes, W. (Eds.). (2009). *The social neuroscience of empathy*. Cambridge, MA: MIT Press.

DeLamater, J. D., & Hyde, J. S. (1998). Essentialism vs. social constructionism in the study of human sexuality. *Journal of Sex Research, 35*(1), 10–18.

Derksen, M. (2010). Realism, relativism, and evolutionary psychology. *Theory and Psychology, 20*(4), 467–487.

Dess, N. (2003). Violence and its antidotes: Promises and pitfalls of evolutionarily aware policy development. In R. W. Bloom & N. Dess (Eds.), *Evolutionary psychology and violence: A primer for policymakers and public policy advocates* (pp. 239–268). Westport, CT: Praeger /Greenwood.

Dess, N. K., & Chapman, C. D. (1998). "Humans and animals"? On saying what we mean. *Psychological Science, 9*(2), 156–157.

Deutsch, M. (1990). Sixty years of conflict. *International Journal of Conflict Management, 1*(3), 237–263.

Diamond, L. M. (2004). Emerging perspectives on distinctions between romantic love and sexual desire. *Current Directions in Psychological Science, 13*(3), 116–119.

Dickinson, J. (2009). The people paradox: Self-esteem striving, immortality ideologies, and human response to climate change. *Ecology and Society, 14*(1), 34.

Dowd, M. (2007). *Thank God for evolution! How the marriage of science and religion will transform your life and our world*. Tulsa, OK: Council Oak Books.

Dunbar, R. I. M. (2003). The social brain: Mind, language, and society in evolutionary perspective. *Annual Review of Anthropology, 32*, 163–181.

Dunlap, K. A., Palmarini, M., Varela, M., Burghardt, R. C., Hayashi, K., Farmer, J. L., & Spencer, T. E. (2006). Endogenous retroviruses regulate periimplantation placental growth and differentiation. *Proceedings of the National Academy of Sciences USA, 103*(39), 14390–14395.

Duntley, J. D., & Shackelford, T. K. (Eds.). (2008). *Evolutionary forensic psychology: Darwinian foundations of crime and law*. New York: Oxford University Press.

Dupré, J. (2003) *Human nature and the limits of science*. New York: Oxford University Press.

Dusek, V. (1999). Sociobiology sanitized: Evolutionary psychology and gene selectionism. *Science as Culture, 8*(2), 129–169.

Eblen, A., Stout Rohrbauck, K., & Lori, W. (2009). Women's portrayal and paradox in peace links' documents, 1981–2001. *Women and Language, 32*(1), 1–11.

Egi, N. (2004). Hand structure in primates: Significance of grasping ability in arboreal life. *Primate Research, 20*(1), 11–29.

Eibl-Eibesfeldt, I., & Salter, F. K. (1998). *Indoctrinability, ideology, and warfare*. New York: Berghahn Books.

Elbert, T., Weierstall, R., & Schauer, M. (2010). Fascination violence: On mind and brain of man hunters. *European Archives of Psychiatry and Clinical Neuroscience, 260*(2), S100–S105.

Eskine, K., Kacinik, N. A., & Prinz, J. J. (2011). A bad taste in the mouth: Gustatory disgust influences moral judgment. *Psychological Science 22*(3), 295–299.

Fagen, R. (2002). Primate juveniles and primate play. In M. E. Pereira & L. A. Fairbanks (Eds.), *Juvenile primates: Life history, development, and behavior* (pp. 182–196). Chicago: University of Chicago Press.

Falger, V. S. E. (1992). Sex differences in international politics? An exploratory study of coalitional behaviour in biopolitical perspective. In J. M. G. van der Dennen (Ed.), *The nature of the sexes: The sociobiology of sex differences and the "battle of the* sexes" (pp. 171–194). Groningen, The Netherlands: Origin Press.

Ferrari, P. F., Paukner, A., Ionica, C., & Suomi, S. J. (2009). Reciprocal face-to-face communication between rhesus macaque mothers and their newborn infants. *Current Biology, 19*(20), 1768–1772.

Fessler, D. M. T. (2006). A burning desire: Steps toward an evolutionary psychology of fire learning. *Journal of Cognition and Culture, 6*(3–4), 429–451.

Fetchenhauer, D., & Dunning, D. (2010). Why so cynical? Asymmetric feedback underlies misguided skepticism regarding the trustworthiness of others. *Psychological Science, 21*(2), 189–193.

Field, T., Diego, M., & Hernandez-Reif, M. (2007). Massage therapy research. *Developmental Review, 27*(1), 75–89.

Figueredo, A. J., Gladden, P., Vásquez, G., Wolf, P. S. A., & Jones, D. N. (2009). Evolutionary theories of personality. In P. J. Corr & G. Matthews (Eds.), *The Cambridge handbook of personality psychology* (pp. 265–274). New York: Cambridge University Press.

Fishbein, H. D., & Dess, N. (2003). An evolutionary perspective on intercultural conflict: Basic mechanism and implications for immigration policy. In R. W. Bloom & N. Dess (Eds.), *Evolutionary psychology and violence: A primer for policymakers and public policy advocates* (pp. 157–202). Westport, CT: Praeger/Greenwood.

Fox, M. F. (1999). Gender, hierarchy, and knowledge in science. In J. S. Chafetz (Ed.), *Handbook of the sociology of gender* (pp. 441–457) New York: Kluwer Academic/Plenum.

Fraser, O. N., Stahl, D., & Aureli, F. (2010). The function and determinants of reconciliation in *Pan troglodytes*. *International Journal of Primatology, 31*(1), 39–57.

Friedman, T. (1993, September 10). Brave new Middle East. *New York Times*, p. A1.

Fry, D. P. (2007). *Beyond war: The human potential for peace*. New York: Oxford University Press.

Fry, D. P., Bonta, B. D., & Baszarkiewicz, K. (2009). Learning from extant cultures of peace. In J. de Rivera (Ed.), *Handbook on building cultures of peace* (pp. 11–26). New York: Springer Science + Business Media.

Fuentes, A. (2004). Revisiting conflict resolution: Is there a role for emphasizing negotiation and cooperation instead of conflict and reconciliation? In R. W. Sussman & A. R. Chapman (Eds.), *The origins and nature of sociality* (pp. 215–234). Hawthorne, NY: Aldine de Gruyter.

Gallo, L. C., & Matthews, K. A. (2003). Understanding the association between socioeconomic status and physical health: Do negative emotions play a role? *Psychological Bulletin, 129*(1), 10–51.

Galtung, J. (2010). Peace studies and conflict resolution: The need for transdisciplinarity. *Transcultural Psychiatry, 47*(1), 20–32.

Gangestad, S. W., Thornhill, R., & Garver-Apgar, C. E. (2005). Adaptations to ovulation. In D. M. Buss (Ed.), *The handbook of evolutionary psychology* (pp. 344–371). Hoboken, NJ: Wiley.

Gardner, W. L., & Gabriel, S. (2004). Gender differences in relational and collective interdependence: Implications for self-views, social behavior, and subjective well-being. In A. H. Eagly, A. E. Beall, & R. J. Sternberg (Eds.), *The psychology of gender* (2nd ed., pp. 169–191). New York: The Guilford Press.

Geary, D. C. (2010). *Male, female: The evolution of human sex differences* (2nd ed.). Washington, DC: American Psychological Association.

Geher, G. (2006). Evolutionary psychology is not evil! (…and here's why…). *Psihologijske Teme, 15*(2), 181–202.

Giberson, K. (2008). *Saving Darwin: How to be a Christian and believe in evolution*. New York: Harper One.

Glass, C., & Minnotte, K. L. (2010). Recruiting and hiring women in STEM fields. *Journal of Diversity in Higher Education, 3*(4), 218–229.

Goldin-Meadow, S. (2005). *Hearing gesture: How our hands help us think*. Cambridge, MA: Harvard University Press.

Goldstein, J. S. (2001). *War and gender: How gender shapes the war system and vice versa*. New York: Cambridge University Press.

The Graduate Institute. (2007). *Small arms survey (2007)*. Geneva, Switzerland. Retrieved January 2011, from http://www.smallarmssurvey.org/publications/by-type/yearbook/small-arms-survey-2007.html

Graham, J., Haidt, J., & Nosek, B. A. (2009). Liberals and conservatives rely on different sets of moral foundations. *Journal of Personality and Social Psychology, 96*(5), 1029–1046.

Gregor, T. (Ed.). (1996). *A natural history of peace*. Nashville, TN: Vanderbilt University Press.

Hagee, J. (2003). *The battle for Jerusalem*. Bentonville, AR: Thomas Nelson Publishing.

Hagee, J. (2010). *Can America survive? 10 prophetic signs that we are the terminal generation*. New York: Simon and Schuster.

Hagee, J. (Producer), & van Heerden, A. (Director). (1998). *Vanished in the twinkling of an eye* [Video recording]. Niagara Falls, NY: Cloud Ten Pictures.

Hagen, E. H. (2005). Controversial issues in evolutionary psychology. In D. M. Buss (Ed.), *The handbook of evolutionary psychology* (pp. 145–173). Hoboken, NJ: Wiley.

Halpern, D. F., Benbow, C. P., Geary, D. C., Gur, R. C., Hyde, J. S., & Gernsbacher, M. A. (2007). The science of sex differences in science and mathematics. *Psychological Science in the Public Interest, 8*(1), 1–51.

Hamber, B. (2009). *Transforming societies after political violence: Truth, reconciliation, and mental health*. New York: Springer Science + Business Media.

Hand, J. (2003). *Women, power, and the biology of peace*. San Diego, CA: Questpath Publishing.

Haque, A. (1973). Mirror image hypothesis in the context of Indo-Pakistan conflict. *Pakistan Journal of Psychology, 6*(1–2), 13–22.

Harness, S. K., & Hall, D. L. (2010). The future of the gender system: An interventionist approach. *Social Psychology Quarterly 73*(4), 339–340.

Harris Poll Interactive. (2010, March 24) *"Wingnuts" and Obama*. Retrieved December 2011, from http://www.harrisinteractive.com/NewsRoom/HarrisPolls/tabid/447/ctl/ReadCustom%20Default/mid/1508/ArticleId/223/Default.aspx

Hegarty, P., & Pratto, F. (2004). The differences that norms make: Empiricism, social constructionism, and the interpretation of group differences. *Sex Roles: A Journal of Research, 50*(7–8), 445–453.

Herman, K. N., Winslow, J. T., & Suomi, S. J. (2010). Primate models in serotonin transporter research. In A. V. Kalueff & J. L. LaPorte (Eds.), *Experimental models in serotonin transporter research* (pp. 288–307). New York: Cambridge University Press.

Hertenstein, M. J., Verkamp, J. M., Kerestes, A. M., & Holmes, R. M. (2006). The communicative functions of touch in humans, nonhuman primates, and rats: A review and synthesis of the empirical research. *Genetic, Social, and General Psychology Monographs, 132*(1), 5–94.

Hill, P. L., Allemand, M., & Burrow, A. L. (2010). Identity development and forgivingness: Tests of basic relations and mediational pathways. *Personality and Individual Differences, 49*(5), 497–501.

Hirschberger, G., & Ein-Dor, T. (2005). Does a candy a day keep the death thoughts away? The terror management function of eating. *Basic and Applied Social Psychology, 27*(2), 179–186.

Hirschberger, G., & Pyszczynski, T. (2011). An existential perspective on violent solutions to ethno–political conflict. In P. R. Shaver & M. Mikulincer (Eds.), *Human aggression and violence: Causes, manifestations, and consequences* (pp. 297–314). Washington, DC: American Psychological Association.

Hobbes, T. (1996). *Leviathan* (J. C. A. Gaskin, Ed.). New York: Oxford University Press. (Original work published 1651).

Hogg, C. L. (2009). Women's political representation in post-conflict Rwanda: A politics of inclusion or exclusion? *Journal of International Women's Studies, 11*(3), 34–54.

Horowitz, F. D. (1995). The nature–nurture controversy in social and historical perspective. In F. Kessel (Ed.), *Psychology, science, and human affairs: Essays in honor of William Bevan* (pp. 89–99). Boulder, CO: Westview Press.

Howell, S., Westergaard, G., Hoos, B., Chavanne, T. J., Shoaf, S. E., Cleveland, A.,...Dee Higley, J. (2007). Serotonergic influences on life-history outcomes in free-ranging male rhesus macaques. *American Journal of Primatology, 69*(8), 851–865.

Hrdy, S. B. (1997). Raising Darwin's consciousness: Female sexuality and the prehominid origins of patriarchy. *Human Nature, 8*(1), 1–49.

Hrdy, S. B. (2009). *Mothers and others: The evolutionary origins of mutual understanding.* Cambridge, MA: Harvard University Press.

Hughes, M. M. (2009). Armed conflict, international linkages, and women's parliamentary representation in developing nations. *Social Problems, 56*(1), 174–204.

Human Rights Watch. (2010). *Trail of death: LRA atrocities in northeastern Congo.* New York: Author.

Iacoboni, M. (2009). Imitation, empathy, and mirror neurons. *Annual Review of Psychology, 60,* 653–670.

Inhorn, M. C. (2007). *Reproductive disruptions: Gender, technology, and biopolitics in the new millennium.* New York: Berghahn Books.

Janson, C. H. (2000). Primate socio-ecology: The end of a golden age. *Evolutionary Anthropology, 9*(2), 73–86.

Johnson, W., & Coffin, J. (1999). Constructing primate phylogenies from ancient retrovirus sequences. *Proceedings of the National Academy of Sciences USA, 96*(18), 10254–10260.

Jones, A. (2009). *Gender inclusive: Essays on violence, men, and feminist international relations.* New York: Routledge/Taylor & Francis Group.

Jones, M. (2007). *Feast: Why humans share food.* New York: Oxford University Press.

Jost, J. T., Nosek, B. A., & Gosling, S. D. (2008). Ideology: Its resurgence in social, personality, and political psychology. *Perspectives on Psychological Science, 3*(2), 126–136.

Kaikkonen, R., Rahkonen, O., Lallukka, T., & Lahelma, E. (2009). Physical and psychosocial working conditions as explanations for occupational class inequalities in self-rated health. *European Journal of Public Health, 19*(5), 458–163.

Kalayjian, A., & Paloutzian, R. F. (Eds.). (2009). *Forgiveness and reconciliation: Psychological pathways to conflict transformation and peace building.* New York: Springer Science + Business Media.

Kaplan, H., & Gurven, M. (2005). The natural history of human food sharing and cooperation: A review and a new multi-individual approach to the negotiation of norms. In H. Gintis, S. Bowles, R. Boyd, & E. Fehr (Eds.), *Moral sentiments and material interests: The foundations of cooperation in economic life* (pp. 75–113). Cambridge, MA MIT Press.

Kappeler, P. M., & van Schaik, C. P. (2006). (Eds.). *Cooperation in primates and humans: Mechanisms and evolution.* New York: Springer.

Karlberg, M., & Buell, L. (2005). Deconstructing the "war of all against all": The prevalence and implications of war metaphors and other adversarial news schema in *Time, Newsweek,* and *MacLean's. Peace and Conflict Studies, 12*(1), 22–39.

Keller, J., & Bless, H. (2004). Evolutionary thought and psychological essentialism: The belief in genetic predispositions and its relationship to basic processes of social cognition. *Journal of Cultural and Evolutionary Psychology, 2*(1–2), 123–141.

Kellert, S. R. (2002). Experiencing nature: Affective, cognitive, and evaluative development in children. In P. H. Kahn, Jr. & S. R. Kellert (Eds.), *Children and nature: Psychological, sociocultural, and evolutionary investigations* (pp. 117–151). Cambridge, MA: MIT Press.

Kendon, A. (1990). *Conducting interaction: Patterns of behavior in focused encounters.* Cambridge, England: Cambridge University Press.

Kenrick, D. T., Maner, J. K., Butner, J., Li, N. P., & Becker, D. V. (2002). Dynamical evolutionary psychology: Mapping the domains of the new interactionist paradigm. *Personality and Social Psychology Review, 6*(4), 347–356.

Kenrick, D. T., Trost, M. R., & Sundie, J. M. (2004). Sex roles as adaptations: An evolutionary perspective on gender differences and similarities. In A. H. Eagly, A. E. Beall, & R. Sternberg (Eds.), *The psychology of gender* (2nd ed., pp. 65–91). New York: The Guilford Press.

Kirschner, S., & Tomasello, M. (2010). Joint music making promotes prosocial behavior in 4-year-old children. *Evolution and Human Behavior, 31*(5), 354–364.

Kjellgren, A., & Buhrkall, H. (2010). A comparison of the restorative effect of a natural environment with that of a simulated natural environment. *Journal of Environmental Psychology, 30*(4), 464–472.

Knoblich, G., & Sebanz, N. (2009). Evolving intentions for social interaction: From entrainment to joint action. In C. Renfrew, C. Frith, & L. Malafouris (Eds.), *The sapient mind: Archaeology meets neuroscience* (pp. 135–152). Oxford, England: Oxford University Press.

Konner, M. (2010). *The evolution of childhood: Relationships, emotion, mind.* Cambridge, MA: The Belknap Press of Harvard University.

Koski, S. E., Koops, K., & Sterck, E. H. M. (2007). Reconciliation, relationship quality, and postconflict anxiety: Testing the integrated hypothesis in captive chimpanzees. *American Journal of Primatology, 69*(2), 158–172.

Krebs, D. L., & Hemingway, A. (2008). The explanatory power of evolutionary approaches to human behavior: The case of morality. *Psychological Inquiry, 19*(1), 35–38.

Kroger, S. M., & Winter, D. D. (2010). *The psychology of environmental problems: Psychology for sustainability* (3rd ed.). New York: Psychology Press.

Krug, E. G., Mercy, J. A., Dahlberg, L. L., & Zwi, A. B. (2002). The world report on violence and health. *Lancet, 360*(9339), 1083–1088.

Kutsukake, N., & Clutton-Brock, T. (2008). Do meerkats engage in conflict management following aggression? Reconciliation, submission and avoidance. *Animal Behaviour, 75*(4), 1441–1453.

Landau, M. J., Solomon, S., Pyszczynski, T., & Greenberg, J. (2007). On the compatibility of terror management theory and perspectives on human evolution. *Evolutionary Psychology, 5*(3), 476–519.

Langford, D. J., Crager, S. E., Shehzad, Z., Smith, S. B., Sotocinal, S. G., Levenstadt, J. S.,...Mogil, J. S. (2006). Social modulation of pain as evidence for empathy in mice. *Science, 312*(5782), 1967–1970.

Lavender, P. (2011). 2012 election: Where GOP presidential candidates stand on evolution. *Huffington Post*, October 24, 2011. Retrieved January 2012, from http://www.huffingtonpost.com/2011/08/24/2012-election-gop-candidates-evolution_n_934045.html#s333316&title=Rick_Perry

Li, S. (2003). Biocultural orchestration of developmental plasticity across levels: The interplay of biology and culture in shaping the mind and behavior across the life span. *Psychological Bulletin, 129*(2), 171–194.

Lickliter, R., & Schneider, S. M. (2006). Role of development in evolutionary change: A view from comparative psychology. *International Journal of Comparative Psychology, 19*(2), 151–169.

Liesen, L. T. (2007). Women, behavior, and evolution: Understanding the debate between feminist evolutionists and evolutionary psychologists. *Politics and the Life Sciences, 26*(1), 51–70.

Lieven, A. (2004). *America right or wrong: An anatomy of American nationalism.* New York: Oxford University Press USA.

Lindner, E. (2010). *Gender, humiliation, and global security: Dignifying relationships from love, sex, and parenthood to world affairs.* Santa Barbara, CA: Praeger/ABC-CLIO.

Livingstone Smith, D. (2007). *The most dangerous animal: Human nature and the origins of war.* New York: St. Martin's Press.

Lloyd, E. A. (2005). *The case of the female orgasm: Bias in the science of evolution.* Cambridge, MA: Harvard University Press.

Long, W. J., & Brecke, P. (2003). *War and reconciliation: Reason and emotion in conflict resolution.* Cambridge, MA: MIT Press.

López-Larrea, C. (Ed.). (2011). *Self and non-self.* Austin, TX: Landes Bioscience.

Lovenduski, J. (Ed.) (2005) *State feminism and the political representation of women.* Cambridge, England: Cambridge University Press.

Maccoby, E. E. (2002). Gender and group process: A developmental perspective. *Current Directions in Psychological Science, 11*(2), 54–58.

MacLennan, B. (2002). Synthetic ethology: A new tool for investigating animal cognition. In M. Bekoff, C. Allen, & G. M. Burghardt (Eds.), *The cognitive animal: Empirical and theoretical perspectives on animal cognition* (pp. 151–156). Cambridge, MA: MIT Press.

MacNeilage, P. F. (1998). The frame/content theory of evolution of speech production. *Behavioral and Brain Sciences, 21*(4), 499–546.

Magee-Egan, P. (2009, April). Psychology's religion problem. *Catholic League: For religious and civil rights.* Retrieved January 2012, from http://www.catholicleague.org/psychologys-religion-problem/.

Majolo, B., Ventura, R., & Koyama, N. F. (2009). Anxiety level predicts post-conflict behaviour in wild Japanese macaques (*Macaca fuscata yakui*). *Ethology, 115*(10), 986–995.

Malafouris, L. (2009). Between brains, bodies and things: Tectonoetic awareness and the extended self. In C. Renfrew, C. Frith, & L. Malafouris (Eds.), *The sapient mind: Archaeology meets neuroscience* (pp. 89–104). Oxford, England: Oxford University Press.

Malka, A., & Lelkes, Y. (2010). More than ideology: Conservative-liberal identity and receptivity to political cues. *Social Justice Research, 23*(2–3), 156–188.

Mallon, R., & Stich, S. P. (2000). The odd couple: The compatibility of social construction and evolutionary psychology. *Philosophy of Science, 67*(1), 133–154.

Man, M. M., & Bond, M. H. (2005). A lexically derived measure of relationship concord in Chinese culture. *Journal of Psychology in Chinese Societies, 6*(1), 109–128.

Marecek, J., Crawford, M., & Popp, D. (2004). On the construction of gender, sex, and sexualities. In A. H. Eagly, A. E. Beall, & R. J. Sternberg (Eds.), *The psychology of gender* (2nd ed., pp. 192–216). New York: The Guilford Press.

Mayton, D. M. (2009). *Nonviolence and peace psychology: Intrapersonal, interpersonal, societal, and world peace.* New York: Springer Science + Business Media.

McClamrock, R. (2008). The emergent, the local, and the epiphenomenal. *Ecological Psychology, 20*(3), 244–251.

McClintock, M. K., Conzen, S. D., Gehlert, S., Masi, C., & Olopade, F. (2005). Mammary cancer and social interactions: Identifying multiple environments that regulate gene expression throughout the life span. *Journal of Gerontology Series B, Psychological Sciences and Social Sciences, 60*(1), 32–41.

McGrew, W. C. (2003). Ten dispatches from the chimpanzee culture wars. In F. B. M. de Waal & P. L. Tyack (Eds.), *Animal social complexity: Intelligence, culture, and individualized societies* (pp. 93–110). Cambridge, MA: Harvard University Press.

McGrew, W. C., & Feistner, A. T. C. (1992). Two nonhuman primate models for the evolution of human food sharing: Chimpanzees and callitrichids. In J. H. Barkow, L. Cosmides, & J. Tooby (Eds.), *The adapted mind: Evolutionary psychology and the generation of culture* (pp. 229–243). New York: Oxford University Press.

McGrew, W. C., Marchant, L. F., Scott, S. E., & Tutin, C. E. G. (2001). Intergroup differences in a social custom of wild chimpanzees: The grooming hand-clasp of the Mahale Mountains. *Current Anthropology, 42*(1), 148–153.

McKinnon, S. (2006). *Neo-liberal genetics: The myths and moral tales of evolutionary psychology.* Chicago: University of Chicago Press.

Melloni, R. H., Jr., & Ricci, L. A. (2010). Adolescent exposure to anabolic/androgenic steroids and the neurobiology of offensive aggression: A hypothalamic neural model based on findings in pubertal Syrian hamsters. *Hormones and Behavior, 58*(1), 177–191.

Mesquida, C. G., & Wiener, N. I. (1996). Human collective aggression: A behavioral ecology perspective. *Ethology and Sociobiology, 17*(4), 247–262.

Mikolajczak, M., Gross, J. J., Lane, A., Corneille, O., de Timary, P., & Luminet, O. (2010). Oxytocin makes people trusting, not gullible. *Psychological Science, 21*(8), 1072–1074.

Milstein, T., & Manusov, V. (2009). Oppositional discourse in Israeli media: Reflections of multiple cultural identities in coverage of the Rabin-Arafat handshake. *The Howard Journal of Communications, 20*(4), 353–369.

Mithen, S. (2007). Key changes in the evolution of human psychology. In S. W. Gangestad & J. A. Simpson (Eds.), *The evolution of mind: Fundamental questions and controversies* (pp. 256–266). New York: The Guilford Press.

Moran, M. H. (2005). Barbarism, old and new: Denaturalizing the rhetoric of warfare. In S. McKinnon & S. Silverman (Eds.), *Complexities: Beyond nature and nurture* (pp. 251–267). Chicago: University of Chicago Press.

Morgan, D. K., & Whitelaw, E. (2008). The case for transgenerational epigenetic inheritance in humans. *Mammalian Genome, 19*(6), 394–397.

Motyl, M., Hart, J., & Pyszczynski, T. (2010). When animals attack: The effects of mortality salience, infrahumanization of violence, and authoritarianism on support for war. *Journal of Experimental Social Psychology, 46*(1), 200–203.

Moyers, B. D. (2006). *Welcome to doomsday*. New York: New York Review of Books.

Musallam, N., Coleman, P. T., & Nowak, A. (2010). Understanding the spread of malignant conflict: A dynamical systems perspective. *Peace and Conflict: Journal of Peace Psychology, 16*(2), 127–151.

Music, G. (2011). *Nurturing natures: Attachment and children's emotional, sociocultural and brain development*. New York: Psychology Press.

Mysterud, I., & Poleszynski, D. V. (2003). Expanding evolutionary psychology: Toward a better understanding of violence and aggression. *Social Science Information/Information Sur Les Sciences Sociales, 42*(1), 5–50.

Nakata, R. (2008). Comparative study about face recognition by new world monkeys and humans: Similarities and differences of facial recognition between squirrel monkeys and humans. *Japanese Journal of Psychonomic Science, 26*(2), 179–185.

Natarajan, D., & Caramaschi, D. (2010). Animal violence demystified. *Frontiers in Behavioral Neuroscience, 4*, 9.

Nathan, O., & Norden, H. (1981). (Eds.). *Einstein on peace*. New York: Avenel Books.

National Academies of Science. (2010). *Expanding underrepresented minority participation: America's science and technology talent at the crossroads*. Washington, DC: National Academies Press.

National Science Foundation (NSF). (2009, December). *SRS doctorate recipients from U.S. universities: Summary report 2007–08*. Retrieved February 2011, from http://www.nsf.gov/statistics/nsf10309/

Navarrete, C. D., McDonald, M. M., Molina, L. E., & Sidanius, J. (2010). Prejudice at the nexus of race and gender: An outgroup male target hypothesis. *Journal of Personality and Social Psychology, 98*(6), 933–945.

Nell, V. (2006). Cruelty's rewards: The gratifications of perpetrators and spectators. *Behavioral and Brain Sciences 29*(3), 211–257.

Nellemann, C., Redmond, I., & Refisch, J. (Eds). (2010). *The last stand of the gorilla—environmental crime and conflict in the Congo Basin. A rapid response assessment. United Nations Environment Programme, GRID-Arendal*. Retrieved Jnauary 2012, from http://www.grida.no/publications/rr/gorilla/

Newman, F., & Holzman, L. (2006). *Unscientific psychology: A cultural-performatory approach to understanding human life*. Lincoln NE: iUniverse.

Newport, F. (2010, December 17). *Four in 10 Americans believe in strict creationism*. Retrieved February 2011, from http://www.gallup.com/poll/145286/four-americans-believe-strict-creationism.aspx

Norrander, B., & Wilcox, C. (2008). The gender gap in ideology. *Political Behavior, 30*(4), 503–523.

Nowbahari, E., Scohier, A., Durand, J.-L., & Hollis, K. L. (2009). Ants, *Cataglyphis cursor*, use precisely directed rescue behavior to free entrapped relatives. *PLoS ONE 4*(8), e6573.

Oatley, K., & Mar, R. A. (2005). Evolutionary pre-adaptation and the idea of character in fiction. *Journal of Cultural and Evolutionary Psychology, 3*(2), 179–194.

O'Leary, D. (2009, February). Post details: Ben Wiker picks 10 books that screwed up the world and explains how. *The ID Report*. Retrieved December 2011, from http://www.arn.org/blogs/index.php/2/2009/02/06/ben_wiker_picks_10_books_that_screwed_up

Oishi, S., & Schimmack, U. (2010). Culture and well-being: A new inquiry into the psychological wealth of nations. *Perspectives on Psychological Science, 5*(4), 463–471.

Oppenheimer, D. M., & Trail, T. E. (2010). Why leaning to the left makes you lean to the left: Effect of spatial orientation on political attitudes. *Social Cognition, 28*(5), 651–661.

Palagi, E. (2009). Adult play fighting and potential role of tail signals in ringtailed lemurs (*Lemur catta*). *Journal of Comparative Psychology, 123*(1), 1–9.

Parish, A. R., & de Waal, F. B. M. (2000). The other "closest living relative": How bonobos (*Pan paniscus*) challenge traditional assumptions about females, dominance, intra- and intersexual interactions, and hominid evolution. In D. LeCroy & P. Moller (Eds.), *Evolutionary perspectives on human reproductive behavior* (pp. 97–113). New York: New York Academy of Sciences.

Parr, L. A., Winslow, J. T., Hopkins, W. D., & de Waal, F. B. M. (2000). Recognizing facial cues: Individual discrimination by chimpanzees (*Pan troglodytes*) and rhesus monkeys (*Macaca mulatta*). *Journal of Comparative Psychology, 114*(1), 47–60.

Patterson, N., Richter, D. J., Gnerre, S., Lander, E. S., & Reich, D. (2006). Genetic evidence for complex speciation of humans and chimpanzees. *Nature, 441*(7097), 1103–1108.

Pellis, S. M., & Pellis, V. C. (2010). Social play, social grooming, and the regulation of social relationships. In A. V. Kalueff, J. L. LaPorte, & C. L. Bergner (Eds.), *Neurobiology of grooming behavior* (pp. 66–87). New York: Cambridge University Press.

Petitto, L. A., & Marentette, P. F. (1991). Babbling in the manual mode: Evidence for the ontogeny of language. *Science, 251*(5000), 1493–1496.

Pezzulo, G., & Castelfranchi, C. (2009). Intentional action: From anticipation to goal-directed behavior. *Psychological Research/Psychologische Forschung, 73*(4), 437–440.

Pichot, A. (2009). *The pure society: From Darwin to Hitler* (D. Fernbach, Trans.). London: Verso.

Pika, S. (2008). Gestures of apes and pre-linguistic human children: Similar or different? *First Language, 28*(2), 116–140.

Pinker, S. (2002). *The blank slate: The modern denial of human nature*. New York: Viking.

Potts, M., & Hayden, T. (2008). *Sex and war: How biology explains warfare and terrorism and offers a path to a safer world*. Dallas, TX: BenBella Books.

Pratto, F., Sidanius, J., & Levin, S. (2006). Social dominance theory and the dynamics of intergroup relations: Taking stock and looking forward. In W. Stroebe & M. Hewstone (Eds.), *European review of social psychology* (Vol. 17, pp. 271–320). New York: Psychology Press.

Pratto, F., & Walker, A. (2004). The bases of gendered power. In A. H. Eagly, A. E. Beall, & R. J. Sternberg (Eds.), *The psychology of gender* (2nd ed., pp. 242–268). New York: The Guilford Press.

Preston, S. D., & de Waal, F. B. M. (2002). Empathy: Its ultimate and proximate bases. *Behavioral and Brain Sciences*, 25(1), 1–20.

Pusey, A., Murray, C., Wallauer, W., Wilson, M., Wroblewski, E., & Goodall, J. (2008). Severe aggression among female *Pan troglodytes schweinfurthii* at Gombe National Park, Tanzania. *International Journal of Primatology*, 29(4), 949–973.

Racine, E., Waldman, S., Rosenberg, J., & Illes, J. (2010). Contemporary neuroscience in the media. *Social Science and Medicine*, 71(4), 725–733.

Rath, R., & Das, J. P. (1958). Study in stereotypes of college freshmen and service holders in Orissa, India, towards themselves and four other foreign nationalities. *The Journal of Social Psychology*, 47, 373–385.

Renfrew, C. (2009). Neuroscience, evolution and the sapient paradox: The factuality of value and of the sacred. In C. Renfrew, C. Frith, & L. Malafouris (Eds.), *The sapient mind: Archaeology meets neuroscience* (pp. 165–186). Oxford, England: Oxford University Press.

Renfrew, C., Frith, C., & Malafouris, L. (Eds.). (2009). *The sapient mind: Archaeology meets neuroscience*. Oxford, England: Oxford University Press.

Robarchek, C. A. (1989). Hobbesian and Rousseauan images of man: Autonomy and individualism in a peaceful society. In S. Howell & R. Willis (Eds.), *Societies at peace: Anthropological perspectives* (pp. 31–44). Florence, KY: Taylor & Frances/Routledge.

Robertson, P. (2002). *The end of the age*. Bentonville, AR: Thomas Nelson Inc.

Rochat, P., & Ferreira, C. P. (2008). *Homo negotiatus*: Ontogeny of the unique ways humans own, share and reciprocate. In S. Itakura & K. Fujita (Eds.), *Origins of the social mind: Evolutionary and developmental views* (pp. 141–156). New York: Springer Science + Business Media.

Roulin, A., Dreiss, A. N., & Kölliker, M. (2010). Evolutionary perspective on the interplay between family life, and parent and offspring personality. *Ethology*, 116(9), 787–796.

Rousseau, J-J. (1997). *The discourses and other early political writings* (V. Gourevitch, Ed.). Cambridge, England: Cambridge University Press. (Original work published 1754).

Sakurai, K., Kawakami, N., Yamaoka, K., Ishikawa, H., & Hashimoto, H. (2010). The impact of subjective and objective social status on psychological distress among men and women in Japan. *Social Science and Medicine*, 70(11), 1832–1839.

Salomon, G., & Cairns, E. (2010). *Handbook on peace education*. New York: Psychology Press.

Sapolsky, R. M. (2004). Social status and health in humans and other animals. *Annual Review of Anthropology*, 33, 393–418.

Sapolsky, R. M. (2006). A natural history of peace. *Foreign Affairs*, 85(1), 104–120.

Sapolsky, R. M., & Share, L. J. (2004). A pacific culture among wild baboons: Its emergence and transmission. *PLoS Biology*, 2(4), E106.

Schaffner, C. M., & Caine, N. G. (2000). The peacefulness of cooperatively breeding primates. In F. Aureli & F. B. M. de Waal (Eds.), *Natural conflict resolution* (pp. 155–169). Berkeley: University of California Press.

Schaffner, C. M., Aureli, F., & Caine, N. G. (2005). Following the rules: Why small groups of tamarins do not reconcile conflicts. *Folia Primatologica*, 76(2), 67–76.

Scheid, C., Schmidt, J., & Noe, R. (2008). Distinct patterns of food offering and co-feeding in rooks. *Animal Behaviour*, 76(5), 1701–1707.

Schubert, T. W., & Koole, S. L. (2009). The embodied self: Making a fist enhances men's power-related self-conceptions. *Journal of Experimental Social Psychology*, 45(4), 828–834.

Seelinger, G., & Seelinger, U. (1983). On the social organisation, alarm and fighting in the primitive cockroach *Cryptocercus punctulatus scudder*. *Zeitschrift Für Tierpsychologie*, 61(4), 315–333.

Shaver, P., & Mikulincer, M. (Eds.). (2011). *Human aggression and violence: Causes, manifestations, and consequences*. Washington, DC: American Psychological Association.

Shtulman, A., & Schulz, L. (2008) The relation between essentialist beliefs and evolutionary reasoning. *Cognitive Science*, 32(6), 1049–1062.

Sidanius, J., & Pratto, F. (2004). *Social dominance theory: A new synthesis*. New York: Psychology Press.

Silk, J. B. (1998). Making amends: Adaptive perspectives on conflict remediation in monkeys, apes, and humans. *Human Nature*, 9(4), 341–368.

Silk, J. B. (2002). The form and function of reconciliation in primates. *Annual Review of Anthropology 31*, 21–44.

Silk, J. B., Brosnan, S. F., Vonk, J., Henrich, J., Povinelli, D. J., & Richardson, A. S. (2005). Chimpanzees are indifferent to the welfare of unrelated group members. *Nature*, 437(7063), 1357–1359.

Silk, J. B., Kaldor, E., & Boyd, R. (2000). Cheap talk when interests conflict. *Animal Behaviour*, 59(2), 423–432.

Silverberg, J., & Gray, J. P. (1992). *Aggression and peacefulness in humans and other primates*. New York: Oxford University Press.

Simaika, J. P., & Samways, M. J. (2010). Biophilia as a universal ethic for conserving biodiversity. *Conservation Biology*, 24(3), 903–906.

Simonton, D. K. (2004). Psychology's status as a scientific discipline: Its empirical placement within an implicit hierarchy of the sciences. *Review of General Psychology*, 8(1), 59–67.

Skinner, B. F. (1985). Toward the cause of peace: What can psychology contribute? *Applied Social Psychology Annual*, 6, 21–25.

Solomon, S., Greenberg, J., & Pyszczynski, T. (2004). The cultural animal: Twenty years of terror management theory and research. In J. Greenberg, S. L. Koole, & T. Pyszczynski (Eds.), *Handbook of experimental existential psychology* (pp. 13–34). New York: The Guilford Press.

Spolsky, E. (2002). *Darwin and Derrida: Cognitive literary theory as a species of post-structuralism*. Baltimore: Johns Hopkins University Press.

Sponsel, L. E. (1996). The natural history of peace: A positive view of human nature and its potential. In T. Gregor (Ed.), *A natural history of peace* (pp. 95–125). Nashville, TN: Vanderbilt University Press.

Staub, E. (1997). The psychological and cultural roots of group violence and the creation of caring societies and peaceful group relations. In T. Gregor (Ed.), *A natural history of peace* (pp. 129–155) Nashville, TN: Vanderbilt University Press.

Stirrat, M., & Perrett, D. I. (2010). Valid facial cues to cooperation and trust: Male facial width and trustworthiness. *Psychological Science, 21*(3), 349–354.

Sue, D. W. (2010). *Microaggressions in everyday life: Race, gender, and sexual orientation.* Hoboken, NJ: Wiley.

Suedfeld, P. (2010). The cognitive processing of politics and politicians: Archival studies of conceptual and integrative complexity. *Journal of Personality, 78*(6), 1669–1702.

Sugden, J. (2006). Teaching and playing sport for conflict resolution and co-existence in Israel. *International Review for the Sociology of Sport, 41*(2), 221–240.

Suomi, S. J. (2003). Social and biological mechanisms underlying impulsive aggressiveness in rhesus monkeys. In B. B. Lahey, T. E. Moffitt, & A. Caspi (Eds.), *Causes of conduct disorder and juvenile delinquency* (pp. 345–362). New York: The Guilford Press.

Suomi, S. J. (2006). Risk, resilience, and gene x environment interactions in rhesus monkeys. *Annals of the New York Academy of Sciences, 1094,* 52–62.

Szyf, M., McGowan, P. O., Turecki, G., & Meaney, M. J. (2010). The social environment and the epigenome. In C. M. Worthman, P. M. Plotsky, D. S. Schechter, & C. A. Cummings (Eds.), *Formative experiences: The interaction of caregiving, culture, and developmental psychobiology* (pp. 53–81). New York: Cambridge University Press.

Taylor, S. E. (2006). Tend and befriend: Biobehavioral bases of affiliation under stress. *Current Directions in Psychological Science, 15*(6), 273–277.

Thayer, B. A. (2009). *Darwin and international relations: On the evolutionary origins of war and ethnic conflict.* Lexington: The University Press of Kentucky.

Thierry, B. (2004). Social epigenesis. In B. Thierry, M. Singh, & W. Kaumanns (Eds.), *Macaque societies: A model for the study of social organization* (pp. 267–290). Cambridge, England: Cambridge University Press.

Thierry, B. (2007). Unity in diversity: Lessons from macaque societies. *Evolutionary Anthropology, 16,* 224–238.

Thornhill, R., & Gangestad, S. W. (2008). *The evolutionary biology of human female sexuality.* New York: Oxford University Press.

Tinbergen, N. (1968). On war and peace in animals and man. *Science, 160*(3835), 1411–1418.

Tomasello, M. (2009). Cultural transmission: A view from chimpanzees and human infants. In U. Schönpflug (Ed.), *Cultural transmission: Psychological, developmental, social, and methodological aspects* (pp. 33–47). New York: Cambridge University Press.

Tse, P. U. (2008). Symbolic thought and the evolution of human morality. In W. Sinnott-Armstrong (Ed.), *Moral psychology, Vol. 1. The evolution of morality: Adaptations and innateness* (pp. 269–297). Cambridge, MA: MIT Press.

Tulogdi, A., Toth, M., Halasz, J., Mikics, E., Fuzesi, T., & Haller, J. (2010). Brain mechanisms involved in predatory aggression are activated in a laboratory model of violent intraspecific aggression. *European Journal of Neuroscience, 32*(10), 1744–1753.

Tybur, J. M., Miller, G. F., & Gangestad, S. W. (2007). Testing the controversy: An empirical examination of adaptationists' attitudes toward politics and science. *Human Nature, 18*(4), 313–328.

van Hooff, J. A. R. A. M., & Preuschoft, S. (2003). Laughter and smiling: The intertwining of nature and culture. In F. B. M. de Waal & P. L. Tyack (Eds.), *Animal social complexity: Intelligence, culture, and individualized societies.* (pp. 260–287). Cambridge, MA: Harvard University Press.

van Schaik, C. P., & Deaner, R. O. (2003). Life history and cognitive evolution in primates. In F. B. M. de Waal & P. L. Tyack (Eds.), *Animal social complexity: Intelligence, culture, and individualized societies* (pp. 5–25). Cambridge, MA: Harvard University Press.

Vandermassen, G. (2005). *Who's afraid of Charles Darwin? Debating feminism and evolutionary theory.* Lanham, MD: Rowman & Littlefield.

Villareal, L. P. (2008). *Origin of group identity: Viruses, addiction and cooperation.* New York: Springer.

Vonk, J., & Shackelford, T. K. (2012). Comparative evolutionary psychology: A united discipline for the study of evolved traits. In J. Vonk & T. K. Shackelford (Eds.), *Oxford handbook of comparative evolutionary psychology* (pp. 547–560). New York: Oxford University Press.

Wallace, C., Haerpfer, C., & Abbott, P. (2008). Women in Rwandan politics and society. *International Journal of Sociology, 38*(4), 111–125.

Weiss, A., King, J. E., & Figueredo, A. J. (2000). The heritability of personality factors in chimpanzees (*Pan troglodytes*). *Behavior Genetics, 30*(3), 213–221.

Westneat, D. F., & Fox, C. W. (2010). *Evolutionary behavioral ecology.* Oxford, England: Oxford University Press.

Wiese, S. L., Vallacher, R. R., & Strawinska, U. (2010). Dynamical social psychology: Complexity and coherence in human experience. *Social and Personality Psychology Compass, 4*(11), 1018–1030.

Wiker, B. (2008). *10 books that screwed up the world: And 5 others that didn't help.* Washington, DC: Regnery Press.

Wilkinson, R. (2004). Why is violence more common where inequality is greater? *Annals of the New York Academy of Sciences, 1036,* 1–12.

Wilkinson, R. G., & Pickett, K. E. (2006). Income inequality and population health: A review and explanation of the evidence. *Social Science and Medicine, 62*(7), 1768–1784.

Wilson, F. (1998). *The hand: How its use shapes the brain, language, and human culture.* New York: Pantheon.

Wilson, D. S. (2005) Evolutionary social constructivism. In J. Gottschall & D. S. Wilson (Eds.), *The literary animal: Evolution and the nature of narrative* (pp. 20–37). Evanston, IL: Northwestern University Press.

Winegard, B., & Deaner, R. O. (2010). The evolutionary significance of Red Sox nation: Sport fandom as a byproduct of coalitional psychology. *Evolutionary Psychology, 8*(3), 432–446.

Winter, D. D., & Cava, M. M. (2006). The psycho-ecology of armed conflict. *Journal of Social Issues, 62*(1), 19–40.

Winter, D. D. N., Pilisuk, M., Houck, S., & Lee, M. (2001). Understanding militarism: Money, masculinity, and the search for the mystical. In D. J. Christie, R. V. Wagner, & D. D. N. Winter (Eds.), *Peace, conflict, and violence: Peace psychology for the 21st century* (pp. 139–148). Delhi, India: Indo American Books.

WorldNews. (2009). *Rep. John Shimkus: God decides when the "earth will end."* Retrieved February 2011, from http://wn.com/shimkus_march_2009

Wrangham, R. W., Wilson, M. L., & Muller, M. N. (2006). Comparative rates of violence in chimpanzees and humans. *Primates, 47*(1), 14–26.

Wrangham, R. (2009). *Catching fire: How cooking made us human.* New York: Basic Books.

Wunsch, S. (2010). Evolution from mammals: Heterosexual reproductive behavior to human erotic bisexuality. *Journal of Bisexuality, 10*(3), 268–293.

Yamagishi, T., & Mifune, N. (2009). Social exchange and solidarity: In-group love or out-group hate? *Evolution and Human Behavior, 30*(4), 229–237.

Yarn, D. H. (2000). Law, love, and reconciliation: Searching for natural conflict resolution in *Homo sapiens*. In F. Aureli & F. B. M. de Waal (Eds.), *Natural conflict resolution* (pp. 54–70). Berkeley: University of California Press.

Yuki, M., & Yokota, K. (2009). The primal warrior: Outgroup threat priming enhances intergroup discrimination in men but not women. *Journal of Experimental Social Psychology, 45*(1), 271–274.

Zihlman, A. L., & Bolter, D. R. (2004). Mammalian and primate roots of human sociality. In R. W. Sussman & A. R. Chapman (Eds.), *The origins and nature of sociality* (pp. 23–52). Hawthorne, NY: Aldine de Gruyter.

Zorn, B., Sucur, V., Stare, J., & Meden-Vrtovec, H. (2002). Decline in sex ratio at birth after 10-day war in Slovenia: Brief communication. *Human Reproduction, 17*(12), 3173–3177.

Zur, O. (1987). The psychohistory of warfare: The co-evolution of culture, psyche and enemy. *Journal of Peace Research, 24*(2), 125–134.

CHAPTER 27

Resource Acquisition, Violence, and Evolutionary Consciousness

Gregory Gorelik, Todd K. Shackelford, *and* Viviana A. Weekes-Shackelford

Abstract

The evolution and development of adaptations result from the gradual selection and inheritance of traits and behaviors that better enable organisms to acquire and maintain resources needed for survival and reproduction. We argue that instances of individual, regional, and global violence are rooted in our adaptations to seek, acquire, maintain, and utilize limited resources, regardless of whether such adaptations are currently successful at doing so. However, violence is not the only strategy employed by organisms to acquire resources; cooperation, reciprocity, and social bonding are behaviors that may likewise prove useful in this endeavor. We speculate about how individual adaptations and their by-products may interact with the adaptations of other individuals and with societal and cultural phenomena, both violently and nonviolently. Finally, we discuss how individual decisions can affect higher level regional and global violence. Individual decisions carry moral weight for the individual in question and for society as a whole. We hope to convince readers that their personal decisions and behaviors have far-reaching consequences on the well-being of others and that an evolutionary consciousness may help us to understand the effects of our personal choices on the existence of individual- and group-level violence.

Key Words: evolution, violence, war, rape, resources, sexual selection, extended phenotype

Introduction

The scourge of brutal violence has gripped humanity from time immemorial. While writing this chapter, the "Arab Spring" uprising of individuals in opposition to ruling despots in North Africa and the Middle East has unleashed unimaginable violence that has left thousands dead. In Libya, Moammar Gadhafi and his supporters are raping and murdering their way through the populace in an attempt to hold onto the reins of power. Cell phone videos confiscated from Gadhafi loyalists depict the brutal physical and sexual torture of Libyan civilians. According to CNN (Razek, Ahmed, & Sidner, 2011):

> It [a confiscated video] shows two men in civilian clothes standing over a naked woman who is bent over with her face on the floor. The man standing behind her is sodomizing her with what appears to be a broomstick.
> "I can't bear it! I can't bear it!" the woman cries.
> "Let's push it farther," a male voice says off camera.
> "No, no, that's enough!" the woman begs.
> Eventually, one of the men puts his sock-covered

This chapter is based on an unpublished manuscript by G. Gorelik, T. K. Shackelford, and V. A. Weekes-Shackelford, entitled "Human violence and evolutionary consciousness," which is currently under editorial review.

foot on her face. In Arab culture, that is considered a major insult.

Farther east, a wave of protests across Syria has sparked genocidal retaliation from Bashar al-Assad's government. Men, women, and children are being tortured and killed for demanding their right to free expression. Hamza Ali al-Khateeb, a 13-year-old boy participating in anti government protests with his family and friends, was shot and tortured by Syrian Airforce Intelligence officers prior to his body being returned to his family. *The Washington Post* (Sly, 2011) reported that Hamza's...

> ...head was swollen, purple and disfigured. His body was a mess of welts, cigarette burns and wounds from bullets fired to injure, not kill. His kneecaps had been smashed, his neck broken, his jaw shattered and his penis cut off.

In Norway, the worst mass shooting since World War II was perpetrated by a right-wing Christian extremist in reaction to the government's support of Muslim immigration and other multiculturalist policies. His bombing of downtown Oslo and his subsequent shooting rampage at a Labor Party youth camp left 76 dead (McLaughlin, 2011).

Meanwhile in Somalia, a widespread famine has led to the starvation and death of nearly 30,000 children and the malnourishment of 13 million Somalis. The situation is exacerbated by Somalia's high fertility rate and violent conflict between various Islamist militants, tribal warlords, and the federal government. Somalia thus exemplifies the fact that overpopulation and resource scarcity fuel much of global violence (Teague, 2011).

Students of history are well aware of the ubiquity of human brutality and sadism throughout the ages. As cited by Van Vugt (Chapter 17, this volume), warfare may have existed early on in human evolution, as anthropologists have uncovered mass graves of mostly male skeletons exhibiting blunt-force trauma dated to around 200,000 years ago (YA). In Provence, France, a rock etching dated to about 22,000 YA portrays a human figure embedded with projectile weapons (Livingstone Smith, Chapter 20, this volume), and numerous geological and archaeological findings from the southwest and northeast United States depict millennia of coalitional warfare between Native American tribes, especially during times of drought and other periods of resource scarcity (Lambert, Chapter 19, this volume). Modern history is bloodied with the horrors of World War I, World War II, the Holocaust, Soviet purges and gulags, the Korean War, the Vietnam War, the Cambodian Killing Fields, the first Gulf War, genocides in Bosnia, Kosovo, Rwanda, and Darfur, the Israeli-Palestinian conflict, and the US-led wars in Iraq and Afghanistan, to name a few.

Although death rates due to war, homicide, and other forms of violence have declined throughout the Western world in recent centuries (even if we include the bloody conflicts of the 20th century; Van Vugt, Chapter 17, this volume), the human capacity to destroy its own species and the rest of the ecosystem is unprecedented. Thus, our penchant to inflict unimaginable harm on one another has kept pace with advances in medicine and innovations in nutrition-yielding technologies. Unless violence is understood with the empirical and conceptual tools of modern science, and evolutionary science in particular, the near future of our species looks bleak.

In keeping with the themes of this volume, we advance an evolutionary perspective on human violence. In addition to discussing the evolutionary and developmental origins and abstract dynamics of individual violence, and violence within and between political, religious, ethnic, national, and other cultural groups, we speculate about the possible applications of evolutionary science to moral and practical choices within the personal domain, which may help one to develop what we term an "evolutionary consciousness." The application of scientific findings to practical matters of human life is not without peril, and the misuse of science to support racial, political, or religious movements is not unheard of. Nonetheless, findings within the evolutionary sciences can inform and guide individual and collective decisions regarding acts of physical and sexual violence. An evolutionary perspective provides a useful heuristic for scholars wishing to understand human violence because humans are biological beings who are related to, and have coevolved with, one another and with other species. Likewise, an evolutionary paradigm can enrich one's understanding of oneself and one's context.

The Problem of Population

In 1798, the English scholar Thomas Malthus published his landmark *An Essay on the Principle of Population*. Within it, Malthus posited his "great law of nature," which states that population levels cannot exceed levels of subsistence production. Thus, because populations grow hyperbolically, while means of production grow arithmetically, a point is inevitably reached at which there is no longer enough food to sustain the growing population.

We now know that Malthus's laws are not immutable, in that population rates may not always surpass or even reach levels of food production, as is the case in many developed nations (Hopfenberg & Pimentel, 2001). However, conflicts over access to limited nutritional and other reproductively relevant resources were a great selection pressure on human and nonhuman populations across evolutionary time. No wonder Malthus's ideas inspired Charles Darwin's formulation of natural selection as the creative factor in biological evolution in the following century. Darwin's addendum to Malthus states that because there are variations between individuals within a population, those individuals who are successful at competing for scarce resources outreproduce less successful individuals, and so pass on the very traits that led to their success. Thus, adaptations such as the heart and the brain are constructed across evolutionary time as randomly appearing variations are inherited that refine and improve an organism's ability to acquire reproductively relevant resources. From single-celled organisms competing for nutrients or hosts to complex multicellular eukaryotes such as plants competing for sunlight, evolutionary success is synonymous with the acquisition and use of resources needed for survival and reproduction, across many levels of analysis.

Reproductive success may be achieved by means other than direct reproduction. For example, helping genetic relatives to reproduce increases the likelihood that some of one's own genes are passed on to the next generation, regardless of whether one has offspring (Hamilton, 1964). This phenomenon may help to explain instances in which individuals sacrifice their lives for relatives, and pseudo-relatives (or "fictive kin") in times of conflict and war, or during acts of terrorism on behalf of one's actual (or nominal) brothers and sisters. As a result of such acts, the self-sacrificed individual's relatives may acquire reproductively useful resources (see Sosis, Phillips, & Alcorta, Chapter 14, this volume). This phenomenon may likewise explain instances of self-inflicted violence and suicide, which is likely to affect individuals of low reproductive value but with fertile family members in need of useful resources that the suicidal individual may be consuming (see Brown & Brown, Chapter 9, this volume).

In this chapter, we apply concepts from evolutionary biology and evolutionary psychology to examine some of the evolved functions of the human mind that are manifested as violent behaviors. Our underlying theme is that violence served the function of enabling organisms to acquire reproductively relevant resources in ancestral environments. For our ancestors, possession of resources served to foster two related, though somewhat orthogonal, reproductive goals. The first was to survive long enough to reproduce. Some of the resources needed to fulfill this goal are food, shelter, warmth, and safe environments. Thus, much of violent conflict in ancestral and modern humans, both within and between groups, can be traced to the scarcity of such resources, all essential for survival. Not so obvious (except to students of evolutionary biology) is the second goal that the acquisition of resources fostered: the chance to acquire a mate—a resource in itself. Resources needed to fulfill this goal are numerous and vary across time and place. Some of the requisite resources are territory, allies, social dominance, status, weaponry, precious natural or human-made objects such as diamonds, body decorations and accessories, and currency. The reason that organisms compete for resources that are seemingly inessential for survival is attributable to sexual selection, a concept from evolutionary biology which posits that survival is not the only hurdle that organisms must surmount to reproduce; they must also defeat their reproductive rivals and attract members of the other sex. Defeating rivals often entails the evolution of traits supporting physical strength and social dominance (which may explain why men are, on average, larger and more violent than women—a correlate of high testosterone; Buss & Shackelford, 1997; Kolbert & Crothers, 2003). Such traits may also be considered attractive by members of the other sex. Thus, although human violence is mostly perpetrated by men of reproductive age against other men of reproductive age, the fact that many women find dominant and aggressive men attractive suggests that no one sex is to blame for the evolution of violent behavior in our species.

In the natural world, conflicts over resources are usually more violent between males than between females. This was the case in human ancestral environments and remains so today (Kruger & Fitzgerald, Chapter 10, this volume). The reason for this is that in most sexually reproducing species, males are less likely to invest in parenting than are females (Trivers, 1972). As a result, it is often in a male's best interest to compete more vigorously with other males for sexual access to females, as he is not burdened by gestation, lactation, and other costs of offspring production and rearing, and can be more reproductively successful by copulating with many females. Females, however, pay higher reproductive costs than males and so avoid indiscriminate mating and injury-causing competition with rival females. Human males are notable in that they make better fathers than most other primates. Thus, for an ancestral woman, mating with a man of low mate value or who was unlikely to assist in childrearing could have imperiled a woman's reproductive prospects by causing injury or death to her child, perhaps due to starvation, disease, predators, or violent conspecifics. Therefore, men are likely to use violence against other men when competing for both short-term mates and long-term mates.

Due to differences between ancestral environments and modern environments, what was adaptive for our ancestors then may not be adaptive for us now. Even if human violence serves an evolved function in modern environments, this does not make it morally defensible. Nevertheless, if we take a cursory look at current local and global conflicts, most are waged over resources. Thus, conflicts over water reservoirs, oil pipelines, and gold and diamond deposits often involve savage forms of violence. It is also easy to see (especially after the 2008 worldwide economic crisis) how more relational or "structural" forms of violence (see Dess, Chapter 26, this volume) over monetary and other intangible economic resources (such as subprime mortgages) may be responsible for much social unrest. This last point suggests that human violence may not only result from struggles over material resources but symbolic ones as well. Therefore, many religiously inspired acts of violence and war may be rooted in a struggle for access to the "belief-sphere" for one's god or gods over the god or gods of others. Of course, religious conflicts may sometimes be about access to tangible resources such as food, territory, and mates, but they are likely to be especially intractable when there is a lack of compromise on "sacred values" by the parties involved (see Sosis et al., Chapter 14, this volume). Next, we discuss the developmental dynamics of violent conflict in humans. To understand the evolution of human violence, its emergence must be tracked across an individual's life span—from its prenatal origins to its global consequences. Although violent behavior varies individually and contextually, its emergence in conflicts over reproductively relevant resources is what unites its varying characteristics.

The Development of Human Violence

Biological adaptations are not preformed but undergo a dynamic and intricate process of development that belies the nature-nurture dichotomy. A complex biological organism begins its existence as an undifferentiated cell. This cell soon divides into two daughter cells. In turn, those two cells divide into two cells, and so on. Throughout this process, the cells differentiate in structure and function into the myriad organs and organ systems that comprise an individual organism. The developmental course of a cell is dependent on where it is physically located within the developing organism and on the timing of its replicative cycle (Carroll, 2005). Although all nongametic cells are genetic clones of one another, they assume different structural and physiological characteristics due to the differential effects of the developmental context upon each cell and its genome. Thus, a biological adaptation (which is a result of natural selection) is dependent upon the developmental context for its emergence and functionality (see Tooby & Cosmides, 1992, for an early and comprehensive argument for the central role of development in understanding adaptations). Factors extrinsic to the developing organism, such as the mother's diet, exposure to biochemicals, and other ecological factors, affect the development of an organism and its adaptive properties (Bjorklund & Pellegrini, 2002; Carroll, 2005). The developmental context is not limited to extragenetic factors, as a gene's expression is dependent on the action of other genes that either suppress or enhance its effects (Carroll, 2005). Interestingly, an organism's own behavior is pivotal for the normal development of species-typical adaptations. For example, a fetus's flailing of its arms and legs is essential for the proper development of its musculoskeletal structures (Rodriguez, Palacios, Garcia-Alix, Pator, & Paniagua, 1988). Likewise, an infant's development of vision, audition, and facial recognition is dependent on its exposure to sights, sounds, and faces (Chang & Merzenich, 2003; Fagiolini, Pzzorusso, Berardi, Domenici, & Maffei, 1994; Nelson, 2001). Adaptations to violent conflict are no different.

Organisms that were successful at acquiring reproductively relevant resources survived long enough to reproduce and thereby pass on the means by which their offspring would develop the adaptations of its parents. Thus, from conception onward, an organism's development is characterized by an ever-increasing ability to acquire and consume resources. Rather than debate which violent traits or behaviors are biological adaptations and which are not, we posit that all acts of physical and sexual violence have an evolutionary history associated with resource acquisition. This is not to say that such acts of violence are currently adaptive or that formerly adaptive behaviors cannot be recombined and refashioned for novel purposes.

Beginning with conception, there is a struggle over nutritional resources between the developing organism and its mother. Among other risky conditions, an expectant mother experiences a decrease in blood insulin as a result of a fetus-induced suppression of insulin production (Salmon, 2007). This is adaptive for the developing fetus, which is in need of glucose, but may lead to gestational diabetes for the mother. Likewise, pregnancy leads to an increase in maternal blood pressure, which is dangerous to the mother but nutritionally beneficial to her fetus (Salmon, 2007). Such parent-offspring conflicts (Trivers, 1974) may have contributed to high rates of maternal mortality, miscarriage, and stillbirth throughout human history and in parts of the developing world today.

As an infant develops, its struggle to acquire nutritional resources may take increasing tolls on its mother and on its current and future siblings. In mammals, conflict over weaning is a classic example (Salmon, 2007; Trivers, 1974). Throughout the weaning period, an infant is adaptively motivated to extract more milk than the mother is willing to apportion. Extracting the maximum amount of milk from the mother is an effective way for the infant to acquire valuable nutrients at minimal cost. The mother, on the other hand, is adaptively motivated to minimize her apportionment of milk to the infant and to invest her energy and resources into other current or future offspring instead. Sibling rivalry over access to parental resources is a related phenomenon that occurs at many dinner tables and playgrounds. Violent conflicts between adult human siblings over parental resources occur as well and may be exacerbated by the accumulation of family wealth, as facilitated by the rise of agriculture (Salmon, Chapter 7, this volume). Nevertheless, contrary to the preceding statements, genetic kin have similar reproductive interests and are more likely to cooperate and care for one another than for someone who is unrelated.

As humans mature through juvenility and adolescence, contexts for resource acquisition increasingly become peer oriented. It is during this formative period that an individual's personality and interaction style develop. Our social adaptations do not arise ex nihilo but are dependent upon life experience for their emergence. Thus, interaction with one's peers during childhood provides stimuli and responses that affect the development of our social adaptations. A host of factors contribute to this development, including genes, rearing influences, ecological factors, developmental history, and the contexts of group interaction. If a group of unacquainted children are made to interact with one another, hierarchical stratification based on dominance occurs rather quickly (Plusquellec, Francois, Boivin, Perusse, & Tremblay, 2007; Savin-Williams, 1976). This stratification emerges via a bottom-up process and does not require centralized planning. Thus, some children become popular, others get shunned, and most find themselves in the middle of the social status hierarchy. A child's position in this hierarchy leads to the development of conditional adaptations (Boyce & Ellis, 2005) that furthered the reproductive success of human ancestors who found themselves in such hierarchical positions in past environments. Because a child's hierarchical position is determined relative to the position of his or her peers, most children develop a combination of submissiveness- and dominance-oriented adaptations, as each child encounters settings in which he or she is either more submissive or more dominant relative to his or her peers (e.g., school, camp, karate class, etc.). Inherited characteristics and contextual factors are also responsible for the formation of stable personalities and dispositions across contexts (Weiss, King, & Figueredo, 2000). The processes of hierarchical status formation and the development of personality traits specific to one's position within that hierarchy can be framed in the language of game theory and evolutionary biology as the development of "evolutionarily stable strategies" (Axelrod, 2006; Dawkins, 1976).

A child's hierarchical position determines his or her access to survival-related or (for older children and young adults) reproductively relevant resources. In Western cultures, where food, clothing, and shelter are generally available, children mostly compete for the approval of their peers. Peer approval is important for the formation of long-term cooperative relationships and the future exchange of resources. Likewise, social popularity in childhood may be predictive of future reproductive success in adolescence (Pellegrini & Long, 2003; Veenstra, Lindenberg, Munniksma, & Dijkstra, 2010). Children employ a host of strategies to acquire material and social resources within peer groups. One of these strategies is bullying, or the repeated harming of a weaker individual by a more powerful individual (Volk, Camilleri, Dane, & Marini, Chapter 16, this volume). In poverty-stricken contexts, the consequences of being victimized by a bully may be more than just the loss of one's lunch money. Bullying may have been a successful strategy by which our juvenile and adolescent ancestors acquired the nutritional and social resources needed for survival and reproduction. Although bullying is one of a few strategies employed by children and adolescents, and although there are individual and situational differences in the use of this strategy (e.g., children who employ a combination of bullying and coalition building are of a higher social status than children who employ only one of the strategies; see Volk et al., Chapter 16, this volume), the historical and contemporary cross-cultural presence of bullying hints at its adaptive role in resource acquisition.

Men achieve greater reproductive success by being socially dominant and aggressive, as they can thereby acquire more female sexual partners. Women, on the other hand, are more likely to use indirect forms of aggression to acquire high-status mates, such as talking behind a female rival's back in order to disparage her looks or sexual reputation (see Volk et al., Chapter 16, this volume). Although there are more similarities between the sexes than there are differences, most acts of physical violence, sexual violence, war, and genocide are perpetrated by men (Daly & Wilson, 1988). Therefore, males, more than females, should exhibit the development of cruel behaviors such as violent bullying in childhood. At a proximal level, the development of behavioral repertoires depends on the principles of operant conditioning, whereby behaviors that are reinforced by some physiological reward (perhaps regulated by dopamine) will be exhibited more often when triggered by particular stimuli associated with that reward. The neurological correlates of operant conditioning entail the strengthening of synapses between neurons detecting particular stimuli (e.g., signs of vulnerability in an individual) and neurons responsible for initiating a conditioned behavioral response to such stimuli (e.g., harassment or torture of that individual). The proximal development of violent bullying, and male aggression in general, may be characterized by such a process. This process highlights our previous point that adaptations are never preformed but depend on contextual factors for their emergence. It may be that males are more physiologically rewarded for cruelty than are females and so are more easily conditioned to engage in it. Even when threatened with punishment or the loss of resources, such children and adolescents may nevertheless engage in cruelty as it may be associated with an internal sensation of pleasure. Such individuals may be diagnosed with oppositional defiant disorder as children and antisocial personality disorder as adults—disorders characterized by a lack of concern for the well-being of others and sometimes even the positive enjoyment of others' distress.

The evolution and development of cruelty and the associated pleasure that some individuals may derive from such behavior are certainly disturbing. That such behavior may have been adaptive in certain contexts, however, does not mean that it has a scientific stamp of approval. On the contrary, approaches to remedy such behavior must take into account its evolutionary and developmental origins. Parents and educators, for instance, must learn to recognize children and adolescents who derive pleasure from inflicting pain on humans and nonhuman animals (for an evolutionary discussion of animal cruelty, see Patterson-Kane & Piper, Chapter 15, this volume) and must somehow dissociate cruel behavior from any internal or external rewards that may be derived from it. An evolutionary paradigm may be useful in this endeavor as it may help to identify contexts in which cruelty is more likely to be exhibited—that is, during competition over reproductively relevant resources. However, situational predictors may not be enough because individuals may be cruel for seemingly intangible rewards, such as an internal feeling of pleasure. Thus, attempts must be made to identify individuals who are more likely to be cruel due to dispositional traits exhibited across different contexts. Heritable factors may explain much of the difference in individual cruelty within a population and the use of behavioral genetic models, genetic screening, and neuroimaging technologies may help to identify and provide treatment for at-risk individuals. As opposed to treating the symptoms of cruelty, such an approach aims to cut it at its developmental roots. Therefore, if we want to live in a more humane society, we must not shy away from employing the tools of modern science to get us there.

Puberty and Beyond

An important paradigm for studying the relationship between evolution and development is life history theory (LHT; Hill & Kaplan, 1999). LHT posits that every developmental stage of an organism is characterized by different reproductive costs and benefits. What this means is that individuals may develop new adaptations and grow out of old ones as they mature. For example, the most immediate concern for an infant is to acquire nutritional resources. Thus, infants develop adaptations such as lovability, cuteness, and eye gazing, all designed by selection to assist them in acquiring nutritional and social resources from their caretakers. However, as individuals approach puberty, they develop adaptations designed to acquire reproductive resources (i.e., mates). In addition to species-typical reproductive development during puberty, both sexes develop secondary sexual characteristics; most men develop increased body hair, upper-body strength, aggression, and an interest in casual sex, while most women develop breasts, buttocks, and a desire for long-term relationships. Some childhood adaptations may still be present and functional (e.g., eye gazing), while others disappear (e.g., infantile features associated with "cuteness"), but puberty marks the emergence of new adaptations designed for mating and childrearing.

With the onset of puberty, aggression and cruelty may become linked with sexual gratification (Malamuth, Check, & Briere, 1986). This phenomenon is witnessed in the most depraved of human behaviors, such as rape and serial killing. The killing of a sexual partner is unlikely to represent an evolutionarily adaptive behavior (see Goetz & Romero, Chapter 4, this volume), but there may be a link between sex and violence (especially in men) and rape may have ensured reproductive success for some of our male ancestors. Thus, cases of sexually motivated homicide may be by-products of evolved sexually aggressive male adaptations.

Not every emotion can occur alongside another emotion within an individual's psychology at the same time because scarce physiological and neurological resources are used to fuel every emotional expression. The basal ganglia may play the proximal role of neural manager by only apportioning neurological resources to cognitive and affective states that are the most biologically urgent within an individual's particular context (Redgrave, Prescott, & Gurney, 1999). For example, an individual is usually not both angry and happy at the same time. However, some emotional states do co-occur, and we may assume that they were either positively selected to co-occur in our evolutionary history, or that their co-occurrence was not selected against. An example of such a co-occurrence may be the presence of both sexual jealousy and anger in males who perpetrate intimate partner violence (Goetz & Romero, Chapter 4, this volume). Another co-occurrence may exist between aggression and sexual motivation. In the following paragraphs, we speculate as to whether there is a psychological link between aggression and sexual motivation/gratification and, if so, we discuss some possibilities as to what reproductive advantages this link may have provided for our male ancestors.

One argument in favor of the aggression–sexual motivation link is that sexual motivation is so common in instances of aggression. Testosterone is associated with an increase in both sexual arousal and aggression in men and women (Glina, 2004; Hermans, Ramsey, & van Honk, 2008; Olweus, Mattson, Schalling, & Low, 1988; Tuiten et al., 2000). Furthermore, most instances of global violence and homicide are perpetrated by young men against other young men (Daly & Wilson, 1988), the same demographic that is disproportionately represented in militaries and coalitional combat units across communities and generations (though most generals, bureaucrats, politicians, leaders, and other "behind the scenes" individuals are usually older; see Browne, Chapter 22, this volume). From an evolutionary perspective, the fact that violence is mostly perpetrated by young men against other young men is not surprising. Men must compete aggressively with other men if they want to gain access to women—a scarce reproductive resource. Thus, sexual motivation may sometimes trigger aggression or cruelty in men. What may be surprising, however, is that men may have evolved a propensity to act aggressively during sexual encounters. Aggression and cruelty pose substantial fitness costs on men's reproductive success if enacted during sexual reproduction, as the mother of their offspring could be injured or killed in such an encounter. That aggression and sexual motivation can simultaneously occupy men's psychology suggests a selective advantage for the link between these two emotional states, an advantage that outweighed whatever fitness costs may have been paid by ancestral men due to the injury or death of their sexual partners.

Assuming the existence of a positively selected link in men between aggression and sexual behavior, we next speculate about the relevant selection pressures that may have led to its evolution. Our discussion will center on two topics from evolutionary biology: sexual conflict and sexual selection. Sexual conflict arises whenever the reproductive interests of one sex exact a cost on the reproductive interests of the other sex (Chapman, Arnqvist, Bangham, & Rowe, 2003). A common result of sexual conflict is a coevolutionary arms race, whereby an adaptation that benefits one sex's reproductive interests but harms the other sex's reproductive interests, leads to the evolution of a defensive or an offensive counteradaptation in the other sex. These coevolutionary relationships can go on indefinitely, sometimes intensifying, other times subsiding. There is much evidence that such a relationship exists between males and females across many different species, including humans. For example, because of females' reluctance to engage in short-term mating due to the costs of maternal investment, males often evolve counteradaptations aimed at circumventing female sexual defenses. Such male adaptations are usually met with counteradaptations in females aimed at further restricting males' sexual access, and so a coevolutionary arms race is born. In most species, males and females need each other to reproduce, and so the majority of coevolutionary relationships between males and females are cooperative. However, there is now mounting evidence for the adaptive value of some forms of sexual coercion in humans (for a review, see Camilleri, Chapter 11, this volume). Thornhill and Palmer (2000) were initially decried for their popularization of the idea that rape may be an adaptive strategy by which some men pursue their reproductive interests. From the ashes of the ensuing controversy arose much evidence in support of an adaptive function of sexual coercion by men of women. For example, a man is more likely to sexually coerce his female intimate partner if he suspects her of sexual infidelity, as her sexual infidelity may increase the risk of rival sperm competing inside of her reproductive tract (Goetz & Romero, Chapter 4, this volume). Furthermore, there is evidence that women may have evolved counteradaptations to deter male sexual coercion, such as being extremely cautious and wary of strange men during ovulation (McKibbin & Shackelford, 2011). Of course, that rape may result from male adaptations does not make it moral or just. The take-home lesson is that we must be careful to not evaluate any controversial or extraordinary scientific findings on the basis of our initial emotional reactions.

One can now see how sexual conflict may lead to a link between sexual behavior and aggression in men. If a woman is reluctant to have sex with a man, then it may be to the man's reproductive advantage to have sex with her by force. Therefore, it may have been reproductively beneficial for some ancestral men to exhibit sexual arousal alongside aggressive behavior, provided that this aggressive behavior was mostly nonlethal to ancestral women. Even in contexts of apparently "consensual" sex, ancestral men may have benefited reproductively by aggressively initiating or prolonging a sexual encounter.

Most men are not rapists, and the use of a sexually coercive strategy is limited to a few contexts. Thus, the link between sexual arousal and aggressive behavior in men requires an additional evolutionary explanation. Although speculative, the concept of sexual selection may supplement our understanding of the co-occurrence of male sexual arousal and aggression. Sexual selection entails the evolution of traits that are seemingly inessential for survival, be it the peacock's tail, or men's propensity to spend much of their paychecks on shiny objects for women (Darwin, 1871; Miller, 2000). Such traits evolve because members of the other sex find them sexually attractive. That such traits are attractive is attributable to what they signal to members of the other sex: I am genetically and developmentally healthy enough to produce and maintain these traits (or procure these objects) and you should mate with me if you want your offspring to be as healthy, sexy, and resourceful as me (see Zahavi & Zahavi, 1996). Therefore, men's standings on these traits provide excellent criteria by which women judge the anatomical, physiological, and psychological states of their suitors. We hypothesize that the co-occurrence of male sexual arousal and aggression may function as a sexually selected fitness signal for women. Perhaps men who engage in aggressive (though consensual) sexual behavior are considered attractive by women because this behavior signals physical and psychological health. Thus, only men who are in control of their bodies and minds can be sexually aroused and aggressive at the same time, without hurting or coercing their sexual partners. Such behavior requires subtlety and finesse on the part of men, and there may be a thin line between sexually aggressive consensual behavior and sexually coercive behavior. Nevertheless, that between 31% and 57% of women engage in erotic "rape" fantasies (Critelli & Bivona, 2008) is evidence for the attractiveness of men's aggressive sexual behavior. Note, however, that such fantasies differ qualitatively from actual instances of rape and that women who engage in such fantasies consider actual instances of rape horrifying. More often than not, erotic rape fantasies are "... viewed as ritual displays of male dominance and female surrender" (Fisher, 1999; quoted from Critelli & Bivona, 2008).

Sexual selection provides a less sinister explanation for the association between violence and sexual behavior in men. Nevertheless, some instances of sexual coercion, rape, and sexually motivated homicide may be the unintended results of a sexually selected co-occurrence of male sexual arousal and aggression. Furthermore, some women may be attracted to sexually coercive men because these men are more likely to sire sexually aggressive sons who will help to pass on their mothers' genes via forced copulations. Likewise, women may find sexually aggressive men attractive because such men may be especially successful in competitions with other men, and so will likely be able to provide for their families. That sexual aggression may sometimes function as a costly fitness signal in the context of a courtship ritual leads us to one of the topics of the next section. In war, as well as in love, exaggerated posturing and deceptive signaling occur as frequently as outright violence.

Society, Culture, and Global Conflict

Many scholars of human evolution have argued that instances of global conflict and war result from evolved male propensities to engage in violent conflict over reproductively relevant resources (Van Vugt, Chapter 17, this volume). Indeed, one of our closest living relatives, the chimpanzees (*Pan troglodytes*), engage in what appears to be coalitional warfare over feeding territories and mates (Wilson & Wrangham, 2003). A coalition of adult males may embark on scouting missions to investigate the territory of a neighboring chimpanzee community. These seemingly logistical encroachments into enemy territory can go on for some time before there is any physical violence. When opposing coalitions are evenly matched, violent coalitional conflict is usually too costly to engage in. In such encounters, members of the two coalitions engage in prolonged bouts of loud and aggressive displays that deescalate intergroup violence (Goodall, 1990). However, during conflicts between individual males within communities, prolonged displays are associated with an escalation of violence. For individual males, engaging in conflict is often necessary because it promotes sexual access to fertile females, a reproductive benefit that is often worth the cost of battle. Loud and aggressive displays between males are indicative of each male's strength and are used to assess the social status of opponents. If a likely winner can be determined ahead of time, then neither individual is likely to benefit from a further escalation of displays, much less actual violence. If rival males cannot determine the likely winner, however, then displays become more prolonged until engaging in violent conflict becomes the only alternative. Thus, prolonged aggressive displays are associated with a de-escalation of coalitional violence but with an escalation of violence between individuals. One can see how individuals may sometimes benefit by deceptively inflating or deflating the volume or aggressiveness of their displays (Dawkins & Krebs, 1978). For example, an *individual* male who *inflates* his displays may dissuade his competitors from engaging in violent conflict and so may deceptively acquire mates and other reproductively relevant resources. The consequences of being exposed as a fraud, however, usually prevent individuals from deceptively exaggerating their aggressive displays. On the other hand, deceptively *deflating* the displays of one's *coalition* may function to lure unwary enemies into attacking and so may hasten the demise of a weaker coalition of rivals. In humans, bluffing and calling others' bluffs may lie at the heart of diplomacy and negotiation. During the Cold War, for example, both the United States and the Soviet Union were flexing their nuclear muscles toward one another so as to prevent the other side from mounting a first strike, the cost of which would have had devastating consequences for the entire world. Similar to aggressive displays between chimpanzee coalitions, nuclear testing may have paradoxically prevented an actual nuclear war. Both countries may have benefited by deceptively inflating their arsenal so as to appear untouchable, but they risked retaliation if exposed as bluffing.

When violence occurs between chimpanzee communities, it usually involves a raid by a coalition of males from one community on a lone member of another community. Such an attack is vividly portrayed by Jane Goodall (1990) in *Through a Window*:

> Humphrey [a member of the attacking group] was the first to grab Godi, seizing one of his legs and throwing him to the ground. Figan, Jomeo, Sherry and Evered pounded and stamped on their victim, while Humphrey pinned him to the ground, sitting on his head and holding his legs with both hands.

Goodall goes on:

> Rodolf, the oldest of the Kasakela males, hit and bit at the hapless victim whenever he saw an opening and Gigi, who was also present, charged back and forth around the melee. All the chimpanzees were screaming loudly, Godi in terror and pain, the aggressors in a state of enraged frenzy
> (pp. 104–105).

Godi subsequently died from his wounds. Such attacks by members of one chimpanzee community against another are not random but serve key biological functions, such as the conquest of fertile land, fertile females, or both (Wilson & Wrangham, 2003). Instances of cannibalism have also been reported among chimpanzees, indicating that the lack of food was perhaps one of the selection pressures responsible for the evolution of primate violence (Goodall, 1990; Wilson, Wallauer, & Pusey, 2004). Cannibalism has similarly been used as a weapon of war by humans living in tribal societies (Lambert, Chapter 19, this volume). Though different, there are similarities between male coalitional violence in chimpanzees and male-perpetrated human warfare, suggesting that male coalitional violence was practiced by the common ancestor of humans and chimpanzees. Whether this is true is still a topic of debate.

To understand the emergence of human warfare, we must first examine the emergence of coalitional behavior, which necessitates a discussion of cooperation. Ironically, without cooperative coalitions, large-scale warfare and genocide would not occur. Cooperative behavior between conspecifics, alongside competitive behavior, is also a product of evolution, and it must have been reproductively advantageous to ancestral individuals to account for the outlay of time and resources on conspecifics. Favoring one's genetic relatives over unrelated conspecifics is a common example of cooperation in nature. For example, ants and termites that are part of the infertile "soldier" caste may nevertheless achieve reproductive success by sacrificing themselves in conflict against rival ant and termite populations. Such sacrifices occur because the resources gained (territory and slaves) benefit the queen of the conquering colony—usually the only colony member that is fertile. Thus, by sacrificing their lives for the colony, infertile soldiers can indirectly spread their genes via their queen. Small-scale tribal warfare in humans is often based on genetic relatedness between the male warriors and between the warriors and the rest of the tribe. Even in modern military and terror-cell settings—where soldiers or terror recruits are usually not genetic relatives—kinship-based terminology is often used to cement each soldier's or jihadist's commitment to his *brother* in arms.

While ants and termites get their marching orders via pheromones, cooperative coalitions of human warriors use other modes of communication. Kinship-based terms such as *brother* may be useful for military cohesion, but cooperation between humans is not only based on genetic relatedness. Most evolutionary explanations for cooperation between unrelated conspecifics involve various types of reciprocity, or the practice of "you scratch my back, I'll scratch yours." Reciprocity can evolve when organisms within a population encounter one another over a prolonged and indefinite period, making long-term cooperation adaptive in such contexts (Axelrod, 2006; Trivers, 1971). Reciprocity can evolve as an indirect strategy, as when individuals with helpful and generous personalities are incidentally rewarded for their help and generosity, and as a direct strategy, as when individuals explicitly expect reimbursement for prior favors. Direct reciprocity is practiced mostly by socially complex organisms with sophisticated nervous systems—organisms who can recognize each other and who can remember the cooperative or uncooperative nature of each relationship. Both direct and indirect reciprocity are practiced by humans and other primates and both set the stage for the emergence of coalitional warfare. Coalitions, however, are more than just aggregates of dyadic relationships based on reciprocity and are better understood from the perspective of group dynamics.

Because selection is stronger on individuals than it is on groups, participating in groups or in group-level behavior must benefit the reproductive interests of individual group members. Animals such as goats and sheep, for example, can lower their risk of being attacked by a predator if they travel together in a herd, as individuals are less likely to be attacked if they surround themselves with their conspecifics. As the saying goes, "You don't have to outrun the bear, just the other guy who's running away." Coalitions, however, are not herds, in that they involve the sophisticated coordination of behavior aimed at achieving a collective goal. A cooperative coalition can often extract more ecological resources per individual than if each individual was to go it alone, and so group behavior may sometimes be favored by selection. Sophisticated group behavior can emerge via a bottom-up process with no centralized planning. Because each individual follows a few simple rules in response to local stimuli, sophisticated group behavior can evolve and develop faster than expected. Once group dynamics emerge, they can influence individuals to behave differently than they would have if they were not part of a group. For instance, otherwise caring and thoughtful people can engage in shockingly callous and ignorant behavior when in a group, as studies in diffusion of responsibility and groupthink have demonstrated (Darley & Latane, 1968; McCauley, 1989). The risks of engaging in such behaviors are lessened by the presence of others who are also engaging in such behaviors, and the benefits associated with the acquisition of reproductively relevant resources may be immense. Thus, instances of looting, raping, and ethnic cleansing are often perpetrated by groups of individuals, as during the lethal raids on Eastern European Jews in the 19th and 20th centuries, campaigns of extermination by German and Japanese troops and widespread sexual violence by Russian troops during World War II, and gang rape and genocide in the Balkans and in war-ravaged parts of Africa more recently. Military culture appears to be especially conducive to the perpetration of sexual violence by male soldiers (Morris, 1996). Thus, for our male ancestors, warfare may have been an acceptable venue in which they could pursue their reproductive interests by raping outgroup women with impunity.

Although group-perpetrated violence can arise without any centralization, charismatic and totalitarian leaders are especially effective at directing group behavior toward horrendous acts of violence and cruelty. The manipulation of one organism by another is a cross-species phenomenon and can be best understood with Dawkins's concept of the *extended phenotype* (Dawkins, 1982). This concept posits that a phenotype (in contrast to the genotype, the phenotype is that property of an organism which is the product of its genes and its nongenetic environment—usually restricted to an organism's bodily frame) does not end with the organism's physical body. Thus, anthills and termite mounds are ant and termite phenotypes, even though they are not parts of ant and termite bodies. Similarly, organisms can evolve manipulative adaptations by which they control the behavior of other organisms—that is, using other organisms as extended phenotypes. For example, our coughing and sneezing can be seen as an adaptive reaction on the part of our bodies to rid ourselves of viruses. Taken from the perspective of a virus, however, our coughing and sneezing may be the best avenues by which it can spread and infect other humans. This makes us, and our coughing and sneezing in particular, extended phenotypic viral adaptations. With the aid of behavioral and psychological mimicry (Chartrand & Bargh, 1999), pheromones, verbal and nonverbal expressions, emotions, ideas, beliefs, and values, humans can manipulate the behavior of other humans in an extended phenotypic fashion and can thereby acquire reproductively relevant resources. Groups of individuals are especially vulnerable to exploitation due to the decrease in self-consciousness that accompanies deindividuation (i.e., the losing of one's self-identity within a group; Morris, 1996).

Manipulators are not always as charismatic or oratorical as was Hitler; they can be as bland and monotonous as convicted child rapist Warren Jeffs, the leader of a polygamist Mormon sect in Utah (CNN Wire Staff, 2011). Jeffs was able to seduce young girls into being his wives and concubines not through charm but through the use of inherited status, religious ideas, and sacred values. This leads us to a discussion of human culture and its relationship to human evolution. For humans, culture provides the symbolic mechanisms by which we can pursue our reproductive interests while communicating our commitment to the larger coalition. Commitment to religious and political coalitions can be communicated by following costly dietary laws, enacting complex rituals, brandishing emotional displays (e.g., having mystical visions and revelations), undergoing reproductively harmful genital mutilation, or risking injury and death in violent coalitional conflict (Atran, 2002; Wilson, 2008). Individuals who cement their commitment to a coalition by enacting such costly displays in front of coalition members may reap long-term reproductive benefits by being part of the coalition. Without cooperative coalitions based on cultural beliefs or symbols, there would be no modern civilization. Thus, a society that is too large to be united by kinship or reciprocity may nevertheless pursue common goals by uniting behind a symbol, a tradition, a moralizing god, or a philosophy. It appears that nothing unites individuals as much as beliefs in the supernatural. Individuals are drawn to minimally counterintuitive beliefs (i.e., beliefs that are realistic enough to be memorable yet strange enough to be attention grabbing—for instance, a god with human-like thoughts and emotions who is also invisible and omnipotent; Atran, 2002). Such beliefs are at the heart of tribal and modern religions and may function to unite individuals into a community of cooperative alliances with large numbers of unrelated individuals. These large-scale coalitions can be reproductively beneficial for some individuals who can thereby acquire social support and long-term access to reproductively relevant resources, including mates. At times, however, manipulators may exploit shared cultural symbols by convincing others to engage in costly acts of group commitment that benefit manipulators but inflict costs on the rest of the community. In such instances, the manipulated group or community can be considered the extended phenotype of the manipulator. Manipulators can thus acquire reproductively relevant resources such as food, territory, money, and mates. The consequences of such instances of group manipulation can range from losing one's money to a religious charlatan, to the instigation of unlawful military campaigns, terrorism, and genocide under the banner of religious or political symbols and ideas.

Cultural beliefs and values have an interesting effect on human evolution. Through culture, modes of behavior may be inherited that may otherwise take millions of years to evolve via the random mutation and natural selection of genes. The mechanisms by which culture affects human behavior and evolution may be illuminated by the somewhat different phenomenon of mother rats licking their offspring. Licking behavior, like human culture, can be inherited across generations without altering the genes of individual rats. Thus, if a newborn female rat whose birth mother was not a licker is raised by a foster mother who licks her pups, the rat will subsequently lick her own pups when she becomes a mother (Meaney, 2001). Having been licked is associated with benefits such as sociability and lowered anxiety (Meaney, 2001). Similarly, the linguistic and cultural environment experienced by humans during childhood may affect their own adult behavior and the behavior of their children. For example, men from populations with a long history of resource scarcity and lawlessness (e.g., the descendants of the Scotch-Irish settlers in the southern and western parts of the United States, and men from herding cultures throughout the Middle East) often develop a "culture of honor" centered on the aggressive defense of one's reputation and manhood (see Brown & Osterman, Chapter 13, this volume). In contexts of resource scarcity and a lack of law enforcement, individuals (particularly men) must develop a reputation for toughness and vengefulness if they are to acquire and maintain reproductively relevant resources, including women. Thus, aggressive behavior associated with a culture of honor may become culturally inherited and may remain within a population even if the original contexts that spawned it have been long gone.

The emergent effects of genetic and cultural evolution can be difficult to predict, as genes and cultural products dynamically interact and cause evolution to spiral into unexplored territories (Cochran & Harpending, 2009). Similarly, much of our ancestral genetic and cultural inheritance may be combined and recombined in many ways that differ from ancestral contexts. Thus, military recruits may take advantage of the "culture of honor" mindset of poor young men by convincing them that their country's honor is on the line and that lawless savages are threatening their family and their resources. When kinship-based terms, sacred values, and religious beliefs are thrown into the mix, individuals may become ready to sacrifice their lives and engage in unimaginable physical and sexual violence. From there, group dynamics and extended phenotypic manipulation of militaries and terror cells may lead to destruction on a global scale. Military conflicts are sometimes inevitable and a just war can be waged. Our evolutionary legacy, however, may not be ready for its lethal combination with weapons of mass destruction. In the following section, we call for an approach by which individuals can understand the evolutionary antecedents of their behavior and the effects of their behavior on the rest of society.

Evolutionary Consciousness

In this section, we do not confine ourselves to abstract evolutionary explanations of human violence. Instead, we personalize some of the ideas discussed in previous sections to better understand our own thoughts, emotions, and behaviors. We do not advocate for any one social or political policy or ideology, save for our deep commitment and endorsement of evolutionary science and its application to issues of human concern. In discussing personal responsibility from an evolutionary perspective, we are cognizant of the fact that individual-level behavior affects societal-level phenomena. Thus, our primary goal is to unveil the extent to which our actions not only influence our immediate context but also society and the world at large. The human extended phenotype may thus be the most extended of any species, as our technological and cultural innovations enable us to influence lives and ecosystems on a global scale. With such power, ignorance of our evolved nature—its strengths and its weaknesses—is morally inexcusable. Therefore, our secondary goal is to help ourselves and our readers to develop an evolutionary consciousness. By evolutionary consciousness, we are not referring to any mystical or new age concept plucked out of a self-help book. Instead, being evolutionarily conscious means being aware of the evolutionary origins of our drives, motivations, desires, emotions, and thoughts. Such awareness may better enable us to understand the moral and ethical implications of our actions and decisions. In advocating for an evolutionary consciousness, we do not posit any code of conduct or ethics. Instead, we hope to empower the reader to make his or her own moral decisions in an evolutionarily informed way. We are not naïve and understand that the application of evolutionary principles to personal matters is not without danger, as social Darwinism and government-instituted eugenics have proven within the last century. Nonetheless, the dangers of not viewing ourselves through an evolutionary lens may be much greater and the price of ignorance may be paid by the unintended effects of our own choices and the choices of others. Thus, we tentatively embark on an exploration of what an evolutionary consciousness is and how it might be applied to matters both personal and public. Our discussion is only the beginning. It is up to educators and policy makers to ensure that no child is made ignorant of the beauty and relevance of biological evolution. Especially in the United States, where science teachers are ridiculed and censured by Evangelical interests, no time is more pressing than now. If we are to understand the biological roots of sexism, xenophobia, war, and genocide, then our society must accept and embrace the evolutionary paradigm.

To understand what an evolutionary consciousness may entail, we return to the concept of the extended phenotype. We assume that most readers of this chapter are not rapists, murderers, and warmongers. However, every decision that we make, as innocuous as it may seem, may contribute to global instances of rape, murder, and war. The reason for this is that over the past 10,000 years (Cochran & Harpending, 2009), human agriculture, technology, and global interconnectedness have extended our phenotypic effects to unprecedented scales. For better or worse, modern civilization has immensely magnified our influence on each other and on our environment. From the products and services that we purchase, to the political, religious, and philosophical stances that we take, the effects of our reproductive interests have been felt by billions of humans and innumerable other species across the globe. Next, we discuss an example of a reproductively relevant resource—the diamond—whose consumption has led to the rape and slaughter of countless individuals and ecosystems. Though not the only such resource (some others include fossil fuels whose extraction supports brutal dictatorships in the Middle East, African and Asian goods manufactured by child-slave labor, and delicacies and products procured from endangered species), the purchasing of diamonds exemplifies an instance in which our reproductive interests as consumers are pitted against the survival and well-being of other humans. We do not focus our discussion on the effects of our decisions on nonhuman animals and ecologies, but the arguments that we make can be readily applied to both. Our goal is to inspire an awareness of the extended phenotypic effects of our daily decisions. This awareness we term "evolutionary consciousness." We hope that such an evolutionary consciousness can enable us to modify our behavior in order to reduce the suffering of those affected by it. However, this hope may carry too much optimism. At the very least, an evolutionary consciousness can enrich our understanding of ourselves, our world, and of the effects that we have on our world. If for no other reason than this, the development of an evolutionary consciousness is a worthy endeavor. Of course, violent sociopaths may also be capable of developing an evolutionary consciousness and benefiting from it—a worrisome possibility for which we admit we have no antidote. By focusing on the ethical implications of human decisions, however, we hope that our discussion can better empower the prosocial among us to cast aside some of the destructive effects of their extended phenotypes.

Presumably, most readers of this chapter do not have to compete for resources that are essential for survival, such as food, water, and shelter. However, many of us engage in economic competition for other reproductively relevant resources that are believed to be useful in acquiring sexual partners, such as extravagant property and superfluous capital (Miller, 2009). This competition over *nonessential* resources contributes to the destruction or redirection of *essential* resources that are needed by millions of destitute individuals, especially those living in underdeveloped nations. For example, men in Westernized societies are culturally conditioned to communicate romantic commitment and devotion to women by buying them lavish products and services. The jewelry industry, with help from the media, has popularized the notion that nothing says "I love you" to a woman as much as a glittering diamond. Thus, many Western men believe that a diamond ring is the quintessential symbol of long-term commitment to a mate, and many Western women consider this gift a necessity for acceptance of men's marital propositions. Such displays of monogamy, however, come at the cost of millions of human lives and irreparable environmental degradation. That otherwise kind and peaceful individuals may be complicit in the genocide, rape, enslavement, and population displacement wrought by the jewelry industry in many parts of sub-Saharan Africa underscores the need for us to examine our purchasing decisions from an evolutionary perspective. Such an examination reveals that our ancient reproductive strategies have gained unprecedented extended phenotypic powers via their utilization of modern-day cultural innovations in technology and global business practices, as exemplified by the diamond industry. Whether such extended phenotypic uses of cultural products lead to reproductive success in modern societies is difficult to determine and, in any case, is beside the point. The point that we are making is that by being evolutionarily conscious of our reproductive behaviors and the economic decisions that they motivate, we can redirect our mating efforts toward more prosocial avenues that do not entail the exploitation of third-world populations and environments. For example, a diamond is used to signal commitment to one's romantic partner. This signal is not only directed toward one's partner but also toward members of one's community (e.g., friends, family, acquaintances, and in-laws) who are used as guarantors to insure that one lives up to the commitment symbolized by that diamond. The same signaling function can be achieved by resources whose global impact is less destructive, and possibly even constructive, such as expensive custom-made jewelry produced by local artisans with materials that are just as sturdy and beautiful but whose extraction and synthesis did not entail the spillage of blood. Thus, rather than attempting to bring down the monolithic jewelry industry, individuals can fundamentally change the marketplace of reproductive goods and services by changing their consumption patterns in a bottom-up fashion.

As discussed in the previous section, human thoughts, emotions, and behaviors can become drastically altered when an individual finds himself or herself surrounded by others. Thus, forms of physical and sexual violence inconceivable by isolated individuals become acceptable in a group setting. For group behavior to emerge, however, one does not have to be in direct contact with other group members as one is in the military or in a soccer riot. Even when in isolation, group mentality may lead one to support religious and political policies that enact brutality and environmental degradation. As discussed by Hudson and Den Boer (Chapter 18, this volume), patriarchal traditions and institutions may be effective cultural tools by which cooperative male coalitions exert extended phenotypic control over women's reproductive interests. The disastrous effects of such male dominance are not only felt by women but by all of society, as patriarchal cultures exhibit increased rates of internal and external violence and discord. Thus, when one supports a religious tradition or a political party that curtails women's reproductive freedom (e.g., policies that often go under code words such as "right to life" or "family values"), one's adaptations that normally function to bring about intragroup reciprocity, group coordination toward resource acquisition, and emotional belongingness to a social network may indirectly bring about deplorable outcomes. Many kind-hearted Catholics, for example, are complicit in the death of millions of Africans by indirectly (or directly) supporting the Catholic Church's policy of not advocating the use of condoms to stem the spread of AIDS. In the political sphere, support for some conservative policies may indirectly bring about militarism, economic and social inequality, and environmental degradation, while support for some liberal policies may lead to the appeasement of brutal despots and dictators, suppression of life-saving agricultural innovations such as genetically modified crops, and the continuation of funding for corrupt and wasteful government institutions. By being evolutionarily conscious of our motivations for aligning ourselves with some of these groups and communities, we can help to reverse the socially and environmentally violent consequences of our support for their policies.

When thinking about an evolutionarily informed consciousness, one is easily reminded of psychoanalytic explorations of hidden drives and unsavory libidinous desires. Although there are similarities between the psychoanalytic and the modern, evolution-informed understanding of the mind (i.e., both posit that the mind is subdivided into modular processes, though to varying degrees), there are also clear differences. For example, unlike the Freudian model of the id, ego, and superego, an evolutionary conception of the mind does not posit that some mental functions are innate or "primal" while others are socialized. All psychological adaptations are innate, in the sense that they have an evolutionary history, are products of natural selection, and that the means of their construction are inherited. Furthermore, all psychological adaptations require environmental input and socialization to develop in a species-typical manner. Thus, mental adaptations that motivate behaviors as diverse as physical and sexual aggression are no more and no less "primal" than human kindness, and all require experience to develop properly. Another difference between the two traditions is that, in contrast to the psychoanalytic conception of the unconscious, one does not need years of psychoanalytic therapy filled with exercises in free association to understand one's own drives and desires. Though many of our mental processes are implicit and function outside of conscious awareness (Greenwald, McGhee, & Schwartz, 1998), by examining our behavior from the perspective of resource acquisition, we can gain valuable insights into our evolved minds. For example, from one perspective, we are writing this chapter to expose readers to evolutionary ideas and hope that the scientific and philosophical frontier is thereby expanded. From an evolutionary perspective, however, our motivation in writing this chapter may stem from our desire to be cited by our academic peers or awarded with tenure by our universities—outcomes that may enhance our social status and help us to accumulate economic resources. Thus, developing an evolutionary consciousness does not require us to analyze our dreams but to shift our own perspective of ourselves.

The psychological struggle against one's inner demons is a common theme in world mythology and much of literature. From the Buddha to Christ, Doctor Faust to Doctor Jekyll, archetypal battles against aspects of oneself may stem from the nature of our evolved minds. Indeed, discoveries in biology, genetics, neuroscience, and psychology have unveiled just how fractionated we are. For example, our mitochondria were once free-living bacteria that invaded our single-celled ancestors and subsequently engaged in a symbiotic relationship with them, as did much of the bacteria that help us to digest our food (Emelyanov, 2001; Hooper, 2004). Likewise, much of our DNA may have been borrowed from viruses that embedded themselves into our ancestors' genomes (Belshaw et al., 2004). In fact, our genes and chromosomes sometimes pursue their own interests at the cost of our well-being, as is exemplified by instances of cancer, Down syndrome (Axelrod, 2006), and conflicts between paternal and maternal genes within an individual organism (Haig, 2000, 2006; Patten & Haig, 2008; Úbeda & Haig, 2003). At the neurological level, our right hands may not always know what our left hands are doing, as is shown by experiments with split-brain patients (Gazzaniga, 2005). Lastly, our modular minds, as posited by evolutionary psychologists, provide evidence for a disconnected network of psychological processes as opposed to a unitary consciousness (Kurzban, 2010). Could it be that our internal struggles with ourselves have a deep evolutionary history? How can we truly understand, much less control, ourselves if there is no real "self" to begin with? Reflecting on our own behavior and its consequences may be a start.

As with any philosophy or mindset, an evolutionary consciousness is not without dangers. Although we believe that holding false beliefs and having the need for a supernatural salvation are immeasurably more dangerous, we do not delude ourselves to the dangers that may arise from perceiving the world through an evolutionary lens. A feeling of anguish may overcome one who sees parasitism and violent coevolutionary arms races as the *raison d'être* of all life—anguish that is perhaps exacerbated by the knowledge that one is not in control of oneself and is possessed by conflicting agendas and influences, both internal and external. This anguish may pale in comparison to the fear of hellfire but is nonetheless worthy of attention. Realizing that your loved ones may be harboring manipulative tendencies or that your romantic relationships may be based on billion-year-old reproductive conflicts between the sexes may be somewhat disenchanting. In consolation, we say this: There is a deep feeling of satisfaction and connectedness that comes from realizing that you are part of a 3.5 billion year saga that biologically connects you to all life on Earth. In addition to traditions, rituals, folk knowledge, and other cultural practices, our ancestors possessed more wisdom than they ever imagined. Via their genetic and developmental legacy to us, they imparted clues as to who we are and where we might be going. Evolutionary consciousness is a romantic idea of the highest caliber and it makes one's love (however love may be defined) reverberate with the knowledge that a very similar feeling was present in our ancestors across millions of generations. In all likelihood, loving others was indispensable for our ancestors' survival and reproduction and may therefore be partly responsible for our very existence. In addition to love and compassion, however, aggression and violence may have been just as indispensable for our ancestors' reproductive success. Therefore, evolutionary consciousness is also a potent tool for plumbing the darkest depths of our bodies and minds, and both explains and suggests remedies for the violence that so plagues our world. Finally, evolutionary consciousness may help to guide the individual on a journey that so many other organisms have taken in the past and are taking again today. Like a compass, the theoretical and empirical framework of evolutionary science may guide us as individuals—and as a species—to the heights of our potential.

Conclusion

We doubt that a chronically violent individual will become peaceful if his or her evolutionary consciousness is expanded. Therefore, our discussion of an evolutionary consciousness should not be read as a remedy for the violence plaguing our world but understood as an approach by which one can better appreciate the ecological and evolutionary effects of one's actions on oneself and on others. The elimination of human violence has been attempted by countless individuals and civilizations throughout the ages—to little avail—and often revolutionaries and utopians who undertake just causes in the name of "peace" become as inhumane as their enemies. Because violence is often the product of evolved mechanisms that enabled our ancestors to acquire reproductively relevant resources over millions of years, it is unlikely to disappear anytime soon. Even if resources are equally distributed within and across populations, humans are likely to find a way to compete for innumerable other resources that are useless for survival but are necessary for the procurement of sexual partners.

Violence can be a moral necessity if used to defend oneself, one's loved ones, or those who are weak or oppressed. Thus, by seeking to eliminate violence (including the propensity for war) from the human behavioral repertoire, we may be eliminating an important means of defense against murderers, rapists, and warmongers—individuals who are ready to prey upon the kindness and peacefulness of others. The reason that eliminating violence may have this effect is that nonviolent societies are vulnerable to invasion and takeover by violent individuals from within and without. Even if human violence is eliminated entirely, selection will favor the reproductive prospects of individuals whose violence would enable them to extract reproductively relevant resources from nonviolent conspecifics. On the other hand, we may be condemning our progeny to endless cycles of violence if some violence is condoned, as the maintenance of morally sanctioned violence within a population can lead to the inadvertent emergence of cruelty and sadism in subsequent generations. One might say that humanity is stuck between the Scylla and Charybdis of making ourselves defenseless against violence by eliminating it, or of doing nothing about it. This may be a false dichotomy. So far, however, there is no obvious pathway toward world peace.

Beginning with the Industrial Revolution, science and technology have blossomed to unprecedented levels. This blossoming may be somewhat equivocal, as along with modern medicine came the Atomic Age. However, death rates due to violent crime, homicide, and war are substantially lower now than they were in our ancestral past (at least in developed nations). This is partly a result of an increase in the quality of life for even the most destitute among us, highlighting the importance of making sure that all individuals have access to resources needed for survival. The relative peace and social harmony prevalent throughout the Scandinavian countries (despite the recent tragedy in Norway) is further proof that providing for everyone's basic needs may benefit all of society (Zuckerman, 2008). However, providing life-sustaining resources to the needy without dealing with the problem of population is fruitless. In later versions of his *Essay on Population*, Thomas Malthus—perhaps influenced by his position as an Anglican curate or by his Colonialist sentiments—stressed that encouraging the lower classes to engage in *moral restraint* was the best remedy for unsustainable population growth. Even for Malthus's time, encouraging poor young men to become celibate may have been a bit naïve (though not too naïve to prevent the Catholic Church from doing so). However, Malthus was right to encourage the delaying of marriage until one had accrued enough resources to sustain a family. For instance, in 18th-century England—Malthus's own setting—the increase in women's marrying age may have been responsible for the educational and economic empowerment of women and the related decrease in male-wrought violence and instability throughout much of Northwestern Europe (see Hudson & Den Boer, Chapter 18, this volume). Couple this with modern birth control practices and society need not resort to *moral restraint* to live sustainably.

With the Industrial Revolution also came a kind of "sublimation" of the violence that was previously perpetrated over reproductively relevant resources. Thus, men are less likely to wage war or engage in Wild West–style shootouts to acquire mates (except in poverty-stricken environments; see Kruger & Fitzgerald, Chapter 10, this volume) than they are to aggressively pursue their reproductive interests in coalitional behavior on the basketball court or on Wall Street (though the latter economic and reproductive playground may be causing much of the structural violence responsible for income inequalities throughout the world). Of course, we are not implying that "shooting hoops" can free the world from senseless brutality, but we do suggest that modifying the contexts in which men compete for reproductively relevant resources may help to decrease levels of violence. Our efforts may also be supplemented with the best tools that modern science has to offer. Along with behavioral modification approaches, future innovations in fields such as genetics and cognitive neuroscience may help to remedy the scourge of human violence on an individual-by-individual basis. In doing so, however, we must confront the ethical and moral dilemma of whether we should value the rights of society over the rights of the individual. Hopefully, we will be able to strike an acceptable balance.

References

Atran, S. (2002). *In gods we trust: The evolutionary landscape of religion*. Oxford, England: Oxford University Press.

Axelrod, R. (2006). *The evolution of cooperation*. New York: Basic Books.

Belshaw, R., Pereira, V., Katzourakis, A., Talbot, G., Paces, J., Burt, A., & Tristem, M. (2004). Long-term reinfection of the human genome by endogenous retroviruses. *Proceedings of the National Academy of Sciences USA, 101*(14), 4894–4899.

Bjorklund, D. F., & Pellegrini, A. D. (2002). *The origins of human nature: Evolutionary developmental psychology*. Washington, DC: American Psychological Association.

Boyce, W. T., & Ellis, B. J. (2005). Biological sensitivity to context: I. An evolutionary- developmental theory of the origins and functions of stress reactivity. *Development and Psychopathology, 17*, 271–301.

Buss, D. M., & Shackelford, T. K. (1997). Human aggression in evolutionary psychological perspective. *Clinical Psychology Review, 17*(6), 605–619.

Carroll, S. B. (2005). *Endless forms most beautiful: The new science of evo devo*. New York: W. W. Norton.

Chang, E. F., & Merzenich, M. M. (2003). Environmental noise retards auditory cortical development. *Science, 300*(5618), 498–502.

Chapman, T., Arnqvist, G., Bangham, J., & Rowe, L. (2003). Sexual conflict. *Trends in Ecology and Evolution, 18*(1), 41–47.

Chartrand, T. L., & Bargh, J. A. (1999). The chameleon effect: The perception-behavior link and social interaction. *Journal of Personality and Social Psychology, 76*(6), 893–910.

Cochran, G., & Harpending, H. (2009). *The 10,000 year explosion: How civilization accelerated human evolution*. New York: Basic Books.

Critelli, J. W., & Bivona, J. M. (2008). Women's erotic rape fantasies: An evaluation of theory and research. *Journal of Sex Research, 45*(1), 57–70.

CNN Wire Staff. (2011, August 12). Court releases Warren Jeffs audio sex tapes. *CNN*. Retrieved December 2011, from: http://articles.cnn.com/2011-08-12/justice/texas.polygamist.jeffs_1_warren-jeffs-sexual-assault-fundamentalist-church?_s=PM:CRIME

Daly, M., & Wilson, M. (1988). *Homicide*. Hawthorne, NY: Aldine de Gruyter.

Darley, J. M., & Latane, B. (1968). Bystander intervention in emergencies: Diffusion of responsibility. *Journal of Personality and Social Psychology, 8*(4), 377–383.

Darwin, C. (1871). *The descent of man, and selection in relation to sex*. London: Charles Murray.

Dawkins, R. (1976). *The selfish gene*. Oxford, England: Oxford University Press.

Dawkins, R. (1982). *The extended phenotype*. Oxford, England: Oxford University Press.

Dawkins, R., & Krebs, J. R. (1978). Animal signals: Information or manipulation? In J. R. Krebs & N. B. Davies (Eds.), *Behavioral ecology: An evolutionary approach* (pp. 282–309). Oxford, England: Blackwell Scientific Publications.

Emelyanov, V. V. (2001). Rickettsiaceae, rickettsia-like endosymbionts, and the origin of mitochondria. *Bioscience Reports, 21*, 1–17.

Fagiolini, M., Pizzorusso, T., Berardi, N., Domenici, L., & Maffei, L. (1994). Functional postnatal development of the rat primary visual cortex and the role of visual experience: Dark rearing and monocular deprivation. *Vision Research, 34*, 709–720.

Fisher, H. (1999). *The first sex*. New York: Random House.

Gazzaniga, M. S. (2005). Forty-five years of split-brain research and still going strong. *Nature Reviews Neuroscience, 6*, 653–659.

Glina, S. (2004). Testosterone and erectile dysfunction. *Journal of Men's Health and Gender, 1*(4), 407–412.

Goodall, J. (1990). *Through a window*. New York: Mariner Books.

Greenwald, A. G., McGhee, D. E., & Schwartz, J. L. K. (1998). Measuring individual differences in implicit cognition: The implicit association test. *Journal of Personality and Social Psychology, 74*(6), 1464–1480.

Haig, D. (2000). The kinship theory of genomic imprinting. *Annual Review of Ecology and systematic, 31*, 9–32.

Haig, D. (2006). Intragenomic politics. *Cytogenetic and Genome Research, 113*, 68–74.

Hamilton, W. D. (1964). The genetical evolution of social behavior (I and II). *Journal of Theoretical Biology, 7*, 1–52.

Hermans, E. J., Ramsey, N. F., & van Honk, J. (2008). Exogenous testosterone enhances responsiveness to social threat in the neural circuitry of social aggression in humans. *Biological Psychiatry, 63*, 263–270.

Hill, K., & Kaplan, H. (1999). Life history traits in humans: Theory and empirical studies. *Annual Review of Anthropology, 28*, 397–430.

Hooper, L. V. (2004) Bacterial contributions to mammalian gut development. *Trends in Microbiology, 12*(3), 129–134.

Hopfenberg, R., & Pimentel, D. (2001). Human population numbers as a function of food supply. *Environment, Development and Sustainability, 3*, 1–15.

Kolbert, J. B., & Crothers, L. M. (2003). Bullying and evolutionary psychology. *Journal of School Violence, 2*(3), 73–91.

Kurzban, R. (2010). *Why everyone else is a hypocrite: Evolution and the modular mind*. Princeton, NJ: Princeton University Press.

Malamuth, N. M., Check, J. V. P., & Briere, J. (1986). Sexual arousal in response to aggression: Ideological, aggressive, and sexual correlates. *Journal of Personality and Social Psychology, 50*(2), 330–340.

McCauley, C. (1989). The nature of social influence in groupthink: Compliance and internalization. *Journal of Personality and Social Psychology, 57*(2), 250–260.

McKibbin, W. F., & Shackelford, T. K. (2011). Women's avoidance of rape. *Aggression and Violent Behavior, 16*, 437–443.

McLaughlin, E. C. (2011). From "privileged" youth to afternoon of carnage. *CNN*. Retrieved December 2011, from: http://

www.cnn.com/2011/WORLD/europe/07/27/norway.breivik.chronology/index.html

Meaney, M. J. (2001). Maternal care, gene expression, and the transmission of individual differences in stress reactivity across generations. *Annual Review of Neuroscience, 24*, 1161–1192.

Miller, G. F. (2000). *The mating mind: How sexual choice shaped the evolution of human nature.* London: Heinemann.

Miller, G. F. (2009). *Spent: Sex, evolution, and consumer behavior.* New York: Viking.

Morris, M. (1996). By force of arms: Rape, war, and military culture. *Duke Law Journal, 45*(4), 651–781.

Nelson, C. A. (2001). The development and neural bases of face recognition. *Infant and Child Development, 10*(1–2), 3–18.

Olweus, D., Mattsson, A., Schalling, D., & Low, H. (1988). Circulating testosterone levels and aggression in adolescent males: A causal analysis. *Psychosomatic Medicine, 50*, 261–272.

Patten, M. M., & Haig, D. (2008). Reciprocally imprinted genes and the response to selection on one sex. *Genetics, 179*, 1389–1394.

Pellegrini, A. D., & Long, J. D. (2003). A sexual selection theory of longitudinal analysis of sexual segregation and integration in early adolescence. *Journal of Experimental Child Psychology, 85*, 257–278.

Plusquellec, P., Francois, N., Boivin, M., Perusse, D., & Tremblay, R. E. (2007). Dominance among unfamiliar peers starts in infancy. *Infant Mental Health Journal, 23*(3), 324–343.

Razek, R., Ahmed, A., & Sidner, S. (2011, June 18). Libyan government denies rape allegations. *CNN*. Retrieved December 2011, from: http://www.cnn.com/2011/WORLD/africa/06/18/libya.rape/index.html?iref=allsearch

Redgrave, P., Prescott, T. J., & Gurney, K. (1999). The basal ganglia: A vertebrate solution to the selection problem? *Neuroscience, 89*(4), 1009–1023.

Rodriguez, J. I., Palacios, J., Garcia-Alix, A., Pastor, I., & Paniagua, R. (1988). Effects of immobilization on fetal bone development: A morphometric study in newborns with congenital neuromuscular diseases with intrauterine onset. *Calcified Tissue International, 43*, 335–339.

Salmon, C. A. (2007). Parent-child conflict. In C. A. Salmon & T. K. Shackelford (Eds.), *Family relationships: An evolutionary perspective* (pp. 145–161). New York: Oxford University Press.

Savin-Williams, R. C. (1976). An ethological study of dominance formation and maintenance in a group of human adolescents. *Child Development, 47*, 972–979.

Sly, L. (2011, May 29). Apparent death of boy reinvigorates Syria's protest movement. *The Washington Post*. Retrieved December 2011, from: http://www.washingtonpost.com/world/middle-east/torture-of-boy-reinvigorates-syrias-protest-movement/2011/05/29/AGPwIREH_story.html

Teague, K. (2011, August 7). Two million East African infants are now starving. *The Independent*. Retrieved December 2011, from: http://www.independent.co.uk/news/world/africa/two-million-east-african-infants-are-now-starving-2333270.html

Thornhill, R., & Palmer, C. T. (2000). *A natural history of rape: Biological basis of sexual coercion.* Cambridge, MA: MIT Press.

Tooby, J., & Cosmides, L. (1992). The psychological foundations of culture. In J. H. Barkow, L. Cosmides, & J. Tooby (Eds.), *The adapted mind: Evolutionary psychology and the generation of culture* (pp. 19–136). New York: Oxford University Press.

Trivers, R. (1971). The evolution of reciprocal altruism. *Quarterly Review of Biology, 46*, 35–57.

Trivers, R. (1972). Parental investment and sexual selection. In B. Campbell (Ed.), *Sexual selection and the descent of man, 1871–1971* (pp. 136–179). Chicago: Aldine-Atherton.

Trivers, R. (1974). Parent-offspring conflict. *American Zoologist, 14*, 249–264.

Tuiten, A., Van Honk, J., Koppeschaar, H., Bernaards, C., Thijssen, J., & Verbaten, R. (2000). Time course of effects of testosterone administration on sexual arousal in women. *Archives of General Psychiatry, 57*, 149–153.

Úbeda, F., & Haig, D. (2003). Dividing the child: Genomic imprinting and evolutionary games. *Genetica, 117*, 103–110.

Veenstra, R., Lindenberg, S., Munniksma, A., & Dijkstra, J. K. (2010). The complex relation between bullying, victimization, acceptance, and rejection: Giving special attention to status, affection, and sex differences. *Child Development, 81*, 480–486.

Weiss, A., King, J. E., & Figueredo, J. (2000). The heritability of personality factors in chimpanzees *(Pan troglodytes)*. *Behavior Genetics, 30*(3), 213–221.

Wilson, C. G. (2008). Male genital mutilation: An adaptation to sexual conflict. *Evolution and Human Behavior, 29*, 149–164.

Wilson, M. L., Wallauer, W. R., & Pusey, A. E. (2004). New cases of intergroup violence among chimpanzees in Gombe National Park, Tanzania. *International Journal of Primatology, 25*(3), 523–549.

Wilson, M. L., & Wrangham, R. W. (2003). Intergroup relations in chimpanzees. *Annual Review of Anthropology, 32*, 363–392.

Zahavi, A., & Zahavi, A. (1996). *The handicap principle.* New York: Oxford University Press.

Zuckerman, P. (2008). *Society without God: What the least religious nations can tell us about contentment.* New York: New York University Press.

INDEX

A
abortion, violent crime rates and, 220
Abrahamism, 459
abuse. *See* animal abuse; child maltreatment
accidental deaths, in cultures of honor, 226
accidental homicide-suicide, 121
ACD. *See* Armed Conflict Dataset
Achebe, Chinua, 420
Ache peoples, 164
  homicide rates for, 396
acquaintance rape, 174
Action-Control theory, 275
Act of Union, 223
Adam Bede (Eliot), 422
adolescents. *See also* bullying, among adolescents; intersexual bullying, in sexual relationships; intrasexual bullying; young male syndrome
  neural development for, 245–246
  religious belief transmission for, 245–246
  religious terrorism among, 246
  rites of passage for, 246
  suicide attempts by, for leverage of parental investment, 138
adolescent limited offenders, in young male syndrome, 181
adoption studies, for suicide, 136
adrenarche, for males, 162
Aeneid (Virgil), 420
Aeschylus, 417
affective aggression, 42
  as hostile, 42
Africa, religious terrorism in, 458
African wild dogs, coalitional aggressive behaviors among, 45
age
  child maltreatment by, 93
  female aggression by, 205, 205–206
  filicide by, 93
  in sibling conflict theory, 112
  suicide by, 133

aggression. *See also* anger; fear; female aggression; impulsivity; male-male competition, violence and homicide from; male warrior hypothesis; sexual aggression
  as advantageous strategy, 198–199
  affective, 42
  child development and, 403–405
  coalitional, in males, 367
  definition of, 23, 42, 254
  emotional role in, 200–201
  evolutionary biology of, 154, 198–200
  evolutionary psychology of, 200–204
  in frustration-aggression hypothesis, for animal cruelty, 256
  by gender, 156, 200–201, 200–204, 375
  indirect, among females, 12–13, 156
  instrumental, 42
  as lexical concept, 479
  in male dominance hierarchies, reinforcement of, 313–314
  in male-male competition, 153
  maternal, 206–207, 207, 212
  parental investment and, 198
  regional differences in, for U.S. males, 226–228
  relational, among females, 12–13, 156
  sexual selection hypothesis for, in males, 513–514
  in social learning theory, 309
  spousal, 156
  in strain theory, 124
  stream analogy for, 124
  violence aggression, 484
aggression, animal models of, 42–46.
  See also coalitional aggression, in animal models; dyadic aggression, in animal models
  costs and benefit assessment in, 43–44
  infanticide in, 44
  lethal, 45, 44–46, 55
  from reproductive access, 43

  RHP and, 43
  for social status, 43
  for territorial access, 43
agricultural societies, early
  afterlife for, 440
  armed combat in, 441
  China, 440
  emigration from, 441
  Jewish Diaspora during, 441
  religion in, 440–442
  religious intolerance in, 441
  socioeconomic conditions for, 440–441
  warfare in, 441–442
Air Force, U.S., 383
alcohol use, IPV and, 66
Alexander, Richard, 313
All the Pretty Horses (McCarthy), 415
altruism
  genetic basis for, 139
  in human-animal bond, 261
  in hunter-gatherer societies, 281
altruistic suicide, 133
  as evolutionary response, 139–140
American Exceptionalism, 443
American Indian Wars, 333
American Psycho (Ellis), 415
An American Tragedy (Dreiser), 424–425
America Right or Wrong (Lieven), 474
The Ancient Contract, 261–262
  domestication history for animals and, 261–262
anger
  aggression and, 201–202
  animal cruelty as result of, 256–257
  approach motivations and, 201
  confidence triggers from, 201
  confrontation triggers from, 201
  in IPV, 66
  neural pathways for, 202
  provocation conditions for, 201
  sympathetic nervous system activity during, 202

525

animal abuse. *See also* human-animal
     bonds; humane treatment of
     animals
  definition of, 255
  evolutionary history of, 255
  future research study for, 265
  religion and, 255
  as social phenomenon, 264
animal cruelty. *See also* human-animal
     bonds; humane treatment of
     animals
  abuser typology, 263
  as adaptive expression, 256–258
  from anger, 256–257
  biological factors for, 263
  companion status of animal and, 256
  compartmentalization and, 263
  competing theories for, 263–264
  as control strategy, 257
  as cruel play, among children, 256
  cultural factors for, 263
  definition of, 255
  as deliberate deviance, 259, 264
  desensitization thesis for, 264
  dissociation as part of, 260–261
  environmental conditions for, 256–257
  evolutionary history of, 255
  as expression of predatory instincts,
     258–259
  from family status of animal, 260
  food production and, 255
  from frustration, 256–257
  frustration-aggression hypothesis for,
     256
  future research study for, 265
  in hunter-gatherer societies, 260
  hunting success and, 258
  incidence rates for, as self-reported, 255
  as inhibition failure, 259–260
  language basis for, 259
  life stage and, 263
  after loss of family status, for animal,
     259–260
  as masculine motivation, among males,
     257–258
  naturalistic fallacy and, 263
  psychiatric foundations for, 263
  religion and, 255
  from rival status, 260
  social acceptability of, 263
  as social phenomenon, 264
  strain theory for, 264
  suffering as reward value, 258–259
  toward cats, 260
  after utility of animal, 259
animals, violence in. *See* violence, in animals
anomic suicide, 133–134
anomie, in strain theory, 124
Antigone (Sophocles), 419
Antilocapra americana. See pronghorn
     antelope
anti-Semitism, Christianity and, 456
  in Catholicism, 458

antisocial behavior
  intersexual bullying and, 279
  sexual offending and, 182
  violence as, 23
Antony and Cleopatra (Shakespeare), 417
anxiety, child development and, 401–402
  as facultative response, 402
  genetic basis for, 401–402
  during Holocaust, as trauma
     bundle, 402
apes. *See also specific species*
  infanticide among, 35
  intersexual NLV among, 29
  intrasexual competition among, 158
  intrasexual NLV among, 29
  LV among, 30–33
  NLV among, 29–30
approach motivations, anger and, 201
Aquila verreauxi. See black eagles, siblicide
     among
Arab-Israeli War, 84
Arafat, Yasir, 493
archaeology, for warfare, 326–334. *See
     also* North America, wars in; Santa
     Barbara Channel area, warfare
     record in; Southwestern U.S.,
     warfare record in
  benefits and limitations of, 326
  environmental exposure in, 327
  future research study for, 335–336
  paleoclimate data in, 330, 331–332,
     334
  paleopathology for, development of,
     335–336
  population profiles in, 327
  during prehistory period, 341
  reconstruction of war, 326–327
  resource conflict data in, 334–335, 335
  settlement data in, 326, 328, 330,
     332–333
  skeletal injury in, 326–327
  through weaponry assessment, 326–327
Arctocephalus galapagooensis. See Galapagos
     fur seals, siblicide among
Armed Conflict Dataset (ACD), 354
armed forces, sexual integration of. *See also*
     cohesion, in combat groups
  aggression, by gender, 375
  combat motivation, by gender,
     378–379
  common assumptions for
     exclusion, 373
  contemporary approaches to, 372–373
  cowardice and, public perceptions
     of, 378
  empathy responses, by gender, 375–376
  fear responses, by gender, 375
  future research study for, 387–388
  group dynamics in, 379–381
  leadership issues in, 385–386, 386
  male bonding and, 379
  male distrust, 386–387
  MWH for, 379–380

  as national policy, 373
  nurturance responses, by gender,
     375–376
  pain tolerance levels, by gender, 374
  physical endurance as factor in, 374
  physical sex differences and, 373–374
  psychological sex differences and,
     374–376
  risk-taking, by gender, 374–375,
     376–377
  self-selection in, by females, 374
  sex difference studies for,
     underestimation of, 376–377
  standards adjustments in, for females,
     374
  strength as factor in, 374
Arnold, Matthew, 421
art. *See* cave art
al-Assad, Bashar, 507
atheism
  global increase in, 443
  Nazism as, 436
  in Soviet Union, 442
  after World War I, 435–436
Atheists, 442
Atta, Muhammad, 237
Austen, Jane, 417, 417
avoidance, fear and, 201
The Awakening (Chopin), 420
Azzam, Abdullah Yusuf, 247

B

baboons, intrasexual competition among,
     158
the Baha'i, 319
"Ballad of Reading Gaol" (Wilde), 424
Balzac, Honoré de, 423
Bamforth, Douglas, 334
band of brothers, 379. *See also* male
     bonding
Barbary macaques, 157–158
Barber, Brian, 245
Barchester Towers (Trollope), 417
Barry Lyndon (Thackeray), 415
Be'eri, Dan, 239
Behavioral and Brain Sciences, 180
behavioral freezing, 202
Beisner, E. Calvin, 473
Beloved (Morrison), 422
Belsky, Steinberg, and Draper (BSD)
     theory, 397–398, 398–399
Berman, Paul, 236–237
La Bête Humaine (Zola), 423
Betzig, Laura, 313
biastophilia, 174, 186
the Bible
  control of females as purpose of, 83
  female infidelity in, punishment for, 78
  good *versus* evildoers in, 82
  Israelite behavior in, 82
  law of divorce in, 79–80, 80, 79–80
  law of jealousy in, 80, 80–81
  literature influenced by, 417

male solidarity reinforced under, 82–83
mass murder of non-virginal woman in, 81–82
Midianites in, 81–82
Old Testament, 459
patrilineal societies' use of, female sexual repression and, 79
stoning in, 77–78
violence, as proactive approach in, 77
virginity in marriage, for females, 78–79
Bierce, Ambrose, 427
Billy Budd (Melville), 427
Bin Laden, Osama, 238, 247
biological philosophy, 346
Biophilia Hypothesis, 260
birth order
 fratricide and, among males, 114–115
 siblicide and, 113–114
 in sibling conflict theory, 107
 suicide attempts and, 139
birth sex ratios, by gender, 317
 infanticide and, 317
Bison Horn Maria of India, 112–113
bistrategic controllers, 274–275
black eagles, siblicide among, 110
black-legged kittwakes, siblicide among, 109
Blanc, Steven, 331
Bleak House (Dickens), 427
"Blood-Burning Moon" (Toomer), 423
Blood Meridian (McCarthy), 416
blue footed boobies, siblicide among, 108, 110
"Blue Laws," 453–454
Boas, Franz, 347
bonobos
 community social structure for, 32
 intrasexual competition among, 159
 LV in, 34
Born to Rebel (Sulloway), 113
brain imaging techniques, for MWH research, 298–299
Brave New World (Huxley), 421
broken window effect, 221
The Brothers Karamazov (Dostoevsky), 418, 422
Browne, Thomas, 132
Browning, Robert, 423
Bryan, William Jennings, 436
BSD theory. *See* Belsky, Steinberg, and Draper theory
Bubulcus ibis. See cattle egrets, siblicide among
Buddhism, 456
bullying, among adolescents. *See also* intersexual bullying, in sexual relationships; intrasexual bullying; psychopathy, bullying and
 as aberrant behavior, misconceptions about, 284
 Action-Control theory for, 275
 as adaptive behavior, 270–271, 283

adaptive social outcomes from, 273–274
by bully-victims, 274, 275–276
in Child Behavior Checklist, 271
classroom context for, 275
cultural differences in, historical data for, 283
in cultures of honor, 225
definition of, 270
formal schooling and, development of, 282–283
future research study for, 283–284
as heritable trait, 271
as heterogeneous behavior, 275
historical data for, 281–283
in hunter-gatherer societies, 279–281
incidence rates for, 270
intervention implications for, 283–284
moderators for, 274–276
in modern society, 271–276
of out groups, 273, 275
pathological perspectives on, 275
personality traits for, 276
psychopathy and, 281–282
resource control theory and, 271, 274–275
sex of victim and, 275
twin studies for, 271
bullying, by adults, 284
by parents, 284
bully-victims, 274, 275–276
burdensomeness, suicide and, 141, 147
 contributions to others, self-perception of, 145
 illness and, 144–145
 interaction studies for, 142–145
 KRP and, 142
 maternal age and, 143–144
 self-harm ideation and, 143
 self-perceptions of, 141, 141–142
 self-preservation motivations and, 145
 social bonding and, 144
Burgess, Anthony, 415
Burmese Days (Orwell), 420
byproduct behaviors
 from rape, 177, 178–179
 from sexual homicide, 187
 for sexual offenders, 190
byproduct hypothesis. *See* slip-up hypothesis, for uxoricide

C

Campbell, Anne, 303
Can American Survive? (Hagee), 474
Canis lupus. See wolves, coalitional aggressive behaviors among
cannibalism, 332
The Canterbury Tales (Chaucer), 423
capitalism
 late marriage as influence on, 315–316
 under moral-creator socioeconomic hypothesis, 436–437
Carrie (King), 426

"The Cask of Amontillado" (Poe), 426–427
Catch-22 (Heller), 418
Cather, Willa, 420, 423
Catholic Church
 anti-Semitism in, 458
 just wars for, 456–457
 organized crime and, 458
 support of Nazism in, 458
cats, animal cruelty toward, 260
cattle egrets, siblicide among, 110
The Causes of Rape (Lalumière/Harris/Quinsey/Rice), 180
Cavan, Ruth, 120
cave art, 342
Cavia aperea f. porcellus. See guinea pigs, sibling competition among
Cervus elaphus. See red deer
Chaney, Christian James, 457
chastity belts, 78. *See also* virginity, for women, in Bible
Chaucer, Geoffrey, 423
cheater strategies, 182
Child Abuse Potential inventory, 98–99
Child Behavior Checklist, 271
child development, violence and war and. *See also* adolescents; aggression; children; puberty
 ancestral conditions and, 395–397
 anxiety and, 401–402, 402
 BSD theory for, 397–398, 398–399
 depression and, 402–403
 emotional security hypothesis for, 400
 exposure to violence and, 393
 exposure to war and, 393–394
 future research study for, 406
 during Holocaust, 400
 inclusive fitness theory for, 394
 insecure attachment in, 400–401, 399–401
 LHT for, 395, 397–399
 MHT in, 394
 pair bonding and, 405–406
 parenting and, 405–406
 phenotypic inertia and, 400–401
 plasticity of, 397–399
 PTSD and, 394
 puberty, timing of, 405–406
 sexual behavior and, 405–406
 time preference analysis for, 405–406
child homicide-suicide, 122. *See also* filicide; infanticide, among humans
 evolutionary perspectives on, 126–127
 in extended suicide, 122
 genetic relatedness and, 122, 127
 mental illness and, 122, 127
 methods of, 122
 by older parents, 122
 reproductive fitness of offspring and, 127
 as revenge, 122

child maltreatment. *See also* filicide
    actuarial risk assessments for, 99
    age factors for, 93
    animal research for, 93
    Child Abuse Potential inventory for, 98–99
    dissociation as result of, 101
    epigenetics and, 100
    externalizing characteristics after, 92, 97–100
    familicide and, 94
    future research study for, 100–101
    genetic studies for, 93
    inclusive fitness theory and, 92
    internalizing characteristics of, 92, 97–100
    intervention strategies for, 98–99, 101
    LHT and, 91, 96
    longitudinal studies for, 93
    marital disharmony and, 97
    mental illness and, 97
    molestation, 174
    parental investment theory and, 91, 92, 96
    parental solicitude and, 96–97
    personal traits and, 97–100
    resilience after, 100–101
    risk assessment for, 98–99
    sexual interference as, 174
    sexual selection hypothesis for, 94, 94–95, 97
    social learning bias and, 92
    socioeconomic stressors for, 93
    as spiteful strategy, 99–100
    suicidal thinking and behaviors from, 137
    therapeutic strategies for, 99
    training and behavioral programs for, 99
    withdrawn behaviors after, 92–93
child molestation, 174
children
    animal cruelty by, as cruel play, 256, 256
    genetic relatedness of, IPV and, 68
    modeling of violence in, from parents, 310
    parental conflict with, 414
    in sibling conflict theory, 112
chimpanzees
    boundary patrols by, 47
    coalitional aggression among, 294
    coalitional violence among, for resources, 8–9
    coalition-building among males, 32–33
    community social structure for, 32, 47
    in comparative primatology, 342–344
    core-area-competition hypothesis for, 53
    female-female violence among, 53–54
    ICEs among, 25
    under imbalance-of-power hypothesis, for violent behaviors, 47

infanticide by, 31, 52, 52–53, 51–53, 53–54
intercommunity LV among, 31–32, 47, 46–48
intracommunity infanticide, 52
intrasexual competition among, 50–51, 158–159
male dominance hierarchies in, 306
male-female violence among, 50–51
male-male violence among, 48–50
non-transferring females, 51
patterns of violence among, 46–47
predation among, infanticide as, 52
reproductive access for, violence between males and, 49
ritualized fighting among, 25
sexual coercion among, between males and females, 51, 52–53
sexual selection by, infanticide as, 52
territorial security by, violence from, 47
transferring females, 51
violence in, 46–54
China
    early religion in, 440
    as world power, 443
Chopin, Kate, 420
Christianity, 456–457. *See also* Catholic Church
    anti-Semitism and, 456
    defeat of Communism by, 461
    pacifist sects within, 457
Christocommunism, 461
Civil War, U.S., in literature, 429
civil wars, 353. *See also* intrastate armed conflicts
Clarissa (Richardson), 427
Clark, William, 372
claustration, 78
A Clockwork Orange (Burgess), 415
coalitional aggression, in animal models, 44–46
    among African wild dogs, 45
    among chimpanzees, 294
    under game theory, 47–48
    intergroup competition and, 45
    among red colobus monkeys, 45
    among spider monkeys, 45
    among spotted hyenas, 45, 45–46
    among wolves, 45
coalitional aggression, in males. *See also* male warrior hypothesis
    in parasite-stress model of sociality, 367
coalitional lethal violence, among mammals, 28
coalitional violence, in animals, 8
    among chimpanzees, 8–9
coalition-building
    among human males, 32–33
    among male chimpanzees, 32–33
coalition formation, in human tribalism, 291–292
coercive controllers, 274–275
coercive intersexual bullying, 277–279

bullies and, 278
    as cuckoldry risk management, 278
    by females, 278–279
    relationship duration with, 277–278
    sexual conflict theory and, 278
cognitive model, for suicidal thinking and behaviors, 134
cohabitation, IPV and, 68
Cohen, Zvi, 236
cohesion, in combat groups, 381–385
    attributes of effective soldiers, 385
    benefits of, 381–382
    emotional bonds and, 381
    hazing practices and, 383–384
    hypermasculinity and, 383
    loyalty and, 381
    moral factors for, 381
    as performance enabling, 382
    psychological homogeneity in, 381
    sexual integration and, 382–383
    studies on, 382
    trust and, 384, 383–385
    in urban warfare, 382
    in U.S. Air Force, 383
Cold War, 443
collectivism, 352
    data methodology for, 356
    ethnocentrism and, 362
    in intrastate armed conflicts, 353
    psychology of, 362–363
    pursuit of conflict and, 363
Colobus guereza. *See* colobus monkeys, intragroup antagonism among
colobus monkeys, intragroup antagonism among, 26
combat motivation
    cowardice label and, 378
    by gender, 378–379
    personnel selection and, 378
Communism, Christianity's defeat of, 461
comparative primatology, 342–344
compartmentalization, animal cruelty and, 263
competition. *See also* male-male competition
    definition of, 478–479
competitively disadvantaged males, 181–182
    biological foundations for, 182
    future research study for, 182
    under micro-mate deprivation hypothesis, 181
    neurological correlates for, 182
complementary socioeconomic security hypothesis, 438
complex hunter-gatherer societies, 341
concord, as lexical concept, 481–482
condition-dependence, in parasite-stress model of sociality, 364
confidence triggers, from anger, 201
conflict resolution
    definition of, 478
    IPV as influence on, 308

528 | INDEX

confluence model of sexual aggression,
     179–180
  correlates in, lack of, 180
  early development of, 179
  evolutionary perspectives in, 179
  feminist theory, 179–180
  limitations of, 179–180
  male hostility in, 179
confrontation triggers, from anger, 201
Conrad, Joseph, 415, 419, 420, 421, 426
Contemporary Pathogen Severity Index,
     355, 355–356
  Global Peace Index and, 365
cooperative breeders, humans as, 199–200
core-area-competition hypothesis, female
     chimpanzees and, 53
corporate-consumer hypothesis, for
     religiosity, 453–454
coups, political, 353
  data methodology for, 354
  results predictions for, 359
Cousin Bette (Balzac), 423
cowardice, 378
Cowden, Jonathan, 319
Creamer, Winifred, 332
crime, violence and. *See also* rape
  in U.S., statistics for, 3
Crime and Punishment (Dostoevsky), 418,
     424
Croatian War of Independence, 165
Crocula crocuta. *See* spotted hyenas
Crow Creek site, 334, 334
cruel play, among children, with animals,
     256, 256
cuckoldry, 13. *See also* paternity
     uncertainty, for males;
     reproduction, in humans
  coercive intersexual bullying and, as risk
     management strategy, 278
  cuckoldry risk hypothesis, 183–184,
     184, 184
  evolutionary considerations of, 64
  FIPC and, 70–71
  karo-kari and, 63
  male-male competition and, 160
  male responses to, 64
  monitoring behaviors and, 65
  post-detection behaviors, for males,
     65–66
  protective guarding behaviors against,
     65–66
  psychological insults as prevention
     strategy, 65
  psychological mechanisms for reduction
     of, 65–66
  punishment for, IPV as, 67
  sexual jealousy as, among males, 65
  in Talmud, 79
cuckoldry risk hypothesis, 183–184
  female infidelity in, 184
  tests for, 184
cultural violence, 309
  patriarchy as foundation of, 309

culture. *See also* intercultural contact
  animal cruelty and, typology for, 263
  definitions of, 219
  evolutionary effects of, 517
  female aggression influenced by, 212
  globalization as influence on, 218
  low-level features of, 219
  MWH influenced by, 294
  rule of law and, 221, 221–222
  violence and, 219
cultures of honor, violence in, 17
  accidental deaths in, 226
  aggressive defense of reputation in, 223
  from bullying, 225
  definition of, 223
  depression rates in, 229
  environmental conditions in, 230
  field studies of, in U.S., 224–226
  foundations of, 219–222
  future research study for, 229–230
  gender roles in, 223
  gun control legislation in, 225
  help-seeking behaviors in, 229
  herding hypothesis for, 230
  historical origins of, 222–223
  intergenerational transmission of,
     228–229
  IPV in, 72, 225
  lab studies of, in U.S., 226–228
  legal permissiveness in, for homicide,
     225
  manhood in, 224, 223–224, 223–224
  overview of, 218–219
  pastoralism and, 230
  patronymic naming in, 229
  precarious manhood hypothesis for,
     224, 223–224
  realistic group conflict theory for, 220
  regional differences in, 226–228
  resource deprivation hypothesis and,
     220, 220–221
  restoration of reputation and, 221–222,
     225
  as retaliatory, 224–225, 225–226, 228
  scarcity of resources in, 219–221
  in school settings, 224–225
  suicide rates in, 229
  for terrorist acts, 225–226
  among Ulster Scots, 222–223
Cummings, J., 473
Cummings, N., 473
cute factor, 262–263

D

Dacelo novaeguineae. *See* laughing
     kookaburras, siblicide among
Dagg, A.I., 474
Dante Alighieri, 417
Darwin, Charles. *See also* natural selection;
     sexual selection, in animals
  evolutionary continuity for, 261
  on evolutionary psychology, 4
  Malthus as influence on, 508

on origins of human tribal nature, 291
Darwin and International Relations
     (Thayer), 307
date rape, 174
deCatanzaro, Denys, 140
Defoe, Daniel, 424
dehumanization, from ethnocentrism, 347
Deists, 442
DeLay, Tom, 473
deliberate deviance, animal cruelty as,
     259, 264
deliberate self-harm (DSH), 138
Delphinidae. *See* dolphins
democracy. *See also* Western democracies,
     religiosity in
  common assessment of, as political
     system, 311
  in Islamic society, economic success
     from, 462
  late marriage as influence on, 316
  parasite-stress model of sociality and,
     352, 356–357, 365–366
  as response to patriarchy, 308
democratic peace theory, 316
De Palma, Brian, 415
depression
  as adaptive value, 137–138
  child development and, 402–403
  in cultures of honor, 229
  DSH and, 138
  ethnic cleansing and, 403
  low moods and, 138
  suicidal thinking compared to, 135
  suicide as byproduct, 137–138
de Rivera, Joseph, 478
desensitization thesis, 264
Deuteronomy, book of, virginity
     requirements in, 77–78
Deutsch, Morton, 477
developmentally disabled, sexual offending
     by, 186
  pedophilia and, 186
dexamethasone suppression test (DST),
     136
Dickens, Charles, 415, 420, 423, 424,
     426, 427
Dipodomys spp. *See* kangaroo rats
direct aggression, among females, 272
direct sexual coercion, 188
dissociation, 101
  animal cruelty and, 260–261
dolphins
  infanticide by, 29
  violence among, 28
domestic abuse. *See* intimate partner
     violence
domestication history, for animals,
     261–262
domestic violence. *See* intimate partner
     violence
dominance hierarchies, female aggression
     within, 199. *See also* male
     dominance hierarchies

INDEX | 529

dominance hierarchies, male, in FEA, 306–307
domination and control hypothesis, 70
Dostoevsky, Fyodor, 418, 418, 422, 424
Dr. Jekyll and Mr. Hyde (Stevenson), 415
The Dram Shop (Zola), 426
Dreiser, Theodore, 424–425
DSH. *See* deliberate self-harm
DST. *See* dexamethasone suppression test
Durkheim, Emil, 235
dyadic aggression, in animal models, 44
    among gelada, 44
    among mandrills, 44
    in red deer, 44
    among yellow baboons, 44

E

Eagley, Alice, 302
early Hominids
    cooperative social structures among, 34
    LV among, 34–35, 40
    NLV among, 34–35, 40
    as peaceful, 33–34
    primate methodology for, for assessment of violence, 40
    violence in, 33–35
early humans
    pair-bonding in social structures, 32
    patrilineal society structures for, 32
educational settings. *See* schools
ego, in homicide-suicide, 125
egoistic suicide, 133
EHHS. *See* European Homicide-Suicide Study
Einstein, Albert, 472
Eisenhower, Dwight, 472
elephant seals, 26–27
    polygyny among, 157
Eliot, George, 422, 424
Ellis, Bret Easton, 415
embodied cognition, 494
emotions. *See also* affective aggression; anger; fear; frustration
    aggression and, 200–201
    function of, 65
    low moods, 138
    psychopathy and, 281–282
    sexual jealousy as, among males, 65
emotional security hypothesis, 400
empathy bias, 263
empathy responses, by gender, 375–376
Empedocles on Etna (Arnold), 421
The End of the Age (Robertson), 473
epigenetics
    for child maltreatment and filicide, 100
    for suicidal thinking and behaviors, 136–137
equestrian hunter-gatherer societies, 341
error management theory, 384
ESS. *See* evolutionarily stable strategy
An Essay on the Principle of Population (Malthus), 507, 521
essence, as concept, 345, 345–346

ethnic cleansing, 395
    ancestral responses to, 396
    depression and, 403
    rape and, 403
ethnocentrism
    collectivism and, 362
    definition of, 347
    dehumanization as result of, 347
    as foundation for war, 347
    parasite-stress model of sociality and, 351–352, 363
    religious terrorism and, 361
Euripides, 420
European Homicide-Suicide Study (EHHS), 128
Evaristti, Marco, 259
evil
    in literature, definition of, 415
    wrong compared to, 82
evolutionarily stable strategy (ESS), 24–25
    for sacred values, 248
evolutionary biology, 306
evolutionary consciousness, 506–507, 517–520
    complicit behaviors and, 519
    extended phenotypes and, 518
    psychological inner struggle within, 520
evolutionary continuity
    for Darwin, 261
    in humane treatment of animals, 260–261
    modern approaches to, 261
evolutionary game theory, 67
evolutionary marriage, 315
evolutionary peace project, 493–495
evolutionary psychology
    of aggression, 200–204
    behavioral justification through, as criticism, 4
    Darwin on, 4
    domain-specific information-processing mechanisms for, 4
    environmental input and, 4
    for fear, 4
    fear stimuli in, 4
    of female aggression, 200–204
    future research applications in, 18–19
    for gender behavior, 306
    genetic determinism through, as criticism, 4–5
    of male-male competition, 200–204
    misconceptions about, 4–5
    output predictions in, 4
    overview of, 4
    for peace, 19, 471–472
    for religious terrorism, 249–250
    stereotyping of, 475
    as unifying approach to psychology, 4
    violence against females and, male reproductive access and, 13
evolutionary theory
    for aggression, 154, 198–200
    for altruistic suicide, 139–140

for child homicide-suicide, 126–127
    in confluence model of sexual aggression, 179
    cultural effects on, 517
    for female aggression, 198–200
    for global conflict, 514–517
    for homicide-suicide, 125–127
    for intimate partner homicide-suicide, 126
    for IPV, 64, 207–208
    for male-male competition, violence and homicide from, 154, 154–156, 198–200
    for paraphilias, 185
    for paternity uncertainty, 64
    for peace, 473–475
    for psychology of law, 188
    for psychopathic bullying, 282
    for rape, costs and benefits of, 174–175
    for religion, 235
    for religious terrorism, 238, 249–250
    for siblicide, 107
    for social conflict, 514–517
    structural patriarchy in, 311–312
    suicidal thinking and behaviors and, 137
    for suicide, as purposeful, 140–141, 141
    for trust, in combat groups, 384
The Evolution of Human Sexuality (Symons), 174–175
exhibitionism, 174, 185
exhibitionistic suicides, 120
existential despair, in literature, 421
The Exploits of Prince Yamoto, 115
extended phenotype, 516–517
    evolutionary consciousness and, 518
extended suicide, 122

F

facultative adaptation, 280
FAH. *See* food amount hypothesis
familial model, for suicidal thinking and behaviors, 134
familicide, 94. *See also* homicide-suicide; infanticide, among humans; intimate partner homicide-suicide; intimate partner violence; parricide; siblicide; uxoricide
    in literature, 422
familicide-suicide, 122–123. *See also* homicide-suicide; infanticide, among humans; intimate partner homicide-suicide; intimate partner violence; parricide; siblicide; uxoricide
    economic demographics with, 123
    from loss of control, 123
    mental illness and, 123
    methods for, 122–123
    as murder by proxy, 123
    as suicide by proxy, 123

families, violence within, 13–15. *See also* suicide
  filicide, 14
  kin selection theory and, 14
  in literature, 422
  between mothers and offspring, 14
  parental investment theory and, 14
  between siblings, 14
fantasy fiction, war in, 430
Far From the Madding Crowd (Hardy), 423
fascism, development of, 442–443
fast life history strategy, violence and, 16–17
Faulkner, William, 423
Fay Tolten site, 334
FEA. *See* feminist evolutionary analysis
fear. *See also* impulsivity
  avoidance triggers from, 201
  behavioral freezing with, 202
  evolutionary psychology for, 4
  neural pathways for, 202
  OT and, 210–211
  provocation conditions for, 201
  relationship establishment and, for females, 211
  risk-taking and, among males, 203
  sex differences in, 202–203, 211–212, 375
  as survival response, 202
  terrorism and, 234
FEE. *See* formative evolutionary environment
females. *See also* armed forces, sexual integration of; female groups; female infidelity; feminism; violence, against females
  aggressive behaviors by, 156, 200–201, 200–204, 375
  chastity belts for, 78
  coercive intersexual bullying by, 278–279
  combat motivation for, 378–379
  control of, as purpose of Bible, 83
  empathy responses for, 375–376
  facial masculinity in males for, 163
  fear for, expressions of, 202–203, 211–212, 375
  foot-binding of, 78
  group attachment and, 380–381
  group formation for, 380–381
  heroic behavior by, 377
  human nature for, 346
  in hunter-gatherer societies, 303
  impulsivity among, 203–204
  infanticide by, in animals, 28
  intergroup aggression among, 296, 298–299
  intersexual bullying by, 277
  intimate partner homicide-suicide by, 121
  intrasexual bullying by, 272
  intrasexual competition between, among humans, 12–13
  late marriage for, 315
  leadership issues for, of males, 385–386
  legal protections for, in nation-states, 305, 305–306
  in nomological theory of human nature, 346
  nurturance responses for, 375–376
  pain tolerance levels for, 374
  in parental investment theory, 6
  peace organizations under, 494
  physical security of, in nation-states, 305, 305–306
  rape and, U.S. statistics for, 3
  relational aggression among, 12–13, 156
  relationship establishment and, fear reduction in, 211
  risk-taking by, 374–375, 376–377
  sexual jealousy among, 65
  siblicide by, 113
  suicide by, 133
  as symbol of peace, 372–373
  valuation of, as offspring, 305
  violence against intimate partners, 18–19
  virginity for, in Bible, 77–78, 78–79
female aggression. *See also* anger; fear; impulsivity; indirect aggression, among females; monogamy; relational aggression, among females
  as advantageous strategy, 198–199
  age factors for, 205, 205–206
  common stereotypes for, 197
  costs of, 199
  cultural influences on, 212
  within dominance hierarchies, 199
  evolutionary biology of, 198–200
  evolutionary psychology of, 200–204
  IPV and, 197, 207–211
  legal ramifications of, 209
  for male partners, 205
  management of, 204–205
  maternal, 206–207, 207, 212
  OT influence on, 211
  parental investment and, 198
  as personal defense behavior, 205
  physical, 205–206
  relationship establishment and, fear reduction through, 211
  for reproductive success, 198–199
  resource competition and, 197, 198, 206
  as self-defense behavior, inconsistency of, 209
  sex ratios as influence on, 206
  from sexual jealousy, 205, 208
  social norms and, 209
  target paradox for, in IPV, 210
female groups
  formation of, 380–381
  as hierarchy-averse, 380–381
  ostracism in, 380
  as talk-dependent, 380
female human nature, 346
female infidelity. *See also* cuckoldry; paternity uncertainty, for males
  in the Bible, punishment for, 78
  in cuckoldry risk hypothesis, 184
  FIPC as response to, 71
  indirect aggression and, 205
  relational aggression and, 205
feminism
  confluence model of sexual aggression and, 179–180
  imagined kinship in, 249
  nationalism and, conflicts with, 309
  synthesized theory of rape and, 180
feminist evolutionary analysis (FEA), 302–306
  evolutionary perspectives in, 304–305
  gender ideology in, development of, 304
  male dominance hierarchies in, 304
  male-male alliances in, 303–304
  parameters of, 302
  patriarchy and, 302
  patrilocality in, 303
  reproductive control in, by males, 303
  resource competition and, 304
feudal societies, siblicide in, 113
feuding, in prehistorical societies, 341
Fielding, Henry, 415
filicide, 14. *See also* infanticide, among humans
  actuarial risk assessments for, 99
  age factors for, 93
  epigenetics and, 100
  familicide and, 94
  future research study for, 100–101
  inclusive fitness theory and, 92
  intervention strategies for, 98–99, 101
  life history strategies and, 91, 96
  in literature, 422
  marital disharmony and, 97
  maternal, 94–95
  mental illness and, 97
  by older adults, as homicide-suicide, 122
  parental investment theory and, 91, 92, 96
  parental solicitude and, 96–97
  paternal, 93–94
  perpetrators of, 93–97
  sexual selection hypothesis for, 94, 94–95, 97
  socioeconomic stressors for, 93
  as spiteful strategy, 99–100
  by stepparents, 95
FIPC. *See* forced in-pair copulation
Fitzgerald, F. Scott, 427
Flaubert, Gustave, 420, 422
food, access to, intrasexual competition for, between animals, 7–9
food amount hypothesis (FAH), 109
Football for Peace, 489
foot-binding, 78

forced in-pair copulation (FIPC), 70–71.
    See also partner rape
  cuckoldry and, 70–71
  female infidelity and, 71
  rape as, 183–184
  sexual jealousy and, among males, 70–71
  sperm competition hypothesis for, 70–71
Ford, Ford Madox, 421
formal schooling, adolescent bullying and, 282–283
formative evolutionary environment (FEE), 302
Frankenstein (Shelley), 426
fratricide, 107
  birth order and, among males, 114–115
  in literature, 422
  by males, 113
Frazer, James, 234–235
frotteurism, 174, 185
frustration
  animal cruelty from, 256–257
  in frustration-aggression hypothesis, for animal cruelty, 256
  in stream analogy, 124–125
frustration-aggression hypothesis, for animal cruelty, 256
fundamentalism. *See* religious fundamentalism

G

Gadhafi, Moammar, 506
Galapagos fur seals, siblicide among, 111
Galsworthy, John, 421
Galtung, John, 308–309
  on cultural violence, 309, 309
  on structural violence, 308–309
game theory
  coalitional aggression in animal models and, 47–48
  evolutionary, for IPV, 67
  uxoricide under, costs of, 69–70
Gaza War, 85
GDP. *See* gross domestic product
Gebusi tribe, 161
gelada, aggressive behaviors among, 44
gender. *See also* females; gender inequality; males
  aggression by, 156, 200–201, 200–204, 375
  birth sex ratios by, 317
  combat motivation by, 378–379
  in cultures of honor, 223
  empathy responses by, 375–376
  evolutionary psychology for, 306
  fear and, aggression and, 202–203, 211–212, 375
  group attachment and, 380–381
  group formation and, 380–381
  heroic behavior and, 377
  as identity marker, 301–302
  ideology, development of, 304
  impulsivity and, 203–204
  inequality, 305
  intergroup aggression by, 296
  intersexual bullying by, 277
  intimate partner homicide-suicide and, 121
  leadership issues and, 385–386
  male surplus, from gender-based infanticide, 317–318
  MWH and, study bias in, 294
  in nation-states, treatment of, 302
  in nomological theory of human nature, 346
  nurturance responses by, 375–376
  pain tolerance levels by, 374
  parental investment theory by, 6
  as primary formative fixed difference, 302
  risk-taking by, 374–375, 376–377
  sexual jealousy by, 208
  siblicide by, 113
  suicide by, 133
  violence by, in animals, 6
  war and, 15–16
gender equality, future enforcement of, 83
gender inequality, 305
  cultural violence and, 309
  structural violence and, 308–309
genetics
  altruism and, 139
  for anxiety, 401–402
  bullying and, 271
  child maltreatment and, studies for, 93
  pleiotropy, 137
  suicidal thinking and behaviors and, 135–136
genetic determinism
  through evolutionary psychology, 4–5
  suicide and, 135–136
genetic relatedness
  child homicide-suicide and, 122, 127
  IPV and, for children, 68
  male-male competition and, 161
  siblicide and, 114
gibbons
  infanticide among, 30
  LV among, 30
GIDEON. *See* Global Infectious Disease and Epidemiology Network
Gissing, George, 420
global conflict, as evolutionary process, 514–517
Global Infectious Disease and Epidemiology Network (GIDEON), 355
globalization
  cultural conflict from, 236
  culture influences of, 218
  intercultural contact influenced by, 236
Global Peace Index, 355, 362
  path analysis with, 357–358
  pathogen severity and, 365
  regression analysis with, 357
Goethe, Johann Wolfgang von, 132
The Golden Bough (Frazer), 234–235
Golding, William, 428
the good, in literature, 415
Goodall, Jane, 514
Goodman, Andrew, 457
"A Good Man Is Hard To Find" (O'Connor), 415
The Good Soldier (Ford), 421
Gopin, Marc, 249
gorillas
  infanticide by, 31
  intrasexual competition among, 158
  LV among, 30–31
  NLV among, 29–30
gossip, as indirect/relational aggression among females, 205, 273–274
Grand Gulch Caves, 331
The Grapes of Wrath (Steinbeck), 426
The Great Gatsby (Fitzgerald), 427
gross domestic product (GDP), 356, 357
group attachment, sex differences in, 380–381
group dynamics. *See also* cohesion, in combat groups; female groups; horizontal cohesion, in male bonding; in-group identification; intergroup aggression; male groups; out groups; vertical cohesion, in male bonding
  in armed forces, 379–381
  group attachment and, sex differences in, 380–381
  group formation and, sex differences in, 380–381
  MWH and, 379–380
  under SSSM, 379
group formation, sex differences in, 380–381
guilt, in literature, 419
guinea pigs, sibling competition among, 108
Gulf War, 85, 247
gun control legislation, in cultures of honor, 225

H

Haas, Jonathan, 332
Hagee, John, 473, 474
Hajnal, John, 315
Hajnal-Hartman thesis, 314–316
  democratic peace theory and, 316
  evolutionary marriage and, modifications to, 315
  late marriage in, 315–316, 315, 316
Hannagan, Rebecca, 303
Hardy, Thomas, 419, 421, 423, 426
Harris, G.T., 180
Hartman, Mary, 312, 315. *See also* Hajnal-Hartman thesis
hazing practices, in combat groups, 383–384
Heller, Joseph, 418

help-seeking behaviors, in cultures of honor, 229
Helsinki Birth Cohort, 405
herding hypothesis, 230
heroic behavior
    gender and, 377
    during Holocaust, 377
hierarchies. *See also* dominance hierarchies; male dominance hierarchies
    in female groups, 380–381
higher-order theories of impulsivity, 203
"him or me" dilemma, 123
Hinduism, 456
Hippolytus (Euripides), 420
Hobbes, Thomas, 476
Hoffman, Bruce, 234
Holocaust
    anxiety during, as trauma bundle, 402
    child development during, 400
    heroic behavior during, 377
Homer, 417, 422–423
homicide. *See also* male-male competition, violence and homicide from; sexual homicide; uxoricide
    among Ache peoples, 396
    as adaptive mechanism, 19
    in cultures of honor, legal permissiveness for, 225
    homicide-suicide compared to, 120
    "hot-blooded," 225
    among Kung San peoples, 396
    of non-virginal woman, in the Bible, 81–82
    among Yanomamö peoples, 155, 396
homicide adaptation theory, 69, 72
homicide-suicide. *See also* intimate partner homicide-suicide; strain theory; stream analogy, for homicide-suicide
    accidental, 121
    classification system for, 120–121
    declines in, 119
    definition of, 118
    demographics for, 120
    ego in, 125
    EHHS studies, 128
    evolutionary perspectives on, 125–127
    exhibitionistic suicides and, 120
    fear of exposure and, 120
    future research study for, 127–128
    homicide compared to, 120
    id in, 125
    incidence rates for, 118–119, 118
    in Japan, 119
    mental illness and, 126
    natural selection and, 125
    nature of, 119–120
    by older persons, 120
    operational criteria for, 117–118, 119–120
    parameters of, 117
    as paranoia-based, 120
    parricide and, 123
    psychodynamic approach to, 125
    psychological autopsy after, 128
    reproductive fitness and, 125
    social integration theory and, 125
    stability of rates for, 119
    suicide compared to, 120
    superego in, 125, 125
    as terrorist act, 120, 121
    theoretical perspectives on, 123–127
    theory-testing for, 127
    in U.S., 119
Hominids. *See* early Hominids
honor killings, as IPV, 72
horizontal cohesion, in male bonding, 379
hostility, in confluence model of sexual aggression, 179
"hot-blooded" homicide, 225
The House of Mirth (Wharton), 420
HPA axis. *See* hypothalamic-pituitary-adrenal axis
Huckabee, Mike, 474
Huckleberry Finn (Twain), 427
human-animal bonds
    altruism in, 261
    as The Ancient Contract, 261–262
    companionship benefits of, 261
    domestication history for animals and, 261–262
    empathy bias in, 263
    evolutionary benefits of, 261–263
    fitness benefits of, 261
    pet-keeping, 262, 262–263
    reciprocity in, 261, 261–262
humane treatment of animals, 260–261
    Biophilia Hypothesis for, 260
    as evolutionary continuity, 260–261
human nature, 344–346
    biological philosophy and, 346
    common characteristics as part of, 345, 346
    essence as concept in, 345, 345–346
    naturalness as concept in, 345
    nomological theory of, 346,
    parameters of, 348
human nature, war and, 346–348
    biological traits for, 347
    comparative primatology for, 342–344
    ethnocentrism as foundation for, 347
    evidence for, 348
    nomological theory for, 346
    as philosophical question, 339–340, 348
    sexual dimorphism, 347–348
human sacrifice, in literature, 427–428
human violence. *See* violence, against females; violence, in humans
Hume, David, 348
hunter-gatherer societies
    altruism through kin selection in, 281
    animal cruelty in, 260
    bullying among adolescents in, 279–281
    childhood mortality in, 279–280
    complex, 341
    dominance establishment in, 280
    equestrian, 341
    facultative adaptation in, 280
    female roles in, 303
    indirect/relational aggression in, 280–281
    intraspecific violence among, 440
    mobility within, 280
    patrilocality in, 303
    religion in, 439–440
    in Santa Barbara Channel area, 328
    shamanism in, 439
    socioeconomic conditions among, 439–440
    tolerance setting for aggression in, 280
    wars between, 340–341
hunting, animal cruelty and, 258
Hurston, Zora Neale, 423
Huxley, Aldous, 421
hypermasculinity, 383
hypothalamic-pituitary-adrenal (HPA) axis, 136

I

ICEs. *See* intercommunity encounters
id, in homicide-suicide, 125
Iliad (Homer), 417
imagined kinship, 249
    in feminism, 249
    in Islamic society, 249
    through patriotism, 249
    religion as, 249
imbalance-of-power hypothesis, for lethal violence, 28
    among chimpanzees, 47, 47
immigration, intercultural contact and, 236
impulsivity
    definition of, 203
    higher-order theories of, 203
    low-order theories of, 203
    risk-taking and, among males, 203–204
    sensation-seeking compared to, 203
    sex differences in, 203–204
incest, 174, 186–187
    avoidance of, as psychological adaptation, 186
    kin detection deficiencies and, 187
    pedophilia and, 186–187
    as reproductive strategy, 187
"Incident at Owl Creek Bridge" (Bierce), 427
inclusive fitness theory, 92
    for child development, 394
    in contemporary environments, 145
    direct tests of, 142
    implications for, 146
    interaction studies for, 142–145
    limitations of, 145–146
    in literature, 413
    methodological limitations of, 146
    for sibling competition, in animals, 108

inclusive fitness theory (cont.)
   sibling conflict theory and, 107
   for suicide, 137, 140–141, 147
   suicide intervention strategies as result of, 146
indirect aggression, among females, 12–13, 156, 205
   through fidelity, 205
   through gossip, 205, 273–274
   in hunter-gatherer societies, 280–281
   as intrasexual bullying, 272
   through physical appearance, 205, 272
indirect sexual coercion, 188
individualism, 356, 362
infanticide, among humans
   birth sex ratios and, 317
   under Canadian Criminal Code, 94
   in literature, 422
   male coalition-building and, 33
   male-male competition and, 161
   male surplus as result of, 317–318
   from mental disorders, 94
   in sexual conflict theory, 188
   by Yanomamö, 161
infanticide, in animals, 9
   among apes, 35
   among dolphins, 29
   in female animals, 9, 28
   by female chimpanzees, 53–54
   by females, 28
   among gibbons, 30
   intracommunity, among chimpanzees, 52, 53–54
   among languars, 28
   as lethal aggression, 44
   as LV, 28–29
   by male chimpanzees, 31, 52, 51–53
   by male gorillas, 31
   as predation, 52
   as reproductive strategy, 29
   as sexual coercion, among male chimpanzees, 52–53
   as sexual selection, by male chimpanzees, 52
   sibling competition and, 109
   by species males, 9, 29
infectious diseases, 367–368. *See also* pathogen exposure
Inferno (Dante), 417
infibulation, 78
infrahumanization, 296. *See also* ethnocentrism
Inglehart, Ronald, 311
in-group identification
   religion and, 17–18
   tribalism and, 292
   war and, 16
inhibition failure, animal cruelty as, 259–260
insecure attachment, in child development, 399–401
   emotional security hypothesis for, 400

intergenerational transmission of, 400–401
   phenotypic inertia and, 400–401
instrumental aggression, 42
Insurance Egg Hypothesis, 109–110
intelligence quotient (IQ)
   psychopathy and, 182–183
   recidivism and, 183
intercommunity encounters (ICEs), 25
intercultural contact, 236–237
   globalization's influence on, 236
   hideous schizophrenia of, 236–237
   immigration and, 236
   stress systems as result of, 236
intergroup aggression, 292, 295–296. *See also* tribalism, among humans
   for females, as research study, 298–299
   future research implications for, 297–298
   by gender, 296
interlocus sexual conflict, 188
international aid, factors for, 367
   infectious diseases exposure, 367–368
intersexual bullying, in sexual relationships, 276–279. *See also* coercive intersexual bullying
   antisocial behavior and, 279
   in courtship, 277–278
   definition of, 276–277
   by gender, 277
   pathways to, 279
   private contexts for, 277
   public contexts for, 277
   sexual maturity and, 277
intersexual competition, in animals
   among apes, as NLV, 29
   among female chimpanzees, 50–51
   sexual selection as, 5–6
intersexual competition, in humans. *See also* male-male competition, violence and homicide from
   for reproductive access, 11–12
intersubjectivity, 494
intimate partner homicide-suicide, 121–122
   common methods of, 121
   as control mechanism, 126
   dependence issues in, 126
   evolutionary perspective for, 126
   gender influences on, 121
   mental illness and, 121–122
   among older adults, 121
   physical abuse history and, 121
   as premeditated, 121
   sexual jealousy as factor in, 122
   socioeconomic stressors and, 121
intimate partner violence (IPV), 63–64, 66–71. *See also* cuckoldry; forced in-pair copulation; partner rape; paternity uncertainty, for males; punishment, IPV as; sexual coercion, IPV and; uxoricide
   acts *versus* outcomes in, 209

   alcohol use and, 66
   anger in, 66
   cohabitation as factor for, compared to marriage, 68
   in cultures of honor, 72, 225
   in evolutionary game theory, 67
   evolutionary perspective for, 64, 207–208
   female aggression and, 197, 207–211
   female behavioral control and, 68
   future research study for, 72, 212
   honor killings as, 72
   intrasexual competition and, 66
   karo-kari, 63
   male-male competition and, 161
   male proprietariness and, 67–68
   manifestations of, 68
   minor *versus* severe acts of, 209–210
   nation-state conflict resolution strategies and, influenced by, 308
   nongenetic offspring as factor for, 68
   paternity uncertainty and, 64–66
   relationship counseling strategies for, 166
   reproductive ability and, 72
   sexual jealousy and, 66, 208
   strategy of attack locations in, 72
   victim demographics, 208
   worldwide incidence rates for, 63
intimidation, by male chimpanzees, 51
intracommunity infanticide
   by female chimpanzees, 53–54
   by males chimpanzees, 52
intralocus sexual conflict, 188
intrasexual bullying, 271–273
   for dating opportunities, 272, 273
   as direct aggression, among females, 272
   by females, 272
   negative perceptions of, 273
   resource control theory and, 271–272
   for social acceptance, 272
intrasexual competition, between animals, 5–6
   among apes, NLV in, 29
   among Barbary macaques, 157–158
   common behaviors in, 157
   for food access, 7–9
   among male primates, 157–159
   reproductive access and, 7
   severity of violence in, 7
intrasexual competition, between humans
   for females, 12–13
   IPV and, 66
   for males, 11–12
   for status, 12
intrasexual competition, in animals, 5–6
   among apes, 158
   among Barbary macaques, 157–158
   among bonobos, 159
   among chimpanzees, violence in, 50–51, 158–159
   among Japanese macaques, 158

among male baboons, 158
among male orangutans, 158
among mountain gorillas, 158
intrastate armed conflicts, 352–353, 366
   collectivism in, 353
   data methodology of, 354
   results predictions for, 358–359
   xenophobic groups and, 352–353
intuitive theism, 243
IPV. *See* intimate partner violence
IQ. *See* intelligence quotient
Iraq War, 85
Islam, expansion of, 237
Islamic society
   democratic secular governments in, 462
   early development of, 237
   imagined kinship in, 249
   Muslim jihad and, 237, 237, 237
   sharia in, 237
Israel, Two State Solution for, 85

J

Jackson, Shirley, 427–428
James, Henry, 420
James VI (King), 223
Japan. *See also* cultures of honor, violence in
   homicide-suicide in, 119
Japanese macaques, 158
jealousy. *See* law of jealousy, in Bible; sexual jealousy
Jebel Sahaba cemetery, 10, 341
Jeffs, Warren, 516
Jewish Diaspora, 441
Jewish Underground, 236, 239
John Paul II (Pope), 458
Johnson, Gary, 249
Jonathan Wilde (Fielding), 415
Judah and Tamar, in the Bible, 78
Judaism
   anti-Semitism, Christianity and, 456, 458
   Jewish Diaspora, 441
Jude the Obscure (Hardy), 421
Julius Caesar (Shakespeare), 417, 425
jurisprudence. *See* psychology of law, for sexual offending
just wars, 456–457

K

Kafka on the Shore (Murakami), 424
kangaroo rats, 26
karo-kari, 63
kashrut laws, 241
Kennewick Man, 327
Khar, Fahkra, 63
al-Khateeb, Hamza Ali, 507
kin detection deficiencies, incest and, 187
King, Stephen, 415, 422, 426
King Lear (Shakespeare), 422
King Solomon's Ring (Lorenz), 24
kin protection, male-male competition and, 159

kin reproductive potential (KRP), 142
kin selection theory, 14
   self-destructive behavior under, 140–141
   sibling conflict theory and, 107
   suicide and, 140–141
Kony, Joseph, 458
Kook, Zvi Yehuda, 239
Korean War, 385
KRP. *See* kin reproductive potential
K-selected species, 164
Kubrick, Stanley, 415
Kung San peoples, 396

L

LaHaye, Tim, 474
Lalumière, M.L., 180
langurs, infanticide among, 28
late marriage, 315–316
   capitalism influenced by, 315–316
   democracy influenced by, 316
   evolutionary marriage compared to, 315
   male control in, 315
laughing kookaburras, siblicide among, 110
lawlessness, broken window effect and, 221
law of divorce, in Bible, 79–80
   alimony payments under, 79–80
   causes under, for males, 80
law of jealousy, in Bible, 80
   punishment under, 80–81
leadership issues, in armed forces
   gender and, 385–386
   stereotyping and, 386
   type of, 386
Leahy, Michael, 372
Lebanon Wars, 85
legal execution, in literature, 427
Lehane, Dennis, 427
lethal aggression, in animal models, 44–46. *See also* coalitional aggression, in animal models; dyadic aggression, in animal models
   future research study directions for, 55, 55
   among primate social groups, 45
lethal violence (LV). *See also* homicide; infanticide, in animals
   among apes, 30–33
   among bonobos, lack of, 34
   among chimpanzees, 31–32, 47, 46–48
   coalitional, 28
   among early Hominids, 34–35, 40
   future research study for, 36
   among gibbons, 30
   among gorillas, 30–31
   imbalance-of-power hypothesis for, 28
   infanticide as, 28–29
   among mammals, 27–28, 35
   as natural behavior, 35

   among social carnivores, 28
   in stream analogy, 124
Leviathan (Hobbes), 476
LHT. *See* life history theory
Liberation Tigers of Tamil Eelam (LTTE), 235, 246–247
Lieven, Anatol, 474
life history theory (LHT)
   BSD theory and, 397–398
   for child development, 395, 397–399
   child maltreatment and, 91, 96
   development period and, 162
   fast life history strategy, violence and, 16–17
   filicide and, 91, 96
   for K-selected species, 164
   male human development under, 162–164
   male-male competition and, 161–165
   parameters of, 162, 397
   for religious terrorism, 242
   reproductive tradeoffs, 162
   for r-selected species, 164
   socioeconomic factors in, 165
   tradeoffs in, 397–398
   trait organization in, 397
   uncertainty responses in, 163–164, 164–165
   for violence, 16–17
   violent tendencies and, individual variations in, 164–165
   war and, 165
literature, violence in. *See also* war, in literature
   ancient Greek influences in, 417
   in ancient literature, 10
   biblical influences on, 417
   from economic inequality, 426
   emotional depiction of, 414
   for ethnic/racial dominance, 426
   evil in, 415
   evolutionary perspectives on suicide in, 418–419
   from existential despair, 421
   against family members, 422
   future research study for, 431–432
   the good in, 415
   from guilt, 419
   as human sacrifice, 427–428
   importance of, 416–418
   inclusive fitness theories in, 413
   interpretation in, 414
   by legal execution, 427
   between lovers, 423–424
   meaning in, 414
   from mental illness, 421
   psychopathic cruelty in, 414–416
   as reciprocation, 425–426
   for revenge, 426–427
   from sexual desire, 422–424
   towards sexual rivals, 422–423
   in Shakespearean works, 417, 420
   social context for, 424–428

literature, violence in (*cont.*)
   for social dominance, 425–426
   from social failure, 419–421
   sociopolitical context for, 416
   suicide in, 132, 418–421
Little Bighorn, Battle of, 333
Little Dorrit (Dickens), 420
Livni, Menachem, 240
Lolita (Nabokov), 426
Lonesome Dove (McMurtry), 415
Lord of the Flies (Golding), 428
Lorenz, Konrad, 24
"The Lottery" (Jackson), 427–428
Love of Shopping is Not a Gene: Problems with Darwinian Psychology (Dagg), 474
low moods, 138
low-order theories of impulsivity, 203
loyalty, in combat groups, 381
LTTE. *See* Liberation Tigers of Tamil Eelam
LV. *See* lethal violence
Lycaon pictus. See African wild dogs, coalitional aggressive behaviors among

M

Machiavellian Intelligence hypothesis, 292
Madame Bovary (Flaubert), 420
Maid in Waiting (Galsworthy), 421
Maimonides, 80–81
males. *See also* competitively disadvantaged males; cuckoldry; male bonding; male groups; male-male competition, violence and homicide from; male warrior hypothesis; manhood, in cultures of honor; paternity uncertainty, for males; young male syndrome
   adrenarche for, 162
   aggressive behaviors by, 156, 200–201, 200–204, 375
   animal cruelty by, as masculine motivation, 257–258
   under biblical law of divorce, 80
   coalitional aggression in, 367
   coalition-building among, 33, 32–33
   combat motivation for, 378–379
   in cultures of honor, 17
   empathy responses for, 375–376
   facial masculinity for, social perception of, 163
   fast life history strategy for, 16–17
   fear for, expression of, 202–203, 211–212, 375
   female reproduction controlled by, 303
   fratricide by, 113, 114–115
   group attachment and, 380–381
   group formation for, 380–381
   heroic behavior by, 377
   hostility towards women, in confluence model of sexual aggression, 179
   human nature for, 346
   impulsivity among, 203–204
   infanticide by, from coalition-building, 33
   infanticide by, in animals, 29
   in-group distinctions between, 16
   intergroup aggression among, 296
   intersexual bullying by, 277
   intersexual competition among, for reproductive access, 11–12
   intimate partner homicide-suicide by, 121
   intrasexual competition among, for reproductive access, 11–12
   in late marriage, 315
   leadership issues for, by females, 385–386
   under LHT, 162–164
   male-male competition as harmful, 157
   in mate-deprivation hypothesis, 176
   neuroendocrine system for, 162
   in nomological theory of human nature, 346
   nurturance responses for, 375–376
   pain tolerance levels for, 374
   in parental investment theory, 6
   rape as sexual preference for, 178, 185
   regional differences in aggression, for U.S. males, 226–228
   resource attributes for, by age, 163
   risk-taking by, 203, 203–204, 374–375, 376–377
   sexual coercion by, in human reproduction, 303
   sexual jealousy for, 65
   sexual selection hypothesis for, violence and aggression in, 513–514
   siblicide by, 113
   social status development among, 162
   in Sociosexual Orientation Inventory, 204
   solidarity among, biblical enforcement of, 82–83
   spousal aggression by, 156
   suicide by, 133
   surplus of, from gender-based infanticide, 318, 317–318
   testosterone levels in, 162–163, 183
   valuation of, as offspring, 305
   violence against females, as learned behavior, 309–310, 310–311
   violence against females, evolutionary psychology and, 13
   violence by, in animals, 6
   wars and, 15–16, 325
male bonding, 379
   horizontal cohesion in, 379
   vertical cohesion in, 379
male dominance hierarchies, 313–314. *See also* Hajnal-Hartman thesis
   among animals, 306
   contemporary influences of, 307
   democracy as response to, 308
   dysfunctionality of, 314, 317
   in FEA, 304, 306–307
   late marriage in, 315–316, 315, 316
   mitigations of, 319
   nationalism and, 309
   out groups and, aggression towards, 307
   patriarchy and, 306
   polygyny in, 313
   power-seeking in, 313
   purpose of, 306
   reinforcement of aggression within, 313–314
   resource accumulation in, 317
   violence against women in, 306–307
male groups
   as activity-dependent, 380
   formation of, 380–381
male human nature, 346
male-male alliances, 303–304
   in social learning theory, 310–311
male-male competition, violence and homicide from. *See also* life history theory; male warrior hypothesis; manhood, in cultures of honor
   as advantageous strategy, 198–199
   aggression in, 153
   in contemporary society, 153–154
   in cycle of life, 153
   early warfare and, 155
   for elimination of sexual rivals, 159
   evolutionary psychology of, 200–204
   evolutionary theory for, 154, 154–156, 198–200
   in foraging societies, 155
   functions of, 159–161
   future research study for, 166
   genetic relatedness and, 161
   as harmful to males, 157
   with infanticide, 161
   for kin protection, 159
   for offspring care, resources for, 155
   paternity uncertainty and, 160
   phylogenetic patterns of, 156–159
   poverty and, 165
   in pre-industrial societies, 153
   to prevent cuckoldry, 160
   for reproductive selection, 154–155, 160, 161
   for resources, 155–156, 160
   for self-protection, 159
   for social status, 160–161
   socioeconomic factors for, 165
   spousal homicide and, 161
   for territorial access, 160
   in uncertainty environments, 164–165
   violence in, 153
   during war, 165
male surplus, from gender-based infanticide, 317–318
   violence increase as result of, 318
male warrior hypothesis (MWH), 291–297. *See also* band of brothers; male bonding
   behavioral science evidence for, 294, 295

brain imaging techniques for, 298–299
cross-species research for, 298
cultural influences on, 294
evolutionary models of, 293–294
external threat and, protection behaviors towards, 293–294
future research study for, 298–299
gender bias in, 294
for group dynamics, 379–380
group-level selection in, 294
hierarchy preferences in, 297
historical data for, 294
infrahumanization under, 296
intergroup aggression in, 292, 295–296, 297–298
multilevel selection theory and, 293
neurobiological mechanisms for, 298
out group prejudice in, 296
parameters of, 293
parental investment theory and, 293
psychological mechanisms for, 295–297
reproductive benefits in, 294
risk contract hypothesis and, 293
social identity in, from tribe, 297
stereotyping in, 296
tribal politics in, support for, 297
Malthus, Thomas, 507, 521
　Darwin influenced by, 508
mammals, violence among. *See also specific mammals*
　coalitional lethal violence, 28
　LV, 27–28, 35
　NLV, 26–27
Manchester, William, 348
Mandela, Nelson, 458
mandrills, aggressive behavior among, 44
Mandrillus sphinx. *See* mandrills, aggressive behavior among
manhood, in cultures of honor, 223–224. *See also* male warrior hypothesis
　under precarious manhood hypothesis, 224, 223–224
manipulators, 516–517
marriage. *See also* late marriage
　evolutionary, 315
　in Hajnal-Hartman thesis, 315–316
　IPV and, compared to cohabitation, 68
　late, 315–316, 315
　patrilocality and, 312
　sexual coercion within, incidence rates for, 70
　under structural patriarchy, 312
Marshall, S.L.A, 348
masculinity
　facial, for females, 163
　hypermasculinity, 383
　in precarious manhood hypothesis, 224
　war and, 372
masked boobies, siblicide among, 108
mass homicide, suicide after, 121
mate-deprivation hypothesis, 175–177. *See also* competitively disadvantaged males

age of male as factor in, 176
cost-benefit approach to, 176
data support for, 180
individual differences within, 180–183
micro-mate deprivation hypothesis, 177, 181
in polygynous mating systems, 176
resource competition and, in animals, 176
sexual aggression and, 176–177
socioeconomic factors in, 176
young male syndrome and, 181
materialism, development of, 451
maternal aggression, 206–207
　future research study for, 212
　OT and, 207
　in rat models, 206–207
maternal mortality, offspring survival rates and, 199–200
Maupassant, Guy de, 423
The Mayor of Casterbridge (Hardy), 419
McCain, John, 474
McCarthy, Cormac, 415, 416
McDermott, Rose, 319
McKinnon, S., 474
McMurtry, Larry, 415
McTeague (Norris), 424
McVeigh, Timothy, 458
meerkats, sibling competition among, 111
Melville, Herman, 427
Men Against Fire (Marshall), 348
Mencken, H.L., 475
mental health theory (MHT), 394
mental illness
　child homicide-suicide and, 122, 127
　child maltreatment and, 97
　dissociation, 101
　familicide-suicide and, 123
　filicide and, 97
　homicide-suicide and, 126
　intimate partner homicide-suicide and, 121–122
　in literature, 421
　suicidal thinking and behaviors from, 134
mercy killing-suicide, 121
MHT. *See* mental health theory
Of Mice and Men (Steinbeck), 427
micro-mate deprivation hypothesis, 177
　competitively disadvantaged males under, 181
Middle East, political instability in, 83–85
　Two State Solution for, 85
Middlemarch (Eliot), 424
Midianites, mass murder of, 81–82
Midrash Rabbah, law of jealousy in, 80, 80–81
Miller, Barbara, 307
Mirounga spp. *See* elephant seals
monogamy, 204
　social, 204
　Sociosexual Orientation Inventory and, 204
　two-way sexual selection and, 204

moral-creator socioeconomic hypothesis, 436–437
　capitalism under, 436–437
　for U.S., 436–437
moral psychology, 364
Morrison, Toni, 422
mortality rates
　economic inequality and, for males, 16–17
　in hunter-gatherer societies, for children, 279–280
　maternal, offspring survival rates and, 199–200
　paternal, offspring survival rates and, 200
Moulay Ismail the Bloodthirsty, 198
Moyers, Bill, 474
Mrs. Dalloway (Woolf), 421
multilevel selection theory, 293
Murakami, Haruki, 424
murder by proxy, 123
murder-suicide, 117. *See also* homicide-suicide
Murdoch, Rupert, 454
Muslim jihad, 237
　development of terrorism, periods of, 237
　Al Qaeda and, 237
Muslim law. *See* sharia
MWH. *See* male warrior hypothesis
Mystic River (Lehane), 427
myth of restraint, 24

N

Nabokov, Vladimir, 426
Napoleonic Wars, in literature, 429
National Counterterrorism Center (NCTC), 354–355
nationalism, patriarchy and, 309
　feminist conflicts with, 309
nation-states. *See also* male dominance hierarchies
　conflict resolution strategies, IPV as influence on, 308
　cultural violence in, 309, 309
　democracy in, development in, 308
　gender treatment in, 302
　legal protections in, for females, 305, 305–306
　physical security of females in, 305
　prohibition of polygyny in, 313
　social diffusion theory for, 308
　structural violence in, 308–309
　Women and Peace Thesis for, 306
natural, as lexical term, 485–486
naturalistic fallacy, 263
natural selection
　homicide-suicide and, 125
　survivability compared to sexual selection with, 5
Nazca boobies, siblicide among, 109–110

Nazism
- Catholic Church support of, 458
- as Darwinian atheism, 436
- theology-based racism and, 458

NCTC. *See* National Counterterrorism Center

negative affect rituals, 244

Neo-Liberal Genetics (McKinnon), 474

nepotism, in parasite-stress model of sociality, 367

Neriene litigiosa. *See* sierra dome spiders, ritualized fighting among

New Grub Street (Gissing), 420

9/11, spiritual rewards for terrorists after, 239

1984 (Orwell), 428

NLV. *See* non-lethal violence

No Country for Old Men (McCarthy), 415

nomological theory, of human nature, 346
- divisions by gender in, 346
- limitations of, 346
- war and, 346

non-lethal violence (NLV)
- among apes, 29–30
- among early Hominids, 34–35, 40
- future research study for, 36
- among gorillas, 29–30
- intersexual, among apes, 29
- intrasexual, among apes, 29
- among mammals, 26–27
- as natural behavior, 35
- among orangutans, 30
- with sibling conflict, 112

non-state wars, 353
- data methodology for, 354
- results predictions for, 359

nontheism. *See* atheism

nonviolence, as lexical concept, 482

Norris, Frank, 424

Norris, Pippa, 311

North America, wars in, 327–334. *See also* Northern Great Plains, warfare record in; Santa Barbara Channel area, warfare record in
- historical record of, 327–328
- Kennewick Man, 327
- paleoclimate data in, 330, 331–332, 334
- settlement data for, 326, 328, 330, 332–333

Northern Great Plains, warfare record in, 333–334
- American Indian Wars, 333
- Battle of Little Bighorn, 333
- Battle of Wounded Knee, 333
- Crow Creek site, 334
- Fay Tolten site, 334
- historical record for, 333
- paleoclimate data for, 334

Nostromo (Conrad), 415, 421

nurturance responses, by gender, 375–376

O

Oates, Joyce Carol, 415
Obama, Barack, 474
Obama, Michelle, 460
obligate strategies, 182
O'Connor, Flannery, 415, 415, 415
The Odyssey (Homer), 422–423
Oedipus Rex (Sophocles), 419
The Old Curiosity Shop (Dickens), 415
older adults, homicide-suicide by, 120
- as filicide, 122
- by intimate partners, 121

Old Testament, slavery in, 459

Oliver Twist (Dickens), 426

One Day in the Life of Ivan Denisovich (Solzhenitsyn), 428

One Thousand and One Nights, 426

O Pioneers! (Cather), 423

orangutans
- intrasexual competition among, 158
- NLV among, 30

Oresteia (Aeschylus), 417

organized crime, Catholic Church and, 458

Orwell, George, 420, 428

ostracism, within female groups, 380

OT. *See* oxytocin

Othello (Shakespeare), 415

Othello Syndrome, 184

Our Mutual Friend (Dickens), 423

out groups
- bullying of, 273, 275
- infrahumanization of, 296
- male dominance hierarchies and, aggression towards, 307
- MWH and, 296
- religion and, 17–18
- religious terrorism against, 239
- stereotyping of, under MWH, 296
- tribalism and, psychology of, 292
- war against, 16

overproduction of offspring, in animals
- Insurance Egg Hypothesis for, 109–110
- sibling competition from, 109

oxytocin (OT), 207
- fear reduction and, 210–211
- female aggression and, 211

P

pain tolerance levels, by gender, 374

paleoclimate data, in archaeological warfare records
- for Northern Great Plains, 334
- for Santa Barbara Channel area, 330
- for Southwestern U.S., 331–332

paleopathology, 335–336

Palestine, Two State Solution for, 85

Palestinian Islamic Jihad, 238

Palin, Sarah, 460

Papio cynocephalus. *See* yellow baboons, aggressive behavior among

paraphilias, sexual offending through, 174, 185–186
- biastophilia, 174, 186
- as courtship disorder, 185
- evolutionary hypothesis for, 185
- exhibitionism, 174, 185
- frotteurism, 174, 185
- pedophilia, 174, 186, 186, 186
- rape as sexual preference, 178, 185
- toucheurism, 185
- voyeurism, 174, 185

parasite prevalence, violence and, 17
- social cooperation and, 17

parasite stress
- Contemporary Pathogen Severity Index for, 355, 355–356
- data methodology for, 355–356
- GIDEON, 355
- religion and, 361

parasite-stress model of sociality
- as casual-effect model, 364–365
- coalitional aggression in, 367
- collectivism and, 352, 353, 356
- condition-dependence in, 364
- control variables for, 356–357
- coups and, 353, 354, 359
- democracy levels and, 352, 356–357, 365–366
- ethnocentrism and, 351–352, 363
- future research study for, 368
- GDP per capita variable, 356, 357
- individualism and, 356, 362
- intrastate armed conflicts and, 352–353, 353, 354, 358–359, 366
- methodology for, 353–358
- moral psychology in, 364
- nepotistic adaptation in, 367
- non-state wars and, 353, 354, 359
- parameters of, 351
- path analysis for, 357–358, 359–360, 365, 366
- for peace, 353, 355, 359
- political conflict under, causes of, 362
- political instability and, 357
- population size variable for, 356
- proximate causes under, for political conflict, 364
- pursuit of conflict under, 363
- regression analysis for, 357, 358
- results predictions for, 358–360, 364
- revolutions and, 353, 354, 359
- scientific foundations for, 362
- warfare under, as adaptation, 363
- within-state terrorism and, 353, 354–355, 359
- world region as variable for, 357
- xenophobia in, 352–353, 363

parents. *See also* child maltreatment; filicide; stepparents
- bullying by, 284
- burdensomeness and, maternal age, 143–144
- child development and, 405–406

child homicide-suicide by, among older parents, 122
conflicts with offspring, 414
modeling of violence from, in children, 310
in parental investment theory, mothers and unborn offspring, 14
in sibling conflict theory, 108
violence and, mothers and offspring, 14
parental investment theory, 6
 aggression and, 198
 child maltreatment and, 91, 92, 96
 filicide and, 91, 92, 96
 by gender, 6
 male control over female reproduction and, 303
 mothers and unborn offspring under, 14
 MWH and, 293
 sibling conflict theory and, 108, 112
 suicide attempts and, 138
parental solicitude, 96–97
parent offspring conflict theory, 108, 108
parricide, 123
 "him or me" dilemma and, 123
 in literature, 422
 separation-individuation development conflicts and, 123
partner rape, 183–184
 as adaptive behavior, 183
 cuckoldry risk hypothesis for, 183–184, 184, 184
 definition of, 174
 psychopathy and, 183
pastoralism, 230
paternal mortality, offspring survival rates and, 200
paternity uncertainty, for males, 64–66
 evolutionary considerations of, 64
 male-male competition and, 160
 monitoring behaviors and, 65
 post-detection behaviors, for males, 65–66
 protective guarding behaviors against, 65–66
 psychological mechanisms for reduction of, 65–66
 sexual coercion as response to, 70
 sexual jealousy as, among males, 65
path analysis
 with Global Peace Index, 357–358
 for parasite-stress model of sociality, 357–358, 359–360, 365, 366
pathogen exposure
 Global Peace Index and, 365
 international aid and, as deterrent to, 367–368
 warfare and, 363
patriarchal family law, 311–312
 in contemporary society, 312
patriarchy. See structural patriarchy
patrilineal societies, female sexual repression in, 79

patrilocality, 303
 in hunter-gatherer societies, 303
 marriage and, 312
patriotism, through imagined kinship, 249
patronymic naming, in cultures of honor, 229
"Paul's Case" (Cather), 420
Paul VI (Pope), 458
Pax Chaco period, 332
peace
 dynamical systems models for, 486
 embodied cognition with, 494
 evolutionary peace project, 493–495
 evolutionary psychology for, 19, 471–472
 evolution theory and, acceptance of, 473–475
 females as symbol of, 372–373
 framework for, 480
 gender-neutral language for, 485
 Global Peace Index for, 355, 357, 357–358, 362
 Hobbesian approach to, 476
 intersubjectivity and, 494
 lexical issues for, 478–486
 organizational levels for, 490–493, 491
 organizations for, female leadership of, 494
 parasite-stress model of sociality for, 353, 355, 359
 perceptions of threats and, 472–478
 positive peace processes, 482
 regional variables for, 361
 relevant ideology for, 472–473
 Rousseau on, 476
 simplicity in approaches to, 475–477
 sustainability of, 495
 systems of, 482
 time scales for, 487–489, 488
peacemaking, 482
pedophilia, 174, 186
 by developmentally disabled, 186
 incest and, 186–187
personal strain, 124
Persuasion (Austen), 417
Peterson, Dale, 306
pet-keeping, 262–263
 cute factor for, 262–263
 as parental care, 262
Phèdre (Racine), 419
phenotypic inertia, 400–401
philosophy. See biological philosophy
physical abuse. See also child maltreatment
 intimate partner homicide-suicide and, 121
physical security, of females
 legal protections for, 305, 305–306
 in nation-states, 305
Physical Security of Women scores, 305
Pichot, A., 474
The Picture of Dorian Gray (Wilde), 419
pigs, sibling competition among, 108
pleiotropy, 137

Poe, Edgar Allen, 426–427
political coups. See coups, political
political psychology, theories for, 307–309
 conflict resolution strategies, influences on, 308
 cultural violence, 309, 309
 social diffusion theory, state security and, 308
 structural violence, 308–309
political revolutions. See revolutions, political
polygynous mating systems
 among elephant seals, 157
 in male dominance hierarchies, 313
 in mate-deprivation hypothesis, 176
 prohibition of, nation-state formation and, 313
 for reproduction, in animals, 157
 warfare and, 313
polytheism, war and, 456
population profiles, 450
 in archaeology, for warfare, 327
 human violence and, 507–509
 for rape, sex ratio as influence on, 188–189
 religious terrorism and, high-fertility factors for, 250
 for Santa Barbara Channel area, in archaeological warfare record, 329–330
"Porphyria's Lover" (Browning), 423
positive peace processes, 482
post-traumatic stress disorder (PTSD), 394
postviolence peacebuilding, 482
poverty, male-male competition and, 165
precarious manhood hypothesis, 223–224
 masculinity and, violent displays of, 224
predation, 24
 infanticide as, in chimpanzees, 52
prehistory, warfare in, 340–344
 archaeological evidence for, 341
 artistic support for, 342
 comparative primatology for, 342–344
 data interpretation dilemma for, 342–343
 definition of war and, 341–342
 feuding as, 341
 forensic support for, 342
 between hunter-gatherer societies, 340–341
 small-scale raiding as, 341, 343
Presbytis spp. See languars, infanticide among
Pride and Prejudice (Austen), 417
primates. See apes; chimpanzees; gorillas; specific species
The Prime Minister (Trollope), 420
Primitive War (Turney-High), 348
The Princess Casamassima (James), 420
process-tracing, in Women in Peace Thesis, 317, 317–318
 criticism of, 318

Procolobus badius temminckii. See red colobus monkeys, coalitional aggression among
pronghorn antelope, 27
psychological autopsy
   after homicide-suicide, 128
   after suicide, 135
psychology. *See also* evolutionary psychology; political psychology, theories for; social learning theory
   evolutionary approach to, 4
   moral, 364
   social, 301–302
   of tribalism, for out groups, 292
   in Women and Peace Thesis, 311
psychology of law, for sexual offending, 188
   evolutionary perspectives in, 188
   for rape, 188
Psychology's War on Religion (Cummings/Cummings), 473
psychopathic cruelty, in literature, 414–416
psychopathy, bullying and, 276
   emotional expression and, 281–282
   evolutionary development of, 282
   historical data for, 276, 281–282
psychopathy, sexual offending and, 182–183
   antisocial behavior and, 182
   as cheater strategy, 182
   heritable coefficients for, 183
   IQ and, 182–183
   neurological correlates for, 183
   as obligate strategy, 182
   partner rape and, 183
PTSD. *See* post-traumatic stress disorder
puberty, timing of, 405–406
   violent behaviors and, 511–512
Pueblo peoples, war among, 331
punishment, IPV as, 66–67
   from cuckoldry, 67
   in evolutionary game theory, 67
   for female infidelity, in the Bible, 78
   severity of, seriousness of offense and, 67
Pure Society: From Darwin to Hitler (Pichot), 474

Q

Al Qaeda, 237
Quinsey, V.L., 180
Quran, slavery in, 459
Qutb, Sayyid, 236, 239

R

Rabin, Itzhak, 493
Racine, Jean, 419
racism, theology-based, 458. *See also* anti-Semitism, Christianity and; slavery, religiosity and

Rantisi, Abdul Aziz, 238
rape. *See also* biastophilia; confluence model of sexual aggression; forced in-pair copulation; mate-deprivation hypothesis; partner rape; sexual coercion, IPV and
   acquaintance rape, 174
   as adaptation, 175
   byproduct behaviors from, 177, 178–179
   costs and benefits of, under evolutionary perspective, 174–175
   date rape, 174
   early evolutionary accounts of, 174–175
   for establishment of relationship, 184
   ethnic cleansing and, 403
   false explanations for, 180
   FIPC and, 183–184
   integrated models for, 179–180
   during Iraq War, 82
   legal definitions of, in U.S., 173, 174
   personal relationships and, 183–185
   prevalence of, variations of, 188–189
   psychology of law for, 188
   sex ratio of populations and, 188–189
   sexual arousal during, 177–178
   as sexual coercive behavior, 178
   sexual jealousy and, 184–185
   as sexual preference, among males, 178, 185
   sexual selection and, for reproduction, 175
   synthesized theory of, 180
   in U.S., statistics for, 3, 70
rat models, for maternal aggression, 206–207
realistic group conflict theory, 220
recidivism, IQ and, 183
reciprocity
   as The Ancient Contract, 261–262
   evolution of, 515
   in human-animal bonds, 261
reconciliation, 485
red colobus monkeys, coalitional aggression among, 45
red deer, 27
   dyadic aggression in, 44
Reformed Zionism. *See* Two State Solution
Regan, Tom, 261
regression analysis, for parasite-stress model of sociality, 357, 358
relational aggression, among females, 12–13, 156, 205
   through fidelity, 205
   through gossip, 205, 273–274
   in hunter-gatherer societies, 280–281
   as intrasexual bullying, 272
   through physical appearance, 205, 272
relationship counseling, for IPV, 166

religion. *See also* atheism; the Bible; Buddhism; Catholic Church; Christianity; Hinduism; Islam, expansion of; Midrash Rabbah, law of jealousy in; moral-creator socioeconomic hypothesis; polytheism, war and; religious fundamentalism; religious terrorism; sacred values; Talmud; Western democracies, religiosity in
   adaptability of, 239, 247–248
   adaptive benefits of, 241
   during adolescence, 245–246
   afterlife in, in early agricultural societies, 440
   animal abuse and, 255
   animal cruelty and, 255
   belief in supernatural agents in, 243–244
   communal participation in, 241–243
   conflict identification within, 238
   counterintuitive concepts in, 243
   definitions of, 234–235
   demands on faithful, 241–242
   in early agricultural societies, 440–442
   in early China, 440
   essentialist perspective on, 235
   evolutionary development of, 235
   extension of community from, 239–240
   fundamentalism in, 241–242
   generational reinterpretation of, 239
   group identity through, 245
   hierarchy of ideas in, 247
   among hunter-gatherers, 439–440
   as imagined kinship, 249
   inflexibility of, as popular misconception, 247–248
   in-group identification and, 17–18
   in literature, declines in, 444
   moral justification from, 238–239
   mythology in, 240
   negative affect rituals and, 244
   out groups and, 17–18
   parasite stress and, 361
   recurrent features of, 235
   rites of passage in, for adolescents, 246
   ritual as feature of, 235, 240, 239–240
   the sacred in, creation of, 244
   signaling models for, 241
   slavery and, 442, 457
   social bonding through, 240
   spiritual rewards from, 239
   superficiality of, 455
   symbolism of, 240
   violence and, 17–18, 455–462
   in Western democracies, declines in, 444–445
   after World War I, 435–436
religiosity. *See also* religious terrorism; Western democracies, religiosity in
   complementary socioeconomic security hypothesis and, 438

corporate-consumer hypothesis for, 453–454
definitions of, 438–439
in early agricultural societies, 440–442
in early China, 440
global declines in, 446
grading of, 438–439
among hunter-gatherers, 439–440
noninternal nature of, 451–452
nonuniversality of, 451–452
science and technology and, 451
slavery and, 442, 457
social regulation through, 437
societal conditions and, 437–438
socioeconomic dysfunctionality hypothesis and, 438
in U.S., declines in, 445–446
violence and, 455–462

religious fundamentalism, 241–242
definition of, 241
exposure to secular values and, 241
multiculturalism as influence on, 241
resource competition as result of, 241–242
signaling theory for, 241–242

religious terrorism. *See also* sacred values
adaptability of, 239
among adolescents, 246
for adolescents, belief transmission for, 245–246
in Africa, 458
benefits to kin through, 242
conflict identification in, 238
contemporary, 236–237
definition of, 234, 235–236
ethnocentrism and, 361
evolutionary perspectives for, 238, 249–250
extension of community from, 239–240
future research study on, 249–250
group identity through, 245
in high-fertility populations, 250
increase in, 233
LHT for, 242
moral justification from, 238–239
by Muslim jihad, 237, 237, 237
mythology for, 240
through negative affect rituals, 244
out group conflicts and, 239
perpetrators of, demographics for, 237–240
political motivations of, 235–236
purpose of, 233–234
as ritual performance, 235, 240, 239–240
the sacred for, creation of, 244
sacrifice of youth as symbol of, 242
social bonding through, 240
social status inconsistencies as factor in, 238
spiritual rewards through, 239, 242–243, 243–244
symbolism of, 240

Renaissance period wars, in literature, 428
reproduction, among animals. *See also* polygynous mating systems
aggression and, 43
among chimpanzees, violence between males, 49
female aggression and, 198–199
incest strategies, 187
infanticide as strategy for, 29
intersexual competition and, among female chimpanzees, 50–51
intrasexual competition for, violence in, 7
in polygynous species, 157
self-destructive behavior and, evolutionary purpose of, 140–141
sexual coercion for, between males and female chimpanzees, 51

reproduction, in humans. *See also* cuckoldry; monogamy
cooperative breeding and, 199–200
facial masculinity and, female perception of, 163
in FEA, 303
homicide-suicide and, 125
intersexual competition for, in males, 11–12
intrasexual competition for, in females, 12–13
intrasexual competition for, in males, 11–12
IPV and, 72
male control over, 303
male-male competition for, 154–155, 160, 161
under MWH, 294
in parental investment theory, 303
rape and, 175
sexual coercion in, by males, 303
siblicide and, 114
status and, 12
suicide and, hypothesis for, 15
violence against females and, evolutionary psychology and, 13
violence and, as catalyst for, 11–13

reproductive tradeoffs, 162
reputation, in cultures of honor
aggressive defense of, 223
restoration of, 221–222, 225
resilience, after child maltreatment, 100–101
Resisting the Green Dragon, 473
resource competition
bullying and, 271
among chimpanzees, coalitional violence in, 8–9
FEA and, 304
female aggression and, 197, 198, 206
for food supplies, 7–9
intrasexual bullying and, 271–272
in male dominance hierarchies, 317
between males, 155–156, 160

in mate-deprivation hypothesis, among animals, 176
reproductive access as, 7
ritualized fighting and, 25
siblicide as result of, 108
resource control theory, bullying and, 274, 274–275
bistrategic controllers in, 274–275
coercive controllers in, 274–275
intrasexual bullying, 271–272
resource deprivation hypothesis, 220, 220–221
in realistic group conflict theory, 220
resource-holding potential (RHP), 43
retaliatory violence, in cultures of honor, 224–225, 225–226, 228
for terrorist acts, 225–226
revenge
child homicide-suicide as, 122
in literature, 426–427
murder by proxy and, 123
by Yanomamö peoples, violence as, 329
revolutions, political, 353
data methodology for, 354
results predictions for, 359
RHP. *See* resource-holding potential
Rice, M.E., 180
Richard III (Shakespeare), 415–416
Richardson, Samuel, 427
risk contract hypothesis, 293
risk-taking
gender differences in, 374–375, 376–377
by males, 203, 203–204, 374–375
Riss, Linda, 63
rituals
negative affect, 244
in religion, 235, 240, 239–240
religious terrorism as, 235, 240, 239–240
ritualized fighting, 24–25
as ESS, 24–25
among male chimpanzees, 25
resource competition and, 25
among sierra dome spiders, 25
Robertson, Pat, 473
Robinson Crusoe (Defoe), 424
"A Rose for Emily "(Faulkner), 423
Rosen, Stephen, 313–314
Rousseau, Jean Jacques, 476
r-selected species, 164
rule of law, violence and, 221–222
broken window effect and, 221
strong state development and, 221
Rushdie, Salman, 236–237

S

Sacagawea, 372
sacred values
during adolescence, 245–246
for adolescents, belief transmission for, 245–246
compromise over, responses to, 245
in conflict resolution, 248

sacred values (*cont.*)
  creation for, 244–245
  emotional significance of, 244
  ESS approach to, 248
  future research study on, 250
  group identity through, 245
  as physical space, 244
  sacrifice from commitment to, 245
Sade, Marquis de, 415
sadism, 174
Sageman, Marc, 237
Sakharov, Andrei, 461
Salammbô (Flaubert), 422
San Suu Kyi, 461
Santa Barbara Channel area, warfare record in, 328–330
  craft specialization and, 330
  hunter-gatherer societies in, 328
  paleoclimate data, 330
  population profiles in, 329–330
  resource shortage assessment in, 330
  settlement data for, 328, 330
  severe injury data for, 328–329
  weaponry in, 329, 330
The Satanic Verses (Rushdie), 236–237
schools
  formal development of, adolescent bullying and, 282–283
  violence in, 224–225
Schwerner, Michael, 457
science and technology, religiosity and, 451
science fiction, war in, 430
The Secret Agent (Conrad), 420, 426
secular terrorism. *See* terrorism, secular
selection bias, 135
self-destructive behavior, evolutionary purpose of, 140–141. *See also* burdensomeness
  burdensomeness and, 141, 141–142
  reproductive fitness and, 140–141
self-harm. *See also* self-destructive behavior, evolutionary purpose of
  burdensomeness and, 143
  DSH, 138
  in literature, 418–421
  suicide and, 15
self-preservation motivations, 145
self-protection, male-male competition and, 159
sensation-seeking, impulsivity compared to, 203
serotonin, suicide and, 136
settlement data, 326
  for Santa Barbara Channel area, 328, 330
  for Southwestern U.S., 332–333
sexual abuse, as legal term, 173. *See also* incest; pedophilia
sexual aggression, 173. *See also* confluence model of sexual aggression
  definition of, 173
  mate-deprivation hypothesis and, 176–177

sexual assault, as legal term, 174
  sexual homicide and, 187
sexual behavior, child development and, 405–406
sexual coercion. *See also* coercive intersexual bullying; forced in-pair copulation; partner rape; rape
  as adaptive behavior, 513
  among chimpanzees, 51
  direct, 188
  in human reproduction, by males, 303
  indirect, 188
  infanticide as, among chimpanzees, 52–53
  rape and, 178
  sexual offending compared to, 173
sexual coercion, IPV and, 70. *See also* coercive intersexual bullying; forced in-pair copulation; partner rape; rape
  in domination and control hypothesis, 70
  in marriage, incidence rates for, 70
  paternity uncertainty and, 70
  sperm competition hypothesis for, 70
sexual conflict theory, 187–188
  coercive intersexual bullying and, 278
  direct coercion in, 188
  indirect coercion in, 188
  infanticide in, 188
  interlocus conflict in, 188
  intralocus conflict in, 188
sexual dimorphism, 303
  in human nature, war and, 347–348
sexual disorders, 185–187
  in sexual offenders, 191
sexual harassment, 276
sexual homicide, 187. *See also* intimate partner homicide-suicide; intimate partner violence; uxoricide
  as byproduct behavior, 187
  sexual assault and, 187
  victim demographics, 187
sexual interference, 174
sexual jealousy. *See also* law of jealousy, in Bible
  female aggression from, 205, 208
  among females, 65
  FIPC and, among males, 70–71
  by gender, 208
  intimate partner homicide-suicide from, 122
  IPV and, 66, 208
  in literature, 422–423
  among males, 65
  Othello Syndrome, 184
  rape and, 184–185
sexual offenders. *See also* developmentally disabled, sexual offending by
  as adaptive behavior, 190
  assessment of, 189
  as byproduct behavior, 190
  through mating efforts, 190

  as opportunistic, 190
  prevention strategies for, 189
  sexual disorders among, 191
  treatment strategies for, 189
  typology of, 190–191, 190
sexual offending. *See also* competitively disadvantaged males; forced in-pair copulation; incest; paraphilias, sexual offending through; partner rape; psychopathy, sexual offending and; rape; sexual coercion; sexual homicide
  acquaintance rape, 174
  child molestation, 174
  in contemporary period, 180–188
  date rape, 174
  definition of, 173–174
  by developmentally disabled, 186
  in early periods, 174–180
  incest, 186–187
  integrated models for, 179–180
  overview of, 173–174
  through paraphilias, 185–186
  psychology of law for, 188
  sexual abuse, 173
  sexual acts in, 173
  sexual aggression in, 173, 173
  sexual assault, 174
  sexual coercion compared to, 173
  in sexual conflict theory, 187–188
  through sexual disorders, 185–187, 191
  sexual interference, 174
  under Standard Social Sciences Model, 174
  three-path model for, 183
  victimization rates for, 174
  young male syndrome and, 181, 181, 181, 181
sexual selection, in animals, 5–6. *See also* intrasexual competition, between animals
  infanticide as, by male chimpanzees, 52
  intersexual competition in, 5–6
  survivability compared to, 5
sexual selection hypothesis
  for child maltreatment and filicide, 94, 94–95, 97
  for rape, 175
  for violence and aggression, in males, 513–514
Shakespeare, William, 415, 415–416, 417
  violence in works of, 417, 420, 422, 425, 427
shamanism, among hunter-gatherers, 439
sharia (Muslim law), 237
Sheehan, Michael, 238
Shelley, Mary, 426
Shimkus, John, 473
The Shining (King), 422, 426
siblicide
  age disparity between siblings, 114
  among animals, 109–111
  birth order as influence on, 113–114

in Bison Horn Maria of India, 112–113
among black eagles, 110
among black-legged kittwakes, 109
among blue footed boobies, 108, 110
as brood reduction, in animals, 109
among cattle egrets, 110
cultural myths about, 112
evolutionary perspectives on, 107
factors for, 113–115
in feudal societies, 113
fratricide, 107, 113
future research study on, 115
among Galapagos fur seals, 111
by gender, 113
genetic relatedness and, 114
historical examples of, 107
in humans, 112–113
incidence rates for, 107
among laughing kookaburras, 110
in literature, 422
among masked boobies, 108
among Nazca boobies, 109–110
parent offspring conflict theory for, 108, 108
proximity factors for, 112
reproductive fitness and, 114
from resource competition, 108
from sibling competition in animals, 108
sibling conflict theory for, 107–108
sororicide, 107
among spotted hyenas, 111
suicide after, 123
in U.S., incidence rates for, 112
sibling competition, in animals, 108–111
FAH for, 109
among guinea pigs, 108
inclusive fitness theory for, 108
infanticide and, 109
among meerkats, 111
overproduction of offspring and, 109
among pigs, 108
for resources, 108
siblicide as result of, 108
sibling conflict theory, 107–108, 112
age differences among siblings, 112, 114
birth order in, 107
children's perceptions of conflict, 112
conflict of interests in, 107
inclusive fitness theory and, 107
kin selection theory and, 107
NLV and, 112
parental investment theory and, 108, 112
parent offspring conflict theory and, 108
siblings, violence between, 14, 106
historical examples of, 107
parent offspring conflict theory for, 108
sibling conflict theory for, 112
sierra dome spiders, ritualized fighting among, 25

signaling theory, 241–242
Sinai War, 85
Singer, Peter, 261
Six-Day War, 85
slavery, religiosity and, 442, 457
in Old Testament, 459
in Quran, 459
slip-up hypothesis, for uxoricide, 69
small-scale raiding, in prehistorical societies, 341
comparative primatology for, 343
by Yanomamö people, 343–344
Smuts, Barbara, 302, 306. See also feminist evolutionary analysis
social bargaining model, suicide attempts and, 139
social bonding, burdensomeness and, 144
Social Brain hypothesis, 292
social carnivores, lethal violence among, 28
social conflict, as evolutionary process, 514–517
social diffusion theory, state security and, 308
social failure, in literature, 419–421
Social Glue hypothesis, 292
social integration theory, 125
social learning theory, 309–311
biological basis for aggression in, 309
immediate reinforcement in, 310
male-male alliances in, 310–311
modeling in, 310
violence as learned behavior, 309–310, 310–311
social monogamy, 204
social navigation hypothesis, 139
social psychology, 301–302
social status. See also reputation, in cultures of honor
male-male competition for, 160–161
for males, development of, 162
religious terrorism and, 238
social status, among animals, aggressive behavior and, 43
socioeconomic dysfunctionality hypothesis, 438
socioeconomic security hypothesis, 452–453
Sociosexual Orientation Inventory, 204
Soloveitchik, Joseph, 248
Solzhenitsyn, Alexandr, 428
The Song of Roland, 428
Sophie's Choice (Styron), 422
Sophocles, 419, 419
sororicide, 107
in literature, 422
Southwestern U.S., warfare record in, 330–333
cannibalism in, 332
Grand Gulch Caves, 331
osteological record of violence in, 331
paleoclimate data, 331–332
Pax Chaco period, 332

among Pueblo peoples, 331
settlement data for, 332–333
severity of violence in, 333
skeletal injury assessment, 333
Soviet Union. See also Communism, Christianity's defeat of
atheism in, 442
Cold War and, 443
sperm competition hypothesis, 70
for FIPC, 70–71
spider monkeys, coalitional aggression among, 45
spiteful strategy, in child maltreatment and filicide, 99–100
spotted hyenas
coalitional aggressive behaviors among, 45, 45–46
siblicide among, 111
spousal aggression, 156
"Spunk" (Hurston), 423
Standard Social Sciences Model (SSSM), 174
mixed sex groups under, 379
Stanford prison experiment, 294
status, reproductive access and, 12
Steinbeck, John, 426, 427
Stendahl, 427
stepparents
filicide by, 95
homicide-suicide by, 127
stereotyping
of evolutionary psychology, 475
of female aggression, 197
leadership and, in armed forces, 386
in MWH, 296
Stevenson, Robert Louis, 415
strain theory, 124
aggression in, origins of, 124
for animal cruelty, 264
anomie in, response to, 124
as personal *versus* social, 124
violence as responsive behavior in, 124
stream analogy, for homicide-suicide, 124–125
for aggressive behaviors, 124
frustration as propulsive emotion in, 124–125
LV in, 124
stress systems, intercultural contact and, 236
structural patriarchy, 311–312
cultural pervasiveness of, 311
cultural violence and, 309
democracy as response to, 308
in evolutionary theory, 311–312
family law under, 311–312, 312
FEA and, 302
as learned behavior, 307
male dominance hierarchies and, 306
marriage arrangements under, 312
nationalism and, 309
patrilocality and, 303, 303, 312
structural violence, 308–309, 480–481

Styron, William, 422
suicidal thinking and behaviors, 133.
    See also burdensomeness
  adoption studies for, 136
  child abuse history and, 137
  cognitive model for, 134
  depression compared to, 135
  diagnostic criteria for, 135
  DST for, 136
  epigenetics and, 136–137
  evolutionary significance of, 137
  familial model for, 134
  future research study on, 147–148
  gene identification for, 136, 137
  genetic foundations for, 135–136
  HPA axis research and, 136
  inclusive fitness theory for, 137, 140–141, 147
  measurement variables for, 134–135
  mental illness as risk factor, 134
  neurochemical correlates for, 136–137
  patient status as influence on, 134–135
  proximate factors in, 133–134
  psychological autopsy methods and, 135
  from psychological disturbances, 134–135
  selection bias in assessment of, 135
  twin studies for, 135–136
suicide, 14–15. *See also* burdensomeness; child homicide-suicide; familicide-suicide; homicide-suicide; intimate partner homicide-suicide
  adoption studies for, 136
  age factors for, 133
  alternative approaches to, 147
  altruistic, 133, 139–140
  anomic, 133–134
  burdensomeness and, 141, 141–142
  as byproduct of depression, 137–138
  child abuse history and, 137
  classification of, difficulties with, 132–133
  in cultures of honor, 229
  as desire, 142
  egoistic, 133
  epigenetics and, 136–137
  as evolved response, 139–141
  exhibitionistic, 120
  extended, 122
  after familicide, 94
  future research study on, 147–148
  by gender, 133
  gene identification for, 136, 137
  genetic foundations for, 135–136
  historical references to, 132
  homicide-suicide compared to, 120
  HPA axis research and, 136
  inclusive fitness theory for, 137, 140–141, 147
  intervention strategies for, 146
  kin selection theory and, 140–141
  in literature, 132, 418, 418–419

  after mass homicide spree, 121
  mercy killing and, 121
  nature of, 132–133
  neurochemical correlates for, 136–137
  reproductive hypothesis for, 15
  as self-destructive behavior, evolutionary purpose of, 140–141, 140–141, 141
  self-harm and, 15
  serotonin levels and, 136
  after siblicide, 123
  twin studies for, 135–136
  universality of, 133
  in U.S., statistics for, 3, 133
suicide attempts
  birth order and, 139
  DSH and, 138
  emotional purposes of, 138–139
  for leverage of parental investment, by adolescents, 138
  leveraging hypothesis and, 139
  selective value of, 138
  social bargaining model and, 139
  social navigation hypothesis and, 139
suicide by proxy, 123
suicide genes, 136, 137
Sula dactylatra. *See* masked boobies, siblicide among
Sula granti. *See* Nazca boobies, siblicide among
Sula nebouxii. *See* blue footed boobies, siblicide among
Sulloway, Frank, 107, 113
Sumner, William Graham, 347
superego, in homicide-suicide, 125, 125
Suricata suricatta. *See* meerkats, sibling competition among
survivability, sexual selection compared to, 5
Symons, D., 174–175
sympathetic nervous system, during anger, 202
synthesized theory of rape, 180
systems of peace, 482

T

A Tale of Two Cities (Dickens), 424
Talmud
  cuckoldry in, 79
  law of jealousy in, 80, 80–81
target paradox, in IPV, 210–211
  female aggression in, 210
Taylor, Charles, 458
The Tea Party, 462
10 Books That Screwed Up the World (Wiker), 476–477
territorial access, animal aggression and, 43
  male-male competition and, 160
terrorism, secular, 246–247. *See also* religious terrorism
  as asymmetric, 361
  civilian victims as focus of, 234

  core features of, 246–247
  against cultures of honor, retaliatory violence by, 225–226
  definition of, 234, 355
  fear as motivation for, 234
  homicide-suicide from, 120, 121
  by LTTE, 235, 246–247
  political motives of, 234
  violent features of, 234
  within-state, 353, 354–355
Tess of the d'Urbervilles (Hardy), 426
testosterone production, in males, 162–163, 183
  in non-industrialized nations, 164
Thackeray, William Makepeace, 415
Thayer, B., 307
theism. *See* religion; religiosity
Thérèse Raquin (Zola), 419
Theropithecus gelada. *See* gelada, aggressive behaviors among
Things Fall Apart (Achebe), 420
Through a Window (Goodall), 514
time preference, child development and, 405–406
Tobach, Ethel, 478
Tolstoy, Leo, 417–418
Toomer, Jean, 423
toucheurism, 185
tradeoffs
  in LHT, 397–398
  reproductive, 162
trauma bundle, 402
tribalism, among humans. *See also* male warrior hypothesis
  coalition formation mechanism in, 291–292
  Darwin on, 291
  as in-group psychology, 292, 292
  intergroup aggression as result of, 292
  Machiavellian Intelligence hypothesis for, 292
  out group conflict psychology with, 292
  proximate causes for, 292
  Social Brain hypothesis for, 292
  Social Glue hypothesis for, 292
  social identity from, 297
  ultimate causes for, 292
Triple Threat, to religiosity in Western democracies, 454
Trollope, Anthony, 417, 420
Truman, Harry, 83
trust, in combat groups, 383–385
  error management theory for, 384
  evolutionary basis of, 384
  as subconscious judgment, 384
Turney-High, H.H., 348
Twain, Mark, 15, 427
twin studies
  for bullying, 271
  for suicide, 135–136
Two State Solution, 85
two-way sexual selection, 204

U

UCDP. *See* Uppsala Conflict Data Program
Ulster Scots, culture of honor for, 222–223
  emigration to U.S., 223
uncertainty, in LHT, 163–164, 164–165
  male-male competition and, 164–165
United States (U.S.). *See also* cultures of honor, violence in; Northern Great Plains, warfare record in; Santa Barbara Channel area, warfare record in; Southwestern U.S., warfare record in
  American Exceptionalism in, 443
  Cold War and, 443
  field studies of violence in, 224–226
  homicide-suicide in, 119
  lab studies of violence in, 226–228
  legal definitions of rape in, 173, 174
  moral-creator socioeconomic hypothesis for, 436–437
  rape statistics in, 3
  regional differences in, for male aggression, 226–228
  religiosity in, declines in, 445–446
  retaliatory violence in, 224–225, 225–226, 228
  siblicide in, incidence rates for, 112
  socioeconomic conditions in, 448–449, 450–451
  suicide in, statistics for, 3, 133
  The Tea Party in, 462
  terrorism and, definition for, 234, 234
  Ulster Scots in, 223, 223
  uxoricide incidence rates in, 68–69
  violent crimes in, statistics for, 3
United States Lifesaving Association (USLA), 376–377
Uppsala Conflict Data Program (UCDP), 354
USLA. *See* United States Lifesaving Association
uxoricide, 68–70
  under game theory, costs of, 69–70
  homicide adaptation theory and, 69, 72
  in literature, 422
  male-male competition and, 161
  as misapplied control tactic, 69
  slip-up hypothesis for, 69
  U.S. incidence rates for, 68–69

V

Vanished in the Twinkling of an Eye, 473
Vatican. *See* Catholic Church
vertical cohesion, in male bonding, 379
Victory (Conrad), 419
Une Vie (Maupassant), 423
Vietnam War, 385
  in literature, 430
violence, against females. *See also* cuckoldry; intimate partner violence; paternity uncertainty, for males; uxoricide
  claustration, 78
  collective undermining of, 314–315
  evolutionary psychology and, 13
  infibulation, 78
  in male dominance hierarchies, 306–307
  as punishment, 66–67
violence, as lexical concept, 479
  violence aggression, 484
violence, in animals, 5–9. *See also* aggression, animal models of; chimpanzees; intrasexual competition, between animals; lethal violence; mammals, violence among; non-lethal violence; resource competition; ritualized fighting; *specific animals*
  behavior characterization for, 42
  coalitional, 8
  competition increase and, 25
  future research studies for, 55
  by gender, 6
  human violence compared to, 42
  through infanticide, 9
  parental investment theory for, 6, 6
  predation and, 24
  as purposeful, 9
  resource competition and, 7–9
  sex-role reverses in, by species, 6
  sexual selection and, 5, 5–6, 5–6
  within species, 5
violence, in humans. *See also* aggression; child development, violence and war and; crime, violence and; homicide; intimate partner violence; literature, violence in; male-male competition, violence and homicide from; violence, in animals; violence, within families; wars
  as aberrant behavior, 24
  animal violence compared to, 42
  as antisocial behavior, 23
  archaeological evidence for, 10–11
  child development and, 393
  cultural, 309
  cultural approach to, 219
  in cultures of honor, 17
  definition of, 3, 42, 254
  development of, 509–511
  in early literature, 10
  early tools for, 10
  evolutionary consciousness for, 506–507, 517–520
  fast life history strategy and, 16–17
  in hunter-gatherer societies, 440
  Industrial Revolution as influence on, 521–522, 521
  LHT for, 16–17
  from male surplus, through gender-based infanticide, 318
  modeling of, from parents, 310
  as moral necessity, 521
  myth of restraint and, 24
  parasite prevalence and, 17, 17
  in popular media, 153–154
  population issues and, 507–509
  puberty as influence on, 511–512
  religion and, 17–18, 455–462
  for reproductive access, 11–13
  retaliatory, 224–225
  in schools, 224–225
  sexual selection hypothesis for, in males, 513–514
  in social learning theory, as learned behavior, 309–310, 310–311
  in strain theory, 124
  structural, 308–309, 480–481
  in Western democracies, contemporary statistics for, 448
violence, within families, 13–15. *See also* child maltreatment; filicide; intimate partner violence; siblicide; siblings, violence between; uxoricide
  familicide, 94
  kin selection theory and, 14
  between mothers and offspring, 14
  parental investment theory and, 14
  between siblings, 106
  suicide, 14–15, 94
violence aggression, 484
The Violent Bear It Away (O'Connor), 415
Virgil, 420
virginity, for women, in Bible, 77–78, 78–79
voyeurism, 174, 185

W

wars, 15–16. *See also* archaeology, for warfare; armed forces, sexual integration of; child development, violence and war and; cohesion, in combat groups; human nature, war and; intrastate armed conflicts; male warrior hypothesis; North America, wars in; Northern Great Plains, warfare record in; prehistory, warfare in; Santa Barbara Channel area, warfare record in; Southwestern U.S., warfare record in; *specific wars*
  child development during, 393–394
  civil, 353
  cultural character of, 343
  death from, in 20th century, 3
  definitions of, 325, 341–342, 479–480
  in early agricultural societies, 441–442
  early archaeological evidence of, 15
  frequency of, 340
  historical patterns for, 325

wars (cont.)
   individual perspectives on causes for, 325
   in-group distinctions and, 16
   just, 456–457
   as male-centered, 15–16, 325
   male-male competition and, 155, 165
   masculinity and, 372
   non-state wars, 353
   under parasite-stress model of sociality, as adaptation, 363
   pathogen exposure and, 363
   polygynous mating systems' influence on, 313
   polytheism and, 456
   as psychological adaptation, 363
   rape during, 82
   trigger incidents for, 325
war, in literature, 428–430
   for eighteenth century wars, 428–429
   emotional intensity of, 430
   in fantasy fiction, 430
   for Napoleonic Wars, 429
   for nineteenth century wars, 429
   for prehistory period, 428
   for Renaissance period, 428
   in science fiction, 430
   for U.S. Civil War, 429
   for Vietnam War, 430
   for World War I, 429
   for World War II, 429–430
War Against Terrorism, 85
War and Peace (Tolstoy), 417–418
War of Attrition, 85
Washington Post, 507
Watchword movement, 442
weathering hypothesis, 405
Welcome to Doomsday (Moyers), 474

Western democracies, religiosity in. *See also* United States
   corporate-consumer hypothesis for, 453–454
   declines in, 444–445, 452–454
   science and technology factors for, 454
   socioeconomic conditions in, 446–448, 448–449, 450–451
   socioeconomic security hypothesis for, 452–453
   Triple Threat to, 454
   in U.S., declines in, 445–446
   violence statistics in, 448
Wharton, Edith, 420
"Where Are You Going, Where Have You Been?" (Oates), 415
Wiker, B., 476–477
Wilde, Oscar, 419, 424
Wise Blood (O'Connor), 415
within-state terrorism, 353
   data methodology for, 354–355
   results predictions for, 359
WITS. *See* Worldwide Incidents Tracking System
wolves, coalitional aggressive behaviors among, 45
women. *See* females
Women and Peace Thesis, 306, 316–319
   empirical support for, 317–319
   future research study for, 319
   historical process-tracing for, 317, 317–318, 318
   psychology in, 311
Woolf, Virginia, 421
Wordsworth, William, 431
World War I
   in literature, 429
   religious belief influenced by, 435–436

   religious conflict over, 442
World War II, in literature, 429–430
Worldwide Incidents Tracking System (WITS), 354
Wounded Knee, Battle of, 333
Wrangham, Richard, 306
Wright, Robert, 313
wrong, evil compared to, 82

X

xenophobia, 352–353, 363. *See also* ethnocentrism

Y

Yanomamö peoples
   homicide rates for males, 155, 396
   infanticide among, 161
   mortality through tribal violence for, 294
   revenge violence by, 329
   skeletal injuries for, through tribal violence, 327
   small-scale raiding behaviors by, 343–344
yellow baboons, aggressive behavior among, 44
Yom Kippur War, 85
Yosef, Ovadia, 248
young male syndrome, 181
   adolescent limited offenders in, 181
   as developmentally flexible facultative mechanism, 181
   expression of, 181
Young Werther's Sufferings (Goethe), 132

Z

Zola, Émile, 419, 423, 426
zoophilia, 174